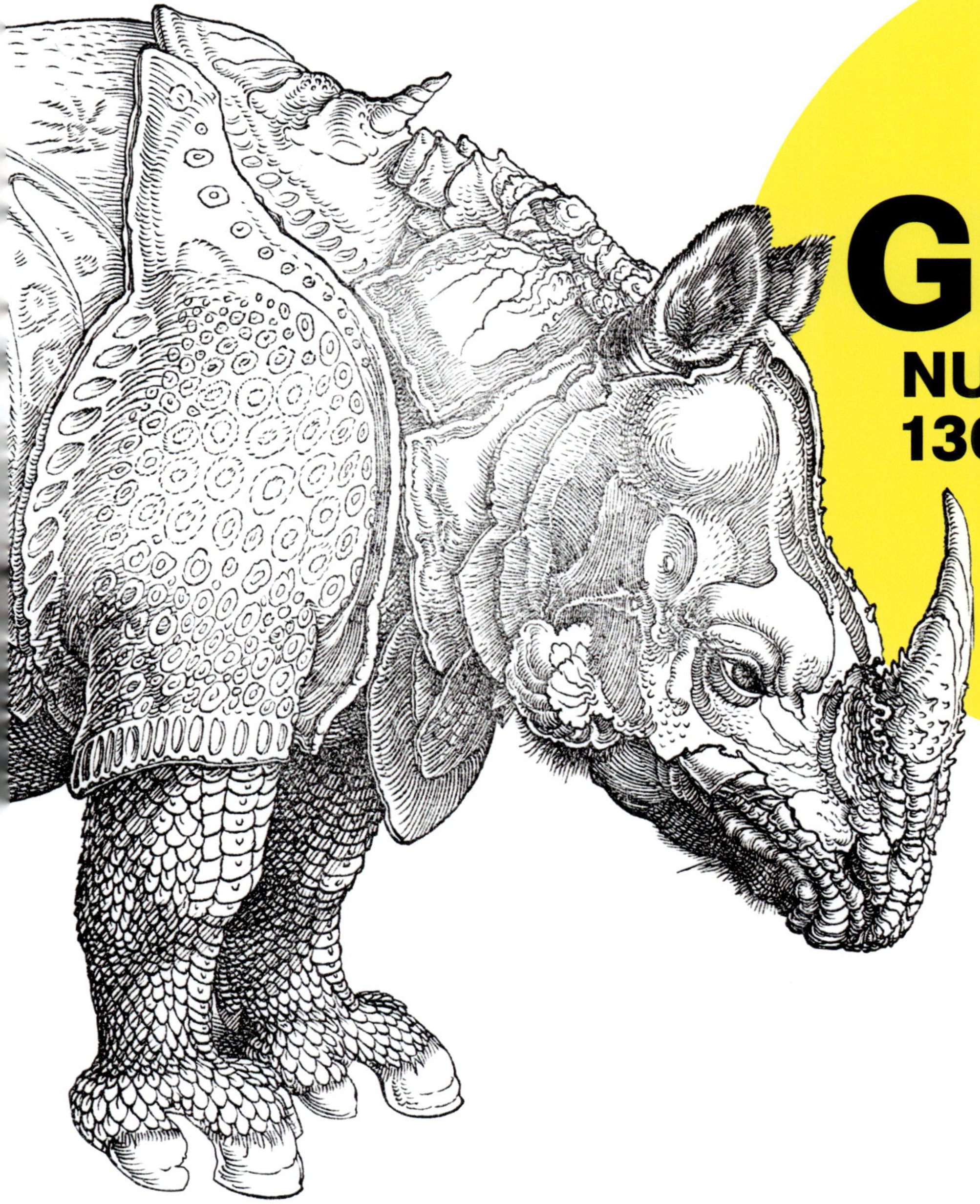

GLOBAL

NUREMBERG 1300–1600

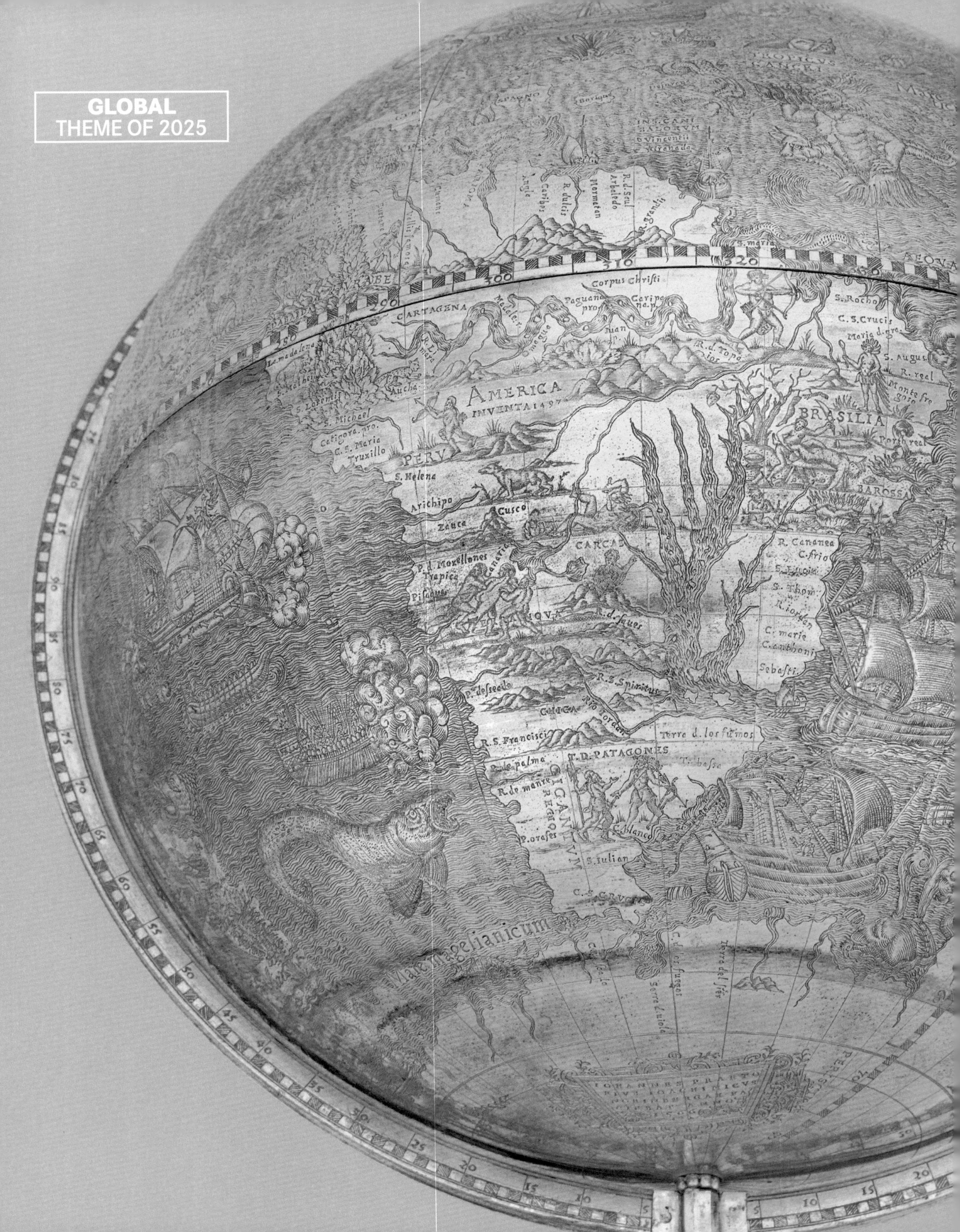
GLOBAL
THEME OF 2025
AMERICA
INVENTA 1497
PERV
BRASILIA
CARTAGENA
Corpus Christi
S. Rocho
C. S. Crucis
S. Augus
R. regal
Porto real
BAROSSA
S. Helena
Arichipo
Cusco
CARCAS
R. Cananea
C. frio
S. Thom
C. marie
C. anthoni
Sebasti
S. Michael
Truxillo
R. S. Spiritus
R. S. Francisci
T. D. PATAGONES
Terra d. los fumos
R. de palma
P. orases
S. Iulian
C. blanco
Mare Magellanicum
Terra del fuego
310
320
300
290

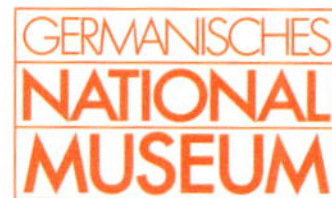

Ein Forschungsmuseum der

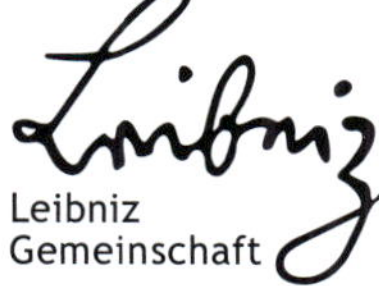

GLOBAL NUREMBERG 1300–1600

Edited by Benno Baumbauer,
Marie-Therese Feist, and Sven Jakstat
Translated by Joshua Waterman

Deutscher
Kunstverlag

CONTENTS

CATALOGUE

APPENDIX

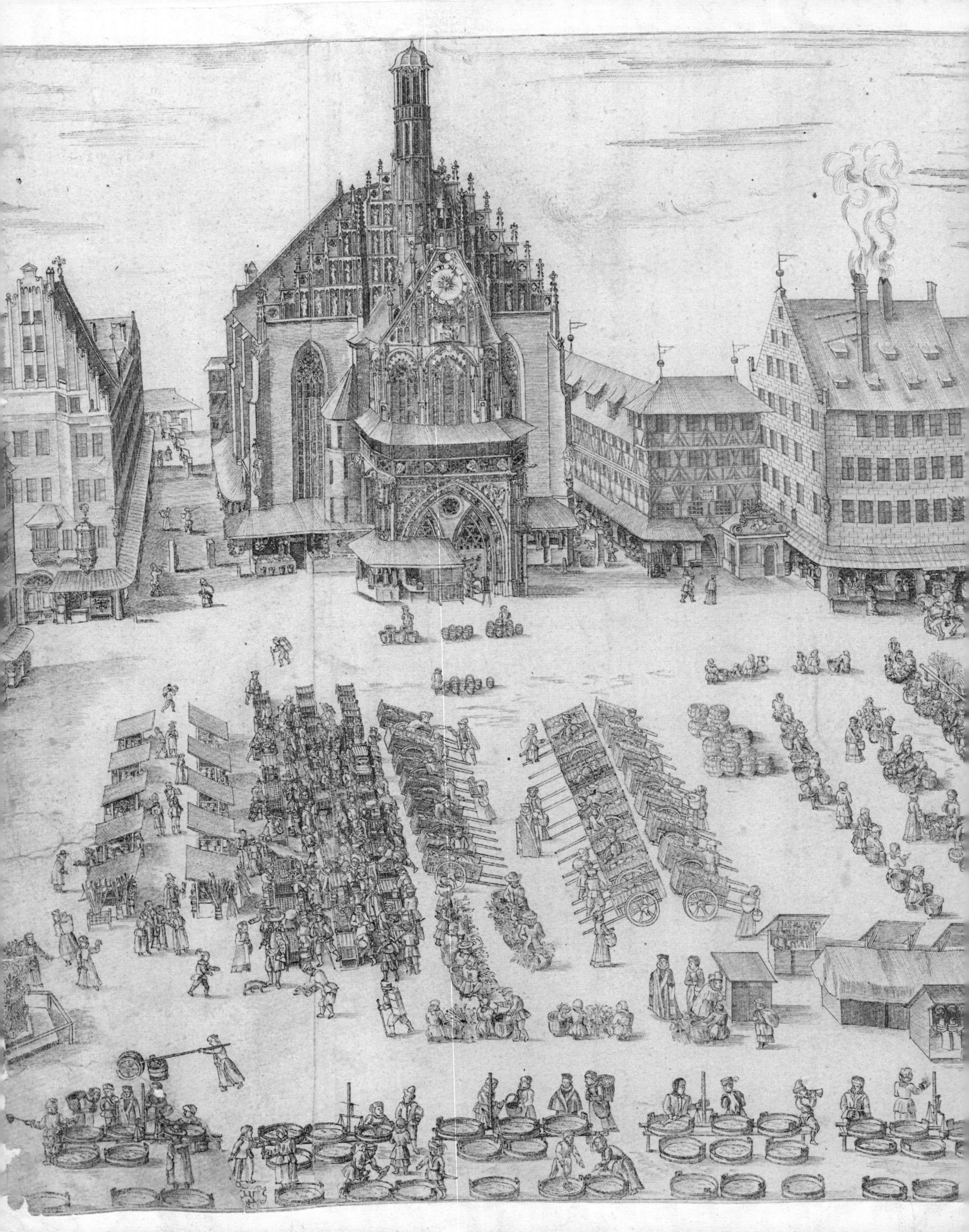

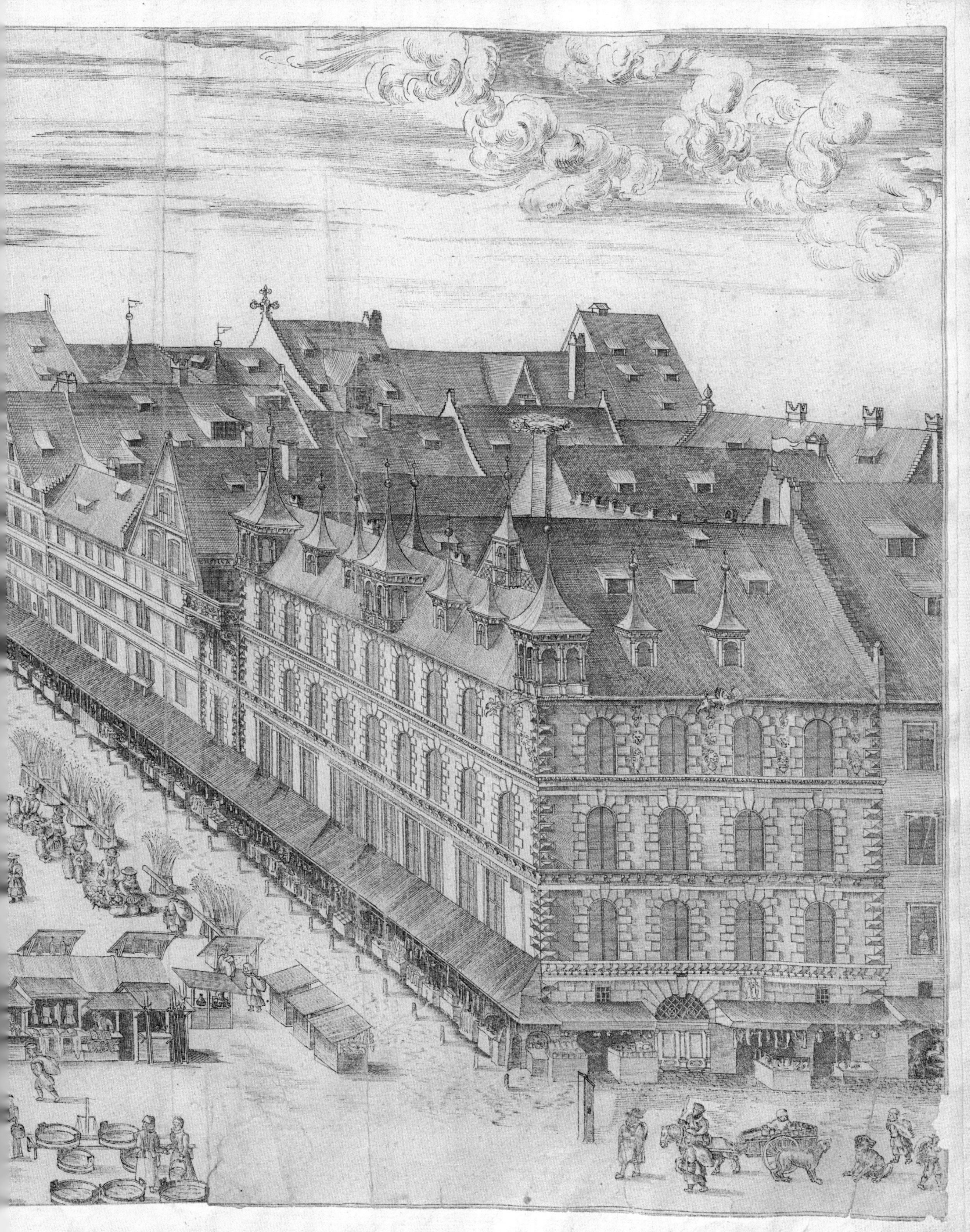

FOREWORD

At the time of the Behaim Globe's creation, Nuremberg was a global city, a hub in the worldwide exchange of knowledge. As made clear in the exhibition *GLOBAL Nuremberg, 1300–1600*, any given view of the world is always shaped by one's own location and scope of knowledge. Understanding globalization means recognizing not only connections but also contradictions. The history of world maps alone suffices to demonstrate the relativity of different perspectives: while the so-called Hereford Mappa Mundi of about 1300 focuses on Christian Jerusalem, the religious geography of Islam in the period locates the world's center in Mecca. The Kangnido Map of 1402, a royal Korean commission, places the territorially superior China at the center and shows the Korean peninsula as the second-largest landmass.

Our Behaim Globe, on the other hand, provides a specifically European view of the world around 1500—a world opened up for global trade after the voyages of Christopher Columbus. The globe shows the world as understood from a European perspective. At the same time, it encapsulates the cultural-historical, technical, and economic knowledge of the period. And with its many errors, it stands as emblematic of the relativity of world knowledge. The world is no longer mapped out as a Christian pilgrimage from Paradise to the Flood, and from Bethlehem and Jerusalem to the Last Judgment, but instead as a global marketplace for newly available resources. The Behaim Globe is thus not only a remarkable document of the profound change from a spiritual-religious to a mercantile-capitalist understanding of the world. It is also a monument to humanity's tendency to misuse broadened horizons for the purposes of power and exploitation.

The relevance and topicality of our exhibition project is underscored by publications such as David Blackbourn's 2023 global history (published in German translation in 2024). That book surveys the German presence in the world across five centuries, in both positive and negative aspects. Germans have been involved in many global activities since the year 1500—as traders, cartographers, financiers, mining technicians, naval gunners, and settlers. Blackbourn repeatedly emphasizes Nuremberg's importance as a global trading center. As a museum with a research mission and holdings that include such key objects as the Behaim and Schöner globes, the Germanisches Nationalmuseum embraces an ongoing critical examination of the European understanding of the world and Nuremberg's role in it. This is particularly necessary at a time when debates over European perspectives are becoming ever more prevalent and when opposing viewpoints about the apparent correctness of various global and postcolonial interpretive approaches are marked by increasing polarization. How can an exhibition adequately address the global history of the early modern period, given that the period not only saw the beginnings of European expansion but also ushered in a Eurocentric historiography that served the purposes of expansion and often became the standard for narrating the history of the subjugated? Who were the actors on this global stage, and what narratives and worldviews shaped them? Given the gaps in our knowledge, how can we tell the story of this early period of European global expansion?

In 2025, as part of a year devoted to "global" themes, the Germanisches Nationalmuseum is addressing these questions in various formats. One of them is a smaller exhibition entitled *Vernetzte Welten / Connected Worlds*, in which objects of global relevance from across the museum's collections are brought together to prompt discussion of globalization's complexity through all time periods and geographic areas. Many of these objects pack quite a punch. Take, for example, the manillas made in Europe beginning in the sixteenth century for the transatlantic slave trade. Manillas served as a "premonetary means of payment" in western Africa until modern times. That unwieldy description touches on the issue of appropriate postcolonial language, for the term "premonetary" has been agreed upon in recent times as a replacement for the pejorative expression "primitive money." These copper or bronze bracelets, manufactured in Europe, were used primarily as a medium of exchange in the slave trade. The recent history of the exemplars now in the Germanisches Nationalmuseum is pertinent to postcolonial discourse. When the African countries under British rule introduced coinage as legal tender as part of the 1948 "Operation Manilla," the manillas were rendered superfluous and sold (back) into the European metal trade as raw materials. Our pieces were acquired at that time by the Nuremberg-based Diehl-Gruppe, one of Germany's largest arms manufacturers. The company allowed the Germanisches Nationalmuseum to select particularly beautiful examples for its collection. With their characteristic shape, manillas are now ubiquitous as "African jewelry." But who is aware that the objects preserved in many museums around the world embody the cruelty and ruthlessness that have accompanied the process of globalization since the sixteenth century? The manillas not only provide tangible material evidence of the slave trade's inhumanity. In their long history, from manufacture to reuse as a cheap raw material, such objects also lack any precise geographical or biographical indicators, therefore opening up space for artistic interventions and creative narratives to help bridge the historical gaps.

Our realization of the ambitious exhibition project *GLOBAL Nuremberg* was made possible by the generous support of a private foundation, which, in addition to financing numerous loans and parts of the catalogue and accompanying programs, also funded a scholarly position to augment the exhibition team. Thanks to the generosity of lending institutions and individuals, we are able to exhibit numerous outstanding objects from Germany and abroad—many of them being shown in Nuremberg for the first time. We wish to express our deep gratitude to all the individuals and institutions listed below. Some deserve special mention: the Staatliche Kunstsammlungen Dresden, represented by Director General Bernd Ebert, made available from the Green Vault the spectacular lavabo set by the Nuremberg goldsmith Nicolaus Schmidt, which features a mother-of-pearl basin made in Gujarat. That lavabo set serves as the introductory work in the exhibition. During a visit to the Österreichische Nationalbibliothek in Vienna, members of the exhibition team had the privilege of holding in their hands the spectacular impression of the woodcut map of Tenochtitlán from the collection of Archduke Ferdinand, a work that was printed in Nuremberg in 1524 and magnificently hand-colored with ultramarine. We owe a great debt of gratitude to Director General Johanna Rachinger and her team for allowing us to present that object in the exhibition. Fascinating evidence of the early reception of Albrecht Dürer and other Nuremberg artists in southern Asia is provided by the motifs borrowed from Dürer on a Sinhalese ivory casket from a private collection and on three leaves from the Jahangir Album in the Staatsbibliothek zu Berlin, Preußischer Kulturbesitz. The famous herbal by Georg Öllinger, from the library of the Friedrich Alexander University of Erlangen and Nuremberg, illustrates how rapidly knowledge of "New World" plants reached Nuremberg. Noteworthy loans came not only from abroad—from Madrid, Siena, Warsaw, and Vienna—but also from the local family foundations that attend to the heritage of the old patriciate: the Alt-Conrad v. Imhoff'sche Familienstiftung; the Stromer'sche Kulturgut-, Denkmal- und Naturstiftung; and the Tucher Kulturstiftung. The exhibition brings into focus not least the importance of the holdings at the Germanisches Nationalmuseum, which houses artifacts of the highest order representing the global horizons of late-medieval and early modern Nuremberg. The numerous objects on long-term loan from the collections of Nuremberg's municipal museums (Museen der Stadt Nürnberg) play a crucial role in this.

Wherever we spoke about our concept for the project, we encountered great interest and active support. In this foreword, it is impossible to acknowledge all our colleagues at universities, museums, and libraries who have supported the project with advice and practical assistance. The catalogue's authors merit special mention. An important aspect of this project was the collaboration with non-European colleagues, some of whom we were able to obtain as authors. These include Elgidius E. B. Ichumbaki, who has long been studying the ruins of the trading city of Kilwa Kisiwani, off the coast of Tanzania, and Dominicus Z. Makukula, both of the University of Dar es Salaam. Their essay makes clear that, in the early sixteenth century, the once flourishing Kilwa Kisiwani was raided and plundered during a Portuguese expedition to India that was backed, in part, by investors from Nuremberg. Today, the remains of the city form part of the UNESCO World Heritage Site "Ruins of Kilwa Kisiwani and Ruins of Songo Mnara." In an essay devoted to a single object, Daniel Astorga-Poblete, from the University of La Serena in Chile, examines the aforementioned hand-colored impression of the map of Tenochtitlán that was intended for Archduke Ferdinand, and he arrives at entirely new perspectives about this object.

Sincere thanks go to all the guest authors and everyone who contributed to this project's success. A special debt of gratitude and recognition is owed to the exhibition team itself, which developed the concept and identified fascinating objects under the leadership of Benno Baumbauer, Curator of Painting before 1800 and Stained Glass, together with the exhibition's co-curator, Sven Jakstat. When, in January 2025, Sven Jakstat departed Nuremberg for the Gemäldegalerie in Berlin (where he assumed curatorial responsibility for Italian and Spanish painting of the sixteenth and seventeenth centuries and French painting of the seventeenth century), the position he left vacant was taken over by Marie-Therese Feist. Thanks to her relevant experience, she was able to ensure that preparations continued seamlessly into the next, highly accelerated phase of the project. Laura Di Carlo, a curatorial trainee, played an active role throughout the entire project. Exhibition registrar Arabelle Herkner as well as Barbara Rök, Birgit Schübel, and Sabine Tiedtke supported the team. The project required a great deal of effort from numerous other departments of the Germanisches Nationalmuseum: the logistics of presenting difficult-to-transport and fragile objects—for example, the sepulchral tapestry of the Holzschuher family, the 1520 Schöner Globe, and Albrecht Dürer's *Kaiserbilder* (the globe and imperial portraits on long-term loan from the Museen der Stadt Nürnberg)—posed special challenges to all the departments and curatorial areas involved. We wish to express deep thanks to all our colleagues who, in addition to carrying out demanding tasks related to the museum's ambitious renovation projects, have also supported *GLOBAL Nuremberg* with exceptional commitment; all of them are named in the list of contributors found on this volume's copyright page.

The exhibition design was the work of Bach Dolder GmbH in Darmstadt (particularly Michiko Bach and Lilly Lieske). Graphic design was carried out by the firm Design Practice, Darmstadt (especially Charalampos Lazos and Maximilian Walter), which also devised a visual solution for displaying critical commentary on topics such as antisemitism, the slave trade, and colonial activities. We owe the banner and poster motif of rotating rhinoceroses and the advertising graphics to the communication agency BOROS in Berlin, which always engages afresh with our wishes and expectations, supporting every project in creative ways. Martina Kupiak, Ilka Backmeister-Collacott, and Edgar Endl made it possible for this catalogue to be published in collaboration with the Deutscher Kunstverlag, in both German and English. For the translations, we wish to thank Joshua Waterman (German to English) as well as Eva Dewes and Martin Baumeister (English to German), and for the English copyediting, Dawn Michelle d'Atri.

In times of increasing polarization and intransigence, it is our hope that this project will help point the way forward for mutually respectful dialogue that broadens our understanding of an often fragmentary, contradictory, and conflict-laden past.

Daniel Hess
Generaldirektor

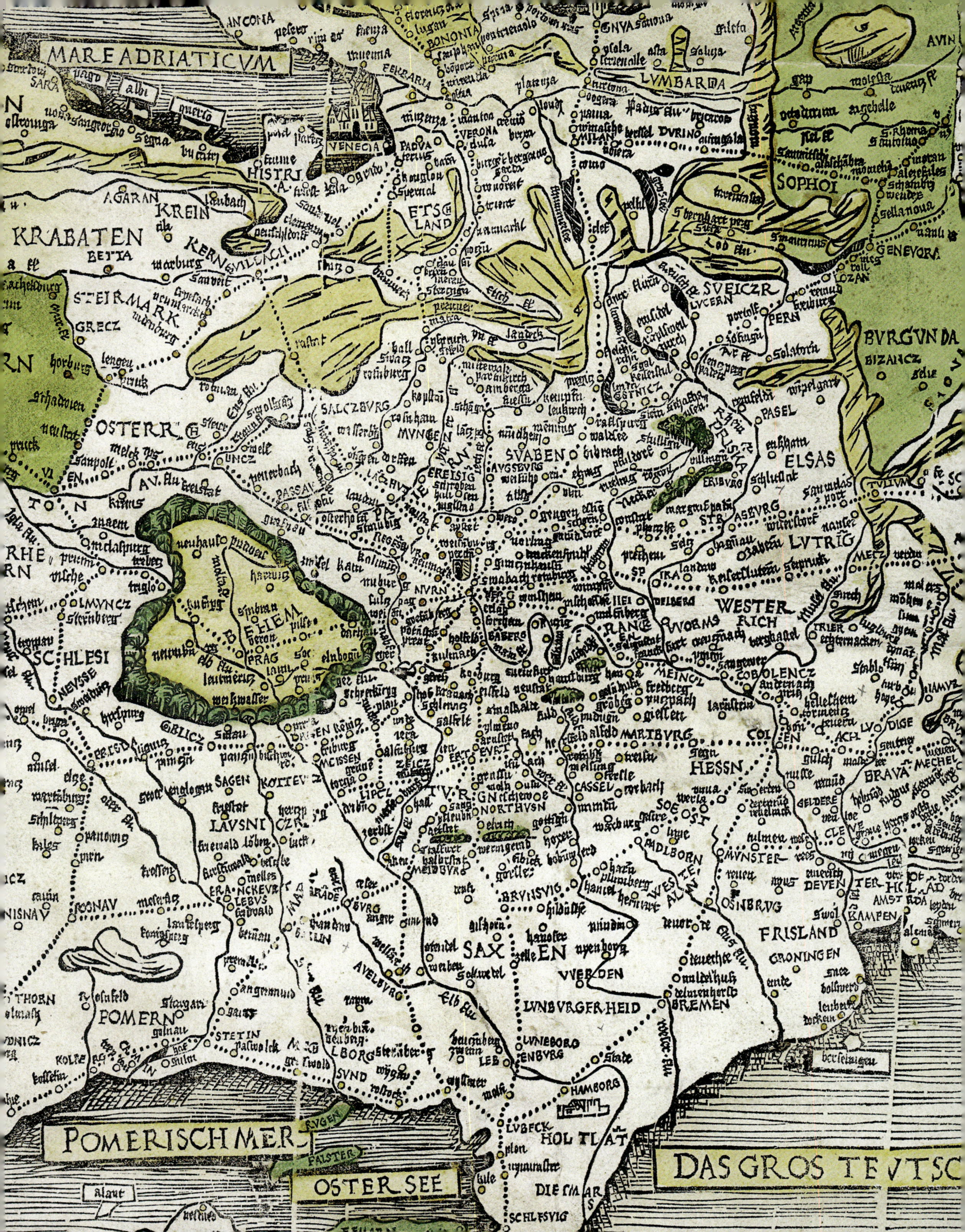

MARE ADRIATICVM
VENECIA
LVMBARDA
KRABATEN
KREIN
STEIRMARK
GRECZ
OSTERR
SALCZBVRG
BEHEM
PRAG
SCHLESI
LAVSNI
POMERN
SAX EN
BRVNSVIG
LVNBVRGER HEID
HAMBORG
LVBECK
SCHLESVIG
BREMEN
FRISLAND
GRONINGEN
HESSN
WESTER RICH
ELSAS
PASEL
BVRGVNDA
BIZANCZ
SOPHOI
GENEVORA
SVEICZR
LVCERN
SVABEN
AVGSBVRG
NVRN
MARTBVRG
COBOLENCZ
ERFFVRT
CASSEL
VVORMS
HOLTLAT
DIETMAR
POMERISCH MER
RVGEN
FALSTER
OSTER SEE
DAS GROS TEVTSC

LENDERS

Many thanks to our lenders

Berlin, Staatliche Museen zu Berlin, Kupferstichkabinett

Berlin, Staatsbibliothek zu Berlin, Preußischer Kulturbesitz

Coburg, Kunstsammlungen der Veste Coburg

Dresden, Staatliche Kunstsammlungen Dresden, Grünes Gewölbe

Erlangen, Universitätsbibliothek der FAU Erlangen-Nürnberg

Gotha, Stiftung Schloss Friedenstein Gotha

Madrid, Museo Nacional del Prado

Madrid, Museo Nacional Thyssen Bornemisza

Munich, Bayerisches Nationalmuseum

Munich, Bayerische Staatsbibliothek

Munich, Universitätsbibliothek der LMU München

Nuremberg, Alt-Conrad v. Imhoff'sche Familienstiftung

Nuremberg, Museen der Stadt Nürnberg, Albrecht-Dürer-Haus

Nuremberg, Museen der Stadt Nürnberg, Kunstsammlungen

Nuremberg, Museen der Stadt Nürnberg, Museum Tucherschloss und Hirsvogelsaal

Nuremberg, Stadtbibliothek im Bildungscampus Nürnberg

Nuremberg, Tucher Kulturstiftung

Private Collection

Siena, Banca Monte dei Paschi di Siena

Stromer'sche Kulturgut-, Denkmal- und Naturstiftung

Vienna, Albertina

Vienna, Österreichische Nationalbibliothe

Warsaw, Muzeum Narodowe w Warszawie / National Museum in Warsaw

Warsaw, Muzeum Wojska Polskiegok

Wolfenbüttel, Herzog August Bibliothek Wolfenbüttel

◂ cat. no. 25.2 (detail)

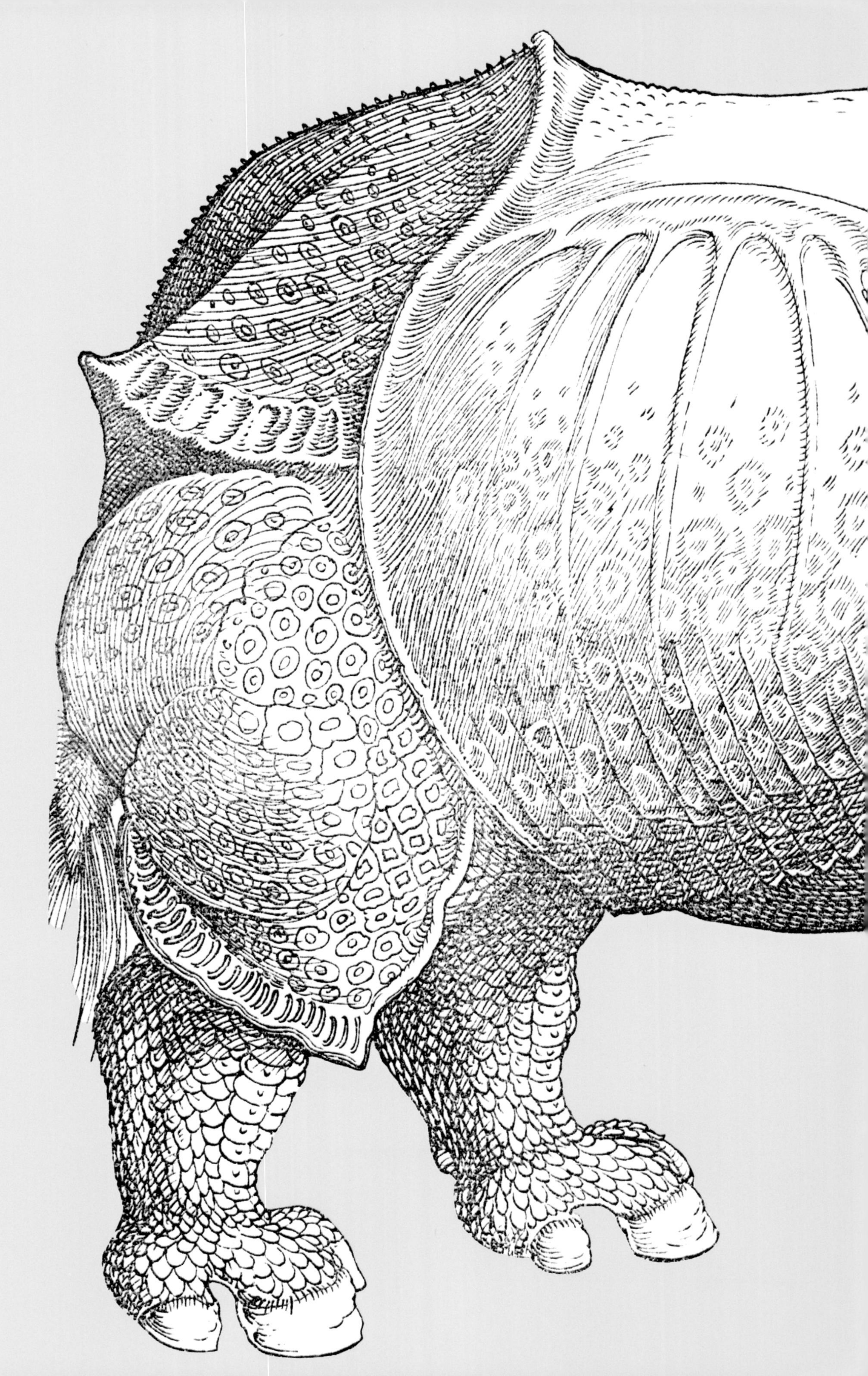

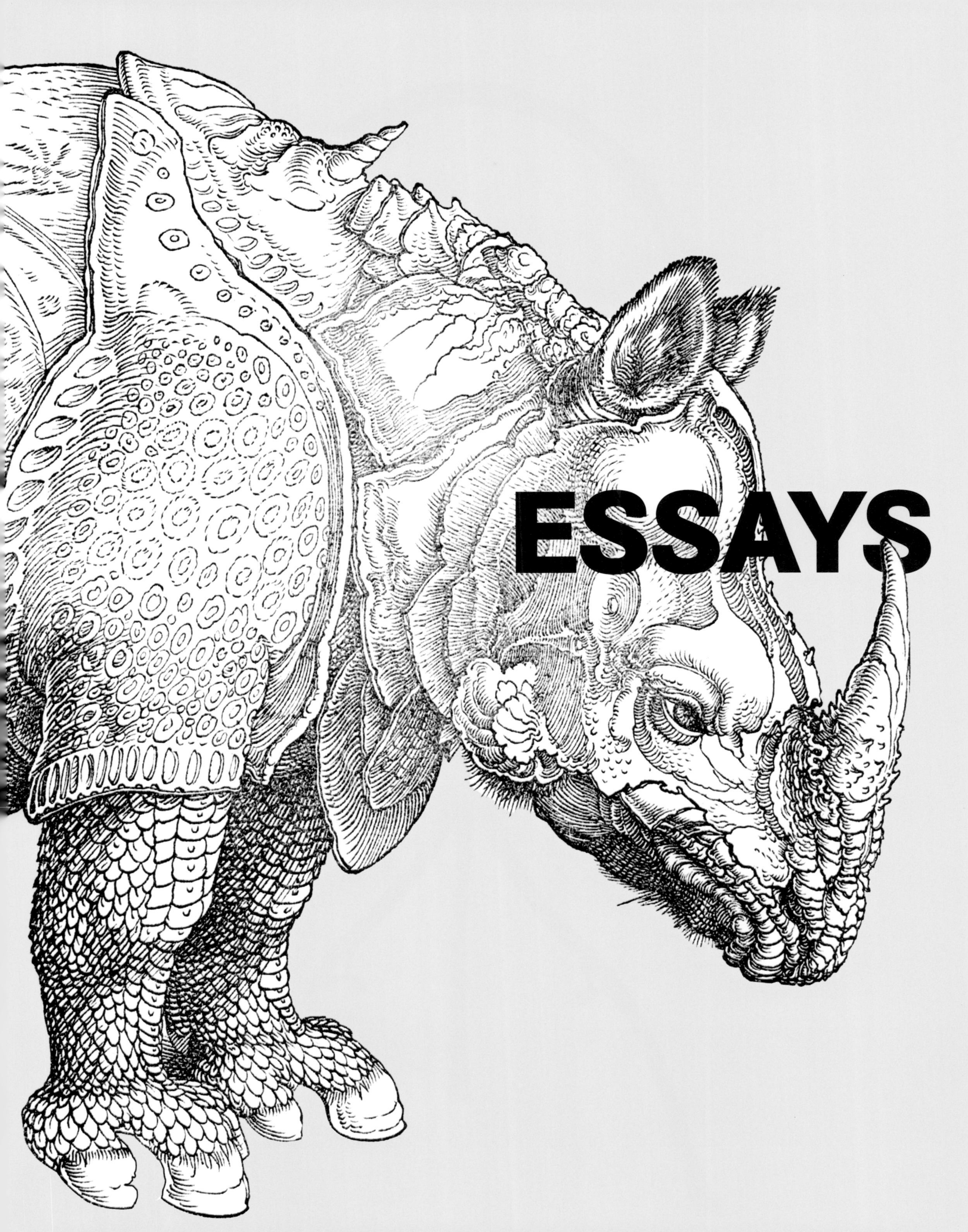

ESSAYS

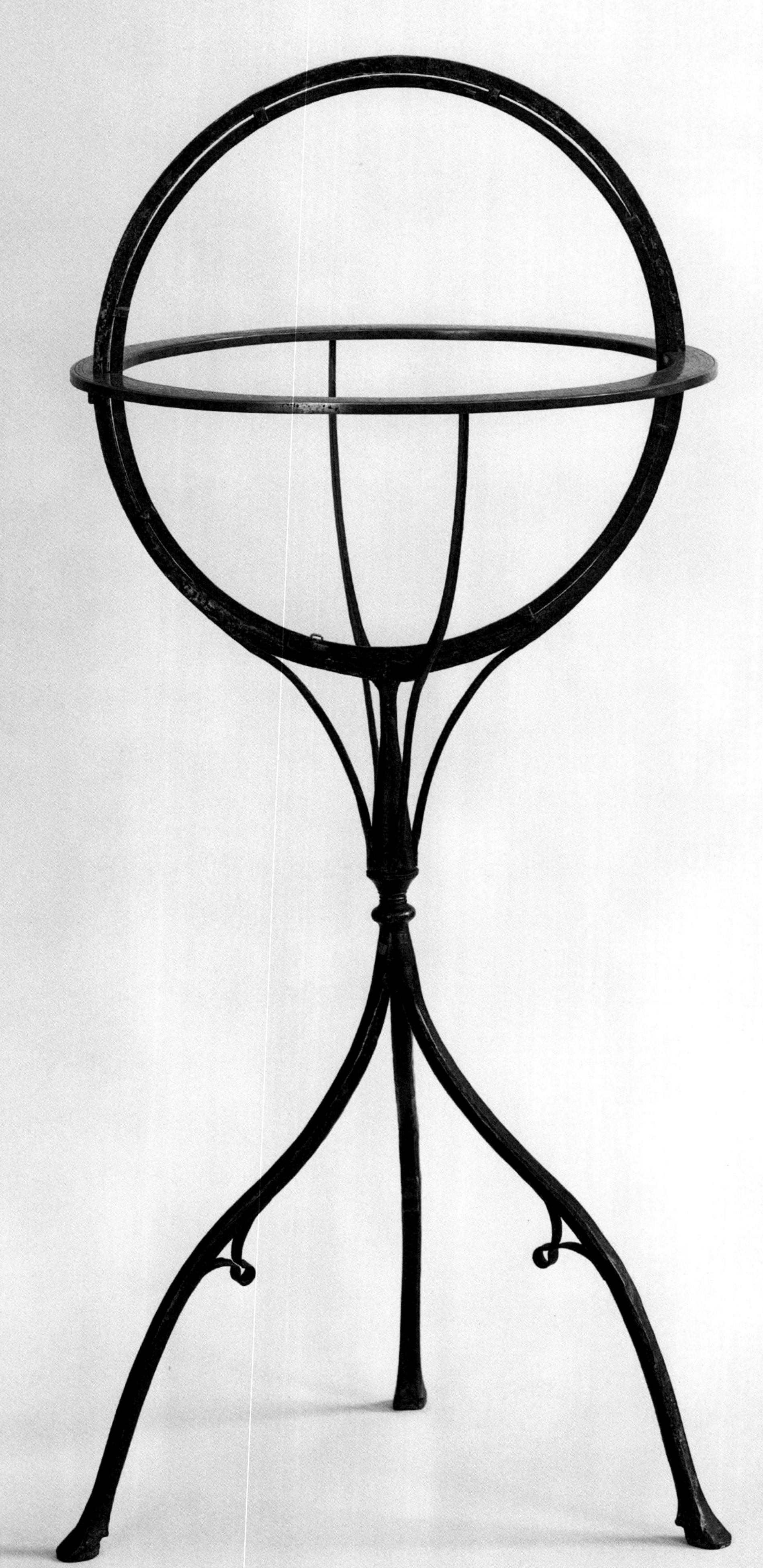

Daniel Hess

THE WORLD IN EXPERIENCE AND CONCEPTION, CIRCA 1500: COORDINATES FOR AN UNDERSTANDING

Fig. 1 Stand of the Behaim Globe, Nuremberg, 1492–94 and 1510, GNM, inv. no. WI 1826 | **cat. no. 1** |

Even a quick glance through the histories of the early modern period recently published in Germany suffices to reveal the complexities and challenges of the present research and exhibition project, "GLOBAL Nuremberg, 1300–1600." This essay places the exhibition in a broader context—first, by offering insight into the controversial discourses surrounding the study of global history, and second, by identifying coordinates that make it possible to navigate one's way, in a historically informed fashion, through images and conceptions of the world from half a millennium in the past. Every view of the world is shaped by one's own location and knowledge, and since no means of comprehending the world exists without presupposition, there is a constant need to clarify the conditions required for sound scholarship. Since no direct and clear path leads from Europe's expansion into the wider world around 1500 to the consolidation of colonial empires in the nineteenth century, there is likewise no such path leading back. Despite certain structural continuities and persistent stereotypes, the coordinate systems are too different to be transferred either one way or the other. At most, only Portugal and Spain can be described as world empires around 1500, having divided the Atlantic sphere between themselves after the Treaty of Tordesillas in 1494. However, their ventures were also intertwined with the struggles for expansion and domination undertaken by other territorial princes, such as Sultan Selim I in the Ottoman Empire. Despite common features and interdependencies, the mercantile systems of Portugal and Spain, which also involved Nurembergers, were fundamentally different: while Portugal developed a worldwide maritime network of port cities and fortified trading posts, Spain, in pursuit of royal interests in Central America, established a colonial system based on land seizure, resource extraction, and forced labor, which remained in existence as the Viceroyalty of New Spain until the early nineteenth century.[1]

Current Global Histories, Controversial Discourses

Recent global histories of Europe place initial emphasis on the territorial expansion that characterized Europe's actions in the world. As Wolfgang Reinhard underscores in his four-volume *Globalgeschichte der europäischen Expansion, 1415–2015* (Global History of European Expansion), published between 1983 and 1990 and reissued in a revised edition in 2016,[2] Europe has always been expansionist, and expansion necessarily involves violence—violence that took on global dimensions with the first voyage of Columbus. Cooperation and physical violence are the leitmotifs of Reinhard's narrative, which spans six centuries and seven continents. In 2023, under the rubric of a "great emergence" (*Der große Aufbruch*), Wolfgang Behringer analyzes the increasing contacts and conflicts that occurred among the world's civilizations with the rise of globalization in the early modern period.[3] Behringer's global history is devoted not only to Europe but also to the spread of other empires and civilizations that interacted on a global scale, such as China and the Ottomans. In a 2024 book on Europe, Peter Sloterdijk introduces, via Goethe, the concept of *Ausdehnung* (expansion) as a way of understanding the "long second millennium" that began with Columbus's voyage.[4] In his view, this expansion was accompanied by power-hungry aggression and greed. Consistent with the *Plus Ultra* (More Beyond) motto of Emperor Charles V, European aspirations extended across all borders and, with Ignatius of Loyola, became imbued with a mandate to perform global missionary work. With that in mind, Sloterdijk in 2001 characterized the modern era as the "age of man-made monstrosity."[5] In a central figure such as Columbus, the pursuit of Christian geographical utopias—for example, the idea of discovering paradise on earth—combined with the quest for treasures that lay not vertically within the earth but instead

1 For an overview, see Flores 2015, pp. 271–96; Behringer 2023, pp. 265–92.
2 Reinhard 2018.
3 Behringer 2023.
4 Sloterdijk 2024. On the concept of "Ausdehnung," see esp. p. 205.
5 Sloterdijk 2001, p. 367 ("Weltalter des menschengemachten Ungeheuren").

at great horizontal distances. In 1959, the philosopher Ernst Bloch likened this to a "horizontal mining for treasure," in which the "digging took place first westward and then eastward, until the discovery of the earth's spherical form made the direction irrelevant,"[6] although it should be noted that the spherical shape of the planet had been known since ancient times.

The enterprise of collecting and trading luxury goods led to war, plunder, destruction, and subjugation. For Serge Gruzinski, therefore, excess and a thirst for power are the leitmotifs of the European globalization that was facilitated by Portuguese and Spanish seafarers. With his book *The Eagle and the Dragon*, originally published in French in 2012, he sought to free historiography from its fixation on national, colonial, and imperial perspectives, as they run counter to any global approach.[7] Gruzinski therefore takes the perspective of the conquered, attempting to relate a history that is as close as possible to the relevant sources from the standpoint of Asia and Latin America. The aim is to overcome the polarization between the victors and the vanquished in order to better understand the complex process of globalization. A major obstacle to this approach was the European monopoly on shaping historical narratives, coupled with a general lack of correctives from the perspective of the "Other," since, after all, history is written by the victors. Therefore, according to Gruzinski, the challenge posed by a non-Eurocentric historiography lies not only in the incomplete record and the one-sided sources, but also in the danger of fusing the different perspectives into a conclusive, teleological overall narrative. This would make global history merely "another variant of Western history."[8] On the other hand, as early as the 1980s, within the new framework of "Subaltern Studies," a group of South Asian scholars, including Gayatri Chakravorty Spivak, Homi K. Bhabha, and Dipesh Chakrabarty, had formed to disrupt the discourses of power and domination ingrained in European historiography about the former colonies. In engagement with Marxist and post-structuralist approaches, the aim was to establish alternative postcolonial theories.[9] In his recent global history of Africa, *Born in Blackness*, published in 2021, Howard W. French calls for a reassessment of that continent's role in the process of globalization. He draws attention to the exploitation and enslavement of Black civilizations, and he highlights the key contribution that Africa made to the economic upswing of the Western world ever since the fifteenth century. For French, the sustained and fundamental omission of Africa is evidence of a "centuries-long process of diminishment, trivialization, and erasure of Africans and of people of African descent from the story of the modern world."[10]

In 2023, Monica Juneja explored the artistic domain that lies beyond grand global narratives and territorial fixations, using transcultural processes of exchange to develop alternatives to the prevailing nationally and culturally determined histories.[11] In the present volume, she illustrates this transculturalism using an example of the global reception of Albrecht Dürer's pictorial inventions. The effects of artistic inspiration and artistic exchange always reach beyond the systems of power in which they are embedded. Art thus cannot be reduced to its role of representing and stabilizing colonial power. Viktoria Schmidt-Linsenhoff argues for a nuanced view in her two-volume *Ästhetik der Differenz* (Aesthetics of Difference) of 2010, in which she offers a history of the European conception of the "Other." In fifteen case studies of various visual media from the sixteenth to the twentieth century, she attempts "to correct the tendency toward broad generalizations characteristic of postcolonial and gender studies and to differentiate such sweeping categories as man and woman, white and black, Orient and Occident, and the Self and the Other by drawing attention to the potentially infinite diversity found in concrete examples."[12] The notion of the Other had existed in

6 Translated from the German in Bloch 1959, vol. 5, p. 884.
7 Gruzinski 2014, p. 299.
8 Translated after the German edition, Gruzinski 2014, p. 80.
9 For a summary, see Chakrabarty 2010, pp. 19–40.
10 French 2021, p. 3.
11 Juneja 2023.
12 Translated from the German in Schmidt-Linsenhoff 2010, vol. 1, p. 15.

Europe as a pejorative and exclusionary concept ever since the Middle Ages. In the sixteenth century, it profoundly influenced views of the newly encountered continents. As Oliver Eberl made clear in 2021, recourse to the medieval catalogue of human oddities and to the mythical figures of the Wild Man and Wild Woman played a key role in this.[13] Intercultural tolerance of the kind expressed by Montaigne in 1580 remained the exception.

With regard to the European capacity for self-criticism, what some still regard as insufficient in all these discourses, reconciliations, and dissensions has for others become too much. Therefore, in addition to tolerance and openness, the ability to critically examine different perspectives and interpretations, especially concerning one's own history and its dark sides, will continue to play an important role in ongoing discussions.

Perceptions of the Self and the Other, circa 1500

Against the backdrop of these controversial debates, our exhibition examines aspects of globalization from the perspective of Nuremberg in the period between 1300 to 1600. Here it must be noted that the collective identity categories that dominated colonial history in the nineteenth century, such as "race" and "nation" (or *Volk* in German), were hardly a factor around 1500. The context of the early period is fundamentally different, as are the genres of texts and images, the historical narratives and constructs, and the personages involved. And even though the source materials available for Nuremberg, compared with the situation both elsewhere in Europe and globally, are particularly promising, the historical texts nevertheless present considerable difficulties of interpretation, since they seamlessly merge world experience with imagination of the world, blending empirical knowledge with literary and artistic fantasy.

Around 1500, Nuremberg was not only one of the most important globally active cities in the German-speaking lands; it was also an extraordinary knowledge center. However, the city was in constant competition, primarily with Augsburg but soon also with such "global players" as Venice and Antwerp—and finally, after the so-called Atlantic turn, with Lisbon and Seville. This affected the new literary medium of city descriptions and encomiums. The genre promoted civic self-assurance and self-representation in a time of intense competition over the display of status, driven by the Habsburg imperial family. Many such texts were produced in Nuremberg around 1500.[14] In addition to city chronicles, the genealogical and memoranda books of leading families (such as the Stromers, Tuchers, Muffels, and Paumgartners) played an important role. The city's identity was therefore not only articulated in town hall furnishings and other collective forms of display; it also found clear expression in the donations to various churches and monasteries made by urban elites, other leading figures, and family associations. Governance, representation, and ennoblement depended on individual office holders and their families. The private and the official were inextricably linked.

In the interest of reviving the classical panegyric tradition, the period's historical sources expressed many literary clichés. They therefore only partially reflect the realities of urban life. Nevertheless, beginning about 1500, authors increasingly endeavored to provide empirical examination and description, as is apparent in such literary works as the *Norimberga* by the humanist Conrad Celtis and in pictorial city views that display ever greater authenticity and realism |**cat. nos. 4, 53, 67**|. Those pictorial representations also served the purpose of civic praise, as did the ambitious projects that produced the Behaim Globe, about 1492–94 |**cat. no. 1**|, and Hartmann Schedel's *Nuremberg Chronicle*, published in 1493 |**cat. no. 4**|. Both the globe and the chronicle use innovative media to

13 Eberl 2021. On European perceptions and imagery of the Indigenous peoples of the Americas, see esp. pp. 112–67.
14 See Meyer 2009.

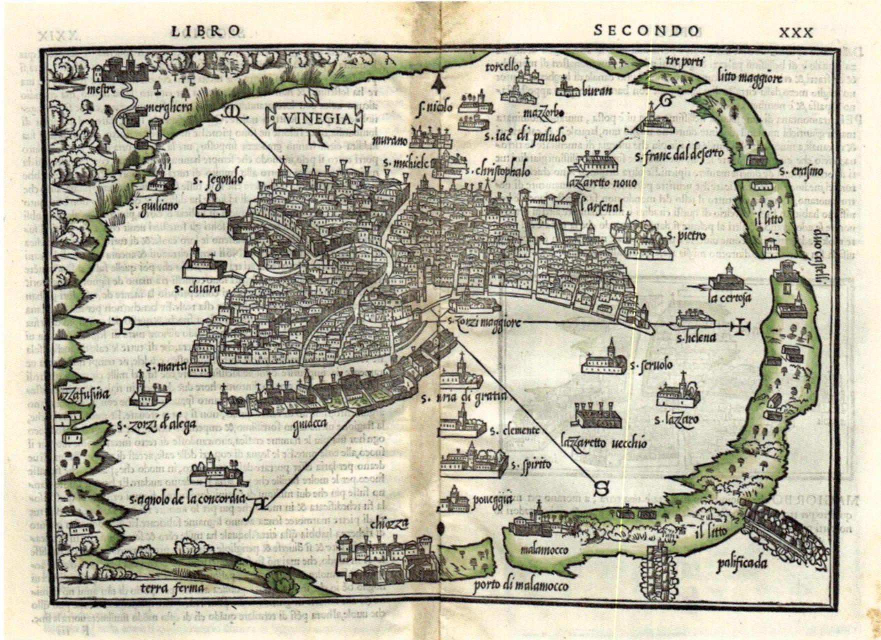

Fig. 2 View of Venice, from Benedetto Bordone, *Isolario*, Venice: Nicolò d'Aristotele, 1528, Universitätsbibliothek Erlangen-Nürnberg, Erlangen, shelf mark H61/2 TREW.F 11 |**cat. no. 106.2**|, fols. 29v, 30r

address the period's geographical and topographical interests. The persons involved were highly educated, greatly respected humanists with broad European networks. Some of them held important municipal offices and had considerable financial resources at their disposal. Their knowledge was obtained from libraries that were unrivaled in the German-speaking sphere, including the one assembled by Schedel. The aim of Schedel's chronicle was to provide a comprehensive description of the origin and nature of the earth. Encyclopedic in its ambitions, the book combines classical and biblical materials with knowledge gained from the new science of geography and *Länderkunde* (regional geography). The chronicle's city views convey historical significance and topographical features as vividly and accurately as possible, to the extent that such information was available. Beyond that, perception was determined by what seemed plausible and what could be meaningfully compared with the realm of experience. Nineteenth-century concepts of truthfulness and objectivity therefore hardly do justice to the humanists' studies in regional geography, as illustrated not only by Schedel's *Nuremberg Chronicle* but also by Conrad Celtis's *Germania illustrata*. With that literary work, the latter sought to elevate the German-speaking area to the status of a cultural landscape for a number of reasons: to be able to describe it in the context of a cosmological-geographical didactic poem, to differentiate it from Italy, and to put it on an equal footing with classical and Italian culture.

Geographico-historical knowledge of the world reached a point of culmination in Nuremberg around 1500, as illustrated by the example of the first schoolbook on geography, written by Johannes Cochlaeus and published in 1512. Cochlaeus, rector of the Latin school by the Lorenzkirche, addressed his *Brevis Germaniae Descriptio* to his students, emphasizing that an understanding of history and mythology was impossible without geography. As book knowledge, literary geography determined and also limited perception of the world at a time when highly dynamic changes were taking place.[15] Anything new was elucidated through analogy, duplication, and mirroring of the known. This subjected empirical knowledge to constant comparison with the traditions of classical and biblical literature, easily leading to confusion and misattribution. Even Columbus's scope of vision was limited to what he knew from books. Like all of his contemporaries, he underestimated Earth's circumference on the authority of ancient authors and, at the same time, overestimated the eastern extent of Asia based on Marco Polo's accounts.[16] As a result, Cuba was considered an extension of Asia until the 1560s, and the Americas were regarded as the easternmost part of the "Orient." Tenochtitlán, the Aztec capital conquered and destroyed by Hernán Cortés in 1521, was identified as the magnificent Chinese city of Quinsai known from the rapturous description by Marco Polo. This elevated Tenochtitlán to the status of an ideal city in the European imagination.[17] In the first printed pictorial representation of the city, which appeared in 1524 in Nuremberg, along with a Latin translation of the letters of Cortés, many of the topographical elements reflect the equation of Tenochtitlán with Quinsai |**cat. no. 105**|.[18] In the map's Venetian second edition, printed in 1528, the Aztec capital shows conspicuous topographical and infrastructural parallels to maps of Venice |**fig. 2**|. According

15 See Piechocki 2019.
16 Reichert 1988, p. 22.
17 Reichert 1988, p. 53.
18 Reichert 1988, pp. 54–55.

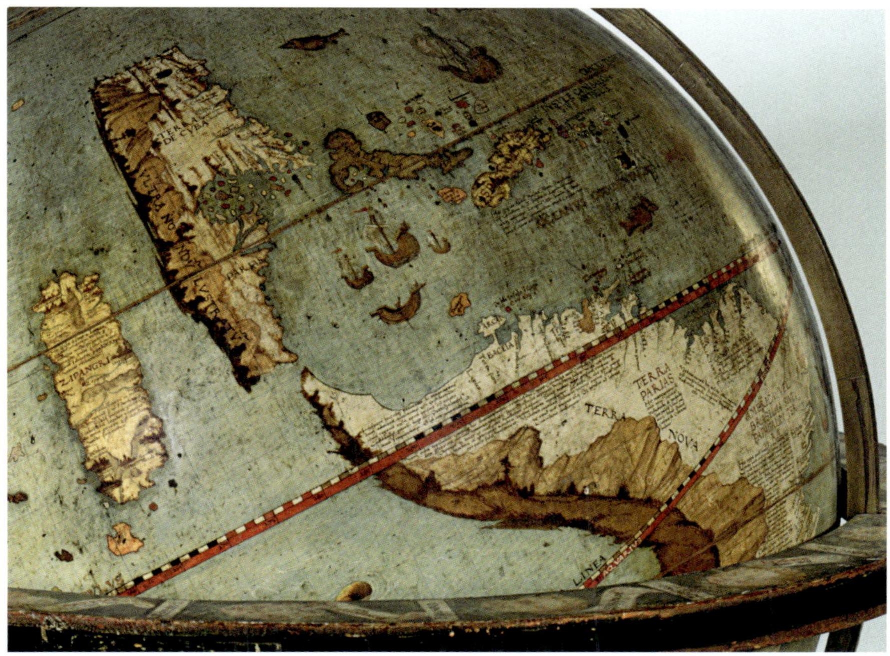

Fig. 3 Terra Nova, Zipangri, and Terra de Cvba on the Nuremberg Schöner Globe, Bamberg, 1520, GNM, inv. no. WI1, on long-term loan from the Museen der Stadt Nürnberg, Kunstsammlungen |**cat. no. 6**|

to David Y. Kim, Tenochtitlán thus became a "dialectical mirror" that reflected both the venerable past and ambivalent future of Venice, which had lost much of its former economic leadership as a result of Portuguese and Spanish seafaring.[19]

Despite all the analogizing and the anchoring of new discoveries in the tradition of book learning, doubts remained, coupled with an awareness of the limitations of one's own knowledge. For example, the Nuremberg astronomer and globe maker Johannes Schöner admitted on his Nuremberg globe of 1520 |**cat. no. 6**|, in an inscription along the east coast of "Cuba" (North America), which is shown adjacent to "Zipangri" (Japan), that he was unable to depict anything more of the land's eastern extent ("ULTRA NONDUM I(L)LUSTRATUM")[20]—a commendable way of mapping fragile knowledge |**fig. 3**|.

For his globe project, Martin Behaim had brought first-hand knowledge to Nuremberg, which explains why he was able to reproduce the western coast of Africa quite reliably. But this knowledge proved inadequate to the task of correctly locating Africa's southern tip, which Bartolomeu Dias had circumnavigated in 1487 |**cat. no. 1**|. Behaim, who placed the southern extremity at Cape Cross in Namibia, was apparently unaware of the geographical knowledge held by Henricus Martellus Germanus, a German cartographer who was active in Florence. About 1490, Martellus drew a world map that was remarkably similar to Behaim's globe but included the entire southern tip of Africa with the "Cap de bona Speranza."

The circumnavigation of the Cape of Good Hope marked a decisive step in the entrenchment of Portuguese maritime trade: what had begun in 1415 in Ceuta, Morocco, under Prince Henry the Navigator led to the sustained conquest and military occupation of the western coast of Africa. Gold, pepper, and ivory were brought home through a long chain of Portuguese trading posts, and the lucrative business model of sugar cultivation and slave trading was developed on offshore islands.[21] First tested in the Gulf of Guinea, the sugar plantation system and slave trade were transferred to Brazil in the 1530s. This capital-intensive business also involved Germans, both as investors and administrators.[22] With their voyages to India, the Portuguese gradually established a dense succession of ports—strategically located but under constant threat—stretching from the eastern coast of Africa to India and on to the Malaysian city of Malacca, the most important hub of the international spice trade. Finally, in 1557, they extended their reach to Macau in China, thus gaining control of trade with East Asia.[23] The merchant families of Nuremberg also benefited from this. Ultimately, however, the far-flung East Asian trading network, which involved numerous players and was under constant renegotiation, proved as unsuccessful for Portugal as did Central America for the Spanish. In the seventeenth century, the Portuguese ceded their rule to the Dutch East India Company. With regard to Spain, the flow of silver from Potosí—set in motion by German mining techniques and technical innovations—forever altered the global economy. It ended the silver shortage in China and halted the need for the inflationary paper money that had been introduced there as a substitute currency. This revolutionized trade within Asia. Spain, however, became hopelessly indebted and declared state bankruptcy in 1557.[24]

19 Kim 2006.
20 The "I" is not clearly legible. An alternative reading might be: "ULTRA NONDUM LUSTRATUM" (no further measurements have yet been taken).
21 For a summary, see Coquery-Vidrovitch and Mesnard 2019, esp. pp. 63–80. See also Hess 2022, pp. 46–48.
22 Blackbourn 2024, pp. 53–54.
23 See Subrahmanyam 2013.
24 See Behringer 2023, pp. 50–55; Blackbourn 2024, pp. 62–63.

In the process of giving an account of the world, early modern global and regional geography always reveals the positionality of the narrator and his community. The same holds true for contemporary travelogues, which became bestsellers from the late medieval period onward and helped to shape the European worldview beyond the contribution made by Columbus |**cat. nos. 68, 81–83, 93, 116**|. The most important ones were (and remain) Marco Polo's *Il Milione*, from the late thirteenth century, and the *Travels of Sir John Mandeville*, written about a hundred years later and subsequently exposed as a fiction. The travelogues written and published in connection with Jerusalem pilgrimages and trade expeditions also interweave personal observations with hearsay, topoi, and stereotypes, and the accompanying illustrations are often likewise of questionable authenticity. The era's characteristically fluid transitions between empirical observation and acquired knowledge manifest in such travelogues, particularly with regard to social relationships and personal networks. For example, Columbus's reports turn a blind eye to the many doubts and perplexities associated with the regions he encountered. They also served the expectations of his patrons, whose unfulfilled hopes for the discovery of urban centers and spices Columbus attempted to compensate with gold and slaves.[25]

Conceptions of the world and knowledge of the world were mutually contingent, and here, too, the boundaries blur between empirical and literary knowledge, between documentation and fantasy. Dürer's famous rhinoceros is illustrative of this |**cat. no. 119**|, as is the travelogue written by Hieronymus Köler the Elder |**cat. no. 110**|, which makes detours into the realm of fiction. Another first-person report is that of Balthasar Springer, who accompanied two ships financed by Augsburg and Nuremberg merchant families (the Fuggers, Welsers, Hochstetters, Gossembrots, Hirschvogels, and Imhoffs) as part of Portugal's seventh and largest India armada |**cat. no. 116**|.[26] The widely read report was published in 1509 with woodcut illustrations by the Nuremberg artist Wolf Traut, based on models by Hans Burgkmair. The report's portrayals of peoples from the western and eastern coasts of Africa and from South Asia put foreignness on display |**fig. 4**|. In these popular illustrations, which were printed in large runs, Burgkmair combined knowledge from reports and other first-hand sources with motifs borrowed from the late medieval pictorial tradition of "Wild People" |**cat. nos. 116, 117**|, thereby contributing to a consolidation of the European sense of superiority.

Apart from disseminating geographical knowledge and telling gripping stories, travelogues also belong to a new narrative form that emerged in the early modern period: the life story.[27] These biographical texts are an expression of a developing awareness of individual identity and of each author's self-placement in the world. Yet they remain fundamentally enmeshed in the Christian concept of a life confession, which traces back to Saint Augustine. With education and experience in the world, one could carve out a career; it was therefore essential that success and social advancement be documented and made public in representative fashion through autobiographical writing. The individuals who wrote about themselves and the world pursued general strategies of portrayal whose narrative patterns differed according to professional group and career path (scholars, merchants, artists). But amongst their compelling stories, one always encounters claims to social prestige as a shared motif.

Global Nuremberg: Gaps and Differences in a Networked World

Regardless of how incomplete, one-sided, and constructed the written sources prove to be, the situation with objects of material culture is by no

25 Reichert 1988, pp. 28–30, 37–38, 43–44.
26 See the essay by Elgidius E. B. Ichumbaki and Dominicus Z. Makukula in the present volume.
27 See Enenkel and Zittel 2013.

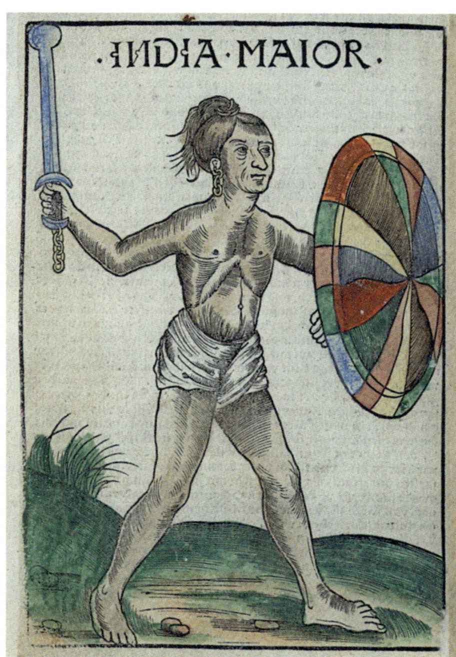

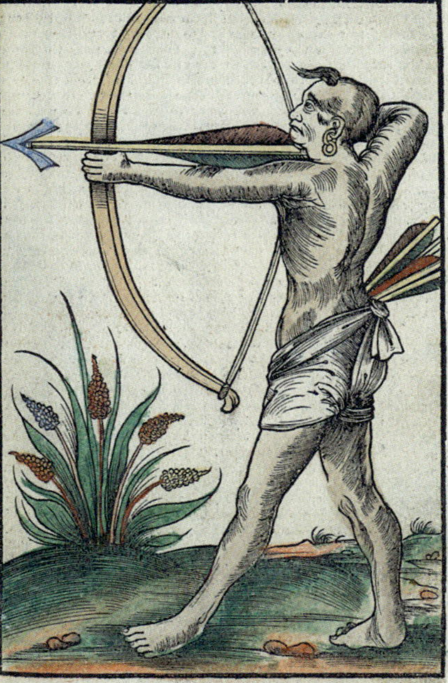

Fig. 4 Attributed to Wolf Traut, People in "India Maior," from Balthasar Springer, *Die Merfart*, Oppenheim: Jakob Köbel, 1509, Bayerische Staatsbibliothek, Munich, shelf mark Rar. 470 |**cat. no. 116**|, fols. 14r, 15v

means better. For example, the mining entrepreneur Hans Tetzel played a leading role in Cuban copper mining before his death in Madrid in 1571; nevertheless, the only surviving object associated with him is a Totenschild (memorial shield) created as part of the Tetzel family's burial site in Nuremberg's Egidienkirche |**cat. no. 108**|. Because the success of an exhibition project hinges on the availability of material evidence relevant to the subject, the many gaps in the corpus of surviving objects are particularly painful. How we would relish showing pieces of the Aztec treasure that Dürer admired in Brussels in 1521![28] At any rate, we can assume that some examples of Aztec art arrived in Nuremberg three years later: it was in Nuremberg, in 1524, that the latest curiosities shipped from the Americas are said to have been handed over to Archduke Ferdinand. That 1524 delivery apparently also contained the model for the famous map of Tenochtitlán, which was then printed as a woodcut in Nuremberg and distributed throughout Europe.[29]

Given the manifold ways in which local and global events and actions are interconnected, the task of studying the cultural history of Nuremberg around 1500 is not merely local or regional in nature. Inquiry into Nuremberg's past inevitably leads to an engagement with the complex and controversial discourses surrounding global history. It is important, therefore, to broaden and deepen our perspective, to overcome monodisciplinary approaches and linear conceptions of development, and to cultivate both a critical awareness of history and a capacity for judgment informed by historical scholarship—particularly in these times of increasing polarization. The world's oldest surviving globe was created in Nuremberg, and together with many other works of global cartography, it clearly shows the extent to which a person's view of the world was (and still is) shaped by their own location and scope of knowledge.[30] One thing to be learned from the history of cartography is that there is no single (correct or binding) view of the world, just as scholarship is unable to provide unconditioned understanding to the world. Scholarship and cartography are united in the concept of difference: difference in perspectives and questions, difference in hypotheses and findings. A project such as "GLOBAL Nuremberg" obliges us to deal responsibly with difference, contradiction, and ambivalence as a way of broadening our horizons and traversing the boundaries inscribed within thought and discussion.

28 See the essay by Manuel Teget-Welz in the present volume.
29 See the essay by Daniel Astorga-Poblete in the present volume.
30 See, for example, Brotton 2014.

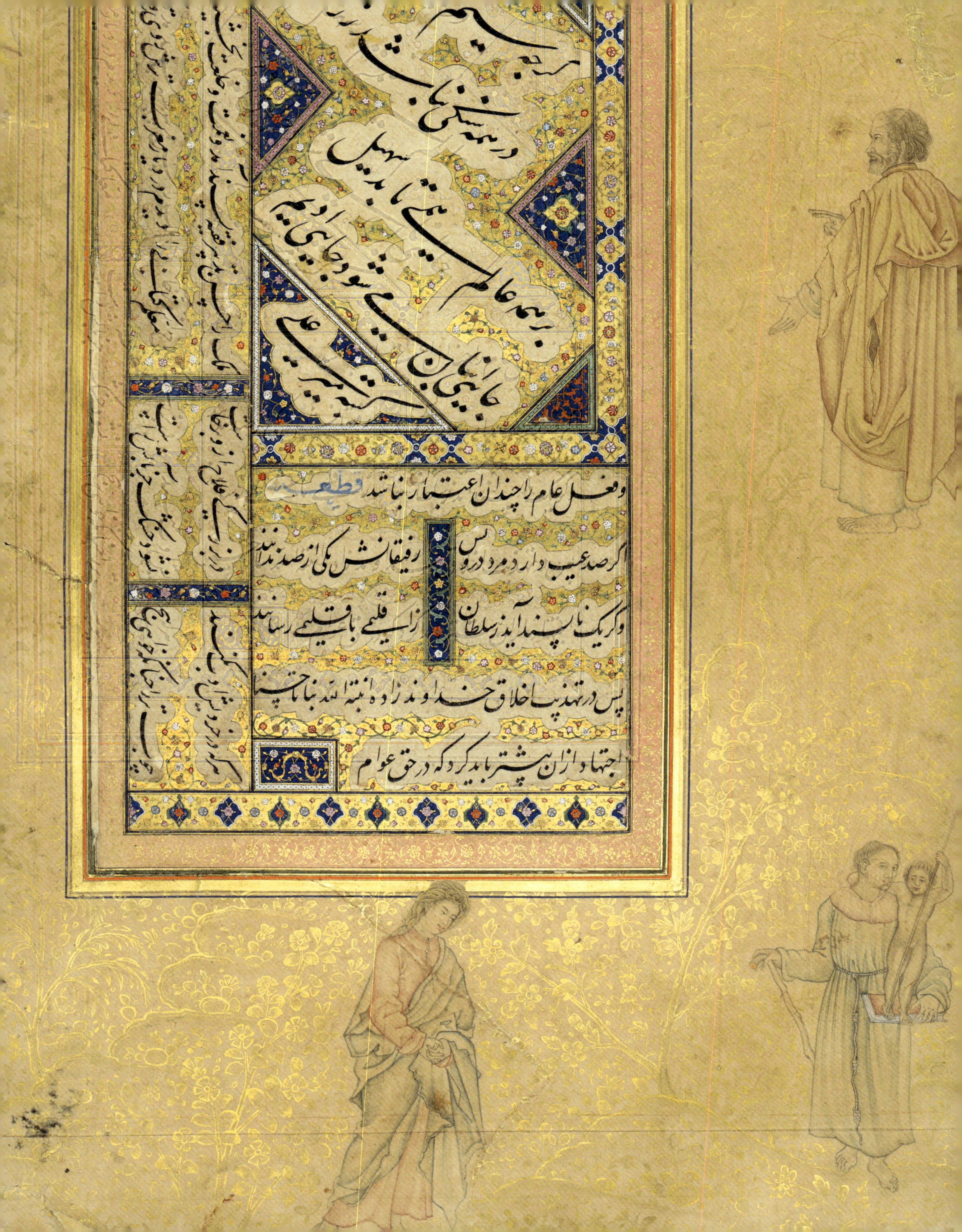

Benno Baumbauer
and Sven Jakstat

NUREMBERG IN THE GLOBAL NETWORKS OF THE EARLY MODERN PERIOD

Albrecht Dürer's *Rhinoceros* of 1515 is an icon of global history |**cat. no. 119**|.[1] The story behind this woodcut is so often told as to require a renewed appreciation of just how sensational it was at the time. Rhinoceroses were surrounded by legend in the European imagination, informed mainly by the ancient author Pliny—that is, until Sultan Muzaffar Shah II of Cambay in India gifted a live specimen to Afonso de Albuquerque, the governor of Portuguese India in Goa. Albuquerque then had the two-ton animal and its Indian keeper shipped along the coast of Africa to Lisbon, where the rhinoceros joined the menagerie belonging to King Manuel I of Portugal. The mere existence of this animal served as living proof to Europeans that the tales told about the wonders of faraway India must be true. News of the rhinoceros reached Dürer's hometown of Nuremberg in a letter sent by Valentim Fernandes, a printer from Moravia who was active in Lisbon.[2] After having undergone all its ordeals, the rhinoceros ultimately drowned off the coast of Liguria while being shipped to Rome as a gift to Pope Leo X. But the creature lived on in Dürer's woodcut, which made it probably the most famous example of cultural exchange between India and central Europe in the early modern period. At the same time, Dürer's *Rhinoceros* is emblematic of our exhibition's objective of telling the story of early globalization from the perspective of Nuremberg—an undertaking that hinges on works of art and related objects with demonstrable historical connections to Nuremberg or to persons active there.

Dürer in India

Comparatively little attention has been paid to the reciprocity of the exchange with India, which is traceable in art and artifacts produced there. The Ashmolean Museum in Oxford has a brush drawing of a young man standing isolated and posed in contrapposto, looking into the distance with a sorrowful expression |**fig. 3**|.[3] His curly hair is subtly modeled, and the drapery folds of his robe are skillfully arranged. According to the note written in Persian at the bottom of the sheet, the drawing was created by Abū'l Hasan, in his thirteenth year, "on the 11th day of the spring month in 1009" according to the Islamic calendar—that is, in the spring of 1600 or 1601 in the European system. Abū'l Hasan became one of the favorite miniaturists of the Mughal emperor Jahangir, who ruled over a vast empire on the Indian subcontinent between 1605 and 1627, including large parts of present-day India, Pakistan, Bangladesh, and Afghanistan. The model for Abū'l Hasan's drawing is found in Dürer's Engraved Passion of 1511: the figure of Saint John the Evangelist in the *Crucifixion* |**fig. 2**|.[4] It is difficult to say what Abū'l Hasan's intentions might have been in extracting exactly this figure from its Christian iconographic setting.[5] In any case, the model's origin in faraway Europe will almost certainly have played a role.[6] Abū'l Hasan was probably also fascinated by the engraving's artistic quality, which, as Mika Natif has argued, he sought to imitate and perhaps even surpass with his fine brushstrokes.[7] But perhaps he also recognized in Dürer's figure a universal visual formula for the expression of human grief and wished to adopt it for his own purposes.

Works on paper by Dürer and other European artists found their way to India through Christian missionaries and merchants, and as diplomatic gifts.[8] The high regard there for such works is evidenced by the Jahangir Album, one of the most prominent examples of Mughal book illumination |**cat. no. 122; fig. 1**|.[9] The intricate ornamentations of the page borders feature several figures based on European prints, including the same Saint John, a Virgin and Child by Dürer, and other saints.[10] These figures, most of which come from Christian images, surround Persian poems written in exquisite calligraphy. Such an intentionally hybrid, col-

Fig. 1 Leaf with figures after Albrecht Dürer, from the Jahangir Album, India (Agra?), ca. 1608–18, Staatsbibliothek zu Berlin, Preußischer Kulturbesitz, Orientalische Handschriften, Libri picturati A 117, fol. 5r |**cat. no. 122.1**|

1 Schoch, Mende, and Scherbaum 2002, pp. 420–24, cat. no. 241 (Yasmin Doosry); Dackerman 2011; Werner 2015, pp. 81–87, 89–90.
2 On Fernandes, see Pohle 2000, pp. 137–38, 219–27; Hendrich 2007, esp. pp. 169–270; Westermann 2009, pp. 53–54.
3 Exh. cat. New York 2011, p. 74, cat. no. 28 (John Guy).
4 See Grebe 2014, pp. 397–99; Keating 2018, pp. 101–4; Natif 2018, pp. 99–107. On the engraving, see Schoch, Mende, and Scherbaum 2001, vol. 1, pp. 143–44, cat. no. 55 (Anna Scherbaum).
5 See Keating 2018, p. 104.
6 See the essay by Monica Juneja in the present volume.
7 Natif 2018, pp. 101, 106.
8 In the case of Dürer's engraved *Crucifixion*, it is assumed that one or more impressions reached the Mughal court in 1580, in the context of a Jesuit mission. See Bailey 1999, p. 115; Keating 2018, p. 101.
9 See Beach 1965; Rice 2009; Grebe 2014, p. 397.
10 See Saviello 2022, pp. 46–49. Bailey 1999, p. 114.

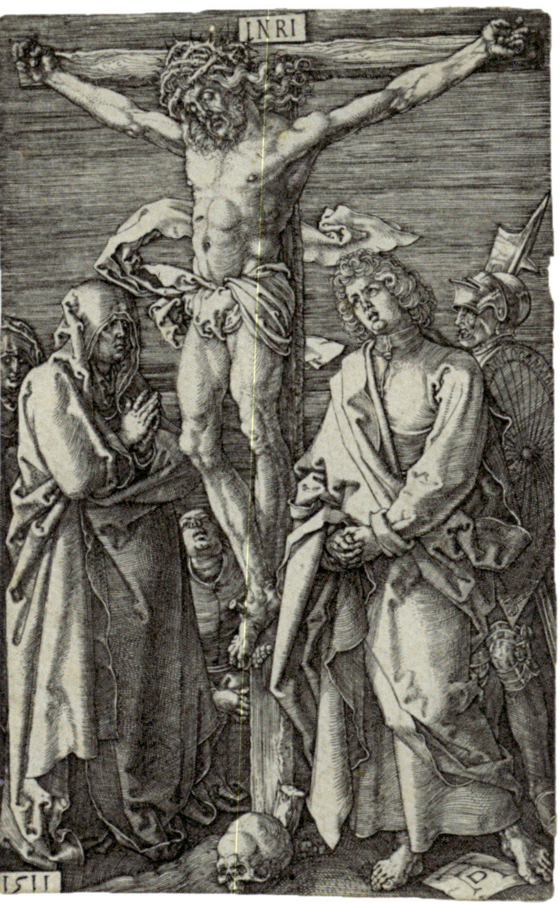

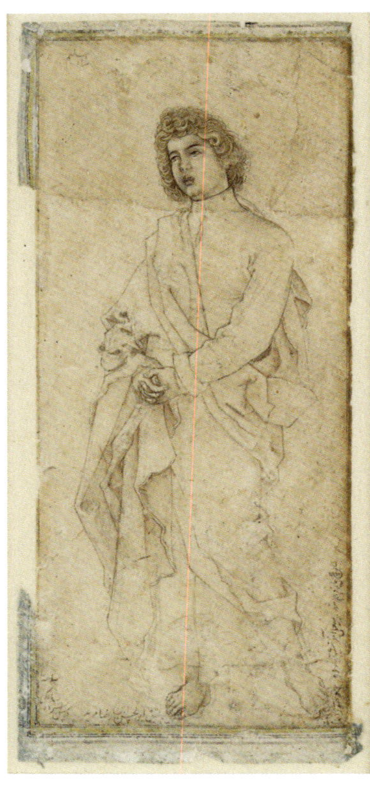

Fig. 2 Albrecht Dürer, *The Crucifixion*, 1511, GNM, inv. no. StN2081, on long-term loan from the Museen der Stadt Nürnberg, Kunstsammlungen |**cat. no. 122.4**|

Fig. 3 Abu'l Hasan, *Saint John the Evangelist*, 1600–1601, Ashmolean Museum, Oxford, inv. no. EA1978.2597

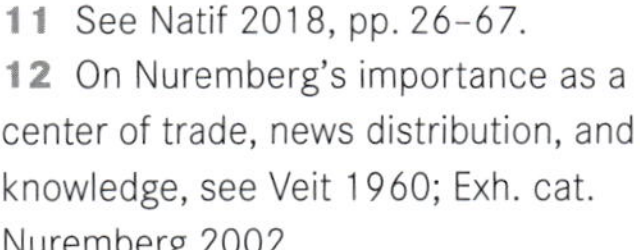

lage-like combination of differently sourced motifs and aesthetics is characteristic of art produced at Jahangir's court and of the emperor's broad interests.[11] At the Mughal court, the presence of works by Dürer and other Nuremberg printmakers, such as Georg Pencz and Sebald Beham, also highlights Nuremberg's role in the period as a hub for the exchange of goods and information.[12]

Global Networks

The historical precondition for these global exchanges is found in the European expansion that began in the late fifteenth century, with the main efforts being launched from the Iberian Peninsula.[13] Ten years before Dürer's *Rhinoceros* woodcut and nearly a century before Abū'l Hasan's drawing, Augsburg trading houses and the Nuremberg branches of the Welser, Hirschvogel, and Imhoff families invested in the great Portuguese expedition to India of 1505–6, led by Francisco de Almeida |**cat. no. 116**|.[14] What historians once fondly recounted as an adventurous trading voyage was in fact also an early colonial enterprise, involving massacres in the international trading centers of Kilwa Kisiwani and Mombasa on the eastern coast of Africa as well as brutal warfare on the western coast of India.[15]

Since then, Nuremberg merchants could be encountered in Calicut (Kozhikode), Goa, and Kochi. A bustling exchange of raw materials and goods developed along a route leading from Calicut to Nuremberg by way of Lisbon and sometimes Antwerp |**cat. nos. 2, 119–22**|.[16] While the southern German trading firms were primarily interested in India's fabled wealth in spices[17] and jewels,[18] their most important trade goods consisted of metalwork of all kinds.[19] This is impressively documented by the wreck of the *Bom Jesus*, a Portuguese ship that sank off the coast of present-day Namibia in 1533. When it was salvaged in 2008, in an area being drained for diamond mining, its cargo included countless metal export products and semifinished

11 See Natif 2018, pp. 26–67.
12 On Nuremberg's importance as a center of trade, news distribution, and knowledge, see Veit 1960; Exh. cat. Nuremberg 2002.
13 For an overview, see, for example, Exh. cat. Berlin 2007; Jordan Gschwend and Lowe 2015. On the participation of entrepreneurs from Nuremberg and southern Germany in overseas expansion, see Bernecker 2000; Pohle 2000, pp. 51–81; Westermann 2009; Häberlein 2021.
14 Pohle 2000, esp. pp. 122–34, 205–11; Horst 2009; Exh. cat. Frankfurt and Vienna 2023, pp. 138–41, cat. nos. 1.18–1.21 (Heidrun Lange-Krach).
15 See Cipolla 1965; Brühne 1992, pp. 149–51; Erhard and Ramminger 1998; Rothermund 1998, pp. 6–7; Rothermund 2004, pp. 27–28. See also the essay by Elgidius E. B. Ichumbaki and Dominicus Z. Makukula in the present volume.
16 Pohle 2000, pp. 151–56.
17 Eser 2010a.
18 Siebenhüner 2018.
19 On the trades involved in nonferrous metalwork in Nuremberg, see Kröner 2023. See also the instructive essays in Exh. cat. Nuremberg 2002.

goods typical of Nuremberg, such as copper and brass wares, pewter plates, nested weights, clasps, rosary beads, and of course weapons.[20]

The exchange via sea routes between South Asia, Africa, and Europe also involved objects of a more rarefied kind. A particularly splendid example is the mother-of-pearl basin crafted in Gujarat that is now kept in the Green Vault in Dresden. It was shipped to Lisbon and then transported to Nuremberg, where it was set into a mount by the goldsmith Nicolaus Schmidt (d. 1609) and later sold to the princely court of Saxony |**cat. no. 2**|.[21]

Lacunae between Nuremberg, Seville, and the Americas

Whereas Lisbon was the starting point for expeditions to India,[22] early-sixteenth-century Seville developed into a hub for European activities in the Americas.[23] In the person of Lazarus Nürnberger, who hailed not from Nuremberg but from the nearby town of Neustadt an der Aisch, there was a well-connected lobbyist in Seville from 1520 to 1564 who became involved in almost every enterprise pursued by southern Germans in the Americas.[24] In 1517–18, he had traveled to India on behalf of the Hirschvogel family from Nuremberg.[25] Among other things, he traded in cane sugar, gold, jewels, pearls, weapons, and enslaved people, and he later invested in the mining of Mexican silver and Cuban copper.[26] Through all these lines of business, he and his partners were implicated in the violent colonization of the Americas and the brutality of the transatlantic slave trade.

Despite Lazarus Nürnberger's importance to the global history of Nuremberg, he exemplifies the dilemma inherent in this exhibition topic—namely, that many of the relevant stories can now only be reconstructed on the basis of textual sources. Material evidence is often lost or can no longer be assigned to specific contexts or events. This discrepancy poses a challenge to an art- and cultural-historical exhibition such as ours, which aims to make history tangible to visitors through the presence of original works of art. The only known art object that can be associated with Lazarus Nürnberger is a massive iron chest with an elaborate locking mechanism kept in the Archivo General de Indias in Seville. Many of the documents and objects in that archive's holdings come from the Casa de la Contratación de Indias, the institution centrally responsible for organizing enterprises in the Americas. Lazarus Nürnberger sold a chest of this type to the Casa in August 1537.[27] However, because such objects were produced and exported in large numbers, it remains uncertain whether the surviving chest is indeed the one mentioned in the sources. In this way, the figure of Lazarus Nürnberger typifies the many gaps in the material record, all nearly impossible to fill with illustrative objects. In the study of the global history of early modern Nuremberg, these lacunae underscore the major discrepancy between the richness of textual sources and the paucity of related works of art and artifacts.[28]

The story of the young trading assistant Hieronymus Köler of Nuremberg, who participated in a failed venture to Venezuela, illustrates the unscrupulous treatment that Lazarus Nürnberger and other agents of early global capitalism meted out even to their own people. Köler recorded his experiences in a richly illustrated genealogical book |**cat. no. 110**|.[29] When Köler arrived in Seville in 1534, Lazarus Nürnberger took him in and convinced him to join an expedition organized by the Welsers, who were colonizing Venezuela on behalf of the Spanish crown.[30] After an extensive recruitment campaign, the fleet set sail from Sanlúcar de Barrameda. However, their attempts to cross the Atlantic failed because they ignored the onset of dangerous autumn storms. In Köler's report, written after his return, his anger over this failure is palpable, especially with regard to the exploitative

20 Knabe and Noli 2012, concerning Nuremberg esp. pp. 69–92, 153–201; Westermann 2013b; Werz 2015.
21 Weinhold and Witting 2024, vol. 3, pp. 808–11, cat. no. 170 (Theresa Witting).
22 Jordan Gschwend and Lowe 2015; Exh. cat. Lisbon 2017.
23 Elliott 1989, p. 18; Bernecker and Pietschmann 2005, p. 106; O'Flanagan 2008, p. 42.
24 See Kellenbenz and Walter 2001, pp. 19–29.
25 On Nürnberger's voyage to India in 1517–18, see Kroell 1980 (Nürnberger's travelogue on pp. 63–71); Pohle 2000, pp. 211–15.
26 Häberlein 2016, pp. 190–94; Otte 1963–64.
27 Otte 1963–64, pp. 129–30, fig. 1 following p. 132.
28 The memorial shield (*Totenschild*) for Hans Tetzel (cat. no. 108) exemplifies this dilemma. Tetzel ran a copper-mining operation in Cuba that depended on the labor of enslaved people, but no artifacts related to that activity survive. See Jakstat 2024.
29 Méndez Rodríguez 2013; Bräunlein 2018; Rublack 2022, pp. 294–99; Amburger 1931 (including a partial transcription of Köler's report, which omits the section on Venezuela).
30 See Kellenbenz and Walter 2001, p. 23. On the Welsers in Venezuela, see Simmer 2000; Denzer 2005.

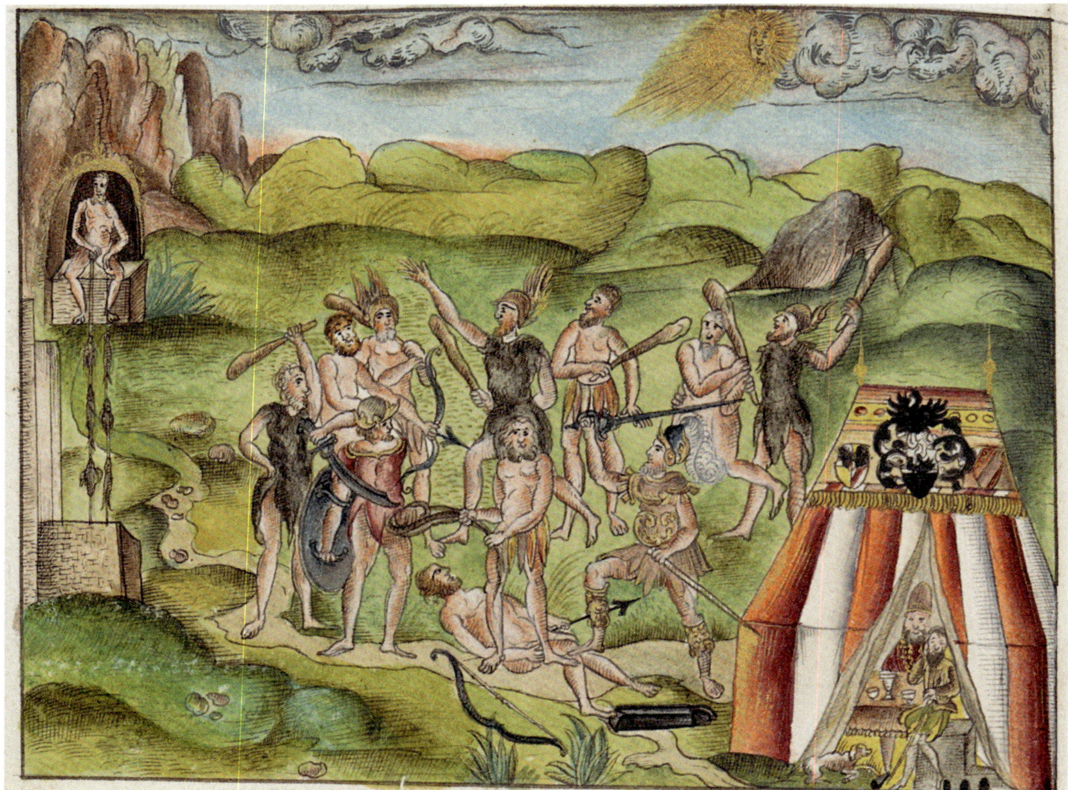

Fig. 4 *Hieronymus Köler in Venezuela*, from Hieronymus Köler, *Family Book*, 1560–65, British Library, London, shelf mark Ms 15217, fol. 40v |**cat. no. 110**|

conditions of the whole enterprise. He also denounces the Europeans' treatment of the Indigenous population of Venezuela, and he cites Christian missionary activity as a pretext for plundering the natural resources of the Americas and exploiting the peoples there. This demonstrates that in sixteenth-century Nuremberg a clear awareness existed of the injustices committed by Europeans in the process of early colonialism.[31] At the same time, many passages in Köler's text reveal the disparaging attitude he himself held toward the Indigenous peoples of the Americas, even though he had never actually arrived there.[32]

Köler never saw Venezuela with his own eyes. Yet that did not prevent him from having his notions about the place illustrated with images drawn from the imagination. While the miniatures in his family book (*Familienbuch*) appear naive at first glance |**fig. 4**|, they reveal much of what characterized such ventures. One sees conquistadores on horseback and Christian ritual objects of the type brought to New Spain by missionaries. Unlike Dürer, Köler had no intention of offering an authentic representation of Indigenous material culture |**see cat. no. 100**|. He imagined the people of Venezuela in the pictorial tradition of "Wild Men," portraying them as primitive, bearded cave dwellers in loincloths, equipped with clubs, slings, and bows. However, the lintels above the entrances to their caves are shown as being made of gold, and large golden cups are situated in the landscape, some being used by inhabitants to scoop water from the sea. Executed by unknown illuminators, these images embody notions and stereotypes about the Americas that became firmly established in Nuremberg and elsewhere through broadsheets, travelogues, and oral communications |**see cat. nos. 98–100, 105**|.[33]

Dürer's *Rhinoceros* in the Andes

This leads us back to Dürer's *Rhinoceros*, which itself arose within the context of news reports about early colonial enterprises in India. This woodcut was one of Dürer's most commercially successful works, becoming a sought-after commodity that circulated throughout Europe. Indirectly, through the medium of a book illustration, the motif even found its way to the Andes, to the city of Tunja in the present-day Boyacá department of Colombia. The learned scribe and bibliophile

31 The best-known example of a contemporary critique of such colonial practices is the widely read *Brevísima relación de la destrucción de las Indias* of 1552 by Bartolomé de Las Casas. See Las Casas 1992.
32 Bräunlein 2018, pp. 332–33.
33 On this phenomenon in general, see Falk 1987; Frübis 2001; Kiening 2006; Massing 2016.

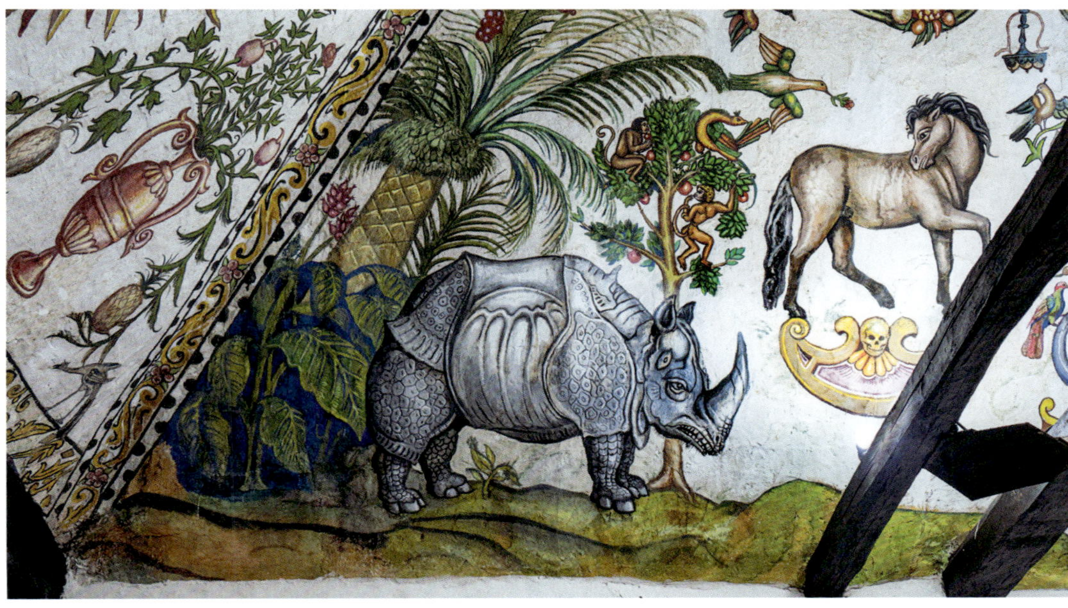

Fig. 5 *Rhinoceros*, after 1585, Casa del Escribano, Tunja (Colombia, Departamento Boyacá)

Juan de Vargas lived in Tunja from 1588 to 1622. In the Casa del Escribano, Vargas's former home and now the site of a museum dedicated to colonial history, he commissioned an elaborate program of grotesques to be painted on the ceiling of the large hall on the second floor. The imagery encompasses Vargas's coat of arms; the monograms of Jesus, Mary, and Joseph; ancient deities; and animals.[34]

These Mannerist paintings, repeatedly reworked up into the twentieth century, also include a rhinoceros that is unmistakably based on Dürer's work |**fig. 5**|. However, the immediate source was most likely not Dürer's woodcut, but rather a reproduction of it that appeared in the artistic treatise *Varia commensuracion para la escultura y arquitectura*, written by the goldsmith Juan de Arfe and published in Seville in 1585. Several copies of the book can be traced to South America in the period.[35] As Patricia Zalamea puts forth, by including the rhinoceros and other animals and objects from faraway places in the ceiling painting at the Casa del Escribano, Juan de Vargas made an imperial claim, relocating the "peripheral" to what was for him the center of the world.[36] Beginning in Gujarat, on the western coast of India, and leading to Lisbon, Nuremberg, and ultimately Tunja, the curious story of the Indian rhinoceros immortalized in Dürer's woodcut spans the entire world known to Europeans at the time. And in doing so, it broadens the horizons of our exhibition.

34 Palm 1956; Schatz 2002, pp. 123–31, 139–40, 151–57, figs. 8–19; Mejía 2005, pp. 59–93; Zalamea 2019.
35 Palm 1956, p. 67; Schatz 2002, pp. 128–30, 140; Zalamea 2019, p. 173.
36 Zalamea 2019, pp. 188–89.

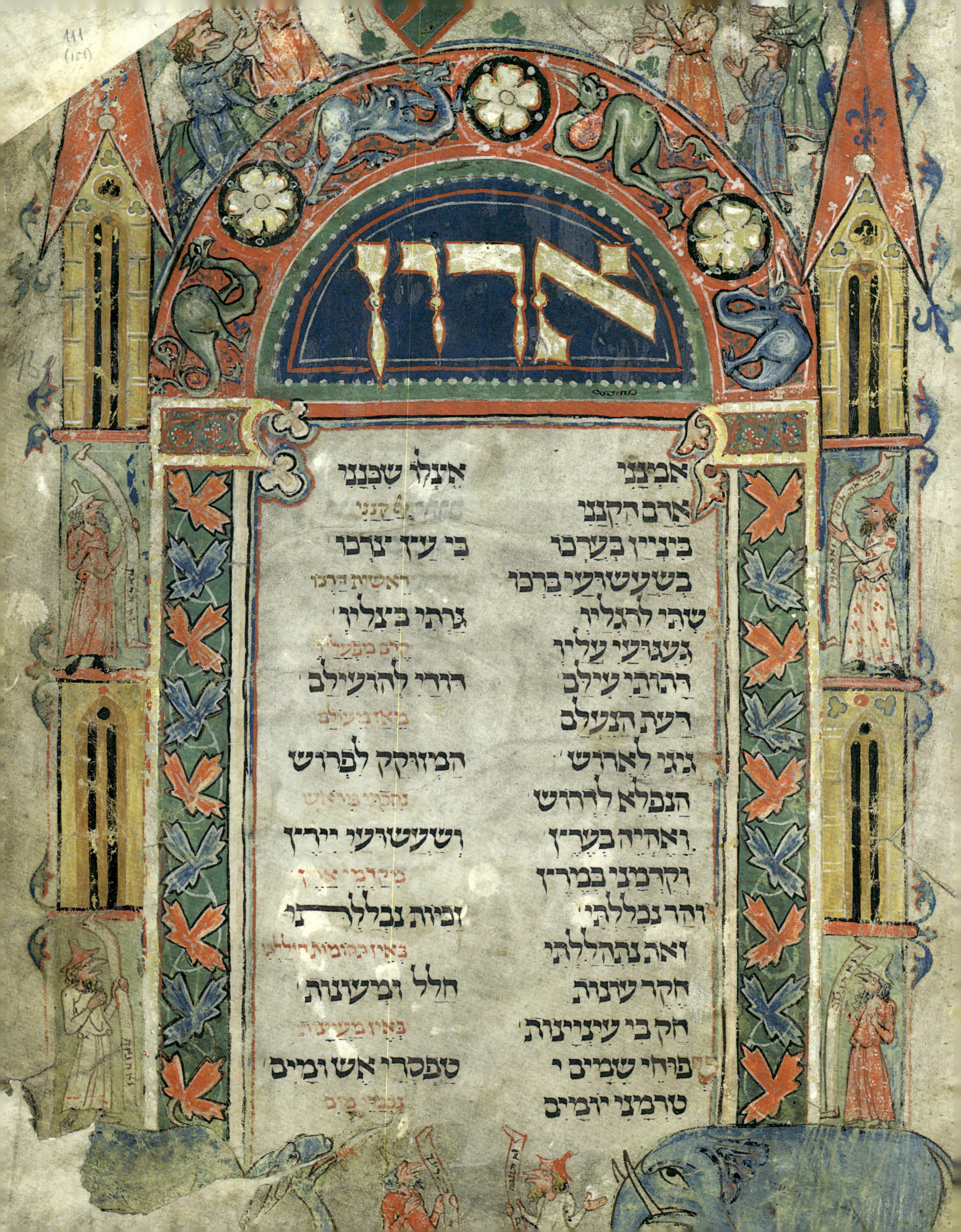

אהרן

Meyrav Levy

CROSSING BORDERS

JEWISH MOBILITY AND URBAN INTEGRATION IN NUREMBERG, 1350–1499

A Jewish settlement in Nuremberg was first documented in the early thirteenth century. During the fifteenth century, the city's Jewish community reached its peak as one of the most significant within Ashkenaz (the Hebrew term for the German-speaking lands). On December 5, 1349, at least 562 Jews were massacred in a pogrom in Nuremberg. This occurred during the broad wave of so-called Black Death persecutions, although at the time there was no outbreak of the plague in Nuremberg. Shortly after, the city took in some survivors, who were soon joined by other Jews from further afield. The new community settled not in the area of the former Jewish quarter, at the Hauptmarkt, but in a less favorable location at the city's eastern edge, extending into the neighborhood called Salzmarktviertel between the streets Judengasse, Wunderburggasse, and Rotschmiedgasse. This quarter comprised sixteen to eighteen houses that formed a closed unit around a large courtyard. It included a synagogue with a women's section, a bathhouse, a mikvah (ritual bath), a cemetery, a dance house, two bakeries, at least one well, and a hospital (*Szelhaus*) for the sick and poor. The community grew steadily and numbered 200 to 250 individuals by 1489.[1]

As in much of Europe, the Jews of Nuremberg endured multifaceted anti-Judaism, including false accusations, massacres, and eventual expulsion in 1499 under King Maximilian I. They suffered from heavy taxation, remission of debts owed to them (*Judenschuldentilgung*, occurring in 1385 and 1390), and restrictions on their occupations and places of residence. Efforts to convert the Jewish community in Nuremberg included sermons given by the Italian Franciscan John of Capistrano in 1452 and by the Dominican Peter Schwarz in 1478, who invited Jews to public theological debates. Anti-Jewish rhetoric was spread by figures such as Hans Rosenplüt, Hans Folz, and Alfonso de Spina, whose *Fortalitium Fidei*—blaming Jews for ritual murders and host desecration—was printed in Nuremberg in 1485 and 1494.[2] Nevertheless, the Jewish community of medieval Nuremberg cannot be defined solely by persecution. While navigating a complex environment of toleration and crisis, it integrated into urban life and contributed to the city's prosperity. Numerous legal records shed light on the community's participation in Nuremberg's economic and cultural evolution. Jews conducted business, undertook legal matters, and saw to everyday affairs outside their quarter, operating in the city court and with the city council.[3] They traded at the local markets with certain restrictions, such as the ban on them being sold fish in the mornings of Christian fasting days and the requirement, renewed in 1458, to wear distinctive Jewish clothing. At the same time, the medieval community engaged with fellow Jews from outside Nuremberg, and its members were highly mobile, either because they were forced to be or because of their economic and intellectual pursuits—all of which illustrates a dynamic interplay of different cultural, social, and geographical spheres.

Medieval Nuremberg afforded Jews a certain degree of tolerance, largely owing to their economic contribution. The predominant Jewish occupation in the city was moneylending. Until 1385, Nuremberg Jews lent money to various entities against promissory notes and pledges. The borrowers included the city, members of the patriciate, and the religious and secular nobility. This established Nuremberg as the key Jewish banking center in southern Germany. The period following the cancellation of debts owed to them (remissions in 1385 and 1390) saw significant economic growth, leading to an increased demand for credit. Jews, however, were no longer involved in the major financial transactions. By the late fifteenth century, because of new restrictions, their moneylending activities became limited to a clientele of artisans and day laborers or involved small-scale pawnbroking. Nevertheless, Jews still enjoyed thriving economic ties with northern Italian cities that utilized

Fig. 1 Simcha ben Jehuda and Schemaja ben Isaac, *The Worms Mahzor*, Würzburg, 1272, The National Library of Israel, Jerusalem, shelf mark MS 4°781, fol. 110v

1 Maimon, Breuer, and Guggenheim 1995, pp. 1001–2; Toch 2003b, pp. 80–91; Weber 2022, pp. 25–50.
2 Weber 2022, pp. 111–42, 328–42.
3 Weber 2022, pp. 53–71, 209–43.

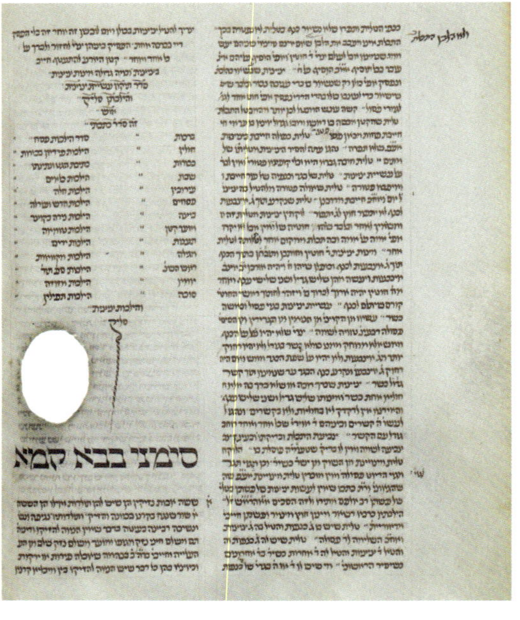

Fig. 2 Jacob ben Asher, *Qitzur pisqei Ha-Rosh*, probably Nuremberg, ca. 1400, Bodleian Libraries, University of Oxford, shelf mark MS. Laud Or. 269, fol. 60v

their banking services, such as the Bernhardi Bank in Venice, and they also engaged in business in cities located along the route to Italy, such as Ulm and Zurich. Jut, the widow of Samuel of Basel, and Jutte, the widow of Jacob Rapp, both of whom operated their family businesses in Nuremberg, lost tens of thousands of guldens during the *Judenschuldentilgung* and fled to Venice with their remaining capital, attempting unsuccessfully to recover their assets.[4]

Financial success elevated prominent Jewish figures who had ties to the centers of Christian power. Together with their families, wealthy Jews received citizenship (*Bürgerrecht*), which allowed them to appeal to the city court for internal disputes and to purchase houses outside their quarter. From about 1464 to 1497, the three wealthiest moneylenders—Meir Johel the Elder, Moses (Mostel) of Schaffhausen, and Simon Sack, who was also a scholar—dominated the Jewish community. They led significant households and received support from both the city and Emperor Frederick III.[5] Owing to their power and connections, the Nuremberg rabbinate was appointed by the emperor to oversee all Jews in the German lands, which enabled them to receive protection from the sovereign. Thus, for example, in 1421 the rabbis of Nuremberg took successful diplomatic steps on behalf of the Jews of Germany to avert the threat of the Hussite Wars.[6] The Nuremberg community even gave alms in support of the Jews of Jerusalem.[7] Evidence of the city's centrality within Ashkenaz is found in the *Nürnberger Memorbuch*, initiated during the construction of the new synagogue in 1296. This memorial book, intended for Yizkor prayers in the synagogue, compiles lists of Jewish martyrs who had perished in anti-Jewish persecutions throughout Ashkenaz, France, and England since the First Crusade. Some of the lists from Franconian towns likely drew from records of Jewish taxpayers maintained by Nuremberg's community.[8]

The community's potency led to it becoming a key rabbinic center within the Ashkenazic scholarly network. Prominent rabbis such as Jacob Weil and Jacob Margoles lived in the city, presided in the Jewish court, and maintained close personal and written communication with rabbis of other communities across Germany, Alsace, Austria, Bohemia, and Poland. They also taught in the two yeshivot (Talmudic schools) of Nuremberg, which attracted students from across Europe and perhaps even from as far away as Constantinople. A unique "Nuremberg" method of interpreting the Talmud's dialectic emerged in these schools.[9] The Jewish scholars in the city owned a variety of Hebrew books. A copy of a treatise on religious law written in Toledo by Rabbi Jacob ben Asher was in the possession of a Nuremberg scholar |**fig. 2**|. At the end of the book, the owner added a lament for the deceased head of the city's community and yeshiva, Rabbi Simon Sack (d. 1447). Another manuscript, this one copied out by Joseph bar Samuel Yaffe from Nuremberg around the same time features a philosophical text in Hebrew by the Andalusian scholar Maimonides.[10]

4 Maimon, Breuer, and Guggenheim 1995, pp. 1004–5, 1015; Toch 2008a, p. 202; Toch 2003a, pp. 283–310; Michelfelder 1967, pp. 243–57.
5 Weber 2022, pp. 209–43.
6 Maimon, Breuer, and Guggenheim 1995, pp. 1013, 1019–21; Weber 2022, pp. 272–79.
7 Yuval 1981, pp. 182–97.
8 Yuval 2006, p. 138; Barzen 2011.
9 Maimon, Breuer, and Guggenheim 1995, pp. 1013–14.
10 Cambridge University Library, MS Add. 1565.

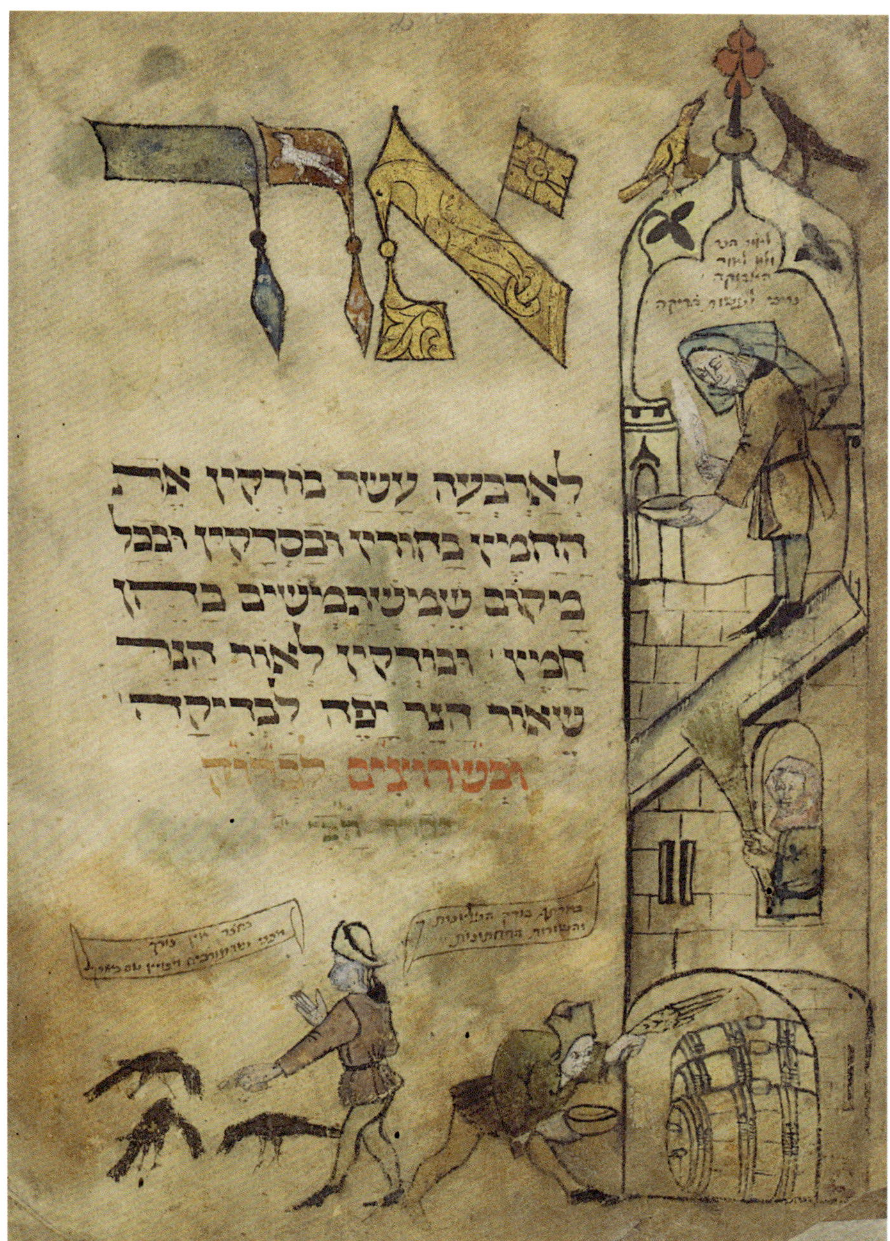

Fig. 3 *The Yahuda Haggadah*, probably Nuremberg, 1460s, The Israel Museum, Jerusalem, shelf mark Ms. 180/50, fol. 2v

Nuremberg's economic growth in the late Middle Ages and the burgeoning of its urban fabric also created opportunities for Jewish merchants and craftspeople. Throughout the fifteenth century, the city council's records mention Jewish traders, both male and female, who dealt in saffron, wine, and fruit. Other Jews worked as physicians, oculists, midwives, and alchemists. One Jew served as the family physician for the municipal master builder (*Ratsbaumeister*) Endres Tucher. Some Jewish gold- and silversmiths were trained by Christians up until about 1488–90, when they were banned from this practice owing to pressure from their Christian counterparts. Moreover, city projects benefited from the contributions of Jewish engineers, including a builder of a mill model in 1426 and a sewerage expert who built a machine for boring wooden well pipes in 1431. In 1445, the Christian burgher Andreas Stromer recommended the Jewish mining specialist Samuel von Kassel to the mayor of Goslar for work on a flooded mine at Rammelsberg. And Jews relied on Christians' services, too: a Christian butcher served the Jewish community, and Christian stonemasons crafted Jewish gravestones with Hebrew inscriptions. The fact that Christians frequently conducted business in the Judengasse and the Jewish bathhouse further demonstrates the interreligious connections that existed.[11]

The shared economic environment of that period is evident in two illuminated Hebrew manuscripts whose production has been localized to Nuremberg in the 1460s: the Yahuda Haggadah |**fig. 3**| and the Second Nuremberg Haggadah. These books narrate the biblical exodus from Egypt and elaborate on the Passover holiday rituals. They exhibit a collaborative production process: one artist created the foundational designs, while others added color and detail. This reflects practices common in contemporaneous Christian manuscript workshops in southern Germany. The decorative elements, such as the animal motifs, draw from a repertoire commonly found in Christian manuscripts, prints, and playing cards of the time. This suggests that Jewish artisans in Nuremberg were well-versed in the visual culture of the region, participating in a shared artistic tradition rather than operating in isolation.[12]

As a free imperial city, Nuremberg not only attracted Jewish craftspeople but also served as a starting point from which they traveled throughout southern Germany and across Europe. As far back as the thirteenth century, in 1272, Simchah ben Yehudah, a scribe from Nuremberg who was assisted by Shema'ayah ben Isaac, "the Frenchman," copied the two-volume illuminated Worms

11 Maimon, Breuer, and Guggenheim 1995, pp. 1005, 1013; Stromer 1963, p. 31.
12 Kogman-Appel 1994, pp. 30–31; Kogman-Appel 2001, pp. 128–29.

Fig. 4 Simcha ben Jehuda and Schemaja ben Isaac, *The Worms Mahzor*, Würzburg, 1272, The National Library of Israel, Jerusalem, shelf mark MS 4°781, fols. 110v–111r

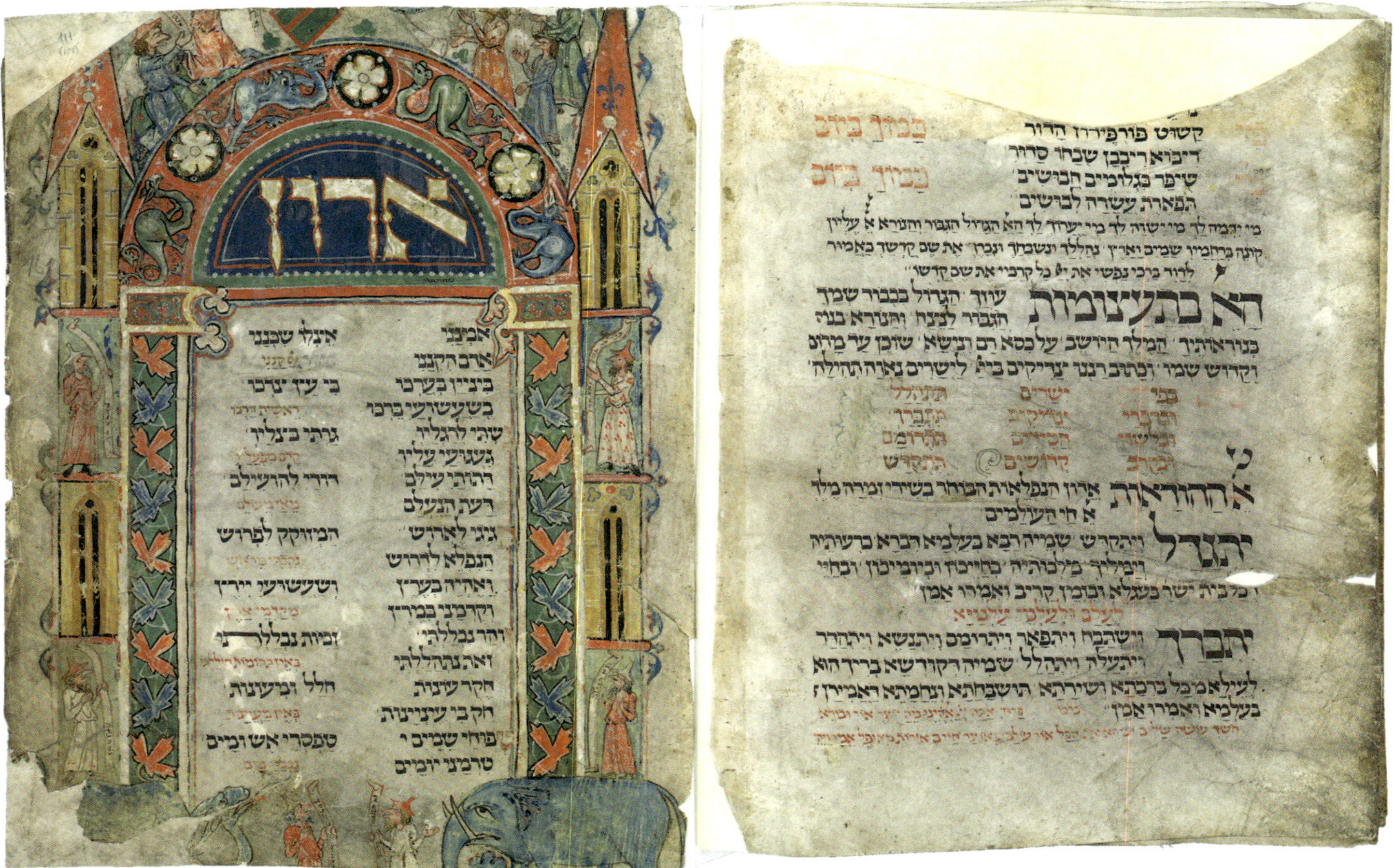

Mahzor for his uncle Rabbi Baruch bar Isaac |**figs. 1, 4**|. This prayer book, which contains the liturgical poetry for all the annual festivals, was intended for the use of the Würzburg community.[13] In addition to such captivating details as illuminations of bird-headed Jewish figures, the manuscript also presents the first documented inscription in Yiddish (fol. 54r). Less than two hundred years later, Meir ben Israel Jaffe of Ulm traveled to Nuremberg. He was a highly skilled Jewish bookbinder and master of the art of cuir ciselé. Likely the son of the renowned scribe Israel ben Meir of Heidelberg, Jaffe worked for wealthy patrons in various cities. He visited Nuremberg twice, binding books for Hans von Thill, a member of the city's *ehrbar* (honorable) rank, and then for the city council, which hired "Meyerlein, Juden von Ulm" in 1468 to bind books in its library.[14] One surviving example of Jaffe's work in Nuremberg is the luxurious binding of a thirteenth-century Hebrew Pentateuch used for Jewish oaths in the city court |**cat. no. 13**|. The piece of paper with the fifteenth-century Jewish oath written in German is still attached to folio 52r |**fig. 5**|. The binding's cut-leather technique (*cuir ciselé*) involved incising and raising decorations in relief on moist leather, a craft

13 Beit-Arié 1985, p. 20.
14 Avrin 2010, p. 313; Husung 1925–26, pp. 29–43.

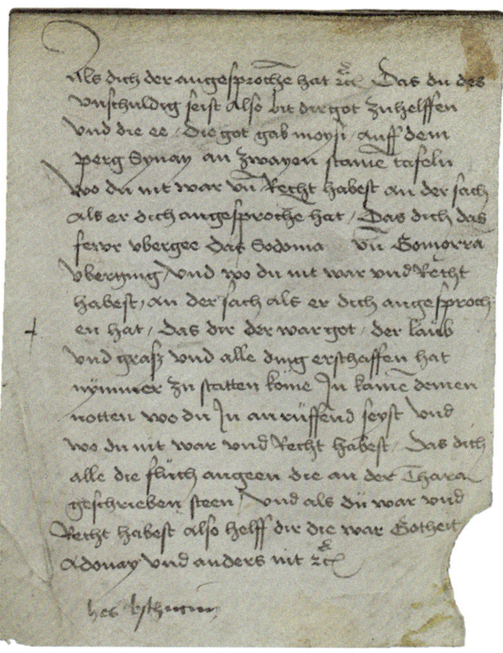

Fig. 5 Oath in the Pentateuch of the Nuremberg City Council, fifteenth century, Bayerische Staatsbibliothek, Munich, Cod.hebr. 212, attached to fol. 52r

introduced to central Europe from Spain and Portugal by Jewish artisans. The front cover features Nuremberg's coat of arms framed by Yaffe's inscription in large Gothic Hebrew script: "The Pentateuch for the council of Nuremberg, [long] may he live Meir Yaffe, the decorator."[15] This hybrid design, combining Christian and Jewish elements, reflects an intricate sociocultural intersection.

Inevitably, interreligious interaction went hand in hand with a loosening of social boundaries drawn along religious lines. Between 1384 and 1499, especially after 1470, some Jews converted to Christianity, motivated by theological persuasion or incentives such as citizenship and job support for converts. Sexual intercourse of Jewish men with Christian women was a frequent matter, often resulting in fines or exile.[16] Court protocols document joint gambling and Christian participation in Jewish celebrations such as Purim and weddings. In March 1483, seven notable patricians were sentenced to house arrest after dancing at a Jewish wedding. Among them were the textile merchant and cartographer Martin Behaim |**see cat. nos. 1, 114**| as well as Sebald Deichsler, Sebald Tucher, and Martin Paumgartner. Interestingly, they were punished not for associating with Jews but for dancing during the Golden Fast days, shortly after Lent began.[17] This showcases the normality of Jewish-Christian intermingling in late-medieval Nuremberg, where economic and cultural exchanges fostered coexistence. The nuanced perspective supported by all these examples highlights how Jews balanced integration and marginalization, thriving as a prominent community within European networks, while demonstrating resilience and adaptability amid adversity.

15 Steimann 2019, pp. 77–102; Sternthal, Cohen-Mushlin, and Levy 2009–14; Katzenstein 1982, pp. 17, 20.
16 Maimon, Breuer, and Guggenheim 1995, pp. 1012–14; Müller 2009a, pp. 19–32.
17 Wenninger 2016, pp. 51–55.

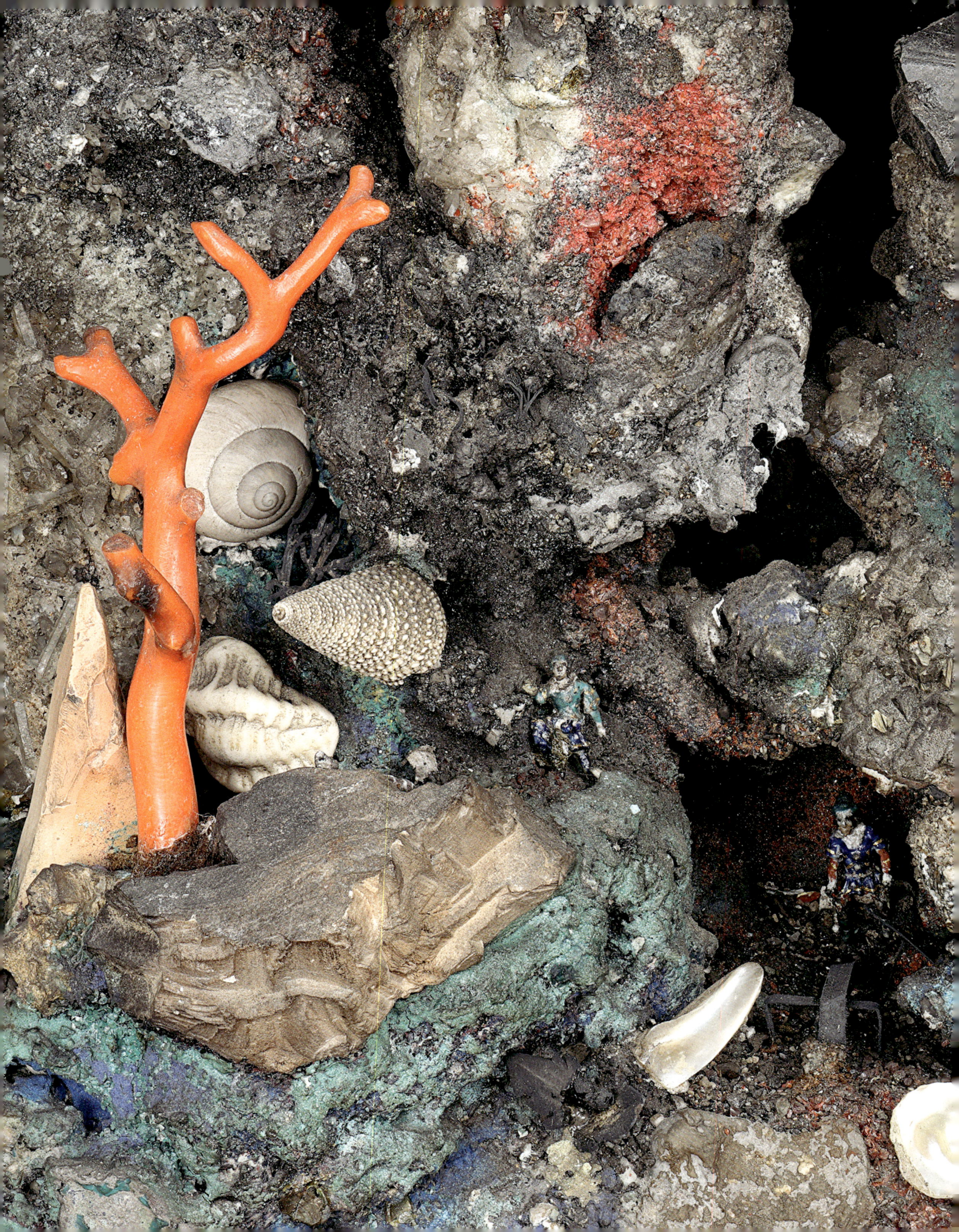

Tina Asmussen

METALS FOR THE WORLD

NUREMBERG'S NETWORKS IN THE EUROPEAN AND GLOBAL MINING INDUSTRY

Mining and the Metalworking Trades

Typefounders, goldsmiths, mintmasters, bell-founders, locksmiths, cutlers, wire-drawers, gunsmiths, brass-smiths, stove-makers, nail-makers, basin-makers, spur-makers, and coppersmiths—all of these metalworking professions were firmly established among the panoply of trades practiced in sixteenth-century Nuremberg. Their activities helped to shape the economic and social fabric of Nuremberg, contributing significantly to the city's widespread renown. It was to these trades that Nuremberg owed its status as an important center of European metalworking.[1]

An impression of the diversity of the metalworking trades can be gained from the so-called *Book of Trades*, published in Frankfurt am Main in 1568 under the title *Eygentliche Beschreibung aller Stände auff Erden* (True Description of All Estates and Trades on Earth).[2] The book is illustrated with 114 woodcuts by Jost Amman (1539–1591), an artist who had been active in Nuremberg since 1561, and each image is accompany by a poem from the pen of Hans Sachs (1494–1576). Twenty-seven metalworking professions are represented in the book, all of which were also present in late medieval and early modern Nuremberg. By 1550, more than 2,000 master metalworkers were active in the city, distributed among about eighty specialized trades.[3] They produced a wide range of articles: arms and armor for warfare, precision mechanical instruments for science and technology, and luxurious works of gold- and silversmithing that were prized at princely courts and in markets far beyond the borders of the Holy Roman Empire. Iron, copper, and brass goods fashioned in Nuremberg were exported to Africa, East Asia, and the Americas.[4] These extensive trading relations and the high degree of specialization among the crafts required a continuous and reliable supply of raw metals. Accordingly, the urbanites of Nuremberg maintained a strong interest in the mining industry; this called for in-depth knowledge of deposits, extraction techniques, and trade routes. The central role played by mining is reflected in the aforementioned *Book of Trades* in the figure of the *Bergknappe*, or miner |**fig. 2**|.

The acquisition of metals such as silver, copper, tin, iron, and calamine (the historical name of certain zinc ores) was among the foremost tasks of Nuremberg's trading and mining companies. Also, many merchant families were involved in the mining industry as *Gewerken* (shareholders) or were actively engaged in the trade in metals. The Nuremberg branch of the Welser family, for example, was involved in mining in central Germany in the sixteenth century and was particularly active in trade connected with the so-called *Saiger* process. In this metallurgical method of separating silver and copper, silver-containing copper ores were smelted with the addition of lead. The silver was thus combined with the lead, leaving behind nearly pure black copper. In the next step, cupellation, the silver was extracted from the lead. The trading and manufacturing companies that organized and controlled this process were referred to collectively as the *Saigerhandel* (Saiger trade). In the decade after 1524, Jakob Welser (1468–1541) |**see cat. nos. 101–3**| headed the important Leutenberg *Saigerhandel* company as its main shareholder. His son Sebastian (1500–1566) |**see cat. no. 104**| and his grandson Hans (1534–1601) were active in the same business sector. In 1581, Hans became the principal shareholder in the Gräfenthal *Saigerhandel* company.[5]

This economic basis allowed Nuremberg to assert its position as a center of the metal industry. The city obtained copper mainly from the important mining districts of Kutná Hora (Kuttenberg) |**see cat. no. 43**| and Mansfeld (in the Harz region), but also from Banská Bystrica (Neusohl) and from both Schwaz and Rattenberg in Tyrol. Calamine, the zinc carbonate used for brass production, came primarily from the Aachen area. Most tin originated in the Ore Mountains and the Fichtel Hills,

Fig. 1 Martin Stieber, *The Scheurl Erzstufe*, Nuremberg, 1563, GNM, inv. no. HG10294 |**cat. no. 27**|, detail: coral and miners

1 Kröner 2023.
2 Sachs 1568.
3 Fumasoli 2017, pp. 110–28, esp. p. 116; Stahlschmidt 1971.
4 Bernecker 2000, esp. pp. 206–14; Müller 2002, pp. 73–79.
5 Westermann 2002, p. 240; Kellenbenz 1977; Hildebrandt 1972.

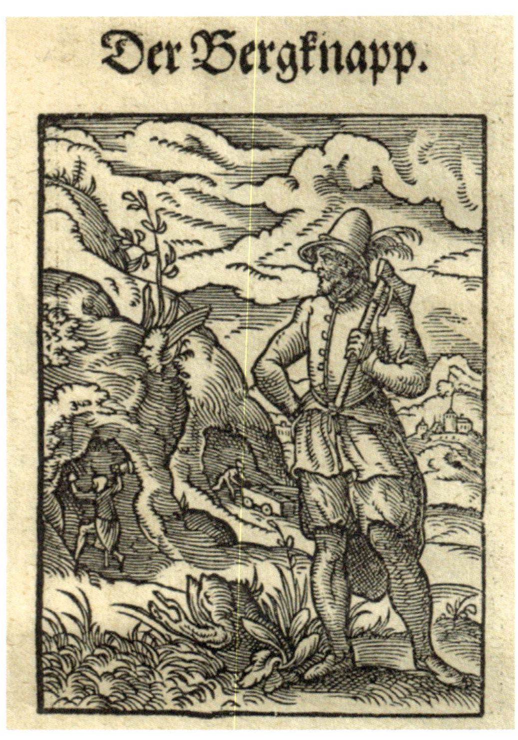

Fig. 2 *The Miner*, from Hans Sachs and Jost Amman, *Book of Trades* (*Ständebuch*), Frankfurt am Main: Sigmund Feyerabent, 1568, GNM, shelf mark 8° L. 2083, fol. 104r

while iron was imported mainly from the Upper Palatinate and Styria.[6] These raw materials enabled the manufacture of a wide range of crafted goods, encompassing everything from simple everyday objects such as nails, kettles, and small bells; semi-finished goods such as wire; and more elaborate items such as weapons, scientific instruments, and numerous luxury goods.[7]

The resources obtained through mining did not come exclusively from central Europe. As early as the sixteenth century, Nuremberg entrepreneurs were taking part in the global trade in raw materials. The transnational reach of Nuremberg's entrepreneurial interests is exemplified by the activities of Hans Tetzel (1518–1571). Born in Nuremberg into a family with a long history in the mining business, Tetzel set out into the colonies of the Spanish Empire about 1541 and ran a copper smelting operation in Cuba for over two decades |**cat. no. 108**|.[8] His involvement in the Caribbean points to the global dimensions of Nuremberg's mining networks. This included not only trade in metals from outside of Europe, but also direct participation in colonial regimes of resource extraction, characterized by violent appropriation, forced labor, and structural exploitation.

Mining and Status

For Nuremberg's artisan and patrician families, however, mining was more than just an economic necessity or profitable investment. For the patriciate, it was also an important means of displaying power, knowledge, and social status. This is evident in works of art that illustrate the close connection between mining and social prestige. In the sixteenth and seventeenth centuries, a type of object that was highly sought after for collections and gifting was the so-called *Erzstufe* (chunk of ore) or *Handstein* (hand stone), typically decorated with miniature mining scenes. Particularly princes who had mining operations in their territories tended to accumulate many such artifacts in their collections. As owners of the mining rights and thus lords over the mineral deposits, they saw the *Erzstufen* as representative of their power.[9] Yet these objects were also collected and put on display by members of the urban elite. An example from Nuremberg is the *Erzstufe* of 1563 from the collection of the city judge Christoph Scheurl III (1535–1592) |**fig. 1; cat. no. 27**|. The renowned Nuremberg goldsmith Martin Stieber (d. 1592) fashioned this magnificent showpiece from a selection of minerals, crystals, corals, and fossils. In addition to a hunting scene consisting of enameled figures, there are mining scenes showing figures breaking stone and hauling ore. Many of these come into view only when one peers into the object's caves and recesses. Apart from its artistic merits, this *Erzstufe* also called attention to the owner's

6 Fumasoli 2017, pp. 173–74.
7 Exh. cat. Nuremberg 2002.
8 Werner 1961, pp. 289–328, 444–502; Werner 1967–68.
9 Haug 2021, pp. 41–193.

interest in geology and his economic ties to the mining industry. The Scheurl family held shares in numerous mines, most notably in Horní Slavkov (Schlaggenwald), Jáchymov (Joachimsthal), and Annaberg. Christoph Scheurl II (1481–1542) had received those shares in return for loans made to Emperor Maximilian I.[10] The Scheurl *Erzstufe* symbolized certain salient rewards of participation in the mining industry—namely, knowledge of raw materials, economic power, and social status.

In addition to featuring in such mineralogical and artisanal showpieces, mining figured as a motif in numerous other kinds of objects. An impressive example is the so-called Imhoff–Holzschuher cup, whose hallmark indicates that it was made by Hans Petzolt (1550–1632) between 1593 and 1602 |**figs. 5, 6; cat. no. 28**|. Petzolt, a goldsmith who came to Nuremberg from the Bohemian mining district of Jáchymov, probably created the cup for Veit Georg Holzschuher (1573–1606) and his wife Regina, née Imhoff (d. 1613). In 1626, years after both of their deaths, their children gave the cup to their uncle Andreas Imhoff, who was the imperial mayor (*Reichsschultheiß*) of Nuremberg, chief administrator of the Eisfeld *Saigerhandel*, and himself a mine owner.[11] The cup's finely worked mining scenes, distributed across six large and three smaller cartouches, are based on designs by Virgil Solis (1514–1562) |**figs. 3, 4; cat. no. 28**|. They depict the main processes of silver mining, from extraction and smelting to subsequent processing techniques.[12] This work exemplifies how economic power and artistic sophistication could come together in prestige objects, giving visual expression to the social aspirations of the urban elite. At the same time, the cup brings into focus the main themes of self-representation in such works: family influence, economic potency, and social status. The artfully staged mining scenes emphasize a form of self-representation primarily concerned with technical knowledge, economic participation, and social distinction, while passing over other aspects of the mining industry. This holds true as well for the *Totenschild* (memorial shield) for Hans Tetzel, made from his family's burial chapel at the Egidienkirche. The panel memorializes Tetzel's social status and familial importance but not his mining ventures in Cuba nor the colonial structures in which they were embedded |**cat. no. 108**|.[13] The global reach of Nurembergers' mining activities was inextricably linked to the colonial reality of the early modern period—a reality based on violent appropriation of resources, exploitation of enslaved laborers, and profound economic dependencies. Yet that dimension is absent from the types of self-representation cultivated by the urban elite.

The interconnection of the mining business, social prestige, and self-representation points to a broader interest in mining that extended beyond symbolic treatments in works of art. As a center of book printing, early modern Nuremberg became a nexus at which economic practice, learned reflection, and journalistic communication intersected. Organizing and carrying out mining-related activities required knowledge of mineral resources, deposits, technical processes, and markets. This knowledge derived not only from practical experience; it was also conveyed in printed form. Publications produced in Nuremberg offer striking evidence of the ways in which knowledge about mining was systematized, preserved in writing, and made accessible to a broader public. A prominent example that underscores how important Nuremberg printers were in this process is Johannes Mathesius's book *Sarepta oder Bergpostill*, which was printed in folio format in 1562 by Johann vom Berg and Ulrich Neuber.[14] Mathesius was a disciple of Martin Luther and worked as a pastor in Jáchymov. He was also an expert on the subject of mining. His mining sermons interweave theological reflection with mineralogical and technical knowledge.[15]

Apart from such long, large-format works, smaller, more easily accessible publications such

10 Haug 2021, p. 57.
11 I thank Birgit Schübel, Nuremberg, for pointing this out.
12 Exh. cat. Bochum 1990, pp. 518–26, cat. no. 230 (Rainer Slotta).
13 Jakstat 2024.
14 Mathesius 1562.
15 Morel 2020.

Figs. 3, 4 Virgil Solis, *Mining Scenes*, Nuremberg, before 1562, SMB, Berlin, Kupferstichkabinett, inv. nos. 815-6, 814-6 |**cat. nos. 28.3, 28.2**|

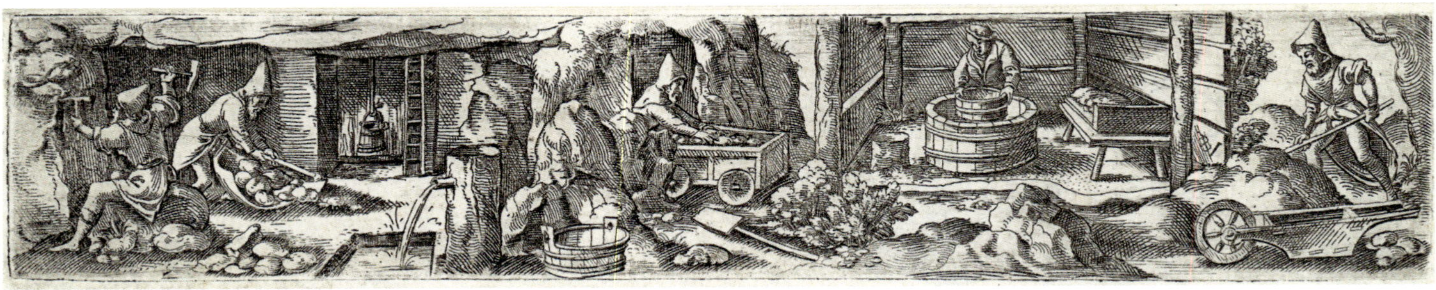

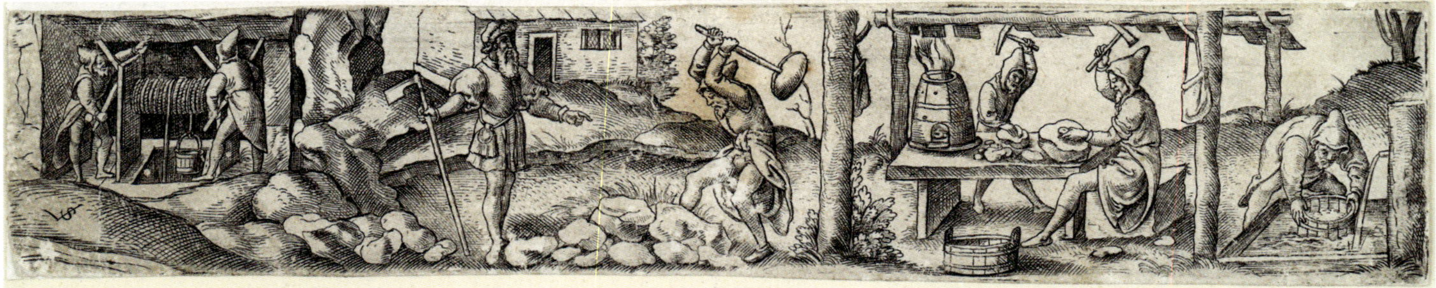

as calendars and prognostications helped to establish Nuremberg as a hub of mining knowledge. Of great interest in this regard is a text by the priest and calendar-maker Georg Kreslin (1563–1628): the thirty-page *Berg-Practica oder Prognosticon diß Bergwerck bawens* (Prognostication on Mining).[16] It was published in 1597 by the Nuremberg printer Valentin Fuhrmann. The *Berg-Practica* instructs shareholders on how to ensure profit from financial investments in mining, dispensing advice on which times of year were particularly profitable for a given metal. Kreslin combines astrological knowledge with economic calculus. For shareholders not only in Nuremberg but also in other centers of the mining business, knowledge of this kind was highly important for assessing risks and maximizing returns on investments. The publications by Mathesius and Kreslin demonstrate that technical treatises were not the only genre that transmitted mining-related knowledge. Rather, such knowledge was conveyed in various forms of print media and addressed to a number of different audiences. In this situation, theological, technical, astrological, and economic topics were closely intertwined.

Nuremberg was therefore much more than a production center for metalwork sold to a global market. The city operated as a junction of economic networks; as an entrepôt for the distribution of technical, economic, and mining knowledge; and as a stage for the self-representation of the urban elite. Mining was closely interlinked with urban society—not only as a resource but also as a central medium of cultural and economic self-affirmation. This manifested in elaborately designed cups, in publications, and in extensive trade and investment networks that extended from the mines and smelteries of central Germany all the way to the Caribbean, Africa, and Asia.

16 Kreslin 1597.

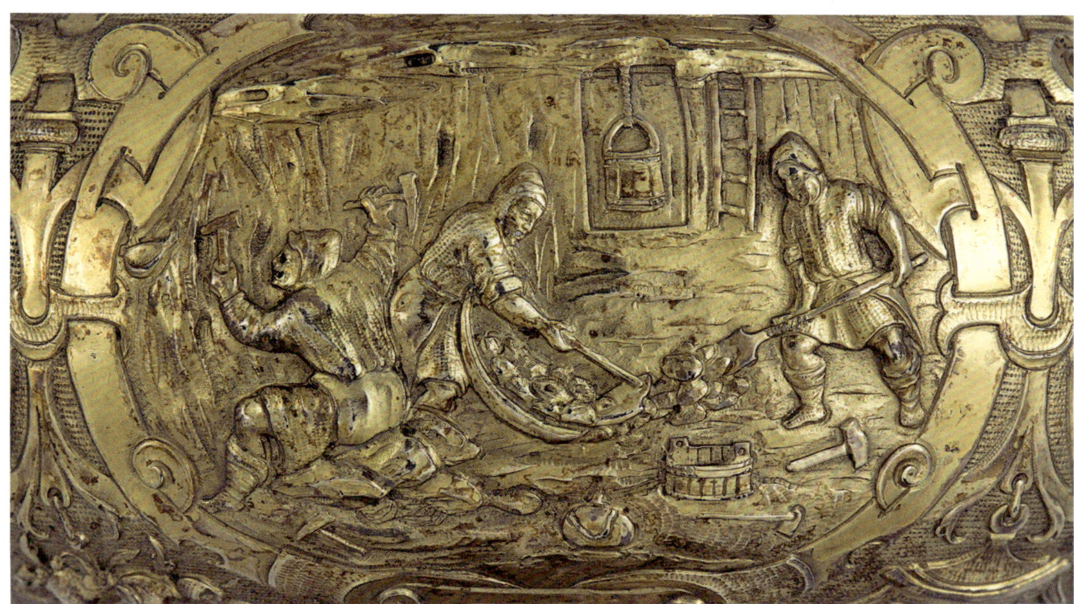

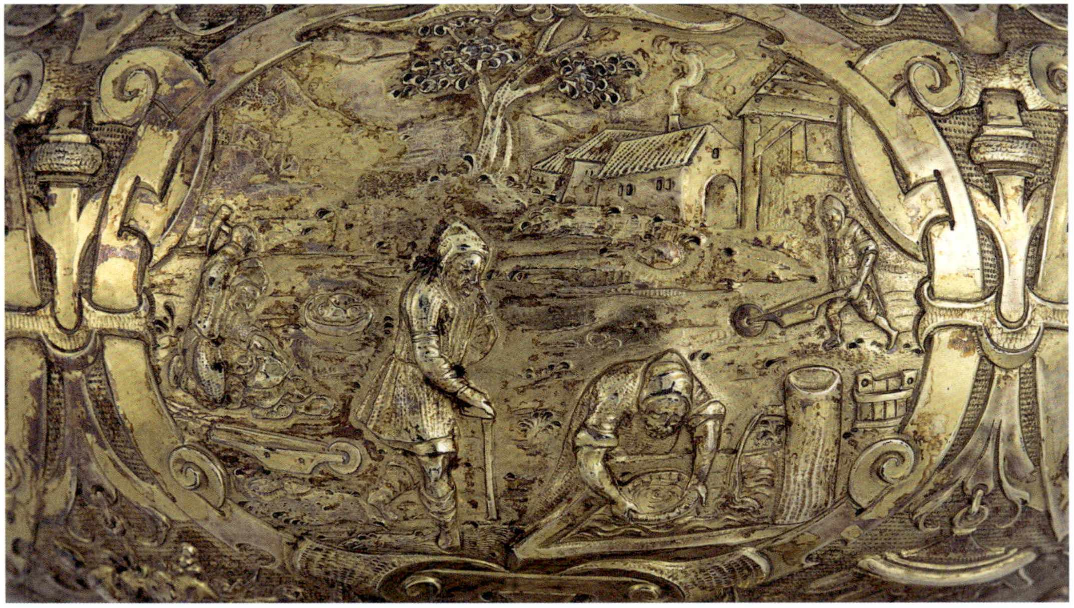

Figs. 5, 6 Hans Pezolt, *The Imhoff-Holzschuher Cup*, details of the medallions *The First Mine* and *The Washworks*, Nuremberg, 1593/1602, Museo Nacional Thyssen Bornemisza, Madrid, inv. no. DEC0972 |**cat. no. 28.1**|

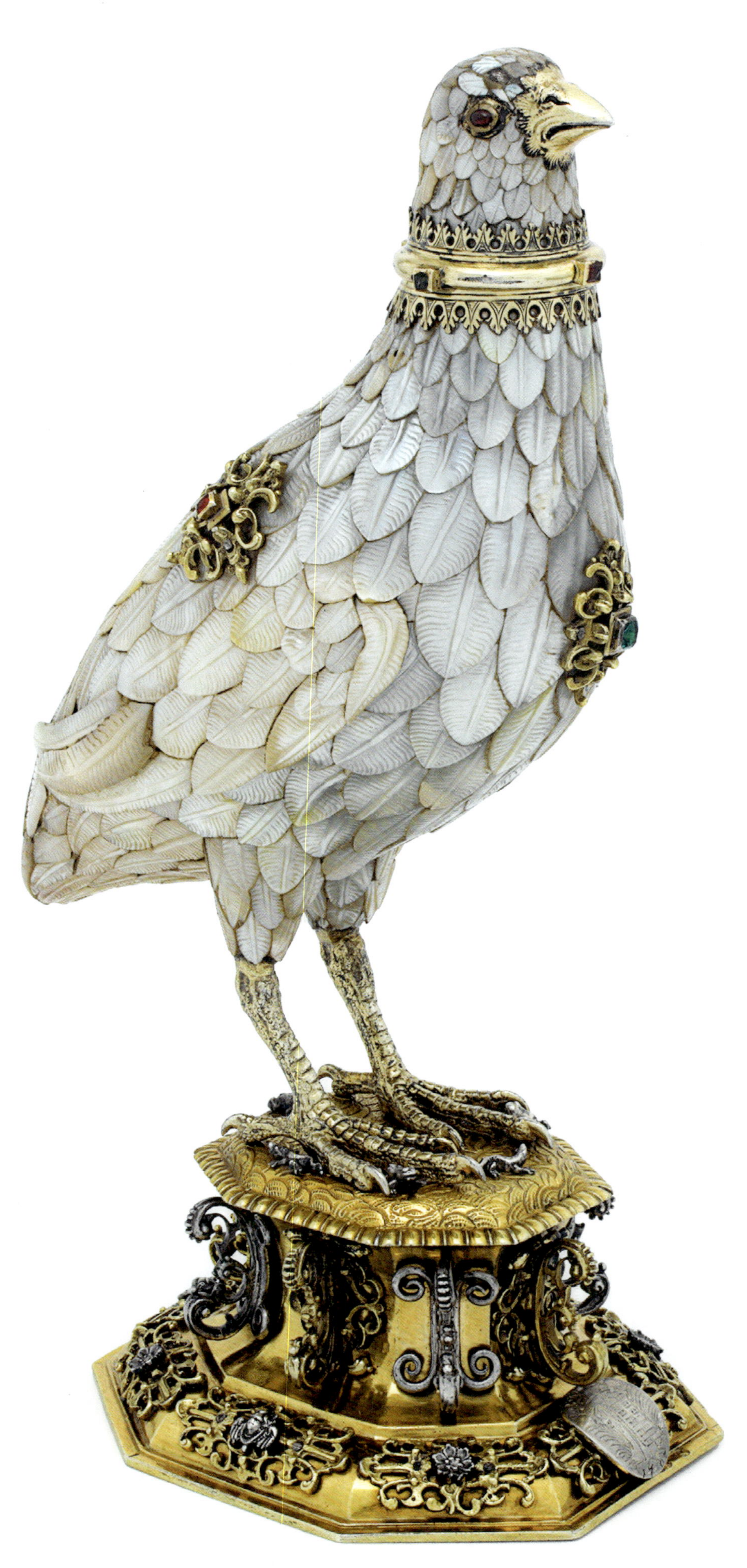

Heike Zech

GLOBAL LUXURY GOODS IN NUREMBERG

Between 1300 and 1600, rare and precious goods obtained through long-distance trade became available to the Nuremberg citizenry in ever-increasing variety and quantity. This essay presents examples of such global luxury goods and sheds light on their use and significance in the period from the fourteenth to the early seventeenth century. As historian Ulinka Rublack notes while discussing the material culture of the European Renaissance, "Objects contributed to shaping the period's sentiments, ideas and practices rather than just representing existing values and aesthetic ideals. Innovative uses of matter, texture and form helped to constitute contexts in which these objects took on meaning."[1] Nuremberg is a place where such contexts were formed. The production and consumption of luxury and premium goods performed important social functions in Nuremberg between 1300 and 1600: such goods were indicative of prestige, wealth, power, and social affiliation; at the same time, owing to their novelty, they could develop an almost subversive power |**cat. nos. 16, 41, 104, 120**|. In addition, the luxury sector supported a number of highly specialized mercantile and craft enterprises, as well as the people associated with those enterprises. For that reason, this essay begins with the Nuremberg goldsmiths and their use of materials from around the globe.

Fig. 1 Georg Rühl I, *Partridge Cup*, 1598–1602, Victoria & Albert Museum, London, inv. no. LOAN:GILBERT.60:1, 2-2008

The Art of Goldsmithing: Refining the World

By the late Middle Ages, the goldsmiths of Nuremberg had established their handiwork—stamped with the city's capital "N" hallmark—as a well-known and sought-after brand throughout Europe. For centuries, the city's Inner Council used works created in Nuremberg as diplomatic gifts, thereby contributing significantly to the trade's success.[2] Along with armor-making |**cat. no. 36**|, goldsmithing became one of the city's flagship crafts, and its fame affected all the local metalworking trades. The *Schlüsselfelder Nef* of 1503 |**cat. no. 97**|, a table centerpiece in the form of a ship, is one of the earliest works on which the Nuremberg "N" hallmark is recognizable. It appears prominently on the bow. One can only speculate about the origin of the work's silver. Before 1492, Nuremberg goldsmiths had access to material from mines owned by Nuremberg trading firms, for example in Kutná Hora (Kuttenberg), Schwaz, Annaberg, and Jáchymov (Joachimsthal). Yet South American silver was probably also used in Nuremberg from an early date, for example from the rich deposits mined from 1545 onward at the Cerro Rico (Rich Mountain) of Potosí.[3]

The goldsmiths' use of global materials was not limited to precious metals. In Nuremberg, fine items from all over the world were among the things mounted in silver: ostrich eggs from Africa and Arabia; coconuts, mother-of-pearl, and sea-snail shells from Asia |**cat. nos. 2, 16, 41, 104, 120**|; and delicate glass vessels from Venice and Antwerp. Mother-of-pearl objects originating in the Gujarat Sultanate in northwestern India seem to have been particularly prized, especially in the late sixteenth and early seventeenth centuries. From the sixteenth century onward, vessels, pieces of furniture, and boxes decorated with sections cut from sea-snail shells were brought from Goa to Europe by Portuguese traders. Indian workshops responded to growing demand by producing objects at varying levels of quality for westward export, destined for ports from the seat of the Ottoman Empire to Portugal. The best works are distinguished by intricately cut pieces of mother-of-pearl whose appearance is reminiscent of fish scales or flower petals. The sections are arranged without any visible gaps and secured to the object's wooden core with small metal pins |**see cat. no. 2**|. A group of bird-shaped drinking vessels made in Nuremberg and featuring mother-of-pearl is strikingly differ-

1 Rublack 2013, pp. 41–42.
2 See NGK 2007.
3 Although evidence remains to be found, the use of such silver in the workshops of Nuremberg seems likely given the massive scale of South American silver mining and the extensive exportation to Europe that is documented beginning in the last third of the sixteenth century. See Hanke 2012; Lane 2019.

Fig. 2 Hans Rappolt I, *Parrot Cup*, 1593–1602, Staatliche Kunstsammlungen Dresden, Grünes Gewölbe, inv. no. III 151

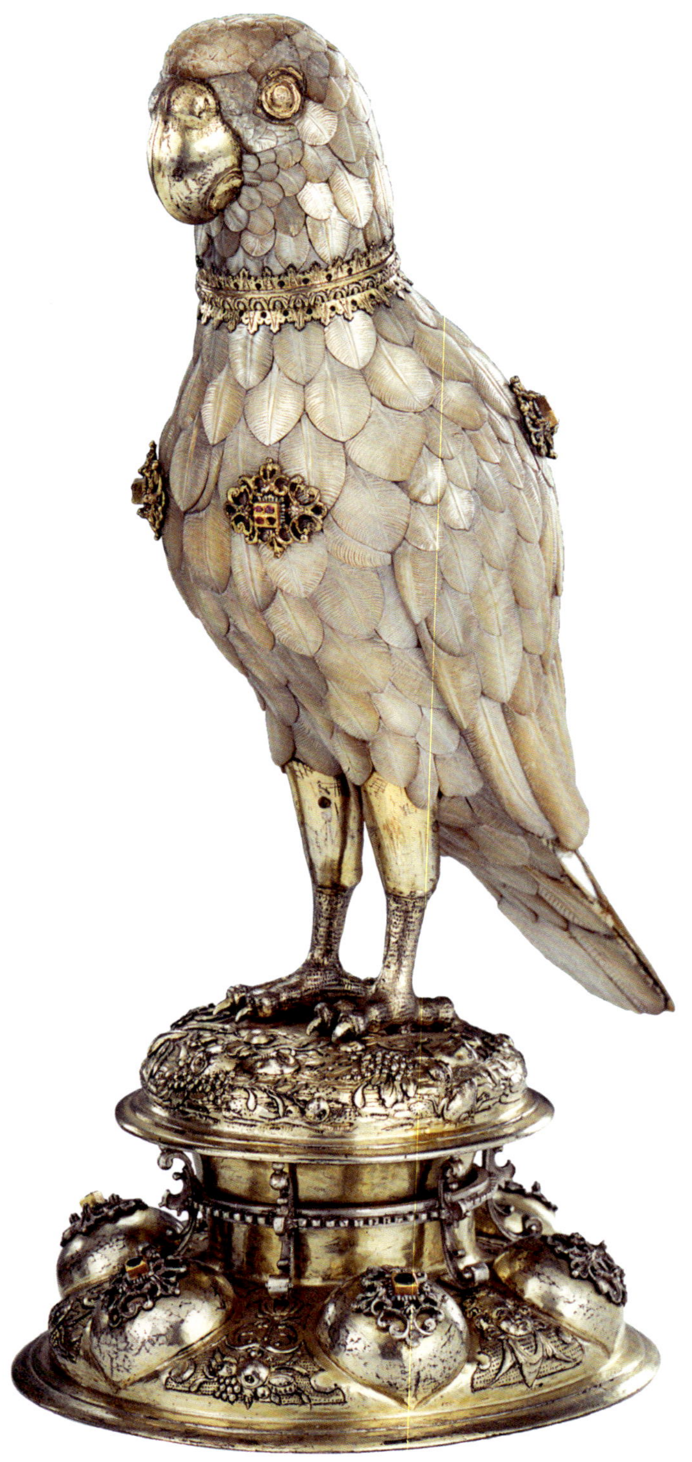

ent. Four partridges and a parrot have survived, all created about the same time |**figs. 1, 2**|. Each bears the Nuremberg hallmark, struck with the same punch, alongside the respective master's mark of a different workshop. Clearly, the precious global resources were shared.[4] The plumage consists of densely arranged pieces of mother-of-pearl, each feather individually cut from a snail shell in appropriate size and curvature. In a subsequent step, the outside surface of each piece was carved to resemble a feather. The pieces were then attached to the silver corpus, overlapping like roof tiles, so that the fastening pins would remain out of sight. The highly similar treatment of the mother-of-pearl on all five cups suggests that the feathers were probably prepared in the same workshop before being applied by the goldsmiths. In their form and fastening, the feathers differ greatly from the mother-of-pearl craftsmanship typical of Gujarat. This suggests that the feathers were carved only after arrival in Europe, perhaps even in Nuremberg. Although it is certain that the mother-of-pearl was mounted onto drinking vessels in Nuremberg, the pieces were not destined to remain there: today, the bird-shaped cups are found in four different countries.

Textiles and Leather: Global Materials, European Trends

Not only goldsmiths took part in working and refining internationally sourced materials. The trades that specialized in textiles, furs, and leathers also relied on a constant influx of goods to produce such items as veils, shoes, and clothing. Casemaking, a historical craft that is often overlooked today, involved the use Moroccan leather or leather tanned in Italy or Spain.[5] Finished fashion accessories were also among the goods imported to Nuremberg. For example, a Spanish origin is possible for a shoe of finest goatskin that Margarethe

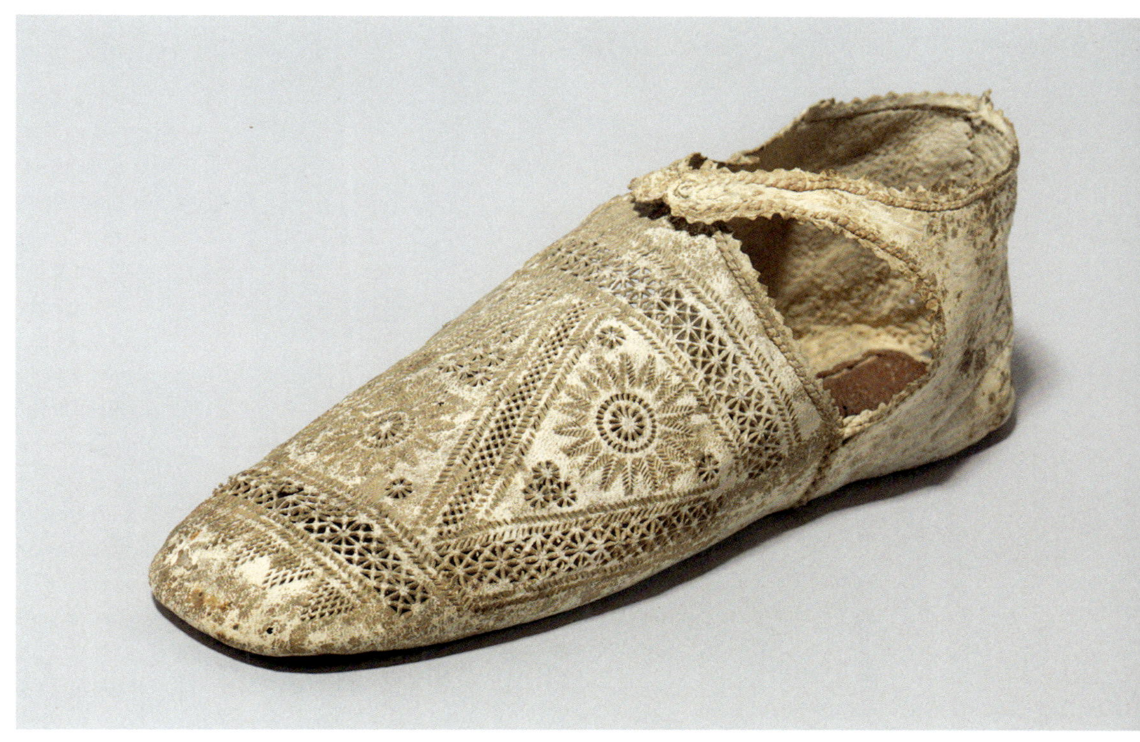

Fig. 3 Shoe made of goatskin, late sixteenth century, GNM, inv. no. T44

Völker, according to family tradition, wore at her wedding to Hans Joachim Nützel (1531–1603) on February 4, 1594 |**fig. 3**|.[6] The velvet beret of Christoph Kress zu Kressenstein (1484–1535), decorated with dyed ostrich feathers, is another such global accessory |**cat. no. 39**|. It is said to have been given to Kress by Emperor Charles V (1500–1558) at the 1530 Diet of Augsburg, which Kress attended as an envoy of Nuremberg.[7] Like the shoe, the imperial gift survived the centuries as a family relic, stored safely in a box. The inside of the hat box is adorned with a posthumous portrait engraving, created in the seventeenth century, showing Christoph Kress wearing this very beret.

In addition to such family treasures, which were accessible to only a select circle and demonstrated the global dimensions of a family's history, large examples of the textile arts also found their way to Nuremberg, where they were seen and admired by a wider public. The memorial tapestry of the Holzschuher family, dated 1495 and measuring nearly three meters in height, must have aroused great astonishment when it arrived in Nuremberg from Brussels |**cat. no. 49**|.[8] At that time, no other artistic genre was more expensive than such tapestries fashioned partly from silk. The only known work that is directly comparable to the Holzschuher panel is a tapestry panel that was made for Queen Isabella the Catholic (1451–1504) on the basis of the same cartoon. Appropriately regal in appearance, it is still kept in the royal collections in Madrid. During this period, Nuremberg families other than the Holzschuhers also acquired southern Netherlandish tapestries for display in churches. For example, four Passion panels that belonged to the Starck family, made about 1510, were hung "on the feast days in the choir" of the Sebalduskirche. Of those, only a single fragment has survived.[9]

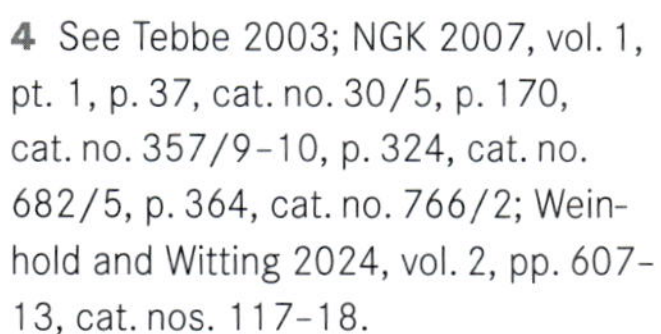

4 See Tebbe 2003; NGK 2007, vol. 1, pt. 1, p. 37, cat. no. 30/5, p. 170, cat. no. 357/9–10, p. 324, cat. no. 682/5, p. 364, cat. no. 766/2; Weinhold and Witting 2024, vol. 2, pp. 607–13, cat. nos. 117–18.
5 See Zander-Seidel 1990. On leather's significance in sixteenth-century Augsburg, see Rublack 2010.
6 See Exh. cat. Nuremberg 2015b, pp. 63–64, cat. no. 30 (Jutta Zander-Seidel), p. 273, cat. no. 30 (technical notes); Exh. cat. Braunschweig 2019, p. 192, cat. no. 120 (Birgitt Borkopp-Restle), ill. p. 193 (shoes, second half of the sixteenth century, Deutsches Ledermuseum, Offenbach). On the Nützel family, see Fleischmann 2008, vol. 2, pp. 733–56.
7 See Zander-Seidel 1990, pp. 221–22; Exh. cat. Nuremberg 2015b, pp. 40–42, cat. no. 11 (Jutta Zander-Seidel), pp. 271–72, cat. no. 11 (technical notes); Hanß 2021b.
8 Since the fourteenth century, Nuremberg itself had been a center of tapestry production, also making use of global materials in the form of silk and metal thread. Tapestry panels owned by the church parishes were brought out for feast days; others were lent by certain families for display in churches. See Zander-Seidel 2006, pp. 40–41.
9 GNM, inv. no. Gew4968. See Zander-Seidel 1997, pp. 184–87.

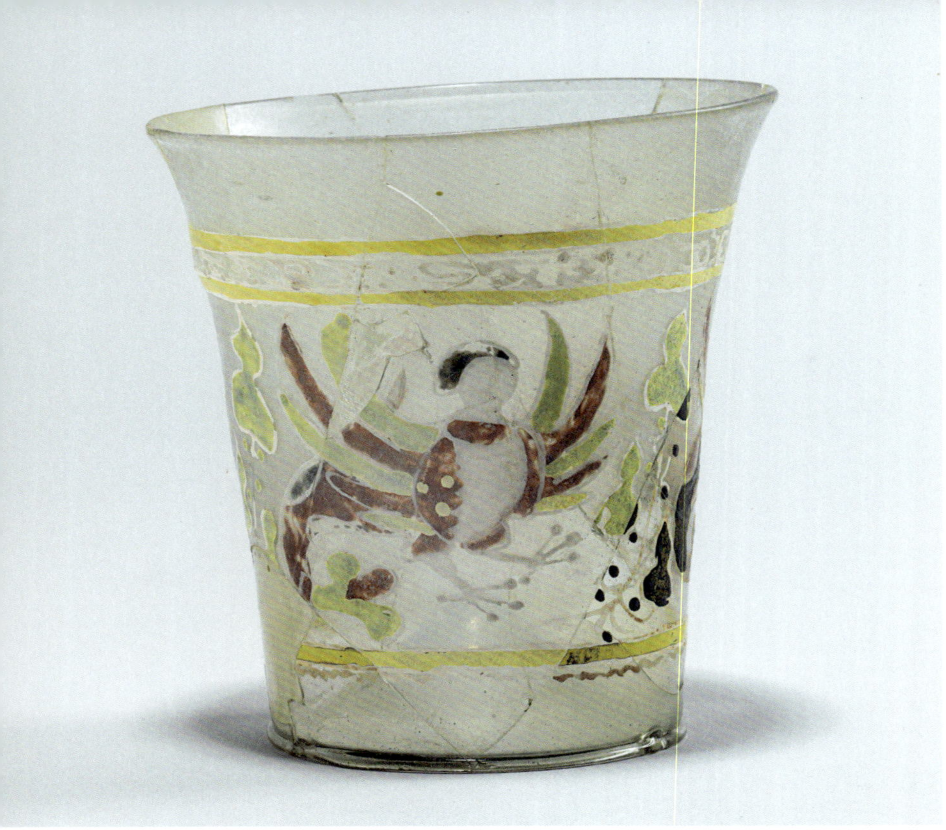

Fig. 4 Glass beaker with painted enamel decoration (reconstructed), second half of thirteenth or early fourteenth century, GNM, inv. no. Gl644

Dishes and Glassware: Italian Lifestyle and Islamic Inspiration

While such splendid works as tapestries were acquired in small numbers, ceramics and glassware made in Italy came to Nuremberg in much larger quantities in the period under consideration. The reasons for their acquisition, however, were often the same as those already mentioned: acts of diplomacy as well as marriages and other family affairs. Fragments of a glass beaker found during excavations in the medieval inn called "At the Wild Man," located on the Hauptmarkt, prove that Venetian drinking glasses reached Nuremberg as early as the fourteenth century |**fig. 4**|. The beaker's almost colorless glass bears an image of a mythical creature painted with delicate brushstrokes. The materials and decorations allow us to assign the beaker to a group of drinking glasses that were made in Venice around 1300 based on models from the Abbasid Caliphate.[10] For centuries, Venice was Nuremberg's closest and most reliable long-distance trading partner south of the Alps.[11] Many merchants from Nuremberg spent their formative years as apprentices in Italian trading firms or at universities such as those in Padua and Bologna. In addition to acquiring knowledge and language skills, they learned to appreciate Italian art and culture—things the Nurembergers did not want to be without after returning home. Despite their fragility, examples of Italian ceramics, glass, and fashion accessories found their way north almost as a matter of course, as demonstrated by maiolica decorated with the coats of arms of Nuremberg patricians |**cat. no. 61**|. Nuremberg craftspeople, in turn, imitated Italian models in various genres, sometimes so closely that later generations believed their work to have come from Italy |**cat. no. 20**|.

The Tucher family's enamel table service, by contrast, resulted from a unique collaboration between metalworkers in Nuremberg and enamel painters in Limoges, France |**cat. no. 52; fig. 5**|. The project was not without problems, however, because the Nuremberg copper vessels that were initially sent to Limoges for decoration were unsuitable for the enamel techniques practiced there. Despite laudable efforts made in the art of enamel painting in Nuremberg, the patrons insisted on obtaining the far superior quality characteristic of Limoges enamels. While all the other groups of "global" objects in Nuremberg are mirrored by comparable examples in other southern German imperial cities and in princely collections, the Tucher service is a unique ensemble and provides testimony to an instance of cross-border collaboration in the European decorative arts of the early modern period.

As maiolica and enamel gradually replaced Nuremberg pewter, they changed the character of the city's banquet tables. These colorful dishes, with their fascinating patterns and complex pictorial programs, enlivened table settings both visually and intellectually. They expressed the host families' connections to a Europe-wide network of elites. Whether created in Nuremberg or simply used and appreciated there, each of these pieces had global aspects that extended far beyond the origins of their materials. For it was also in their form and decoration that these works clearly distinguished themselves from the everyday objects traditionally produced in the region. This made it possible to put wealth and international networking on conspicuous display.

10 Exh. cat. Nuremberg 1984; Kahsnitz 1984. On the attribution and dating, see Ward 2015.
11 See the essay by Henry Kaap in the present volume.

Fig. 5 Pierre Reymond and Wenzel Jamnitzer, *Limoges Table Service of the Tucher Family*, ca. 1553–62, on long-term loan from the Tucher Kulturstiftung to the Museum Tucherschloss und Hirsvogelsaal, Museen der Stadt Nürnberg, inv. nos. HI Kh 001–HI Kh 010

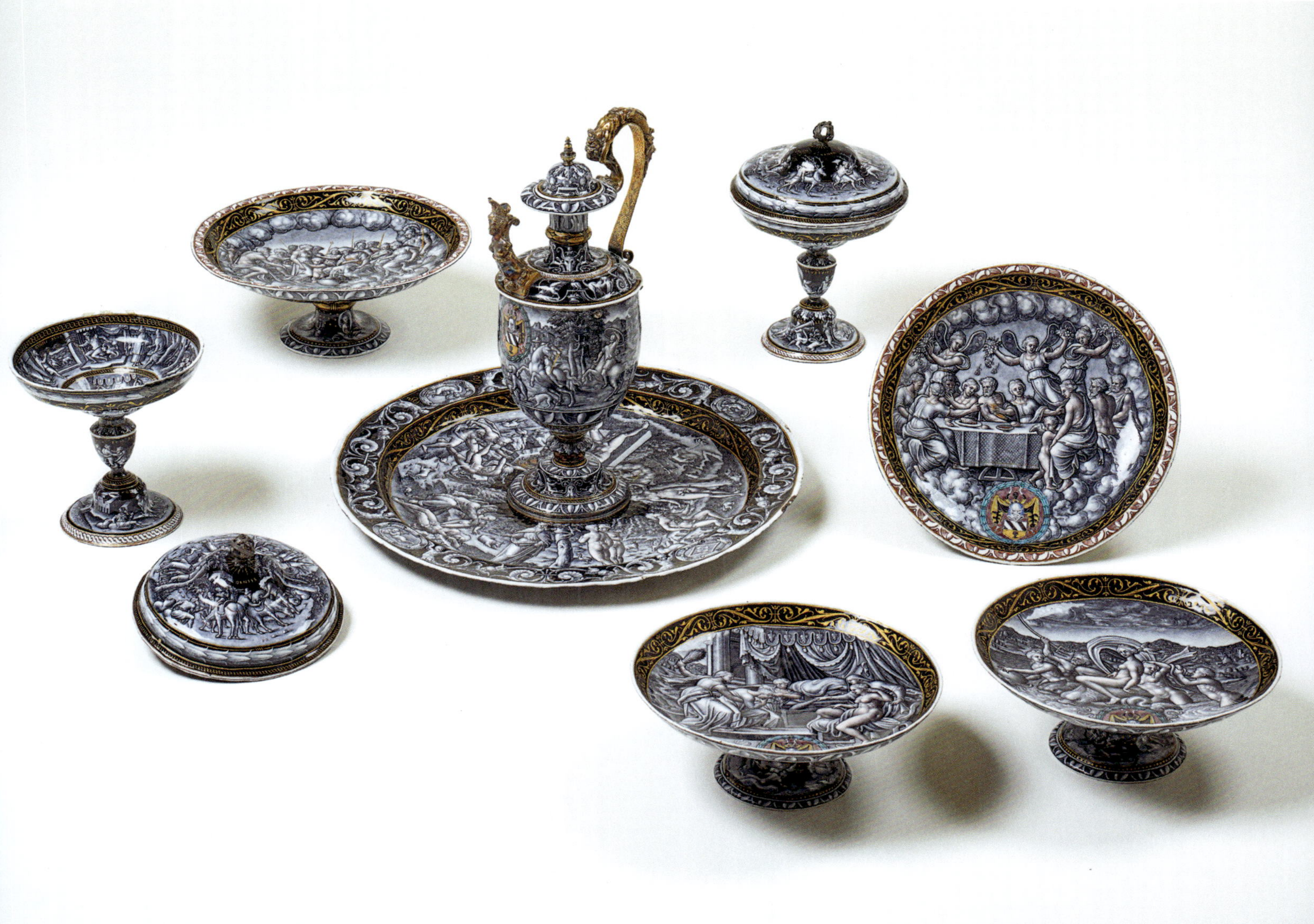

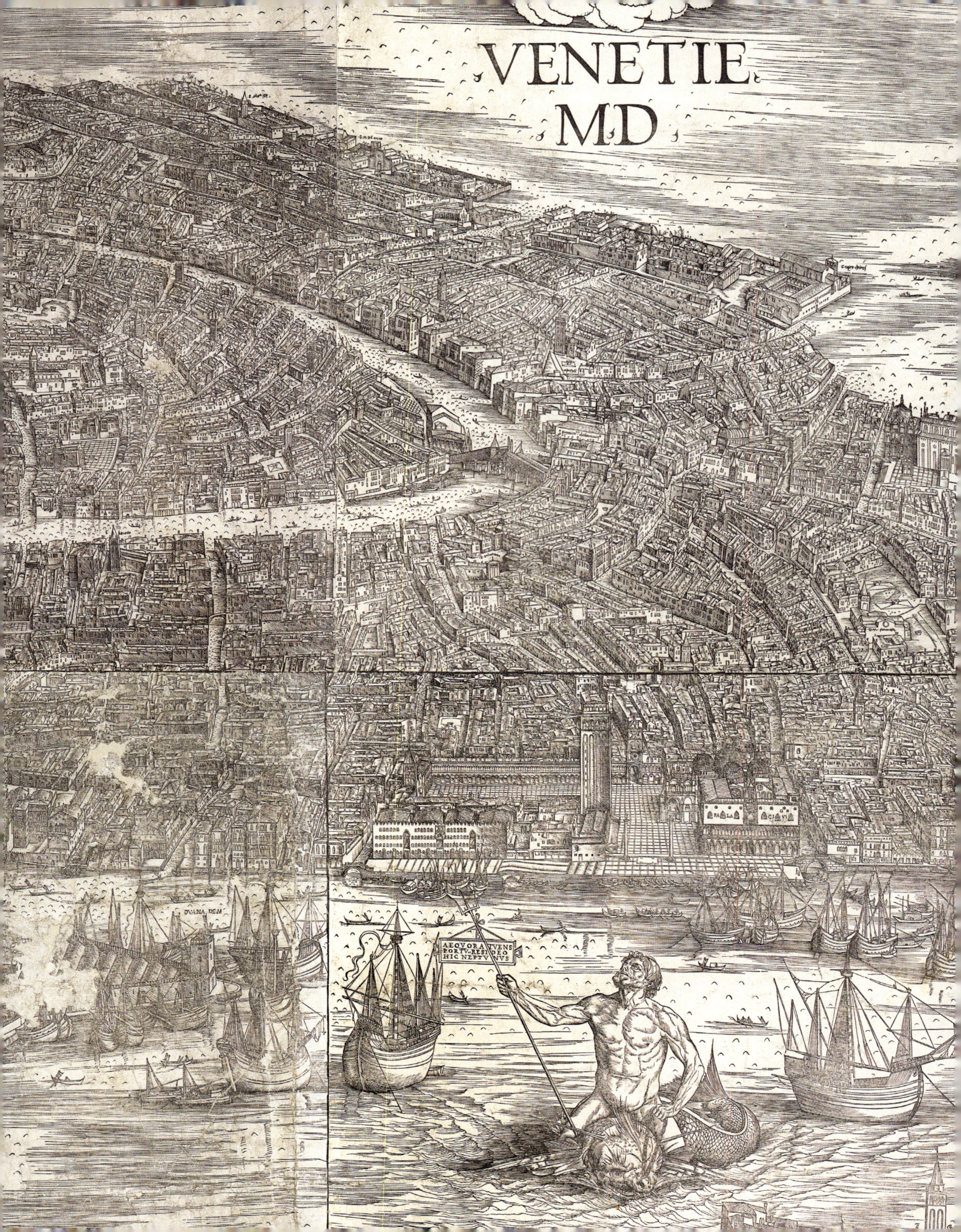
VENETIE
MD
AEQVORA TVENS
PORTV RESIDEO
HIC NEPTVNVS

Henry Kaap

VENICE AS NUREMBERG'S GATEWAY TO THE WORLD

If you want to see the world, go to Venice! Sayings of this sort applied to more than just the pilgrims who crossed the Alps to board a ship in Venice bound for the Holy Land. In the fifteenth century, the Serenissima was the Mediterranean's leading commercial and maritime center. The city stood at the beginning and end of important trade routes to and from Asia and the Middle East, and it was a crucial entrepôt for the movement of goods throughout Europe. At the same time, Venice itself had many marvels to offer—not just to Holy Land pilgrims, but also to merchants, artisans, and artists arriving from the North. About 1450, Fra Mauro, a monk belonging to the Camaldolese monastery of San Michele di Murano, created a world map that gave expression to the city's special role as a global hub of goods, ideas, and information |**fig. 2**|.[1] This *mappa mundi*, which Giovanni Ramusio (1485–1557) referred to as the "miracle of Venice," is far more than just an image of the world as known at the time: measuring 196 centimeters in diameter and containing more than 3,000 annotations, it is a monumental testimony to the currents of knowledge and commerce that shaped Venice during the late medieval and early modern periods. As a synthesis of intellectual traditions of the Middle Ages and empirical innovations of the Renaissance, the map incorporates knowledge from Aristotelian natural philosophy, Christian cosmology, portolan nautical charts, and the travelogues of Venetian merchants such as Marco Polo (d. 1324). At the same time, the representation encompasses maritime trade routes, geographical discoveries, and descriptions of cities, ships, and ports. From the sea as a cosmological entity all the way to specific trade routes—this multiplicity of different categories of knowledge would have been inconceivable if Venice had not played a major part in the collection and distribution of global information. It is therefore no accident that this *mappa mundi* was created in Venice. Through its cosmopolitan perspective and its fusion of diverse sources of knowledge into a comprehensive "image of the world," the map indirectly reflects the self-perception of Venice as a "gateway to the world." Fra Mauro's work thus not only illustrates geographical features; it also renders an image of the cultural and economic dynamics that made Venice a key participant in European and worldwide trade networks.

For Nuremberg, a center of art and commerce in the heart of Europe, the fourteenth century marked the beginning of a period of economic and cultural flowering. It is therefore unsurprising that Nuremberg merchants, craftspeople, and artists journeyed to Venice to participate in the global exchange of knowledge and goods.[2] Routes such as the Via Norimbergi provided good connections. Around 1500, hurried travelers could move between the two cities in just four days, but the journey normally took two weeks.[3] The cities held each other in mutual esteem, for Venice also benefited from Nuremberg, whose favorable geographical location ensured access to important raw materials such as precious and non-precious metals. Because of the diversity of trades practiced in Nuremberg around 1500, the city became the most important European center for precision mechanical products, including the types of astronomical and nautical instruments that were particularly sought after in Venice.[4] The Behaim Globe, which was begun in 1492, is the oldest surviving three-dimensional model of the earth (excluding the Americas) |**cat. no. 1**|. It is also a tour de force of the collaborative working processes of Nuremberg craftspeople. In terms of its cartography and cosmography, it may well have aroused admiration similar to that expressed for Fra Mauro's world map. The relationship between Nuremberg and Venice was therefore not merely economic but also cultural and technological. The two cities represented two different but complementary roles in the global networks of the early modern period. While Venice served as a hub of trade between Europe, North Africa, the Middle East, and Greater Central Asia, Nuremberg

Fig. 1 Jacopo de' Barbari and Anton Kolb (publisher), *View of Venice* (detail), 1500, GNM, inv. no. SP5903 |**cat. no. 53**|

1 Cattaneo 2010.
2 Pfotenhauer 2016; Schmitz-Esser 2023, p. 185.
3 Stauber 2000, pp. 127–28.
4 Stauber 2000, pp. 135–36; Pfotenhauer 2016, pp. 258–98.

Fig. 2 Fra Mauro, *Mappa mundi*, ca. 1450, Biblioteca Nazionale Marciana, Venice, shelf mark 106173

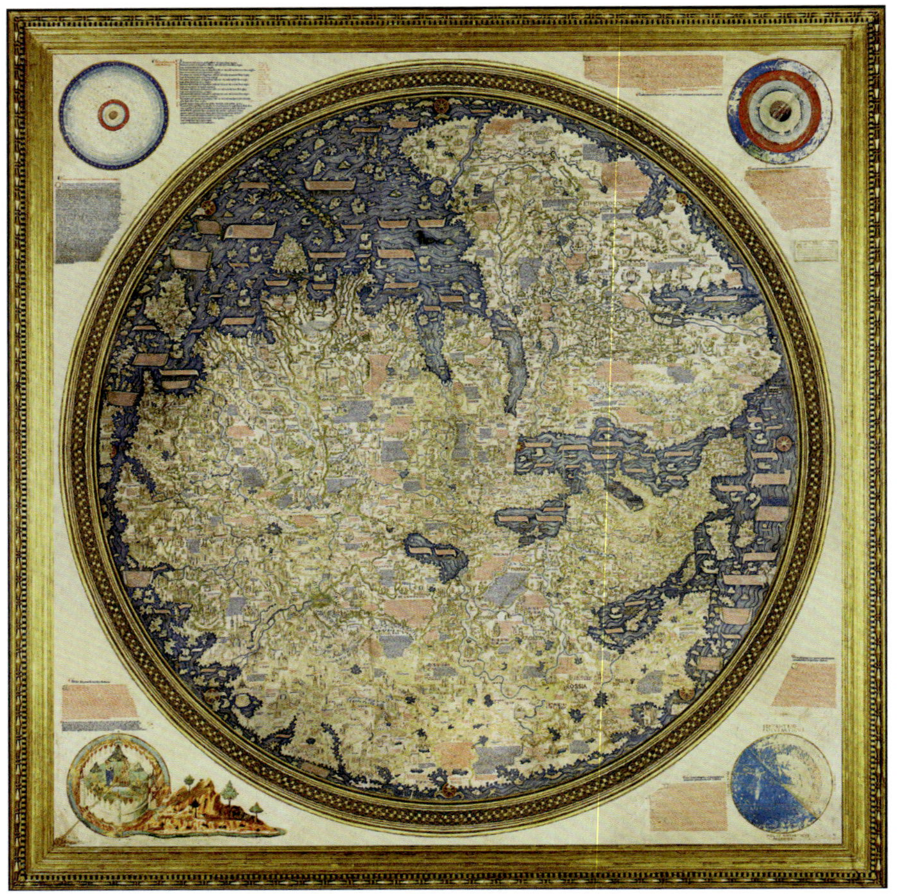

was a center of technical and artisanal innovation. Connections between the cities manifested even in civil engineering, as demonstrated by the design of of Nuremberg's Fleischbrücke, which is similar in construction to the Rialto Bridge in Venice |**cat. nos. 54, 55**|.

The woodcut *View of Venice* by Jacopo de' Barbari (d. 1516) is emblematic of the two centers' economic and cultural interconnectedness |**cat. no. 53**|.[5] This monumental city view was begun by the Italian artist in 1497, at the behest of the Nuremberg merchant and publisher Anton Kolb (1471–1541), who had lived in Venice since 1493, where he was a distributor of *Schedel's Weltchronik* (commonly known in English as the *Nuremberg Chronicle*) |**cat. no. 4**|.[6] The *View of Venice* was printed from six blocks and measures about 135 by 280 centimeters, making it the largest and most detailed view of a European city at the time. Titled "VENETIE MD" (Venice 1500), it shows the metropolis from the southwest, in a bird's-eye view, a then novel method of representation which combines technical precision with artistic mastery. The view focuses on the *bacino*, the harbor basin, rimmed by central buildings such as the Doge's Palace and the Basilica di San Marco. These sites embody the political and religious power of Venice, while emphasizing the city's maritime identity. A feature of particular importance is the Arsenal, one of the world's largest shipbuilding centers at the time. It was the backbone of Venetian naval and commercial power. The inclusion of mythological elements, such as the god Neptune situated in the harbor basin, underscores the portrayal of Venice as the undisputed maritime superpower of the Mediterranean.

Jacopo de' Barbari's cityscape is thus not only a cartographic masterpiece but also a programmatic representation of a complex urban structure—one that formed its identity through the interplay of commerce, religion, politics, and art. The prospect of the city from a viewpoint above the sea presents Venice as a place of passage and of the imagination. Canals, bridges, and palazzi with small private docks are features of an urban network that had to continually remake itself at the edges. This dynamic interplay between nature and culture, between water and architecture, makes Venice a threshold city—a place where the boundaries between land and water, and also between "Orient" and "Occident," are always being crossed.[7]

The painter Gentile Bellini (1430–1507), for instance, was sent in 1479 as a Venetian ambassador to Istanbul, the capital of the Ottoman Empire. The impressions he gained at the court of Mehmed II (1432–1481) were formative not only for his own art but also for that of his brother Giovanni (d. 1516)

5 Huffman 2024.
6 Martin 1994, p. 89.
7 Baader and Wolf 2014, pp. 36–39.

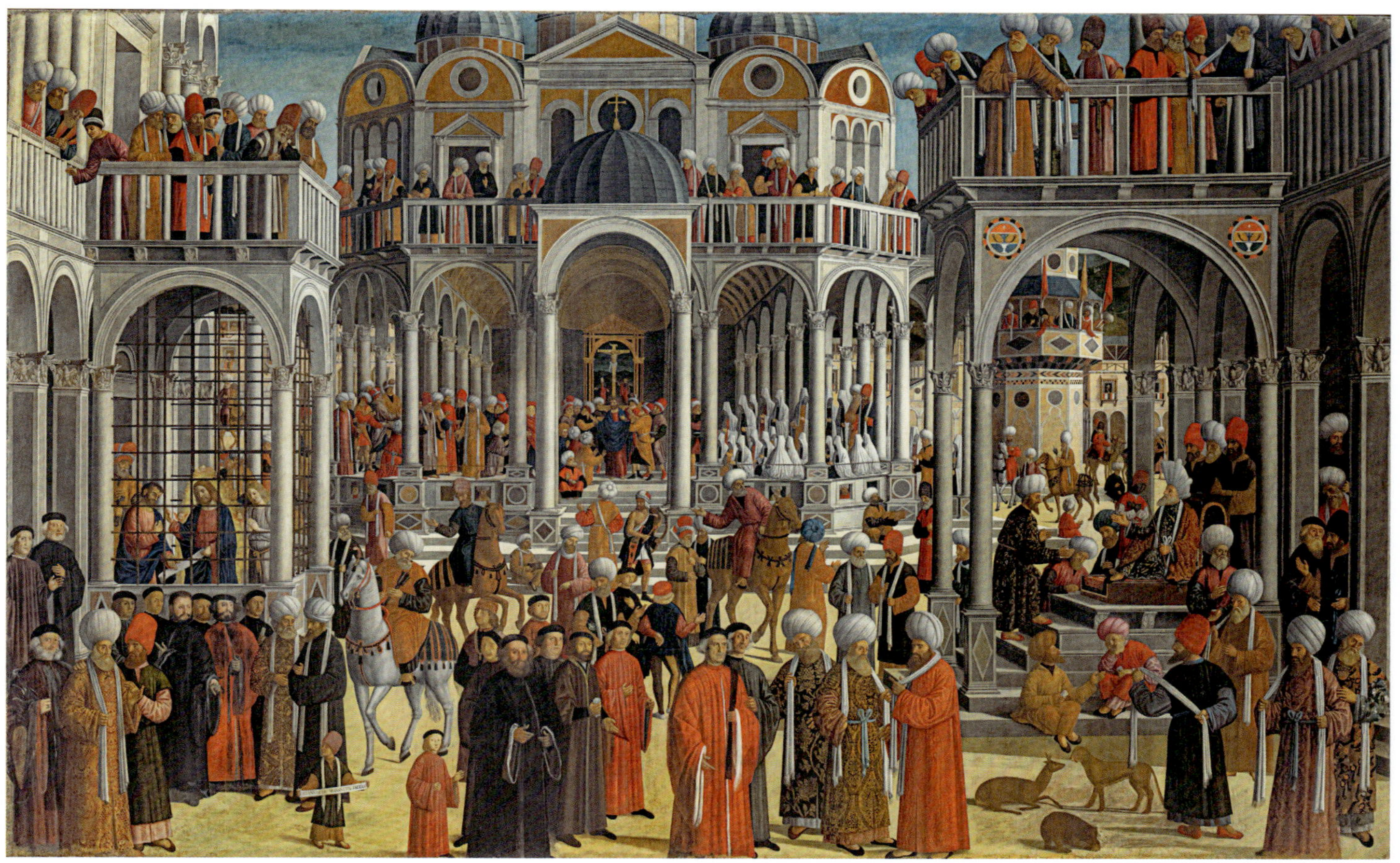

Fig. 3 Giovanni Mansueti, *Scenes from the Life of Saint Mark*, 1525, Gallerie dell'Accademia, Venice, inv. no. 562

and their workshop assistants, such as Giovanni Mansueti (ca. 1465–1527) |**fig. 3**|.[8] Their works contribute to an understanding of the cultural interaction between the Ottoman world and the Venetian early Renaissance, which in turn left traces in the oeuvre of Albrecht Dürer (1471–1528), as can be seen in his drawing of an Ottoman horseman |**cat. no. 58**|.

In the 1490s, Dürer made the acquaintance of both Gentile and Giovanni Bellini, and Giovanni is known to have greatly admired the German's work. Later, Dürer came into contact with Jacopo de' Barbari, who lived in Nuremberg for a short time (1500–1502).[9] Although Dürer was of two minds about de' Barbari's skill as a painter, both artists shared certain art-theoretical views, particularly with respect to the rules of proportion and perspective.[10] In this regard, the precision that de' Barbari employed in his *View of Venice* to capture the city's overall architectural form and character speaks volumes. The aforementioned Anton Kolb, who published de' Barbari's city view in 1500, would have been one of the people whom Albrecht Dürer was in contact with during his stays in Italy. Merchants from Nuremberg formed the largest group among the German traders in Venice who were there to acquire valuable goods from the Middle and Far East, such as spices, silk, and gemstones, while at the same time bringing artworks and handicrafts from the North to Venice.[11] The Venetian Republic closely monitored the merchants' activities. For that purpose, the Republic used the Fondaco dei Tedeschi, a business establishment meant for merchants from all regions then considered "German-speaking," including people not just from the German and Austrian territories but also from Bohemia and the Low Countries.[12] The word *fondaco* derives from the Arabic *funduq*, which refers to a caravansary, a type of combined warehouse, shop, and inn that existed in eastern and northern African port cities for use by itinerant traders.[13] The Fondaco dei Tedeschi was distinguished not only by its impressive size but also by its strategic location near the Rialto, the main business district in Venice. Merchants who were unable to find lodgings at the Fondaco could

8 Exh. cat. London 2005; Belting 2018; Ilg 2024.
9 Pfisterer 2013; Böckem 2016; Yoon 2024.
10 Schmitz-Esser 2023, p. 188; Monteleone 2024.
11 Stauber 2000, p. 131; Schmitz-Esser 2023, p. 183.
12 Oakes 2009; Backmann 2010; Bergdolt 2011, pp. 25–38; Pfotenhauer 2016, pp. 96–116.
13 Schmitz-Esser 2023, p. 186.

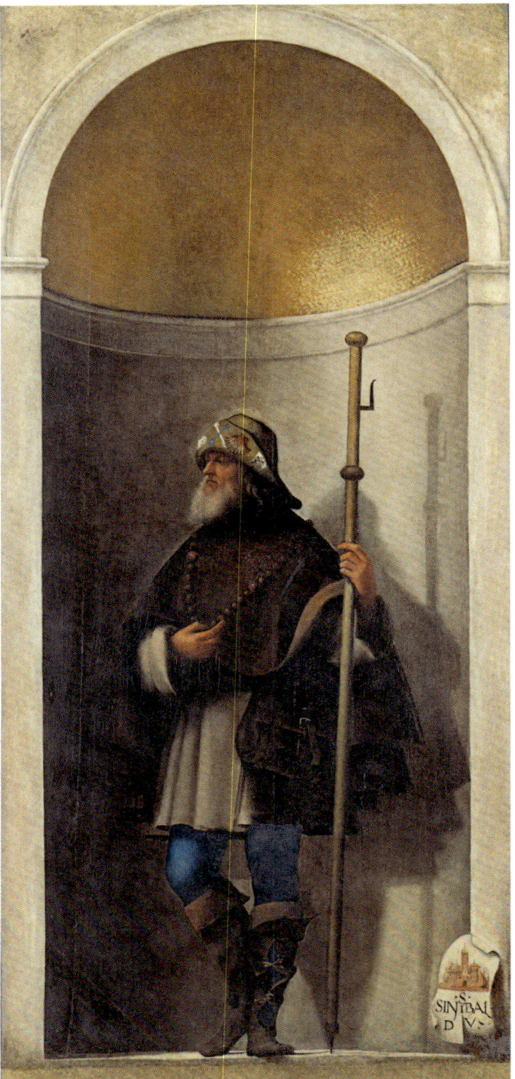

Fig. 4 Sebastiano del Piombo, *San Sinibaldo*, ca. 1509, Gallerie dell'Accademia, Venice, inv. no. 1804b

stay at specially designated inns. The northerners' dealings were mediated by Venetian brokers, the so-called *sensali*.[14] In order to carry out their work, the *sensali* first had to learn foreign languages. A language school located near the Fondaco and run by a certain Georg of Nuremberg ("maister Jorg von Nurmberck") provides an example of how German and Italian were taught in the fifteenth century.[15] Surviving language primers from the period show that translations took into account cultural aspects alongside linguistic ones. The Fondaco thus served as a kind of cultural hub in Venice, and it was the place from which Albrecht Dürer gained access to the wider city.

In order to be able to call upon their local patron saint for assistance, even from afar, the merchants of Nuremberg erected an altar dedicated to Saint Sebaldus in San Bartolomeo, which was the church used by the Germans, located not far from the Fondaco dei Tedeschi. In 1509, the Venetian painter Sebastiano del Piombo (d. 1547) adorned one of the organ shutters in San Bartolomeo with a depiction of Saint Sebaldus |**fig. 4**|.[16] Three years earlier, Albrecht Dürer had created an altarpiece painting for the same church: *The Feast of the Rose Garlands*, his most important work done in Venice |**fig. 5**|.[17] It was commissioned by the Confraternity of the Rosary, which was comprised of members of the German community. With this work, the Germans in Venice made their mark as patrons of the arts. The painting shows Emperor Maximilian I (1459–1519) and a pope, probably Julius II (1443–1513), in symbolic roles as patrons of the confraternity. Depicted kneeling before the Virgin and Child, each is being crowned with a garland of roses—the emperor by the Virgin Mary and the pope by the Christ Child. Important contemporaries, including Dürer, are grouped around the central scene. In this prestigious context, Dürer made an impressive display, visible to the Venetian public, of the community of merchants of the Holy Roman Empire. He proudly noted that the painting was marveled at by the doge and the patriarch of Venice, the city's highest secular and religious dignitaries.[18] Their visit to San Bartolomeo, a church of such great importance to the German community, can be seen more broadly as a symbolic tribute to the multilayered commercial and cultural ties that existed between Venice and the North. And whereas Dürer emphasized the close ties between the German merchants and their Venetian surroundings in *The Feast of the Rose Garlands*, in works done after his return to Nuremberg he transmitted the cosmopolitan flair of Venice to his hometown by incorporating motifs such as the Ottoman horseman found in the Holzschuher *Lamentation of Christ* |**cat. no. 57**|.

14 Stauber 2000, p. 132; Bergdolt 2011, p. 26.
15 Stauber 2000, p. 134; Schmitz-Esser 2023, p. 187.
16 Pfotenhauer 2016, pp. 202–16; Exh. cat. Berlin 2008, pp. 114–17, cat. no. 10 (Mauro Lucco).
17 Exh. cat. Prague 2006; Bergdolt 2011, pp. 42–43.
18 Schmitz-Esser 2023, p. 186.

Fig. 5 Albrecht Dürer, *The Feast of the Rose Garlands*, 1506, Národní galerie, Prague, inv. no. O 1552

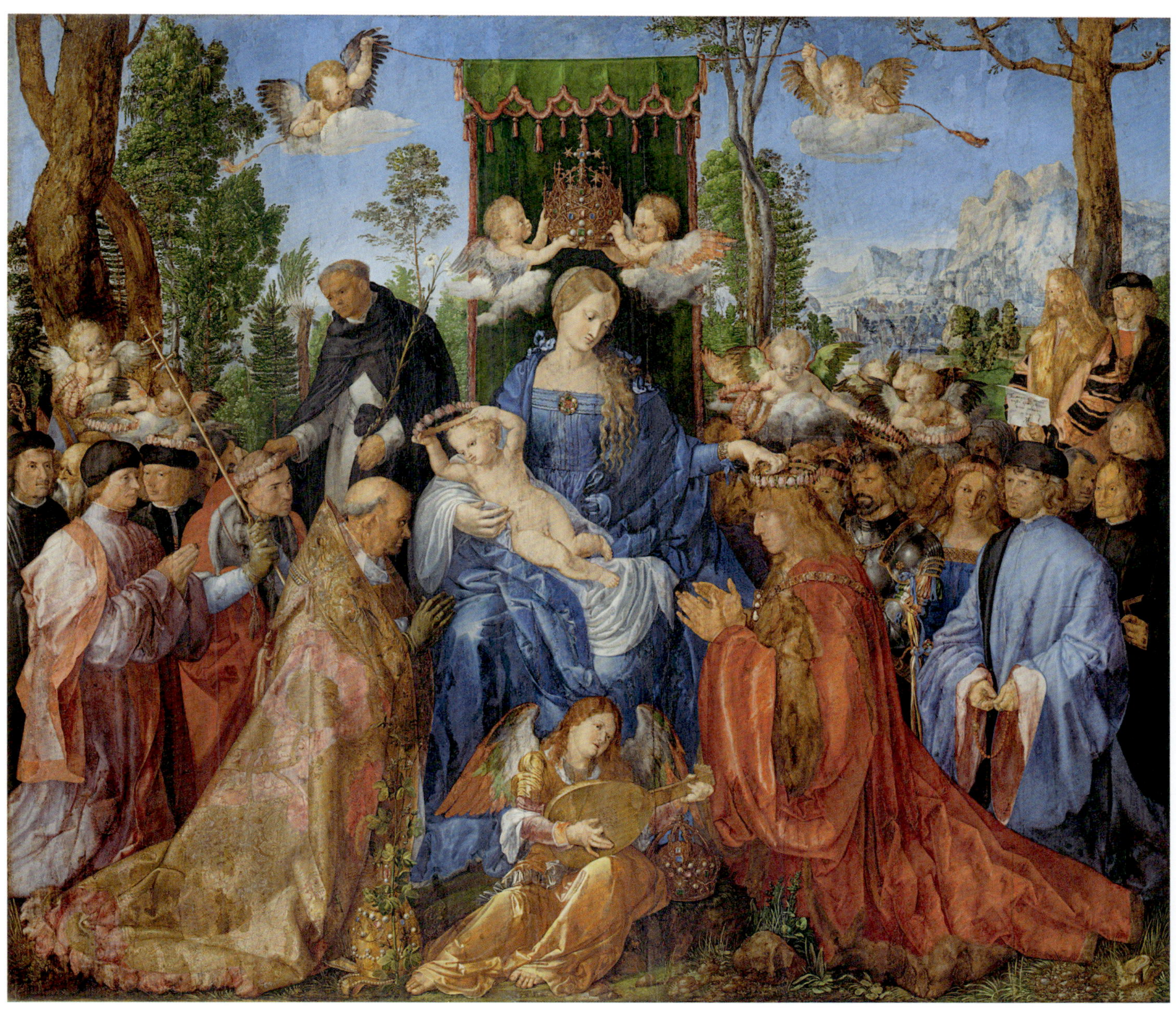

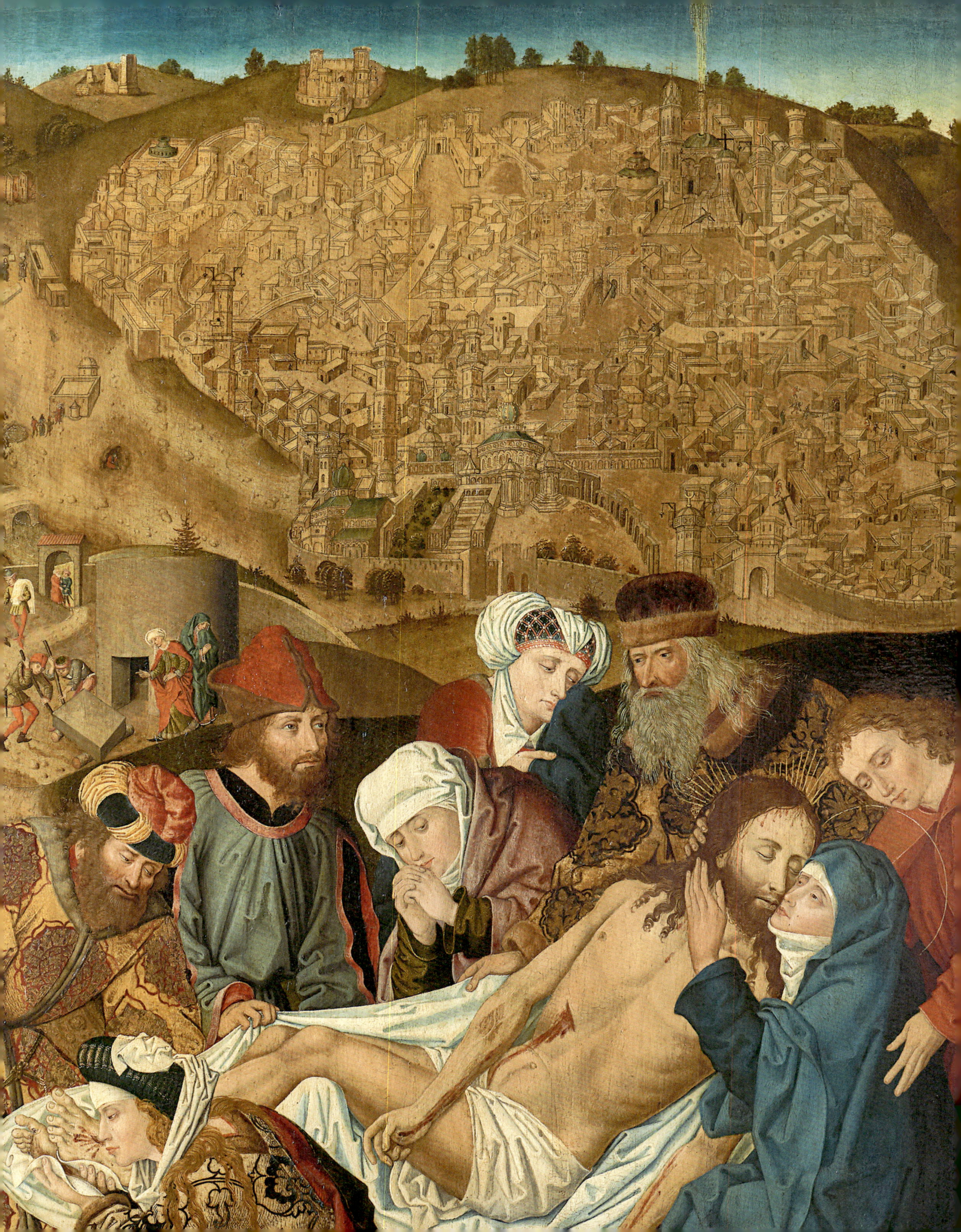

Florian Abe

NURENBERG AND JERUSALEM

BETWEEN THE *QUASI CENTRUM EUROPAE* AND THE NAVEL OF THE WORLD

The Nuremberg patrician and Holy Land pilgrim Hans Tucher VI (1428–1491) chose a remarkable way of making the Church of the Holy Sepulchre in Jerusalem intelligible to readers of his pilgrimage report |**cat. no. 68**|: he equated the faraway sanctuary with Nuremberg's Sebalduskirche. Just as Franciscan friars had guided him through the Church of the Holy Sepulchre, Tucher takes his readers on a step-by-step tour through the local church situated adjacent to the town hall. Familiar areas of the Sebalduskirche assume the roles of significant locations within the topography of Christ's Passion: the southern Three Kings Portal corresponds to the entrance of the Holy Sepulchre Church; the western chancel, known as the Katharinenchor, is recast as the dome of the Anastasis (Resurrection) at the Jerusalem church's west end; and the sacrament house marks the place where soldiers are said to have thrown dice for Christ's robe during the Crucifixion.[1]

Tucher's act of projecting the *loca sancta* (holy sites) onto his native land seems also to have worked in the opposite direction. It appears that buildings familiar to him shaped his perception of sites in the Holy Land. According to Tucher, the Holy Sepulchre in Jerusalem closely resembled its replica in Eichstätt, and he recognized the dome of the Anastasis as corresponding in width and overall size to the church of the Scots Monastery in Eichstätt, which houses the Holy Sepulchre replica. This merging of distance and proximity, of Holy Land and homeland, and of the biblical past and the world of the present is characteristic of how late-medieval Europeans conceptualized the story of Christian salvation.[2]

The Holy Land came into view in Europe not only in the mind's eye. Jerusalem was made physically present in European cities—in buildings, images, and processions. Of central importance to this phenomenon was the Passion of Christ, the suffering through which Jesus, according to Christian belief, reconciled humanity with God. Over the course of the Middle Ages, the biblical narrative of the Passion became increasingly embellished with detail in devotional and biographical texts, as for example in the mid-fourteenth-century *Vita Christi* by Ludolf of Saxony. This development heightened the need to commemorate the story of Christ's suffering at Holy Land sites that were considered authentic. In some cases, as with the Stations of the Cross in Jerusalem, this prompted the first attempts to assign the episodes to concrete locations.[3] Those places, in turn, were often reflected in European art and urban design. The sites of Christ's Passion thus also became prominent features of Nuremberg's cityscape—from Christ's entry into Jerusalem on Palm Sunday |**cat. no. 73**|, to his prayer at the Mount of Olives before his arrest |**cat. no. 74**|, all the way to his carrying of the cross and crucifixion. With a suitable devotional infrastructure, Nuremberg—referred to in the period as *quasi centrum europae*, "more or less the center of Europe"—could simulate Jerusalem, the medieval *umbilicus mundi* or "navel of the world."

Heaven on Earth

Jerusalem—no other city cast such a spell over European Christians of the Middle Ages. The name is associated both with the terrestrial city in the Holy Land and with the Heavenly Jerusalem promised in the Book of Revelation: a city of pure gold, its walls adorned with jewels (Rev. 21:18–19).[4] It was there on earth, in Jerusalem, that Jesus walked his path of suffering and died on the cross; it was there that he rose from the dead and ascended into heaven. For believers, the story of salvation was inscribed in the city's stones: the crack in the rock at Golgotha, the blood-soaked Stone of Anointing, the final footprint of Christ in the Chapel of the Ascension. Traces such as these were understood to corroborate the biblical narratives.

Fig. 1 Wolfgang Katzheimer the Elder and workshop, *Memorial for Adelheid Tucher, née Gundlach* (detail), ca. 1483, on long-term loan from the Tucher Kulturstiftung to the Museum Tucherschloss und Hirsvogelsaal, Museen der Stadt Nürnberg, inv. no. HI Gm 004 |**cat. no. 67**|

1 Herz 2002, pp. 390–405.
2 See Kiening 2016.
3 On this, see Zwijnenburg-Tönnies 1998.
4 Kurmann 2002.

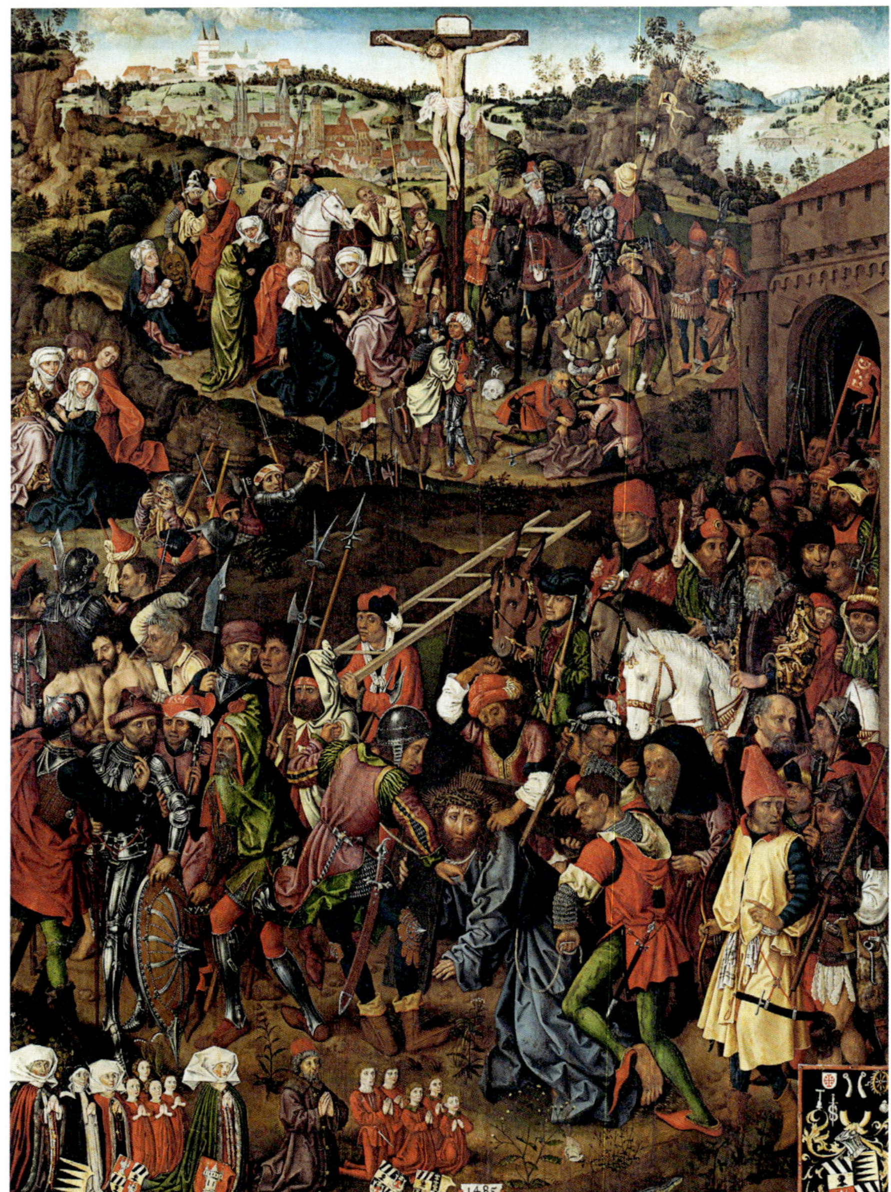

Fig. 2 Wolfgang Katzheimer the Elder and Master L. Cz., *Memorial for Barbara Tucher, née Ebner*, 1485, Sebalduskirche, Nuremberg

For most Europeans, however, Jerusalem was a locus of yearning that remained far out of reach. And although Christian pilgrims had been visiting the holy sites and the monuments erected under Emperor Constantine (such as the Church of the Holy Sepulchre in Jerusalem and the Church of the Nativity in Bethlehem) ever since the fourth century, the situation for Christians in Jerusalem became increasingly complicated after the Muslim conquest in the year 639 (ultimately leading to the destruction of the Holy Sepulchre Church shortly after the turn of the first millennium). The Crusades briefly returned the area to Christian control, including with the short-lived Kingdom of Jerusalem, established in 1099 |**see cat. no. 68**|. By 1187, however, Jerusalem was once again under Muslim rule, making access much more difficult for European Christians.

Nurembergers in the Holy Land

Yet the Holy Land was not completely closed to Christian pilgrims. Beginning in the late Middle Ages, a number of Nuremberg citizens, mainly people of wealth, visited the holy sites. The available sources allow an estimate of about fifty Holy Land pilgrims from Nuremberg in the period between the fourteenth and sixteenth centuries.[5] Given that the city's population lay just under 38,000 around the year 1500, those travelers represented a tiny minority. But they were still highly important to the transmission of concrete knowledge about the Holy Land, knowledge that informed their reports and artistic commissions, thereby shaping the image of Jerusalem in Nuremberg.

Hans Tucher's aforementioned travelogue, the *Reise ins gelobte Land* (Journey to the Promised Land), was the first German-language pilgrimage report to have been conceived as a print publication, with wide distribution and a broad readership in mind. Tucher describes the Holy Land and individual buildings in detail. This knowledge appears to have been incorporated into a work of art that is thought to contain the earliest topographically accurate view of Jerusalem in the medium of panel painting: the memorial panel for Hans's sister-in-law Adelheid Tucher |**fig. 1; cat. no. 67**|.[6] Shown in its late-fifteenth-century form, the city of Jerusalem rises vision-like within the sloped landscape background. In contrast to earlier, fanciful views, this depiction accurately represents such structures as the Dome of the Rock and the Golden Gate, as well as such features as the Via Dolorosa (the route on which Christ carried his cross), which leads from the Lion's Gate to the Church of the Holy

5 Herz 2005, p. XI.
6 On the parallels between Tucher's descriptions and the painting, see Schulz 2015.

Sepulchre. In a letter that Hans Tucher sent from the Holy Land to his brother Endres, the husband of the Adelheid Tucher commemorated in the painting, Hans confirms that the length of the Via Dolorosa corresponds exactly to the distance covered by the Stations of the Cross running from the Neutor gate to the Johannisfriedhof (Saint John's Cemetery) outside Nuremberg's western walls.[7] A full-scale Via Dolorosa must therefore have been present in Nuremberg by at least the second half of the fifteenth century.

The placement of the Passion in a hometown setting also found its way into pictorial form |**fig. 2**|. In the memorial panel for Hans Tucher's first wife, Barbara Ebner, in Nuremberg's Sebalduskirche (also containing portraits of Hans, his children, and his second wife, Ursula Harsdörffer), the Carrying of the Cross and the Crucifixion take place in front of a view of Bamberg, the seat of the bishop responsible for Nuremberg. Such representations transferred the events of the Passion and their salvific significance into the viewer's realm of experience.[8]

Both this painted Tucher memorial and a stone Ketzel-family memorial located on the Sebalduskirche's exterior (for Heinrich Ketzel and his son Heinrich the Younger) display insignia of chivalric orders joined during pilgrimage to the Holy Land: the Aragonese Order of the Jar, the Order of Saint Catherine, the Cyprian Order of the Sword, and the Order of the Holy Sepulchre with the sign of the Jerusalem cross. Even though Nuremberg lacked a confraternity of Knights of the Holy Sepulchre (as present, for example, in the Netherlands and France), the symbols of that order were nevertheless displayed in many of the city's churches, where they contributed to the remembrance—and social standing—of entire branches of families.[9]

Of all the Nurembergers who traveled to Jerusalem, the Ketzel merchant family was among the most active, with eight pilgrims to the Holy Land |**cat. nos. 69, 70**|. In 1459, Jörg Ketzel had a replica of the Chapel of the Holy Sepulchre built on Schütt Island, in the churchyard of the Heilig-Geist-Spital, which was destroyed in World War II |**fig. 3**|. The structure was distinctive both for its visual similarity to the original—not a matter of course for medieval architectural copies—and for the dimensions of the interior features. Ketzel is said to have taken its measurements directly from the Holy Sepulchre.[10]

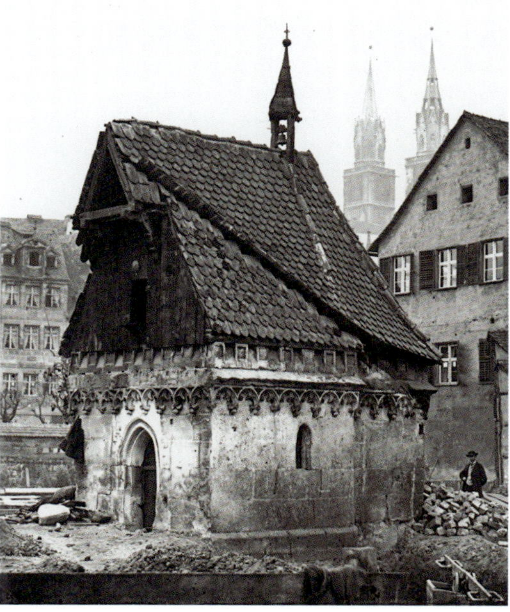

Fig. 3 *Chapel of the Holy Sepulchre*, Nuremberg, churchyard of the Heilig-Geist-Spital, built in 1459, destroyed in World War II, and cleared away after 1945; photograph by Ferdinand Schmidt, before 1871, Stadtarchiv Nürnberg, inv. no. A 47 Nr. KS-79-13

Situated near the church of the Heilig-Geist-Spital, Ketzel's chapel was furthermore in close proximity to the place where the regalia of the Holy Roman Empire were kept from 1424 to 1797 |**cat. no. 8**|. The regalia included precious relics of the Passion: pieces of the tablecloth of the Last Supper and of the True Cross, as well as the Holy Lance. Because of those relics, the Passion of Christ was not only symbolically represented in Nuremberg but also materially present.

Nuremberg as Jerusalem

In addition to the annual display of the imperial relics on the Hauptmarkt in Nuremberg |**see cat. no. 7**|, other forms of public presentation situated the Passion of Christ symbolically within the urban fabric. Beginning in the high Middle Ages, these presentations included processions and liturgical dramas. The latter, in the form of Passion plays staged up until 1498, appear to have been

7 Herz 1997, p. 77.
8 On this, see also Schock-Werner 1986.
9 See the Rieter family window at the Lorenzkirche; Scholz 2019, vol. 1, pp. 221–44. See also the heraldic window panels with arms of the Ketzel family from the Heilig-Geist-Spital, now at the GNM, inv. nos. MM197–MM201, on long-term loan from the City of Nuremberg; Hess and Hirschfelder 2010, p. 388, cat. no. 8.
10 See Aign 1961, p. 68.

Fig. 4 Johann Alexander Böner, *Johannisfriedhof (Saint John's Cemetery) with Crucifixion Group, Stations of the Cross Relief, and Holzschuher Chapel*, early eighteenth century, GNM, inv. no. SP8870

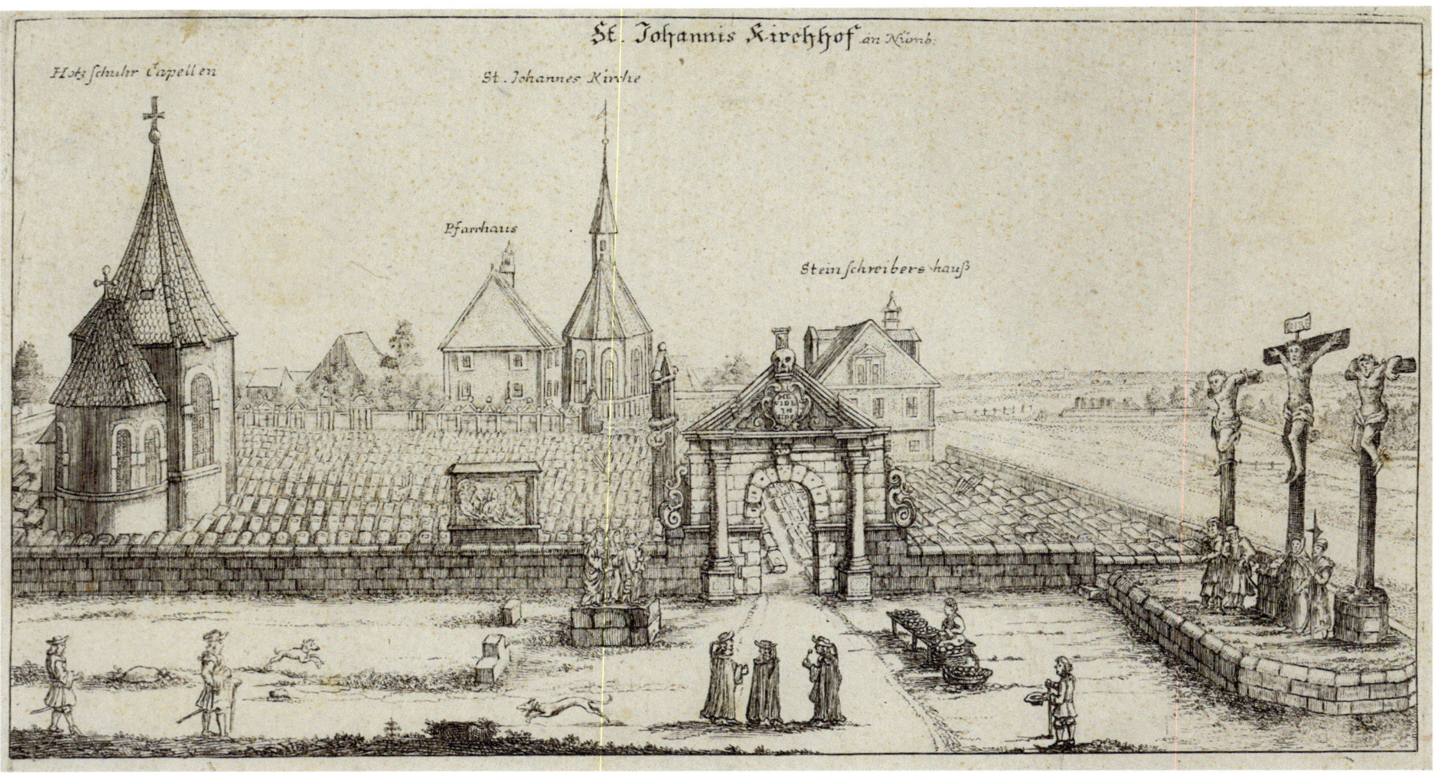

greeted with a certain hesitancy by Nurembergers.[11] Yet the Palm Sunday processions that marked the beginning of Holy Week proved especially popular and also incorporated theatrical elements. Nuremberg was one of many places where so-called "palm donkeys" (*Palmesel*) were put to use—sculptures that commemorated Christ's entry into Jerusalem, showing him riding a donkey mounted on a wheeled platform |**cat. no. 73**|. Such works are documented in the holdings of the churches of Saint Sebaldus, Saint Lawrence, and Saint Catherine, and of the Frauenkirche. It is known of the *Palmesel* used at the Sebalduskirche that the figure of Christ was adorned with a crown and a scepter before being wheeled out of the church and processed through the streets. The use of these figures ceased in Nuremberg in 1523, with the arrival of the Reformation.[12]

These mobile forms of commemorating the Passion all involved the projection of sites of the Passion onto the local cityscape, much like their immobile counterparts such as sculptures of the Agony in the Garden and the Crucifixion |**cat. no. 74**| or architectural replicas of the Holy Sepulchre. Through such rituals, objects, and built structures, biblical events were made physically present in the everyday world.

This concept culminated in the Stations of the Cross ensembles that were laid out in the late fifteenth and early sixteenth centuries—static objects serving mobile worshippers in their devotions to the Way of the Cross. The ensembles employed various means of visualizing the Passion of Christ to enable people to tread the path of Jesus to Golgotha in a location close to home. The faithful could walk from one stopping-point to the next along distances

11 Grafetstätter 2013, p. 18.
12 Weilandt 2007, p. 460.

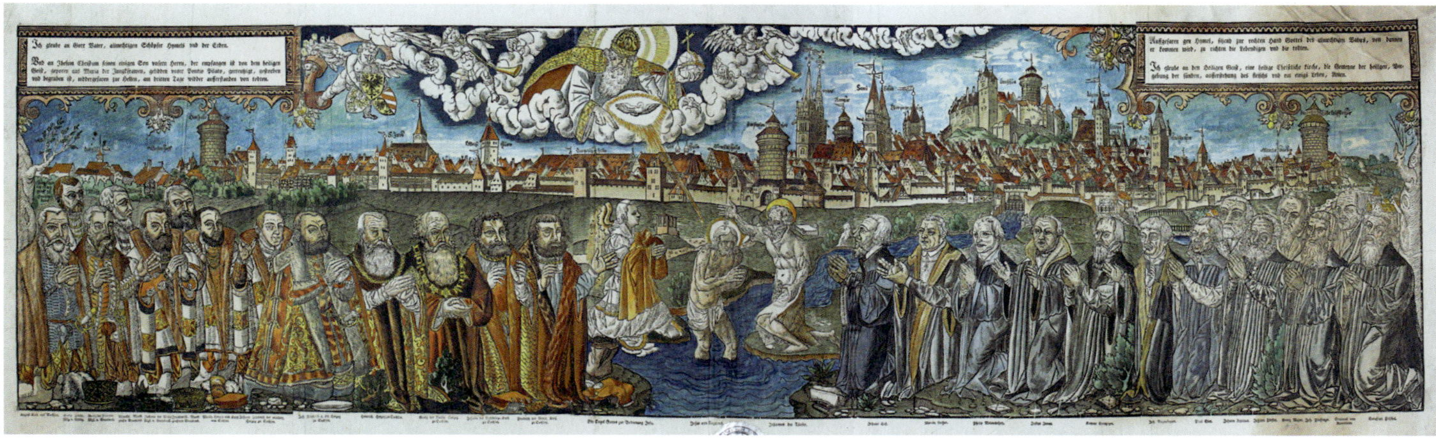

Fig. 5 *Allegory of the Reformation in Nuremberg*, Nuremberg (?), 1559, Museen der Stadt Nürnberg, Kunstsammlungen, inv. no. Gr.A. 12632

that in some instances matched those in Jerusalem. This might involve a veritable dramaturgy of different media—wayside shrines with Passion scenes, sculpted Crucifixion groups, and replicas of the Holy Sepulchre. The intertwining of the distant with the local was achieved to particularly great effect when existing buildings were assigned the role of structures in Jerusalem. City gates became the Lion's Gate; town halls or churches served as the house of Pontius Pilate.

About 1508, in a series of sculptures ranged along a path leading from the Tiergärtnertor to the Johannisfriedhof, Adam Kraft created one of the most elaborate Stations of the Cross known today |**fig. 4**|.[13] The special feature of this ensemble, which it shares with other Franconian examples such as those in Bamberg and Volkach, are the inscriptions at each station that indicate the distance in paces from the path's starting point, the "house of Pilate" (*Pilatushaus*). This clearly demonstrates the aspiration of transferring the original measurements of the Via Dolorosa in Jerusalem to the local context, something to which Hans Tucher had attested thirty years earlier in reference to the previous Stations of the Cross route between the Neutor and the Johannisfriedhof. Kraft's sculptures for most of the stations consist of reliefs. The Crucifixion group, sculpted fully in the round, stood just outside the Johannisfriedhof, opposite a group of figures comprising followers of Jesus and Roman soldiers. When Nurembergers who walked the Stations of the Cross stepped into the space between the Crucifixion's sculptural groups, they could imagine themselves as witnesses to the event.

The final station is located inside the chapel known today as the Holzschuherkapelle. Unlike the Ketzel chapel formerly on Schütt Island, this building was not intended to precisely imitate the model in the Holy Land. Nevertheless, a 1515 letter of indulgence clearly refers to it as the "Capella Sancti Sepulchri"—the Chapel of the Holy Sepulchre.[14] Kraft's slightly over-life-size Entombment group is sculpted in the round. The wall niche behind the sculptures displays a distinctive feature of the chapel: a painted panorama of the Holy Land. The mural presents a detailed topography of Jerusalem, containing all the episodes of the Passion. Thus, at the end of the Nuremberg Stations of the Cross, the faithful were able to immerse themselves once again in the concrete space of the Holy Land, which they had just finished traversing mentally along the full-scale route outside.

Even after the official introduction of the Reformation to Nuremberg in 1525, the practice of equating the city with the Holy Land continued. Indeed, the association became almost programmatically linked with the new confession. This is apparent in the anonymous monumental woodcut of 1559 entitled *Allegory of the Reformation in Nuremberg* |**fig. 5**|. The print depicts a key scene from the New Testament: the baptism of Jesus by Saint John in the Jordan River, blessed from above by God the Father and the Holy Spirit. Yet the act is also attended by a group of important reformers and princely patrons, and it takes place in the Pegnitz River, clearly recognizable as such by the detailed view of Nuremberg in the background. [15] In this image that was created only a few years after the Religious Peace of Augsburg of 1555, Nuremberg becomes a new Jerusalem, while also staging itself as one of the homes of the Reformation—thus once again linking the "navel of the world" with Nuremberg as *quasi centrum europae*.

13 See Weingärtner 2020.
14 Zittlau 1992, p. 93.
15 See Exh. cat. Nuremberg 2015a, pp. 182–83, cat. no. 87 (Thomas Schauerte).

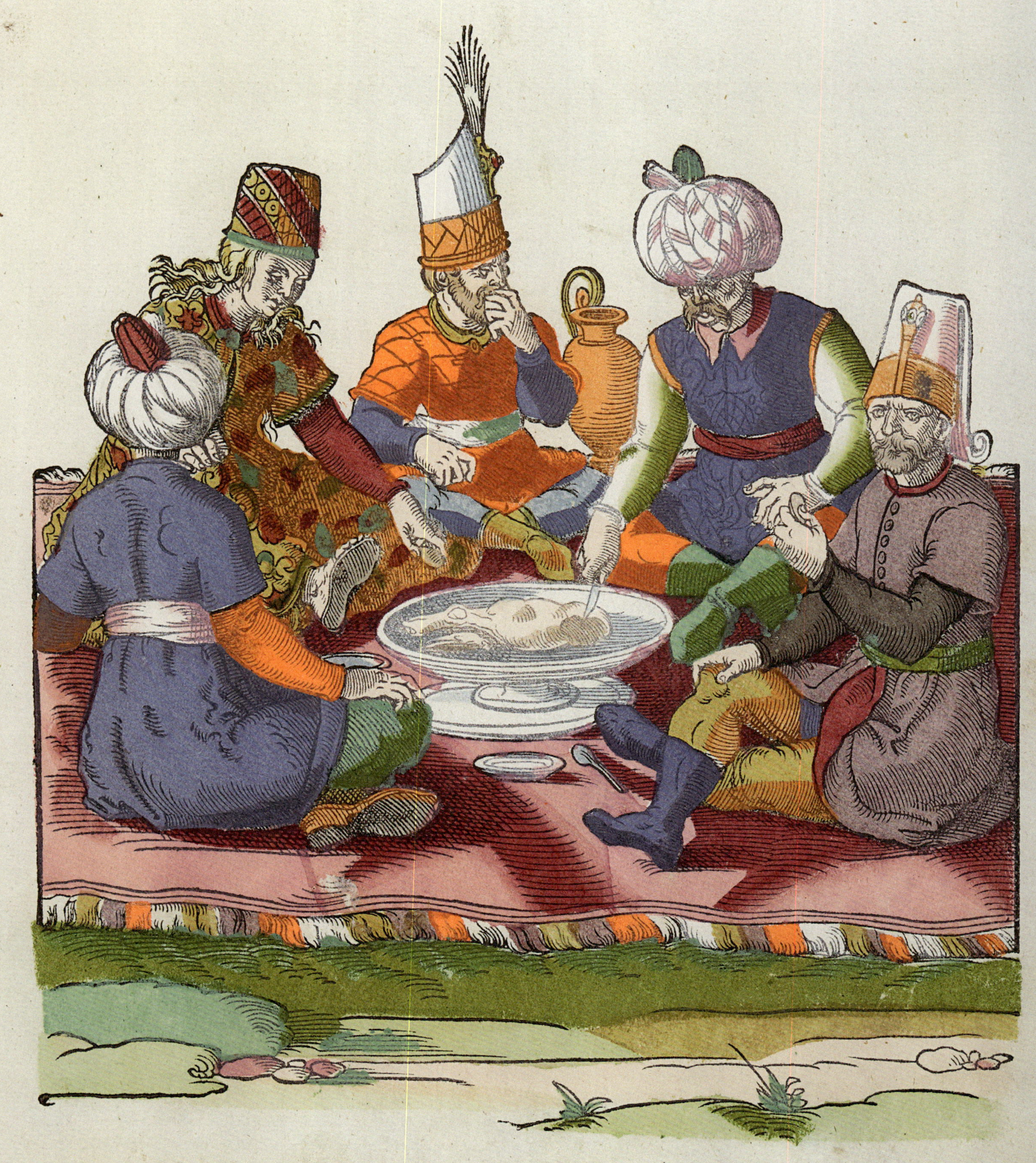

CCXV.

Wie die Türcken essen.

WAnn die Türcken mit Weib vnd Kindt/
Wöllen essen vnd hungrig sindt.

So sitzen sie rumb auff der Erden/
Vnd haben darob kein beschwerden.

Stefan Hanß

FEAR AND FASCINATION

NUREMBERG AND THE OTTOMAN EMPIRE

On October 26, 1571, the sounds of gunshots and tolling church bells took the people of Nuremberg by surprise. News had arrived from Venice about the devastating defeat of Ottoman forces at the Battle of Lepanto. Members of the patriciate soon organized a celebration of the Eucharist. The city's Inner Council immediately shared the news with Bamberg, Brandenburg-Ansbach, Mainz, and Würzburg. Nuremberg printers and newswriters hastened to spread the word of "a great Christian victory" unseen in "many hundreds of years since the arrival of the Turk, the archenemy."[1] On Sunday, October 28, worshippers crowded into Nuremberg's churches and, with tears of joy, sang the hymn "Lord God, we praise you" to the sound of tolling bells.[2]

In this bustling news hub, information on Ottoman affairs was a profitable business, straddling politics and commerce. Christoph Scheurl (1481–1542) and the Imhoff family regularly received news from Istanbul and Hungary, and Nuremberg's elite micromanaged the exchange of information with German authorities concerning Ottoman advances. Nuremberg merchants, artisans, and patricians ran prosperous news agencies that distributed information about Ottoman affairs to places as far-flung as England, Poland, and Prussia. The exchange of such news fostered political alliances and bolstered Nurembergers' reputation, personal wealth, and mercantile success at a time when the city's merchants were engaging in global commerce.[3]

News from the Levant had circulated throughout Europe for centuries, but it was the conquest of Constantinople (1453) that caused a rapid escalation of concern over the spread of the Ottoman Empire. Hartmann Schedel's *Nuremberg Chronicle* (1493) |**cat. no. 4**| details that event alongside a woodcut view that invites readers to imagine Constantinople's fall |**fig. 2**|: "That is how God's sacred houses and temples were terribly and cruelly stained and dishonored, and how much inhuman malignity and misdeed was carried out against Christian blood by raging Turks."[4] Increasing demand for stories from the Ottoman realm and the emphasis placed in publications on "Turkish cruelties" promised considerable profits and fueled the development of moveable type printing in its early stages—after all, anti-Ottoman crusade pamphlets are the earliest dated publications issued by Johannes Gutenberg (d. 1468). Publications on Ottoman topics (*turcica*) rate among the most popular bestsellers of the time |**cat. nos. 81–83**|.[5] While both Christians and Muslims committed horrendous crimes in this age of Habsburg-Ottoman imperial rivalry, the focus in Nuremberg publications on "Turkish" atrocities connected politics with anxieties about religious purity and military expansion as a means of fueling demand among the readership. Depictions of "Turks" slaughtering women and impaling children echoed images of the Massacre of the Innocents and late medieval anti-Judaic tropes of child sacrifice |**cat. nos. 14, 35**|. This was a way of stigmatizing Ottoman rule as "Turkish tyranny" and undermining the overall legitimacy of Ottoman dominion in southeastern Europe |**fig. 3; cat. no. 80**|. Ottomans had become "useful enemies," so to speak.[6]

The notion of a "Turkish menace" situated Nuremberg society in opposition to Ottoman advances, both politically and spiritually. In 1529, Nuremberg was the only city in the Holy Roman Empire actively involved in the defense of Vienna |**cat. no. 76**|.[7] Bells rang routinely in support of the fight against "the Turks." Since biblical scenes were set in what had become Ottoman territory, stereotyped portrayals of "Turks" populated Nuremberg's churches |**cat. no. 57**|, marketplaces, and homes. Nuremberg printers distributed some of the most impactful anti-Ottoman zealotry, written by leading Protestant reformers who considered the military prowess of the Ottoman "Antichrist" a sign of the Apocalypse. Meanwhile at the churches of Saint Lorenz and Saint Sebaldus, Andreas Osiander

Fig. 1 *How the Turks Eat (Wie die Türcken essen)*, from Jost Amman and Hans Weigel, *Book of Costumes (Trachtenbuch)*, Nuremberg: Hans Weigel, 1577, Trinity College, Cambridge, L.11.33, fol. CCXV

1 Sächsisches Hauptstaatsarchiv Dresden (SächsHStA Dresden), 10024 Geheimer Rat (Geheimes Archiv), 203. Zeitungen, Loc. 10696/12, 24v; *Zeittungen, Von dem Grossen Christen Sieg* ... (Nuremberg, 1571).
2 Hanß 2017, pp. 198–207.
3 Sporhan-Krempel 1968, pp. 32, 39–40, 79, 81–83, 86, 89; Munro 2007.
4 Hartmann Schedel, with Michael Wolgemut and Wilhelm Pleydenwurff, *Das buch der Chronicken vnd gedechtnus wirdigern geschichte[n]* ... (Nuremberg, 1493), fol. CCXLIXr.
5 Göllner 1961–78; Dackerman 2024, p. 13.
6 Höfert 2003a; Johnson 2011, pp. 42–56; Malcolm 2019.
7 Landois 2020, p. 171.

(1498–1552) and Veit Dietrich (1506–1549) preached anti-Turkish sermons.[8] Nuremberg delivered both manpower (soldiers and galley slaves) and money (the so-called Turkish tax) to fight Ottomans in the Mediterranean and southeastern Europe. In fact, Johann Neudörffer (1497–1563) **|cat. no. 19|** was keen to publish calculations detailing enormous sums available for military action if Christians would indeed meet their tax liabilities.[9]

Fear also channeled fascination as more and more stories that facilitated knowledge about Ottoman culture came into circulation. Costume albums, for instance, established "moral geographies"[10] while showcasing clothing of unmatched quality along with associated Ottoman customs **|fig. 1; cat. no. 84|**. Nuremberg astronomers edited Arabic and Persian treatises, and citizens who had been taken captive by Ottomans in southeastern Europe published autobiographical prints peppered with ethnographic anecdotes.[11] Gunsmith Jörg of Nuremberg's *History of Turkey* (ca. 1482–83), for instance, discusses politics alongside religious topics **|cat. no. 81|**. Rituals of washing the body were of particular interest, as cleanliness undermined ideas of a supposed moral corruption of "the Turks," with hygiene being reframed as the Devil's cunning trick to lure Christians into idolatry.[12] Nuremberg soldier and former Ottoman slave Johann Wild (b. 1585) published the very first European description of Islamic holy sites in Mecca and Medina in 1613 **|cat. no. 83|**. The publication was supervised by Salomon Schweigger (1551–1622), minister at Nuremberg's Frauenkirche and former Lutheran chaplain at the imperial embassy in Istanbul (1577–81). Schweigger's *Reyßbeschreibung* (Description of a Journey, 1608), a bestseller on Ottoman affairs, was dedicated to Nuremberg patricians who had made pilgrimages to Ottoman Jerusalem, fought "the Turks," and served at the imperial embassy in Istanbul **|cat. no. 82|**. Schweigger also authored the first complete German translation of the Quran in 1616, a polemic response to the Nontrinitarianism being propagated at nearby Altdorf Academy.[13] Humanists, merchants, noblemen, and theologians cultivated a wider interest in Near Eastern lands and languages. In 1487, in fact, Schedel approached a "Turkish" visitor in Nuremberg, a man who claimed to be the brother of Sultan Mehmed II (1432–1481), to inquire if the Ottoman-language terms used in a former European captive's publication were rendered faithfully.[14]

Knowledge exchange also facilitated the mobility of Ottoman material culture. The circulation of textiles, manuscripts, plants, antiquities, weapons, and craft products shaped a shared taste.[15] Nuremberg silverware, armor, and clocks, for instance, were gifted to sultans, and high-ranking Ottoman court officials commissioned Nuremberg artisans to produce personalized clocks. Islamic metalware, in turn, influenced the early experiments in engraving and woodcutting **|cat. no. 92|** carried out by Albrecht Dürer (1471–1528) and craft designs by Peter Flötner (d. 1546).[16] A precious cup decorated with splendid arabesques, for example, was held in high esteem by Stephan Praun II (1513–1578); and Stephan Praun III (1544–1591) purchased several Ottoman items while serving as imperial secretary in Istanbul (1569–76), including a pair of leather shoes that testify to the appreciation of foreign craftsmanship and fashion in Nuremberg **|fig. 4|**.[17] Ottoman objects in fact "afforded Europeans new cultural possibilities of self-expression."[18] With regard to footwear, the sudden fashionability of high heels imposed postures and movements associated with wealth, power, and distinction.[19] This positioned Stephan Praun III at the forefront of innovation in fashion, lending grace and sophistication to his presence. In general terms, Praun's interest in the pair of Ottoman shoes reflects an overall increase in demand for leather products with rich sensory impact. In Renaissance Nuremberg, these shoes, like many other Ottoman items, were provocative objects: they prompted Nurembergers

8 Kaufmann 2008; Grimmsmann 2016, pp. 51–52; Thomas 2022, pp. 115–81.
9 Wolder and Neudörffer 1558; Schulze 1978, pp. 31, 190; Hanß 2017, pp. 247–66.
10 Rublack 2010, p. 146. See, for example, Nicolay 1572; Weigel 1577.
11 Al-Farghānī and al-Battānī 1537; Māshā'allāh and Heller 1549.
12 Jörg of Nuremberg ca. 1482–83; Höfert 2003b.
13 Wild 1613; Schunka 2016.
14 Hanß 2021c, p. 9.
15 Hanß 2021d.
16 Faroqhi 2016, pp. 1, 14; Hanß 2021d, p. 260; Radway 2023, p. 202; Wouk 2023; Dackerman 2024.
17 GNM, inv. no. T555, on long-term loan from the Friedrich von Praunsche Familienstiftung; Schürer 2010, pp. 263–65; Hess and Hirschfelder 2010, pp. 437–38, cat. no. 464.
18 Bevilacqua and Pfeifer 2013, p. 112.
19 Riello 2006, p. 62; Rublack 2013.

der werlt Blat CCXLIX

¶ Von beſtreitung der ſtatt Conſtantinopel im .M.cccc.liii.iar beſchehen.

COnſtantinopel die ſtatt ein ſtůl des orientiſchen kaiſerthumbs vnd ein einige behawſũg kriechiſcher weißheit iſt in diſem iar am̃ andern tag des monats Junij von Machumeto dem fürſten d Türckẽ fünfzig tag belegert mit gewalt vnnd waffen beſtritten. verwůeſtet vnd befleckt worden im dritten iar des reichs deſſelben Machumets. der dañ diſe ſtatt zu land vnd waſſer vmbſchrencket vnd vil vnzallich körbe mit weydẽ gezeündt damit ſich die feynd bedeckten an die graben rucket vnd den thurn bey ſant Romans thor mit einer großẽ mechtigen büchßen zertrüedet vnd nyderſchoße alſo das der einfal des erckers oder der worweere den grabẽ außfüllet vnd alſo ebnet das die feind darüber einen weg haben mochten. Als aber der Türck die mawrn an dreyen orten mit ſtaynen verletzet vnd ſchier verzweiflet do vnderſtund er ſich auß ertrachtung eins treülofen verheyten criſten ſchife von der höhe vber einen pühel abzelaſſen. Nw hett die ſtatt ein lange vnd enge pforten gegen dem auffgang der ſunnen aneinander gepundne ſchiff vnd mit einer ketten befeſtigt. daſelbſt hinein zekomen den feyndẽ nicht müglich was. vnd auff das aber d Türck die ſtatt noch mer einzwengen vnd vmblegerñ möcht ſo ließe er in der höhe auf dem pühel den weg ebnen vnd die ſchiff auß vnderlegten faſſen wol bey. lxx. roßlawfen ſchieben vnd machet vom̃ geſtadt gegen Conſtantinopel ein prugk bey. xxx. roßlawffen lang von holtz mit weyn faſſen vnderlegt darauff das heer zu der mawrn lawffen mocht. Alſo wardt die ſtatt Conſtantinopel vnnd auch Pera geſtürmet. die mawr vnd die thor beſchoßen. vnd die öber mawr erſtigen. alſo das die feinnd die burger in der ſtatt mit ſtaynwerffen ſer beſchedigten vnd in dem einlawff der pforten bey achthunndert rittern auß den Lateiniſchen vnd Kriechiſchen ermörten vñ erſchlůgen vnd eroberten die ſtatt. Alda warde der Kriechiſch kayſer Conſtantinus paleologus enthawbt. alle menſchen ſechs iar vnd darüber alt erſchlagen. die brieſter vnd alle cloſterlewt mit mancherlay marter vnd peyn getödt. vnd das ander volck mit dem ſchwert ermordt. vnd ein ſölchs plůtvergießen das plůtig beche durch die ſtat fluß. So warden die heilligen gotzhewßer vnnd tempel erbermdlich vnd grawſamlich befleckt vñ enteeret vnd vil vnmenſchlicher boßheit vñ myßtat durch die wůetenden Türcken gegen dem criſtenlichen plůt geübt. vnd das geſchahe nach erpawung der ſtatt Conſtãtinopel M.c. xxx. iar. oder da bey.

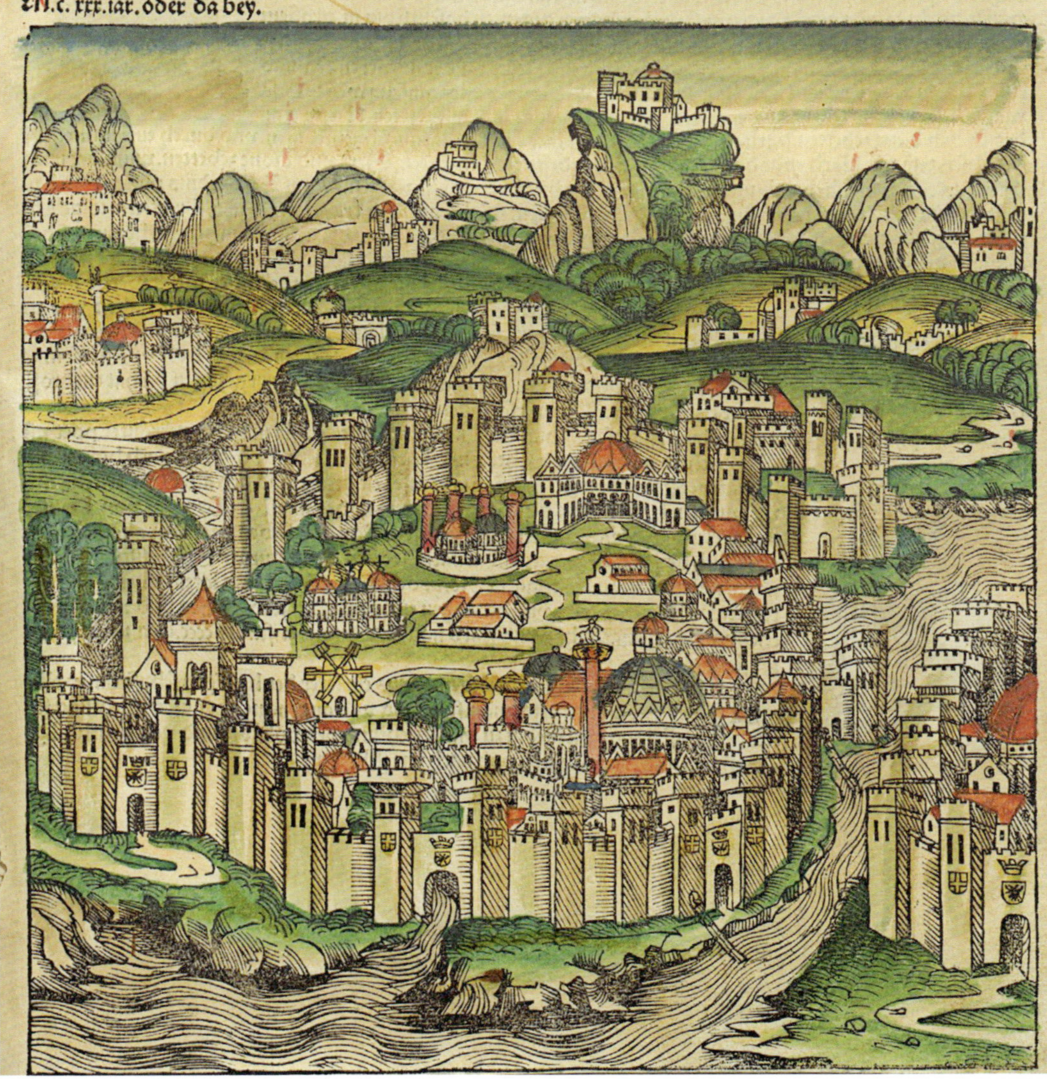

Fig. 2 "On the Conquest of the City of Constantinople," from Hartmann Schedel, Michael Wolgemut, and Wilhelm Pleydenwurf, *The Nuremberg Chronicle*, Nuremberg, 1493, GNM, shelf mark Inc. 2° 266, fol. CCXLIXr

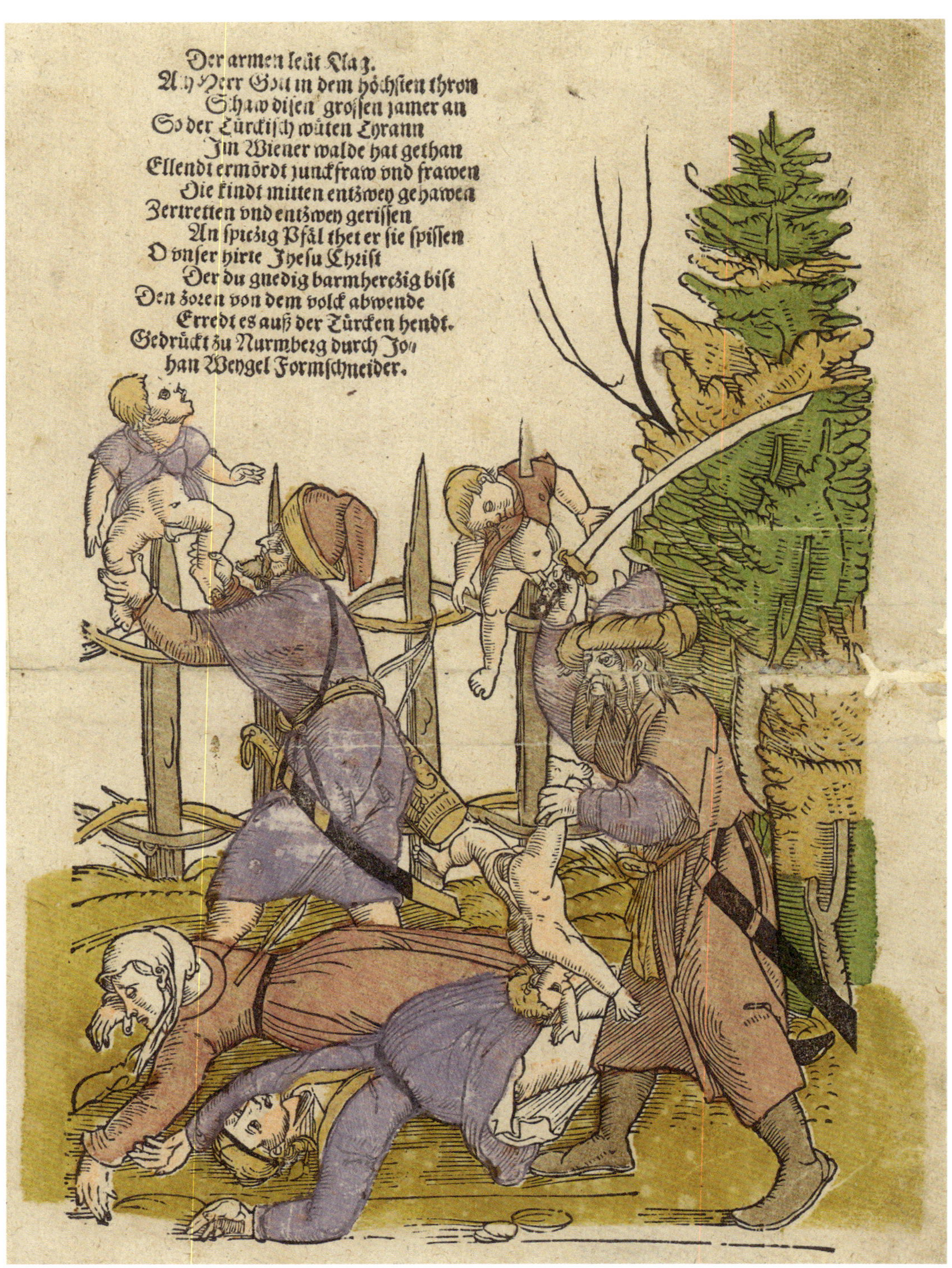

Fig. 3 Erhard Schön and Hans Sachs, "The Poor People's Lament," Nuremberg: Hans Weigel, no date, Zentralbibliothek, Zurich, Graphische Sammlung, shelf mark PAS II 2/4

Fig. 4 *Pair of Ottoman Leather Shoes*, acquired by Stephan Praun III during his time as imperial secretary in Istanbul (1569–76), GNM, inv. no. T555,0, on long-term loan from the Friedrich von Praun'sche Familienstiftung

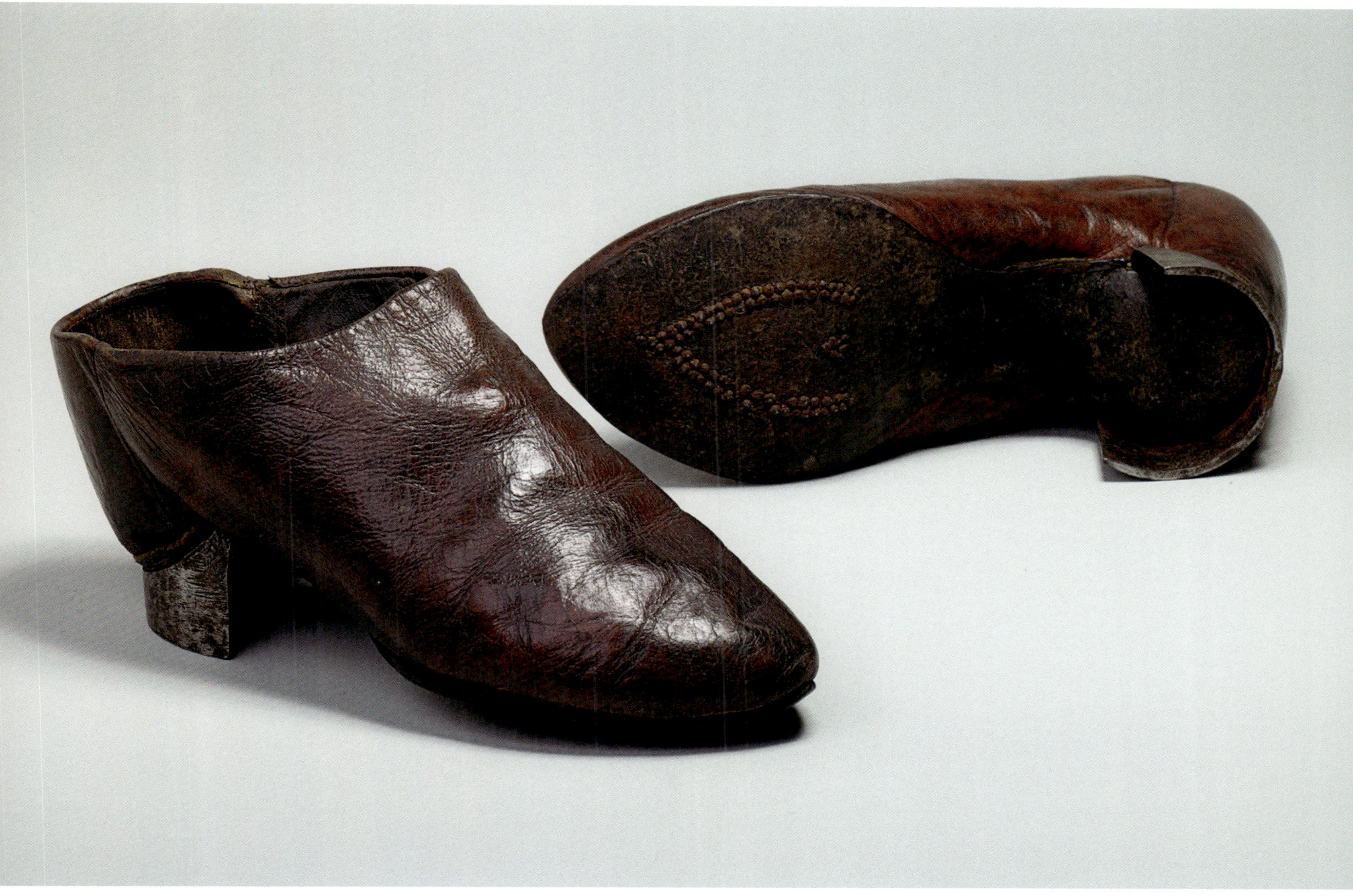

to imagine what shoes were capable of as material, visual, and biographical expressions. They widened Stephan Praun's cultural repertoire of self-fashioning by foregrounding his experience of travel, possession of a refined taste, and knowledge about foreign lands, particularly as gained during his career in diplomatic service—achievements that he clearly wished to be remembered over generations. We must situate these shoes, like so many objects on display in this exhibition, both in the Ottoman world and in that of Nuremberg, for they speak to us about a connected and shared world that was shaped by experiences beyond fear and fascination.

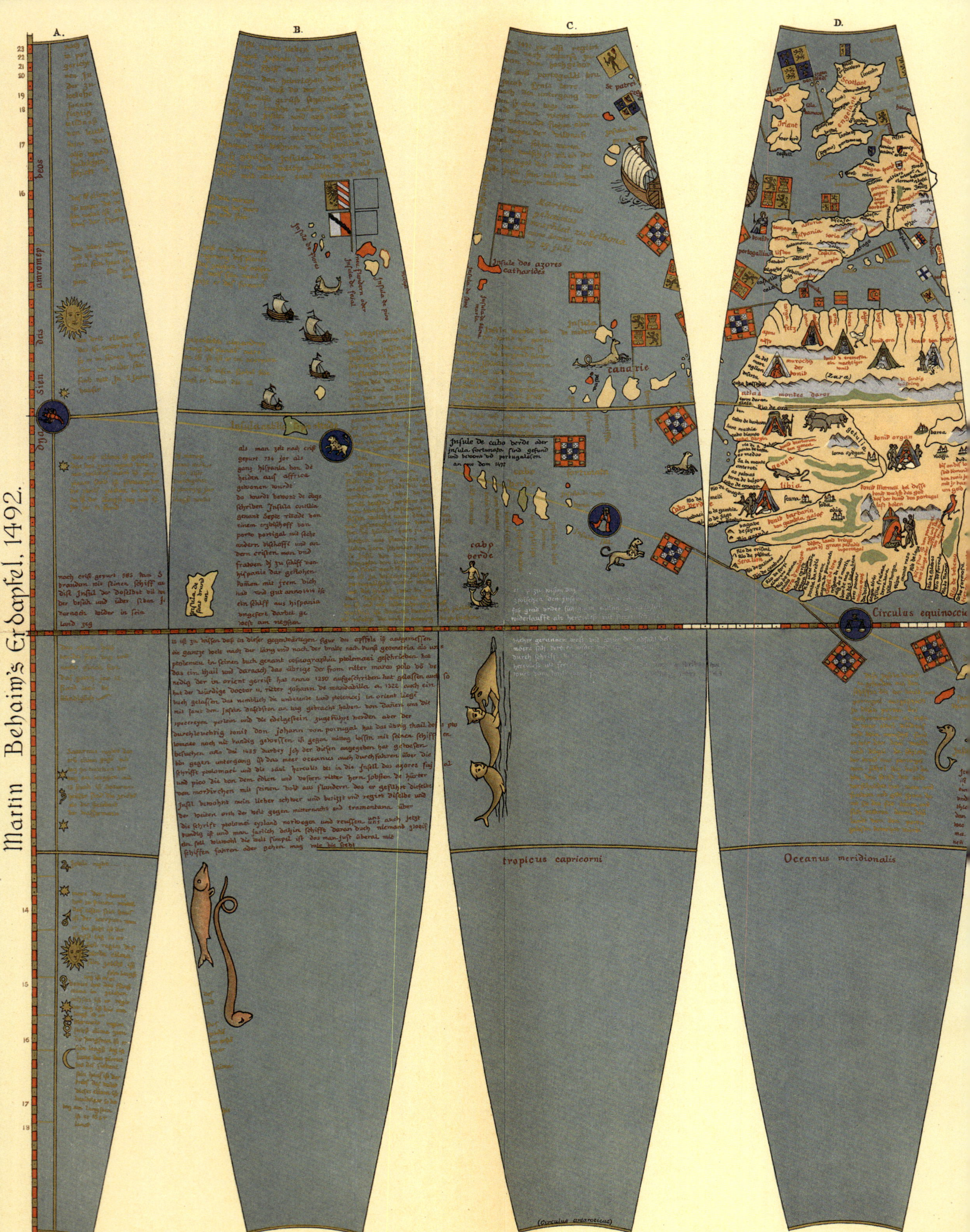

Martin Behaim's Erdapfel, 1492.

Sven Jakstat

NETWORKS AND PROTAGONISTS

NUREMBERG AND THE IBERIAN PENINSULA IN HIERONYMUS MÜNZER'S TRAVELOGUE (1494–95)

From September 1494 to February 1495, the scholar Hieronymus Münzer (d. 1508), who was the municipal physician of Nuremberg, traveled through the Iberian Peninsula in the company of three young merchants. By his own account, he had fled an outbreak of the plague that was ravaging Nuremberg at the time, though his wife and daughter remained behind. The journey, made on horseback, took Münzer via Lyon, Barcelona, Valencia, Granada, Seville, and Lisbon to Santiago de Compostela. From there, he returned to Nuremberg via Salamanca, Toledo, Zaragoza, Paris, Ghent, and Antwerp |**fig. 2**|. At a stop in Évora he met King John II of Portugal, and in Madrid he had an audience with the Catholic Monarchs of Spain, Isabella of Castile and Ferdinand of Aragon. It is therefore assumed that Münzer took the journey with economic and diplomatic aims in mind. His travelogue, written in Latin, is preserved in a copy that Hartmann Schedel transcribed for his own library |**cat. no. 93**|.[1] The text was fully edited and translated into German for the first time in 2020.[2]

In his travelogue, Münzer comments on economic activities in the regions he visited, describes goods that seemed promising for trade, and addresses social and political topics.[3] His curiosity is apparent in his examinations of local flora and fauna as well as in his reflections on scientific subjects, religious practices, and art and culture.[4] Münzer's travelogue also offers remarkable testimony to the networks that existed between Nuremberg and the Iberian world at the time.[5] In many places, Münzer encountered fellow countrymen—German-speaking clerics, soldiers, printers, artists, craftspeople, nobles, and merchants—who shared their knowledge and helped him to establish further contacts.[6] He related much of what he saw on his journey to things he knew from his homeland.[7] Therefore, in the present exhibition the numerous objects that illustrate Nuremberg's connections to the Iberian Peninsula can be viewed in relation to Münzer's observations and experiences.

From Nuremberg via Lisbon to the Eastern Coast of Asia

We are relatively well informed about the life of Hieronymus Münzer.[8] Born in Feldkirch, in the modern Austrian state of Vorarlberg, he studied in Leipzig (1464–74) and Pavia (1476–77) as a young man. He then worked as Nuremberg's municipal physician (*Stadtarzt*). His progress through life is remarkable for its rise from humble beginnings to the highest levels of society in Nuremberg. One indication of his elevated status is that his only daughter, Dorothea, married Hieronymus Holzschuher, whose prestigious family had the distinction of being *ratsfähig* (eligible to serve on the city council). This was the same Hieronymus Holzschuher whose portrait was painted by Dürer in 1526.[9] In addition to his profession as municipal physician, Münzer was also a partner in a trading company that operated in southern Germany and northern Italy.[10]

Münzer was closely associated with the scholarly milieu surrounding Hartmann Schedel, and he contributed to Schedel's famous chronicle of the world (or *Nuremberg Chronicle*, as it is commonly known in English) |**cat. no. 4**|.[11] He was responsible for the chronicle's map of western, central, and eastern Europe and for a lengthy passage concerning Portuguese conquests along the West African coast. Münzer's knowledge of Portuguese colonial ventures is said to have come from Martin Behaim |**see cat. nos. 1, 114**|, who had lived in Lisbon since 1484 but was back in Nuremberg around the time of the chronicle's preparation. During that time, Behaim was occupied with creating his now famous globe |**cat. no. 1**|, made for the Nuremberg city council, a project that also involved Münzer and Schedel.[12]

It was in this context in Nuremberg that Münzer wrote a letter to King John II of Portugal.[13] Dated July 14, 1493, the letter brings into focus the complexity of the networks that existed between

Fig. 1 Facsimile of the Behaim Globe, leaf 1: *Iberian Peninsula and Atlantic Ocean*, from Ravenstein 1908, p. 124

1 Exh. cat. Munich 2014, pp. 149–51, cat. no. 7.3 (Juliane Trebe).
2 Herbers 2020; Münzer and Herbers 2020.
3 Classen 2003.
4 On Münzer's observations about art, see Tammen 1996.
5 For an overview of Nuremberg's economic connections to the Iberian Peninsula and the Americas, see Bernecker 2000 (with references to earlier literature) and Kellenbenz 1967.
6 Jaspert 2002.
7 Herbers 2000.
8 See, most recently, Herz 2018; Münzer and Herbers 2020, pp. XIII–CXXXVIII.
9 Gemäldegalerie, Staatliche Museen zu Berlin, cat. no. 557E.
10 Herz 2018, pp. 157–59.
11 Herz 2018, pp. 131, 134, 186–92; Münzer and Herbers 2020, pp. XXXVII–XLI (Klaus Herbers).
12 Herz 2018, pp. 176–80.
13 A fragment of the letter is preserved in a copy transcribed by Schedel and bound into a volume of

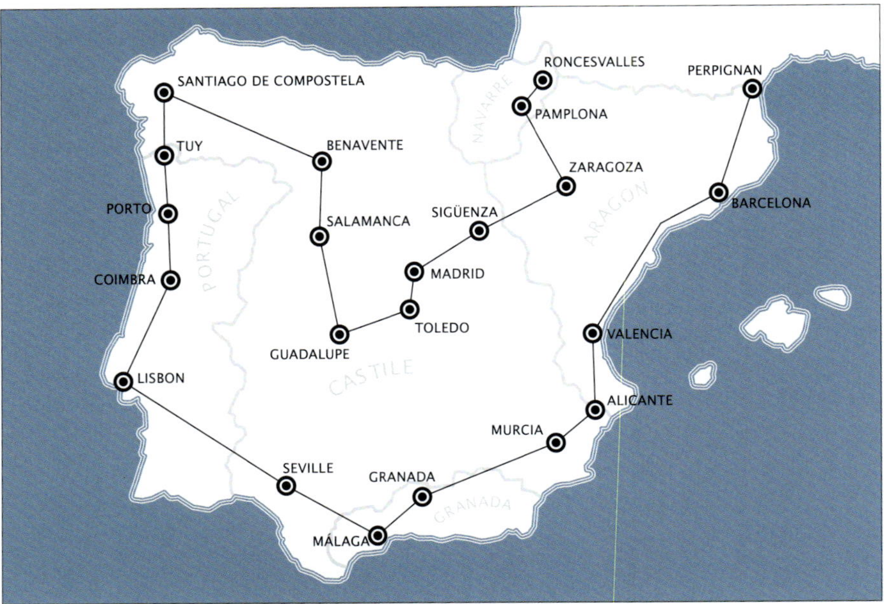

Fig. 2 Hieronymus Münzer's journey through the Iberian Peninsula, 1494–95; itinerary and map by Kraus Lazos Design Practice, based on Herbers 2020

Nuremberg and Portugal at that time. Münzer's aim was to convince the king of the economic advantage of establishing a sea route to the eastern coast of Asia—to "Chatai" (China)—by crossing the Atlantic. As a suitable companion for such an undertaking, he recommended none other than Martin Behaim.[14] When Münzer later met the king of Portugal in Évora, their communication was translated by Valentim Fernandes, a book printer from Moravia who, because of his privileged position at court, acted as a kind of intermediary for the southern German merchants based in Lisbon.[15] More than a decade later, a letter sent to Nuremberg by Valentim Fernandes prompted Albrecht Dürer to create his Rhinoceros woodcut |**cat. no. 119**|. During Münzer's time in Lisbon, he stayed at the home of Martin Behaim's father-in-law, Joost de Hurtere, governor of the Azorean islands of Faial and Pico.[16]

Münzer's letter to the Portuguese king coincided not only with the publication of the Latin edition of Schedel's world chronicle but also, by a lag of just a few months, with Columbus's return from his first Atlantic crossing. The aforementioned Behaim Globe |**cat. no. 1; fig. 1**|, created about the same time in Nuremberg, illustrates that the route from western Europe to the eastern coast of Asia, as promoted by Columbus, was considered feasible in those years, for the globe does not include the land masses of the Americas. A direct Atlantic sea route from Europe to China was therefore regarded as a realistic and commercially promising alternative to the established overland route.[17]

Santiago de Compostela

Despite the close trade relations that existed between Nuremberg and the Iberian Peninsula by the fifteenth century,[18] the Behaim Globe's representation of that region is surprisingly imprecise |**fig. 3**|. And although the globe's surface is replete with pictograms, only one representation adorns the Iberian Peninsula: an enthroned figure of Saint James. Placed in the far northwest of Spain, the figure marks one of the most important pilgrimage destinations in Christianity, Santiago de Compostela—the place where the apostle's mortal remains are kept. Münzer arrived there on December 13, 1494.[19]

Even prior to Münzer, pilgrims who traveled from Nuremberg to Santiago de Compostela had written reports about their journeys. One such report is by the patrician Gabriel Tetzel, who went to Santiago from 1465 to 1467 in a group of about fifty persons accompanying the Bohemian knight Jaroslav Lev ("Leo") of Rožmitál, a brother-in-law of the king of Bohemia.[20] Some pilgrims from Nuremberg even commissioned works of art there—for example, Peter Rieter, who during his 1428 journey had a large painting of the Crucifixion with Saint James installed in the cathedral's choir. Several years later, the painting was refreshed on the order of Peter Rieter's son Sebald and augmented with additional family donor figures and their coats of arms.[21]

Apparently, Münzer's expectations of this legendary place at the far western end of Europe were only partially fulfilled. Like other travelers, he criticized the exploitation of pilgrims by the locals and expressed skepticism about the authenticity of the relics venerated there: "There is always such a racket in the church that one feels as if on a market square. The veneration taking place there is undistinguished. The holy apostle truly deserves to be venerated with greater respect. It is believed that he is buried with his two disciples beneath the

Plutarch's writings now kept at the Bayerische Staatsbibliothek, Munich, Inc. c. a. 424. See Exh. cat. Nuremberg 1992, vol. 2, p. 735, cat. no. 3.20 (Johannes Willers). Also, a Portuguese translation is available in a nautical guidebook published in 1509 and 1516: Biblioteca Pública, Évora, Res. 404 - ans. 676, and Bayerische Staatsbibliothek, Munich, Rar. 204. See Exh. cat. Berlin 2007, p. 391, cat. no. V.II.5 (Philipp Billion and Michael Kraus).

14 Pohle 2000, pp. 87–96; Herz 2018, pp. 180–86.
15 Hendrich 2007, p. 46.
16 Westermann 2009, p. 55.
17 Eser 2010a, pp. 142–45.
18 Kellenbenz 1967; Kellenbenz 1970a; Ammann 1970; Stromer 1970; Bernecker 2000; Jaspert 2002.
19 Herbers and Plötz 1996, pp. 135–50.
20 Herbers and Plötz 1996, pp. 99–128.
21 Walleit 2020, pp. 376–77; Herbers and Plötz 1996, pp. 68–77, esp. p. 72.

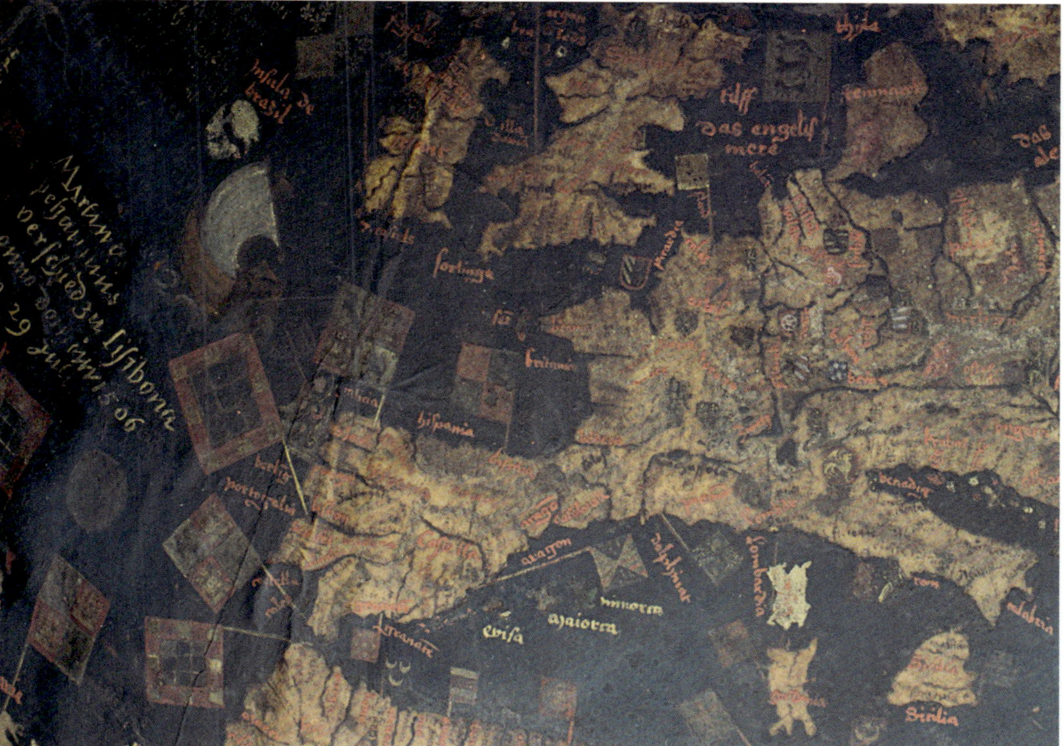

Fig. 3 The Iberian Peninsula on the Behaim Globe, Nuremberg, 1492–94, GNM, inv. no. WI1826 |**cat. no. 1**|

high altar … . Yet no one has seen the body, not even the king of Castile when he visited in the year of our Lord 1487. It is by faith alone, through which we humans are saved, that we trust in the saint's presence."[22]

Despite such skepticism, the relics of Saint James remained a popular destination for pilgrims from Nuremberg, even after the Reformation, which was introduced in the city in 1524–25. With the set of pilgrim's attire worn by Stephan Praun |**cat. no. 96**|, made about 1571, the GNM has in its collection a unique ensemble that testifies to the status gained by male members of the social elite through participation in pilgrimage.[23]

The Trade in Enslaved People

The involvement of Nurembergers in the trade in enslaved people is a topic that has thus far escaped systematic scholarly investigation. As discussed elsewhere in the present volume, the entanglement of Lazarus Nürnberger and Hans Tetzel |**cat. no. 108**| in the transatlantic slave trade illustrates the subject's relevance to the global history of sixteenth-century Nuremberg and the need for its critical examination.[24]

Münzer was witness to the trade in enslaved people during his journey. In Valencia, he spoke with a slave trader (*patronus schlavorum*) who recounted his activities. Münzer's comments give only a rudimentary idea of the inhumane and degrading conditions suffered by the men, women, and children who were subjected to physical violence, coercion, and humiliation as objects of trade and sources of forced labor. At the same time, Münzer's words make clear how condescendingly he himself viewed and judged these people: "In a certain house, I saw people of both sexes destined for sale, including children and older boys. They came from Tenerife, one of the Canary Islands in the Atlantic Ocean … . There was a merchant from Valencia who brought eighty-seven people on a ship, fourteen of whom died because they could not withstand the sea, air, and climate … . The men were dark-skinned, not black, but Berbers [in the Latin original, 'Barbari' in reference not to 'barbarians' but to the peoples of northern Africa]. The women were well built, with strong limbs, and quite tall … . They are prepared to accept our religion, and they have taken to wearing clothing, like we do. Oh, what faith and solicitude can do to make gentle people out of animals in human bodies! If I had not seen many of them, I would not

22 Translated after the German in Herbers 2020, p. 138.
23 Zander-Seidel 2010; Exh. cat. Nuremberg 2015, pp. 117–18, cat. no. 58 (Jutta Zander-Seidel).
24 See the essay by Benno Baumbauer and Sven Jakstat in the present volume, as well as Jakstat 2024.

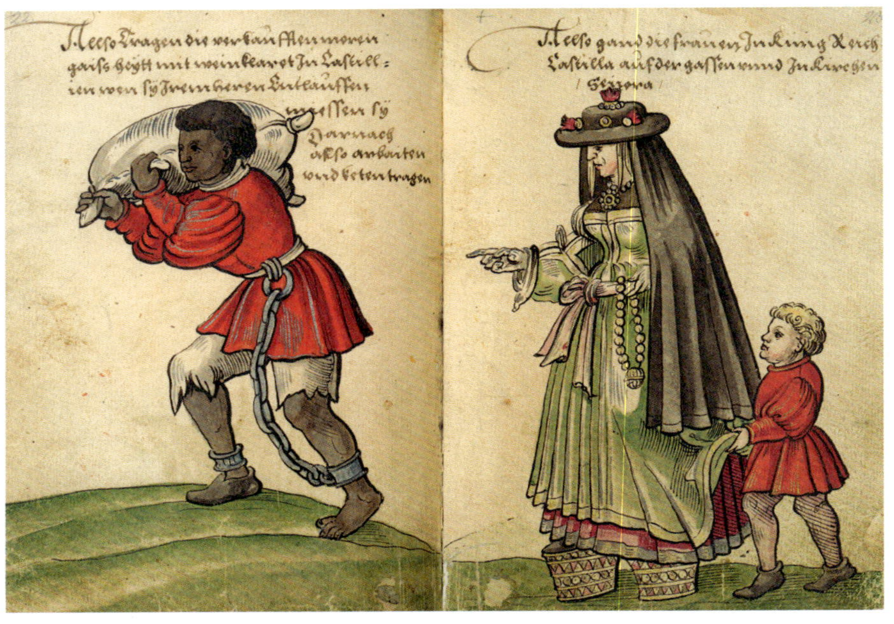

Fig. 4 *Black Slave in Castile* and *Woman and Child in Castile*, from Christoph Weiditz, *Costume Book (Trachtenbuch)*, Augsburg, ca. 1530–40, GNM, shelf mark Hs22474 |**cat. no. 109**|, fols. 22v–23r

dare to write such things … . I saw many captives in iron chains and behind bars, who were forced to do very hard work."[25]

In the period covered by the present exhibition, there are hardly any pictorial representations with links to Nuremberg that directly address the Atlantic trade in enslaved people. Rare exceptions are two pen-and-ink drawings in a costume book (*Trachtenbuch*) of about 1530–40 that is usually attributed to Christoph Weiditz |**cat. no. 109**|.[26] Copies made in Nuremberg after those drawings, only a few decades later, prove that they must have been known in the imperial city from early on.[27] Folio 22 of the costume book shows a Black man carrying a bulging wineskin |**fig. 4**|. Large manacles are fastened to his ankles, and a thick chain attached to one of the manacles connects to his belt. He wears only one shoe, and his white trousers are tattered. According to the accompanying inscription, he was observed this way in Castile. He is described as one of the "sold Moors" (*verkaufften moren*) who was put in chains for having once escaped from his master. This is one of the earliest known depictions of a Black man chained up and subjected to forced labor by Europeans.[28]

A Printer from Nuremberg in Granada

A few weeks after having witnessed the trade in enslaved people in Valencia, Münzer arrived in Granada. A mere two and a half years earlier, Queen Isabella and King Ferdinand had captured the city from the Nasrids, the last Muslim rulers on the Iberian Peninsula. Münzer's travelogue is one of the earliest descriptions of the city from the period immediately after the conquest. He was particularly amazed by the Alhambra, the palace of the Muslim rulers, with its elaborately designed ceilings and rich ornamentation: "Nothing like it exists in all of Europe. It is all so magnificent, so wonderful, and built from so many different materials that one imagines oneself to be in paradise."[29] Presumably the enthusiasm for arabesque decoration in Nuremberg |**cat. nos. 90–92**| had one of its origins in such experiences.

In this former capital of the Nasrid emirate, Münzer also experienced Muslim worship and entered several mosques. Two Germans he encountered, an Andreas from Fulda and a Johannes from Speyer, explained the customs of the local population. Only a few years after Münzer's stay in Granada, the Muslims there met the same fate as Jews had in 1492, being forced to choose between converting to Christianity or leaving the territories of the Catholic Monarchs forever.[30] It is relevant in this context that Münzer met several German book printers in Granada who presumably worked in the shop run by Johann Pegnitzer of Nuremberg and Meinhard Ungut (d. 1499).[31] Pegnitzer belonged to a group of printers active in Seville beginning in 1490, who referred to themselves in their books as *compañeros alemanes*.[32] In Granada, Pegnitzer and Ungut printed several books for the first archbishop of the newly founded diocese, Fray Hernando de Talavera (ca. 1428–1507), including Talavera's reworking of the *Vita Christi* treatise by Francisco Eiximenis[33] and Talavera's own *Breve y muy provechosa doctrina cristiana* |**cat. no. 94**|. These incunabula are very probably the first books printed in Granada after the conquest of the emirate by the Christian queen and king. As Queen Isabella's confessor, Talavera was one of the most influential clerics in the milieu of the Catholic

25 Translated after the German in Herbers 2020, pp. 57–58.
26 Erichsen 2024, with references to earlier literature. On the problems surrounding the attribution, see cat. no. 26.
27 See the album of Sigmund Heldt, Kunstbibliothek, Staatliche Museen zu Berlin, Lipp Aa 3 mtl R. See also Rublack 2022, pp. 302–12, esp. p. 305.
28 Lowe 2005, pp. 25–26.
29 Translated after the German in Herbers 2020, p. 79.
30 For the broader historical context, see Nirenberg 2007.
31 Herbers 2020, p. 95; Herbers 2000, pp. 175–77; Jaspert 2016, p. 80. On German book printers in the Iberian Peninsula, see Häbler 1900, pp. 498–99; Kehrer 1953, pp. 64–67. On the introduction of book printing in Spain and Seville, see Griffin 1988, pp. 1–19.
32 Walter 2001, p. 19.

Monarchs. He was also among the notables whom Münzer met while staying in Granada. For Talavera, these books were essential tools to be used in the instruction of local clerics who were tasked with helping to convert the Muslim population to Christianity.[34]

The presence of German printers in Andalusia was not the region's only book-related link to Nuremberg. Seville played a central role for Nuremberg in a closely associated context. Fernando Colón (1488–1539), a son of Christopher Columbus, assembled one of the world's largest private libraries in Seville in the first half of the sixteenth century.[35] In the winter of 1521–22, he bought several hundred books in Nuremberg alone.[36] Those purchases are traceable because Colón noted in his books the place and date of purchase and often the price paid. In Nuremberg, he acquired not only many locally published books, but also numerous publications printed in other European cities such as Paris and Milan. These books offer remarkable evidence of Nuremberg's importance as a major European center of publishing, printing, and bookselling.

Epilogue

Münzer's travelogue was never published during his lifetime, and it is unclear how many people even had access to it. However, in its many-sidedness and often astonishing subjectivity, it provides unique and wide-ranging insight into the world of the Iberian Peninsula at the end of the fifteenth century. Indirectly, the travelogue also illustrates a fundamental lacuna in narratives about early globalization: owing to the social norms of the time, the ability to become a protagonist in far-flung undertakings and to create textual or pictorial records of one's doings was almost exclusively the prerogative of male members of high-ranking families. In view of those conditions, the concluding passage of Münzer's travelogue appears in a different light: "On April 15 [1495, we] finally arrived at Nuremberg, our longed-for harbor and the end of our journey. As mentioned, I was in the best of health and found both my wife and my only daughter, and the whole family, to be doing well."[37] In contrast to Münzer, his wife and daughter, because of their sex, had no possibility of journeying to the Iberian Peninsula to escape the plague and thus had no chance at becoming protagonists in the narrative of Nuremberg's global history.

33 Eiximenis 1496.
34 Pereda 2007, pp. 254–87, esp. pp. 278–80; Biersack 2010, pp. 289–93.
35 On Fernando Colón's activities as a collector, see McDonald 2004.
36 Kollinger and Pommeranz 2001; Pommeranz 2002.
37 Translated after the German in Herbers 2020, p. 275.

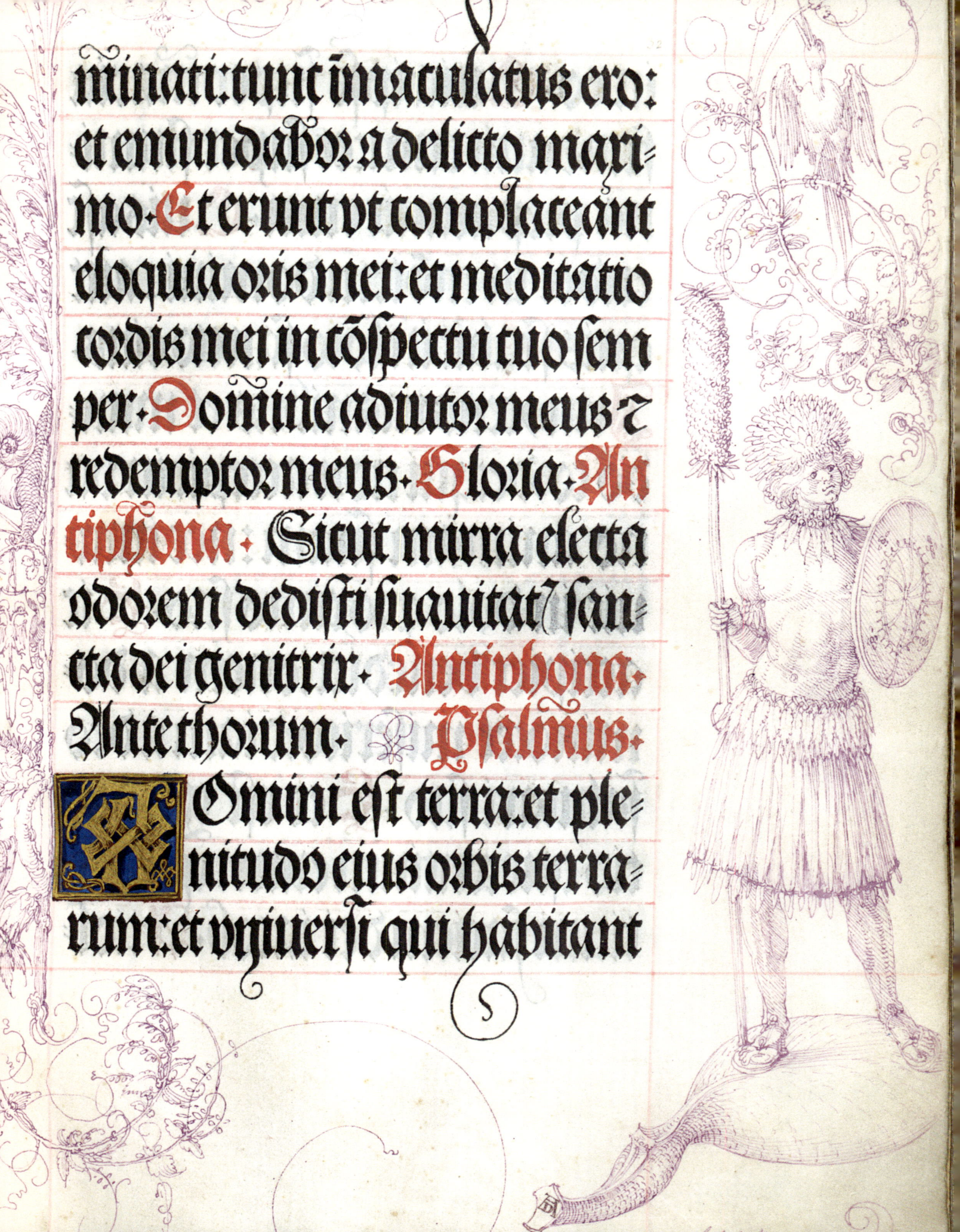

minati: tunc īmaculatus ero:
et emundabor a delicto maxi-
mo. Et erunt vt complaceant
eloquia oris mei: et meditatio
cordis mei in cōspectu tuo sem
per. Domine adiutor meus ⁊
redemptor meus. Gloria. An
tiphona. Sicut mirra electa
odorem dedisti suauitat⁊ sancta dei genitrix. Antiphona.
Ante thorum. Psalmus.
Domini est terra: et ple-
nitudo eius orbis terra-
rum: et vniuersi qui habitant

Manuel Teget-Welz

DÜRER AND THE INDIGENOUS PEOPLES OF THE AMERICAS

PERCEPTUAL FRAMEWORKS FOR THE UNKNOWN IN RENAISSANCE NUREMBERG

Fig. 1 Albrecht Dürer, *A Tupinambá*, from the Prayer Book of Emperor Maximilian I, Nuremberg, 1515, Bayerische Staatsbibliothek, Munich, shelf mark 2 L. impr.membr. 64 |**cat. no. 100**|, fol. 41r

Amerigo Vespucci and the "New World" in Nuremberg

In 1505, the Nuremberg printer Wolfgang Huber (documented ca. 1504–14) published a pamphlet titled "Von der neu gefunnde[n] Region die wol ein welt genannt mag werden" (On the Newly Discovered Region Which May Rightly Be Called a World) |**cat. no. 98.2**|. It is a German translation of the *Mundus Novus*, a report written by the Florentine merchant and explorer Amerigo Vespucci (1454–1512). In that widely read text, which appeared in about sixty editions between 1502–3 and 1529,[1] Vespucci offers an elegantly styled description of his third expedition, which took place from May 10, 1501, to September 7, 1502. The expedition took him to the east coast of South America (Brazil) on behalf of the king of Portugal. At the very beginning of his text, Vespucci emphasizes the novelty of the regions he visited: "And these we may rightly call a new world. Because our ancestors had no knowledge of them, and it will be a matter wholly new to all those who hear about them."[2] The natural world he describes is paradisal in character and includes the then widespread notion of gold in abundance. Vespucci also discusses the habits and customs of the Tupinambá people. He portrays them in largely pejorative terms by devoting special attention to subjects that clashed with European norms, particularly nakedness, cannibalism, and licentiousness.[3] As Karl-Heinz Kohl notes, "The New World is thus made to seem like a world gone topsy-turvy."[4] Such a framing of the Indigenous people probably also served to justify Vespucci's own colonial practice.

Also in 1505, Georg Stuchs (1460–1520) of Nuremberg printed a broadsheet containing Vespucci's description of the Tupinambá from the *Mundus Novus*. This broadsheet includes a woodcut illustration of the "newly discovered people or nations, in their form and appearance" |**cat. no. 98.1**|. The three men shown in the left foreground from the "new land and islands" wear feathered crowns and skirts. As described by Vespucci, their chests and faces are marked by various piercings: "[T]hey bore their cheeks, lips, noses and ears. ... They stop up these holes of theirs with blue stones, bits of marble, very beautiful crystals of alabaster, very white bones, and other things artificially prepared according to their customs."[5]

At the same time that the aforementioned pamphlet and broadsheet appeared in Nuremberg, an illustrated broadsheet based on the *Mundus Novus* was published in Augsburg by Johann Froschauer (d. 1523) |**fig. 2**|.[6] Its woodcut stages cannibalism in a particularly sensationalist manner.[7] Following Vespucci, the caption explains, "They also eat one another ... and hang up the flesh to be smoked." One can certainly concur with Frauke Gewecke's assessment of how such images affected European viewers of the time: "Those ... who drew their knowledge of the Americas primarily ... from illustrations and maps must have been all the more strongly and lastingly influenced by the stereotype of the 'naked man-eater,' since almost any type of information conveyed in visual form has greater suggestive power than does a text."[8]

Albrecht Dürer (1471–1528) appears to have been familiar with such "New World"[9] pamphlets and broadsheets. This is supported by a marginal drawing that he made about 1515 in the Prayer Book of Emperor Maximilian I |**cat. no. 100; fig. 1**|. There, in the depiction of a young warrior wearing feathered clothing and standing on an overturned spoon, the figure's dress and pose recall the aforementioned Nuremberg illustration; and the adornments on the neck and upper arm are similar to those found in the Augsburg broadsheet. While Dürer omitted piercings of stone and bone on the chest and face, he added a shield and a staff-like club. As Jean Michel Massing has noted, the club was probably based on a real Tupinambá weapon brought back from South America and recorded by Dürer with almost scientific precision.[10] This recognizably

This essay is based on the lecture I gave on April 3, 2024, at the University of California, Riverside, titled "Meeting the Unknown: Albrecht Dürer and the Aztecs."

1 Of these sixty editions, there were fifteen German editions printed between 1505 and 1509. See Briesemeister 1992, p. 197.

2 Translation cited after Vespucci 1916, p. 1.

3 Wallisch 2012, pp. 25–29. In describing the Indigenous peoples, Vespucci was doubtlessly less interested in ethnological objectivity than he was in confirming European notions. His tendency to exaggerate is exemplified by his claim that the people he encountered could live up to 150 years. Wallisch 2012, pp. 29, 128.

4 Exh. cat. Berlin 1982, p. 285 (Karl-Heinz Kohl).

5 Translation cited after Vespucci 1916, p. 5.

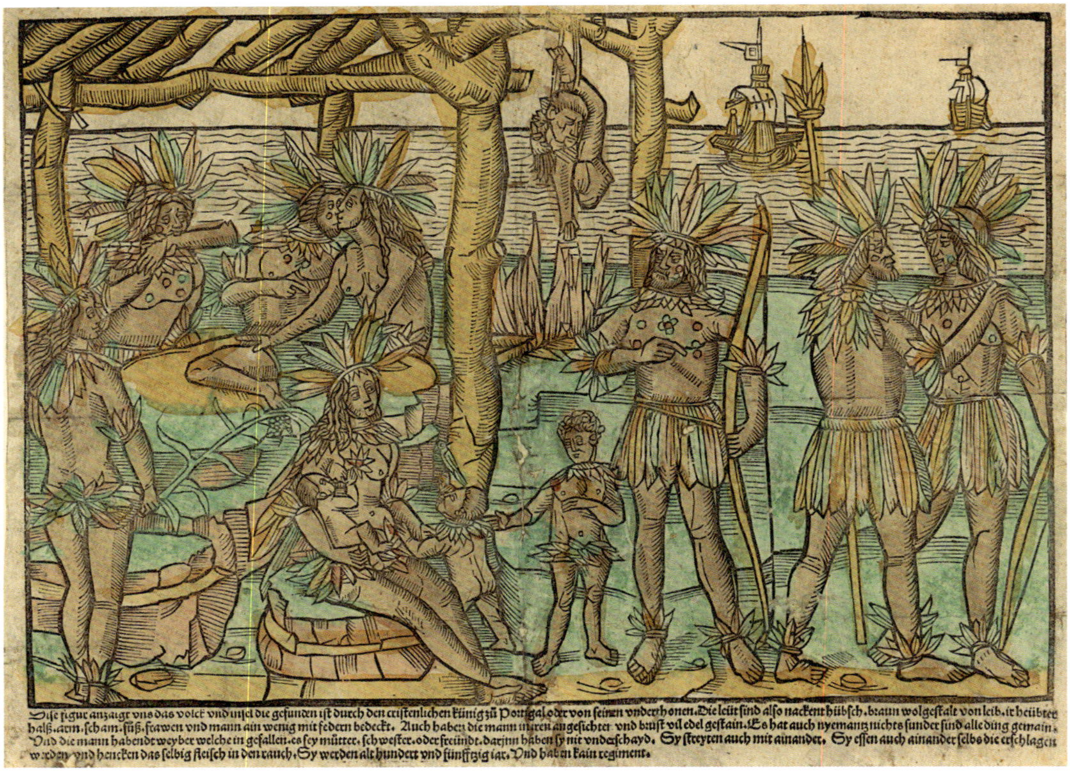

Fig. 2 Johann Froschauer, Broadsheet based on the *Mundus Novus*, 1505, Bayerische Staatsbibliothek, Munich, shelf mark Einblattdruck V,2

non-European figure illustrates the first verse of Psalm 24 in the prayer book: "The earth is the Lord's and the fulness thereof, the world and those who dwell therein."[11]

Albrecht Dürer and the Aztecs

On March 17, 1520, the Nuremberg publisher Friedrich Peypus (1485–1534) issued a hastily assembled pamphlet containing spectacular news from overseas |**cat. no. 99**|. Titled *Ein auszug ettlicher sendbrieff dem aller durchleüchtigisten großmechtigiste[n] Fürsten und Herren Herren Carl* (An Extract from Several Letters to His Most Serene and Mighty Highness, the Prince and Lord Charles), this thin booklet reports on expeditions carried out by the Spanish conquistadors Francisco Hernández de Córdoba (d. 1517), Juan de Grijalva (1490–1527), and Hernán Cortés (1485–1547). Cortés's arrival at the southern end of the Gulf of Mexico on April 21, 1519, effectively marked the beginning of the Aztec Empire's ruin. The text published in Nuremberg is supplemented by a section devoted to geography and culture, in which the anonymous author, in a way similar to Vespucci, emphasizes Indigenous practices that ran contrary to norms held by European readers. Particular attention is paid to "idolatry" and human sacrifices, which, according to this text, claimed five thousand lives per year.[12]

The Nuremberg pamphlet also notes that Cortés received from the Aztecs "a tapestry made of silk, decorated with gold ornaments." This is an abbreviated reference to the gifts that Moctezuma II (ca. 1465–1520), the last Aztec emperor, presented to the Spaniards in late April 1519.[13] The conquistador Bernal Díaz del Castillo (1495/96–1584) witnessed this presentation of gifts and later recounted it in great detail, making special mention of the numerous artifacts consisting of precious metals, including a gold and a silver disk.[14] The Annals of Tlatelolco, written by an Indigenous chronicler, also mention Moctezuma II's gifts: "When he [Cortés] arrived at Tecpan Tlayacac, the Huaxtecs greeted him by giving him Golden Suns (one of gold and one of silver), a cross mirror, golden helmets, golden snail-shaped vessels to be worn on the head, green feather ornaments of the coastal people, and shell shields."[15] According to Bernardino de Sahagún (1499/1500–1590), who recorded the accounts of Indigenous informants, the

6 Among the extant impressions, see for example BSB, Munich, Einbl. Dr. V,2. Colin 1988, pp. 186–87, cat. no. B. 10; Exh. cat. Munich 1992, p. 29, cat. no. 15.
7 On the iconography of cannibalism in early German prints, see for example Colin 1992, esp. pp. 179–80; Massing 2016.
8 Gewecke 1986, p. 149.
9 The term "Neue Welt" (New World) is used by Christoph Scheurl in a 1506 letter to Sixtus Tucher: "You know that fourteen years ago, on behalf of the Spanish monarchy and under the leadership of Christopher Columbus, a new world, so to speak, was discovered, and within it six hundred islands." Translated from the German citation in Schultheiß 1955, p. 194.
10 Massing 1991, p. 516.
11 Holy Bible, Revised Standard Version. See Massing 1991, p. 515; Freigang 2009, p. 89.
12 On the subject of Aztec human sacrifice, see for example the recent studies Jansen and Jiménez 2019, esp. pp. 259–64; Rodriguez 2019, pp. 237–47.
13 Riese 2011, pp. 266–67; Rinke 2022, pp. 120–21.
14 Narciß 1988, p. 88.
15 Translated based on the German translation in Riese 2011, p. 266.

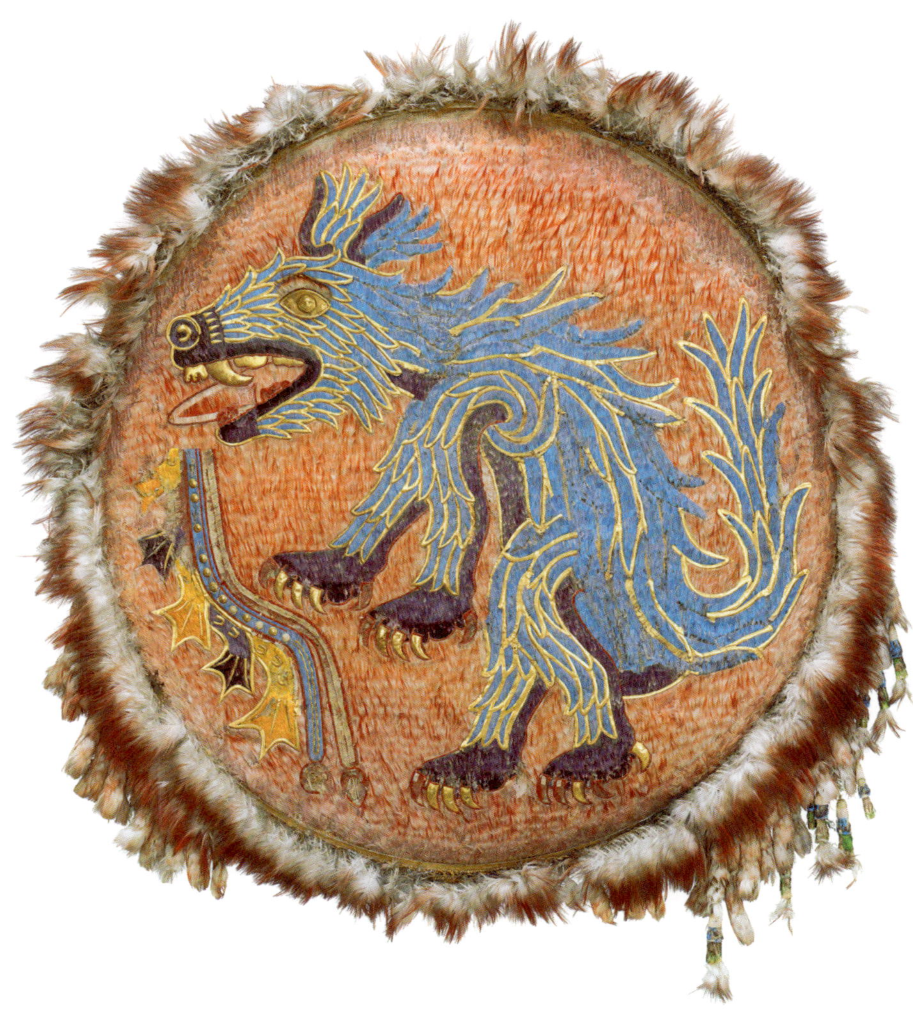

Fig. 3 Featherwork shield with a coyote, ca. 1500, Weltmuseum Wien, Vienna, inv. no. 43380

gifts encompassed mainly four sets of garments for Aztec deities, consisting of featherwork items, mosaic masks, precious stones, gold disks, and the like.[16] However, the conquistadors were uninterested in the objects' religious significance. According to Sahagún, their interest lay only in the precious metals: "The Spaniards delighted in the gold, they grabbed at it like monkeys, because they hunger for gold, they root after gold like pigs."[17]

Cortés sent Moctezuma's gifts, along with other artifacts, to King Charles (1500–1558; Emperor Charles V) in Spain, where they arrived on November 5, 1519.[18] The Aztec treasure was then exhibited in Seville and Valladolid, where it was viewed by Peter Martyr d'Anghiera (1457–1526), and later in Brussels. On August 20, 1523, most of the objects were given to Charles's aunt, Margaret of Austria (1480–1530), who was the governor of the Habsburg Netherlands. Margaret displayed the items as "exotica" in her library in Mechelen.[19]

Of these gifts, the only surviving item appears to be a turquoise mosaic shield formerly kept in the Kunstkammer (Chamber of Art and Wonders) at Ambras Castle, which was founded by Ferdinand II (1529–1595), Charles V's nephew.[20] Although other parts of the Ambras Mexicana collection did not belong to the gifts of 1519, they nevertheless give an impression of the high quality of Aztec craftsmanship, as is apparent, for example, in the featherwork shield decorated with a coyote figure, which arrived in Europe around 1522 |**fig. 3**|.[21] Furthermore, a mosaic mask of the type that, according to Sahagún, belonged to the Aztec deities' garments has been preserved with an old Medici provenance.[22] Any gold objects that fell into the hands of the conquistadors were melted down for the value of their raw material. However, at least one Mixtec ring, an item mentioned in the 1598 inventory of the ducal Kunstkammer in Munich, appears to have survived to the present day |**fig. 4**|.[23]

16 Nowotny 1960, pp. 9–10; Litterscheid 1989, pp. 246–48.
17 Translated based on the German translation in Braun 1982, p. 41.
18 A packing list has survived from the shipment. See Nowotny 1947, pp. 213–18; Nowotny 1960, pp. 20–25.
19 Vandenbroeck 1992, pp. 104–5, 115; Eichberger 2002, pp. 182–84.
20 Weltmuseum, Vienna, inv. no. 43379. Nowotny 1960, pp. 38–41; Feest 1990, pp. 24–25.
21 Weltmuseum Vienna, inv. no. 43380. Nowotny 1960, pp. 54–56; Feest 1990, pp. 14–17.
22 Museo delle civiltà, Rome, inv. no. MPE 4213. See Exh. cat. Washington 1991, p. 356, cat. no. 377 (Michael D. Coe); Exh. cat. Munich 1992, vol. 2, pp. 909–11, cat. no. 5.90 (Ferdinand Anders).
23 Schatzkammer of the Residenz, Munich, inv. no. Res. Mü. Schk. 1257 (WL). See Exh. cat. Hildesheim and Munich 1986, vol. 2, pp. 374–75, cat. no. 352 (Wolf-Günter Thieme); Exh. cat. London, Berlin, and Bonn 2003, p. 443, cat. no. 177 (Sabine Heym).

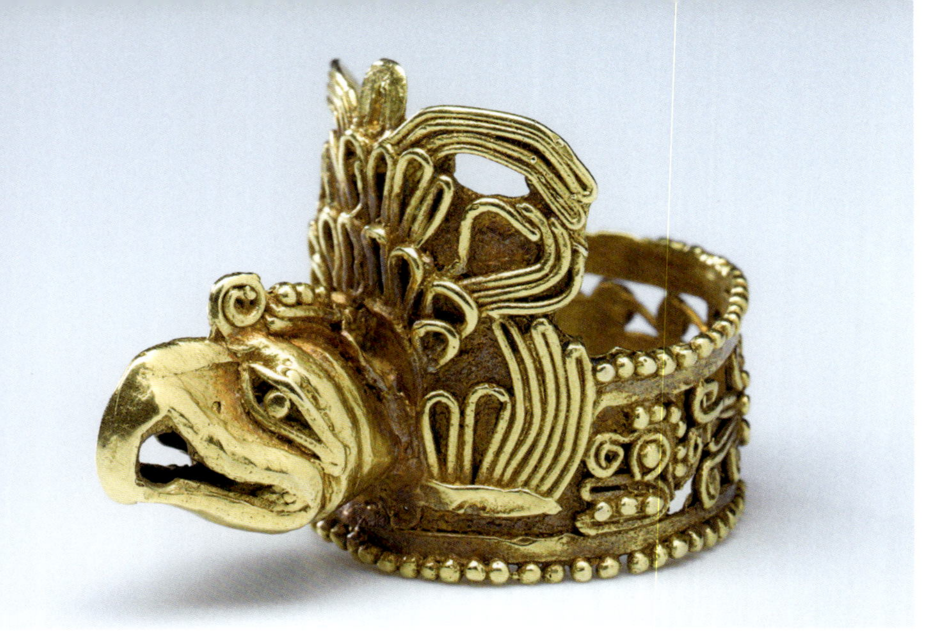

Fig. 4 Mixtec ring, fifteenth century, Schatzkammer der Residenz, Munich, inv. no. 1257

In Brussels, on the occasion of Charles V's coronation in Aachen, the gifts were displayed over a number of weeks in several halls of the court palace.[24] It was there that Dürer saw the items sometime between August 27 and September 2, 1520, as follows from a much-quoted entry he made in the diary of his travels in the Low Countries: "I also saw the objects which men have brought back for the king from the new Land of Gold: a sun made all of gold, a good six feet across, likewise a moon of pure silver, of the same size, also two rooms full of those natives' armour, all manner of their weapons, military gear and missilery, amazing shields, curious costumes, bed coverings and every kind of spectacular things for all possible uses, more worth seeing than the usual prodigies. These things are all so precious that they are valued at a hundred thousand gulden. I have never in my life seen anything that gave my heart such delight as these things, for I saw amongst them marvellously skilful objects and was amazed at the subtle ingeniousness of people in foreign lands. I cannot find words to describe all those things I found there."[25]

The diary entry's extraordinary length is immediately striking. Usually, Dürer was satisfied with jotting down just a few words as reminders of things he had seen, even in the case of works of art by famous masters.[26] The long entry suggests a genuine interest in the gifts on display "from the new Land of Gold." Dürer's enthusiasm—"I have never in my life seen anything that gave my heart such delight"—becomes clearer when one considers that he had probably formed a preconception of the Aztecs based on the type of primitive man-eaters popularized by Vespucci. In fact, however, the "people in foreign lands" clearly possessed "subtle ingeniousness"—something that Dürer would not have expected. The highly elaborate pieces of iridescent featherwork must have impressed him, given his past investigations of the optical effects of feathers, for example in his study of the wing of a European roller, created about 1500 |**fig. 5**|.[27] And as the son of a master goldsmith, Dürer was equipped with knowledge to expertly assess the material and technical properties of the "sun made all of gold" and the "moon of pure silver"—the items he listed first.[28] But he was at a loss for words when it came to objects of other kinds, probably owing in part to a lack of expertise and technical vocabulary: "I cannot find words to describe all those things I found there."

Dürer was in contact with numerous scholars. In Brussels, for example, he met Erasmus of Rotterdam (1466/69–1536).[29] With that in mind, as Christian F. Feest has pointed out, it is hardly surprising that Dürer's diary entry on the Aztec gifts shows clear parallels in content and language to other reports on the treasure.[30] At the court in Brussels, Dürer may have heard statements made by the royal historiographer Peter Martyr,[31] who wrote in the fourth book (1520) of his *Decades*: "If ever artists of this kind of work have touched genius, then surely these natives are they. It is not so much the gold or the precious stones I admire, as the cleverness of the artist and the workmanship, which much exceed the value of the material and excite my amazement. I have examined a thousand figures which it is impossible to describe. In my opinion I have never seen anything, which for beauty could more delight the human eye."[32]

However great it may have been at first, Dürer's enthusiasm for the gifts of Moctezuma II was ultimately short-lived. After his return to Nuremberg from the Low Countries, he was influenced above all by the normative power of classical antiquity, a subject that had fascinated him from early on. In that way, he was a typical man of the Renaissance,

24 See Veth and Muller 1918, vol. 2, pp. 100, 105.
25 Translation cited after Ashcroft 2017, p. 560. See also Klingelhöfer 1972, p. 375; Freigang 2009, p. 84.
26 For example, the wall paintings by Rogier van der Weyden (1399/1400–1464) in the town hall of Brussels, which Dürer saw prior to viewing the Aztec treasure. See Rupprich 1956, p. 155, and Unverfehrt 2007, p. 67, among other sources.
27 Vienna, Albertina, inv. no. 4840. Winkler 1936–39, vol. 3, pp. 58–59, cat. no. 614; Exh. cat. Vienna 2019, p. 451, cat. no. 56.
28 See Feest 1992, p. 116; Feest 2013, pp. 367–68.
29 See, for example, Rupprich 1956, p. 156; Unverfehrt 2007, p. 63.
30 Feest 1992, pp. 120–21; Feest 2013, pp. 367–68.
31 Eichberger 2002, pp. 182–83.
32 Translation cited after Martire d'Anghiera 1912, vol. 2, p. 46. See also Klingelhöfer 1972, p. 375; Freigang 2009, p. 84.

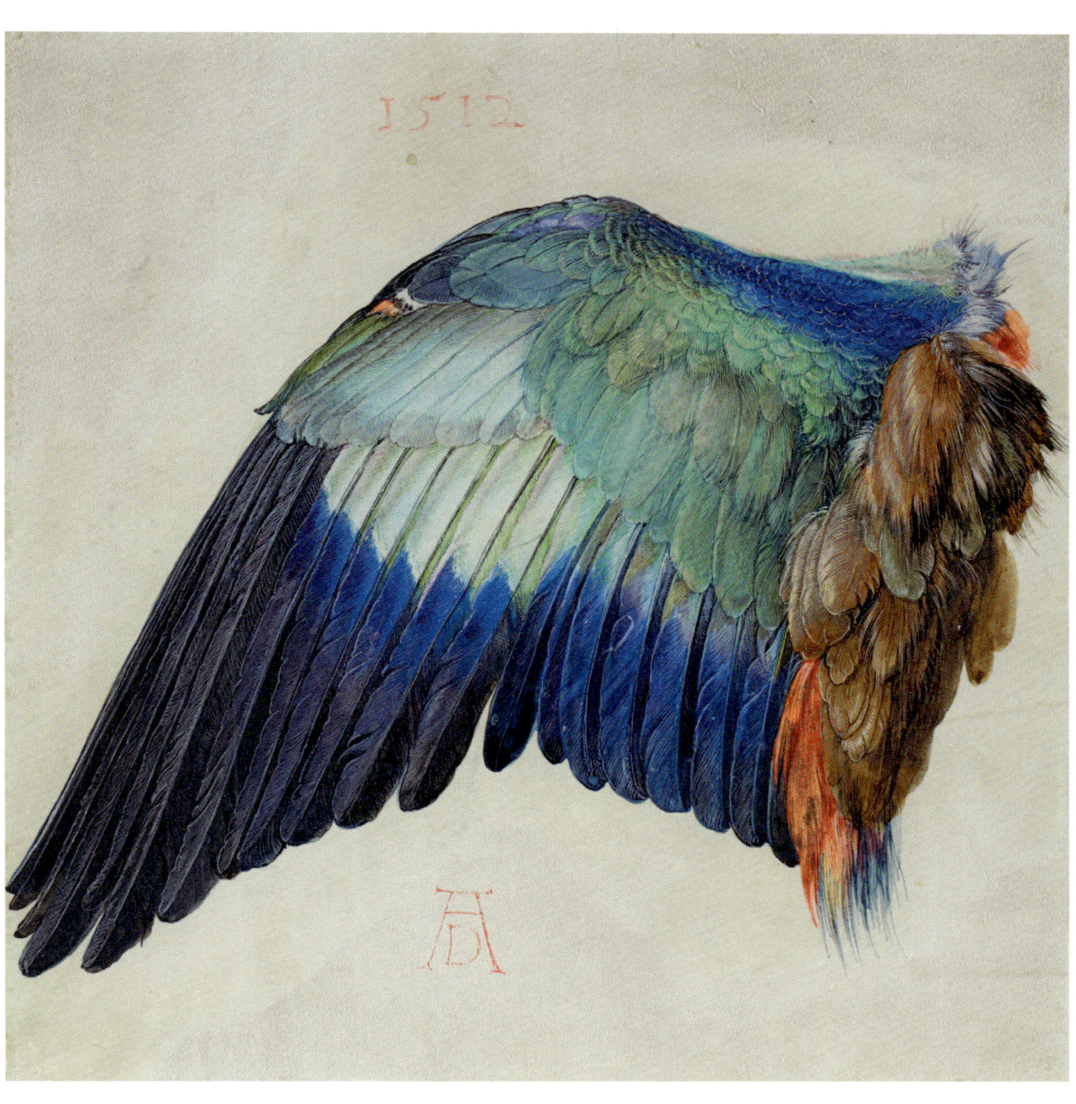

Fig. 5 Albrecht Dürer, *Wing of a European Roller*, ca. 1500, Albertina, Vienna, inv. no. 4840

shaped in a milieu of humanism. For example, in 1522, for the redecoration of the Great Hall in Nuremberg's town hall, he designed a wall painting showing the Calumny of Apelles.[33] This was a new staging of a lost ancient painting described by the Greek author Lucian. And in the "Aesthetic Excursus" of Dürer's treatise on human proportions (*Vier Bücher von Menschlicher Proportion*), published in 1528, he makes it unmistakably clear that more *ingenium* resided in the ruins of ancient Roman buildings than in the art of his day.[34] The "marvellously skilful objects" from the Aztec Empire had no place in that Eurocentric narrative. Instead, these items were integrated into cabinets of curiosities, where they were admired as "exotica."[35]

33 See the preserved design by Dürer, now at the Albertina, Vienna, inv. no. 3177. Schauerte 2012, pp. 216–20; Exh. cat. Vienna 2019, p. 464, cat. no. 197.
34 As kindly pointed out to me by Thomas Schauerte, Aschaffenburg; private communication, February 21, 2024.
35 In Nuremberg, the so-called "Vitziputzli" (cat. no 112), a Mexican statuette of a monkey, was kept in the city library's collection of *Memorabilien*.

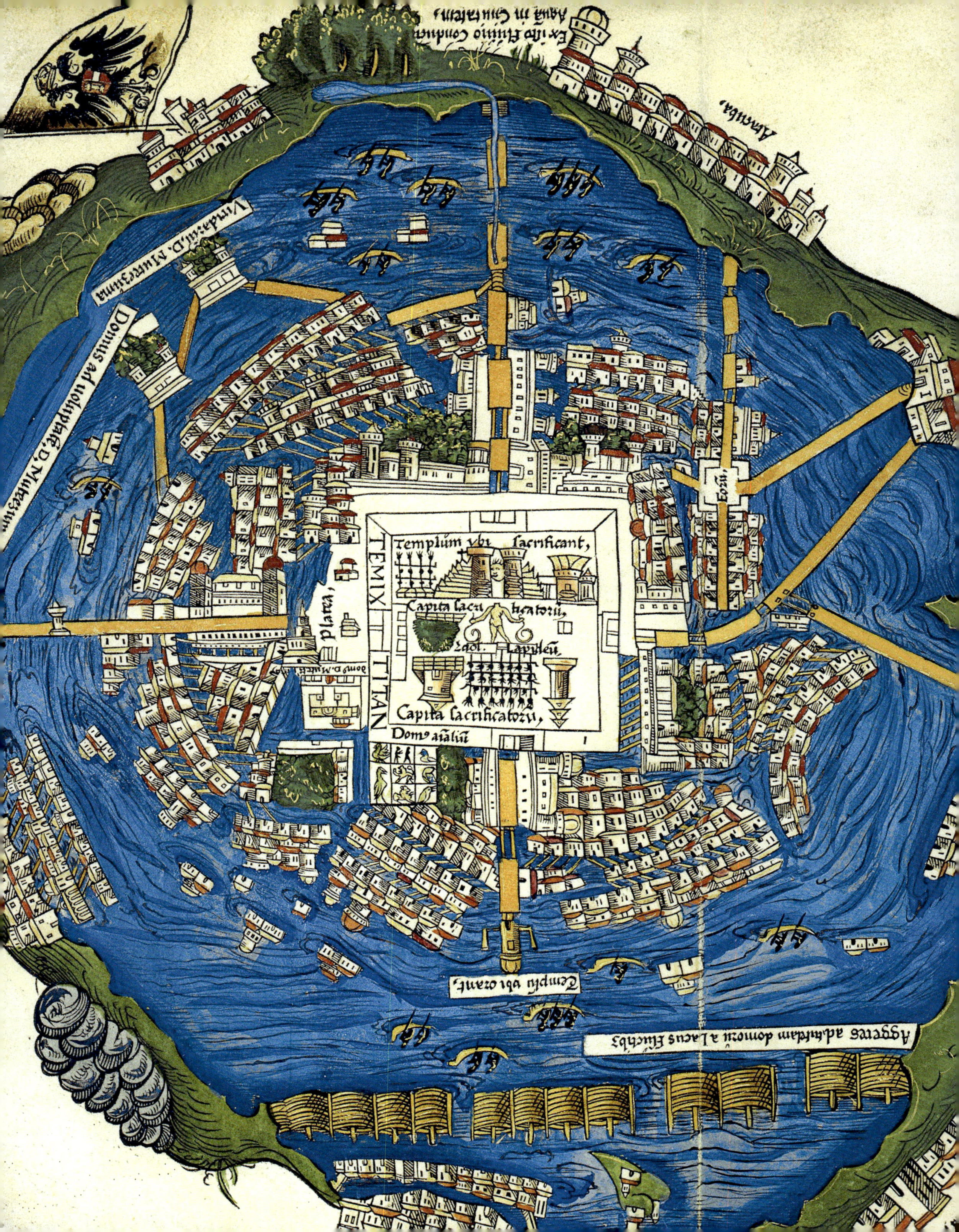
Templum vbi sacrificant,
TEMIXTITAN
Plaza
Capita sacrificatoru,
Dom' aialiu
Templu vbi orant
Domus ad voluptate D. Muteczume

Daniel Astorga Poblete

TENOCHTITLÁN 1524

THE FIRST MAP OF AN AMERICAN CITY, PUBLISHED IN NUREMBERG

The woodcut *Map of Tenochtitlán and the Gulf of Mexico* |**cat. no. 105**| is Europe's oldest known depiction of an American city. It is included in the text *Praeclara Ferdinandi Cortesii de Nova Maris Oceani Hyspania Narratio*, published in 1524 by the Nuremberg printer Friedrich Peypus (1485–1535). This publication is a Latin translation of the second and third letters of the conquistador Hernán Cortés (1485–1547) addressed to Emperor Charles V (1500–1558), in which Cortés narrates his expedition to the Mexica city of Tenochtitlán and the city's subsequent capture. Numerous copies of the 1524 map of Tenochtitlán are preserved in libraries throughout Europe and the United States. Two impressions of the woodcut are noteworthy owing to their decoration in color: one in the Newberry Library in Chicago and another in the Österreichische Nationalbibliothek (Austrian National Library) in Vienna |**fig. 1 and fig. p. 329**|. The latter impression constitutes an *avant la lettre* presentation copy, printed on parchment and illuminated with luxurious bright blue (containing ultramarine, a highly expensive pigment) and gold heightening done in shell-gold paint. This specific copy, presented to Archduke Ferdinand of Austria (1503–1564), was integrated into the collection of the imperial Hofbibliothek (Court Library).

The woodcut features two cartographic representations. The one on the left shows the Gulf of Mexico, while the one on the right depicts Tenochtitlán. Positioned at the upper left is a laudatory poem in Latin, honoring Charles V and his dominion over the New World. This essay will first focus on the depiction of the Aztec capital and, second, on the reasons why it was created in Nuremberg, of all places.

Fig. 1 *Map of Tenochtitlán*, luxury impression for Archduke Ferdinand (detail), Nuremberg: Friedrich Peypus, 1524, Österreichische Nationalbibliothek, Vienna, shelf mark 394471-C KAR MAG |**cat. no. 105.1**|

Description of the Map

The map of Tenochtitlán presents the city in a circular layout from directly above. The image can be divided into four segments from the center outward. The first segment shows the ceremonial heart of the city |**fig. 1**|. The central structure on the plan is the Templo Mayor, with its two towers dedicated to the gods Huitzilopochtli and Tlaloc. The image of the sun between the two towers alludes to the astronomical and historical motivations behind the Templo Mayor's construction.[1] The woodcut designer included the brief description "Templum ubi sacrificant" (temple where they sacrifice) above the Templo Mayor in reference to the rituals practiced there. To the left of the temple, we see a grid-like *tzompantli* labeled with the inscription "capita sacrificatorum" (the sacrificed heads). The *tzompantli* were structures fitted with spikes, on which the severed heads of those sacrificed in the Templo Mayor were displayed. To the right of main temple is the Temple of Tezcatlipoca.[2] Below, there is a headless sculpture of a woman posed in contrapposto, holding a snake in each hand and accompanied by the caption "idolo lapideum" (stone idol). This figure may represent the goddess Coyolxauhqui, given that a sculpture of her was indeed located at the Templo Mayor, at the base of the staircase leading to the tower devoted to Huitzilopochtli.[3] Below the idol is another *tzompantli*, flanked on the left by the *Calmecac* (college for the Tenochca elite) and on the right by the Temple of the Sun.[4] Just beyond the perimeter of the ceremonial precinct, at the lower left, one encounters the palace of Moctezuma (*Domus Moctezuma*) and, below, the ruler's zoo (*Domus animalium*).

The second segment depicts the *chinampas* (floating gardens) along with the houses that surrounded them, which include some of Moctezuma's buildings, such as his pleasure house (*Domus ad voluptatem*) and his gardens (*viridarium*). The designer positioned the market of Tlatelolco (*Forum*) in the upper right corner of this section. Tlatelolco was Tenochtitlán's twin city, located on an islet northwest of the Aztec capital |**fig. 2**|.

1 Mundy1998, p. 16; Boone 2011, p. 36.
2 Matos Moctezuma 2009, p. 94.
3 Boone 2011, p. 35.
4 Matos Moctezuma 2009, p. 94.

The third segment illustrates the intricate network of causeways and dikes in Tenochtitlán. These causeways created a quadripartite layout, dividing the city into four neighborhoods: Moyotlan, Teopan, Tzacualco, and Cuepopan-Tlaquechiuhca. The causeways extended toward Churubusco (on the plan, toward the left) and Tacuba (toward the top). The latter facilitated the transfer of fresh water from the forests of Chapultepec. Two routes on the right lead to the towns of Tenayuca and Tepeyacac.[5] Near the bottom, we see the impressive dike of Nezahualcoyotl, which controlled the flow of saltwater from Lake Texcoco into the freshwater of the Laguna of Mexico.

The fourth and final segment features the cities along the shores of Lake Texcoco. Only three cities are labeled with their names: "Tesqua" (Texcoco) and "Atacuba" (Tlacopan), which were part of the so-called "Triple Alliance," and "Iztapalapa" (Ixtapalapa), the first city Cortés encountered upon entering the Valley of Mexico. Lastly, the cluster of buildings that scholarship has recognized as Tacubaya displays the banner of the Habsburgs, featuring the double-headed eagle of the Holy Roman Empire, along with the emblems of Charles V's Castilian and Burgundian territories.

An Aztec Map in Nuremberg?

But how did it come about that the plan was published in Nuremberg, of all places? In recent decades, there has been extensive discussion regarding the plan's origin. Eduardo Matos Moctezuma, Barbara Mundy, and Elizabeth Hill Boone have argued that the woodcut image is based on an Indigenous prototype that came into Spanish hands and was later redesigned in European style. One specific detail, the sun appearing between the two towers of the Templo Mayor, references the astronomical use of the temple during the equinox.[6] Mundy and Boone note that this information about the temple did not circulate in Europe, making it unlikely that a German artist would have included that detail independent of a prototype by an Indigenous designer. They also point out that the circular view of the city closely resembles extant representations of the Aztec capital made by native inhabitants. Certain pre-Colonial representations of Tenochtitlán, including those present in the *Codex Boturini* and *Codex Aubin*, as well as other colonial records such as the *Codex Mendoza* |**fig. 3**| and the *Lienzo de Tlaxcala*, also depict the city in a rounded manner.

In his letters to Charles V, Cortés mentions a depiction of the city of Tenochtitlán that he had sent to the emperor.[7] This was possibly the Indigenous prototype for the 1524 map. Even more interesting is the observation made by the chronicler Peter Martyr d'Anghiera (1457–1526), who observed a collection of Indigenous artifacts brought from the Central Valley of Mexico. By the end of 1522, Peter Martyr had encountered one of Cortés's agents in Valladolid, Juan de Ribera, who presented him with a small map of Tenochtitlán by an Indigenous creator. This image showed the city with its temples, bridges, and lakes.[8]

In my opinion, the prototype for the map published in Nuremberg in 1524 was none other than the native image seen by Peter Martyr in 1522. The source image would most likely have arrived in the imperial city toward the end of 1523 or the beginning of 1524. I believe that the image reached Nuremberg thanks to Charles V's agent Henry du Hemricourt, who was tasked with delivering a number of Aztec artifacts to Archduke Ferdinand of Austria. Ferdinand was meant to have these artifacts in his possession by the time of the 1524 Imperial Diet of Nuremberg, which was set to commence at the beginning of the year under Ferdinand's direction.

As Martín de Salinas notes in his letters to the archduke and to Gabriel de Salamanca (1489–1539), Ferdinand was keenly interested in receiving news

5 Tyrakowski 1997, pp. 96–97.
6 Aveni, Calnek, and Hartung 1988, p. 293; Šprajc 1999, pp. 74–75.
7 Cortés 1998, p. 174.
8 Martire d'Anghiera 1912, p. 201.

Fig. 2 *Map of Tenochtitlán and the Gulf of Mexico*, Nuremberg: Friedrich Peypus, 1524, Universitätsbibliothek der LMU, Munich, shelf mark 0014/W 2 H.aux. 52 | **cat. no. 105.2** |

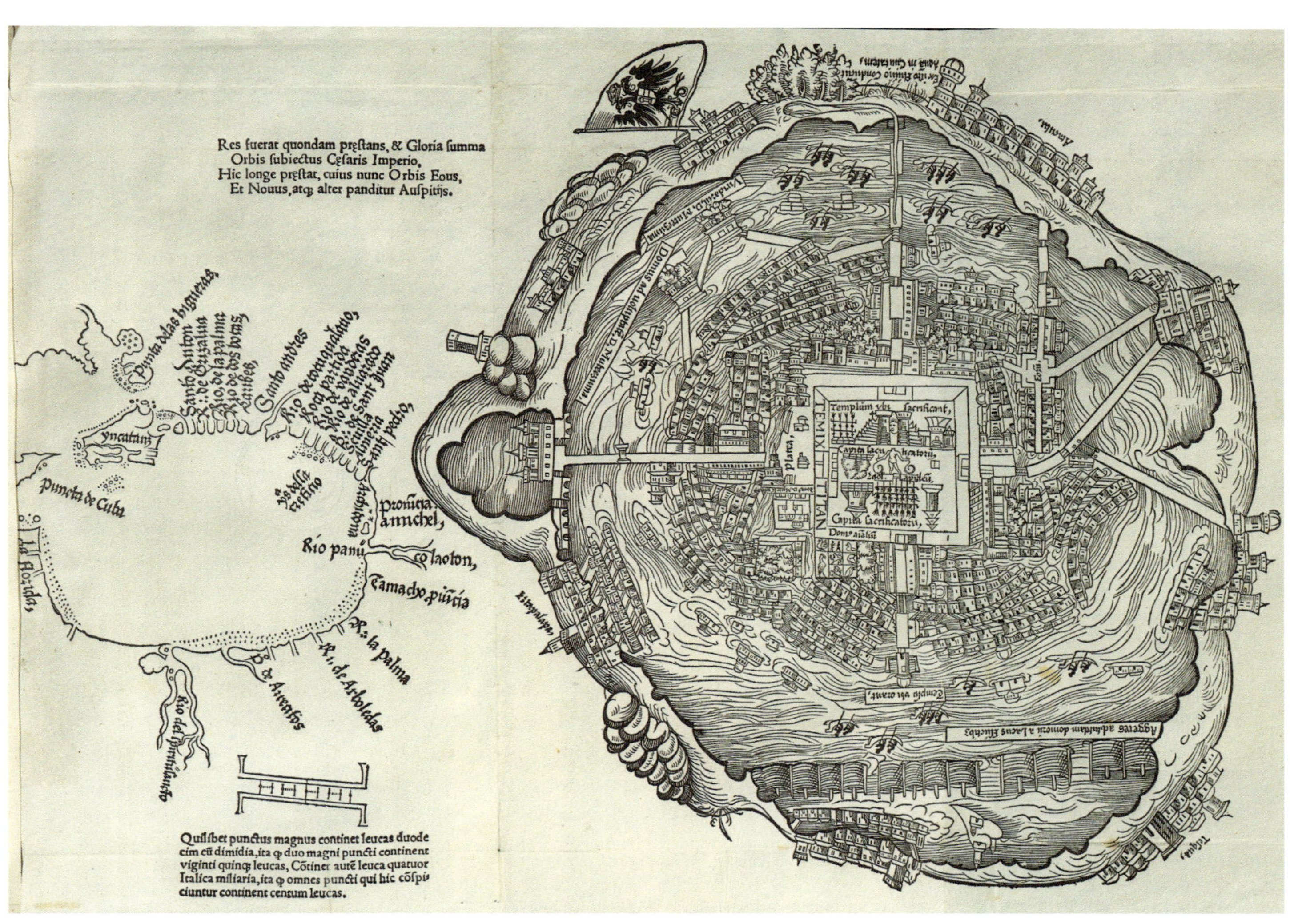

about the lands discovered in the Americas.[9] Therefore, Hemricourt departed from Burgos on August 20, 1523, carrying a treasure from Charles intended for Ferdinand. Due to adverse weather conditions, Hemricourt was unable to arrive before the end of the year. As documented in the inventory of Ferdinand's chamberlain, Martín de Paredes, Hemricourt met with the archduke in Nuremberg no later than January 12, 1524.[10] That inventory contains several entries in which Paredes notes that he received featherwork (*plumarios*), shields (*rodelas*), and Indigenous leather clothing from New Spain while the archduke's court was in Nuremberg.[11] These artifacts are among the treasures described by Cortés in the inventory sent with his third letter to the emperor.[12] The items traveled on the ship *La Rábida* under the protection of Juan de Ribera, who showed them to Peter Martyr during the aforementioned 1522 encounter.[13] Paredes's inventory does not explicitly mention the reception of maps or images, as it was intended as a register of jewelry, clothing, and

9 Salinas 1903, p. 312.
10 "Rationes cottidianarum expensarum: 1521–1524 imperatoris Caroli V. a camerario hispanico conscriptae," Österreichische Nationalbibliothek, 1521–24, fol. 197.
11 Rationes 1521–24, fols. 197–99.
12 Martínez 1990, pp. 316–40.
13 Martire d'Anghiera 1912, pp. 195–98.

weapons. However, this document does indicate that Ferdinand received at least "three books from New Spain," which were taken to Vienna by Antonio Calvo and only recorded on August 24, 1524, several months after Hemricourt arrived in Nuremberg and three months after Ferdinand's departure for the Austrian capital.[14] It is worth noting that the "books" mentioned in Paredes's inventory may well have included pre-Hispanic codices, since that was the term (*libros*) the Spaniards used for such objects. This leads us to believe that Hemricourt delivered to Nuremberg not only featherwork, shields, and clothing but also codices from the Central Valley of Mexico, also known as *amoxtli*. Maps of a type similar to the one on folio 2r of the later *Codex Mendoza* would plausibly have been included. Additionally, copies of Cortés's letters could also have been brought to Nuremberg by Hemricourt.

In Nuremberg, members of Archduke Ferdinand's court—particularly Johann von Revellis (d. 1529) and Pietro Savorgnano—played a crucial role in producing the 1524 *Praeclara Narratio*, containing the map of Tenochtitlán. Savorgnano, a native of Friuli and Revellis's secretary, translated both of Cortés's letters from Spanish to Latin. Revellis, meanwhile, was the newly elected bishop of Vienna during the Diet of Nuremberg but also held significant positions at Ferdinand's court. Known in the Spanish world as Juan de Granada, Revellis served as the almoner, confessor, and preacher at Ferdinand's court until 1530 and was a prominent figure in the archduke's inner circle. Peter Martyr informs us that Revellis, while in Germany, advocated for the translation of Cortés's letters.[15]

The identity of the map's designer and woodcutter has been a matter of extensive discussion. Although some scholars have attributed the image to a putative woodcutter named Martin Plinius, said to have been active in Nuremberg, there is no record of this artist. Heinrich Röttinger ascribed the map to Erhard Schön (1491–1542), a frequent collaborator of the printer Peypus.[16] Nevertheless, recent studies have discarded that attribution.[17] Hans Sebald Beham (1500–1550) has been considered in various studies related to the map, and not without good reason.[18] Firstly, Beham has been associated with a coat of arms prepared for Revellis in Nuremberg in 1524. Secondly, he played a role in the design of the map of Vienna published in 1530 by Niclas Meldemann (d. 1552), which has in common with the map of Tenochtitlán a circular layout in a view from directly above |**cat. no. 76**|. The similarities between the two maps may suggest that Beham participated in creating the woodblock of the map of Tenochtitlán. However, no conclusive documentation is currently available to resolve the attribution of this woodblock printed in Nuremberg. I propose that one or more artists in Nuremberg from the circles of Erhard Schön and Hans Sebald Beham prepared the final design and woodblock of the map of Tenochtitlán from the Indigenous prototype, adding certain elements familiar from the city views contained in the 1493 *Nuremberg Chronicle* |**see cat. no. 4**|. The creation of the *Map of Tenochtitlán and the Gulf of Mexico* in Nuremberg calls attention to the German city's role as a hub for the distribution of news and artifacts from the Aztec Empire.

14 Rationes 1521–24, fols. 49–50.
15 Martire d'Anghiera 1912, p. 212.
16 Röttinger 1925, p. 61.
17 Hollstein German 47; Gresle-Pouligny 1999, pp. 37–38.
18 Steinhilper 2016, pp. 396–97.

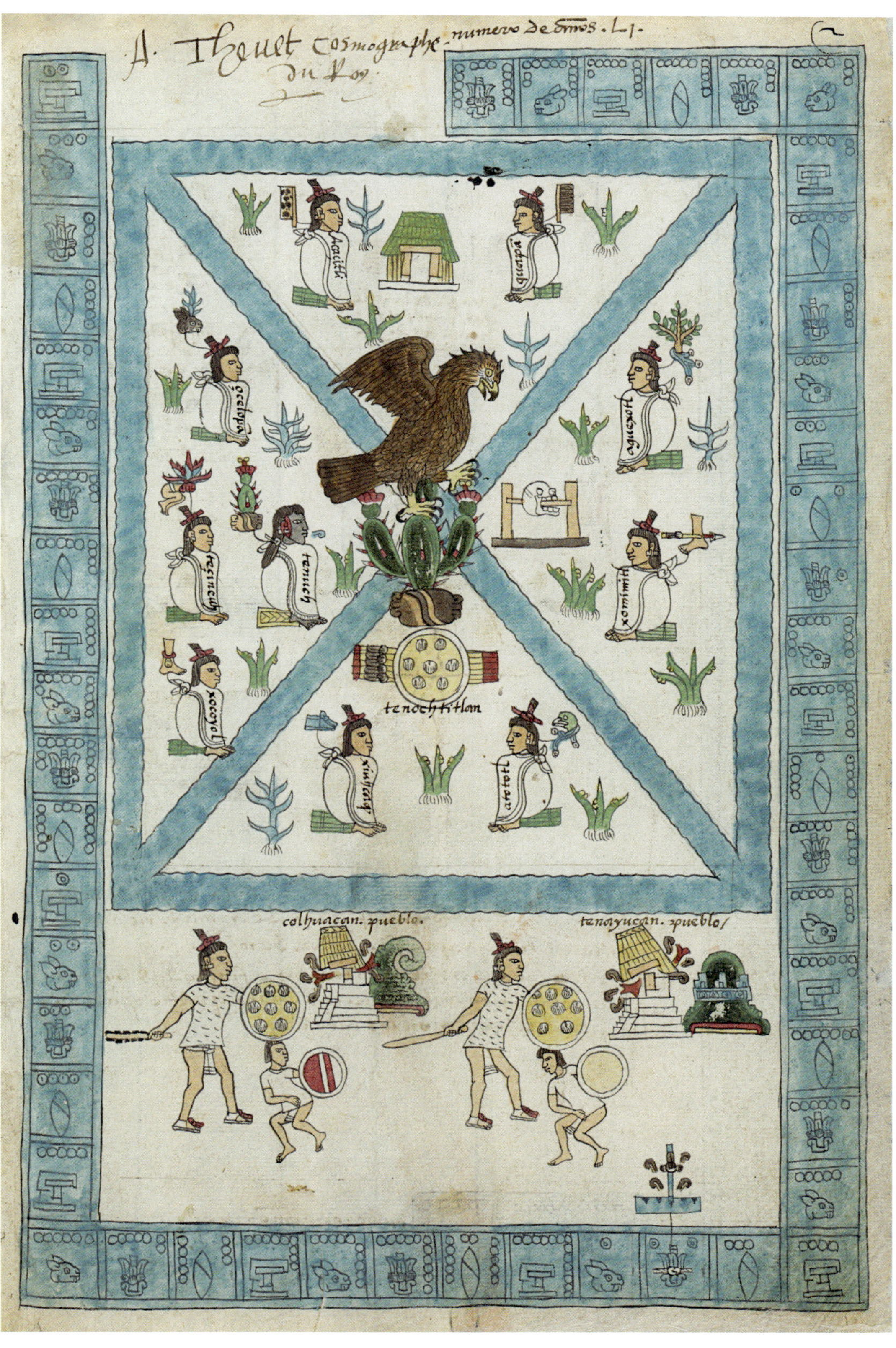

Fig. 3 *The Foundation of Tenochtitlán*, from the Codex Mendoza, Mexico, 1541–42, fol. 2r, Bodleian Libraries, University of Oxford, shelf mark MS. Arch. Selden A. 1

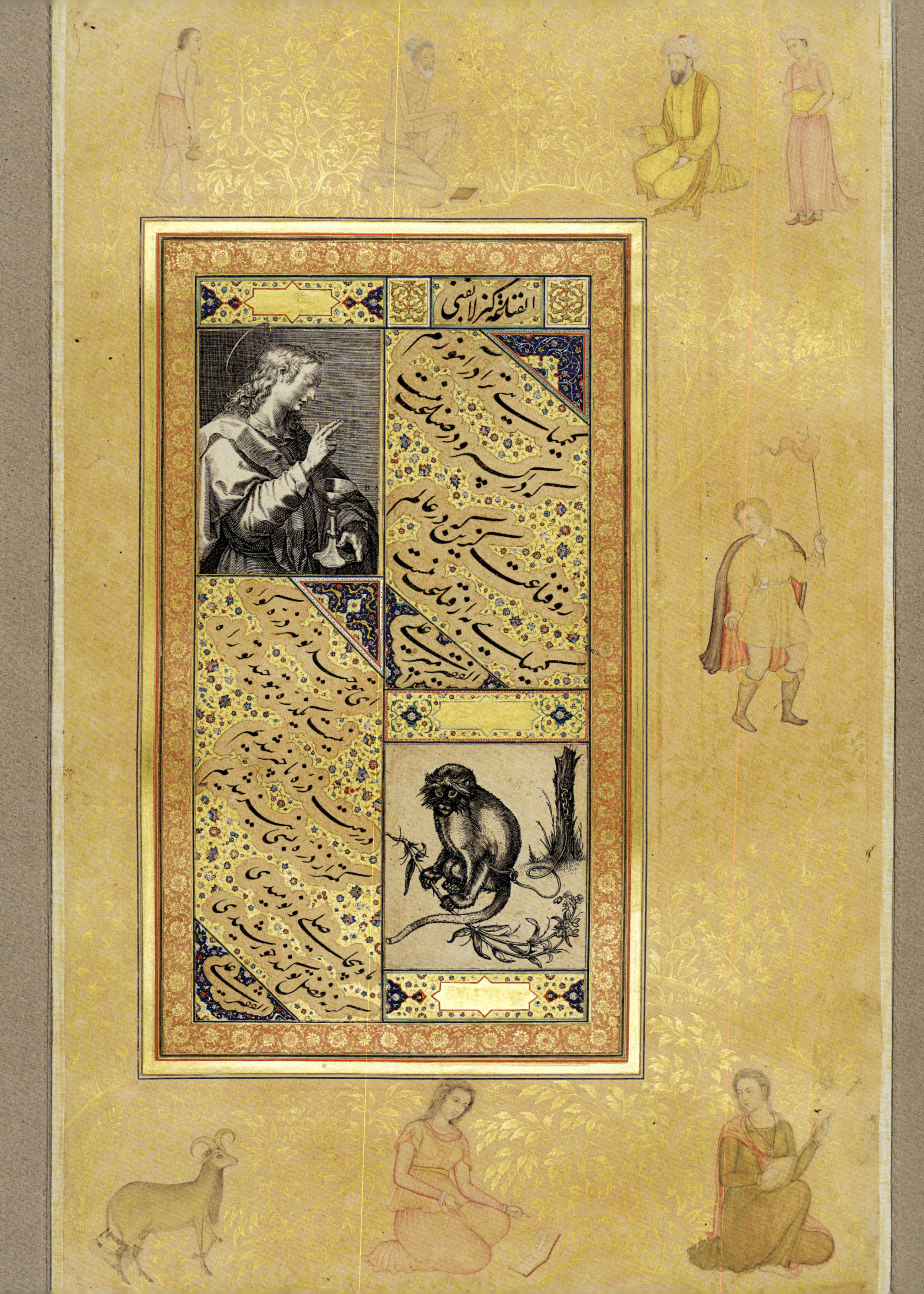
القناعة کنز لا یفنی

Monica Juneja

ALBRECHT DÜRER: THE "MASTER FROM *FIRANG*" IN MUGHAL INDIA

Fig. 1 Leaf with prints by Raphael Sadeler the Elder and after Albrecht Dürer, from the Jahangir Album, India (Agra?), ca. 1608–18, Staatsbibliothek zu Berlin, Preußischer Kulturbesitz, Orientalische Handschriften, Libri picturati A 117, fol. 5r |**cat. no. 122.2**|

Since the early modern period, European printed books, compact and easily reproducible, epitomized an "aesthetic of portability."[1] Likewise, printed images, because of their ability to replicate and thus enhance the mobility of larger works of art, were instrumental in bringing Christian imagery to faraway peoples and places. Though intended by Jesuit missionaries as tools for converting the "heathens" to Christianity, biblical imagery abroad served instead as a source of artistic inspiration. Outside of Europe and the Christian sphere, the engagement with alien motifs and pictorial practices could generate unforeseen experiments in reconfiguration, ultimately giving rise to reflection on the meanings and ways of image-making.

Prints heralded a new mobility of images across geographic and temporal boundaries, as well as between media. The printed image was more than a simple substitute for an already existing work in another, more highly valorized medium, such as painting or sculpture. Rather, it also functioned as an active agent in the new settings to which it traveled. The "knowledge" that the print's narrative content was intended to disseminate may or may not have been assimilated according to the expectations of its makers. Instead, by making visible and knowable the plurality of pictorial practices, printed images served as a locus for material creativity and inventiveness.

While prints from Europe rarely carried the names of the artist-engravers who produced them, those made by Albrecht Dürer, the famed artist of Nuremberg, are an exception. His works, even those copied by other artists and printmakers, all carried his *AD* monogram, which functioned as a kind of trademark. At the courts of the Mughal rulers in sixteenth-century India, Dürer was apparently perceived as an outstanding European artist who could bear comparison to those included in the canon of artists from Persia and India, whose names were compiled in Mughal chronicles. Nowhere, however, do textual sources refer to Dürer by his name. Instead, in accordance with the customary practice of designating artists as masters from specific regions, he has been described as a renowned European artist, a master from *firang* (the Persian term for Europe), whose works exercised a particular magnetism. Dürer's print series and individual engravings seem to have evoked a particular curiosity within the *taswirkhana*, the artists' workshop at the Mughal court, as is evident from several painterly responses to the prints in the form of copies or adaptations.[2]

Yet the engagement with Dürer's work and its Christian content involved more than a simple act of emulation. Invariably, a reinterpretation took place, often effected through a recalibration of individual details, which at first glance might appear too small to matter. When a seventeenth-century Mughal artist created a painted "reproduction" of Dürer's print *Virgin and Child Seated by a Tree* (1513), he provided the viewers of his work with an altered perception of the relationship between the Virgin Mary and the infant Jesus to conform with an Islamic interpretation of this bond. Recalibrations of color, a different treatment of the surrounding vegetation, and an altered facial expression all worked to transform the image of a sorrowing mother into an idyllic scene of maternal love.[3]

Beyond these models of emulation and adaptation, we can uncover a deeper, less immediately visible, engagement with the work of Albrecht Dürer on the part of artists at the Indian courts. This relationship may be described as a mode of transculturation, in which the encounter with a visual practice that is alien, and yet not incommensurable, generates a self-reflection on the nature of visual representation and the position of the artist.[4]

These issues engrossed the Mughal art world into which Dürer's works had entered. While the organizational structures and practices of art-making in the royal workshops give us insight into the position of the patron and the hierarchies within

1 The term draws on Shalem 2016, pp. 250–61.
2 For this approach, see Grebe 2014, pp. 389–402; Saviello 2022.
3 Extensively discussed in Saviello 2022, pp. 46–54.
4 For an elaboration of transculturation as a theoretical paradigm for art history, see Juneja 2023.

the artists' workshop, the voice of the artist can be heard through only a handful of self-reflexive representations built into the image. Such a mode of theorizing one's own position and praxis emerged through a transcultural dialogue with the work of an esteemed artist from *firang*.

The widely held vision of the painterly profession in early modern South Asia, as transmitted by earlier histories, characterizes the painter as a nameless craftsperson confined within the twin prisons of patronage and caste. Although today we indeed know more about the employment and status of court artists, and have even recovered many of their names, found in inscriptions and marginal notes within manuscript folios, many questions still remain open. What kind of individual presence can we plausibly invest the work with, when we study a particular artist's production? Art-making took place within a workshop organized hierarchically according to the functions performed by different members. These functions included preparing the paper, drawing the outlines, creating a composition, applying colors, drawing faces, designing the margins, and so on. A painted folio was the product of several hands. The division of labor among the artists was recorded in the margins or on the reverse of the page by the librarian or another official of the workshop. During the seventeenth century, even as image-making continued to be a collective enterprise, the practice of recording the various contributors declined in favor of citing a single artist, whose name was frequently inscribed by no less than the emperor's hand.[5]

The evolution of the system to privilege a notion of the master artist suggests an enhanced valorization of connoisseurship within an imperial structure of artistic production. The connoisseur's eye could claim the special power to discern talent and endow its bearers with high-sounding titles such as "Wonder of the Age" or "Golden Pen."[6] Imperial etiquette prescribed that an artist's self-description be cast in self-abnegation and humility in the face of his powerful patron: the same artist whom the emperor designated as "Wonder of the Age" would, in his inscriptions, describe himself as "slave," "servant of the exalted house," or "dust of the patron's feet." Pictorial self-representations, on the other hand, frequently seek to bypass this rhetoric of subservience and to confer a quiet dignity on the unique skills with which the artist—and he alone—could transform earthly materials (pigment, ink, paper) into transcendent aesthetic value. Such representations invariably allude to image-making by including depictions of materials and tools of work in the picture, as well as their product, a painting or a bound manuscript, all integrated caringly across the picture plane.

Dürer's work emerged in this context as a repository of both symbols and practices that could be productively harnessed to make a pictorial argument about the "artist's art."[7] The following example will give us an insight into how an artist reflected on his skills and chose to represent them, together with his individual persona, perhaps as an indexical trace in the work's matrix. A detailed examination will enable us to unravel the more reflective and less direct mimetic interaction with Dürer's art in Mughal India.

The work in question, *A Sufi Sage*, is by the artist Farrukh Beg (1540 – after 1615), done in 1615, when he was seventy years old |**fig. 2**|. Though it ostensibly offers a portrait of an old Sufi, the work is at the same time replete with references to the artist's persona, his biography, and, not least, his skill in making images. It might therefore be described as a convergence between a portrait and a self-portrait, wherein the person of the artist fuses with that of a Sufi, whose figure in turn was drawn from a representation of a Christian saint. Indeed, this image grew out of multiple intersections and interweavings of traditions and practices, making it a site of intense transcultural negotiations. The initial impulse for the painting came from two sources: Dürer's *Saint Jerome in His Study*, repre-

5 These issues are discussed in detail in Juneja 2023, pp. 107–13.
6 Thackston 1999, pp. 268–69.
7 Juneja 2023, p. 107.

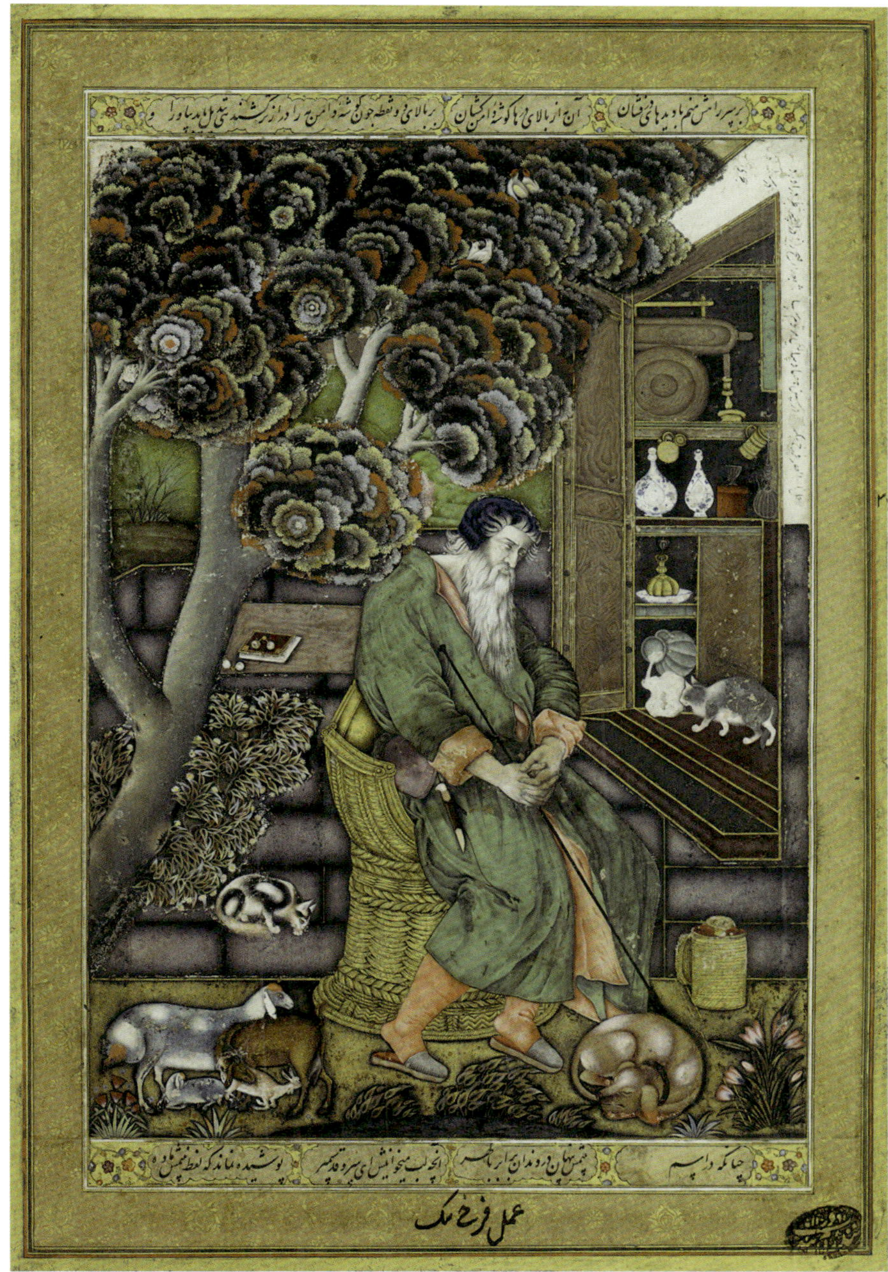

Fig. 2 Farrukh Beg, *A Sufi Sage* (single leaf), Agra, ca. 1615, The Museum of Islamic Art, Doha, shelf mark MS.44.2007

senting the contemplative life of a Christian saint |**fig. 3**|, and a composition by the Flemish artist Marten de Vos (1532–1603) entitled *Dolor (Sorrow)*, which was conceived as a homage to Dürer. Farrukh Beg's familiarity with de Vos was mediated through an engraving by Raphael Sadeler (1560–61 - 1628–32) that had made its way to the Mughal atelier from Antwerp |**fig. 4**|.

Farrukh Beg spent his early career in Shiraz, Khurasan, and then Kabul. In 1580, he was employed by the Mughal emperor Akbar as a member of the imperial workshop of painters. The arrival of European works of art at the Mughal court meant that the Persianized idiom practiced by Farrukh Beg declined in importance, leading him to migrate further south in search of new patrons. He spent many years at the court of the Sultan of Bijapur in southern India, and returned in 1609 to the Mughal capital of Agra, on the invitation of Akbar's successor Jahangir.[8] The painting *A Sufi Sage*, possibly Farrukh Beg's last work, presents the sole instance in which the artist made a more or less direct copy of a European work. Yet he did so in a manner that engaged with several sources, resulting in a complex example of transcultural negotiation that grafted visual biographical references onto a selection of materials. References to his praxis as an artist, distributed across the composition, include a miniature album of paintings with a red and gold lacquer binding and a pair of spectacles, an object often deployed by calligraphers and painters as a mark of their profession.

The motif of the cat approaching a puddle of spilt milk, taken from the Sadeler engraving, has been reconfigured in this image as a reference to the artist's activity: it alludes to one of the important tools of Mughal image-making, the fine paintbrushes made of cat hair, sometimes only a single one. Referencing the material aspects of art production functioned as a recognizable trope within the self-representation of artists and calligraphers. It referred to the power wielded by the artist alone, his skilled use of material substances to create immaterial aesthetic value. Contemporary texts often draw a parallel between this creative process and the way the Sufi used bodily experience to reach God.[9] The animals in the painting are partly taken from de Vos and Dürer—for example, the sleeping dog, an animal associated with both erudition and melancholy. On the other hand, the motif of the goat suckling its young, an addition by Farrukh Beg, recurs in many variants in Mughal painting as a means of drawing attention to the cycles of life and changing generations—a reference again to this artist's own advanced stage in life.

8 Farrukh Beg's biography has been studied by Skelton 1957, pp. 393–411; more recently by Seyller 1995, pp. 319–41.

9 Abu'l Fazl and Blochmann 2001, vol. 1, p. 115.

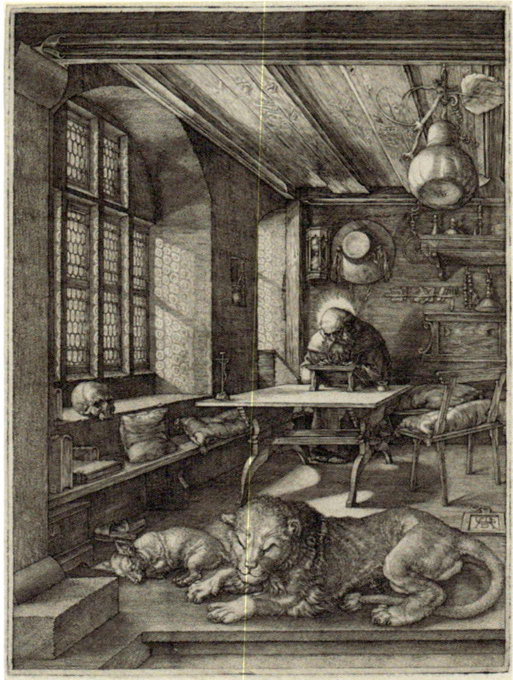

Fig. 3 Albrecht Dürer, *Saint Jerome in His Study*, Nuremberg, 1514, GNM, inv. no. MS1527, on long-term loan from the Paul Wolfgang Merkel'sche Familienstiftung

Beyond appropriating and relocating symbols and motifs, the image discussed here is the product of a dialogical encounter between Farrukh Beg and the works of Dürer and de Vos. Dürer's extraordinary artistic achievement lay in the way he used the engraver's burin and the graphic medium to recreate material textures: of wooden planks, of wall surfaces, of animal fur, and of greenery, as in the Saint Jerome engraving. Farrukh Beg's response, akin to a literary-cum-musical mode of improvisation in Indo-Persian tradition, is to translate into paint and color Dürer's particular mode of rendering texture. He accomplishes this using a single-hair brush and paint, as in his treatment of the animals' coats. Each hair of the dog, for example, is highlighted by a deft golden stroke. Further instances of the selective use of new representational practices can be observed in the brushwork of the wicker chair, in the graining of the wood panels of the desk and cabinet, and not least in the subtle and mottled painterliness of the stones, tree trunk, and foliage.

The billowing sleeves, the cuffs, and the swelling folds of the sage's/painter's robe create further connections with Dürer's practice, as for example in the engraving *Melencolia I*. We might speculate as to whether the idea of an artist as creator, a figure of loneliness and saturnine melancholy, has managed to seep in through the layers of this portrait, causing the artist and the Sufi sage / Christian saint to merge into each other. The pictorial organization of the painting, however, registers a refusal of the Albertian perspective that Dürer strictly adhered to in his work. Farrukh Beg's composite portrait gestures for a moment in the direction of the principle separating inner and outer space that marks the Saint Jerome images in their several variants, including the one by de Vos that provided the initial impulse for the present work.

Here, however, a separation is barely suggested by the extension of the wall from one end of the composition to the other, only then to be discarded in favor of a wondrous and highly ambiguous space traversed by a fantastical tree. The tree, seemingly infinitely expanding and populated by colorful birds, enters into the lonely space of the artist/Sufi and imposes a different sense of spatial order. The placement of the tree follows a frequent compositional convention in Persian painting—that of the overarching plane tree standing for the tree of life. The tree here is evocative of Farrukh Beg's roots in Shiraz and Khurasan, where he started his life as a court artist and managed, unlike most of his counterparts, to retain a loyalty to Persianate idioms throughout his peripatetic existence. Yet unlike any other tree painted by a Persian, Mughal, or European artist of the time, this one is a product of a unique fantasy. Its bright red, orange, yellow, and green foliage, burgeoning into cabbage-like shapes, rejects any concern for botanical observation or anthropocentric exactitude, features that had become standard in the depiction of plant and animal life, especially under the patronage of the emperor Jahangir.

This unusual work, which in many ways is a condensation of a lifetime's experience, is also a statement about the artist's positioning in a field regulated by the predilections of changing patrons. To a certain extent, it represents the artist's struggle to retain a sense of his own constancy. Interestingly, he is able to make this statement in a work that goes beyond its sources, negotiating

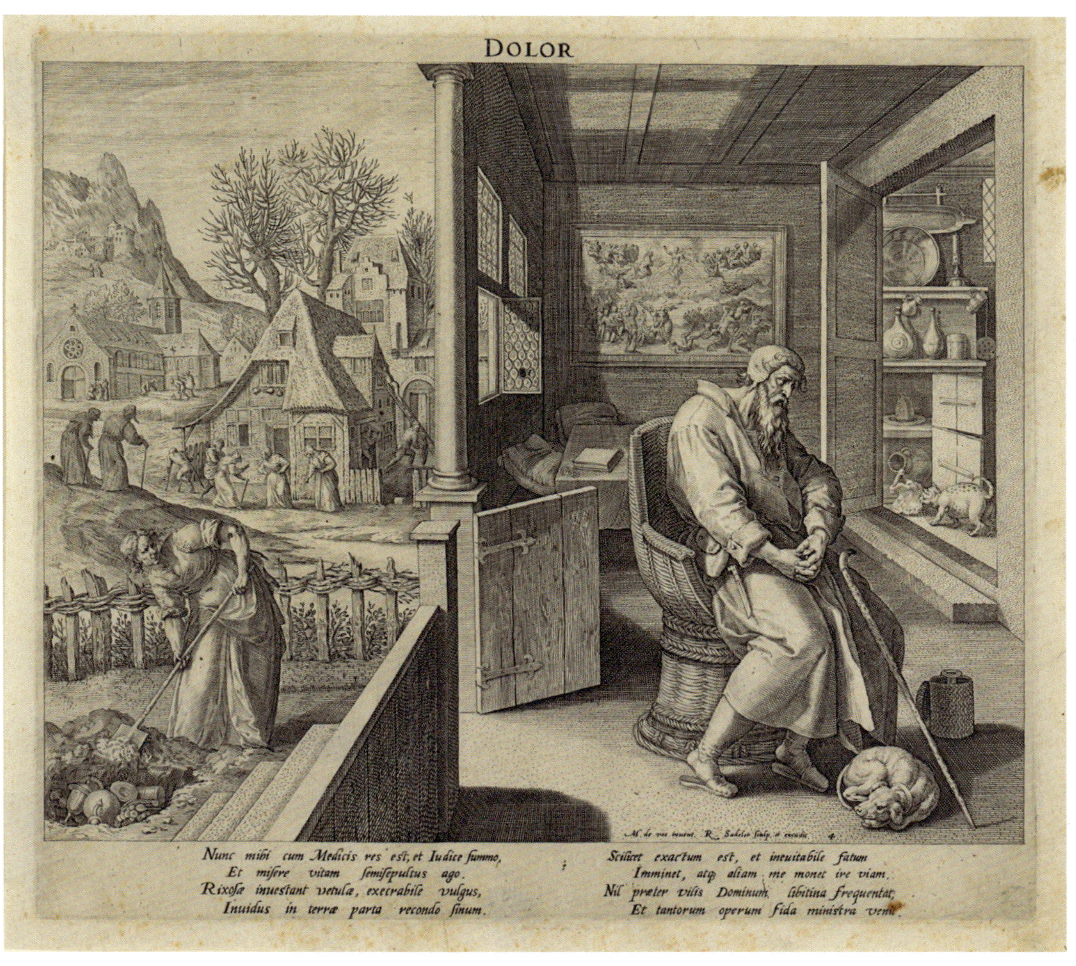

Fig. 4 Raphael Sadeler the Elder after Marten de Vos, Dolor (Sorrow), Munich, 1591, GNM, inv. no. K 1508

with different modes of image-making and their signifying processes, and using a combination of the mimetic and the dialogical to generate a surplus of meaning.

The engagement with Dürer's work that unfolded in the artists' workshops of the northern Indian courts during the early modern period complicates what we understand by emulation, imitation, or appropriation. The transcultural encounter involves a mediation between different worlds, visual modes, and symbolic systems, bringing forth a fresh discourse. In that sense, we might posit not only that mimetic desire is drawn to the power of that which it imitates or appropriates, but also that it enters into a relationship that induces reflection on the instability of canons and knowledge. In doing so, such encounters make the image into a charged object.

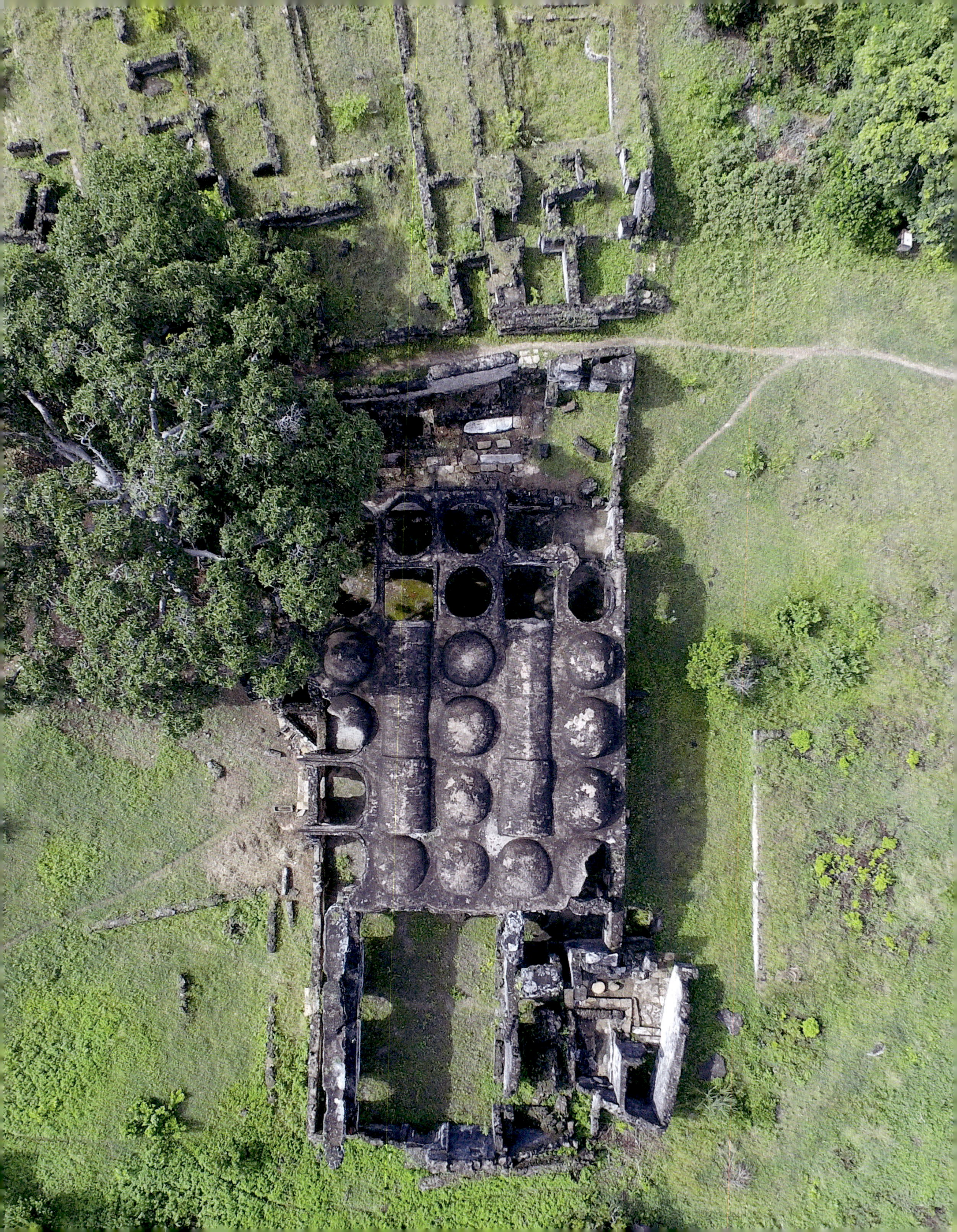

Elgidius E. B. Ichumbaki and Dominicus Z. Makukula

GLOBALISM ON THE COAST OF EAST AFRICA AND THE CONSEQUENCES OF "SPRINGER'S *MEERFAHRT*"

For nearly two millennia, the coastal area of East Africa popularly known as the Swahili coast has interacted with other parts of the maritime world of the Indian Ocean and places beyond. This essay will first introduce the development of culture and society in this part of coastal East Africa over the several centuries leading up to the period around 1500. Using the port city of Kilwa Kisiwani as a case study, it will then discuss how Portuguese and a number of German ships destined for India, attacked several eastern African trading centers, thus ending the civilization that had been established in the area.[1]

The imperialistic Portuguese and German companies in question collaborated to carry out conquest and to plunder resources that had made the trading centers on the East African coast recognized worldwide. The expedition—sometimes referred to as "Springer's *Meerfahrt*" (Springer's Sea Voyage), after the travelogue written by the participant Balthasar Springer |**cat. no. 116**|—involved twenty-two ocean vessels with over 1,500 soldiers navigating the Swahili coast in the years 1505 and 1506. These conquerors pillaged wealth that had been accumulated over a period of more than five hundred years. Nuremberg trading companies such as those of the Welser, Imhoff, and Hirschvogel families took part in this, and other voyages of plunder done under the auspices of the Portuguese crown.

The Swahili Coast of Eastern Africa

The term "Swahili coast" applies to the coastal areas of the present-day countries of Somalia, Kenya, Tanzania, and Mozambique. It also includes the island country of Comoros and the northern part of Madagascar. Additional islands such as Unguja (Zanzibar) and Mafia also belong to this region. As stone tools from the Middle Stone Age found in the Kilwa Basin vicinity indicate, human settlement on the coast of East Africa dates back over 40,000 years.[2] The area—especially the approximately 3,000 kilometers of coastline stretching from Mogadishu in Somalia to Imbane in Mozambique—developed trade with other parts of the Indian Ocean. Ancient writings such as those of Periplus and Ptolemy[3] inform us that the Swahili coast was a part of the world economy well before the AD era. The exchange of traded goods such as cassia, cinnamon, and metal objects among the Swahili people and southwest Asians is a testimony of what has been referred to as "Swahili globalism."[4]

The East African coastal region was active in international trade during the fifth century BC or even earlier.[5] The voyage of Pharaoh Necho and his group from Egypt into the Red Sea, the Indian and Atlantic Oceans, and the Mediterranean Sea sometime between 610 and 594 BC provides evidence for such trade.[6] Trade along the Swahili coast expanded tremendously toward the end of the first and beginning of the second millennium AD. It involved the export of minerals, skins and horns of animals, and forest resources such as mangrove poles. Imports to the Swahili coast included spices, silk, beads, ceramics, and glass.

The seasonal monsoon winds facilitated trade, enabling easy navigation. Various localities emerged as commercial centers characterized by monumental buildings constructed of coral blocks bonded with lime mortar. While some of the trade centers, such as Kilwa Kisiwani in present-day Tanzania and Manda in present-day Kenya, comprised areas as large as fifteen hectares, a few towns, such as Kaole in Tanzania, were smaller than a hectare in size.[7] The centers were scattered across eastern Africa's coastline and were connected by both large and small ports.[8] Although a few places developed their own harbors, others depended on nearby ports for the import and export of goods.

In terms of populations, the centers attracted many people, ranging from 5,000 to 20,000 inhabi-

Fig. 1 The Great Mosque, Kilwa Kisiwani, twelfth to thirteenth century

This chapter was made possible (in part) by the Preparing Outstanding Social Science Investigators to Benefit Lives and Environments in Africa initiative (POSSIBLE Africa) [POS-2024-01], an initiative of the Science for Africa Foundation (SFA Foundation) enabled by the support of Carnegie Corporation of New York. The statements made and the views expressed are solely our responsibility and not necessarily those of the SFA Foundation and her partners.

1 Kusimba 1999.
2 Beyin et al. 2025.
3 Casson 1989.
4 Kusimba 2024.
5 Lacroix 1998.
6 Cary and Warmington 1963; Lacroix 1998.
7 Kusimba 2024, p. 21.
8 Pollard and Ichumbaki 2017.

tants. These included residents, traders, artisans, workers, gardeners, administrators, religious leaders, and visitors. Recent studies on the Swahili peoples' ancient ancestries have noted that many East African women married men of either Asian or Persian origin.[9] This intermarriage fostered peaceful trading activities and the development of prosperous trading centers. Because most people residing in and visiting these coastal centers were Muslims, many mosques were constructed.[10] The Islamic religion and the common language, Kiswahili, strengthened trade and social relations among residents and visitors in much of the area. Consequently, a distinctive culture developed, commonly referred to as "Swahili civilization," characterized by such things as monumental architecture, maritime trade, Islamic religion, and the minting of coins.[11]

Beginning in the eleventh century, several towns developed their trading activities in a more organized and formalized manner. Trading centers expanded in size, building types, leadership structure, commitment to the Islamic religion, and many other aspects. Several centers on the coast emerged as key players in international trade, including Kilwa in present-day Tanzania, Manda and Shanga in present-day Kenya, Mogadishu in present-day Somalia, and Sofala in present-day Mozambique.[12] Traders and commercial ships regularly moved between these and many other centers in East Africa, and they frequently set sail for "the Shiraz"—that is, the region of the Persian Gulf and southern Arabia. For example, in 1232, as described by Ibn al-Mujawir (d. 1292), Kilwa Kisiwani emerged as a staging point on the route from the city of Aden in Yemen to al-Qumr (the Arabic term for Madagascar). Generally, between 1000 and 1500, the region of East Africa conducted international trade marked by a high level of globalism.

Some visitors to the great trading centers—for example, Ibn Battuta, who was in Kilwa in 1331, and Zheng He, who visited Kilwa and other centers along the Swahili coast between 1405 and 1433—documented these places as being beautiful and elegantly built. Because of the vast number of centers, it is impossible to deal with all of them in this essay. We will therefore focus on Kilwa Kisiwani, off the southern coast of Tanzania, which is now part of the UNESCO World Heritage Site "Ruins of Kilwa Kisiwani and Ruins of Songo Mnara."[13]

Kilwa Kisiwani and Its Surroundings

Kilwa Kisiwani, or Kilwa for short, had a well-organized leadership of sultans who controlled trade in the region. Records such as those left by the historian and geographer al-Masudi indicate that, during the tenth century, Kilwa controlled the trade in blue-green glazed ceramics, also known as celadon, imported from China. The discovery of Indo-Chinese stone anchors along the Kenyan and Tanzanian coasts, dating between the eleventh and fourteenth centuries, confirms the existence of long-distance international trade in the region.[14] This commerce is also corroborated by such material-culture objects as spherical storage vessels dating between the twelfth and fifteenth centuries and Islamic monochrome ceramics from between the ninth and fifteenth centuries.[15] At the time, Kilwa minted copper and gold coins, a big step in trading activities during the time. The town's sultans used this coinage to buy beads, porcelain, and spices.

As a major Swahili trading city, Kilwa derived its prosperity from the control of Indian Ocean trade, especially from the eleventh to the sixteenth century. Kilwa traded with the Arabic world, India, and China, surpassing the rival eastern African coastal towns of Sofala, Mombasa, and Mogadishu.[16] Kilwa's prosperity reached its zenith in the fifteenth century, after the city gained control not only of the lucrative trade in gold but also of the exchange of exotic goods such as aromatic gums, spices, tortoise shells, coconut oil, ivory, mangrove poles, ebony

9 Brielle et al. 2023.
10 Steyn 2023.
11 Ichumbaki and Pollard 2021.
12 Horton and Middleton 2000.
13 Ichumbaki and Munisi 2024.
14 Pollard et al. 2016.
15 Chittick 1974.
16 Chittick 1968, pp. 105–6; Mathew 1963, p. 95.
17 Chittick 1974.
18 See, for example, Fleisher 2004; Wynne-Jones 2016, pp. 55–88; Ichumbaki and Pollard 2021; Ichumbaki and Munisi 2024.
19 Ichumbaki and Pollard 2021.
20 Maugham 1906.
21 Maugham 1906.
22 Liesegang 1972; Roque 2017.
23 Horst 2009; Pohle 2000.
24 Kunstmann 1861; Staub 2021.
25 Singer and Jopp 1967.

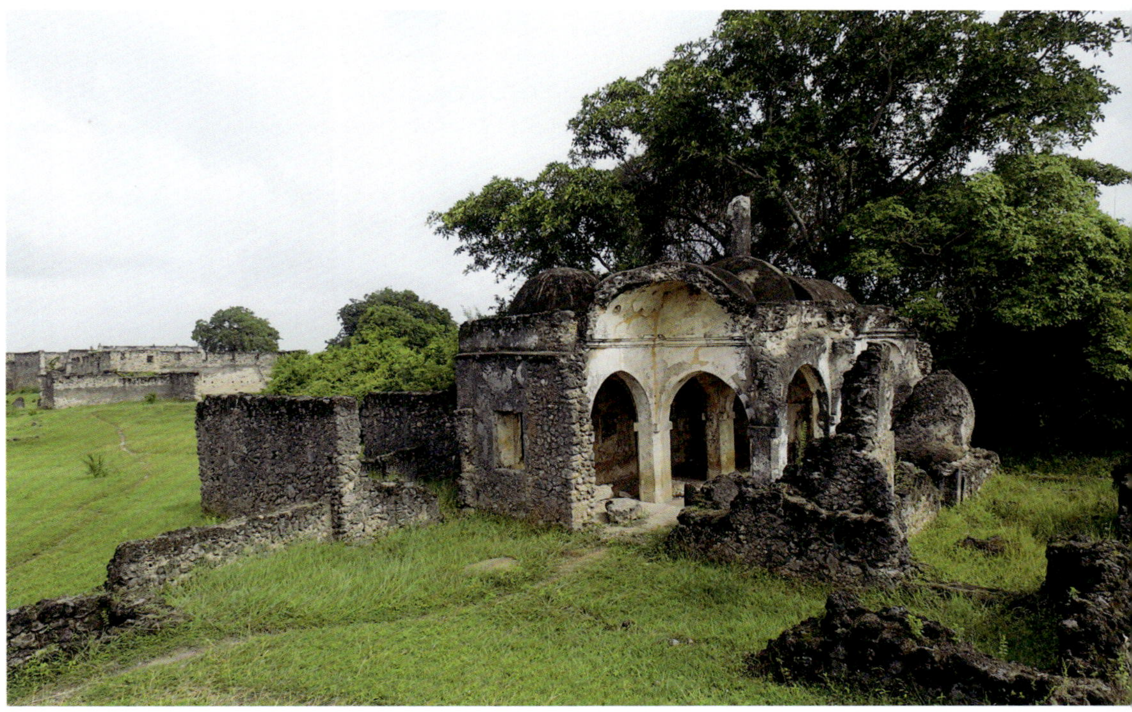

Fig. 2 The Small Mosque, Kilwa Kisiwani, mid-fifteenth century

timbers, animal skins, and minerals. The primary trade goods, including gold and ivory from the mainland in present-day Zimbabwe, were exchanged for silver, carnelians, perfumes, Persian faience, and Chinese porcelain. As time passed, Kilwa stopped relying solely on the exchange of goods for other goods and introduced its own minted currency, which circulated widely in the region between the eleventh and fourteenth centuries.

Owing to its international trade, Kilwa developed an elaborate built infrastructure, as can be observed in substantial surviving monuments such as the Husuni Kubwa and Husuni Ndogo palaces and the Great and Small Mosques |**figs. 1, 2**|. These majestic buildings were constructed of coral blocks and lime mortar and roofed with domes and vaults. Many buildings of the time were decorated with embedded Chinese porcelain, as is found, for example, at the Husuni Kubwa palace, built about 1310–33, a spacious structure with several rooms and a large octagonal bathing pool.[17] The entire city was constructed using coral stones bonded with lime mortar. Whereas the doors were framed with hardwood timbers, the roof structure was framed with coral blocks, supported by wooden joists and mangrove poles. Kilwa had well-positioned settlements, narrow paved streets, and open spaces.[18] Indeed, based on what is visible and known today, there is no doubt that between the eleventh and fifteenth centuries Kilwa was a major center of international trade on the coast of East Africa.[19] It must have served as an important hub of Swahili coastal culture, of the Islamization of East Africa, and of the prosperous Indian Ocean trade.

Unfortunately, in the early sixteenth century, a Portuguese marine convoy, which included German participants, conquered Kilwa and plundered all its wealth, leading to its decline. Today, many of the city's old buildings are in a ruinous state, but a few have been renovated and now serve as tourist

26 Elkiss 1973, p. 126.
27 Elkiss 1973.
28 Strandes 1989.
29 Pollard 2016.
30 English translation cited after Jeff Bowersox, "Balthasar Springer Pillages

destinations. Whether operational or abandoned, these monuments are testimonies to the growth and development of Swahili culture, which was dealt a severe blow by the early-sixteenth-century invasions. How did this happen, and what consequences did it bring? The next section answers these questions.

Portuguese Invasion of the East African Coast

Vasco da Gama's voyage in 1497–98 from Lisbon, Portugal, to India by way of the southern tip of Africa was certainly the first Portuguese expedition into East Africa. Multiple narratives have been published about its aftermath, both with regard to southern Africa, including the Cape of Good Hope and the town of Sofala, and with respect to the coastal mercantile centers of eastern Africa, such as Kilwa, Mombasa, Malindi, and Mogadishu.[20] Despite Vasco da Gama's purported economic interests, the purpose of his expedition must be scrutinized more closely, as all subsequent Portuguese expeditions had both imperialist and financial motives. Ever since 1498, invasion became the sole method of Portuguese imperialism along East African trade routes and into the political systems of most trading centers there, including Kilwa, Zanzibar, Mombasa, Lamu, and Pate.[21]

This scenario is demonstrated by the coerced tribute paid by the ruling sheikhs and sultans to Portuguese authorities, who operated from fortresses that had been seized from the Arabs and rebuilt to accommodate Portuguese merchants and administrators. The forts that were turned into Portuguese command posts include the Gereza or Fort Santiago in Kilwa (rehabilitated and renamed by the Portuguese after the invasion in July 1505), the Saint Cajetan Fortress in Sofala (1505–6), and Fort Jesus in Mombasa (1593–96), to name a few notable examples.[22] Despite the voluminous publications about Vasco da Gama's expedition in East Africa, only a scant amount of literature, if any, informs on the artifacts, cultural objects, and valuable raw materials that were presumably plundered during the expedition. The present article initiates the agenda and calls for the necessity of further research on the topic.

Continuing his predecessors' ambitions, in 1505 King Manuel I of Portugal organized another expedition to reach India via southern and eastern Africa, in addition to Vasco da Gama's explorations |**fig. 3**|. The King appointed the soldier and explorer Francisco de Almeida as the first governor and viceroy of the state of Portuguese India. Tristão da Cunha was the commander of Almeida's fleet of twenty-two ships that sailed in the expedition to Africa and India. The enterprise received financial support from a consortium of southern German merchants led by the Welser trading company, a few individual entrepreneurs from Augsburg and Nuremberg, and some Genoese and Florentine merchants, including support for shipbuilding. Three of the ships that sailed on Almeida's voyage—the *Hieronymus*, the *Raffael*, and the *Lionarda*—were German merchants' ships built for a sum of 65,000 cruzados.[23]

Although previous economic relationships had existed between the German lands and Portugal, this was the first time that Germans had directly participated in Portuguese mercantile ventures to the East.[24] Unlike their trading partners in Portugal and Spain, the Germans lacked direct access to the Mediterranean Sea. The Welser and Fugger trading companies, based in southern Germany, were represented by Balthasar Springer and Hans Mayr. Springer and Mayr were pioneering German "merchants" interested in trading and accumulating wealth from the "newly discovered" regions of Africa and Asia as a means of expanding their trading networks beyond the borders of Europe.[25] According to Springer's *Meerfahrt*, the travelogue he published in 1509 |**cat. no. 116**|, he and Mayr

East African Cities (1509)," on the website "Black Central Europe," accessed September 10, 2025, https://blackcentraleurope.com/sources/1500-1750/balthasar-springer-pillages-east-african-cities-1509/,

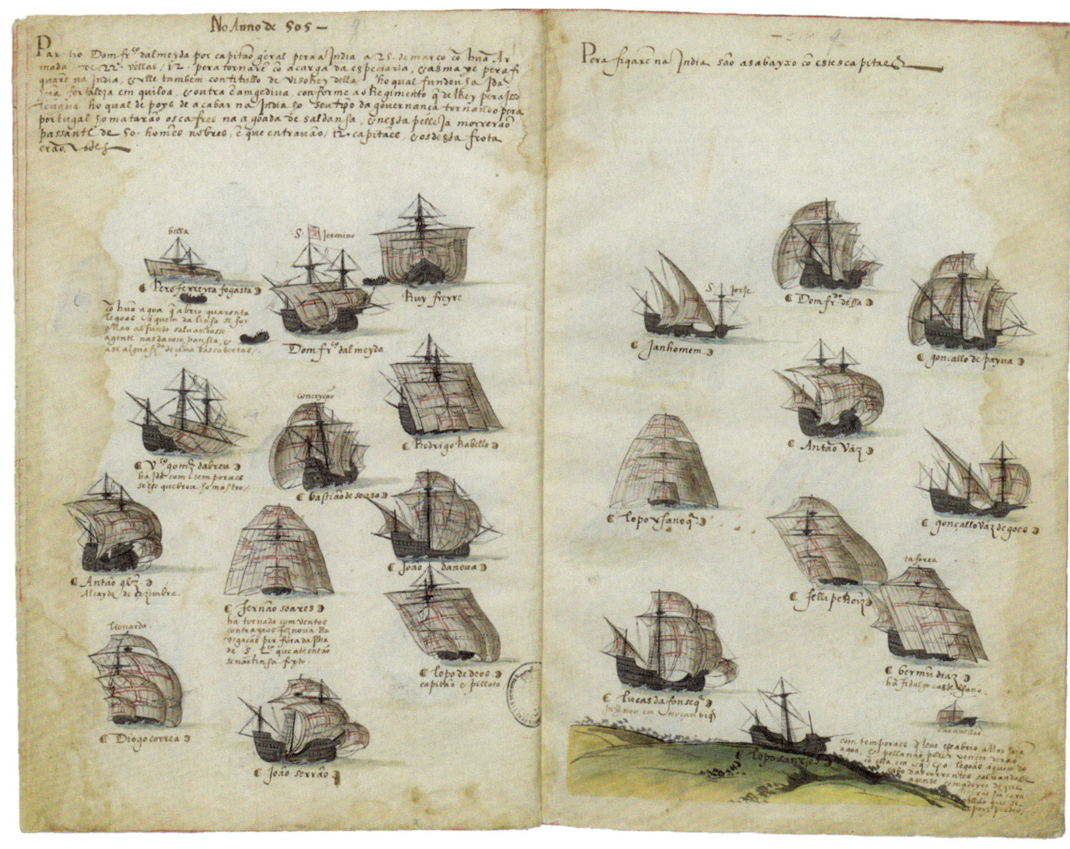

Fig. 3 The fleet of Francisco de Almeida in the years 1505–6, from the *Livro das Armadas*, ca. 1568, Academia das Ciências de Lisboa, Lisbon, shelf mark Azul 588, pp. 8–9

participated in several pillaging sprees in East African ports while traveling in Francesco de Almeida's fleet in 1505 and 1506.

The Invasion and Plundering of Kilwa Kisiwani

By the late fifteenth century, stories of Kilwa Kisiwani's luxurious lifestyle, trade successes, and magnificent infrastructure had spread throughout the world.[26] The city's affluence gave rise to ever-increasing trade ties as well as rivalry with neighboring eastern African sultanates, such as Mombasa and Mogadishu.[27] This prosperity also attracted hordes of avaricious traders interested in plunder. In July 1505, a fleet of Portuguese warriors accompanied by German "traders" invaded Kilwa Kisiwani, killing several counter-attacking natives and pillaging the city's treasures.[28] The Portuguese and German invaders seized hundreds of coffers containing Kilwa coins, gold bars, gemstones, and royal wooden and ceramic artifacts. They also took possession of utilitarian objects such as domestic utensils and furniture, ivory tusks, mangrove poles, and valuable timbers.[29] An account of the incident appears in Springer's *Meerfahrt* travelogue as follows:

"On the 14th of August in the afternoon we came to the city. There they fired with bows and rifles and threw rocks at us and seriously wounded quite a few of our crew. But it was all in vain. We

which is based on the modern edition by Erhard and Ramminger 1998, pp. 40–45.

31 Fleisher et al. 2012.

shot fire into the city in two places and burned many of them out of their houses. Before we did this, they defiantly drove—in order to frighten us—twelve elephants all around at us. We also found three camels in the city and in front of it on the field. The strongly secured city with narrow alleys was almost not to be taken. But, calling for the help of God the Almighty, we formed two units and attacked our enemies in the city with great courage and on the fifteenth of August braved the storm. As we passed through the narrow streets and alleys of the city, no one wanted to give any ground to the other. But without delay we forced our way through with force.

The moors and heathens threw themselves against us so inhumanly that we could have thought that it would be impossible to get into the city if it had not been the clear will of God. But through God's providence and determination there was left many a heathen dead, of our own only two met their end. We conquered and occupied the city with great joy and thanked God the Almighty. When we had secured the city and gotten ready to plunder, we noticed that the king had gotten himself out of the city and there strengthened his force with several moors and heathens. We had to take care in order not to get immediately thrown back out of the city again. We ordered that the streets had to be patrolled so that we could not be ambushed unawares and began to plunder. We found the previously mentioned great treasures, so much that it is impossible to count it all up. God be praised forever and to Him be glory and honor, amen."[30]

The destruction and plundering mentioned above is clearly confirmed by historical and archaeological evidence. For example, both archaeological excavations and geophysical surveys carried out across large parts of Kilwa Kisiwani have recorded the presence of several buried foundations.[31] Indeed, the absence of elaborate buildings and streets, features mentioned in the historical documents, is an indication that the Portuguese and Germans plundered the city's wealth and ensured its complete destruction. Several excavations have brought to light nearly complete ceramics, strings of beads, and a number of coins that are suggestive not of planned disposal but of urgent departure because of the invasion. Also, the complete collapse of the city and the establishment of new settlements on nearby islands are further evidence of the invasion.

A close examination of Balthasar Springer's report reveals that the India-bound merchant fleet of Admiral Francisco de Almeida was also a plundering expedition. It had been meticulously planned several years before, based on reports about the riches of Kilwa Kisiwani brought back from earlier Portuguese voyages, including Vasco da Gama's visits of 1498 and 1502. Springer's travelogue does not mention any consignment brought by Mayr and Springer, as representatives of southern German trading companies, for commercial purposes while in East Africa, but other sources corroborate the plundering of great wealth. It seems clear that the plunder of Swahili treasures was among the prospects motivating Springer's group to leave Germany and join the Portuguese expedition.

Furthermore, there are clear indications that Francisco de Almeida's objectives included taking over Swahili merchants' trade, strengthening Portuguese control over shipping routes in the Indian Ocean, and turning Kilwa into a Portuguese gateway to and from the East African mainland |**fig. 4**|. Based on Springer's testimony, the profit they gained from Kilwa alone amounted to more than double their total investments.[32] Within less than two years, Portuguese and German invaders destroyed the commercial connections that had been established over centuries along the eastern African coast. Unfortunately, even post-invasion initiatives could not fully revive the commerce that had led to the trading centers' growth and expansion. Consequently, much of the city of

32 Erhard and Ramminger 1998, pp. 40–45.

Fig. 4 Kilwa Kisiwani, Festung, 16. Jahrhundert, Aufnahme 2018

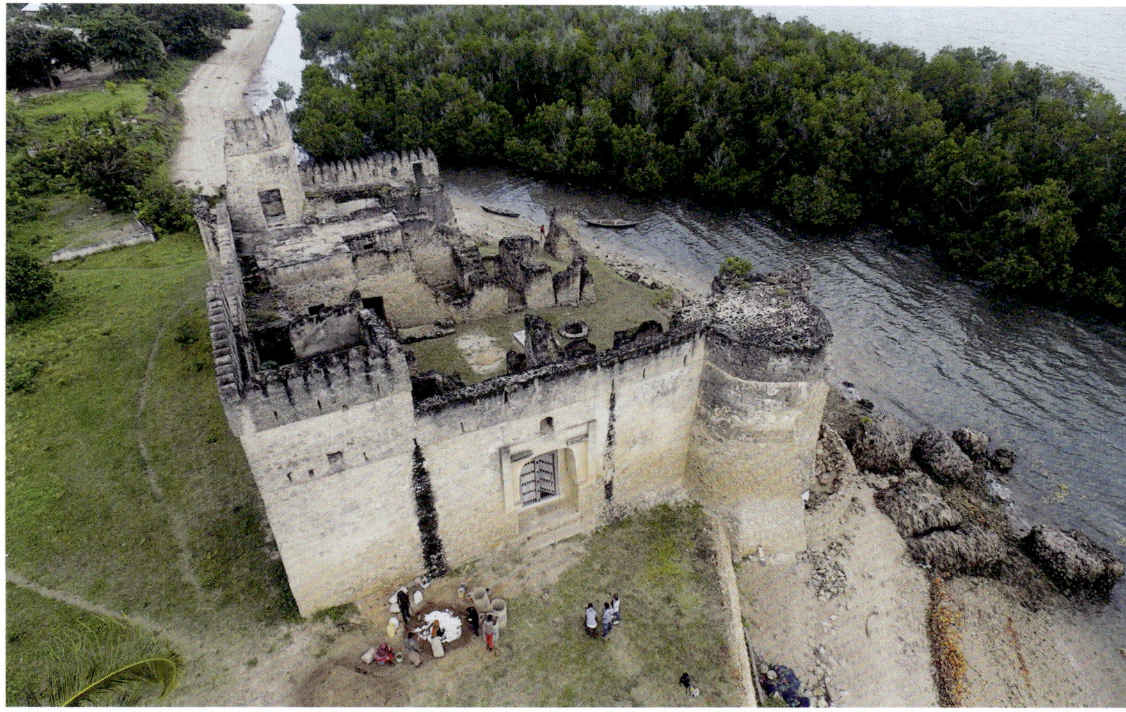

Kilwa collapsed completely and never regained its former prosperity.

In conclusion, we are of the view that although the harms inflicted during the existence of the colony of German East Africa (1885–1918) have entered public awareness, it is essential that the looting, killings, and other atrocities that the Portuguese and German invaders committed during the sixteenth century also be more widely recognized—and remain in memory for generations to come. As the present and future generations of Portugal and Germany, as well as others responsible for wrongdoings in the region, continue to enjoy their high levels of development, they must become aware of the looting and destruction their forefathers committed during the early sixteenth century. It is also impossible to disconnect the killings and destruction carried out from the current levels of poverty and suffering in East Africa.

Germany and Portugal would do well to acknowledge the atrocities committed and even take measures to bridge the developmental gap, which would help to ensure goodwill and mutual understanding between Africans and Europeans in the present and future. Tendering an open apology, as well as negotiating compensation, certainly would calm the anger of East Africans.

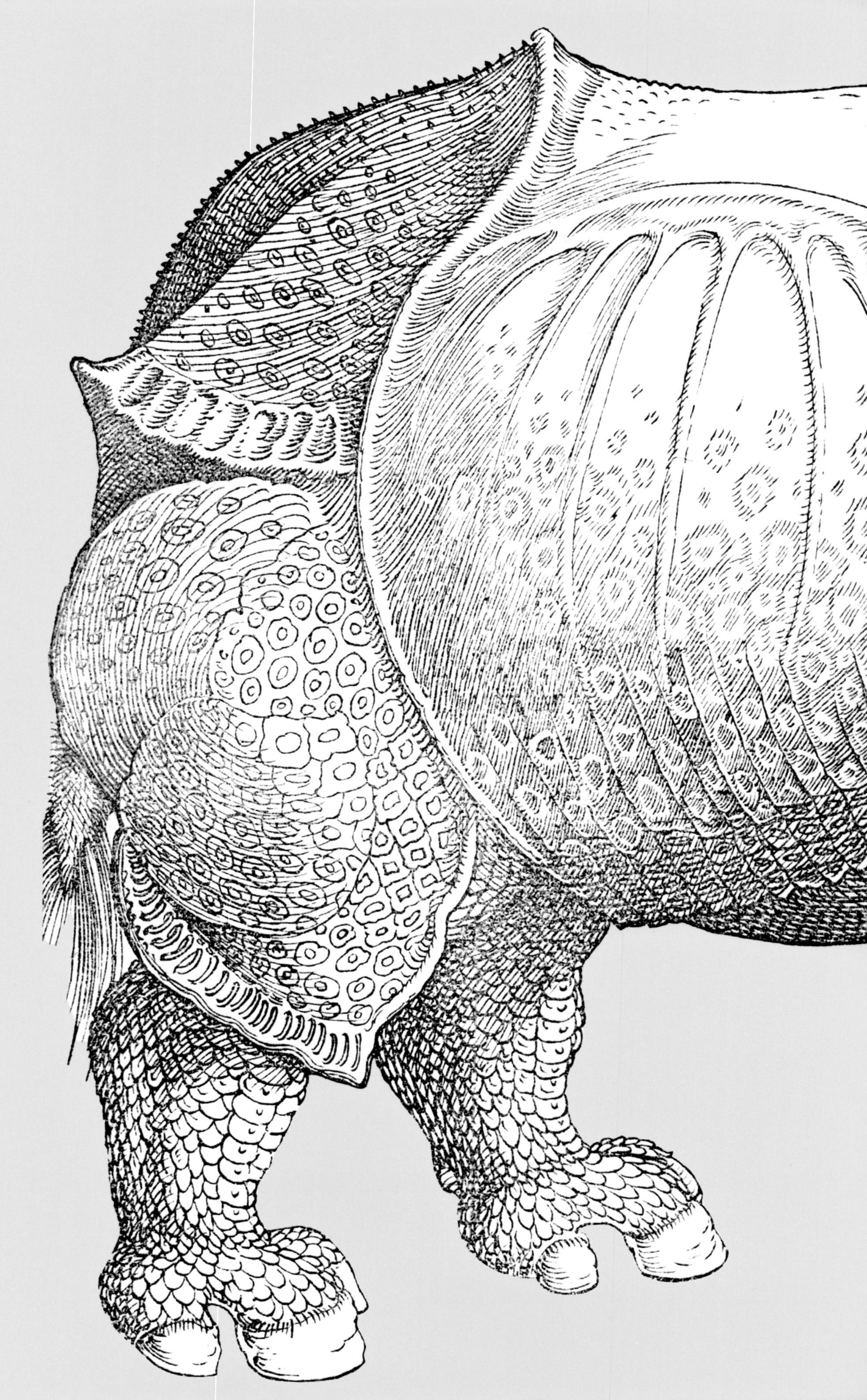

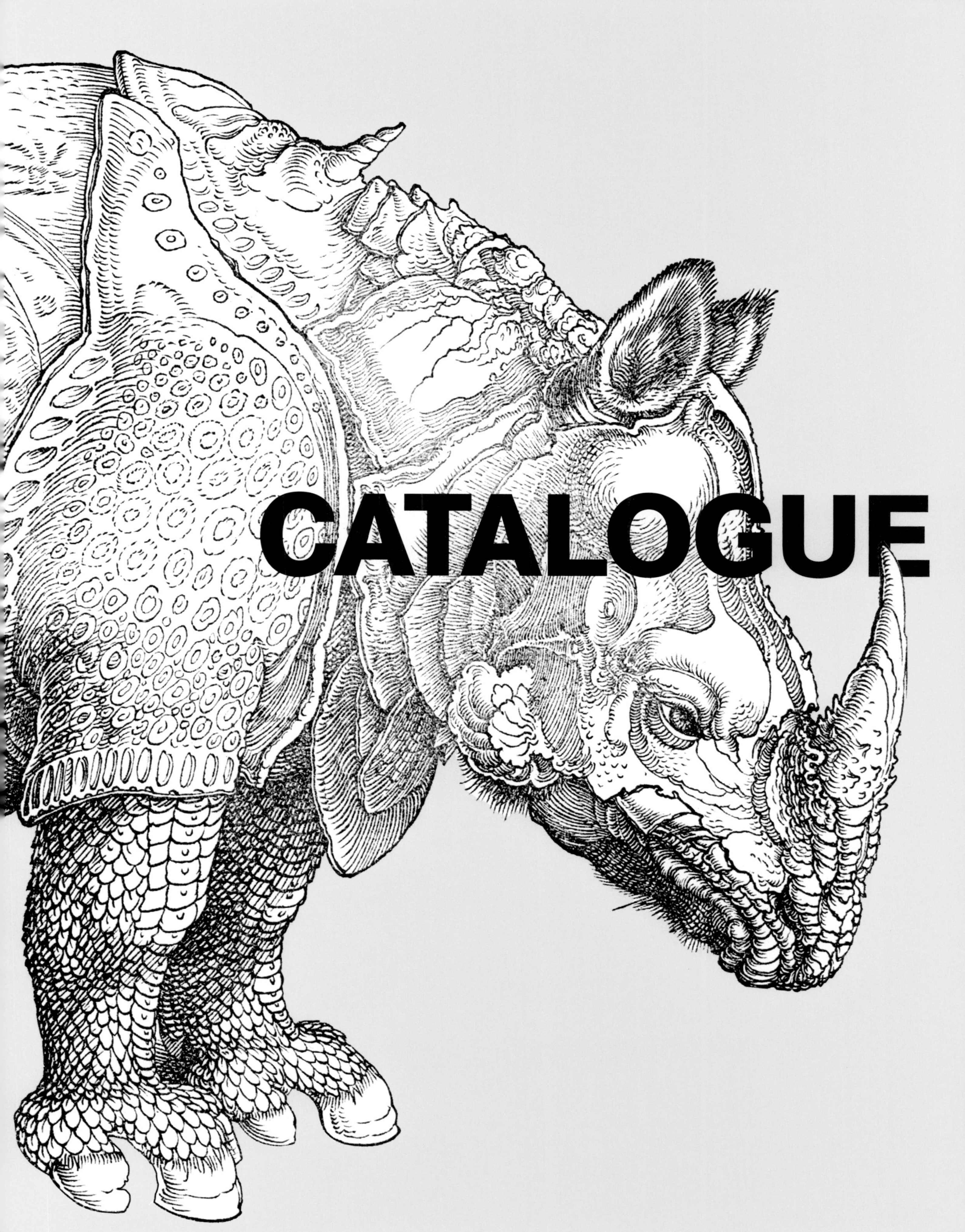

CATALOGUE

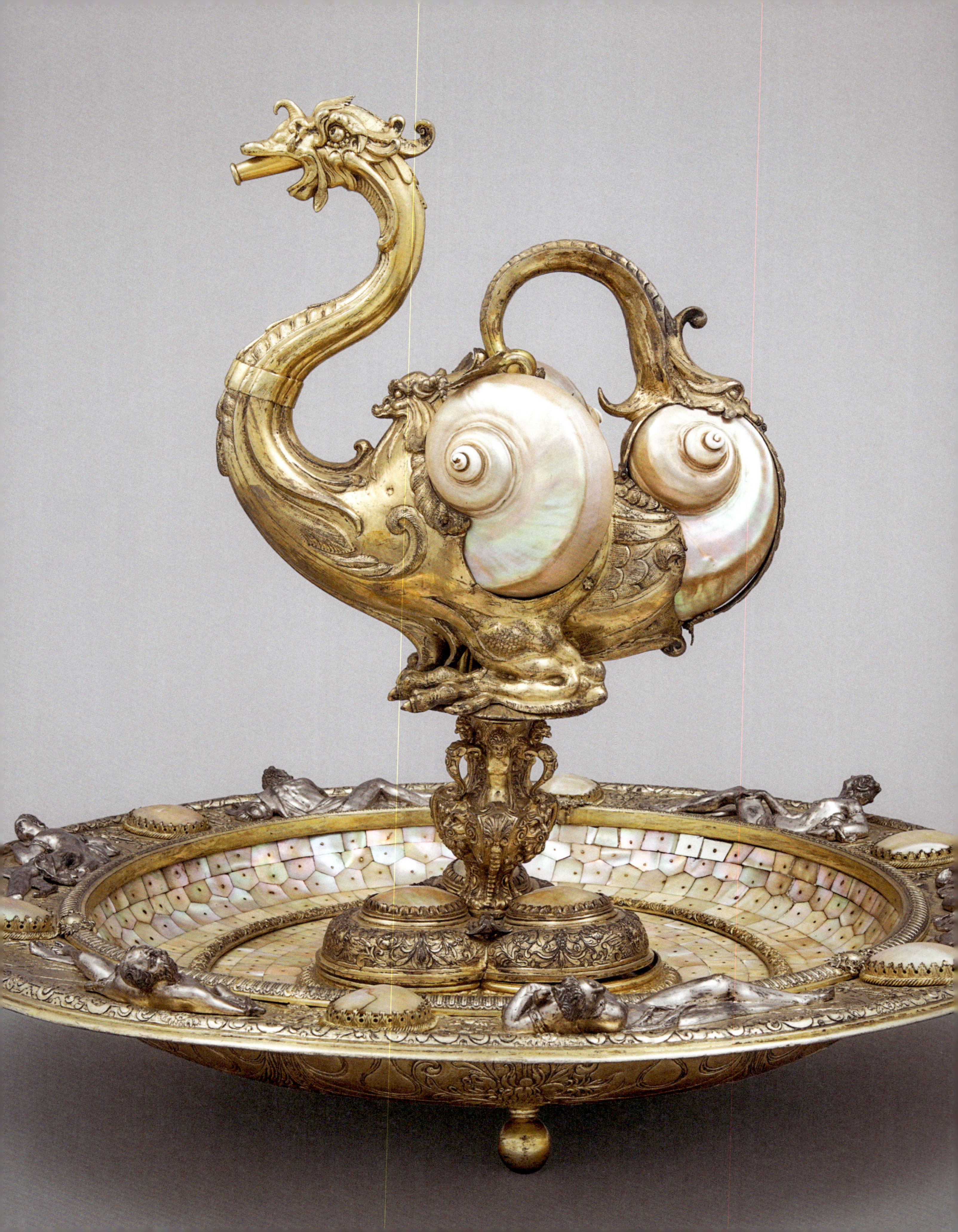

PROLOGUE

How can the history of Nuremberg between 1300 and 1600 be told from a global-historical perspective? Two artifacts that draw together many of the common threads running through the exhibition are the Behaim Globe—the oldest surviving globe in the world—and a magnificent lavabo set from the Green Vault in Dresden that is distinguished by its global genesis.

The Nuremberg city council's placement of the Behaim Globe in the town hall shows that the act of visualizing the world was important to the city's self-conception. Through the medium of the globe, the city expressed its claim to a share in distant parts of the world and, in particular, to the raw materials that are noted in various areas. The globe also embodies the enduring effort to gain new insight into the world's appearance and expanse. The great irony of this globe's creation is that it occurred at precisely the time when Christopher Columbus was making his first voyage across the Atlantic in 1492: the Americas are absent from the Behaim Globe.

The claim on worldwide resources made with the globe is to a certain extent realized in the lavabo set from the Green Vault: the set's ewer, made in the bizarre shape of a basilisk, contains three iridescent turban shells from the Indian Ocean. The magnificent basin consists of a wooden body decorated with hundreds of mother-of-pearl sections applied by artisans in Gujarat, India. Long-distance traders brought the sea snail shells and mother-of-pearl basin from India to Lisbon, and then on to Nuremberg. There, the goldsmith Nicolaus Schmidt set these items into extravagant Mannerist-style mounts.

The showpiece on loan from Dresden is juxtaposed in the exhibition with nine brass basins typical of Nuremberg. In contrast to the numerous works on exhibit representing the highest stratum of luxury, the brass basins call attention to the fact that mass-produced goods were exported from Nuremberg in far greater numbers, especially metalwork objects of all kinds.

Benno Baumbauer

◀ cat. no. 2 (detail)

1

THE BEHAIM GLOBE

Martin Behaim (design)
Georg Glockendon the Elder (painted decoration)

Nuremberg, 1492–1494

Cloth, parchment, and paper, glued and painted; wrought iron, painted; brass, cast, punched, engraved

H. 133 cm; Diam. 51 cm

GNM, inv. no. WI1826

References:
Ravenstein 1908; Dekker 2007, pp. 141–47, fig. 6.4; Eser 2010a; Schmieder 2021, passim; Hess 2022, pp. 44–48.

Every view of the world is shaped by one's own location and scope of knowledge. The Behaim Globe surveys knowledge about the world from the perspective of Nuremberg and Portugal at the very point in time when Christopher Columbus was making his first voyage to the Americas on behalf of the "Catholic Monarchs," landing in the Bahamas on October 12, 1492. Because Martin Behaim (1459–1507) of Nuremberg worked in service to the crown of Portugal |**see cat. no. 114**|, his globe gives special emphasis to the western coast of Africa, which is shown dotted with Portuguese insignia. From the conquest of Ceuta, in 1415, to the rounding of the Cape of Good Hope in 1488, Portugal had systematically explored that coastline and established trading posts along it. Behaim's placement of the southern tip of Africa at the level of Cape Cross, in southern Namibia, demonstrates the relativity of cartographic knowledge during this period, even in the best-informed circles.

As the oldest surviving globe—on the UNESCO Memory of the World Register since 2023—Behaim's creation is the last European cartographic object to lack a representation of the Americas. The news of Columbus's landing at the "Indian" islands, transmitted to Europe in a letter of March 1493 and then disseminated in print publications, reached the makers of this globe too late for inclusion. Apart from its unique historical status, the Behaim Globe is remarkable for being the first European world map to include neither the earthly paradise nor the birthplace of Christ or other locations important to the story of Christian salvation, features that had been standard on late-medieval maps of the world (*mappae mundi*). And while Behaim was content to show Mount Ararat and Prester John, he omitted the sites of ancient legends. The world appears as described by Marco Polo and as rendered in the travelogue purported to have been written by Sir John Mandeville (but later exposed as a forgery). With motifs such as the monopod and other such curiosities, the globe draws upon knowledge contained in even further bygone works of medieval prose—for example, the *Lucidarius* of about 1190.

A completely new aspect of this representation of the earth is its focus on global resources and the question of maximally profitable logistics—concerns that continue to dominate the world's economic activities to this day. In addition to gold and precious stones, spices such as pepper, saffron, and nutmeg played a leading role thanks to their great profitability |**see cat. no. 38**|. Long text passages inscribed on the globe propagate the idea of transporting these luxury goods directly to Europe to avoid costs associated with intermediaries and the payment of duties. Commissioned by the Nuremberg city council and originally kept at the town hall, the globe was intended to motivate Nuremberg's patricians, who were already versed in European commerce, to engage in maritime trade, an undertaking that was financially and operationally risky. The new medium of the terrestrial globe made it easier to conceive of a world grown larger. Around 1500, Nuremberg understood itself not only as a site of industry and knowledge production, but also as one of the centers of an increasingly globalized trade, with all the attendant negative aspects, including the sugar-plantation economy and the slave trade. Beginning in 1471, the fateful "triangular trade" began to take shape, initially involving the Gulf of Guinea and later, from about 1518–20 onward, expanding to encompass the Caribbean and then Brazil. In the Treaty of Tordesillas of 1494, Spain and Portugal divided the known world between themselves. World exploration and world conquest went hand in hand.

Daniel Hess

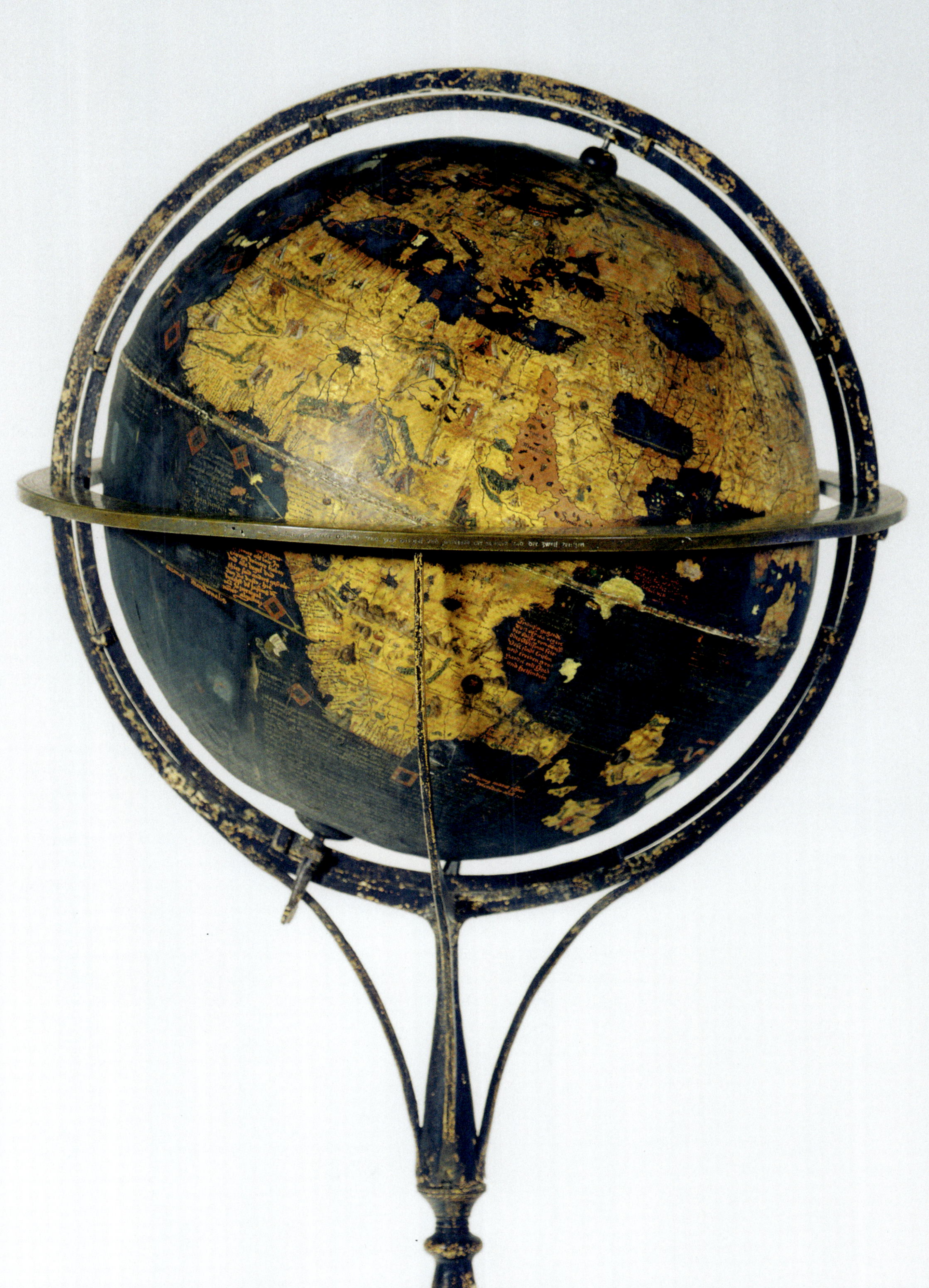

2

LAVABO SET WITH MOTHER-OF-PEARL

Unknown artists in Gujarat (mother-of-pearl work and painted decoration)
Nicolaus Schmidt (silversmith's work)

Gujarat, ca. 1540–80
Nürnberg, ca. 1592–94

Silver, repoussé, cast, chased, engraved, gilded; turban shells, polished (ewer); mother-of-pearl cabochons, mother-of-pearl, cut, teak, lacquered (basin)

Ewer: H. 40 cm; basin: Diam. 56 cm

Staatliche Kunstsammlungen Dresden, Grünes Gewölbe, inv. nos. IV 157 (ewer), IV 248 (basin)

References:
NGK 2007, vol. 1, pt. 1, pp. 379–81, cat. no. 809.05; Weinhold and Witting 2024, vol. 3, pp. 806–11, cat. no. 170 (Theresa Witting); Witting and Weinhold 2024, p. 62.

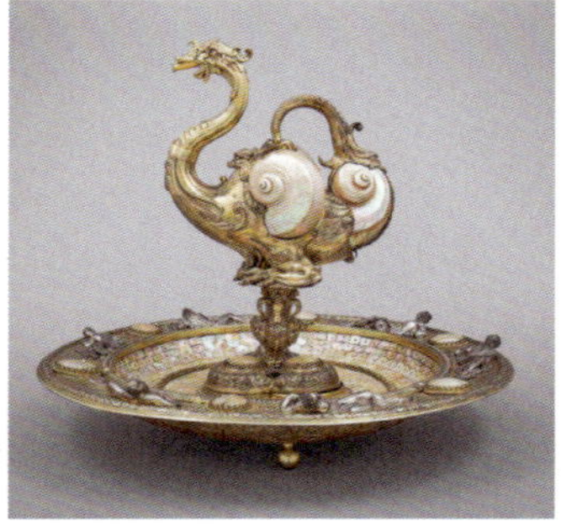

Ewer and basin, see fig. p. 100

This spectacular lavabo set is truly global in its genesis. Formerly part of the cabinet of arts (*Kunstkammer*) of the Saxon electors, the set is now kept in the New Green Vault at the Residenzschloss in Dresden. The basin was made in Gujarat, on the western coast of India, probably in the third quarter of the sixteenth century. The technique practiced in Gujarat, which involved using metal pins to secure differently shaped mother-of-pearl sections to a wooden support, creates a visual effect that is at once homogeneous and vibrant. Between about 1592 and 1594, the Nuremberg goldsmith Nicolaus Schmidt (master in 1582, d. 1609) set this Indian creation into an elaborate silver mount that completely covers the original reverse, which shows animal motifs painted on a red ground. Schmidt, who specialized in mother-of-pearl work, created a fanciful, dragon-shaped ewer out of three turban shells—a tour de force of Mannerist goldsmithing. The combination of materials in the ewer probably did not allow for a tight seal between the shells and the metal mounts. This suggests that the ewer was not intended to hold liquid; instead, like the basin, it was probably used purely for show.

Schmidt fitted the basin with a wide rim, decorated with cast figures of river gods and water nymphs. Also, he applied thin strips that divide up the basin's surface and form the trefoil rest for the ewer at the center. The use of a contemporary Nurembergian vocabulary of form and the inclusion of three small, cast lizards (made from natural specimens) served to adapt the Indian basin to central European taste and, with the addition of the ewer, to repurpose it into a familiar lavabo set. At about the same time, Schmidt created an even more elaborately designed set, with a basin whose mother-of-pearl decoration was made entirely in Europe, in imitation of southern Asian models.[1] That set's purchase by the imperial court in Vienna is confirmed by a 1592 invoice recorded in an imperial account book. Schmidt presumably executed the two ensembles with different degrees of decoration in order to appeal to a broader group of potential buyers. The less ornate metal mount of the set in Dresden may have been deliberately chosen to better showcase the Indian mother-of-pearl work. Such exclusive Indian work was highly prized, apparently in contrast to the painted elements done in India, which are concealed beneath the European mounts.

The Saxon ruling family did not acquire this lavabo set in Nuremberg, but instead from the merchant Veit Böttiger (before 1585, d. after 1600). Böttiger specialized in the trade of shells and objects fashioned from shells, which he sold at the triannual Leipzig Fair. Between 1585 and 1610, his name appears repeatedly in invoices and inventories related to gifting celebrations held at the Saxon court. One such invoice from 1602 lists a large group of mother-of-pearl works, encompassing two lavabo sets (including the present one), a gaming table, three small boxes, and five drinking vessels. The Augsburg patrician and art dealer Philipp Hainhofer (1578–1647) explicitly mentions this spectacular purchase in his report on his visit to the Dresden cabinet of arts.[2]

Theresa Witting

1 Kunsthistorisches Museum, Vienna, inv. nos. KK 1124 (ewer), KK 1138 (basin); see Exh. cat. Vienna 2000, p. 295, cat. no. 229 (Helmut Trnek), ill. p. 297.
2 Doering 1901, p. 171.

BRASS BASINS ("ALMS DISHES")

Nuremberg, fifteenth to sixteenth century

3

"Ein Beckschlager bin ich genannt/ Mein Beckn fuehrt man in weite Land"[1]

These lines open a poem by Hans Sachs (1494–1576) about basin-makers, published in his 1568 volume commonly known as the *Book of Trades* or *Eygentliche Beschreibung Aller Stände auff Erden* (True Description of All Estates and Trades on Earth). In the fifteenth and sixteenth centuries, the trade of the *Beckenschläger*, literally "basin beater," referred to producers of brass dishes, often called "alms dishes" in English. The basin-makers decorated their wares with figural or ornamental designs, frequently borrowed from prints. Religious motifs, foliate scrolls, banderoles, and mouchette-patterned rosettes were formed by hammering the brass into a mold from behind. This technique made it possible to produce decorated basins almost in a serial manner, since the individual motifs could be reproduced by the thousands and freely combined. Works such as these underscore that the metalworking trades in Nuremberg were responsible not only for exclusive und unique luxury objects, such as the Gujarat basin now in Dresden |**cat. no. 2**|, but also for mass-produced goods.

Brass basins had many uses. In a sacred context, they functioned as baptismal fonts. Pieces that were later engraved with Hebrew inscriptions indicate their use in Jewish rituals, such as the consecration of priests and circumcision.[2] In the secular sphere, the basins adorned tables and sideboards at patrician banquets, formed parts of washbasin sets, and hung on walls as decoration. Ordinary burghers used them as dishes and decorative objects. They may also have served as midwives' or barbers' basins and possibly as bloodletting bowls. Other uses were as drip pans beneath oil lamps[3] or as reflectors on wall sconces. A dish that found its way to Siena Cathedral was repurposed as a halo for a marble statue of Saint Peter.

Brass basins with embossed decorations were a Nuremberg specialty.[4] As early as 1485, thus even before the basin-makers were incorporated as an oath-bound trade (1493), there was a street named after them in the city, Beckschlagergasse. The trade was a restricted one, meaning that apprentices had to be from Nuremberg, journeymen were not allowed to travel, and masters were not permitted to move away. This strict policy of isolation was intended to keep the mold-based production technique secret, as it gave Nuremberg an international advantage over other locations.

Nuremberg brass basins are global objects. This began with the raw materials. The zinc and copper required to produce brass were obtained through long-distance trade. For example, the calamine from which zinc was extracted was imported from the area between the Maas and Rhine rivers. The finished basins were sought-after export items; they were indeed "sold far and wide," in the words of Hans Sachs. For instance, it was probably a brass dish, described as a "beautiful raised basin" (*schön erhaben beck*), that the Nuremberg merchant Hans Praun acquired in 1471 to sell in Italy.[5] The presence of pieces throughout Europe, from Spain to Sweden, attests to the productivity and international reach of Nuremberg's metalworking trades.

Verena Suchy

Brass, pressed and embossed

Diam. 25.4–47.5 cm

GNM, inv. nos. HG466, HG468, HG470, HG471, HG485, HG1440, HG1450, HG3394, HG8063 (cat. nos. 3.1–3.9, from top left to bottom right)

References:
Egyeki-Szabó 2008; Tiedemann 2018.

1 English translation: "A basin beater is what I'm called, my basins are sold far and wide." Sachs 1568, sig. V1r.
2 Egyeki-Szabó 2008, p. 14.
3 Tiedemann 2018, p. 23, adduces examples from Catalonia.
4 Klaus Tiedemann has shown that all the brass basins known to him use varying combinations of a limited set of motifs. Among the pieces he examined, there is not one that exhibits exclusively unique designs. He therefore posits that all of them were made in Nuremberg. See Tiedemann 2018, p. 11. A research project underway since 2020 at the Royal Museums of Art and History in Brussels is using technical investigation to illuminate the production contexts of such copper-alloy basins.
5 Tiedemann 2018, p. 39.

cat. no. 2

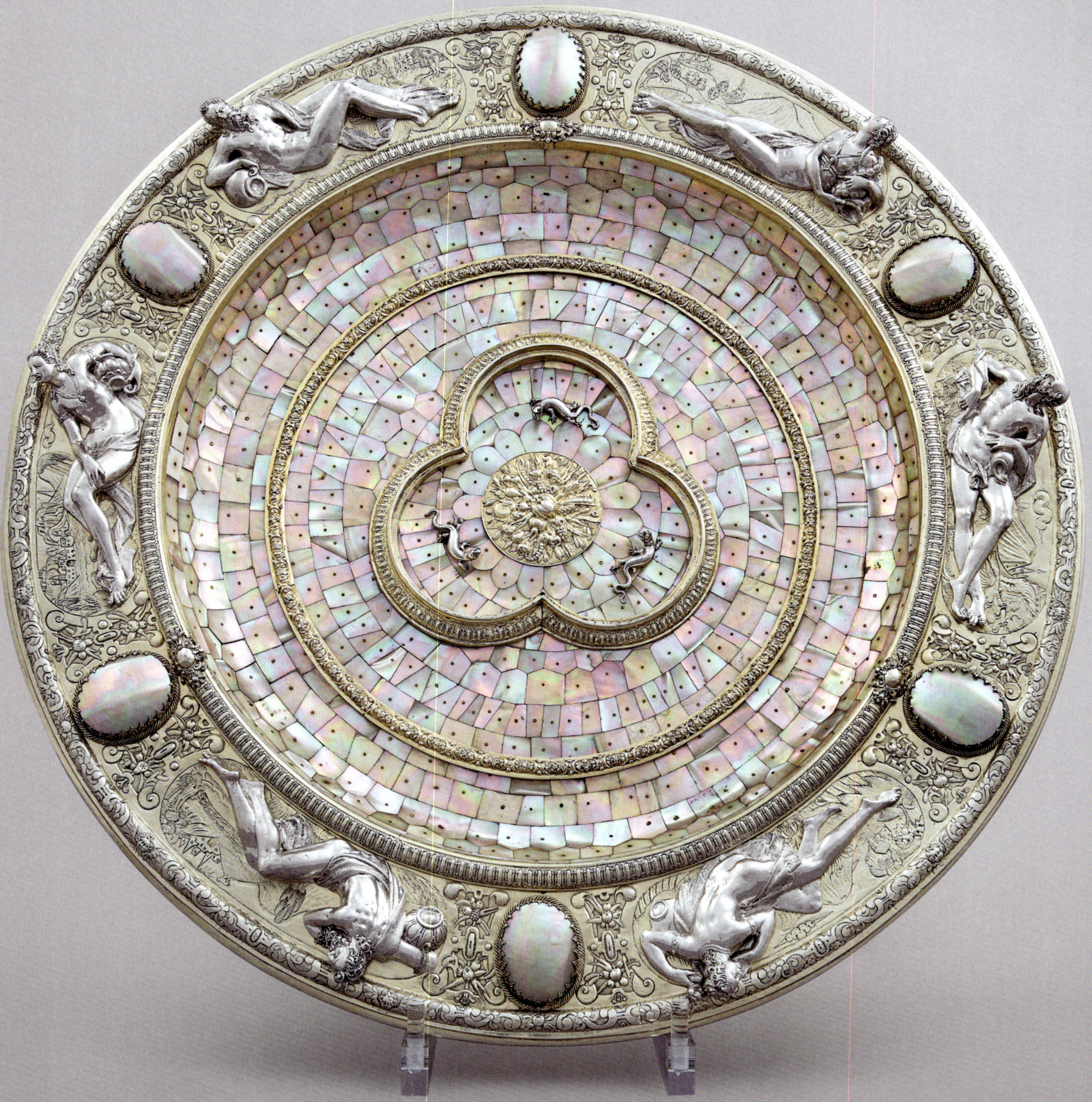

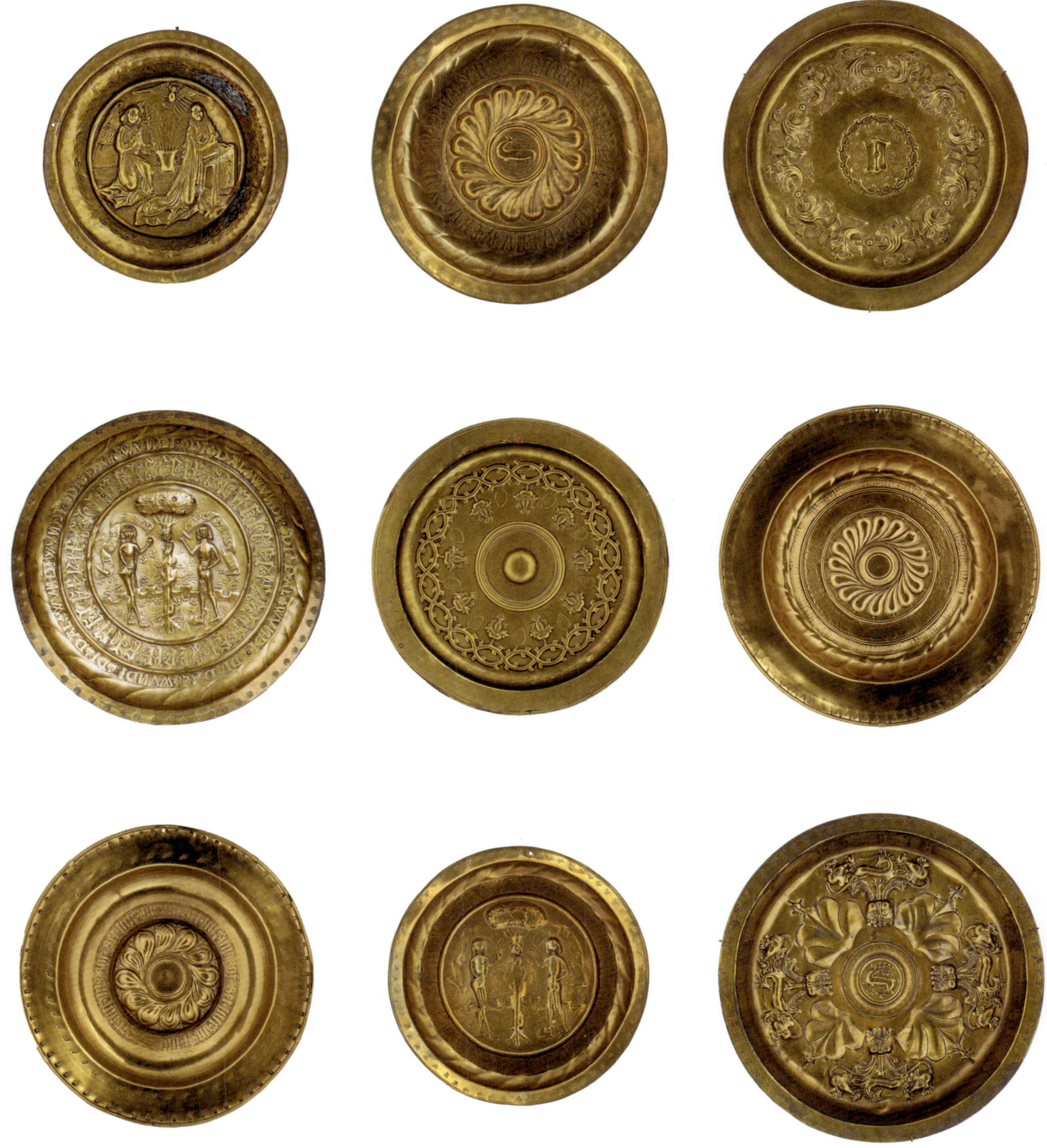

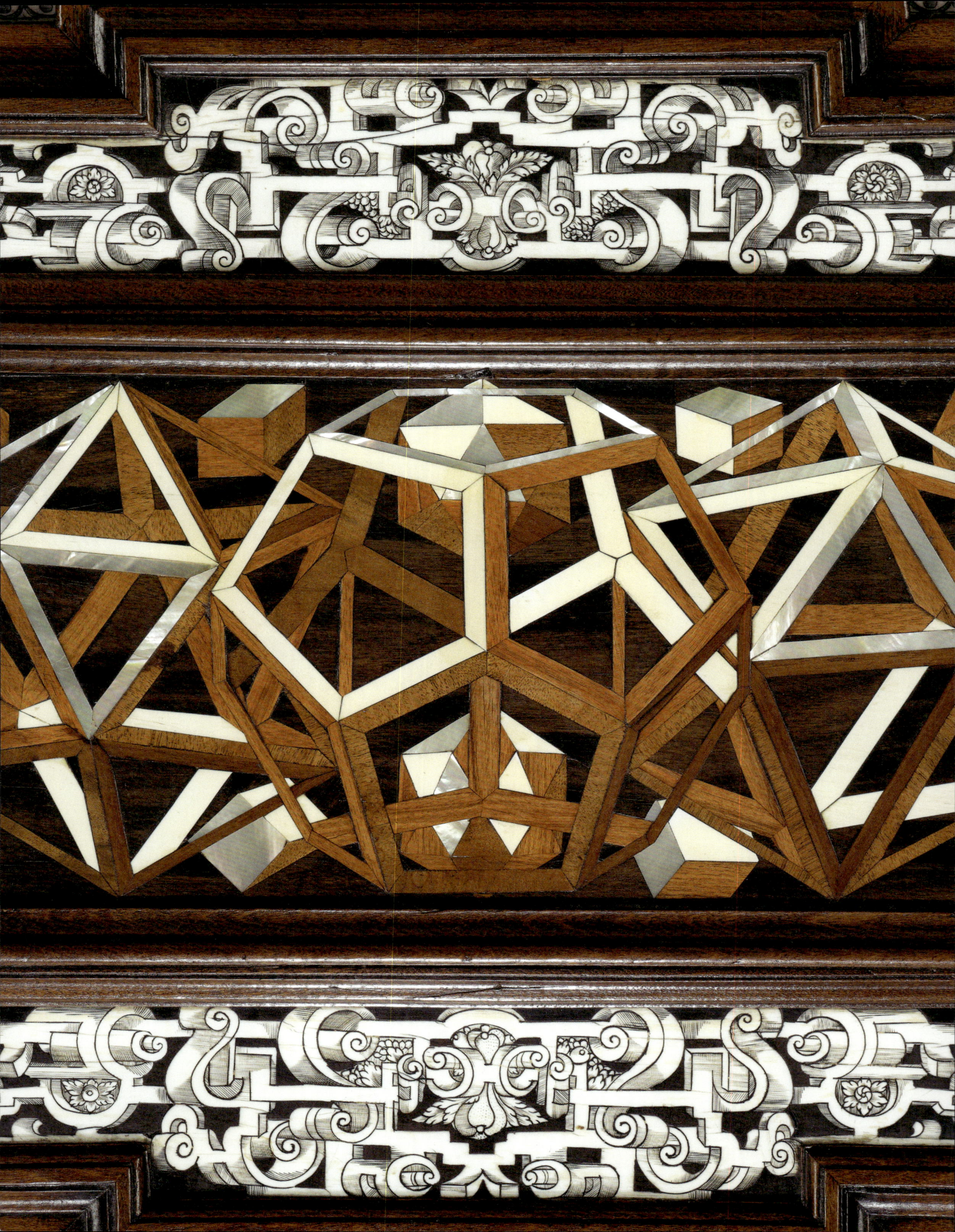

NUREMBERG: PORTRAIT OF A CITY

Nuremberg's rise to prominence owed much to the kings and emperors of the Holy Roman Empire. Ever since the High Middle Ages, those rulers had supported the city by granting it wide-ranging privileges. Influential personalities from far and wide were drawn to Nuremberg thanks to the regular visits of the royal court and, as codified in the Golden Bull of 1356, the meetings of the Imperial Diet. In 1424, Emperor Sigismund confirmed Nuremberg's status as a royal city by decreeing that the imperial regalia—the holy relics and coronation insignia of the Roman-German kings—were to be kept in Nuremberg permanently.

An exclusive circle of patrician families steered the city's course. They amassed great wealth through various business ventures. The close connection between political influence and financial potency enabled the patricians to develop networks that became increasingly global in scope. In all of this, economic factors intertwined with politics, culture, and the exchange of information. Nuremberg's growing prosperity made it a center of the arts, printing, and the sciences. The elite families who served on the city council put their status on display by commissioning ambitious works of art.

Political and economic power in Nuremberg was concentrated in the area of the Hauptmarkt (main market square). This was the location of important churches, the town hall, the Schöner Brunnen (Beautiful Fountain), and merchants' residences. The Hauptmarkt also serves as a reminder of the fate of Nuremberg's once flourishing Jewish community. For centuries, the freedoms afforded to Jews were determined by contrary forces of integration and exclusion. The community produced important scholars, economic success stories, and sophisticated works of art. In 1349, one of the bloodiest in a series of pogroms took place in Nuremberg. At least 562 Jews were murdered. The city council then had the Jewish quarter demolished and built the Hauptmarkt in its place.

Benno Baumbauer

◄ cat. no. 20 (detail of casket lid)

4

NURENBERG CHRONICLE

Hartmann Schedel

Woodcuts by **Michael Wolgemut** and **Wilhelm Pleydenwurff**

Nuremberg: Anton Koberger, 1493

Incunable, 326 leaves, woodcut illustrations

4.1 Liber chronicarum
(Latin edition)

H. 48.5 cm; W. 34 cm

GNM, Sign. Inc.117013a

Open to fols. 99v–100r: View of Nuremberg

4.2 Das Buch der Chroniken
(German edition)

Translated from Latin to German by Georg Alt

H. 47.5 cm; B. 33.5 cm

GNM, Sign. Inc.5539

Open to fols. 12v–13r: World map

References:
Hellwig 1970, p. 254, cat. no. 830 (Inc.117013a), p. 255, cat. no. 832 (Inc.5539); Herz 2019; Exh. cat. Nuremberg 2019b, pp. 318–20, cat. no. 95 (Randall Herz); Worm 2021, pp. 371–481.

Nuremberg was one of early modern Europe's most important centers of printing and news distribution. The city's printers and publishers were networked throughout the continent and maintained branch offices in numerous cities, from Kraków to Seville |**cat. no. 94**|. Among the most successful was Anton Koberger (d. 1513), the godfather of Albrecht Dürer.

In 1493, Koberger's workshop printed a chronicle of the world, now widely known in English as the *Nuremberg Chronicle*. This publication stands as the most lavishly illustrated book produced in the early stages of printing, in the period up to 1500. The work's 652 pages contain a universal history of mankind written from a Christian, Eurocentric perspective, from the biblical creation story to the Last Judgment. The book concludes with a treatise on Europe. A total of 1,804 woodcut illustrations, including the famous 116 city views, are arranged in sophisticated layouts with more than 2,000 texts. Work on the *Nuremberg Chronicle* began in 1490 at the latest. The first contract dates from December 1491, an agreement reached between the project's humanist backers and the painter-entrepreneur Michael Wolgemut (1433/34–1519)—who was Dürer's teacher—along with Wolgemut's stepson Wilhelm Pleydenwurff (d. 1494). The texts were compiled by the humanist Hartmann Schedel (1440–1514) in collaboration with Hieronymus Münzer (d. 1508), both of whom were working on the Behaim Globe at the time |**cat. no. 1**|.

The book's woodcut view of Nuremberg is prominently placed, given a full double-page opening at leaf "C" (100). Within the chronology, the depiction appears only a few pages into the chapter devoted to the Sixth Age of the World, which begins with the life of Jesus. Appropriately, the accompanying text recounts the myth of the city's ancient foundation, an event that was sorely lacking for Nuremberg compared to some of its trade rivals, including Augsburg. Viewed from the south, the city is presented as an intricate cluster of buildings marked by numerous church spires and defensive towers. The lines of sight all lead to the Imperial Castle, situated on the hill after which Nuremberg was named (the "Norenberc," or rocky hill). Although only a few of the most prominent buildings were rendered in recognizable form, this depiction has shaped the perception of medieval Nuremberg's appearance like no other.

While the Nuremberg woodcut bespeaks the chroniclers' identification with their hometown, the world map reflects their view of the world. Jerusalem, consistent with its status as a holy city, appears at the center. By comparison, Europe, at the upper left, inscribed with "Francia," among other labels, seems almost withdrawn from view. Nuremberg is not indicated at all—unlike on the Behaim Globe, a product of the same intellectual milieu. Yet like its spherical sibling, this world map—an "unfurled" globe, so to speak—also refers back to the image of the earth formulated by the late antique geographer Ptolemy. The task of reconciling contemporary cartographic findings with biblical and classical conceptualizations is apparent in the three figures that present the map: the three sons of Noah, from whom, according to biblical exegesis, the inhabitants of the three known continents descended. Each of them appears as a bearded *white* man. At the same time, the legendary creatures at the left, such as the centaur and the crane-necked man, belong to the regular cast of characters found in medieval encyclopedias. Within the dynamics of this early period of globalization, such creatures are only ostensibly incongruous with the rapid expansion of Europe's understanding of the world, which, for all its discoveries, also generated new myths.

Benno Baumbauer

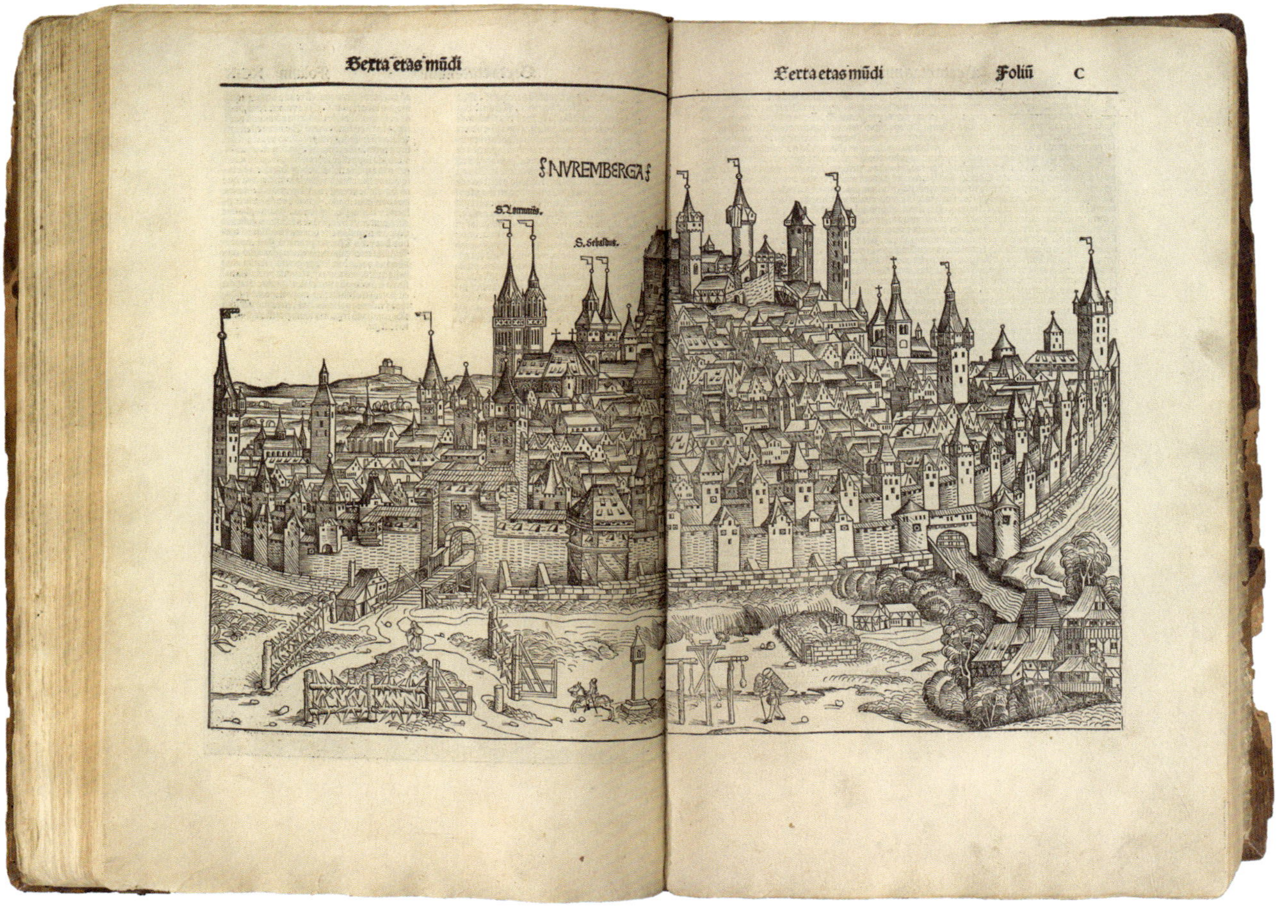

Sexta etas mūdi

Sexta etas mūdi Foliū C

NVREMBERGA

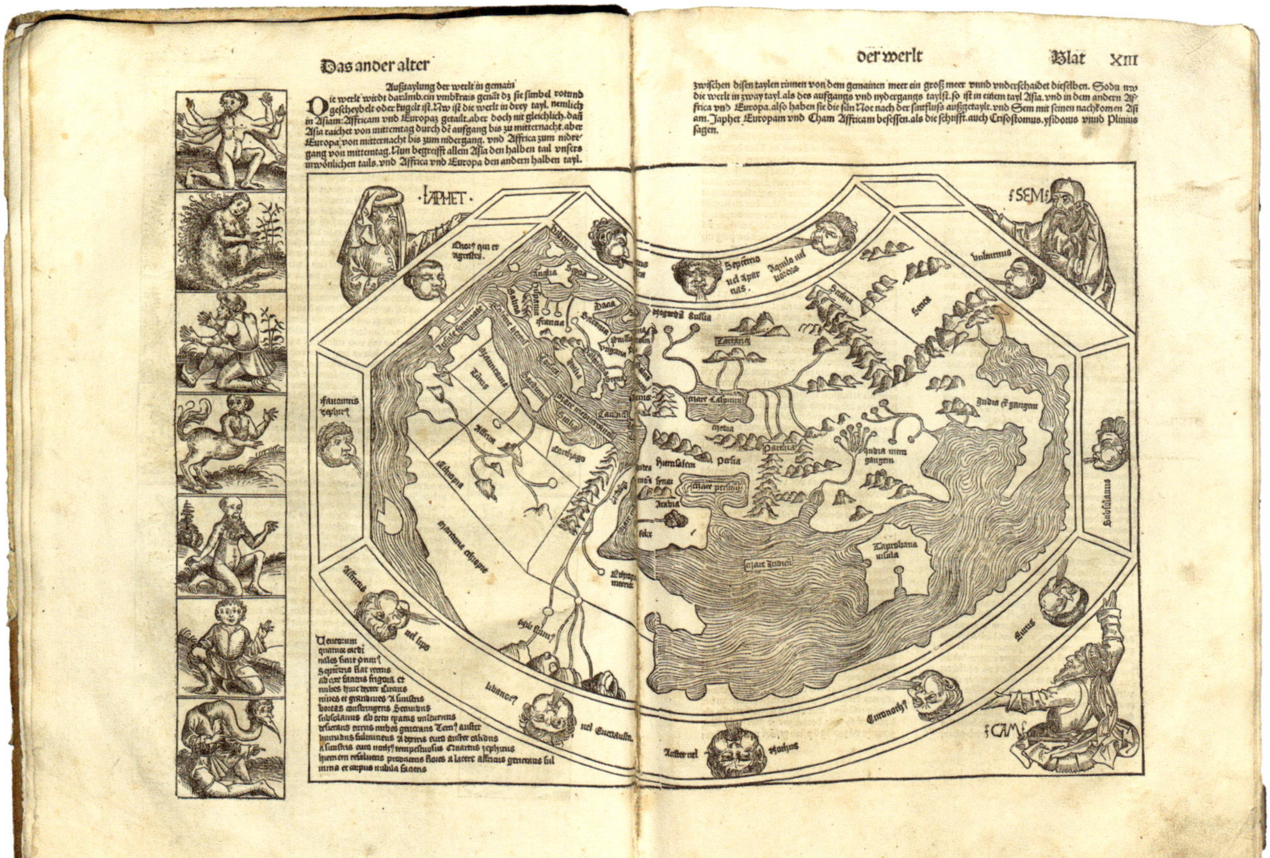

S. Laurentii.

S. Sebaldus.

Das ander alter

der werlt Blat XIII

Außtaylung der werlt in gemain

Die werlt wirdt darumb ein umbkrais genãt dz sie simbel rotund geschaybelt oder kugelt ist. Nw ist die werlt in drey tayl, nemlich in Asiam: Affricam vnd Europaz getailt. aber doch nit gleichlich. dañ Asia raichet von mittemtag durch dẽ aufgang bis zu mitternacht. aber Europa von mitternacht bis zum nidergang. vnd Affrica zum nidergang von mittemtag. Nun begreifft allein Asia den halben tail vnsers inwonlichen tails. vnd Affrica vnd Europa den andern halben tayl.

zwischen disen taylen rinnen von dem gemainen meer ein groß meer vnnd vnderschaidet dieselben. So du nw die werlt in zway tayl. als des aufgangs vnd nydergangs taylst. so ist in einem tayl Asia. vnd in dem andern Affrica vnd Europa. also haben sie die sün Noe nach der sintfluss außgetaylt. vnd Sem mit seinen nachkomen Asiam. Japhet Europam vnd Cham Affricam besessen. als die schrifft. auch Crisostomus. ysidorus vnnd Plinius sagen.

IAPHET

SEM

CAM

5

MODEL OF THE CITY OF NUREMBERG

Sigmund Pfreundtner and **Alfred Baumann**

Copy after the original by **Hans Baier**, Nuremberg, 1540[1]

München, 1941/42

Wood, with polychromy

H. 63.5 cm; W. 78.5 cm; D. 6.7 cm

Museen der Stadt Nürnberg, Kunstsammlungen, inv. no. Pl 0387

References:
Exh. cat. Nuremberg 2000a, pp. 138–39, cat. no. 4 (Matthias Mende); Schiermeier 2006, pp. 18, 30, 46–47, 51, 66–67; Grieb 2007, vol. 1, p. 52; Hoppe 2014, pp. 258–60, 266.

On September 11, 1540, the painter and sculptor Hans Baier received 40 gulden from the Nuremberg city council "for the likeness [Contrafactur] of Nuremberg, set on a board, with all the houses, alleys, and other things, etc."[2] The "likeness" being referred to is the oldest surviving model of the city. The work shown in the present exhibition is a faithful copy, produced after the failed 1940 attempt by Nuremberg's Nazi mayor, Willy Liebel, to claim the original model, then kept at the Bayerisches Nationalmuseum in Munich, for his hometown.[3] As the "City of the Nazi Party Rallies," Nuremberg played a central role in Nazi ideology, leading to the almost complete destruction of the town's historic center just three years after this copy was finished.

Baier's model must have required an extensive surveying campaign. Although the individual buildings are represented only schematically, their distribution within the urban fabric is highly precise. The main topographical features are clearly visible. The Pegnitz River divides the city into two parishes, that of the Sebalduskirche in the north and that of the Lorenzkirche in the south. The model shows the city walls as they appeared before the gate towers were enlarged in 1556–64, when they received their colossal, round forms |**see cat. no. 9**|. In the sixteenth century, 40,000 to 50,000 people lived within the area enclosed by the walls.

The area around the Hauptmarkt, north of the Pegnitz, was in many respects the nucleus of Nuremberg's global trading activities |**fig. pp. 6–7**|. Yet the Hauptmarkt, the site of the medieval Jewish quarter, owed its creation to an atrocity: the pogrom of 1349, during which 562 Jews were murdered. Afterward, the Inner Council had large parts of the quarter demolished, while the remaining properties were sold to the pogrom's Christian instigators. At the behest of Emperor Charles IV, the Frauenkirche was erected in place of the destroyed synagogue, as a monument to Christian triumph |**cat. no. 11**|. Diagonally opposite the church, the council had the Schöner Brunnen built, a fountain with a sculptural program of encyclopedic pretensions |**cat. no. 10**|. From that time onward, the grand house facades of Nuremberg's leading merchant families began to line the square.

In the Hauptmarkt's immediate vicinity stand both the town hall and the Sebalduskirche, which contains the tomb of Nuremberg's patron saint and was sometimes dubbed the "city-council church." Like the city's second parish church, the Lorenzkirche, south of the Pegnitz, the Sebalduskirche was one of the main places where the local elite put their status on display. The Imperial Castle, temporary residence of numerous kings and emperors during the Middle Ages, stands at the far north. The model shows the construction site of the bastions north of the castle complex, built between 1538 and 1545 by the Maltese architect Antonio Fazuni. The hospital church of the Heilig-Geist-Spital, on the north bank of the Pegnitz, was also of central importance to the emperor and empire, for it served as the repository of the imperial regalia from 1424 onward |**cat. no. 8**|. The annual presentation of the regalia, including sacred relics, on the Hauptmarkt—a major event that attracted visitors from far and wide—had been discontinued by the time of Baier's model, owing to the introduction of the Reformation |**cat. no. 7**|.

Baier's "likeness" of Nuremberg is an important testimony to the art of surveying in the early modern period. It is the "oldest surviving scale model of a European city."[4] Probably for reasons of secrecy, the city council instructed Baier "never to carve or paint a replica."[5]

Benno Baumbauer

1 The original is on display at the Imperial Castle, Nuremberg, on long-term loan from the Bayerisches Nationalmuseum, Munich, inv. no. Modell 7.
2 Translated from the citation in Grieb 2007, vol. 1, p. 52.
3 I thank Sybe Wartena, Bayerisches Nationalmuseum, for pointing this out.
4 Hoppe 2014, p. 258.
5 Translated from the citation in Grieb 2007, vol. 1, p. 52.

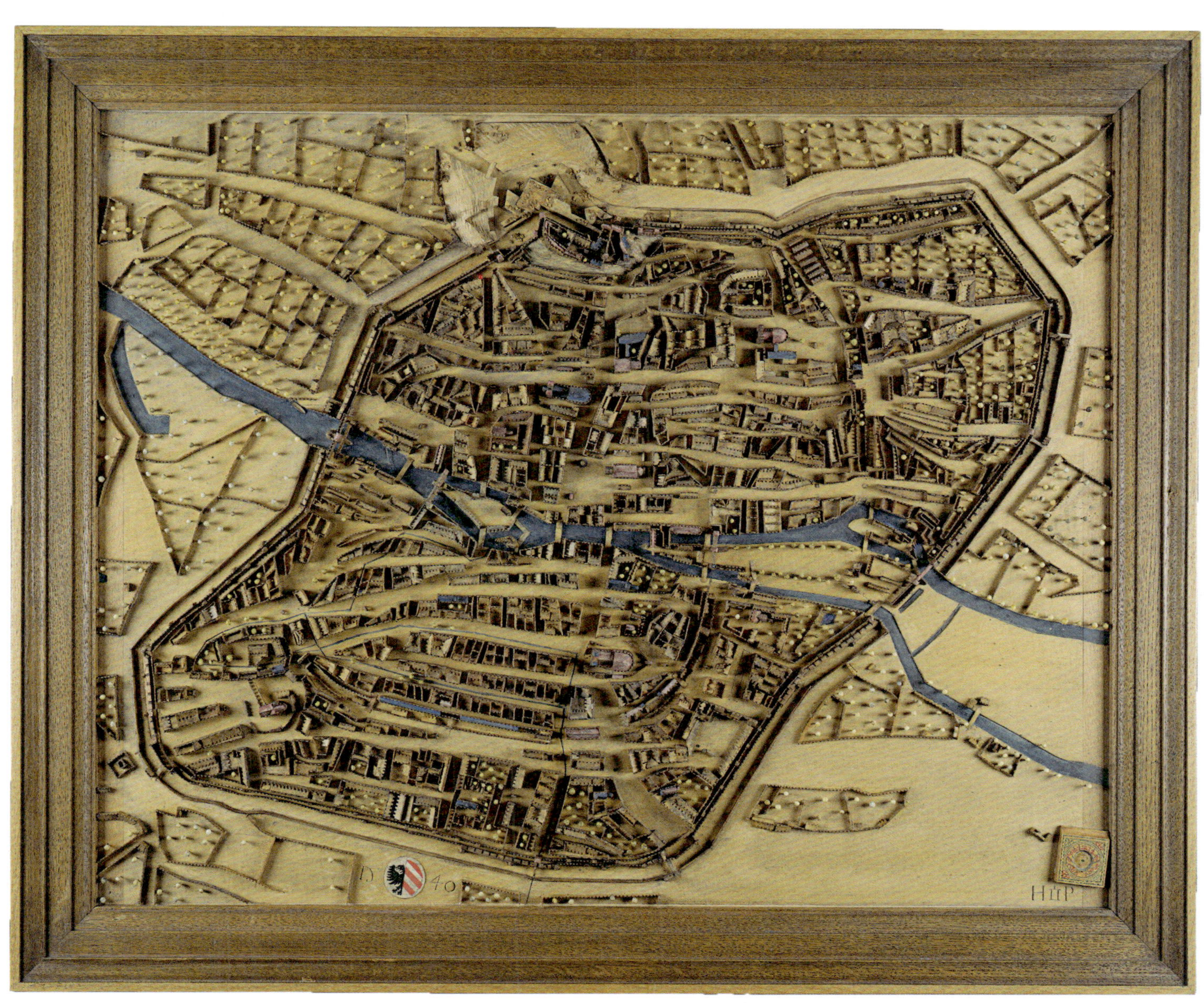
D 40
HüP

6

THE NUREMBERG SCHÖNER GLOBE

Johannes Schöner

Bamberg, 1520

Molding material, chalk and gypsum ground, polychromy, wood

H. 129 cm; Diam. 89.7 cm

GNM, inv. no. WI1, on long-term loan from the Museen der Stadt Nürnberg, Kunstsammlungen

References:
Exh. cat. Nuremberg 1992, vol. 2, pp. 673–74, cat. no. 2.30 (Norbert Holst); Maruska 2008, pp. 156–57; Eser 2013; Sauer 2021a, pp. 55–64, fig. 2.36.

This Schöner Globe, so named after its creator, Johannes Schöner (1477–1547), testifies to the dynamism that characterized Europe's view of the world in the decades around 1500. The period was increasingly filled with news about regions previously unknown to Europeans, something that posed enormous problems in the production of globes. Schöner, a clergyman from Bamberg, took up the challenge. His surviving body of work includes several globes from the years 1515 and 1533, all made from printed map segments. The 1520 globe, by contrast, is a unique object that Schöner created for his benefactor Johannes Seiler, who was a mayor of Bamberg. Shortly after Seiler's death in 1530, his heir Johann Eck donated the globe to the city of Nuremberg, where Schöner had been teaching for several years at the gymnasium recently founded at the former monastery of the Egidienkirche. The city council's placement of the globe in the municipal art collection is indicative of the work's significance.

Schöner made important contributions to the ongoing discussion and evaluation of the western landmasses discovered since the time of Christopher Columbus. Schöner used the term Terra Nova for those places, meaning—from a European perspective—"New World." Nearly three decades after Columbus's first landing, key questions remained unanswered: Was it merely a set of islands that had been "found," or a whole continent? Or did the discovery involve two new continents, separated by a waterway? If so, what kind of sea lay beyond the *Terra Nova*? Was it the eastern part of the Indian Ocean or a larger, previously unknown ocean? Were the landmasses bounded by oceans on both sides, or were they an extension of eastern Asia? Or was only the northern part an extension of northeastern Asia?

Schöner's "toolbox" for the production of globes has been preserved in the form of a bound collection of cartographic materials compiled by him.[1] Of particular importance to Schöner were two monumental woodcut maps by Martin Waldseemüller (d. 1520): one from 1507 and another, called the *Carta marina*, from 1516. The Waldseemüller maps are themselves indicative of the dynamics of knowledge production at the beginning of the early modern period, when cartographers were repeatedly revising and adapting their understanding based on the most recent findings. In the world map of 1507, Waldseemüller was the first to label the new continent with the term "America." In his 1516 *Carta marina*, however, he abandoned both that term and the interpretation of the landmass as a separate entity. This was also relevant to the Pacific Ocean, which is no longer contained in the 1516 map.

Schöner's 1520 globe follows Waldseemüller's world map of 1507 in certain fundamental aspects, including the wide expanse of the Eurasian landmass, the elongated Mediterranean Sea and flattened coastline of northern Africa, and the small scale of the Indian subcontinent. Schöner also depicted the Americas as an independent continent, bounded by the Pacific in the west; he adopted the new name "America" and, in an inscription quoting from Amerigo Vespucci's *Mundus Novus* letter |**cat. no. 98**|, noted the 1492 landing of Christopher Columbus. Other inscriptions provide information about places, inhabitants, nature, and resources, while also spreading early stereotypes about the inhabitants ("Canibalorum Terra"). Schöner's works belong to the initial approximations of the cartographic form of the Americas, which would gain ever greater definition in the following decades.

Susanne Thürigen

1 Library of Congress, Washington, DC. See Hessler 2013.

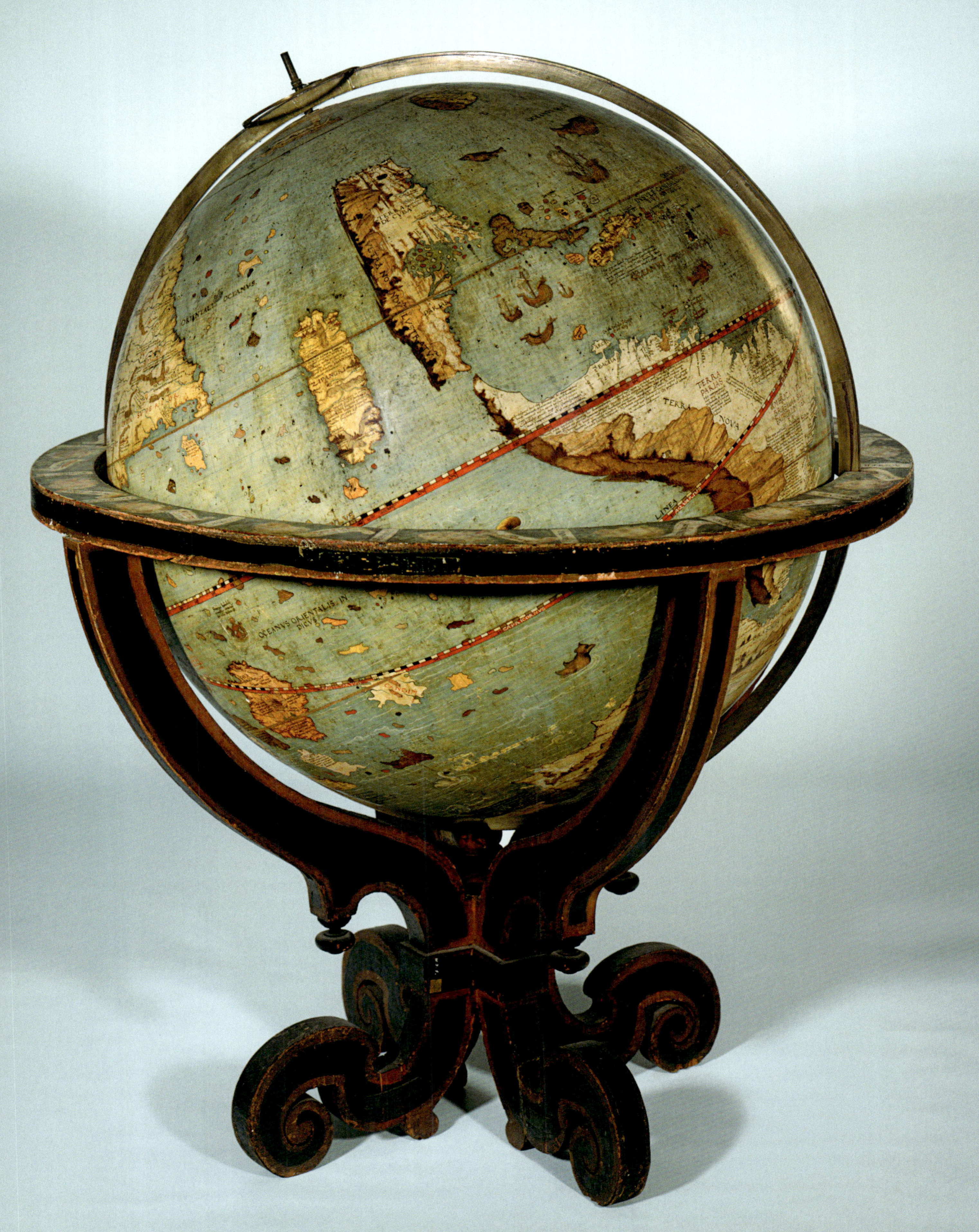
OCEANVS ORIENTALIS IN
DICVS
TERRA NOVA

7

THE "KAISERBILDER" (IMPERIAL PORTRAITS)

Albrecht Dürer

Nuremberg, ca. 1510–13

Paint on limewood

7.1 Charlemagne

H. 214.2 cm; W. 115.0 cm (including original frame)

GNM, inv. no. Gm167

7.2 Emperor Sigismund

H. 213.1 cm; W. 115.1 cm (including original frame)

GNM, inv. no. Gm168

On long-term loan from the Museen der Stadt Nürnberg, Kunstsammlungen

References:
Exh. cat. Nuremberg 1971, p. 138, cat. nos. 251–52 (Ludwig Veit); Anzelewsky 1991, pp. 235–40, cat. nos. 123–24; Löcher 1997, pp. 203–10; Exh. cat. Nuremberg 2004, pp. 58–59 (Daniel Hess); Exh. cat. Nuremberg 2013, pp. 174–76, cat. nos. 5.15a–5.15b (Thomas Schauerte).

During the late Middle Ages, Nuremberg was more closely associated with the kings and emperors of the Holy Roman Empire than nearly any other imperial city. In return for the considerable taxes it paid, the prosperous mercantile center benefited from numerous imperial privileges. In 1219, Frederick II issued the Great Charter of Freedom (*Großer Freiheitsbrief*), which placed the citizens of Nuremberg under his sole protection and guaranteed them advantages in policy relating to coinage and customs. In 1356, Charles IV decreed in the Golden Bull that the first Imperial Diet of each newly crowned king would be held in Nuremberg. And in 1424 Sigismund had the imperial regalia (*Reichskleinodien*) transferred from his residence in Buda (Ofen) to Nuremberg for permanent safekeeping. The regalia, consisting of both rulership insignia and holy relics |**cat. no. 8**|, were presented to the public in an annual spectacle held on the Hauptmarkt. This was done not only to demonstrate Nuremberg's close ties to the empire but also for religious reasons, since almost all the items among the regalia had the status of relics.

On the day before the imperial regalia were put on view each year, they were brought from their repository in the hospital church of the Heilig-Geist-Spital to the Schopperhaus (Hauptmarkt 15), in front of which a monumental, multilevel display platform was erected (the *Heiltumsstuhl*). Inside the Schopperhaus, the regalia were stored in a wall cabinet. About 1510, Albrecht Dürer was commissioned to paint new doors for the cabinet, showing likenesses of the emperors Charlemagne (left) and Sigismund (right) in three-quarter length, a job for which he received 149 guldens in total. Dürer executed these works with almost archaeological precision, outfitting both rulers with items that belonged to the regalia, such as the imperial crown and orb, ceremonial sword, eagle-patterned dalmatic, and coronation robe in the Charlemagne portrait. In a number of preparatory studies, Dürer made meticulous renderings of the insignia. Detailed pictorial documents of this sort, depicting the imperial crown and orb and the ceremonial sword, are preserved at the Germanisches Nationalmuseum.[1] His next step in the process, a kind of "test run" for the paintings, was to draw full studies for the figures; one of those survives showing Charlemagne dressed in the same dalmatic and robe.[2]

Owing to the advent of the Reformation in Nuremberg, which caused the veneration of relics to fall into disfavor, the imperial regalia were no longer publicly displayed on the Hauptmarkt after 1523. As a result, Dürer's likenesses of the two emperors lost their original function. In 1526, they were moved to the town hall, where they could be admired as works of art and collector's items. These paintings were also valued as historical documents in the early modern period, and numerous copies were made in various formats. Georg Pencz is known to have painted replicas for Elector John the Steadfast of Saxony in 1532.[3] Another set of copies, the carefully worked, bust-length pair now in Berlin, has at times been ascribed to Dürer himself.[4]

Manuel Teget-Welz

1 Inv. nos. Hz2574, Hz2575, Hz2576. See Zink 1968, pp. 74–78, cat. nos. 53–55.
2 Albertina, Vienna, inv. no. 3125. Koschatzky and Strobl 1971, p. 274, cat. no. 74.
3 Dyballa 2014, p. 432, document no. 35.
4 Stiftung Deutsches Historisches Museum, Berlin, inv. nos. Gm 2003/8, Gm 2003/9.

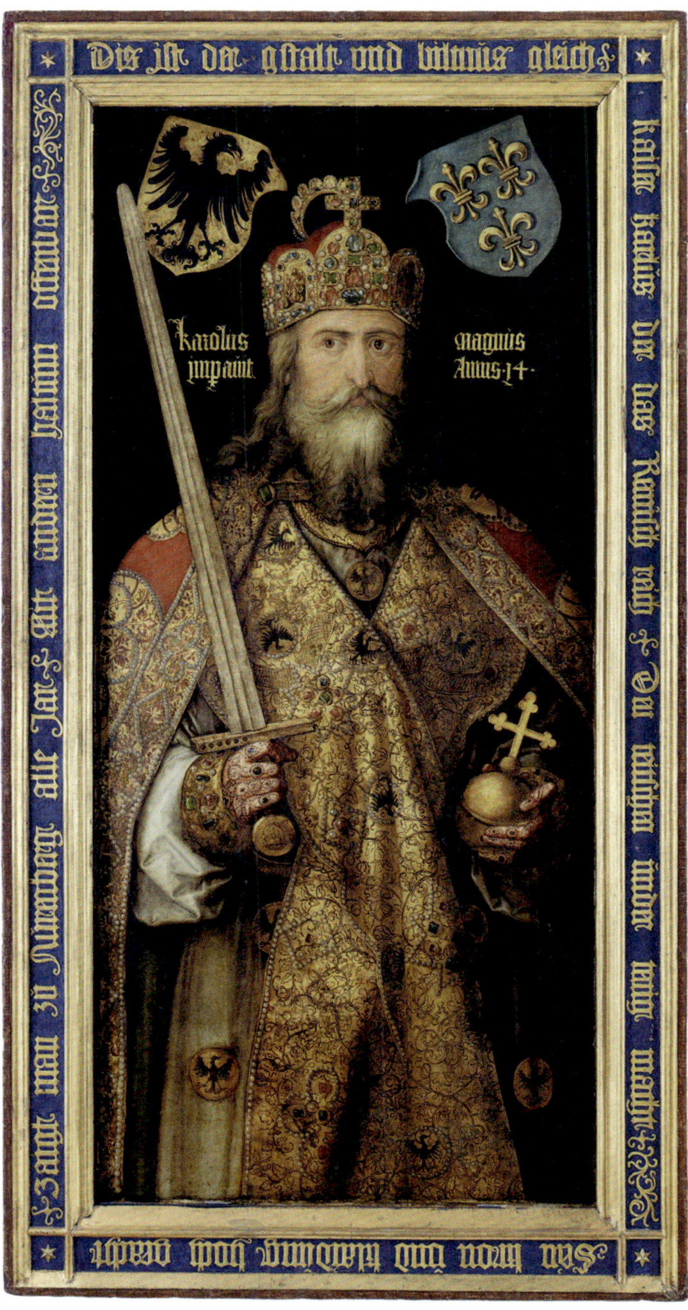

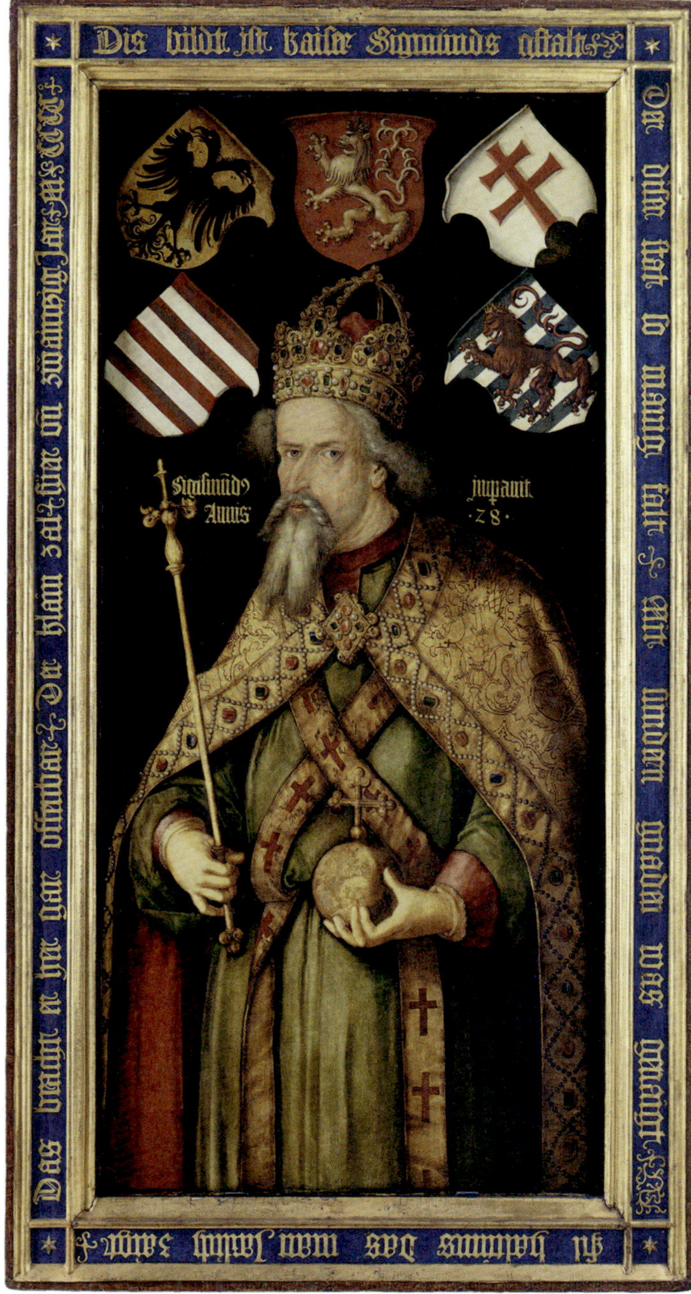

8

THE IMPERIAL RELICS

Attributed to **Friedrich Juvenel**

Nuremberg, ca. 1645

Oil on canvas

H. 120 cm; W. 90 cm

GNM, inv. no. Gm557, on long-term loan from the Museen der Stadt Nürnberg, Kunstsammlungen

References:
Murr 1801, p. 373, no. 21; Tacke 1995, pp. 129–32, cat. no. 58; Tacke 2001b, pp. 79–83; Grieb 2007, vol. 2, p. 739.

At the behest of Emperor Sigismund of Luxembourg (1368–1437), the imperial regalia were transferred to Nuremberg for permanent safekeeping in 1424. In addition to rulership insignia and the coronation vestments of the Roman-German kings and emperors, the regalia included the sacred relics depicted in this painting. The rightful ruler had to be in possession of these objects—also known as the "imperial treasure" (*Reichskleinodien*)—at the time of his coronation. The presence of these highly important imperial artifacts in Nuremberg not only underscored the city's central significance to the emperor and empire, but it also lastingly influenced Nuremberg's self-image and widespread renown. The distinction of being one of the foremost imperial cities was a decisive impetus for Nuremberg's development into a global center of culture, art, and trade.

The painting contains life-size depictions of the containers in which the imperial relics were kept and displayed. These reliquaries were crafted at different times. The top row in the painting includes two reliquaries made by Hans Krug (d. 1519) in Nuremberg in 1518, each adorned with small figures of the city's patron saints, Sebaldus and Lawrence. The vessels are said to have contained pieces of the tablecloth from the Last Supper and of the apron Christ wore while washing his disciples' feet. Together with the reliquary of the tooth of John the Baptist, they stand silhouetted against the painting's black background. The reliquaries further down purportedly held a piece of wood from the Christ Child's crib; chain links associated with the apostles Peter, Paul, and John the Evangelist; a fragment of John's robe; pieces of the True Cross; and an arm bone of Saint Anne. The immediate foreground is occupied by the Holy Lance, the weapon with which Longinus was said to have stabbed the side of the crucified Christ.

The reliquaries are depicted with a high degree of realism. The display table, covered with a dark red cloth, appears to tilt forward so that all the details of the shining, golden containers are visible in their entirety, without overlapping. In this way, the painting gives the impression of being a pictorial inventory. Inscriptions facilitate the relics' identification.

The painting is neither signed nor dated, and its original function is unknown. In light of stylistic similarities to related drawings by the Nuremberg artist Friedrich Juvenel (1609–1647)—twelve pen-and-ink studies done after the reliquaries, now at the Staatsarchiv in Nuremberg—the painting is attributed to him. As we know from an 1801 publication by Christoph Gottlieb von Murr, the painting was at that time displayed in the town hall's *Schöner Saal* (Beautiful Hall). Yet it could just as well have been painted for the Heilig-Geist-Spital, where the relics were stored in the *Heiltumsschrein*. The shrine hung suspended in the hospital church's chancel, out of the reach of visitors.[1] If the painting was displayed at the Heilig-Geist-Spital, its realistic, life-size renderings would have conveyed to viewers a sense of the objects' real proximity—physically present in the space but hidden from view in the shrine.

Sven Jakstat

1 The *Heiltumsschrein* is now exhibited as part of the permanent collection of the GNM (inv. no. KG187, on long-term loan from the Evangelisch-Lutherische Kirchengemeinde Nürnberg – St. Lorenz). The reliquaries depicted in the painting are now kept in the Imperial Treasury at the Hofburg in Vienna.

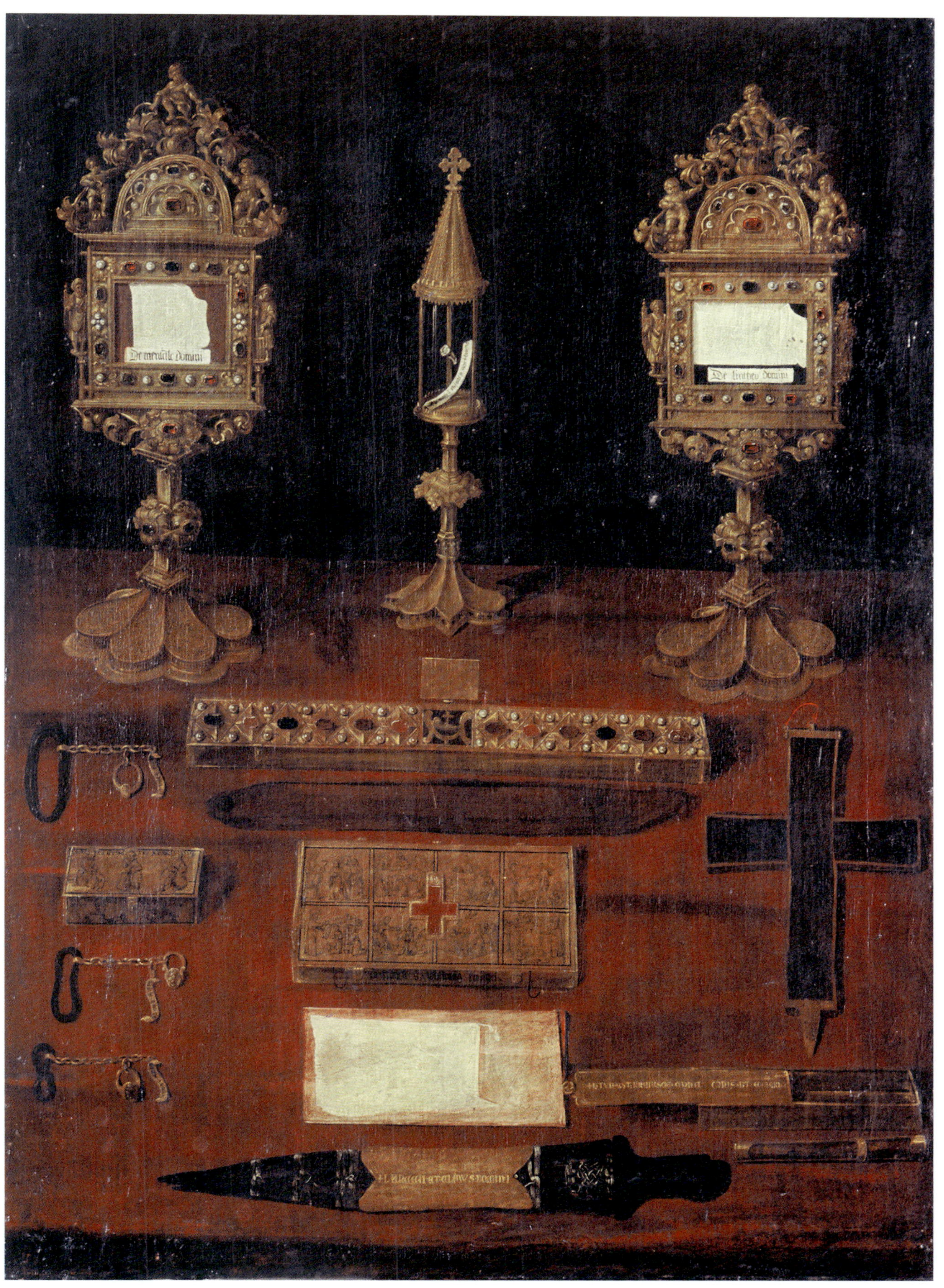

9

THE BURDEN OF CITY GOVERNMENT IN NUREMBERG

Jost Amman or his circle

Nuremberg, ca. 1575–80

Pen and ink, watercolor, heightened with gold

H. 34.4 cm; W. 46.6 cm

Stadtbibliothek im Bildungscampus, Nuremberg, Grafikkästen, inv. no. Nor. K. 6143, no. 333

References:
Exh. cat. Nuremberg 1979, p. 17, cat. no. 6 (Gerhard Hirschmann), ill. p. 19; Tipton 1996, pp. 119, 562 n. 36; Exh. cat. Nuremberg 2000a, pp. 154–55, cat. no. 11 (Matthias Mende); Fleischmann 2008, vol. 1, p. 1, ill. p. 3.

The three elegantly dressed men in this drawing represent Nuremberg's municipal government. The seated patrician at the center supports a model of the city on his shoulders, giving visual expression to the burden of administrative responsibility. His lavish attire—a fur-lined cloak, jewelry, and a beret decorated with gold cords—identifies him as one of the *septemviri*, the seven most powerful city councilors of Nuremberg. He probably stands for the Chief Tax Administrator (*Vorderster Losunger*), the official who presided over the Inner Council, the city's main governing body. The two men accompanying him are clearly lower in rank.[1] The one on the left wears no jewelry or other ornament and appears entirely in black, a fashion that originated at the Spanish royal court. Since he assists the *Losunger* in carrying the model of the city, he was possibly meant to stand for a lower-ranking councilor, such as one of the so-called younger mayors (*Jüngere Bürgermeister*). Those officials likewise came from patrician families but held less-influential posts.[2] The man wearing a beige coat on the right has been identified in the literature as an artisan delegate.[3] Despite the importance of the crafts to Nuremberg's economy, only eight of the Inner Council's forty-two members represented the artisan class, and those eight served in a merely advisory capacity. This interpretation of the figure on the right seems plausible, given that he is not shown supporting the city model.

The depiction primarily emphasizes the Nuremberg city council's good governance. This is indicated by the two attributes that are positioned above the figures and accentuated with delicate gold heightening: a sword standing for high justice (*Blutgerichtsbarkeit* or "blood justice"), including capital punishment, and a pair of scales representing righteous judgment. At the same time, the composition assigns each of the three men a fixed place in the hierarchy of Nuremberg's ranks, as determined by birthright and office. This essentially oligarchic system emerged in Nuremberg in the fourteenth century and became deeply entrenched by the sixteenth century. The patriciate, the class entitled to serve on the Inner Council, recruited representatives from about forty wealthy entrepreneurial families. They formed a kind of municipal aristocracy. It was often members of those families who were networked beyond Nuremberg's vicinity and active in long-distance trade. For them, politics, commerce, and a quasi-aristocratic sense of status were inseparable. Women and members of less privileged social classes were excluded from participation in that patriarchal system of politics.

Little is known about the drawing's function. Susan Tipton compared it with a woodcut from the *Officia Ciceronis* published in Augsburg in 1540, demonstrating that compositions of this sort were not unprecedented in the sixteenth century.[4] One conjecture has been that the Nuremberg sheet was associated with a lost wall painting, but both the former location and the very existence of such a work remain a matter of mere speculation. The drawing entered the collections of the Nuremberg Stadtbibliothek as part of a volume compiled by the chronicler Georg Paul Amberger (1789–1844).[5]

Benno Baumbauer

1 For that reason, the interpretation of the figures as representing Nuremberg's triumvirs fails to convince. In the "Rieter Geschlechterbuch" (StANbg, D 14, B 24, fol. 231r), for example, the *septemviri* are all dressed consistently in fur-lined cloaks and berets. Classifying the two lateral figures with certainty will require a more extensive study of costume.
2 It is also possible that the figure represents a merchant belonging to the category of *Ehrbarkeit* (honorability), a wealthy class that, unlike the patriciate, was not eligible to hold seats on the Inner Council.
3 Exh. cat. Nuremberg 2000a, p. 154, cat. no. 11 (Matthias Mende).
4 Tipton 1996, pp. 118–19, 563, fig. 37.
5 On Amberger, see Grieb 2007, vol. 1, p. 20.

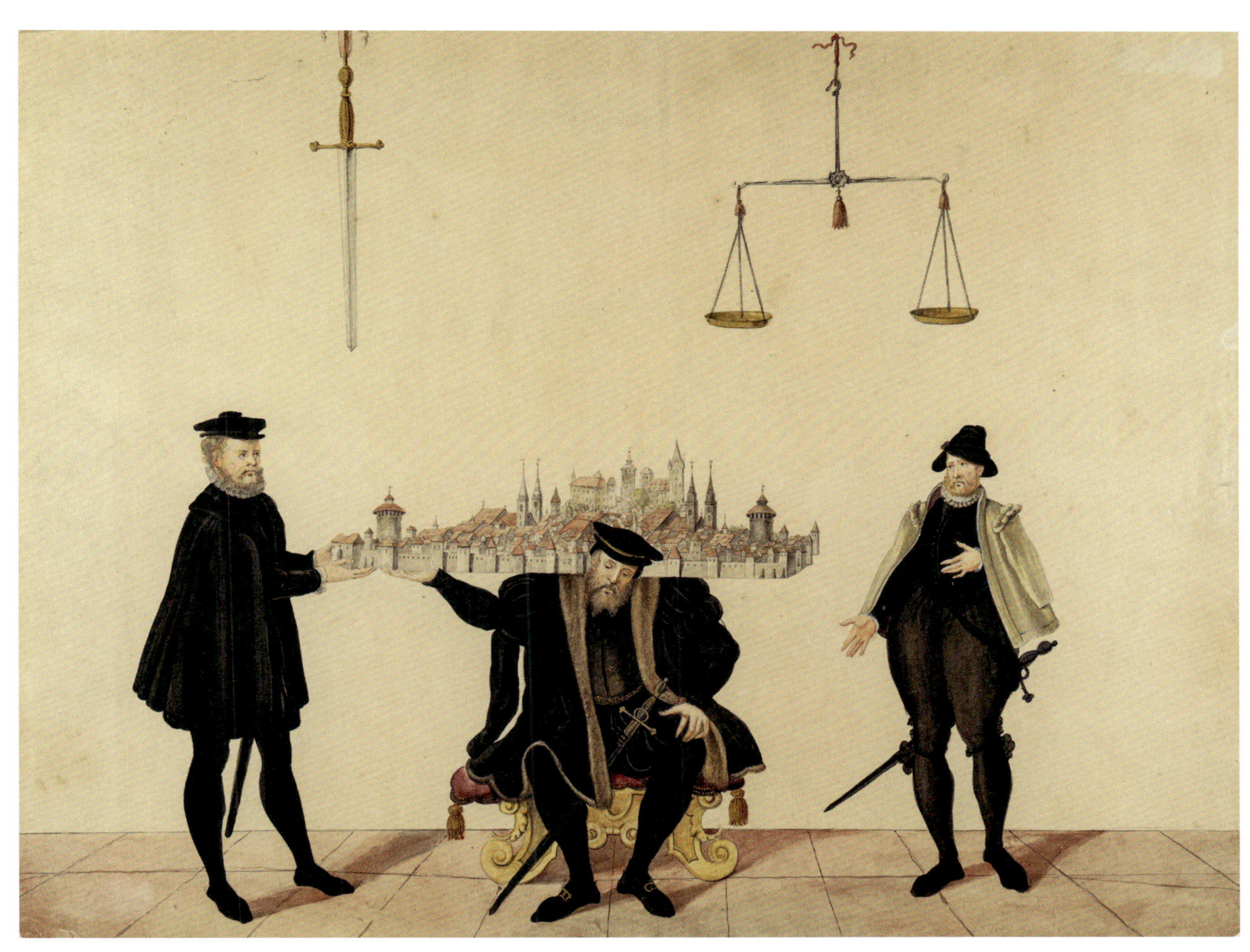

10

MOSES AND FOLIATED CONSOLE, FROM THE SCHÖNER BRUNNEN

Nuremberg, 1385–1396

Gray sandstone

10.1 Moses

The lower third, up to knee height, nineteenth-century reconstruction in plaster

H. 91 cm; W. 34 cm; D. 23 cm

GNM, inv. no. Pl.O.261

10.2 Console

Surface reworked with a glossy substance

H. 30.5 cm; W. 24 cm; D. 27 cm

GNM, inv. no. Pl.O.282

On long-term loan from the Museen der Stadt Nürnberg, Kunstsammlungen

References:
Wilder 1824; Bergau 1871; Gümbel 1906; Exh. cat. Nuremberg and New York 1986, pp. 132–35, cat. no. 14 (Rainer Kahsnitz); Weilandt 2019.

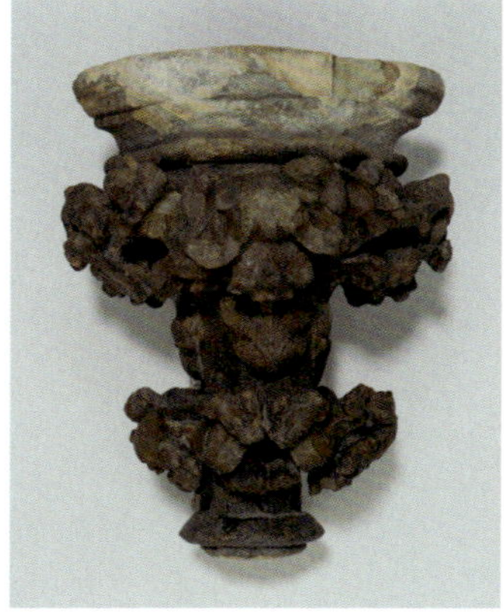

cat. no. 10.2. Console

As a monument to the imperial city's self-image, the *Schöner Brunnen* (Beautiful Fountain), commissioned by the Nuremberg city council and erected on what was then called the Herrenmarkt, is a counterpart to the Frauenkirche |**cat. no. 11**|. While chronicles report that construction began in 1362, the surviving invoices fall between the years 1385 and 1396. The invoices also reveal the name of the creator, "Master Heinrich, the *Parlirer* [construction foreman]"—most likely Heinrich Beheim the Elder.

The fountain's tower, which rises 17.3 meters above the water basin, is designed as an octagonal, buttressed pyramid. It consists of three tiers and culminates in a slender pinnacle supporting a cruciform finial at the top. Each level is constructed according to the same principle: an octagonal parapet of open tracery has pinnacled columns at the corners that rise up and are spanned by pointed arches. Ornamental gables crown the arches and overlap the boundaries between the tiers. The stepped diminution of each tier's ground plan causes the structure to taper. Further pinnacles, freestanding but connected by buttresses to the pyramid's core, elegantly conceal the abrupt setbacks from one tier to the next.

The architectural framework displays an extensive sculptural program that visualizes the historical and conceptual context in which Nuremberg existed as a free imperial city. In the tower's bottom tier, the figures of the seven electors and "Nine Good Heroes"—first individually identified by Hans Rosenplüt in 1447 (published in 1490)—personify the imperial order and good rulership. The sculptures in the tier above and at the level of the water basin expand the program to encompass universal history and the history of Christian salvation: above, Moses and seven biblical prophets; below, the evangelists, church fathers, and eight exemplary thinkers and authors of antiquity (originally unspecified). This program, which reflects the city's endeavor to situate itself in the religiopolitical order and in the course of history, is characteristic of municipal self-representation in the late Middle Ages.

At the same time, the bold, towering architecture underscores the major engineering achievement represented by the *Schöner Brunnen*, Nuremberg's first municipal fountain. In contrast to wells, which often provided water of dubious quality, the fountain was supplied with fresh spring water. An ingenious system of pipes carried the water to the city center over a distance of nearly three kilometers. The so-called Schönbrunn pipeline, built in 1388, ran from the spring at Gleißhammer castle to a chamber directly beneath the fountain, from where the water was then distributed via lead pipes to a total of sixteen outlets. Meticulous descriptions by Heinrich Scharpf (1459) and Endres Tucher (1464) of the double wood-log piping and all the associated features—including masonry channels that conveyed the water to the piping, collection basins, drains, inspection openings, and tapping points—gives an idea of the great effort required to supply the city with drinking water.

To protect the fountain from being soiled or vandalized, a surrounding grating was installed from the very beginning (renovated by Paulus Kuhn in 1587). However, despite all the protective measures and continual maintenance, the fountain had to undergo extensive restoration from 1821 to 1824, at which time only a sixth of the original parts were reused. From 1897 to 1902, a complete copy was erected. With the exception of three prophets' heads, the surviving original parts—about half of the sculpted figures and architectural sculpture and about 40 percent of the tracery and canopies—were placed on loan to the Germanisches Nationalmuseum by the city of Nuremberg.

Markus T. Huber

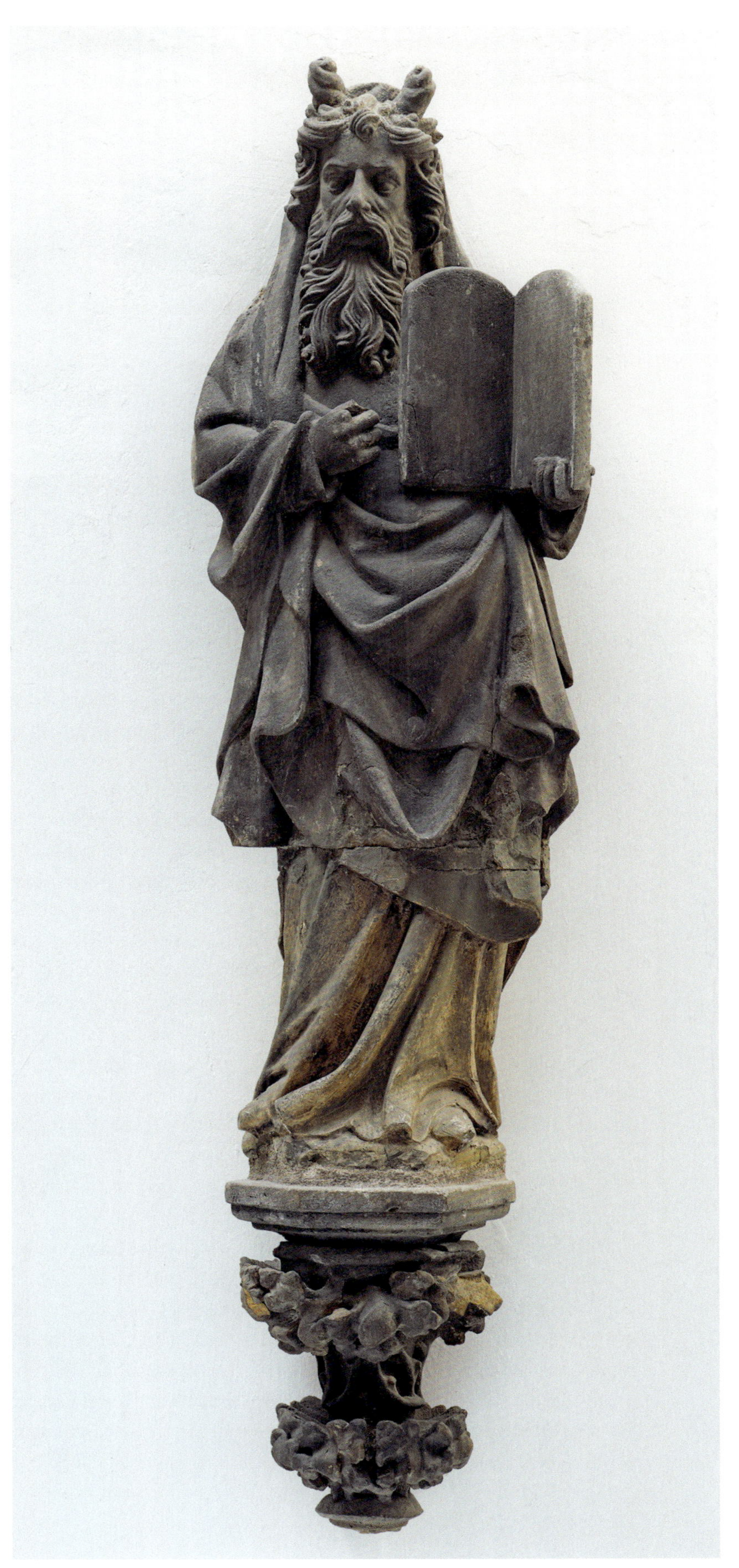

11

THE ANNUNCIATION, FROM THE SOUTHERN PORTAL OF THE FRAUENKIRCHE

Nuremberg, ca. 1355–60

Sandstone

11.1 The Virgin Mary

1879–80, hand positions of the Virgin Mary changed

H. 139.5 cm; W. 35 cm; D. 35 cm

GNM, inv. no. Pl.O.2426

11.2 Angel

1879–80, wings and inscription on the banderole reconstructed

H. 146.5 cm; W. 47 cm; D. 33 cm

GNM, inv. no. Pl.O.2425

References:
Bräutigam 1961; Exh. cat. Nuremberg and New York 1986, pp. 118–19, cat. no. 5 (Rainer Kahsnitz); Weilandt 2013; Hörsch 2019, pp. 63–75; Srovnal 2019.

The power of the Holy Roman Emperor is put on display in the grand facade of the Frauenkirche, the church first mentioned as the *capella regia* (royal chapel) in 1361 |**fig. pp. 6–7**|. The church's construction was preceded by an atrocity: the pogrom on December 5, 1349, in which 562 Jews were murdered. Charles IV had helped to incite the pogrom in a document issued on November 16 of that year. His decree contained the plan to destroy the Jewish quarter, located in the city center, in order to make room for two market squares and the Frauenkirche (Church of Our Lady), which would replace the demolished synagogue. Putting the new church under the patronage of the Virgin Mary was done with express purpose, for she was regarded as personifying the allegorical triumph of the Church (*Ecclesia*) over the Synagogue.

The Frauenkirche's foundation stone was laid shortly after the demolition of the Jewish quarter. Construction began with the chancel, simple and unadorned, and continued westward. Although initiated by the emperor, this was a building project of the Nuremberg city council. On his return from being crowned emperor in Rome on July 8, 1355, Charles carried out the official act of foundation. He appointed a small council of canons subordinate to the Prague Cathedral chapter. With Charles's foundation formalized in a document, the building took on an increasingly imperial character. That aspect found visual expression on the western facade, with its lavish ornamentation and sculptural decoration, its magnificently designed vestibule, and the Saint Michael's choir, which served as an imperial oratory. The Frauenkirche became part of the rulership symbolism cultivated by Charles. This is confirmed by a presentation of the imperial relics |**see cat. no. 7**| that took place in 1361 on the balcony of the vestibule; the occasion was the baptism of Charles's son Wenceslas, the heir to the throne. Even in the emperor's absence, the church building projected his authority.[1] The coats of arms of the electors, the empire, and the city of Rome which are displayed on the parapet above the portal represent the imperial constitution that Charles established in the Golden Bull of 1356.

Charles must have followed the Frauenkirche's construction with great interest. Even the choice of architect—presumably Heinrich Parler the Elder, the builder of the Heilig-Kreuz-Münster in Schwäbisch Gmünd—may have been influenced by the emperor. There is much to suggest that Heinrich Parler's extraordinarily talented son Peter oversaw the project for a time. Peter appears to have performed that task so brilliantly that Charles appointed him, at the young age of only twenty-three, probably in 1356, as imperial master builder in Prague. By the time the imperial foundation was confirmed by the bishop of Bamberg, on January 11, 1362, construction of the Frauenkirche was probably finished or at least near completion.[2]

The church has a remarkably complex iconographical program, with striking emphasis on the incarnation and infancy of Christ. It is unlikely, however, that this iconography should be understood as a personal statement of Charles IV;[3] rather, the program was probably developed by a member of the council of canons around the fundamental theological notion of Christ's incarnation.[4] The architectural sculpture contains more than four representations of the annunciation to the Virgin Mary by the archangel Gabriel. The Annunciation group from the southern portal is distinguished by its emphasis on the moment of Jesus's conception in Mary's womb. This rare formulation of the subject has parallels in art made for the imperial court in Prague. The figures also differ stylistically from earlier sculpture produced in Nuremberg. They closely resemble the sculptures located inside the vestibule, which reflect the style of the Parler milieu.

Markus T. Huber

1 Hörsch 2019, p. 73.
2 Hörsch 2019, p. 67.
3 Compare, however, Weilandt 2013.
4 Srovnal 2019, p. 390.

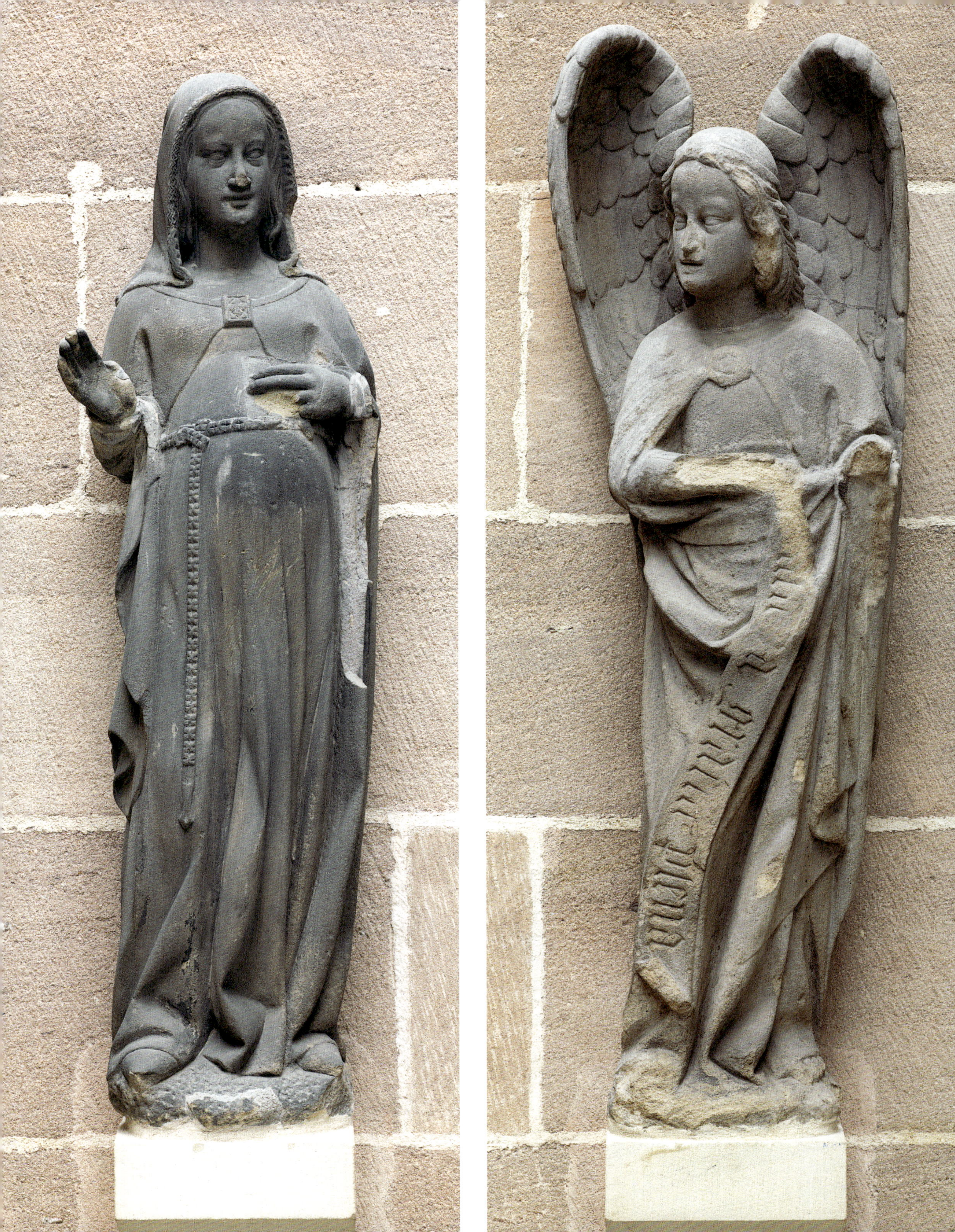

12

TOMBSTONE OF JOCKLIN

Nuremberg, 1464 (repurposed in 1499)

Sandstone

H. 99.5 cm; W. 81 cm; D. 18.5 cm

GNM, inv. no. A3163

References:
Frommann 1875, col. 182; Seidl 1983, pp. 64–66, cat. no. 16; Hoppe 2002, pp. 71–72; Kammel 2018, pp. 13–14; Purin and Selheim 2025, pp. 214–15, cat. no. 66 (Bernhard Purin).

Jocklin. / This stone that I erected is / a monument at the head of the old man, the honorable / Jakob, son of Abraham, who was buried on the eighth / day of the month Shevat in the year 5000 / and 224 to the counting [January 18, 1464]. – May his soul be bound in the bundle of life / Amen – Selah[1]

This tombstone, elegantly decorated with a trefoil arch, bears a Hebrew inscription honoring a man by the name of Jocklin (Jakob), a notable Jewish figure who lived in Nuremberg in the mid-fifteenth century, an important period for the city and its Jewish community. This Jakob was Jakob of Schweinfurt (before 1394–1464), and his extended family is well documented. He was the son of Abraham of Coburg, the brother of the Ulm-based Rabbi Seligmann of Coburg, the husband of Gutlein (d. 1465), the father of Abraham, Mair, David, Seligmann, Maitalein, Gutlein, and Mindlein, and the father-in-law of Rabbi David Frank and Jossel of Hof.[2] Jakob was a prominent moneylender and merchant, attested in Schweinfurt from 1434 to 1439, where he appears to have been the head of the local Jewish community. He spent the years 1442 to 1447 in Würzburg. Then, until his death, although not without interruption, he lived in Nuremberg, where he owned houses and had citizen status. He held protective charters issued by the city of Nuremberg and regional authorities, and his network comprised significant figures such as bishops, members of the nobility, and municipal officials throughout Franconia.

Jakob's life is also marked by his engagement in the Jewish community. In January 1455, the authorities in Nuremberg approved his position as a Dajan, or judge, in the city's Jewish council: "He should also be of legal standing to citizens and foreigners, who may have a right to appeal to the court and council or to the Jewish Council of Nuremberg, where the matter is heard."[3] In a conflict of 1458 over rabbinical authority in Nuremberg, Jakob supported his son-in-law, Rabbi David Frank, as an alternative to Rabbi David Sprintz—a move that sparked debate and involved influential rabbis from across the German-speaking lands as well as the Nuremberg city council.[4] Tensions of this sort underscore the political and religious complexity of Jewish life in medieval Nuremberg and reflect the central role that figures like Jakob played in shaping the community dynamics.

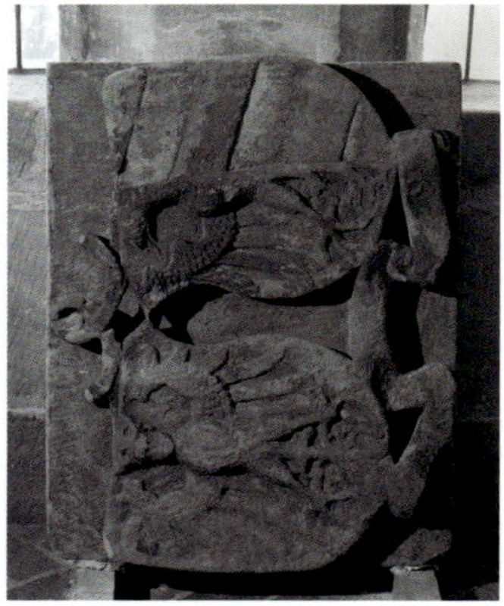

Back of the tombstone

While the front of the tombstone reflects a success story of Jewish life in fifteenth-century Nuremberg, the back gives an indication of the community's tragic end. The stone's reverse, rotated by 90 degrees, bears the date "1499" alongside Nuremberg's two municipal coats of arms: the "greater" one with the *Königskopfadler* (eagle with the head of a king) and the "lesser" one. Following the 1499 expulsion of Jews from the city, the Jewish cemetery near the Münz- and Manggasse, where the gravestone initially stood, was destroyed. In the aftermath of expulsions of Jews throughout Europe during the fourteenth and fifteenth centuries, many cities demolished Jewish cemeteries by repurposing the tombstones as building materials for houses, churches, and public structures. Jakob's grave marker, too, was put to new use for an official municipal building. It was incorporated into a wall of the inn "Zum Roten Ochsen" (At the Red Ox), formerly located across from the Mauthalle, near the address Königstraße 41. In 1875, while the inn was being demolished, Jakob's gravestone and another, this one belonging to a woman named Pessl, daughter of Rabbi Menachem (d. 1477), were rediscovered and transferred to the Germanisches Nationalmuseum.

Today, Jakob's tombstone not only commemorates the life of a notable Jewish burgher of Nuremberg but also serves as a witness to the multilayered history of Jewish–Christian relations in the city. Through its secondary use as building material, the stone is emblematic of the marginalization and erasure of Jewish presence within the urban landscape.

Meyrav Levy

1 We know lines 6 and 7 only from the documentation of 1875. This translation of the Hebrew inscription is based on those found in Seidl 1983, p. 64, and Purin 2025, p. 131.
2 Seidl 1983, pp. 64–66.
3 Salfeld and Stern 1894–96, p. 294 (translated by Meyrav Levy).
4 Maimon, Breuer, and Guggenheim 1995, p. 1017.

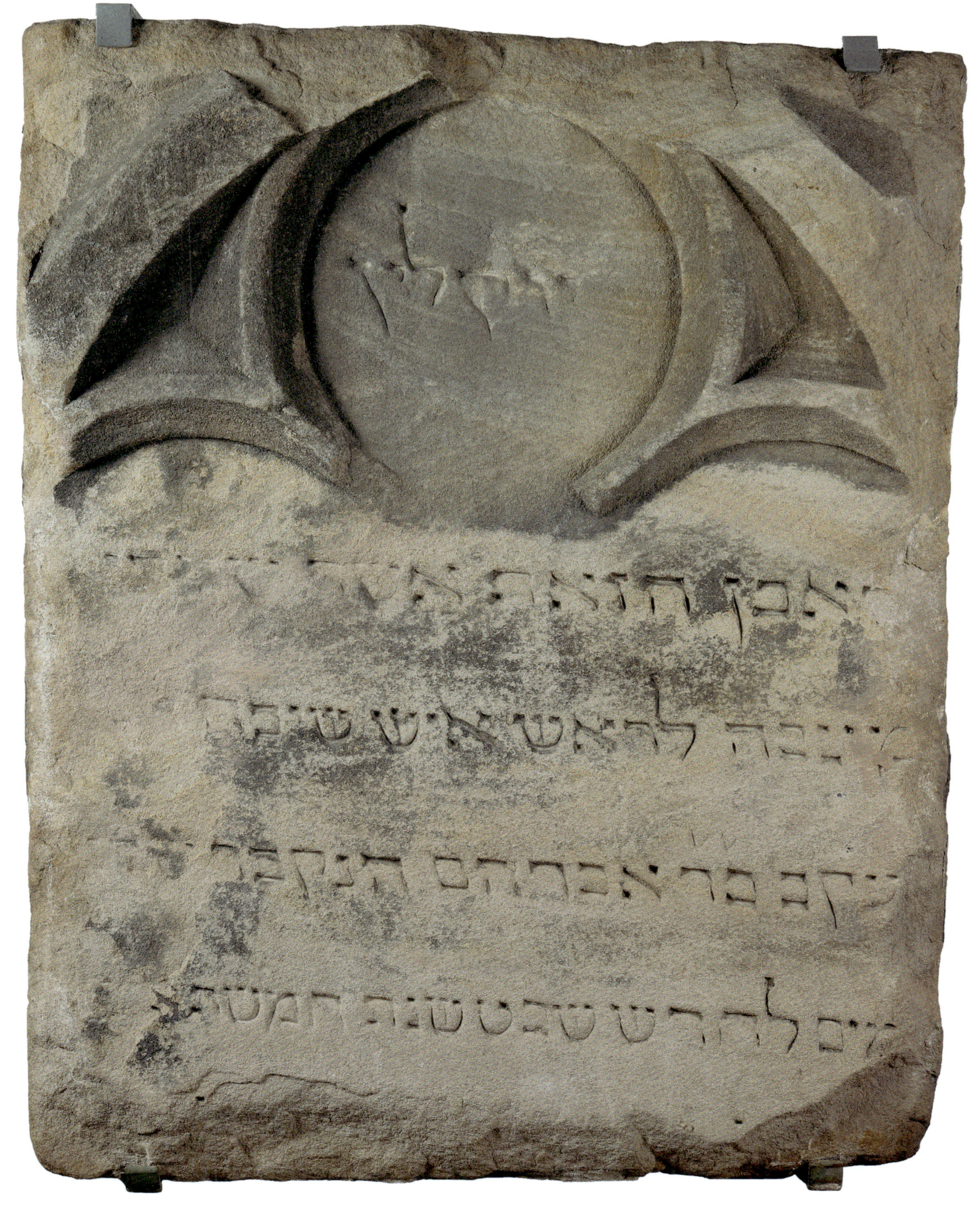

13

PENTATEUCH FOR THE NUREMBERG CITY COUNCIL

First half of thirteenth century

Binding: **Meir ben Israel Jaffe of Ulm**

Nuremberg, ca. 1468

Parchment, 151 leaves, cut-leather technique (cuir ciselé)

H. 23.5 cm; W. 18 cm

Bayerische Staatsbibliothek, Munich, Cod.hebr. 212

References:
Steinschneider 1895, p. 94, no. 12; Husung 1925–26, pp. 29–43; Katzenstein 1982, pp. 17, 20; Sternthal, Cohen-Mushlin, and Levy 2009–14; Steimann 2019, pp. 77–102.

This exquisite leather binding, crafted by the Jewish bookbinder, scribe, and illustrator Meir ben Israel Jaffe of Ulm, stands as a testament to the remarkable mobility of Jewish artists in Europe during the Middle Ages—and to their dynamic coexistence with Christian society. Although details of Jaffe's personal life remain elusive, it is assumed that he was the son of Israel ben Meir of Heidelberg, the celebrated scribe of the Darmstadt Haggadah.[1] In the latter half of the fifteenth century, Jaffe journeyed widely, binding and copying manuscripts. He visited Nuremberg at least twice: first to do work for Hans von Thill, a member of the city's *ehrbar* (honorable) rank, and later in service to the city council. A decree from July 4, 1468, records that the council commissioned "Meyerlein, Juden von Ulm" to bind several volumes for its library, permitting him a four-month stay, until November 11 of that year.[2]

The luxurious binding presented here is the sole surviving example of Jaffe's work in Nuremberg. It covers a thirteenth-century Ashkenazi Hebrew Pentateuch, or Torah.[3] Originally kept in the city council's library, this Pentateuch allowed Jews to take a ceremonial oath (the *Judeneid* or Jewish oath) on the Five Books of Moses in Christian court. A sheet attached to the front of folio 52 bears a fifteenth-century Jewish oath in German, invoking the name of the God of Israel and Old Testament curses against falsehood |**fig. p. 35**|. Such oaths were sworn in the context of lawsuits and for the conferral of citizenship status to Jews ("Judenburckrecht" or *Judenbürgerrecht*), which typically had to be annually renewed.[4]

The binding is adorned in the traditional cut-leather technique (cuir ciselé), in which delicate ornaments and figures are incised into moistened leather and then brought into relief by compression of the surrounding areas. This craft, which flourished in the fourteenth and fifteenth centuries, was likely introduced to central Europe from Spain and Portugal by Jewish artisans.

The front cover features a frame inscribed in Gothic Hebrew script by Meir Jaffe: "החומש להעיצה מנירנבערקא שיחי מאיר יפ[ה] המצייר" (The Pentateuch for the Council of Nuremberg, [long] may he live, Meir Jaffe, the decorator). The central panel displays Nuremberg's coat of arms and, below, a deer raising its right foreleg, both set against a background of vine scroll decoration. This intriguing fusion of Gothic Hebrew script with the official emblem of a Christian city encapsulates the integral role of Jews in the urban fabric, particularly with regard to the municipal authorities' acceptance and regulation of Jewish economic activities and legal status, and with regard to Jewish contributions to the local artistic idiom.

Meyrav Levy

1 Universitäts- und Landesbibliothek Darmstadt, Cod-Or-8.
2 Avrin 2010, p. 313; Husung 1925–26, pp. 29–43.
3 "Ashkenaz" is the Hebrew term for the German-speaking lands.
4 Steimann 2019, pp. 77–102; Sternthal, Cohen-Mushlin, and Levy 2009–14.

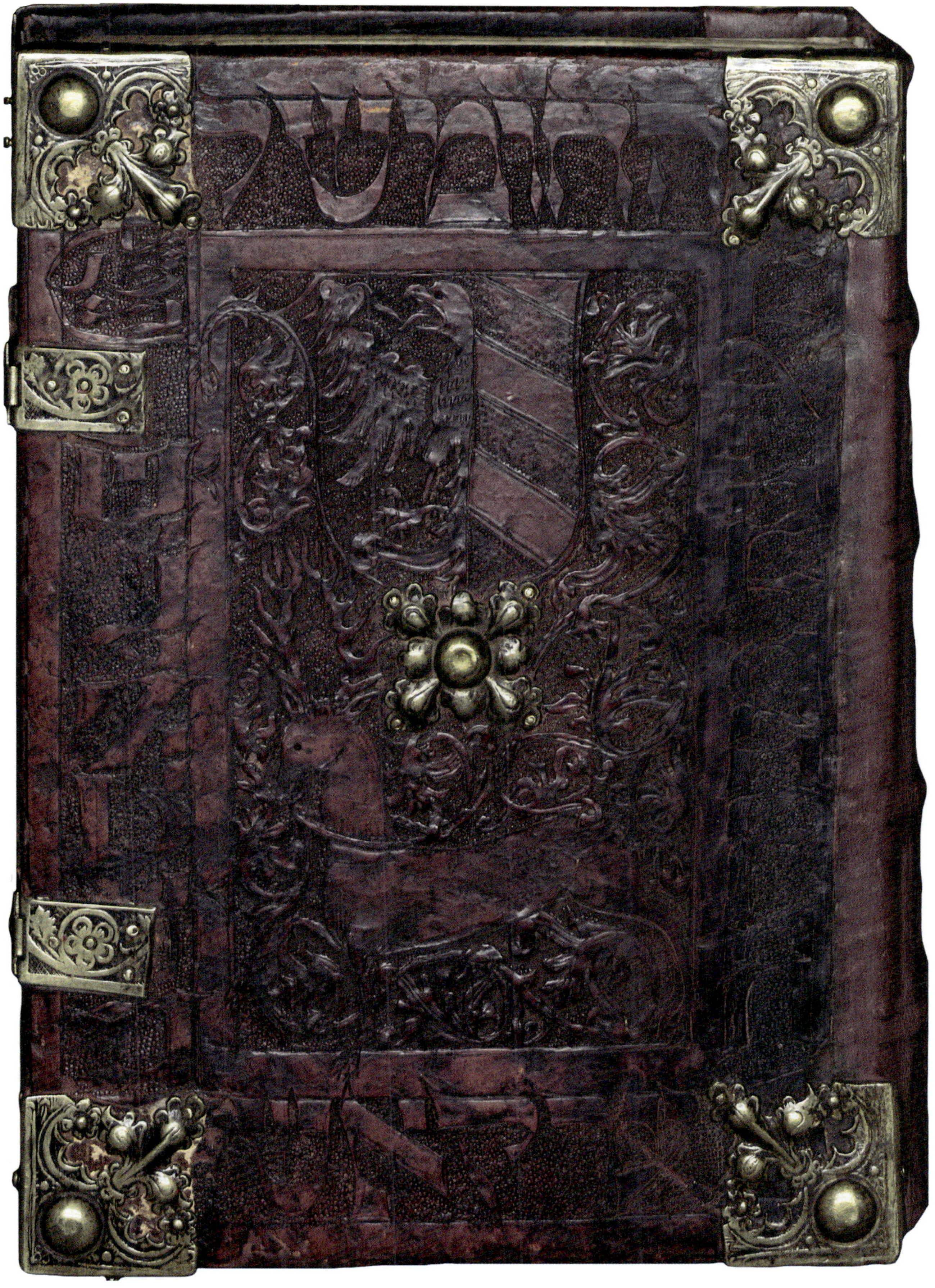

14

NURENBERG CHRONICLE

Hartmann Schedel
Translated from Latin to German by Georg Alt
Augsburg: Johann Schönsperger, 1496

Incunable, 317 leaves, woodcut illustrations

H. 43 cm; W. 29 cm (opened)

GNM, Inc. 4° 5540

Open to fols. 296v–297r: The alleged ritual murder of Simon of Trent

References:
Hellwig 1970, pp. 255–56, no. 833; Treue 1996, pp. 308–45, 371–72; Esposito 2003, p. 133; Teter 2020, pp. 14–42; Maxwell 2022, pp. 41–43.

The so-called *Nuremberg Chronicle*, first published in 1493, was one of the most influential works of the early age of printing |**cat. no. 4**|. Its blend of texts compiled by Hartmann Schedel and vivid woodcut illustrations created by Michael Wolgemut and Wilhelm Pleydenwurff reached a wide audience. However, unauthorized versions also appeared. This increased the reach of the work as a whole, including one of its images that is emblematic of the era's deep-seated antisemitic sentiments: the illustration depicting the alleged ritual murder of Simon of Trent. The unauthorized Augsburg edition of 1496, produced in smaller format, reproduces the scene in a far more schematic woodcut than that of the original.

In 1475, the death of a two-year-old named Simon in the northern Italian episcopal city of Trent gave rise to false accusations against members of the local Jewish community—namely, that they had murdered Simon to use his blood for ritual purposes. Accusations of this sort, known as blood libels, had long circulated in Europe. Although entirely unfounded, the allegation against the Jews of Trent triggered instances of brutal torture, forced confessions, and, ultimately, the execution of nineteen Jews. Their families were expelled, their property was confiscated, and the story of Simon's supposed martyrdom rapidly took on a life of its own, amplified by local clergymen and perpetuated in works of art and texts. Simon was venerated as a saint in parts of Europe, which fueled hostilities and served to justify the oppression of Jewish communities. This was the reason for illustrating the scene in the *Nuremberg Chronicle*, where it appears in a series of representations of saints' martyrdoms.

Compared with the image of Simon's alleged murder in the original Nuremberg edition, which was based on a 1475 woodcut published by Albrecht Kunne in Trent, the depiction in the Augsburg edition is smaller, reversed, simplified, and less gory. Nevertheless, the fiendish visual mechanisms operating in the image remain clear to see. Simon is shown surrounded by a group of Jewish men and one woman, who cut him with a knife, stab him with a large needle, and collect his blood in a bowl. The perpetrators are marked with the ring-shaped badge (yellow in real life) that Jews were forced to wear, and they are labeled with Old Testament and Ashkenazic names. Such imagery powerfully reinforced stereotypes of Jews as dangerous outsiders, fueling the spread of antisemitic narratives far beyond Trent. The composition's calculated resemblance to images of the Circumcision of Christ is particularly malicious, as it stigmatizes that Jewish ritual by playing on Christians' visual experience.

The *Nuremberg Chronicle* remains a testament to the complex legacy of the era of early print, when technology's power to disseminate knowledge also became a tool for spreading destructive ideologies. The woodcut was part of a broader development in which fear and prejudice against Jews found expression in widely circulated images and texts. These narratives had devastating, long-lasting effects on Jewish life and gave rise to recurrent persecutions of Jews, including their mass expulsions from European cities throughout the fifteenth and sixteenth centuries. In 1499, only six years after the initial publication of Schedel's world chronicle, all Jews were expelled from Nuremberg |**see cat. no. 12**|.

Meyrav Levy and Benno Baumbauer

gen durch Lumbardiam vnd Tusciam gān
rom gezogen vnd von allen fürsten. herrñ. vnd
der commun regierern mit großen eren vnnd
züchten empfangen worden. Zů rom kam im
die wierdig samlunge der cardinel entgegen.
Darnach ward er von babst Sixto dem vier
den gar erlichen empfangen. vnd mit der gul
din rosen (die die bābst alle jar am suntag czů
mittfasten einem cristenlichen fürsten pflegē
zegeben) zů sunderer ere begabet. Daselbst fieg
en an von gemaynem frid cristenlicher fürstē
zehandlen vnnd einen gemaynen zuge wider
dye türcken zebewegen. Aber nach dē er nichtz
geschaffen mocht do keret er durch die welsch
en stet allēthalb erlich gehalten wid' anhaims
Alda lebet er ettliche jar in gůttem tugentlich
en leben vnnd ebenpild der heyligkeyte bis in
sein ennde. Diser Cristiernus hat zů einer eege
mahel gehebt die durchleüchtigen Dorotheã
geborne marggreffin zů brādenburg die noch
mals in leben ist

CArolus hertzog zů bürgundi belegeret
die statt Neüße vnderhalb Cöln am
Rhein gelegen. Aber als kayser Fride
rich mit mechtiger heerßkrafft des gantzē rö
mischen reichs den belegerten czů hilffe kome
do machet der hertzog mit dē kayser ein pünt
nuße vñ zoh mit seinem heer vor neüß ab.

GNadenreich jar vō babst Paulo auff
gesatzt ward vō babst Sixto jm. M
cccc. jar gehalten vnnd durch den kü
Ferdinandum auch gān Rome deßmales ko
mende zwischen den welschen fürsten vñ com
munen auß verwilligūg des babsts ein pünt
nus fürgenomen. vnd der künig für den ersten
darinn bestymbt vñ eingeschriben.

Hercules hertzog
zů Ferraria

HErcules estensis
marggrafen Ni
clasen sun vnnd
des Borsij brůder der and'
hertzog zů ferraria hat nitt
on großen widerstand sein
vetterlich herrschafft diser
zeit annemende bißhieher
geregiert. ei güter. synreich
er vnd ritterlicher sachē ge
übter man. Diser Hercules hat helionorā des
künigs Ferdinandi tochter gar ein behertztes
weib zů eegemahel genomen. vnd auß jre vier
sün vñ zwů töchter empfangen. Diser Hercules ward auß seines schwehers rat vñ anreg-
ung beweget sich von den Venedigern zewen
den vnnd in desselben seines schwehers vnnd
andrer seiner mituerwanten püündtnus vñ ge-
selschafft zekomen. vnnd der venediger pünt-
nus vnnd freyheit zeuerletzen. Demnach ver-
folgten die venediger disen herculem zů lande
vnd zů wasser vñd entwendeten jm villands
also wo alphunsus der hertzog Calabria des
künigs Ferdinandi sun gar ein streytper man
mit der waffen. vnd der babst mit dem pann
nit ob disem Hercules gehalten hetten so wār
es vmb in geschehen gewest. Als aber darna
chent die sachen vnder jnen allen gestilt ward
do hat er seydher die stat ferrariā mit vil schönen gepeüwen erleüchtet gemacht.

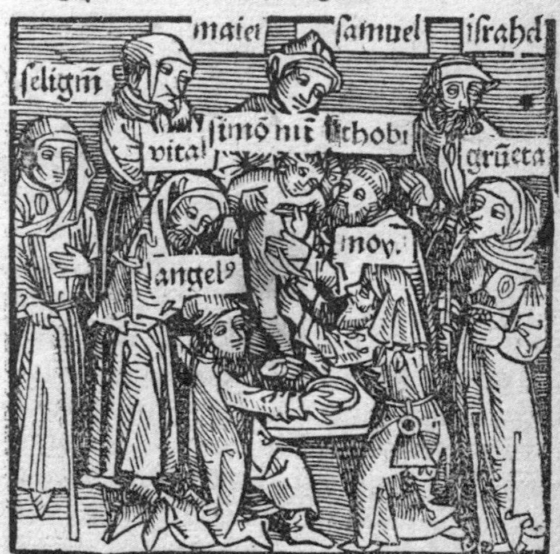

SImon das sellig kindlein zů Trient
ist am. xxj. tag des mertzen nach der
geburt Cristi. M. cccc. lxxv. jar in der
der heyligen marterwochen in der stat Trient
von dē judē getödt vñ ein marter cristi wordē
dañ als die judē in d' selbē stat wonēde jr oster
nach jrm sittē begeen woltē vñ doch kain cri-
stēlichs plůt zů geprauch jrs vngeseürtē prots
hettē do brachtē sy diß kindlein verstolēs in sa
muelis eins judē hauß in solcher gestalt. an dē
dritten tag vor ostrens vmb die vesperzeit saß
diß kindlein vor seines vatters thüre in abwe-
sen seiner eltern do nāhnet sich Thobias ein jü
discher verrāeter zů disem kindlein dz noch nit
dreymal zehen monat alt wz. dem redet er mitt
schmaichelworten zů vnnd trůg es pald in dz
hauß Samuelis. Als nün dye nacht herfiel do
frewetē sich. Samuel. Thobias Vitalis Moy
ses Jsrahel vnnd Mayer vor d' synagog über

15

THE ADORATION OF THE MAGI

Hans Pleydenwurff and workshop

Bamberg or Nuremberg, ca. 1455–60

Paint on fir

H. 150.0 cm; W. 71.3 cm

GNM, inv. no. Gm132

References:
Hess, Hirschfelder, and Baum 2019, pp. 379–93, cat. no. 27 (Beate Fücker and Dagmar Hirschfelder); Exh. cat. Nuremberg 2019b, pp. 164–65, cat. no. 6 (Dagmar Hirschfelder).

In 1457, the painter Hans Pleydenwurff (d. 1471–72) relocated his workshop from the episcopal city of Bamberg to nearby Nuremberg. Around roughly the same time, he completed an altarpiece devoted to the Virgin Mary that was probably intended for the burial site of Canon Georg von Löwenstein (d. 1464) in Bamberg Cathedral. This *Adoration of the Magi*, showing the Three Kings bringing gifts to the Christ Child seated on the Virgin's lap, was located on the inner side of the altarpiece's right wing, visible when the ensemble was opened.

Apart from its religious content, the Adoration scene can also be interpreted from a global-historical perspective. In the fifteenth century, the magi were construed as representatives of the three continents known to Europeans at the time. While Pleydenwurff did not clearly distinguish between the two figures that stand for Asia and Europe, he depicted the African magus as Black and equipped him with attributes that were associated with Africa. These include a golden earring |**see cat. no. 118**| and a crown suggestive of helmets worn in northern Africa. He is presenting the Christ Child with a precious vessel made from an ostrich egg.[1]

Ostrich egg settings often served as exclusive diplomatic gifts in late-medieval Europe. The connection with the Black magus illustrates the types of associations conveyed by luxury goods of this sort |**see cat. no. 16**|. As also demonstrated by the Behaim Globe |**cat. no. 1**|, on which a large ostrich marks northern Africa, Europeans strongly associated these birds with the African continent. There was also a religious connotation, since eggs, whose pristine shells bear new life, symbolized the inviolate womb of the Virgin Mary.

Pleydenwurff's African magus leaves open the question of whether the artist used a Black man as a model or based the figure on other works of art. As far as we know, the motif of a Black magus first appears in the art of Nuremberg about 1450, in the Kleinschwarzenlohe Altarpiece.[2] The extent to which Pleydenwurff himself may have met Black people in Nuremberg or Bamberg is a topic that requires further study.[3] Yet such encounters could well have happened in the Burgundian Netherlands, where Pleydenwurff is certain to have worked for a time.

Even in the early sixteenth century, the presence of Black Africans in Nuremberg was probably still not an everyday occurrence. It is noteworthy that during Albrecht Dürer's stay in Antwerp in 1521, he drew a portrait study of a woman named Katharina, a Black servant of Dürer's Portuguese host. However, as with Dürer's drawing of an unidentified Black man (now at the Albertina in Vienna), nothing is known about why the artist made these portraits. While Katharina presumably came to Flanders involuntarily and enslaved, there are other relevant aspects to European contact with Africans—for example, the diplomacy cultivated with Christian Ethiopia, which had been intensifying since the mid-fifteenth century.[4] Europeans' awareness of an African empire comprised of Black Christians lent further plausibility to the figure of the Black magus.

Pleydenwurff evidently wished to provide his representative of Africa with a special air of authenticity. Yet in the combination of various prop-like items associated with that continent, he ultimately created a stereotypical figure. This culminates in the inscription on the crown of the Black magus: "MELICHAR REX DE ORIENT S[UM]" (I am Melchior, king from the Orient).

Benno Baumbauer

1 The Dürer monogram on the ostrich egg is a later forgery.
2 GNM, inv. no. Gm1225, on long-term loan from the Museen der Stadt Nürnberg, Kunstsammlungen.
3 See, however, the forthcoming dissertation by Carolin Alff. For Europe as a whole, see Exh. cat. Baltimore and Princeton 2012.
4 Krebs 2021.

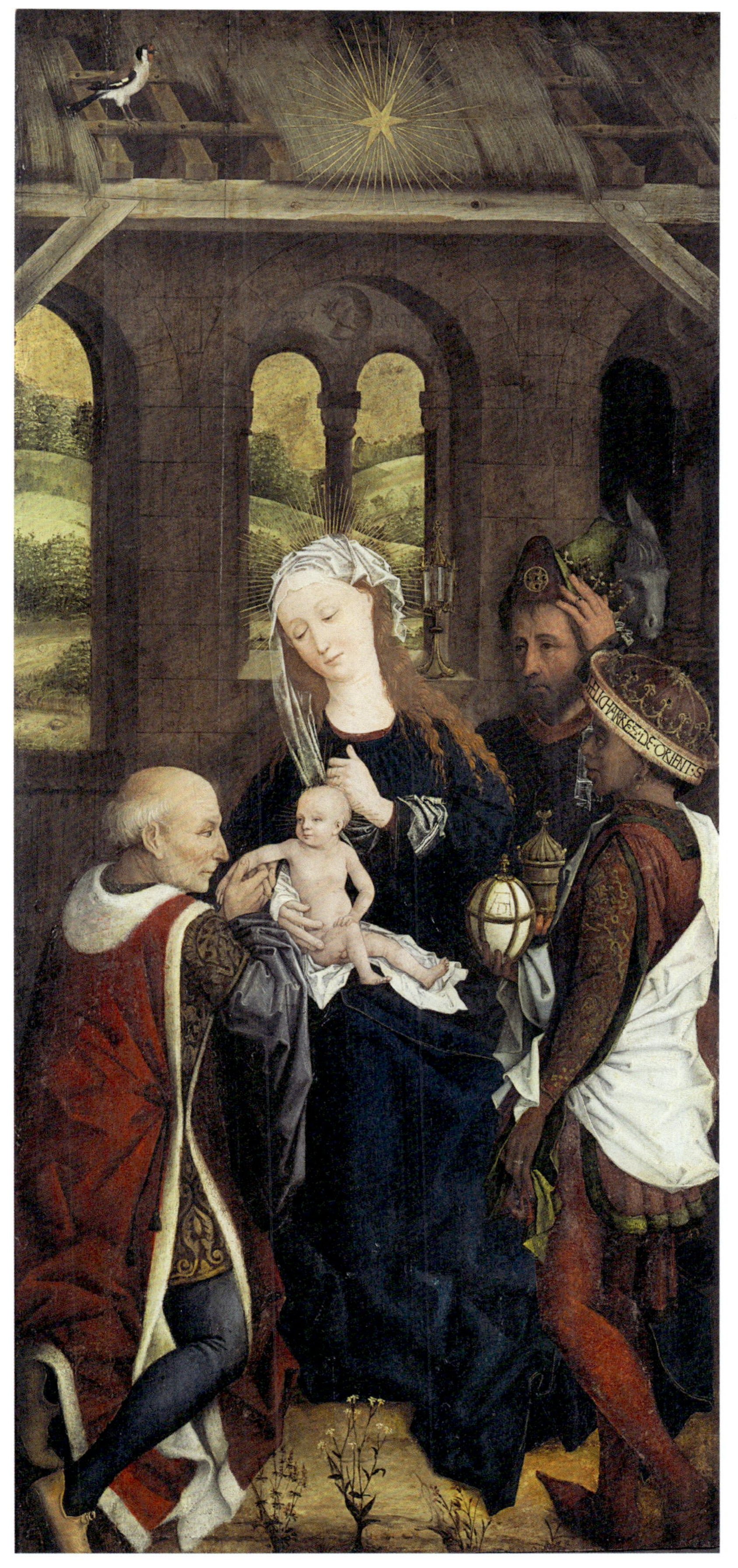
ELCHARREX·DE·ORIENT·S

16

OSTRICH EGG CUP

Georg Rühl I

Nuremberg, ca. 1615

Ostrich egg, cut, polished; silver-gilt, chased, cast, punched, etched

H. 50.5 cm; Diam. max. 15.7 cm

GNM, inv. no. HG11771, on long-term loan from the Freiherrlich von Scheurlsche Familienstiftung

References:
Exh. cat. Nuremberg 1985, p. 269, cat. no. 97; Exh. cat. Nuremberg 1992, vol. 2, pp. 863–64, cat. no. 5.37 (Peter J. Bräunlein); Bock 2005, p. 261, cat. no. 86; Tebbe 2007, pp. 162–63, fig. 127.

During the heyday of goldsmithing in Nuremberg, from the mid-sixteenth to the early seventeenth century, extraordinary drinking vessels were created by a number of masters who appear to have specialized in "exotica." In addition to mother-of-pearl |**cat. no. 2**|, nautilus shells, and turban shells |**cat. no. 120**|, ostrich eggs were also used by these artists. Through ownership of works fashioned from such materials, art patrons were able to showcase their access to global luxury goods.

Georg Rühl I (master in 1596, d. before 1635) produced a large oeuvre of highly elaborate works. About 1615, he created a cup from an ostrich egg encased by three openwork straps. The figural stem alludes to the ostrich egg's African origin; it takes the form of a kneeling Black archer wearing a feathered skirt and equipped with a bow, arrows, and a quiver. The vessel's tall metal rim depicts an ostrich hunt taking place on foot and on horseback. The cut-off end of the egg forms the cover, surmounted by a small ostrich figure holding a horseshoe in its beak. This iconographical detail has its origin in the *Physiologus*, the medieval period's standard text on animal symbolism. Since, according to the *Physiologus*, the ostrich could eat iron, in the early modern period this bird became a symbol of strength. That the cup was indeed used for drinking is suggested by the silver-gilt lining fitted into the eggshell.

Beginning in the eleventh century, ostrich eggs became increasingly sought-after collector's items, first as parts of church treasuries and later, in the early modern period, as *naturalia* in princely cabinets of curiosities.[1] In religious paintings, they appear as symbols of the virgin birth of Jesus, and in depictions of the *Adoration of the Magi*, ostrich egg vessels serve to emphasize the African origin of the Black king |**cat. no. 15**|. In Nuremberg, as early as the mid-fifteenth century, the city council presented ostrich egg cups as gifts to visiting dignitaries and emperors.[2]

Ostrich eggs entered Europe through northwestern Africa and Spain, and from there they were transported further north. Other paths to Europe, similar to those taken by ostrich plumes |**cat. no. 39**|, ran along trade routes leading from the areas around Timbuktu and Darfur to northern Africa, especially Egypt.[3] The Nuremberg patrician Christoph Fürer, during his journey to the Holy Land in 1565–66, remarked while visiting the market in Cairo, "One also finds beautiful ostrich eggs for 3 medini."[4] Around 1600, ships brought ostrich eggs, along with other "exotica," from Alexandria to Venice, and from there merchants transported them to Nuremberg, as well as to the great trade fairs at Frankfurt and Leipzig. Ostriches were also native to the Arabian Peninsula and Sinai before being hunted to extinction in those places in the first half of the twentieth century.[5] Thus, travelers, pilgrims, and crusaders to the eastern Mediterranean brought back ostrich eggs as exclusive souvenirs. Closer to their places of origin, the eggs were used—unworked or as parts of vessels and lamps—in Orthodox and Coptic churches and in mosques.[6]

Birgit Schübel

1 Bock 2005, p. 173.
2 Meißner 2018, p. 24; StAN, Rst. Nbg., AstB 316, fol. 4.
3 Rublak 2021, p. 24.
4 Fürer von Haimendorf 1646, p. 135.
5 Bohms 2024, vol. 2, p. 600.
6 Green 2006, pp. 35–36.

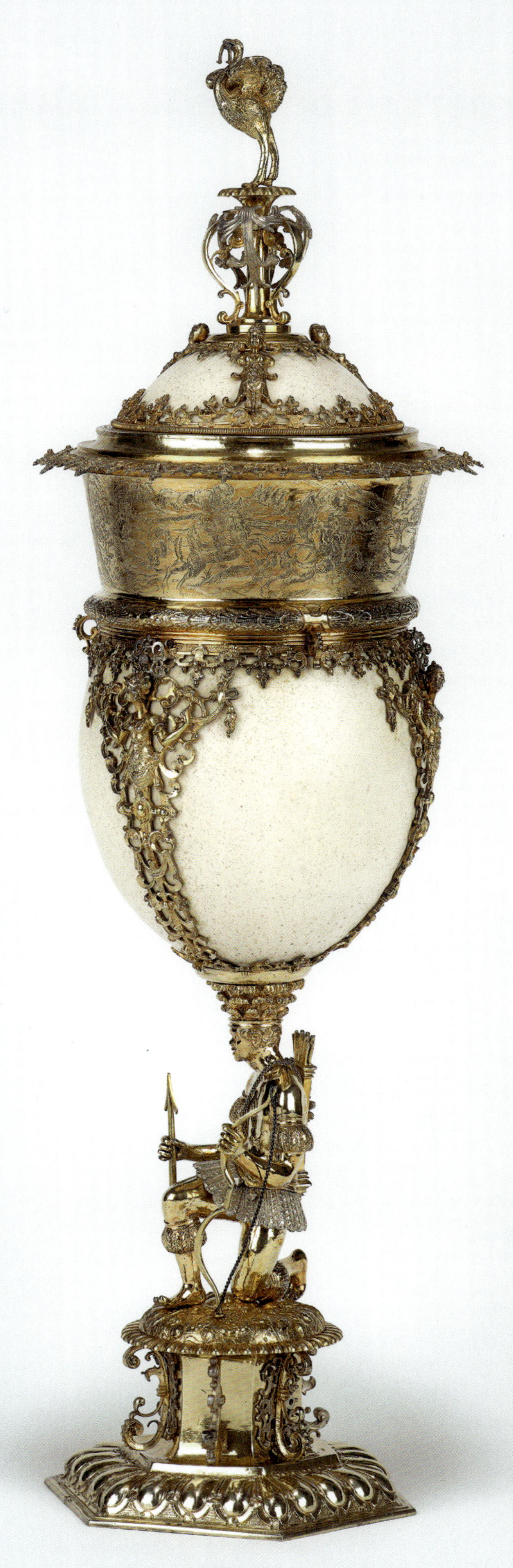

17

PORTRAIT OF BARBARA DÜRER, NÉE HOLPER

Albrecht Dürer

Nuremberg, 1490

Paint on fir

H. 47.2; W. 35.7

GNM, inv. no. Gm1160

References:
Hess, Hirschfelder, and Baum 2019, pt. 1, pp. 570–83, cat. no. 42 (Dagmar Hirschfelder and Oliver Mack).

This portrait of Barbara Dürer (1452–1514), the mother of Albrecht Dürer (1471–1528), is regarded as the earliest surviving painting made by Dürer after the completion of his apprenticeship. It therefore represents an important point of departure for understanding the career of this Nuremberg artist. Several aspects of the portrait are typical of Nuremberg as an artistic center. Barbara's stylized facial features and the drapery folds of her veil are derived from female figures found in the workshop repertoire of Albrecht Dürer's teacher, the painter Michael Wolgemut. Yet, however much Dürer's art was initially based on the collaborative production methods of the large Wolgemut workshop, in which individual artistic expression was of little importance, he increasingly departed from that tradition.

The present panel formed one half of a portrait diptych, together with the likeness of Barbara's husband, Albrecht Dürer the Elder (d. 1502), now found in the Uffizi Gallery.[1] The elder Albrecht Dürer, a goldsmith, hailed from Ajtós in the Kingdom of Hungary. Before settling in Nuremberg, he spent time working in the Burgundian Netherlands.[2] Fifteenth-century Nuremberg was an artistic melting pot that attracted specialist craftspeople from far and wide. The fluid character of the city's artistic scene contributed significantly to the flourishing of the arts there. Albrecht Dürer the Elder's marriage to Barbara (Holper) was in part motived by professional interest, as she was the daughter of the renowned goldsmith Hieronymus Holper (d. 1478). The elder Dürer also became highly esteemed for his art. However, as is characteristic for Nuremberg goldsmiths of the period, no surviving work can be securely attributed to him.

Although Barbara's role in her husband's studio is undocumented, as is true for nearly all women in artistic families of the period, it seems plausible that she would have had certain workshop responsibilities. We know that her daughter-in-law Agnes (1475–1539) was at the very least involved in selling prints made by the younger Albrecht Dürer.[3] Kunigunde Glockendon (d. 1534) received payment for her work on the Behaim Globe |**cat. no. 1**|.[4] And Anna Storch, widow of the goldsmith Hans Storch (d. 1514), temporarily ran her deceased husband's workshop; and in 1518 she certified the completion of a pupil's apprenticeship.[5]

The portrait also offers insight into the material culture of Nuremberg. Barbara Dürer holds a rosary made of precious coral beads |**see cat. no. 18**|. This luxury item was not only meant to indicate her piety but, as is apparent from the frequency of coral rosaries in patrician-class portraits and donor likenesses |**cat. nos. 24, 45**|, it also served to suggest that Albrecht Dürer's parents shared company with high-ranking families.

The function of this portrait diptych remains a matter of debate. While some have proposed that the young Albrecht Dürer used it as a demonstration piece in proof of his artistic mastery,[6] that function alone fails to explain Dürer's handling of portraits of his closest relations and associates. In addition to the diptych of his parents, he also kept in his possession his painted likeness of the aged Michael Wolgemut. If one also considers drawings such as Dürer's moving portrait of his mother in old age and, furthermore, his act of supplementing the portrait of Wolgemut with an inscription detailing the circumstances of the sitter's death, there is much to suggest that Dürer regarded these works as parts of a personal memorial gallery.

After Dürer's death, the portraits of his parents came into the possession of Willibald Imhoff (1519–1580), a patrician who, in his house on the Egidienplatz, accumulated Renaissance Nuremberg's most important private art collection.[7] Centuries later, two entries in Imhoff's inventories made it possible to identify the sitter in this portrait as Barbara Dürer.

Benno Baumbauer and Marie-Luise Kosan

1 Galleria degli Uffizi, Florence, inv. no. 1086.
2 Schauerte 2014.
3 Schleif 1999.
4 Timann 2007a, p. 60.
5 Timann 2007b, pp. 34–35.
6 On this, see Hess, Hirschfelder, and Baum 2019, pt. 1, p. 582.
7 Pohl 1992; Budde 1996.

CORAL ROSARY

18

Nuremberg (?), ca. 1500

Strings of rosary beads serve to guide recitation of the Rosary prayer.[1] This exemplar, from about 1500, consists mainly of small coral beads. It also has two larger, golden beads, in the form of stylized pomegranates, and four pendants, cast in silver and gilded. The pendants represent Saint Sebastian, the Annunciation, and a skull, with a crucifix forming the final element.

The rosary was discovered in the nineteenth century in the Georgskirche at Kraftshof, a village near Nuremberg. Although the previous owners cannot be determined with certainty, in view of the discovery site, a connection to the patrician family Kress is probable. The Kresses held lordship over Kraftshof and had the church built as a family burial place.[2] The use of a precious material, coral, suggests at the very least that the original owner was a person of rank. Coral was a favored material for prayer beads in the fifteenth century. While it remains unclear where this rosary was made, the technique and provenance point to Nuremberg. Alongside Nördlingen, Nuremberg was one of the main centers for the production of coral rosaries.

Coral was one of the most highly valued imported goods in the fifteenth century. The harvesting of corals took place mainly in the waters of the Levant.[3] From there, coral reached Nuremberg either via Barcelona or Venice. The coral trade through Barcelona began as early as the twelfth century. Distribution to Nuremberg was first documented in the late fourteenth century and increased afterward. Along with saffron and silver, coral was one of the most valuable commodities. Nuremberg merchants conducted their business either directly in Barcelona or from Nuremberg.[4] There was also a lively mutual exchange between Venice and Nuremberg. Coral was traded northward from Venice, and Nuremberg produced rosaries for export back to Italy.[5] In fact, corals that had been worked in Nuremberg reached not just Venice but all of Europe.[6]

Apart from their use as aids to prayer, coral rosaries were also carried as precious fashion accessories, especially by women of high social status. Coral was believed to have healing and protective properties, but the substance's material value was the main reason why such rosaries became status symbols. This is evidenced by the presence of coral rosaries in numerous portraits and depictions of donor figures |**cat. nos. 17, 24, 45**|. Accordingly, rosaries also served as diplomatic gifts in the medieval and early modern periods. And missionaries brought coral rosaries on their travels, for example to central Africa, where elites would carry rosaries as an unusual accessory, expressive of religious affiliation and social status.[7]

After the Reformation, coral rosaries became signs of denominational allegiance. But even Protestant families admired them as valuable objects. As such, they found their way into the cabinets of arts (*Kunstkammer*) of both burghers and the nobility.[8]

Marie-Luise Kosan

Coral, gold, silver-gilt

L. 54 cm

GNM, inv. no. KG298

References:
Exh. cat. Nuremberg 2000b, pp. 287–88, cat. no. 122 (Frank Matthias Kammel); Prummer 2016.

1 See the extensive discussion in Prummer 2016. Also see Nuremberg 2000b, pp. 287–88, cat. no. 122 (Frank Matthias Kammel).
2 Rusam 2000.
3 Pfotenhauer 2016, p. 271. Vázquez de Prada 1986, p. 730, cites coral harvesting carried out along the present-day Costa Brava and off the coasts of Sardinia and Tunis.
4 Vincke 1959, pp. 127–28; Stromer 1970, p. 157; Ammann 1970, pp. 136, 139; Coulon 2002, pp. 155, 272, 423, 425. Although Vázquez de Prada 1986, p. 730, postulates that Barcelona held a near-monopoly over coral works, that remains unproven.
5 Pfotenhauer 2016, pp. 271, 288–89.
6 Veit 1960, p. 21.
7 Siebenhüner 2021, pp. 84–85.
8 Siebenhüner 2021, p. 94.

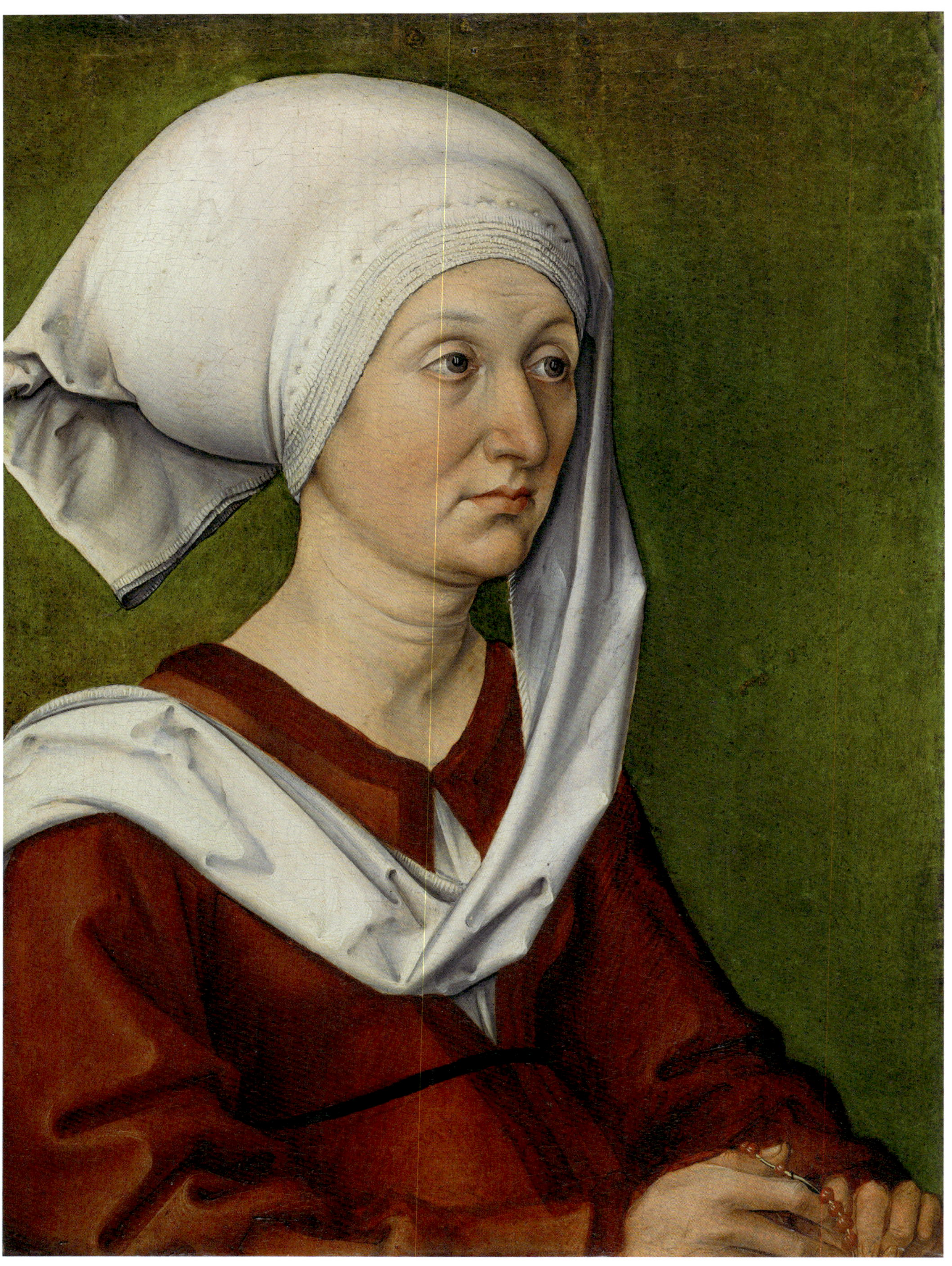

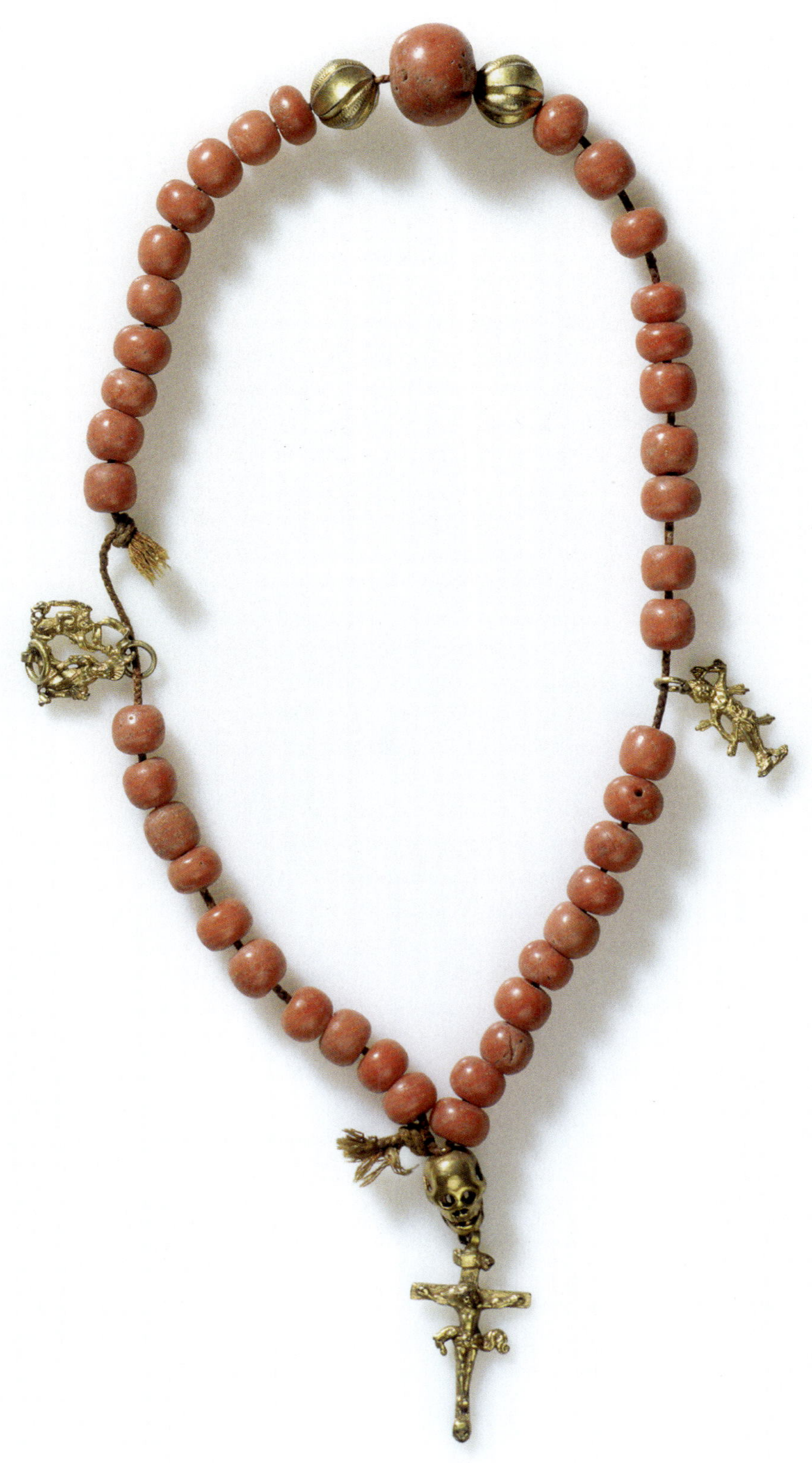

19

PORTRAIT OF JOHANN NEUDÖRFER WITH A PUPIL

Nicolas Neufchâtel

Nuremberg, 1561

Oil on canvas

H. 120 cm; W. 112 cm (including original frame)

GNM, inv. no. Gm1836, on long-term loan from the Bayerische Staatsgemäldesammlungen

References:
Smith 1983, pp. 69–70; Löcher 1995, pp. 328–30.

Nicolas Neufchâtel's sensitive portrait of the master calligrapher and mathematician Johann Neudörfer (1497–1563) with a pupil, dated 1561, is a striking work, both for its psychological depth and the subtlety with which the sitters emerge from the dark background. While Neudörfer concentrates on measuring a dodecahedron, the pupil records his aging teacher's lessons in a notebook. Another geometric figure, a cylindrical sundial, and writing implements round out the composition. The inscription on the original frame praises Neudörfer as an influential scholar, celebrated by his many former students throughout Europe. Unusually large for its subject matter, the painting is a sophisticated representation of the union of the arts and sciences, a topic characteristic of mid-sixteenth-century Europe.

Neudörfer, a man of varied interests, described himself as a master arithmetician (*Rechenmeister*). During his lifetime and beyond, he was one of the most esteemed intellectuals in the German-speaking world of the Renaissance. Furthermore, he can be regarded as Nuremberg's first art historian inasmuch as he wrote short biographies of seventy-nine of the city's "artists and people adept in the arts" (1547).[1] In those texts, which are unencumbered by later hierarchies of medium, Neudörfer does not make distinctions of rank among painters, sculptors, goldsmiths, table-fountain makers, screw makers, and other craftspeople. An increasing separation between the media, accompanied by a persistent dismissiveness toward the crafts, would come only with the emergence of art academies. The sixteenth century took a much more inclusive view of artistic techniques, in all their variety. For example, perspective studies, as practiced by Neudörfer and his pupil in this painting, appear in almost all media—a particularly exceptional specimen being the magnificent casket by the Master of Perspective that was acquired by the Germanisches Nationalmuseum in 2024 |**cat. no. 20**|.

The present painting stands as one of many testimonies to the attraction that Nuremberg, as a center of the arts and sciences, exerted on artists across Europe. The painter Nicolaus Neufchâtel, who trained in Antwerp under Pieter Coecke van Aelst, probably came to Nuremberg as a Calvinist refugee. It cannot be ruled out that he may have relocated on the recommendation of a Nuremberg merchant active in Antwerp. One candidate for such a situation is Lazarus Tucher I (1491–1563), who had established his own branch of the Tucher family in Antwerp.[2] In Nuremberg, Neufchâtel became the preferred portraitist of the city's upper class, but he came into conflict with the city council over certain religious statements.[3] The Neudörfer portrait is Neufchâtel's only signed work. He gave it to the Inner Council as an artistic manifesto, so to speak, and it was displayed in the town hall. In 1564, the council rewarded him for the painting with a payment of 32 guldens. Although the inscription on the frame emphasizes that Neufchâtel made this gift as a grateful guest ("HOSPES GR[ATUS]"), the act followed in the tradition of notable artistic predecessors, including Albrecht Dürer and Georg Pencz |**see cat. nos. 7, 75**|, and it secured Neufchâtel's memory at the governmental heart of the city. Together with other portraits of famous Nuremberg artists and scholars kept at the town hall, Neufchâtel's painting became one of the cornerstones of the municipal art collections.[4]

Benno Baumbauer

1 Neudörfer 1875.
2 Grote 1961, pp. 37–39; Harreld 2004, pp. 73, 88, 91, 111–12, 135.
3 Smith 1990–91, pp. 153, 155–56; Hagen 2001, p. 525.
4 Schwemmer 1949, pp. 97–103; Valentin 2019.

CASKET

Master of Perspective

Nuremberg, 1565

20

Ebony, yew, walnut, manna ash, and other European and non-European woods; ivory, alabaster, mother-of-pearl; fittings of brass and fire-gilt metal

H. 34.5 cm; W. 53 cm; D. 36 cm

GNM, inv. no. HG13639, acquired in 2024 with funding from the Erbschaft Renate und Theodor Schimann and with the support of the GNM's Förderkreis e. V.

References:
Catalogue Glasgow 1882–83, p. 49, cat. no. 718; Laue 2018; Spenlé 2018; Andrews 2022, pp. 16–17.

This small piece of furniture, a rectangular casket dated 1565, offers outstanding testimony to global aspects of Nuremberg's cultural history. Its imagery and exquisite materials draw upon the fifteenth-century tradition of the Italian *studiolo*, the type of wood-paneled study that showcased power, scholarship, and taste. The Nuremberg casket, a kind of portable *studiolo*, is certainly worthy of a mid-sixteenth-century prince. Also, comparable chests were used by Nuremberg's guild-like craft organizations for storage of their valuables, ranging from documents and money to ceremonial cups and masterpieces.[1] Yet this object is smaller than those and has an additional socle area. The casket's elaborate design makes it a treasure in itself—less a functional piece of furniture than a showpiece and collector's item. Furthermore, the casket is also the only dated piece in a group of ten stylistically matching works distinguished by geometric intarsia patterns, all of which have been localized in Nuremberg and attributed to the artist known as the Master of Perspective.

As noted by Virginie Spenlé, the casket exemplifies Nuremberg's self-image as a city of the arts and sciences.[2] The imagery presents two subjects—seemingly unrelated at first—that occupied the arts and crafts of the imperial city in equal measure: geometry and the theory of the four temperaments. Representations of geometric solids are combined here with allegories of the temperaments[3] and associated subjects,[4] as well as two each of the cardinal and theological virtues.[5] The subjects are represented in various materials, some of which arrived in Nuremberg from distant lands. Inlays of native and tropical woods and of mother-of-pearl form the geometric solids, while the figural scenes are engraved in ivory |**fig. p. 108**|.

The work shows stylistic influences from central and southern Europe, combined to create an overall impression typical of Nuremberg. Sixteenth-century engravings from Nuremberg and elsewhere in central Europe, by such artists as Virgil Solis and Heinrich Aldegrever, served as models for the allegories and scenes. However, the first early modern specimens of polyhedral intarsia are found in Italy—for example, in the *studioli* of Federico da Montefeltro in Urbino and formerly at Gubbio, both from the second half of the fifteenth century.[6] From the early sixteenth century onward, published scholarly treatises made geometric knowledge and its philosophical interpretation accessible even in German, for example, studies by Augustin Hirsvogel (*Geometria*, 1543) and Wenzel Jamnitzer (*Perspectiva*, 1568) printed in Nuremberg.

Although no evidence remains of the casket's earliest owners, by about 1730 the work was in England, where a stand was made for it.[7] The object was first exhibited in Glasgow in 1882, on loan from the Marquess of Lothian. At that time, it was regarded as Italian.[8] Only recently has the oeuvre of the Master of Perspective been localized in Nuremberg, demonstrating the city's close artistic exchange with Italy.

Heike Zech

1 For example, GNM, inv. no. Z1289, dated 1595.
2 Spenlé 2018.
3 Front: the melancholic and phlegmatic types; back: the sanguine and choleric types.
4 Front: Sophonisba and Masinissa; right: Aristotle and Phyllis; back: Herkinbald and his nephew; left: Samson and Delilah.
5 Right: fortitude and prudence; left: faith and hope.
6 Clough 1995.
7 GNM, inv. no. HG23640.
8 Catalogue Glasgow 1882–83, p. 49, cat. no. 718.

cat. no. 19

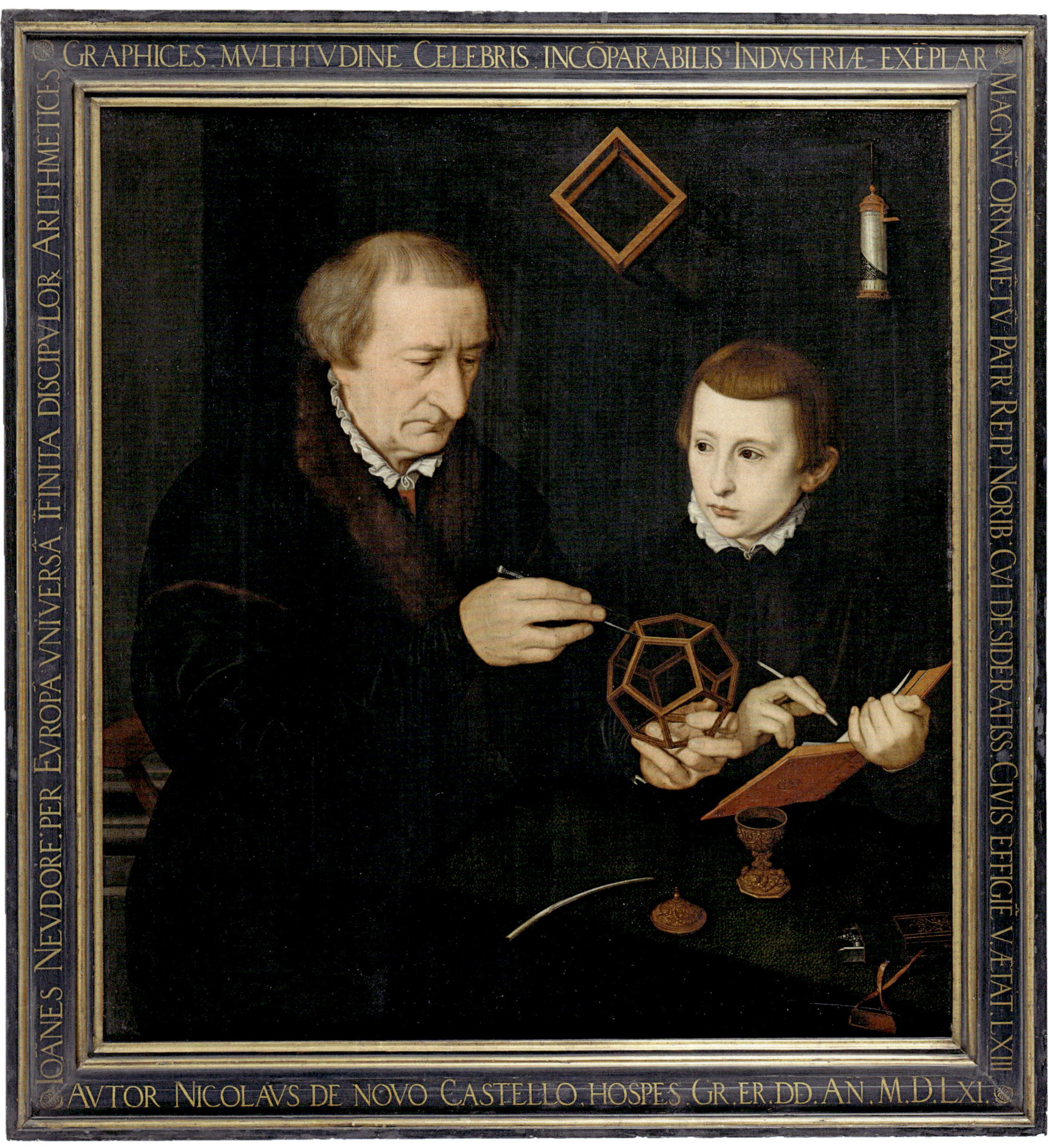
GRAPHICES MVLTITVDINE CELEBRIS. INCŌPARABILIS INDVSTRIÆ EXĒPLAR
MAGNV ORNAMĒTV PATR. REIP. NORIB. CVI DESIDERATISS. CIVIS EFFIGIE V. ÆTAT. LXIII
AVTOR NICOLAVS DE NOVO CASTELLO. HOSPES GR. ER. DD. AN. M.D.LXI.
IOANES NEVDORF. PER EVROPÂ VNIVERSÂ, IFINITA DISCIPVLOR. ARITHMETICES

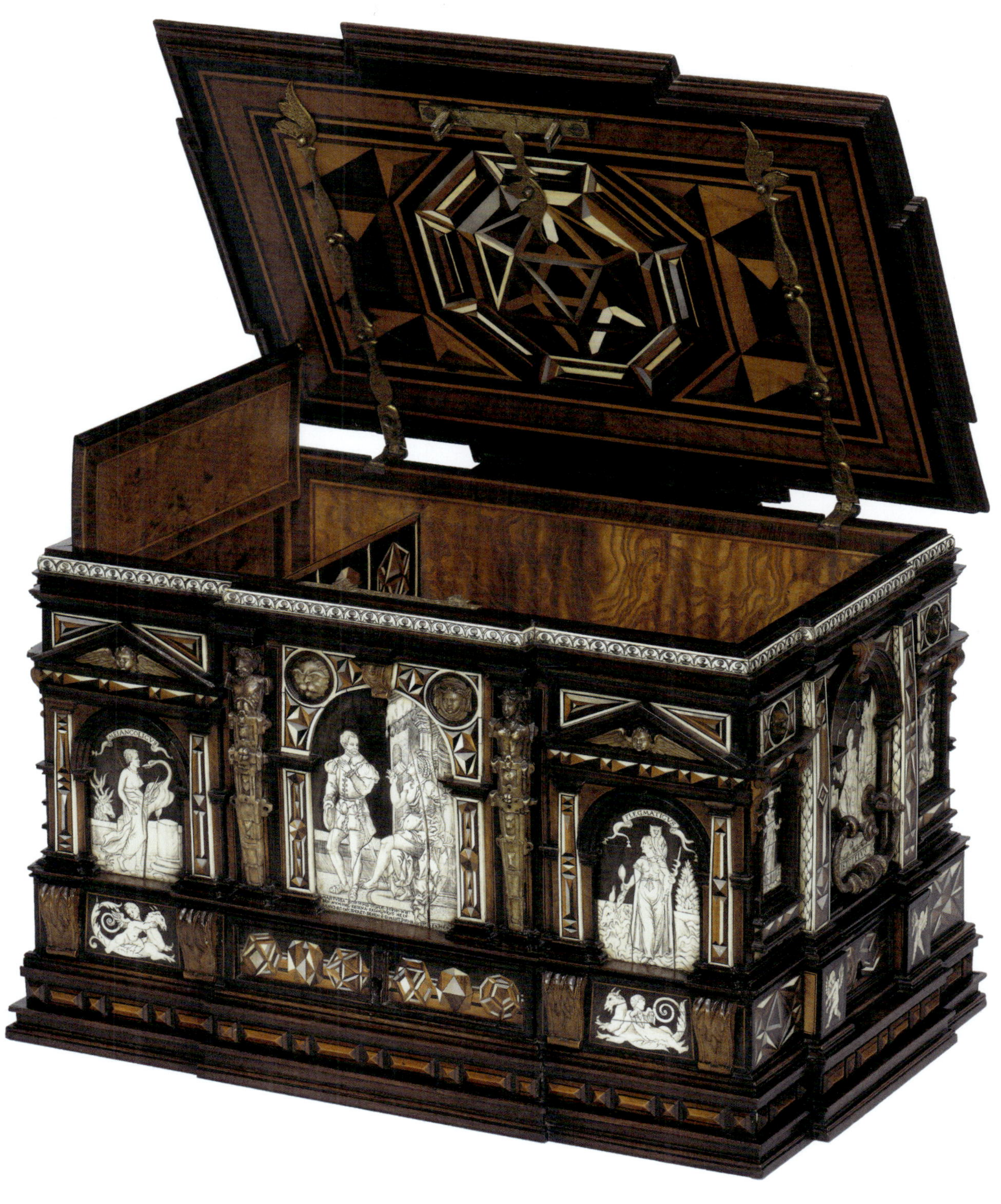

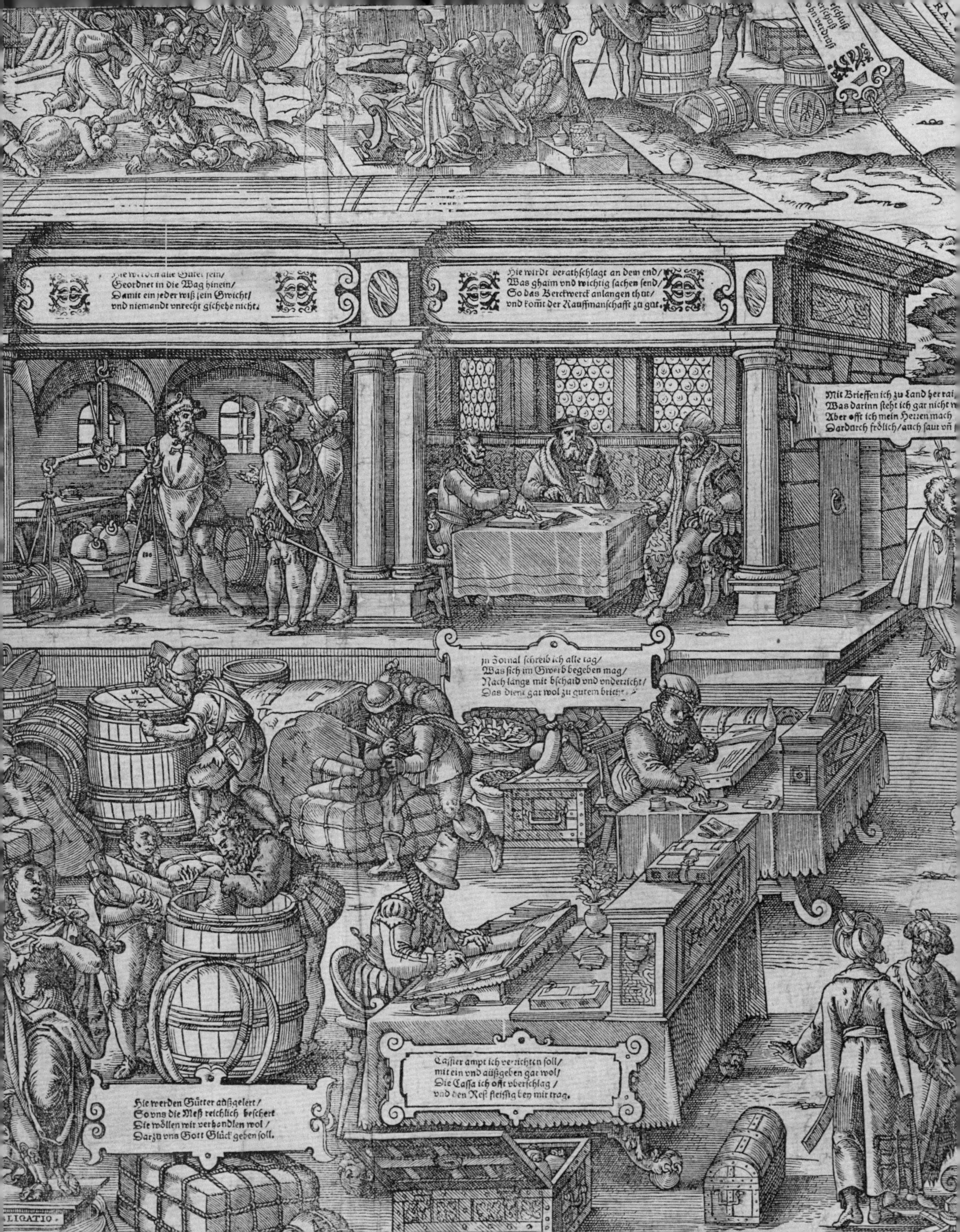
Geordnet in die Wag hinein/
Damit ein jeder wiß sein Gwicht/
vnd niemandt vnrecht gschehe nicht.
Hie wirdt berathschlagt an dem end/
Was ghaim vnd wichtig sachen send/
So das Berckwerck anlangen thut/
vnd kombt der Kauffmanschafft zu gut.
Mit Brieffen ich zu Land her rai
Was darinn steht ich gar nicht w
Aber offt ich mein Herren mach
Dardurch frölich/auch saur vñ
In Zornal schreib ich alle tag/
Was sich im Gwerb begeben mag/
Nach länge mit bschaid vnd vnderricht/
Das dient gar wol zu gutem bricht.
Cassier ampt ich verrichten soll/
mit ein vnd außgeben gar wol/
Die Cassa ich offt vberschlag/
vnd den Rest fleissig bey mir trag.
Hie werden Gütter außgelert/
So vns die Meß reichlich beschert
Die wöllen wir verhandlen wol/
Darzu vns Gott Glück geben soll.
LIGATIO.

ART, TRADE, AND ECONOMICS

Long-distance trade, mining, and financial dealings contributed significantly to Nuremberg's economic success and the development of its global networks. The city was conveniently located in Europe's center, at a crossroads of important trade routes. A comprehensive system of royal exemptions from customs helped to foster the long-distance trade undertaken by Nuremberg patrician families. Their activities spanned the entire continent and beyond, reaching ever more distant parts of the world.

The most innovative and intensive business sector was the mining industry. Mining offered a rapid route to major profits. Nurembergers were involved as owners or shareholders in almost all the mining districts of central Europe. To process the extracted ore, they maintained state-of-the-art, water-powered hammer mills and smelting furnaces, which consumed enormous quantities of charcoal. Another area in which Nuremberg's entrepreneurs were active was finance. Ever since the fourteenth century, the business of lending money to kings and princely houses had enabled wealthy Nurembergers to accumulate more and more trading privileges.

Economic activities were rarely depicted in images, especially in the period before the Reformation, which was dominated by sacred art. Yet by commissioning works of art, wealthy entrepreneurial families had a way of spending their profits while also putting their economic success on display. From the late fifteenth century onward, depictions of mining became increasingly widespread. In works containing mining imagery, economic issues of interest to the urban elite became interwoven with subjects of natural philosophy that were highly topical at the time. In 1585, Jost Amman created the ultimate tableau of early modern economics with his monumental *Allegory of Trade* woodcut.

Benno Baumbauer

◂ cat. no. 21.1 (detail)

21

ALLEGORY OF TRADE

Caspar Brinner (text)
Jost Amman (design of the image)
Augsburg: Wilhelm Peter Zimmermann, 1622

Woodcut from six blocks

21.1
H. 110.7 cm; W. 74.0 cm
GNM, inv. no. H128

21.2 (not illustrated)
H. 108.8; W. 73.6 cm
Kunstsammlungen der Veste Coburg, inv. no. I,330,2614

References:
New Hollstein German 5.2, p. 81; Pilz 1974; Pietrzak and Schilling 2018, pp. 48–49 (Hanns-Peter Bruchhäuser).

The highly detailed *Allegory of Trade* by the Nuremberg printmaker Jost Amman (1539–1591), first published in Augsburg in 1585, provides a comprehensive overview of the practices of early modern commerce. In its interplay of image and text, the monumental woodcut conveys both theoretical principles and practical instructions. Various personifications illustrate the virtues of "good" trading practices. The figure of Fortune, standing on a winged globe, serves as a reminder that economic success depends largely on the vagaries of luck—with careful bookkeeping being no less important a factor.

The text columns explain how to use the various accounting books that figure prominently in the picture. The daybook, or journal, is placed at the top of the central column and aligns with the fulcrum of the balance scale above, held by Mercury. The scale is shown in perfect equilibrium between the ledger of assets, in the left weighing pan, and the ledger of liabilities, in the right pan. The column rises from the center of a large fountain basin, which itself is supported by an aedicula housing the *Geheimbuch*, the record of confidential matters. A trading company manager, dressed in a fur coat, is seated directly below. He is surrounded by numerous figures performing a variety of activities, including weighing, taking inventory, packing, stamping trademarks, inspecting, and collecting payments. In the foreground space, four desks are arranged facing center: a cashier's desk and three other desks at which bookkeeping operations are being carried out. As described in the associated texts, the debts listed in the daybook are transferred to the debt register and to the *Capus*, or general ledger, and the cashbook is also updated.

The first textbooks on double-entry bookkeeping, the rational basis of the capitalist economic system, appeared in Italy during the fifteenth century, and these were later printed in translation in Nuremberg.[1] In sixteenth-century Augsburg, Matthäus Schwarz (1497–1574), chief accountant for the Fugger family, worked methodically to commit German-language descriptions of the various accounting methods to paper.[2] The *Allegory of Trade* woodcut was probably commissioned by a merchant from Augsburg or Nuremberg. Judging from the view of Antwerp in the background, the patron may have had a branch office in that Flemish metropolis.[3]

The woodcut's nine-line header identifies Caspar Brinner (d. 1610), a master arithmetician (*Rechenmeister*) from Augsburg, as the author of the verses that appear in the margins and on numerous cartouches. The reference to Brinner's teacher Johann Neudörfer (1497–1563) |**cat. no. 19**| as the project's initiator is regarded as being merely a rhetorical device to lend the publication greater authority.[4] Neudörfer, who died twenty years before the woodcut was first printed, was a Nuremberg master calligrapher and arithmetician, as well as a teacher of bookkeeping. Regardless of whether Neudörfer contributed, the print illustrates the serious thought and social relevance involved in theories of bookkeeping at the time.

Laura Di Carlo

1 On double-entry bookkeeping, see Lang 2020, pp. 83–112; Stromer 1967, pp. 757–59.
2 See Häberlein 2010, pp. 2–3.
3 See Pilz 1964, p. 25; Pietrzak and Schilling 2018, p. 48 (Hanns-Peter Bruchhäuser).
4 Pilz 1964, p. 33; Pietrzak and Schilling 2018, p. 48 (Hanns-Peter Bruchhäuser).

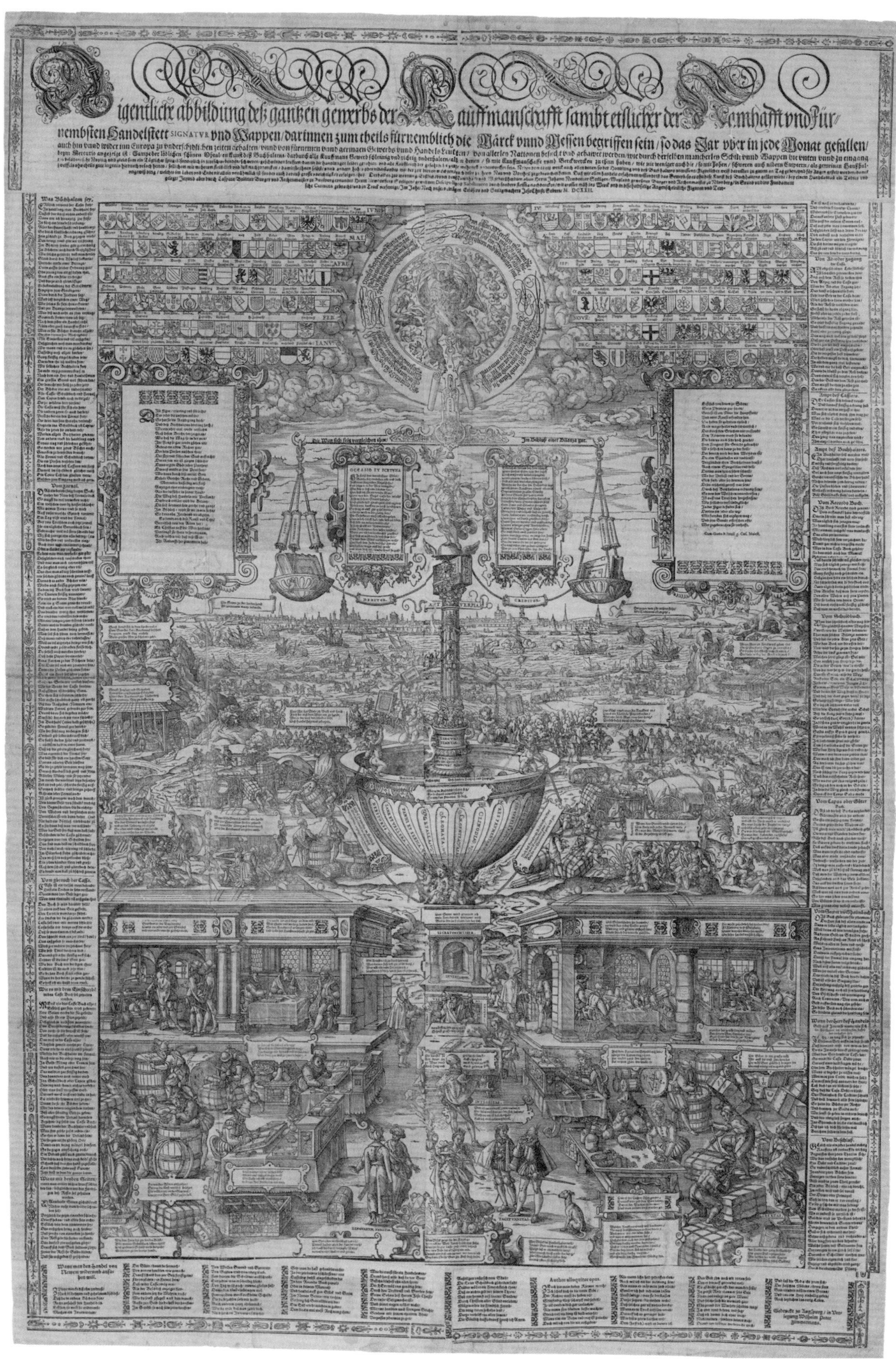

cat. no. 21.1

22

NINE RECKONING COUNTERS (*RECHENPFENNIGE*)

Hans Krauwinckel (22.1–8)
Wolf Lauffer (22.9)

Nuremberg, sixteenth century

Copper, brass, and bronze

Diam. 2.35–2.9 cm

GNM, inv. nos. ZJ1783, ZJ88, ZJ1782, ZJ3347, ZJ1776, ZJ1780, ZJ1792, ZJ1785, ZJ4926 (cat. nos. 22.1–22.9, from top left to bottom right)

References:
Gebert 1917; König 1935; König and Stalzer 1989; Press and Bauch 2013; Groenendijk and Levinson 2015.

Reckoning counters or jetons (*Rechenpfennige* in German), which were once essential to the culture of European commerce, were produced in huge numbers in Nuremberg. Despite their similarity to coins, counters were not intended for making payments. Their main use was in the calculation of accounts, which was usually done on a table, board, or cloth marked with lines for counting. This practice is even depicted on certain counters. One made by Hans Krauwinckel shows a bearded man seated at a table, performing a calculation by arranging counters on lines marked on the tabletop |**cat. no. 22.1**|.

Whereas in fifteenth-century Europe reckoning counters were still produced in various locations, during the sixteenth century production became concentrated mainly in Nuremberg. Some Nuremberg makers memorialized themselves on their products. For example, the aforementioned counter with an image of an accountant bears the name of both the maker and the place of origin: "HANNS KRAVWINCKEL IN NVR[NBERG]" |**cat. no. 22.1**|.[1] Another counter by Krauwinckel displays a rhyme that begins on the front and ends on the back: "HANNS KRAVWINCKEL BIN ICH BEKONT / IN FRANCKREICH VND AVCH IN NIDERLONT" (Hans Krauwinckel, I am known / in France and also in the Netherlands) |**cat. nos. 22.2, 22.3**|.

As the latter inscription indicates, a considerable proportion of the counters produced in Nuremberg were intended for export. Their motifs were often specially designed for that purpose. For example, the counters decorated with three crowns and three fleurs-de-lis refer to the French royal house |**cat. no. 22.5**|.[2] The motif of an imperial orb surrounded by a trefoil |**cat. no. 22.4**| is a reference to the place of manufacture, for it alludes to the orb that belonged to the regalia of the Holy Roman Empire |**see cat. no. 7**|, kept in Nuremberg at the time. The interpretation of the ship motif is more complicated; it is thought to derive from the English noble, a gold coin |**cat. no. 22.6**|.[3] Even city views could be stamped on the counters, despite their small size. An example by Hans Krauwinckel with a ship on the front shows a view of Nuremberg on the reverse, with Mercury, the messenger god, hovering above the city as a symbol of economic prosperity |**cat. no. 22.7**|. A counter by Wolf Lauffer shows a view of Paris |**cat. no. 22.9**|. The so-called Saint Mark's counters bear an image of a winged lion |**cat. no. 22.8**|, the symbol of Saint Mark the Evangelist, who is the patron saint of Venice. By the mid-seventeenth century, with the increasing adoption of the Indo-Arabic numeral system for arithmetic, the practice of calculating on line systems, with counters, became less and less widespread. Consequently, the production of counters gradually ceased. However, in terms of both their iconography and broad distribution, the surviving examples are illustrative of Nuremberg's importance as an international center of trade.

Sven Jakstat

1 It is often unclear whether the counters marked with the name Hans Krauwinckel are by Hans Krauwinckel I (master from 1562 to 1586) or his son Hans Krauwinckel II (master from 1586 to 1635).
2 Gebert 1917, p. 32.
3 Gebert 1917, p. 32.

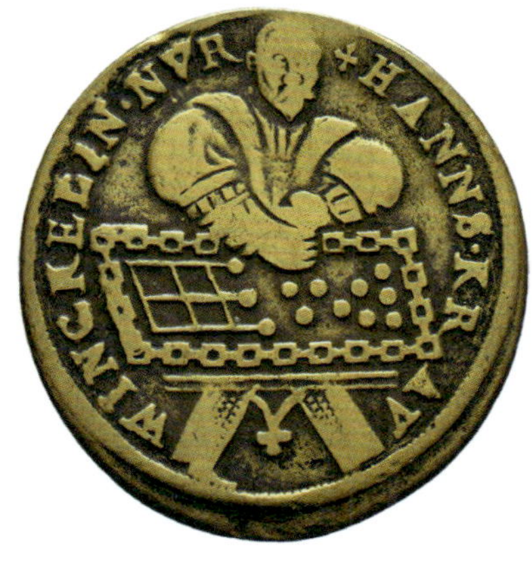
HANNS·KRAV
WINCKELIN·NVR

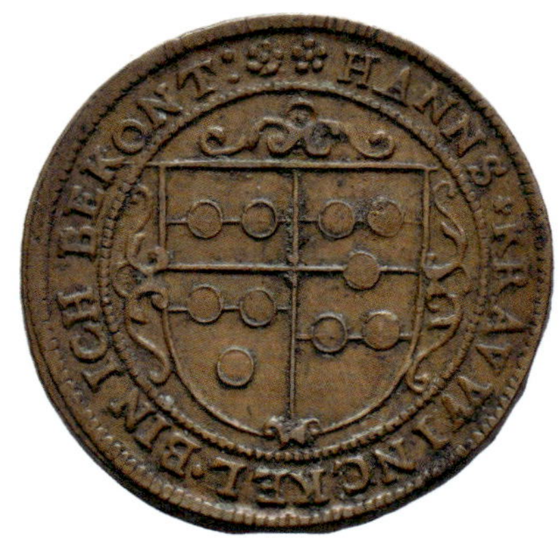
HANNS·KRAVWINCKEL·BIN·ICH·BEKONT:

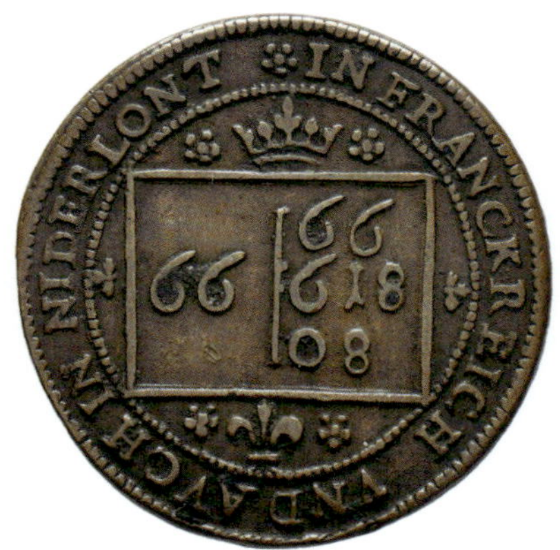
IN FRANCKREICH VND AVCH IN NIDERLONT

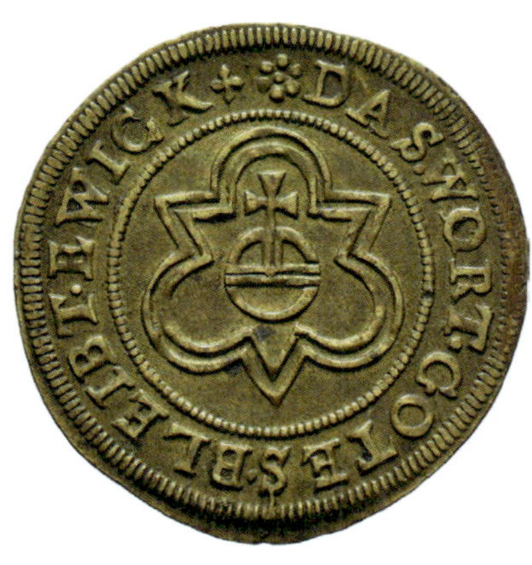
DAS·WORT·GOTES·BLEIBT·EWICK

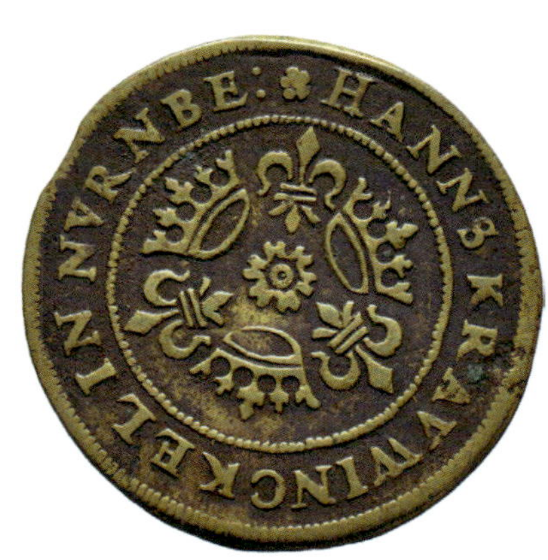
HANNS KRAVWINCKELIN NVRNBE:

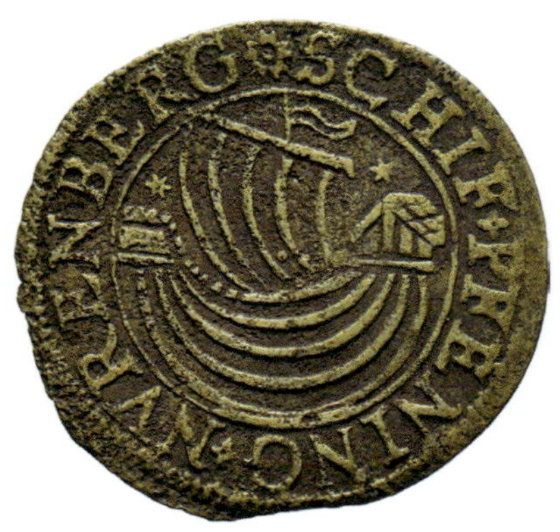
SCHIF·FRENING·NVRENBERG

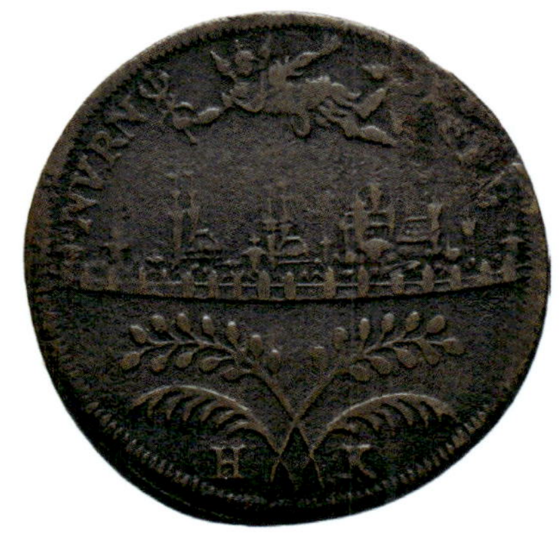

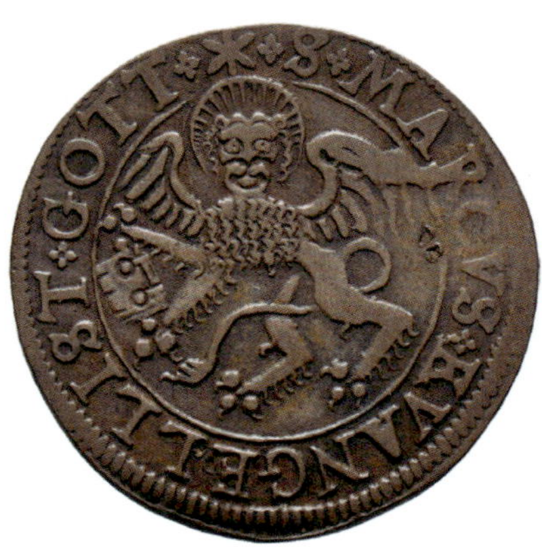
MARCVS EVANGELIST GOTT

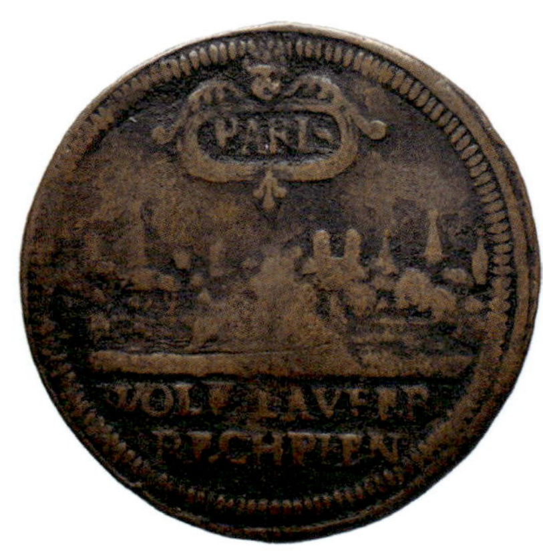
PARIS

23

THE VOTIVE PAINTING OF STEPHAN PRAUN

Nuremberg (?), 1511

Paint on limewood

H. 84.8 cm; W. 51.7 cm (with frame)

GNM, inv. no. Gm196

References:
Murr 1801, p. 151; Löcher 1997, pp. 306–9; Hess 2019, pp. 78, 80; Exh. cat. Nuremberg 2019a, p. 129, cat. no. 35.

This panel depicts the hazards faced by the Nuremberg merchant Stephan Praun I (1478–1532) during a business trip to northern Italy in 1511. According to the picture's inscription (probably refreshed in 1738), Praun and the goods he was transporting survived rough waters on Lake Garda ("Garztse"), only to be threatened by a group of Venetian mercenaries once back on land. Praun is shown kneeling on the lakefront, his hands lifted in prayer. His coat of arms and that of his first wife, Anna Gall (d. 1520), appear beside him. On the lake, a boat crew struggles to steady their vessel in the storm. Two of the boatmen reach skyward, directing their pleas for help to an apparition of the Holy Family in the clouds above. In the right foreground, four mercenaries on horseback, carrying colorful banners, gallop out of the picture. The inscription relates that Praun, in distress, appealed to the "Mother of God at the 'Twelve Brothers' here in Nuremberg," whereupon he was "mercifully helped."

This narrative depiction of a contemporary "merchant adventure" is highly unusual for a painting created in the age of Dürer, when most such works represented standard sacred subjects. The reason why the incident was considered worthy of painting at all was because Praun attributed his survival to the Virgin Mary's help. As a sign of gratitude, he dedicated the painting to the "Mother of God" located in the chapel of the Mendel Twelve Brothers' House, a charitable home. The reference is to a clay relief representing the Holy Family, which seems to have been venerated as a miraculous image, and to which Praun believed he owed his deliverance from danger. That makes the painting one of the earliest of all votive images; it was still hanging in the Twelve Brothers' Chapel when described by Murr in 1801.

Praun's confrontation with Venetian mercenaries probably occurred within the context of the period's battles for supremacy in northern Italy, then being fought in changing alliances such as the League of Cambrai and the Holy League. The ubiquitous wars of the early modern era hampered long-distance commerce—a situation emphasized in Jost Amman's *Allegory of Trade* |**cat. no. 21**|. The votive painting's inscription refers to the mercenaries as stradiots. These were light cavalrymen from the Peloponnese who had fought in service to Venice since the republic's wars against the Ottomans in the fifteenth century. Stradiots carried pennant-adorned lances, sabers, maces, and daggers, and they were feared for their lightning-fast attacks. Venetian sources emphasize the stradiots' ruthlessness.[1] A compositionally similar group of horsemen appears in one of Jörg Breu's woodcuts for the *Entry of Charles V into Augsburg* of about 1530.[2] Usually interpreted as Hungarian lancers, they likewise wear tall, cylindrical caps and carry bannered pikes. The painter of the votive panel thus appears to have used stock horseman figures, meant to be construed as vaguely eastern European in type.

With regard to authorship, the past attempts to attribute the painting to Hans von Kulmbach or Paul Lautensack (the latter active in Nuremberg from 1527) are both untenable on stylistic grounds. Comparison with another work from 1511, the altarpiece in Gutenstetten, painted largely by Albrecht Altdorfer's brother Erhard, likewise does not solve the problem.[3] Nevertheless, the votive panel exhibits characteristics of the so-called Danube Style, like the work in Gutenstetten. Future investigations into the picture's authorship will be necessary.

Benno Baumbauer

1 Pappas 2008.
2 New Hollstein German 7, p. 26, no. 28; Exh. cat. Braunschweig 2019, pp. 164–65, cat. no. 79 (Marcus Pilz).
3 On Gutenstetten, see Sturm and Teget-Welz 2022, pp. 91–94.

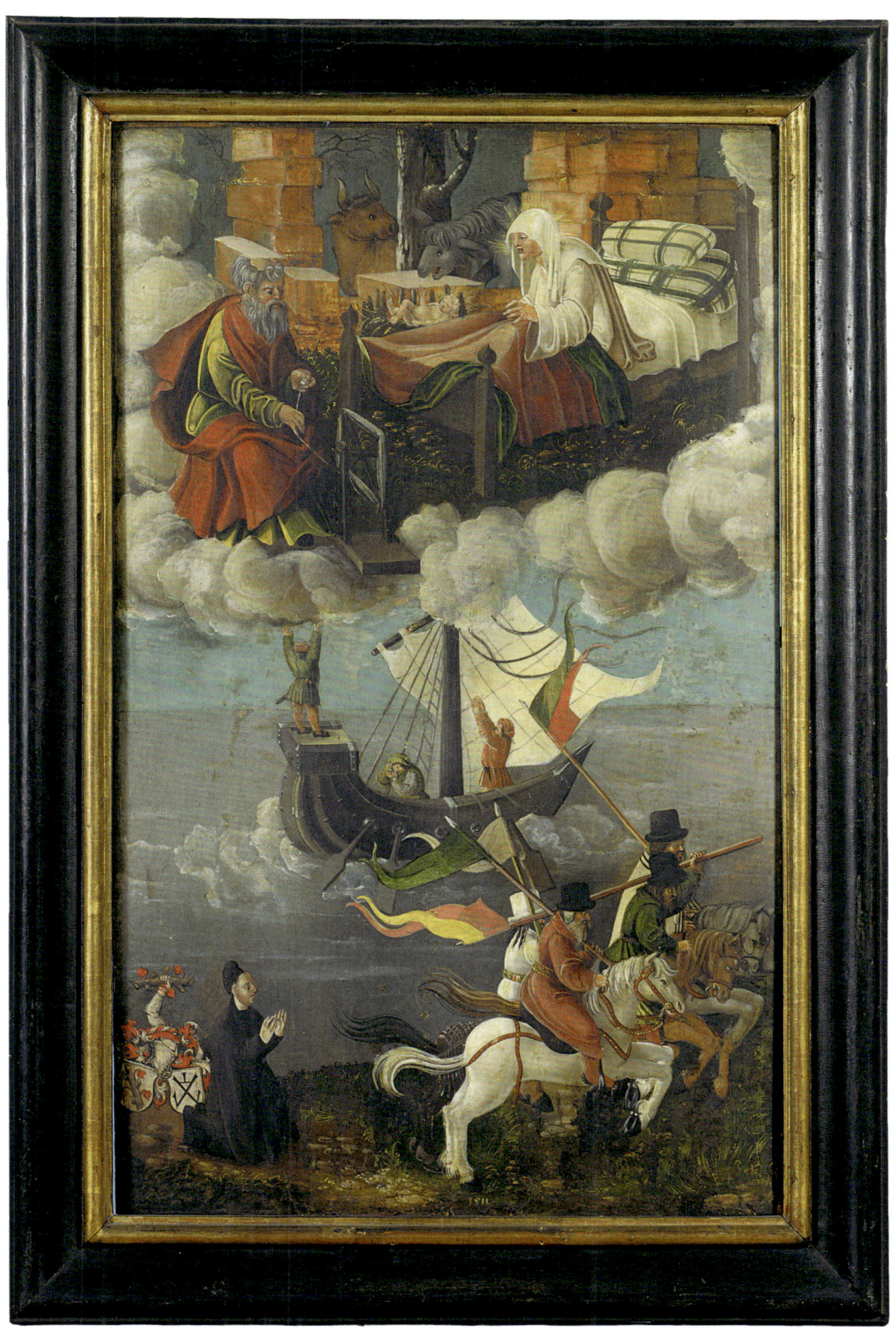

24

MEMORIAL FOR PETER VOLCKAMER I ("PIETÀ SERRISTORI")

Master of the Osservanza (Sano di Pietro or workshop?)

Siena, 1432 or shortly after

Paint on wood

H. 101 cm; W. 71 cm

Banca Monte dei Paschi di Siena, inv. no. 381476

References:
Erffa 1976, pp. 3–7; Exh. cat. Siena 2010, pp. 258–59, cat. no. C.31 (Andrea de Marchi); Angelini 2012, pp. 20, 21 n. 25, pl. 1; Kovács 2018, pp. 228–29; Exh. cat. Massa Maritima 2024, pp. 112–15, cat. no. 28 (Vittoria Pipino).

This painting, in early fifteenth-century Italian style, shows the dead Christ lying in his grieving mother's lap, his body spanning the picture's full width. To the right of the Virgin Mary, a gray-haired man with a moustache kneels in adoration. He wears a fur-trimmed tabard and holds a string of coral prayer beads |**see cat. no. 18**|. This figure is a memorial representation of a deceased person. The saint standing behind him, dressed in pilgrim's attire and holding a church model, serves as an intercessor, recommending the deceased man to the Virgin and Christ. Instruments of the Passion visualize Christ's suffering: the Holy Cross with nails, the scourge, the Holy Lance, and the vinegar sponge set on a staff. An inscription identifies the saint as "S. SIBALDUS" (Sebaldus), the patron saint of Nuremberg. Two coats of arms at the bottom of the painting identify the man who is being memorialized as a member of a Nuremberg patrician family: he is Peter Volckamer I, who died in Siena in 1432.

The memorial panel calls attention to the riskiness of long-distance travel before the modern era. Unlike the journey taken by Stephan Praun |**cat. no. 23**|, Volckamer's mission ended in death. He was traveling as a royal counselor and an envoy of the city of Nuremberg to King Sigismund's imperial coronation in Rome. Volckamer initially accompanied Sigismund as far as Feldkirch, at which point he left to participate in negotiations associated with the Hussite War. He rejoined Sigismund's entourage and army in Siena but died there on September 5, 1432. He was buried in Siena Cathedral, together with a certain Heinz Fuchs of Speckfeld, who had been shot near Acquapendente.[1] The explanation of why Volckamer was granted such a venerable burial place, despite being a foreigner, probably lies in his position at the royal court. Hans Martin von Erffa notes that the painting was probably commissioned by Peter Volckamer's son Berthold, who had been accompanying his father, along with a servant, some mercenaries, a cook, and a messenger, all financed by the Nuremberg city council.[2]

Peter Volckamer's memorial panel belongs to a group of works attributed to the Master of the Osservanza, so named after a triptych in the Basilica dell'Osservanza in Siena. Owing to stylistic and technical similarities to works by the Sienese artist Sano di Pietro (1405–1481), scholars have debated whether the two painters were collaborators, whether the anonymous artist was active in Sano's workshop, or whether the group of works in question might even represent an early stage of Sano's own production.[3] Apart from its style, the Volckamer panel also differs from memorials produced in Nuremberg in the scale of the person being commemorated. Contemporary Nuremberg memorials typically show the figures of the deceased much smaller than the holy figures, often in a separate area of the composition. Berthold Volckamer was able to have his father memorialized in a more prominent way in Siena than would have been acceptable at home. The inclusion of Saint Sebaldus, the hometown patron saint, is characteristic of works of art commissioned by Nurembergers abroad |**see also fig. p. 52**|.

Benno Baumbauer

1 "Item in demselben jar da rait der Peter Volkhaymer zu dem kunig gen der Hohen Syn und beleib da innen und starb am freitag vor unser frawen tag, als sy geporen ward. und zu derselben zeit ward Heincz Fuchß da innen derschossen, und ligen bede bey einander begraben zu der Hohen Syn zu unser frawen in dem thum." Kern 1862, p. 385. See also Erffa 1976, p. 6 n. 22; Kovács 2018, pp. 180–81, 228.
2 On the traveling entourage, see Kern 1862, p. 385 n. 2; Kovács 2018, p. 77.
3 Fattorini et al. 2012.

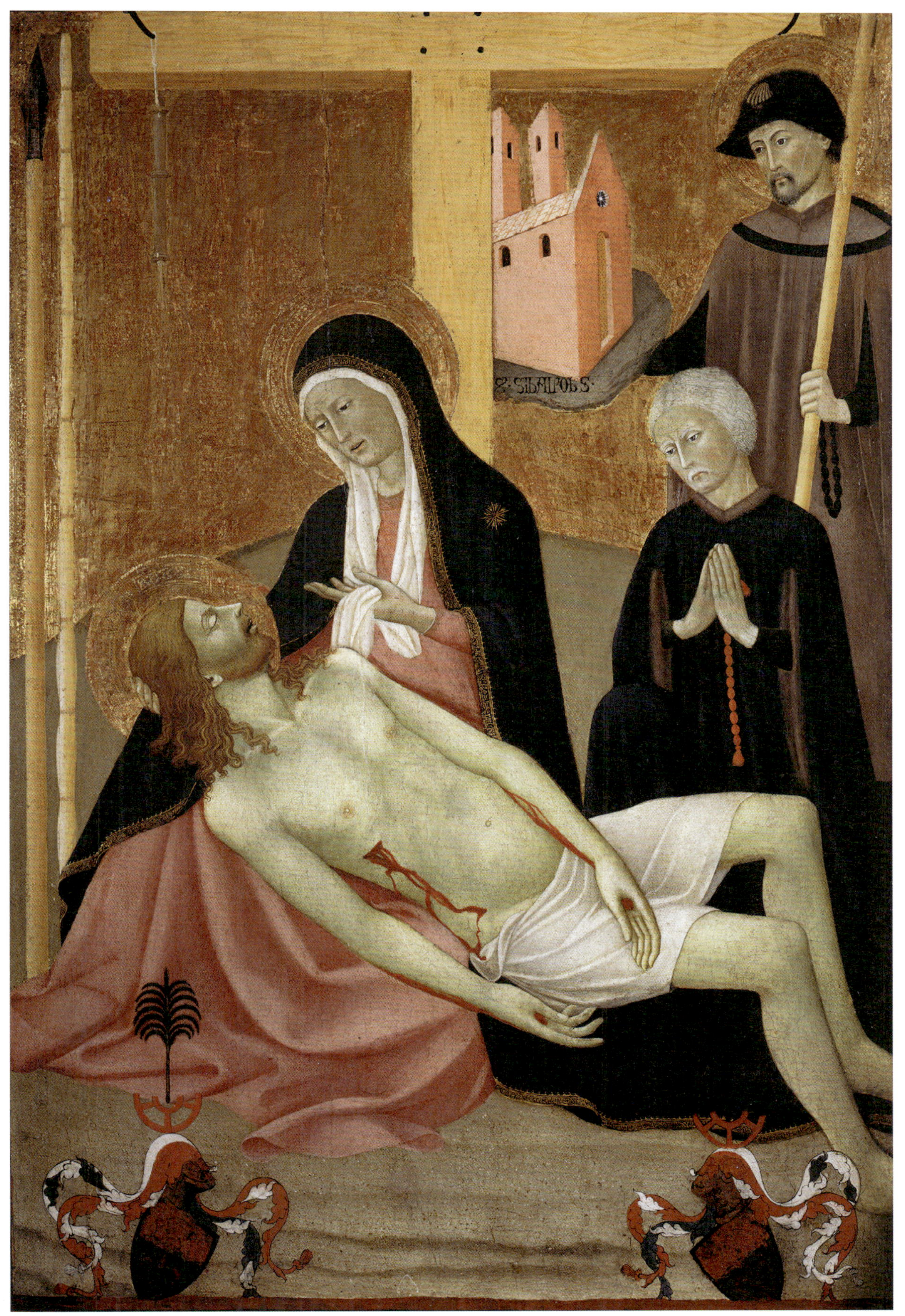

25

ROAD MAPS

Erhard Etzlaub (designer)

"This is the way to Rome through the German lands, mile by mile as indicated by points marked from one city to the next" (Das ist der Rom Weg von meylen zu meylen mit puncten verzeichnet von eyner stat zu der andern durch deutzsche lantt).

25.1 The "Way to Rome" Map (*Romwegkarte*) (not illustrated)

Nuremberg: Kaspar Hochfeder, 1499

Woodcut

H. 41.7 cm; W. 29.5 cm

GNM, inv. no. La142

25.2 Road Map of the Holy Roman Empire

Nuremberg: Albrecht Glockendon the Elder, 1533

Woodcut, hand-colored

H. 56.8 cm; W. 42.0 cm

GNM, inv. no. La217

References:
Exh. cat. Munich 1984, pp. 89–90, cat. no. 124 (Sigrid Canz); Exh. cat. Washington and Nuremberg 2005, pp. 204–6, cat. no. 56 (Rainer Schoch); Schneider 2004, pp. 21–23; Denzler 2023, pp. 109–12.

So goes the title at the top of the so-called *Romwegkarte*, a map designed in south-up orientation by Erhard Etzlaub (d. 1532) and printed in 1499. Within this depiction of Europe, the city of Nuremberg, where the woodcut was first published and received several reprints, lies exactly at the center. The map is superbly illustrative of how Nuremberg's location favored its strategy of networking with other trading centers.

The *Romwegkarte* or "Way to Rome" Map is Europe's oldest surviving printed road map.[1] From places as far away as Ribe on the North Sea, Nieuwpoort in Flanders, and Kraków in Poland, the map shows the distances between the most important cities and pilgrimage sites along the various routes to Rome. In the south, the Italian peninsula extends to Monte Sant'Angelo in Puglia. Across all the regions represented, the main morphological features of the terrain, such as mountain ranges and plateaus, are included. A compass dial is shown at the bottom center, accompanied by text that explains how a compass can be used to correctly read the map. Etzlaub, himself a compass maker, made significant contributions to that device's development as a scientific instrument |**cat. no. 26**|.[2]

This innovative map was probably originally conceived for planning trips to Rome in the Holy Year of 1500, when the city was Europe's main pilgrimage destination. In later editions, the map was expanded to include additional roads, making it a practical tool for all travelers, including merchants.[3] The map's utility in planning journeys—especially ones beginning in Nuremberg—is demonstrated by the additional routing depicted on the hand-colored impression from 1533.[4] From Nuremberg, given special emphasis with its municipal coat of arms, eight roads radiate outward, showing the accessibility of all of Europe within a densely branched network. Following the southern route via Schwabach, travelers could choose between two Alpine passes on the way to Italy. Heading west, the road through Rothenburg branched into further routes that connected Nuremberg with northern France, Flanders, and even England. To the north, Nuremberg's Buch and Bayreuth roads led respectively to the North Sea and Baltic Sea and further to Scandinavia or, via Saxony, to Bohemia, Silesia, Poland, and the Baltic lands. The long-distance trade route that departed Nuremberg in the east, in the direction of Sulzbach, ran through southern Poland and Lviv all the way to the Black Sea and thus to Constantinople. The road through Neuburg and Regensburg brought travelers to Salzburg and Carinthia.[5]

Laura Di Carlo

1 Exh. cat. Washington and Nuremberg 2005, p. 206, cat. no. 56 (Rainer Schoch).
2 Schneider 2004, p. 23.
3 Exh. cat. Munich 1984, pp. 89–90, cat. no. 124 (Sigrid Kanz).
4 See Denzler 2023, p. 111.
5 On Nuremberg's long-distance trade routes, see Diefenbacher 2000, p. 280.

MARE TIRENVM
MARE LIGVSTICVM
MARE ADRIATICVM
WINDEN
BOSSEN
KRABATEN
HVNGERN
POLEN
SCHLESI
PREISSN
POMERISCH MER
OSTER SEE
DEVTSCH MER
DAS GROS TEVTSCH MER
WVESTER SEE
SCHOTLANT
DENMARCK
DEN MARK
CELIDONIA SILVA
DELPHINAT
BVRGVNDA
FRANCA
FLAND
Albrecht Glockendon Illuminist. 1533

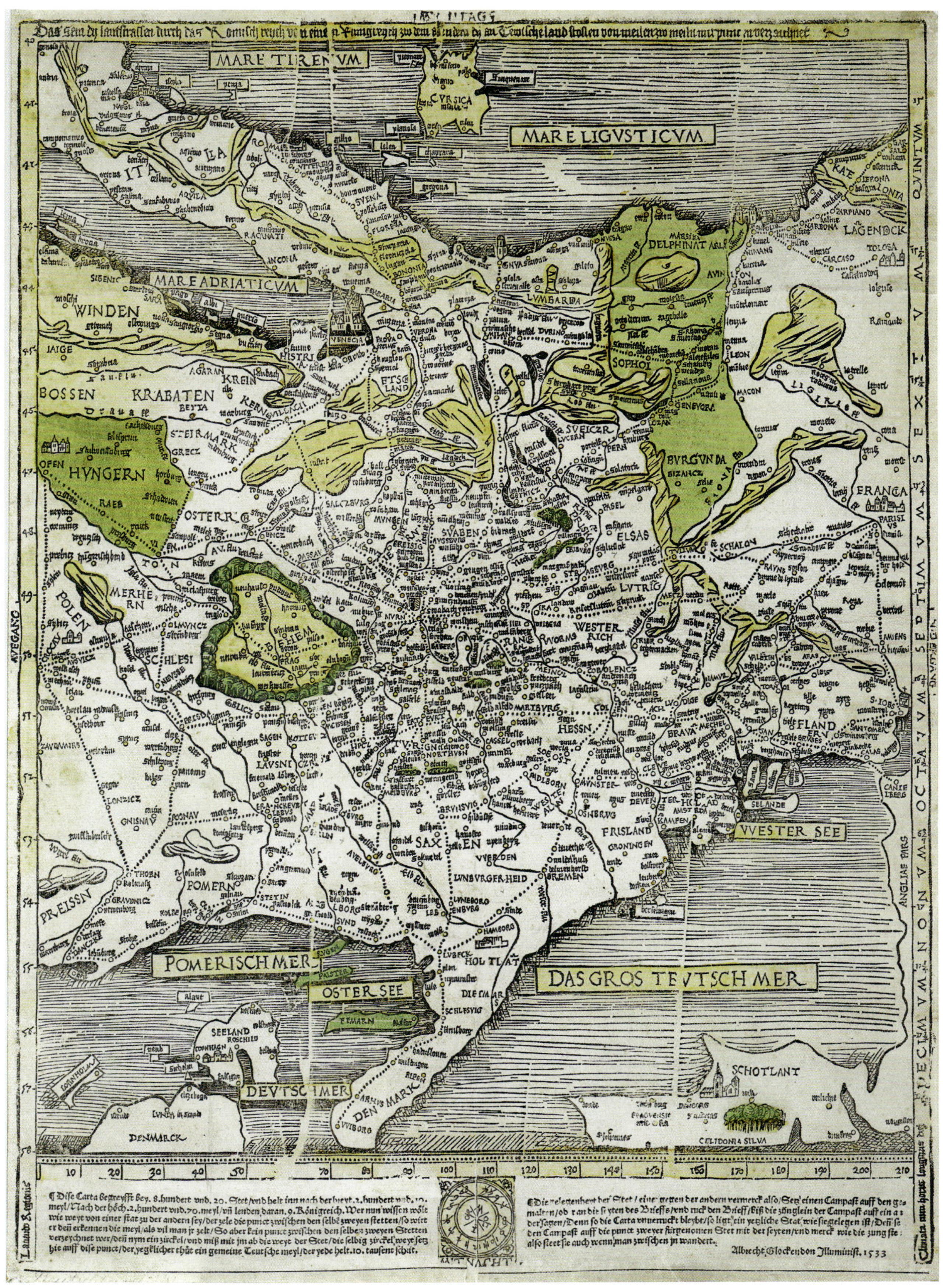

cat. no. 25.2

26

DIPTYCH SUNDIALS FROM NUREMBERG

26.1 Diptych Sundial with Map

Erhard Etzlaub

Nuremberg, 1511

Boxwood, cut, punched, filled in with color; brass

H. 12 cm (opened); W. 8.4 cm; D. 11.4 cm

GNM, inv. no. WI28, on long-term loan from the Museen der Stadt Nürnberg, Kunstsammlungen

26.2 Diptych Sundial, Ivory

Hans Tucher II

Nuremberg, ca. 1580

Ivory, engraved, punched, cut; brass; traces of red, blue, and black paint

H. 10.3 cm (opened); W. 5.4 cm; D. 1 cm

GNM, inv. no. WI1965

References:
26.1: Zinner 1967, p. 310; Exh. cat. Nuremberg 1992, vol. 2, pp. 670–71, cat. no. 2.27 (Johannes Willers); Meurer 2001, vol. 1, p. 135; Schewe and Goll 2019, pp. 13–14.
26.2: Eser 2014, p. 184, cat. no. 53.

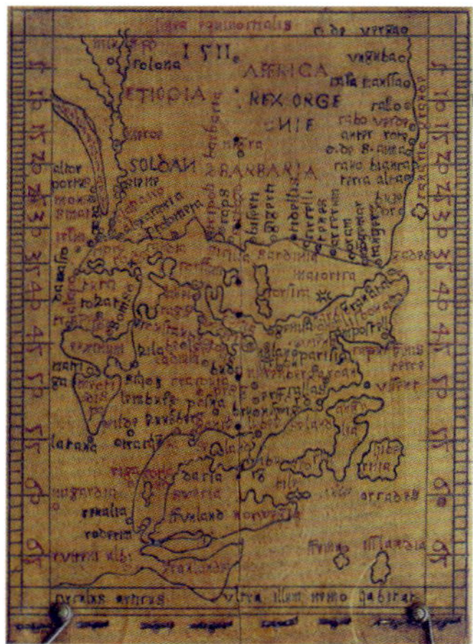

cat. no. 26.1
Back side of the cover panel

In the medieval period, information about travel routes, the distances between places, and the durations of journeys was more widely available and comprehensive than one might assume. One type of item that aided travelers was a guide called an *itinerarium*, containing lists of routes. It was a guide of this sort, by the name of *Den Weck und meylen von Erffort uß bys gen Rom* (The Way and Miles from Erfurt to Rome), that the compass maker and cartographer Erhard Etzlaub (d. 1532) used for the routes delineated on his map showing the ways to Rome (before 1499) |**cat. no. 25**|. The first half of the fifteenth century saw the introduction and refinement of another travel aid in Europe, this one not for directions and routes but rather for determining the time required to traverse a distance: the portable horizontal and vertical sundial, referred to in English as a "diptych sundial."

Etzlaub's diptych sundial, dated 1511, is one of the earliest surviving examples. It combines a number of fifteenth-century innovations. These include, firstly, a gnomon (the shadow-casting part) consisting of a string that stretched between the two dial faces when the device was opened. The string gnomon could be aligned with the Earth's axis and also allowed the sundial to be easily folded shut and transported without damaging the dials. Secondly, small holes in the cover panel enabled adjustment of the string gnomon for various northern latitudes. The Etzlaub sundial could thus be used at different locations: the inner face of the cover panel has dials for the latitudes 24°, 30°, 36°, and 49°30', while the horizontal panel features dials for 42°, 49 ½°, and 54 ½°. The respective latitudes correspond to place-names given on a south-up oriented map located on the outside of the cover panel. The map shows Europe and northern Africa—from Scandinavia to Ethiopia, and from the west coast of Africa to the east coast of the Black Sea. Thirdly, a compass embedded in the horizontal panel was used for north-south orientation. Compasses significantly increased the precision of portable sundials by taking into account the phenomenon of magnetic variation—that is, the deviation between magnetic north and true north, which became known in the mid-fifteenth century. When the sundial was opened, aligned north-south, and the string gnomon was set according to the local latitude, then the shadow cast by the sun on the dial indicated the current time. Both the formal similarity to Etzlaub's "Way to Rome" Map and the special emphasis given to Mount Sinai support the assumption that this diptych sundial was used on pilgrimages.

The information marked on the diptych sundial made by Hans Tucher II (d. 1615) is less specific, suggesting that the device was intended for use both by pilgrims and by merchants involved in long-distance trade. Another highly "communicative" object, this ivory sundial does not skimp on advice and instructions about its use. The cover panel contains a vertical dial meant to indicate day length, an important factor for travelers. Below that are four small holes marked with the latitudes 45°, 48°, 51°, and 54°, accompanied by the following instruction: "Attach the string to the hole corresponding to your location's latitude" (den faden duh [*sic*] in das löchlein des lands polus grad). Instead of a tabular list of places with their respective latitudes, as is commonly found on diptych sundials in the second half of the sixteenth century, this example has a running text that lists broad regions and cities corresponding to the latitudes 48° and 45°. The horizontal panel features a sundial for the latitudes marked on the cover panel.

Elephant ivory was a particularly suitable material for diptych sundials because of its hardness and its white color, which yielded clear shadows. After having been scarce in Europe throughout the Middle Ages, ivory became more widely available, including in Nuremberg, as new trade routes opened to West Africa, India, and Southeast Asia.

Susanne Thürigen

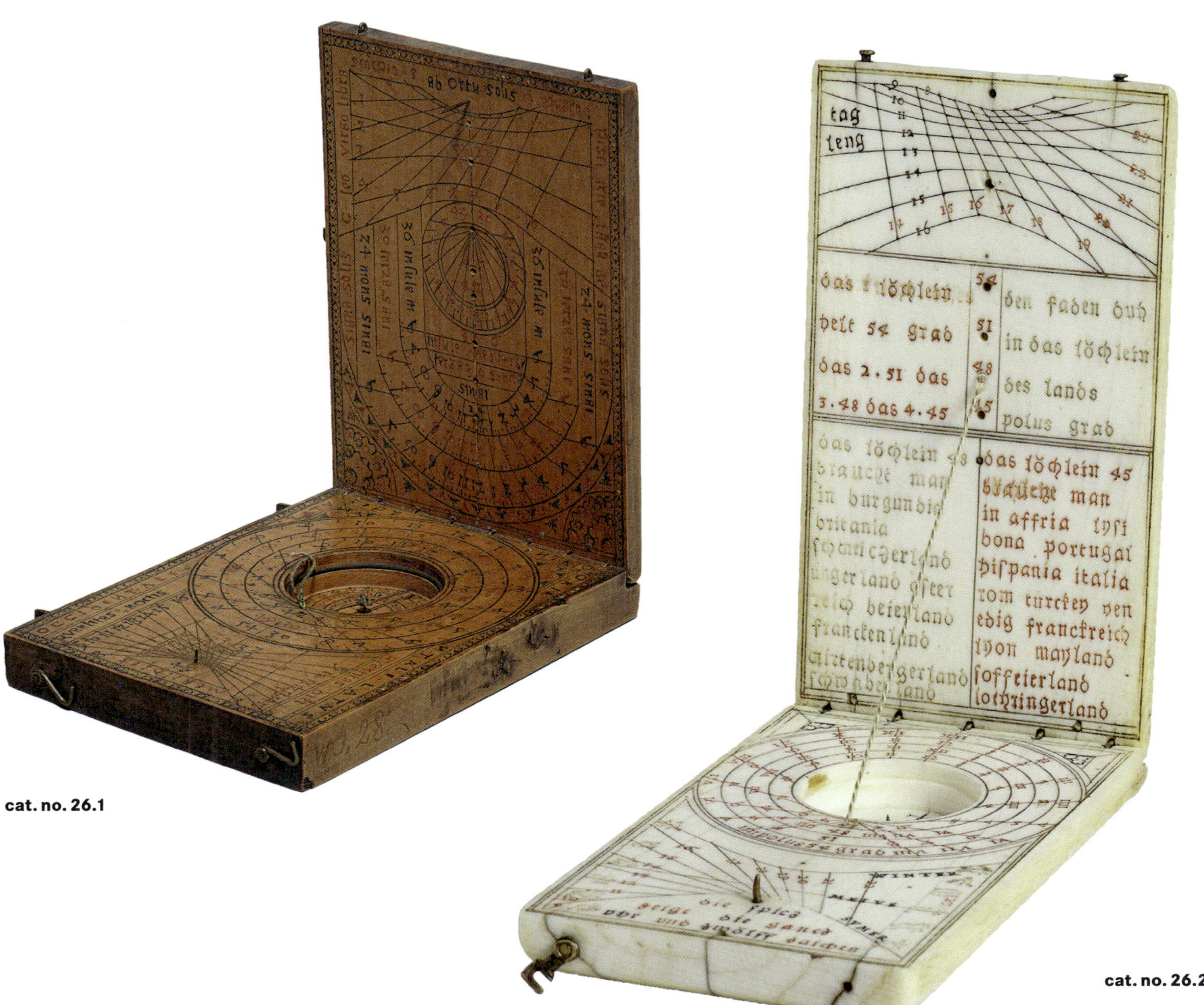

cat. no. 26.1

cat. no. 26.2

27

THE SCHEURL *ERZSTUFE*

Martin Stieber

Nuremberg, 1563

Ores, minerals, corals, mother-of-pearl, snail shells, silver, enamel, base added after 1950

H. 29.5 cm; W. 35.0 cm; D. 24.0 cm

GNM, inv. no. HG10294

References:
Slotta 1990, pp. 47–48; Exh. cat. Bochum 1990, pp. 562–79, cat. no. 244 (Rainer Slotta); Exh. cat. Nuremberg 2004, pp. 131–32 (Barbara Dienst); Kammel 2010a, p. 236; Exh. cat. Nuremberg 2024, pp. 81–82, cat. no. 25 (Heike Zech).

At first glance, the Scheurl *Erzstufe* (literally, "chunk of ore") appears to be a natural stone formation. Yet a closer inspection reveals this miniature mountain to be a man-made object composed of a variety of ores and minerals, including silver ore, quartz, amethyst, fluorite, cassiterite, malachite, azurite, petrified wood, and carnelian. Among the other natural materials and objects found here are pieces of mother-of-pearl, snail shells, and coral branches made to look like trees. Small enameled figures arranged in scenes bring the miniature landscape to life. In the main view, one sees hunters and their dogs cornering a stag, while elsewhere a crossbowman takes aim at a chamois. The crevices at the sides and back reveal further figures still: miners extracting ore and transporting it above ground in mine carts. These scenes illustrate the mining techniques used to extract the very materials from which this work of art was made. The work's creator, the Nuremberg goldsmith Martin Stieber (d. 1592), added a silver crucifix near the top and various delicate plant forms, possibly cast from natural specimens. These have lost their former luster as a result of corrosion.

In the second half of the sixteenth century, such collectible ore specimens and compositions—referred to either as *Erzstufen* or *Handsteine* (hand stones)—found their way mainly into mineral collections as well as art and curiosity cabinets in the princely sphere. In those contexts, the objects invited viewers not only to marvel but also to exchange mineralogical and mining knowledge. For potentates whose territories included significant mining operations, *Erzstufen* served as prestige objects. Such works allowed rulers to display the riches of the earth provided by God and nature, while also showcasing the rulers' skill in overseeing the extraction of resources.

Although the Scheurl *Erzstufe* does not come from a princely collection, it represents a comparable desire for the display of status. The Scheurls of Nuremberg were a family of merchants. According to their family chronicle, it was Christoph Scheurl III (1535–1592) who collected the materials for this *Erzstufe*. The alabaster lion at the work's pinnacle bears a shield with a Scheurl coat of arms. This figure was probably a later addition; at the time of the work's creation, a clock occupied that space at the top. The *Erzstufe* originally stood on a base equipped with a "drawer containing cast portraits"—presumably portrait medals made of precious metal, another representative product of the mining industry.

The Scheurls owed their wealth to long-distance trade and particularly to mining. Christoph Scheurl I (1457–1519), the grandfather of Christoph III, had moved from Wrocław (Breslau) to Nuremberg around 1480. The family remained in possession of mining rights in the Bohemian mining districts of Horní Slavkov (Schlaggenwald) and Jáchymov (Sankt Joachimsthal). Christoph III used the *Erzstufe* to showcase his family's far-reaching trade relations and entrepreneurial prowess. In doing so, he adopted forms of self-representation characteristic of the nobility. This helped to consolidate his family's position in relation to Nuremberg's patrician class, to which the Scheurls gained admission only in 1729. Beyond the immediate family context, the *Erzstufe* underscores the fact that Nuremberg's prosperity in the sixteenth century and the florescence of its arts and crafts derived to no small extent from the mining industry.

Verena Suchy

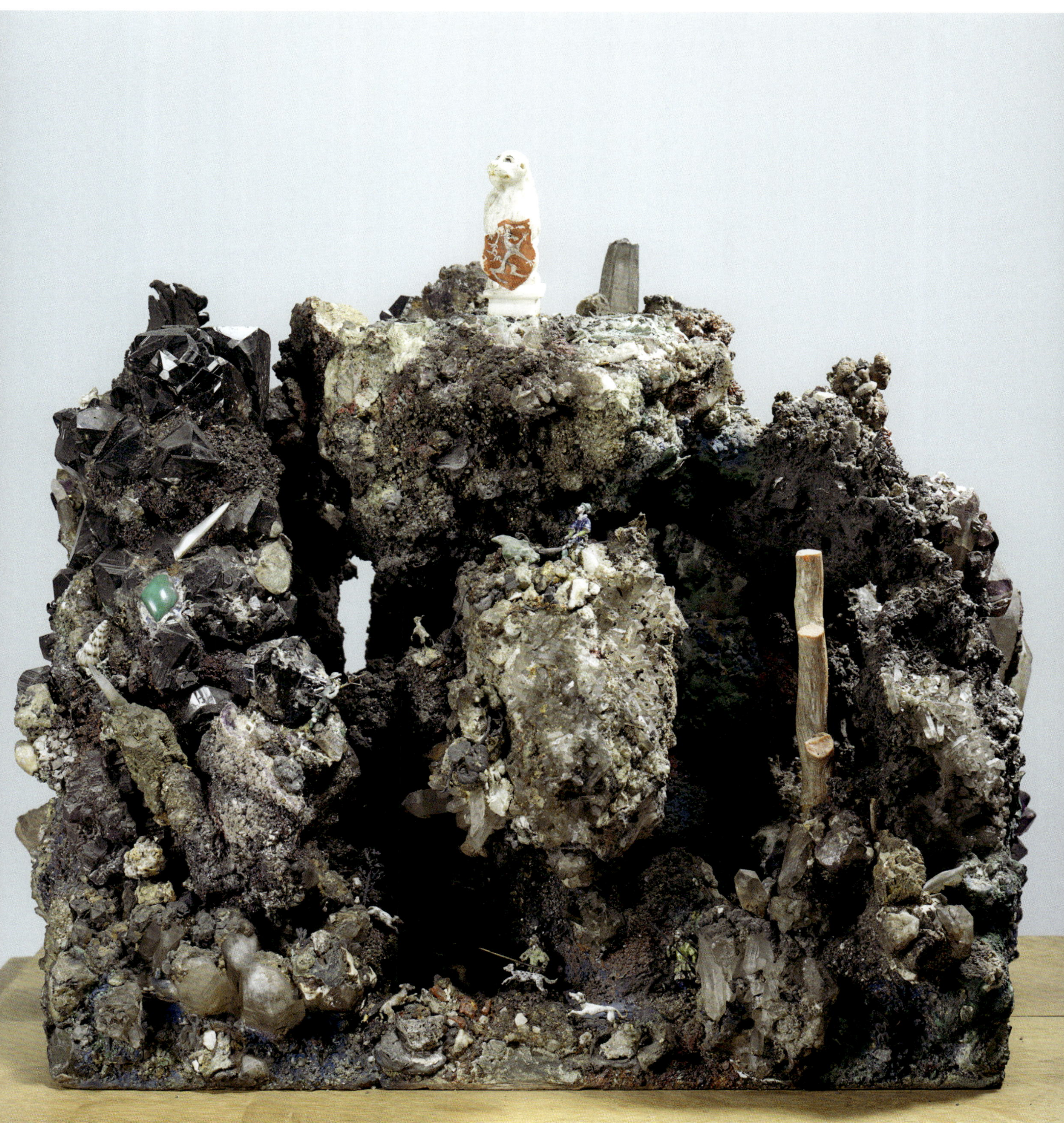

28

THE IMHOFF–HOLZSCHUHER CUP AND MINING SCENES

28.1 The Imhoff-Holzschuher Cup

Hans Pezolt

Nuremberg, 1593/1602

Silver-gilt, repoussé, cast, engraved, chased, etched, punched

H. 46.3 cm; Diam. 12.4 cm (stem); Diam. 11.8 cm (bowl)

Madrid, Thyssen-Bornemisza Collections, inv. no. DEC0972

28.2–3 Mining Scenes
(figs. p. 40)

Virgil Solis

Nuremberg, before 1562

Etchings

28.2: H. 3.2 cm; W. 16.9 cm

Kupferstichkabinett, Staatliche Museen zu Berlin, inv. no. 814-6

28.3: H. 3.3 cm; W. 17.1 cm

Kupferstichkabinett, Staatliche Museen zu Berlin, inv. no. 815-6

References:
Pittioni 1969, pp. 1–37; Exh. cat. Nuremberg 1985, p. 255, cat. no. 74 (Günther Schiedlausky); Müller 1986, pp. 194–99, cat. no. 58; Exh. cat. Bochum 1990, pp. 518–26, cat. no. 230 (Rainer Slotta); Tebbe 2007, p. 176.

The so-called Imhoff-Holzschuher Cup is supported by a foot with representations of the four elements. The stem is formed by the heraldic animal of the Nuremberg patrician family Imhoff: a lion with a fish's tail. The bell-shaped bowl, rising above a surround of stylized foliage, displays nine relief scenes depicting mining activities and the processing of ores.[1] The domed cover, showing allegories of the four seasons, supports an obelisk-like structure that culminates in another Imhoff "sea lion."

By the mid-sixteenth century, the Imhoff family was one of Nuremberg's most important large-scale traders in metals. Among other things, the family was a shareholder in the *Saigerhandel* company of Gräfenthal, which sold copper and silver smelted there by means of the so-called *Saiger* process.[2] The scenes on the cup's bowl probably refer to this involvement in the mining industry. This work's creator, the goldsmith Hans Pezolt (ca. 1551–1633), hailed from the mining town of Jáchymov (Sankt Joachimsthal). While he based some of the cup's scenes on prints by Virgil Solis (1514–1562) |**fig. p. 40**|, he appears also to have implemented pictorial ideas of his own.

The lip of the cup displays a poem in praise of mining. Beneath that, six inscriptions identify the scenes located on the large lobe of the bowl |**fig. p. 41**|. "The First Mine" (*Das Erste Bergkwerckh*) shows work happening down in a mine chamber.[3] While one miner hammers at the wall, others are filling a tray with ore. "The Second Mine" shows operations both below and above ground, with one worker on a ladder and another pulling a filled tray, whilst, above ground, another miner processes chunks of ore. "The Third Mine" illustrates ore conveyance: two miners operate a hoist to draw a bucket from the shaft; another pushes a cart out of a tunnel. The fourth scene is devoted to the "Weighing of Ore" (*Ertzwegen*) and shows crushed pieces of ore being put on the scales. The fifth step in the process is described as "The Washworks" (*das Wäschwerckh*): a miner, under the watch of a supervisor, rinses a bucket of crushed ore at a fountain. The sixth scene, labeled "Refining Furnace" (*TreibOfen*), depicts the aforementioned *Saiger* process, in which silver was extracted from copper ore by the addition of lead. The three smaller, uncaptioned scenes on the lower part of the bowl illustrate further steps in processing ore. Two of the scenes concern the melting down of ore and the sampling of alloys. The third shows metal being weighed.

A plaquette attached to the inside of the lid is engraved with a depiction of the Calling of Saints Peter and Andrew. The image is surrounded by the names of three members of the Holzschuher family: "ANNA REGINA. GEORGIUS ET VITUS GEORGIUS HOLZSCHUCHERI." Another plaquette, this one on the underside of the foot, bears a Holzschuher coat of arms and an inscription indicating that these three Holzschuher siblings, wards of their uncle "ANDREAE IM HOFF" (Andreas Imhoff III, 1572–1637), had given the cup to their uncle in 1626 as a token of thanks. Andreas Imhoff had become their guardian after the deaths of their parents. At the time of the gift, he was involved in mining as the chief administrator of the Eißfeld *Saiger* operation.[4] As indicated by the hallmark stamped on the work, which was valid from 1593 to 1602, Hans Pezolt must have created this cup earlier than scholars had originally thought.[5] It could not have been commissioned by any of the three Holzschuher siblings, who were all born after 1602. They probably inherited it from their mother, Regina (1580–1613). She was Andreas Imhoff's sister and held investments in the Gräfenthal *Saigerhandel* company. The two plaquettes, which had been decisive for the incorrect dating, must therefore be later additions, attached to the cup for the purpose of gifting it to Andreas Imhoff.

Birgit Schübel

1 Exh. cat. Bochum 1990, pp. 518–26, cat. no. 230 (Rainer Slotta); Pittioni 1960, pp. 1–37.
2 Hildebrandt 1977, p. 223; Kalus 2010, pp. 92–93.
3 Müller 1986, pp. 194–99, cat. no. 58.
4 Krauß 1732, p. 16.
5 NGK 2007, vol. 1, pt. 1, p. 305, cat. no. 640.17.

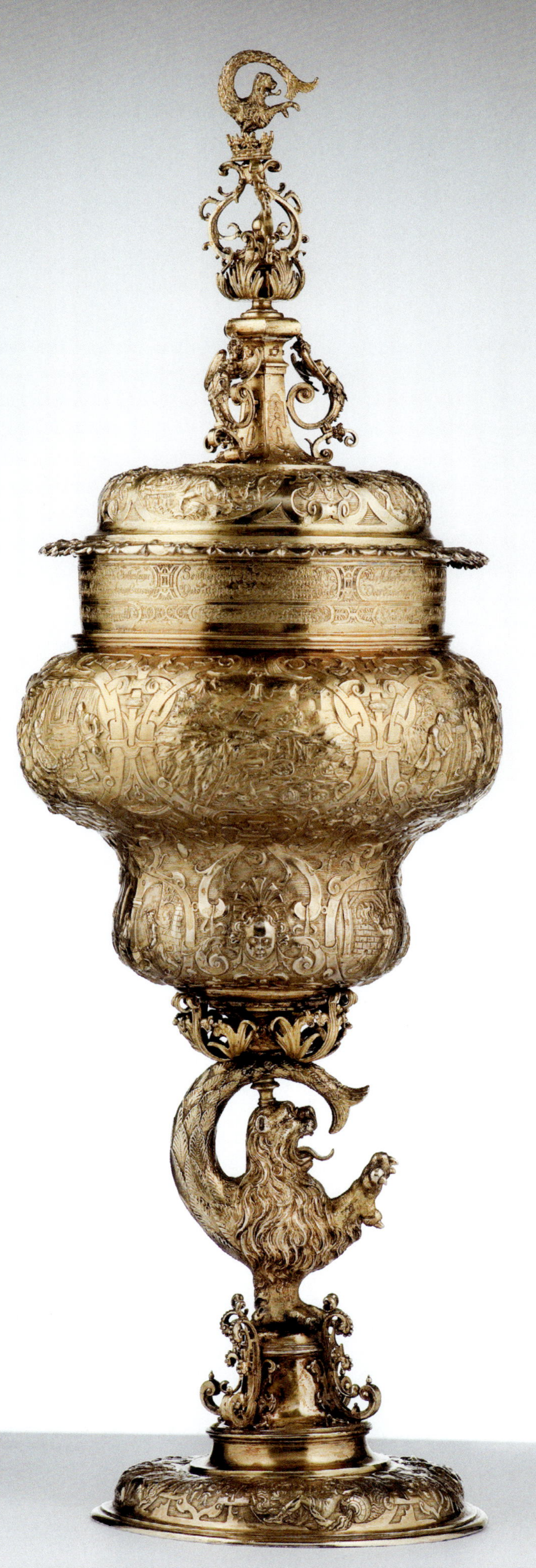

29

KEYSTONE FROM THE HEILIG-GEIST-SPITAL IN NUREMBERG

Nuremberg, ca. 1335

Sandstone, polychromed and gilded
H. 52 cm; W. 67 cm; D. 42 cm
GNM, inv. no. A3929

References:
Kammel 2007, pp. 222–23; Hess et al. 2007, p. 416, cat. no. 322.

This keystone from a vaulted ceiling was recovered from the postwar ruins of Nuremberg's Heilig-Geist-Spital (Holy Spirit Hospital) in May 1946.[1] The stone is carved in relief with a Vera Icon, a "true image" of Christ. The work's style dates it to the period of the hospital's construction, which began after 1331, when Konrad Groß I (d. 1356) founded the institution, and was completed in 1339.

Groß was by all accounts the wealthiest citizen of Nuremberg. Through shrewd investments, he maximized the income from the extensive property holdings he had inherited from his father, Heinrich. As a financial trader and entrepreneur, Groß amassed one of the largest capital and real-estate fortunes of the time. By 1333 at the latest, he had established a close relationship with Emperor Louis (Ludwig) the Bavarian (r. 1314–47), who often stayed with Groß when in Nuremberg. Groß operated as a court banker and financier for the emperor, who was plagued by financial shortcomings. In return, in 1339, Louis pledged Groß the office of *Reichsschultheiß* (imperial mayor) as well as customs and minting authority in Nuremberg.[2]

Groß's wealth presented am impediment to his salvation as a Christian, since the financial dealings he took part in blatantly violated the church's prohibition of usury. He therefore devoted a considerable portion of his wealth to religious endowments. He summed up his motivation as follows: "How salutary it is to assist the poor; while endeavoring to help one's neighbor in his current misery, one earns salvation from eternal misery."[3]

For his hospital project, Groß acquired a plot of land along the Pegnitz River, in the affluent Saint Sebaldus parish. Construction began in 1332, and the finished complex had room to accommodate two hundred patients and residents. Together with Groß's endowment for the institution's permanent upkeep, this was one of the largest charitable foundations of the Middle Ages. The Spitalkirche (hospital church) was especially important as a place of worship because the hospital residents were required to pray for the salvation of the founder's soul. In the church's furnishings and personnel, Groß manifested his desire for the display of status: this included six altars with their own benefices and twelve choir boys who, under the direction of a schoolmaster, accompanied the liturgy with song.[4] After his death in 1356, Groß was buried in the most exclusive location in the Spitalkirche, in the chancel, before the high altar. His resting place was marked by an elaborate table tomb, which is now situated in the hospital courtyard.

After the hospital's wartime destruction in 1945, a keystone with a representation of the Agnus Dei was recovered from the ruins of the chancel in December of that year.[5] The Vera Icon keystone was found during a follow-up excavation in the rubble of the sacristy, on the south side of the former chancel. Given their similarity in size, profile, and polychromy, both keystones must come from the same structural context.[6] Each shows the beginnings of double-grooved ribs. The ribs' number and arrangement indicate irregular vault forms: while the Vera Icon marked the intersection of three ribs, the Agnus Dei was positioned in an irregular four-part rib vault. The vault of the chancel can be ruled out as the original location, because the ribs there were pear-shaped in profile. These keystones can therefore be assigned to the former sacristy vault.

Markus T. Huber

1 Report, "Bericht über die 17. Sitzung des Komitees zur Erhaltung der Nürnberger Denkmäler, Kunstwerke, Bibliotheken und Archive … am Mittwoch, den 8. Mai 1946," fol. 2, Historisches Archiv, GNM A-000593.2, GNM, Nuremberg.
2 Exh. cat. Nuremberg 1989, pp. 41–43 (Michael Diefenbacher); Fleischmann 2008, vol. 2, pp. 457–59.
3 Translated from the citation in Löhlein 1963–64, p. 67.
4 Exh. cat. Nuremberg 1989, pp. 43–47 (Michael Diefenbacher); Böckel 1990, esp. pp. 13–16; Stolz 2007, pp. 6–12.
5 GNM, inv. no. A3928.
6 Report, "Bericht Nr. 5 des Bergungstrupps Gruber vom 7.12.1945," Historisches Archiv, GNM A-000593.7, GNM, Nuremberg. See also Kammel 2007, pp. 222–23.

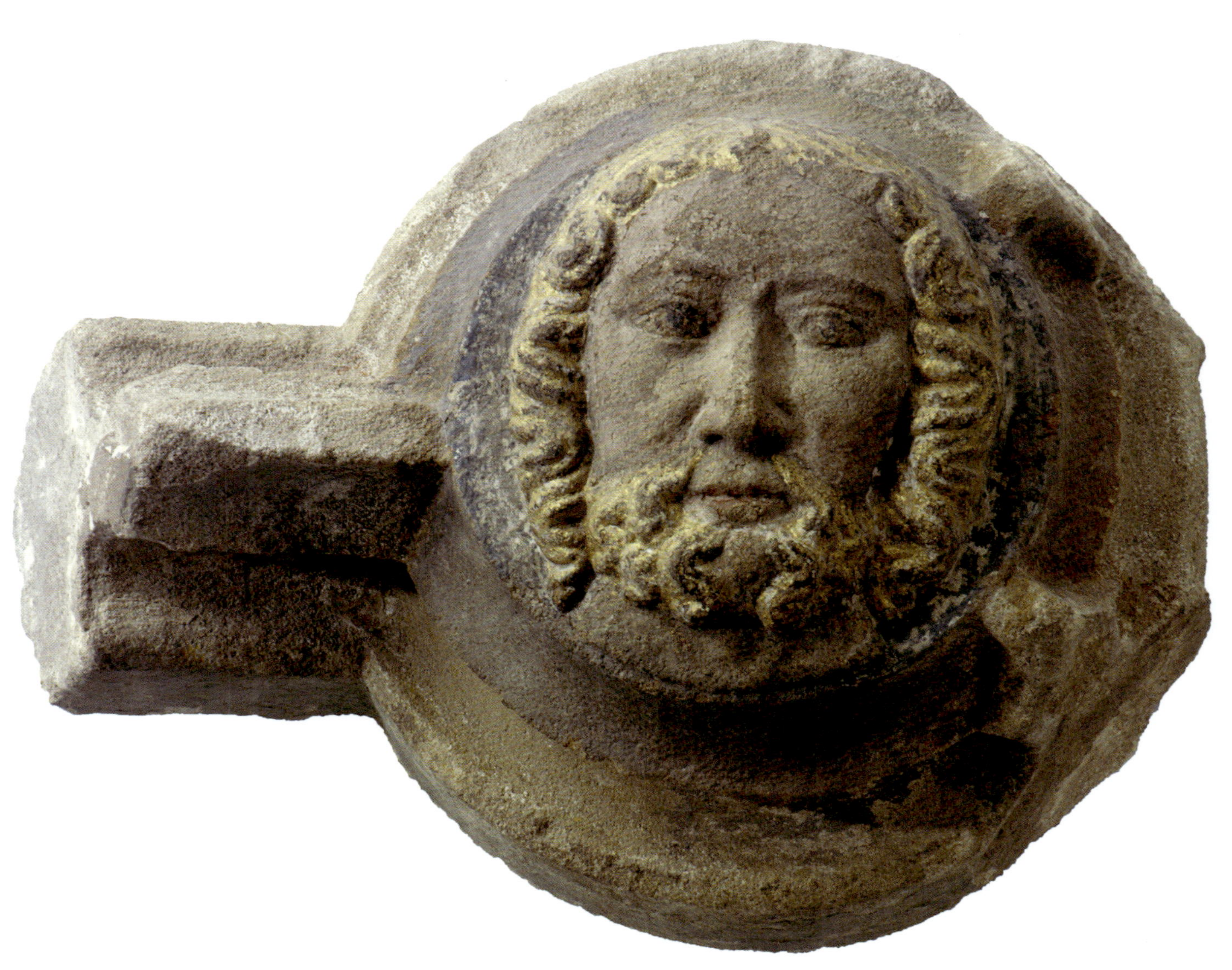

30

THE MASS OF SAINT GREGORY

Unknown painter, active in Nuremberg (circle of Hans Traut?)

Nuremberg, ca. 1500

Paint on fir

H. 187.9; W. 138.2 cm

GNM, inv. no. Gm154

References:
Flurschütz da Cruz 2014, pp. 94–111; Hess, Hirschfelder, and Baum 2019, pt. 2, pp. 928–41, cat. no. 64 (Katja von Baum and Esther Meier); Meier 2021.

In the year 1500, Heinrich Wolf von Wolfsthal (d. 1504) was one of Nuremberg's wealthiest citizens, with an estimated fortune of 100,000 guldens. That year, death claimed his wife, Katharina, daughter of the Nuremberg goldsmith Sylvester Mayr. In her memory, Heinrich Wolf commissioned this painting of the Mass of Saint Gregory and had it installed in the Dominikanerkirche in Nuremberg. The subject, a popular one during the late Middle Ages, is based on a legend that tells of Christ's miraculous appearance before Pope Gregory the Great (d. 604) while Gregory was celebrating Mass at Santa Croce in Gerusalemme in Rome. The saint is shown kneeling at an altar, before a half-length figure of Christ as the Man of Sorrows displaying the stigmata.

To distinguish his picture from other paintings of the same subject, Heinrich appears to have ordered the painter to create a work of exceptional opulence. Not only is the panel unusually large, but the Mass is also staged in a particularly splendid manner, with five other saints positioned around the altar and Gregory accompanied by a bishop and two deacons, all dressed in the most sumptuous vestments, embroidered with pearls and precious stones. Also, the Arma Christi, the instruments of suffering that allude to Christ's Passion, are strikingly numerous in the upper half of the painting. The impression of opulence and splendor culminates in the lavish use of shimmering silver and gold leaf.

In the late Middle Ages, memorial pictures such as this *Mass of Saint Gregory* not only expressed the piety of those who commissioned them, but they also reflected patrons' financial and social status |**see cat. no. 49**|. As a newcomer to Nuremberg, Heinrich was keen to assert his high social standing. Born into a merchant family that was involved in long-distance trade and active in Antwerp, Poland, and Venice, Heinrich moved from Nördlingen to Nuremberg in 1469, thereafter quickly establishing himself as one of the city's leading textile and spice merchants. His most important and lucrative business, however, was in the trade in metals. The shares he owned in the silver mines at Schneeberg and Schwaz enabled him to engage in large and at times risky financial operations involving notable personalities. For example, he lent considerable sums to the future Emperor Maximilian I and also supplied Maximilian with Milanese weapons and armor.

Heinrich's wealth and excellent contacts enabled him to join Nuremberg's Greater Council in 1475 and to buy an impressive house near the Hauptmarkt toward the end of the century. He married off his daughters to members of the patrician families Haller and Tucher.[1] Yet his political ambitions were greater still. Although he did not belong to one of the families long represented on the city council, his connections to Maximilian I enabled him to be appointed a delegate to the Inner Council, the city's highest governing body, in 1499. When his son Balthasar was ennobled by Maximilian at a meeting of the Imperial Government (*Reichsregiment*) in Nuremberg (1500–1502), the family was at the peak of its prestige. Heinrich Wolf's commissioning of this costly *Mass of Saint Gregory* painting is therefore also a testimony to his and his family's newfound sense of status as merchants who could henceforth grace their name with the noble addition "von Wolfsthal."[2]

Judith Hentschel

1 Fleischmann 2008, vol. 2, pp. 1165–67.
2 The Wolfs also had a family tree prepared in the context of their ennoblement. See Flurschütz da Cruz, Vroom, and Zander-Seidel 2017.

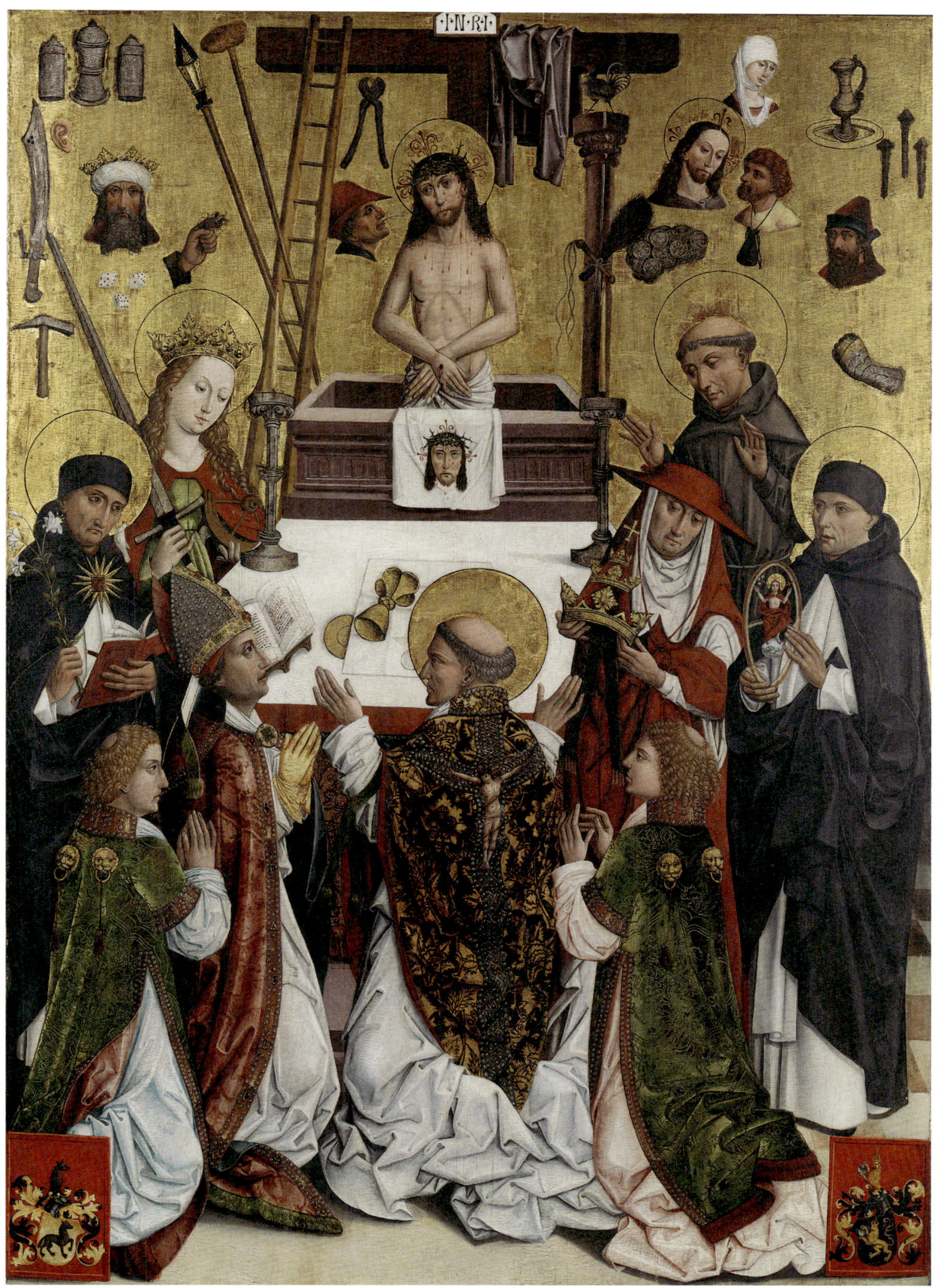
·I·N·R·I·

31

CHRIST DRIVING THE MONEY LENDERS FROM THE TEMPLE

Albrecht Dürer

Nuremberg, ca. 1508–9

Woodcut

31.1

H. 12.7 cm; W. 9.8 cm

GNM, inv. no. H7617, Kapsel 19e

31.2 (not illustrated)

H. 12.5 cm; W. 9.7 cm

GNM, inv. no. H211, Kapsel 16

References:
Schoch, Mende, and Scherbaum 2002, pp. 296–97, no. 192 (Erich Schneider).

This print illustrates an episode from the Gospel of John (2:13–16): "Jesus went up to Jerusalem. In the temple he found those who were selling oxen and sheep and pigeons, and the money-changers at their business. And making a whip of cords, he drove them all, with the sheep and oxen, out of the temple; and he poured out the coins of the money-changers and overturned their tables. And he told those who sold the pigeons, 'Take these things away; you shall not make my Father's house a house of trade.'"

Albrecht Dürer's woodcut indicates the setting, the Temple in Jerusalem, with just a few architectural elements. A receding row of columns lends depth to the space, but the overall impression is one of oppressive confinement. A single candle burns at the back wall, its light barely penetrating the prevailing darkness. Only the foreground figures are brightly illuminated. With precision and economy of line, Dürer lent great plasticity and volume to Christ's robe. Yet the figure of Christ is marked by a certain ambiguity: on the one hand, Christ appears solid, steady, and still; on the other hand, he seems to be charging energetically forward. He raises the whip with his right arm, about to strike the man lying motionless on the ground. The raised arm hides half of Christ's face and shrouds the rest of his countenance in shadow. Two gleaming white dots are the only indications of his eyes. This makes Christ seem strangely distant, while at the same time intensifying his apparent fury. Dürer devoted great attention to rendering the facial expressions and gestures of the surrounding men. Their faces reflect fear, astonishment, horror, and panic. An overturned table and bench indicate the force with which Christ cleaves through the crowd of merchants. A bulging sack of coins has fallen to the ground at the lower right, and loose coins are scattered beside it. Dürer placed his famous monogram in the corresponding position at the lower left.

The woodcut belongs to Dürer's *Small Passion* series (no. 7). With thirty-seven scenes, it was the most extensive print cycle in his oeuvre. It was published in Nuremberg in 1511, with Latin texts by Benedictus Chelidonius. An edition was printed in Venice in 1612. Entries in Dürer's diary suggest that he brought copies of the Small Passion on his trip to the Low Countries. In light of Nuremberg's position as a globally networked center of trade, Dürer's depiction of Christ expelling the money lenders can also be understood as a subtle commentary on the business affairs of his fellow citizens.

Sven Jakstat

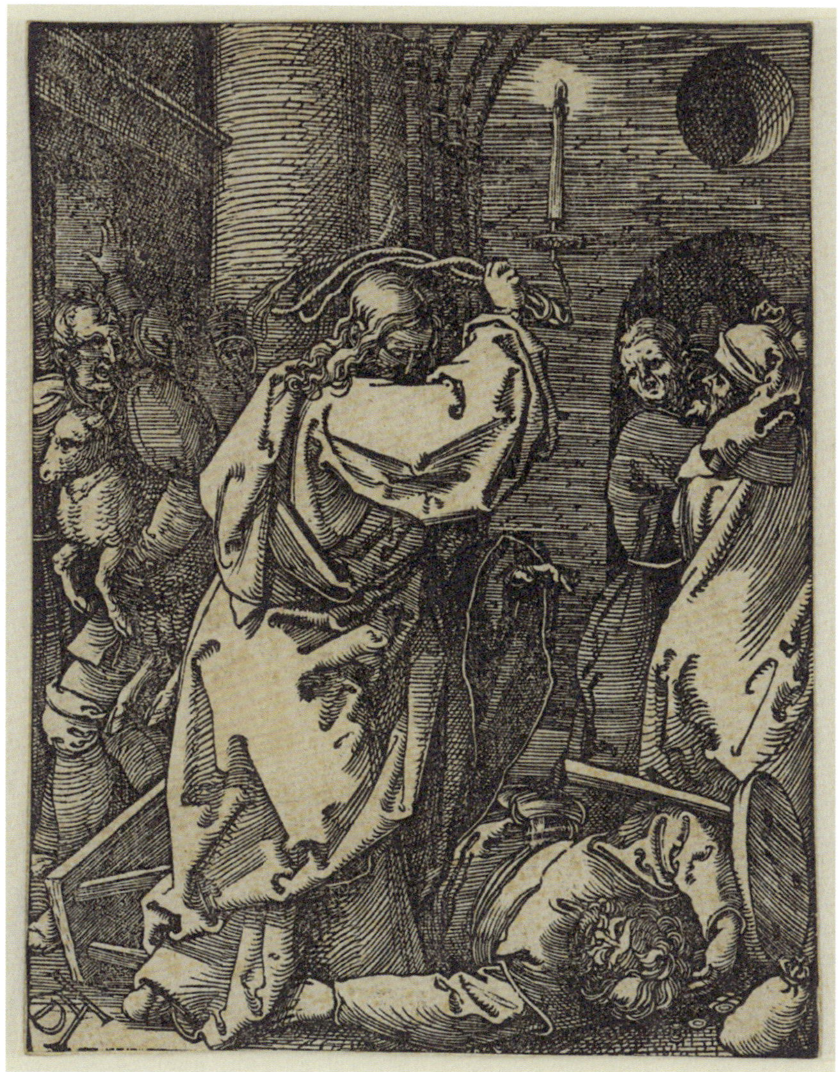

cat. no. 31.1

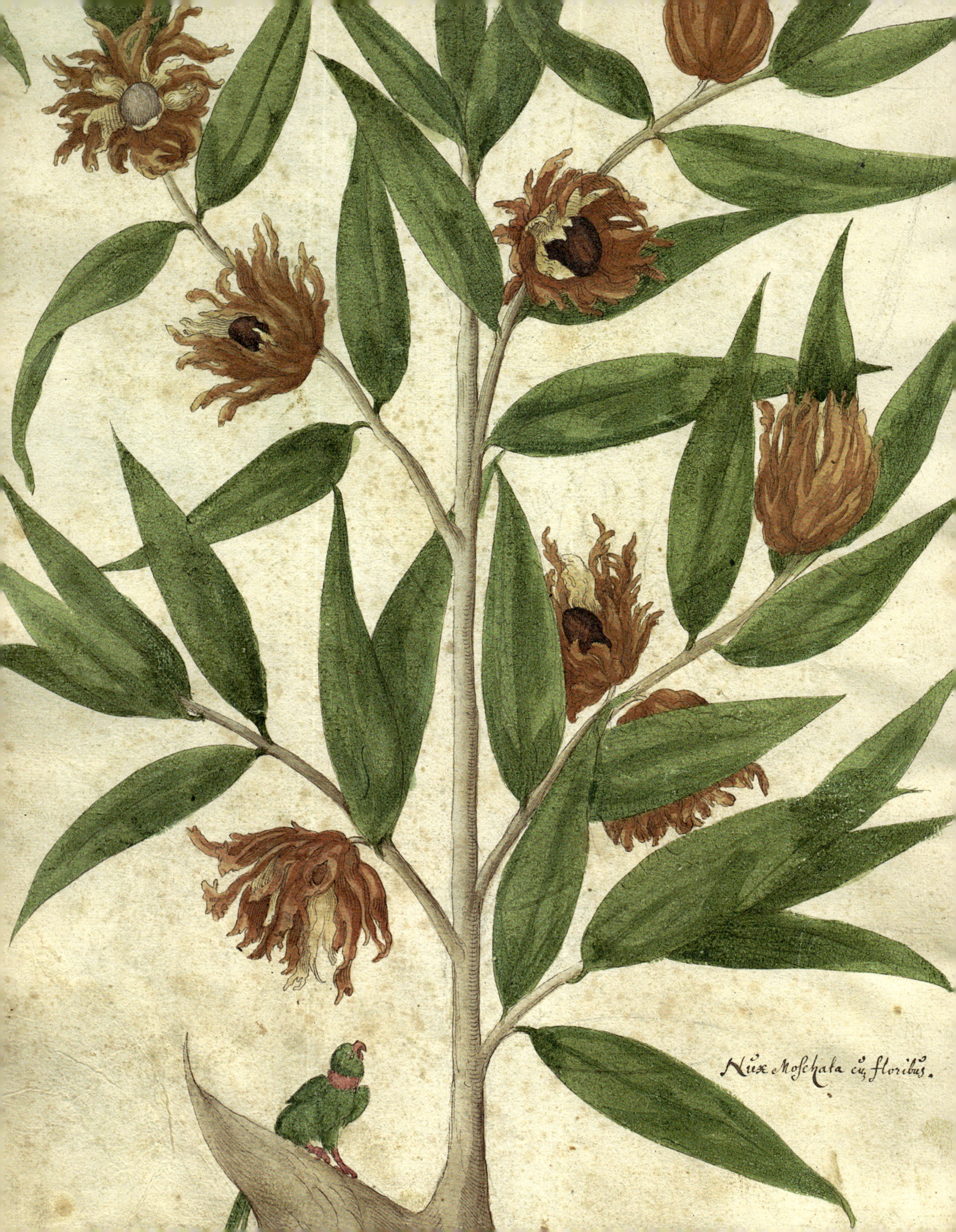
Nux Moschata cũ floribus.

LUXURY AND VIOLENCE

Spices from India, ostrich feathers from Africa, and stuffed birds of paradise from Oceania—such were the precious goods that global long-distance trade brought to Nuremberg. The spice trade in Nuremberg is documented in written sources as early as about 1300. Vivid pictorial evidence is found in the full-page illustrations of spice plants in the herbal created about 1553 for the apothecary Georg Öllinger.

Access to raw materials and artifacts from distant parts of the world signified luxury. Removed from their original contexts and construed as "exotica," these items were transformed by Nuremberg artists into extravagant accessories as well as virtuoso pieces for cabinets of arts (Kunstkammer). Among their many implications, such objects served to showcase the global interconnectedness enjoyed by their owners.

One of the incongruities of the era is that this luxury was financed at least in part by the trade in arms and armor. Luxury goods and articles of war even shared many of the same trade routes. Nuremberg was a leading center of arms and armor production. Shirts of mail manufactured in Nuremberg were widely recognized and highly sought-after exports. Suits of plate armor, which were much quicker to produce and also offered greater protection, regularly left the city in large quantities.

Arms and armor from Nuremberg were sold and put to use in combat on a global scale. The constant presence of war and violence—a source of wealth for Nuremberg families that traded in armaments—is vividly brought to mind by the memorial panel for Anton Imhoff, a young soldier killed in action.

Benno Baumbauer

◄ cat. no. 38 (nutmeg tree, detail)

32

NUREMBERG SHIRT OF MAIL

Nuremberg, late fourteenth or fifteenth century

Steel, drawn into wire, bent, riveted; copper alloy, cast, riveted, embossed; leather (modern)

H. 80 cm; W. 60 cm; D. 32 cm

GNM, inv. no. W2944

References:
Mraz 1983; Rose 1929; Zils 1927, pp. 115–17.

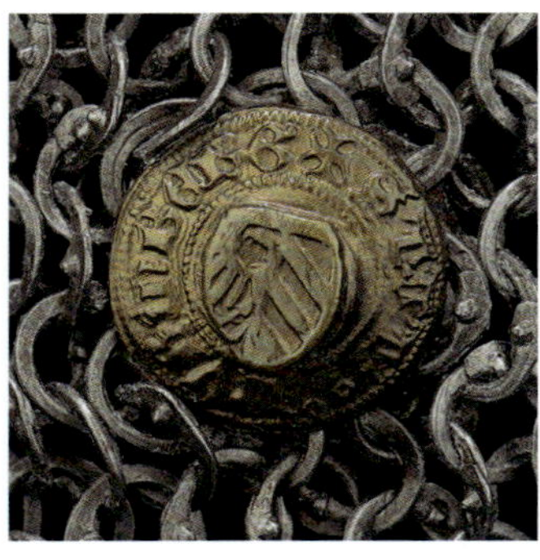

Nuremberg mark on the chest of the shirt of mail

This long-sleeved shirt of mail is slightly fitted at the waist, overlaps at the front to be fastened closed, and has a narrow tail that extends forward between the legs. Each of the mail rings is oval in section and closed with a rivet. A ring cast from copper alloy is attached at the center of the chest. It bears the following raised inscription bounded by two beaded border lines: "✠ STAT °₀° NVRMBERG" (City of Nuremberg). A slightly more reddish rivet of copper alloy is pushed through the center of the inscribed ring from the back; it is stamped on the front with Nuremberg's municipal coat of arms. The principle here is similar to that of the type of lead seal of quality that was affixed to pieces of cloth at the time. The same mark is also found on a mail vest at the Germanisches Nationalmuseum[1] and on the mail shirt at the Museum Luzern (Lucerne) that is said to have belonged to Archduke Leopold III of Austria, who fell in the Battle of Sempach in 1386.[2] A similar seal that was in use bears the inscription "✠ ZV + NVERENBERG ∴"; also, simple brass rings exist that are inscribed "✿ NVRNBERCK" or "✠ NVRENBERCK" or "✠ czv+nvrnberg+".

The Nuremberg mail makers (*Panzermacher,* also known as *Salwürker*) are first mentioned in the will of the Nuremberg citizen Hermann von Stein, dated January 13, 1295. Presumably this craft was present in Nuremberg decades earlier.

According to the 1536 regulations governing the Nuremberg mail makers, each master was allowed to employ one journeyman, two apprentices with three years of training, and up to three pieceworkers. Each finished piece had to be inspected by sworn masters and marked with the city's insignia—one of the types of copper alloy rings described above. This made the mail armor recognizable everywhere as a certified product of Nuremberg. The master could also hang a ring inscribed with his name on the piece, as is known from several examples produced in Nuremberg. Furthermore, he was allowed to entrust his housemaid with a number of tasks. Their description gives insight into the manufacturing process: "bending and cutting the rings, and cutting the rivets, beating them flat, and sealing them with a stamp" (*ringlein winden, claffen, neglein schneiden, die klopffen und stempffen*).[3] The complex production process took a considerable amount of time. In 1565, journeymen were allowed six months for the completion by their own hands of a "masterpiece," a mail shirt required to become qualified as a master. In contrast to mail armor, the plate armor that was produced in Nuremberg |**cat. no. 36**| was significantly faster and cheaper to manufacture in large quantities, and it also offered better protection.

Like other wares that bore the mark of the city, Nuremberg mail armor was known throughout Europe. From 1435 to 1439, the Castilian nobleman Pero Tafur (d. before 1490) journeyed through large parts of the then known world. In the travelogue he later penned (ca. 1453–57), he noted that Nuremberg was home to many craftspeople, particularly in the metalworking crafts, and that they produced mail shirts commonly known as "those from Nuremberg."[4] Mail armor from Nuremberg found its way not only to Spain but also to France (King Charles VIII, 1488) and Austria (the arsenal in Graz, 1577–79). Even Emperor Rudolf II ordered a shirt of mail from Nuremberg: made by Michael Kobolt in 1590, it was sent to the Ottoman commander Sinan Pasha (1512–1596) along with pieces of plate armor and handguns.

Fabian Brenker

1 Inv. no. W2172.
2 Inv. no. HMLU 00026.
3 Zils 1927, pp. 115–17.
4 "Biven en ella muchos artesanos, especialmente de toda lavor de alatón, e aquí se fazen los jaceranes que dizen de Nirumberga." Tafur and Pérez Priego 2018, p. 299.

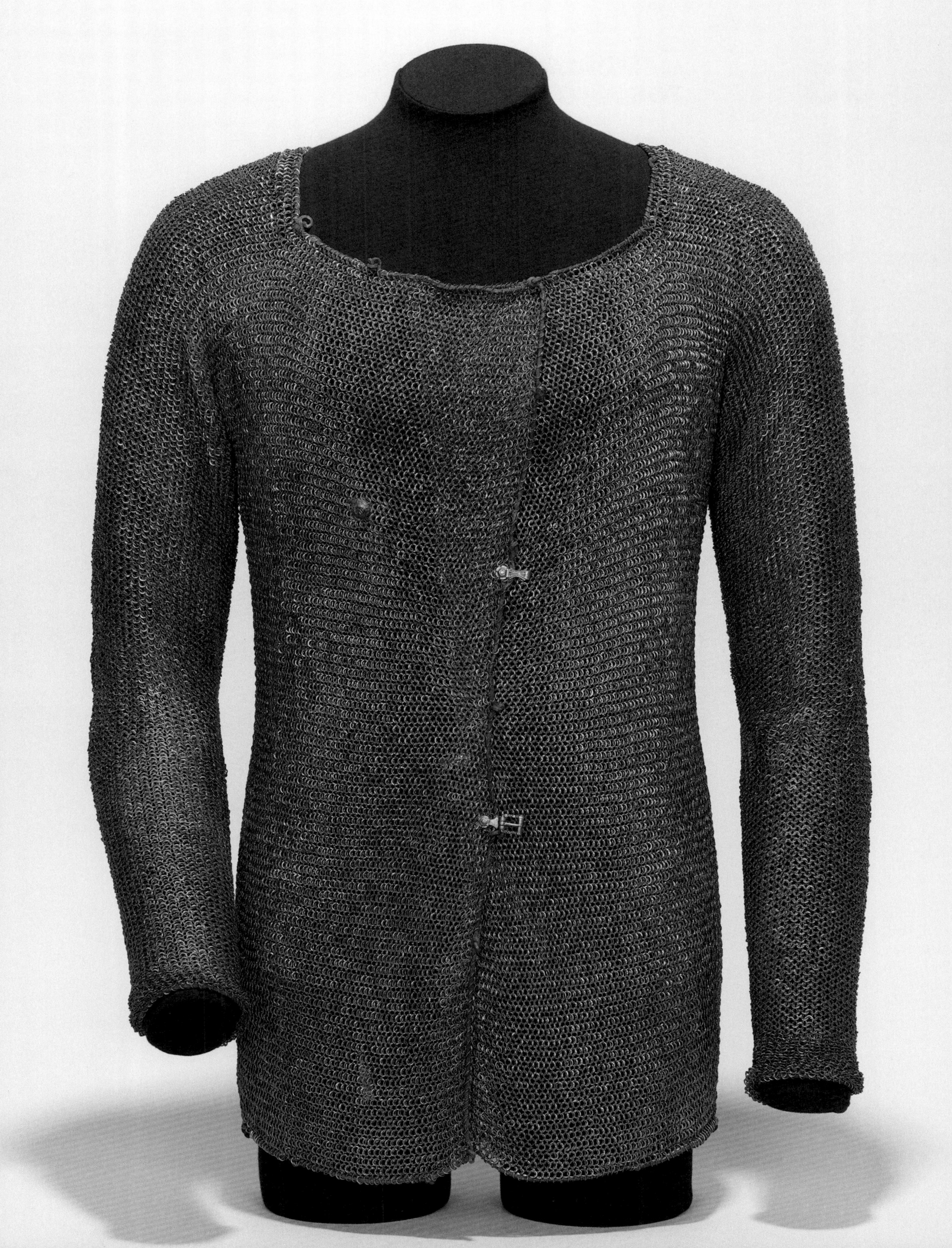

33

MEMORIAL PANEL FOR ANTON IMHOFF

Master of the Deocarus Altarpiece (workshop)

Nuremberg, ca. 1449–50

Paint on spruce
H. 30 cm; W. 98.3 cm
GNM, inv. no. Gm511

References:
Hess, Hirschfelder, and Baum 2019, vol. 1, pp. 192–99, cat. no. 12 (Beate Fücker and Judith Hentschel).

This panel was painted in remembrance of Anton Imhoff, who, according to the inscription, died of injuries sustained near Fürth on November 12, 1449.[1] This occurred during the First Margrave War, in a battle between the city of Nuremberg and Margrave Albrecht Achilles of Brandenburg-Ansbach. The deceased, who had probably not reached adult age, is shown kneeling in prayer, dressed in a suit of plate armor, with sword at his hip. He has placed his iron helmet on the ground in a sign of reverence for the Virgin and Child. The object of his devotion becomes apparent when one considers that this panel was created as a supplement to the so-called Imhoff Madonna at the family's burial site in the Lorenzkirche. It was originally mounted beneath the Madonna painting.[2]

This depiction is unique for its time in Nuremberg, since memorials for members of the city's upper class usually showed them in their church-going clothes. The inscription's mention of the precise circumstances of death is also exceptional. It is not known whether more examples of this type of memorial once existed; no evidence has survived. In essence, this inconspicuous panel is perhaps the oldest surviving war memorial in Nuremberg. At the same time, it is worth noting that memorial paintings and reliefs were reserved for city-council families, the clergy, and a few other types of elites, while the vast majority of the victims of war were forgotten.

1 "Anno d[omi]ni·m°·cccc°·xlviiii° iar do / he[re]n un[d] stet mitenand[er] krigten / nam antoni crista[n] im hoff sun / schade[n] bey fürt am neste[n] mitw / och noch martini d[er] hy beg[ra]be[n] leit" (In 1449, when the princes and the cities were at war with each other, Anton, Christian Imhoff's son, sustained injuries [i.e., perished] near Fürth on the Wednesday after Saint Martin's Day; he lies buried here).
2 Hess, Hirschfelder, and Baum 2019, vol. 1, pp. 194–97 (Beate Fücker and Judith Hentschel), fig. 12.3 (p. 195).

The person who commissioned the Imhoff Madonna was presumably Anton's father, Christian Imhoff, warden of the Lorenzkirche. The Madonna panel commemorates Christian Imhoff's wife Margarethe, who died on July 2, 1449. Christian probably also ordered the memorial panel for his son. The reason why he chose this way of portraying his war-fallen son is well explained by Judith Hentschel and Beate Fücker: "The public commemoration of Anton Imhoff's military service for the city of Nuremberg was surely intended to contribute to the family's social prestige."[3]

The fate of Anton Imhoff takes on a note of ambivalence when one considers that the Imhoff family participated in the international arms trade. Anton's uncle Konrad—who also died in 1449, a year marked by war and pestilence—and other relatives traded not only in mining products, chemicals, textiles, wine, spices, and handicrafts, but also in armaments.[4] In fact, in light of the arms industry's potency in Nuremberg, the admonition that war is detrimental to commerce found in Jost Amman's *Allegory of Trade* |**cat. no. 21**| would seem to cut both ways.[5] In later decades, the Imhoffs increasingly came to specialize in the spice trade |**see cat. no. 38**|.

Benno Baumbauer

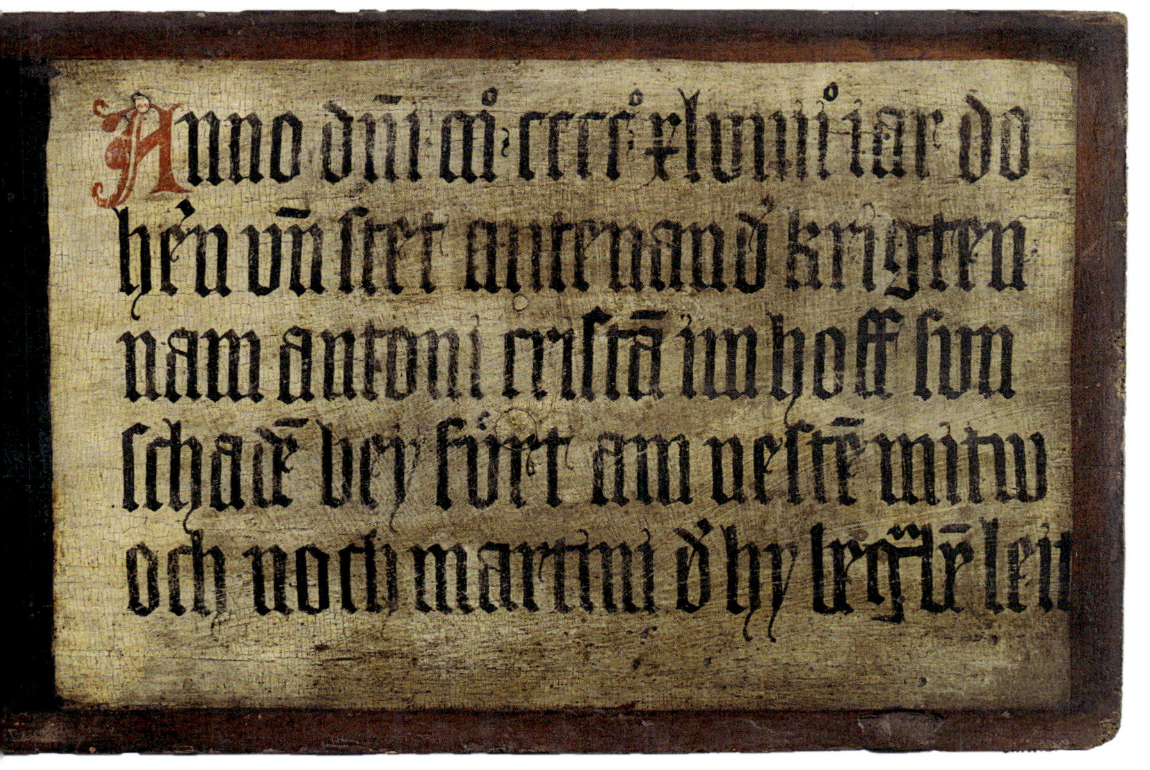

3 Translated from the German in ibid., p. 197.
4 Imhoff 1974. See also Jahnel 1950, p. 32.
5 On the trade in weapons in Nuremberg, see Willers 2002.

34

SHAFTED WEAPONS WITH ETCHED DECORATIONS

Southern or central Germany, second half of the sixteenth century or early seventeenth century

34.1 Halberd with Coat of Arms of the Kress Family

Iron, forged, hardened, ground, polished, etched, blackened; shaft: wood; tassels: textile

L. 240 cm

GNM, inv. no. W2856

34.2–3 Watchmen's Spears from the Municipal Construction Yard in Nuremberg

Iron, forged, ground, etched; shaft: wood with leather straps nailed on

L. 218.5 cm (cat. no. 34.2); L. 218 cm (cat. no. 34.3)

GNM, inv. nos. W948, W949, on long-term loan from the Museen der Stadt Nürnberg, Kunstsammlungen

References:
Essenwein 1883 (on cat. no. 34.2); Diener-Schönberg 1904 (on boar spears); Van Dijk 2020 (on halberds); Westphal 2024, p. 169, cat. no. 108 (on cat. nos. 34.2–3).

In the late Middle Ages and Renaissance, Nuremberg was well-known for the manufacture of mail armor, plate armor, and handguns. By the sixteenth century at the latest, all those items were inspected by sworn masters and then marked with the municipal coat of arms. That way, buyers everywhere knew when they were holding a Nuremberg-made product in their hands. For shafted weapons, particularly spears and halberds, the city council never introduced a proof mark. Accordingly, no authentic shafted weapons bearing the city's mark are known. However, written sources indicate that halberds and spears were produced in Nuremberg. But most of the sources merely mention the sale of spears and halberds by local merchants, without specifying whether those items had been produced in Nuremberg or were merely sold there. The etched ornamentation of the present three weapons shows, at any rate, that they were decorated for Nuremberg buyers. While it seems likely that they were forged and etched in Nuremberg, this cannot be proven.

The etched decoration of the halberd |**cat. no. 34.1**|, a weapon used exclusively by foot soldiers, shows the coat of arms of the Nuremberg patrician family Kress von Kressenstein on both sides. The surfaces are otherwise filled with vine scrolls, animals, weapons, and musical instruments on a dotted ground. This type of decoration was widespread in the second half of the sixteenth century. The overall form and construction are typical of that period as well as of the early seventeenth century. A blacksmith's mark is stamped on the hook on the back. Highly similar marks are found on halberds in the Solothurn arsenal and in many modern collections. A halberd with a similar mark at the Royal Armouries in Leeds bears the date "A. D. [16]05."[1] Etched halberds were popular as parade weapons during the Renaissance.

The two short spears were discovered by August von Essenwein (1831–1892) in a chamber at the municipal construction yard (*Werkhof* or *Bauhof*) in Nuremberg. One of the spearheads is etched with strapwork and vine scrolls on a blackened background |**cat. no. 34.2**|. Decorations of that type were particularly common in the second half of the sixteenth century and in the early seventeenth century. The other spearhead is considerably plainer in decoration |**cat. no. 34.3**|. A third example, now at the Landesmuseum für Kunst- und Kulturgeschichte in Oldenburg, bears the date "1585" above the coat of arms of Nuremberg.[2] All three show the small Nuremberg coat of arms on one side and the inscription *Gehördt aůff die peünt* (belongs at the Peunt) on the other. The "Peunt" was the municipal construction yard in the city's southern half. The three weapons therefore originally belonged precisely where Essenwein found them. The Nuremberg *Zeugbuch* (book of armaments) of 1578–80 lists corresponding weapons for the construction yard: "In addition, in this small chamber there are ... old halberds ... [and] old boar spears which are provided daily to the gatekeepers and watchmen etc."[3] The small triangular hole in the hexagonal socket of each of the spears indicates that they were all indeed once boar spears (*Sauspieße* or *Knebelspieße*). Through the hole, a short lug, probably made of horn, was once perpendicular to the wooden shaft. The boar spear was a common hunting weapon. The perpendicular lug was intended to prevent the spear from penetrating too deeply into the flesh, stopping the raging boar from working its way up the shaft. It remains unclear why the gatekeepers and watchmen of the construction yard chose to use hunting weapons. As is known from the so-called *Schembartbücher*, participants in the Nuremberg Schembart Carnival also carried boar spears, equipped instead with steel lugs.

Fabian Brenker

1 Inv. no. VII.1028.
2 Inv. no. 24.630. Westphal 2024, p. 169, cat. no. 108.
3 "Item mehr sindt jn diesem Kemmerlein ... allt Hellmparten ... allt Knebelspiess dauon man den Thorsperrern vnnd wächtern etc. teglichs gibt." Essenwein 1877, p. 146.

THE MASSACRE OF THE INNOCENTS

35

Master of the Nuremberg Marian Altarpiece

Nuremberg (?), ca. 1400–1410

The *Massacre of the Innocents* shows the brutal reality of weapons in action. At the left, King Herod, seated on his throne, orders the slaughter of all boys under two years of age in Bethlehem and vicinity. He does so out of fear of Christ, the recently born child prophesied to become "king of the Jews." To the right of Herod, the bloody deed is shown in a disturbing scene: the king's soldiers are killing infants, while the mothers are trying in vain to protect them. The depiction of two children whose naked bodies are pierced by a sword and a halberd is incredibly violent.

The panel comes from a large winged altarpiece that was created about 1400–1410 for the high altar of the Frauenkirche in Nuremberg. It serves to commemorate the feast day of the "Holy Innocents," which had special significance in that church: the treasury included a relic that was venerated as "the whole head of one of the Innocents."[1]

The episode described in the Gospel of Matthew is generally considered fictional, but this image can still be read as an artistic treatment of the existential extremes of human experience. The display of brutality is primarily religious in motivation: the Holy Innocents were considered the first martyrs to lose their lives in the name of Christ. Ostentatious violence is a deliberate pictorial strategy here, since it lies at the core of any ideology of martyrdom. The greater the barbarism of the martyr's death and the more defenseless he appears, the more glaring is the contrast with his innocence, the stronger is the identification of followers with him, and the more united is the rejection of the common enemy.

The scene appears even more lurid when contrasted with other paintings from the former altarpiece. Next to the charming depiction of the infants Jesus and John playing together with a porridge pot in the scene showing the Virgin Mary and Saint Elizabeth at the spinning wheel,[2] the sight of the murdered and impaled children of Bethlehem is all the more shocking.[3]

The layers of meaning in this altarpiece cannot be fully understood without an awareness of the violent history of the Frauenkirche itself, even though the events in question occurred half a century before the work's creation. The church had been built as a Christian symbol of triumph over Judaism; it replaced the Nuremberg synagogue, which had been torn down during the bloody pogrom of 1349. In the course of the pogrom, Christian Nurembergers had murdered 562 Jews |**cat. no. 11**|.[4] In the altarpiece's pictorial program, this anti-Judaism is evident alongside the history of violence inscribed in the church, most explicitly in the painting of the Twelve Apostles bearing the Virgin Mary's body to the tomb, which, following an apocryphal legend, shows the procession being attacked by Jews.

The types of pictorial mechanisms at work in the *Massacre of the Innocents* are so effective that they were also exploited for other purposes. In the sixteenth century, for example, identical motifs were used to demonize the people of the Ottoman Empire as wartime enemies. In Peter Flötner's deck of playing cards of about 1540, the King of Hearts appears as a sultan accompanied by a warrior who is sheathing his sword, while three murdered infants lie at their feet |**cat. no. 66**|. The infiltration of such explicit depictions of violence into the culture of everyday life offers a clear example of how the labeling of entire groups of people as brutal and barbaric could become normalized.

Benno Baumbauer

Paint on spruce
H. 91.3 cm; W. 122.1 cm
GNM, inv. no. Gm114

References:
Hess, Hirschfelder, and Baum 2019, vol. 1, pp. 95–117, cat. no. 5 (Beate Fücker and Daniel Hess).

1 "der unschuldigen kindlein ein gantz heuptlein"; Schuler and Metzner 1869, p. 34; Hess, Hirschfelder, and Baum 2019, vol. 1, p. 116, cat. no. 5 (Beate Fücker and Daniel Hess).
2 For both theological and philological reasons, the previous interpretation of this scene as showing a squabble between Jesus and John needs to be called into question. I thank Markus Huber, Nuremberg, for pointing this out.
3 On expressive tendencies in the art of the Beautiful Style, see Vlachos 2018, esp. pp. 243–44.
4 Stromer 1978.

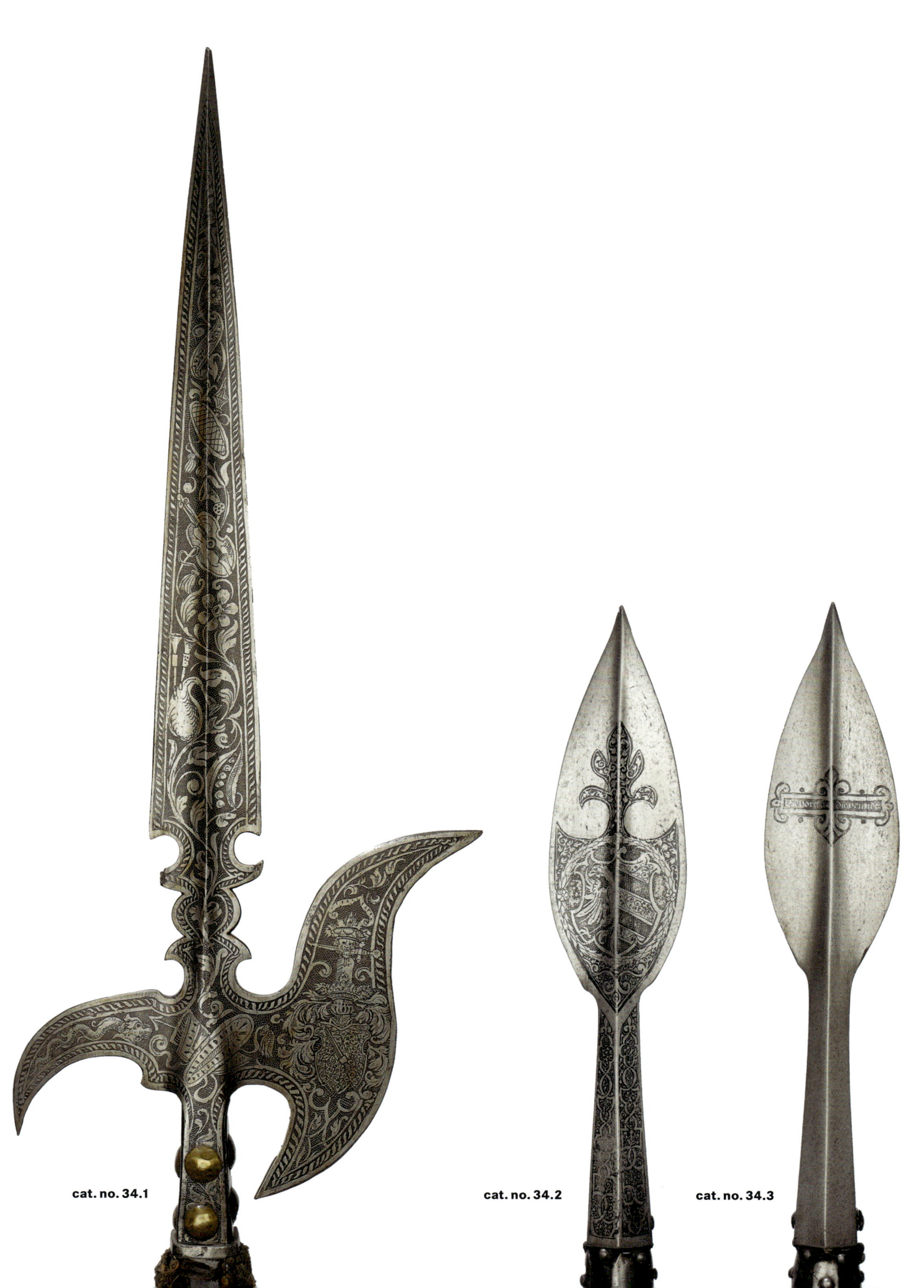

cat. no. 34.1

cat. no. 34.2

cat. no. 34.3

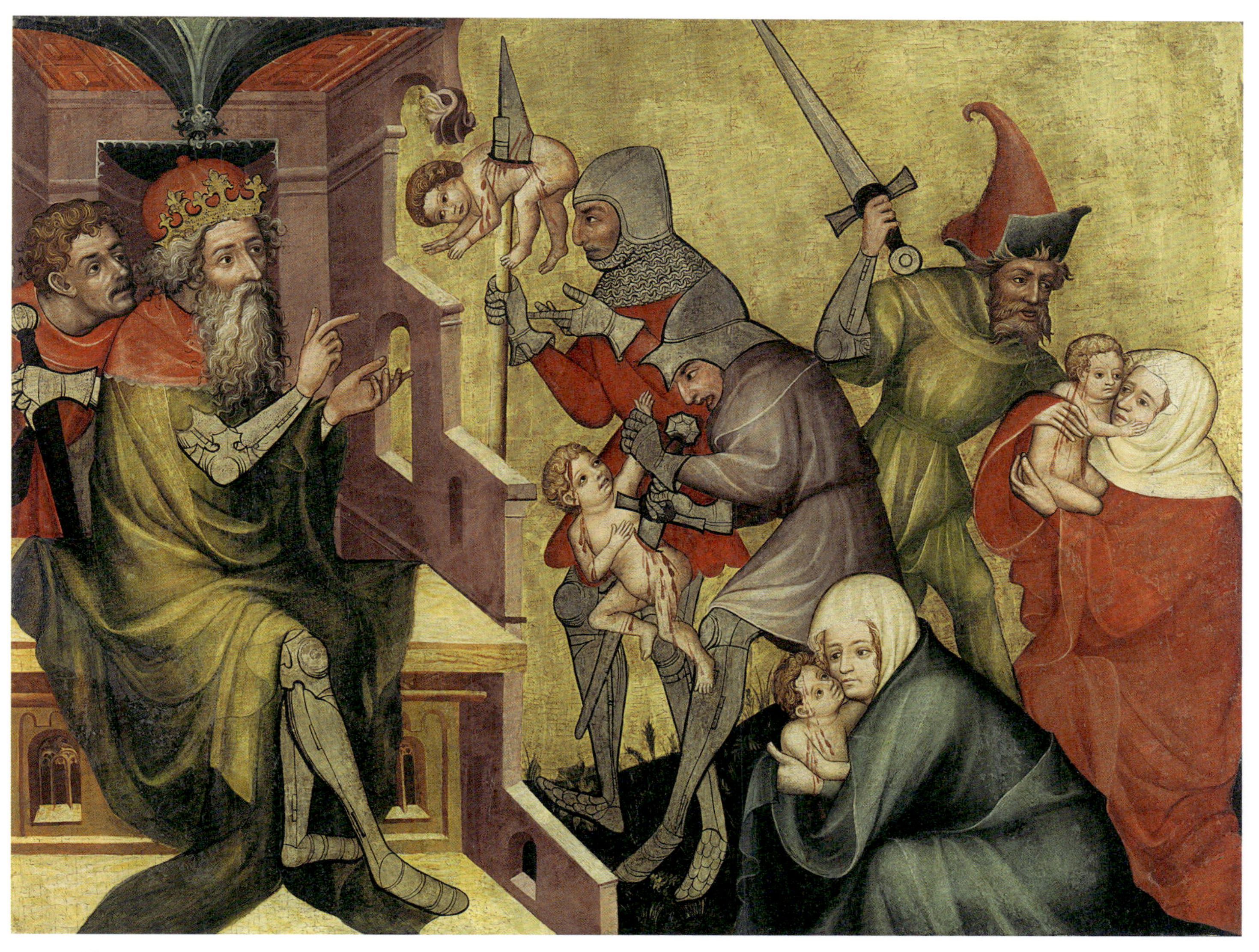

cat. no. 35

36

INFANTRY ARMOR FROM THE CIVIC ARMORY IN VIENNA

Unknown Nuremberg armorer, Augustin Hirsvogel (etcher)

Nuremberg and Vienna, 1546

Steel, forged, filed, ground, polished, etched; leather

H. 95 cm; W. 68 cm; D. 31 cm

GNM, inv. no. W1120

References:
Uhlirz 1894, p. 116; Exh. cat. Schallaburg 1977, pp. 95–96, cat. nos. 213–20, fig. 36; Williams 2003, p. 632 (with incorrect illustration).

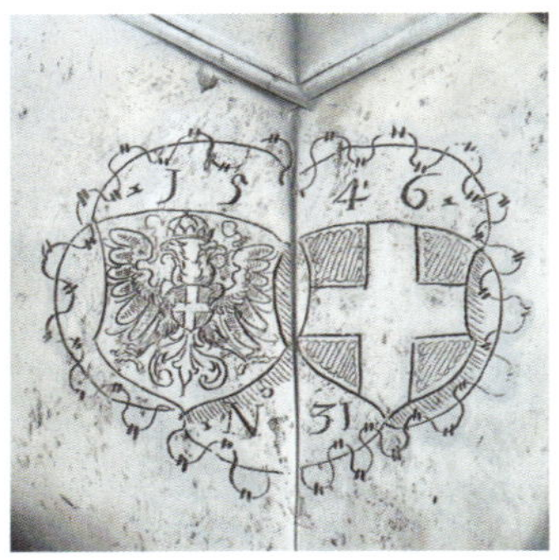

Etching on the breastplate

The breastplate and backplate were acquired by the Germanisches Nationalmuseum in 1873, together with unrelated parts, as a gift from the city of Vienna. They were originally housed in Vienna's civic arsenal (*Bürgerliches Zeughaus*). The bottom ends of the thigh defenses are stamped with an emblem of a shield charged with a cross. This is the proof or ownership mark of the city of Vienna. Both the breastplate and the backplate are etched with two forms of Vienna's coat of arms, the year 1546, and the number 31. The armor can thus be associated with a 1546 invoice in the city's account books, which reads as follows: "On October 22, I paid Georg Zimerman, citizen here, 450 guldens for 60 cuirass back- and frontplates, together with pauldrons [shoulder defenses] and burgonets [helmets], having previously purchased more of these as well as 8 cuirasses. Augustin Hirsvogel was paid 17 guldens, 2 shillings, and 18 pfennigs to etch the city coat of arms, numbers, and dates on the pieces."[1] The city had therefore bought sixty new armors and, together with eight existing ones, had them etched by Augustin Hirsvogel (1503–1553). Further breastplates and backplates,[2] along with other parts of this series, are preserved today in the Wien Museum in Vienna. The helmet, gorget (collar), and pauldrons originally belonging to the present armor are now missing.

The municipal coat of arms of Nuremberg is stamped at the upper edge of both breastplate and backplate. This well-known coat of arms was easy to recognize and confirmed to the buyer that the piece of hardened steel armor originated in a Nuremberg workshop. (Technical examinations of the breastplate have revealed, however, that it was not in fact hardened.)

Augustin Hirsvogel was the son of the Nuremberg glass painter Veit Hirsvogel (1461–1525). After the market for stained-glass windows collapsed with the coming of the Reformation, Augustin earned his living as a cartographer and etcher. He settled in Vienna in 1543 |**see cat. no. 47**|. The etching techniques employed by goldsmiths and armorers played a decisive role in the development of etching as a printmaking process. It is not known why the group of armors in question were acquired and etched in Vienna in 1546. In addition to the constant need to adapt to new technologies of weaponry and changing fashions in armor, a connection with the Schmalkaldic War of 1546–47 has also been suggested as a possible reason.

For those who wanted to buy as many armors as possible in a short period of time, Nuremberg was the producer of choice in southern Germany. Orders of hundreds of pieces for major clients are repeatedly documented from the fourteenth century onward. Individual armorers, known as *Plattner*, were present in almost all German-speaking cities, including Vienna. In Nuremberg, more than five hundred master armorers are known by name from the fourteenth to the seventeenth century. Yet only a few Nuremberg masters made armor of the highest quality for wealthy patrons, as was also done in Augsburg, Landshut, and Innsbruck. In general, quantity prevailed over quality in Nuremberg. As a result, many of the Nuremberg armorers lived under the threat of poverty, worked primarily on large orders for the city, and did not have their own master's mark. This includes the anonymous maker of the present armor. The pieces were typically hammered into shape in a few hours, filed, and then finished in grinding mills. Flanged edges, ridges, and grooves were fashioned as minimal decoration in keeping with the period's tastes. Only in this way could Nuremberg armorers produce several hundred pieces within a few weeks' time, ensuring an adequate supply for all of southern Germany. In terms of quantity, the sixteenth century was perhaps the heyday of the suit of plate armor, even though over the course of the century the parts became largely limited to breastplates, backplates, gorgets, and helmets.

Fabian Brenker

1 "Georgen Zimerman Bürger alhie zalt ich den 22/10 umb 60 Harnisch Rük und Krebs sambt den Achseln und Sturmbhauben 450 fl. dn., mer von denselben und noch 8 Harnischen so zuvor erkauft. Augustin Hirschvogel von der Stadtwappen, Numero und Jarzal darein zu etzen 17 fl. 2 sh. 18 dn." Uhlirz 1894, p. 116.
2 These are etched with the numbers 14, 18, 29, 39, 55, 66, 67, and 68.

SHELL OF A SEA TURTLE WITH COAT OF ARMS OF THE STROMER FAMILY

37

Nuremberg, ca. 1600 (or nineteenth century?)

This painted shell of a green sea turtle has been preserved from the collections of the patrician Stromer family.[1] The paint was applied directly to the orange shell without any further surface preparation. The full heraldic achievement of the Stromers appears at the center. It consists of three white (meaning silver) lilies on a red shield, topped by a helmet with mantling spread at either side. A male attendant figure dressed in armor stands to the right, on a patch of grass, resting his left hand on a blank shield and holding a herald's staff in his right hand. An uninscribed banderole floats above. Along the shell's edge, there is a painted white beaded pattern with a silvered surround, heavily darkened. Openings and damages in that area have been lined with a textile material.[2]

Although the inventory of the Stromer collection written in the 1990s dates the piece to the sixteenth century, the loose brushwork and the attendant figure's trappings may indicate that the decoration was carried out in the first third of the seventeenth century or later. It remains unknown which member of the family commissioned the painted decoration, nor is it known how and from where the shell found its way to Nuremberg. This type of sea turtle is native to the waters of the Caribbean, Pacific, and Mediterranean. A comparable piece that once belonged to the Behaim family is thought to be of Italian provenance.[3] It can only be surmised whether the present shell might have been purchased in Bologna or Venice by the well-traveled Wolf Jacob Stromer (1561–1614) or whether it was perhaps acquired by Philipp Jacob Stromer (1624–1694), whose collection Joachim von Sandrart mentioned as a "famous art cabinet."[4]

The nutritious meat of the sea turtle made it a popular ocean catch. With the expansion of Portuguese maritime trade, the shells became increasingly sought-after commodities. Albrecht Dürer, during his trip to the Low Countries, received a turtle shell as a gift from the Fugger agent Bernhard Stecher.[5] While the tortoiseshell material obtained from turtle carapaces was used for luxury goods, complete shells were displayed in cabinets of art and curiosities—including in Nuremberg, as evidenced by the illustrated inventory of Basilius Besler's natural history cabinet dating from 1616.[6] The size, durability, and hardness of sea turtle shells were all considered remarkable.[7] The interpretation of such shells as weapons was based on ancient texts and contemporary descriptions. That notion found pictorial expression in Dürer's engraving *The Sea Monster*.

Painted turtle shells began entering European collections in the early sixteenth century. The oldest known example, dating from 1510, is first mentioned in an inventory of the collections of Ferdinand II. It features a magnificent painted scene, probably by a northern Italian artist.[8] The shells are more often decorated with coats of arms—for example, the aforementioned specimen from the Behaim collection and one dated 1600 bearing the arms of Frederick I, Duke of Württemberg.[9] The turtle shells that were refashioned in shield form were probably not used as defensive arms.[10] Instead, they most likely served as prestige objects displayed in cabinets of art or family chapels.[11]

Marie-Therese Feist

Dorsal shell of a green sea turtle (*Chelonia mydas*); paint; textile linings; metal grip (nineteenth century?)

H. 82 cm; W. 64 cm; D. 22 cm

Stromer'sche Kulturgut-, Denkmal- und Naturstiftung, inv. no. 3/8

References:
Inventory of the Stromer Foundation (Stromer'sche Kulturgut-, Denkmal- und Naturstiftung).

1 For the identification, we thank Gabriel S. Ferreira, Tübingen.
2 Thanks go to Benjamin Rudolph and Markus Raquet for this observation.
3 The Art Institute of Chicago, inv. no. 1982.2457.
4 Sandrart 1679, pt. 3, p. 69.
5 Rupprich 1956, p. 175.
6 Besler 1616.
7 See, for example, Gessner 1606, fols. 170r, 171v.
8 Possibly Amico Aspertini. See Exh. cat. Vienna 2000, p. 290, cat. no. 223 (Sylvia Ferino-Pagden). A similarly lavish decoration is found on the shell with an equestrian portrait of Frederick Henry, Prince of Orange (1584–1647) at the Rijksmuseum, Amsterdam. See Bikker 2007, pp. 502–3, cat. no. 434 (Yvette Bruijnen); Hermens and Van Laar 2024.
9 Landesmuseum Württemberg, Stuttgart, inv. no. E 2417. Further specimens with coats of arms are found, for example, at the Rijksmuseum, Amsterdam, and the Museum Naturalienkabinett, Waldenburg.
10 The metal grip on the back of the Stromer piece is probably a later addition. In any case, it is unsuited for use in battle.
11 See Saviello 2018b, p. 119 n. 52; Nickel 1995.

cat. no. 36

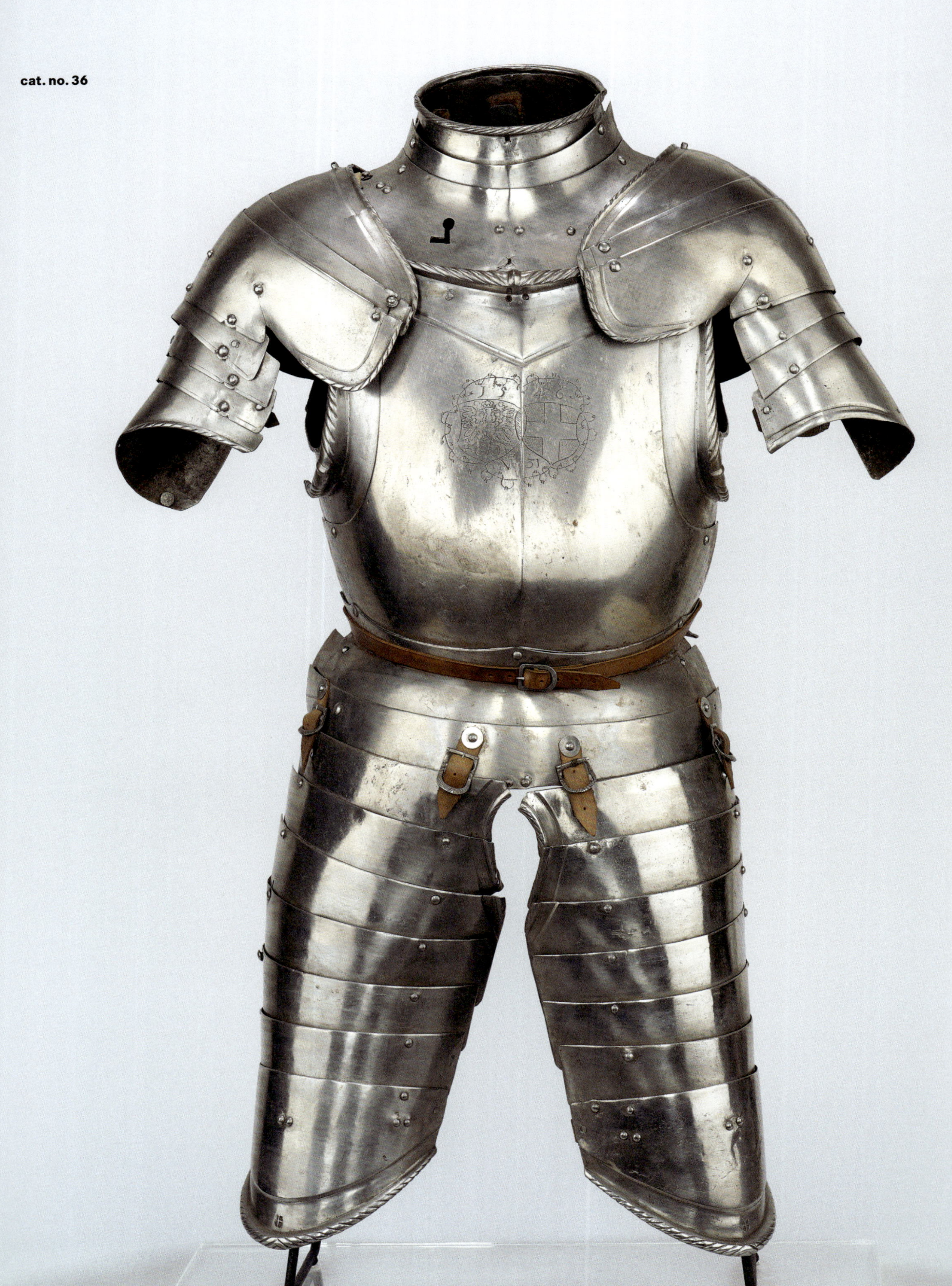

cat. no. 37

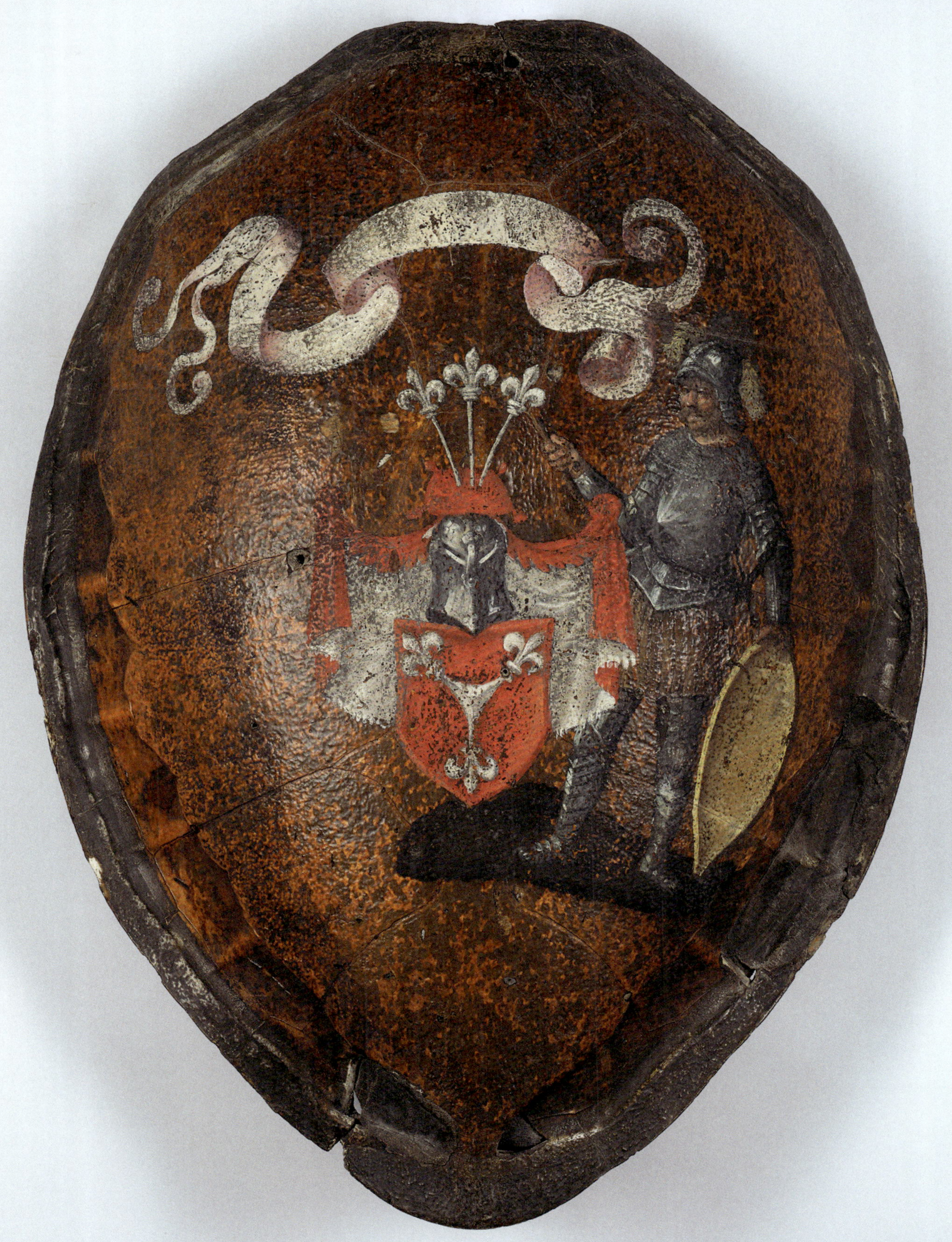

38

SPICE PLANTS FROM SOUTH ASIA

From Georg Öllinger, *Magnarum medicine partium herbariae et zoographiae imagines*

Nuremberg, ca. 1553

Pen and ink, brush and ink, watercolor

Each illustration H. 48 cm; W. 32.5 cm or 65 cm

Universitätsbibliothek der FAU Erlangen-Nürnberg, Erlangen, inv. no. MS 2362

Plates 6–7: Chinese cinnamon; plate 14: nutmeg tree (fig. p. 168); plate 118: ginger; plates 138–39: pepper; plate 529: clove tree

References:
Olariu 2023.

In 1553, after many years of work on his book of mostly botanical illustrations, the Nuremberg apothecary Georg Öllinger (1486/87–1558) had Samuel Quichelberg design a title page for the work |**cat. nos. 89, 111**|. This compendium is global in scope: the 680 watercolors depict plants and a number of animals from all parts of the world. Öllinger had cultivated some of the plants in his own garden, described by Conrad Gessner as the most distinguished garden in Nuremberg (*Norimbergae celeberimmus … hortus*).[1] Other depictions in the book are based on earlier botanical illustrations. The full-page and sometimes double-page drawings place equal emphasis on precise observation and aesthetic appeal. Only at a later date, probably about 1600, were the identifying inscriptions added.

The book contains numerous illustrations of spice plants, which is instructive given the importance of the spice trade in Nuremberg. This globally organized line of business was crucial to the wealth of many of the city's merchant families. Important varieties of spice that were imported from South Asia and Indonesia included ginger, nutmeg, pepper, cloves and cinnamon. Öllinger's exquisite depiction of the nutmeg plant gives equal emphasis to the seeds and the flowers, both of which are used as spices |**fig. p. 168**|. The two-part depiction of a Chinese cassia tree (a source of cinnamon) is enhanced with parakeets and guenon monkeys. In contrast, the black pepper plant (filling an entire double-page spread) and the clove tree owe their appeal to their ornamental qualities. The two symmetrically arranged ginger roots are notable for their bizarre shape.

These spices were known in Nuremberg well before the sixteenth century. The trading account book of the Holzschuher family documents the buying and selling of pepper, ginger, and nutmeg shortly after 1300.[2] An order placed by Albrecht Scheurl of Wrocław (Breslau) with a Nuremberg business partner in 1444 shows that Nurembergers were selling spices at large scale to the eastern parts of central Europe by that time.[3] Merchants involved in the speculative spice trade had to keep themselves informed about what was happening in the ports of southern Europe. A 1446 cargo list in the Imhoff Archive (GNM) concerns two Venetian galleys loaded with goods from Beirut and Alexandria; the cargo included large quantities of pepper, ginger, cinnamon, cloves, and nutmeg (seeds and blossoms).[4] In correspondence from 1561, the cousins Lazarus, Linhart, and Lorenz Tucher discuss a spice galley that landed in Lisbon and four other ships still in India, noting their impact on pepper prices.[5]

The spice trade was one of the main motivations driving Nuremberg merchant families to become involved in the Portuguese voyages of expansion. The Behaim Globe advertises the availability of spices in numerous locations in Africa and Asia |**cat. no. 1**|; and the 1505–6 Portuguese expedition to India, cofinanced by Nuremberg trading firms |**see cat. no. 116**|, brought enormous quantities of pepper to Europe, along with other goods.[6] While visiting Goa in 1579–80, Gabriel Holzschuher reported that he was able to purchase spices at the local markets without intermediaries.[7]

Benno Baumbauer

1 Gessner 1561, fol. 239v. On Öllinger's garden, see Olariu 2023, pp. 19–22.
2 Chroust and Proesler 1934, pp. 78, 117.
3 Stromer 1963, p. 169, appendix 7.
4 Eser 2010a, p. 137.
5 StadtAN, E29/IV nos. 300, 424.
6 Jahnel 1950, pp. 103–4; Eser 2010a, p. 145.
7 StadtAN, E 49/II no. 717.

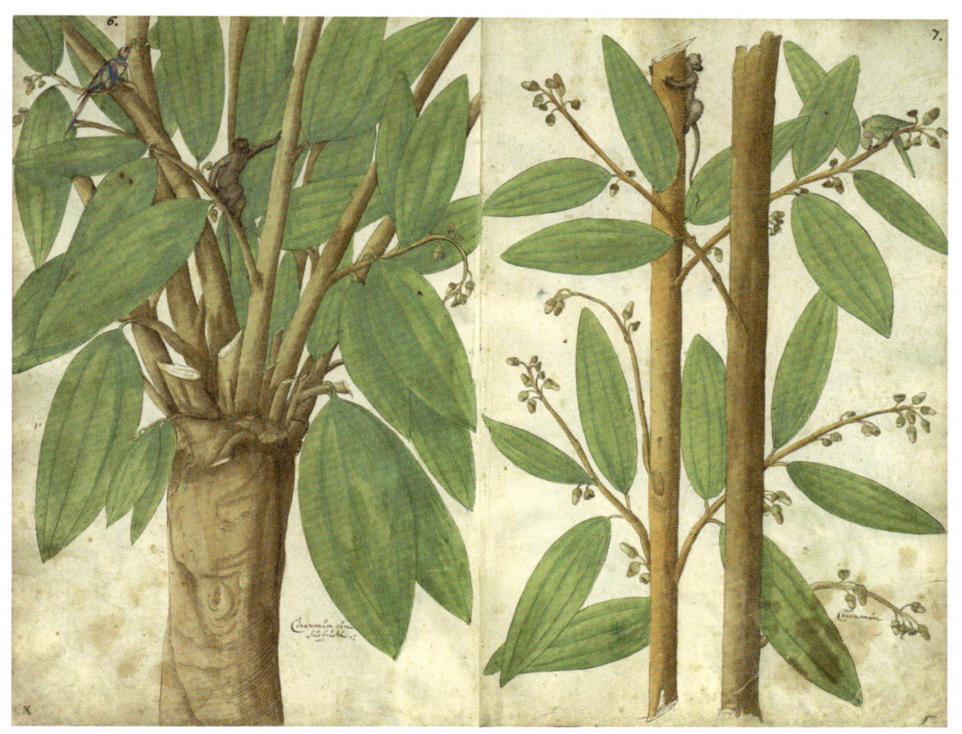

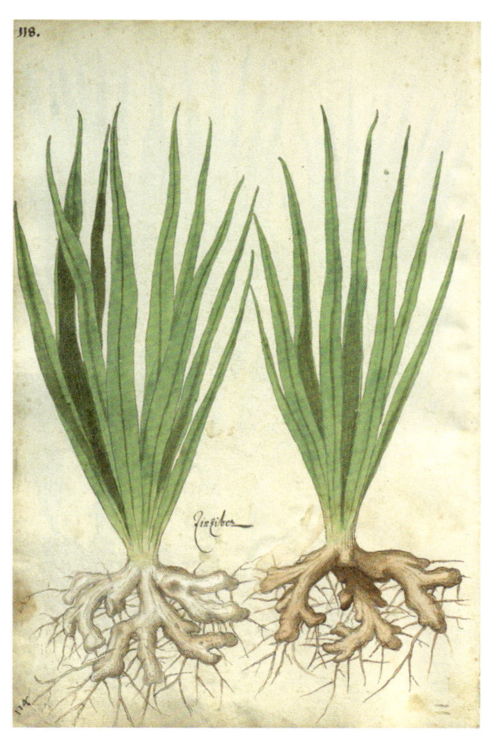

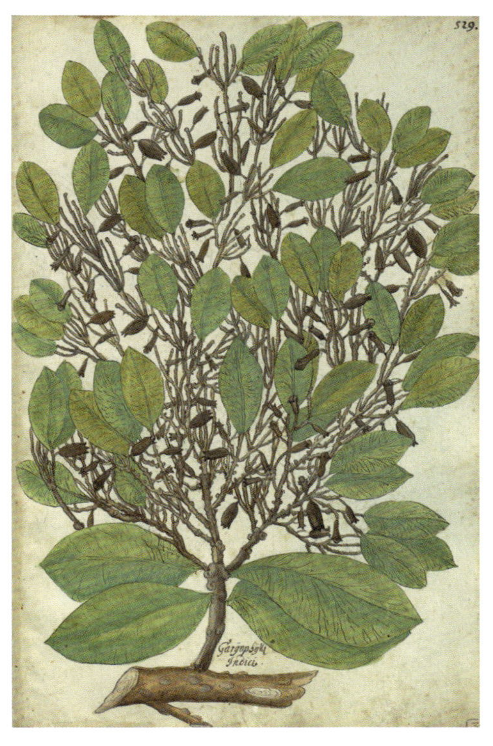

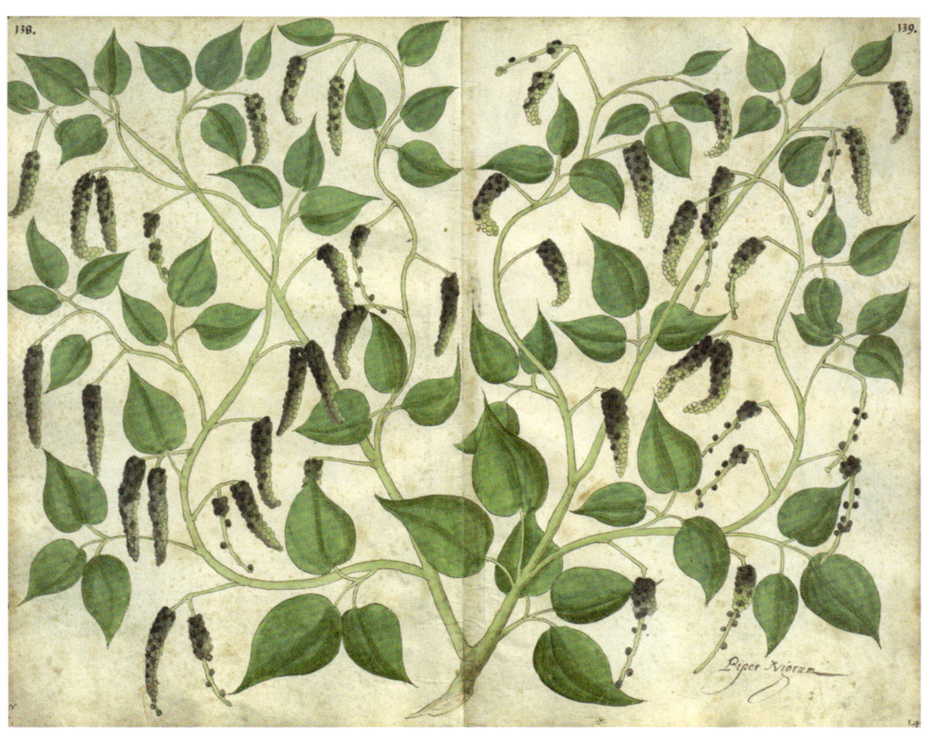

39

BERET OF CHRISTOPH KRESS ZU KRESSENSTEIN

Nuremberg, ca. 1530 and later

Silk velvet, ostrich feathers, spangles, lining: silk taffeta

Diam. 55 cm

GNM, inv. no. T3784,0

References:
Neuhaus 1935; Nuremberg 2015b, pp. 40–42, cat. no. 11 (Jutta Zander-Seidel), p. 271, cat. no. 11a (Sabine Martius), p. 272, cat. no. 11b (Ilona Stein and Frank Heydecke); Rublack 2021, pp. 32, 34; Hanß 2021a, pp. 153, 155–56.

In early modern Nuremberg, feathers imported from distant parts of the world were a coveted mark of social exclusivity. This owed to their rarity as well as their aesthetic and material properties. Attached to headgear and other garments, decorative plumes communicated wealth and prestige.[1] Because of their softness and luster, ostrich feathers imported from Africa, were among the most sought-after kinds of feathers. Great effort was involved in sourcing them. Ostriches were not domesticated until the nineteenth century. Hunting the birds was a laborious endeavor, as is illustrated by the pictorial program of the Scheurl family's ostrich egg cup |**cat. no. 16**|. Ostrich feathers were mainly obtained in northern and western Africa and then shipped via Mediterranean ports to central Europe. They often had to be transported along trade routes that ran through the Sahara Desert, on the way to ports on Africa's northern coast. In cities such as Nuremberg, these feathers were crafted into products or sold as raw materials.[2] The commercial significance of ostrich feathers and eggs is evidenced by the prominent representation of such a bird on the Behaim Globe |**cat. no. 1**|, in northern Africa |**fig. p. 66**|.

The plumed beret originally belonging to the Nuremberg patrician Christoph Kress zu Kressenstein is a rare surviving example of the use of ostrich feathers in early sixteenth-century clothing. Owing to the fragility of such feathers, only very few comparable pieces have survived from the period. However, pictorial representations, such as those in prints and paintings, indicate widespread use and confirm the importance of ostrich feathers as coveted status symbols. According to family tradition, the beret was a gift from Emperor Charles V. He is said to have presented it to Christoph Kress at the Imperial Diet of Augsburg in 1530, which Kress attended as an official envoy of the city of Nuremberg. However, it has not been possible to confirm this spectacular account on the basis of contemporary sources. The beret is first documented in a book of family genealogy compiled by Georg Jacob Kress between 1708 and 1732. Preserved together with its accompanying hatbox, it never left the family's possession. In 1933, it entered the Germanisches Nationalmuseum on long-term loan from the Kress family.

The current state of preservation only hints at the beret's original appearance. Technical studies have shown that while most of the feathers are original, at an unknown later date they were mounted on a smaller beret, with the result being that a strand of feathers now hangs like a tail at the back. The small tassels of metallic thread and their attached spangles appear to be original. An engraved likeness of Christoph Kress, made by Hans Troschel after 1600, may give a sense of the beret's former appearance. A copy of that engraving was glued down to the inside of the hatbox. Despite the many changes, it is still possible to imagine the former splendor of this sensational garment. When the beret was worn, the combined effect of the shimmering, gently rippling feathers and the glittering spangles must have been as awe-inspiring as the awareness of the feathers' distant origin and rarity.

Sven Jakstat

1 Hanß 2021a.
2 Rublack 2021, p. 24.

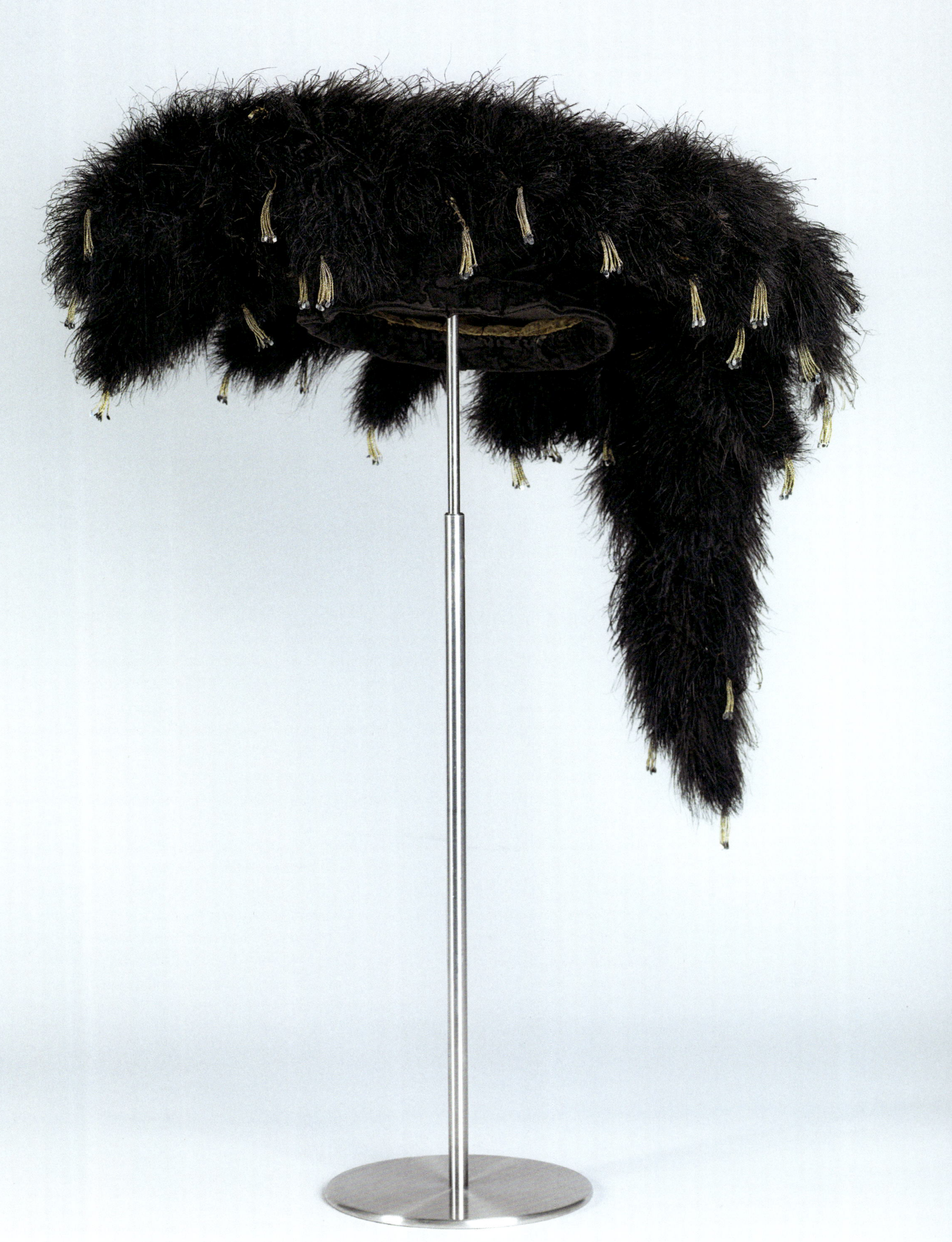

40

BIRDS OF PARADISE

40.1 Two Studies of a Bird-of-Paradise Specimen

Nuremberg (?), ca. 1550–60

Pen and dark brown ink over watercolor and bodycolor, white heightening, on paper

H. 59.5 cm; W. 37.5 cm

Universitätsbibliothek der FAU Erlangen-Nürnberg, Erlangen, inv. no. H 62 / B 164

40.2 Bird of Paradise

Virgil Solis, workshop (designer), and Stefan Hamer (printer)

Nuremberg, before 1554

Woodcut, hand-colored

H. 26.6 cm; W. 39.1 cm

Stiftung Schloss Friedenstein, Gotha, inv. no. 36.8

References:
40.1: Exh. cat. Nuremberg 2008, pp. 206–7, cat. no. 81 (Rainer Schoch); Dickel 2014, p. 220, cat. no. 337 (Iris Brahms).
40.2: Schäfer, Eydinger, and Rekow 2016, vol. 2, pp. 385–86, cat. no. 523.

In the sixteenth century, Nuremberg was an important hub for the trade in feathers.[1] Much profit could be made from the sale of feathers from distant parts of the world. The presence of rare feathers in Nuremberg not only shaped people's imagination of far-flung regions and the animals that lived there, but it also changed ideals of preciousness and luxury. In addition to ostrich feathers from Africa |**cat. no. 39**| and featherwork objects from the Americas, bird specimens from the Australasian region were also traded in early modern Nuremberg.

An impressive and rare piece of evidence for this is an illustrated broadsheet |**cat. no. 40.2**| that was printed by Stefan Hamer in Nuremberg, showing a bird of paradise suspended from a branch. The "exotic" bird, with long, colorful wing feathers and a striking green throat area, spans the entire width of the hand-colored sheet. The placement of the tree trunk in the immediate foreground makes the bird's body appear almost to project forward, out of the picture plane. This sense of closeness and presence is further enhanced by the background strip of landscape in the lower quarter of the image. The text flanking the bird's head provides information about this type of animal. It describes the "long, delicate translucent wings" and repeats the then common belief that birds of paradise lacked legs and therefore remained in permanent flight. Because of their rarity, such specimens were extraordinarily valuable. *Grosse herren* (great men) sometimes wore them as *Federpusch* (headgear plumes). And in the lower section of text it is stated that "Whoever wants to see or buy this bird specimen should go to Hanns Kramer," who would sell it for the handsome sum of 100 thalers.

Opportunities in Europe to see birds of this type, which looked almost as if they had come straight from the Garden of Eden, were indeed extremely rare. Their natural habitat lies several thousand kilometers from Nuremberg, on islands in the South Pacific. The first five known specimens arrived in Europe in 1522, aboard the first ship that successfully circumnavigated the globe, beginning and ending in Seville—the last remaining vessel in the Magellan expedition. At that time, specimens of birds of paradise were used as gifts or traded in exchange for goods, and the preparation process involved removal of the feet. Birds of paradise were among the rarest treasures kept in Renaissance cabinets of curiosities.[2]

The hand-colored broadsheet was therefore a kind of "advertising brochure" for the specimen then being offered for purchase in Nuremberg. The sale of this coveted object appears to have attracted attention even far outside the city. The naturalist Conrad Gessner, in Zurich, mentioned the broadsheet in a compendium he published in 1555.[3] Rainer Schoch was the first to suggest that the specimen on the broadsheet could be the same animal that is shown in front and back view in a drawing kept at the Universitätsbibliothek in Erlangen, a work of great virtuosity by an unknown draftsperson |**cat. no. 40.1**|. Owing to its high artistic quality, the drawing was initially attributed to Albrecht Dürer—that is, until the paper's watermark was identified as one not in use before the mid-sixteenth century. Hans Hoffmann has also been proposed as the creator.

Sven Jakstat

1 Hanß 2021a, pp. 140–49; Rublack 2021, p. 36.
2 Freigang 2009.
3 Gessner 1555, p. 611.

cat. no. 40.1

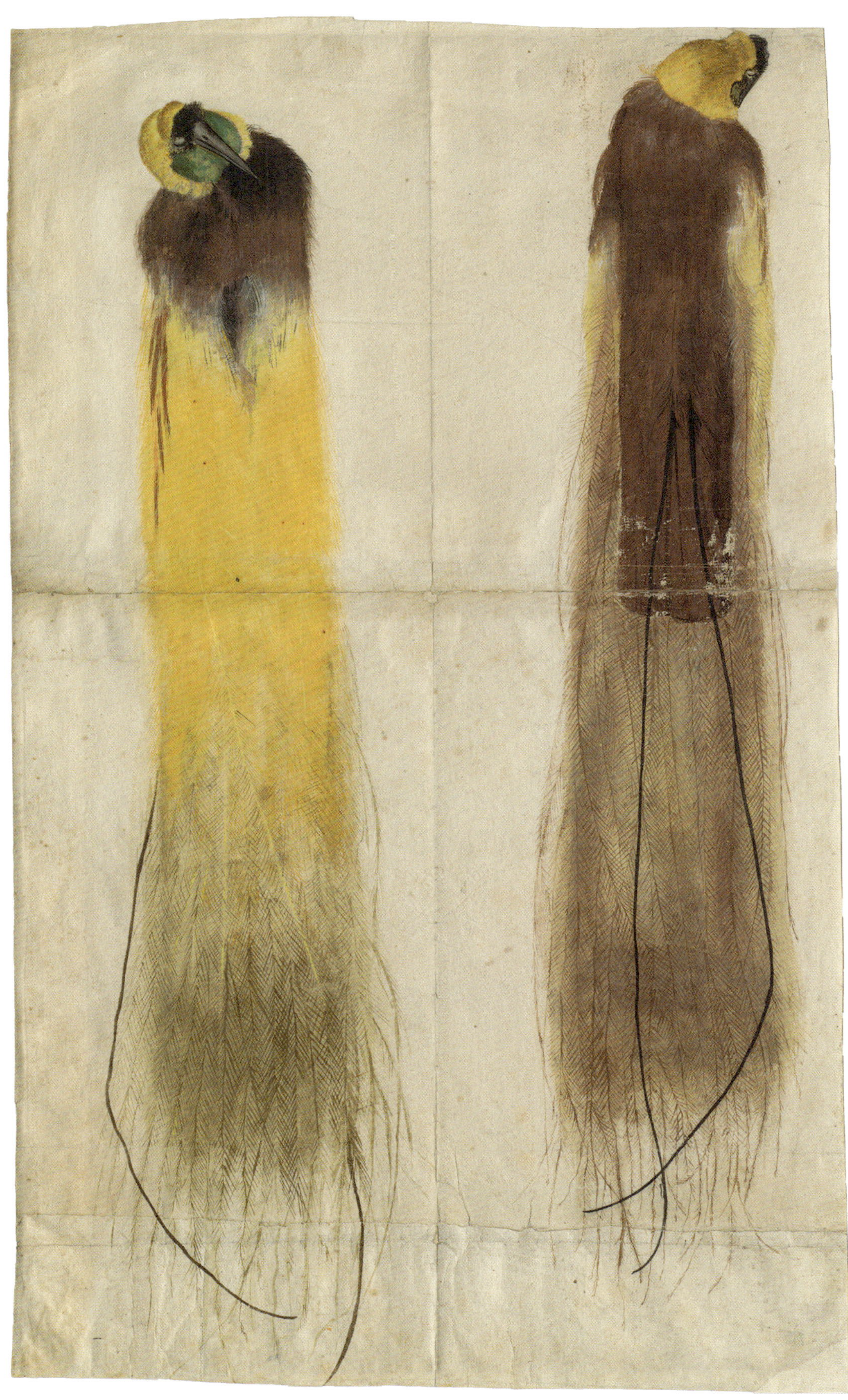

cat. no. 40.2

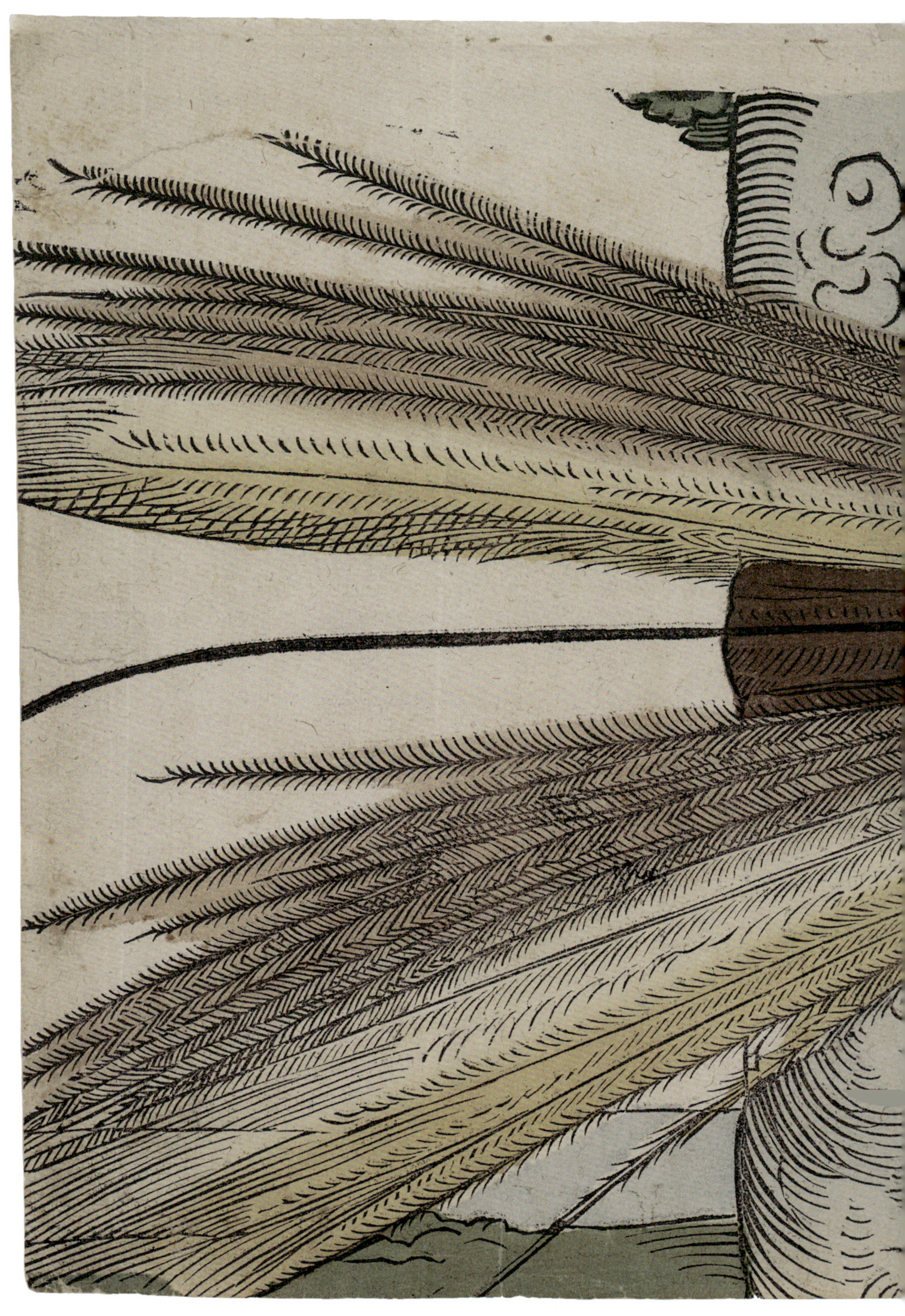

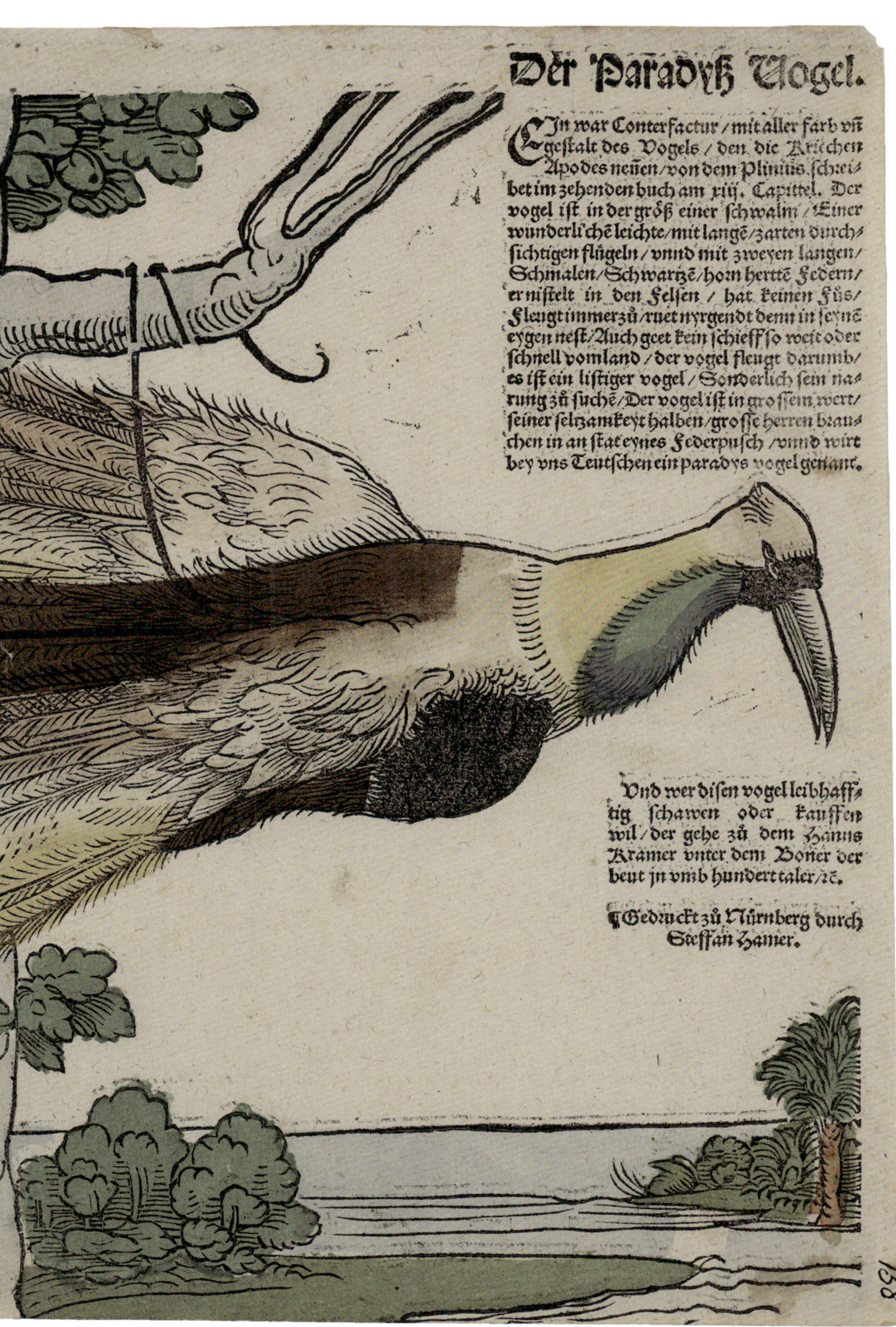

Der Paradyß Vogel.

Ein war Conterfactur / mit aller farb vñ
geſtalt des Vogels / den die Kriechen
Apodes neñen / von dem Plinius ſchrei=
bet im zehenden buch am xiij. Capittel. Der
vogel iſt in der grôß einer ſchwalm / Einer
wunderliche̅ leichte / mit lange̅ / zarten durch=
ſichtigen flügeln / vnnd mit zweyen langen /
Schmalen / Schwartze̅ / horn hertte̅ Federn /
er niſtelt in den Felſen / hat keinen Fůs /
Fleugt immerzů / ruet nyrgendt denn in ſeyne̅
eygen neſt / Auch geet kein ſchieff ſo weit oder
ſchnell vom land / der vogel fleugt darumb /
es iſt ein liſtiger vogel / Sonderlich ſein na=
rung zů ſuche̅ / Der vogel iſt in groſſem wert /
ſeiner ſeltzamkeyt halben / groſſe herren brau=
chen in an ſtat eynes Federpuſch / vnnd wirt
bey vns Teutſchen ein paradys vogel genant.

Vnd wer diſen vogel leibhaff=
tig ſchawen oder kauffen
wil / der gehe zů dem Hanns
Kramer vnter dem Boner der
beut jn vmb hundert taler / 2c.

¶ Gedruckt zů Nürnberg durch
Steffan Hamer.

41

THE HOLZSCHUHER CUP

Melchior Baier I (goldsmith)
Attributed to **Peter Flötner** (sculptor)
Nuremberg, 1535–41 (according to the hallmark)

Silver, gilded, cast, repoussé, chased; coconut shell, carved

H. 43.5 cm; Diam. 17 cm (bowl)

GNM, inv. no. HG8601, on long-term loan from the Museen der Stadt Nürnberg, Kunstsammlungen

References:
Lange 1896, pp. 226–35; Kohlhaussen 1968, pp. 477–79, cat. no. 469; Dienst 2002, pp. 138–50; Exh. cat. Nuremberg 2014a, pp. 108–11, cat. no. 24 (Barbara Dienst); Pfisterer 2018.

Like sea shells |**cat. nos. 2, 120**| and ostrich eggs |**cat. no. 16**|, coconuts belonged to the category of "exotic" natural objects that were set into metal mounts by goldsmiths |**cat. no. 104**|. Their presentation at feasts and celebrations served to showcase the owners' access to luxury goods from all over the world. Known in the early modern period as the "sea nut" (*Meernuß*) or "Indian nut" (*Indianische Nuss*), the coconut initially arrived in Europe from South Asia and Africa, and was later also obtained from Central and South America.[1]

This piece, known as the Holzschuher Cup, is an outstanding example of the transformation of a coconut shell into a luxury drinking vessel. While the cup's exquisite goldsmithing is attributed to the Nuremberg master Melchior Baier I, its intricate reliefs are regarded as the work of the sculptor Peter Flötner, who was probably also responsible for the overall design. The cup's imagery is striking for its explicit eroticism.

The foot of the cup takes the form of a rocky mound, and several figures are arranged around it: a putto bearing the Holzschuher coat of arms, a copulating pair of goats, a nymph covering her face, and another nymph fondling a drunken man. In the stem, two gnarled grapevines growing out of the rocky terrain support a node of burst pea pods. The coconut bowl, enclosed within silver-gilt straps, is carved with a relief representing a triumphal procession of Bacchus, divided into three panels. The god of wine is shown seated on a goat-drawn cart, surrounded by naked, carousing satyrs. A man in sixteenth-century dress, armed with a sword and carrying a tall, cylindrical glass, is included somewhat incongruously in the mythological setting. In the second panel, a man reaches between the legs of the woman standing at the center, shown from behind. A woman lying on the ground at the left grips her partner's penis while vomiting. All around, followers of Bacchus are drinking, urinating, and heaving. In the third panel, at the left, a bearded man is being steadied by two female companions; the area of his lower abdomen is badly damaged. At the right, a woman on all fours is being flogged by a goat-horned figure. A putto sticks a peacock feather in her behind, and a satyr with an erect penis approaches, carrying a bellows.

The lid is topped by the figure of a satyr pouring wine into the mouth of a man lying naked on the ground. The three coconut segments on the lid are later additions, probably inserted at the same time that an augmented Holzschuher coat of arms, dated 1593, was added to the underside of the lid. The lid's three reliefs, mining scenes, differ in style from the carvings on the bowl. In the first one, a miner pushes a cart out of a tunnel. In the second, a miner shoulders a pan containing a jug, while another hammers the wall. In the third, next to a hoisting mechanism, a vessel is being forged on an anvil.

It remains unclear which member of the Holzschuher family commissioned the cup and on what occasion the mining scenes were added.[2] The family was involved in the mining business, and the inclusion of those scenes creates a new layer of interpretation. The formation of ores in the earth's interior was a common subject of contemporary discourse surrounding mining. In keeping with the understanding of nature at the time, there was widespread belief that minerals formed in root- or vein-like underground structures, following seasonal growth cycles the same way as plants.[3] Thus, the many small indications of roots on the cup's foot, the vegetal forms of the stem, and the bluntly pornographic imagery would have provided abundant material for conversation among the drinking company. The Holzschuhers and their guests would surely have been able to recognize connections between their mining operations and subjects of natural philosophy. The topics of conversation that prevailed presumably depended in large part on the amount of drink consumed.

Laura Di Carlo and Birgit Schübel

1 Fritz 1983, pp. 8–9.
2 Lange 1897, pp. 98–100.
3 See Asmussen 2020, pp. 381–82.

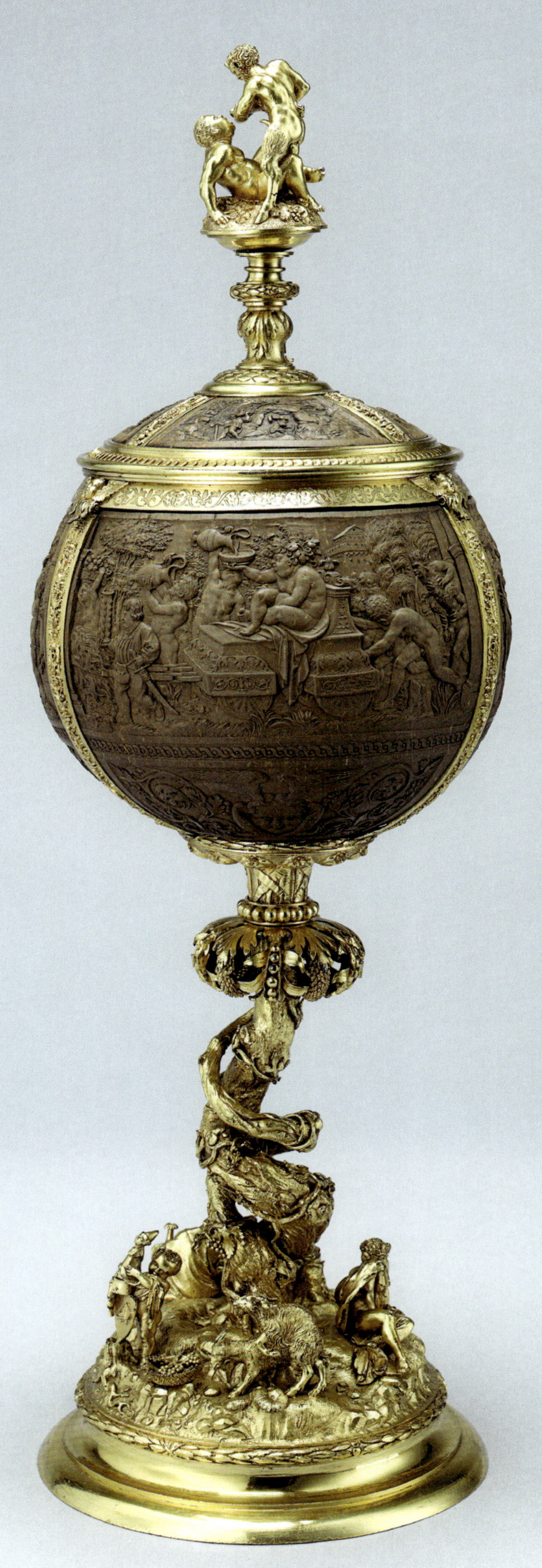

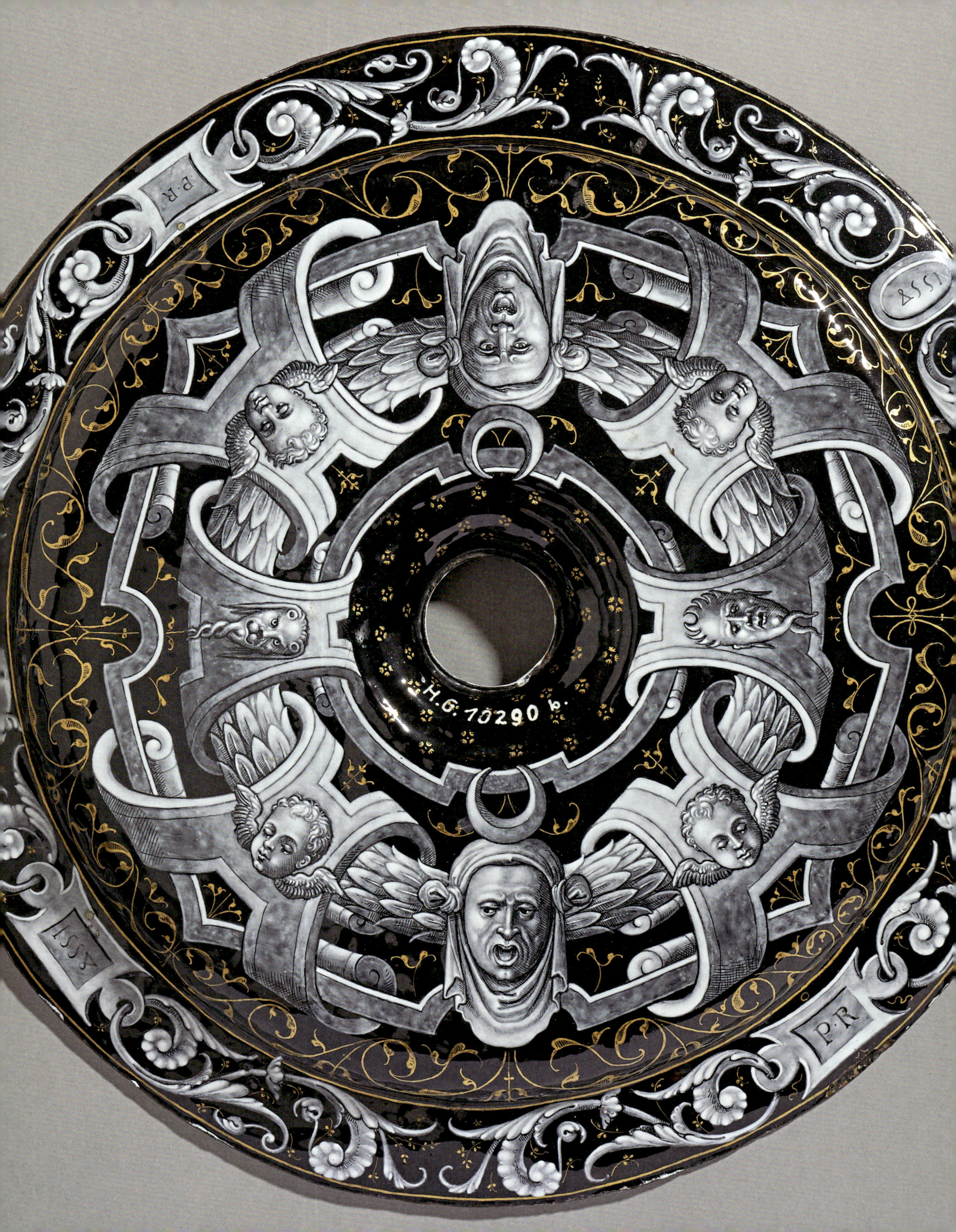
P·R
1555
H.G. 10290 b.

NETWORKS BETWEEN WEST AND EAST

Nuremberg was a juncture in the complex network of exchanges between western and eastern Europe. Merchants from Nuremberg were involved in the cloth trade with economic centers in Flanders and Brabant. They engaged in the silver mining industry in Bohemia and supplied spices to Silesia. The prestigious artistic commissions on which they spent their capital were located both in Nuremberg and abroad.

Illuminated manuscripts from Paris, tapestries from Brussels, and stained-glass church windows from Strasbourg were highly prized in Nuremberg. The city's workshops exported winged altarpieces and bronze sculptures to Prague, Wrocław, and Lviv.

Exchanges between the west and the east were highly dynamic and encompassed both material and immaterial aspects of culture. For example, around the middle of the fourteenth century, supporters of Emperor Charles IV brought the cult of Wenceslas, the patron saint of Bohemia, to Nuremberg. Nearly two centuries later, a bronze candle stand depicting Saint Wenceslas was made in Nuremberg by the Vischer workshop, and it went the opposite direction: to Prague Cathedral.

Nuremberg's role as a conduit between the west and the east is particularly well illustrated by Hans Pleydenwurff's *Descent from the Cross*, a panel from the former high altarpiece of Saint Elizabeth's in Wrocław. Pleydenwurff, who hailed from Bamberg, had traveled to the Burgundian Netherlands and learned firsthand the painterly innovations of the *ars nova* being practiced there. After settling in Nuremberg, he exported to Wrocław the monumental altarpiece for Saint Elizabeth's, thereby spreading the "new style" of painting to Silesia.

Benno Baumbauer

◂ cat. no. 52 (underside of basin, detail)

42

CASTING MODEL FOR THE SAINT WENCESLAS CANDLESTAND IN PRAGUE

Workshop of Hans Vischer the Younger

Nuremberg, 1532

Limewood, monochrome painted finish

H. 148 cm (with lance); H. 112 cm (without lance); W. 42 cm; D. 37 cm

GNM, inv. no. Pl.O.216

References:
Exh. cat. Nuremberg and New York 1986, p. 424, cat. no. 233 (William D. Wixom); Kammel 2010b, p. 64; Smith 2013, pp. 127, 132–33, n. 50.

This wooden sculpture shows Saint Wenceslas dressed in Maximilian-type armor, wearing a ducal crown and holding a lance and shield. The monochrome finish, in a color suggestive of bronze, gives a clue to the original function: the figure served as the model for the bronze candlestand that Hans Vischer the Younger (d. after 1549) cast in 1532 for the brewers' and maltsters' guild of Prague. The guild commissioned it in memory of the Hussite Wars. The candlestand was intended for the Saint Wenceslas Chapel in Prague Cathedral, where it is still found today.[1] Except for the banner, lance, and shield (with the raised letters SPR, probably for "Senatus Pragensis"), the casting very closely follows the model.[2] In the completed work, the candle spike and drip pan crown a richly ornamented baldachin supported by three Corinthian columns, into which the figure of Saint Wenceslas is set. The saint is flanked by angels, and there are lions bearing heraldic shields at the base.

The commission to create a sculpture of Bohemia's patron saint for what is perhaps the holiest site in the land was awarded to the Vischer workshop in Nuremberg for good reason: at the time, the Vischer foundry was an exclusive address where "secular and ecclesiastical lords from Magdeburg, Kraków, Würzburg, Bamberg, Eichstätt, Wrocław, Berlin, and Poznań ordered tombs and memorial sculptures."[3] The artist responsible for carving the wooden model remains unidentified. The handling is of the highest quality, distinguished by the figure's calm and commanding posture, the convincing realization of bodily volume fully in the round, and the finely worked details such as those of the hair and face. Although the Vischer workshop regularly collaborated with highly skilled sculptors in the design of models, only Peter Flötner (d. 1546) is known by name among them.[4]

The city of Nuremberg was well aware of the value of such casting models. The city council assembled a collection of wooden models from various workshops. In the seventeenth century, the collection was transferred to the municipal bell foundry, and in the early nineteenth century, parts of it were put on display at the art school in the Imperial Castle. The Saint Wenceslas figure is the only model from the Vischer workshop to have survived to this day.[5] The special appreciation shown to this model may be attributable to the quality of execution, but it may also be related to Nuremberg's close connection with Saint Wenceslas. The cult of the Bohemian patron saint spread to Nuremberg during the reign of Emperor Charles IV of the House of Luxembourg, whose residence was in Prague. Several fourteenth-century altar patronages and artistic representations established the saint's presence in Nuremberg, testifying to the city's close ties with Bohemia.[6] The casting model for the Prague candlestand figure of Saint Wenceslas is exceptional in many respects. Not only does it attest to the extraordinary, far-reaching importance of Nuremberg and the Vischer workshop to bronze casting in the eastern parts of central Europe; it also sheds light on the appreciation over time of models created by sculptors who are now mostly shrouded in anonymity.

Britta Dümpelmann

1 Exh. cat. Nuremberg and New York 1986, p. 424, cat. no. 233 (William D. Wixom); Kammel 2010b, p. 64.
2 Exh. cat. Nuremberg and New York 1986, p. 424, cat. no. 233 (William D. Wixom).
3 Citation translated from the German in Weihrauch 1944. See also Smith 2013, p. 127.
4 Kammel 2010b, p. 64. However, see the discussion surrounding Peter Vischer the Elder and Simon Lainberger in Baumbauer 2021, pp. 213–16.
5 Schwemmer 1949, pp. 109, 154; Hauschke 2006, p. 50. It remains a subject for future investigation as to whether the monochrome painted finish, evocative of bronze, was applied when the sculpture went on exhibit at the art school—perhaps to emphasize the work's function as a casting model—or was only renewed there.
6 Fajt 2019, p. 52 and passim.

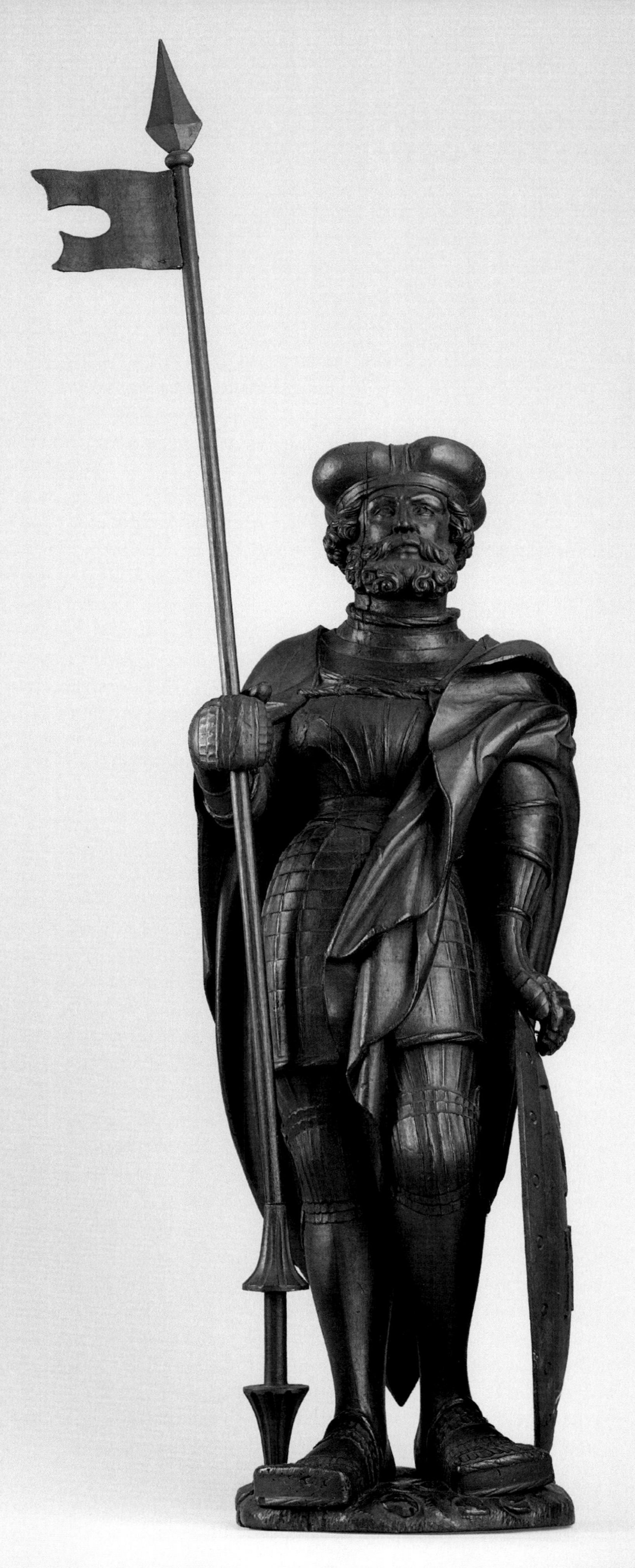

43

THE HARSDORFFER GOLD AND GEM SCALE

Unknown goldsmith; painted decoration attributed to **Jakob Elsner**

Nuremberg, 1497

Wood, painted; paper, painted; iron; silver, partly gilt; lead; thread; a pearl

Wooden case: L. 17.4 cm; W. 10.3 cm; H. 2.5 cm; small box for weights: L. 5.8 cm; W. 3.8 cm; scale, assembled: H. 24 cm; W. 14.5 cm; weight for height adjustment: L. 2.2 cm; W. 2 cm; H. 1.4 cm; weighing pans: Diam. (each) 2 cm; tweezers: L. 14.2 cm

GNM, inv. no. HG11161, on long-term loan from the Freiherrlich von Harsdorf'sche Familienstiftung

References:
Exh. cat. Nuremberg and New York 1986, pp. 218–19, cat. no. 77 (Rainer Kahsnitz); Fajt, Hörsch, and Jaeger 2011, pp. 13–17; Exh. cat. Potsdam 2013, p. 158 (article on Hans Harsdorfer II), cat. no. III.11, ill. p. 156 (Jiří Fajt et al.); Hentschel 2018, p. 5.

This medieval scale is probably the oldest surviving example meant expressly for weighing gold and gems. The silver base, weighted with lead and designed with multi-chamfered edges, is engraved with the allied coats of arms of the Nuremberg patrician families Harsdorffer and Nützel. The two-part stem supports a gilded, movable crossarm, from which the balance beam, pointer, and two weighing pans are suspended. A weight attached by a cord to the back end of the crossarm allows the balance beam to be lifted so that the pans hang freely. The device can be disassembled for storage in a wooden box, its lid decorated on both sides with paintings done on pasted-down paper.[1] On the exterior of the lid, two Wild Men surrounded by green vines are engaged in a sword fight. The date "1.4.9.7" is inscribed on a small panel at the lower center. On the lid's interior, two landsknechts wearing ostrich-plumed hats support a shield encircled by a laurel wreath. The shield bears another image of the Harsdorffer–Nützel arms of alliance. The meanings of the initials "AT" and "KAG" on the landsknechts' shirts have not yet been determined. The case contains a smaller box that originally held twenty-seven weights. Further compartments in the case indicate that the set originally included additional weighing pans. The accompanying tweezers are engraved on one side with a line from the Gospel of Luke that often served as a protective blessing; the other side displays a verse from the imperial coronation rite.[2] Also included with the ensemble is a sixteenth-century parchment recounting the life of Hans Harsdorffer (before 1464–1511), the device's original owner.

The Harsdorffers had been active in the Bohemian mining industry and metal trade since 1460. Hans Harsdorffer belonged to a Bohemian branch of the family based in Malešice (Malesitz) near Plzeň (Pilsen).[3] In 1481, he married Margarete Nützel, the daughter of Gabriel Nützel (1444–1501), who himself would later become Nuremberg's chief tax administrator (*Vorderster Losunger*) and thus the city's most powerful councilman. In the late 1480s, Hans and Katharina commissioned an altarpiece |**cat. no. 44**| for the Katharinenkirche in Nuremberg, the church where the Harsdorffers had their family burial site. King Vladislav II of Bohemia (1456–1516) appointed Hans as the chief mint master of the realm in 1496. From his post at Bohemia's main mint, located in the mining town of Kutná Hora (Kuttenberg), Hans Harsdorffer was responsible not only for controlling the minting of coins but also for overseeing the rich silver and copper mines that had been in operation there since the thirteenth century.[4] In 1497, on the occasion of a visit by King Vladislav, Hans commissioned three altars with retables created in Nuremberg for the so-called Italian Court, the royal residence in Kutná Hora.[5] The corresponding year inscribed on the case of the gold and gem scale suggests that the apparatus may have had some connection to the royal visit. The scale was not merely a tool but also a status symbol. This is confirmed by the motto engraved on the tweezers: "Christ conquers, Christ reigns, Christ commands" (*Xpvs Vincit, Xpvs Regnat, Xpvs Imperat*), which is the opening line of the so-called Royal Acclamations hymn (*Laudes regiae*). The inscription surely alludes to Harsdorffer's special connection both to King Vladislav and to the royal minting and mining operations he administered.

In 1498, Hans Harsdorffer inherited from his uncle Endres |**see cat. no. 51**| shares in the smeltery and copperworks in Enzendorf, near Nuremberg. That is presumably one of the reasons why, in 1499, he relinquished the privileged and lucrative position of chief mint master in Kutná Hora and moved to Nuremberg, where later, in 1505, he was elected senior mayor (Älterer Bürgermeister). All in all, Harsdorffer's career demonstrates that involvement in silver mining and proximity to kings and rulers were enormously important to the economic success of Nuremberg families.

Birgit Schübel

1 Hentschel 2018, p. 5.
2 Luke 4:30. See Reither 2009, pp. 40, 42.
3 Harsdorf 1958, pp. 31–35.
4 Harsdorf 1958, p. 29; Paehr 2018, p. 22.
5 Exh. cat. Potsdam 2013, p. 156 (Jiří Fajt et al.).

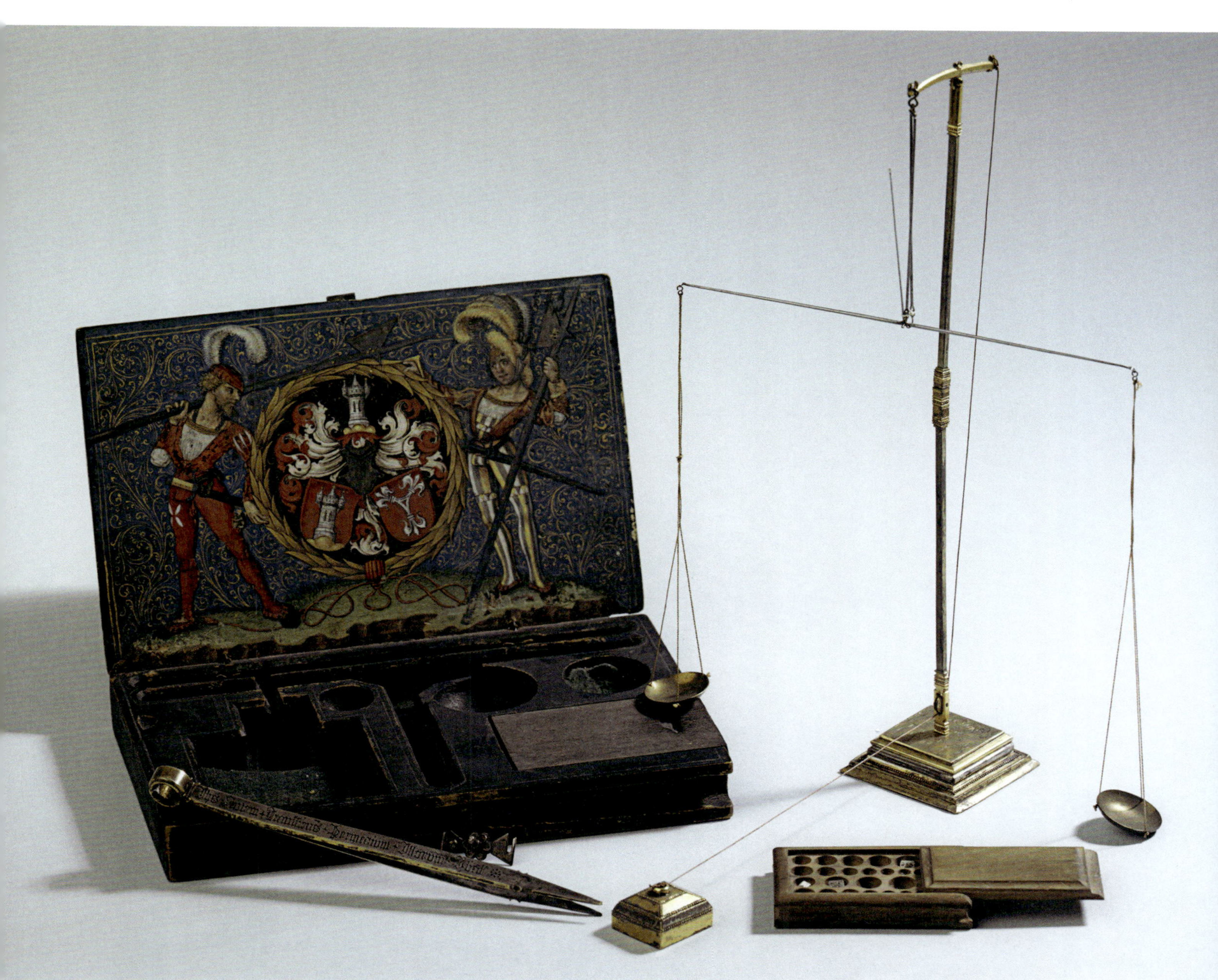

44

WING PANELS OF THE AGONY IN THE GARDEN ALTARPIECE FROM THE KATHARINENKIRCHE IN NUREMBERG

Hans Traut and/or workshop

Nuremberg, ca. 1485–88

Paint on fir

44.1 The Agony in the Garden

H. 111.2 cm; W. 77 cm

GNM, inv. no. Gm159a, on long-term loan from the Museen der Stadt Nürnberg, Kunstsammlungen

44.2 The Resurrection

H. 111.2 cm; W. 76.7 cm

GNM, inv. no. Gm1110, on long-term loan from the Bayerische Staatsgemäldesammlungen, Munich

References:
Carbach 1733, p. 122; Hess, Hirschfelder, and Baum 2019, vol. 2, pp. 653–72, cat. no. 44 (Beate Fücker and Dagmar Hirschfelder); Baumbauer 2019, p. 111, n. 44.

The church of the Dominican convent of Saint Catherine in Nuremberg contained an altar that was dedicated to Christ's agony during his prayer in the Garden of Gethsemane.[1] The retable that stood on the altar showed the Carrying of the Cross in its lost central section, now known only from old descriptions. The wings, when opened, displayed the Agony in the Garden on the left. Hans Traut (d. 1516) depicted the scene in an atmospheric nighttime setting. The disciples Peter, John, and James, who had resolved to keep watch with Jesus through the night, have fallen asleep. An angel appears to Jesus, showing him the cross that would serve as the instrument of his execution. In the background, a group of soldiers approaches to take him captive. They are led by the traitor Judas—a motif that was inherently anti-Jewish. On the right altarpiece wing, Hans Traut achieved an effective tonal contrast with the brightly lit depiction of the Resurrection. Here, the staging before the backdrop of the rock tomb is highly similar to that of the Agony in the Garden, but Traut bathed the scene in the hopeful light of a sunrise, thus establishing a cosmic parallel with the Resurrection. When the altarpiece's wings were closed, the Flagellation of Christ and the Crowning with Thorns completed the program.[2]

According to the description of the Katharinenkirche published by Carbach in 1733, the altarpiece originally featured "a Harsdorffer coat of arms in the lower right and a Stromer coat of arms in the lower left" (the viewer's left and right, respectively).[3] Until recently, this gave rise to an incorrect identification of the patrons. Since there was no marriage between a male Harsdorffer and a female Stromer at the time of the work's creation, the coats of arms were assigned to Ortolf Stromer and his wife Katharina Harsdorffer, even though this would have meant a reversal of the traditional left-right positions of the male and female coats of arms. However, because the patrician family Nützel had the same coat of arms as the Stromers, the commission can be traced instead to Ortolf Stromer's brother-in-law Hans Harsdorffer (d. 1511) and his wife Margarete Nützel (d. 1531).[4]

Hans Harsdorffer amassed great wealth through mining operations in Bohemia |**see cat. no. 43**|. This paved the way for his marriage in 1481 to Margarete, the daughter of the powerful city councilor Gabriel Nützel.[5] Hans and Margarete Harsdorffer commissioned their altarpiece in the Katharinenkirche about a decade before King Vladislav II of Bohemia appointed Hans to the positions of mint master and chief supervisor of the royal mines in Kutná Hora (Kuttenberg). This is a striking example of how capital generated by mining in Bohemia flowed into the creation of prestigious works of art in Nuremberg. Traut's paintings are distinguished by their impressive artistic quality. Moreover, the altarpiece's placement in the church was highly prominent. It stood in a central location, at the entrance to the chancel, a busy traffic junction within the sacred topography of Saint Catherine's. This is also noteworthy because the Harsdorffer family was represented at another altar in the same church, in a roughly contemporary altarpiece commissioned by Hans's uncle Andreas and his wife Ursula Behaim |**see cat. no. 51**|.[6] Thus, the Harsdorffer family had a considerable presence in the convent church—something that was meant to foster their salvation while also displaying their social prestige.[7]

Benno Baumbauer

1 On devotion to the Agony in the Garden, see Kahsnitz 1983, pp. 218–58, cat. no. 20 (Rainer Kahsnitz).
2 The Flagellation has been split off from its formerly double-sided panel. GNM, inv. no. Gm159b, on long-term loan from the Museen der Stadt Nürnberg, Kunstsammlungen.
3 Carbach 1733, p. 122: "unten zur rechten Hand ein Harsdörfferisches, zur lincken ein Stromerisches Wappen."
4 As first noted in Baumbauer 2019, p. 111, n. 44.
5 On Harsdorffer, see Harsdorf 1958, pp. 31–35; Exh. cat. Potsdam 2013, pp. 156–58 (Jiří Fajt et al.).
6 Exh. cat. Nuremberg 2019b, pp. 243–45, cat. no. 48 (Dagmar Hirschfelder).
7 Given that the *Totenschild* memorials for Andreas and Hans Harsdorffer also hung in the church, it is highly likely that the two men were buried there. See Stadtbibliothek, Nuremberg, Nor H 185,2, "Fragmentarisches Verzeichnis der Monumente in der Katharinenkirche," fol. 5r.

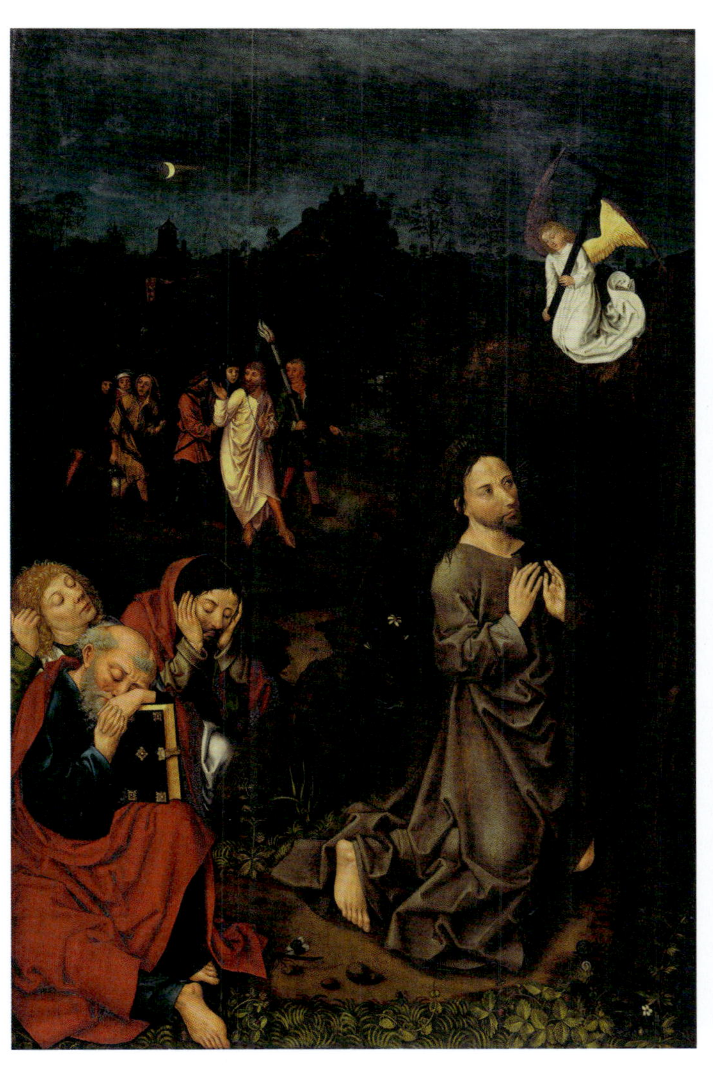

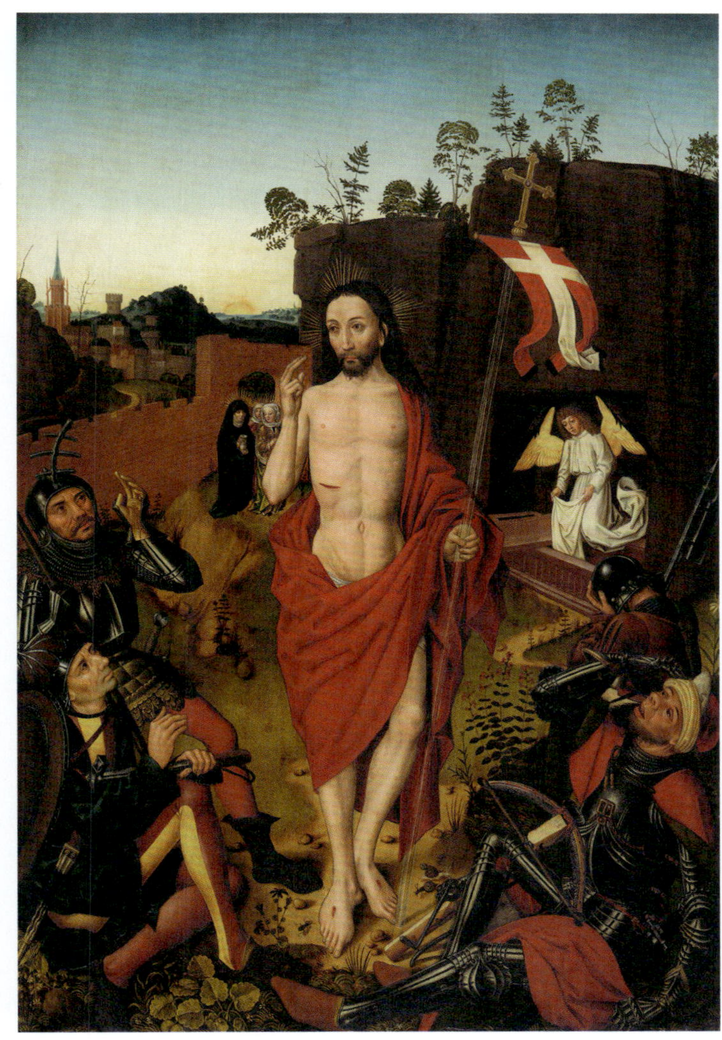

45

MARIAN ALTARPIECE OF THE IMHOFF FAMILY FROM THE CHURCH OF SAINT ELIZABETH IN WROCŁAW

Master of the Wolfgang Altarpiece

Nuremberg, ca. 1445–50

Paint on spruce

Center panel: H. 178–149.5 cm; W. 120 cm; left wing: H. 176.5–149.5 cm; W. 59.5 cm; right wing: H. 178.5–149.5 cm; W. 59.5 cm

Muzeum Narodowe, Warsaw, inv. no. Śr.91/1–3 MNW

References:
Imhoff 1975, pp. 20–22; Stromer 1975, p. 1098; Strieder 1993, pp. 46–51, 188, cat. no. 31; Patała 2019, pp. 188–89, cat. no. 26; Exh. cat. Besançon, Colmar, and Dijon 2024, p. 90, under cat. no. 10 (Benno Baumbauer).

This ogive-arched triptych offers an early example of a large work of art being exported from Nuremberg, a phenomenon that became particularly prevalent along the main trade routes. The work depicts important episodes from the life of the Virgin Mary. The closed wings show the Visitation; when opened, they reveal the Annunciation on the left and the Adoration on the right. The central panel shows the Assumption of the Virgin. All three scenes in the triptych's open state are adorned with gold backgrounds. In the Assumption, the Virgin floats above an open sarcophagus and a nearby bier, rising up to be received by Christ. He wears a crown and carries a scepter, and the Virgin is being crowned as the Queen of Heaven by an angel. The concept of Mary's bodily assumption into heaven comes not directly from the Bible but instead from apocryphal accounts and legends. Those texts also describe the apostles being summoned from all corners of the earth to gather at her deathbed.

This retable, which is now kept in Warsaw, is one of the finest works produced by the Master of the Wolfgang Altarpiece, who was active in Nuremberg around 1450. He is named after a work in the Lorenzkirche in Nuremberg; and his tentative identification as Valentin Wolgemut, Michael Wolgemut's father, has yet to be proven. Clearly he was known and active outside the region around Nuremberg, since he created this Marian altarpiece for the Church of Saint Elisabeth in Wrocław (Breslau), which lies some five hundred kilometers away from his hometown |**see cat. no. 46**|.

The figure of the work's wealthy patron appears in the lower left of the central panel, depicted in adoration among the apostles, in somewhat smaller scale. His distinctive coat of arms showing a lion with a fish's tail identifies him as a member of the Imhoff patrician family of Nuremberg. Because no wife is present, it is assumed that the man is Melchior Imhoff, who was first mentioned in Wrocław in 1445–46 and died there, unmarried, in 1457.[1] The triptych was probably commissioned for memorial purposes while he was still alive.

By the end of the fourteenth century, the Imhoff family had succeeded in building a trading empire that spanned across Europe.[2] Trade with Venice and with clients to the east laid the foundation for their success. Hans Imhoff III (d. 1398), Melchior's grandfather and the founder of the first Imhoff trading firm, secured the family an important position in the exchange of goods with the eastern parts of central Europe. In addition, Hans acquired lucrative shares in mining operations in Silesia, Bohemia, and Moravia.

The descendants of Hans Imhoff expanded the trading network, which by 1505 extended even as far as India |**see cat. no. 116**|.[3] They consolidated the family's wealth and became known as patrons of lavish works of art—particularly in Nuremberg but also in the places where they had branch offices. In the second quarter of the fifteenth century, the Imhoffs cofounded an altar dedicated to Saint Sebaldus in the Venetian church of San Bartolomeo, the same altar for which Albrecht Dürer would later paint his *Feast of the Rose Garlands* |**fig. p. 53**|.[4] In Wrocław, where Melchior Imhoff managed the family's operations in the surrounding region, the parish and city-council church of Saint Elizabeth was regarded by all "foreign" merchants from the German lands as a preferred location for memorial works and the public display of status.

It remains unknown exactly why Melchior Imhoff commissioned an artist from his faraway hometown to paint this triptych. About twenty years later, the painter Hans Pleydenwurff of Nuremberg was commissioned to create another altarpiece for Saint Elizabeth's, which suggests that, alongside personal preferences, political and diplomatic networks played a role in these long-distance orders |**cat. no. 46**|.

Judith Hentschel

1 Also, his brother Balthasar (d. 1483) is recorded as being in Wrocław in 1450. See Imhoff 1975, pp. 11, 17, 20–23.
2 Imhoff 1987b, pp. 11–44; Pohle 2000, esp. pp. 122–34, 205–11.
3 Imhoff 1987b, pp. 11–44; Pohle 2000, esp. pp. 122–34, 205–11.
4 Pfotenhauer 2016, pp. 202–16.

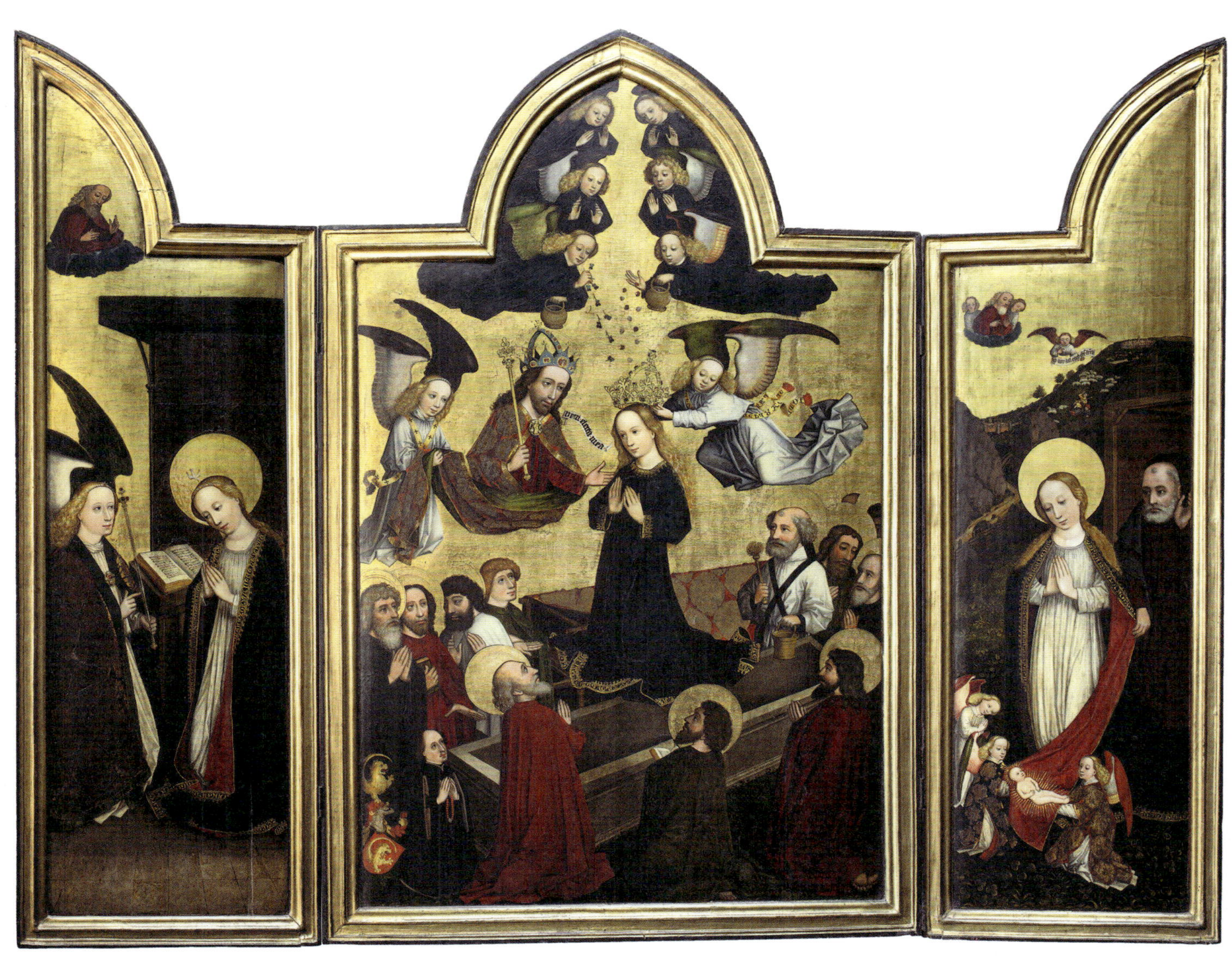

46

THE DESCENT FROM THE CROSS, FROM THE HIGH ALTARPIECE OF THE CHURCH OF SAINT ELIZABETH IN WROCŁAW

Hans Pleydenwurff

Nuremberg and Wrocław, ca. 1462

Paint on limewood
H. 286 cm; W. 142 cm
GNM, inv. no. Gm1127

References:
Hess, Hirschfelder, and Baum 2019, vol. 1, pp. 364–78, no. 26 (Beate Fücker and Dagmar Hirschfelder); Patała 2019.

In 1462, the painter Hans Pleydenwurff (d. 1471/72) of Nuremberg created a winged retable for the high altar of the parish church of Saint Elizabeth in Wrocław (Breslau), the chief city of the region of Silesia. Although the altarpiece survives only in fragments, it must have been highly impressive, as it measured more than three meters tall and six meters wide. The wing panel preserved at the Germanisches Nationalmuseum depicts the dead Jesus being taken down from the cross by his followers Joseph of Arimathea and Nicodemus. The Virgin Mary, Saint John, and their companions stand below, waiting to receive the corpse. The background offers a deep view into a landscape with a river and mill, and the sky area is gilded.

Pleydenwurff is regarded as the most important Franconian painter of the time before Albrecht Dürer. He came from a family of painters in Bamberg[1] and spent his journeyman years in the Low Countries, where, in addition to acquiring a refined use of color, he learned innovative methods of representing spatial depth in landscapes, portraying individualized figures, and depicting realistic surface textures. Back in Franconia, from 1457 onward he ran a flourishing workshop in Nuremberg with a sphere of operation that extended far beyond the region. Painters such as Hans Schüchlin from Ulm, Johannes Siebenbürger from Vienna, and the Silesian Master of the Years 1486–1487 came to Nuremberg to work in Pleydenwurff's shop.[2]

The altarpiece created for Wrocław occupies an important position in Pleydenwurff's oeuvre, for it is his only securely documented work. Through this major commission, Nuremberg became a hub through which the artistic innovations of early Netherlandish painting were transmitted from the west to urban centers in east-central Europe. Furthermore, the written sources provide insight into the types of financial transactions involved in the export of art at the time. For example, in June 1462, Pleydenwurff was in Wrocław to take payment from the city council and presumably also to supervise the altarpiece's installation. Upon his return to Nuremberg, however, he wrote to the church administrators in Wrocław, complaining that he had been paid 200 Hungarian guldens—not the agreed-on 200 Rhenish guldens. He had incurred a loss when exchanging the currency in Nuremberg and was now requesting compensation for the difference.

The reason why the high altarpiece of Saint Elizabeth's in Wrocław was commissioned across such a great distance—from a painter some five hundred kilometers away in Nuremberg—probably lies not only in Pleydenwurff's fame but also in initiatives taken by merchants from Nuremberg who had settled in Wrocław. The Silesian metropolis served as the gateway to trade with the eastern part of central Europe. Therefore, Nuremberg patrician families such as the Imhoffs, Holzschuhers, and Hallers had established a presence there, as had certain burgher families, who managed to join Wrocław's civic elite by conducting business, purchasing property, and networking.[3] As the city's most important parish church, Saint Elisabeth's was the center of religious life for Nurembergers who lived in Wrocław. They used four of the church's chapels; venerated Saint Sebaldus, the patron saint of Nuremberg, at three or more altars; and served as church administrators. They also ordered memorial works and altarpieces from Nuremberg artists, as shown by the Imhoff-family retable painted by the Master of the Wolfgang Altarpiece |**cat. no. 45**|. However, the high altarpiece by Pleydenwurff set a new benchmark for the size and cost of such endeavors. Apparently, this commission also required diplomatic efforts at the highest level, for in a letter of July 1462, the mayors and city councilors of Nuremberg thanked their counterparts in Wrocław for their patronage of Pleydenwurff and their generous payment to him.

Judith Hentschel

1 Hirschfelder 2014.
2 Suckale 2009, vol. 1, pp. 166–98, 247–56. On the artistic reception of Pleydenwurff in Silesia, see Patała 2018a.
3 Stromer 1975; Patała 2018b.

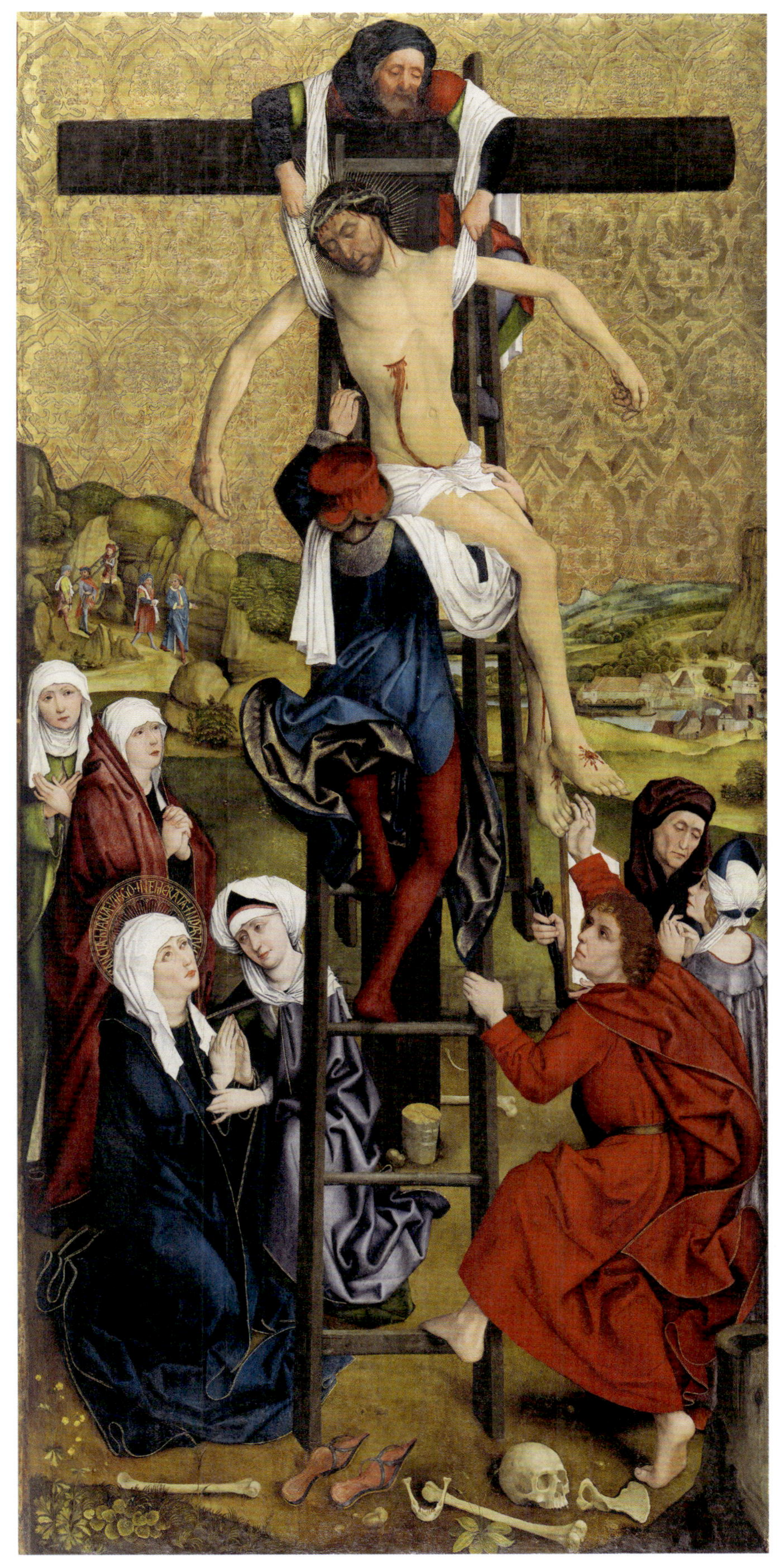

47

RERVM MOSCOVITICARVM COMMENTARII

Sigmund von Herberstein
Illustrations by **Augustin Hirsvogel**

47.1 Hand-Colored First Edition

Vienna: Johann Singriener the Elder (his heirs), 1549

Post-incunable, etchings, hand-colored

H. 30.1 cm; W. 23.8 cm

Universitätsbibliothek der LMU, Munich, shelf mark 0017/2 Hist.prof. 330

47.2 Moscovia der Hauptstat in Reissen (German edition)

(not illustrated)

Vienna: Michael Zimmermann, 1557

Post-incunable, 15 woodcut illustrations

H. 32 cm; W. 42 cm (opened)

GNM, shelf mark 4° G. 12753

References:
Nehring 1897; Schwarz 1917, pp. 29–35; Novgorod Geography 2022, no. 5.3; Kollmann 2024, pp. 67–116.

From 1516 to 1518, Sigmund Freiherr von Herberstein (1486–1566) traveled to the court of the grand prince in Moscow as a Habsburg envoy on behalf of Emperor Maximilian I. The goal was to mediate between Poland and Russia. From 1526 to 1527, Herberstein visited Russia again, this time on behalf of King Ferdinand, Maximilian's grandson. Those experiences gave rise to the travelogue *Rervm Moscoviticarvm Commentarii* (Notes on Muscovite Affairs), first published in Latin in 1549 and illustrated with several etchings by Augustin Hirsvogel (1503–1553), a Nuremberg-born artist who had moved to Vienna. In later editions, the designs of the etchings were transferred to woodcuts. A German edition followed in 1567 under the title *Moscovia der Haupstat in Reissen* (Moscovia, the capital of Russia).[1]

The map of Russia contained in the book had already been published separately in 1546. It was probably one of the first illustrations that Herberstein commissioned from Hirsvogel, who was known for his cartographic work.[2] Hirsvogel signed this etching at the right, below a bar scale in German miles: "HANC TABULAM ABSOLVIT AUG HIRSFOGEL VIE: AUS: CUM GRA ET PRIVI IMP" (This plate was executed by Augustin Hirsvogel in Vienna, Austria, with the favor and patent of the emperor).[3] The title at the upper left and the Herberstein coat of arms at the lower left identify Herberstein as the map's designer. The detailed indications of place names, rivers, and forests present Russia as an accessible part of the Christian world. Only the northeastern corner, beyond the Urals, near the mouth of the Ob River, is differently characterized: marked by the pagan idol of the Golden Woman (*Zlata baba*), it is a mysterious region of myths and wonders, so far east that it borders China (*Kytay*).[4]

On the whole, Herberstein's account is distinguished by its "eyewitness character and faithfulness in interpretation."[5] Some of Hirsvogel's etchings are so accurately observed as to give the impression that he designed them on-site. One of those is the detailed portrayal of three cavalrymen with short stirrups, quilted coats, and light helmets, armed with maces and Mongolian bows.[6] In fact, for these precise depictions, Hirsvogel was able to study the numerous objects that Herberstein brought back from his travels, consisting not only of the military articles that appear in the aforementioned image. The items included other weapons, ceremonial robes and costumes, a carriage, a sleigh, and specimens of an aurochs and a bison. Herberstein conveyed Muscovite geography, regional knowledge, and warfare techniques in the form of oral reports and written records, while the realia he imported corroborated his eyewitness accounts and gave his central European audience a glimpse of Muscovite culture in the form of original objects.[7] The characteristic sleigh on the opposite page, in which Herberstein appears as the passenger, is probably based on the object he imported. Although designed by Hirsvogel long after the event and at great distance from where it occurred, the scene brings Herberstein's diplomatic mission to life, almost as if it were happening in the here and now.

Britta Dümpelmann

1 Herberstein 2007.
2 Nehring 1897, p. 35; Schwarz 1917, p. 30; Kollmann 2024, pp. 82–83.
3 See Nehring 1897, p. 23.
4 Kollmann 2024, pp. 90–91; Novgorod Geography 2022, no. 5.3.
5 Translated from the German in Bergstraesser 1969, p. 579.
6 Kollmann 2024, pp. 87–90.
7 Nevinson 1967, p. 70; Kollmann 2024, pp. 87–88.

MOSCOVIA SIGISMVNDI LIBERI BARONIS IN HERBERSTEIN NEIPERG ET GVTNHAG. ANNO M.D.XLIX.
HANC TABVLAM ABSOLVIT AVG HIRSFOGEL VIE: AVS: CVM GRA: ET PRIVI IMP

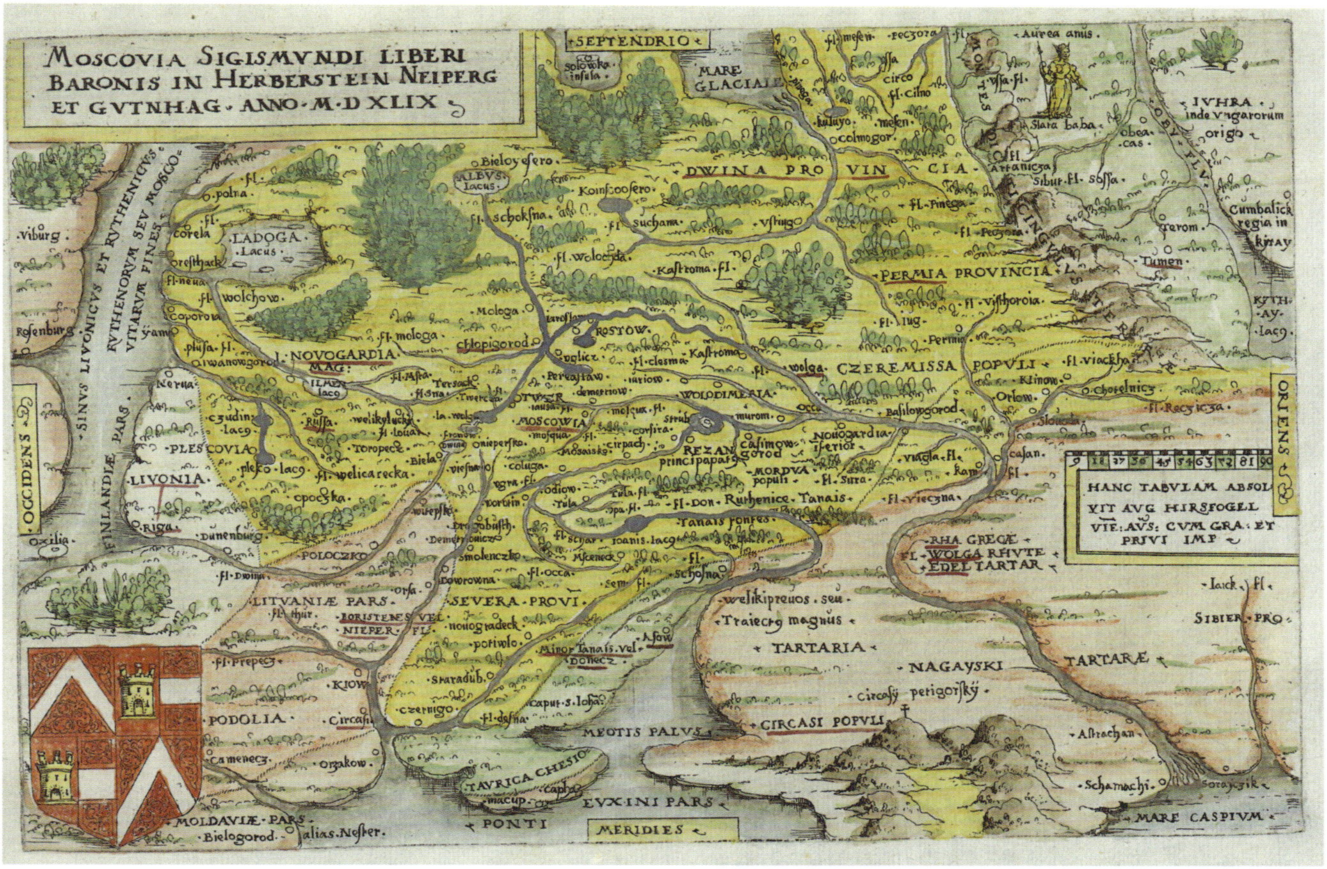

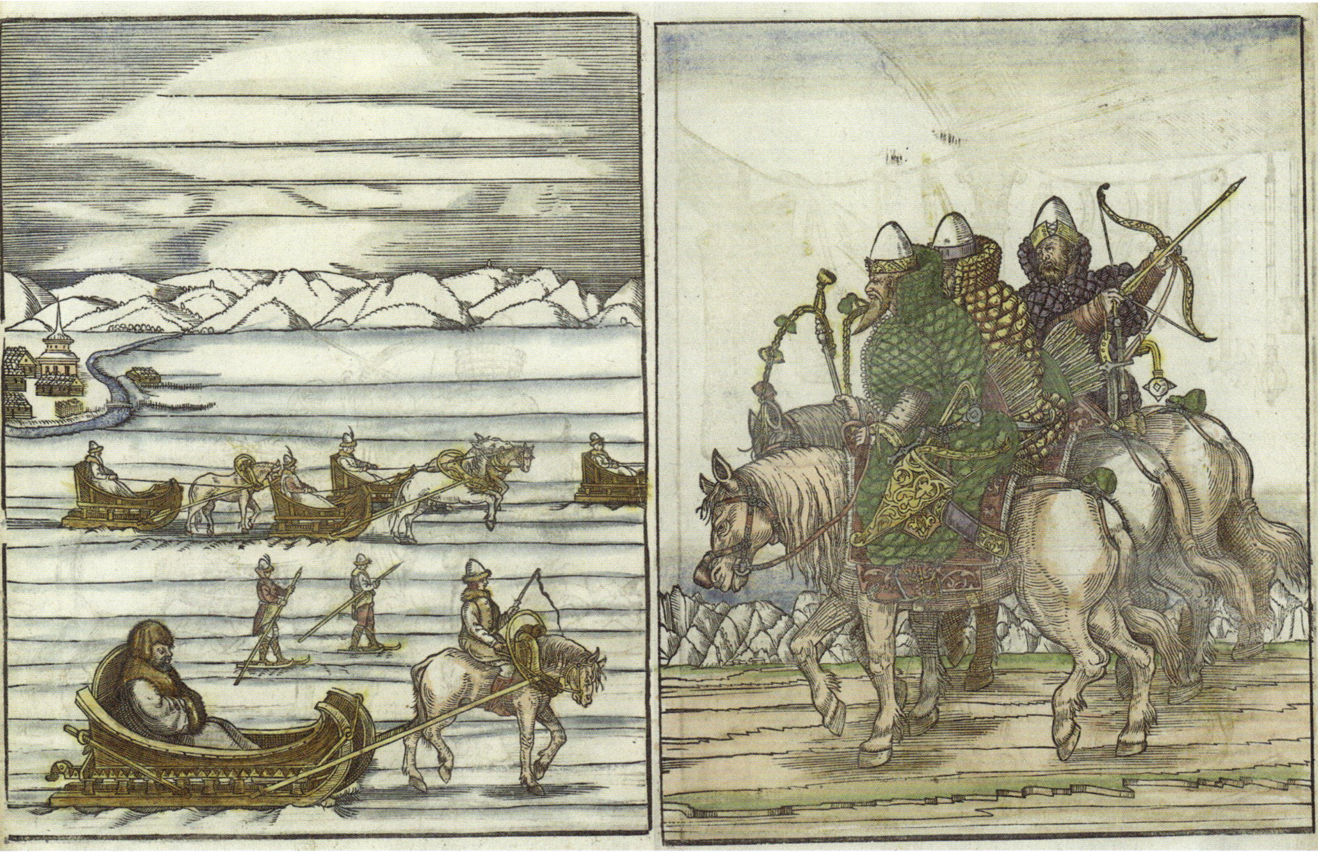

cat. no. 47.1

48

CASTING MODEL FOR THE TOMB EFFIGY OF MIKOŁAJ HERBURT-ODNOWSKI

Workshop of **Pankraz Labenwolf**

Nuremberg, 1550–51

Limewood, polychrome finish; the polychromy now visible is from the nineteenth century

H. 65 cm; W. 213 cm; D. 15.5 cm

GNM, inv. no. Pl.O.3196

References:
Timann 1996; Kammel 1997; Hess and Kammel 2010, pp. 300–302.

This flat, relief-like wooden sculpture shows the reclining figure of a man dressed in armor, his head resting in his left hand and his legs outstretched. The work served as the casting model for the brass tomb effigy in Lviv Cathedral of the Polish nobleman Mikołaj Herburt-Odnowski, who died in 1555. Herburt-Odnowski commissioned the sculpture in 1551 from Pankraz Labenwolf (1492–1563).[1] Lviv (Lwów in Polish, Lemberg in German) had been the capital of the Polish province of Ruthenia since 1353, and Herburt-Odnowski, descendant of a Galician family of magnates, had been the chief starost there since 1537—that is, a liege man of the Polish king and head of both the city and province. Closely connected with the Polish royal family, he was promoted to the office of starost of Sandomierz in 1553 and voivode of Kraków the following year.[2]

For this work, the choice of form and material and the selection of a foundry in Nuremberg, more than a thousand kilometers away, resulted from the multifaceted cultural ties that existed between Nuremberg and Lviv. These factors provide insight into the memorial ambitions that a high-ranking Polish nobleman in the mid-sixteenth century associated with the creation of a tomb that combines Italian innovation and Polish tradition. With regard to form, the design of the Herburt-Odnowski tomb follows the type consisting of a reclining figure with the head supported by a hand which became com-

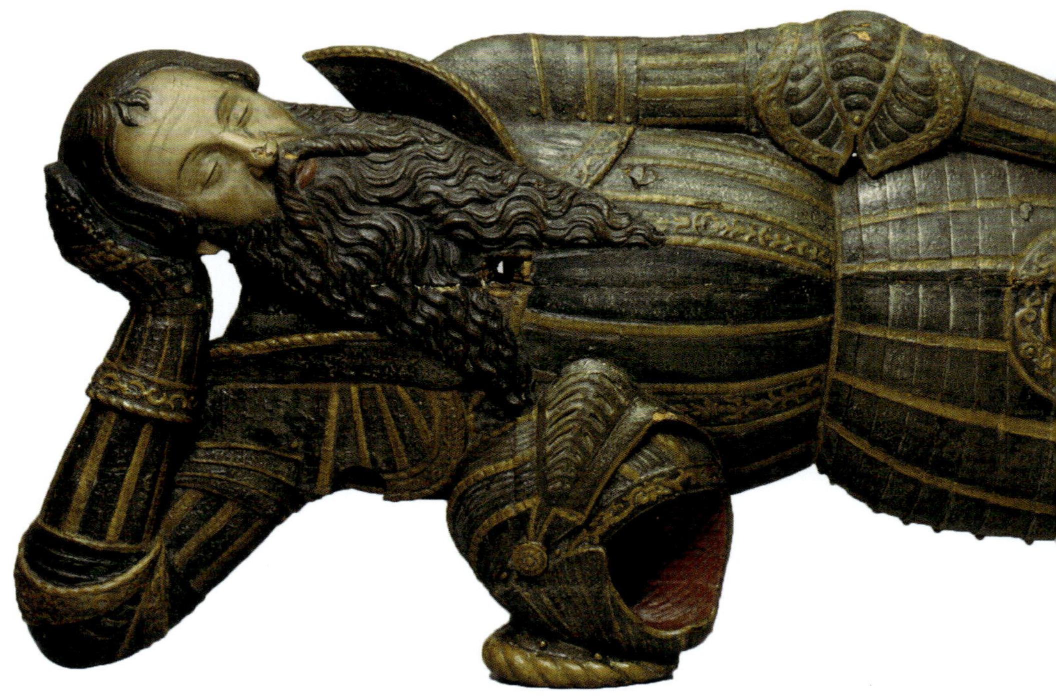

1 As documented in a receipt for payment in the amount of 245 guldens for the casting, preserved in a transcription in the Stadtarchiv, Nuremberg. See Kammel 1997, p. 13; Timann 1996, p. 98.
2 Kammel 1997, pp. 12–13; Timann 1996, pp. 105–9.

mon at the royal court in Kraków in the sixteenth century (and into the next). It was regarded as the "tomb form befitting the high aristocracy."[3] This type was introduced from Italy; in Kraków, the stone used was the so-called red marble typical of the region.[4]

While the legs of figures of this tomb type are normally elegantly crossed, those of the effigy of Herburt-Odnowski are extended in a peculiar fashion. In some of the literature, this has been attributed to a misunderstanding in the course of the motif's transfer from Lviv to Nuremberg.[5] However, it seems much more likely that this aspect was based on an older local tradition—namely, the wall tombs with standing effigies that were widespread in Poland and often cast in metal.[6] The outstretched legs of Herburt-Odnowski could thus be explained as a ninety-degree rotation of the type of figure found in the standing-effigy tradition. There are certain similarities here with the tomb figures of Severin and Zofia Boner in Saint Mary's Church in Kraków, which date from the 1530s and were probably also cast by Pankraz Labenwolf in Nuremberg.[7] Therefore, contrary to previous assumptions, the present wooden model may not necessarily have been carved in Nuremberg and was possibly even made by a sculptor active in or around Lviv itself.[8]

Britta Dümpelmann

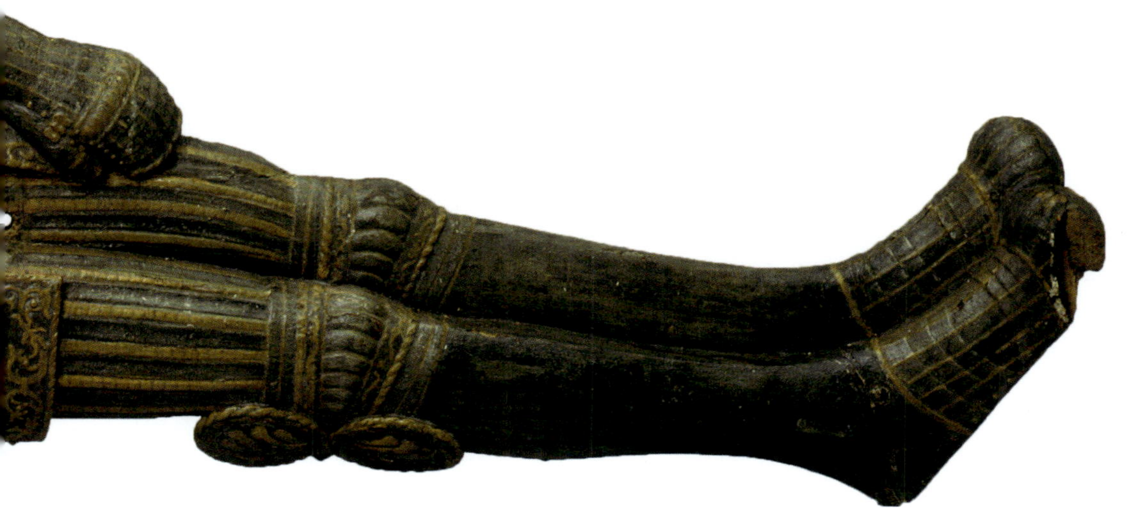

3 Citation translated from the German in Hess and Kammel 2010, p. 301.
4 For a seminal example of this type in Italy, see Andrea Sansovino, *Tomb of Ascanio Sforza*, ca. 1505–9, Santa Maria del Popolo, Rome; Timann 1996, p. 100, fig. 9.
5 Timann 1996, pp. 101–2; Hess and Kammel 2010, p. 302.
6 Chrzanowski 1986, pp. 147–48; Timann 1996, p. 109.
7 That tomb is mentioned in Hauschke 2006, p. 40. See also Walczak 2018, pp. 132–33, fig. 10.
8 Timann 1996, p. 102; Hess and Kammel 2010, p. 302. As a precedent, see the delivery from Kraków to Nuremberg of the wooden model by Veit Stoss for the Callimachus memorial, which was cast in the Vischer workshop. Hauschke 2006, pp. 229–34, cat. no. 49.

49

SEPULCHRAL TAPESTRY OF THE HOLZSCHUHER FAMILY, SHOWING THE MASS OF SAINT GREGORY

Attributed to **Colyn de Coter** (cartoonist)
workshop of **Pieter van Edingen Aelst** (weaver)

Brussels, 1495

Tapestry weave: wool, silk

H. 296 cm; W. 247 cm

GNM, inv. no. Gew679

References:
Wilckens 1983; Meier 2006, pp. 239–41; Weilandt 2007, pp. 100–101, 239, 449; Tammen 2014, pp. 7–11; Henkelmann 2021, pp. 316–17, 320.

This sepulchral tapestry is an impressive manifestation of the ties that Nuremberg had with Brussels, one of the main hubs of art and commerce in Flanders. The date and coat of arms in the tapestry's lower right indicate that it was made in 1495 for the Holzschuher family of Nuremberg. The sources of the family's wealth included the trade in textiles with Flanders. The elite level at which the Holzschuhers purchased art abroad is illustrated by the fact that, only a few years later, Joanna I of Castile presented her mother, Queen Isabella I, with a tapestry created from the same design. That work, now part of the royal collections in Madrid, displays the letters "BRVXEL" on the border of Saint Gregory's chasuble.[1] The proud mention of the place of manufacture on that version supports the traditional account of the Holzschuhers having acquired their tapestry in Flanders, through the Nuremberg merchant Nikolaus Selbitzer.[2] The example in Madrid, which unlike the one in Nuremberg contains gold and silver threads, is attributed to the famous workshop of Pieter van Edingen Aelst, who is documented in Brussels from 1493. The cartoon is said to have been created by the painter and draftsman Colyn de Coter, who was also active there.[3] Despite the earlier date and the different types of threads used, the same attribution is conceivable for the Nuremberg tapestry.

This tapestry was used in the Sebalduskirche during Holzschuher family memorial Masses.[4] The subject matter is consistent with that function. It shows the apparition of Christ as the Man of Sorrows at a Mass being celebrated by Pope Gregory. In the context of commemoration of the dead, the Man of Sorrows was regarded as the embodiment of "misericordia," representing the invocation of God's mercy toward the souls of the deceased.[5]

The composition, which draws upon older depictions of the subject in early Netherlandish painting, is richly detailed in its staging. The symbols of the Passion are arranged around the figure of Christ, against a gold background. Nineteen figures crowd around the altar, variously standing or kneeling. The scene takes place in a spacious interior defined by several pillars, a wooden ceiling, and, on the back wall, five windows. The perspectival foreshortening and the dense layering of the figures create a suggestion of spatial depth that is characteristic of paintings. Yet, unlike in a painting, the tapestry's impression of depth results from the additive juxtaposition of different colored threads, woven line by line through the warp. The weaver's artistic achievement in testing the boundaries of the medium is further emphasized by the fictitious frame surrounding the scene, which gives the appearance of being decorated with precious stones. With this import from Brussels, a work of outstanding artistic quality, the Holzschuher family was able to put its economic potency and refined taste on display during liturgical celebrations in one of Nuremberg's most prestigious churches.

Sven Jakstat

1 On the tapestry in Madrid, see Junquera de Vega and Herrero Carretero 1986, p. 32; Exh. cat. Brussels 2000, pp. 14–17, cat. no. 2 (Cecilia Paredes); Herrero Carretero 2004, pp. 29, 38–41.
2 Wilckens 1983, p. 206.
3 Exh. cat. Brussels 2000, p. 16 (Cecilia Paredes).
4 The theories concerning its liturgical use are contradictory in parts. See Meier 2006, pp. 240–41; Weilandt 2007, p. 100; Tammen 2014, pp. 8–9; Bauernfeind 2018, pp. 94–98.
5 On the meaning of the Man of Sorrows, see Weilandt 2007, pp. 85–109.

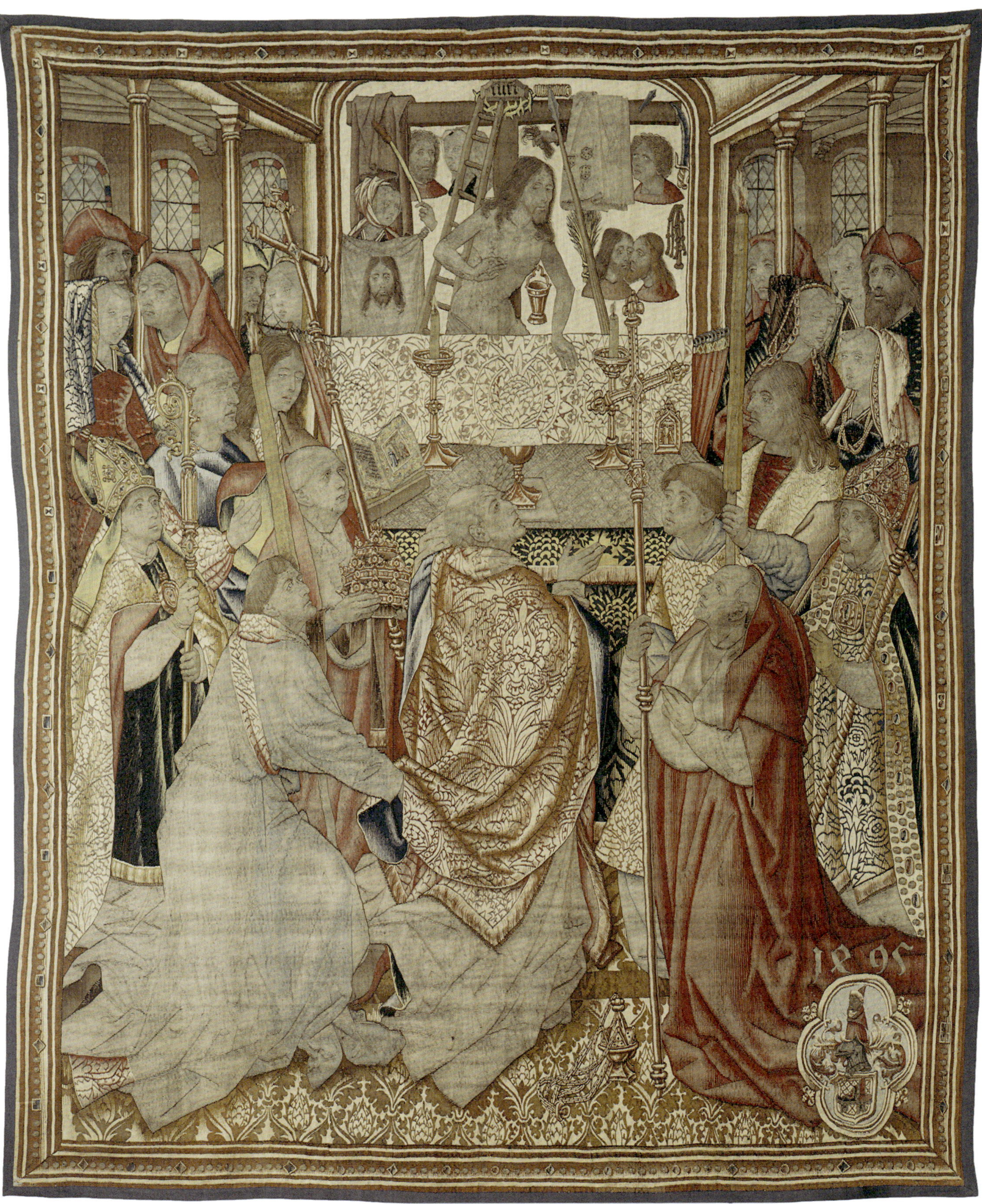

50

VIRGIN AND CHILD ON A CRESCENT MOON, WITH TWO ANGELS

Strasbourg Workshop Cooperative

Strasbourg, ca. 1480

Pot-metal glass with black vitreous paint and silver stain; the left arch with its two figures is a restoration

H. 46 cm; W. 35 cm

GNM, inv. no. MM116

References:
Exh. cat. Ulm 1995, pp. 146–47, cat. no. 34 (Hartmut Scholz); Exh. cat. Nuremberg 2000b, pp. 263–64, cat. no. 91 (Daniel Hess).

About 1481, the patrician Peter Volckamer III (1431–1493) commissioned a stained-glass window measuring 7.4 by 4 meters for the newly built chancel of the Lorenzkirche in Nuremberg.[1] With its masterfully composed Tree of Jesse, it is one of the finest examples of glass painting from the fifteenth century. Still today, the brilliant colors of the Volckamer window outshine the church's three central windows, which had been created shortly before by the workshop of Michael Wolgemut in Nuremberg. The window exhibits all the technical refinements of late Gothic stained glass. At the time, such quality was not available from the local Nuremberg workshops, which explains why Volckamer took the trouble to order this impressive work from Strasbourg, more than 250 kilometers away.

In that bustling artistic center on the Upper Rhine, the five stained-glass painters Peter Hemmel von Andlau, Lienhart Spitznagel, Hans von Maursmünster, Theobald von Lixheim, and Werner Störe joined forces in 1477 to form a collective: the so-called Strasbourg Workshop Cooperative.[2] This allowed the workshops to pool their resources. They drew upon a shared stock of drawings, invested jointly in raw materials, deployed their employees more flexibly than before, and expanded their export radius. Their coveted windows—"Stroßburg finster" in the parlance of the period—went to locations hundreds of kilometers distant from Alsace, such as Frankfurt am Main, Munich, Salzburg, and of course Nuremberg.

Probably about the same time the Volckamer window was produced, the Strasbourg Workshop Cooperative fashioned a panel of exquisite quality depicting the Virgin and Child standing on a crescent moon, flanked by two angels. The creators pulled out all the stops on this small surface. The technique of stained-glass painting revolves around the use of hatchings and glazes in vitreous paint to control the light passing through the colored glass. This allowed for the creation of highly subtle, three-dimensional effects in the modeling of light and shade. The hatching on the present panel is comparable to what one finds in engravings by Martin Schongauer.

Equally masterful here is the use of glass flashing, a technique in which a colorless glass base is overlaid and fused with a layer of colored glass. Blue flashed glass appears in the Virgin Mary's robe, violet and red in the robes of the angels. Using acid, patterns were etched into the colored coatings, allowing clear light to shine through and creating the effect of brocaded fabric. The range of color, especially in the violet robe, was expanded through the use of silver stain, which produces tones of yellow. For the angel on the right, the combination of a red overlay, black vitreous paint, and silver stain made it possible to create a figure of highly varied colors from a single piece of glass. The Strasbourg glass painters achieved sophisticated chromatic effects by drawing in silver stain on the colored glass, for example in the peacock-feather patterns on the angels' wings. Another astonishing effect awaits in the face of the Virgin Mary, where the glass curves slightly outward.

All these artistic subtleties are perceptible only at close range. The panel may therefore have been installed in a private chapel or a house's bay window. However, there is also a degree of plausibility to the theory that the workshop used this window as a presentation piece for potential clients.[3] Owing to the Nuremberg provenance, which goes back to at least 1874,[4] and the great stylistic similarity to the Volckamer window, it is conceivable that the panel was produced in the context of the larger work's creation.

Benno Baumbauer

1 Window number "South III." Scholz 2019, vol. 1, pp. 197–220. I wish to thank Martha Hör, Fürth.
2 See Scholz 1995.
3 Exh. cat. Nuremberg 2000b, pp. 263–64, cat. no. 91 (Daniel Hess).
4 The panel was acquired by the GNM in 1874 as a gift from the Herdegen family.

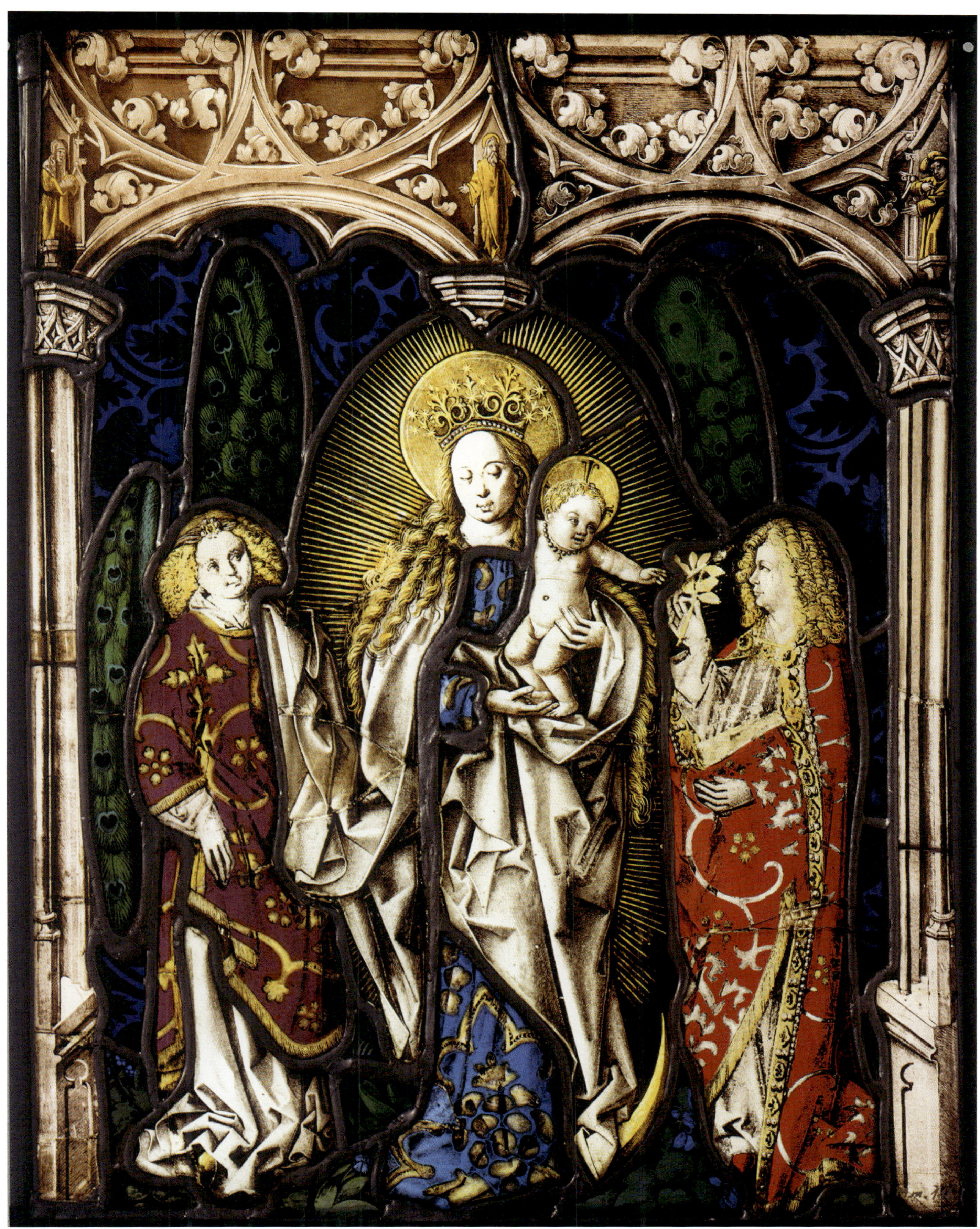

51

BOOK OF HOURS OF URSULA BEHAIM AND ANDREAS HARSDORFFER (Hortulus Animae)

Workshop of Maître François

Paris, after 1474

Parchment, 374 leaves

H. 13.5; W. 10 cm

Herzog August Bibliothek, Wolfenbüttel, shelf mark Cod. Guelf. 296 Blank.

Open to fols. 293v–294r: The Martyrdom of Saint Catherine

References:
Cermann 2010, pp. 9–11, 15–16, 20–21, 23–24.

As revealed by the allied coat of arms on the first page of text (fol. 3r), this small book of hours now kept in Wolfenbüttel was originally owned by the patrician couple Ursula Behaim (1436–1483) and Andreas Harsdorffer (d. 1498). It belongs to a group of eight German-language manuscripts created toward the end of the fifteenth century in the circle of the Maître François, a leading Parisian illuminator.[1] Not only the miniatures but also the fine parchment and the coat of arms of the French kings (fol. 242r) point to Paris as the place of origin.

There are several indications that in Paris in the second half of the fifteenth century, German-language books of hours were produced specifically for the Nuremberg market. These were not individual commissions but rather "high-quality, mass-produced items that ... were made to stock."[2] It is therefore likely that the couple who owned the book had their coats of arms and the date of 1470 added later. The occasion for their purchase is unknown. It was presumably an event that had taken place years before, since the calendrical calculations contained in this book of hours date its production no earlier than 1474.

Although there were skilled illuminators in Nuremberg, a great demand existed for prayer books from Paris. The books of hours created in Nuremberg were primarily in Latin, with the production of vernacular works being left to the Parisian workshops. The prayer texts in the Wolfenbüttel example are written in *Nordbairisch*, the northern Austro-Bavarian dialect. Presumably the scribe was a native speaker and either sold the manuscript to the Parisian illuminators or was even based in Paris himself. The fact that he intended it for the Nuremberg market is indicated not only by the dialect but also by the inclusion of both Saint Sebaldus and the calendar for the diocese of Bamberg. Illuminators working in Nuremberg subsequently borrowed pictorial ideas from the Parisian books of hours.

German-language books of hours were also imported to Nuremberg from European cities other than Paris. Purchases in Florence, Venice, and Pavia are documented. However, those volumes were printed in Italy and later illuminated and bound in Nuremberg.[3] The German-language versions offered certain advantages for private devotion. At the same time, they were probably considered luxury goods, much like coral rosaries |**see cat. no. 18**|. With only sixteen miniatures, however, the Wolfenbüttel manuscript belonged to a rather modest price segment.[4] Its illustrations and prayer texts correspond with each other. For example, Saint Catherine, whose martyrdom is depicted (fol. 194r), is addressed as a Holy Helper in the accompanying prayer.

The Behaim and Harsdorffer families are not known to have had connections with Paris. Yet business relations definitely existed between the two metropolises. They are documented for Nuremberg armorers, goldsmiths, and silversmiths, among other trades.[5] The patrician Fütterer family engaged in monetary transactions with Paris.[6] The book printer, dealer, and publisher Anton Koberger (d. 1513) established an office there. He and other entrepreneurs expressly promoted the exchange of goods between the two cities.[7]

Marie-Luise Kosan

1 On the following, see Cermann 2010.
2 Translated from the German in Cermann 2010, pp. 13–14.
3 See Exh. cat. Nuremberg 2015c, pp. 50–54, cat. nos. 19–21 (Christine Sauer).
4 See Cermann 2010, p. 14.
5 Willers 2002, p. 154; Schürer 2002, p. 185; Maué 2002, pp. 330–31; Hauschke 2002, p. 378.
6 See Fleischmann 2008, vol. 1, pp. 250–51, vol. 2, p. 407. The university in Paris was another attraction for Nuremberg patricians.
7 See Cermann 2010, p. 21.

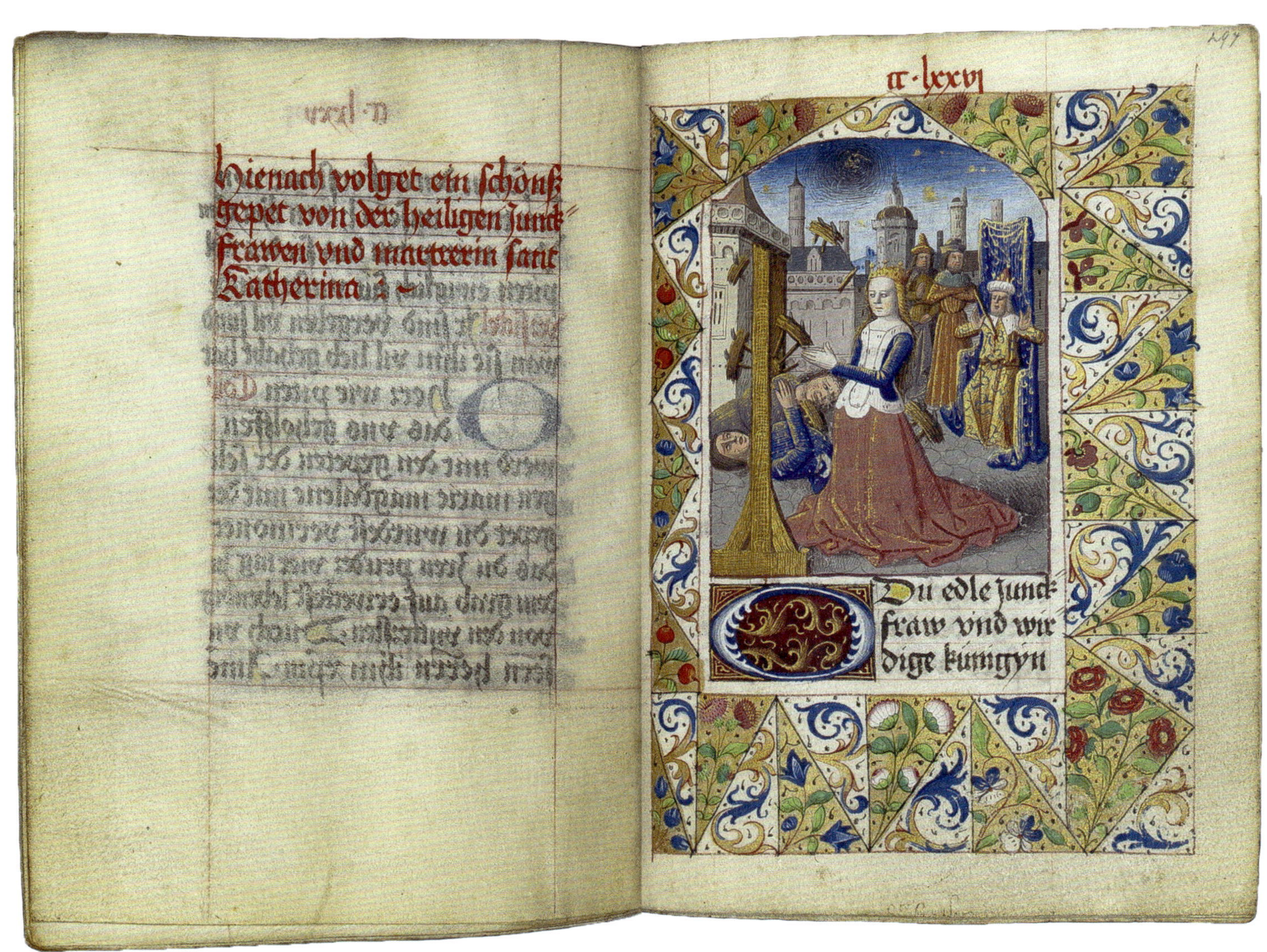
Hienach volget ein schöns gepet von der heiligen junckfrawen vnd marterin sant Katherina

cc·lxxvi

Du edle junckfraw vnd wirdige kungyn

52

LIMOGES TABLE SERVICE OF THE TUCHER FAMILY (BASIN AND EWER)

Pierre Reymond, Wenzel Jamnitzer (ewer)

Nuremberg and Limoges, 1558 (basin), 1562 (ewer)

Copper, silver-gilt, painted enamel

Basin: Diam. 45.4 cm (maximum); H. 5.3 cm; ewer: H. 37.7 cm; W. 20.5 cm (including handle and spout); D. 14.3 cm

On long-term loan from the Tucher Kulturstiftung to the Museum Tucherschloss und Hirsvogelsaal, Museen der Stadt Nürnberg, inv. nos. HI Kh 009, HI Kh 010

References:
Weingärtner 2008; Däubler-Hauschke and Weingärtner n.d.

On September 6, 1560, the master calligrapher and mathematician Johann Neudörfer (1497–1563) |**see cat. no. 19**| sent thanks to the Nuremberg patrician Linhart Tucher (1487–1568) for allowing him to see "excellent works" (*trefflich werckh*), declaring that he had "never seen more appealing pieces" (*nye keine lieblichere stück gesehen*).[1] These exquisite works of art were a basin and two lidded dishes decorated with Limoges enamel painting.

The basin seen by Neudörffer is the one presented here. Its inner surface shows episodes from the Book of Genesis based on prints by Lucas van Leyden: the Creation of Eve, the Fall of Man, and Cain Killing Abel. It is dated 1558 and signed with the initials of the Limoges enameler Pierre Reymond (1513–1584). One of the lidded dishes that Neudörffer saw displays episodes from the biblical story of Joseph (Gen. 42–44), while the other depicts scenes involving Neptune, Amphitrite, and Fortuna from classical mythology.

One can only conjecture whether it was Neudörfer's effusive praise that prompted Linhard Tucher to order a ewer (shown here) and four tazzas from Limoges to complete the table service |**fig. p. 47**|. A letter by Linhart's son Herdegen Tucher (1533–1614), dated December 6, 1561, provides insights into how the commission was realized. At the time, Herdegen was based at the Tucher trading firm's office in Lyon and thus was able to oversee the work on-site. His father had had copper vessels made in Nuremberg and then sent to Limoges to be enameled by Pierre Reymond. However, those proved to be too thick-walled for the enameling process. While the four tazzas were able to be hammered thinner on-site in Limoges, the ewer had to be sent back to Nuremberg and replaced with a newly fashioned one, which was then sent to Reymond.[2]

The Tucher family's international trading network thus provided the framework for this collaborative project between Nuremberg coppersmiths and Limoges enamelers. The ewer's spout and handle, both made of gilded silver, bear the marks of the Nuremberg goldsmith Wenzel Jamnitzer (1507/08–1585). This gave rise to the assumption that Jamnitzer also made the ewer's copper core,[3] but this theory is substantiated neither by written sources nor by any evidence on the object itself. It is altogether possible that Jamnitzer produced only the silver-gilt parts that are mounted on the enameled body of the vessel.

Despite the fact that the pieces were made at different times, the service has the appearance of a stylistically uniform ensemble. Aesthetically, it is particularly impressive because of the outstanding quality of the Limoges enamel painting and the subtly elegant color scheme consisting of grisaille on a black background with gold accents |**fig. p. 192**|.

It is unclear whether Linhart Tucher specified the motifs that appear on the ewer and tazzas, or whether Pierre Reymond selected them from his workshop's stock of patterns. The ewer shows a bear hunt and a deer hunt. The tazzas feature scenes from the myth of Cupid and Psyche based on engravings by the Master of the Die. With this combination of biblical, mythological, and secular scenes, the dinner service presents a disparate pictorial program. It does not appear to have been assembled according to a coherent overall narrative. This thematic variety must have appealed to the Tuchers and their banqueting guests precisely because of its kaleidoscope of subtle and allusive references, which encouraged multilayered interpretations and provided ample fodder for conversation.

Verena Suchy

1 StadtAN, E 29/IV no. 1626. Cited after Weingärtner 2008, p. 66.
2 See Weingärtner 2008. On the technique of Limoges enamel painting, see Speel 2008.
3 Weingärtner 2008, p. 91.

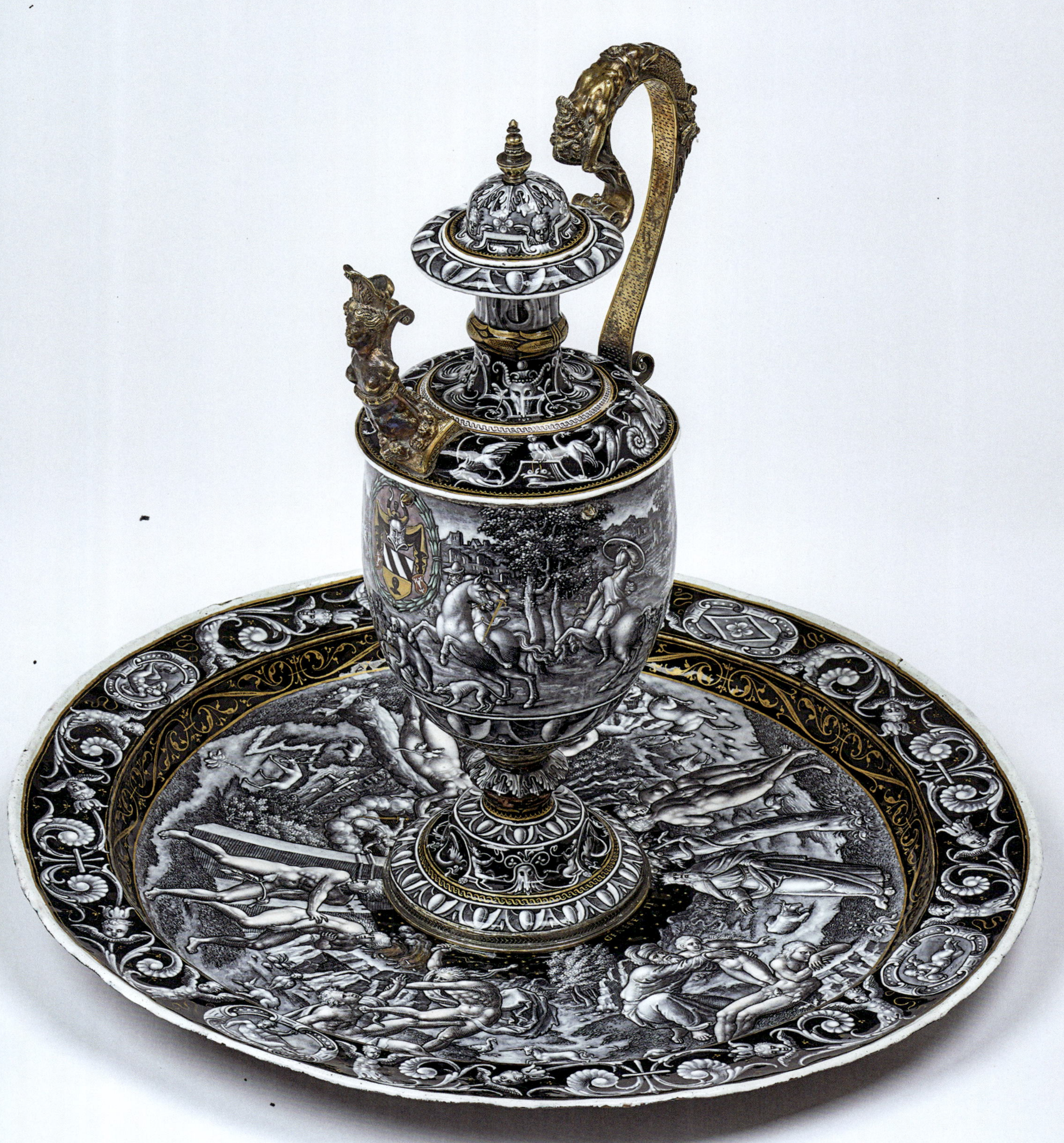

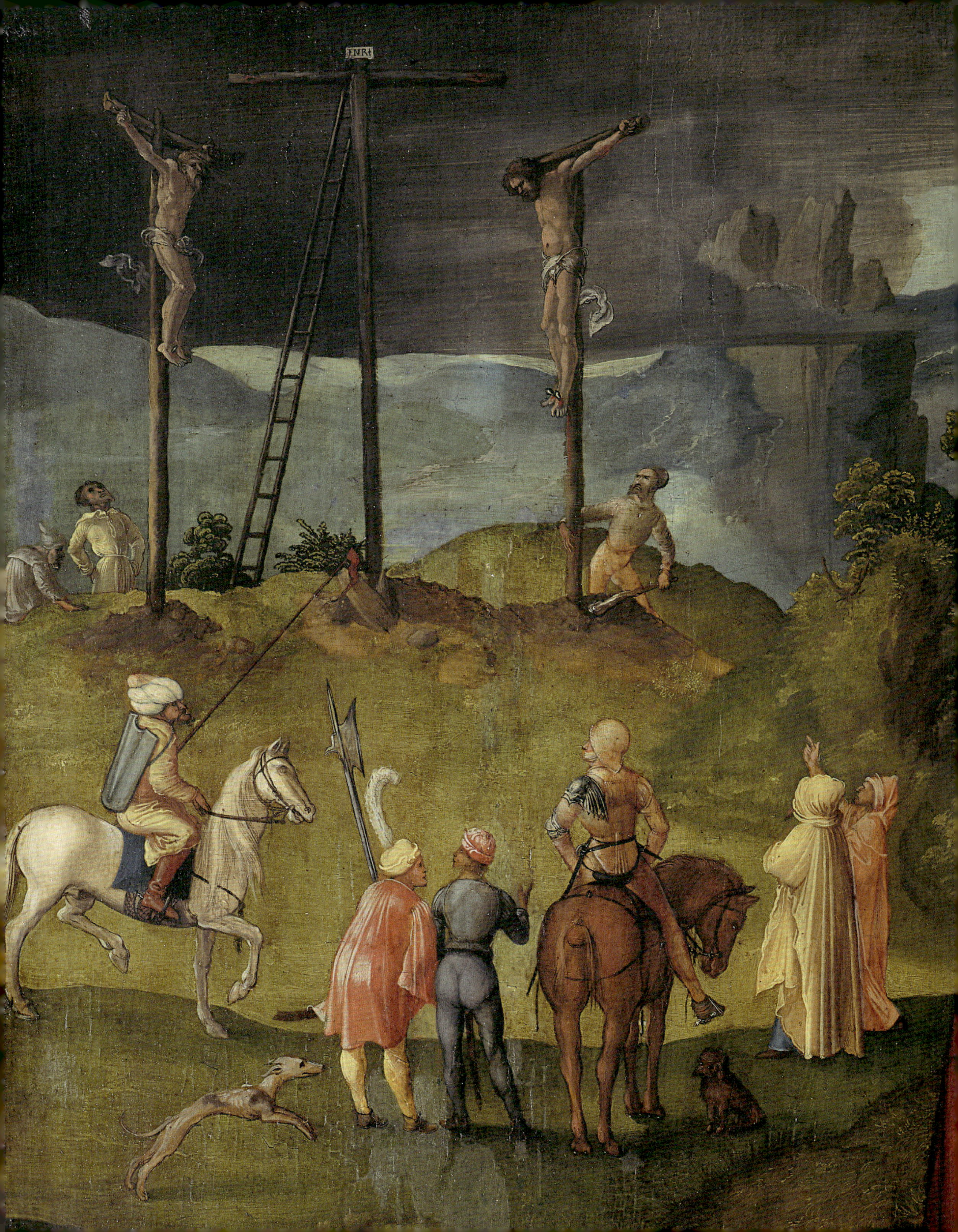
INRI

ACROSS THE ALPS

Nuremberg enjoyed close cultural and economic ties with the cities of northern Italy. Merchants such as Raffaele Torrigiani of Florence and Paulus Praun II of Nuremberg maintained offices on opposite sides of the Alps, respectively, mainly in the lucrative silk trade. Spices and luxury goods from the Mediterranean region, and even further away, were imported to Venice and from there brought to Nuremberg, making the German city an important center for the trade in precious goods. However, not only goods but also knowledge and artistic motifs were in circulation northward and southward across the Alps.

In 1516, Torrigiani commissioned Veit Stoss to carve a *Raphael and Tobias* group for the Dominikanerkirche in Nuremberg, based on Florentine models. Decades later, Praun hired the artist Lavinia Fontana in Bologna to paint his portrait. Fontana's painting shows Praun as an erudite cosmopolitan—as a Nuremberger who felt at home in Bologna. In pursuit of humanist ideals of education, many Nurembergers traveled to the Italian peninsula, where they were able to study both contemporary art and the remains of classical antiquity.

Albrecht Dürer's trips to Venice exemplify the multidimensional dynamics and multifaceted nature of cultural exchange. While Dürer's prints spread throughout Italy and were greatly admired there, he himself in turn absorbed pictorial concepts from Italian art. At the same time, in the art of the Venetian painter Gentile Bellini, Dürer studied depictions of Ottoman figures, which he later creatively integrated into his own works.

Pictures, writings, and other objects from the period demonstrate not only the great extent to which Nuremberg was networked with northern Italy; they also show the lasting effects that this exchange had on Nuremberg's visual and material culture.

Laura Di Carlo

◄ cat. no. 57 (detail)

53

VENETIE MD (View of Venice)

Attribed to **Jacopo de' Barbari**
Anton Kolb (publisher)
Venice, 1500

Woodcut from six blocks
H. 137 cm; W. 284 cm
GNM, inv. no. SP5903

References:
Martin 1994, pp. 84–94; Exh. cat. Venice 1999a; Exh. cat. Nuremberg 2012, pp. 395–97 (Yasmin Doosry); Böckem 2016, pp. 32–58; Pfotenhauer 2016, pp. 429–31.

This large map of Venice in bird's-eye view was published there in 1500 by the Nuremberg entrepreneur Anton Kolb (1471–1541). It impressively conveys the importance of Venice as a trading center in the early modern period. The choice of a view from the south situates the shore of the Gulf of Venice on the horizon, thereby connecting the island city perspectivally with the mainland. The narrow strip of coast along the upper edge of the image is backed by an imposing wall of mountains. But even that natural barrier is shown to be permeable: just left of the cloud-borne figure of Mercury, the god of merchants and travelers who watches over the city's affairs, a trade route runs through the Alps. An inscription identifies the location of this mountain pass: "Seraval," referring to Serravalle, a village situated on the road that led to the Brenner Pass. This route, known as the *Via Norimbergi*, brought travelers to and from Nuremberg, among other destinations in the north.[1] The inscription surrounding the god of commerce states, "I, Mercury, shine favorably on this above all other emporiums,"[2] thus emphasizing the economic prominence of Venice.

Afloat in the harbor in the lower half of the image, the god Neptune gazes upward, along a vertical axis that connects him with the figure of Mercury. It is as if the two classical deities were coordinating their influence over the city's affairs. The element of water, ruled over by Neptune, was indeed the

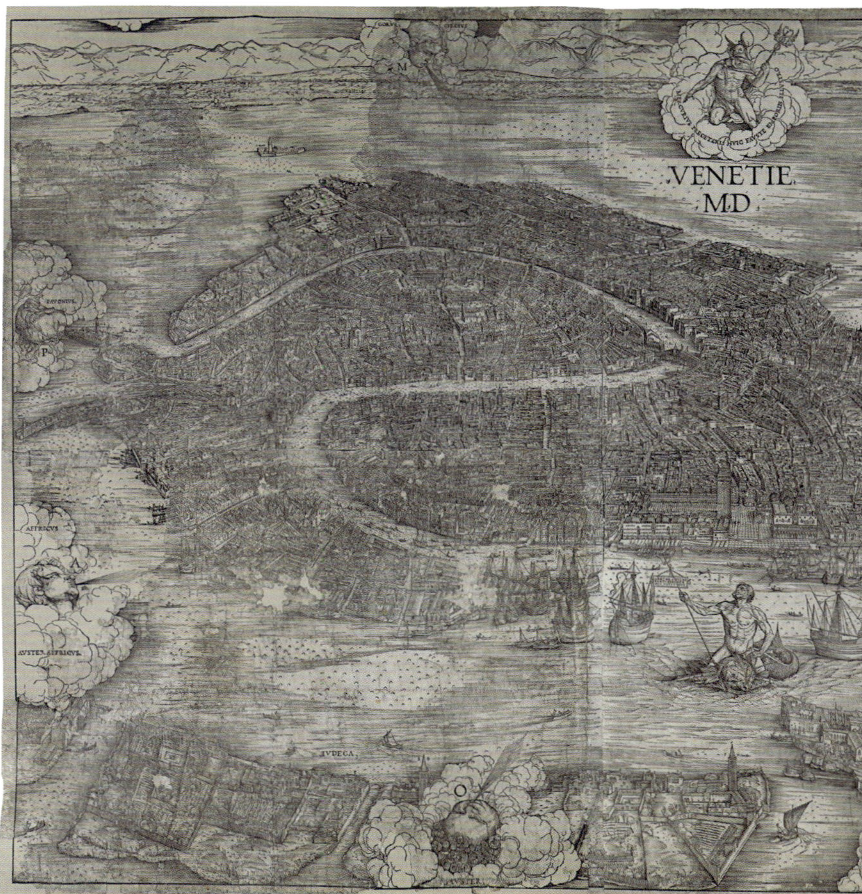

1 See Martin 1994, p. 92; Pfotenhauer 2016, pp. 430–31.
2 MERCVRIVS PRECETERIS HVIC FAVSTE EMPORIIS ILLVSTRO.

source of the maritime republic's wealth. By about 1500, Venice had become the most important hub for long-distance trade in the Mediterranean sphere. The role that German mercantile firms played in this can hardly be overestimated, especially with regard to the transalpine distribution of goods arriving in Venice from an extensive network of trade routes.[3] Accordingly, the warehouse where the Germans carried out most of their business, the Fondaco dei Tedeschi |**fig. p. 48**|, is prominently situated within the urban topography. In the *View of Venice*, it is clearly visible and identified with an inscription. Only a few buildings further south stands the campanile of San Bartolomeo, the parish church frequented by German merchants, especially those from Nuremberg. With an altar dedicated to Saint Sebaldus, this church was the most important place of worship for the community of Nurembergers in Venice. The map's publisher, Anton Kolb, along with numerous members of the Imhoff, Tucher, Tetzel, and Hirschvogel families, are documented there as altar administrators.[4]

The Venetian artist Jacopo de' Barbari (d. before 1516) played an undeniable role in the complex process of creating this city view, even though the extent of his contribution remains uncertain. Shortly before the woodcut was printed, he moved temporarily to Nuremberg.[5] At the time, Nurembergers were fascinated not only with the image of the "Floating City" but also with the art produced there. Over the course of the sixteenth century, comparisons between the two cities featured in learned treatises, becoming a topos of humanist erudition. In this context, the history of the creation and reception of the *View of Venice* reflects the multidimensional dynamics of cultural exchange that existed between Venice and Nuremberg in the early modern period.

Laura Di Carlo

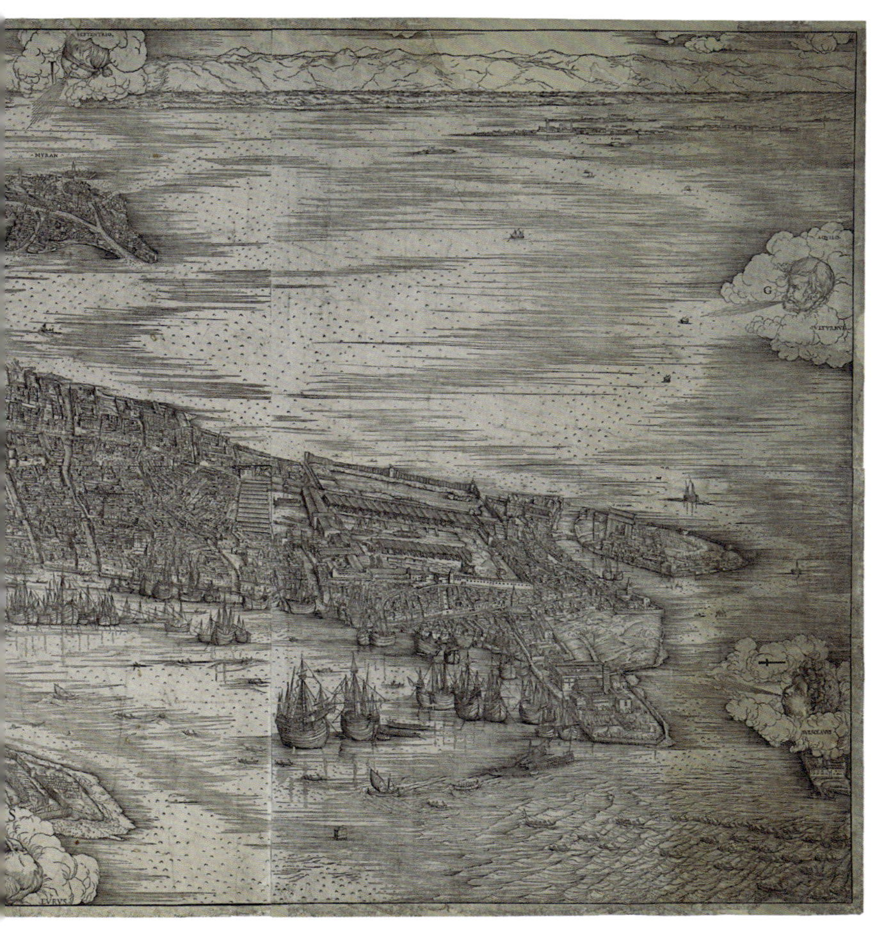

3 See Matthew 1999, p. 61.
4 See Pfotenhauer 2016, pp. 203–14.
5 See Böckem 2016, pp. 50–53, 108.

54

CONSTRUCTIONAL MODEL OF THE RIALTO BRIDGE IN VENICE

Venice, late sixteenth century

Hardwood, paper, iron

Model: H. 31 cm; W. 70 cm; D. 27 cm; case: H. 35 cm; W. 75 cm; D. 29 cm

Stromer'sche Kulturgut-, Denkmal- und Naturstiftung, inv. no. F 38

References:
Stromer 1997, p. 174; Exh. cat. Füssen and Augsburg 2010, p. 108, cat. no. F 39 (Benno Baumbauer); Chinellato 2017, pp. 74–75.

This model of the Rialto Bridge in Venice, in 1:100 scale, was probably owned by the Nuremberg municipal master builder Wolf Jacob Stromer (1561–1614). It now forms part of the Stromer Foundation collections. Because the model was designed to be dismantled, it clearly illustrates the construction methods chosen for building Venice's most important bridge. The parts include the wooden support (the "centering") used for erecting the arch, the rows of shop spaces, the arched span, and the abutments situated below street level. Given the bridge's proximity to the Fondaco dei Tedeschi, where the German merchants had their warehouses |**cat. no. 53**|, its construction could not have escaped the attention of Nurembergers.

The model arrived in Nuremberg in a custom-made wooden case. The side of the case that opens is decorated with a depiction of the bridge. The ensemble also includes a wooden ruler, scaled in Venetian feet. A compass that was provided to take measurements of the model's proportions is no longer preserved. Both ruler and compass are the traditional attributes of architects and master builders.

Designed by the architect and engineer Antonio da Ponte (1512–1597), the single-arch Rialto Bridge was erected over the Grand Canal between 1588 and 1591, with a span of 28.5 meters. Unlike its wooden predecessor, shown in Jacopo de' Barbari's *View of Venice* of 1500 |**cat. no. 53**|, the new bridge was built of stone, which posed great challenges: the ground beneath at either end was swampy; the existing buildings had to be incorporated; and the arch's heavy load needed to be transferred. These problems were overcome with stone abutments resting on piles driven into the bed of the lagoon.

The historian Wolfgang von Stromer conjectured that the model was submitted by Antonio da Ponte as part of the competition to select the bridge's architect.[1] Yet there is no record of who commissioned the piece or which cabinetmaker constructed it, so the exact origin remains unclear. It is possible that Wolf Jacob Stromer, the aforementioned Nuremberg master builder, acquired the model in Venice from someone in Antonio da Ponte's circle or that he had a copy made after a now lost original.[2] In addition to the model, the belongings that Stromer left behind upon his death include more than a thousand drawings, among which there are many architectural sheets that give a detailed idea of the planning and construction of Nuremberg's Fleischbrücke |**cat. no. 55**|. But no drawings of the Rialto Bridge are included. The Fleischbrücke (Meat Bridge) was built as a single-arch stone span, reaching 27.5 meters across the Pegnitz River. While the dimensions are similar to those of the Rialto Bridge, the Fleischbrücke intentionally lacks rows of shops and steps, thus enabling goods to be transported across the Pegnitz in carts and carriages. This necessitated a flatter segmental arch, and the result is an architectural masterpiece.

While overseeing construction of the Fleischbrücke, Stromer faced challenges similar to those that the Venetians had encountered in building the Rialto Bridge, and he was surely interested in the engineering solutions used there. In 1579, he had studied in Bologna and traveled throughout northern Italy, where he acquired extensive knowledge of architecture and engineering. A stay in Venice is documented in 1582. This would have given him the opportunity to follow discussions about the Rialto Bridge's construction on-site and possibly to see drawings and models.[3] The constructional model of the Rialto Bridge offers remarkable testimony to the transmission of knowledge between Venice and Nuremberg in the late sixteenth century, which took place in spoken communication, in texts, in drawings, and in three-dimensional objects.

Alexander Rácz

1 Stromer 1997, p. 174.
2 Chinellato 2017, pp. 74–75.
3 Sporhan-Krempel and Stromer 1962, p. 275; Chinellato 2017, p. 75.

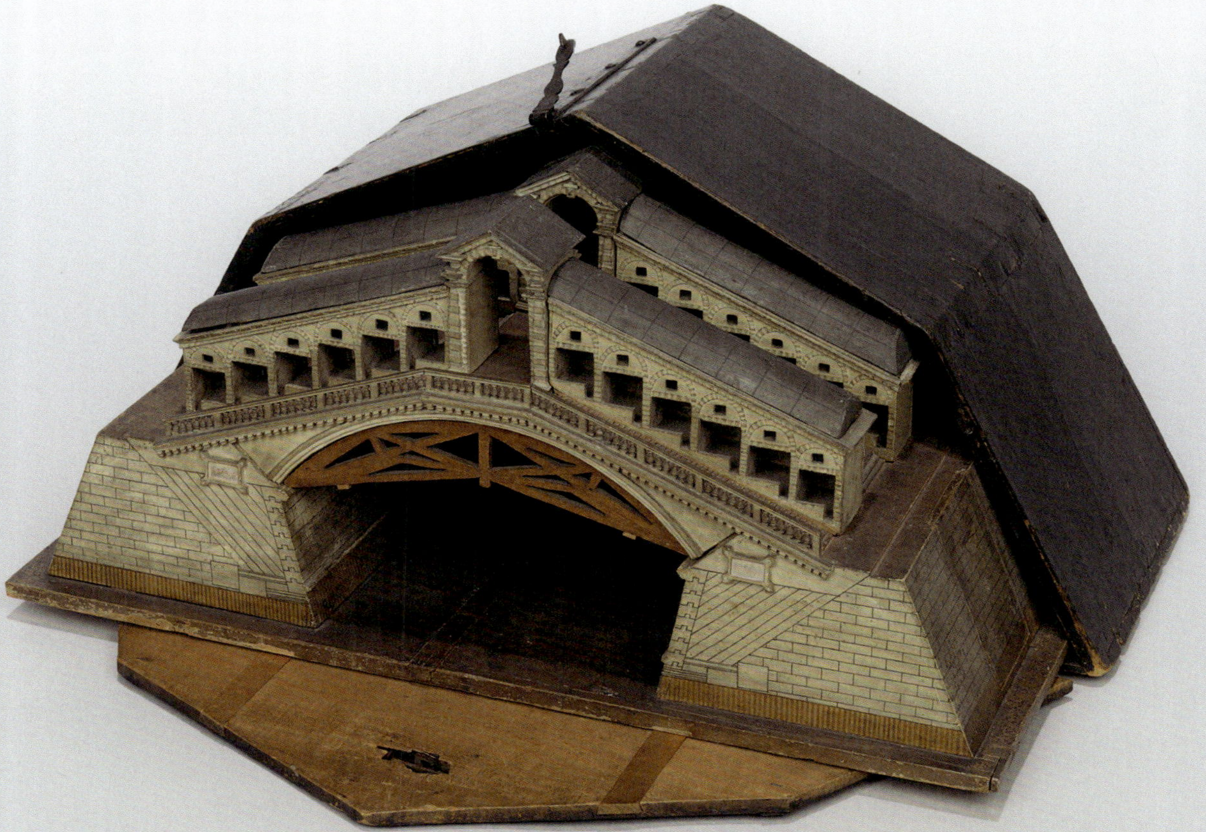

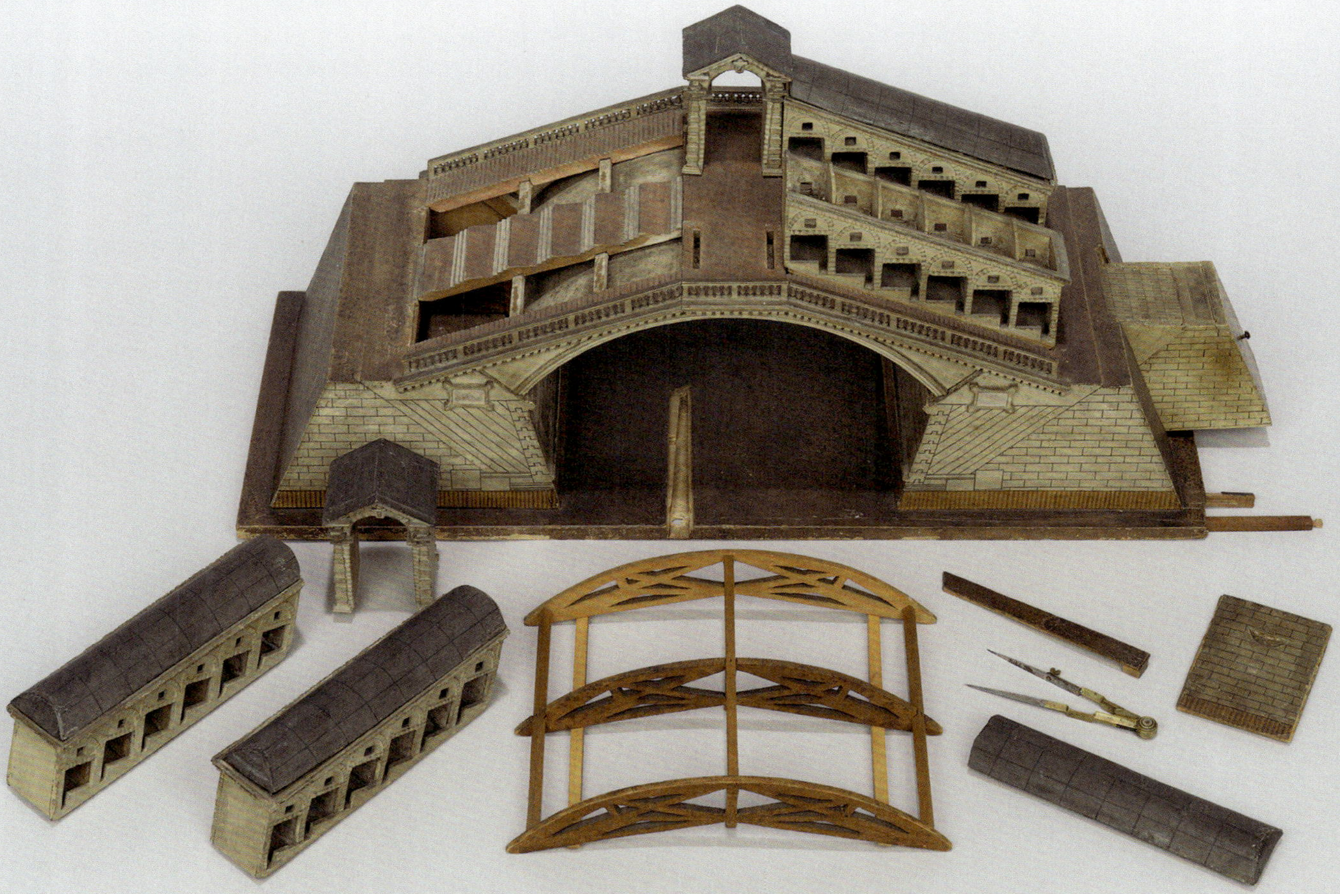

55

ARCHITECTURAL DRAWINGS FOR THE FLEISCHBRÜCKE IN NUREMBERG

Nuremberg, 1595–96

Pen and black and brown ink, colored washes

55.1 Pile Foundation and Elevation

H. 37.5 cm; W. 61.8 cm

GNM, inv. no. HB1403

55.2 Pile Foundation

H. 47.7 cm; W. 60.3 cm

GNM, inv. no. HB1406

55.3 The Four Elements

H. 21.1 cm; W. 33.3 cm

GNM, inv. no. HB1434

55.4 The Four Seasons

H. 21.1 cm; W. 33.2 cm

GNM, inv. no. HB1435

References:
Pechstein 1975, p. 76; Exh. cat. Nuremberg 1996, pp. 154–55, cat. no. 79 (Werner Broda); Kaiser 2005.

The Fleischbrücke (Meat Bridge) was Nuremberg's most important crossing over the Pegnitz River, the main connecting point between the city's northern and southern halves. It was also part of the prestigious "Via Triumphalis," the route by which the emperor made ceremonial entries into the city. The new structure replaced a double-arch stone bridge of 1487–88, which had been ruined by a devastating flood on February 28, 1595.[1] To make the new bridge less vulnerable to torrential waters, it was designed with only one arch, with an enormous span of 27.5 meters. The surviving designs provide great insight into the planning process, as it developed from 1595 to 1596, and into the persons involved. The names of more than twenty workmen and master builders are known who entered the competition to bring the new Fleischbrücke to fruition.[2]

Construction was carried out under the supervision of Wolf Jacob Stromer von Reichenbach (1561–1614), Nuremberg's municipal master builder (*Ratsbaumeister*). Jakob Wolff the Elder (1546–1612) from Bamberg was entrusted with the stonemasonry work, while the master carpenter Peter Carl (1541–1617) was responsible for making the foundation and the temporary wooden support for the arch. The two perspectival architectural drawings very closely resemble the Fleischbrücke as ultimately constructed |**cat. nos. 55.1, 55.2**|. The foundation in the riverbed was particularly innovative. It consists of a dense grid of more than two thousand wooden piles—some driven vertically, some at angles—which support the arch's abutments. Metal crossbars stabilize the structure and transfer the load of the arch's radially coursed masonry into the ground. This complex construction method was the result of an intensive exchange of expertise, some of it acquired from Italy: Stromer's architectural books contain views of Italian bridges, and he owned a model of the Rialto Bridge in Venice |**cat. no. 54**|. Also, the city council obtained an expert opinion from the Florentine architect Pietro Cecini, who advised a single-arch solution.[3]

In addition to the engineering that was required, decoration also played a role in the planning. Two sheets contain colored designs for medallion-shaped reliefs showing the Four Elements and the Four Seasons, framed by laurel wreaths with decorative ribbons |**cat. nos. 55.3, 55.4**|. The Four Elements are personified by female figures with symbolic attributes: Fire with flaming hair, Water holding a cornucopia, Air blowing on a cloud, and Earth with a castle on her head. Among the seasons, the first two are female figures: Spring shown holding flowers and Summer bearing a sheaf of corn and a sickle. The season of Fall is represented by Bacchus, holding grapes, while Winter is a bearded old man wearing a cape and a crown. These designs were never realized, as evidenced by several views dating from the period shortly after the Fleischbrücke's completion.[4]

Alexander Rácz

1 Kaiser 2005, vol. 1, pp. 82–85. A sketch of the old Fleischbrücke is preserved in the chronicle by Wolff Neubauer the Younger, 1601, StadtAN, F1, no. 42.
2 Pechstein 1975; Kaiser 2005, vol. 1, pp. 86–87. See especially the preparatory drawing accompanying the design brief by Peter Carl (Museen der Stadt Nürnberg, Graphische Sammlung, inv. no. Hopf 5584).
3 Kaiser 2005, vol. 1, pp. 94–96.
4 See, for example, *The Fleischbrücke with a Triumphal Column during the Entry of Emperor Matthias*, ca. 1612, pen-and-ink drawing with colored washes and gold heightening (H. 27.3 cm; W. 40 cm), Stadtarchiv Nuremberg, Bildsammlung, no. 35.26.

cat. no. 55.1

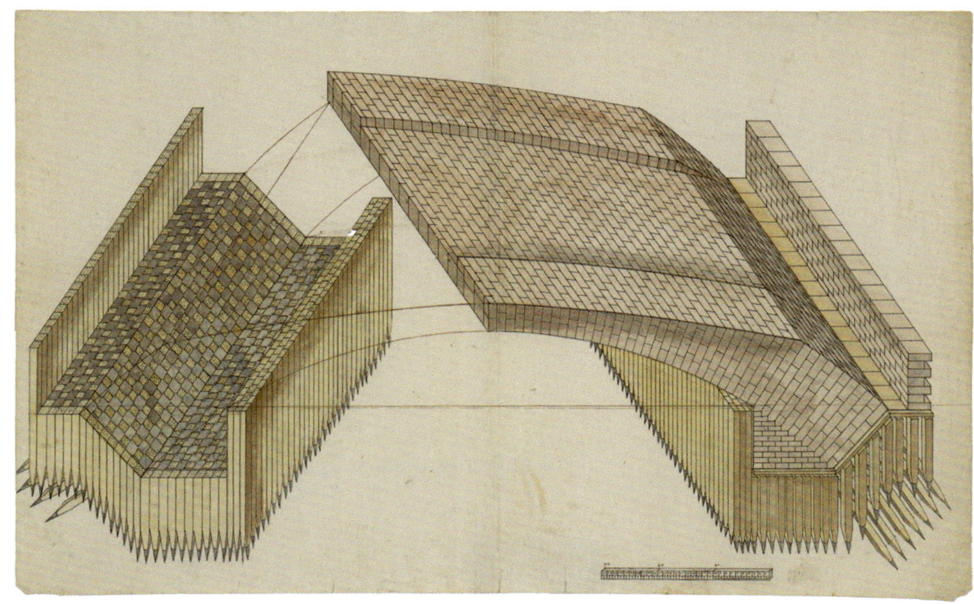

cat. no. 55.2

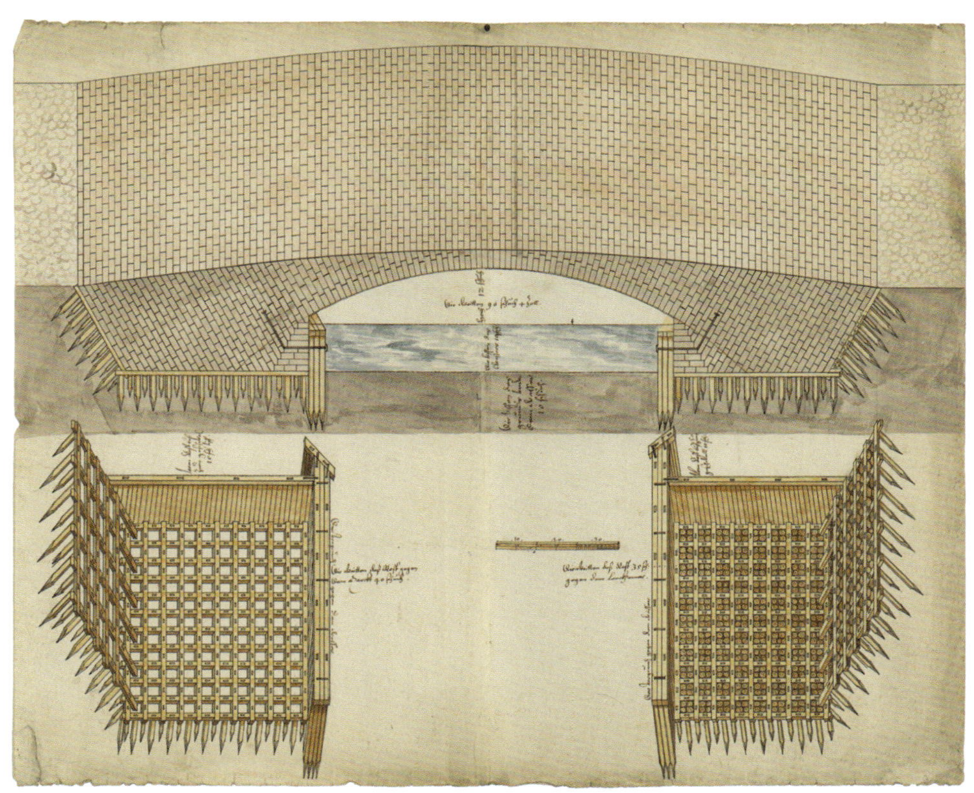

cat. no. 55.3

cat. no. 55.4

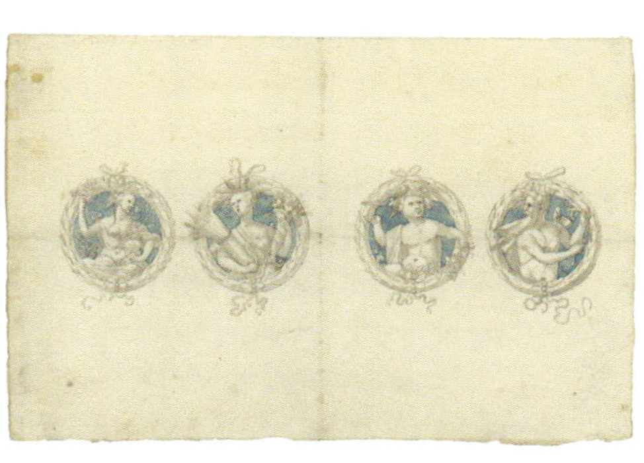

56

SPECULUM ROMANAE MAGNIFICENTIAE

Antonio Lafreri

Rome, 1544–73

Album of 112 leaves of engravings and etchings, leather binding

H. 51 cm; W. 74 cm (opened)

Stromer'sche Kulturgut-, Denkmal- und Naturstiftung

Open to fols. 17v–18 r: The Colosseum

References:
Sporhan-Krempel and Stromer 1962, p. 276.

This album of 112 prints from the *Speculum Romanae Magnificentiae* (Mirror of Roman Magnificence) was owned by the Nuremberg municipal master builder Wolf Jacob Stromer von Reichenbach (1561–1614) and has remained within the family. On the leather binding, the Stromer coat of arms appears along with the motto *Dum spiro spero* (As long as I breathe, I hope). The prints mainly depict ancient monuments, statues, and buildings in the Eternal City. These sights were an endless source of fascination for travelers to Rome—above all the Colosseum, whose enormous size and continuous visibility over the centuries made it the most stunning of all ancient monuments. Images of the Colosseum were highly sought after by collectors. On the sheet from the *Speculum*, this vast amphitheater fills almost the entire picture plane. The viewpoint chosen and the broad elevation offer a generous view into the architecture of the building's interior, with its numerous arcades and corridors.

The *Speculum Romanae Magnificentiae* was one of the most important printing projects contributing to the Europe-wide dissemination of the imagery of ancient Rome in the early modern period. In the sixteenth century, a lucrative market developed for such prints. A central supplier for that market was the engraver and publisher Antoine Lafrery (d. 1577), who hailed from the Franche-Comté region and settled in Rome in 1544, where he became known as Antonio Lafreri. His *Speculum* project is distinctive for having been conceived not as a self-contained series with a fixed order but instead as loose sheets. In 1575, Lafreri began publishing an index listing his prints according to subject. At the same time, his publishing house issued four illustrated title pages which matched the main thematic categories of his enormous supply of prints. These were intended to serve as introductions to hypothetical assemblages of his prints. The individual sheets could be compiled into unique albums, each reflecting the personal interests and focuses of a given collector.[1]

It is impossible to reconstruct when and where Stromer acquired the sheets contained in his album, including the illustrated title page. He matriculated at the university in Bologna in 1579 and is known to have been in Venice in 1582.[2] A stay in Rome would have been consistent with the ideals of humanist education, but Stromer could just as well have acquired the prints elsewhere. In his role as Nuremberg's municipal master builder, he became increasingly interested in Italian architecture |**cat. no. 54**|. This *Speculum* album from Stromer's collection is a vivid example of how prints, owing to their reproducibility, became a precedent-setting medium in humanist circles of the early modern period, fostering transalpine studies as well as the visual reception of Roman antiquity.[3]

Laura Di Carlo

1 See Rubach 2013, pp. 69–72; Rubach 2016, pp. 100–104.
2 See Sporhan-Krempel and Stromer 1962, pp. 275–76.
3 On the role of prints in the reception of antiquity both south and north of the Alps, see Exh. cat. Göttingen 2013, Exh. cat. Tübingen 2018, and Di Carlo et al. 2024.

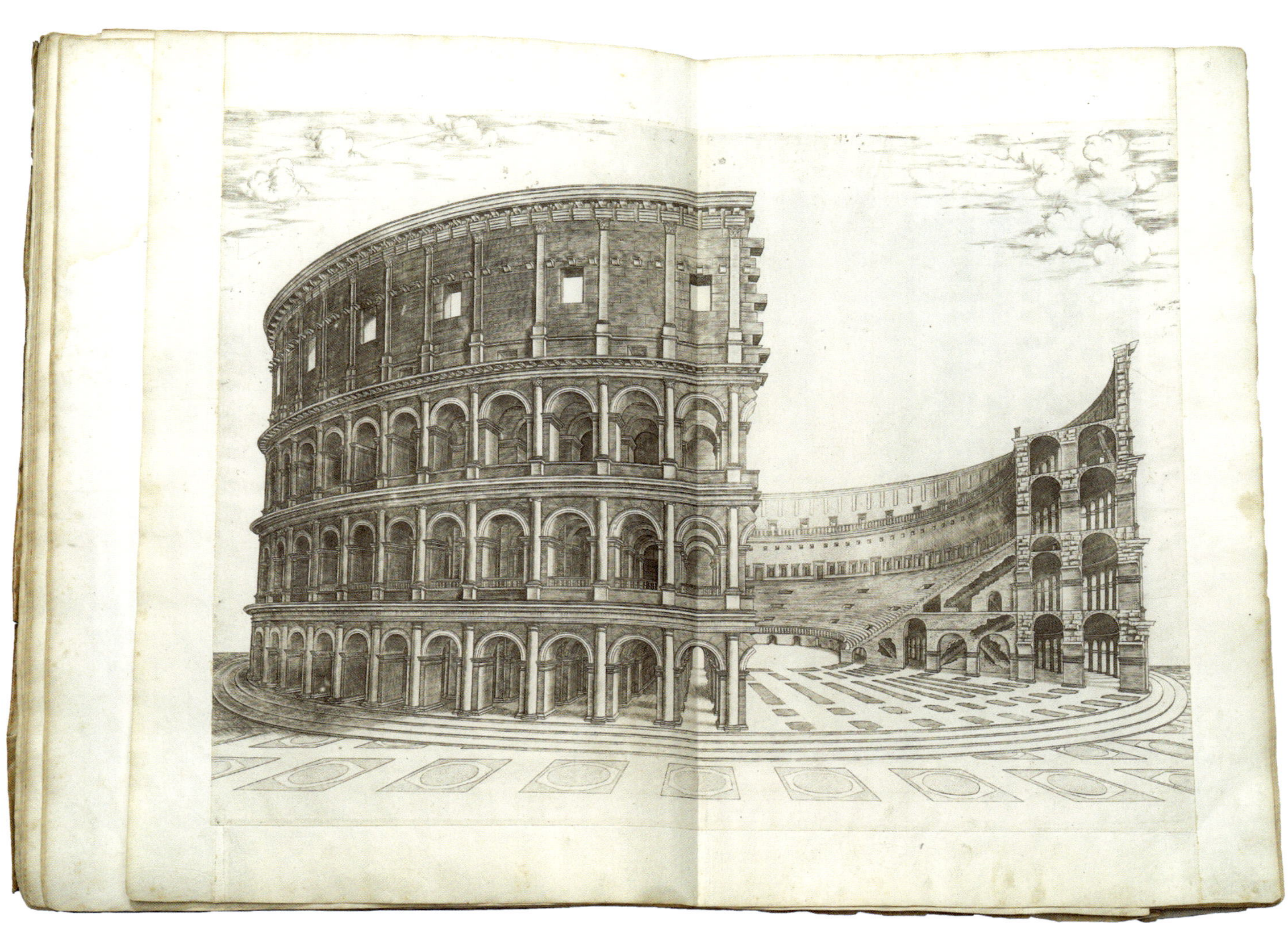

57

THE HOLZSCHUHER LAMENTATION

Albrecht Dürer

Nuremberg, ca. 1499

Paint on fir

H. 150 cm; W. 120.6 cm

GNM, inv. no. Gm165, on long-term loan from the Bayerische Staatsgemäldesammlungen

References:
Anzelewsky 1991, pp. 160–62, cat. no. 55; Löcher 1997, pp. 192–97; Exh. cat. Nuremberg 2004, pp. 98–99 (Daniel Hess); Exh. cat. Nuremberg 2012, pp. 416, 420, cat. no. 107 (Daniel Hess); Teget-Welz 2021, pp. 67–68 (Benno Baumbauer).

Albrecht Dürer painted this *Lamentation of Christ* as a memorial panel for the Holzschuher patrician family of Nuremberg. He situated the event in the foreground of an impressive landscape. The dead body of Jesus, taken down from the cross, dominates the composition. It serves as a reminder of the widespread veneration of the *Corpus Christi* (in German, *Fronleichnam*) in the late Middle Ages. The crown of thorns is prominently placed at the lower center of the painting, flanked by the donor family kneeling in prayer. One gets the impression that this important relic of Christ may have played a special role in the Holzschuher family's piety.

The persons depicted are Karl Holzschuher III, who died in 1480, and his widow Gerhaus, née Gruber, together with their children. Karl Holzschuher's marriage had enabled him to become a partner in the internationally operating wholesale company run by his father-in-law, Hans Gruber. Gerhaus herself managed important business documents and securities for the firm.[1] It was probably on the occasion of her death, in 1499, that the Holzschuher family ordered the memorial panel, which was intended for display at their long-standing burial site in the Sebalduskirche. The painting was later transferred to the Chapel of the Holy Sepulchre at the Johannisfriedhof, which was also used as a Holzschuher burial place.

The subject of the Lamentation of Christ is well suited to commemoration of the dead. Prior to Dürer, the workshop of his teacher, Michael Wolgemut, had used it for the memorial panel for Georg Keiper, who died in 1484.[2] In contrast to that earlier picture, Dürer moved the three crosses from the foreground to the rear left. There, on Golgotha, he gathered several small staffage figures, including a highly evocative one that has received no attention in scholarship thus far: a man on horseback with a long mustache, wearing a large turban, and equipped with a lance and a pavis. This figure is meant to represent an Ottoman horseman.

Beginning in the mid-fifteenth century, Ottoman-themed motifs increasingly found their way into depictions of the Passion of Christ in central Europe. Another prominent example from the Sebalduskirche is the stone memorial relief that Veit Stoss completed in 1497 for the Volckamer family.[3] There, one of the henchmen in the scene of the Arrest of Christ appears as an Ottoman soldier with a turban, mustache, and scimitar.

This artistic phenomenon was linked to the expansion of the Ottoman Empire and the concomitant feeling of threat within the Holy Roman Empire. It therefore stands to reason that equipping Christ's torturers with attributes construed as Ottoman was intended to demonize the enemy. Dürer's figure, however, gives off something of a more "casual" air. It may be expressive of the general fascination in central Europe with the material culture of the Ottoman Empire in its abundance of forms. At the same time, the inclusion of this figure reflects the historical fact that Jerusalem, the site of Christ's Passion, was under Muslim control during Dürer's lifetime.[4]

It has gone unnoticed until now that the likely prototype for this small horseback figure is preserved in Dürer's oeuvre—namely, in the drawing of an Ottoman horseman at the Albertina in Vienna. The drawn figure—in reverse and in slightly different form than the one in the painting—was probably copied by Dürer from a model in Gentile Bellini's workshop during his first stay in Venice in 1494–95 |**cat. no. 58**|. Bellini had served as an envoy to the court of Mehmed II in Istanbul and had recorded his impressions in a series of studies. Dürer appears to have been fascinated by Bellini's treasure trove of imagery from the Ottoman sphere.

Benno Baumbauer and Manuel Teget-Welz

1 Stromer 1963, esp. pp. 18, 26, 51–52, 83, 90–91, 126–27, no. 65, p. 156, no. 136.
2 Lorenzkirche, Nuremberg. See Exh. cat. Nuremberg 2019b, pp. 211–13, cat. no. 32 (Benno Baumbauer).
3 Kahsnitz 1983, pp. 218–58, cat. no. 20 (Rainer Kahsnitz).
4 See the essay by Stefan Hanß and the section on the Ottoman Empire (pp. 265–301) in the present volume.

OTTOMAN RIDER

58

Albrecht Dürer

Venice, ca. 1494–95

Brush and black ink, with watercolor

H. 30.5 cm; W. 21 cm

Albertina, Vienna, inv. no. 3196

References:
Winkler 1936–39, vol. 1, pp. 59–60, cat. no. 79; Exh. cat. Nuremberg 1971, pp. 107–8, cat. no. 183 (Terisio Pignatti); Koschatzky and Strobl 1971, pp. 144–45, cat. no. 15; Meyer zur Capellen 1985, pp. 171–72, cat. no. E 19; Grote 1998, p. 34.

Albrecht Dürer traveled to Venice for the first time in 1494–95 and captured his impressions of the city in drawings.[1] These include the sketch of a Venetian woman's attire now at the Albertina in Vienna and the first-hand study of a lobster now at the Kupferstichkabinett in Berlin.[2] Through his acquaintance with the Venetian painter Gentile Bellini (d. 1507), he apparently gained access to an extraordinary treasure trove of pictorial models. In 1479, Bellini had traveled as a Venetian diplomat to the court of Sultan Mehmed II (1432–1481) in Istanbul—the city that had been conquered by Mehmed in 1453 and made the capital of the Ottoman Empire. Bellini's stay there left numerous traces in his work.

During his stay in Venice, Dürer apparently made a number of drawings after Bellini's workshop stock of motifs. The surviving sheets suggest that Dürer attributed special authority to Bellini's eyewitness depictions of the Ottomans. For example, in the famous sheet in London showing three Ottoman men,[3] Dürer copied a figural group that appears in slightly varied form in Bellini's *Procession in Saint Mark's Square* of 1496.[4] As transmitted through Dürer's drawing, the motif of the three Ottomans was also taken up in separate works of art in Nuremberg |**cat. no. 89**|.

Another Ottoman-themed drawing that Dürer appears to have copied after Bellini ended up serving as the basis for a figure in the *Holzschuher Lamentation*, which Dürer painted in Nuremberg about 1499 |**cat. no. 57**|. In that painting, an Ottoman horseman wearing a prominent turban appears on Golgotha in the left background. The model was probably Dürer's *Ottoman Rider* from the Albertina, rendered in reverse and with minor changes in the painting. The Albertina rider figure also wears a large turban but, unlike the horseman in the *Holzschuher Lamentation*, is equipped with a mace. Detailed correspondences between the two figures are found in such elements as the mustache and the spurs.

Even though this Ottoman horseman does not appear in Bellini's surviving oeuvre, and despite the claim that a medal by Costanzo da Ferrara (d. after 1524) depicting Mehmed II may have served as the model for Dürer's drawing,[5] there are further arguments in favor of the motif having originated in Bellini's workshop: the Albertina drawing was executed in the same media and technique as the sheet with three Ottomans in London, and the Venetian artist Giovanni Mansueti (d. 1527) is also known to have borrowed the motif. The same horseman appears as a staffage figure in the background of Mansueti's monumental *Episodes from the Life of Saint Mark* painted for the Scuola Grande di San Marco |**fig. p. 51**|.[6] Mansueti is documented as having trained under Gentile Bellini, and he probably assisted the master in carrying out history paintings in the Doge's Palace, which were destroyed in 1577.[7] This artistic juncture supports the assumption that Dürer's *Ottoman Rider* was based on Bellini's stock of models.

As with Dürer's woodcuts depicting knot patterns |**cat. no. 92**|, this example shows that his engagement with motifs from the sphere of Islamic culture was in large part mediated through his contacts with Italy, and particularly with Venice. For a short time, Bellini's studio in Venice became a "gateway to the world" for Dürer.

Benno Baumbauer and Manuel Teget-Welz

1 On the following, see Teget-Welz 2020, p. 10.
2 W. 69, 70, 91.
3 W. 78. The British Museum, London, inv. no. 1895,0915.974. See Winkler 1936–39, vol. 1, pp. 58–59, cat. no. 78.
4 Gallerie dell'Accademia, Venice, inv. no. 567. See Meyer zur Capellen 1985, pp. 133–35, cat. no. A 19.
5 See Exh. cat. London and Boston 2005, pp. 71–73, cat. nos. 16–18 (Susan Spinale).
6 Gallerie dell'Accademia, Venice, inv. no. 562. We thank Christof Metzger, Vienna, for pointing this out.
7 See most recently Humfrey 2024, p. 39.

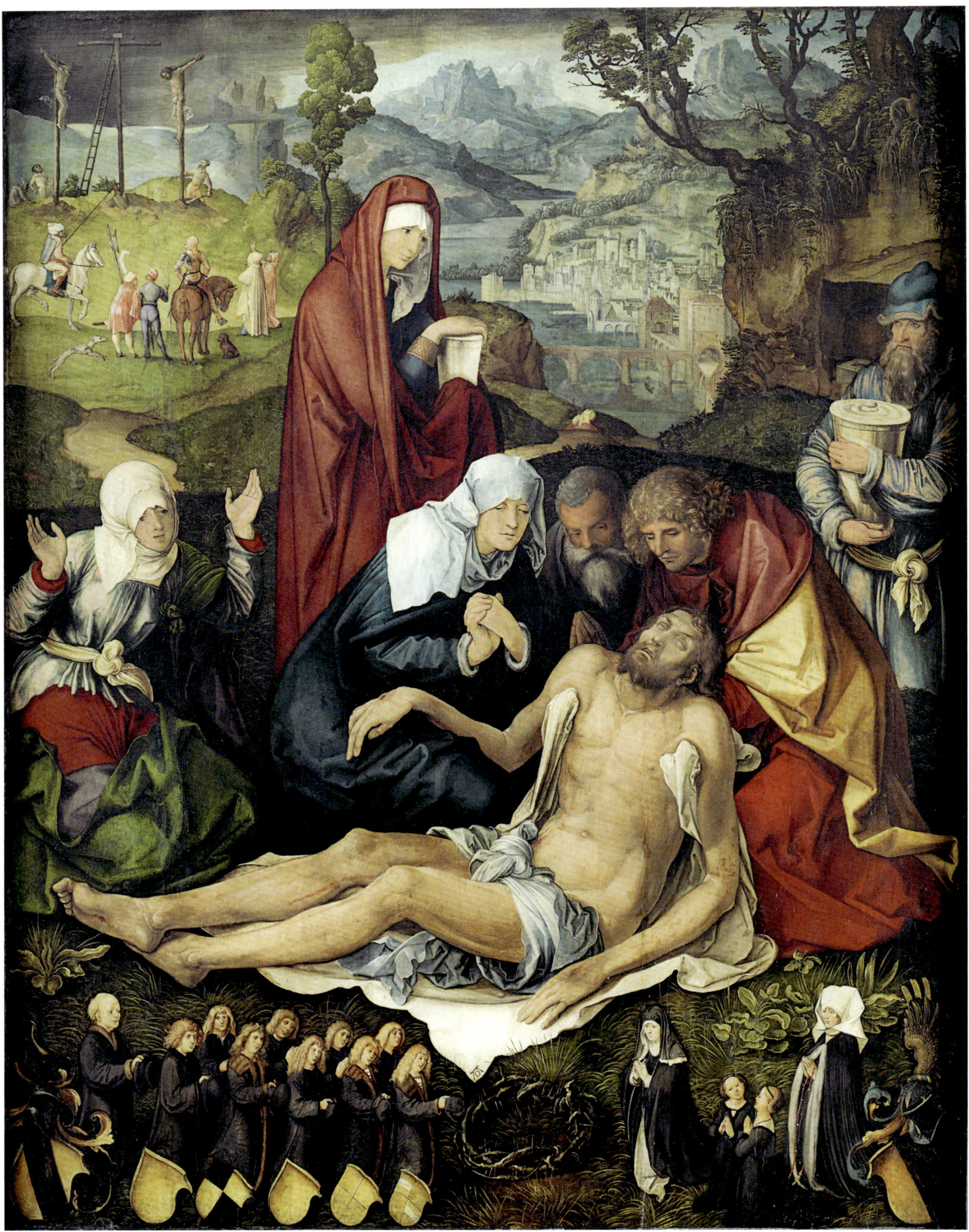

cat. no. 57

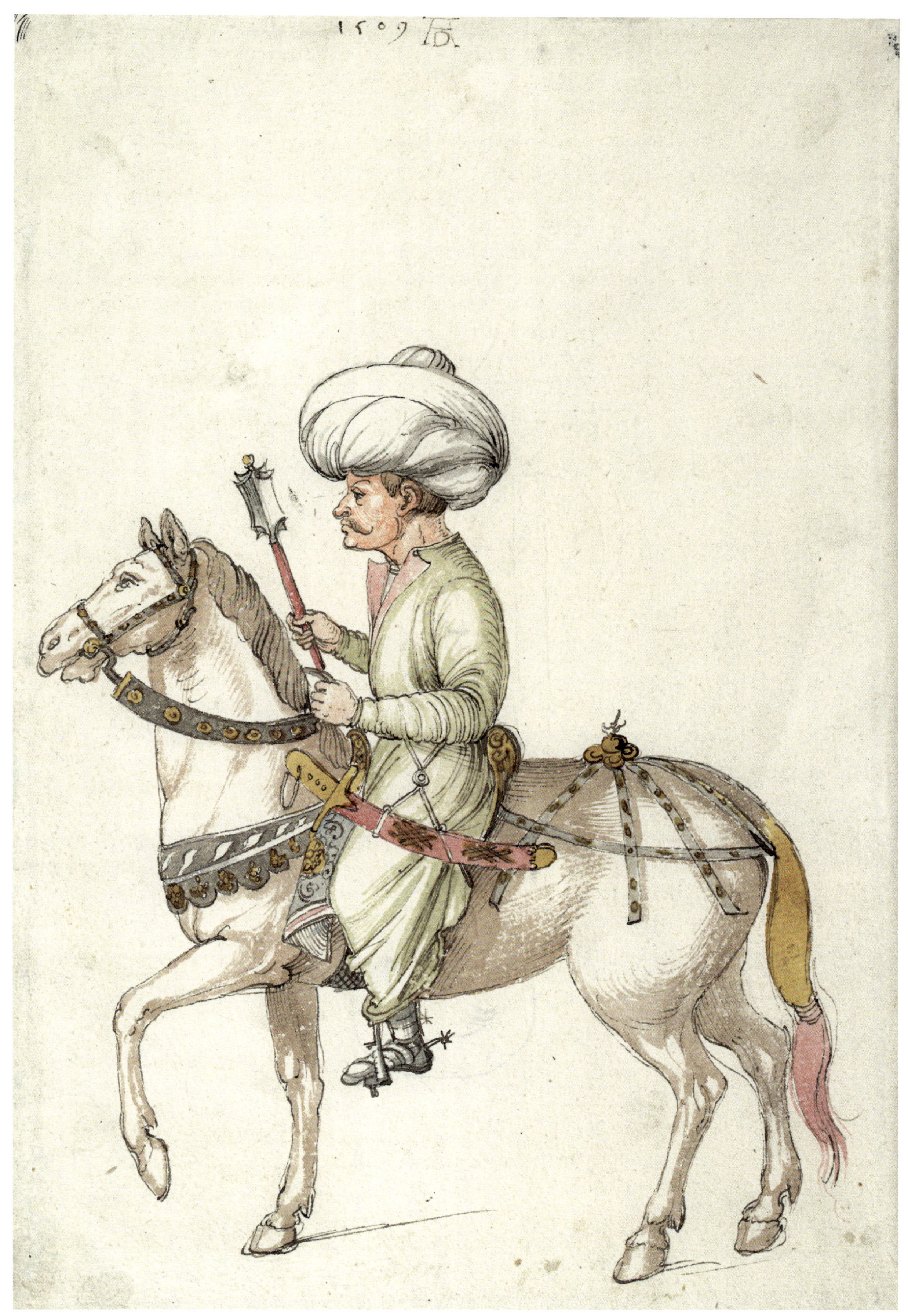

cat. no. 58

59

THE WHORE OF BABYLON

Albrecht Dürer

Nuremberg, ca. 1496–97 (printed in 1511)

Woodcut

59.1

H. 39.6 cm; W. 28.3 cm

GNM, inv. no. StN2234, on long-term loan from the Museen der Stadt Nürnberg, Kunstsammlungen

59.2 (not illustrated)

H. 40.8 cm; W. 28.4 cm

GNM, inv. no. H7701, on long-term loan from the Sammlung Bernhard Hausmann

References:
Böckem 2012, pp. 52–64; Exh. cat. Berlin 2023, p. 65, cat. no. 17 (Silvia Massa); Spinks 2023, p. 41; Dackerman 2024, pp. 8–9.

Albrecht Dürer's *The Whore of Babylon* is the thirteenth image in his series of woodcuts on the *Apocalypse*, first published in 1498. The titular woman of Babylon dominates the composition, despite occupying only the lower right quarter of the picture. She is depicted as a richly bejeweled woman seated on a seven-headed monster and holding aloft a precious lobed cup. The centrally positioned cup, described in the Book of Revelation (17:4) as "full of abominations," forms the focal point of the composition. Its intricate design calls to mind the art of gold- and silversmithing in Nuremberg, reflecting the city's importance as a production center for premium metalware |**see, for example, cat. nos. 41, 97**|. Such elaborate drinking vessels that combined functionality with highly refined craftsmanship were an important part of Nuremberg's material culture. The woman's clothing is meant to represent fashion of utmost splendor. She wears Venetian dress, an element that underscores Dürer's engagement with Italian culture. In its characteristic opulence and ornate design, Venetian fashion symbolized wealth and sophistication—qualities often associated with Venice more generally. By dressing his "Babylonian woman" in Venetian attire, Dürer also conveys moral ambiguity. At the same time, the image's presentation of metalwork and textile art calls attention to the cultural exchange that existed between Nuremberg and Venice.

The lower left of the composition is occupied by figures representing of various social classes and cultures. By displaying her ornate cup to them, the woman identifies herself as an allegory of sensual temptation. This interpretation is reinforced by the monstrous creature's many and varied heads, both in a visual and a linguistic sense (the Latin *monstrum* means "portent"). The contrast between the group of people being subjected to temptation and the heavenly throng directly above creates a visual tension between the earthly and the divine. One of the angels hovering above the cup points to the burning city of Babylon, an allusion to the downfall of earthly corruption and excess—central themes of the Apocalypse narrative (Rev. 17–19). The cup thus symbolizes both the lofty attainments of human artistry and the latent danger of moral depravity when accompanied by worldly excess. The same holds true for the cultural significance attached to fashion. In Nuremberg, clothing was regulated by strict sumptuary laws that were intended to uphold social hierarchies and moral norms by dictating what certain social groups, and women in particular, were allowed to wear. Venice, although not free of such regulations, was distinguished by a greater liberality. Moreover, the Italian city was a hub for the trade in luxury goods. This difference underscores the symbolic nature of the Babylonian woman's clothing: evoking excess and transgression, it links her with cosmopolitan Venice and contrasts her with the burgher morals and ideals characteristic of Nuremberg. Her clothing thus becomes a site of cultural negotiation, reflecting both the fascination and ambivalence with which Dürer and his contemporaries viewed Venice.

Henry Kaap

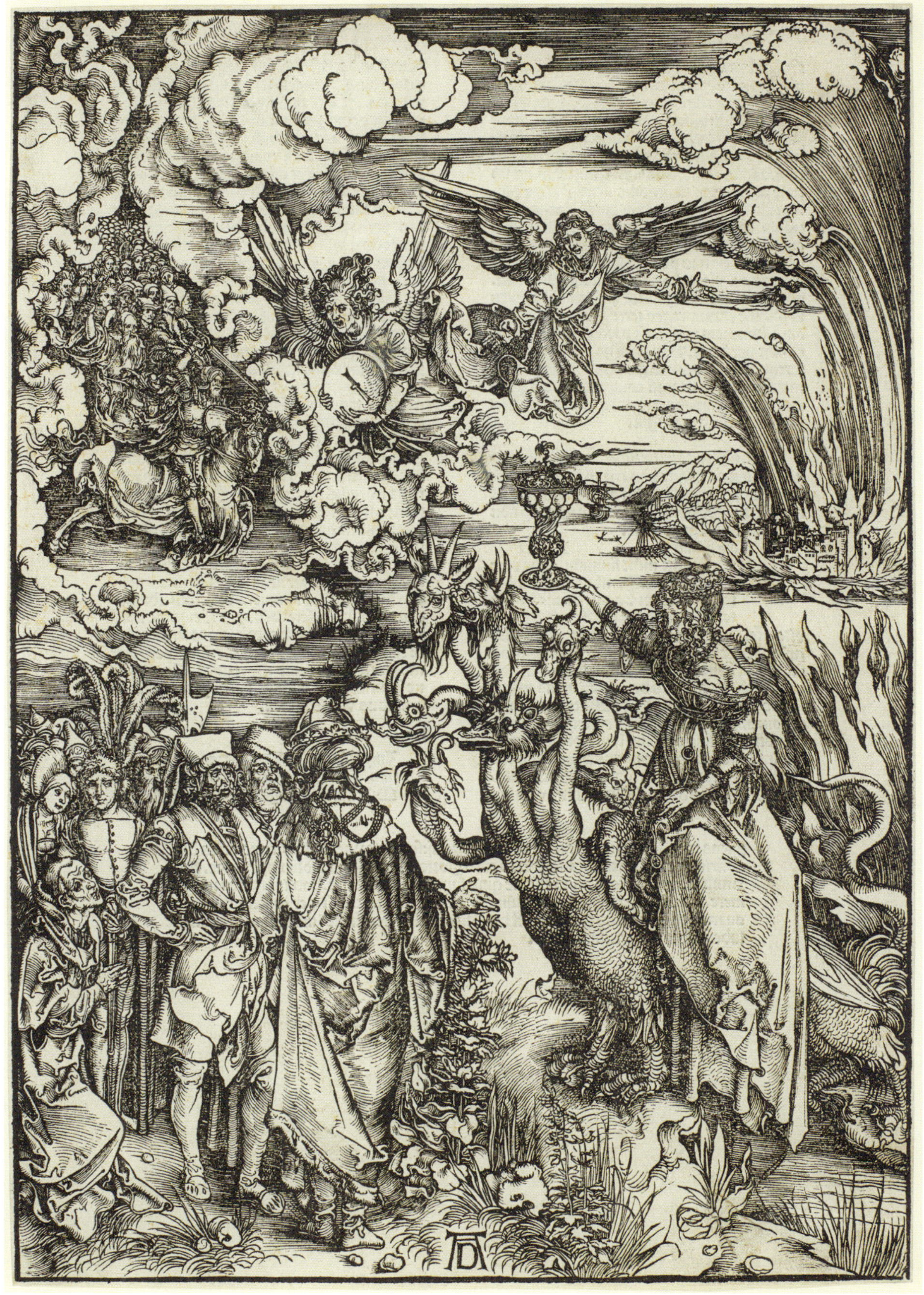

cat. no. 59.1

60

HABITI ANTICHI ET MODERNI DI TUTTO IL MONDO (COSTUME BOOK)

Cesare Vecellio, with woodcuts by **Christophoro Guerra**

Venice: Giovanni Bernardo Sessa, 1598

Printed book, woodcut illustrations

H. 17 cm; W. 11 cm (sheets)

GNM, shelf mark 8° Lr 159/1

Open to fols. 330v–331r: "Sposa ornata di Norimberga" (Adorned Bride of Nuremberg)

References:
Kuhl 2008, pp. 150–59; Paulicelli 2008, pp. 24–53; Jones 2017, pp. 248–69; Riello 2019, pp. 281–317; Rublak 2022, passim

The costume book *Habiti antichi et moderni*, first published in Venice in 1590 and then in an expanded edition of 1598, is one of the most important documents in the history of early modern fashion. With woodcut illustrations designed by the painter Cesare Vecellio (d. 1601), a relative of Titian, it presents a comprehensive survey of dress from Europe, Asia, Africa, and the Americas.

The first edition of 1590, entitled *De gli habiti antichi et moderni di diversi parti del mondo* (Ancient and Modern Clothing of Different Parts of the World), was published by Damiano Zenaro and contains 420 woodcuts, of which 361 feature European dress, while the remaining 59 show attire from elsewhere. The woodcuts, based on drawings by Vecellio, were executed by Christophoro Guerra (Christoph Krieger, d. shortly before 1590), who hailed from Nuremberg. This edition is divided into two parts: one on European fashion and the other on Asian and African fashion. The woodcuts, printed on the verso pages, are surrounded by ornamental frames and accompanied by short captions. The texts on the recto pages provide detailed descriptions of the clothing as well as cultural and geographical notes. An important element of the first edition is its introductory *Discorso*, in which Vecellio sets out his thoughts on historical and cultural influences pertaining to clothing. In addition, a description of the city of Venice (*Breve descrittione*) introduces the illustrations of Venetian fashion. The description is supplemented by a view of Saint Mark's Square, emphasizing the connection between fashion and urban culture.

The second edition, published in 1598 by Giovanni Bernardo Sessa under the title *Habiti antichi et moderni di tutto il mondo* (Ancient and Modern Clothing of the Entire World), underwent a significant redesign. In an effort to present the costumes of the "entire world," this version received many new illustrations, increasing the total to 506, including twenty depictions of Indigenous American peoples from places such as Florida. The second edition was made more broadly accessible by being published in both Italian and Latin. The two alphabetical indexes give this version more the character of a reference work than the first edition. Together with the greater number of illustrations, the reference character explains the significant reduction in the amount of text, most notably through the omission of the *Discorso*. The second edition divides the world of fashion into twelve parts, again arranged regionally: Italy comes first, followed by other European lands and then the non-European regions. Vecellio differentiates according to social class, occupation, age, and marital status, which is particularly evident in the illustrations of female dress, such as the image of an "adorned bride of Nuremberg" (*Sposa ornata di Norimberga*). Among the depictions of German dress, which form the second largest group after Italy, the illustrations of Nurembergers are especially noteworthy. Vecellio depicts a broad spectrum of Nuremberg society, reflecting—from the perspective of Venice—the close cultural and economic ties between the two cities. Conversely, Nurembergers' interest in the particularities of Venetian fashion is evident in Albrecht Dürer's *The Whore of Babylon* woodcut from his Apocalypse series |**cat. no. 59**|.

The title pages of both editions of Vecellio's book are illustrated with an elaborately ornamented compartment. The four corners of the allegorical depiction feature personifications of the four continents known in the period. The attributes associated with these figures follow established visual conventions that are also found in other contemporary costume books, such as the *Habitus praecipuorum populorum* by Hans Weigel and Jost Amman |**cat. no. 84**|.

Henry Kaap

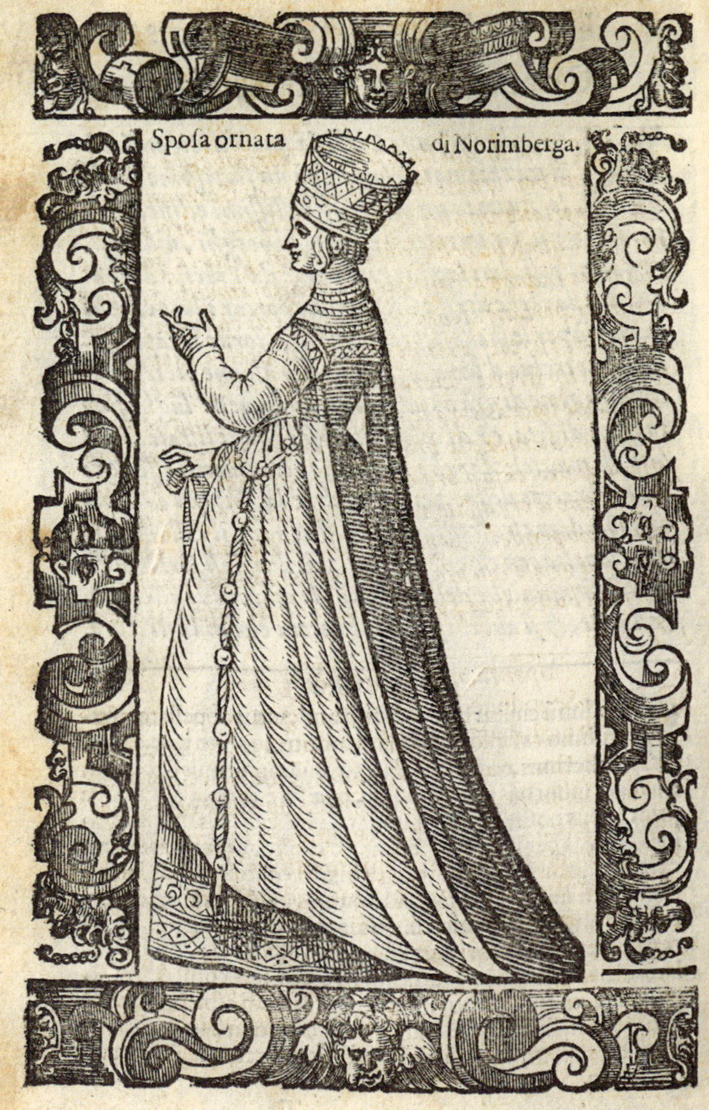

Sposa ornata di Norimberga.

Le spose di questa Città di Norimberga vanno più ben'ornate di tutte l'altre di Germania; & portano una berretta alta di lama d'oro ben lauorata cō qualche bella gioia legataui, sotto la quale acconciatura cadono alcuni capelli gratiosamente giù per le tempie. portano alcune vesti di seta di color di iacinto, ò porpora strette assai nel busto, dal quale cadono alcune maniche strette foderate di pelli bianchissime, & gētili si come sono ancora le meze maniche di essa ueste, le quali uestono meze le braccia. di sotto portano alcune sottane di broccato d'oro, ò di seta, cō grandi opere: si cingono catene d'oro assai grosse, & ben fatte, le quali da un capo fanno pender giù per le uesti. si ornano il collo di perle assai grosse con più doppi, & portano alcuni fregi attorno il busto della sopraueste, il quale lascia il collo scoperto.

Sponsa ornata Segodunensis.

Sponsæ Segodunenses omnium, quæ in Germania sunt ornatissimę incedunt. capitium est ex aurea lamina confectum, cœlatum, & aliqua gemma decoratum, sub quò capilli aliquot iuxta auriculas uenustè cadentes uisuntur. uestes è serico confectæ, sunt uel hyacintini coloris, uel choclyatę: thoraces, quorum manicæ haud latæ pellibus candidissimis munitæ sunt, ad cingulum anguste. interiores tunicę sunt ex aurea, pictaque tela contextę, & aurea, solidaque pręcinguntur catena; cuius unica pars ferè ad humum usque decidit. uniones plurimos collo appendunt; thoracemque, quo collum non prorsus tegitur, limbis, lacinijsque exornant.

61

LAVABO SET WITH THE SCHEURL–FÜTTERER ARMS OF ALLIANCE

Faenza or Cafaggiolo, ca. 1532–34

Maiolica, painted in underglaze colors

Ewer: H. 22.2 cm; Diam. 10.2 cm (mouth); Diam. 11 cm (foot); basin: H. 5 cm; Diam. 40.2 cm

GNM, inv. nos. Ke2838a, b, on long-term loan from the Freiherrlich von Scheurlsche Familienstiftung

References:
Schiedlausky 1973; Glaser 2000, p. 62, cat. no. 59; Lessmann 2004, p. 239.

The ewer and basin of this Italian lavabo set each bear an identical allied coat of arms and Latin motto that allow the set's date of acquisition to be determined with relative precision. In translation, the text reads, "But for me it is good to be near God" (Ps. 73:28; 72:28 in the Vulgate). This motto was used from about 1533 by Christoph Scheurl II (1481–1542), a consultant to the Nuremberg city council (*Ratskonsulent*). Scheurl had strong ties to Italy. He studied law in Bologna from 1498 to 1507 and traveled in the Italian peninsula between 1500 and 1504. While there, he received minor orders, and back in Nuremberg he remained Catholic even after the city became officially Protestant. He took up the position of consultant to the city council in 1512. In that capacity, he saw to the needs of important official guests of the city of Nuremberg, including secular and ecclesiastical princes, some of whom were Italian. He also undertook diplomatic missions on behalf of the city and the emperor. In 1519, he married Katharina Fütterer (1495–1543), whose family coat of arms appears alongside Scheurl's on both pieces of the lavabo set. It is presumed that the set's painted decoration was carried out for the baptism of the couple's son and heir Christoph III (1534–1610) |**see cat. no. 27**|.

In the sixteenth century, works of Italian maiolica arrived in Nuremberg in relatively large numbers. Between March 1534 and March 1535, Scheurl's account book contains entries for the purchase of this type of ceramics, probably including this set: "For 2 Milanese earthen hand basins, 2 ewers, 4 bowls, 2 salt cellars, 11 plates with the Scheurl and Fütterer coats of arms, 9 guldens and 13 pfennigs."[1] The mention of Milan may be a general reference to Italy, as no maiolica was produced in that city. The color of the clay, quality of the glaze, and the blue foliate decoration are comparable to works produced in Faenza and in a much smaller workshop located on the grounds of the Medici villa in Cafaggiolo.

Nurembergers of the time would probably have easily recognized these pieces as unusually valuable, high-quality works specially commissioned from an Italian workshop. As early as the first decades of the sixteenth century, heraldically decorated dish sets were being produced in Italy for members of Nuremberg's patrician class—for example, the seven pieces created between 1518 and 1525 that bear the arms of Andreas Imhoff (1491–1579) and his wife Ursula Schlaudersbach (1501–1525).

The allied coat of arms of the Scheurl and Fütterer families on the lavabo set was probably transferred by means of pouncing from a woodcut attributed to Erhard Schön: the design's outlines are partly dotted, and the sizes of the motif in the print and on the maiolica match exactly. For the blue-on-white decoration, referred to as *alla porcellana*, the painters took inspiration from designs found on faience ware that had been produced only slightly earlier in present-day İznik in Anatolia. Such works found their way to Italy by trade. The models for the Anatolian faience, in turn, were Chinese hard-paste porcelain objects decorated in blue on white. These began arriving in the Levant, via India, in the fifteenth century. The art of producing fine, hard-paste porcelain, with white clay, remained a well-kept Far Eastern secret until well into the eighteenth century. The Scheurl lavabo set proves to be an unexpectedly global object, which brought to a Nuremberg household forms and decorations from several different—some highly distant—places of origin.

Heike Zech

1 "fhur 2 Maylendische Irdene hantpeck, 2 giskandl, 4 schaln, 2 salzvhass, 11 teller mit Scheurl und futerer woppen 9 fl. 13 d." Cited after Schiedlausky 1973, p. 11.

SET WITH THE IMHOFF-SCHEURL ARMS OF ALLIANCE

62

Venice, ca. 1546

This lavabo set, consisting of ewer and basin, is distinguished by its color scheme of dark blue, white, and green enamel together with decorations in gold leaf. The colors, ornamentation, and full coating with opaque painted enamel are characteristic of an entire group of basins, ewers, bowls, salt cellars, candlesticks, and similar functional objects which are now found in museums and private collections in Europe and the United States.[1] These works, which appear to have a common origin, were all made in northern Italy between the late fifteenth and mid-sixteenth century. It is even possible that they were produced by a single workshop in operation over several generations. Since the nineteenth century, art historians have presumed that Venice is the most likely place of manufacture, but there is also evidence to suggest that these works were created in Milan or Florence.[2]

The ewer and basin are each decorated at the center with the allied coat of arms of the Imhoff and Scheurl families of Nuremberg. They were probably acquired in connection with the marriage of Albrecht Scheurl VI (1525–1580) and Magdalena Imhoff (1526–1598) on August 3, 1546.[3] Unlike the Imhoffs, the Scheurls did not belong to the group of families eligible to serve on Nuremberg's city council in the sixteenth century, so for the Scheurls this marriage represented a move one step closer to joining the city's patrician class. Both families had attained wealth and prestige through long-distance trade. They each maintained trading posts in Venice, among other places, which gives reason to believe that the lavabo set was commissioned on-site in Italy. The delicate enamelwork's good state of preservation suggests that the set was not used regularly and served mainly as a display piece within table settings. In the festivities surrounding the marriage of Albrecht and Magdalena, the set may have featured on a banquet table or sideboard as a showpiece of patrician power and cosmopolitanism.

It remains uncertain whether the copper bodies of the vessels were made in Italy or were sent from Nuremberg for enameling, as was done with the table service belonging to Linhard Tucher II (1487–1568), which was dispatched to Limoges to be enameled |**cat. no. 52**|. While the basin, which is decorated with a radial pattern of elongated lobes known as "gadroons," is strikingly similar in shape and size to Nuremberg "alms dishes" (*Beckenschlägerschüsseln*) |**cat. no. 3**|, the ewer, with its smooth, egg-shaped body, is reminiscent of ancient examples. The ewer and basin thus form a visual ensemble mainly through their uniform color scheme, rather than their formal characteristics. It is questionable, however, whether alms dishes—a popular export from Nuremberg—were indeed enameled in Italy. That the present basin was at the least produced as part of a series, much like the alms dishes, can be inferred from a basin at the Victoria and Albert Museum in London, for its size and ornamentation match those of the Nuremberg piece.[4]

The lavabo set testifies in two ways to Nuremberg's position within European networks. First, it shows that the Imhoffs and Scheurls, through their extensive trading relations, were familiar with the latest Italian taste for such vessels and were able to order precious painted enamel directly from Italy. Second, in the juncture of Nuremberg alms dishes with the work of enamelers in northern Italy, the set illustrates the interconnectedness of European craft centers.

Verena Suchy

Painted enamel on copper

Ewer: H. 31.2 cm; Diam. 12.0 cm (maximum); Diam. of the foot, 9.6 cm; basin: H. 4.6 cm; Diam. 44.8 cm (maximum)

GNM, inv. nos. HG2088, HG2089

References:
Barbe, Caselli, and Dantan 2019, vol. 2, p. 101, cat. no. 56, p. 167, cat. no. 234; Borrelli 2019, pp. 28–29; Warren 2019, pp. 60–61.

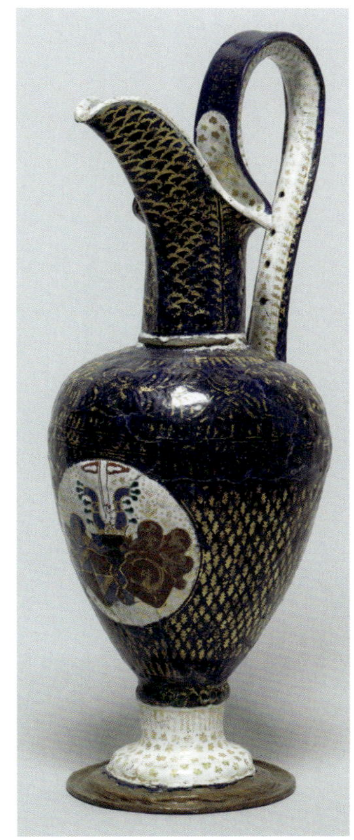

1 See Barbe, Caselli, and Dantan 2019, vol. 2.
2 See Warren 2019, p. 55.
3 Borrelli 2019, p. 29.
4 Inv. no. 580-1899.

cat. no. 61

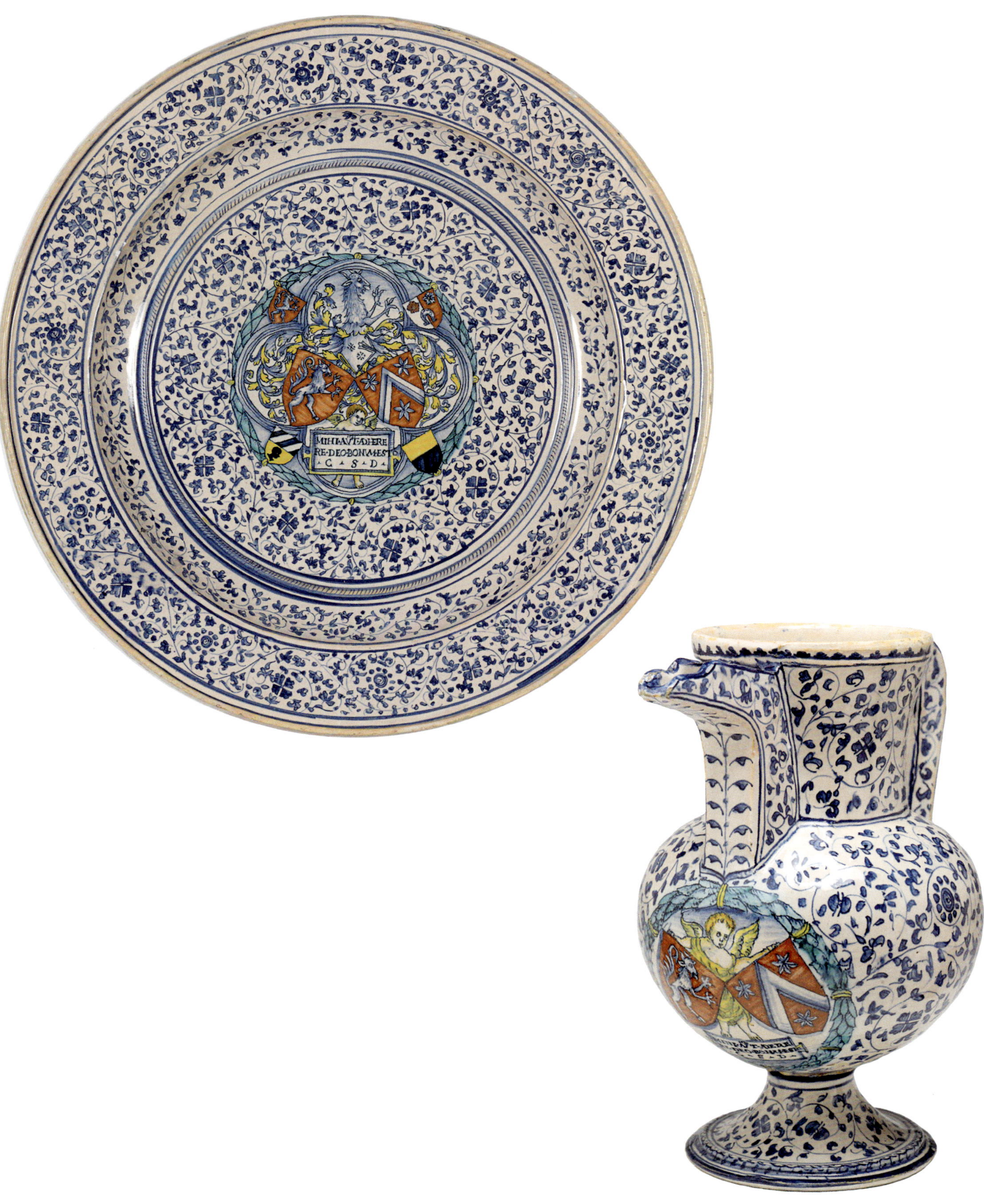

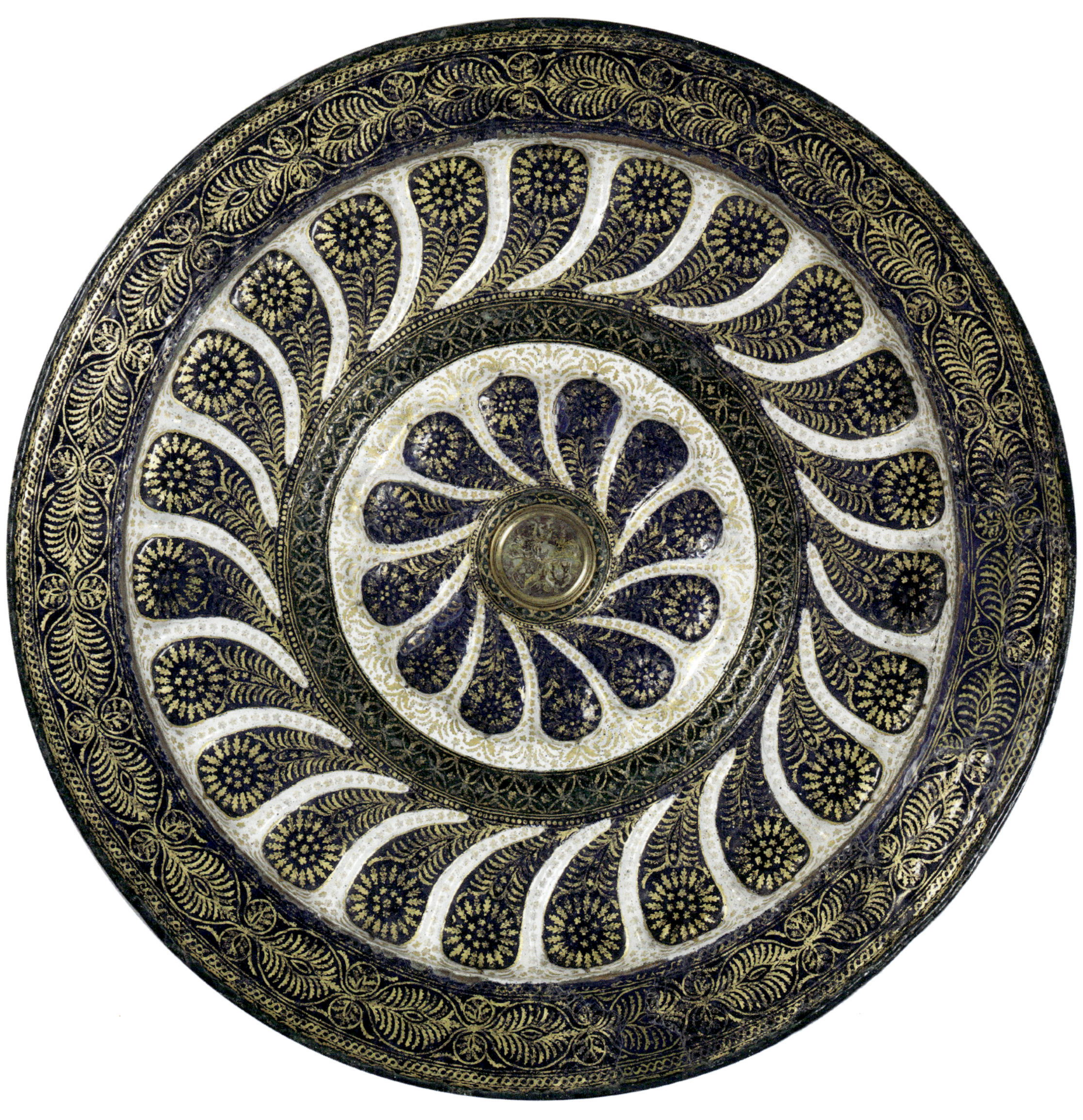

63

THE ARCHANGEL RAPHAEL AND TOBIAS

Veit Stoss

Nuremberg, 1516

Limewood, in its original, unpolychromed state

63.1 Raphael

H. 94.5 cm; W. 48 cm; D. 38 cm

GNM, inv. no. Pl.O.2720, on long-term loan from the Evangelisch-Lutherische Kirchengemeinde St. Jakob, Nuremberg

63.2 Tobias

H. 84.5 cm; W. 34.5 cm; D. 31 cm

GNM, inv. no. Pl.O.1834, on long-term loan from the City of Nuremberg

References:
Kahsnitz 1983, pp. 142–49, cat. no. 8 (Jörg Rasmussen); Exh. cat. Nuremberg and New York 1986, pp. 249–52, cat. no. 93 (Rainer Kahsnitz); Exh. cat. Washington and New York 1999, pp. 260–63, cat. no. 25 (William D. Wixom); Eser 2002, pp. 58–60; Exh. cat. Nuremberg 2002, p. 465, cat. no. 8.

The pair of sculptures *Raphael and Tobias* was created by Veit Stoss (d. 1533) in 1516 for the Florentine jewel and silk merchant Raffaele Torrigiani (1480–1545). It was originally placed in the Dominikanerkirche in Nuremberg, installed not far from the chancel, on the first column on the nave's southern side. The Torrigiani coat of arms, the patron's initials RT, and the date 1516 were displayed on the support beneath the work.[1] Torrigiani is first documented in Nuremberg in 1507, and his Nuremberg branch office that specialized in gold-threaded silk is mentioned beginning in 1521.[2] His son Andrea, born in 1526, ran a fine cloth shop on the Hauptmarkt under the German name "Endres."[3] Understandably, with this commission Raffaele Torrigiani wanted to bring "a piece of home" with him to Franconia, while at the same time placing himself under the protection of the archangel Raphael, his name saint and the patron saint of travelers.

This sculptural group reflects Nuremberg's complex ties with the great northern Italian artistic center of Florence. The Old Testament scene of the archangel Raphael accompanying the young Tobias in a foreign land appeared commonly in Florentine artworks, but it was virtually unknown north of the Alps. Previous scholarship has referred only to paintings as models. However, in and around Florence there are also a number of sculpted terracotta groups from the second half of the fifteenth century.[4]

Instead of importing the work of a Tuscan artist, Torrigiani commissioned Veit Stoss, the best sculptor in Nuremberg at the time, to translate this typically Florentine subject into the local idiom of wooden sculpture, in his characteristically florid style and virtuoso handling. Stoss's mastery is apparent in the deep undercutting of the limewood, which in some areas is remarkably thin, as well as in the textures and details that he convincingly rendered using only carving tools, without the aid of a polychrome finish. The emphatically elaborate execution is not an end in itself but rather serves to focus attention on the contrasting characters' interaction. With his billowing, almost classical-style robe, the archangel seems to float weightlessly while guiding Tobias, who is extravagantly dressed and appears somewhat disoriented owing to the crossed positioning of his legs.[5]

It may have been Raffaele Torrigiani from whom Veit Stoss received another Italian commission—namely, to carve the *Saint Roch* for the Florentine church of Santissima Annunziata, which Giorgio Vasari praised as a "miracle of wood" and a consummate exemplar of wood carving.[6]

Britta Dümpelmann

1 Eser 2002, p. 59; Kahsnitz 1983, p. 143 (Jörg Rasmussen), where the description by Johann Jakob Schwarz (1737) is cited.
2 Eser 2002, p. 59; Bruscoli 1999, p. 83.
3 Eser 2002, pp. 59–60.
4 Andrea della Robbia, Biblioteca Roncioniana, Prato; Luca della Robbia, Santa Croce, Florence. See also the example attributed to Sandro di Lorenzo di Smeraldo at the Szépmüvészeti Múzeum, Budapest, inv. no. 2047. Scholarly opinion is divided over whether Stoss's archangel was originally equipped with wings. See Kahsnitz 1983, p. 142 (Jörg Rasmussen); Exh. cat. Nuremberg and New York 1986, pp. 249–50 (Rainer Kahsnitz); Exh. cat. Washington and New York 1999, p. 262 (William D. Wixom).
5 Kahsnitz 1983, pp. 142–46 (Jörg Rasmussen); Exh. cat. Washington and New York 1999, p. 262 (William D. Wixom).
6 Kahsnitz 1983, p. 146 (Jörg Rasmussen); Exh. cat. Nuremberg and New York 1986, pp. 250–51 (Jörg Rasmussen); Eser 2002, pp. 58–60.

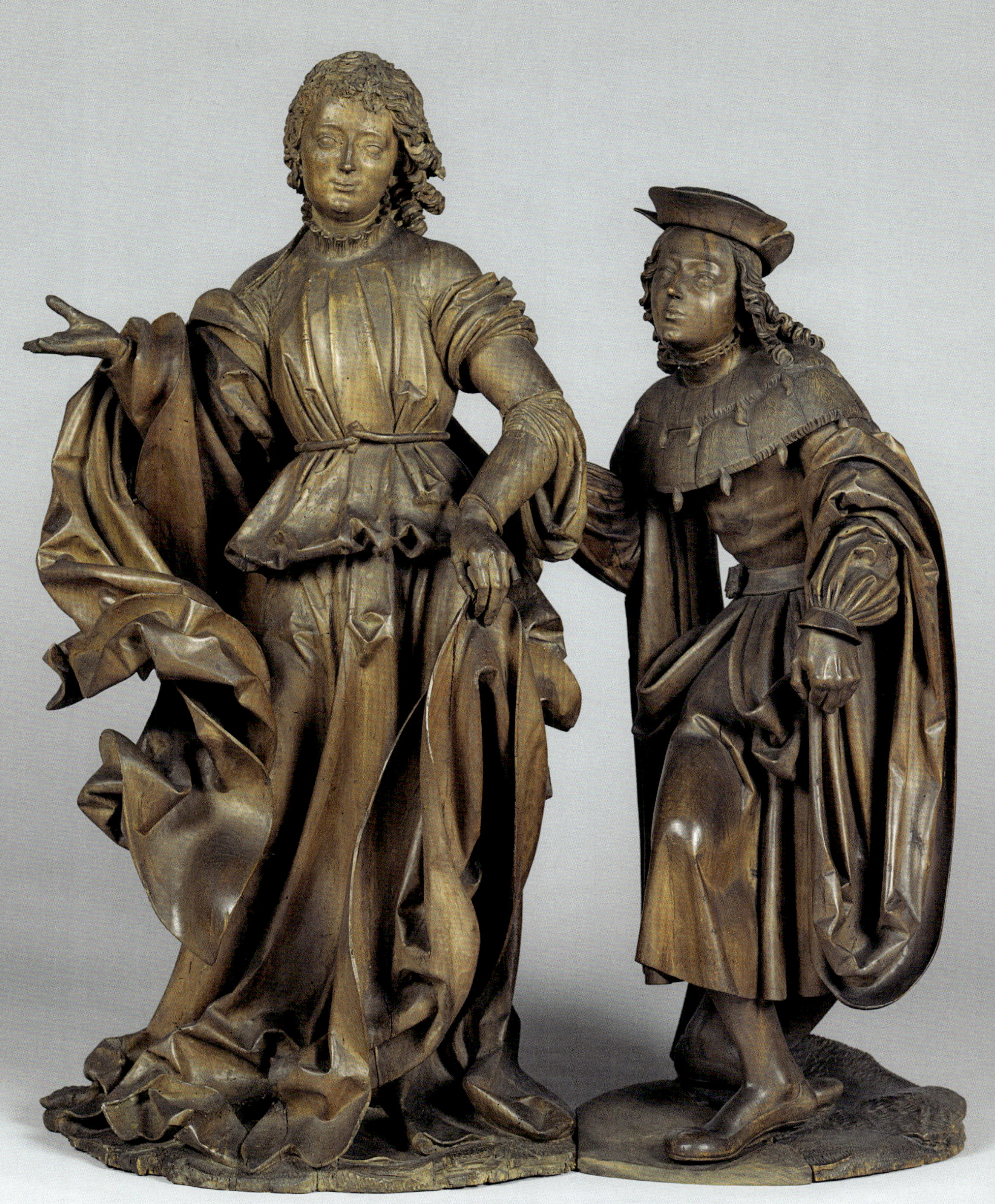

64

HERALDIC STAINED-GLASS PANEL FOR CARLO ALBERTINELLI

Attributed to **Andreas Stein**

Nuremberg, 1595

White glass, black vitreous paint, silver stain, enamel

H. 27 cm; W. 21 cm

Kunstsammlungen der Veste Coburg, inv. no. Gm.004

References:
Lehfeldt and Voss 1907, p. 442; Gast and Syrer 2020.

The cartouche in amber yellow (standing for gold) at the center of this stained-glass panel is charged with the head of a Black man with a white headband, facing to the viewer's left. Set against a blue, foliate-patterned background and flanked by pillars with columns in front of them, the central motif rests upon a base bearing an inscription that reads, "C. · A. / . ANNO . M . D . XCV." The garden scene at the top shows two amorous couples and a man playing a lute against the backdrop of an espalier.

The window's patron, referred to by the initials CA in the inscription, has only recently been identified. He was Carlo Albertinelli, who was born in Florence in 1552 and joined the Nuremberg branch of the Torrigiani trading firm |**see cat. no. 63**| in 1568, at the young age of sixteen. The coat of arms on his seal matches exactly: it, too, shows the left-facing head of a Black man with a headband, and it is accompanied by the initials CA above.[1] Given the window panel's date of 1595, it is unclear why Albertinelli did not have it decorated with the augmented, four-part family coat of arms (Albertinelli–Strozzi) that Emperor Rudolf II had authorized for use by him and his brother Mario on January 12, 1586.[2] It is precisely the augmented coat of arms that identifies Carlo Albertinelli as the patron of one of the most important works of German goldsmithing from the time around 1600, the lidded cup with the head of a Black man by Christoph Jamnitzer (1563–1618).[3]

The Torrigiani firm's branch office in Nuremberg was centrally located on the Hauptmarkt and offered all manner of luxury goods as well as monetary transactions.[4] There, Albertinelli was responsible for establishing and maintaining contacts with princely courts. Over the course of the 1590s, he developed a close personal relationship with Maximilian III, Archduke of Austria (1558–1618) and with Archduke Ferdinand of Inner Austria (1578–1637), later Emperor Ferdinand II. After Albertinelli had become Ferdinand's counselor and principal financier about or after 1607, he apparently encountered financial difficulties. This forced him to flee Nuremberg in 1609 and settle in Graz. Thanks to the connections he had previously established, he became a successful merchant there and remained so until his death in 1620.

Carlo Albertinelli's window panel must originally have been installed in a secular building, undoubtedly together with a formally identical panel bearing the coat of arms of the Italian merchant Benedetto Giorgini (d. 1625), who also worked for the Torrigiani firm.[5] The secular scenes on both windows would have been unsuitable for a sacred building. It remains uncertain whether the original location was the Torrigiani trading house, the gentlemen's tavern (*Herrentrinkstube*) where merchants gathered,[6] or a private home. However, the panel's attribution to the Nuremberg glass painter Andreas Stein (1566–1625) can be made with greater certainty, since Stein's signed album leaf for the guardianship-office scribe Johann Georg Schwingsherlein, dated 1592, is closely related in style.[7]

Uwe Gast

1 Stadtarchiv, Nuremberg, A 1 Nr. 1591-12-23. See Gast and Syrer 2020, p. 15, fig. 5.
2 Frank 1967, p. 11.
3 Bayerisches Nationalmuseum, Munich, inv. no. 2000/81.1-2. Gast and Syrer 2020, pp. 24–29, figs. 11, 13–15.
4 On the Torrigiani family in Nuremberg, see Peters 1994, pp. 531–36; Mazzei 1999, pp. 59–72.
5 Kunstsammlungen der Veste Coburg, inv. no. Gm.148. See Gast and Syrer 2020, pp. 10–14, fig. 1.
6 Beer 2000.
7 Staatsbibliothek, Bamberg, shelf mark I Qc 31. See Gast and Syrer 2020, pp. 20, 22, fig. 10.

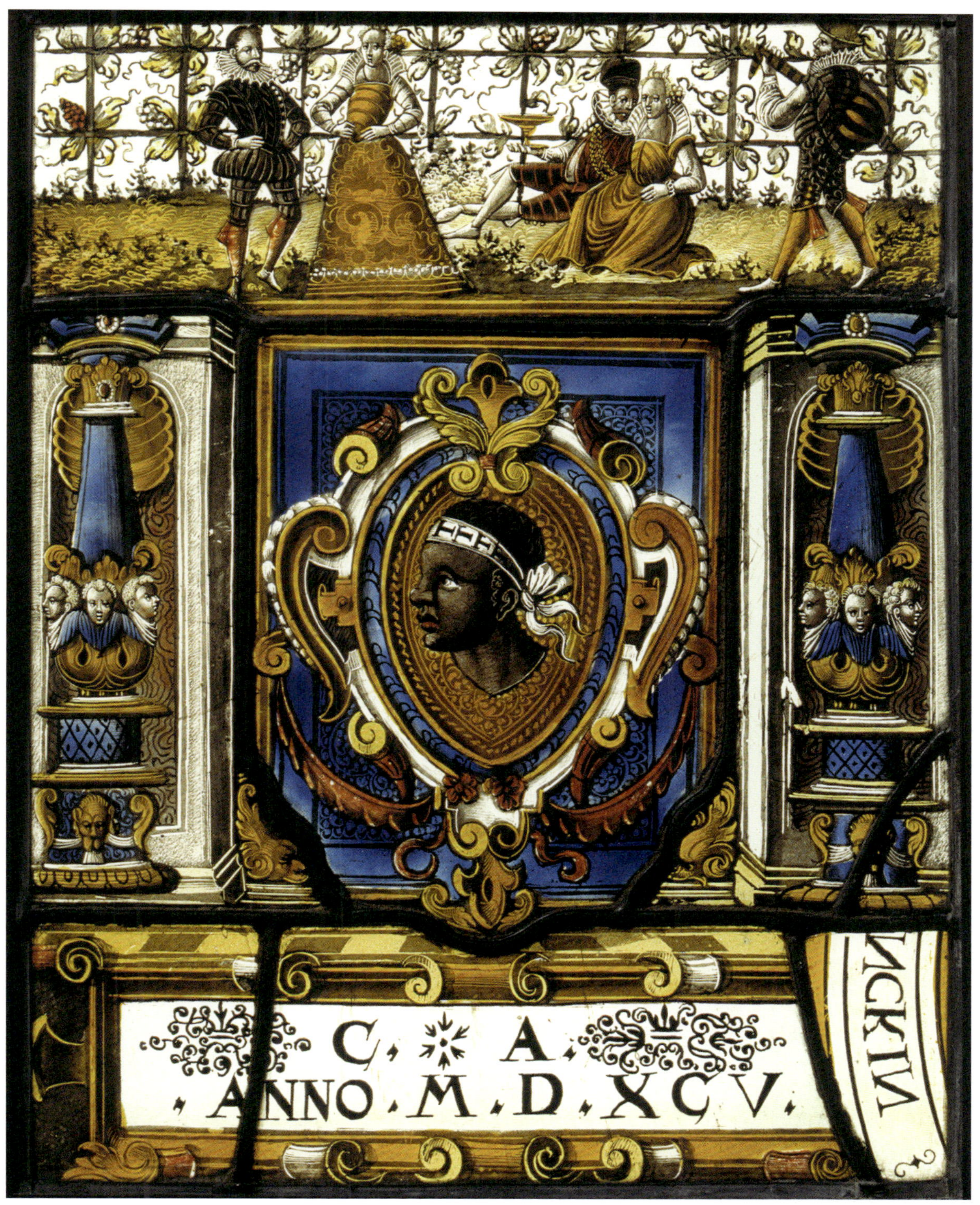
C. A.
ANNO.M.D.XCV.

65

PORTRAIT OF PAULUS PRAUN II

Lavinia Fontana

Bologna, before 1604

Oil on canvas

H. 95.6 cm; W. 74.6 cm

GNM, inv. no. Gm1573, on long-term loan from the Friedrich von Praun'sche Familienstiftung

References:
Exh. cat. Nuremberg 1994, p. 349, cat. no. 176 (Andreas Tacke); Tacke 1995, pp. 86–88, cat. no. 36 (Andreas Tacke).

The sitter in this portrait is the Nuremberg silk merchant Paulus Praun II (1548–1616). He is shown in half-length and three-quarter profile, seated on an armchair turned to the right. His right hand grasps the knob of the armrest, and in his left hand he holds a folded letter, on which his name is displayed as the addressee: "All mag. Signo Brun sua casa Bologna." In Bologna, where he settled in 1600, he used the Italianized name "Paolo Bruni." The doublet that he wears, in fashionable Spanish black, stands out only slightly from the dark background. This makes his large white ruff and lacework cuffs all the more striking in appearance.

The Prauns, a Nuremberg merchant family, derived their wealth from trading operations begun in the fifteenth century. The following century, they focused on the trade in silk with cities in northern Italy, and Bologna held a special position.[1] A center of learning, commerce, and art, the city had developed a tradition of proto-industrial silk manufacture owing to the early introduction there of water-powered spinning machines.[2] Like his younger brothers Hans VII (1556–1608) and Jakob I (1558–1627), Paulus Praun II specialized in that line of business, whereas his elder brother, Stephan III (1544–1591), took other pathways in life |**cat. nos. 68, 87, 96**|.

By the time Paulus had his portrait painted by Lavinia Fontana (1552–1614) in Bologna, he had already assembled most of his art collection. After his death it remained in Nuremberg as a family foundation under the name "Praunsches Kabinett." This was one of the most extensive non-princely art collections north of the Alps.[3] Praun's appreciation of Lavinia Fontana's work is attested by the fact that four paintings by her, including the present one, are documented in the collection's inventories. Fontana made a brilliant career for herself in Bologna before moving to Rome in 1604, where she came under papal patronage and was made an honorary member of the Accademia di San Luca. Not only did she establish herself in the portrait market by taking commissions from academics, clergymen, and members of the nobility; she was also the first professional female painter to receive prestigious commissions for religious paintings in public spaces.[4]

With its Accademia degli Incamminati, founded in 1582 by the Carracci brothers, and its numerous prominent painters, Bologna became an important center of art and art theory by the end of the sixteenth century. Praun's interest in contemporary art theory is evident in his library, which contained instructional books and treatises by authors ranging from Albrecht Dürer (1471–1528) to Giorgio Vasari (1511–1574).[5] The character of his collection reflected the artistic canon that was taking shape at the time. In systematic fashion, Praun brought together objects representing various artistic genres from both north and south of the Alps. Ancient coins and gems rounded out the holdings owned by this humanistically informed collector who had a genuine interest in art.

Praun, the Nuremberger in Bologna, was a man of learning and, through his correspondence, a well-connected cosmopolitan—just as he is portrayed in Fontana's painting. He entrusted the artistic representation of his self-image to the most sought-after female portraitist of the time: Lavinia Fontana, painter from Bologna.

Laura Di Carlo

1 See Weber 1983, pp. 133–38.
2 See Exh. cat. Nuremberg 1994, p. 321, cat. no. 159 (Christiane Lukatis).
3 On the history of the Praun collection, see Achilles-Syndram 1994a; Achilles-Syndram 1994b, pp. 35–43.
4 See Bohn 2021, pp. 42–52. On Fontana's career in Rome, see most recently Morselli 2025, pp. 23–28.
5 See Weber 1983, pp. 176–77.

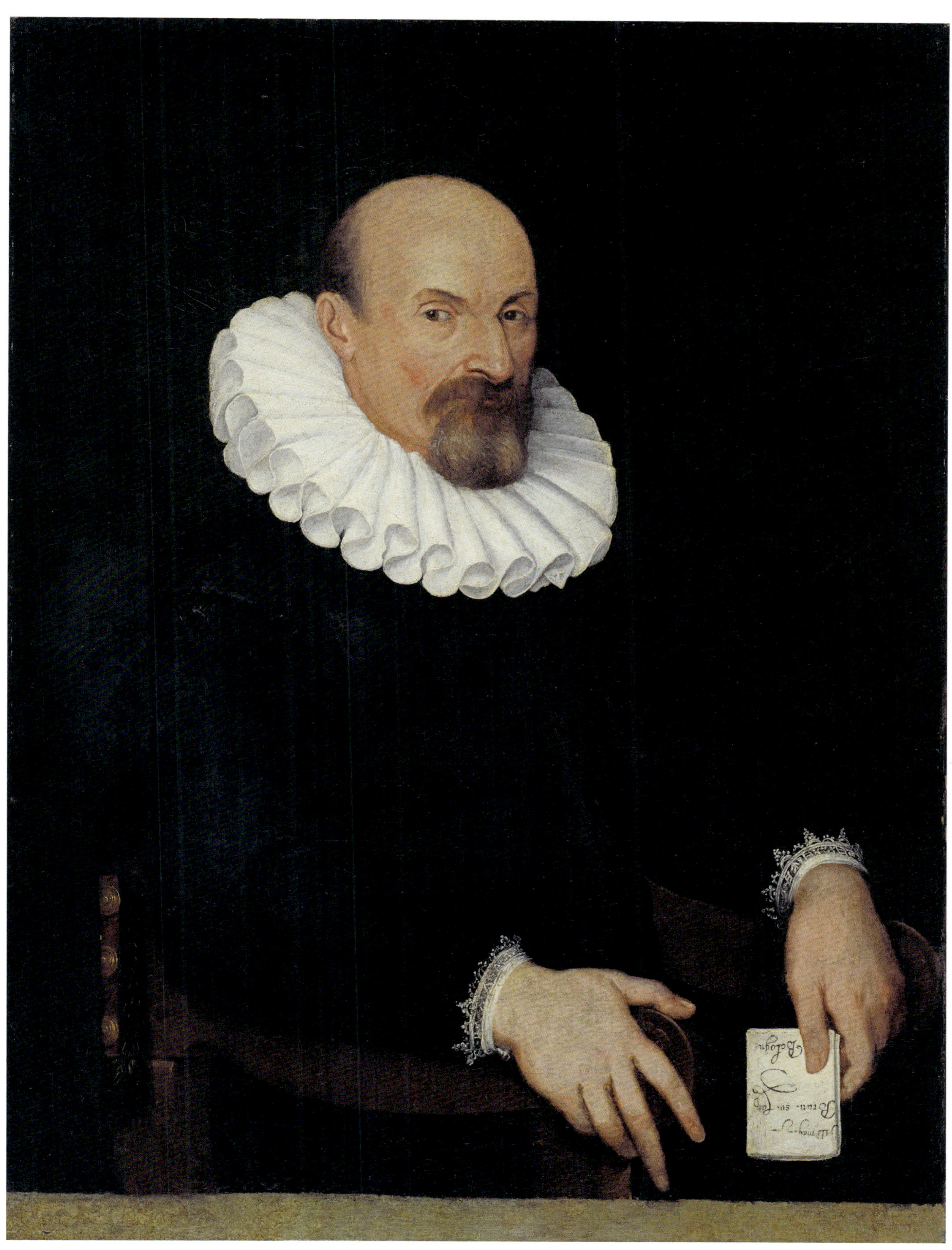

66

DECK OF PLAYING CARDS

Peter Flötner

Nuremberg, ca. 1540

Forty-seven playing cards: woodcuts, hand-colored; the three aces: on the front, pen-and-ink drawings, on multilayer card paper

H. 10.5 cm; W. 5.9 cm (each card)

GNM, inv. no. Sp7418

References:
Schoch 1993, pp. 70–74; Eser 2002, pp. 65–67; Exh. cat. Nuremberg 2014a, pp. 146–47, cat. no. 47 (Thomas Schauerte); Husband 2015, pp. 102–25.

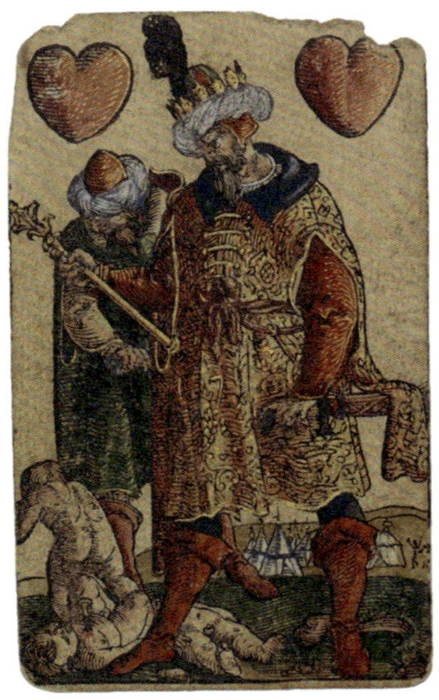

King of Hearts

This deck of woodcut playing cards designed about 1540 by Peter Flötner (d. 1546) is one of the finest examples of a popular genre that has enjoyed a firm place at distinguished gatherings from the Renaissance to the present day. Flötner's deck consists of four suits: Bells, Acorns, Leaves, and Hearts, each with twelve cards. The hand-colored deck preserved in Nuremberg contains forty-seven of the original forty-eight cards. Only the Ace of Acorns is missing. The aces (more properly *Däuser* or deuces) are pen-and-ink drawings showing the coat of arms of the Italian House of Este. Francesco d'Este (1516–1578) stayed in Nuremberg during a reception held for Emperor Charles V in 1541, and he was probably the intended recipient of this impression of the playing cards, with its individualized pen-and-ink drawings.

Flötner's deck of cards is famous primarily for the obscene, sexually suggestive, or scatological nature of many of its depictions. The Acorn suit, for example, is populated by pigs serving up piles of excrement in various ways for their own delectation. The sinful behavior that the cards displayed to players was symbolic of the general category of dissolute and morally reprehensible doings, including the very act of playing card games, which was denounced as a form of gambling.

The characters committing these unchaste and irreverent deeds are watched over by kings, whom Flötner depicts as rulers of world empires, in part using ethnic stereotypes. While the kings of Acorns and Leaves, based on their costumes, can be associated with Christian European dynasties, the kings of Hearts and Bells are portrayed as monarchs from outside the Christian and European sphere, evincing an artistic engagement with the notion of the foreign. Flötner's King of Hearts is depicted as an Ottoman sultan. He and his servant have just sheathed the sabers with which they murdered the children lying dead at their feet.[1] Owing to the great cruelty represented on this card, the sultan can be read as a stereotypical embodiment of the constant threat that Europeans had ascribed to the Ottoman Empire at least since the conquest of Constantinople in 1453. Albrecht Dürer gave visual expression to the same sentiment in his *Landscape with a Cannon* etching of 1518 |**cat. no. 86**|. On the card, the narrative of threat is reinforced by the tents visible in the background, which suggest impending military action.

The King of Bells, together with his servant dressed in feathered clothing, represents a non-European cultural context. In verses written for this deck of cards, the Nuremberg poet Hans Sachs (1494–1576) described the king as being "from India" (*aus Indian*).[2] The figures are meant to be members of the Tupinambá people of present-day Brazil. The Tupinambá became famous in Europe because of their magnificent, intricately crafted featherwork attire. The king's red mantle is strongly reminiscent of the type of feathered cloak (*Manto Tupinambá*) worn by leaders, examples of which are preserved in collections in Florence, Milan, and Basel, among other places.[3] Flötner's inspiration for this image may have come from prints and drawings with similar subjects by artists such as Albrecht Dürer and Hans Burgkmair |**cat. no. 100**|.

Johannes Gebhardt

1 For Christians, this image also called to mind the iconography of the Massacre of the Innocents (see cat. no. 35 in the present volume).
2 Sachs 1895, p. 131.
3 Buono 2015, pp. 179–81.

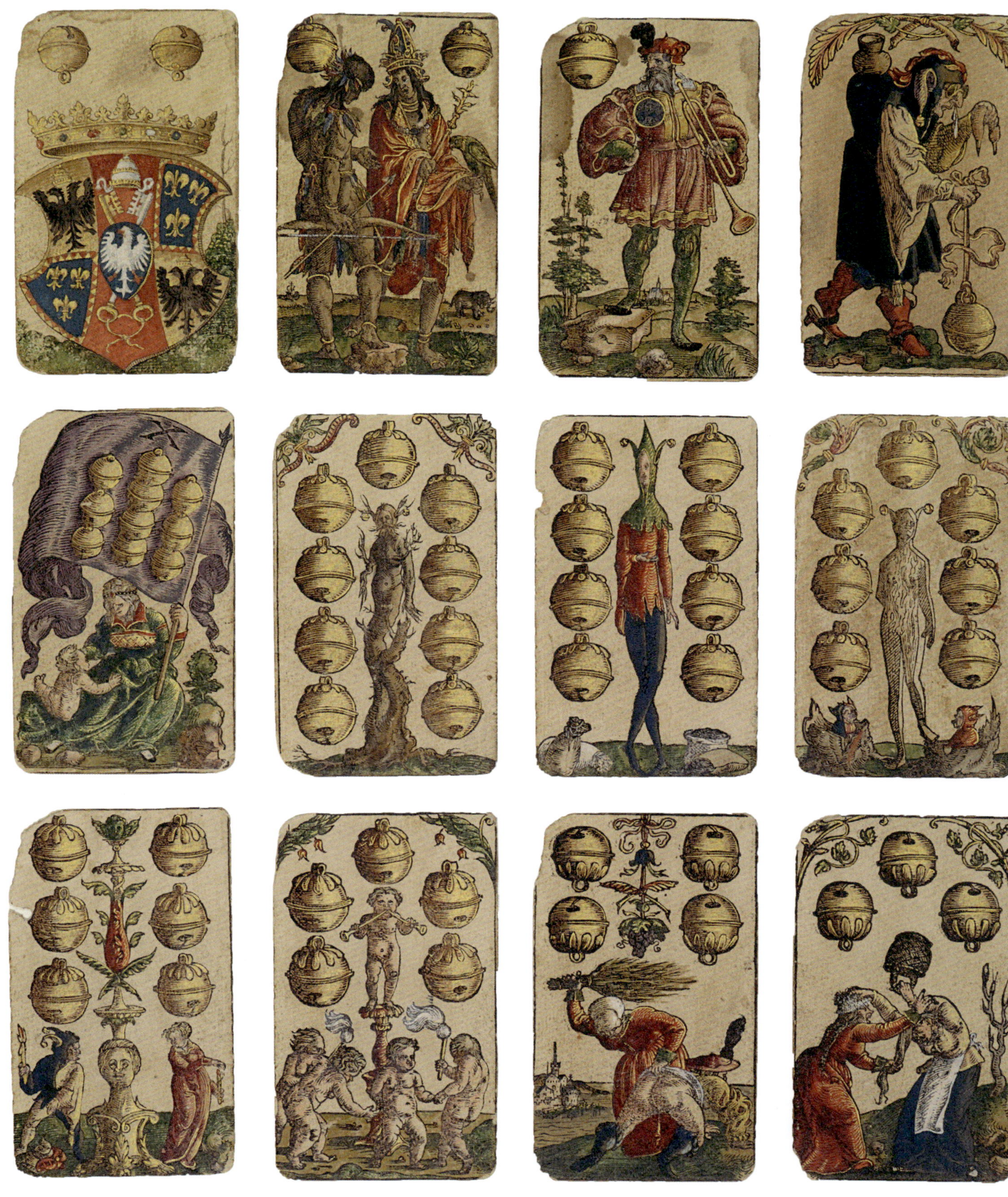

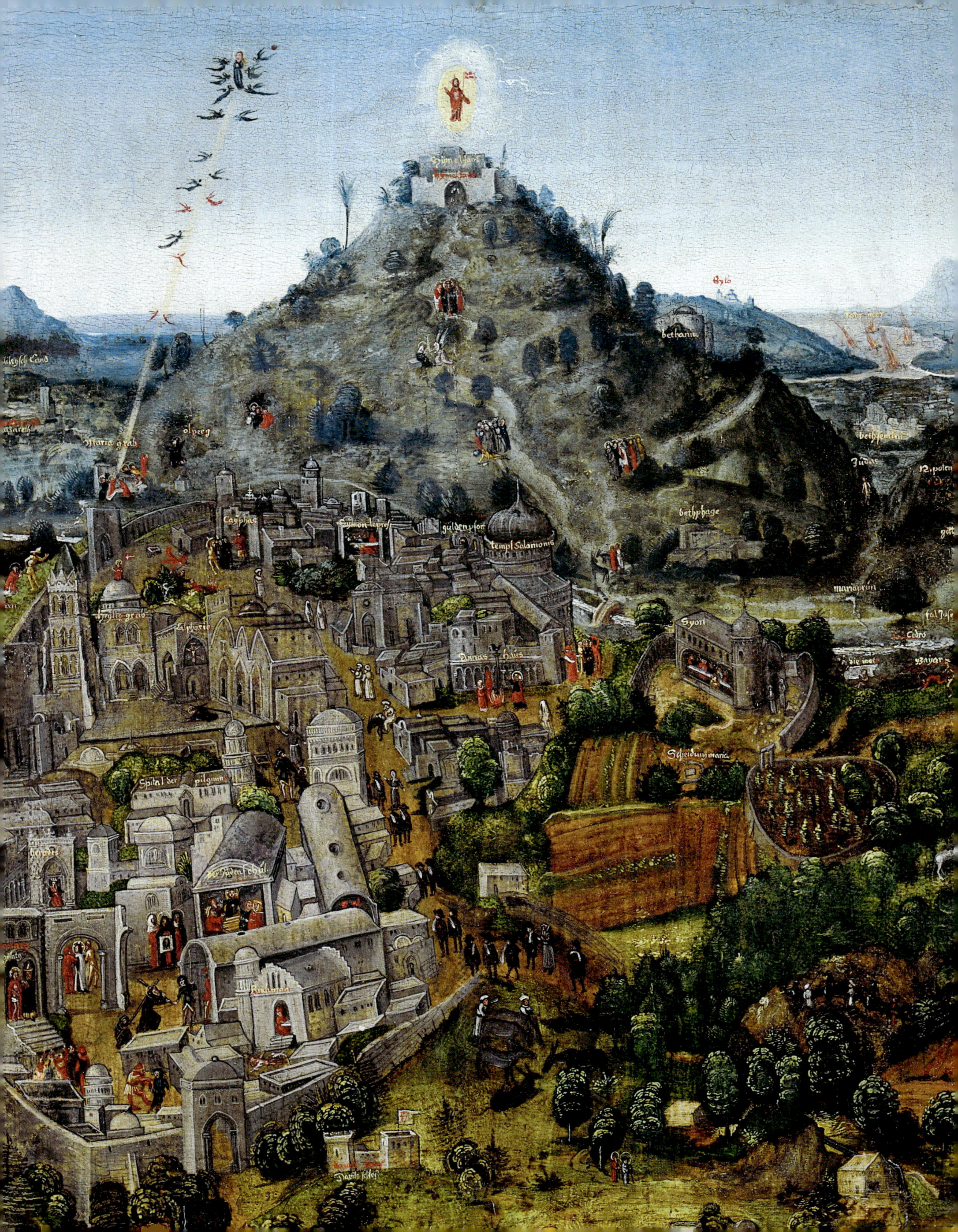
olperg
Maria grab
Cayphas
gulden port
templ Salamonis
heylig grab
Annas haus
bethania
bethsemini
Judas
bethphage
mariaprun
Syon
Cedro
Scheidung maria
Spital der pilgram
herodes
pilatus
der Juden schul

LONGING FOR THE HOLY LAND

Ever since the rise of Christianity, Jerusalem has been one of the religion's most important pilgrimage destinations. It is the site of the ministry and Passion of Jesus. The city's outstanding religious and symbolic significance is reflected in medieval world maps, which often place Jerusalem at the center. Yet at the same time, the Holy Land also marked the outer edge of the conceivable world for many Europeans living in the period covered by the present exhibition.

The chance to visit the sites associated with Jesus motivated people to undergo the risks of long-distance travel. In addition to this religious motivation, social prestige also played a role. Many pilgrims left records of their journeys in the form of travelogues and works of art. A prominent example of the latter are the elaborately designed pilgrimage panels of the Ketzel family of Nuremberg. Some objects brought back from pilgrimages were surrounded by wondrous legends, as is the case with the Byzantine icon depicting Saints Constantine and Helena with the True Cross of Christ, which was displayed at the Saint Sebastian Hospital in Nuremberg.

Fascination with the Holy Land also found expression in other kinds of art objects. Jerusalem was one of the first places that people attempted to depict in art with topographical accuracy. As a way of transmitting the power of Jerusalem's holy sites to Nuremberg, Stations of the Cross ensembles, Holy Sepulchre chapels, and stone sculptural groups depicting the Agony in the Garden were erected in the city. With the help of movable sculptures, episodes from the life of Jesus were reenacted in the context of liturgical feasts. Monumental works of art such as Adam Kraft's reliefs of the Stations of the Cross resulted from a desire to project the holy sites onto the reality of everyday life.

Benno Baumbauer and Sven Jakstat

◄ cat. no. 69 (detail)

67

MEMORIAL FOR ADELHEID TUCHER, NÉE GUNDLACH

Wolfgang Katzheimer the Elder and workshop

Bamberg (?), ca. 1483

Paint on softwood

H. 133.7 cm; W. 104 cm

Museum Tucherschloss und Hirsvogelsaal, Museen der Stadt Nürnberg, inv. no. HI Gm 004, on long-term loan from the Tucher Kulturstiftung

References:
Haussherr 1987–88, pp. 63–66, 68–69; Suckale 2009, vol. 2, pp. 161–66; Worm 2011, pp. 198–201; Schulz 2015, pp. 92–98; Hess, Hirschfelder, and Baum 2019, pp. 746–47, 751, 754, 756, under cat. no. 50 (Beate Fücker and Daniel Hess).

The memorial panel for Adelheid Tucher, née Gundlach (d. 1482), combines an emotional depiction of the Lamentation of Christ with a detailed view of Jerusalem. The latter is considered the earliest topographically accurate representation of the Holy City in panel painting |**fig. p. 54**|. The city view is from an elevated eastern perspective. Particular structures stand out: the Golden Gate and the Dome of the Rock appear in the foreground, along with the Al-Aqsa Mosque, shown as a domed basilica. Numerous crescents above various buildings mark the Muslim presence in the Holy Land, which had been under Mamluk rule since 1291, making it a place where Christian pilgrimage was strictly regulated. Only the Church of the Holy Sepulchre, with its two rooftop crosses, is marked as a Christian shrine. It is further distinguished by a stage-like forecourt and a fountain of light emitting from the dome, probably a sign of Christ's resurrection. The southern view of the Holy Sepulchre Church diverges from the overall eastern perspective on the city. This combination of views on the Tucher panel would soon become standard, and it—or the models on which it was based—probably influenced the view of Jerusalem in the *Nuremberg Chronicle* |**cat. no. 4**|.[1]

The streets are mostly empty. Only on closer inspection does one discover six tiny scenes of Christ carrying the cross along the Via Dolorosa that leads from the Lion's Gate to the Church of the Holy Sepulchre. The way in which Christ's path is embedded within the architectural setting may rely on descriptions and a drawing that the Jerusalem pilgrim Hans Tucher VI (1428–1491) |**see cat. no. 68**| had sent just a few years earlier from the Holy Land to his brother Endres (1423–1507)—the husband of the Adelheid immortalized by this panel.[2] Even the buildings outside the city walls incorporate episodes of the Passion, serving as settings for the Last Supper and the interrogations of Christ before Caiaphas and Annas.

The group of mourners in the foreground is connected to the city by a path that passes by the open Holy Sepulchre. Despite this spatial linkage, Jerusalem looks clearly separated from the foreground figures, rising steeply behind them. Not only does this image merge the historical events of the Passion with a contemporary—that is, late medieval—view of Jerusalem; the city rising up from behind the hills also has the appearance of a rapturous vision. This reflects the dual nature of Jerusalem in the medieval Christian imagination: it was both a place on earth and the Heavenly Jerusalem prophesied in the Book of Revelation (Rev. 21:2). The foreground mourners combine elements of the iconography of the Lamentation and the Bearing of Christ's Body.[3] At the same time, the way in which the body of Christ is presented, with Adelheid Tucher shown in prayer next to the bleeding wound in his hand, calls to mind the Eucharist.

A lack of reliable sources has made it impossible to determine where the memorial panel was originally displayed. Some authors propose that it hung in the cloister of the Jakobskirche in Bamberg. Endres and Adelheid Tucher had no children, and they had lived separated since 1476. Endres had joined the Carthusian monastery in Nuremberg as a lay brother, and Adelheid had returned to her hometown of Bamberg. Despite this separation, a memorial service attended by Endres and his fellow brothers, among others, was held for Adelheid at Nuremberg's Sebalduskirche, the location of the Tucher family's burial site.

The painting was made in the workshop of the Bamberg artist Wolfgang Katzheimer (d. 1508). Robert Suckale sees a stylistic resemblance to an *Entombment of Christ* painted in Bamberg.[4] Other works that are related in technique and style are the high altarpiece of the Stadtkirche in Hersbruck and a *Crucifixion* acquired by the Germanisches Nationalmuseum in 2013.[5]

Florian Abe

1 See Worm 2011, pp. 198–201.
2 On these parallels, see Schulz 2015, pp. 91–98.
3 Suckale 2009, vol. 2, p. 161.
4 Staatsgalerie, Bamberg, inv. no. L 1556. Suckale 2009, vol. 2, pp. 161, 166.
5 The latter: inv. no. Gm2413. See Hess, Hirschfelder, and Baum 2019, p. 756 (Beate Fücker and Daniel Hess).

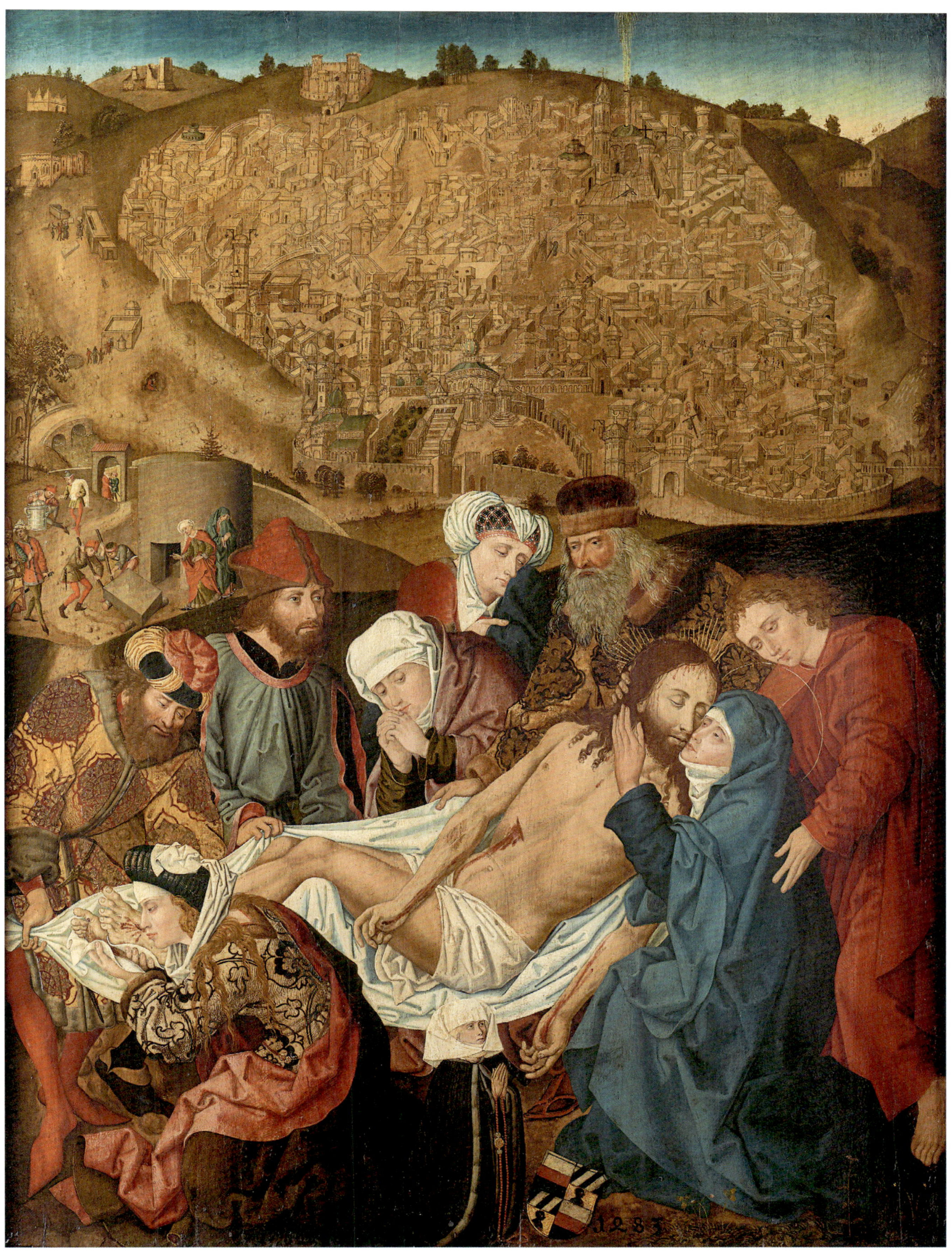

68

JOURNEY TO THE PROMISED LAND

68.1 Reise in das gelobte Land (Journey to the Promised Land)

Hans Tucher

Augsburg: Johann Schönsperger, 1482

Incunable, seventy-five leaves, woodcut illustrations

H. 25.7 cm; W. 18.5 cm (book block)

GNM, shelf mark Inc. 4° 6320

Open to fols. 13v–14r

68.2 Miniature Replica of the Tomb of Godfrey of Bouillon

Jerusalem (?), ca. 1585

Bone, engraved; engraved grooves painted

H. 0.5 cm; L. 2.9 cm; D. 1 cm

GNM, inv. no. KG1234_1, on long-term loan from the Friedrich von Praun'sche Familienstiftung

References:
68.1: Hellwig 1970, p. 279, cat. no. 910; Herz 2002; Herz 2005, pp. 115–16.
68.2: Exh. cat. Nuremberg 2004, pp. 90–91 (Ralf Schürer); Zander-Seidel 2010, p. 176.

The Holy Land held a great fascination for many Nurembergers. In the period before the Reformation, more than fifty of the city's residents had gone on pilgrimages there, and ten wrote travelogues about their experiences.[1] One of them was the patrician and junior mayor Hans Tucher VI (1428–1491). From May 6, 1479, to April 10, 1480, he explored the holy sites in Palestine, Sinai, and Egypt, arriving by sea on a boat that sailed from Venice to Jaffa.

Tucher's book *Reise in das gelobte Land* (Journey to the Promised Land) was meant to serve as a practical guide for pilgrims. In addition to diary-like entries about the itinerary, the book contains helpful appendices such as a *Regimen Sanitatis*—a manual of medicinal recipes compiled by the Nuremberg physician Hermann Schedel (1410–1485)—and a copy of Tucher's contract with a Venetian shipowner concerning the journey's organization.

While most pilgrimage reports circulated in a small number of handwritten copies and therefore served mainly as private forms of remembrance, Tucher's text was conceived from the outset to be printed and thus widely distributed. With this book, Tucher established the tradition of the printed German-language travelogue.[2]

The first edition exhibited here, printed in Augsburg by Johann Schönsperger, comes from the collection of the founder of the Germanisches Nationalmuseum, Hans Freiherr von und zu Aufseß (1801–1872).[3] This edition, however, contains numerous errors, unauthorized changes, and omissions by the publisher—much to Tucher's displeasure. He immediately commissioned a revised edition to be printed in Nuremberg. In just the first five years after its initial publication, the report appeared in six editions.[4]

In addition to writing travelogues, pilgrims also commonly brought back mementos. For example, it is recorded that Tucher took an impression from one of the thirty pieces of silver belonging to the so-called "Blood money of Judas" (*Judaslohn*) that he saw on the island of Rhodes. He used the impression to make silver coins that he distributed to friends.[5] Through contact with relics or with the *loca sancta* (the holy sites), objects could be charged with holiness and thereby transformed into secondary relics. The miniature replica of the tomb of Godfrey of Bouillon, who is said to have touched the Holy Sepulchre, belongs to that category.[6] Made of bone and engraved with inscriptions and ornaments, it was owned by Stephan Praun III of Nuremberg (1544–1591) |**see cat. nos. 87, 96**|. Praun traveled to Jerusalem in 1585, thus offering an example of the continuity of pilgrimage even after the Reformation. The famous crusader Godfrey of Bouillon (d. 1100) established the Christian Kingdom of Jerusalem in 1099 and was buried in the Church of the Holy Sepulchre—a site also visited by Hans Tucher. Praun's tomb souvenir bears an inscription that reads, "HIC IACET INCLITUS GODEFR[I]DUS DE BVILON QVI TOTAM ISTAM TERRAM ACQVISIVIT CVLTVI CHRISTIANO CVIVS A[N]I[M]A CUM CHRISTO REQVIESCAT AMEN" (Here lies the renowned Godfrey of Bouillon, who won all this land for the Christian faith. May his soul rest with Christ. Amen). Preserved along with this object is a piece of paper bearing a broken seal, probably the tomb replica's wrapper.[7]

Florian Abe

1 Herz 2005, p. XI.
2 Herz 2002, p. XIII.
3 Herz 2005, pp. 115–16.
4 On the different editions, see Herz 2005.
5 Fabri 1998, p. 299.
6 Exh. cat. Nuremberg 2004, p. 91 (Ralf Schürer).
7 GNM, inv. no. KG1234_2.

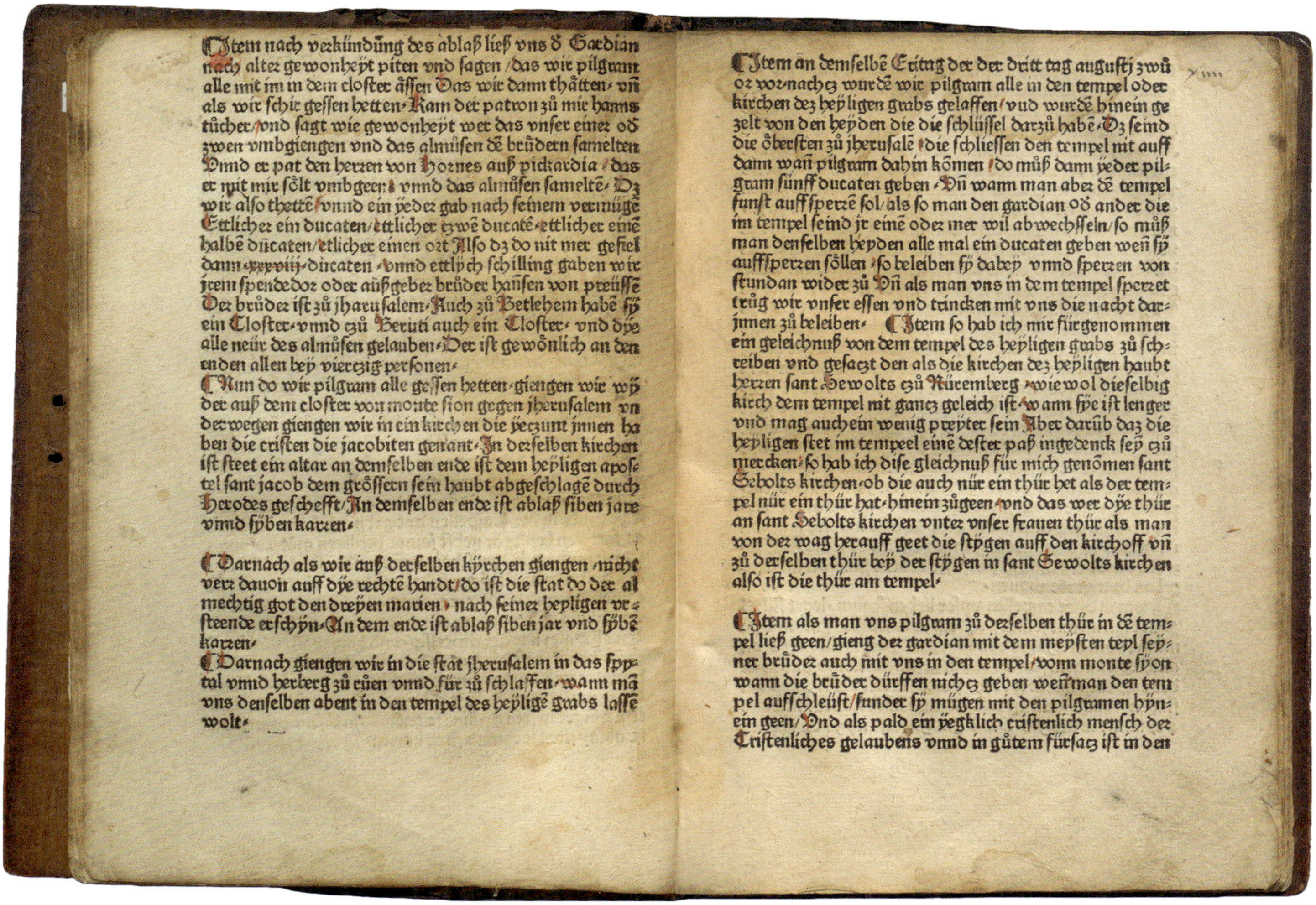

¶ Item nach verkündung des ablaß ließ vns d Gardian nach alter gewonheyt piten vnd sagen / das wir pilgram alle mit im in dem closter ässen Das wir dann thätten · vñ als wir schir gessen hetten · Kam der patron zů mir hanns tůcher / vnd sagt wie gewonheyt wer das vnser einer od zwen vmbgiengen vnd das almůsen dē brůdern samelten Vnnd er pat den herren von Hornes auß pickardia · das er mit mir sölt vmbgeen · vnnd das almůsen samelte · Dz wir also thettē / vnnd ein yeder gab nach seinem vermügē Ettlicher ein ducaten / ettlicher zwē ducatē · ettlicher einē halbē ducaten / etlicher einen ort Also dz do nit mer gefiel dann ·xxviij· ducaten · vnnd ettlych schilling gaben wir irem spendedor oder außgeber brůder hansen von preüssē Der brůder ist zů iharusalem · Auch zů Betlehem habē sy ein Closter · vnnd zů Beruti auch ein Closter · vnd dye alle neür des almůsen gelauben · Der ist gewönlich an den enden allen bey viertzig personen ·

¶ Nun do wir pilgram alle gessen hetten · giengen wir wyder auß dem closter von monte sion gegen iherusalem vn derwegen giengen wir in ein kirchen die yetzunt innen haben die cristen die iacobiten genant · In derselben kirchen ist steet ein altar an demselben ende ist dem heyligen apostel sant iacob dem grössern sein haubt abgeschlagē durch Herodes geschefft / In demselben ende ist ablaß siben iare vnnd syben karren ·

¶ Darnach als wir auß derselben kyrchen giengen · nicht verr dauon auff dye rechtē handt / do ist die stat do der almechtig got den dreyen marien · nach seiner heyligen ersteende erschyn · An dem ende ist ablaß siben iar vnd sybē karren ·

¶ Darnach giengen wir in die stat iherusalem in das spytal vnnd herberg zů růen vnnd für zů schlaffen · wann mā vns denselben abent in den tempel des heyligē grabs lassē wolt ·

¶ Item an denselbē Eritag der der dritt tag augusti zwů or vor·nachtz wurdē wir pilgram alle in den tempel oder kirchen dez heyligen grabs gelassen / vnd wurdē hinein gezelt von den heyden die die schlüssel darzů habē · Dz seind die obersten zů iherusalē · die schliessen den tempel nit auff dann wañ pilgram dahin kōmen / do můß dann yeder pilgram fünff ducaten geben · Vñ wann man aber dē tempel sunst auffsperrē sol / als so man den gardian od ander die im tempel seind ir einē oder mer wil abwechsseln / so můß man denselben heyden alle mal ein ducaten geben weñ sy auffsperren söllen · so beleiben sy dabey vnnd sperren von stundan wider zů Vñ als man vns in dem tempel sperret trůg wir vnser essen vnd trincken mit vns die nacht darinnen zů beleiben · ¶ Item so hab ich mir fürgenommen ein geleichnuß von dem tempel des heyligen grabs zů schreiben vnd gesatzt den als die kirchen dez heyligen haubt herren sant Sewolts zů Nüremberg · wie wol dieselbig kirch dem tempel nit gantz geleich ist · wann sye ist lenger vnd mag auch ein wenig preyter sein Aber darūb daz die heyligen stet im tempeel einē dester paß ingedenck sey zů mercken · so hab ich dise gleichnuß für mich genōmen sant Sebolts kirchen · ob die auch nür ein thür het als der tempel nür ein thür hat · hinein zů geen · vnd das wer dye thür an sant Sebolts kirchen vnter vnser frauen thür als man von der wag herauff geet die stygen auff den kirchoff vñ zů derselben thür bey der stygen in sant Sewolts kirchen also ist die thür am tempel ·

¶ Item als man vns pilgram zů derselben thür in dē tempel ließ geen / gieng der gardian mit dem meysten teyl seyner brůder auch mit vns in den tempel / vom monte syon wann die brůder dürffen nichtz geben weñ man den tempel auffschleüst / sunder sy mügen mit den pilgramen hynein geen / Vnd als pald ein yegklich cristenlich mensch der Cristenliches gelaubens vnnd in gůtem fürsatz ist in den

cat. no. 68.1

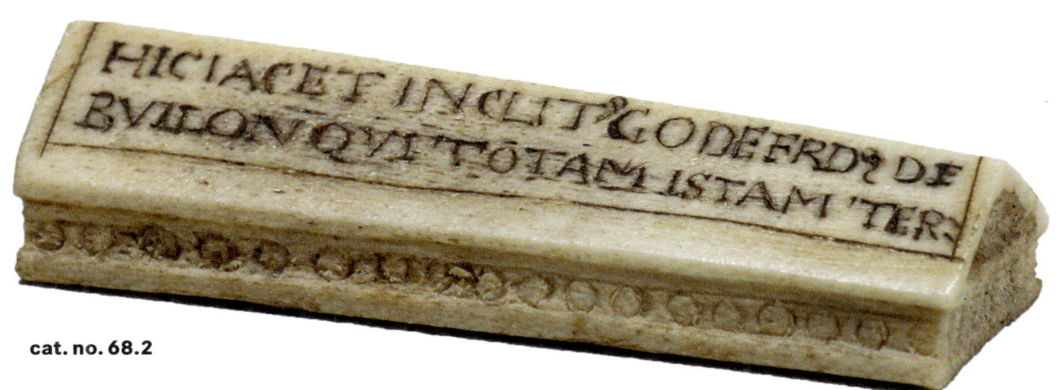

cat. no. 68.2

69

PILGRIMAGE PANEL OF FREDERICK THE WISE

Nuremberg (?), after 1503

Paint on spruce

H. 68.8 cm; W. 80 cm

Stiftung Schloss Friedenstein, Gotha, inv. no. SG77

References:
Bruck 1903, pp. 202–5; Rudy 2001, pp. 216–20; Fey 2006, pp. 152–54, 160; Arad 2020, pp. 92–94; Exh. cat. Lüneburg and Stade 2020, pp. 223–25, cat. no. 4.1.a (Mordechay Lewy).

At first glance, the pilgrimage panel of Elector Frederick the Wise of Saxony (Frederick III, 1463–1525) resembles a seek-and-find picture. Numerous figures populate this vast view of the Holy Land, which reaches from the Mediterranean Sea in the foreground to the Dead Sea in the background, and from Nazareth on the left to Bethlehem on the right. The only figures that stand out clearly are the Virgin Mary and Christ at the upper left, both ascending heavenward, and, directly below them at the lower left, Elector Frederick kneeling in prayer next to his coat of arms. The inscription beneath him indicates that the panel commemorates the journey he made "to the Holy Sepulchre" in 1493 (*Friderich Von gottes gnaden / Hertzog Zu Sachsen und churfürst / Zug Zum Heylige[n] grab 1493*). Frederick's pilgrimage gave rise to numerous artistic commissions and also enabled him to enlarge the enormous collection of relics he kept at the Schlosskirche in Wittenberg.

The other figures are identifiable only on closer inspection. This work presents a Christological panorama in which the history of salvation—mainly from the New Testament but including David's battle with Goliath—is set in the places of its occurrence. Christ himself makes many appearances: at the Mount of Olives and on the streets of Jerusalem alone, there are twenty-three Passion scenes taking place |**fig. p. 246**|.[1] Inscriptions identify important *loca sancta* (holy sites) and people. While contemporary pilgrims and people in "oriental" headdress appear alongside the historical-biblical figures, they do not interact with them. This temporal layering is also reflected in Jerusalem's urban fabric: the cross-bearing Christ makes his way toward the Church of the Holy Sepulchre, a structure built more than three hundred years after his death, under the Emperor Constantine. Thus, while representing the subject of pilgrimage, the panel offers viewers themselves the opportunity to embark on an imaginary pilgrimage by becoming engrossed in the biblical landscape, the scenes, and the inscriptions.

Neither the work's creator, nor place of origin, nor the patron have been identified with any certainty. An earlier attribution to the Nuremberg artist Jakob Elsner has been rejected in recent scholarship, as has the former association with Lucas Cranach, who was once wrongly assumed to have accompanied Frederick to the Holy Land. Although the dating is also uncertain, the stylistic evidence points to the first quarter of the sixteenth century and thus to a time significantly after Frederick's pilgrimage. Recent research suggests that Frederick's figure was added later, possibly on the occasion of his 1507 visit to Nuremberg, where the panel may have been presented to him as a gift. The possibility of a later reworking is corroborated by a separate painted panorama of the Holy Land: that picture, which was probably destroyed in the 1974 fire at Powerscourt House (Ireland), had a provenance from Nuremberg and was identical in many details, but it lacked a figure of Frederick. The year 1503 is regarded as the terminus post quem for the creation of the Gotha panel, owing to a series of portraits located on the reverse. They depict eight Jerusalem pilgrims from the Nuremberg merchant family Ketzel, the last one having made his journey in 1503. Furthermore, Wolff Ketzel is identified as a participant in Frederick the Wise's pilgrimage. It is possible that the Ketzels used this panel to thank Frederick for issuing a heraldic grant of arms in 1507 to the brothers Georg II and Wolff and their cousins Sebald the Younger and Martin the Younger.[2] The portrait series shows great similarities to the Ketzel pilgrimage panels at the Germanisches Nationalmuseum |**cat. no. 70**|.[3]

Florian Abe

1 Arad 2020, p. 93.
2 Exh. cat. Lüneburg and Stade 2020, pp. 223–24, cat. no. 4.1.a (Mordechay Lewy).
3 GNM, inv. nos. Gm581, Gm582_a, Gm582_b.

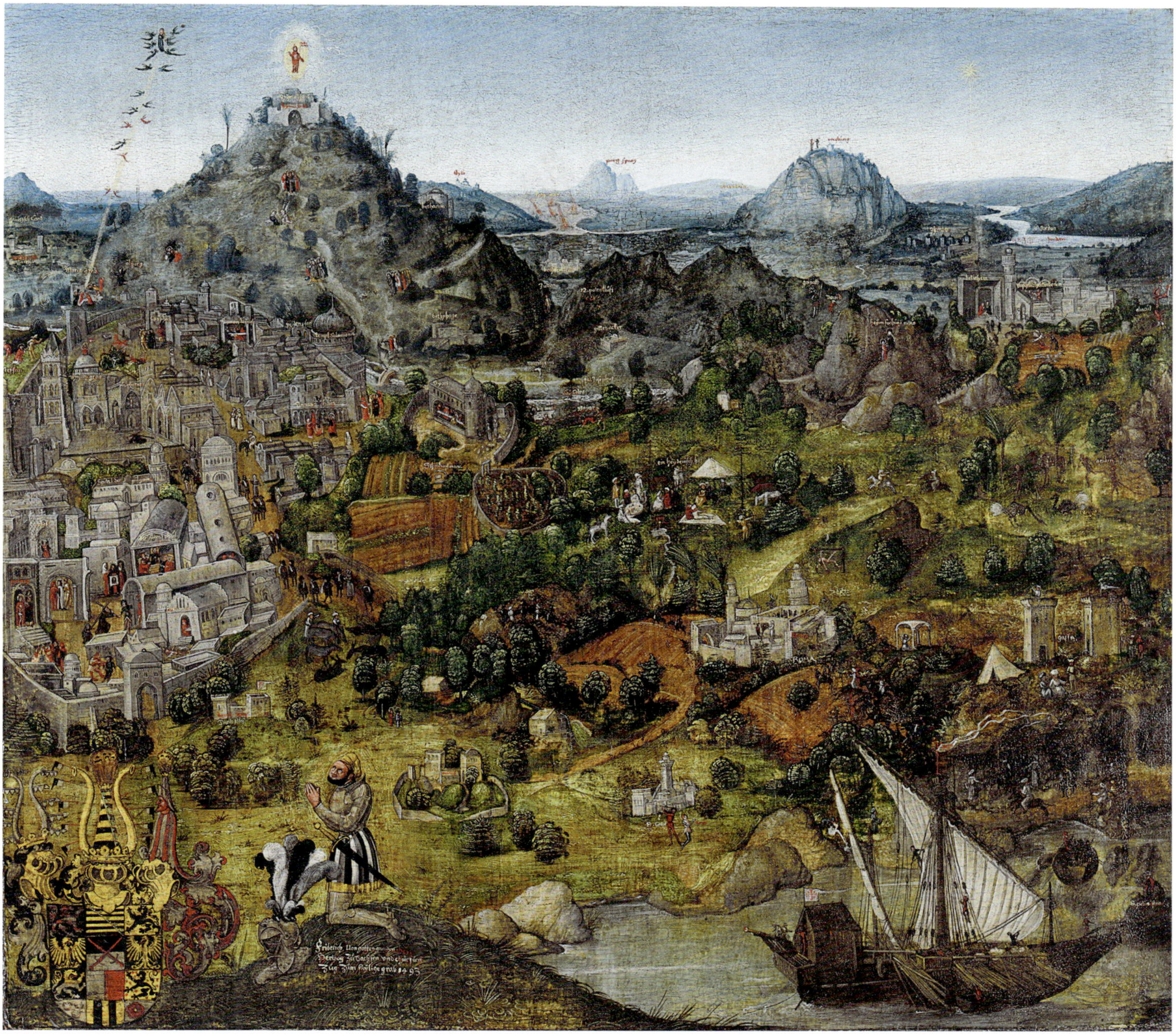

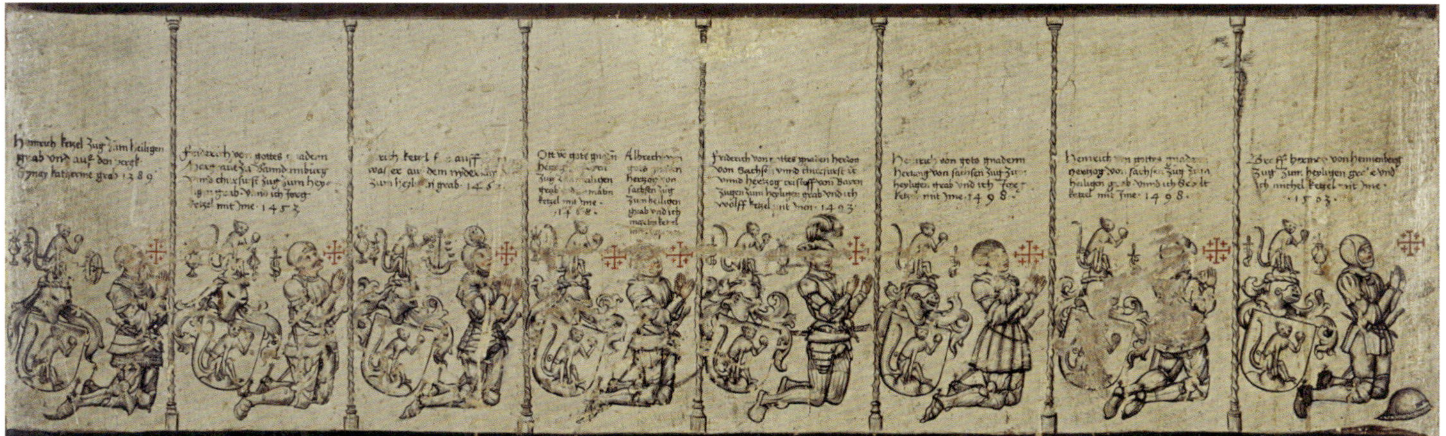

Detail of the reverse

70

GENEALOGICAL PANEL OF THE KETZEL FAMILY

Nuremberg, dated 1595

Paint on pine

Upper half: H. 92.5 cm; W. 176 cm; lower half: H. 92.5 cm; W. 176.5 cm (including frames)

GNM, inv. nos. Gm582_a, Gm582_b

References:
Aign 1961, pp. 80–81; Löcher 1997, pp. 372–77.

Among the more than fifty Nurembergers who made pilgrimages to the Holy Land in the late Middle Ages, the Ketzel family occupies a prominent position. Eight members of the family set out for Jerusalem between 1389 and 1503, and they left numerous traces of their journeys in Nuremberg. As a merchant family, the Ketzels belonged to the social class that was designated "honorable" (*ehrbar*) but, unlike the patricians, was not eligible to serve on the city council. Nevertheless, the present family tree represents the same ambition of displaying status through ancestry that is found in numerous genealogical panels and books created for patricians in the sixteenth century.[1]

The Ketzel panel consists of two hinged halves, each in horizontal format. The lower half bears the date 1595. The family's two progenitors appear at the very top, flanking the Virgin and Child on a crescent moon. An inscription introduces them as follows: "In the year 1389 after the birth of Christ, I, Heinrich Ketzel traveled to the Holy Sepulchre and Mount Sinai. Afterward, in 1391, I married Anna Igelbrecht in Augsburg, and with her I had three sons: Heinrich, Endres, and Martin Ketzel. This Heinrich Ketzel died in the year 1433; may God have mercy on him."[2] The couple is accompanied by their coats of arms, and Heinrich is furthermore shown with insignia of the chivalric orders he joined during his pilgrimage (Order of Saint Catherine, Aragonese Order of the Jar, Cyprian Order of the Sword, Order of the Holy Sepulchre). The family tree that issues from Heinrich and Anna is populated by half-length figures above heraldic shields. These comprise 116 descendants (51 men, 63 women, and 2 deceased children) and 36 persons who belonged to the family by marriage (22 men and 14 women).[3] The figures' clothing reflects developments in fashion: on the men, from the medieval suit of armor to the cloak; on the women, from the bonnet to the beret; and in general, from colorful attire to the introduction of dark Spanish fashion with high ruffs.[4]

The lower panel concludes with the following inscription: "Thus ends the whole Ketzel lineage; they all lived and died in honor and virtue, etc., in praise of God. May the almighty God grant them and us all a joyous resurrection through Jesus Christ, his dear son, our Lord. Amen."[5] The date is noted in the lower right corner: "Completed on the last day of August 1595" (*Verfertigt im letzten Augusti 1595*). The changing character of the script from top to bottom may indicate that the family tree was painted or augmented in stages—a subject worthy of future investigation. The Ketzel family extinguished in the male line with the death of Paulus in 1588. Paulus's sister Maria (1559–1621) may have commissioned this work. Or perhaps the patron was her husband, Hans Christoph von Ploben, who may have wished to demonstrate his wife's respectable origins.[6]

That same ambition is apparent on the lower panel's exterior, which was displayed when the pair was folded shut. It is divided into two rows of nine fields, with the rightmost fields remaining empty. In the lower row, the eight Ketzels who made Holy Land pilgrimages are represented by coats of arms and orders of chivalry. Inscriptions identify each one by name, destination, year of travel, and the respective prince each accompanied—this last item being most important for claims of status. Seven of the princes are represented in the upper row by coats of arms, orders, and inscriptions. The upper left field contains a highly condensed miniature view of the Holy Land, from the Mediterranean coast to the Dead Sea, dominated by the Mount of Olives. Small scenes from the New Testament story of salvation are visible in the landscape. The view is based on earlier Holy Land panoramas, not least the Gotha pilgrimage panel of Frederick the Wise, on whose reverse the eight Ketzel pilgrims appear in portrait |**cat. no. 69**|.[7]

Florian Abe

1 On such genealogical works, see for example Kuhn 2010.
2 "Nach Christi geburt M° ccc° lxxxviiij Jar zuge ich Heinrich Ketzel zum heiligen grab und auf den Berg Synay zue. Darnach M° ccc° lxxxxj ward ich verheirat Anna Ygelbrechtin zu Augspurg, mit der gebar ich drey Sunn Heinrich, Endres und Mertin Ketzel. Dieser Heinrich Ketzel starb im M° cccc° xxxviij Jar, dem got genad."
3 Aign 1961, p. 80.
4 See Löcher 1997, p. 375.
5 "Also endt sich der gantze Ketzel Stam, die alle Gott lob in Ehr vnd Tugent gelebt vnd gestorben etc. Der Allmechtige Gott wöll Ihnen vnd vns allen ein fröliche aufferstehung verleyhen / Durch Jesum Christum seinen lieben Sohn vnsern Herrn. Amen."
6 See Löcher 1997, p. 372.
7 See also the other Ketzel panel in the GNM, inv. no. Gm 581.

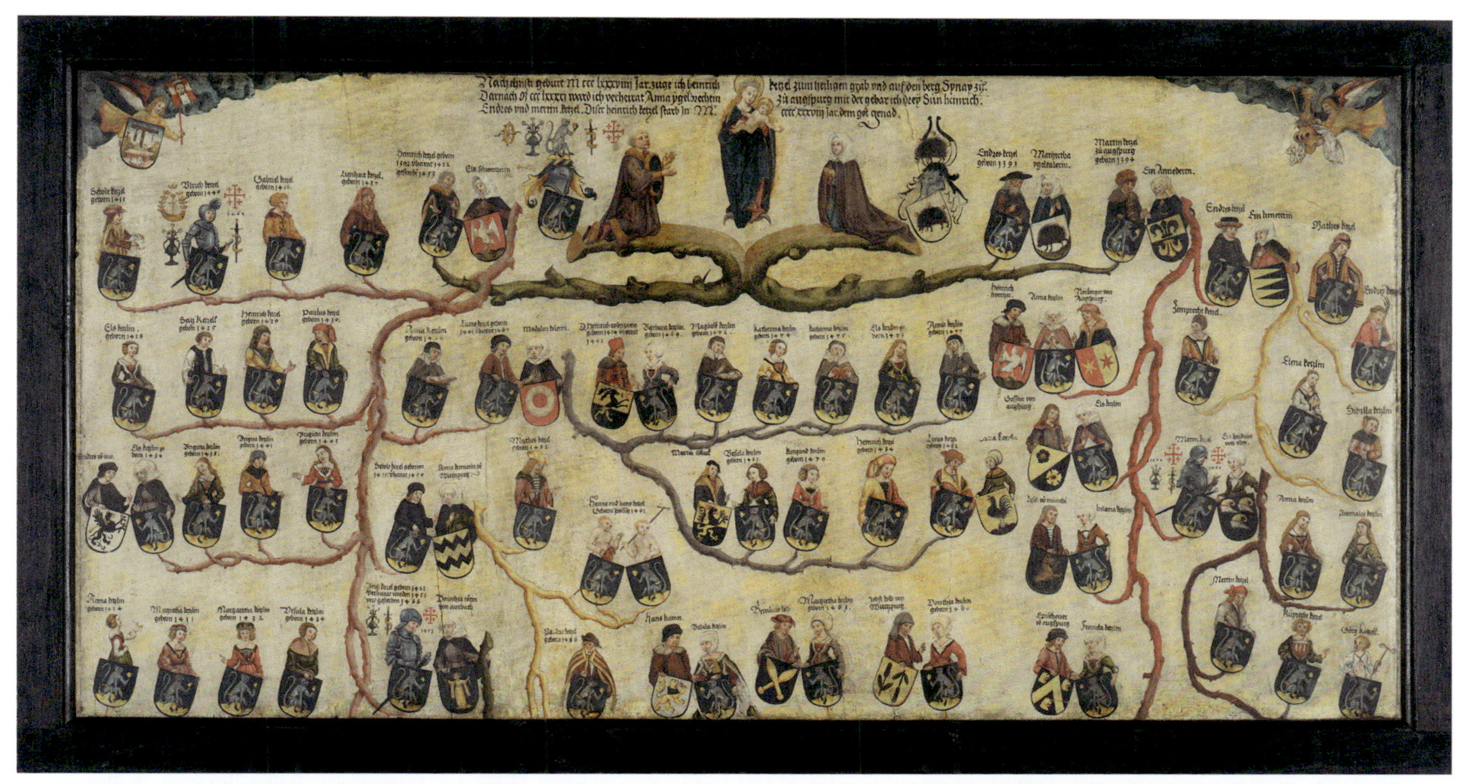

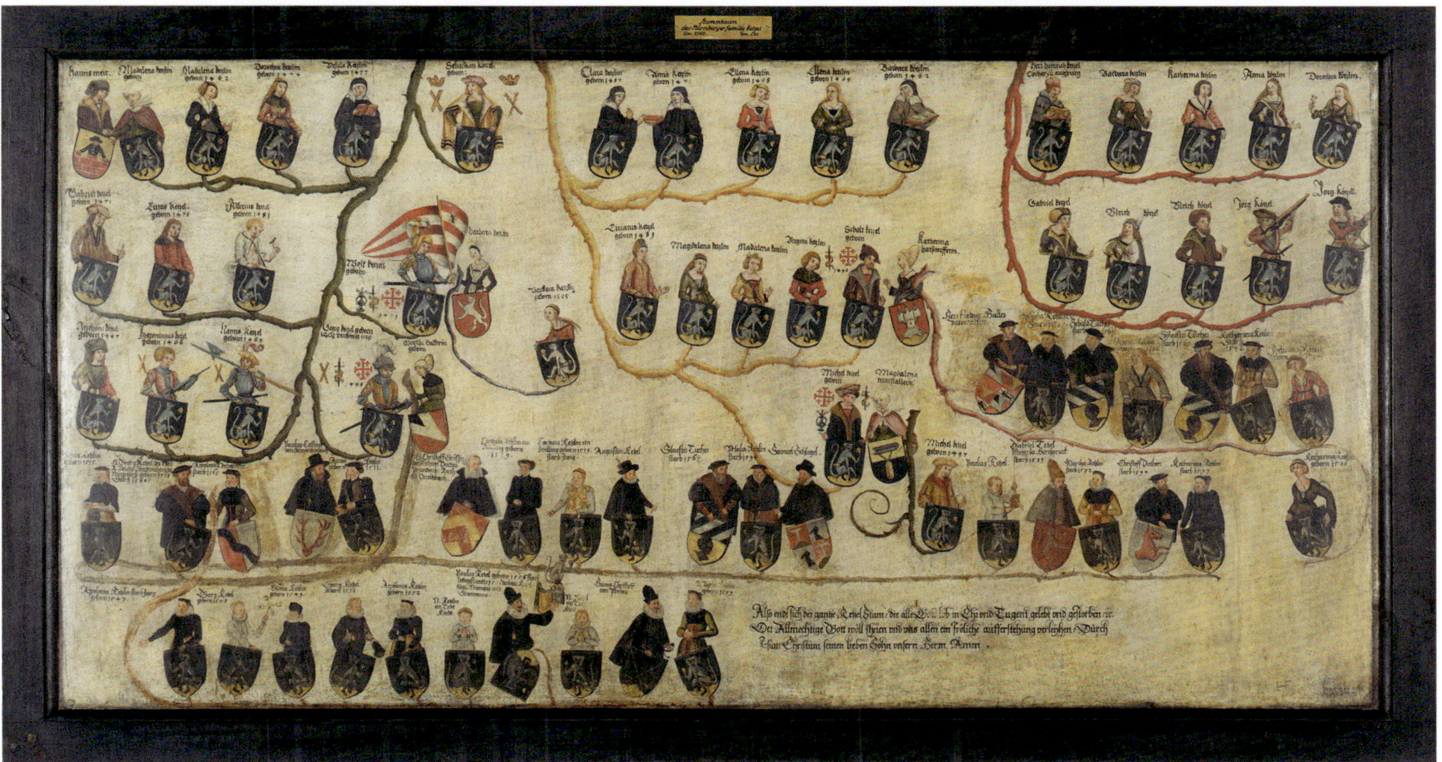

71

SAINTS CONSTANTINE AND HELENA WITH THE TRUE CROSS

Eastern Mediterranean region, late fourteenth or first half of the fifteenth century

Paint on limewood

H. 102 cm; W. 77 cm

GNM, inv. no. Gm507, on long-term loan from the Museen der Stadt Nürnberg, Kunstsammlungen

References:
Murr 1778, pp. 151–52; Timann 2005; Hess 2014, pp. 249–50, cat. no. 96, fig. 140; Heher 2018, p. 44; Exh. cat. Schallaburg 2018, p. 49, cat. no. 3.2, ill. p. 47 (Martina Horn).

This icon depicts Emperor Constantine and his mother, Empress Helena, holding the "True Cross" of Christ. According to legend, it was Helena who discovered the True Cross. In a departure from the usual pictorial type, this example includes a youthful figure of Christ blessing the two protagonists from above. Constantine and Helena wear crowns and imperial garments (*loroi*) and are accompanied by inscriptions in Greek. The panel's construction and the painting itself leave no doubt as to the provenance from the Byzantine cultural sphere. In its present condition, the painting shows several reworkings in the gold ground and garments. Originally, the garments' textures were more differentiated and the highlights were more pronounced. Yet the finely modeled faces are exceptionally well preserved. Overall, the figures must once have given an impression of greater magnificence. Details such as the slanting lower beam of the cross (in place of the suppedaneum) emerged in the late eleventh century but were most common in the fourteenth century.[1] The inspiration for the design and the inclusion of the Christ figure came directly from imperial portraits. A recently proposed alternative identification of the imperial pair as Constantine XI (r. 1448–53) and his mother, Helena (Jelena) Dragaš, is essentially based on a legend that traces back only to the eighteenth century.

The first documentation of the icon in Nuremberg is found in the *Hausbuch* of Anton Tucher II (1458–1524), the city's chief tax administrator (*Vorderster Losunger*): on April 18, 1517, Veit Stoss was commissioned to install this picture, with saints "portrayed from life" (*in irem leben abconttrafett*), in an "altar panel with wings and a superstructure" (*einczufassen in ein alltertafel mit flugeln und einem uberschwaiff*).[2] The painting could therefore have been set within a winged, retable-like enclosure made by Stoss. Traces left by nails at the top and bottom, visible in the X-radiograph, could conceivably be remnants of that mounting. The practice of incorporating old paintings (including miraculous images) into familiar altarpiece formats is known from a number of examples. This altarpiece was installed in the chapel of the Sebastianspital (Saint Sebastian Hospital) in Nuremberg.

After the chapel's destruction in 1552, the panel was moved to the Heilig-Geist-Spital (Holy Spirit Hospital). In 1778, Christoph Gottlieb von Murr cited an inscription formerly associated with the altarpiece, which gave the icon's place of origin as "Chettelin" (Mytilene on the island of Lesbos) and stated that the painting had been brought to Venice under highly adverse conditions. Earlier, in 1733 and 1757, both Johann Jacob Carbach and Andreas Würfel had also taken note of the same inscription. Close ties existed between Mytilene and Constantinople. Caterina Gattilusio, the second wife of Constantine XI, belonged to the Genoese dynasty that ruled Lesbos at the time. Recent considerations of the icon's portrait-related aspects and its potential origin in the Byzantine capital are informed by these connections. However, legends about the provenance of old paintings and icons are known to have proliferated in the eighteenth century. Ultimately, the figures on this panel bear only a vague resemblance to surviving portraits of Constantine XI and his mother Helena Dragaš. It remains unclear whether Anton Tucher acquired the icon himself or, as is often assumed, Hans Tucher VI (1428–1491) brought it back from his journey to the Holy Land (1479–80) |**see cat. no. 68**|. Venice is certainly possible as the place of acquisition, since according to fifteenth- and sixteenth-century sources the city served as a veritable entrepôt for the trade in icons.

Barbara Schellewald

1 See the wall paintings from about 1300 in the Church of the Apostles in Peć.
2 Loose 1877, pp. 143–44.

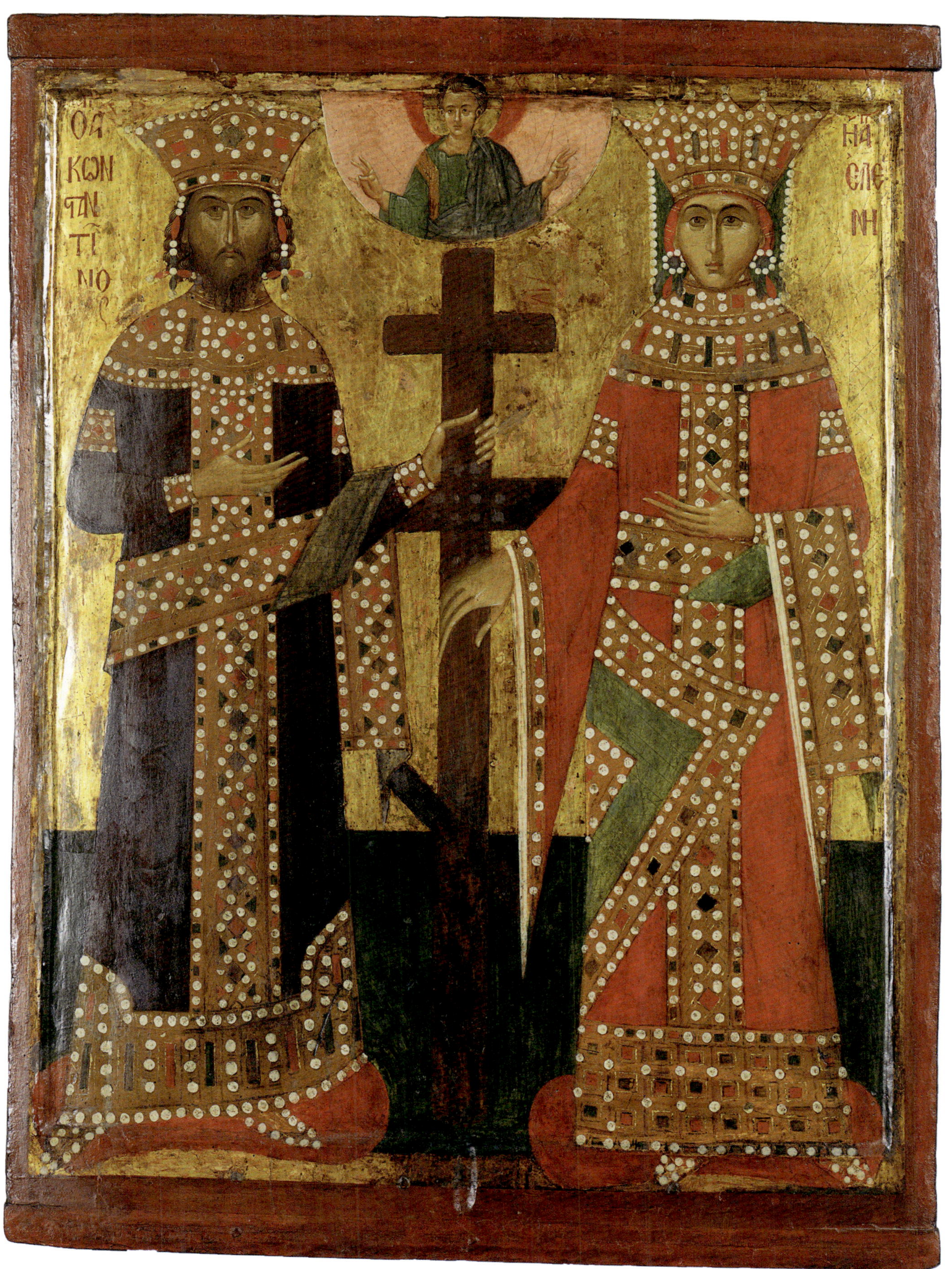

72

DIE GEYSTLICH STRASS (THE SPIRITUAL ROAD)

Nuremberg: Jobst Gutknecht, 1521

Post-incunable, forty unnumbered leaves, woodcut illustrations

H. 18.9 cm; W. 14.9 cm (book block)

GNM, shelf mark [Postinc.] 8° Rl. 3510 c

Open to the eleventh "walk" or chapter: *Der aylfft gang ist bis zum fall des herrn* (The eleventh walk proceeds to Christ's fall [under the cross])

References:
Strauss 1984, pp. 90–103; Freigang 2015, pp. 134–36; Kiening 2016, pp. 312–14.

If you feel like going to the Holy Land / You'll find what's there right here in your hand" (*Hastu lust zum heyligen landt / Was da sey findst auch zuhandt*). This little book, *Die geystlich straß* (The Spiritual Road), published in Nuremberg in 1521, invites readers to walk the path of Christ's sufferings from Bethany to the Holy Sepulchre, in a journey composed of images, prayers, and descriptions of places. The seventeen chapters (fifteen "walks," or *Gänge*, and two stations) are modeled on Stations of the Cross complexes from that period, which often consisted of wayside shrines displaying Passion scenes. These ensembles were meant to allow an experience of Jerusalem's Via Dolorosa close to home, often in distances matching those of the original. In Nuremberg, not many years before the publication of *Die geystlich straß*, an elaborate complex of stone Passion reliefs by Adam Kraft had been erected between the Tiergärtnertor and the Johannisfriedhof, and it surely provided inspiration for the book |**fig. p. 58**|.[1]

The multilayered purpose of this book is formulated on the above-cited title page and in a preface. The pictures and texts were intended to enable a mental pilgrimage and to serve the clergy in daily devotions. The book was also meant as a guide for "the wealthy" (fol. 2v) in setting up new Stations of the Cross ensembles or individual wayside shrines. At the same time, the text contains a critique of images that reflects the influence of Reformation thought, noting that such public images tempted some people simply to admire the workmanship of the sculptures without considering the content. Nevertheless, it is also pointed out that even some of the "common, simple folk" (fol. 1v) were moved to devout prayer by such images displayed in the streets. The woodcuts depict wayside shrines, thereby presenting the Passion scenes at a remove, so to speak–as pictures within pictures. This distancing fosters an inner experience of the Passion story.[2]

Each chapter consists of the same four or five elements: first, a woodcut of a wayside shrine depicting either one or three scenes from the Passion of Christ; second, an introduction to the meaning of each station; third, the corresponding Gospel text, if the scene is described in the Bible; fourth, psalms for prayers appropriate to the station; and fifth, a description of the Holy Land site, sometimes with remarks on other *loca sancta* (holy sites) in the vicinity. *Die geystlich straß* thus combines different genres of text–the personal devotional manual, the biblical source text, and the pilgrimage report–in order to serve its manifold purpose.[3]

The illustrations of wayside shrines were created by the Nuremberg printmaker Erhard Schön.[4] Although the book's author remains anonymous, and clues to his identity are lacking in the text, scholars have often identified him as Nikolaus Wanckel, a Franciscan who probably hailed from southern Germany. Wanckel's 1517 guide for pilgrims, *Ein kurtze vermerckung der heyligen Stet des heyligen landts* (A Brief Record of the Holy Sites in the Holy Land) (VD16: W 1169), was likewise published in Nuremberg by Jobst Gutknecht.[5]

Almost two dozen copies of *Die geystlich straß* have survived to this day. Because it was published at the advent of the Reformation, the book failed to fully realize its purpose of serving as a model for newly erected Stations of the Cross.

Florian Abe

1 See Exh. cat. Nuremberg 2018.
2 Freigang 2015, p. 135.
3 On this, see Kiening 2016, p. 314.
4 Each is printed from two blocks, one for the stand (H. 81–101 mm) and the other for the top part (H. 81–94; W. 57 mm). See Strauss 1984, pp. 90–103.
5 On Wanckel, see Herz 1999.

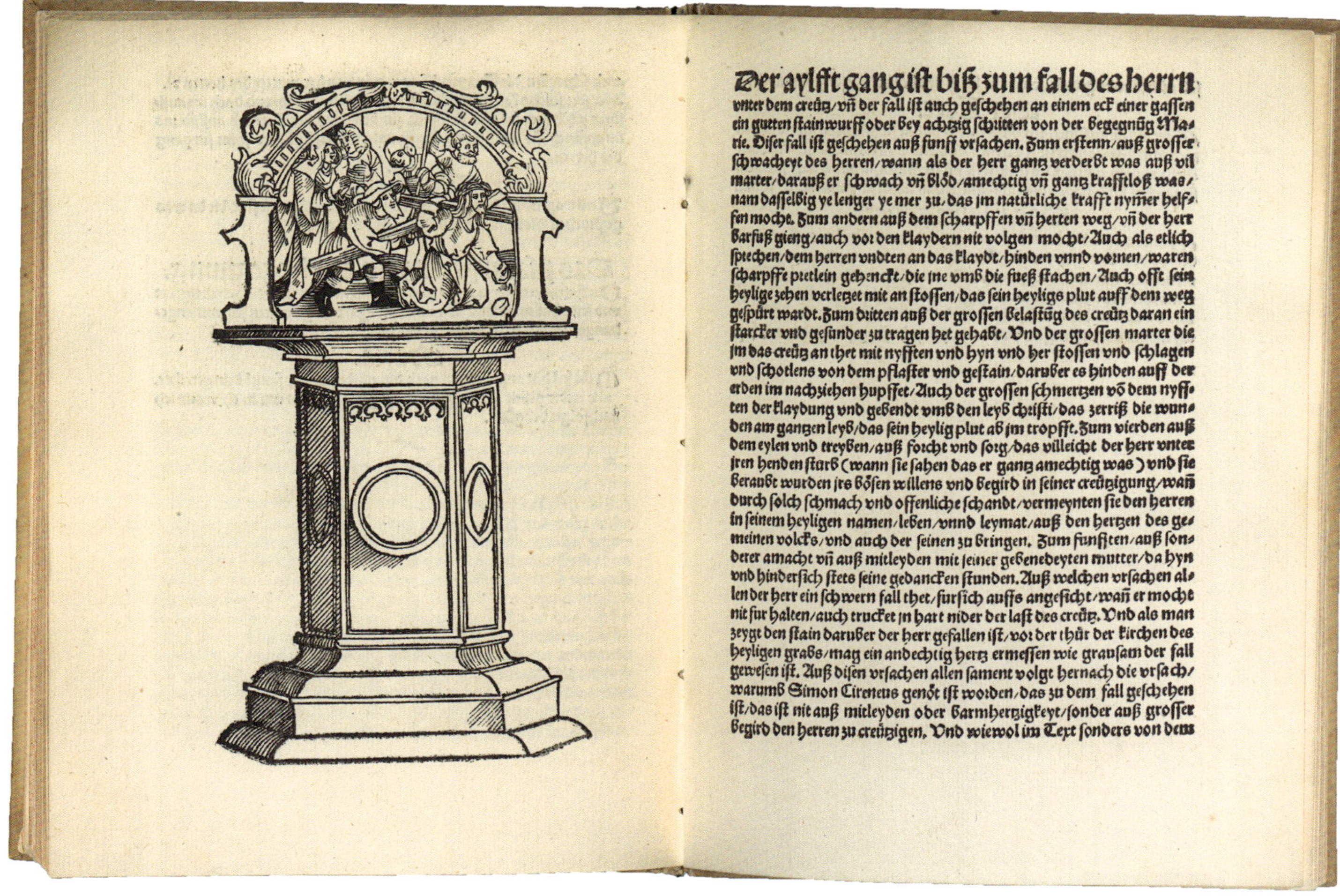

Der aylfft gang ist biß zum fall des herrn

vnter dem creütz/vñ der fall ist auch geschehen an einem eck einer gassen
ein gutten stainwurff oder bey achtzig schritten von der begegnüg Marie. Diser fall ist geschehen auß funff vrsachen. Zum erstenn/auß grosser
schwacheyt des herren/wann als der herr gantz verderbt was auß vil
marter/darauß er schwach vñ blöd/amechtig vñ gantz krafftloß was/
nam dasselbig ye lenger ye mer zu/das im natürliche krafft nym̄er helf-
fen mocht. Zum andern auß dem scharpffen vñ herten weg/vñ der herr
barfuß gieng/auch vor den klaydern nit volgen mocht/Auch als etlich
sprechen/dem herren vndten an das klaydt/hinden vnnd vornen/waren
scharpffe pretlein gehenckt/die jne vmb die fueß stachen/Auch offt sein
heylige zehen verletzet mit an stossen/das sein heyligs plut auff dem weg
gespürt wardt. Zum dritten auß der grossen belastūg des creütz daran ein
starcker vnd gesünder zu tragen het gehabt/Vnd der grossen marter die
jm das creütz an thet mit nyfften vnd hyn vnd her stossen vnd schlagen
vnd schotlens von dem pflaster vnd gestain/daruber es hinden auff der
erden im nachziehen hupffet/Auch der grossen schmertzen vō dem nyfften der klaydung vnd gebendt vmb den leyb christi/das zerriß die wun-
den am gantzen leyb/das sein heylig plut ab jm tropfft. Zum vierden auß
dem eylen vnd treyben/auß forcht vnd sorg/das villeicht der herr vnter
jren henden sturb (wann sie sahen das er gantz amechtig was) vnd sie
beraubt wurden jrs bösen willens vnd begird in seiner creützigung/wañ
durch solch schmach vnd offenliche schandt/vermeynten sie den herren
in seinem heyligen namen/leben/vnnd leymat/auß den hertzen des gemeinen volcks/vnd auch der seinen zu bringen. Zum funfften/auß sonderer amacht vñ auß mitleyden mit seiner gebenedeyten mutter/da hyn
vnd hindersich stets seine gedancken stunden. Auß welchen vrsachen allen der herr ein schwern fall thet/fursich auffs angesicht/wañ er mocht
nit fur halten/auch trucket jn hart nider der last des creütz. Vnd als man
zeygt den stain daruber der herr gefallen ist/vor der thür der kirchen des
heyligen grabs/mag ein andechtig hertz ermessen wie grausam der fall
gewesen ist. Auß disen vrsachen allen sament volgt hernach die vrsach/
warumb Simon Cireneus genöt ist worden/das zu dem fall geschehen
ist/das ist nit auß mitleyden oder barmhertzigkeyt/sonder auß grosser
begird den herren zu creützigen. Vnd wiewol im Text sonders von dem

73

CHRIST ON A "PALM DONKEY" (*PALMESEL*)

Nuremberg, ca. 1370–80

Alder (sculpture), willow (base), parts of the figure reconstructed, original polychromy

H. 172.5 cm; L. 169 cm; W. 61.5 cm

GNM, inv. no. Pl.O.153, on long-term loan from the Museen der Stadt Nürnberg, Kunstsammlungen

References:
Hess et al. 2007, p. 434, cat. no. 460, fig. 455; Lutz 2007, p. 340; Brückner 2010, pp. 43–44; Harris 2019, pp. 178–79; Juckes 2021, pp. 177–78.

A total of four medieval *Palmesel*, or "palm donkeys," are now in the collections of the Germanisches Nationalmuseum.[1] The term *Palmesel* derives from Christ's ride into Jerusalem on the back a donkey, greeted by a crowd waving palm fronds. Tradition holds that the event to which the sculpture group refers, which is depicted in all four Gospels, took place five days before the Crucifixion (Good Friday).[2] The existence of such sculptures in several Nuremberg churches is corroborated by written sources.[3] The present example, which dates from the second half of the fourteenth century, very likely came from a church in Nuremberg. It was first documented as part of the municipal art collections housed in the town hall. From there, it was transferred to the museum in 1872, on long-term loan from the city.

The sculpture is just under life-size. Christ sits bolt upright on the back of the donkey. His right hand is raised in a gesture of blessing. The object he once held in his left hand, presumably a palm frond or the reins of the donkey's bridle, is missing. He faces forward, in a strict frontal posture. At the same time, the supple forms of his facial features convey a sense of vitality. The drapery folds of the red robe and golden mantle, lined with blue, are carved with great care. Although the original polychromy was uncovered in 1948–49, the former vibrancy of the colors and subtlety of the flesh tones, which imbued the figure with a lifelike quality, can only be guessed at today.

As noted, the sculpture refers to Christ's entry into Jerusalem in the time leading up to his crucifixion and subsequent resurrection. The event is described in all four Gospels. As the historical site of Christ's Passion, Jerusalem was one of the most important pilgrimage destinations in Christendom. Numerous pilgrims from Nuremberg were among those who made the journey to see the holy sites with their own eyes |**cat. nos. 68, 70**|.[4] Also, in Nuremberg and many other places in medieval and early modern Europe, efforts were made to project the places and events of the Passion onto local cityscapes. This was a way enabling those who could not travel to Jerusalem to experience the Passion of Christ. Cities such as Nuremberg were "sacralized" by establishing local parallels with the Holy City. Well-known examples from Nuremberg are Adam Kraft's Stations of the Cross and the monumental Agony in the Garden scenes |**cat. no. 74**| that were erected outside a number of churches. The *Palmesel* sculptures served the same purpose of making the Passion feel present: the platform on which this example is mounted once had wheels, which made it possible to set the sculpture in motion during liturgical celebrations, thereby activating it.[5] This type of use of a sculpted object not only rendered the story of the Passion more comprehensible to viewers; it also allowed people to experience the events as reenacted in the present. In Nuremberg, as elsewhere, *Palmesel* sculptures like this one were processed through the streets during Palm Sunday celebrations that commemorated Christ's entry into Jerusalem.

Sven Jakstat

1 Apart from the present example, see inv. nos. Pl.O.152 (currently on loan to the Stadtkirche, Hersbruck), Pl.O.154, and Pl.O.1875.
2 Matt. 21:1–11; Mark 11:1–10; Luke 19:29–39; John 12:12–19.
3 The sources refer to examples in the Sebalduskirche and Lorenzkirche (1831), the Frauenkirche (1442), and the Katharinenkirche (1436). See Juckes 2021, p. 192, n. 3.
4 On this, see the essay by Florian Abe in the present volume.
5 On this type of sculpture and its use, see Tripps 2000, pp. 95–121; Kunz 2019, pp. 141–42. On the use of a *Palmesel* on Palm Sunday in Nuremberg's Lorenzkirche, see Juckes 2019, p. 177.

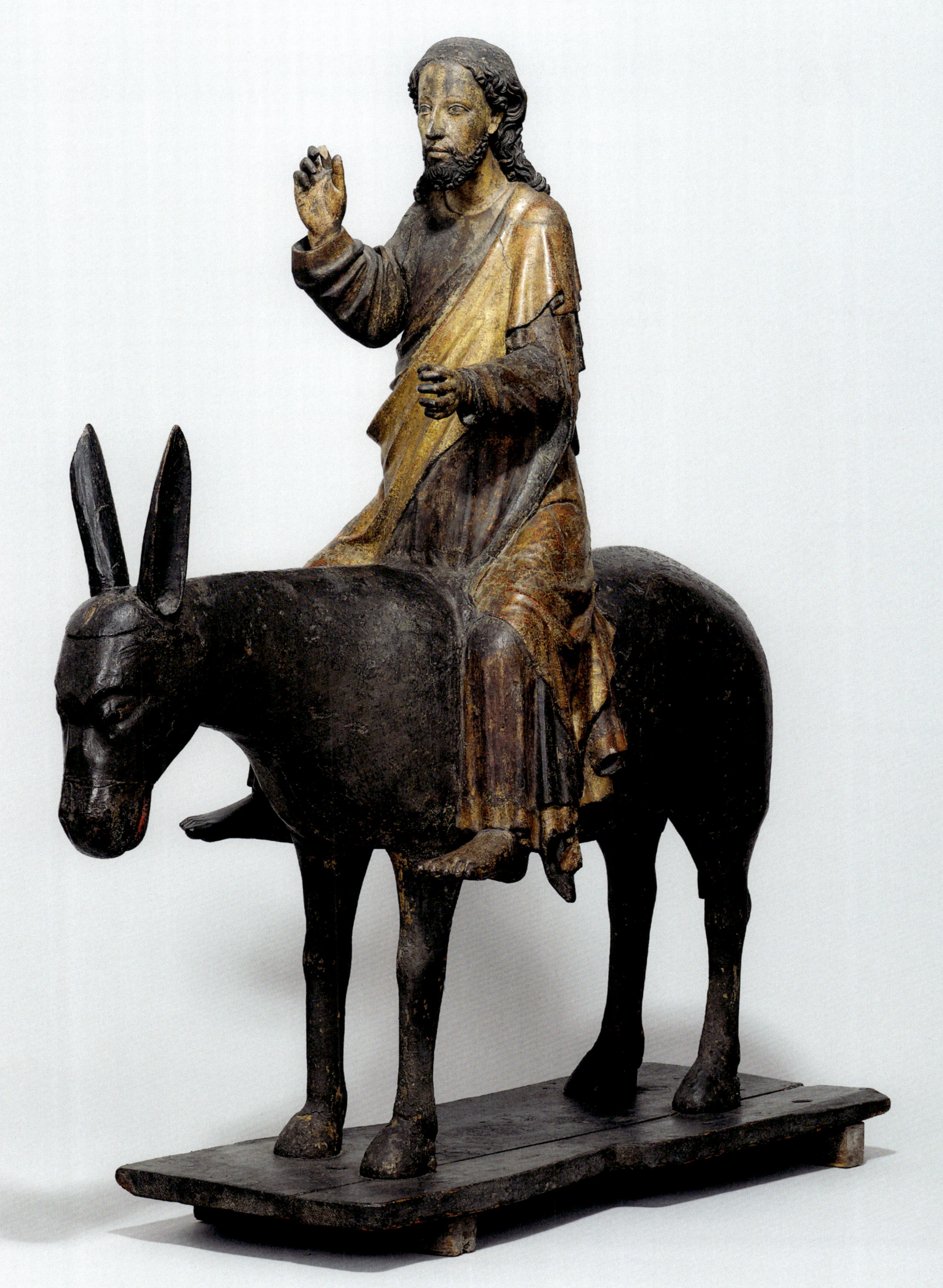

74

THE AGONY IN THE GARDEN, FROM THE KLARAKIRCHE IN NUREMBERG

Workshop or circle of Adam Kraft

Nuremberg, ca. 1500/1505

Sandstone

74.1 Saint Peter

Broken into two pieces

H. 84 cm; W. 74 cm; D. 55 cm

GNM, inv. no. Pl.O.2312

74.2 Saint John

Broken into three pieces

H. 55 cm; W. 120 cm; D. 44 cm

GNM, inv. no. Pl.O.2311

74.4 Saint James

H. 93 cm; W. 60 cm; D. 50 cm

GNM, inv. no. Pl.O.2313

74.4 Christ

Hands reconstructed in plaster, nineteenth century

H. 141 cm; W. 83 cm; D. 50 cm

GNM, inv. no. Pl.O.2310

74.5 God the Father

Germanisches Nationalmuseum, on long-term loan from the Katholische Kirchenstiftung Unsere Liebe Frau, Nuremberg

References:
Stern 1916, p. 154; Schulz 1924; Exh. cat. Nuremberg 2007, pp. 82–86, cat. no. 8 (Frank Matthias Kammel).

Ever since late antiquity, Christians had cultivated the desire to visit the authentic sites of Jesus's ministry. Yet only a small, elite section of society ever had the means or opportunities to travel to the Holy Land. This meant that acquiring the religious indulgences associated with such a journey—thus reducing one's temporal punishment for sins (time spent in Purgatory)—was out of reach for most people. That situation soon gave rise to the idea of replicating faraway sacred sites locally, as a way of providing nearby substitutes for the experience of Holy Land pilgrimage.

Such substitutes included representations of the *Agony in the Garden* (Christ's prayer at the Mount of Olives). Usually displayed on church exteriors, scenes of the Agony in the Garden comprised such types of works as small-scale relief sculptures, mural paintings (sometimes covering large areas of wall), and even life-size sculptural groups installed in chapel-like architectural settings. In the fifteenth century, a number of large-scale portrayals of the subject were sculpted in stone in Nuremberg and its environs.

The present five sculptures come from the *Agony in the Garden* made for Nuremberg's Klarakirche. Long-standing scholarly consensus places this group in close proximity to the work of Adam Kraft, the leading stone sculptor in Nuremberg in the period around 1500.[1] Nevertheless, based on the sculptures' appearance alone, it is impossible to determine whether they were created by a member of Kraft's workshop or by an independent sculptor who had trained under the master. The group was installed on the southern side of the chancel's exterior and thus belonged to the space of the cemetery. In that location, it was meant to encourage pious reflection on the finite nature of life and to vicariously experience the agony that Christ suffered on the Mount of Olives | **see cat. no. 44** |.[2] According to the Gospels,[3] this episode of the Passion took place in the evening of Maundy Thursday, after the Last Supper. Christ

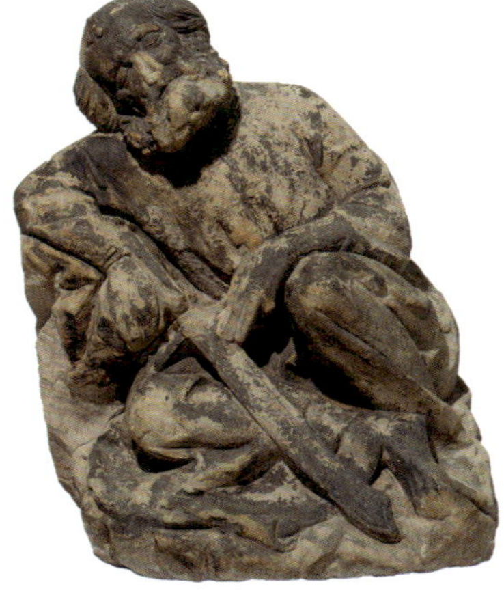

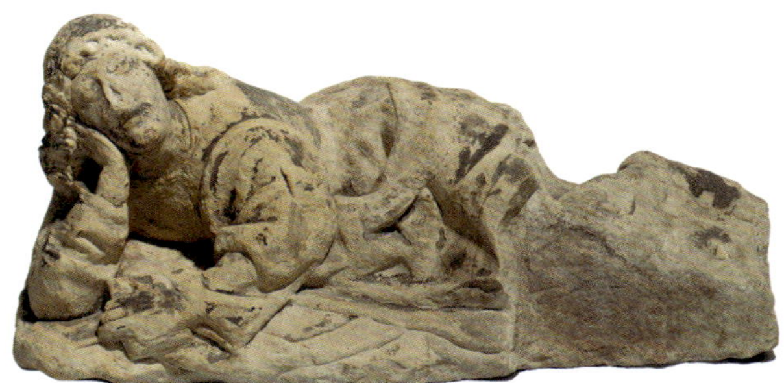

From left to right cat. nos. 74.1–5

1 Stern 1916, p. 154; Schulz 1924, esp. p. 37; Exh. cat. Nuremberg 2007, pp. 82–86, cat. no. 8, esp. p. 84 (Frank Matthias Kammel).
2 Kahsnitz 1983, pp. 218–58, cat. no. 20 (Rainer Kahsnitz); Exh. cat. Nuremberg 2007, pp. 82–86, cat. no. 8 (Frank Matthias Kammel).

is shown gripped with agony over the cruel fate that awaits him. He pleads with God the Father, who is shown in half-length, emerging from a cloud and making a gesture of blessing in reaffirmation of his will. Christ accepts his destiny: to reconcile humanity with God through his own sacrificial death, thus providing redemption from original sin. Meanwhile, Saints John, Peter, and James, the disciples who had accompanied Christ to watch and pray with him, are lost in sleep.

The site of this occurrence, the Garden of Gethsemane, was known to all who traveled to Jerusalem. It was an essential stop on tours lead by friars from the Franciscan monastery at Mount Zion, the institution entrusted with the care of pilgrims. The garden is located at the foot of the Mount of Olives, east of the Jerusalem's Old City, across the Kidron Valley. After exiting the city through the Lion's Gate, one can reach the garden in a matter of minutes. In the Nuremberg sculptural group, the rough stone slabs supporting the figures of Jesus and the disciples give some suggestion of the rocky terrain of the Mount of Olives. The exposed knee of Christ is particularly noteworthy. According to Ute Verstegen, this motif could refer to a story that was told to pilgrims about the Garden of Gethsemane, namely that certain indentations found in the rock there were left by Christ's knees.[4]

These five stone sculptures are the only remaining parts of the Klarakirche's *Agony in the Garden*. It is therefore unknown whether the next episode in the story, the Arrest of Christ, was alluded to with an approaching group of henchmen led by Judas, as is typical for this subject matter. The surviving sculptures are heavily weathered and show signs of vandalism. The noses have been knocked off, apparently with the intention of disfiguring the faces. The present condition allows only a general idea of the former quality of the workmanship.

Markus T. Huber

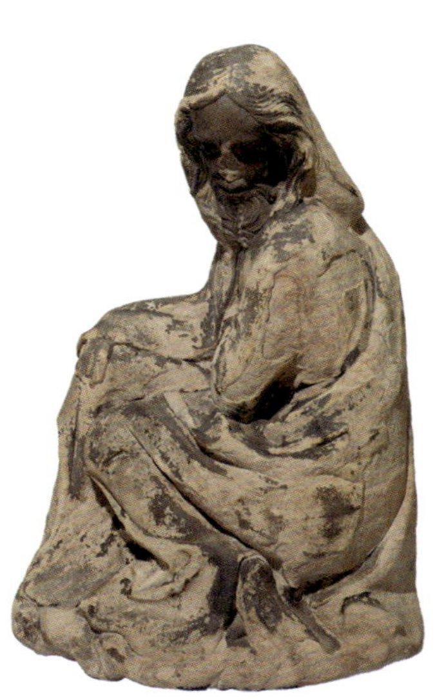

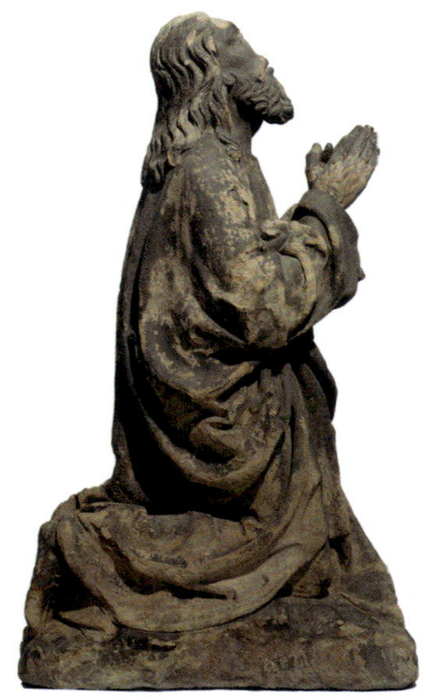

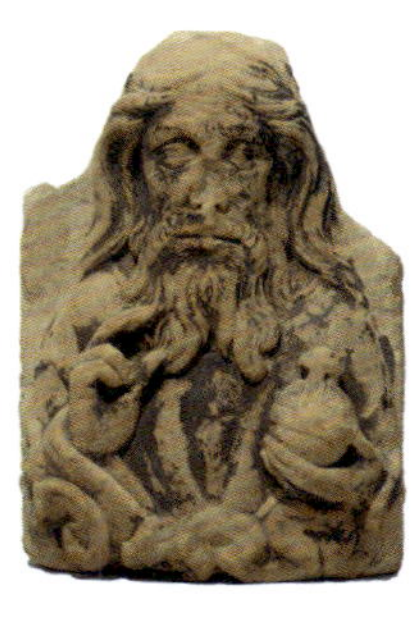

3 Matt. 26:36–46, Mark 14:32–42, Luke 22:39–46, John 18:1–2.
4 Noted by Ute Verstegen in a lecture held at the thirty-seventh German Congress for Art History, Erlangen, March 3, 2024.

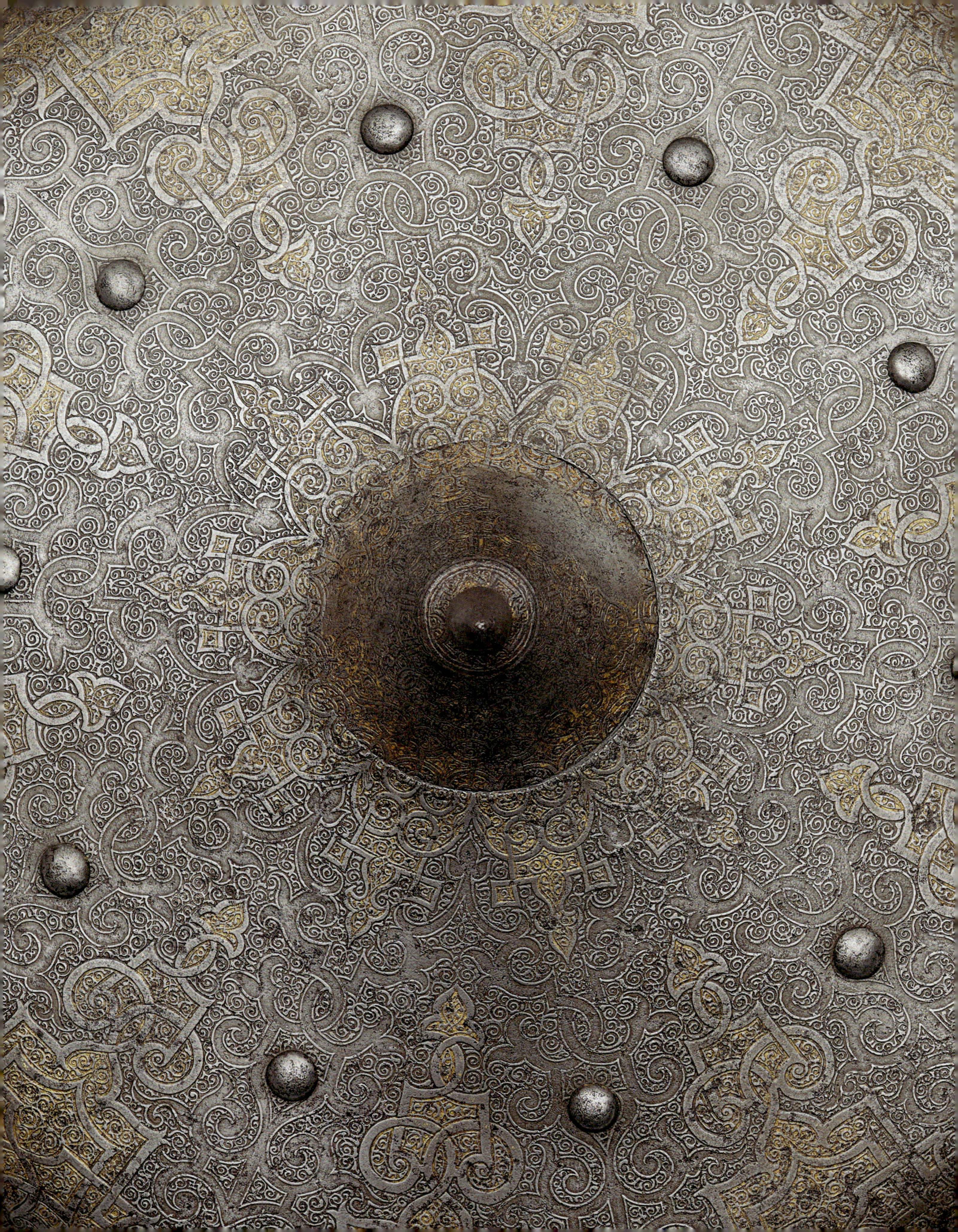

OTTOMAN AFFAIRS

With the conquest of Constantinople by Sultan Mehmed II in 1453, the Ottoman Empire became a major actor on the stage of European power. In Nuremberg, the expansion pursued by the new superpower was followed with close attention. The siege of Vienna by Ottoman troops in 1529 marked a decisive juncture for the Holy Roman Empire and its monarch.

Ottoman expansionism was a source of great fear in central Europe. Nuremberg supported the Habsburg war against the Ottoman Empire by contributing soldiers, weapons, and payment of the "Turkish tax." Printers in Nuremberg found a ready market for news reports and propagandistic broadsheets that accused the Ottoman army of committing unilateral atrocities. These publications employed pictorial mechanisms that remain in use today in comparable ways.

Despite the feelings of hostility that were being fomented, many Nurembergers had a deep fascination with Ottoman culture, as attested by numerous writings and artifacts. The travelogues of prisoners of war and diplomats from Nuremberg fostered interest in the lands of the Ottoman Empire and their inhabitants. Ottoman works of decorative art, textiles, and weapons found their way to Nuremberg, while goldsmiths' works and clocks made in the city were presented as diplomatic gifts at the Sublime Porte, the seat of Ottoman government in Constantinople.

Benno Baumbauer

◂ cat. no. 91 (detail)

75

PORTRAIT OF SEBALD SCHIRMER, MILITARY COMMANDER IN NUREMBERG

Georg Pencz

Nuremberg, 1545

Paint on limewood

H. 123.8 cm; W. 96 cm

GNM, inv. no. Gm206, on long-term loan from the Museen der Stadt Nürnberg, Kunstsammlungen

References:
Löcher 1997, pp. 397–400; Hauschild 2004, pp. 105–14; Exh. cat. Nuremberg 2004, pp. 158–59 (Daniel Hess); Hirschfelder 2010, p. 248; Dyballa, 2014, pp. 305–8.

Sebald Schirmer bore brave arms for the celebrated hometown, attacking the Turks and the margravial troops. This man's spirited features were captured in portrait by Pencz, incomparable in the art of design. But the artist donated this likeness to the city, which is well aware of his loyalty in heart, blood, and hand. He wishes the city felicitous times of peace, or else successful leaders in righteous wars."[1]

This Latin inscription on the frame of Georg Pencz's large-scale portrait of the military commander Sebald Schirmer (1501–1560) points out the merit demonstrated by the sitter in war, including against the Ottomans. The painting shows Schirmer, a *Feldhauptmann* (literally, "field captain"), in three-quarter length, seated in front of a wall niche, confidently posed and dressed in a suit of armor. Like other works by Pencz (d. 1550), this portrait is heavily influenced by Italian pictorial traditions. While that would seem to suggest that the artist spent time in Italy, there is no documentary evidence of any such trip.[2] Pencz made a deliberate display of his painterly skill by including a reflection of Schirmer's head in profile on the helmet.[3]

The portrait has the character of a monument to Schirmer as a war commander in service to the city of Nuremberg. The city council called upon him for military service several times from 1534 onward. He led a company of soldiers in Emperor Ferdinand I's war against the Ottomans at Buda.[4] Later, he fought in the Second Margrave War and commanded the Nuremberg garrison at Plassenburg Castle near Kulmbach.

Although Schirmer came into conflict with the city council over his fondness for drunken revelry, he otherwise seems to have been held in high esteem. In the portrait, Schirmer's monumental bearing and other elements of the picture emphasize his importance. On his left hand, he wears a signet ring marked with his initials and coat of arms, showing the profile head of a Black man with a headband. The same heraldic motif appears in the relief decorating the pilaster at the right. It is unknown how Schirmer gained the right to bear a coat of arms—perhaps as an honor for military service, but that remains unproven.

In any case, Schirmer's reputation as a fighter against the Ottomans lingered long after his passing. His death in 1560 was surrounded by a legend that cast him as a long-suffering war hero: he was said to have died from an operation to remove an Ottoman bullet that had been lodged in this thigh since 1534.[5]

By commissioning his portrait, Schirmer allotted himself a position of prominence in Nuremberg society. According to the inscription on the frame, the painter gifted the work to the city council. It received a place of honor in the town hall, initially in the so-called Beautiful Hall (*Schöner Saal*). In 1711, it is mentioned by Georg Jacob Lang among the furnishings of the "Corner Parlor" (*Eckstube*).[6]

With this portrait, the city council added to its gallery the likeness of a distinguished military commander dressed in armor, a subject matter that had previously been customary mainly in Italy.[7] By hanging such a portrait, Nuremberg presented itself as a city capable of self-defense. Nuremberg provided both financial and military support to the campaigns against the Ottomans. Even the 1529 siege of Vienna involved troops from Nuremberg |**see cat. no. 76**|.

Marie-Therese Feist

1 For transcriptions of the Latin original and German translations, see Löcher 1997, p. 397; Gmelin 1961.
2 Dyballa 2014, p. 79.
3 Hauschild 2004.
4 Müllner 2003, p. 665.
5 Gmelin 1961, p. 98. The unverifiable legend is recorded in a handwritten note made in a copy of Johann Gabriel Doppelmayr's *Historische Nachricht von den Nürnbergischen Mathematicis und Künstlern* (Nuremberg, 1730), p. 197, n. dd.
6 Georg Jacob Lang, *Ausführliche Beschreibung aller auf dem Rathaus in den obern schönen Zimmern befindlicher gross- und kleinen Gemälden*, 1711. Transcription in Mummenhoff 1891, pp. 290–94, with the passage in question on p. 290.
7 Löcher 1997, p. 398.

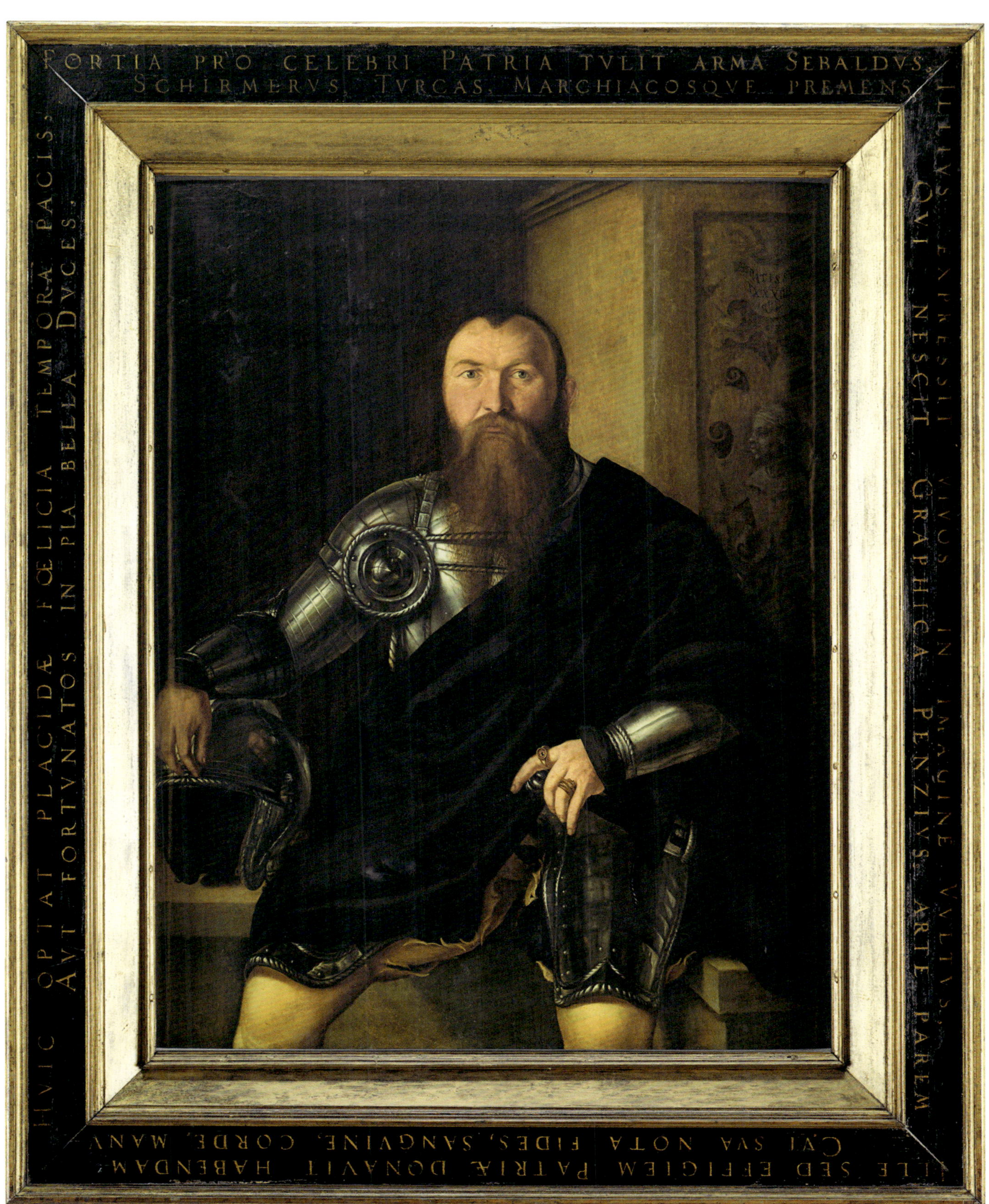

FORTIA PRO CELEBRI PATRIA TVLIT ARMA SEBALDVS,
SCHIRMERVS, TVRCAS, MARCHIACOSQVE PREMENS
ILLIVS ENPRESSIT VIVOS IN IMAGINE VVLTVS,
QVI NESCIT GRAPHICA PENZIVS ARTE PAREM
ILLE SED EFFIGIEM PATRIÆ DONAVIT HABENDAM:
CVI SVA NOTA FIDES, SANGVINE, CORDE, MANV
HVIC OPTAT PLACIDÆ FŒLICIA TEMPORA PACIS,
AVT FORTVNATOS IN PIA BELLA DVCES.

76

THE SIEGE OF VIENNA ("THE MELDEMANN MAP")

Sebald Beham (design)

Nuremberg: Nicolaus Meldemann, 1530

Woodcut from six blocks, the segment at the lower right partially hand-colored in green

H. 80 cm; W. 86 cm

Albertina, Vienna, inv. no. DG1960/1197

References: Timann 1993, pp. 120–47; Exh. cat. Tübingen 2014, pp. 384–85, cat. no. 166 (Christine Bozler); Opll and Scheutz 2020.

The so-called Meldemann Map, a view of Vienna in circular form named after its compiler and publisher, Nicolaus Meldemann, is one of the most prominent pictorial records of the 1529 Ottoman siege of the city. It is a monumental woodcut, comprising six sheets. As a panoramic view of a historical event in roundel form, with Saint Stephen's Cathedral at the center, this work is remarkable in design. The city itself, reduced to the main architectural landmarks, forms the core of the representation. The all-embracing character of the image reflects the comprehensive nature of the siege itself. Numerous attack and battle scenes, sometimes gruesome in detail, encircle the beleaguered city.

Much more than a mere record of topographical and documentary information, Meldemann's map presents a political message. The coats of arms of Hungary, Bohemia, Austria, Vienna, and Nuremberg are arranged around the city. The relationship between Nuremberg and the Holy Roman Emperor had become heavily strained following the official introduction of the Lutheran Reformation in Nuremberg. As noted by Antonia Landois: "In the period of confessional rupture, one's position with regard to the *Türkengefahr* [Turkish threat] ... took on special significance."[1] Nuremberg distinguished itself as one of the most important centers of printing and news distribution, producing a particularly large number of "Turkish prints" that propagated the unity of Christendom against the so-called *Erbfeind* (eternal enemy). But in addition, unlike other imperial cities, Nuremberg made a decisive military contribution to the Habsburg conflict with the Ottomans in Hungary and Austria, actively supporting the defense of Vienna by supplying personnel in the form of landsknechts and weapons.[2]

Soon after news of the siege's end reached Nuremberg, the city council granted the illuminator and publisher Nicolaus Meldemann exclusive printing rights to a pictorial representation of the events. Also, the council supported the project's completion with a loan of fifty guldens.[3] On April 30, 1530, the council noted the receipt of a "portrayal of the siege (neatly colored),"[4] presumably a hand-colored impression.[5] In a dedicatory pamphlet addressed to the council, Meldemann explains the work's elaborate process of creation and manner of representation.[6] Once the siege was over, he had departed Nuremberg for Vienna to conduct research, so as to base his print on sources that were as authentic as possible. In addition to using a detailed report by the war secretary Peter Stern von Labach, which Meldemann later revised and published,[7] he availed himself of drawings by a "famous painter in Vienna."[8] As Meldemann notes, the unnamed artist had witnessed the siege from an elevated vantage point in Saint Stephen's Cathedral. The map's circular layout provides a comprehensive view of events as observed from the center. Scholarship has long regarded Sebald Beham of Nuremberg as the artist who provided the drawing for the woodcut.[9] Ursula Timann has proposed Jacob Seisenegger as the creator of the prototypes. Among the influences that underlie the map's circular form, a city map of global character may well have played a role—namely, the representation of the Aztec capital of Tenochtitlán that was published by Friedrich Peypus in Nuremberg in 1524, showing the city arranged around a religious center |**cat. no. 105**|. Presumably, Meldemann was familiar with that woodcut.[10]

Marie-Therese Feist

1 Landois 2020, p. 170.
2 Landois 2020, p. 171.
3 The official financial backer was the municipal scribe Lazarus Spengler. See Timann 2020, p. 62.
4 Timann 2020, p. 63: "contrafacten belegerung (sauber ausgestrichen)."
5 Also mentioned are seven impressions meant for members of the privy council (the Ältere Herren). The only fully hand-colored impression to survive is at the Wien Museum, Vienna, inv. no. 48068.
6 Timann 2020, p. 64.
7 Stern von Labach and Meldemann 1530.
8 Nicolaus Meldemann, *Ein kurtzer bericht vber ... belegerung der Stat Wien* [Nuremberg, 1530], sig. A1r: "ein berümbter Maler zu Wien." Copies available at the Österreichische Nationalbibliothek, Vienna, shelf mark 64.H.29.(10); Bayerische Staatsbibliothek, Munich, shelf mark Res 4°Turc 81/23.
9 Timann 2020, esp. from p. 78 onward. The attribution to Beham first appeared in Röttinger 1921, p. 6.
10 Timann 1993, p. 141.

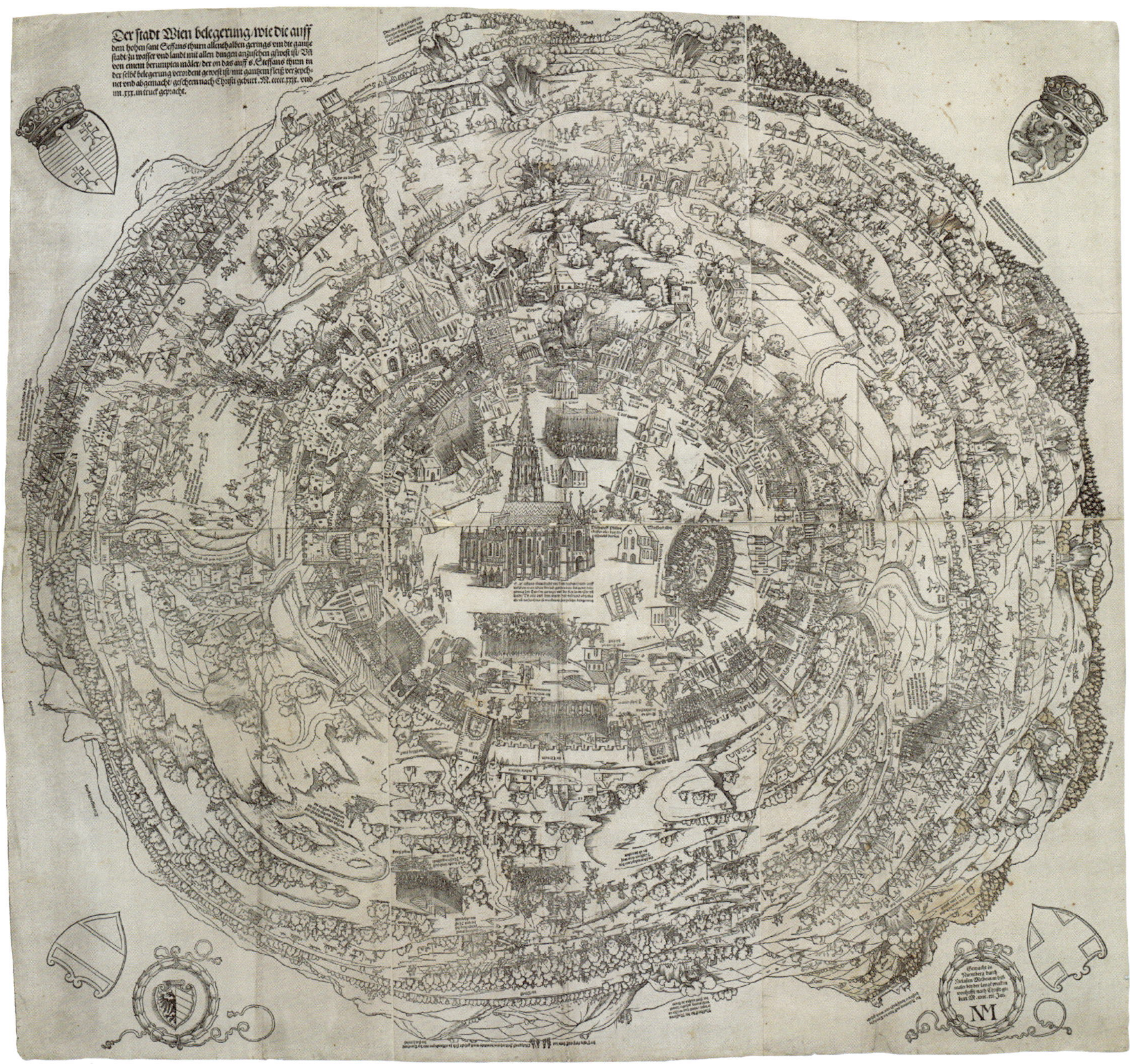
Der stadt Wien belegerung/wie die auff
dem hohen sant Steffans thurn allenthalben gerings vm die gantze
stadt/zu wasser vnd landt mit allen dingen anzusehen gwest ist/ Vñ
von einem berumpten måler/der on das auff s. Steffans thurn in
der selbē belegerung verordent gewest ist/mit gantzem fleiß verzeychnet vnd abgemacht/geschehen nach Christi geburt. M. cccc. xxix. vnd
im. xxx. in truck gepracht.

77

MAMLUK ON A DROMEDARY

Attributed to **Erhard Schön** (design)
Text by **Hans Sachs**
Nuremberg: Hans Guldenmund, 1530

Woodcut, hand-colored, letterpress text

H. 37.4 cm; W 26.7 cm

Stiftung Schloss Friedenstein, Gotha, inv. no. 49,5

References:
Hollstein German 47, p. 19, no. 146 (Ursula Mielke); Exh. cat. Brussels and Kraków 2015, p. 216, cat. no. 117 (Robert Born); Schäfer, Eydinger, and Rekow 2016, pp. 92–93, cat. no. 166 (Matthias Rekow).

This hand-colored woodcut depicting an Ottoman military slave riding a dromedary belongs to a series of fifteen illustrated broadsheets that were published in Nuremberg by Hans Guldenmund (d. 1560) beginning in 1529.[1] The series deals with various aspects of the siege of Vienna by Ottoman troops that same year, an attack that was successfully repelled by Habsburg forces |**see cat. no. 76**|. Some of the broadsheets, in propagandistic fashion, portray the Ottoman army committing horrific acts of violence against the civilian population. Others are devoted to recording the structure of the enemy military, presenting its most important personages and units. This reflects a cultural-anthropological interest, on the part of the broadsheets' audience, in the organization, physical appearance, costumes, and customs of the Ottomans.[2]

The print depicting a "Mammaluck"—as the rider is identified in the print's rhyming couplets at the upper right—testifies to a special fascination for the dromedary, an animal that would certainly have been regarded as a curiosity in Nuremberg. Both the poem and the prose text printed along the top deal mainly with this animal, focusing on its behavior and usefulness to humans. The text at the top is a discussion of camels taken from Pliny the Elder's (d. AD 79) *Natural History*, which emphasizes the utility of female dromedaries in war. The poem's twelve verses address the Ottoman army's use of the animal, "Which carries the Turk into battle / Along with his weapons of war." In fact, the Nuremberg landsknechts who participated in the defense of Vienna brought back a camel as a trophy. It was made available for viewing at the printshop of Hans Guldenmund for the price of three pfennigs.[3] This broadsheet thus disseminated knowledge based on ancient writings about an animal that in Nuremberg was highly unusual and deeply fascinating—an animal that at the time of publication was present in the city in a single specimen. This made more tangible the reality of distant places that seemed to be edging ever closer.

Laura Di Carlo

1 See Hollstein German 47, p. 18, no. 146 (Ursula Mielke).
2 See Exh. cat. Brussels and Kraków 2015, p. 216, cat. no. 117 (Robert Born).
3 See Schäfer, Eydinger, and Rekow 2016, p. 93, cat. no. 166 (Matthias Rekow).

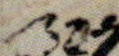

¶ Plinius spricht/Eyn Camel ist eyn vngeschaffen thier/hochfertig /hat eynen langen halß/knörichte payn/vnnd eyn langsamen gang /ist vast eyn
vnreyn thier. Soman sie will ladē/schlecht man sie eyn wenig auff die knye/als bald neygt es sich zů der pürd mit dem halß vñ dem rück. Es trinckt
nicht geren lauter wasser / aber das trüb/von seyner narung wegen. So es zürnet/zanklafft es grausamlich /das es etwan auch vnsinnig wirt/vnd ge-
wint das Podogra oder Zypperla /darvon sie leychtlich sterben. Mit grossen schmertzen sind sie bekümert/so sie lange herte weg gehen. Gersten essen
sie geytzig vnnd gantz / damit sie am widerdewen die nacht zů essen haben. Das recht Camel hat eyn hoger auff dem rücken. Aber es ist noch eyn ge-
schlecht/das man nennet Dromedarios/sind stercker/vnd eyns schnellern lauffs / die haben auch zwey hörner auff dem rück/Die weybleyn aber sind
besser in krieg/dann die mendleyn. Vnd so man sie verschneydet/werden sie nicht fayst. So sie eyn weg eyn mal sind gangen /den wissen sie wider / ob
er gleych vom windt mit santt oder schnee verworffen were. Das Camel geht alle drey Jar eyns in die prunst/dann ist es gar böß gegen den mensch-
en vnnd dem viech doch schont es seyner mütter / die berürts nicht / wie andere thier. Es tregt seyn frucht eyn jar lang/Vnd vier tag mag es on trunck-
en seyn/ Vnd leben lang/Biß in hundert jar/so sie nicht verwarlost werden. Vñ ye jünger die Camel sind /ye gröber vnnd zotteter/ye älter ye liechter
sie werden.

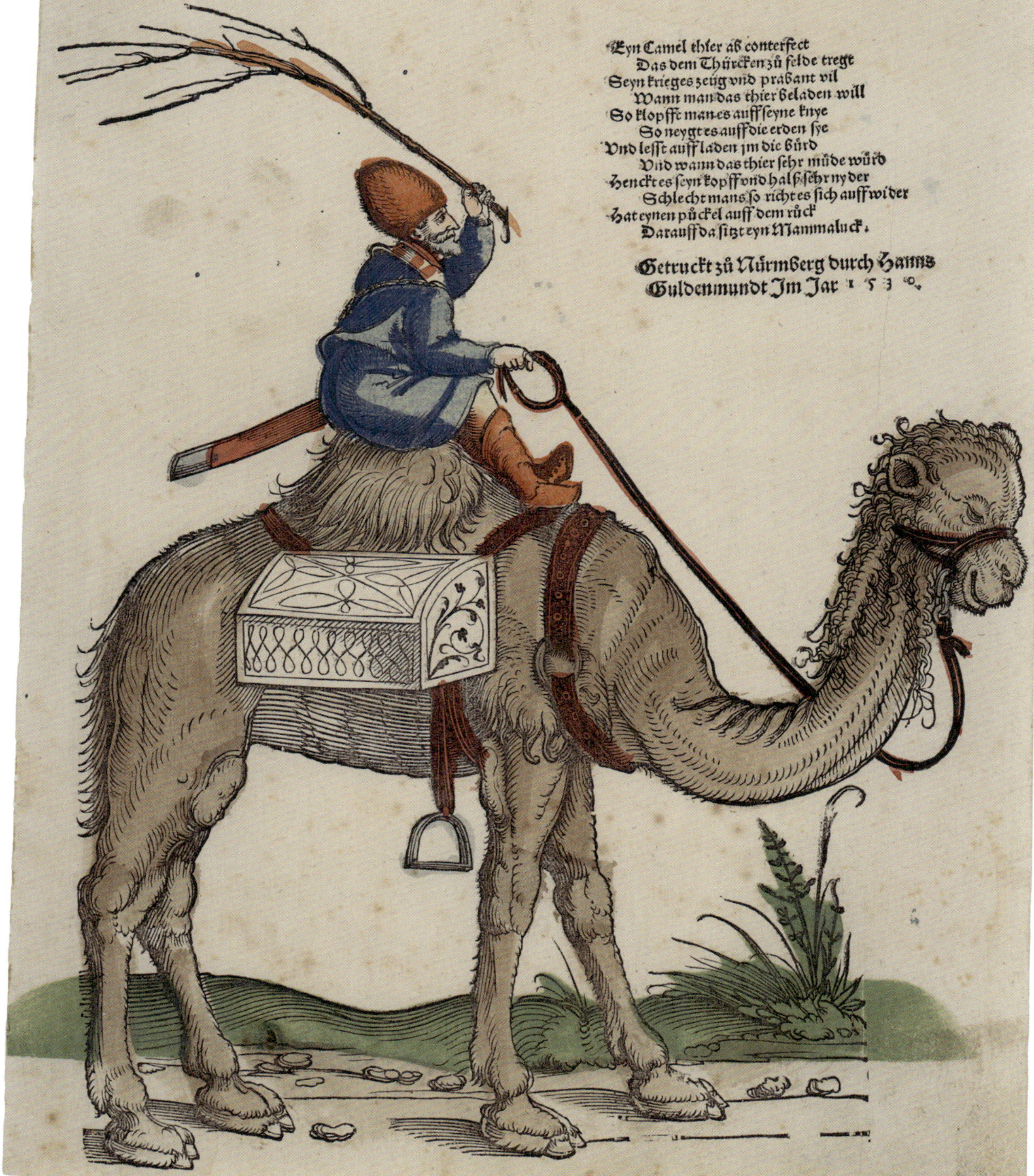

Eyn Camel thier ab conterfect
Das dem Thürcken zů felde tregt
Seyn krieges zeüg vnd prabant vil
Wann man das thier beladen will
So klopfft man es auff seyne knye
So neygt es auff die erden sye
Vnd lesst auff laden jm die bürd
Vnd wann das thier sehr müde würd
Henckt es seyn kopff vnd halß sehr nyder
Schlecht mans so richt es sich auff wider
Hat eynen pückel auff dem rück
Darauff da sitzt eyn Mammaluck.

Getruckt zů Nürmberg durch Hanns
Guldenmundt Jm Jar 1 5 3 0.

78

FIREWORKS AT NUREMBERG CASTLE

Erhard Schön (design)

Nuremberg: Stefan Hamer, 1535

Woodcut, hand-colored, letterpress text

H. 40.1 cm; W. 28 cm

Stiftung Schloss Friedenstein, Gotha, inv. no. G35,15

References:
Gulyás 2014, pp. 219–20; Schäfer, Eydinger, and Rekow 2016, p. 193, cat. no. 193 (Bernd Schäfer); Ziegler 2020, pp. 127–28.

The sucessful siege and capture of Tunis by Charles V in 1535 ranks among the most broadly publicized campaigns waged by the emperor against the westward advance of the Ottoman Empire. In connection with the propagandistic discourse in the period's press about the so-called *Türkengefahr* (Turkish threat),[1] Charles's victory over the army led by the Ottoman corsair Khair ad-Din (d. 1546), alias Barbarossa, became firmly anchored in the collective memory of the Holy Roman Empire. Nuremberg was one of the places where public celebrations were held. On September 13, 1535, spectacular pyrotechnic displays marked the triumph over the Ottoman "infidels,"[2] stylized as pagans.[3] The same year saw the appearance of two broadsheets conceived by Erhard Schön. While one of them describes the fireworks display at Nuremberg Castle in rhyming couplets by Hans Sachs, the other depicts it in a woodcut.

In Sachs's poem, the sequence of events shown in the woodcut is related in detail. On the grounds of Nuremberg Castle, a two-story wooden castle was erected, on top of which stood a large figure of the "Turkish commander with a red beard" (*Türckisch Haubtmann in rotem Bart*), together with "ten small Turkish servicemen" (*zehen klein Türckischen mannen*).[4] The giant, bearded figure of Barbarossa holding a crescent-moon banner is clearly visible in the woodcut. During the fireworks, the smaller figures representing Ottomans were blasted into the air, landing among the spectators below. Ultimately, the temporary wooden castle was set ablaze, causing the figure of the "great Turkish commander" to go up in flames, sending his burning red beard "flying to the heavens."[5] In this macabre spectacle, the enemy defeated in the northern African coastal city of Tunis was made physically present in Nuremberg and killed in a public mock execution, a symbolic *executio in effigie*.

While the prose text below the woodcut summarizes the historical context of the Tunis campaign and briefly describes the sequence of fireworks, the image itself focuses on the active participation of spectators, and thus on the collective aspect of this mock execution. An intact Ottoman figure can be seen soaring overhead, among crisscrossing rockets. Below, groups of Nurembergers swarm two fallen figures of Turks, beating and tearing at them. In the lower of the two groups, one person is shown with fist raised, about to strike a blow to the effigy. Further down in the image, two spectators fight over a crescent-moon banner that had been hurled from the castle.

This sort of collective physical confrontation with, and overpowering of, a staged "enemy" is paradigmatic of the "psychological relief function"[6] served by such public events held in urban spaces. The woodcut *Fireworks at Nuremberg Castle* thus reflects the social relevance of early modern festival culture, in which issues of power, identity, and otherness became the subject of performance and spectacle.

Laura Di Carlo

1 On the phenomenon of the *Türkengefahr* in the media, see the fundamental study Höfert 2003a. See also the essay by Stefan Hanß in the present volume.
2 "Twenty thousand Christian slaves were freed / By His Imperial Majesty / And many infidels were converted to the faith" (*Zweintzig tausent gfangen Christen hat / Erlost Keyserlich Maiestat / Vil vnglaubig zum glauben bracht*); Stiftung Schloss Friedenstein, Gotha, inv. no. G35,14, cited after Schäfer, Eydinger, and Rekow 2016, p. 117, cat. no. 192.
3 On the stylization of Ottomans as heretics, see Born 2024, p. 50.
4 Cited after Schäfer, Eydinger, and Rekow 2016, p. 116, cat. no. 192.
5 Translated from Hans Sachs's verses cited in Schäfer, Eydinger, and Rekow 2016, p. 116, cat. no. 192.
6 Ziegler 2020, p. 127 (*psychologische Entlastungsfunktion*).

das freuden ffeuer zu nurmberg.

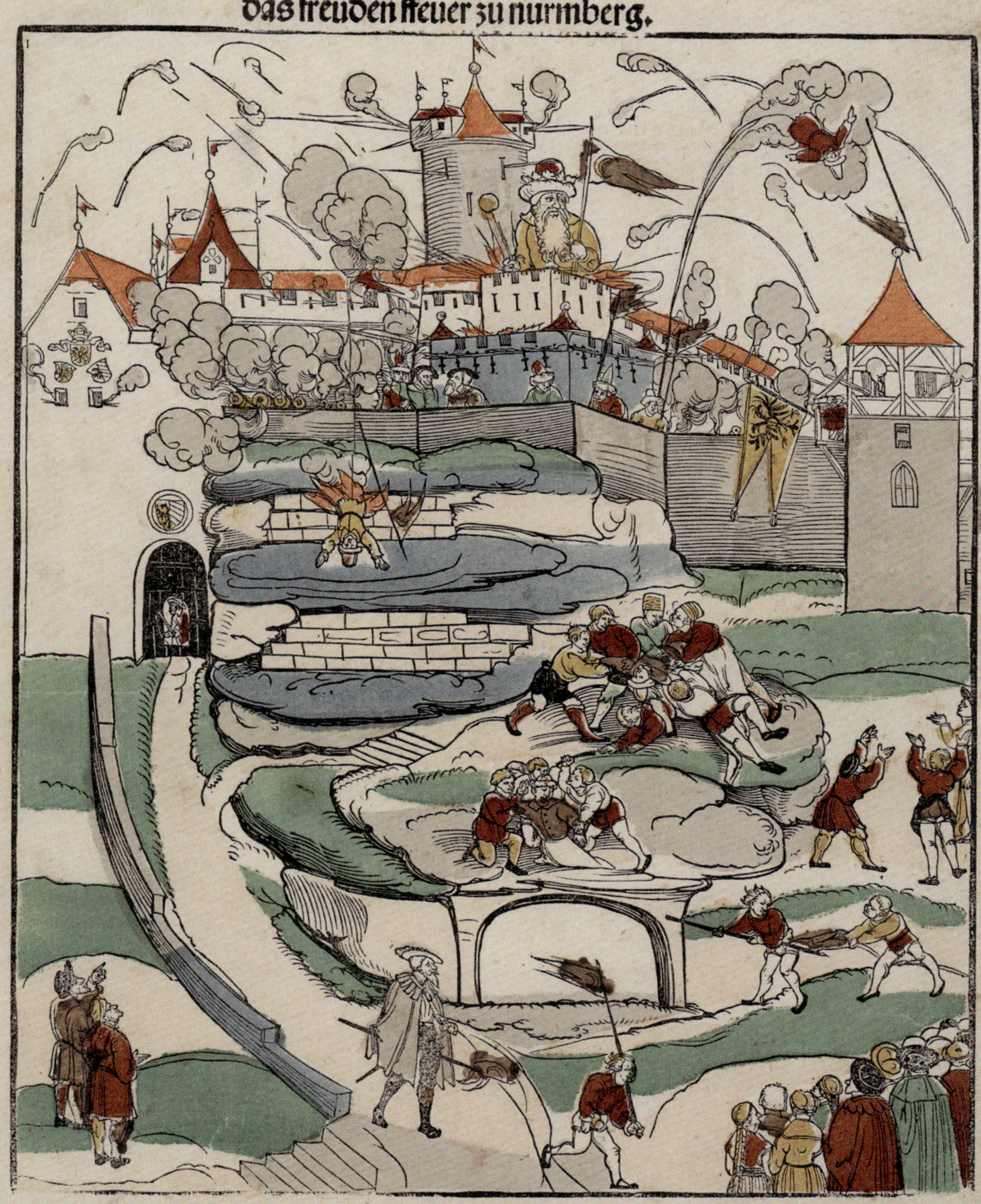

Als man zalt nach der geputt Jessus Cristi M D xxxv iar hat got dem grossmechtigen cristlichem keisser karolo vnsserem heren den
sig geben das er selbst mit in eygner person gezogen ist vnd das gros mechtig kunigreich thunis in affryca ein genümen vnd gebünen
hat vnd sünst mer otten in welchen er pei zbinzig thaussen cristen erlediget hatvnd ander fölcker zum glauben angenümen vbm we
lches sigs wilen den im got geben hat das er auß gepreyt wirt hat man ein freuten feüer geschürt zu nürmberg auff der fessten am drei
tzehent tag septtembris vnd ist gebest wie oben verzeichent ist ein turckiser keisser in eimschlos gestanden das hat gehabt sechtzehen hü
ndert schüs vnd drey hündert steigente feürer dar nach zechen grosse stuck vnd fieter poler dar auß hat man zechen turckisch mender g
eworffen vnder das volck vnd die zechen stuck hat man ab lassen gan zu dem dritten mal mit sampt dem gechütz vnd stücken auff all
en thürnen vnd hat alle glocken gelent vnd got zu lob vnd er in allen kirchen gesüngen welcher den sig vnd die krafft alein geit dem sey
ebig lob vnd preis geben A E getruckt zu nurmberg durch steffan hamer

79

TURKISH SLAVE MARKET

Erhard Schön (design)
Marx Eisenkern (text)

Nuremberg: Nicolaus Meldemann, 1532

Woodcut, letterpress text

H. 29.2 cm; W. 40.5 cm

Stiftung Schloss Friedenstein, Gotha, inv. no. 44,7

References:
Geisberg 1974, p. 1224, cat. no. G.1274; Hollstein German 47, pp. 62–63, cat. no. 21; Messerli 2008, p. 158; Schäfer, Eydinger, and Rekow 2016, pp. 98–99, cat. no. 173 (Matthias Rekow).

How the Turks Trade in Captured Christians, Buying or Selling Them"—thus reads the title of this illustrated broadsheet published by Nicolaus Meldemann in Nuremberg. The woodcut shows a multifigured scene against a backdrop of houses. In the image, the two groups mentioned in the title are clearly distinguishable from one another: armed men—some standing, some on horseback, identified as "Turks" by their clothing, headgear, and distinctive beards—harass and threaten the "captured Christians," some of whom have been disrobed. In the leftward direction of the figures' movements and gazes, the image develops a dynamic narrative of the trade in human beings as a brutal and degrading process. The crowded group of captives at the far right, watched over by guards, is headed by two women trying to hide their nakedness after having just been stripped of their clothes. Expressions of terror mark their faces as they observe the incident unfolding at the center: the captors are driving two naked Christians across the square, raising canes to strike them. At the left, a number of Ottoman soldiers wait casually. The naked man in their midst seems to make eye contact with the beholder.

The triple-column text below takes up central motifs of the image. It gives a first-person, eyewitness account by a certain "Marx Eysenkern," who was taken captive after the Battle of Mohács. He describes the humiliating disrobing taking place in the image as a brutal act of quality assessment that was performed on human merchandise, regardless of status or sex. The conditions of enslavement, not immediately visible in the image, are also described in the text: hard physical labor while being hungry, thirsty, and cold, as well as cruel treatment such as having one's nose cut off or being branded.

The broadsheet must be seen primarily in the context of the anti-Ottoman press that flourished in the wake of the siege of Vienna in 1529. Stories and images of the horrors of war were in high demand. These were based not only on current events but also on older sources. The broadsheet's text has numerous similarities to George of Hungary's *Tractatus de Moribus*, published in 1481, which was widely read in the years following the Habsburg-Ottoman conflict over Hungary and the siege of Vienna; later editions include one issued in Nuremberg by Friedrich Peypus under the title *Chronica und Beschreibung der Türckey* (Chronicle and Description of the Turks).[1] The broadsheet therefore offered little new information to its readers; rather, its visual and textual narrative represented an emotionally engaging condensation of the *Türkengefahr* (Turkish threat), reinforced by the topos of eyewitness experience.[2] In a way similar to the monumental woodcut depicting the siege of Vienna (printed not long before by Meldemann) |**cat. no. 76**|, the broadsheet showing the Turkish slave market not only conveys a scenario of threat by revealing explicit violence;[3] it also evokes a situation of hopelessness in the compositional arrangement, which shows no way out for the imperiled Christians.[4]

Marie-Therese Feist

1 Messerli 2008, pp. 163–64; Schäfer, Eydinger, and Rekow 2016, p. 99, cat. no. 173 (Matthias Rekow).
2 This propagandistic message leaves unmentioned that Nurembergers also profited from the enslavement of people. See cat. no. 109.
3 Meldemann's map of Vienna and a series of fifteen illustrated broadsheets published by Hans Guldenmund (based on designs by Erhard Schön) both contain far more explicit images of violence, for instance the impalement and cutting up of victims. See cat. no. 77.
4 Topkaya 2020, p. 249.

Wie die Türcken mit den gefangenen Christen handlen so sie die kauffen oder verkauffen.

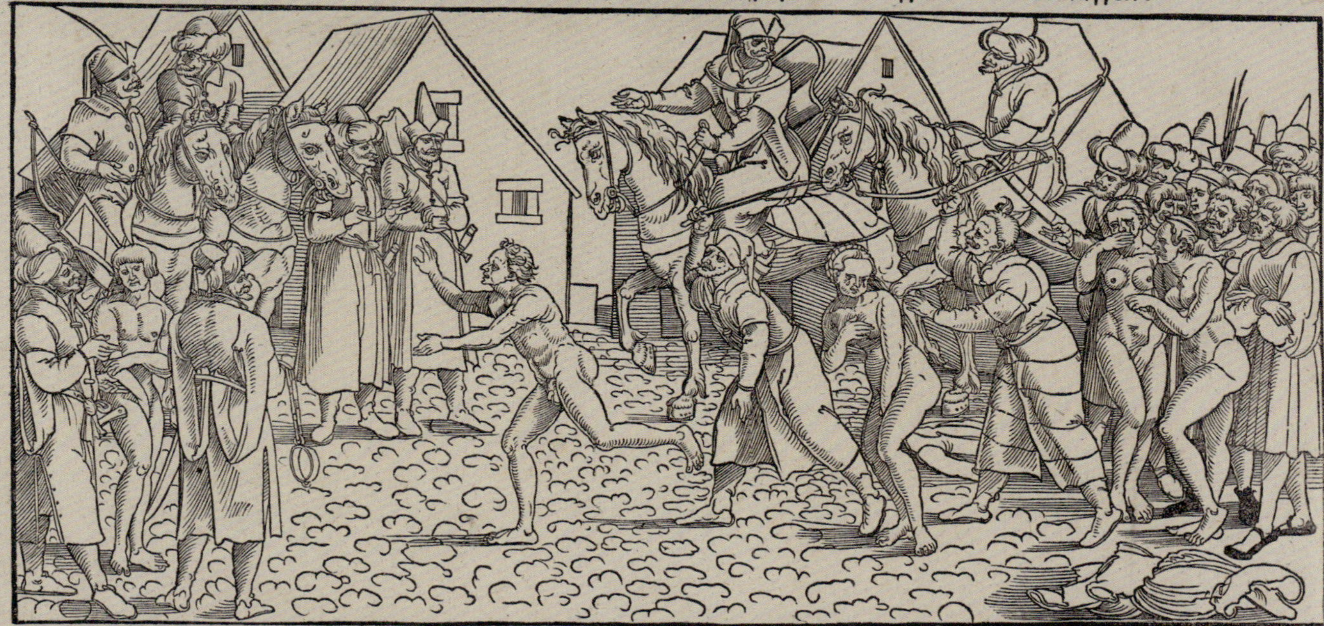

Jch Marx Eysenkern von Pada hab soliche obengemalte vnmenschliche hantirung vnd kauffmanschafft mit den armen gefangen Christen personlich mit grossem schmertzen erfaren vñ erstanden/Nemlich funff jar vnd drey monat lang/Seyder der schlacht vor Mohatz/da der Künig Ludwig von hungern/ erschlagen ward/desselben mals im .26. jar/ also mit andern armen gefangnen hingefürt zusamen gepunden vnd getribẽ wie das vihe oder jaghund/die es doch zum tail in etlichen sachen besser hatten denn wir. Also sein wir von einander getailt worden in etlich hauffen/einer zu der stadt/der ander zu jener/wie nachuolgt/Biß das ich in die viedtẽ hand gekaufft vñ verkaufft worden pin. Aber nach solcher zeit vñ vil elendem leyden /bin ich erledigt durch die hilff/ vñ gnad Got des almechtigen/dẽ ich mein lebenlang nimer gnug lob vñ danck sagen kan. der wunderbarlichen erledigung/das ich widerumb in mein vatterland komen/welchesich doch yetzt an vil orten/ jemerlich vnd erbermlich/mit schmertzẽ verderbet ansihe/got erbarm sich vber dz arm volck. Wie aber vñ was sich in der zeyt alles mit mir verloffen hat/wer wol ein sonderlich histori von zu schreibẽ/würt dißmal vnterlassen. Volgt nu was gstalt die gefangen Christen gehalten werden/Vnnd nemlich durch die groß freyheit der kauffherren von dem Türckischen Keyser gegeben/ darumb sie jm auch den zehend gebẽ nemlich die jungen knabẽ bey. 10. 12. vñ. 15. jaren Die andern gefangẽ Christẽ kauffẽ verkauffen lösen versetzẽ verpfenden sie nach außweysung jrer regalien. ziehen sie auch in die läger mit jhren knechten/ vñ kauffens von dẽ kriegs volck/binden vnd kupelns zusamen treibens also mit yhnen biß in yhr Lande/Da ist auch in einer yeglichen stadt/ein sonderer platz verordnet zu den gefangen/daselb die Türckischẽ kaufleut/ vber das/das sie die leut im ansehen aller jrer natürlichen geschicklickeit vnd eygenschafft sie im anplick võ stundan erkennen kündẽ doch so werden gantz műter nacket abgezogen weyb vnd man würt auch keiner Junckfrawen verschonet/ müssen also auff dem platz lauffen vnnd springen/Das man auch offenlich sehen möge den mangel/ob es gesund oder kranck krumb oder lam sey. Vnd wo etwan ein schamhafftigs ist/so würt es mit ruten vnd geyßlen dartzu gezwungen. Es würt auch da keines standts/ wirde/erbarkeyt/noch kunst verschonet/der paur gilt ebẽ so vil als der edelman/rc. Welche person dañ verkaufft würd etwan in eins verzweyfeltẽ bűben hauß/würd alle arbeit des gantzen hauß auff yn gelegt/welche er mit grossem hunger /dürst/frost kelte vñ hitz/ auch offt darűber gegayselt/ tragẽ műß. Wo sie deñ võeinẽ versteen od merckẽ sol chẽ jamer vñ elend zű entrinnen/Brauchen die türcken erst alle grausamkeit/also/das sie den gefangen kűgel an die fűß/odder keten an die helß hencken/oder die sparradem breñen das sie lam werden/Etlichen schneyden sie die nasen vnd ohren ab/das sie heßlich sehen/vnd das man sie kenne wo sie hin kumen/das es gefangen seind/auch ettlich breñen sie durch die backen vnd stirn/ettlich schlahen sie gar zű tod. Solchs alles hab ich obgemelter Marx Eysenkern nit on vrsach (dann ich kan nit vergessen was die armen elenden leydẽ vñ gedulden műssen) wöllen in schrifft vñ gemelde zű verfassen angegeben/sonder das solch grausame handlũg augẽscheinlich fürgebild/einẽ yglichen frumẽ christẽ zű einer erinnerung mitleydens zűtragen mit denen die noch also bey dem Türcken gefangen seind/Vnd keinen trost haben dann was sie von Gott verhoffen yhn zű helffen/Darumb solchs zu yhrẽ gedechtnus junck vnd alt vor sie zu bitten den almechtigen Got das er ynen sein gnad vnd barmhertzigkeyt mit teylen wölle vnd sie erledigen von der ewigen gefencknuß Amen

Niclas Meldeman zű Nürmberg bey der langen prucken.

325

80

ERSCHRÖCKLICHE ZEITTUNG AUSS NEUHEUSSEL, CARELSTAT UND RAB (TERRIFYING NEWS FROM NOVÉ ZÁMKY, KARLOVAC, AND GYŐR)

Nuremberg: Lucas Mayer, 1592

Woodcut, hand-colored with stencil and watercolor, letterpress text

H. 31.6 cm; W. 38.7 cm

GNM, inv. no. HB252, Kapsel 1341

References:
Strauss 1975, vol. 2, p. 704; Schilling 1990, pp. 175–77, fig. p. 451; Exh. cat. Nuremberg 2017, p. 190, cat. no. 110a (Stephanie Armer).

This illustrated broadsheet from the workshop of Lucas Mayer (d. 1610) appeared in the run-up to the so-called Long Turkish War (1593–1606), during which anti-Ottoman propaganda reached new heights in the Holy Roman Empire.[1] The text reports on Ottoman raids carried out on Hungarian territory in October 1592, painting a picture of seemingly hopeless inferiority in the face of the enemy's military might. Although most readers and viewers were not directly threatened by the hostilities in question, the broadsheet addresses its audiences in Nuremberg and elsewhere in the Empire as people affected by a concrete danger.

The woodcut illustration ensures quick comprehension by means of uncomplicated symbolism and schematic coloring. A multilevel panorama of atrocities unfolds in the Ottoman-dominated scene. In the left foreground, men present to the sultan as trophies the severed heads of their victims, mounted on spears. The walled city behind them is labeled "Constantinobel," and burning villages mark the hills in the right background. Near the upper center, a wagon full of children is being drawn toward the city, presumably in allusion to the dreaded *devshirme*, the abduction of Christian children for recruitment as janissaries.[2] At the center, soldiers herd toward the city a group of captives, male and female, young and old, followed by a mixed group of farm animals and wagons loaded with plundered foodstuffs. The rows of tents in the right foreground are suggestive of a military siege. In addition to this pictorial display of violence, dead bodies, destroyed homes, plunder, siege, and captivity, the text points to the danger of war disrupting trade routes that were relevant to Nuremberg.[3]

The main scene in the foreground makes clear that violence is approved and normalized at the highest level of society. The *Erbfeind*, or "eternal enemy," as the Ottoman Turk is called in the title, is portrayed as fundamentally cruel. The text concludes with an appeal to its Christian readers to pray in order to avert the divine punishment represented by the Ottoman menace.

With such emotional appeals and drastic depictions, the producers of illustrated broadsheets sought to attract buyers from a large swath of society. The authorities were well aware of this medium's great power, and, when in doubt, they intervened with censorship. In this case, however, the pointed message was probably in the interest of the Nuremberg city council, given that a major military conflict would increase Nuremberg's tax burden—a foreseeable result of the city's support for the emperor. In light of that, this broadsheet could well have been recognized as a way of appealing to the people's loyalty and showing them the purpose of financial sacrifice and austerity.[4]

Marie-Therese Feist

1 Exh. cat. Nuremberg 2017, p. 190, cat. no. 110a (Stephanie Armer).
2 Schilling 1990, p. 176.
3 Schilling 1990, p. 176.
4 Schilling 1990, p. 176; on this, see also Schulze 1978, p. 35.

Erschröckliche Zeytung ausz Neüheuszel/ Careisstat/ vnd Rab/ den 11. 13. 14. Octobris von dem Wütenden/ Erbfeindt dem Türcken dises 1592. Jars. ꝛc.

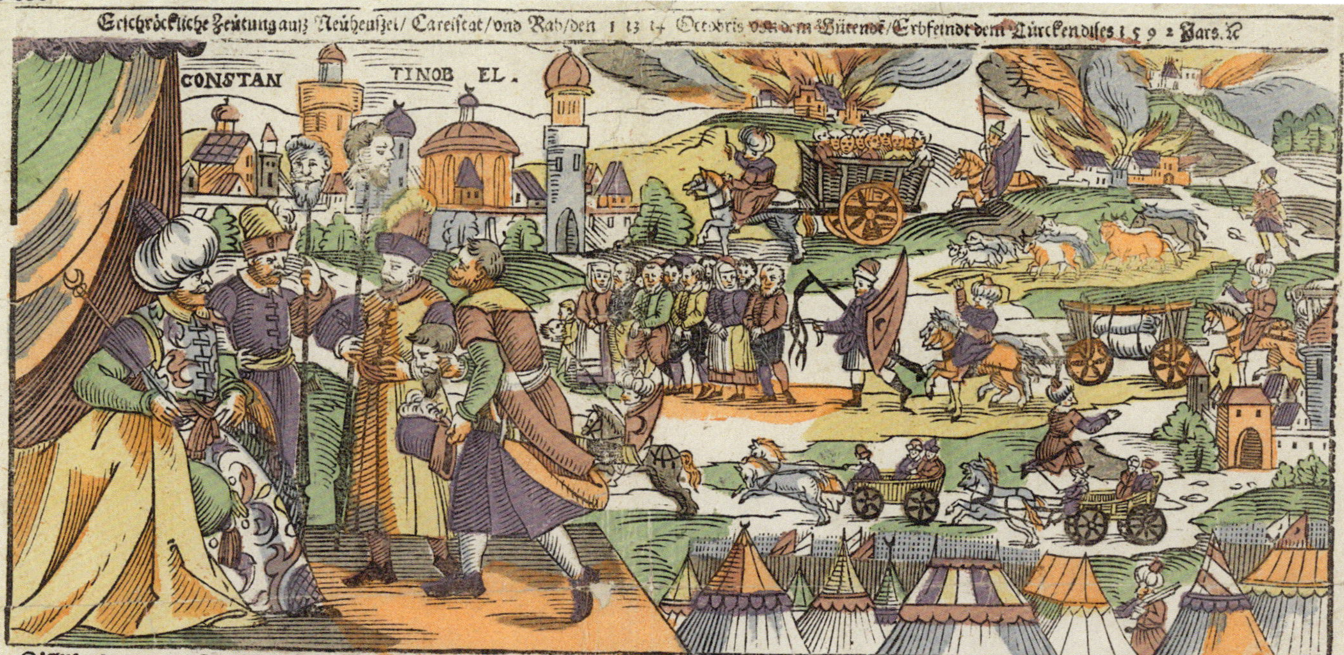

Wyr haben gewise Küntschafft/ das die Türcken mit groszer macht vber 2 mal hūdert Tausent starck beysamē/ da wir Hergegen mit all vnser Macht/ nit vber 40000 starck sein. Der Türckische Keiser/ hat vnserm Keiser den fridt gantz vnd gar vfgeschriben/ will auch kein Tribüt oder Präsent mehr annemen. So ist aúch Zeitúng/ das der Basza ausz Boszna 11000 Lebendige Seelē vnd 4000 Köpff so er in kürtz zusamen gebracht/ sampt etlichen Kärren mit Jungen kindern/ welche er den Christen genommen vnd gen Constantinopel geschickt/ dem Grosz Türcken daselbsten verehrt. Bemelter Basza hat aúch einen starcken straiff auff Düropaliam gedon vū ob 40 dörffer auch zwen grosze Marck/ Chiose vnd Goiritz geblündert/ dieselben in grundt verbrandt gleichfals bey zwey Tausent Christen/ sampt einer grossen anzal Viechs vnd ob 1000 füder Getraydts hinwek gefürt. ausz Canisa habē wir/ das die Türcken Den 11 October zwischen S. Nicolaw vnd witschaw/ vmb miternacht mit 18 Fenlein Füszknecht/ an der Müer Das Castel/ S. Görgen/ mit starcker macht eingenommen die darinligend nidergehaüen/ eins theils von jungen vnd alten personen/ bey 150 gefangē hinweck gefürt/ doch zuvor gedachte Castel In gründt abgebrandt. So sein vor dato/ zwen Beegen gegen Kreditsch gerent/ von denselbē Türcken ist einer gefangen gehn Carelstat eingebracht worden der zeigt an/ der Basza von Boszna solle/ 7 Sangtoché vnd Beegen bey sich haben/ welche samptlich in 36000 starck zu Rosz vnd füsz sein vū halt sich gedachter Basza/ diser zeit In der person auf seiner neüen Vestē petrouna an der Culpa/ vnd sey vorhabens noch 2 Monet alda zuverharrē/ vnd einen auszfal nach dem andern zuthun/ bisz er alle vmbligende Landschafft/ (wo fern man jhme nit hüldige) verhöre vnd verderb/ wie er dan albereit vmb mer grosz Geschütz/ gen warnalúca geschickt in mainung sich vmb Siszegk vū Tretschin ernstlich anzunemē herzwischen hab er alle kleine Schlöschlein/ vnd Edelmans Höffe an der Cúlpa herauff gegen hie ab brenen/ vū nicht nachlassen wollen bisz er alles was sich der hüldigúng verwegert vnder sich bringe dañ er sich keines widerstands/ von fremdē Völcks auff vnser seiten befürcht/ vnd woll waisz das jme die Gräntzen für sich allein zum wider standt viel zu schwach sendt. Ausz Grätz wirt an dē Maúener zu Roeman geschreibē was vorhabens gemelter Basza auff die bayde ordt Zeng vū Syszegk sey/ das möchte aber die zeit baldt endckē/ da er dañ Zeng eröbern solte würdt es vmb Friaúl die Grafschafft Görtz vū andere Ort daselbst herumb/ ellent vnd erbärmlich genug zugehn/ wie dañ der Feindt diser tag dürch ainen Beegen/ bey Siszegk widerumb in die 600 Personen hinweck gefürt aber wir schlaffen noch darbey/ der Almechtige Gott komme vns armen Christen leüten in vnseren grossen Nöhten zu hülff vnd Streidte fur vns.

Ausz Rab haben wir Zeitúng/ das der Basza von Offen/ ist den 13 October zwischē 2 vnd 3 vhr mit 5000 man zu Rosz vū füsz/ sampt Tausent Bütschen/ gen Stulweyszenbürg ankommē/ hat 4 Beegen bey sich/ sampt 10 Fenlein Füszvölck/ welchem die von Weiszenbürg/ bisz in 2000 Man zu Rosz vnd Füsz entgegen gezogen/ haben auch etliche/ Stück Feldt Geschutz bey jnen/ die sag geht vnder den gemeinen Türcken/ er werde gen Wesprin/ aber die Küntschafft lauten/ er wölle einen straiff auff des Herren Nadastzoüter than/ Gott helffe es den armmen Leüten vberwinden. So sollen auch die Türcken bisz in 300. Wägen mit Proúiant/ vnd andere Notdorfft geladen (welche vnserm Kriegsvölck nach den Crabatischen Grentzē zugehn wöllen) abgenommen haben/ ist also ein arme sach. Darumb jhr lieben Christen last vns vnsere mit Christen in vnserm gebet befholen sein das Gott die straff gnedich abwendte.

Zu Nürmberg/ bey Lucas Mayr

81

GESCHICHT VON DER TURCKEY (HISTORY OF TURKEY)

Jörg of Nuremberg

Nuremberg: Peter Wagner, 1500

81.1

Edition with expanded appendix

Incunable, 78 leaves, 1 woodcut

H. 20.4 cm; W. 30 cm (opened)

Bayerische Staatsbibliothek, Munich, shelf mark 4 Inc.c.a. 1780 w

Open to sig. a1v: Title page

81.2 (not illustrated)

Incunable, 78 leaves, 1 woodcut

H. 21 cm; W. 29.5 cm (opened)

Staatsbibliothek zu Berlin, Preußischer Kulturbesitz, shelf mark 8° Inc. 1928.25

Open to sig. A1v: Title page

References:
Göllner 1983, pp. 107–20; Johanek 1983, cols. 867–69; Prinzing 2009, pp. 59–75; Döring 2013, pp. 155–64, 435.

Reports from the Ottoman Empire were often written in connection with diplomatic missions. But some also recount the experiences of people from simpler walks of life who worked in service to the Ottomans, either as captives or voluntarily. The *Geschicht von der Turckey* (History of Turkey) was penned by a master gunsmith. Apart from his profession, all that is known of the author today are his first name and his place of origin. In the text's first sentence, he refers to himself as "Jörg of Nuremberg, now master gunsmith to Our Holy Father, the Pope." Jörg's experiences speak to the mobility of experts from Nuremberg, which was one of the most important centers of arms manufacturing at the time. Having initially served the Bosnian duke Stjepan Vukčić Kosača, Jörg was abducted by Ottomans in 1460. His skills as a maker of firearms and cannons made him useful for technical assistance in military operations. Like a number of European specialist craftsmen, this Nuremberg native joined the army of Sultan Mehmed II for "good pay" (*guten soldt*) and fought for twenty years on the side of the Ottomans in their campaigns in the Balkans and elsewhere.[1]

With the help of Venetian merchants, he managed to escape at Alexandria in 1480. Subsequently, he worked for Pope Sixtus IV. It is unclear whether he later returned to Nuremberg. Yet his text eventually did: written in German in 1481, shortly after the death of Mehmed II, it was initially printed in two editions by Albrecht Kunne in Memmingen in 1482–83 and 1496, with a third edition appearing in Nuremberg in the year 1500.[2]

Jörg's concise text, comprising only eight leaves in the first edition, contains the following parts: a preface with a table of contents; a chronicle of the Ottoman Turks; a section on religion, rites, and customs; and, finally, a discussion of his employer's treatment of captives. Although Jörg's own fate is woven into the text, it remains unclear how much of the report is based on his personal experiences.[3]

The Nuremberg edition adds a long appendix that expands the text of the first edition into a compendium consisting of seventy-eight leaves.[4] For this, the editor drew most extensively from Bernhard von Breydenbach's pilgrim report, *Peregrinatio in terram sanctam*, which is used in heavily excerpted form. Moreover, the Nuremberg edition makes reference to recent events. The Ottoman siege of the Venetian fortress of Modon in August 1500 had caused a stir in Nuremberg. The humanist Sebald Schreyer reported on the conquest in a letter to Conrad Celtis, dated October 18, 1500, and also sent Celtis a related broadsheet.[5] The Nuremberg publisher integrated that very broadsheet into his edition of Jörg's text. On the lucrative market for so-called *Türkendrucke* (Turkish prints), the Nuremberg edition enterprisingly promised not only the latest news but also the text by the "eyewitness" Jörg of Nuremberg enriched with additional detail.

Marie-Therese Feist

1 Western artillery masters were actively recruited and, as Jörg of Nuremberg mentions, well paid. This type of work for the Ottomans did not necessarily follow from abduction and captivity; in many cases, specialist craftsmen went voluntarily into Ottoman service. See Müller 2005, pp. 339–40.
2 The reprint with commentary by Carl Göllner is based on the first edition. A new edition with commentary by Günter Prinzing is in preparation but was not available before publication of the present volume. See Göllner 1983, pp. 107–20.
3 Prinzing 2009, p. 68.
4 Döring 2013, p. 163. The broader subject matter that goes beyond the main topic of the "Turks" is particularly emphasized by Johanek 1983, col. 869.
5 Rupprich 1934, pp. 425–28. On this, see most recently Döring 2013, p. 164.

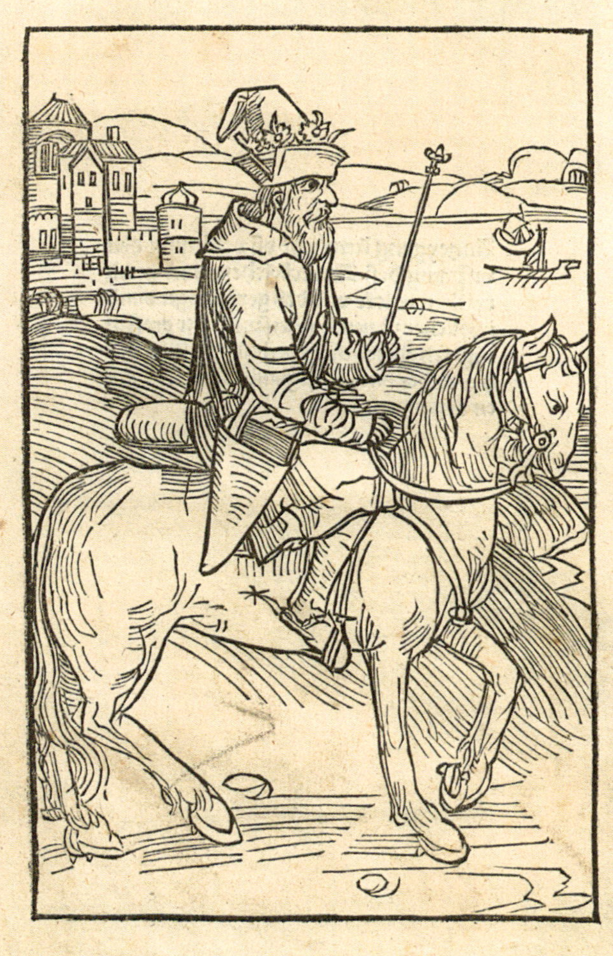

Es iſt zů wiſſen das mayſter Jórg von Nürnbergk yetz vnſers hayligen vaters des Babſt büſchſenn mayſter dyſe her nach geſchybne geſchicht võ der Türckey hat gemacht. wann er bey. xxx. iaren dar innen gewonet hat ¶ Itē zů dem erſtē wie die Türcken auff kumen ſein. Itē zů dē anderñ wie ain yetlich er Türckiſcher kayſer ſein volbracht. vnd was landt vñ ſtet vñ anders rc. ge-wunnē hat. Itē zů dē dritten ein wienig võ irem geſatz oder glauben vaſten vñ beten Itē zů dē vierden wie ſie die armē gefangen behalten kauffen vnd verkauffen.

Itē zů dē erſten. wie die Türckē auff kumē ſein. Ein ſchloß gelegē in dem landt Natolia mit nomē Ottmañ. da võ ein ye-tlicher kayſer den nomen behalten hat. Jndem ſchlos waren ettlich bauren der oberſt bawr was vaſt reych vnd erſamen vñ gieng mit ſechs oder ſibenn bawrenn in einem tal zů acker vñ weñ er eſſen wolt ſo blies er ein horeñ das es die anderenn mochtē hóren vnd zů im komen dar nach ſo lebten ſie mit ein ander als die brůder. 1

Itē auff dez andern teyl waren die kriechen võ des ſelbigen ertrichs wegē zů ſehē. da ſlugen ſie ſich an einander aber die kriechen behielten den ſtreyte des vertroſe die türcken vñ zugē eins nachts vñ verbrenten den kriechē drew oder vier dórffer vnd erſlugē vnd furtē die kinder mit ine vnd ſch encktens irez herreñ mit namen Karaman· der hette ein groß wol geuallen an den kinderñ vñ gab in vrlaub das ſie den kriechen das boſ-eſt ſolten beweiſen als ſie dan theten.

dar nach der obgenant bawer Ottman ſamlet ettlich volck vnd zog in das land Bifa. vñ furte vil volcks auch kinder hin weg aus vil dorfferñ vnd ſchenckte die kind aber ſeinem her-en Karaman der ſprach zů im was gefelt dir von mir wil ich dir auch ſchencken. Er antwort vnd ſprach ich beger anders nit dan ain zaychē võ euch als pald ſchnyde er ab einē ermell võ ſeinē regen mātel vnd ſetzt im den auff ſein haubt als dan noch ettlich tragē weyſſe hůte von leder gemacht mit ab hāg enden widergepogen zipfelñ die heyſſen kepeneck vñ die Tür

a ij

cat. no. 81.1

82

EIN NEWE REYSSBESCHREIBUNG AUSS TEUTSCHLAND NACH CONSTANTINOPEL UND JERUSALEM (A NEW DESCRIPTION OF TRAVEL FROM GERMANY TO CONSTANTINOPLE AND JERUSALEM)

Salomon Schweigger

Nuremberg: Katharina Lantzenberger, 1608

Printed book, 9 folding plates, numerous woodcut illustrations

H. 19.8 cm; W. 31.4 cm (opened)

GNM, shelf mark 4° H. 1944

Open to pp. 232–33: Travel permit issued by the sultan

References:
Schunka 2016, cols. 590–97;
Kula 2014.

The Protestant preacher Salomon Schweigger, originally from Haigerloch in Swabia, settled in Nuremberg only relatively late in his life. In Nuremberg, he was appointed to the Frauenkirche in 1589, where he served as a preacher until his death in 1622. Trained in Lutheran theology and having studied in Tübingen, Schweigger would also have been recognized by Nuremberg's patrician upper class as an expert on Jerusalem and the Orient.[1] Not only did he belong to the elite circle of people who had made a pilgrimage to the Holy Land |**see cat. nos. 68–70**|, but he also had firsthand knowledge of Ottoman culture. In 1577, he succeeded the theologian Stefan Gerlach as a member of the Habsburg mission to the seat of government in Istanbul, led by Joachim Freiherr von Sintzendorff. Schweigger remained in Istanbul until 1581, serving as a chaplain to Protestant captives and as a preacher for the delegation, while also fostering contact with the Greek Patriarchate.

Interest in descriptions, images, and artifacts related to Ottoman culture was not limited to the humanist and Protestant circles in which Schweigger moved,[2] and he put that interest to advantage in his *Reyßbeschreibung*. Shortly after his return to Württemberg, Schweigger used his travel notes to write the report, which is decorated with numerous colorful pen-and-ink drawings.[3] Almost thirty years later, in 1608, the first printed edition was issued in Nuremberg by Katharina Lantzenberger. Numerous reprints followed. The copiously illustrated book was meant to serve the needs of a learned readership. In many respects, it follows the rules of apodemics that developed in the sixteenth century.[4] The book begins with a preface, dedicatory poems in Latin and Greek, and a detailed table of contents. The body of the text consists of three main parts, arranged chronologically and equipped with numerous marginal glosses: a description of the journey from Tübingen to Constantinople; an extensive treatment of customs, political culture, religion, and language, as observed in Istanbul; and a shorter section about a pilgrimage along the Aegean coast via Rhodes to Alexandria and the Holy Land.

The beginning of the third part contains a copy, in Arabic script, of the sultanic document that permitted Schweigger and his noble companions to travel from Istanbul to Jerusalem.[5] The accuracy of the transcription and the ensuing discussion of the document's content demonstrate Schweigger's interest in the materiality of script and the description and study of languages, as is evident in several other passages of the book.[6]

Nevertheless, Schweigger's curiosity about the linguistic, religious, and cultural diversity of Istanbul and the Ottoman Empire was only unbiased to a limited extent.[7] His text clearly follows patterns of polemical disparagement and partial exoticization typical of *Turcica* literature.[8] That ambivalence is evident not only in the travelogue, but also in Schweigger's translation of the Quran, which was likewise printed in Nuremberg.[9] As the first translation of the Quran into German (based on an Italian edition), it opened up new possibilities for the study of Islamic source texts, yet Schweigger's preface is polemical in the extreme.[10]

Marie-Therese Feist

1 Schunka 2016.
2 Schunka 2012, p. 16.
3 Salomon Schweigger, *Constantinopolische vnd Jerüsalemische Raisbeschreibungen*, 1592, Schottenstift, Vienna, Codex 647; see Isler 2019, p. 214.
4 Kula 2014.
5 Mordtmann 1921–22.
6 Stein 1987; Hanß 2019.
7 Özsoy 2024.
8 Neuber 2000, pp. 263–64; Kula 2014, pp. 15–16.
9 Schweigger 1616.
10 See Bobzin 2010, p. 15; Isler 2019, p. 212.

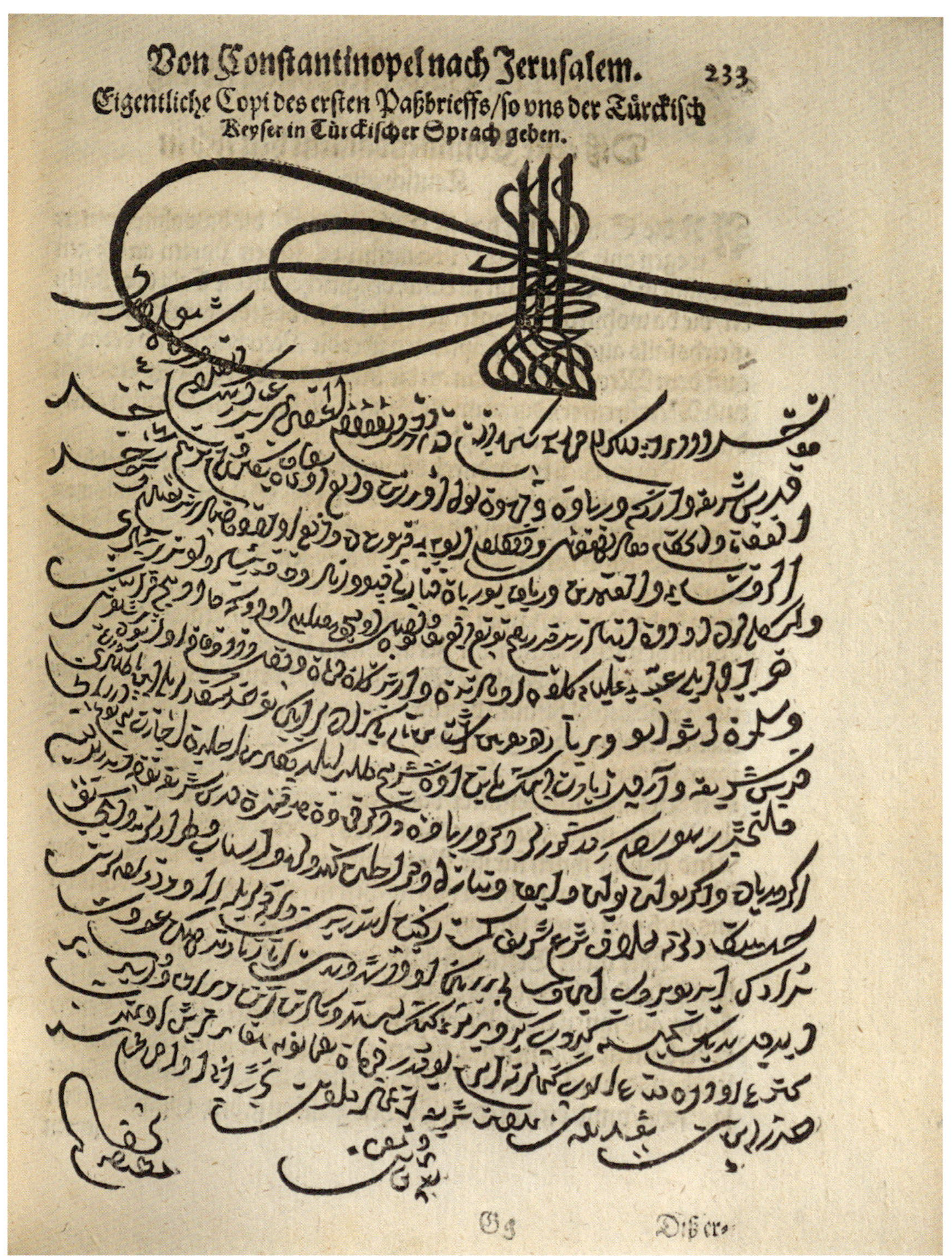

Eigentliche Copi des ersten Paßbrieffs/so vns der Türckisch Keyser in Türckischer Sprach geben.

Gg Diser-

83

NEUE REYSBESCHREIBUNG EINES GEFANGENEN CHRISTEN (NEW TRAVELOGUE OF A CAPTURED CHRISTIAN)

Johann Wild

83.1

Nuremberg: Balthasar Scherff, 1613

Printed book, 1 portrait engraving, 1 woodcut map

H. 20 cm; W. 15 cm (closed)

Staatsbibliothek zu Berlin, Preußischer Kulturbesitz, shelf mark Uk 2992

Open to map, before p. 1, showing Asia, Germania, Italia, Africa, et cetera

83.2 (not illustrated)

Nuremberg: Ludwig Lochner, 1623

Printed book, 1 portrait engraving, 1 woodcut map

H. 18.7 cm; W. 17 cm (closed)

Staatsbibliothek zu Berlin, Preußischer Kulturbesitz, shelf mark Uk 2872

References:
Hantzsch 1897; Teply 1964; Kula 2014; Burschel 2009.

In 1604, the nineteen-year-old soldier Johann Wild, a native of Nuremberg, was fighting on behalf of Austria against the Ottomans when he was taken captive by Hungarian troops and then sold into Ottoman slavery.[1] This marked the beginning of a seven-year odyssey that took him, under various masters, to Constantinople and Egypt, and then on to Mecca and Medina, Yemen, Abyssinia, Sinai, Jerusalem, and Damascus.

Shortly after his return to his hometown in 1611, Wild published a travelogue, first printed by Balthasar Scherff in Nuremberg.[2] The book contains two illustrations: an engraved author portrait and a woodcut map. Readers were surely impressed by the great distance Wild had covered, as represented in the map. Even Salomon Schweigger, the preacher at the Frauenkirche who himself had traveled extensively in the Ottoman Empire, considered Wild's journey remarkable. A few years earlier, Schweigger had published his own travelogue about a journey to Constantinople and Jerusalem |**cat. no. 82**|, and he was called upon to author the preface to Wild's book. There, Schweigger draws attention to Wild's reports from Mecca and Medina as important new sources of knowledge. Because there were hardly any firsthand Christian accounts of those places, the stories that had circulated were often fantastical, such as one about the purportedly floating iron coffin of Mohammed, which Wild exposes as a "fable" (*Fabelwerck*).[3]

Wild's fate as a slave plays a major role in his text: the experience of being sold as a commodity with a quantifiable value is a recurring theme, as are Wild's ever-changing living conditions in total dependence on a series of different masters. In that context, Wild's cultural and linguistic adaptations resemble a survival strategy. The perilous journey and the happy homecoming form a narrative framework that is familiar from comparable accounts. It lends meaning to the suffering endured, as a test imposed by God.[4] The travelogue served not least as proof of the steadfastness of Wild's Christian faith, after the chapter of his life spent among the "enemy."[5]

Wild's firsthand experience of everyday life abroad lent support to his repeated claim that his descriptions of foreign customs, religious rites, and culture were authentic.[6] Nevertheless, for some of his travelogue's content, he probably relied on passages in Schweigger's book, which was surely available to him.[7] Gülbeyaz Kula has identified matching passages in the description of a first visit to a bathhouse.[8] In any case, both authors repeatedly gauge the "foreign" based on the world of experience they shared with their Christian, European readership. For example, to give an idea of the size of Cairo, Wild uses his hometown as a point of reference: citing Sebastian Münster's statement, in Münster's *Kosmographie*, that Cairo is five times the size of Paris, Wild writes: "But I would say that it is four times the size of Nuremberg."[9]

Marie-Therese Feist

1 Knowledge of Wild's biography is based almost exclusively on his own report. Born in Nuremberg, he is recorded as having been baptized at the Sebalduskirche on October 19, 1585. His parents were Hans and Katharina Wild. See Teply 1964, p. 26.
2 Published a second time in 1623, followed by editions in 1636 and 1764 (in excerpts).
3 Salomon Schweigger in Wild 1613, sig. c1r; see also Hantzsch 1897.
4 Burschel 2009, p. 173.
5 Burschel 2009, p. 176.
6 See Amin 2013, p. 261.
7 Müller 2009b, p. 275.
8 Kula 2014, p. 17.
9 Wild 1613, pp. 234–35 ("so sag ich doch daß sie vier mal so groß sey als Nürnberg").

Polanica.
Siebenbürg.
Pont. Euximus.
GERMANIA
Böhem.
Nürnberg
VNGARI
Constant.
Troia
ASIA
Donaw flu.
Ofen.
Adalia
Damasco
Cÿpern
Rhodis
Ierusalem
Sinai.
Alexandr.
Sues.
Dimiat.
AFRICA.
EGYPTEN
Medina.
Cairo.
ARABIA.
Mecha.
Nilus fl.
ROT MOR
GEMEN
Zibia
Machai.

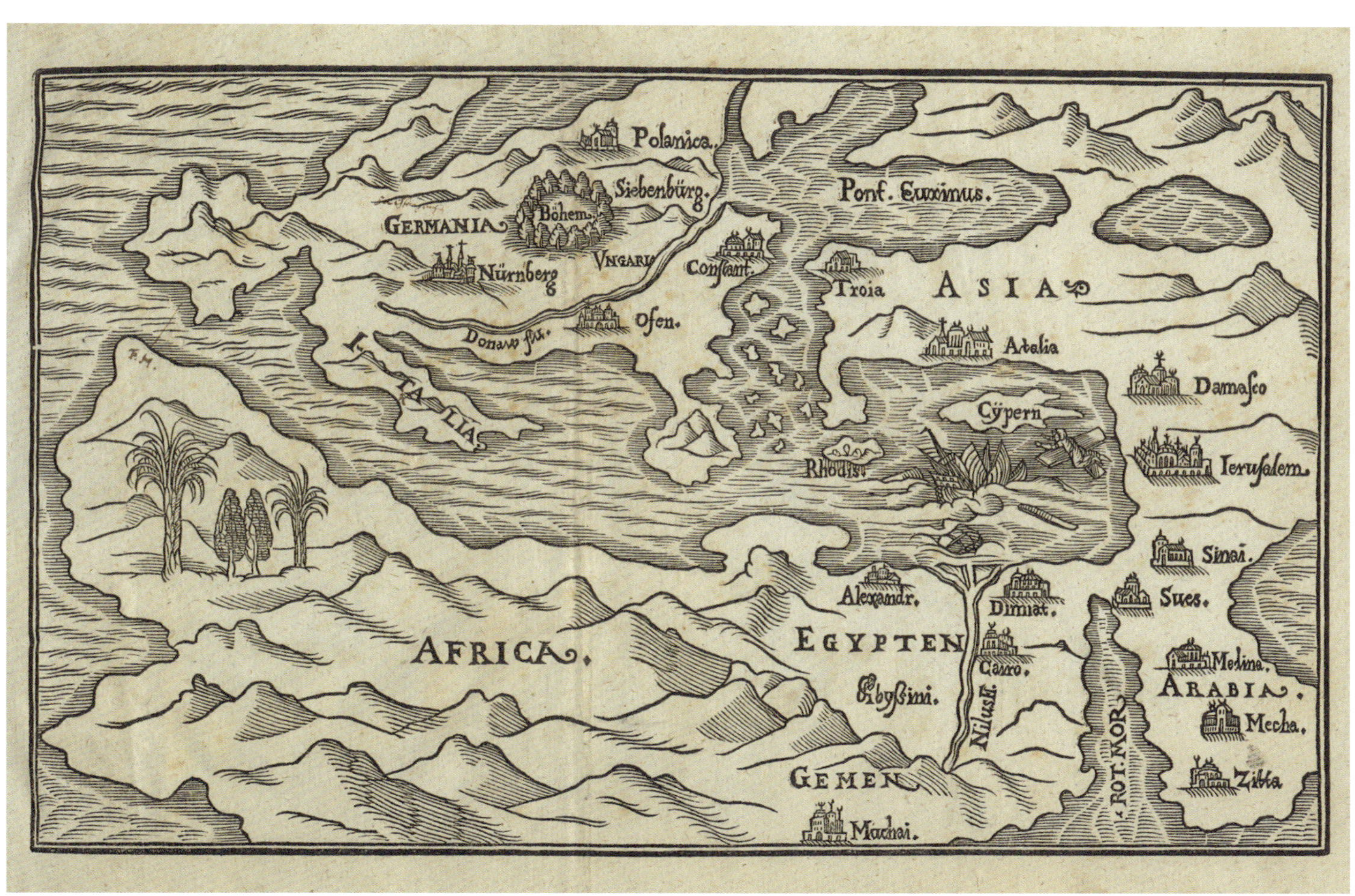

cat. no. 83.1

84

BOOK OF COSTUMES

Attributed to **Jost Amman** (designer)
Hans Weigel (block cutter)
Nuremberg: Hans Weigel, 1577

Printed book, 219 woodcuts
H. 32.5 cm; W. 20.7 cm
GNM, shelf mark 4° Lr 157/1
Open to pl. 209: TVRCICA MVLIER IN BALNEIS

References:
Büttner 2008, pp. 104–5, 115; Rublack 2010, pp. 146–61; Exh. cat. Nuremberg 2015b, pp. 173–74, cat. no. 95 (Jutta Zander-Seidel); Riello 2019, pp. 289–90, 296, 302, 308.

This extensive costume book, printed in Nuremberg in 1577, reflects a truly global ambition. The elaborately illustrated title page describes the contents as follows (in translation): "Book of Costumes, in Which the Clothing Worn by the Men and Women of Almost All Nations Known Today, Including the Most Distinguished, is Depicted with Great Care; Very Amusing and Entertaining to See." With its 219 full-page woodcuts, each accompanied by short verses,[1] this costume book was more comprehensive than any other previously published in Europe. The artist Jost Amman is thought to have supplied the designs for the woodcuts. Amman, who hailed from Zurich, arrived in Nuremberg in 1561, initially working for the printmaker Virgil Solis. He became one of the most successful draftsmen and print designers of the second half of the sixteenth century |**see cat. no. 21**|.

The book is arranged mainly according to geographical criteria and social hierarchies, with emphasis on Nuremberg, the German-speaking territories, and neighboring European lands. But it also includes costumes from Asia, Africa, and, to a lesser extent, the Americas. Leafing through the volume, one notices that the image-text combinations are designed, among other things, to contrast the ideal of German clothing, described as modest, with, on the one hand, the extravagance of Italian and French fashion and, on the other hand, the supposed "primitiveness" of places located further away from Europe. According to Rublack, a comparison with other costume books shows that "Weigel's depiction of clothing thus turns out to have been a renewed attempt to picture an ideal of comportment in order to construct a positively patriotic sense of civilized urban German behavior, especially for women."[2] Rublack thus describes costume books such as Weigel's as "moral geographies in print, which would then orient people's dress styles."[3]

That interpretation is supported by the depictions of inhabitants of the Ottoman Empire, which form a prominent thematic focus in the last third of the book. A particularly telling sequence of two images shows the traditional clothing habits of "simple Turkish women" (labeled "PLEBEIA FOEMINA TVRCICA" and "Ein schlechte [i. e., *schlichte*] Fraw"). Plate 208 presents a fully veiled woman turned to the side, with a caption that reads, "A veil covers her face. / When she goes to market by day, / And buys what is needed for the home" (*Ein netz verdeckt ir Angesicht. / Wann sie beim tag zu Marct gehnt auß, / Und kauffen was man darff zu ha[u]ß*). In the next illustration, it becomes clear that such images were used to reinforce clichés and prejudices associated with the anti-Ottoman propaganda in circulation at the time |**cat. nos. 78–80**|. It is surely no coincidence that the fully veiled woman is followed, on plate 209, by the frontal depiction of a woman clothed only in a transparent chemise. By turning the page, one could, so to speak, undress the veiled woman and fix one's eyes upon an almost naked female body. The caption reads: "When the Turks are at the bath, / They dress in gossamer linen. / They cover the head with a hat, / As shown in this figure" (*Wann die Türcken sindt in dem Bad, / Sinds anthan mit zarter Leinwandt. / Haben auff irem habt ein hut, / Wie die Figur anzeigen thut*). Such deliberately voyeuristic depictions reinforced widespread stereotypes about the bathing habits of "Oriental" women, thus catering to the fantasies of a presumably mostly male European readership.[4]

Sven Jakstat

1 Jutta Zander-Seidel regards the block cutter and printer Weigel as the author of the verses. See Exh. cat. Nuremberg 2015, p. 173, cat. no. 95.
2 Rublack 2010, p. 149.
3 Rublack 2010, p. 146.
4 See Büttner 2008.

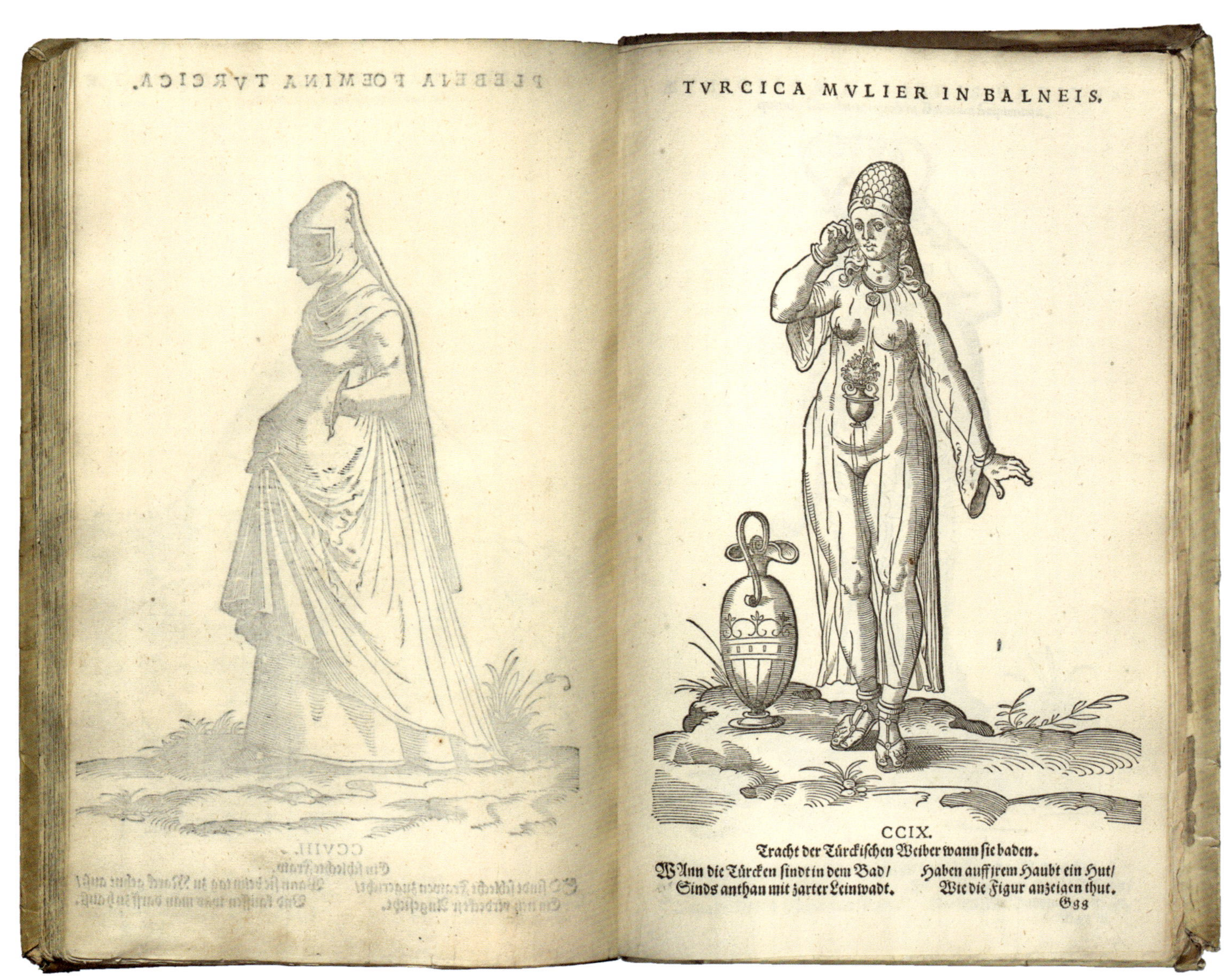
TVRCICA MVLIER IN BALNEIS.
CCIX.
Tracht der Türckischen Weiber wann sie baden.
WAnn die Türcken sindt in dem Bad/
Sinds anthan mit zarter Leinwadt.
Haben auff jrem Haubt ein Hut/
Wie die Figur anzeigen thut.
Ggg

85

ROMANI FAMILY

Albrecht Dürer

Nuremberg, um 1496

Engraving

85.1

H. 11.2 cm; W. 8 cm

GNM, inv. no. StN2186, on long-term loan from the Museen der Stadt Nürnberg, Kunstsammlungen

85.2 (not illustrated)

H. 11.2 cm; W. 7.8 cm

GNM, inv. no. MS1556, on long-term loan from the Paul Wolfgang Merkel'sche Familienstiftung

References:
Schoch, Mende, and Scherbaum 2001, pp. 53–54, cat. no. 12 (Rainer Schoch); Exh. cat. Brussels and Kraków 2015, p. 214, cat. no. 115 (Guido Messling); Born 2024, pp. 52–53; Dackerman 2024, pp. 33–35.

When this small-scale engraving was first discussed in art-historical literature, it was thought to show a "Turkish" family. That has since been corrected: the figures represent a Romani family.[1] The initial identification demonstrates the extent to which images of the "Other" in the early modern period gave rise to cultural stereotypes that had a lasting influence on European habits of viewing. Aspects of the male figure's clothing probably formed the sole basis for calling the family Turkish.

Indeed, certain attributes of dress became visual paradigms of "Otherness." Headgear in particular was frequently used to signify the "Other," especially with regard to religion.[2] Turbans often featured in Passion scenes as a way of stylizing Muslims as perpetrators.[3] At the same time, figures, objects, and textiles from the Ottoman sphere fascinated painters such as Dürer and, before him, Gentile Bellini |**see cat. nos. 57, 58**|. Europeans projected onto the turban their ideas and artistic fantasies of an undifferentiated "Orient"—an image that proliferated and became entrenched thanks to the reproducibility and easy distribution of prints.

Dürer's engraving, one of a number of orientalizing depictions by the artist, was created in that context.[4] Although the caftan and dolman worn by the male figure can be associated with Ottoman dress, the curly locks escaping from beneath the man's bonnet—itself an atypical feature—argue against the Ottoman identification.[5] However, it is the iconography of the female figure that most clearly identifies the family as Romani. Barefoot, bare-breasted, wearing a turban-like headdress, and holding a baby on her left arm, she appears to stride along the path indicated below. The blanket draped over her shoulders and secured with a knot is one of the central motifs and markers of "Otherness" found in contemporary depictions of Romani women, particularly in genre images.[6] In keeping with a myth of the Romani people's origin that situated their ancestors in Egypt, the Romani became part of the European construction of an "iconography of the Orient."[7]

Dürer's engraving thus participated in a discourse of great social relevance, articulated in various visual media of the period. The arrival of Romani people in European cities is documented from the early decades of the fifteenth century. By the end of the century, in resolutions issued at the Imperial Diet in 1497 and 1498, the Romani were declared outside the protection of the law.[8] This was another step in a process of marginalization that had probably already begun with their exclusion from the Peloponnese and the Balkans. Within the aforementioned "iconography of the Orient," a hybridization occurred in which attributes that signified Romani people were amalgamated with those typical of Ottoman figures. Nevertheless, from today's perspective, the former title of this engraving, referring to a "Turkish" family, can be jettisoned. Yet that designation has tended to persist, despite its proven inaccuracy, thereby continuing to render a minority invisible.[9]

Laura Di Carlo

1 First suggested by Erwin Panofsky; see Panofsky 1971, p. 68 (reprint of 4th ed., 1955). Fully elucidated by Anzelewsky 1983, pp. 57–65.
2 See Friedman 2008, pp. 173–77.
3 See Madar 2023, pp. 61–71.
4 See Messling 2015, pp. 53–55.
5 See Anzelewsky 1983, p. 60.
6 See Bell 2015, pp. 253–62; Pokorny 2005.
7 Bell 2015, p. 250.
8 Schoch, Mende, and Scherbaum 2001, p. 53, cat. no. 12 (Rainer Schoch), with references to earlier literature.
9 Guido Messling rightly indicated the new identification by using the title "Gypsy Family (so-called Turkish Family)." See Exh. cat. Brussels and Kraków 2015, p. 214, cat. no. 115.

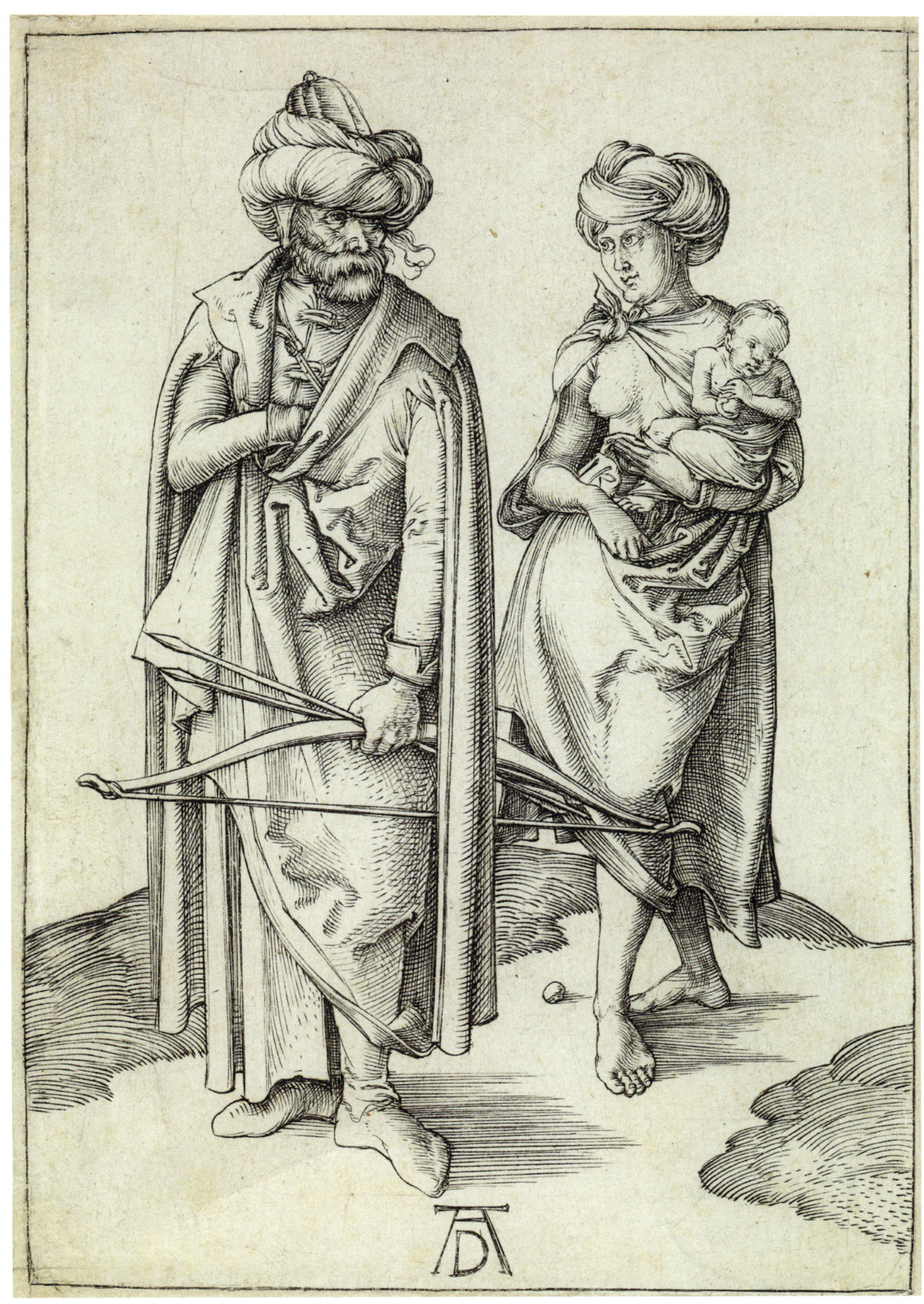

cat. no. 85.1

86

LANDSCAPE WITH A CANNON

Albrecht Dürer

Nuremberg, 1518

Etching

86.1

H. 22.7 cm; W. 33.3 cm

GNM, inv. no. StN13170, on long-term loan from the Museen der Stadt Nürnberg, Kunstsammlungen

86.2 (not illustrated)

H. 21.9 cm; W. 32.2 cm

GNM, inv. no. MS1582, on long-term loan from the Paul Wolfgang Merkel'sche Familienstiftung

References:
Schoch, Mende, and Scherbaum 2002, pp. 210–12, cat. no. 85 (Rainer Schoch); Exh. cat. Vienna 2019, pp. 134–37, 450, cat. no. 45 (Christof Metzger); Hommers 2021, pp. 79–81; Madar 2023, pp. 82–86; Dackerman 2024, pp. 122–59.

Albrecht Dürer's print *Landscape with a Cannon*, created in 1518, is regarded by art historians as an "incunabulum of landscape etching."[1] At the same time, it is a further example of Dürer's enduring interest in depicting people from non-Christian cultures |**see cat. nos. 57, 58, 85, 100**|.

The foreground shows a cannon mounted on a cart, positioned on the stony terrain of a hill. An armored landsknecht leans casually against the barrel, while a group of five men approaches from the right. Further back, an idyllic village is nestled in the valley below, and a range of hills skirts the horizon. The village is Eschenau, which lies a short distance northeast of Nuremberg.[2] Dürer's characteristic *AD* monogram is located in the upper left corner, above the view of a harbor.

Based on their clothing, the figures gathered at the right can be assigned to different regions of the Ottoman Empire, making the group a kind of international delegation. The elderly man with a turban, depicted in profile, stands out as the group's leader. For this figure, Dürer drew inspiration from a study he made in the 1490s of three Ottoman officials; for that study, he copied a model by Gentile Bellini that he saw during a visit to Bellini's workshop in Venice |**see cat. nos. 58, 89**|. Although scholars have attempted to explain the foreign-looking entourage in Dürer's etching as an artistic expression of concern about the constant threat posed by the Ottoman Empire, the scene has an air of calm and peacefulness. The encounter between the landsknecht cannoneer and the Ottoman group is by all appearances a nonviolent one. That interpretation is supported by the type of cannon depicted. As historical studies of weaponry have shown, this model of cannon was obsolete by the time the etching was made. Dürer, who was well versed in military technology, probably included the cannon more as a museum piece than as an operational defensive weapon.[3]

Even though nothing overtly threatening is taking place on this hill above a Franconian village, Dürer nevertheless leaves us with an atmosphere of ambivalence. This has made it difficult for scholars to decipher not only the concrete intention of this highly unusual assemblage of protagonists but also the overall message of the print. It is possible that Dürer deliberately left room for the multiplicity of meanings that might arise in an encounter between people from different cultural contexts. Viewers would thus have been free to imagine various scenarios with uncertain outcomes. For that reason, the *Landscape with a Cannon* will remain indispensable to the study of cultural identity and diversity both in Dürer's oeuvre and in early modern northern Europe in general.[4]

Johannes Gebhardt

1 Quotation translated from the German in Schoch, Mende, and Scherbaum 2001, p. 212, cat. no. 85 (Rainer Schoch).
2 Exh. cat. Vienna 2019, p. 136, cat. no. 45 (Christof Metzger).
3 Hommers 2021, p. 80.
4 Madar 2023, pp. 82–86.

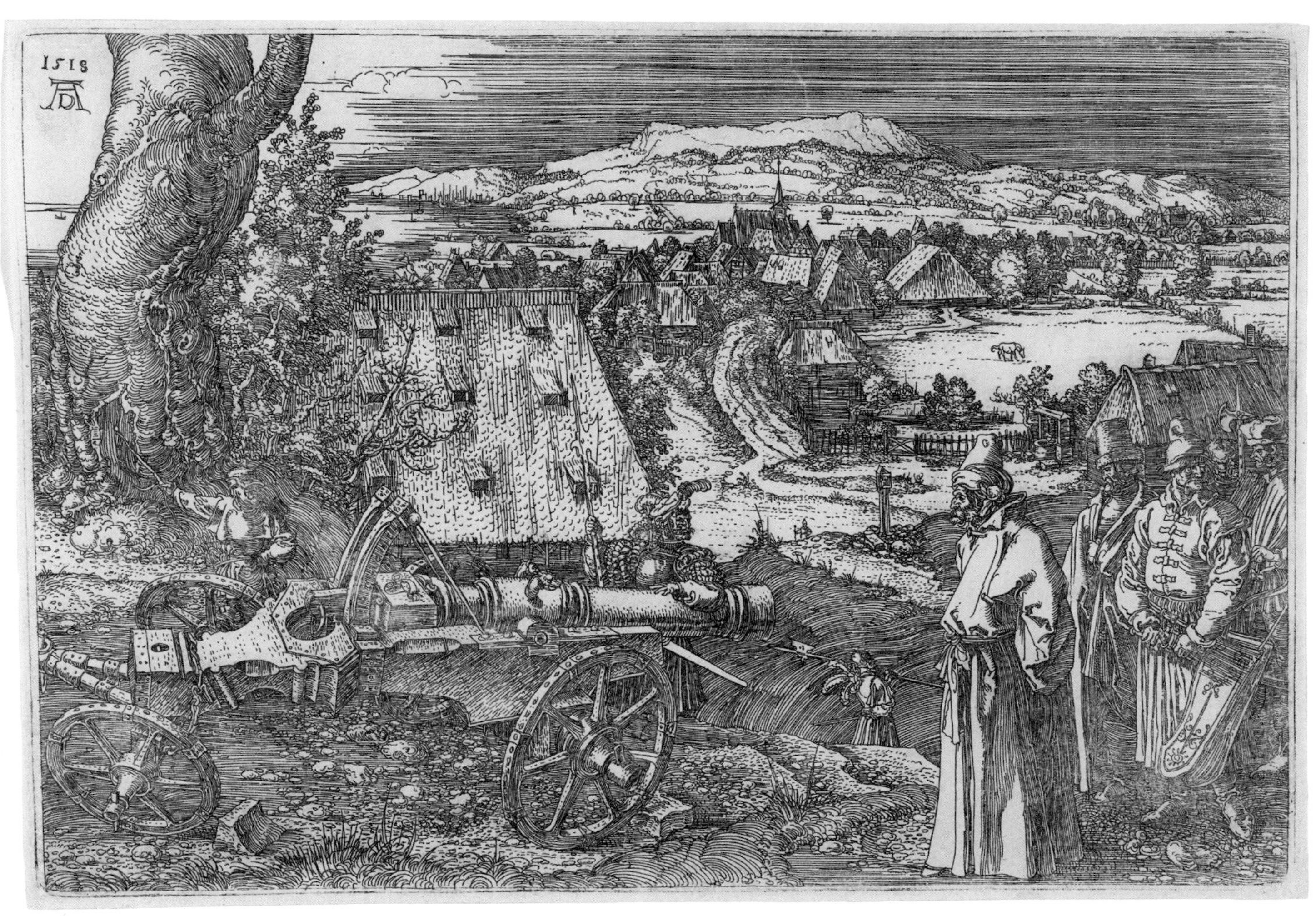

cat. no. 86.1

87

OTTOMAN BOW OF STEPHAN PRAUN III

Ottoman Empire, second half of the sixteenth century

87.1 Bow

Wood, buffalo horn, sinew, glue, lacquer

H. 67 cm; W. 25 cm (unstrung)

GNM, inv. no. W1220

87.2 Bow Case

Leather, wood, gilding, paint

H. 67 cm; W. 30.5 cm

GNM, inv. no. W1217

87.3 Quiver with Arrows

Leather, wood, gilding, paint

H. 86 cm; W. 19 cm (with arrows)

GNM, inv. no. W1218

On long-term loan from the Friedrich von Praun'sche Familienstiftung

References:
Schürer 2010, p. 265; Hess and Hirschfelder 2010, p. 438, cat. nos. 466–68; Achilles-Syndram 1994a, p. 174, no. 17, fig. 79; Hanß 2021d, p. 274.

Stephan Praun III came from a wealthy and broadly networked merchant family of Nuremberg. Even as his parents' eldest son, he showed from early on that his path in life would lead away from the family business. To the great displeasure of his parents, he took up traveling. His work in service to various rulers took him to Constantinople, Jerusalem, and Santiago de Compostela, and eventually to northern Syria, Palestine, Cairo, Tunisia, and Algiers, among other places. The extensive art collection founded by his brother Paulus Praun II |**see cat. no. 65**| contained several items that Stephan had acquired as mementos during his travels. These include a miniature replica, made from bone, of the tomb of Godfrey of Bouillon in Jerusalem |**cat. no. 68**|, a set of pilgrim's clothing |**cat. no. 96**|, and, as listed in the appendix to the collection's 1616 inventory, "Turkish items" (*Turkische sachen*).[1] Among these objects were a bow with a leather case and an arrow-filled leather quiver, as well as a pair of leather riding boots |**see fig. p. 65**|.[2]

It is assumed that Stephan Praun came into possession of these items during his stay in Constantinople. He was there during the reign of Selim II (r. 1566–74), as a member of the 1569 embassy of Emperor Maximilian II, led by Caspar von Minkwitz. Praun's notes on his journey not only allow a reconstruction of the route and the places visited during his stay; they also demonstrate his interest in the culture and wares of the city now known as Istanbul.[3] The exact circumstances surrounding his acquisition of the archery set nevertheless remain unknown.

The bow is of the reflex type and composite in construction, made of wood, horn, and sinew, with a lacquer finish and delicate ornamentation. The leather cases for the bow and the arrows are decorated with gold leaf. Owing to its relatively compact size, this bow was particularly suitable for use on horseback. The bow case and arrow quiver would have been worn at the hip. The high quality of the chosen materials and workmanship would certainly have been reflected in the price paid by Praun, if he acquired the ensemble by purchase. As demonstrated by numerous depictions of Ottomans with composite bows, this weapon was an important component of the central European conception of Turkish men |**see cat. nos. 86, 88**|.

Praun was not alone in collecting Ottoman objects: in parallel with the rise of propaganda that portrayed the Ottomans as the "eternal enemy" (*Erbfeind*) of Christians, a keen interest in Ottoman culture developed in Nuremberg. This is evident not only in the popularity of travelogues |**see cat. nos. 81–83**|, but also in the apparent passion with which collectors acquired weapons, writings, clothing, and many other types of objects associated with the Ottomans.[4] The reception of Ottoman culture is also reflected in various works by Nuremberg artists such as Albrecht Dürer and Peter Flötner |**see cat. nos. 57, 58, 66, 86, 92**|.[5]

This interest was mutual. For example, as part of tribute payments tendered to the Ottoman Empire, diplomatic gifts made in Germany were presented at the sultan's court. Stephan Praun lists such items in detail in his writings about his journey.[6] Objects from Nuremberg such as clocks, weapons, and armor were highly popular as gifts.[7] As expounded by Stefan Hanß, this exchange contributed significantly to the development of a "shared taste" in the sphere of material culture.[8]

Marie-Therese Feist

1 Achilles-Syndram 1994a, p. 174, no. 17.
2 GNM, inv. no. T555,0.
3 Published in summary in Praun 1916–17.
4 See the essay by Stefan Hanß in the present volume.
5 Hanß 2021d, p. 260.
6 Praun 1917, pp. 49–52.
7 Exh. cat. Karlsruhe 2019, p. 364, cat. no. 193 (Stefan Krause).
8 Hanß 2021d.

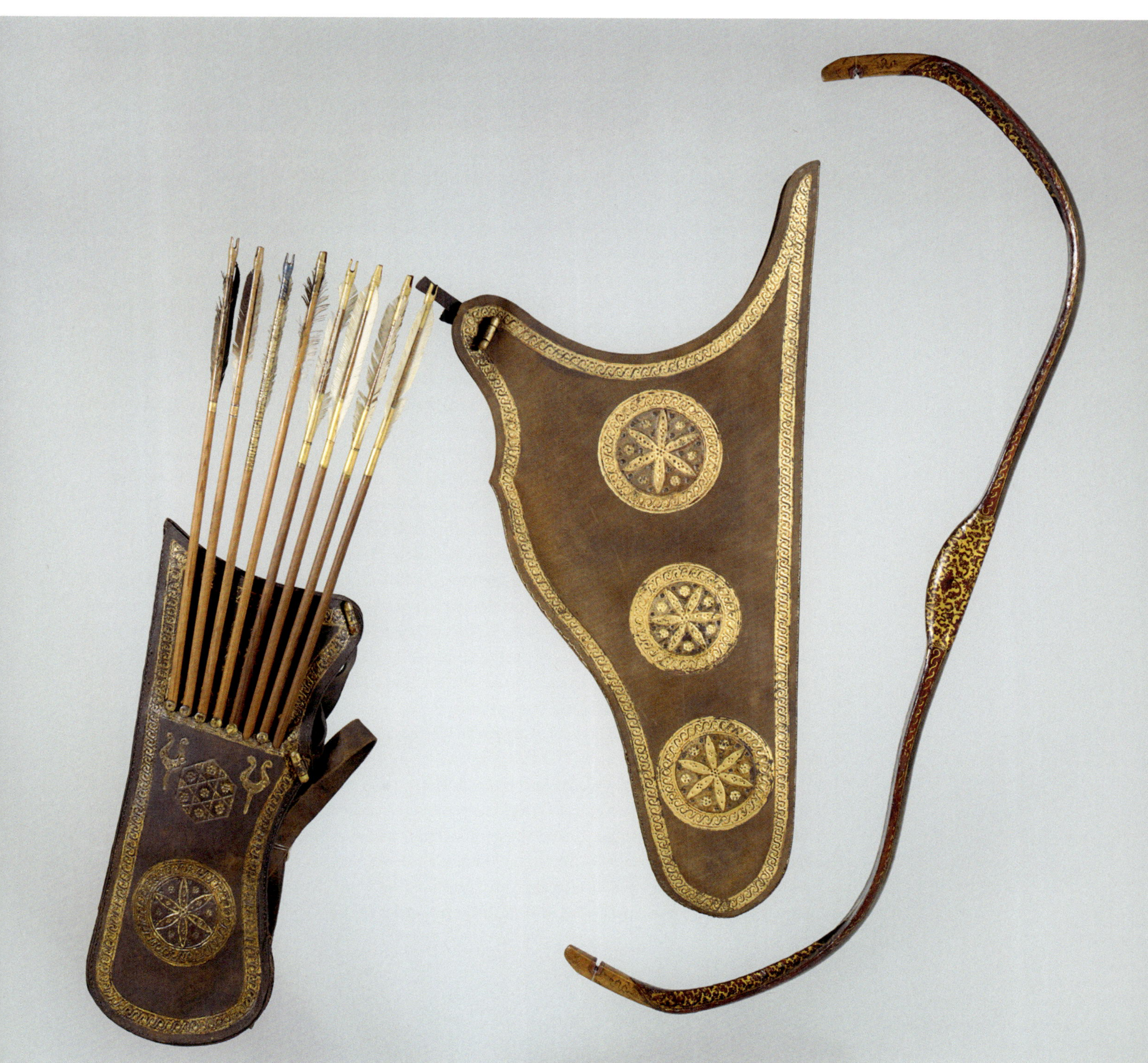

88

OTTOMAN ARCHER

Hans Peisser (model), **Pankraz Labenwolf** (cast)

Nuremberg, ca. 1540

Bronze, solid cast

H. 22.4 cm; W. 14.5 cm; D. 6.5 cm

GNM, inv. no. Pl.O.2948

References:
Exh. cat. Dresden and Bonn 1995, p. 78, cat. no. 33b (Holger Schuckelt); Exh. cat. Brussels and Kraków 2015, p. 222, cat. no. 119 (Raphael Beuing); Exh. cat. Nuremberg 2017, p. 190, cat. no. 111 (Marina Rieß); Söding 2023, pp. 301–11; Kim 2024, pp. 19–58.

This bronze statuette shows an archer training his short, tightly drawn bow on an unseen target. He appears to stride forward resolutely, his forward foot extending beyond the front edge of the oval base. The artist took particular care to characterize the warrior as a representative of the Ottoman Empire, using pictorial formulas and motifs that were common at the time. These include the weapon—a reflex bow, the Ottomans' most dreaded instrument of war—and the costume, consisting of a turban wrapped around a tall cap, a tunic bound with a sash at the waist, a pair of knee breeches, and shoes that leave the ankle exposed. The mustache is another typical element of this iconographic repertoire.

In sixteenth-century Nuremberg, small-scale works in bronze or brass, including statuettes, medals, plaquettes, and everyday objects, were important export goods. After the official introduction of the Reformation and the accompanying decline in commissions for church furnishings, many artists turned to the production of such works. One of them was Hans Peisser (d. after 1571), thought to be the creator of the *Ottoman Archer*. Another cast of the same model is preserved at the Bayerisches Nationalmuseum in Munich.[1] As with the Nuremberg piece, great care was taken in the cold work, that is, the working of the surfaces and details after the casting process.

Together with a bronze statuette representing a swordsman, also at the Germanisches Nationalmuseum,[2] the *Ottoman Archer* has mostly been regarded as part of a once larger group of figures that may have been conceived for a fountain. It is assumed that these statuettes were either themselves fountain figures or that they served as models for a large fountain, comparable to the multifigured *Neptune Fountain* made by Georg Labenwolf from 1576 to 1583 for Kronborg Castle (Elsinore, Denmark), on which the basin rim was decorated with six similar warrior figures.[3]

However, that interpretation is questionable. Models for large sculptures are unlikely to have involved such extensive cold work. At the same time, the lack of any pipework for water speaks against these figures having been intended for installation on a smaller fountain. Furthermore, the warrior's format is suitable neither for a large fountain nor a table fountain but instead lies exactly in between. Dasol Kim therefore recently proposed that the *Ottoman Archer* was an autonomous work of art intended for a cabinet of arts (*Kunstkammer*) or *studiolo*. Several factors support that idea: the format and material, the detailed workmanship, the classic style of a statuette with a base reminiscent of ancient models, and not least the highly topical theme, in the years around 1540, of the threat posed by the Ottoman Empire.[4]

The violent incursion by the army of Sultan Suleiman I into the territory of the Holy Roman Empire and the siege of Vienna in 1529 had precipitated a collective trauma in Christian Europe. In the *Ottoman Archer* statuette, the figure's forceful, border-crossing footstep is evocative of invasion. Yet, especially among the humanist elite, fear of the Ottomans existed alongside an interest in and admiration for the Ottoman Empire and its military. This is exemplified by the fact that original Turkish bows and arrows eventually became coveted collector's items |**cat. no. 87**|.[5]

Markus T. Huber

1 Inv. no. 13/175.
2 Inv. no. Pl.O.2851.
3 Söding 2023, pp. 76–82, 301–3, with references to earlier literature.
4 Kim 2024, pp. 19–58.
5 Kim 2024, pp. 19–58.

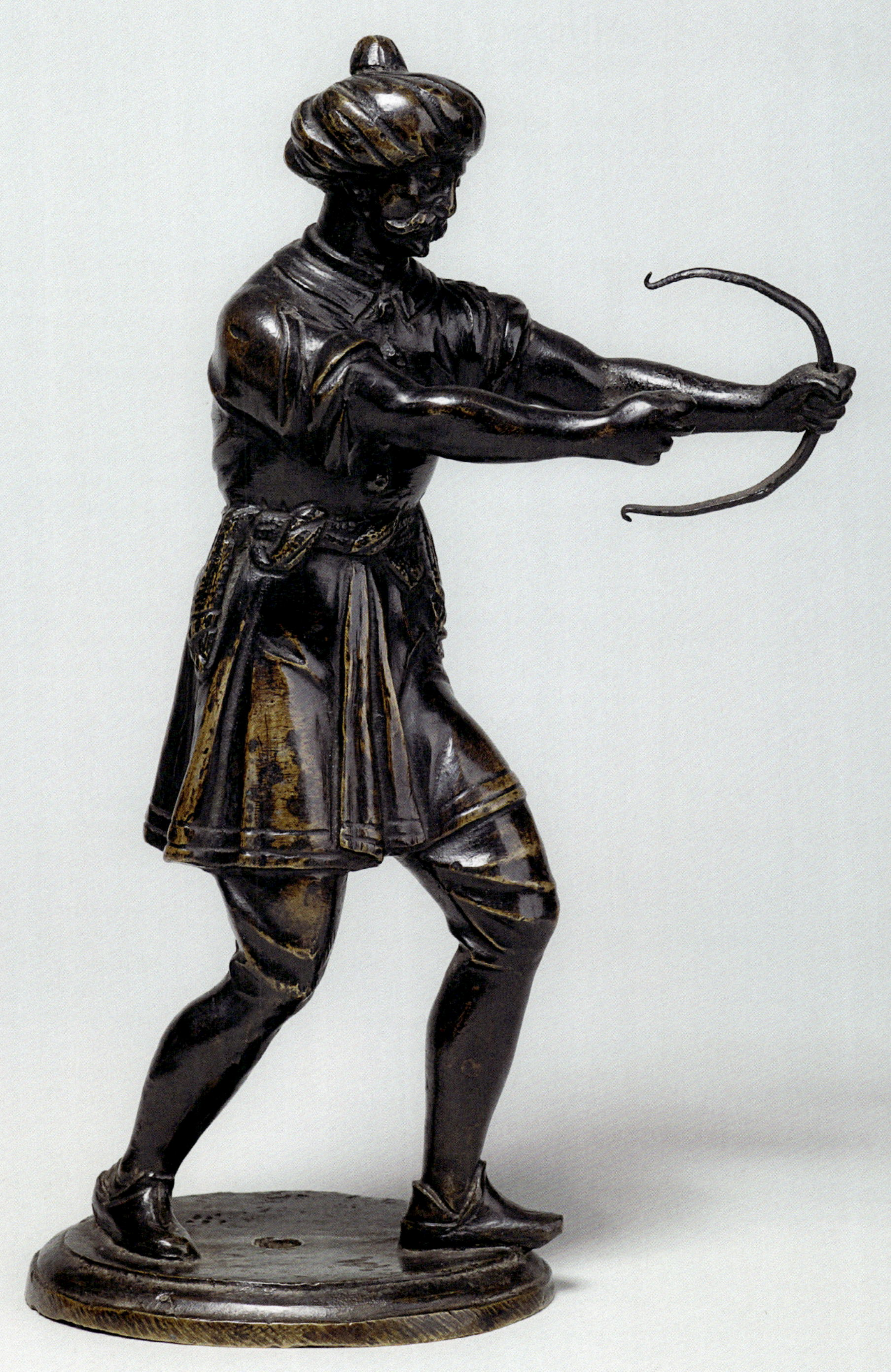

89

RHUBARB PLANT AND AN ALBARELLO

From Georg Öllinger, *Magnarum medicine partium herbariae et zoographiae imagines*

Nuremberg, ca. 1553

Pen and ink, brush and ink, watercolor

Each H. 48 cm; W. 32.5 cm (fol. 10r) and 65 cm (plates 618–19)

Universitätsbibliothek Erlangen-Nürnberg, Erlangen, inv. no. MS 2362

Fol. 10r: Albarello; plates 618–19: Rhubarb

References:
Olariu 2021, pp. 258–61; Olariu 2023, pp. 30–32, 69 (fol. 10r); pp. 41–43, 322–23 (plates 618–19).

The herbal created by the Nuremberg apothecary Georg Öllinger offers a profuse compendium of botanical drawings |**cat. nos. 38, 111**|. Although it provides only scant textual information on the plants' origins and medicinal uses, the work is enriched with numerous pictorial elements that communicate far more than the characteristic physical forms of the plants. In addition to landscape motifs, there are many depictions of animals and humans, including a number of orientalizing figures.

One example of this is in the unfinished double-page illustration of a rhubarb plant, which was never colored. In the right half, the rhubarb's large root and rounded leaves fill most of the page, hovering above a bed of flowers. In the lower right are two male figures dressed in long robes and turbans, shown small in scale in relation to the rhubarb. The left half contains an enlarged view of the rhubarb's upper section of root and leaves.

The two male figures derive from a hand-colored pen-and-ink drawing by Albrecht Dürer, known today under the title *Three Orientals*. Dürer copied the motif during his first trip to Venice in 1495–96. He encountered it in the workshop of Gentile Bellini, who had been keenly interested in Ottoman clothing ever since his visit to Istanbul |**see cat. no. 58**|.[1] The present sheet shows similarities to a woodcut based on Dürer's drawing.[2] However, the artist responsible for the illustration in Öllinger's work made significant changes: he reduced the group to two figures and varied the men's gestures and the direction of their gazes. The man on the left points to the plant, and both look toward it. There are also clear changes in the beards. Dominic Olariu notes that the figures are reminiscent of depictions of learned physicians found in herbals.[3]

Throughout this compendium, Öllinger demonstrates not only his expertise on plants but also his broad knowledge of the relevant source materials. The model for the rhubarb image, an illustration in an herbal by Johannes Kentmann, furthermore suggests that Öllinger intended the rhubarb to allude to the Ottoman cultural sphere:[4] Kentmann reports in his treatise that the rhubarb he shows was drawn after nature in the garden of Scipione Perotto del Belvedere, the caretaker of the Vatican gardens, who had obtained the rare plant's seeds in "Turcia."[5]

Another example of a plant with a distant provenance being connected with exoticized figures is found toward the beginning of Öllinger's work. The herbal begins with eight full-page illustrations of display and apothecary vessels. One of them shows a colorful, elaborately painted albarello with the head of a man wearing a turban framed at the center. The use of such figures in the decoration of Italian maiolica became widespread in the sixteenth century. While some examples are clearly identified as Ottomans, others allude to Arab authors as sources of medical knowledge.[6] The inscription on the illustrated albarello refers to contents whose rarity was consistent with the vessel's exclusivity: "chebuli [con]diti," pickled myrobalan fruits, a precious medication probably imported from Syria and Egypt.[7] Presumably, the fine vessels in the illustrations were not items that Öllinger had in his pharmacy in Nuremberg. Rather, they were probably meant to represent Öllinger's success and the global breadth of his pharmaceutical knowledge.

Marie-Therese Feist

1 The Dürer drawing: British Museum, London, inv. no. 1895,0915.974. The motif in a painting by Bellini: Gallerie dell'Accademia, Venice, inv. no. 567. See Madar 2023, pp. 49–50.
2 Among the woodcut's impressions, see, for example, the one at the British Museum, London, inv. no. 1895,0122.786.
3 Olariu 2023, p. 43.
4 *Codex Kentmanus*, 1547–49, Herzogin Anna Amalia Bibliothek, Weimar, MS Fol 323, fol. 93v.
5 Olariu 2023, p. 53, n. 190.
6 Adıgüzel 2021, p. 366; Exh. cat. Brussels and Kraków 2015, p. 173, cat. no. 73 (Alberto Saviello).
7 Olariu 2023, pp. 31–32.

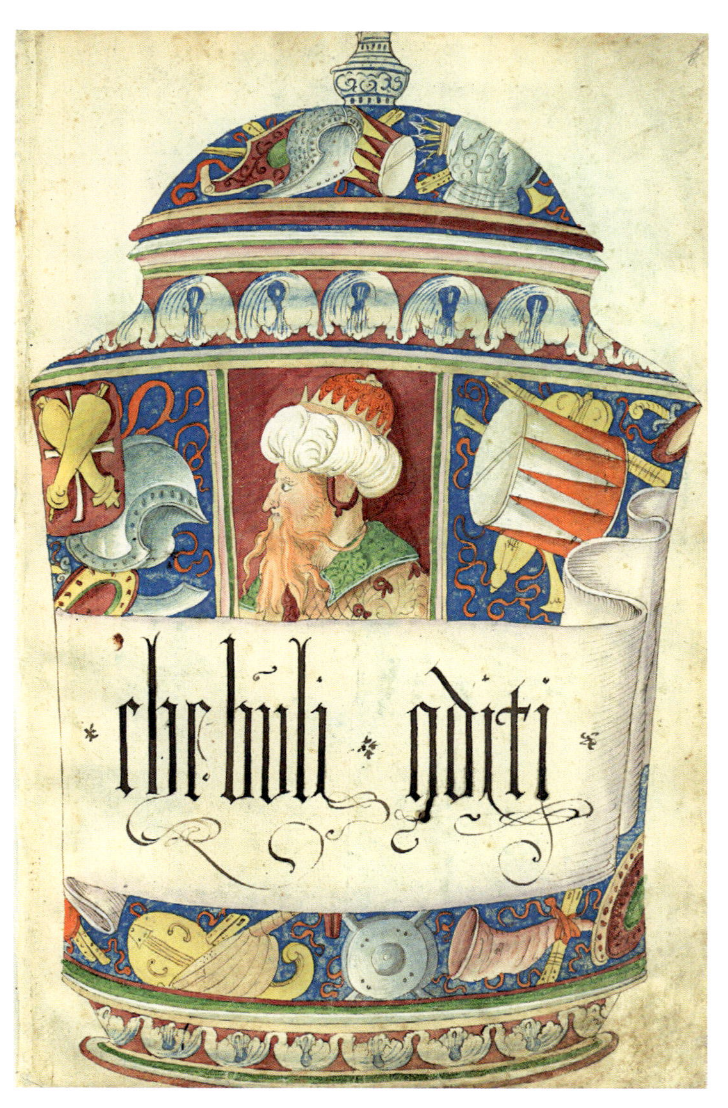
chr·buli · gditi

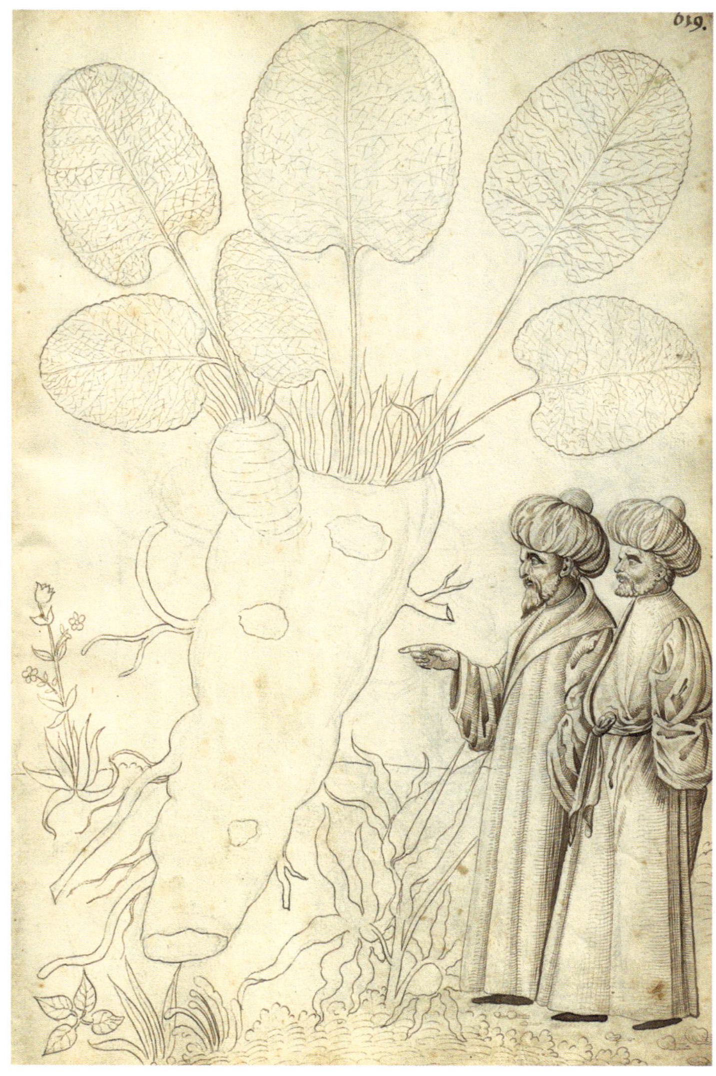

90

PLATE WITH MORESQUE ORNAMENTATION

Nicolaus Horchaimer

Nuremberg, second half of the sixteenth century

Pewter, cast

Diam. 22 cm

GNM, inv. no. LGA792, on long-term loan from the Freistaat Bayern

References:
Mory 1975, p. 322, fig. 50; Bornfleth 1989, p. 112.

The rim and center of this pewter plate are decorated with geometric patterns of interlaced bands in low relief. Vines, blossoms, and leaves fill the spaces around the bandwork. The ground has a fine matte texture. At the exact center of the plate, there is a pitcher motif accompanied by the letters "NH"—a master's mark. Also, the lesser coat of arms of the city of Nuremberg is nestled among the vines on the rim. That, together with the master's mark, points to the Nuremberg pewterer Nicolaus Horchaimer (master in 1561, d. 1583). Horchaimer is known for making pewter objects from etched molds; he may even have invented that technique.[1] The process involved etching figural or purely ornamental designs into a negative mold. This eliminated the need to decorate each piece individually by hand, since the design was already a part of the casting. Because of the resulting woodcut-like appearance, the etched-mold technique is commonly referred to as the *Holzstockmanier* (woodblock manner). It was practiced in Nuremberg until the early seventeenth century. After that, relief-decorated pewter (*Reliefzinn*) was obtained from engraved molds.

Among Horchaimer's works, those with figural decoration predominate over the ornamental ones. The latter include this plate with moresque, or arabesque, ornamentation. Scholarship is not entirely in agreement about which term to use for the ornament. Indeed, it is impossible to make a historical distinction between moresque and arabesque patterns. The origins of both lie in the ancient acanthus scroll pattern. Through the import of handcrafted goods made of metal, textiles, leather, and ceramics from the Islamic world, this type of ornament spread into Europe, where it was imitated from the late fifteenth century onward.[2] In the first half of the sixteenth century, the pattern books *Opera nuova* and *Esamplario nuovo* by Giovanni Antonio Tagliente include knot-like ornaments described as *Groppi moreschi et arabeschi*.

It remains unclear to what extent the two terms were used to indicate different variants or dissimilar origins.[3] In any case, Europeans perceived these patterns as "exotic" and were clearly fascinated by them. Ornamental engravings ensured the patterns' widespread distribution and served as models for various artists and artisans, including pewterers.

Six woodcuts by Albrecht Dürer bespeak an encounter with ornaments from the Islamic cultural sphere |**cat. no. 92**|. Within a round outer contour, each shows complex, symmetrically arranged geometric patterns or "knots" of interlaced white bandwork on a black background. The design concept is reminiscent of a dish or plate viewed from above. It is possible that direct or indirect inspiration came from brass plates with silver inlays in the "Veneto-Saracenic" style.[4] Luxury items of that type were produced in Egypt and Syria in the late fifteenth and early sixteenth centuries. In them, the silver interlacing stands out as brighter in tone than the surrounding brass, much like the bands in Dürer's woodcuts. A similar effect is achieved on the pewter plate by the fine matted finish of the background. Another shared aspect of the Veneto-Saracenic brass dishes is the low relief and the resulting tactile quality. In Dürer's woodcuts, it results from the printing technique; on the pewter plate, from the ornamentation being created in relief in a casting mold.

Sabine Tiedtke

1 Haedeke 1963, p. 180.
2 Irmscher 1984, pp. 266–67.
3 See Irmscher 1984, p. 268.
4 Dackerman 2024, pp. 96–97.

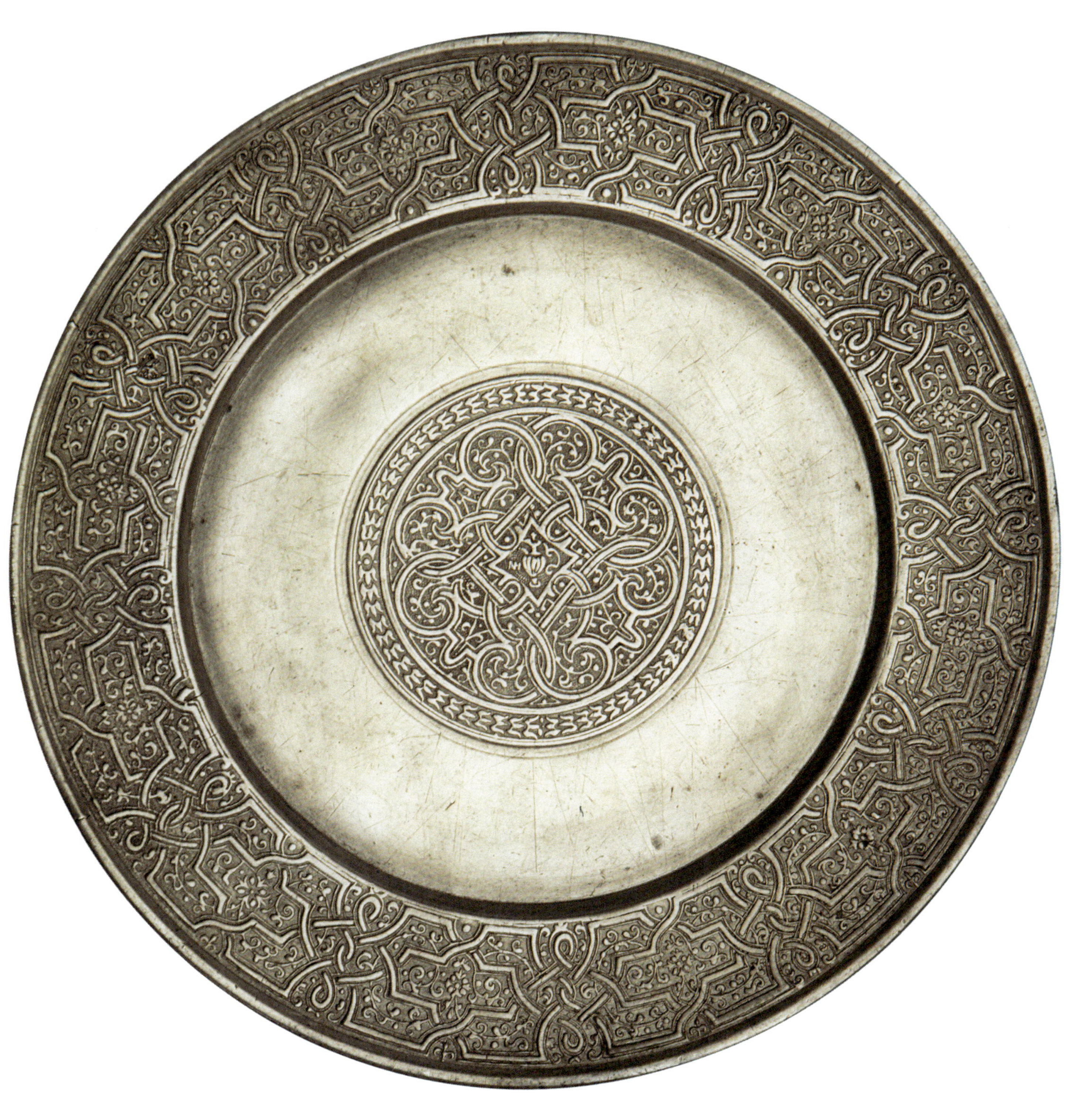

91

SHIELD OF SIGISMUND II AUGUSTUS, KING OF POLAND AND GRAND DUKE OF LITHUANIA

Kunz Lochner

Nuremberg, ca. 1555

Iron, etched

Diam. 60.5 cm

Muzeum Wojska Polskiego, Warsaw, inv. no. MWP 34385

References:
Exh. cat. Nuremberg and New York 1986, pp. 468–69, cat. no. 278 (Martin Angerer); Willers 2002, p. 147; Exh. cat. Nuremberg 2002, p. 469, cat. no. 44.

This shield is thought to have been part of a parade armor owned by Sigismund II Augustus, king of Poland and grand duke of Lithuania (1520–1572). The work's royal provenance and the quality of its craftsmanship are indicative of the global standing enjoyed by Nuremberg's armorers in the Middle Ages and the Renaissance. Round shields such as this one belonged to types of armor garnitures that were worn primarily in tournaments, as lavish symbols of princely power. Only a small number of workshops in Europe were able to produce them at this level of quality. Craftspeople from the German-speaking lands led the market, and some even set up shop abroad, as was the case with the Royal Almain Armoury in Greenwich, England, founded in 1511. In Nuremberg, Kunz Lochner (1510–1567) was the most important armorer of his generation and received commissions from throughout Europe. His works are preserved in private and public collections worldwide.

With this shield, Kunz Lochner demonstrated his knowledge of prevailing trends: elements of Levantine design and warcraft had become sought-after models for European armor. For the shield's form, technique, and decoration, Lochner drew inspiration from prototypes originating in the Levant, though not always at first hand. Arabesque decoration was quite popular in Nuremberg even in the generation of Albrecht Dürer, including in works by Dürer himself |**see cat. no. 92**|. Lochner may therefore have relied on local models for this shield. However, not only the shield's ornamentation but also its etching technique, carried out here to perfection, probably developed in the ancient period in what is now the Middle East. Knowledge of the technique found its way to northern Europe via Italian armorers.

A contemporaneous armor made by Lochner for Mikołaj Radziwiłł IV (1515–1565), a confidant of Sigismund II Augustus and his grand marshal in Lithuania, is comparable in design to the present shield. It still features elaborate painted strapwork in red, gold, and black. Consistent with the fashion of the day, the Warsaw shield must originally have been similarly colored. However, that is now only vaguely discernible, owing to the shield's state of preservation after half a millennium. Recent studies of polychromy on English armor[1] and sixteenth-century works of goldsmithing[2] offer further comparable examples of the contemporary practice of decorating metalwork in multiple colors.

Shortly after the death of Sigismund II Augustus, his sister and successor to the throne, Anna Jagiellon (1523–1596), likewise childless, donated most of the armor garniture to her brother-in-law John III Vasa, king of Sweden (1537–1592). His son—the nephew of the armor's original owner—would become ruler of Poland and Lithuania in 1566, as Sigismund III. This transfer of the royal garniture can be interpreted as a sign of the queen's desire to secure the royal crown for the Jagiellonian dynasty. Except for this shield, the armor is now preserved at Livrustkammaren (The Royal Armory) in Stockholm.[3]

Heike Zech

1 Patterson 2009.
2 Dix and Schübel 2020.
3 Inv. nos. 26043–65.

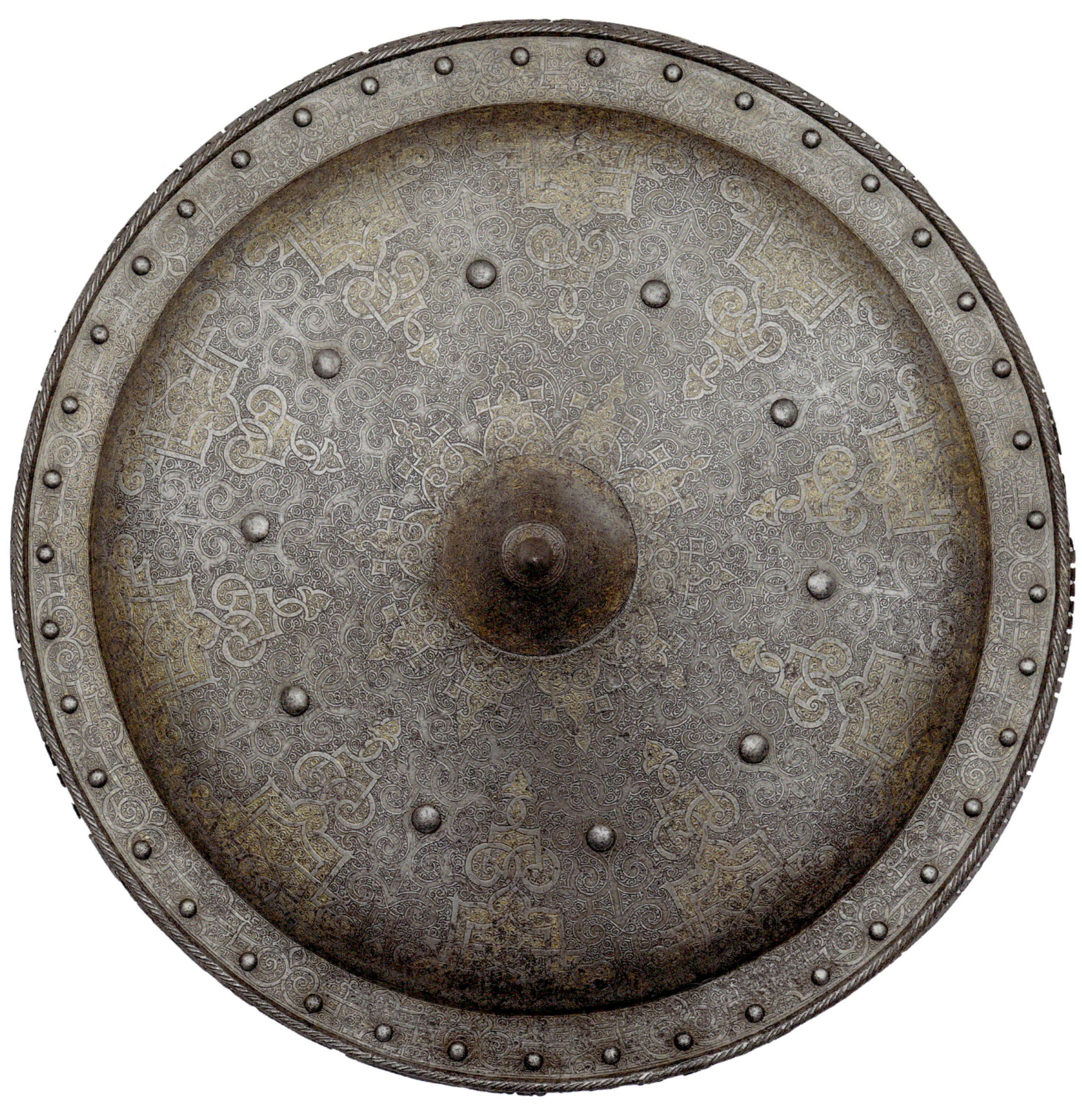

92

SIX KNOTS

Albrecht Dürer

Nuremberg, after 1506

Woodcuts

H. 27–27.4 cm; W. 21–21.4 cm

GNM, inv. nos. H7593, H7595, H7597, H7599, H7601, on long-term loan from the Sammlung Bernhard Hausmann; GNM, inv. no. StN2298, on long-term loan from the Museen der Stadt Nürnberg, Kunstsammlungen

References:
Schoch, Mende, and Scherbaum 2002, pp. 145–57, cat. no. 147 (Matthias Mende); Belting 2012, pp. 47–54; Exh. cat. Frankfurt and Hamburg 2013, pp. 74–76, cat. no. 32 (Werner Busch); Dackerman 2024, pp. 76–121.

These woodcuts, designed by Albrecht Dürer after 1506 as a six-part series, consist of delicately interlaced white bands whose complex flourishes form symmetrical, knot-like networks on black roundels. Even though Dürer's characteristic "AD" monogram is missing from the prints, his authorship is firmly documented: in a 1521 entry in the diary of his journey to the Low Countries, he notes that he gave the "6 knots" (*6 knodn*) as a gift to Dirk Vellert, a glass painter and dean of the Antwerp Guild of Saint Luke.[1] Dürer's "knots" have long held the attention of art historians, for their function appears to go beyond the purely ornamental. To this day, scholars are still engaged in an attempt to untangle the web of meanings associated with these designs.

The *Six Knots* woodcuts are slightly varied copies of engravings from the circle of Leonardo da Vinci (1452–1519). In Italy, these types of ornamental motifs became widespread in various pictorial media in the fifteenth century. Dürer came into contact with them at the latest by 1505–6, during his second trip to Italy. Owing to the engraved originals' connection with Leonardo, scholarship has assumed that Dürer approached his adaptations as a kind of artistic competition (*paragone*), in order to measure himself against the most famous Renaissance artist south of the Alps, a status held by Leonardo even at that time. In contrast to the Italian knot designs, executed as engravings, Dürer chose the medium of woodcut, a more technically demanding process for such intricate patterns, which ultimately enabled him to surpass Leonardo.

However, the analysis of Dürer's *Six Knots* falls short if it is limited to the European art-theoretical discourse of the period. For the knot series can also be understood as a microcosm of the transcultural interconnectedness of artistic production around 1500: both Dürer's designs and their Italian counterparts take inspiration from ornamentation that is familiar from the art of the Islamic world. In Persia, this type of infinite strapwork pattern, termed *girih*, the Persian word for "knot," became an integral part of the Islamic vocabulary of form as early as the twelfth century.[2] In Dürer's time, elaborately crafted metalwork that was heavily decorated with such motifs was commonly found in Venice. Those works frequently came from the Mamluk Sultanate in Syria and Egypt, with which Venice maintained strong trade relations. Examples that entered Europe were most often associated with the name of the artist Mahmud al-Kurdi, who was well known for his metal inlay decorations. During his stays in Venice, Dürer is likely to have encountered works by Mahmud al-Kurdi or similar objects.

The abstract interlacing designs characteristic of the Islamic sphere are not purely ornamental in nature; in Islam, they are understood as universal patterns expressive of the divine order. A similarly transcendent claim to universality underlies Dürer's *Six Knots*, which, due to their mathematical perfection, can be interpreted as a Christian "likeness of divine perfection."[3]

Johannes Gebhardt

1 Schoch, Mende, and Scherbaum 2002, p. 145 (Matthias Mende).
2 Belting 2012, p. 50.
3 Quotation translated from the German in Exh. cat. Frankfurt and Hamburg 2013, p. 74, cat. no. 32 (Werner Busch).

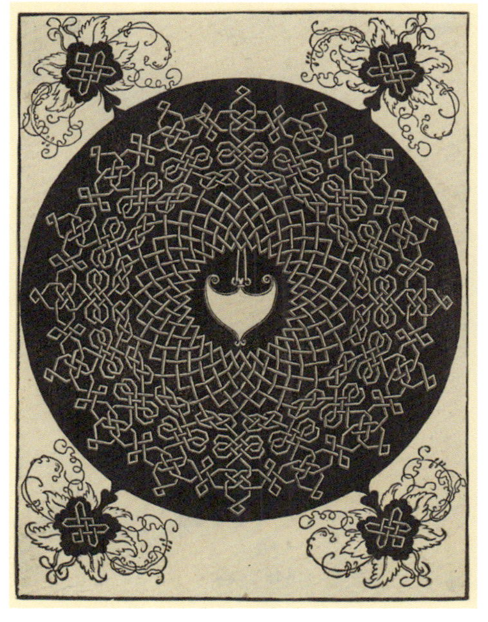
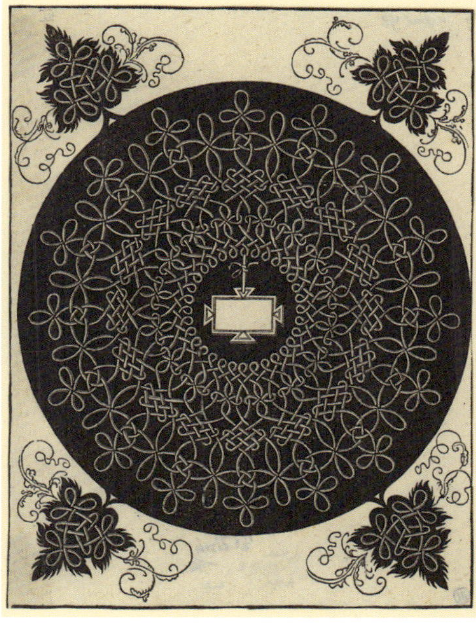
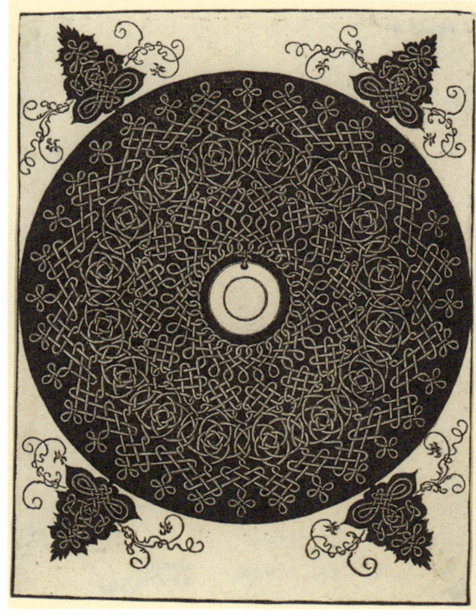
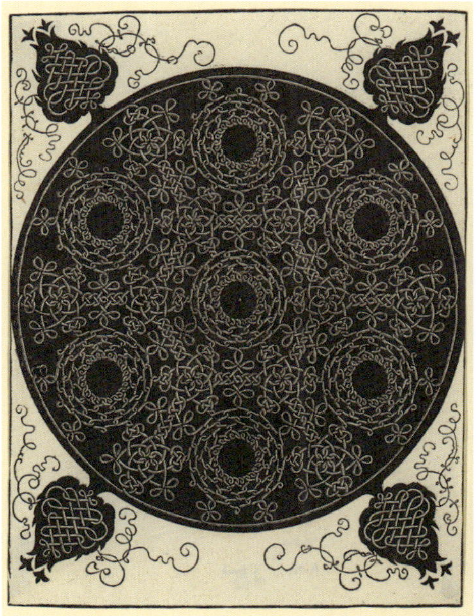
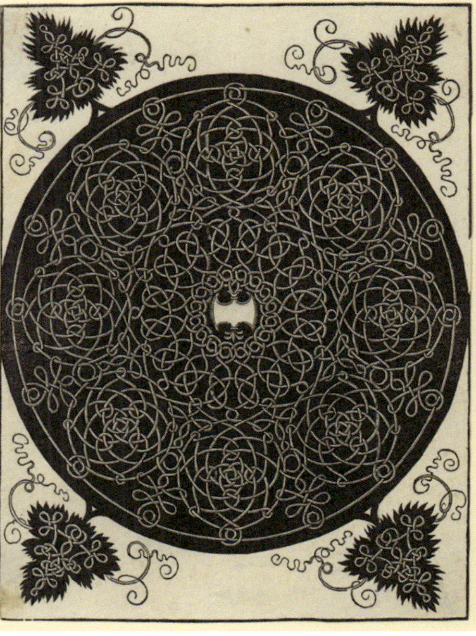
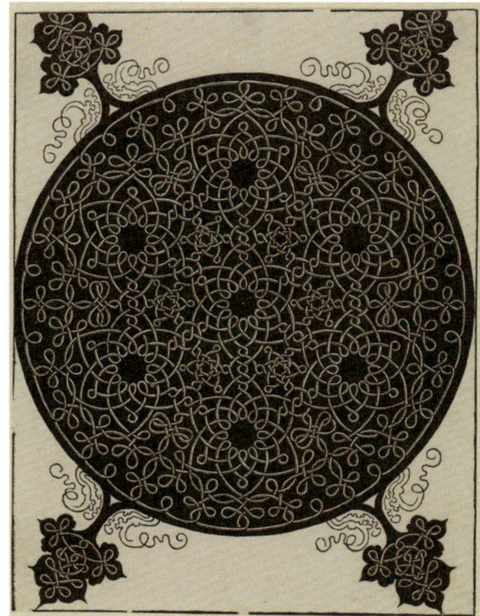

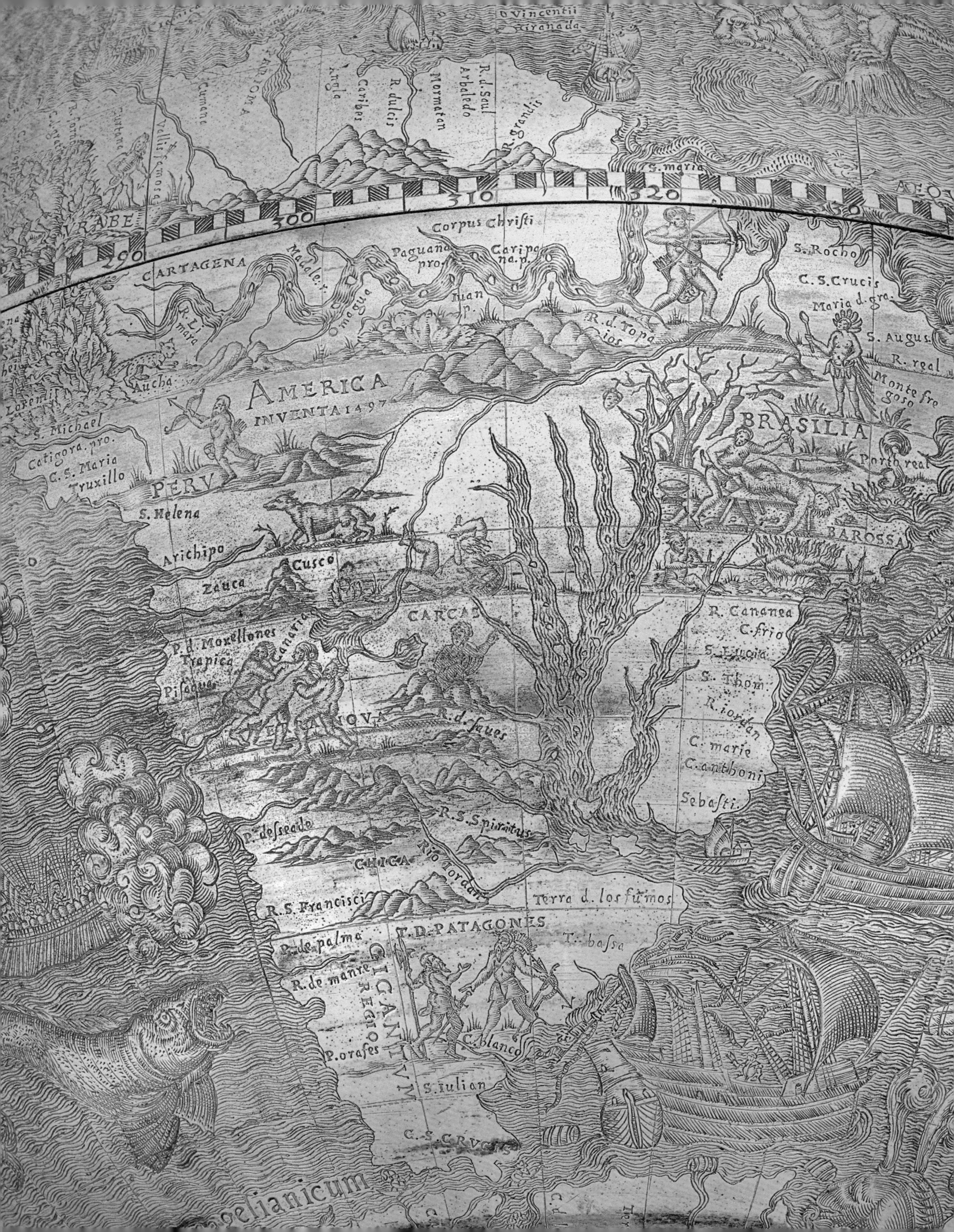
Granada
Cumane
Caribes
Angla
R. dulcis
Mormatan
R. d. Saul
Arbaledo
R. grandis
S. maria
VRABE
290
300
310
320
Corpus Christi
CARTAGENA
Paguana pro.
Caripo na. p.
S. Rocho
C. S. Crucis
Maria d. gra.
S. Augus.
R. real
Monte fre goso
AMERICA
INVENTA 1497
S. Michael
Catigora. pro.
C. S. Maria
Truxillo
PERV
BRASILIA
Porto real
S. Helena
BAROSSA
Arichipo
Cusco
Zauca
CARCAS
R. Cananea
C. frio
P. d. Morellones
S. Thom.
R. iordan
C. marie
C. anthoni
Sebasti.
R. S. Spiritus
P. desseado
CHICA
Rio iordan
Terra d. los fumos
R. S. Francisci
T. D. PATAGONES
T. bassa
P. de palma
R. de manre
GIGANTVM REGIO
C. blanco
P. orafes
S. Iulian

TO THE AMERICAS VIA THE IBERIAN PENINSULA

Nuremberg maintained close ties with the Iberian Peninsula in the fifteenth and sixteenth centuries. The travelogue of the Nuremberg humanist Hieronymus Münzer bears witness to that relationship, as does the presence of printers from Nuremberg in Seville and Granada, along with the early reception of Dürer's prints in Spanish art. With the conquest of Granada in 1492 and Columbus's voyage that same year, cities such as Seville became particularly attractive as hubs for global trading enterprises. The Treaty of Tordesillas, signed in 1494, gave the Spanish crown exclusive rights to the western territories of the "New World," leading to a greater focus on colonial ventures in the American continents.

Entrepreneurs from Nuremberg participated in these expansionist activities in the Americas. In Seville, the lobbyist Lazarus Nürnberger worked as a crucial facilitator and coordinator. Nuremberg merchants sent ships to Brazil, operated copper mines in Cuba, and were involved in the colonization of Chile and Venezuela. Yet we often know about these undertakings only from archival records. Related artistic objects are rare. This applies in particular to Nurembergers' involvement in the economic and ideological processes of European expansion and to the roles they played in colonial power structures.

Profits generated from the use of enslaved people or from the appropriation of Indigenous resources presumably flowed—at least indirectly—into the production of works of art in Nuremberg. This section therefore contains a group of works commissioned by the globally active Welser trading firm. At the same time, reports, broadsheets, and illustrated books printed in Nuremberg significantly influenced European perceptions of the "New World." Also, as Indigenous artifacts made their way through Europe, some changed hands in Nuremberg. The illustrated herbal produced by the apothecary Georg Öllinger attests to the rapid spread of knowledge about plants, both useful and ornamental, that were imported from overseas.

Benno Baumbauer and Sven Jakstat

◂ cat. no. 107 (detail)

93

ITINERARIUM (REPORT ON THE JOURNEY TO THE IBERIAN PENINSULA, 1494–95)

Hieronymus Münzer (author)
Hartmann Schedel (transcription)

Nuremberg, ca. 1497–1501

Manuscript on paper, 305 leaves

H. 21.6 cm; W. 16.1 cm (each leaf)

Bayerische Staatsbibliothek, Munich, Clm 431, fols. 94r–275v

Open to fols. 345v–346r: Ground plan of Santiago de Compostela Cathedral

Not exhibited

References:
Exh. cat. Munich 2014, pp. 149–51, cat. no. 7.3 (Juliane Trede); Münzer and Herbers 2020, pp. CXV–CXXXVII (Klaus Herbers).

From August 1494 to April 1495, the Nuremberg municipal physician and scholar Hieronymus Münzer traveled through large parts of western and southwestern Europe |**fig. p. 68**|. His account of that journey is preserved solely in the present copy made by the humanist Hartmann Schedel.[1] Münzer's travelogue forms the main portion of an omnibus manuscript containing other transcriptions in Schedel's hand. That volume, once part of Schedel's famous library in Nuremberg,[2] has a splendid calfskin binding made in Nuremberg about 1500. It is unclear whether the travelogue was intended exclusively for the humanist circle around Schedel in this town or whether a print publication was planned.

Compared with other early modern travelogues dealing with the Iberian Peninsula, Münzer's text contains an unusually broad range of information. It not only offers insight into the practicalities of travel but also deals with topics from the areas of religion, economics, culture, and politics. All this was based on Münzer's own observations and the information he received from his local contacts. His report thus provides considerable evidence about the types of networks available around 1500 to a traveler who belonged to Nuremberg's upper class. In numerous places, he met people who informed him about local conditions and customs and helped him to establish further contacts.[3]

To give readers an idea of the size and importance of cities or buildings he visited, Münzer repeatedly cites Nuremberg as a point of reference.[4] He describes Murcia as roughly the same size as Nuremberg, Salamanca as "slightly larger," and Lisbon, Toledo, and Zaragoza as significantly larger. He estimates Seville and Barcelona to be two to three times the size of his hometown, and he judges Valencia, which he likens to Nuremberg in its status as a regional trade center, to be twice the size of Barcelona—that is, four times the size of Nuremberg.[5]

Münzer's journey through the kingdoms of the Iberian Peninsula took place at a time of profound social, political, and cultural change. When he arrived in Granada in the fall of 1494, only two and a half years had passed since the Catholic Monarchs, Isabella of Castile and Ferdinand of Aragon, had captured the city from the last Muslim ruler on the Iberian Peninsula, Abu Abdallah Muhammad XII. With the Alhambra Decree of March 31, 1492, Ferdinand and Isabella had ordered the expulsion or forced assimilation of the Jewish population living in their territories. And in the agreement signed on April 17, 1492, in Santa Fe, a short distance from Granada, they had assured Christopher Columbus of their support for his westward expedition across the Atlantic. When Münzer met Isabella and Ferdinand in person in Madrid, a few months after his stay in Granada, he praised them for such acts. These undertakings would prove decisively influential to the history of early globalization and the genesis of European expansion.

Sven Jakstat

1 On Münzer's travelogue, see also the essay by Sven Jakstat in the present volume. For a modern edition of the Latin text, see Münzer and Herbers 2020; for a translation into German, see Herbers 2020; for a translation into English, see Firth 2014.
2 The volume is first documented in the 1507 inventory of Schedel's library (the previous inventory dates from 1498). The library's holdings are preserved nearly in their entirety in the Bayerische Staatsbibliothek. See Exh. cat. Munich 2014.
3 See Jaspert 2016.
4 See Herbers 2000.
5 Herbers 2020, pp. 45, 56, 66, 104, 114, 145, 157, 174.

pulus adeo portanus Et habet plures portas
qui sunt in bono merito Et pigre est quod ad
tuere tene magis mendit ut plurimum ex questu
peregrinorum vivunt. Habent aetem bonum,
et intra muros / similiter extra muros multa
monasteria: ut monasterium S. domini in quo
homo doctissimus predicator qui mihi multos
tenuit. Item monasterium S. benedicti quod ab
atem Rex in Castella [illegible] dum fecit
[illegible] dissipatorem bonorum. Item monasterium S. Clare, Carmelitarum, Fratrum minorum
Rex autem mendit reformationem Augustini
Quem diu protegat deus in longum.

De Ecclesia S. Iacobi

Ecclesia S. Iacobi una de tribus principalibus
ecclesiis est ut post Romanam Et ephesina
in asia que nunc periit. Edificata est autem
a Karolo magno rege francorum et imperatore
almanie: Quam (ut ex post de bellis cum audires) eam
fabre fecit ex spoliis et donis et manubiis sa-
racenorum. Et est stupendum opus ad modum
crucis. Longitudo sepulcri est 100. passuum.
Longitudo brachiorum 120. Latitudo brachiorum 14. Latitudo sepulcri 32. Longitudo
totius sepulcri et capitis. 140. Et est tota
de quadro Et fortissimo lapide fabricata
et testudinata: Et habet duo latera ut ecclesia S.

Sebaldi. Et in capite in circuitu capellas. Et te-
cta est fortissimum opus: Et habet in 4 angu-
lis 4 turres fortissimas Et hodie fortissime
turres edificantur. [illegible]

Ymago Ecclesie S. Iacobi.

Capelle
Altare
Chorus
Turris
Turris
Meridies
·12 pass
=
brachium
Ianua
Stallum
100
passus
34
Turris
Occidens
Turris

Capelle 12 circa chorum Et testudo capitis
crucis est altissima In cuius medio [illegible]
mensam de latere in longum brachiorum [illegible]

94

BREVE DOCTRINA

Hernando de Talavera

Granada: Johann Pegnitzer and Meinhard Ungut, ca. 1496

94.1 De las ceremonias de la misa

Incunable, 30 leaves

H. 20.5 cm; W. 29 cm (opened)

Staatsbibliothek zu Berlin, Preußischer Kulturbesitz - SPK, shelf mark 8° Inc. 4963.6

Open to fols. 2v–3r: Provisions regarding the altar

94.2 Del vestir y calzar

(not illustrated)

Incunable, 48 leaves

H. 20.5 cm; W. 29 cm (opened)

Staatsbibliothek zu Berlin, SPK, shelf mark 8° Inc. 4963.7

References:
Resines 1993, pp. 63–65; Pereda 2007, p. 278; Biersack 2010, p. 370; Johnston 2013; Gilbert 2024, p. 4.

Johann Pegnitzer of Nuremberg and his business partner Meinhard Ungut (d. 1499) were among the first printers to set up publishing houses in Granada, the former capital of the Nasrid dynasty, after the city's conquest by the Catholic Monarchs. Fray Hernando de Talavera (d. 1507), the first archbishop of the newly established Archdiocese of Granada, was early to recognize the great potential of letterpress printing—a relatively new technology—and he quickly engaged printers for his projects. The texts printed for him in Granada played a central role in his efforts both to convert the predominantly Muslim population to Christianity and to influence the education and habits of priests who served in the diocese.[1] The book *Breve y muy provechosa doctrina cristiana* (Short and Very Beneficial Christian Doctrine) emerged in that context. It comprises various treatises by Talavera,[2] including the present two fascicles from the holdings of the Staatsbibliothek in Berlin: one treatise explaining the components of the Christian Mass (*De las ceremonias de la misa*) and the other dealing with dress codes (*Del vestir y calzar*).

The sociocultural context surrounding Talavera's texts is vividly illuminated by the travelogue written by the Nuremberg physician and scholar Hieronymus Münzer |**cat. no. 93**|. When Münzer visited Granada in the fall of 1494, the population was predominantly Muslim.[3] He describes the rites and customs of Granada's Muslims with a mixture of fascination, suspicion, and skepticism. Talavera, as confessor to Isabella of Castile, was one of the most influential clerics and intellectuals in the circle of the Catholic Monarchs. Unlike other Spanish theologians, he wanted to convert Muslims not by force but by persuasion. He saw the education of the clergy as playing a key role in this process. After Münzer met him in Granada, he described Talavera's educational ethos and desire to effect conversions as follows: "Never in all Spain have I seen a man more learned in theology and philosophy. . . . He welcomed me warmly, like a father, and informed me about the things I asked. He is highly regarded by His Royal Majesty and has accepted this esteem. He converts many Saracens to our faith, protects them, and imparts knowledge to them."[4]

In Granada, Münzer also met with German printers, probably employees of Pegnitzer and Ungut.[5] Although the *Breve doctrina* contains no mention of the printer's name or the date of publication, the book was almost certainly issued by the Pegnitzer-Ungut shop in Granada. It uses the same typefaces as are found in Talavera's edition of the *Vita Christi* by Francisco Eiximenis. In a copy of that book in the Biblioteca Nacional in Madrid, the colophon not only lists the place of publication (Granada), the client (Talavera), and the date of printing (1496), but it also names "Meynardo vngut" and "Joha[n]nes de nure[n]berga alemanes" as the printers.[6]

Sven Jakstat

1 Pereda 2007, pp. 254–87, esp. pp. 278–80.
2 On the contents, see Folgado García 2011.
3 On this, see the essay by Sven Jakstat in the present volume and also Münzer and Herbers 2020, pp. 103–43.
4 Translated after the German in Herbers 2020, pp. 95–96.
5 Herbers 2020, p. 95. On this, see also Herbers 2000, pp. 175–77; Jaspert 2016, p. 80.
6 Eiximenis 1496.

las primeras oraciões. ⁊ adonde ſe dize la epiſtola. E llamaſſe parte derecha aq̃lla en que ſe dize el euangelio: ⁊ todo lo al.

Por que eſta el altar hazia oriente.

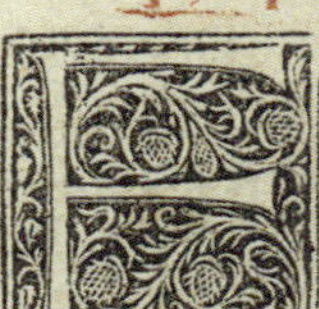

Eſta pueſto el altar hazia oriente: porque el redẽptor nueſtro que por el altar en alguna manera es repreſentado: fue nombrado oriente ſegun ſe eſcribe en zacharias propheta. E Por qne la ſancta cruz en que padeſcio fue pyeſta hazia oriente. E avn por que quando alos cielos ſubio lleuaua ſu dulce cara hazia oriente. E final mẽte por nos deſuiar dela cerimonia del pueblo judiego: que le tenia hazia occidente.

Del frontal ⁊ ornamentos del altar.

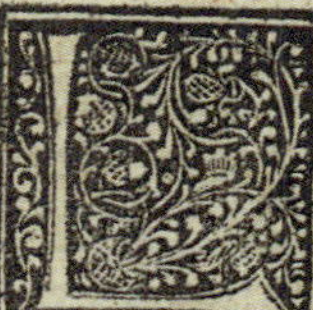

Los ornamẽtos ⁊ paños de ſeda ⁊ de lino de q̃ el altar cubrẽ: repreſentã los precioſos ⁊ ſagrados miẽbros de ihesu chriſto que conpuſieron ⁊ adornaron aquella ſancta cruz. ⁊ las gracias ſin medida ⁊ dones infinitos de que ſu ſancta humanidad fue apoſtada. Los buenos exemplos ⁊ actos de grandes virtudes de que la ſancta yglesia que es la confradia ⁊ ayuntamiẽto de los fieles eſta llena ⁊ adornada.

Delos candeleros que ponen enel altar.

Los candeleros q̃ ſe ponen eñl altar: repreſentan al angel que apareſcio alos paſtores judios ⁊ la eſtrella. que pareſcio alos reyes magos gentiles quãdo ihesu chriſto naſcio. ¶ Pues quando vieremos el altar compueſto para la miſſa: paſſen eſtas coſas: o algunas dellas por nueſtro penſamiẽto deziendo entre nos: o como mas deuocion ouieremos. Bendicta ſeñor aquella ſancta meſa en que tan excellente pan de vida ⁊ tan ſuaue beuer a tus ſanctos diſcipulos diſte. El qual ordenaſte que a nos miſerables ⁊ flacos fueſſe dado. Bendicta ſea la ſancta cruz en que al padre con tanta karidad por nos te offreciſte. Bendicta la ſanctiſſima humanidad que para nos redemir ⁊ glorificar tan pura ⁊ tan delica-

cat. no. 94.1

95

SAINT ANNE, THE VIRGIN, SAINT ELIZABETH, SAINT JOHN AND THE CHRIST CHILD

Fernando Yáñez de la Almedina

Almedina, Ciudad Real, ca. 1524

Paint on pine

H. 142.4 cm; W. 119 cm (incl. frame)

Museo Nacional del Prado, Madrid, inv. no. P2805

References:
Exh. cat. Madrid 2006, pp. 240–49, cat. no. 17 (Maite Jover de Celis and Carmen Garrido); Exh. cat. Madrid 2011, pp. 240–49, cat. no. 171 (Pedro Miguel Ibáñez Martínez); Mozzati 2020, pp. 117–19; López Camarillas 2021. On Dürer: Schoch, Mende, and Scherbaum 2002, pp. 232–34, cat. no. 169 (Anna Scherbaum).

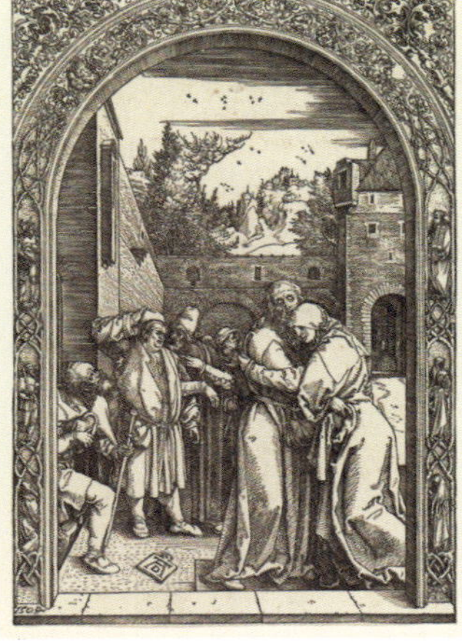

95.2 Joachim and Anne Meeting at the Golden Gate

Albrecht Dürer, Nuremberg, 1504

Woodcut | H. 29.9 cm; W. 21 cm

GNM, inv. no. StN2254, on long-term loan from the City of Nuremberg, Kunstsammlungen

This painting by Fernando Yáñez de la Almedina (d. about 1537) entered the holdings of the Museo Nacional del Prado in 1941. It came from the parish church of Almedina, the artist's birthplace, in the Ciudad Real region of Spain, which lies roughly halfway between Murcia and Madrid.[1] The painting's genesis and Yáñez's biography both exemplify the mobility of artists and their works at the turn of the fifteenth to the sixteenth century. At the same time, this picture is a prominent example of the early reception of Albrecht Dürer's prints in Spain.[2]

At an unknown date early in his career, Fernando Yáñez left Spain for Italy, where he worked with Leonardo da Vinci in Florence. He is usually identified as the painter mentioned in Leonardo's account books under the name "Ferrando Spagnolo dipintore." After returning to Spain, in 1506 he began work on the wings of the high altarpiece of Valencia Cathedral, together with his namesake Fernando de Llanos. Even the earlier history of this altarpiece is of interest for reconstructing transregional networks between southern Germany and the Iberian Peninsula: during his visit to Valencia in October 1494, the Nuremberg municipal physician and scholar Hieronymus Münzer |**see cat. no. 93**| witnessed work on the altarpiece's central section, made of silver (to which the painted wings by Yáñez and Llanos were later attached).[3] Münzer even spoke personally with an unnamed German silversmith from Lauingen an der Donau who was involved in the production process.[4]

Yáñez's paintings frequently exhibit notable similarities in style and motif to those of Leonardo. In the present work, this is particularly true of the Virgin Mary. Her facial features, expression, and gestures are strongly reminiscent of Leonardo's various treatments of the Virgin. In the background, Yáñez included a depiction of Joachim and Anne meeting at the Golden Gate. That event described in the *Legenda Aurea* was interpreted as proof of the Virgin Mary's immaculate conception, since Catholic doctrine held that Anne became pregnant with Mary at the moment of her embrace with Joachim. Yáñez based his rendition of the subject on the woodcut in Albrecht Dürer's Life of the Virgin series,[5] borrowing Dürer's pictorial invention with only a few changes. Because of its visual isolation from the painting's foreground scene, the Meeting at the Golden Gate looks almost like a picture within a picture. This raises the question of whether Yáñez made use of the print simply because he regarded Dürer's depiction as particularly striking and worthy of imitation, or whether he intended a kind of visual quote, a deliberate citation of the Nuremberg artist and his work. In the latter case, the painting would make reference to two of the most famous artists in Europe at the time—Dürer and Leonardo—who clearly served as role models for Yáñez in his own artistic practice. This would be consistent with a statement made by Johannes Cochläus in 1512 concerning Dürer's Engraved Passion: Cochläus described that print series as "executed so well and in such correct perspective that merchants from all over Europe buy it as a model for their artists."[6] In the sixteenth century, the reception of Dürer's works occurred even outside of Europe, as demonstrated by examples from India, Sri Lanka, and South America |**cat. nos. 121, 122; fig. p. 29**|.

Sven Jakstat

1 López Camarillas 2021.
2 On the reception of Dürer in Spain, see Silva Maroto 2008; Ortuño Molins 2002.
3 On Münzer's travelogue, see the essay by Sven Jakstat in the present volume.
4 Kehrer 1953, p. 119.
5 Silva Maroto 2008, p. 199; Ortuño Molins 2002, p. 258.
6 Translated after the citation in Ortuño Molins 2002, p. 253.

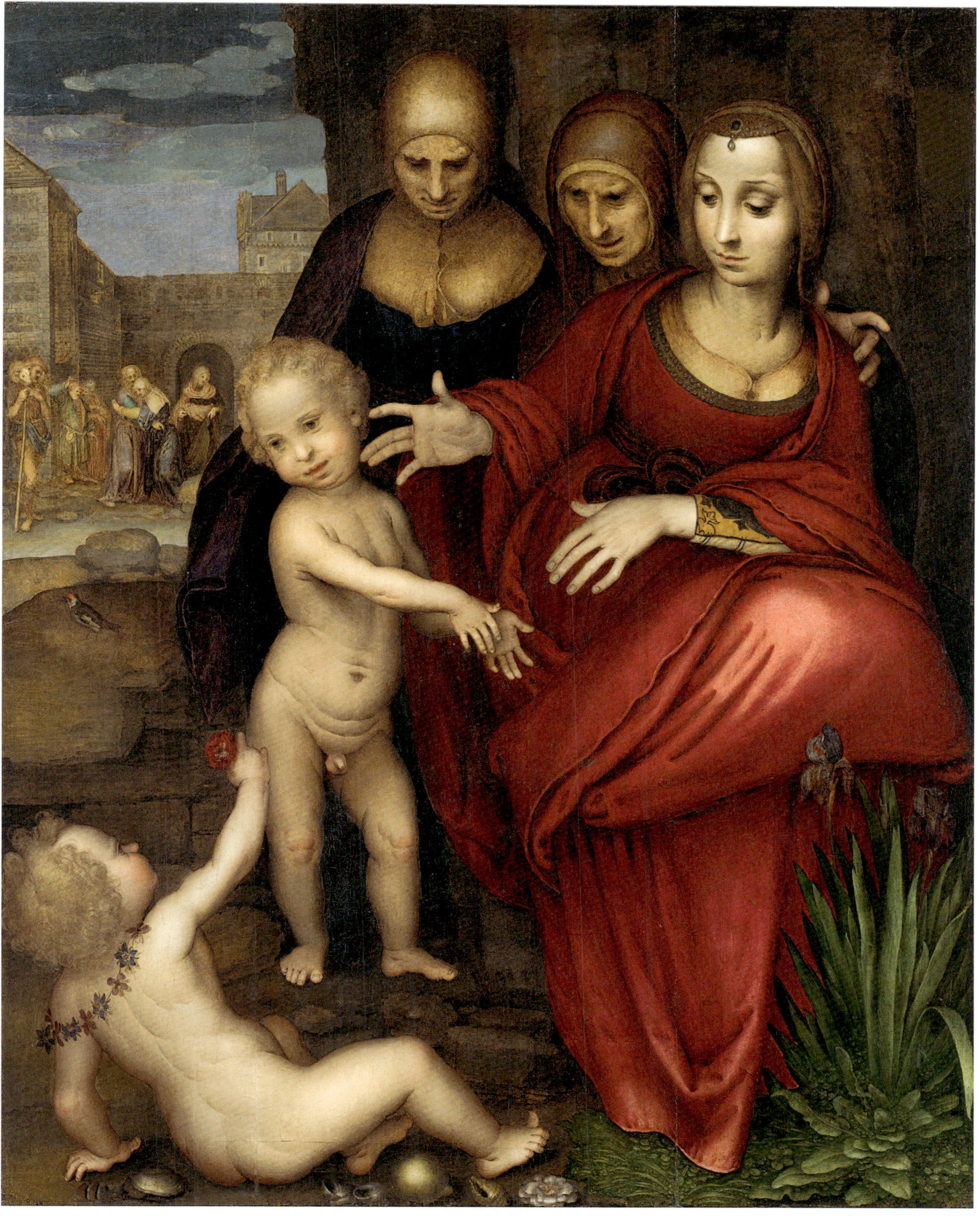

cat. no. 95.1

96

PILGRIM'S CLOAK OF STEPHAN PRAUN III

Spain (?), before 1571

Leather (black), scallop shell, bone

H. 64; W. 105; D. 86 cm

GNM, inv. no. T551, on long-term loan from the Friedrich von Praun'sche Familienstiftung

References:
Praun 1916–17; Achilles Syndram 1994a, p. 174, cat. no. 17 (Kunstsammlung Praun, inventory 1616, appendix), fig. 80; Grebe 2005, pp. 4–5, figs. 1–2.

Stephen Praun III was born in Nuremberg in 1544, the first son of a respected merchant family. He spent almost half of his life away from his hometown, at various places in Europe, the Middle East, and North Africa |**see cat. nos. 68, 87**|.

Travel was a routine part of business for all male members of the Praun family. As traders in spices and silk, they had branch offices in Bologna |**see cat. no. 65**|, Venice, Ferrara, and Florence. But Stephan Praun III was drawn to other forms of travel; from early on, he distanced himself from the duties of the family business. In 1569, at the age of twenty-five, Praun, who was baptized a Lutheran, accompanied the Holy Roman Emperor Maximilian II on a mission to the Turkish court in Constantinople, where he served as secretary to the imperial deputation.

The next stage of his eventful life began in 1570, at the court of King Philip II of Spain. There Praun joined the Order of Santiago, which was subordinate to the crown. In March 1571, he set out from Madrid on horseback for a pilgrimage to Santiago de Compostela. Although the precise motivations for his pilgrimage are unknown, membership in the Order of Santiago probably required it of him. The pilgrimage also served as a symbolic act that elevated Praun's social status.

Praun's set of pilgrimage garments and accoutrements is preserved in the family's ownership and has been on long-term loan to the Germanisches Nationalmuseum ever since 1876. It is one of the few surviving examples of this kind of clothing. The safekeeping of this ensemble adorned with symbols of pilgrimage was meant to perpetuate the memory of Praun's prestigious journey. This type of short leather cloak—rain- and windproof, equipped with a high collar, and open at the front—is often found in pictorial sources as a piece of protective outerwear worn by merchants and horsemen. A posthumous full-length portrait of Praun dressed as a Santiago pilgrim, created about 1600, shows him in precisely this cloak.[1] In that painting, the dark leather cloak is worn over another cloak made of pale wool felt. A wool cloak with toggle fasteners, different in some respects, and a wool hood have also been preserved in the family collection and are on permanent display at the Germanisches Nationalmuseum.[2]

It was not until Praun reached Santiago di Compostela that his black leather cloak was decorated with the prestigious scallop symbols that distinguish pilgrims to the shrine of Saint James. Scallop shells are attached in two places: at the collar, a small shell that serves as part of a fastener; and in the area of the wearer's heart, a large shell combined with two stylized bottle forms carved from bone. The large shell was meant to be recognizable from afar as a pilgrim's symbol.

Praun's activities later in life took him still further away from Nuremberg. Having traveled to Portugal, he assisted King Sebastian in a battle against the sultan of Morocco in 1578 and then helped António, prior of Crato, a claimant to the throne of Portugal, in a battle against the Spanish in 1580—both failed endeavors. Impoverished, Praun returned to Franconia for a time. While there, he took legal action, unsuccessfully, against the will of his father, who had completely disinherited him before his death in 1578. In 1585, we find Praun among a group of German noblemen in the Holy Land, where he was dubbed a knight of the Holy Sepulchre. He then traveled to northern Syria, Asia Minor, Egypt, Tunisia, and Algeria. From 1588, Praun lived at the papal court in Rome, where he contracted the plague in 1591, dying at the age of forty-seven. His brothers brought back his body and possessions to Nuremberg. They preserved his memory by placing his pilgrim's clothing and portrait in the family's cabinet of arts (*Kunstkammer*), the famous Praun Cabinet.

Adelheid Rasche

1 GNM, inv. no. Gm655.
2 GNM, inv. no. T550.

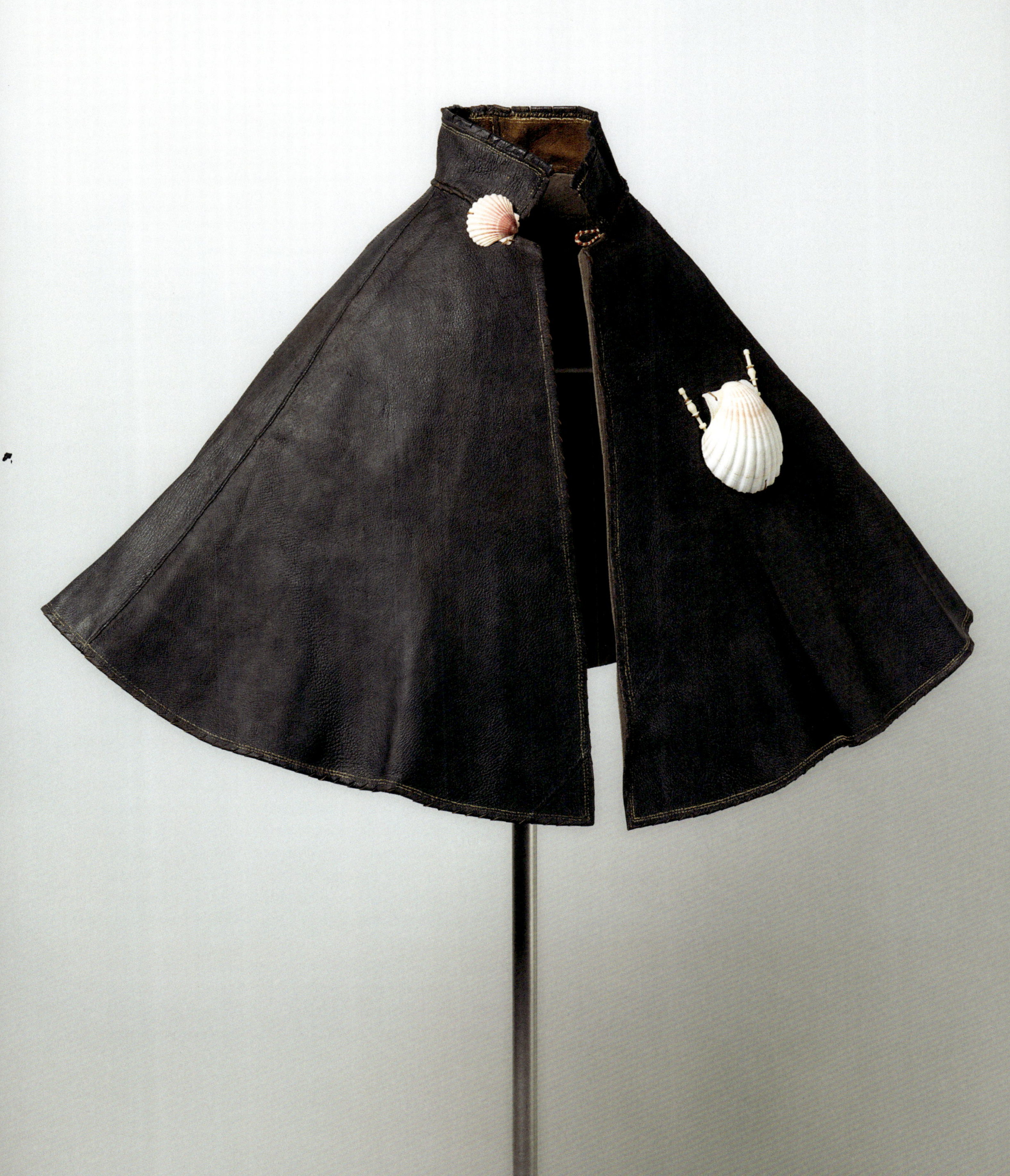

97

THE SCHLÜSSELFELDER SHIP

Nuremberg, dated 1503

Silver, largely gilded, repoussé, cast; enamel; figures partially polychromed

H. 79 cm; W. 43.5 cm; D. 28 cm

GNM, inv. no. HG2146, on long-term loan from the Johann Carl von Schlüsselfelder'sche Familienstiftung

References:
Exh. cat. Nuremberg 2004, p. 84 (Ralf Schürer); Eser 2010b, pp. 38–40; Scherner 2023, p. 30; Schommers 2024, pp. 32–35.

More than almost any other type of ship, the carrack played a crucial role in the process of European expansion during the "Age of Discovery."[1] In these three- or four-masted, ocean-going vessels, people sailed from Venice to the Holy Land, traveled the sea routes to Africa, India, and the Americas, and even attempted to circumnavigate the globe.

The Schlüsselfelder Ship, made of partially gilded silver, represents a carrack in meticulous detail. Seventy-four human figures, some polychromed, constitute the crew, lending a touch of narrative to the work. A festive banquet taking place at the stern alludes to the ship's function: it is a table centerpiece with a removable upper part. With the top removed, the ship's hull becomes a drinking vessel that holds a good two liters.

The Schlüsselfelder Ship follows in the tradition of medieval table ships, which originated in courtly dining culture, where they marked the prince's place at the table. The patron who commissioned the present work, the Nuremberg merchant and mining entrepreneur Wilhelm Schlüsselfelder the Elder (d. 1504), was thus adopting courtly practices of status display. In the Schlüsselfelder Ship, medieval tradition combines with the early modern fondness for unusual and fanciful drinking vessels. Beakers, "welcome cups" (*Willkommenspokale*), and table centerpieces in the form of apples, animals, maidens, lanterns, and, of course, ships were specialties of Nuremberg goldsmiths.[2]

Depictions of carracks were in high demand in the visual arts around 1500. This type of ship is found, for example, in a 1468 engraving by the Netherlandish artist known as the Master WA, in Bernhard von Breydenbach's travelogue *Peregrinatio in terram sanctam* (1486), and in works from the circle of Albrecht Altdorfer (d. 1538). In the 1490s, carracks appear in the work of Albrecht Dürer (1471–1528): as background details in his engraving *The Sea Monster* and in some of the woodcuts in the Apocalypse series. The flagship of Christopher Columbus (1451–1506), the *Santa Maria*, was repeatedly depicted as a carrack, even though he himself referred to it as a "nao."[3] In the period around 1500, the carrack came to symbolize a number of things: the conquest of the oceans, the discovery of the "New World," the qualities of sophistication and daring, and economic success. The stem supporting the Schlüsselfelder Ship, in the form of a double-tailed siren, underscores those layers of meaning. It embodies the sea as a place of wonder, both full of promise and potentially deadly.

Charged with such connotations, the carrack was compatible with the strategies used by Nuremberg's elites to promote their status—especially considering that Nuremberg merchants were involved from early on in the exploitation of the Americas and the precious metals found there. Hans Tetzel (1518–1571) founded copper mines in Cuba |**cat. no. 108**|, and Egidius Arnold (1550–1608) amassed a fortune in Peru, possibly even as a trading-post agent at the Andean silver mine founded in Potosí in 1545. Slavery, grueling working conditions, and reckless environmental destruction were distinctive features of the Potosí mining operations, which are now regarded as emblematic of European greed and brutality in the Americas.[4]

Probably no American silver was used for the Schlüsselfelder Ship. Although Wilhelm Schlüsselfelder the Elder did invest in silver mining, the operations he backed were in Tyrol, not overseas. Nevertheless, with its ostentatious display of precious metal—nearly six kilograms of silver in total—and its maritime iconography, the Schlüsselfelder Ship seems almost to foreshadow later developments in the Americas.

Verena Suchy

1 See Priesterjahn 2024, pp. 147–53.
2 See Scherner 2023.
3 See Walde 2018.
4 See Bendikowski 2016.

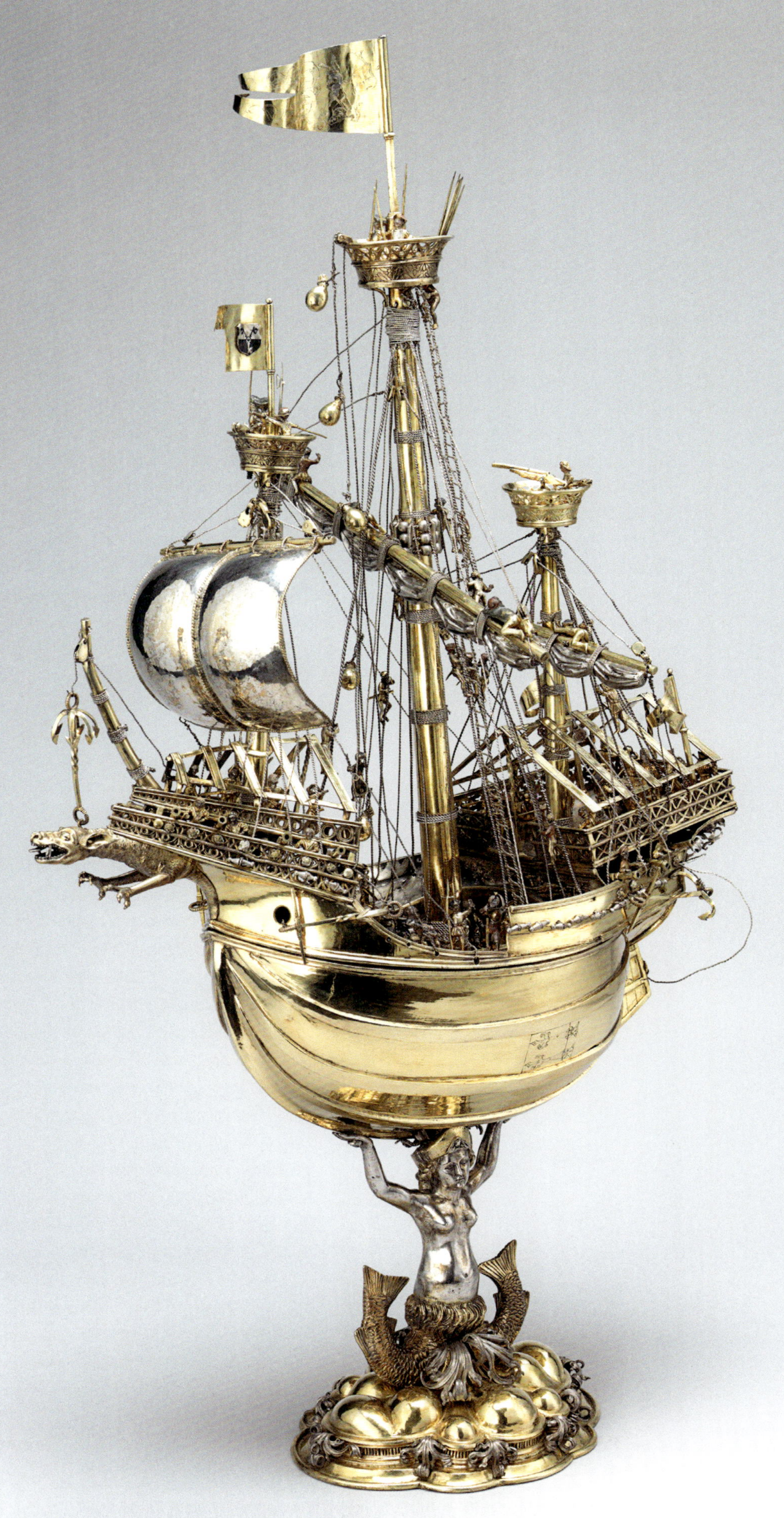

98

MUNDUS NOVUS

98.1 Das sind die new gefunde[n] mensche[n] oder volcker In form un[d] gestalt (These Are the Newly Discovered People or Nations, in Their Form and Appearance)

Nuremberg: Georg Stuchs, 1505

Illustrated broadsheet, hand-colored, leather binding

H. 40.5 cm; W. 29 cm

Herzog August Bibliothek, Wolfenbüttel, shelf mark QuH 26 (5)

98.2 Von der new gefunnde[n] Region die wol ein welt genennt mag werden (On the Newly Discovered Region Which May Rightly Be Called a World)

Nuremberg: Wolfgang Huber, 1505 (?)

Pamphlet, 11 pages, woodcut-illustrated title page

H. 19.6 cm; W. 14.4 cm

Universitätsbibliothek der LMU, Munich, shelf mark 0014/W 4 Itin. 123

References:
Exh. cat. Wolfenbüttel 1976, p. 44, cat. no. 3 [cat. no. 98.1]; Exh. cat. Berlin 1982, p. 286, cat. no. 2/2 [cat. no. 98.1]; Falk 1987, pp. 40–41 [cat. no. 98.1]; Obermeier 2003 [cat. nos. 98.1, 98.2]; Exh. cat. Berlin 2007, p. 360, cat. no. IV.18 (Michael Kraus) [cat. no. 98.2].

From May 1501 to September 1502, the Florentine merchant and astronomer Amerigo Vespucci took part in a Portuguese expedition along the coast of Brazil led by Gonçalo Coelho. Vespucci's impression of the area was that it seemed like a whole "new world."[1] His travelogue, presented in the form of a letter to Lorenzo di Pierfrancesco de' Medici, was first printed in Paris in 1502 or 1503. Entitled *Mundus Novus*, it garnered widespread and lasting attention. Among the factors that contributed to the travelogue's success were Vespucci's elegant prose style and his tendency to exaggerate in effective ways. This is apparent, for example, in his description of the customs and traditions of the Indigenous Tupinambá people, whom he associated with nudity, sexuality, and cannibalism.

An excerpt from Vespucci's *Mundus Novus* appeared in German translation in 1505, as part of an illustrated broadsheet published by Georg Stuchs in Nuremberg. As indicated by the heading, the passage in question concerns "the newly discovered people or nations" (*die new gefunde[n] mensche[n] oder volcker*). Only two impressions of this broadsheet have survived. The woodcut depicts a river flowing into the foreground, being navigated by three Portuguese ships. The Indigenous men at the left are shown with gemstone piercings on their chests and faces, consistent with Vespucci's account. The men's prominent beards, however, are an invention of the illustrator. The addition of beards situates these people in the pictorial tradition of so-called Wild Men, forest-dwelling outsiders of European legend. The feathered skirts could possibly have resulted from a misunderstanding about feathered crowns. These skirts reappear in the *Triumphal Procession* woodcut frieze for Emperor Maximilian I, in the clothing of Hans Burgkmair's "people of Calicut" (*kalikutisch leut*), a collective reference to the inhabitants of Africa, the Americas, and India.[2]

Probably also in 1505—or 1506 at the latest—the complete text of the *Mundus Novus* appeared in German translation in Nuremberg, published by Wolfgang Huber.[3] The title-page illustration **|cat. no. 98.2|** showing a young man in knight's armor is far less spectacular than the image on the broadsheet. As suggested by the publication's subtitle, the depicted crown and scepter, and the Portuguese coat of arms, this figure probably represents King Manuel I of Portugal.

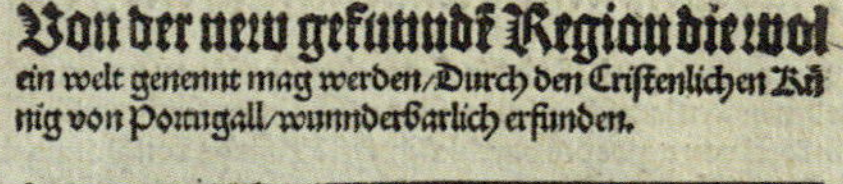

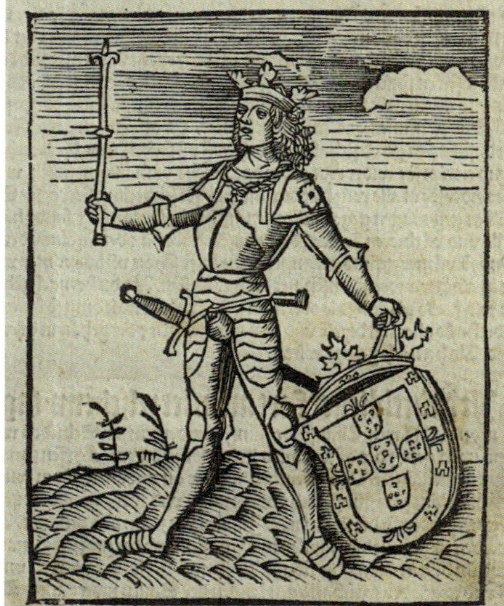

cat. no. 98.2

Three years later, Georg Stuchs issued a publication entitled *Newe unbekanthe landte und eine newe weldte in kurtz verganger zeythe erfunden* (New and Unknown Lands and a New World Discovered in Recent Times). This was a translation, supplied by the Nuremberg municipal physician Jobst Ruchamer, of texts published in 1507 by Fracanzano da Montalboddo under the title *Paesi nuovamente retrovati*. The volume's six books contain various seafaring travelogues, including Vespucci's *Mundus Novus* and descriptions of Christopher Columbus's first three voyages.[4] The appearance of these publications in rapid succession underscores Nuremberg's importance as a distribution center for news from the "New World."

Manuel Teget-Welz

1 See Wallisch 2012, p. 17.
2 See, for example, Feest 2013, pp. 368–69.
3 Colophon: "Gedruckt zu Nuremberg durch Wolffgang Hueber."
4 See, for example, Exh. cat. Berlin 2007, p. 360, cat. no. V.II. 8 (Cornelia Timm); Ankebauer 2010.

Das sind die new gefundē menschē od volcker In form vñ gestalt Als sie hie stend durch dē Cristenlichen Künig von Portugall/ gar wunderbarlich erfunden.

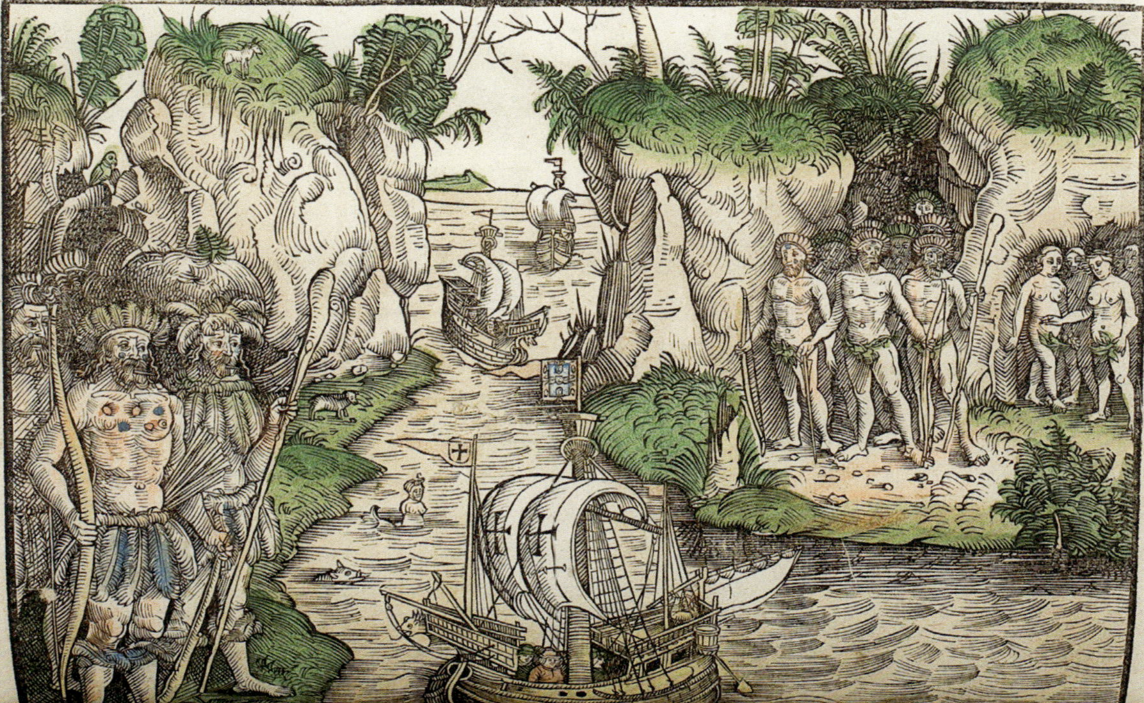

gestümigkeyt des meres biß auff den sibendē tag des monats Augusto/ des obgemeltē jars gefundē ein grosses Landt vñ Reygiō/ vñ so grosse völcker/ scharen vñ leüt/ dz die nyemant erzelē mocht als man list in Apocalpsis/ Ein volck sach ich/ ein mildt güetig vñ hantweysig/ vñ gend all nackent/ beyde weyb vñ man/ vnnd gantz on bedeckung jrer leibē an allē enden/ wie sie auß muter leib kumē/ also gend sie biß sie sterbē/ dan sie sind groß vō leib vierschrötig/ wol geschickt guter schön er glidmaß vñ geferbt etlicher maß gegē rotem/ das ich mein dise vō ð vrsach kumē das sie nacket gond vñ von der sunē bescheinē/ also geferbt werdē sie haben weit vñ groß harlöck vñ schwartz sie sind in irē gang vñ mit spil treibē thetig vñ gering/ vñ gütiger vñ schoner antlitzē die sie doch inē selbs heßlich machē vñ vngestalt dan sie porē jnen selbs löcher in die packē/ die mundlefftzē vñ die nasen vñ die oren. Du solt auch nit gedenckē dz solche löcher klein sein/ od sie eins alein habē dan ich etlich gesehē hab die in irem antlytz alein sibē löcher/ der yegliches so groß was das ein kriech od haselnus wol in eins gen möcht/ sie vstossen inē selbs solche löcher mit plabē steinen/ Cristallē/ Marmor vñ Alabaster gar hübsch vñ schön/ vnnd mit weyssen gebein/ vñ mit andern dingē/ so mit künstē gemacht werdē/ nach jrer gewonheit/ Vnd ob du also sehest ein so fremd vngewont ding/ so mit grossem seltzamē vwundungē/ Nemlich einen menschē der do het in dē backen/ allein vñ in den lefftzen/ siben stein ð etlicher in der leng einer halbē span/ du würdest nit on grosse vwundung sein. Dan ich hab dick wargenumē vñ vber schetzt/ dz sibē solch er stein am gewicht habē. xvj. lot vber/ vñ on das sie in dē oren/ die mit dreyen löchren durch stochē sind/ sie noch ander stein tragē/ die in ringen hangē vñ dise weiß vñ sittē ist allein der manē/ dan die frawen zerstechē jnen selbs ir antlytz nit also mit löcherung/ dan allein ir oren. Ein ander sitt vñ weiß/ ist auch vnd vñ bey inē ge nueg abweysig/ vñ wider alle menschliche glaubung. Das ir frawē die eben gelüstig vñ gayl sind/ vñ irn manē machen das jnen ire mendliche glit geschwellen in solicher vber dick das sie vngestalt vñ schmelich erscheinē/ vñ das thon sie mit etlichē gifftigē thierlen/ vnd vō solcher sach geschicht dz inen vil ir gemecht vderben die in von mangels wegē der artzeney faulē/ vnd beleiben on gemecht. Sie habē kein thuech noch deck/ weder leines noch baumwolles/ dan sie es nit bedürffen vñ haben kein aygen gut. Sunder alle ding seind vnder jnen gemein/ sie habē auch keinen künig oder regierer. Sunder ein yeder ist im selbs ein herr/ souil weiber nemen sie so vil sie wöllē/ vñ der sun mit der mutter/ vñ der bruder mit ð schwester/ vñ der erst mit ð ersten/ vñ der begegner mit der begegnerin. Vnd veinigen sich als dick als sie wöllē/ scheidē sie die ee vñ halltē gantz kein ordenung/ darumb haben sie auch keinen tempel vñ haltē kein gesatz/ vñ seind nit abgötter/ Was soll ich mer sagē sie leben nach der natur dz sie wol Epicuri bauchfuller genant werdē mügen dan Senici. Bey jnen seind kein kaufleüt noch kauffmans guet. Die scharē des volcks haben auch krieg vñ an kunst vñ ordnung/ jre eltern mit jren rethen vñ geboten vnder biegen die jungē zuthon was sie wöllē/ vñ rüsten sich zustreytē/ In solchem sie einand grausamlich zu tod schlahen/ vñ welche sie also im krieg vñ streit fahen die furen sie hin/ domit sie die bey lebē lassen/ vñ sie behaltē das sie dar vō mestig en vñ sie essen dan einer den andern der do obligt/ vñ vnder anderm fleysch ist yr menschē fleysch ein speyß/ Es hat der vater sein sun vñ sein weyb gessen ich hab einē gesehen von dem sagt man er het wol von dreyhundert menschē leyben geessen/ ich bin gewesen an einem end da hab ich gesehen gesaltzen menschē fleysch vñ auff gehenckt zu derren/ wie hie bey vns das schweinē fleysch/ sie verwundn sich warumb wir vnser veint fleysch nit auch essen in vnser speyß/ dan sie meinē dz es das aller beste fleysch sey/ ir waffen seind pogē vñ pfeyl vñ wen sie streiten/ so bedeckē sie sich nit/ Wir rieten in von solcher pöser weyß zulassen/ vñ sie vhiesen vns dar von zulassen/ vñ ob die frawē schön ploß vñ nacket gend/ so haben sie doch ir leib hübsch vñ wol gestalt vñ sauber vñ send nit so schentlich als einer gedenckē möcht wan sie gemueg leibig seind/ so wirt ir scham mindert gesehen vns nam wund das vnder inen keine gesehen ward die do lampend prüst het oder die gekindet heten dz der selben bauch anderst gestalt werdē dan ð junckfrwē vñ die nye gekindet/ vñ on andern glidern vñ enden des leybs der geleichē vmerckt ward/ das ich alles von ersamkeit weyter vngeendert laß/ dan wan sie sich möchten zu den Cristen menschē gefiegen als sie auß der massen gayl sind/ so legtē sie alle scham vō in zu volbringē böse werck. Sie leben hundert vñ funfftzig jar vñ werden seltē kranck/ vñ ob sie etwan kranck werdē so heylen sie sich selber mit wurtzlen/ vñ mit gutē kreütern vñ so vil ich von in vsteen vñ erkenen mocht/ so ist in jrem land nymer kein pestilentz oder ennicherley siechtagē/ die vō bösem lufft kumend/ vñ wo sie nitt mit freuel on einander todt schlüeg so möchten sie lange zeyt leben/ ich mein das in dem land alle zeyt die mittegigē wind wehen vñ vorab allermeist/ den wir nenē etwen der inen also ist wie vns der mitnechtig wind genant Aquilo sie seind kunstreych mit Fischfahen/ dan auch das selbig meer Fysch reych ist/ vñ wen ich wolt alle vñ yegliche ding erzellen/ die in disem land seind/ von seltzamē fogeln vñ thieren von edlem gestein/ das wer ein ding gar zulang vñ on maß/ vnd ich glaub das vnser Plinius dem thausent theyl nit zu kunnen sey. Des volckes der sickustē/ vñ der andern vogel vñ thieren in disem land mit so mancherley vnderscheyd der ant-lytz von frawen/ das der volkumnestē leüt maller kunst beriembt meister Pollicletus die ab zemalen erligē müsten/ vñ on zweyffel halt ich ob das irdisch paradeis auff erdtrich das dz nit verr von diser lantschafft sey. So ist kuntlich vñ offenbar dz wir den vierdē theyl der welt durch schyfft haben. Vnd dise Epistel auß Ytalischer sprach in Latein/ vñ yetz gedeütsch. Der hübsch tholmetsch gezogē hat. Vmb das alle lateiner vñ deütschē vstanden/ wie vil grosser vñ wunderlicher dingē von tag zu tag gefunden/ vñ offenbar werden. Vñ diß missiue in deütsch gezogē/ Auß dem exemplar das von Pariß kam ym Mayen monat. Nach Cristi geburt Fünfftzehenhundert vñ funff Jare. 1505

cat. no. 98.1

99

EIN AUSZUG ETTLICHER SENDBRIEFF (AN EXTRACT FROM SEVERAL LETTERS)

Nuremberg: Friedrich Peypus, 1520

Pamphlet, 8 pages including the illustrated title page

H. 21 cm; W. 15 cm

Universitätsbibliothek der LMU, Munich, shelf mark 0014/W 4 Hist. 2973#15

Open to title page

References:
Saville 1920, pp. 18–20; Wagner 1929, pp. 182–83, 186–98; Colin 1988, p. 192, cat. no. B. 20; Exh. cat. Munich 1992, p. 30, cat. no. 20 (Hans Wolff); Briesemeister 1992, pp. 204–5.

In the spring of 1520, the Nuremberg printer Friedrich Peypus published a hastily compiled pamphlet entitled *Ein auszug ettlicher sendbrieff* (An Extract from Several Letters).[1] The short text describes recent invasions carried out in present-day Mexico by the Spanish conquistadors Francisco Fernández de Cordoba, Juan de Grijalva, and Hernán Cortés. Mention is also made of the precious artifacts that the Aztec ruler Moctezuma II had presented to Cortés as a kind of diplomatic gift around the time of Easter 1519. These were the same objects seen by Albrecht Dürer in Brussels late in the summer of 1520.[2] The pamphlet concludes with a geographico-cultural sketch describing aspects of Indigenous society that clashed with European norms, in particular idolatry and human sacrifice.[3]

The Nuremberg pamphlet is based on a report issued on July 10, 1519, by the governing body of Villa Rica de la Vera Cruz (today's Veracruz).[4] That report, in the form of a letter addressed to Charles V, arrived in Seville on November 5, together with the gifts from Moctezuma II. An early copy is preserved in an omnibus volume in the Österreichische Nationalbibliothek in Vienna.[5] The Vienna volume contains further texts with news from the "New World," including Cortés's second and third reports, which in 1524 were also published by Peypus in Nuremberg |**cat. no. 105**|.

The woodcut illustration on the title page of the 1520 pamphlet shows a ship full of armed Spaniards landing on a mountainous coast. In the background, a group of armed Indigenous people in feathered clothing wait on the shore. The group of European soldiers at the bottom right, dressed in Landsknecht attire and holding their weapons poised, appear not to welcome the new arrivals. While the meaning of this illustration is difficult to interpret, the pictorial concept seems to derive from the illustrated broadsheet published by Georg Stuchs in 1505 based on Amerigo Vespucci's *Mundus Novus* |**cat. no. 98**|.[6]

Reports on the conquest of the Aztec Empire were circulated not just in printed form but also in handwritten newsletters. On November 15, 1519, Dr. Christoph Scheurl (1481–1542), a diplomat and consultant to the Nuremberg city council, reported the following from Spain to Nuremberg: "Yesterday, a letter arrived for King Charles from his captain in Seville, saying that his men had found another island in addition to the others, this one called Mejico, which they captured. It is said to be 150 to 200 miles wide. A great deal of gold, precious stones, and pearls, as well as various spices and other things are to be found there. The people worship the sun and moon and stamp them on their coins. So that His Majesty might see that this is true, they sent him the island's commander together with three pieces of gold, each weighing 60 pounds, along with some pearls and other items, which pleased everyone very much. They also report to His Majesty that more than 100,000 ducats in gold can be extracted on this island annually."[7] Scheurl's letter illustrates one way in which news that was later printed in Nuremberg reached the city.

Manuel Teget-Welz

1 Colophon: "Gedruckt in der keiserlichen Stat Nürmberg durch FrydErichen Peypus / und seligklich volend am.17.tag Marcij / des jars do man zalt nach Christi unsers lieben herren geburt.M.D.XX."
2 See the essay by Manuel Teget-Welz in the present volume.
3 On the contents, see also Briesemeister 1992, pp. 204–5. The recurring narratives of idolatry and cannibalism common to texts about the "New World" also feature in Marco Polo's late-thirteenth-century travelogue, in his description of "Cipangu" (Japan). The first printed edition of Marco Polo's text appeared in Nuremberg in 1477, published by Friedrich Creussner. See Reichert 1993, pp. 25–26.
4 See Wagner 1929, pp. 182–83.
5 Codex Vindobonensis S. N. 1600. See the edition by Stummvoll, Gibson, and Unterkircher 1960.
6 See also Colin 1988, p. 192, cat. no. B. 20.
7 Translated after the German in Müller 1907, pp. 324–25, n. 1.

Ein außzug ettlicher sendbrieff dem aller durchleüchtigisten großmechtigistē Fürsten vnd Herren Herren Carl Römischen vnd Hyspanischē König ꝛc. vnserm gnedigstē hern durch ire verordent Hauptleut/ von wegen einer newgefundē Inseln/ der selbē gelegenheit vnd jnwoner sitten vn̄ gewonheitē inhaltend vor kurtzuerschinen tagen zugesandt.

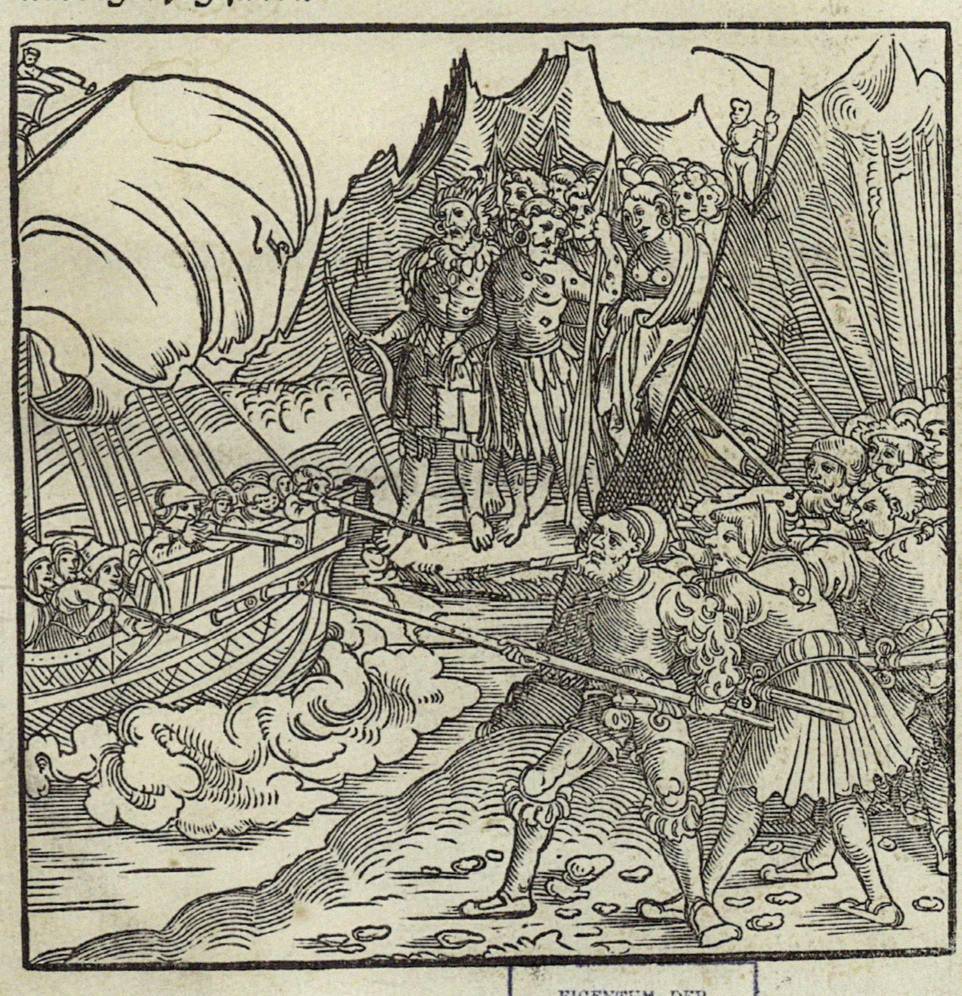

100

PRAYER BOOK OF EMPEROR MAXIMILIAN I (MUNICH SECTION)

Augsburg: Johann Schönsperger, 1513

Albrecht Dürer and Lucas Cranach the Elder (illustrators)

Nuremberg and Wittenberg, ca. 1515

Post-incunable, parchment, 157 leaves, pen-and-ink drawings

H. 28.0 cm; W. 19.5 cm

Bayerische Staatsbibliothek, Munich, shelf mark 2 L.impr.membr. 64

Open to fols. 40v–41r: Albrecht Dürer: Tupinambá figure

Not exhibited

References:
Massing 1991, pp. 515–16; Feest 2013, pp. 369–70; Lange-Krach 2018a; Lange-Krach 2018b; Lange-Krach 2025.

In late 1513, Johann Schönsperger in Augsburg printed a prayer book on parchment meant for knights of the Order of Saint George. The patron was none other than Emperor Maximilian I. About 1515, the margins of one of the copies were decorated with pen-and-ink drawings in various colors by several of the leading artists of the time: Albrecht Altdorfer, Hans Baldung Grien, Jörg Breu, Hans Burgkmair, Lucas Cranach the Elder, and Albrecht Dürer.[1] The illumination project was coordinated by the Augsburg town clerk (*Stadtschreiber*) and imperial counselor Konrad Peutinger, who distributed the book's sections among the artists and probably also provided guidelines for subject matter.[2] The illuminated copy was intended to serve as a model for an illustrated printed edition, but it ultimately remained unfinished. The copy later came into the possession of Cardinal Antoine Perrenot de Granvelle, whose collection also included Dürer's *Martyrdom of the Ten Thousand*.[3] The front section, containing drawings by Dürer and Cranach, was probably acquired by Duke Maximilian I of Bavaria between 1598 and 1600. Today, it is one of the absolute gems of the Bayerische Staatsbibliothek in Munich.[4]

Dürer's marginal drawings in the prayer book are of utmost elegance and iconographic sophistication. Among them, on folio 41r, there is a full-length depiction of a young man standing in contrapposto, wearing various pieces of feathered clothing characteristic of the Tupinambá people of the Atlantic coast of South America. The figure is associated with Psalm 24:1, which appears on the same page: "The earth is the Lord's and the fulness thereof, the world and those who dwell therein." This serves as an allusion to the universal missionary claim of the Catholic Church. Dürer probably took inspiration for this figure from an early illustrated broadsheet concerning the so-called New World. A particularly likely source is the Vespucci broadsheet printed in Nuremberg in 1505 under the title *Das sind die new gefunde[n] mensche[n] oder volcker In form un[d] gestalt* (These Are the Newly Discovered People or Nations, in Their Form and Appearance) |**cat. no. 98**|. At the same time, the ethnologically accurate and scientifically precise rendition of the man's shafted weapon suggests that this item was drawn after a real-world model.[5]

Years later, in August 1520, Dürer saw the diplomatic gifts of the Aztec ruler Moctezuma II in Brussels. Yet he may already have studied such non-European objects in the collection of Peutinger, the prayer book's coordinator.[6] Peutinger, who was related by marriage to the Welser merchant family |**see cat. nos. 101–104**|, owned a large collection of so-called exotica. The 1597 inventory of the Peutinger family's movable property lists, among other things, "Indian featherwork," "bedcovers made of feathers," and "tufts with old shells made of wood"—all possibly ritual objects.[7] In 1507, Peutinger wrote to Sebastian Brant that he had received a talking parrot from "India," presumably a scarlet macaw from South America,[8] as well as a bow, pieces of wood, and other items. That Augsburg was the place where Dürer observed the shafted weapon is also suggested by the presence of what appears to be the same object in a woodcut illustration by Jörg Breu in *Die Ritterlich und lobwirdig rayß* (The Knightly and Laudable Journey), a 1515 edition of Ludovico de Varthema's *Itinerario*.[9] It is noteworthy that, despite the great interest Dürer later showed in the Moctezuma treasure, the drawing in the prayer book is his only surviving depiction of an artifact from the Americas.

Manuel Teget-Welz

1 An anonymous associate of Altdorfer was also involved.
2 See Herberger 1851, p. 27, n. 84.
3 Kunsthistorisches Museum, Vienna, inv. no. Gemäldegalerie, 835.
4 The back section is now in the Bibliothèque municipale, Besançon, Étude 67633. See Exh. cat. Frankfurt and Vienna 2014, pp. 258–59, cat. no. 145 (Jochen Sander).
5 See for example Massing 1991, pp. 515–16.
6 I thank Heidrun Lange-Krach, Königsbrunn, for pointing this out.
7 These translations are after the German published in Lange-Krach 2018c, pp. 116–18. The original source: Bayerische Staatsbibliothek, Munich, Clm 4021d.
8 See Exh. cat. Augsburg 2019, p. 233, cat. no. 36 (Heidrun Lange-Krach).
9 As already noted by Feest 2013, p. 370.

1 Translated from the German in Neudörfer 1875, p. 124.
2 Translated from the German in Bauernfeind 2009, p. 225.
3 See Pickl 1970, pp. 20–21.
4 See Bauernfeind 2009, pp. 242–43.

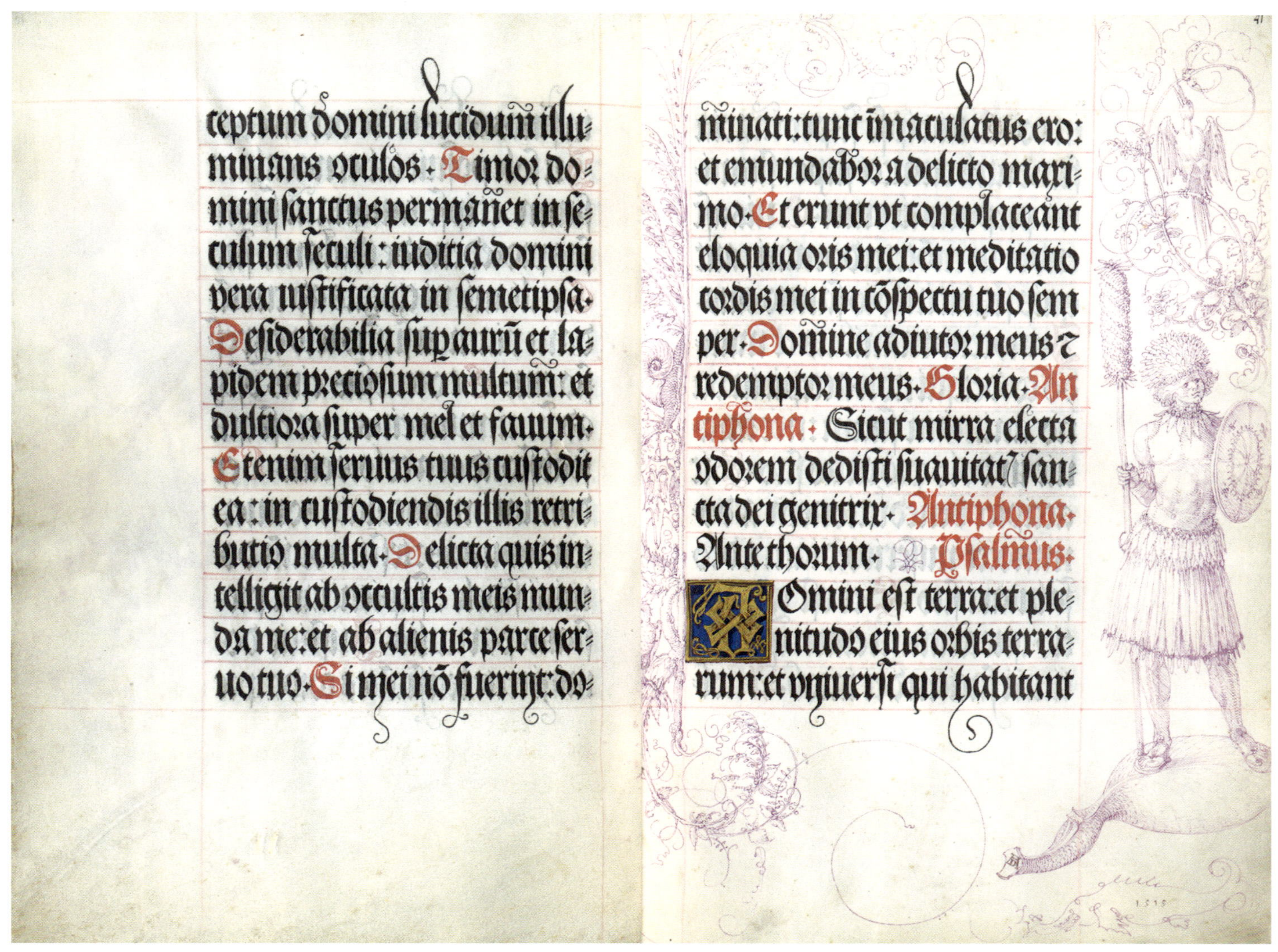
ceptum domini lucidum illu-
minans oculos. Timor do-
mini sanctus permañet in se-
culum seculi: iudicia domini
vera iustificata in semetipsa.
Desiderabilia sup aurū et la-
pidem preciosum multum: et
dulciora super mel et fauum.
Etenim seruus tuus custodit
ea: in custodiendis illis retri-
butio multa. Delicta quis in-
telligit ab occultis meis mun-
da me: et ab alienis parce ser-
uo tuo. Si mei nō fuerint: do-

minati: tunc ĩmaculatus ero:
et emundabor a delicto maxi-
mo. Et erunt vt complaceant
eloquia oris mei: et meditatio
cordis mei in cōspectu tuo sem-
per. Domine adiutor meus ⁊
redemptor meus. Gloria. Antiphona. Sicut mirra electa
odorem dedisti suauitat̃ sancta dei genitrix. Antiphona.
Ante thorum. Psalmus.
Domini est terra: et ple-
nitudo eius orbis terra-
rum: et vniuersi qui habitant

101

MEDAL OF JAKOB WELSER I

Hans Schwarz

Nuremberg, 1519

Cast bronze

Diam. 5.7 cm

GNM, inv. no. Med8009

References:
Habich 1906, p. 44; Habich 1929, p. 31, cat. no. 162; Exh. cat. Nuremberg 1985, p. 437, cat. no. 577 (Hermann Maué); Maué 1989, pp. 26, 30, cat. no. 7; Kastenholz 2006, pp. 183–84, cat. no. 52.

About 1519–20, the Augsburg sculptor Hans Schwarz (d. after 1526) spent time in Nuremberg. He lodged at the parsonage of the Sebalduskirche, with Provost Melchior Pfinzing. As Johann Neudörffer noted in 1547, Schwarz was regarded as "the best portraitist of his time."[1] Nuremberg's elites were among the clients who commissioned medals from Schwarz. One of them was the wealthy merchant Jakob Welser (1468–1541), who in 1494 was admitted to the city's Greater Council and ten years later to the Inner Council, which was reserved for members of the patriciate. In 1511, Lazarus Holzschuher wrote the following about Welser: "Jacob Welser conducts trade with all lands on a scale never before accomplished by any merchant or citizen of Nuremberg."[2]

Like Schwarz, Welser hailed from Augsburg. He settled in Nuremberg in 1493 and married Ehrentraud Thumer, the daughter of a merchant. When he acquired citizenship that same year, he pledged to remain a resident in Nuremberg for the next ten years. Welser's father-in-law, Hans Thumer (d. 1498), known as "der Reiche" (the Rich), had moved to Nuremberg from Styria in 1477. His fortune, amassed through trade in livestock with Italy, is said to have amounted to 100,000 guldens—an enormous sum for the time.[3] During his first years in Nuremberg, Welser probably worked as a kind of junior partner to Thumer.[4]

After the death of his father-in-law, Welser likely invested at least part of his capital in the Welser-Vöhlin company, founded in 1496.[5] A statement made by Christoph Scheurl in 1508 confirms that Welser was a shareholder in that firm. In 1505–6, the Welser-Vöhlin company, together with other German and Italian merchants, contributed three ships to the Portuguese expedition to India led by Francisco de Almeida (d. 1510) |**see cat. no. 116**|. The amount invested in that voyage of trade and conquest was 20,000 cruzados. After the fleet's return, a profit of 150 to 175 percent was achieved. King Manuel I of Portugal later prohibited any further direct investments by foreign entrepreneurs in Portuguese expeditions to India.[6]

In 1517, because of a dispute over profit distribution, Jakob Welser left the Welser-Vöhlin company and founded his own firm in Nuremberg with his sons. His involvement in global overseas trade continued. In some of the related literature, he is said to have supplied manillas—copper bracelets that served as currency in African trade—and other Nuremberg metal goods to western Africa; however, this is disputed.[7] In 1534, a trade agent by the name of Hans Schwerczer worked for Welser in Goa and Vijayanagara in India.[8]

Jakob Welser was also active in the early trade with the Americas. In 1535, he contributed a ship to an expedition to the Río de la Plata led by the Spanish conquistador Pedro de Mendoza. As reported by the German adventurer Ulrich Schmidel, one of the ships "belonged to Sewastian Neithart (Augsburg) and Jacob Welser of Nuremberg."[9]

Jakob Welser was one of the most powerful merchants in Nuremberg at the turn of the fifteenth to the sixteenth century. His commercial activity and patronage of the arts exemplify the interconnectedness of economics, trade, and culture in the context of Nuremberg's global history |**cat. nos. 102, 103**|.

Manuel Teget-Welz

5 See Stromer 2006, p. 216.
6 See Häberlein 1998, pp. 27–29.
7 See Westermann 2013b, pp. 462–63.
8 See Walter 2014, p. 67.
9 Translated from the German in Budde 1987, p. 80. See also Bernecker 2000, pp. 207–9.

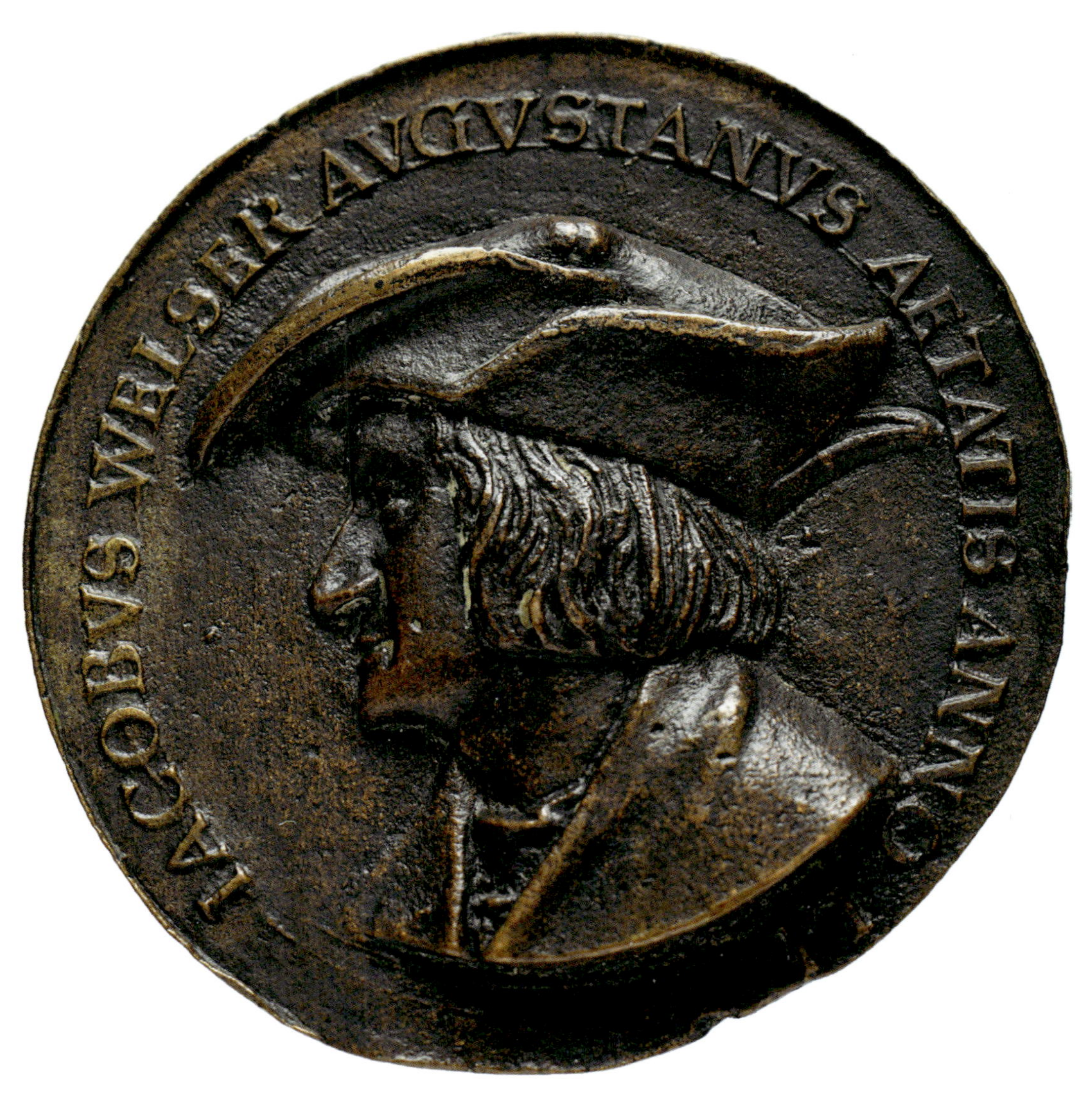
IACOBVS WELSER AVGVSTANVS AETATIS ANNO

102

TWO WING PANELS FROM THE FORMER HIGH ALTARPIECE OF THE FRAUENKIRCHE IN NUREMBERG

Barthel Beham (?)

Nuremberg, ca. 1522–25

Paint on limewood

Each H. 243 cm; W. 122 cm

GNM, inv. nos. Gm187, Gm188, on long-term loan from the Evangelisch-Lutherische Gesamtkirchengemeinde of Nuremberg

References:
Rasmussen 1974, pp. 80–91; Dettenthaler 1976, pp. 160–65, 178–80, cat. no. 12; Löcher 1997, pp. 63–68; Löcher 1999, pp. 214–16, cat. no. 71; Teget-Welz 2022, pp. 45–46.

As a new member of Nuremberg's civic elite, the merchant Jakob Welser I |**cat. no. 101**|, who hailed from Augsburg, was keen to raise his local profile. That ambition was probably one of the reasons why in 1493, the year he was granted citizenship in Nuremberg, he commissioned a relief of Christ's Entry into Jerusalem for display in a prominent place: as part of the Passion cycle on the chancel buttresses of the Sebalduskirche, the church frequented by members of the city council. In that relief, sculpted by Veit Wirsberger (d. after 1534),[1] the fleur-de-lis coat of arms of the Welser family is clearly visible at the bottom center. Jakob Welser later became active in global trade with India and the Americas.

In the 1520s, the artistic patronage of Jakob and his wife Ehrentraud, née Thumer, was mainly devoted to refurbishing the chancel of the Frauenkirche in modern style |**see cat. no. 11**|. The church is located on the Hauptmarkt, only about two hundred meters from Welser's home and offices at Theresienstraße 7, a building that had been expanded into an imposing four-winged complex between 1509 and 1512 (probably by Hans Beheim the Elder).[2] In 1522, Jakob Welser and Ehrentraud Thumer commissioned Veit Hirsvogel the Elder to install a new stained-glass window in the chancel of the Frauenkirche. It featured a Virgin of Mercy (*Schutzmantelmadonna*) and included family donor figures.[3] Hans von Kulmbach was responsible for the window's spectacular design, with its seemingly floating Renaissance architecture.[4]

Probably contemporary with the window project—and certainly before the official introduction of the Reformation in Nuremberg in 1525—Jakob Welser and Ehrentraud Thumer commissioned a new altarpiece for the church's high altar. This was the largest altarpiece of its time in Nuremberg. Although dismantled about 1806, its appearance is preserved in a 1696 engraving by Johann Ulrich Krauß after a drawing by Johann Andreas Graff. The multitiered structure with rows of classicizing columns is reminiscent of a triumphal arch. It immediately calls to mind Renaissance altarpieces created by Augsburg artists, such as the one commissioned in 1518 from Adolf Daucher (d. 1523) for the high altar of the Annenkirche in Annaberg.[5] This aspect of the Frauenkirche altarpiece may be interpretable as a visual reference to Welser's Augsburg origins.

The altarpiece had two pairs of folding wings. Only the outer pair has survived. It comprises four vibrantly colorful scenes from the life of the Virgin Mary on the inside (the open view) and a single scene of the Lamentation of Christ on the outside (the closed view). The painter has not been definitively identified. He was clearly influenced by Albrecht Dürer, and certain elements of his style point to Barthel Beham (1502–1540), who later worked in Munich as a court painter to Duke Wilhelm IV (1493–1550). Of the altarpiece's surviving sculptural decoration, which is attributed to Hans Peisser (d. after 1571), a putto dressed in armor is now at the Germanisches Nationalmuseum.[6] Similarly attired "Italianate putti" (*welsche Kindlein*) are found on the Annaberg high altarpiece, where they appear as heraldic shield bearers. This supports the theory that the Welser altarpiece followed precedents set by the Augsburg Renaissance.

Although the subjects depicted on the former altarpiece came exclusively from the domain of religion, the commission itself nevertheless bears indirect witness to global enterprises: of the money that Jakob Welser and Ehrentraud Thumer spent on the furnishings of the Frauenkirche, some presumably derived from overseas trade.

Manuel Teget-Welz

1 On buttress number "North V." The damaged original is kept at the GNM, inv. no. Pl.O.1846. See Baumbauer 2014, pp. 247–49.
2 The erstwhile "Haus zur goldenen Rose" (House at the Golden Rose), previously owned by the Stromer family. See Schwemmer 1977, pp. 247–48.
3 Now preserved in only small fragments (window number "Chancel, south II, 4a–c/5a/c"). See Scholz 2013, pp. 433–36.
4 Kulmbach's drawing is at the Kupferstich-Kabinett, Dresden, inv. no. C 2254. See Butts 2006, p. 197, cat. no. A120.
5 See most recently Kiesewetter 2022.
6 Inv. no. Pl.O.2724. See Hamm, Taube, and Lorenz 2008, p. 56. Further sculptures from the altarpiece are kept at the Frauenkirche and the Jakobskirche in Nuremberg.

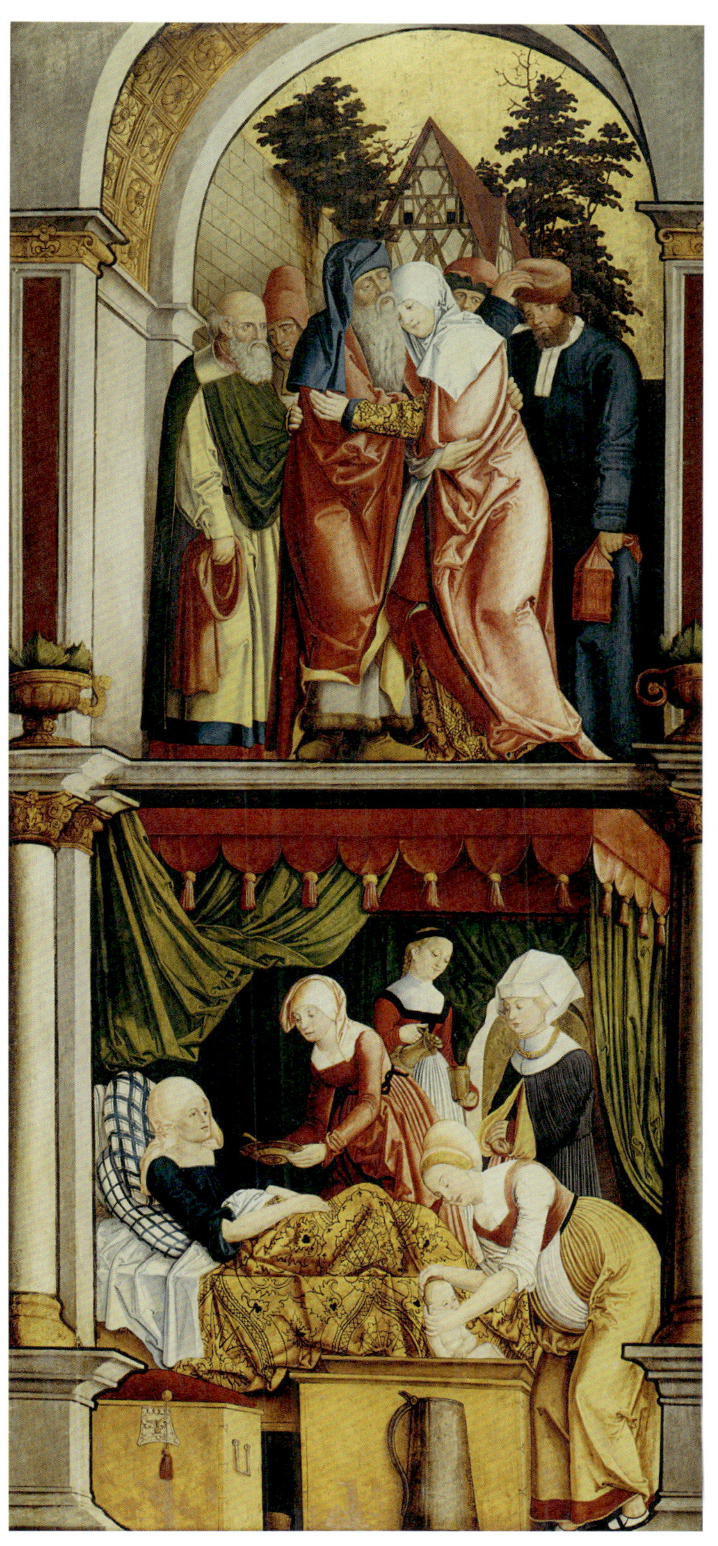

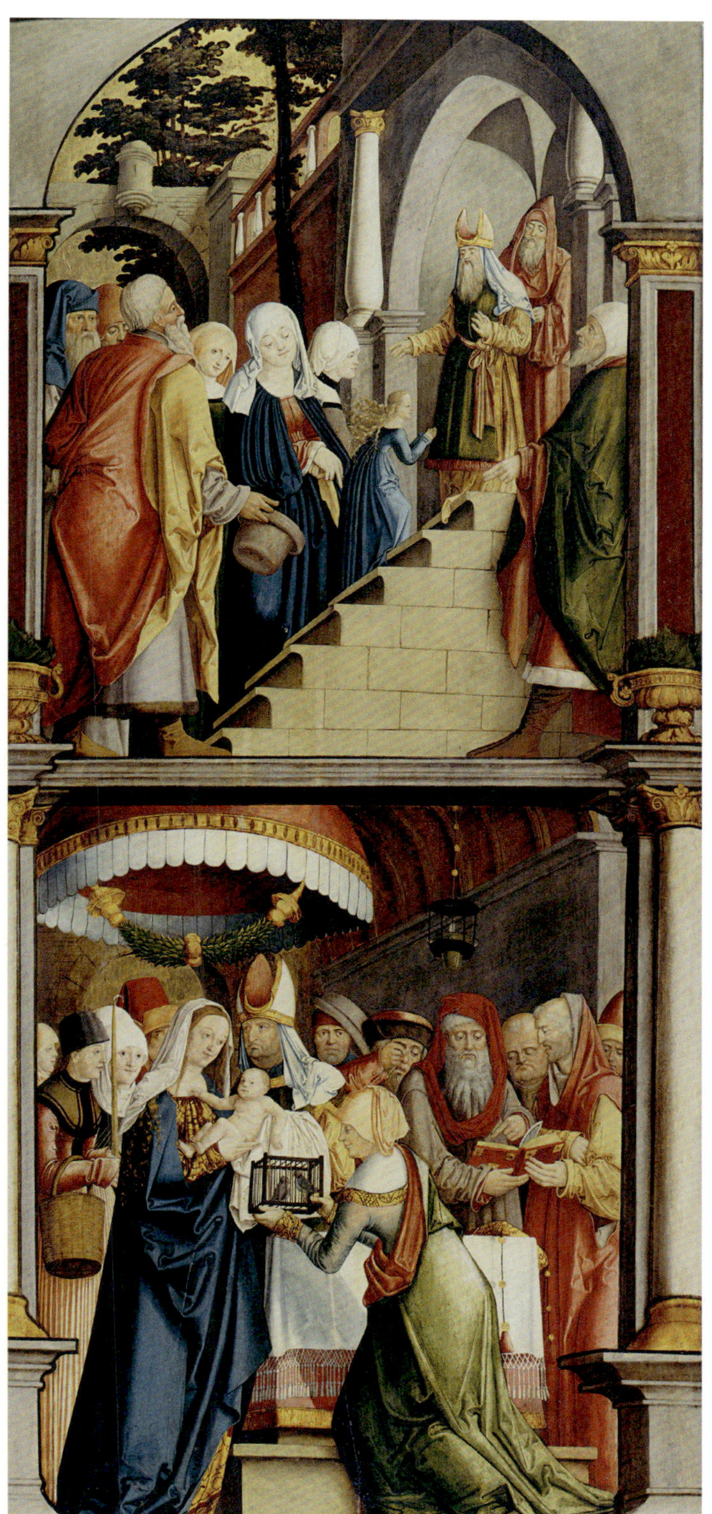

103

NEW TESTAMENT, OWNED BY JAKOB WELSER AND EHRENTRAUD THUMER

Martin Luther | woodcut illustrations by **Hans Schäufelin**
Illuminations added by **Peter Flötner (?)** and **Nikolaus Glockendon (?)**
Augsburg: Johann Schönsperger the Younger, 1523 | Nuremberg, 1523–29 (illuminations)

Post-incunable, 266 leaves; 1 leaf of parchment

H. 31 cm; W. 21.5 cm (book block)

GNM, shelf mark [S] 4° Dk 152/2, acquired with funds from a private foundation

Open to fols. 39v, 40r (Ephesians)

References:
Exh. cat. Augsburg 1955, p. 72, cat. no. 391; Kießling 1997, p. 34; Exh. cat. Augsburg 1997, p. 116, cat. no. 34 (Hubert von Welser); Merkl 1999, pp. 381–84, cat. no. 63.

In 1523, Johann Schönsperger the Younger (d. 1543) in Augsburg printed a new edition of Martin Luther's Bible translation under the title *Das buch des Newen Testaments Teütsch: Mit schönen Figuren* (The Book of the New Testament in German: With Beautiful Illustrations).[1] The folio-size volume is magnificently illustrated with ten woodcuts by Hans Schäufelin, municipal painter of Nördlingen (d. 1539 or 1540).[2] While the depictions of the Four Evangelists and the Apostle Paul are new creations, the five illustrations for the Apocalypse are copies after woodcuts made by Lucas Cranach the Elder (1472–1553) for Luther's "September Testament" of 1522.

A copy of *Das buch des Newen Testaments Teütsch* came into the possession of Jakob Welser and Ehrentraud Thumer, a merchant couple in Nuremberg who had amassed great wealth through global trade |**see cat. nos. 101, 102**|.[3] They had the book decorated in a manner consistent with their social status. First, all the initial letters, capital letters, and woodcuts were hand-colored using watercolor and bodycolor. Then a full-page illumination of the allied Welser–Thumer coat of arms, on parchment, was inserted at the front of the book. Finally, the margins of thirty-three pages were decorated with lively, loosely executed drawings in pen and ink with the addition of watercolor, bodycolor, and gold accents. These include biblical subjects such as the Raising of Lazarus (fol. 91v) as well as grotesques. The latter frolic within a lavish decorative scheme of floral vine scrolls, candelabras, dragons, birds, and other Renaissance motifs.

The parchment sheet with the Welser–Thumer arms of alliance appears to have been designed by an experienced illuminator active in Nuremberg. The cherubim heads in the spandrels are reminiscent of the style of Nikolaus Glockendon (d. 1534). The book's marginal illuminations are undoubtedly by a different hand. This illuminator was a creative and technically skilled draftsperson who surely belonged to the milieu of Nuremberg artists of the 1520s. Ulrich Merkl saw in this hand a talented unknown collaborator of Albrecht Dürer, but his argument remains vague.[4] The supposed parallels with four drawings in pen and ink and watercolor found in the "Kunstbuch Albrecht Dürers" (Albrecht Dürer's art book) are ultimately unconvincing.[5]

A plausible alternative attribution for the miniatures is to Peter Flötner (d. 1546) |**see cat. no. 66**|. Flötner was not just a sculptor; he also worked as an illustrator, for example in a copy of Luther's translation of the Five Books of Moses.[6] In the Welser miniatures, a number of stylistic aspects seem to point to Flötner. These include the playful, perspectivally demanding poses; the physiognomies, in which the eyes, nose, and mouth of each face form a tight grouping; and the high-contrast color scheme, which helps to emphasize the figures' physicality. An additional similarity is found in the illuminator's humorous inventiveness. Drawings by Flötner that immediately suggest themselves for comparison include the design for a grotto fountain in Berlin[7] and the six roundels with half-length female figures in Erlangen.[8]

Manuel Teget-Welz

1 Colophon (fol. 119r): "Gedruckt in der Kayserlichen Stat Augspurg durch Hanns Schönsperger."
2 See Schreyl 1990, pp. 147–48, cat. nos. 870–79.
3 The copy later passed to their grandson Hans Welser (1534–1601). See Merkl 1999, p. 382, n. 376.
4 See Merkl 1999, pp. 383–84, cat. no. 63.
5 Kunsthistorisches Museum, Vienna, Kunstkammer, inv. no. 5127. See Exh. cat. Vienna 1994, pp. 94–101, cat. no. 4 (Helmut Trenk).
6 Universitätsbibliothek Erlangen-Nürnberg, Erlangen, Graphische Sammlung, inv. nos. B 324 – B 355. See Dickel 2014, pp. 93–97, cat. nos. 133–64 (Iris Brahms).
7 Kupferstichkabinett, Berlin, inv. no. KdZ 1263. See Exh. cat. Nuremberg 2014a, pp. 112–15, cat. no. 26 (Barbara Dienst).
8 Universitätsbibliothek Erlangen-Nürnberg, Erlangen, Graphische Sammlung, inv. nos. B 375 – B 380. See Dickel 2014, p. 101, cat. no. 168 (Iris Brahms).
1 See Bauernfeind 2009, p. 251.

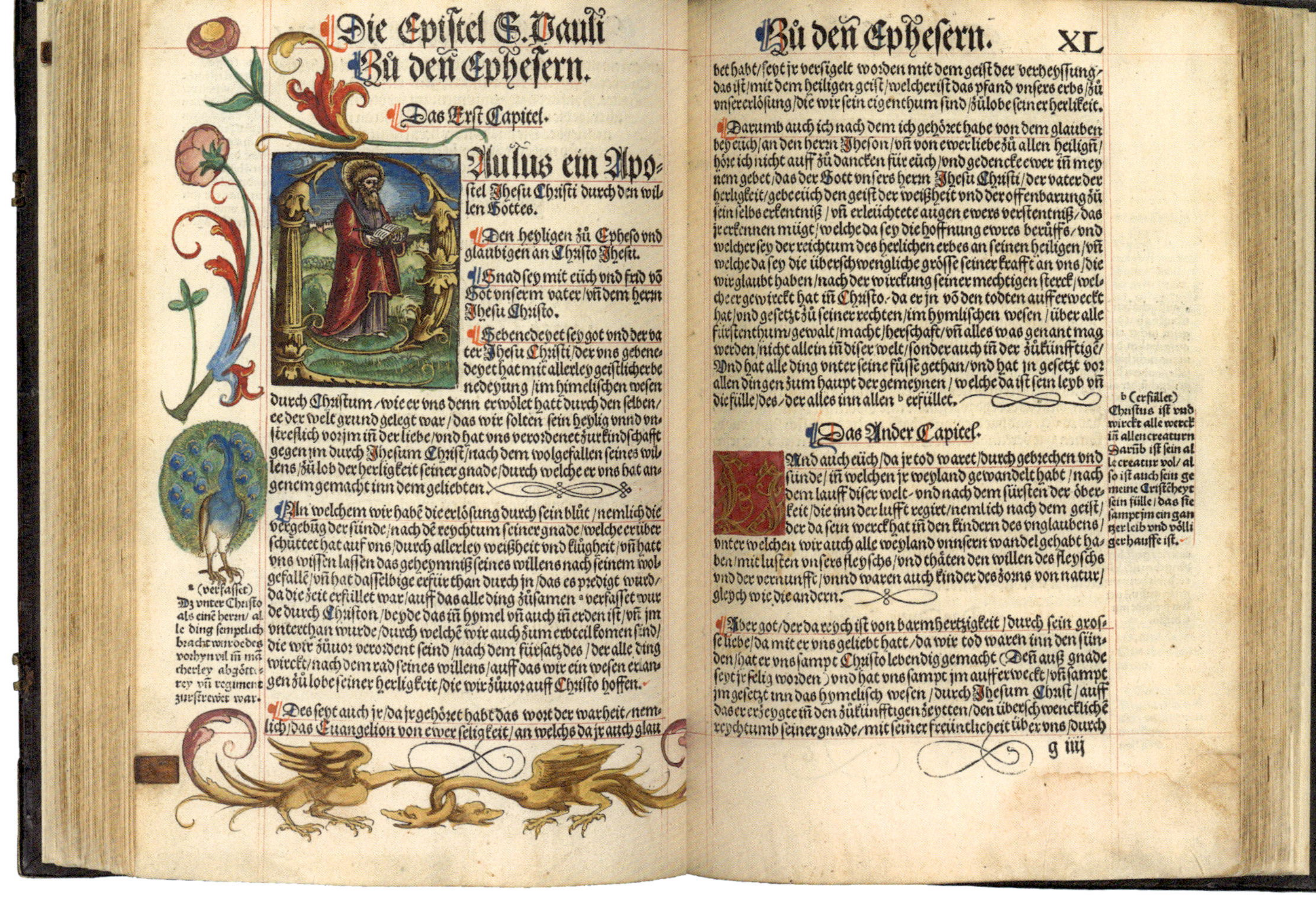

Die Epistel S. Pauli Zů den Ephesern.

Das Erst Capitel.

Paulus ein Apostel Jhesu Christi durch den willen Gottes.

Den heyligen zů Epheso vnd glaubigen an Christo Jhesu.

Gnad sey mit eüch vnd frid võ Got vnserm vater/vñ dem herrn Jhesu Christo.

Gebenedeyet sey got vnd der vater Jhesu Christi/der vns gebenedeyet hat mit allerley geistlicher benedeyung/im himelischen wesen durch Christum/wie er vns denn erwölet hatt durch den selben/ee der welt grund gelegt war/das wir solten sein heylig vnnd vnstreflich vor jm iñ der liebe/vnd hat vns verordenet zur kindschafft gegen jm durch Jhesum Christ/nach dem wolgefallen seines willens/zů lob der herligkeit seiner gnade/durch welche er vns hat angenem gemacht inn dem geliebten.

An welchem wir habẽ die erlösung durch sein blůt/nemlich die vergebũg der sünde/nach dẽ reychtum seiner gnade/welche er überschüttet hat auf vns/durch allerley weißheit vnd klůgheit/vñ hatt vns wissen lassen das geheymniß seines willens nach seinem wolgefallẽ/vñ hat dasselbige erfür than durch jn/das es predigt würd/da die zeit erfüllet war/auff das alle ding zůsamen [a] verfasset wurde durch Christon/beyde das iñ hymel vñ auch iñ erden ist/vñ jm vnterthan wurde/durch welchẽ wir auch zum erbteil komen sind/die wir zůvor verordent seind/nach dem fürsatz des/der alle ding wirckt/nach dem rad seines willens/auff das wir ein wesen erlangen zů lobe seiner herligkeit/die wir zůvor auff Christo hoffen.

[a] (verfasset) Dz vnter Christo als einẽ herrn/alle ding semptlich bracht wurde des vorhyn vil iñ mancherley abgötterey vñ regiment zurstrewet war.

Des seyt auch jr/da jr gehöret habt das wort der warheit/nemlich/das Euangelion von ewer seligkeit/an welchs da jr auch glaubet habt/seyt jr versigelt worden mit dem geist der verheyssung/das ist/mit dem heiligen geist/welcher ist das pfand vnsers erbs/zů vnser erlösung/die wir sein eigenthum sind/zů lobe seiner herlikeit.

Darumb auch ich nach dem ich gehöret habe von dem glauben bey eüch/an den herrn Jheson/vñ von ewer liebe zů allen heiligñ/hör ich nicht auff zů dancken für eüch/vnd gedencke ewer iñ meynem gebet/das der Gott vnsers herrn Jhesu Christi/der vater der herligkeit/gebe eüch den geist der weißheit vnd der offenbarung zů sein selbs erkentniß/vñ erleüchtete augen ewers verstentniß/das jr erkennen mügt/welche da sey die hoffnung ewres berůffs/vnd welcher sey der reichtum des herlichen erbes an seinen heiligen/vñ welche da sey die überschwengliche grösse seiner krafft an vns/die wir glaubt haben/nach der wirckung seiner mechtigen sterck/welche er gewirckt hat iñ Christo/da er jn võ den todten aufferweckt hat/vnd gesetzt zů seiner rechten/im hymlischen wesen/über alle fürstenthum/gewalt/macht/herschaft/vñ alles was genant mag werden/nicht allein iñ diser welt/sonder auch iñ der zůkünfftigẽ/Vnd hat alle ding vnter seine füsse gethan/vnd hat jn gesetzt vor allen dingen zum haupt der gemeynen/welche da ist sein leyb vñ die fülle/des/der alles inn allen [b] erfüllet.

[b] (erfüllet) Christus ist vnd wirckt alle werck iñ allen creaturn Darũb ist sein alle creatur vol/also ist auch sein gemeine Cristẽheyt sein fülle/das sie sampt jm ein gantzer leib vnd völliger hauffe ist.

Das Ander Capitel.

Vnd auch eüch/da jr tod waret/durch gebrechen vnd sünde/iñ welchen jr weyland gewandelt habt/nach dem lauff diser welt/vnd nach dem fürsten der oberkeit/die inn der lufft regirt/nemlich nach dem geist/der da sein werck hat iñ den kindern des vnglaubens/vnter welchen wir auch alle weyland vnnsern wandel gehabt haben/mit lusten vnsers fleyschs/vnd thäten den willen des fleyschs vnd der vernunfft/vnnd waren auch kinder des zorns von natur/gleych wie die andern.

Aber got/der da reych ist von barmhertzigkeit/durch sein grosse liebe/da mit er vns geliebt hatt/da wir tod waren inn den sünden/hat er vns sampt Christo levendig gemacht (Deñ auß gnade seyt jr selig worden) vnd hat vns sampt jm aufferweckt/vñ sampt jm gesetzt inn das hymelisch wesen/durch Jhesum Christ/auff das er erzeygte iñ den zůkünfftigen zeytten/den überschwencklichẽ reychtumb seiner gnade/mit seiner freüntlicheit über vns/durch

g iiij

104

COCONUT CUP OF SEBASTIAN WELSER I

Gregor Türck (goldsmith)
Monogrammist MS (medalist)

Nuremberg, after 1566

Coconut shell, silver, gilded, repoussé, cast, punched, engraved (cup); silver, gilded (medal)

H. 24.5 cm

Bayerisches Nationalmuseum, Munich, inv. no. R 260

References:
Fritz 1983, pp. 105–6, cat. no. 107; Exh. cat. Nuremberg 1985, pp. 235–36, cat. no. 32; Seelig 2006, pp. 387, 391; Exh. cat. Berlin 2007, p. 540, cat. no. IX.48 (Lorenz Seelig); NGK 2007, vol. 1, p. 420, cat. no. 901.

Sebastian Welser I (1500–1566) was the third son of Jakob Welser I |**cat. no. 101**|. In 1529, Sebastian became a delegate of the Greater Council of his hometown of Nuremberg, and in 1530, a member of the city's Inner Council, thus succeeding his father, who had resigned his post in municipal administration that same year.[1] In 1537, Sebastian took over management of the family trading firm in Nuremberg. Like his father, he was involved in overseas commerce. An entry in his daybook, begun about 1530 and now in the Staatsarchiv in Nuremberg, exemplifies the global dimensions of his enterprises: the entry concerns a ship that the Nuremberg Welser firm lost in Brazil;[2] captained by a certain Heinrich von Ende, the ship had been sent across the Atlantic presumably to bring back coveted raw materials such as brazilwood |**see cat. no. 113**|.[3]

Sebastian Welser died in 1566 and was immortalized that same year in a medal by the Monogrammist MS (active in Nuremberg ca. 1556–72).[4] The medal shows a bust-length portrait of Welser in three-quarter profile, with an inscription indicating his age and the year of creation—"SEBASTIAN WELSER · Æ · S · 66 · A° · 66 ·"—while the reverse bears the Welser family coat of arms.

The present coconut-shell cup, acquired by the Bayerisches Nationalmuseum in the nineteenth century, incorporates a gilded silver cast of the 1566 Welser medal on the underside of the lid.[5] The master's mark on the cup identifies it as the work of the Nuremberg goldsmith Gregor Türck (d. 1569).[6] The cup also bears the letter "N" hallmark of Nuremberg. Since Türck died in 1569,[7] this object must have been commissioned shortly after Sebastian Welser's death, presumably by his relatives in memory of him.

The cup's arched foot, with figures represented in relief on an earthen terrain, and its stem are made of gilded silver. Parts of two coconut shells form the bowl and lid. The coconut bowl is enclosed within three ornamented straps and encircled by a tall rim. The lid is topped by a baluster-shaped knob. Sebastian Welser's involvement in overseas trade may have influenced the choice of coconut, a precious non-European material, for this commemorative work. Unlike the intricately carved coconut shell in Peter Flötner's Holzschuher Cup |**cat. no. 41**|, the surface of the present bowl was left largely unworked and raw, an unusual treatment that emphasizes the aesthetics of the material itself. The inside of the coconut shell is polished and lacquered. Thus, Welser's cup could potentially have been used as an actual drinking vessel.[8]

Manuel Teget-Welz

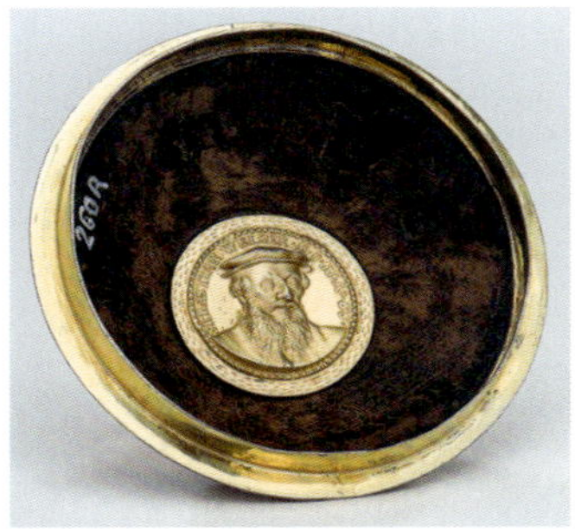

Medal on the inside of the lid

2 Geuder-Rabensteiner-Archiv, vol. 146.
3 Sebastian Welser's financial loss amounted to 894 goldguldens, and Heinrich von Ende was apparently killed by Indigenous locals. See Werner 1967, p. 552; Bernecker 2000, p. 207.
4 See Habich 1931, p. 247, cat. no. 1753.
5 Acquired before March 25, 1867. I thank Annette Schommers, Munich, for this information.
6 The initials "GT," ligated. See NGK 2007, vol. 1, p. 420, fig. MZ0901.
7 See Exh. cat. Nuremberg 1985, p. 497; NGK 2007, vol. 1, pp. 420–21, cat. no. 901.
8 See Exh. cat. Berlin 2007, p. 540, cat. no. IX.48 (Lorenz Seelig).

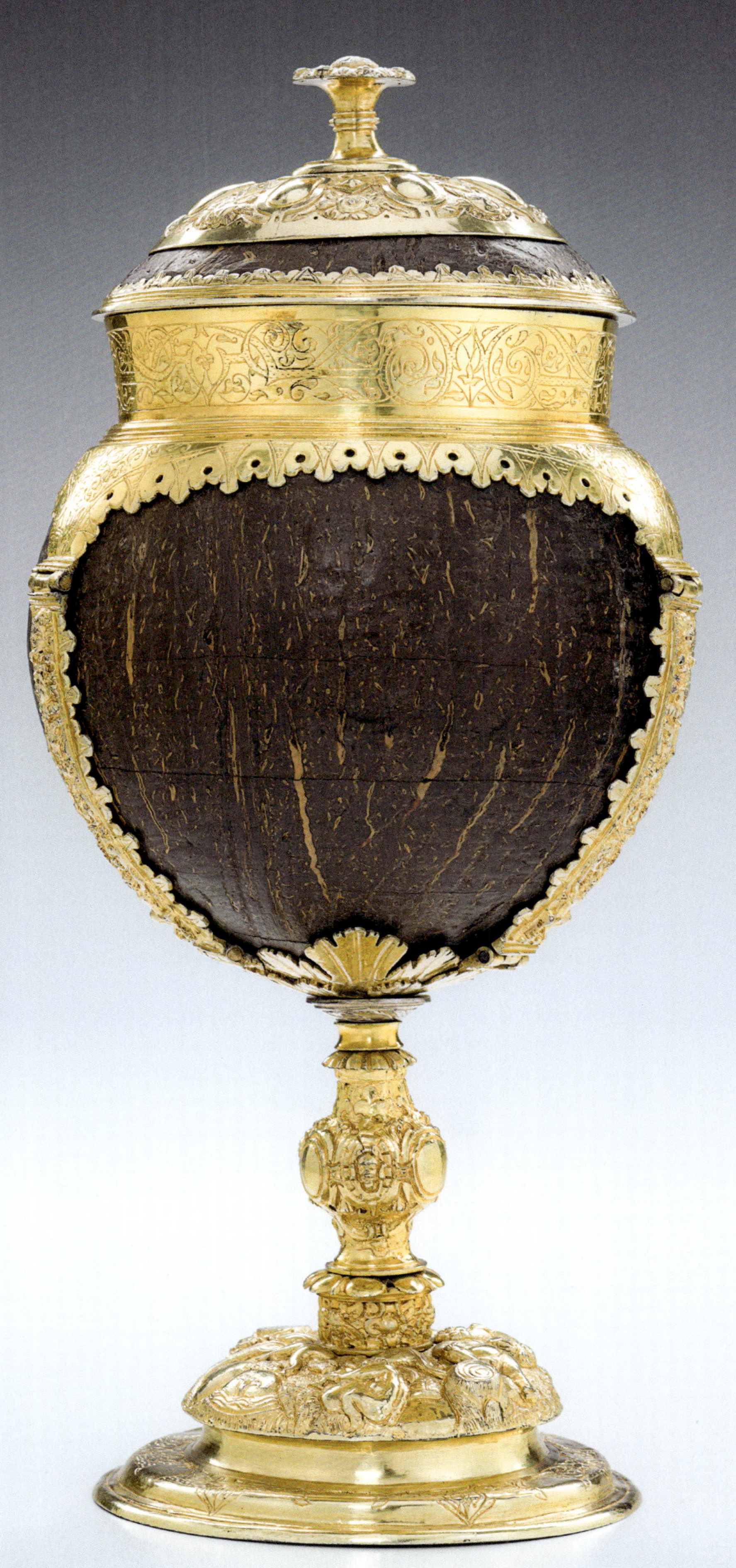

105

MAP OF TENOCHTITLÁN AND THE GULF OF MEXICO

In *Praeclara Ferdinandi Cortesii de Nova maris Oceani Hyspania Narratio*

Hernán Cortés

Nuremberg: Friedrich Peypus, 1524

105.1

Post-incunable, parchment, woodcuts, hand-colored

H. 30.5 cm; W. 21 cm (closed)

Österreichische Nationalbibliothek, Vienna, shelf mark 394471-C KAR MAG

105.2 (fig. p. 81)

Post-incunable, paper, woodcuts

H. 32.8 cm; W. 20 cm (closed)

Universitätsbibliothek der LMU, Munich, shelf mark 0014/W 2 H.aux. 52

References:
Tyrakowski 1997; Mundy 1998; Boone 2011; Astorga Poblete 2021; Astorga Poblete 2025.

Tenochtitlán, the precursor of Mexico City, was the capital of the Aztec Empire. In August 1521, it was captured by the Spanish conquistador Hernán Cortés (1485–1547) and largely destroyed. In several letters to Emperor Charles V, Cortés reported about his conquests in what is now Mexico. In 1522, Cortés's second letter was printed in Seville by Jakob Cromberger; two years later, that letter and the third one were translated from Spanish into Latin and published in Nuremberg by Friedrich Peypus (1485–1535) under the title *Praeclara Ferdinandi Cortesii de Nova maris Oceani Hyspania Narratio.* That edition includes a highly abstracted woodcut map of Tenochtitlán, showing the city immediately before its destruction by Cortés. The map, which includes a separate representation of the Gulf of Mexico and the Mississippi Delta, is considered the earliest European depiction of a city in the Americans.[1]

The impression of the map now in Vienna differs significantly from all other known examples.[2] It is the only one printed not on paper but on parchment. In addition, it was hand colored with expensive, premium-quality pigments. The intense blue of the lagoon was achieved partially with ultramarine, and numerous details were accented with shell gold. This is clearly apparent, for example, in the rowboats shown out on the water and in the building complex of the Templo Mayor. Gold accents also shimmer on the trees, the meadows, and the large flag with the Habsburg double-headed eagle. Owing to its material splendor, this magnificent impression of the map is thought to have been made and decorated specially as a gift for Archduke Ferdinand, the brother of Emperor Charles V.

The circumstances of the map's creation stand as an extraordinary example of the interdependencies present within global networks of the period. Crucial roles were played both by the bishop of Vienna at the time, Johann von Revellis (d. 1529), who is mentioned on the publication's title page, and by his secretary Pietro Savorgnano, who supplied the translation of Cortés's letters from Spanish into Latin. Savorgnano was in contact with the Nuremberg humanist Willibald Pirckheimer (1470–1530) and accompanied Revellis to Nuremberg in late 1523 for the Imperial Diet that took place there in 1524.[3] Revellis, for his part, had close contacts in Spain. Before becoming confessor to Archduke Ferdinand, he was a canon in the Archdiocese of Granada. That is of particular interest because some of the printed editions of the *Praeclara Narratio*, including the Vienna copy, are accompanied by the text *De rebus et Insulis noviter repertis* authored by Peter Martyr d'Anghiera (1457–1526). Peter Martyr was prior of Granada Cathedral and must have met Revellis there. Before the woodcut map was produced in Nuremberg, Peter Martyr had seen an Indigenous map of Tenochtitlán in Valladolid, among Aztec artifacts that Cortés had sent to Spain. That map could have been one of the objects from the Americas that were transported from Burgos to Nuremberg as gifts for Ferdinand in the run-up to the 1524 Imperial Diet. As Daniel Astorga Poblete suspects, that map by an unknown Indigenous creator, now lost, may have served as the model for the woodcut map of Tenochtitlán.[4]

Sven Jakstat

1 On the details of what is represented on the map, the map's genesis, and the question of its designer, see the essay by Daniel Astorga Poblete in the present volume.
2 See Astorga Poblete 2025. I thank the author for sharing his manuscript of this study.
3 Schottenloher 1910, pp. 34–35.
4 Mundy 1998 makes the foundational argument for the use of an Indigenous map as a model.

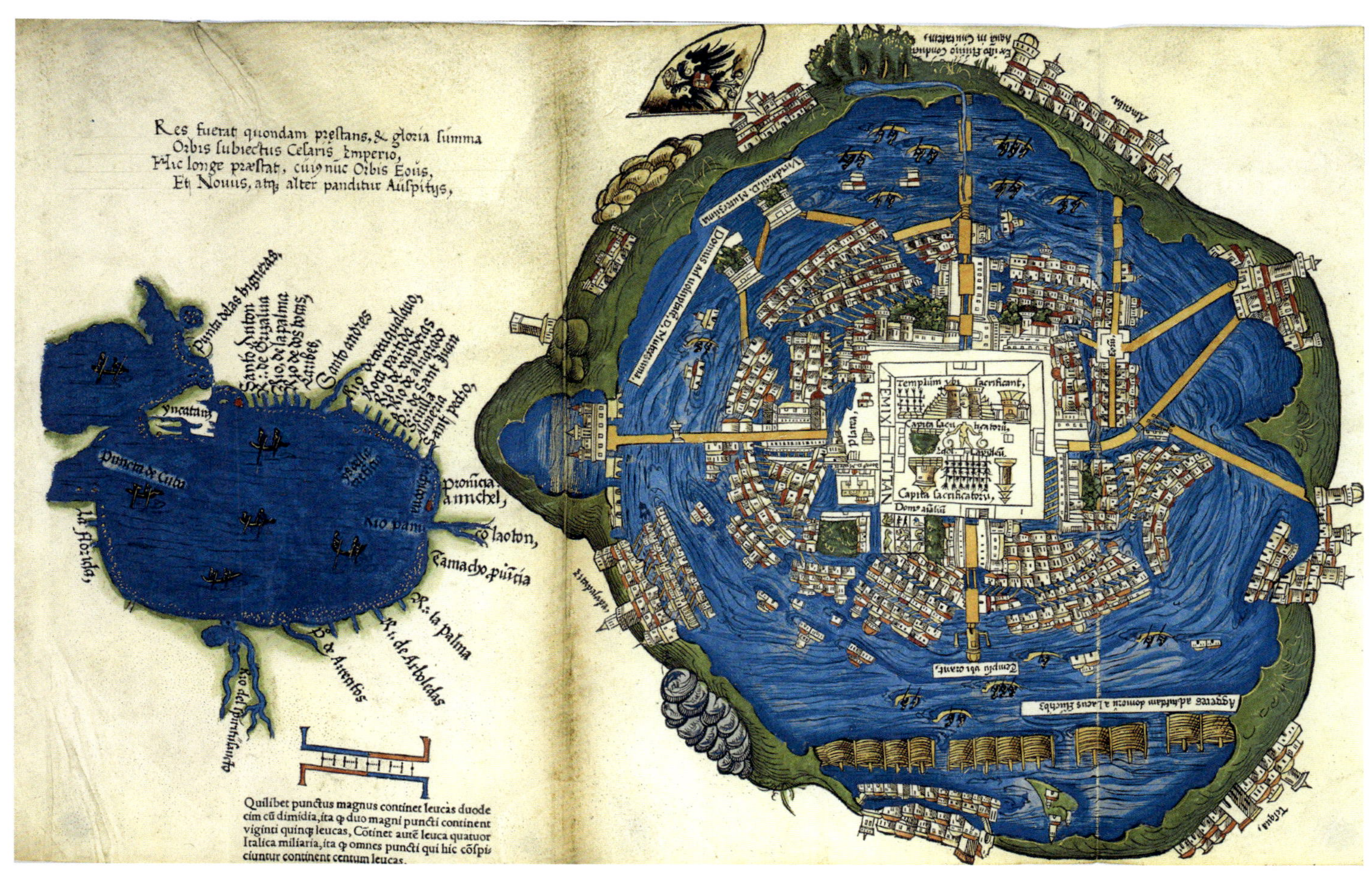
Res fuerat quondam prestans, & gloria summa
Orbis subiectus Cesaris Imperio,
Hic longe præstat, cuius nũc Orbis Eoũs,
Et Nouus, atq; alter panditur Auspitys,
Yucatan
Ri. la palma
R. de Arboledas
Quilibet punctus magnus continet leucas duode
cim cũ dimidia, ita q duo magni puncti continent
viginti quinq; leucas, Cõtinet autẽ leuca quatuor
Italica miliaria, ita q omnes puncti qui hic cõspi
ciuntur continent centum leucas.
TEMIXTITAN
Templum vbi sacrificant,
Capita sacrificatoru,
Platea

cat. no. 105.1

106

ISOLARIO

Benedetto Bordone

Venice: Nicolò d'Aristotele, 1528

106.1

73 pages, woodcuts, hand-colored

H. 30.9 cm; W. 21.8 cm (book block)

Bayerische Staatsbibliothek, Munich, shelf mark 2 Mapp. 34 m

Open to p. X: Tenochtitlán

106.2 (fig. p. 20)

73 pages, woodcuts, hand-colored

H. 31 cm; W. 20 cm (book block)

Universitätsbibliothek der FAU Erlangen-Nuremberg, Erlangen, shelf mark H61/2 TREW.F 11

References:
Armstrong 1996, pp. 80–83; Kim 2006; Tolias 2007, pp. 270–71; Tolias 2012, pp. 39–41; Stazzone 2024.

In the sixteenth century, printers in Nuremberg issued treatises and broadsheets about the Americas that had Europe-wide circulation. The map of Tenochtitlán produced in Nuremberg in 1524 garnered great interest |**cat. no. 105**|. Copies and adaptations of it are found in numerous publications, including Benedetto Bordone's so-called *Isolario*, a book about the world's islands whose lengthy full title reads, *Libro di Benedetto Bordone: nel qual si ragiona de tutte l'isole del mondo, con li lor nomi antichi & moderni, historie, fauole, & modi del loro uiuere, & in qual parte del mare stanno, & in qual parallelo & clima giacciono* (Book of Benedetto Bordone: In Which All Islands of the World Are Discussed, with Their Ancient and Modern Names, Histories, Myths, and Ways of Life, and in What Part of the Sea They Are, and in What Parallel and Climate They Lie).

Bordone, who died in 1531, was a miniature painter, cartographer, and printer who ran a flourishing workshop in Venice. The *Isolario*, his most famous work, presents 111 islands in texts and illustrations. As a kind of systematic representation of the islands known by Europeans at the time, including those in the Atlantic and Indian Oceans, it allowed readers to learn about distant parts of the world.

Only two of the illustrations in the *Isolario* concern "island cities": Venice and Tenochtitlán.[1] The depiction of the Aztec capital is clearly based on the aforementioned map published in Nuremberg in 1524 along with letters of Hernán Cortés |**cat. no. 105**|. Remarkably, the form of Venice, Bordone's hometown, is made comparable to that of Tenochtitlán as represented on the Nuremberg map |**fig. p. 20**|. In this striking visual resemblance between the two cities in the *Isolario*, David J. Kim recognized an intentional comparison that was meant to highlight similarities and differences in urban character and structural organization. He interpreted this as follows: "For Venice, Tenochtitlán was a 'dialectic mirror,' exhibiting images of like and unlike, the ideal and the damned. The New World city dramatized a utopian future for the Republic [of Venice], yet at the same time characterized a hedonistic and destroyed civilization."[2]

Sven Jakstat

1 Kim 2006, pp. 83–85.
2 Kim 2006, p. 91. See also the essay by Daniel Hess in the present volume.

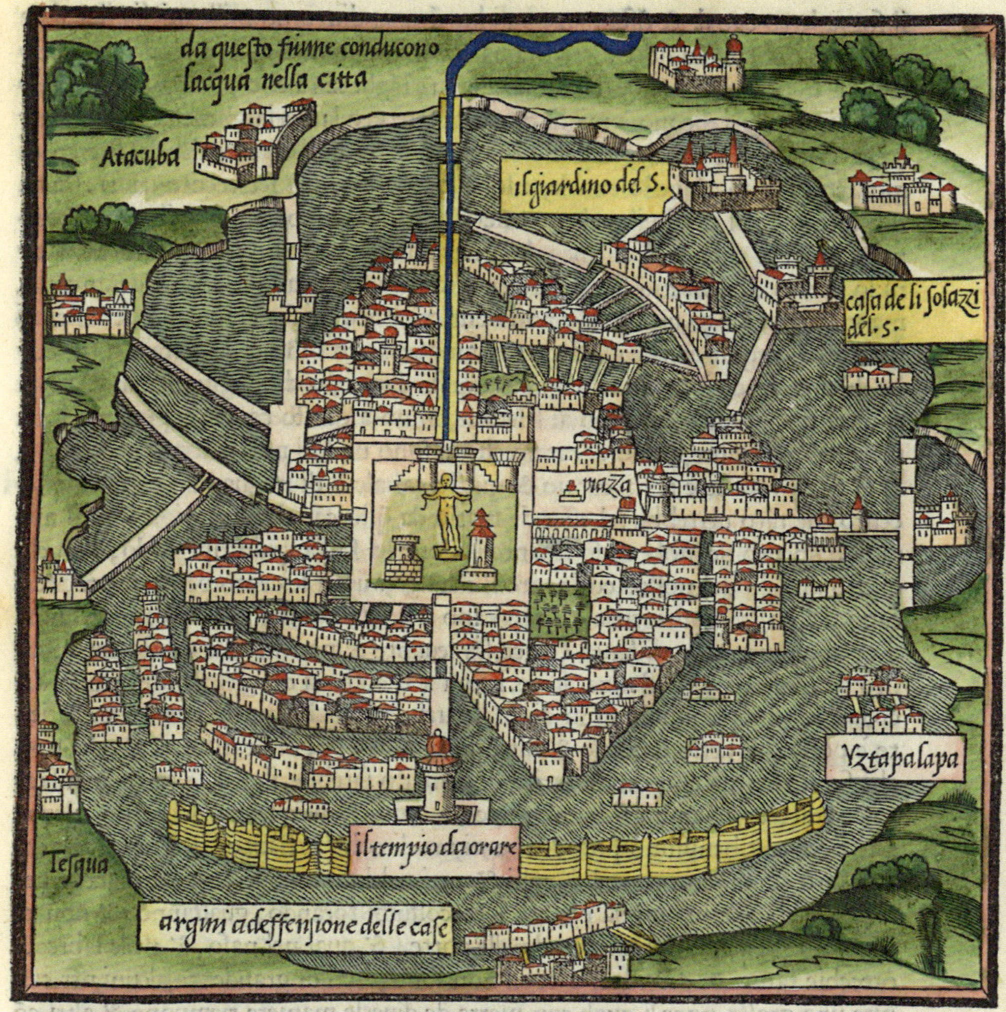

La gran citta di Temistitan.

TERRA di sancta Croce ouer mondo nouo, fu la prima di tutte queste isole, che trouata fusse, & benche alcuni hebbeno ferma openione, che al nostro cōtinēte cōgiunta fusse, nōdimeno al presente possono esser certi, esser grādissima isola, percio, che da uno capitano del re de spagna, una & laltra parte è stata ueduta, cio è la costa, che uerso tramōtana è posta, & laltra, che allostro giace, alla q̃le per giorni sei passando mōti, ualle, & fiumi cō lo esercito suo puenne, Hor dūque noi sciamo certi esser isola & nō col nostro cōtinente contenuta, & il principio suo hauere uerso l'oriēte, laquale ha forma di angulo, & uerso ostro & garbino inchlina, & laltra parte, che al settētrione siede, uerso ponente si stēde miglia tre mila, & doppo uerso tramōtana piega, & cō terra del laboratore (sopradetta) fanno

cat. no. 106.1

107

TERRESTRIAL GLOBE FROM THE AYRER KUNSTKAMMER

Designed by **Johannes Praetorius** (full signature); executed by **Hans Epischofer** (ligated monogram); casting attributed to **Wenzel Jamnitzer**; gilding attributed to **Erasmus Hornick**

Nuremberg, dated 1566

Brass, engraved, punched, gilded

H. 47 cm; Diam. 28 cm

GNM, inv. no. WI3, on long-term loan from the Museen der Stadt Nürnberg, Kunstsammlungen

References:
Exh. cat. Nuremberg 1992, vol. 2, pp. 638–40, cat. no. 1.125 (Johannes Willers); Exh. cat. Nuremberg 2017, p. 122, cat. no. 59 (Thomas Eser); Sauer 2021a, pp. 55–64, fig. 2.29.

This elaborately engraved, gilded brass globe combines the look of a precious cabinet of arts (*Kunstkammer*) piece with the most up-to-date cartographic knowledge of the time. For the representation of North and South America, the globe's designer, Johannes Praetorius, relied on an engraved map by Diego Gutiérrez entitled *Americae Descriptio*, which had been published by Hieronymus Cock in Antwerp in 1562.[1] That monumental engraving, consisting of six sheets, was the largest-ever map of the Americas at the time. Gutiérrez was cosmographer at the Casa de la Contratación de Indias in Seville, the organizing body of Spanish overseas trade. The Casa's numerous responsibilities included cartography, the purpose of which was not only to record new discoveries in North and South America but also to mark out Spanish spheres of influence. For the Nuremberg globe, Praetorius borrowed from Gutiérrez's map the broad divisions of South America into Patagonia in the south, Cartagena in the north, Brazil in the east, and Peru in the west. Major landmarks include various mountain ranges, the Amazon, and the branching river systems around the Paraná River in the Río de la Plata basin. The depictions of legendary Patagonian "giants" and several terrifying scenes of cannibals in Brazil are also based on the engraved map. The figures of unclothed archers, the animals, and the subjects from classical mythology are derived from different sources.

The globe's inscription "America inventa 1497" is based on a longer textual passage found on Gutiérrez's map. The year refers to the maiden voyage of the Spanish merchant and navigator Amerigo Vespucci, who was the first European to set foot on the American mainland and to become convinced that this landmass was a "new" continent |**see cat. no. 98**|. In the following decades, that proposition was the subject of intense debate among cartographers |**see cat. no. 6**|. Gutiérrez shows South America as a peninsula-like landmass. At the southern end, the Strait of Magellan ("Estrecho de Magellanes") separates the mainland from the Tierra del Fuego archipelago. Central and North America, on the other hand, are shown as extensions of northeastern Asia, as on the present globe.

An engraved cartouche at the bottom of the globe indicates that it was created in Nuremberg in 1566. Praetorius lived in Nuremberg from 1562 to 1569. During that time, he created several scientific instruments, including this globe, for the Nuremberg municipal physician and astronomer Melchior Ayrer. After a number of years spent in Wittenberg, in 1576–77 Praetorius took up the first professorship of mathematics at the newly founded university in Altdorf.

How did Praetorius come into possession of Diego Gutiérrez's *Americae Descriptio* map, which appeared only four years before the globe's creation? In the first place, close trade relations existed between Nuremberg and Antwerp, where the map was printed in the workshop of Hieronymus Cock. Another avenue may have been through Seville. Nuremberg printers had been active in Seville since the late fifteenth century |**see cat. no. 94**|.[2] And Nuremberg merchants were present there beginning in the second decade of the sixteenth century. The most prominent of them was Lazarus Nürnberger, who in 1517–18 joined the fleet of António de Saldanha to voyage from Lisbon to eastern India, Goa, Kannur, Kolkata, and Kochi. In 1520, Nürnberger moved to Seville, where he was involved in overseas trade, facilitating local contact with southern German trading firms up until his death in 1564. To some extent, maps were among the goods traded by Nürnberger: he is known to have procured several *cartas de marear* (nautical charts) for the Nuremberg patrician Caspar Nützel.

Susanne Thürigen

1 Buisseret 2007.
2 Kellenbenz 1967. See also the essay by Sven Jakstat in the present volume.

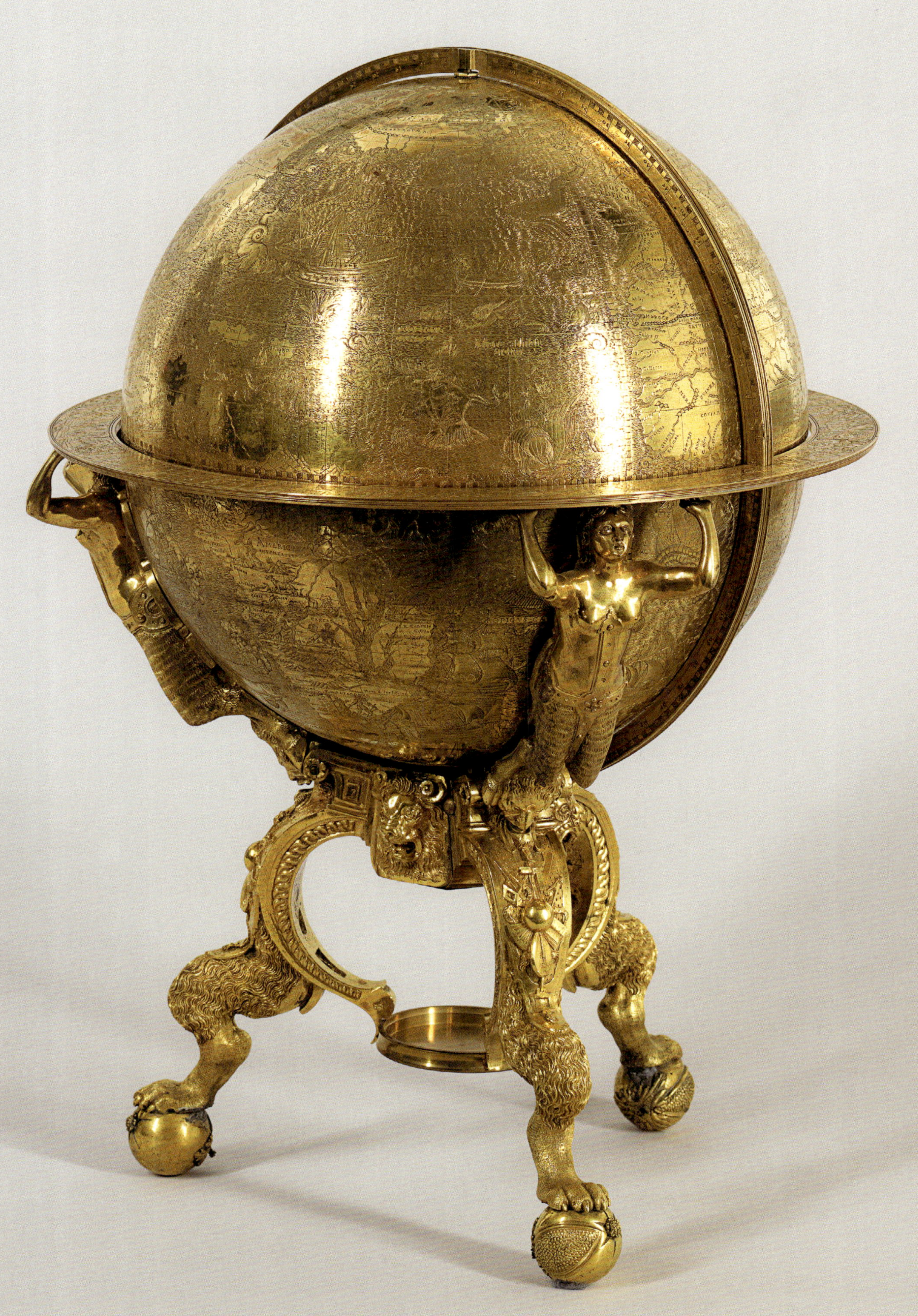

108

MEMORIAL SHIELD (*TOTENSCHILD*) FOR HANS TETZEL

Nuremberg, after 1571

Paint on limewood

H. 70.7 cm; W. 45.5 cm

GNM, inv. no. KG1371

References:
Putzer 2020a, p. 233; Jakstat 2024.

This memorial shield from the Egidienkirche in Nuremberg is the only surviving artifact associated with the Nuremberg mining entrepreneur Hans Tetzel. Between 1535 and 1571, Tetzel operated mines in Cuba that were dependent on the labor of enslaved Black people.[1] Apart from the indication that Tetzel died in Madrid, the memorial panel offers no clues to a life that is highly relevant to the early history of globalization, particularly with regard to the brutal injustices of the transatlantic slave trade.[2]

The design of Tetzel's memorial shield adheres to the directives issued in 1495 by Nuremberg's Inner Council to prevent such memorials from becoming too ostentatious.[3] As prescribed, the upper third is reserved for the inscription, while the lower portion displays the deceased's family coat of arms. The Tetzel coat of arms consists of a red shield charged with a silver cat rampant. Thus, with the exception of particulars found in its inscription,[4] this memorial matches other post-1495 memorial shields for male members of the family created for display in the fourteenth-century Tetzel Chapel at the Egidienkirche.

By the time Hans Tetzel was born, in 1518, three years after the founding of Santiago de Cuba, his family had already achieved prominence in the mining business. Around 1538, he traveled to Seville. It was then, at the latest, that fellow southern German merchants and entrepreneurs would have informed him about the difficulties of producing copper from ore extracted in Cuba. In 1541, Tetzel sailed to Cuba. Forty-nine years earlier, Christopher Columbus had claimed the island for Isabella I of Castile and Ferdinand II of Aragon, and some thirty years earlier, between 1511 and 1515, Diego Velázquez de Cuéllar had conquered it on behalf of King Ferdinand. When Tetzel arrived there, the Indigenous population had shrunk to just a few hundred families through war, malnutrition, and disease. A year and a half after he arrived in Cuba, Tetzel returned to Europe with ore samples so that specialists in his homeland could develop new smelting processes for the Cuban material. An agreement reached with the Spanish crown in 1546 entitled Tetzel to operate ten mines in Cuba and to bring German metallurgists and miners with him for that purpose. Soon after his return to Cuba, he encountered resistance from the local Spanish mine owners, who refused to pay him the contractually agreed prices for smelting the ore they mined. A settlement was reached in 1550, stipulating, among other things, that Tetzel had to teach the art of smelting Cuban ore to the "Black slaves" (*esclavos negros*) who worked for the mine owners. Tetzel's contract ended in 1566, and he returned to Spain in 1568 to negotiate new licenses in Madrid. In 1571, he died in Madrid at the age of fifty-three.

The memorial shield was probably commissioned shortly afterward by his bereaved relatives. It was customary in Nuremberg create local memorials for family members who died far away from home. However, the panel provides no information about Tetzel's activities in Cuba and his involvement in the transatlantic slave trade or the suffering of Cuba's indigenous population.

Sven Jakstat

1 On Tetzel, see Werner 1961; Werner 1967–68; Acosta Cuellar 2022; Schöntag 2023.
2 See the extensive discussion in Jakstat 2024.
3 Putzer 2020b, p. 289.
4 "Anno domini 1571 den / 5 tag Octobris verschid der Er / bar und vest Hanns Tetzel zu / Madrit In Hispania dem Got / genedig sey a[men]" (In the year of our Lord 1571, the honorable and courageous Hans Tetzel died on October 5 in Madrid in Spain. May God have mercy on him. Amen).

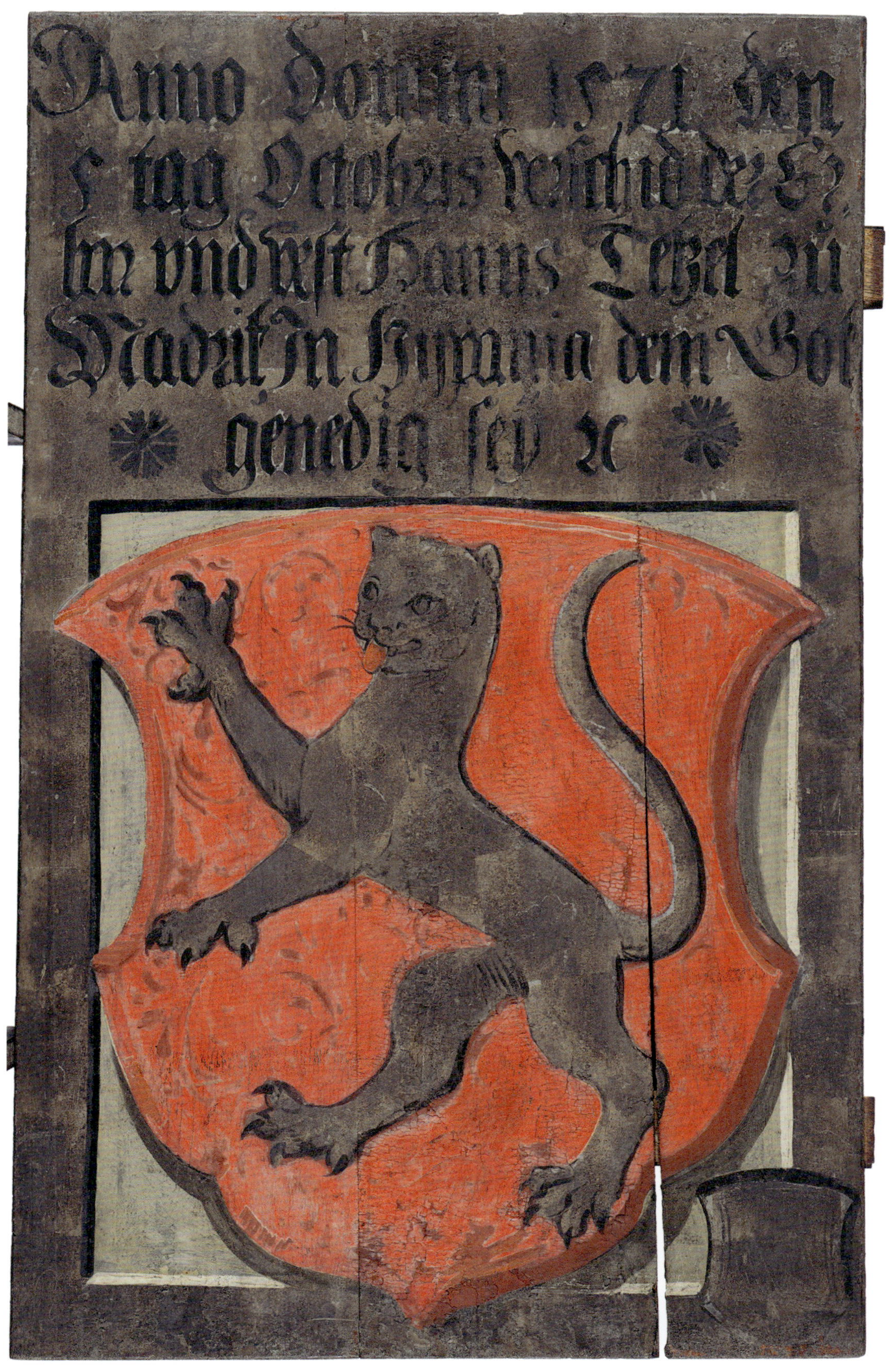
Anno domini 1571 den
5 tag Octobers verschid der Er-
ber und vest Hanns Tetzel zu
Madrit in Hyspania dem Got
genedig sey etc.

109

COSTUME BOOK

Christoph Weiditz (?)

Augsburg, ca. 1530–40

Illuminated manuscript, 154 leaves, pen-and-ink drawings with colored washes

H. 19.5 cm; W. 14.5 cm

GNM, shelf mark Hs22474

Open to fol. 22v: Black slave in Castile (fig. p. 70); fols. 73 v–74r: Black slaves in Barcelona

References:
Hampe 1927; Exh. cat. Washington 1991, p. 572, cat. no. 406 (Jean M. Massing); Lowe 2012, pp. 15–16; Exh. cat. Nuremberg 2017, p. 123, cat. no. 62 (Stephanie Armer); Erichsen 2024.

People from Nuremberg became involved in the emerging transatlantic slave trade by the early sixteenth century. Only a few pictorial sources from the period bear witness to the trade's inhumane conditions and systemic injustices. This underscores the brutality underlying two drawings of Black people forced to work in chains found in the so-called Weiditz Costume Book.[1]

In 1528 or 1529, Christoph Weiditz (1498–1559), a medalist and creator of small-scale sculptures, joined the armorer Kolman Helmschmied on a journey from Augsburg via Portugal to the court of Charles V in Spain. Weiditz was granted a charter from the emperor allowing him to work as a master goldsmith. During this and subsequent journeys, in part in the imperial entourage, he seems to have recorded his impressions in a kind of pictorial diary, which then served as the basis for his costume book. The earliest surviving version of the book is at the Germanisches Nationalmuseum. It is difficult to determine whether Weiditz executed the drawings himself or left his preliminary sketches to another artist for development into the costume book. Although this manuscript was created in Augsburg, the reception of certain motifs in Nuremberg sources, including the costume book of Hans Weigel |**cat. no. 84**| and that of the tax scribe Sigmund Heldt II from about 1560–80,[2] proves that the illustrations were known in Nuremberg.

Weiditz's stay at the court of Charles V gave him the opportunity to create portrait medals of important personalities, including a medal of Hernán Cortés, the conquistador who returned from Mexico in 1528.[3] In addition, presumably in Madrid, Weiditz also attended a showing of Aztec people whom Cortés had brought to Europe along with animals and artifacts. The credibility of the costume book's depictions is corroborated by an eyewitness account preserved in the Scheurl family archive;[4] evidently people in Nuremberg were also aware of the events taking place at the imperial court.

While on the Iberian Peninsula, Weiditz also witnessed the transatlantic slave trade. One scene in the costume book, observed in Castile according to the caption, shows a man said to be one of the "sold Moors" (*verkaufften moren*) who were made to carry large wineskins |**fig. p. 70**|. A heavy iron chain, intended to prevent the man from escaping, is attached to his belt and a leg shackle. The brutality is evident not least in the inscription: "If they run away from their masters, they are made to work like this and wear chains." Another drawing shows two Black men in Barcelona at a well, drawing drinking water for ships and galleys. They, too, are fitted with iron shackles indicative of their enslavement.

Scholarship has devoted only scant attention to the involvement of Nurembergers in the trade in enslaved people during the early modern period. Yet examples are known. In Seville, Lazarus Nürnberger, a well-connected lobbyist for southern German trading firms, sold twenty white female slaves in 1536. Then, in 1537, Nürnberger obtained the right to transport to America as a slave a Christian man born in Portuguese India. And in 1544, he acquired a permit to buy twenty men and five women in Cape Verde and have them brought to America (which ultimately never happened).[5] Black slaves worked in the Cuban mines that were operated by the Nuremberg patrician Hans Tetzel from 1542 |**cat. no. 108**|.[6] Although little is known about the individual fates of these people, they were undoubtedly subjected to coercion and violence.[7]

Benno Baumbauer and Manuel Teget-Welz

1 Lowe 2005, pp. 25–26; Lowe 2012, pp. 15–16; Rublack 2022, pp. 292–93.
2 Kunstbibliothek, Staatliche Museen zu Berlin, shelf mark 14138017. See Rublack 2022, pp. 302–12.
3 See Habich 1929, p. 61, cat. no. 376.
4 Codex B 2, fols. 122r–123r. See Exh. cat. Nuremberg 2017, supplement (Stephanie Armer).
5 Otte 1963–64, pp. 143–44.
6 Jakstat 2024.
7 On the conditions of slavery in the Caribbean, see Zeuske 2004. See also Lowe 2012.

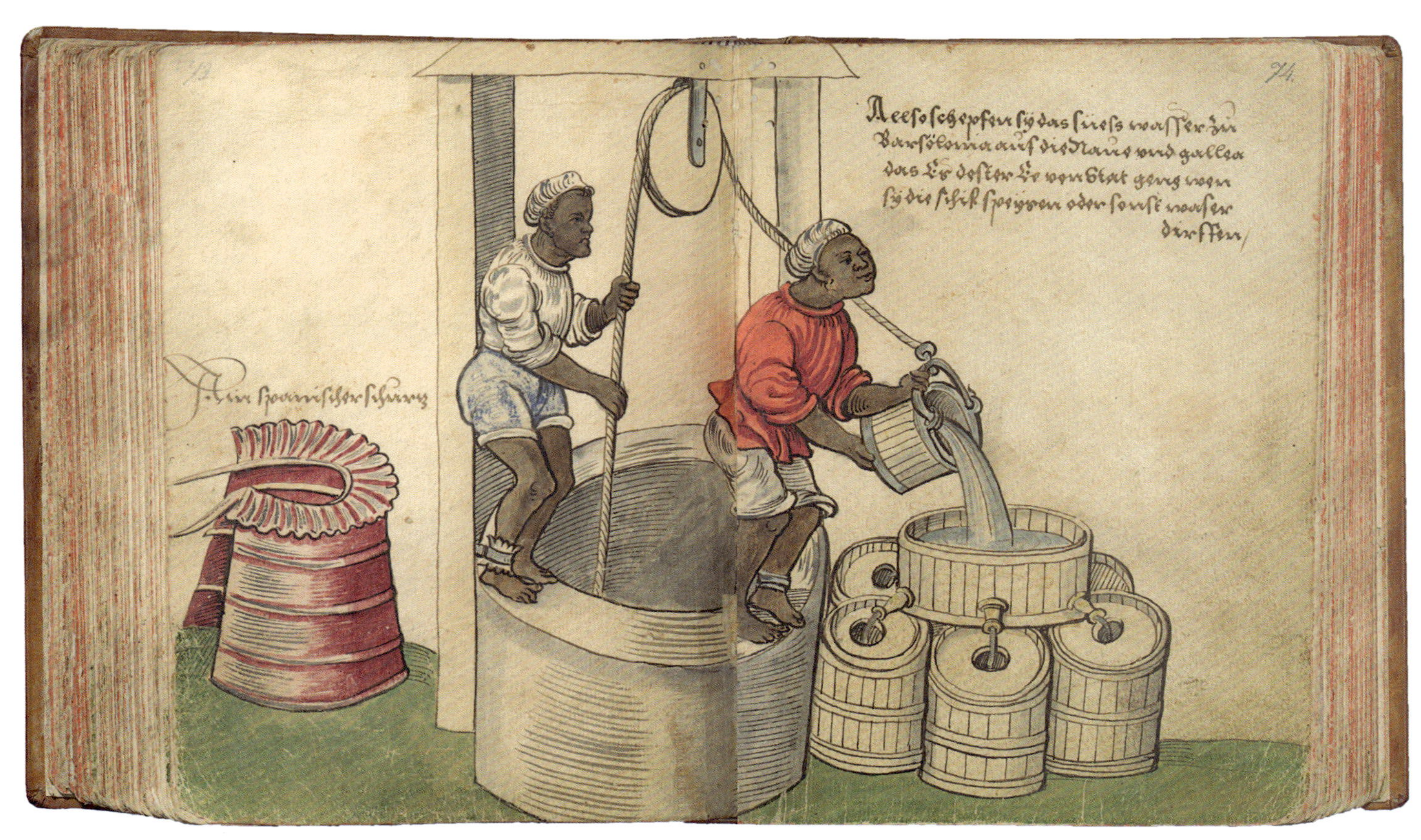
73
Ain spanischer schurz
74
Alsso schepfen sy das süess wasser zu
Barsolonia auf die Naus und gallea
das Er dester Er von Stat geng wen
sy die schif speyßen oder sonst waser
dirffen/

110

KÖLER FAMILIENBUCH ("FAMILY BOOK")

Hieronymus Köler

Nuremberg, 1560–65

Manuscript, 83 leaves, numerous illustrations

H. 30.5 cm; W. 23.3 cm (leaf dimensions)

British Library, London, shelf mark Ms. Add. 15217

Open to fols. 38v–39r: "Unser ander gearmiertes Schiff" (Our other armed ship) and "Gewisser form und gestalth der Inssel Vinicole" (The form and appearance of the island of Venezuela); fols. 39v–40r: "Bestallung zirlicher und scheinparlicher dinng, do man dismals in die Inssel Vinicöle kommen were" (An assemblage of beautiful and splendid things that one would see upon coming to the island of Venezuela) and "Ordnung der Nackenden Indianer" (Characteristics of the naked Indians)

Not exhibited

References:
Welser 1874; Amburger 1931; Méndez Rodríguez 2013; Bräunlein 2018; Rublack 2022, pp. 294–99.

In early 1536, the Nuremberg trading assistant Hieronymus Köler (1507–1573) returned to his hometown after a four-year journey. By the following year at the latest, he began writing down his personal recollections, which then formed the basis for an illustrated *Familienbuch* (family book) created from 1560 to 1565.[1] It is open to question whether the drawings are by Köler himself. While their amateurish appearance could suggest as much,[2] it is more likely that they were done by a *Briefmaler*-type illuminator (literally, "letter painter") who was well acquainted with the stylistic tendencies of the day, as found, for example, in the art of Jost Amman.

The city views in Köler's manuscript allow his route to be traced as far as Seville, where he arrived in 1534. At that time, the port city on the Guadalquivir River was the main point of departure for the Spanish crown's undertakings in the Americas. As Köler reports, he met the influential networker Lazarus Nürnberger in Seville and was persuaded by him to join a fleet headed for Venezuela. In exchange for large loans, King Charles (Emperor Charles V) had granted the Augsburg-based Welser company the governorship over the colony of Klein-Venedig ("Little Venice," the literal meaning of "Venezuela"). The Welsers were obliged in return to settle three hundred colonists there, build fortresses, and establish an administration. In reality, however, the conquistadors mainly engaged in brutal raids and kidnapping.[3]

Because the fleet in which Köler sailed was forced to depart in the fall, it became caught in several storms. Köler bought himself out of his contractual obligations for a high fee. He later cursed the contractual situation and the conditions on board as "torment, exploitation, and drudgery."[4] He also denounced the Europeans' treatment of the Indigenous peoples: "they berate the poor people, strangle them, and rob them of everything just for a shameful bit of gold and silver."[5]

Köler never reached South America. Nevertheless, his descriptions and illustrations of Venezuela are highly revealing, for they convey ideas about the little-known land and its people that were in circulation in Nuremberg at the time. In Köler's imagination, the Indigenous inhabitants of Venezuela went about their lives completely naked. They are shown harvesting wild beets (which Köler describes as inedible for Europeans) and fishing in the sea, among other activities. The text reports that native people were armed with clubs, slings, and bows with poisoned arrows. Unlike in works by artists such as Burgkmair, Dürer, Weiditz, and Amman |**cat. nos. 84, 100, 109, 117**|, no effort appears to have been made to depict the material culture of the Indigenous people in an authentic fashion. Nevertheless, the text does reveal an awareness of certain costume traditions of Indigenous cultures: Köler mentions, among other things, beardlessness, long black hair, hair ornaments made of horsehair, gemstone piercings, and feather decorations. Yet none of this is shown in the illustrations.

The depictions devote great attention to the notion of gold in abundance. Large gold vessels stand in the landscapes; some are shown being used to scoop water. Even the lintels at the entrances to the people's cave dwellings are covered in gold. Details such as these reflect the El Dorado myth, the legend of a "gilded" land or city that became amplified by the rich Incan plunder brought to Spain by Hernando Pizarro in 1534.[6]

Köhler's imaginings take a reflective turn in an illustration where he projects himself into a military tent in Venezuela |**fig. p. 28**|. In this figure, he presents himself as guarantor of the credibility of his own fictions.

Benno Baumbauer

1 Bräunlein 2018, p. 321. The author portrait on fol. 1r is marked with Köler's initials "HC" and the date 1565. The title on fol. 2v refers to the year 1560. For a description of the manuscript, see Priebsch 1901, pp. 128–32, cat. no. 150.
2 Bräunlein 2018, p. 322.
3 Simmer 2000; Denzer 2005; Häberlein 2016, pp. 116–31. Noteworthy in this context is the founding of "Neu-Nürnberg" (New Nuremberg), the present-day city of Maracaibo.
4 Welser 1874, p. 327 (*fretterey, schmarotzerey und schintterey*).
5 Welser 1874, p. 328 (*da man die armen leutt uberpoldttertt, erwürgtt und inen das Ir nymptt allain umb ein wenig schenttliches goldes und silbers willen*).
6 Bräunlein 2018, p. 326.

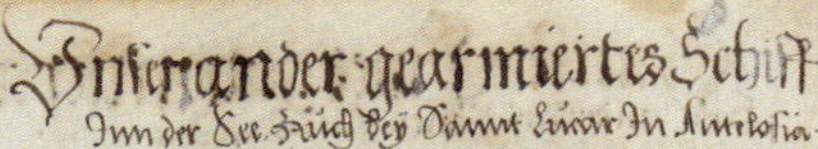

Im der See Zuch des Diamantaz In Antrolia

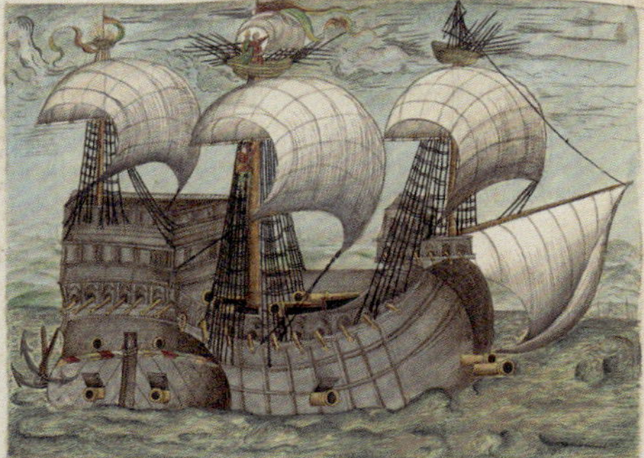

Gewisser form vnd gestalth der Innsel Vinicole

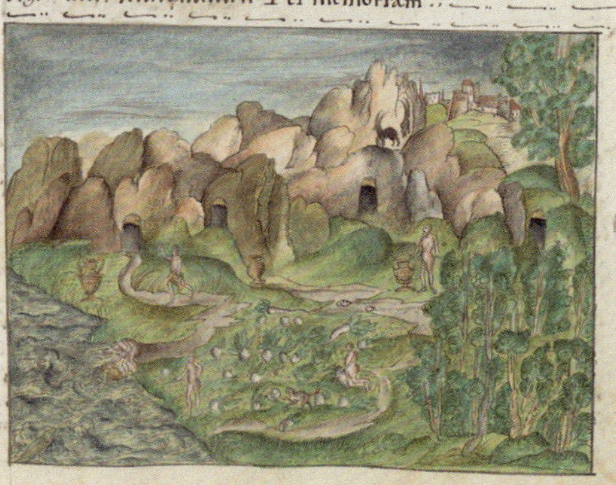

Bestallung zirlicher vnd Schein parlicher dinng, do man dißmals In die Innsel Vinicole kummen wore.

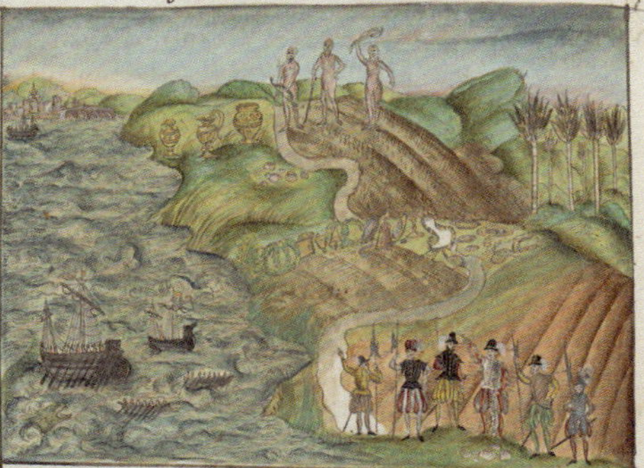

Ordnung der Nackenden Indianer

Zu sahen, Klaiden, Begaben, vnnd widerumb ledig lauffen zu lassen, Do man Inslandt kemen wer.

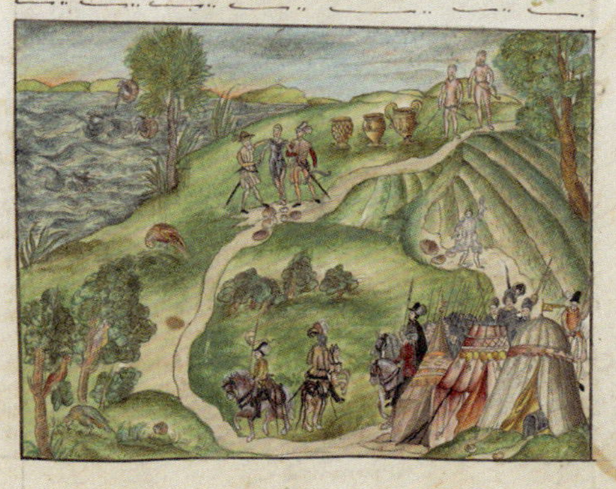

111

CROP PLANTS AND A GUINEA PIG FROM THE AMERICAS

From: Georg Öllinger: *Magnarum medicine partium herbariae et zoographiae imagines*

Nuremberg, ca. 1553

Pen and ink, brush and ink, watercolor

Each H. 48 cm; W. 32.5 cm or 65 cm

Universitätsbibliothek Erlangen-Nürnberg, Erlangen, inv. no. MS 2362

Plates 90–91 and 510–511 (fig.): gourds; plate 106 (fig.): corn; plate 289 (fig.): chili peppers; plates 541 (fig.) and 543: tomatoes; plate 641 (fig.): guinea pig

References:
Exh. cat. Nuremberg 1992, vol. 2, pp. 928–35, cat. no. 5.120a (Werner Dressendörfer); Olariu 2023.

The "herbal" created by the Nuremberg apothecary Georg Öllinger (1487–1557) |**see also cat. nos. 38, 89**| contains numerous images of ornamental, medicinal, and useful plants imported to Europe from the Americas, such as gourds, corn, tomatoes, marigolds, chili peppers, and prickly pears.[1] Some of the illustrations are the earliest known depictions of these plants in Europe.[2] Such is the case for tomatoes, which are native to Central and South America; Öllinger shows three different specimens. The images of marigolds are also the first in Europe. And, from the animal kingdom, no earlier European depiction of a guinea pig is known.

It is unclear whether all the plant species depicted were cultivated by Öllinger in his famous garden in Nuremberg, which was laid out about 1520. After all, he is known to have borrowed a number of motifs from other sources: "Öllinger had part of the illustraticns done from nature and the other part copied after existing depictions."[3]

As noted by Dominic Olariu, a special feature of Öllinger's watercolor plant studies is that they were designed not only to meet the demands of botany, but also to be aesthetically pleasing. The single-page and sometimes double-page illustrations usually fill the entire available space. The captions were added only later, around 1600. The flowers, leaves, and fruits of the gourd plants and the branching vines of the tomato plants are arranged in such a way as to create symmetrical patterns, resulting in an ornamental overall effect. At the same time, the individual fruits are often depicted at different stages of growth and from various perspectives. For example, the tomatoes on one sheet are shown from the side, from below, and from above. In this way, tomato growth can be traced all the way from the blossom to the ripe, bright red fruit, with the unripe green fruit in between. This dual ambition to satisfy the interests of both science and art is confirmed by the contents summary that is found on the illustrated title page designed by Samuel Quiccheberg (1529–1567) after completion of the illustrations. There, the book is said to contain "An extraordinary number of excellent images from the main fields of medicine, namely botany and zoology; presented in this book in admirably vivid paintings and at great expense by the widely acclaimed Mister Georg Öllinger, citizen of Nuremberg, apothecary, and merchant."[4]

In its entirety, with over 700 pages and a total of 635 depictions of plants and animals, the book clearly conveys an ambition to present plants from all parts of the world then known to Europeans in all their chromatic and ornamental splendor. In its claim to completeness, this compendium's global aspect is comparable to only a few other book projects of the period, for example Hans Weigel's costume book |**cat. no. 84**|, another work produced in Nuremberg. The captions added about 1600 show that even at that time, the plants' exact origins were not always known and were subject to error. For example, corn, which Columbus brought to Europe from the Americas, is described as "Triticum Turcicum" (Turkish wheat).[5]

Sven Jakstat

1 Olariu 2023, p. 33.
2 Olariu 2023, p. 44.
3 Translated from the German in Olariu 2023, p. 38.
4 See also Olariu 2023, p. 25.
5 Exh. cat. Nuremberg 1992, vol. 2, p. 931, cat. no. 5.120a (Werner Dressendörfer).

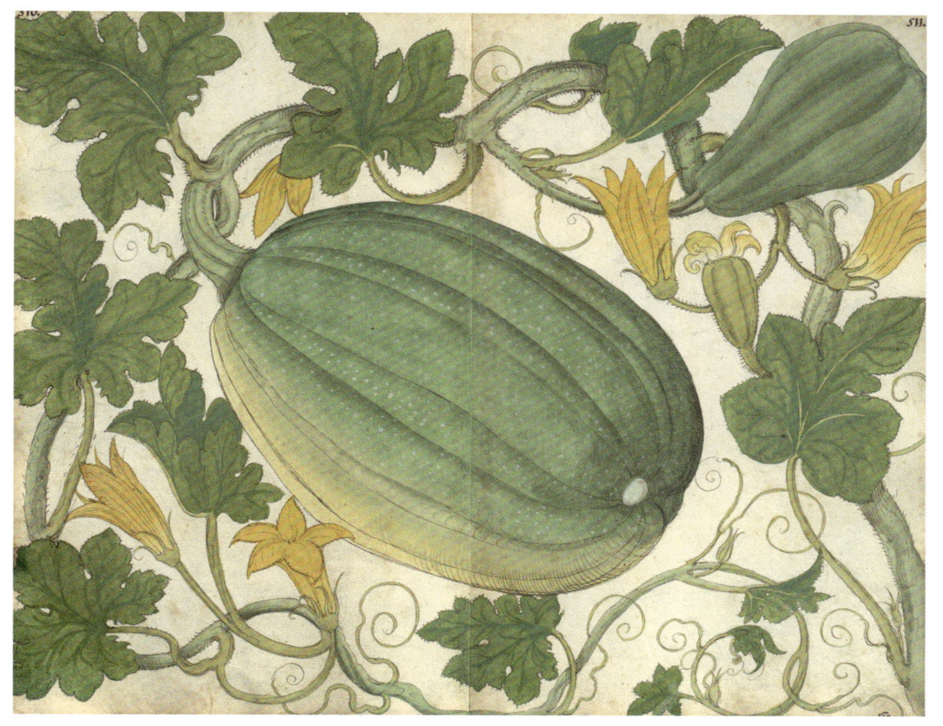

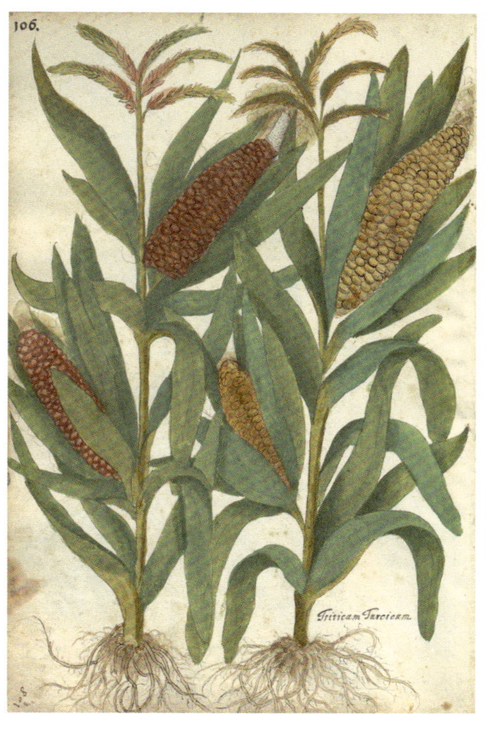
106.
Triticum Turcicum

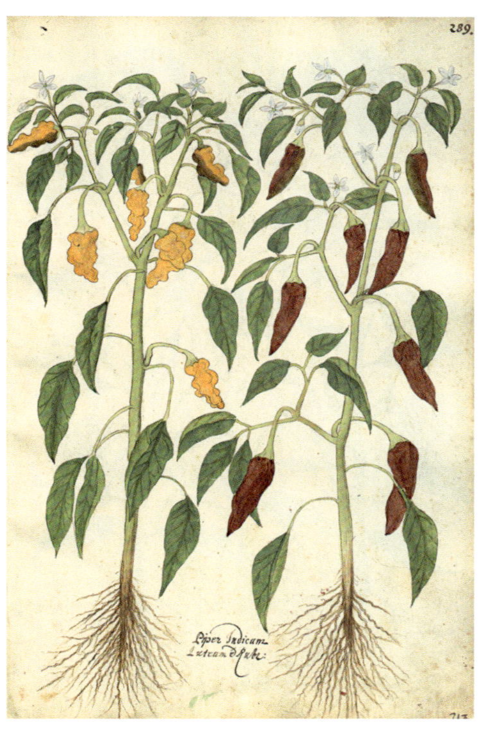
289.

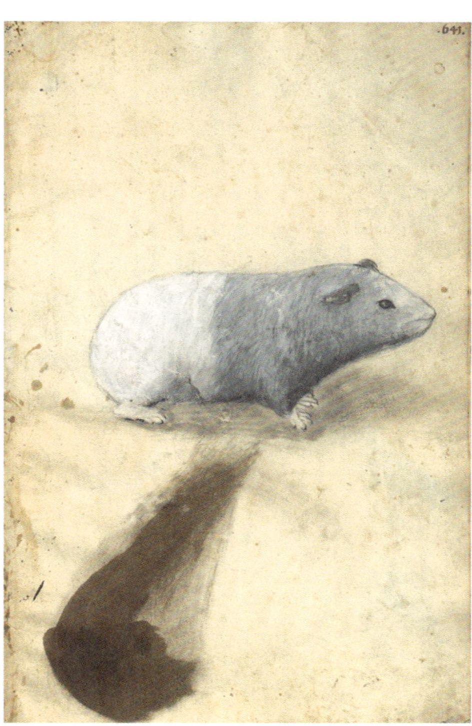

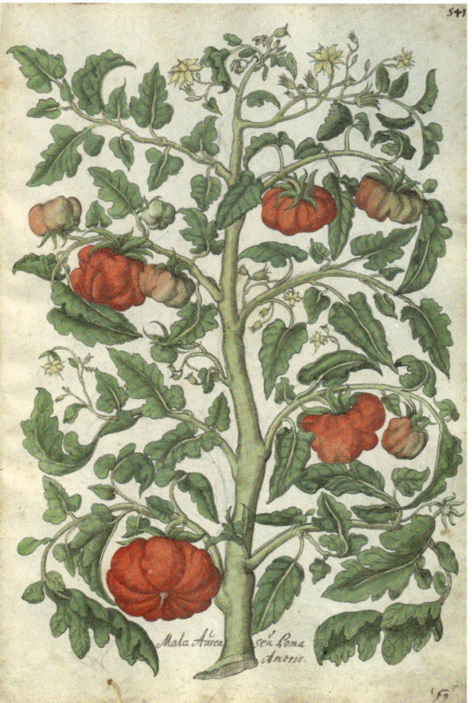
541
Mala Aurea seu Poma Amoris.

112

"VITZLIPUTZLI" (MYTHOLOGICAL MONKEY WITH MIRROR)

Mesoamerica, ca. 1550–1600 (?)

Hollow-cast silver, gilded, 3 pearls, pyrite

H. 7.5 cm; W. 6.0 cm; D. 6.5 cm

Museen der Stadt Nürnberg, Kunstsammlungen, inv. no. Pl 1248

Not exhibited

References:
Exh. cat. New York 1970, unpag., cat. no. 305; Exh. cat. Berlin 1982, p. 343, cat. no. 10/1; Exh. cat. Nuremberg 1992, vol. 2, pp. 887–90, cat. nos. 5.67–5.69 (Ferdinand Anders); Exh. cat. Nuremberg 2017, p. 124, cat. no. 67 (Thomas Eser); Sauer 2021a, pp. 44–45.

Historically, the Nuremberg Stadtbibliothek (city library) contained a large collection of noteworthy objects referred to as "memorabilia." This included a small number of items in the category "exotica," that is, objects from distant lands. A first overview of that collection was published in 1674 by the University of Altdorf student Johann Jacob Leibnitz (1653–1705). In that text, Leibnitz presented a "Mexican idol" that, although beautifully crafted from gold, pearls, and precious stones, he considered uniquely ugly in form.[1] In 1662, the municipal librarian Johann Michael Dilherr (1604–1669) had described this statuette as a "likeness of an Indian idol."[2] He identified it as "Vitzliputzli", by which he meant Huitzilopochtli, the Aztec sun and war god. The accompanying illustration shows a group of Indigenous Americans worshipping a monumentalized rendition of the "Vitzliputzli" statuette, a scene reminiscent of the Old Testament episode of the worship of the golden calf.

In his text, Dilherr was presumably drawing on a local tradition of knowledge about the artifact's Central American origin. Monkeys appear in the pantheon of Aztec deities as companions of the god Xochipilli. An Aztec relief of a monkey wearing the jewelry of Xochipilli is kept at the Musée de l'Homme in Paris.[3] In that work, as in the Nuremberg "Vitzliputzli," the wide-eyed face suggests that the primate being represented is a Geoffroy's spider monkey (*Ateles geoffroyi*), a species native to Central America. The shield on the statuette's back, which served as a kind of mirror, finds a parallel in an Aztec stone figure of the god Tonatiuh at the Museum der Kulturen in Basel.[4]

The statuette is remarkable for having a provenance dating back to the seventeenth century. Many works of Mesoamerican goldsmithing were melted down by European colonizers. In addition to archaeological finds, written sources bear witness to the technical mastery of Aztec goldsmiths. For example, the Spanish missionary Bernardino de Sahagún (d. 1590) describes the production of hollow-cast figures done fully in the round, using a lost wax process—the same technique used to create the "Vitzliputzli."[5]

Technical findings suggest that the gilded silver statuette dates from after the Spanish conquest. The practice of gilding silver figures was probably adopted from European goldsmithing. Although gilding techniques were known in pre-Columbian times, figures made fully in the round were usually cast entirely from gold.[6] Not only was gold more common than silver in the period before the establishment of large silver mines by the Spanish, but it was also regarded as having great symbolic and spiritual value: in the Nahuatl language, it was called *teocuitlatl*, meaning "divine excrement."[7]

The use of three Baroque pearls is further evidence of exchange between Indigenous and European goldsmiths. There were hardly any traditions of pearl fishing and processing in the Americas. It was the Europeans who forced Indigenous Americans to hunt for pearls (under brutal conditions) and who introduced techniques of pearl processing to the Americas. Thus, the "Vitzliputzli" can be seen as a hybrid object that combines Aztec subject matter with techniques imported from Europe.

Verena Suchy and Manuel Teget-Welz

1 See Leibnitz 1674, pp. 22, 43, fig. following p. 20; see also Sauer 2021a, pp. 44–45.
2 See Dilherr 1662, pp. 469–70, plate VII.
3 Inv. no. M.H.87.159.143. See Exh. cat. London, Berlin, and Bonn 2003, p. 424, cat. no. 101 (Leonardo López Luján and Marie-France Fauvet Berthelot).
4 Inv. no. IVb 634. See Exh. cat. Washington, DC, 1991, pp. 542–43, cat. no. 358 (Michael D. Coe).
5 See Saville 1920, pp. 123–42.
6 On pre-Columbian goldsmithing, see Jones and King 2002.
7 King 2002, p. 6.

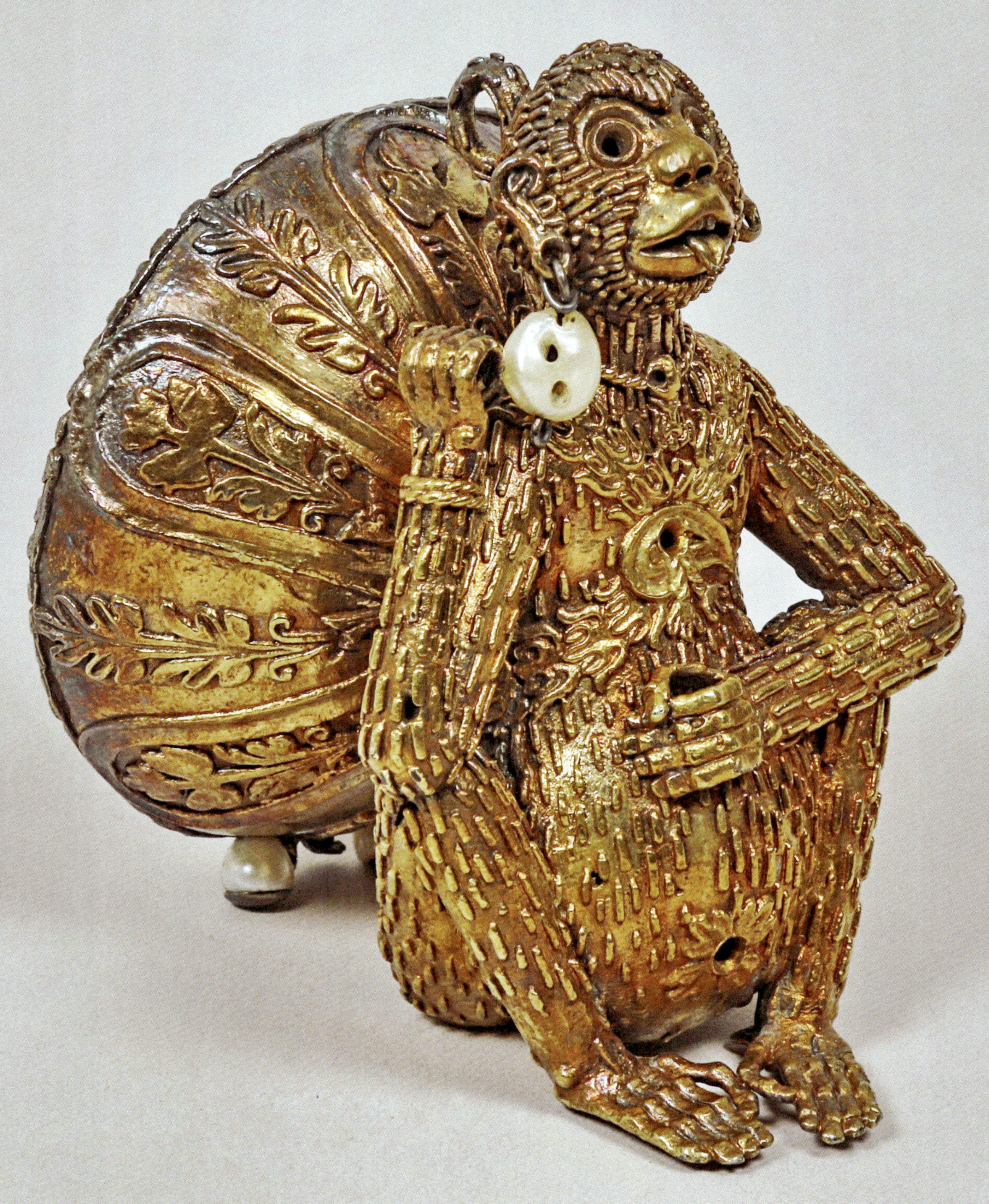

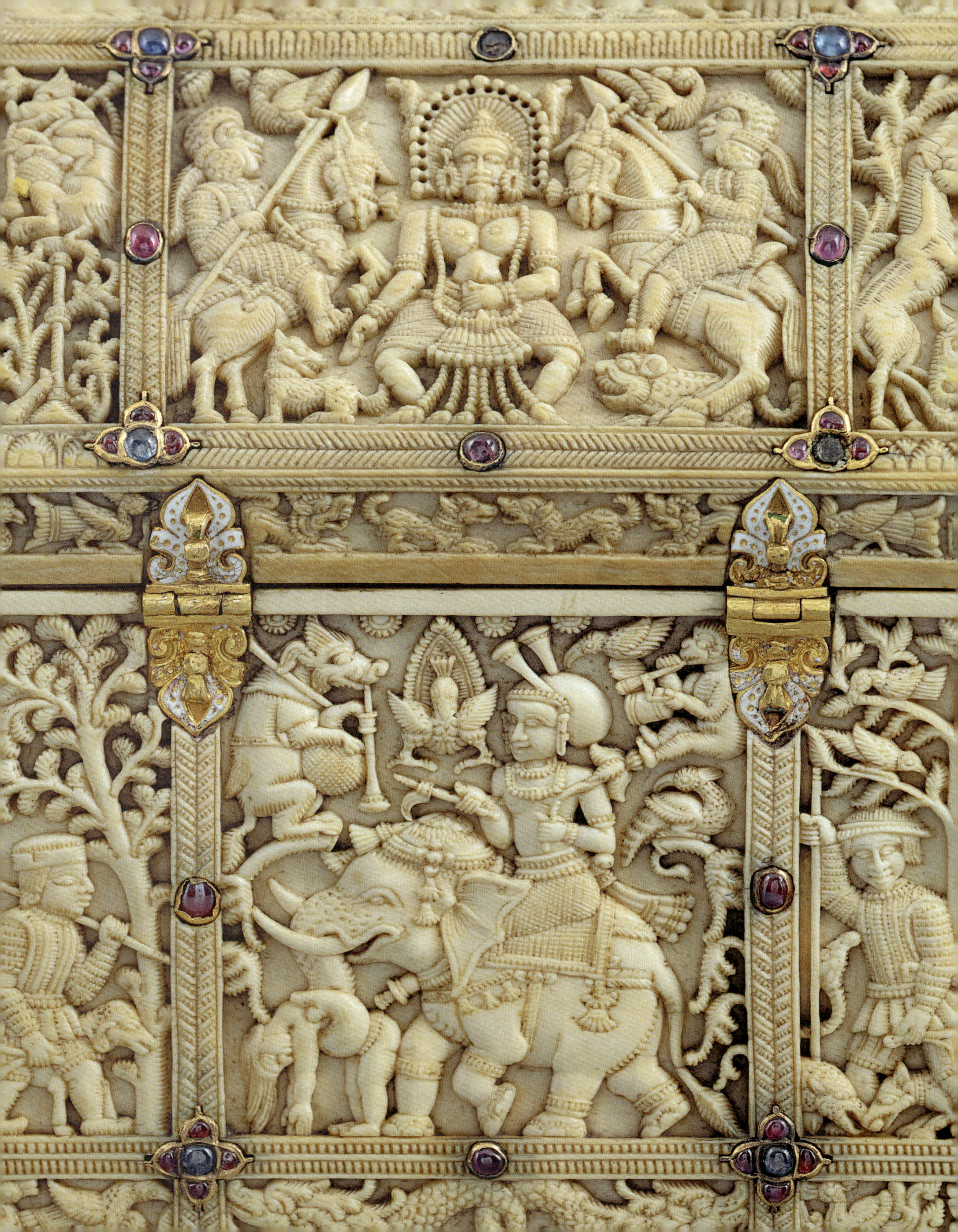

NUREMBERG–LISBON–CALICUT

Martin Behaim, the creator of the famous Behaim Globe, is regarded as the most prominent representative of Nuremberg business enterprises in Lisbon. The establishment of a sea route to India along the African coast, pressed ahead by Portugal, opened up new areas of activity for Nuremberg trading firms. A pamphlet published in 1505 explicitly praises the economic advantages of the Nuremberg–Lisbon–Calicut route (with Calicut being present-day Kozhikode).

Albrecht Dürer's Rhinoceros woodcut exemplifies the cultural exchange that took place along that route. The live rhinoceros had been shipped from Gujarat, India, to the royal court of Portugal. Based on a description and drawing sent from Lisbon, Dürer created his iconic woodcut in Nuremberg. Less well known is that his prints became a medium of transmission in the opposite direction. Christian missionaries, diplomats, and merchants brought images by Dürer to the Mughal court in India. There, the prints underwent artistic adaption by court painters and were integrated into lavish albums. In the movement of goods from southern Asia to Europe, mother-of-pearl vessels from Gujarat and turban shells from the Indian Ocean reached Nuremberg via port cities such as Lisbon and Antwerp, ultimately being crafted by local gold- and silversmiths into magnificent luxury objects.

It is often overlooked that this fascinating early chapter in the history of global interrelations was marked by violence and exploitation. Along the sea route between Portugal and India, European entrepreneurs—sometimes with the involvement of investors from Nuremberg—waged bloody trade wars and plundered flourishing cities on the eastern coast of Africa.

Sven Jakstat

◄ cat. no. 121 (detail)

113

MEMORIAL SHIELD (*TOTENSCHILD*) FOR HEINRICH GRUNDHERR

Nuremberg, ca. 1379

Spruce, fir, and limewood; woven fabric and sheet iron (added); with polychromy

H. 72.2 cm; W. 63.2 cm; D. 13.0 cm

GNM, inv. no. KG33, on long-term loan from the Grundherr'sche Familienstiftung, Nuremberg

References:
Kammel et al. 2020, vol. 2, pp. 370–81, esp. pp. 376–81, cat. no. 3 (Anna Pawlik and Astrid Roth); Taube, Sanyova, and Roth 2023.

Many decades before Vasco da Gama opened up the sea route from Portugal to India, Nurembergers had access to raw materials from South Asia. The memorial shield for Heinrich Grundherr confirms this in an unexpected way. Grundherr was a highly wealthy cloth merchant, city councilor, and financier to Emperor Louis the Bavarian. After his death in 1351, he was buried in front of the altar of Saint Mary in the Sebalduskirche. In the following generations, a permanent family memorial site was created nearby, made visible from afar by a stained-glass window that was donated by Heinrich's son Michael (d. 1388), the church's administrator. Michael Grundherr was probably also the one who commissioned memorial shields to be hung there in memory of his father and other male family members.

The triangular shield for Heinrich Grundherr is one of the oldest and most artistically outstanding examples of its type. Such memorial panels were displayed on walls near the tombs or commemorative sites of Nuremberg families that were eligible to serve on the city council. This shield's motif, the Grundherr coat of arms, consists of a field of red (decorated with a lighter red foliate pattern) charged with a sculpted demi-lion with large claws. The lion, which nearly fills the whole area of the shield, is painted light gray, its tongue red. The inscription, in black on a white background, with word separators in red, names the deceased and his date of death. Although the paint now visible dates from after the work's creation, its color scheme corresponds to the original heraldic tincture and overall design. The original polychromy is preserved beneath several layers of overpaint. In it, the whole surface is covered with silver leaf. The silver was left exposed on the lion and in the inscribed border area, while the shield's background was colored using a red glaze, whose transparent character made the red areas also appear metallic.

A global-historical dimension is revealed by analysis of the glaze, which shows that brazilwood (redwood, sappanwood [*Caesalpinia sappan* L.]) was used as red dye.[1] Brazilwood had been imported to Europe from India and Southeast Asia since the twelfth century. It was used primarily for dyeing textiles but also as a colorant in manuscript illumination and panel painting.[2] The wood was traded in large blocks, which were ultimately rasped to shavings or chips and then ground. Adding the shavings or powder to water and mixing them with alum produced the red dye extract.

Flanders-based trade in brazilwood is documented in Nuremberg as early as 1361, but the material also arrived in the city by way of Venice,[3] which had access to the Silk Road and the Middle East via the Mediterranean Sea. The so-called Nuremberg *Kunstbuch* (after 1450) contains some of the period's most detailed recipes for dyeing textiles with brazilwood, and it provides the use of the material in the region.[4] Evidently, brazilwood was traded as a luxury good. For example, in 1519 the jewel merchant Jörg Pock in Lisbon gave Martin Behaim the Younger two pieces of brazilwood along with "some bitter-orange water," an "Indian nut in its shell," and other items to bring to Nuremberg.[5] In 1594–95, the armory director Hans Löhner wanted to build a mill at the Dutzendteich reservoir in Nuremberg for grinding brazilwood (among other things).[6] Moreover, the local processing of brazilwood is reflected in an illustration in the *Hausbücher der Nürnberger Zwölfbrüderstiftungen* (House Books of the Nuremberg Twelve-Brothers Foundations) depicting a craftsman known as a *Prisilgstoßer* (brazilwood shaver).[7] By the time the illustration was created, in 1592, the redwood that is shown would probably have been imported from Central or South America. In the sixteenth century, trade shifted away from Asia because of the abundance of brazilwood trees in the Amazon region, which is how Brazil got its name.

Elisabeth Taube and Benno Baumbauer

1 Taube, Sanyova, and Roth 2023.
2 Servais 2024, p. 21.
3 Burmester and Krekel 1998, p. 81.
4 Ploss 1967, p. 114.
5 Kellenbenz 1967, p. 473.
6 Stadtarchiv, Nuremberg, B 1/II no. 990.
7 Landauer I, fol. 63r, at the Stadtbibliothek, Nuremberg, Amb. 279.2°. See Taube, Sanyova, and Roth 2023, p. 5, fig. 8.

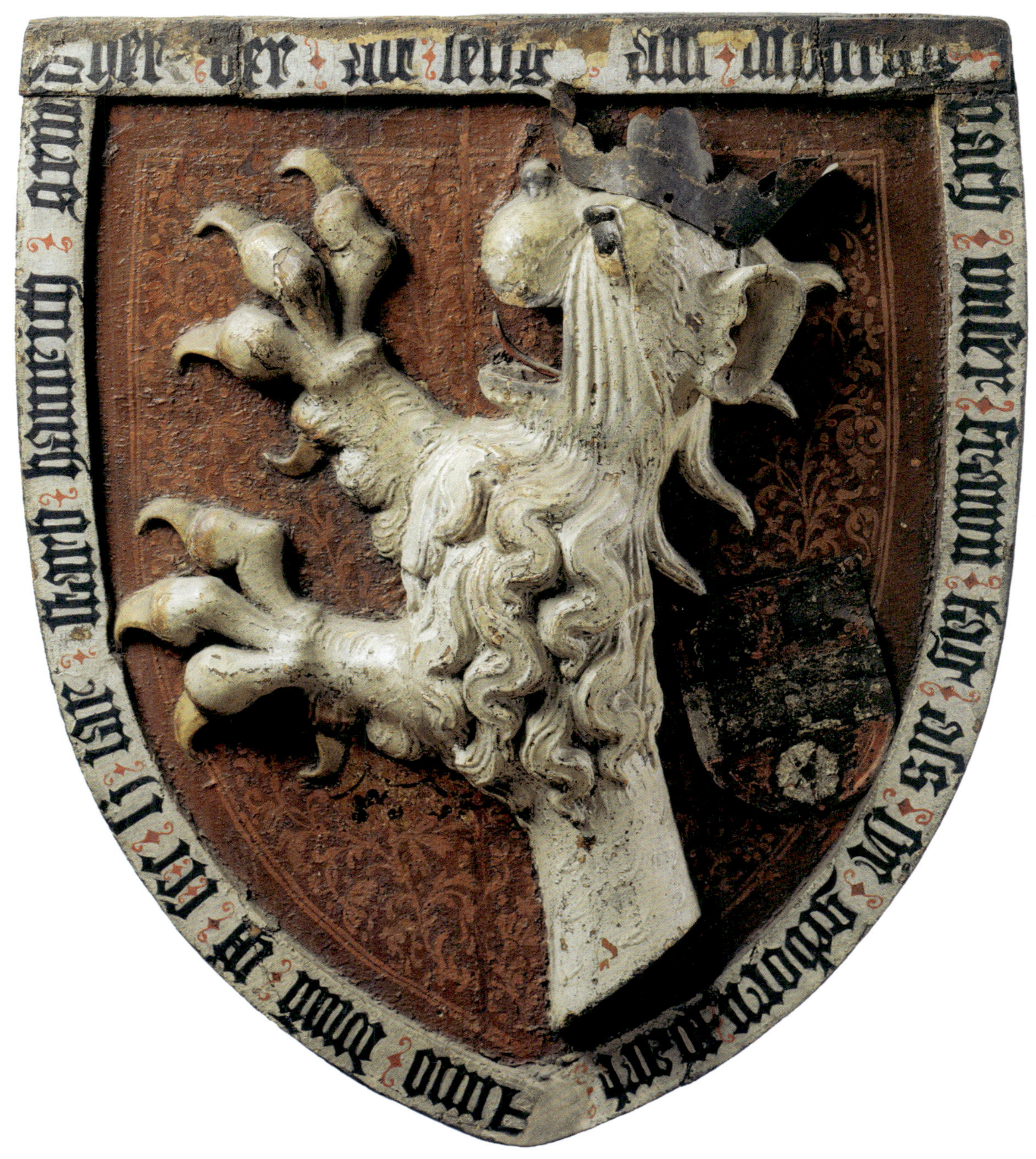

114

THE BEHAIM CHANDELIER

Nuremberg, 1490–94

Wood, painted; sheet iron, forged, stamped; wrought iron

H. 114 cm; Diam. 56 cm and 51 cm (without candle branches); Diam. 85 cm (with candle branches)

GNM, inv. no. KG246

References:
Exh. cat. Nuremberg 1992, vol. 2, pp. 729–32, cat. no. 3.16 (Johannes Willers and Eugen Schöler); Scholz 2005, pp. 278–79; Jacob 2007, pp. 40–41; Exh. cat. Magdeburg 2008, p. 162, cat. no. II.10 (Britta Kusch-Arnhold); Northemann 2011, pp. 194–95.

Martin Behaim (1459–1507), the designer of the eponymous globe |**cat. no. 1**|, was one of the most respected individuals at the Portuguese royal court from the 1480s onward. This chandelier, consisting of two hexagonal panels connected by rods, is one of the few extant objects that traces back directly to Behaim, and it also features his "portrait."

The underside of the lower panel displays the coats of arms of Behaim and his wife, Joãna de Macedo, along with the date 1490. Above the coats of arms, a figure of Joãna is accompanied by a banderole with a Latin inscription that translates to "With longing I have desired you."[1] The panel's edge is inscribed as follows: "Martin Behaim, golden knight of His Most Serene Highness the King of Portugal, fought bravely against the Africans and Moors and married beyond the borders of the world."

The underside of the upper panel shows Martin Behaim and his wife kneeling in prayer. He wears a gilded suit of armor, she a precious robe. The banderole beneath them bears the inscription "In memory of him." The couple's allied coat of arms at center is surmounted by a half-length figure that possibly represents their son, Martin Behaim the Younger, born in 1489 at the latest. At the top, above a band of clouds, the Virgin and Child are accompanied by Saint Catherine at the left, receiving a ring from the infant Jesus, and Saint Barbara at the right. The panel's edge, faced with iron plates and decorated with tracery at the top, bears the inscription: "Johanna, daughter of the captain of the Kingdom of Portugal, the Lord of New Flanders and the islands of the Azores or Catherides, wife of Lord Martin Behaim, knight, of happy memory."

Despite some renewed elements, such as the inscriptions around the edges, the branches, and the suspension, the chandelier is fairly well preserved. However, eighteenth-century descriptions mention that the chandelier housed a representation of a mountain with a figure of Saint Catherine, probably a depiction of the saint's burial on Mount Sinai. As this work belongs to the category of tabernacle chandeliers, it is possible that the aforementioned representation of a mountain, which is an unusual feature for this type of chandelier, was added later. Originally, there may have been a double figure at the center of the chandelier, probably combining representations of the Virgin Mary and Saint Catherine.

The two inscriptions around the edges can be read as a short biography of Behaim, focusing on his role as a knight who rendered great service to King John II of Portugal in the war against the "heathens" and who married a woman of a distinguished family—Joãna being the daughter of Joost de Hurtere, governor of Faial and Pico. The staging of Behaim's life story was intended to contribute not merely to his fame but also to his memoria—that is, to the acts of remembrance and prayers done by the living to ensure Behaim's salvation in the afterlife. The chandelier, surely together with an endowment for candles, served as a material means of ensuring that his *memoria* was preserved. Contrary to the assumption that the chandelier was gradually created between 1490 and 1507/1519 with the involvement of Martin Behaim's son or wife, it is more likely that Martin Behaim himself commissioned the chandelier in a Nuremberg workshop in 1490. However, owing to errors in the wife's coat of arms, it is likely that completion was delayed until shortly after his departure for Lisbon in 1494.

Behaim donated this prestigious object, part of his provisions for the afterlife, to the Katharinenkirche in Nuremberg, to whose patron saint it made visual reference. The chandelier was hung in the chancel, above the tomb of the convent church's founder, Konrad von Neumarkt (d. 1296), and near a tomb of the Behaim family, located on the chancel's north side. Martin Behaim, who died in Lisbon in 1507, probably already knew by 1490 that he would not be buried in the Katharinenkirche. With the chandelier, the well-traveled patrician secured for himself an impressive object of pious remembrance in his hometown.

Vera Henkelmann

1 All the inscriptions presented below are translated from Latin.

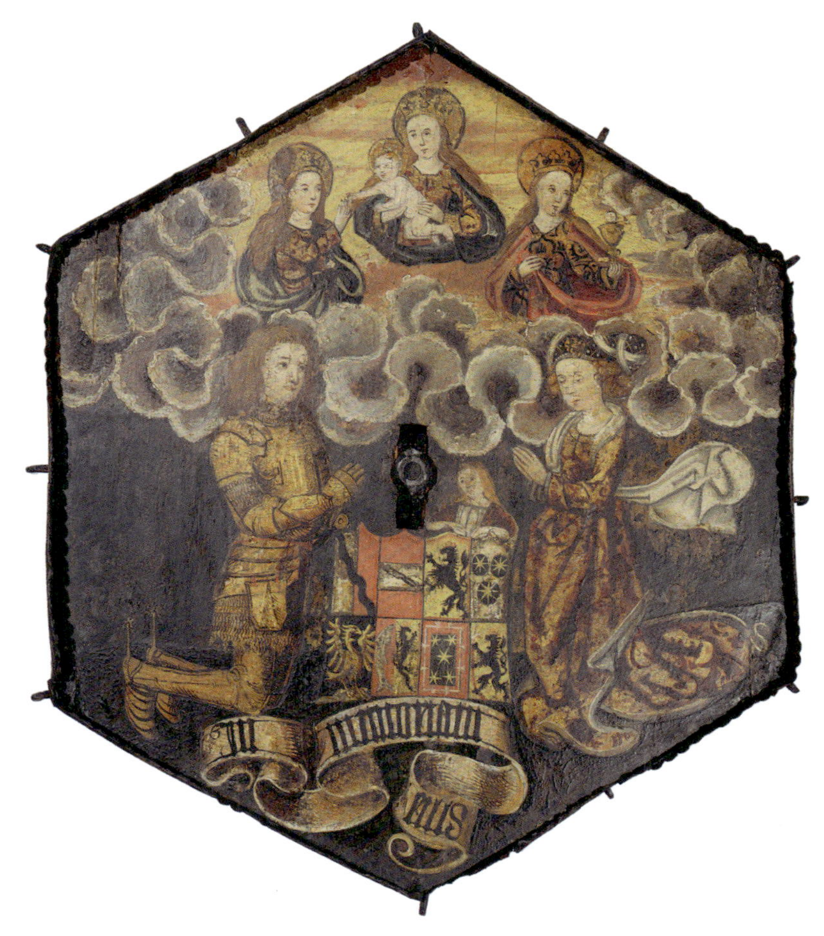

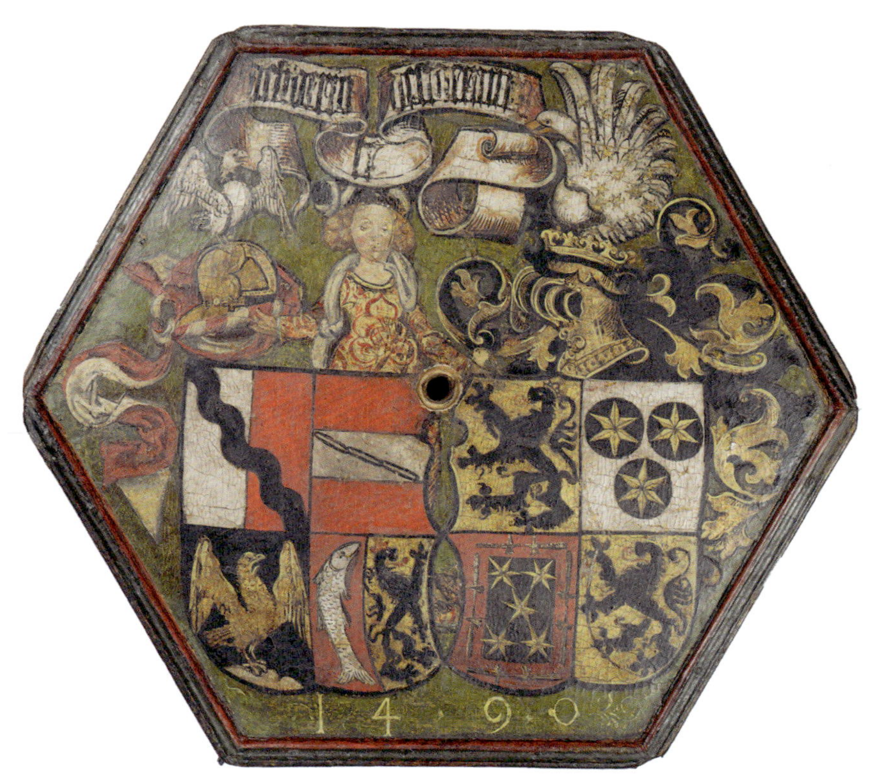
1 4 9 0

115

DEN RECHTEN WEG AUSS ZU FAREN (THE RIGHT ROUTE TO TRAVEL)

Nuremberg: Wolfgang Huber, 1505 or 1506

Pamphlet, 4 leaves

H. 20.2 cm; W. 16 cm (leaf dimensions)

Universitätsbibliothek der LMU, Munich, shelf mark 4° H. aux. 1270:7=W

Open to the world map

References:
Parker and Prottengeier 1956; Bezzel 1995, pp. 32–35; Borowka-Clausberg 1999, pp. 1–9, 192–96 (transcription); Leitch 2009, pp. 138–39; Pápay 2021.

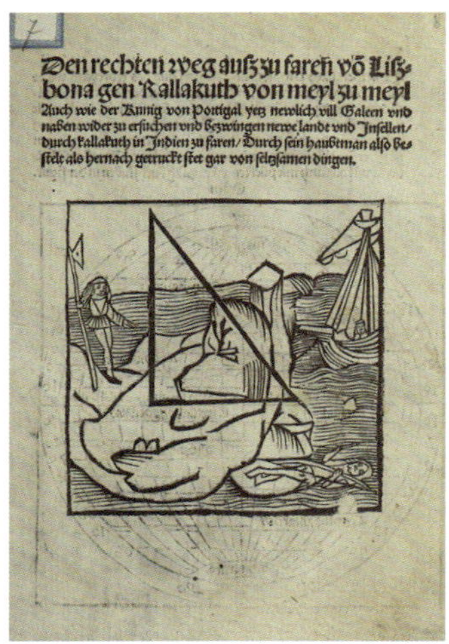
Den rechten weg auſz zu farē vō Liſz-
bona gen Kallakuth von meyl zu meyl
Auch wie der Kunig von Portigal yetz newlich vill Galeen vnd
naben wider zu erſuchen vnd bezwingen newe lande vnd Inſellen/
durch kallakuth in Indien zu faren/ Durch ſein haubtman alſo be-
ſtelt als hernach getruckt ſtet gar von ſeltzamen dingen.

Title page

This pamphlet was printed in Nuremberg not many years after the Portuguese crown had first charted a sea route to India (1498). The text is one of the earliest German-language descriptions of the route that ran from Lisbon to Sumatra along the African and Indian coasts. In addition to indicating distances and giving practical advice, such as how to obtain drinking water along the way, the pamphlet contains information about the latest colonial ventures of the Portuguese in these parts of the world. The author is thought to have been a Nuremberg merchant based in Lisbon.[1] The text also mentions an upcoming expedition of twenty ships destined for Sumatra and for Malacca in present-day Malaysia, scheduled to begin in April 1506 under the leadership of an experienced admiral. This must have been Afonso de Albuquerque (d. 1515), the later governor and viceroy of India,[2] the same official who presented King Manuel I with the rhinoceros that Dürer immortalized in a woodcut |**cat. no. 119**|.

The pamphlet furthermore lists goods that were arriving in Lisbon from Asia at the time. These include not only ginger, cloves, nutmeg, pepper, cinnamon, and coconuts, but also medicines, pearls, precious stones, carpets, and musk deer, described in the text as a kind of dog or cat. Their trade promised lucrative profits. Evidently the pamphlet was intended to attract wealthy entrepreneurs for participation in Portuguese expeditions. Its publication coincided roughly with Francisco de Almeida's expedition |**cat. no. 116**|, which had been cofinanced by several Nuremberg merchant families.

Although no facts of publication are indicated in the pamphlet (neither place, nor date, nor printer), the events mentioned in the work allow us to narrow down the years to 1505 or 1506.[3] The present edition of the pamphlet, which exists in another version with different typefaces, is ascribed to the Nuremberg printer Wolfgang Huber.[4]

The included map proves that the pamphlet was explicitly addressed to a Nuremberg readership. The woodcut shows the continental landmasses of Europe, Africa, and Asia in rudimentary form, with the *Polus arcicus*, at the top, incorrectly labeled *Osten* (east). Only three cities are indicated: Calicut (present-day Kozhikode on the western coast of India), Lisbon, and Nuremberg, represented by the letters *K*, *L*, and *n*, respectively. The text states: "On the map, one also finds *Nurnberg*, *Lißbona*, and *Kallakuth* marked with dots and single letters." This map, marked with the equator and lines of longitude, is one of the earliest known examples to use a globular projection. Gyula Pápay traces it back to a lost prototype by Amerigo Vespucci (1454–1512) which served as a model for still further prints.[5]

The other illustration in the pamphlet shows an amorphous landmass being approached by ship. It is meant to represent Africa, Europe, and Asia. A right triangle is superimposed on it. At the left, next to the triangle's vertical side, stands a man dressed in European clothing and carrying a halberd. At the lower right, parallel to the horizontal edge of the triangle, lies a man armed with a bow and arrow, wearing only a loincloth. The image was clearly meant not only to express the geographical relationship between Europeans and the people living south of the equator, but also to provide an arrogant civilizational contrast between the "upright" and "civilized" on the one hand and the "indolent" and "half-naked" on the other.[6]

Sven Jakstat

1 Bezzel 1995, pp. 32–33.
2 Bezzel 1995, p. 33.
3 On the dating, see Bezzel 1995, pp. 34–35; Parker and Prottengeier 1956, p. 8.
4 VD16, no. R 491; https://gateway-bayern.de/VD16+R+491 (31.7.2025).
5 Pápay 2021, p. 6.
6 On the interpretation of this image, see Leitch 2013; Bezzel 1995, pp. 33–34; Borowka-Clausberg 1999, pp. 2, 7.

¶ Dise spere nach Ptholomeus beschreybung des erdreychs wirdt euch lernen vnd vnderweysen die gelegenheyt der landen bey welcher linien vnd grads Auch ist die nach gesetzt figur/in jr halten alle nach geschribne ding von newen Inseln vnd landen die man yetz in kurtz gefunden hat/das dan den Philosophi lange zeyt verborgen ist gewesen. Man findt auch darin verzeychnet Nurnberg/Lißbona vñ kallakuth mit pũckten vñ einzalig buchstaben in der figur.

Osten

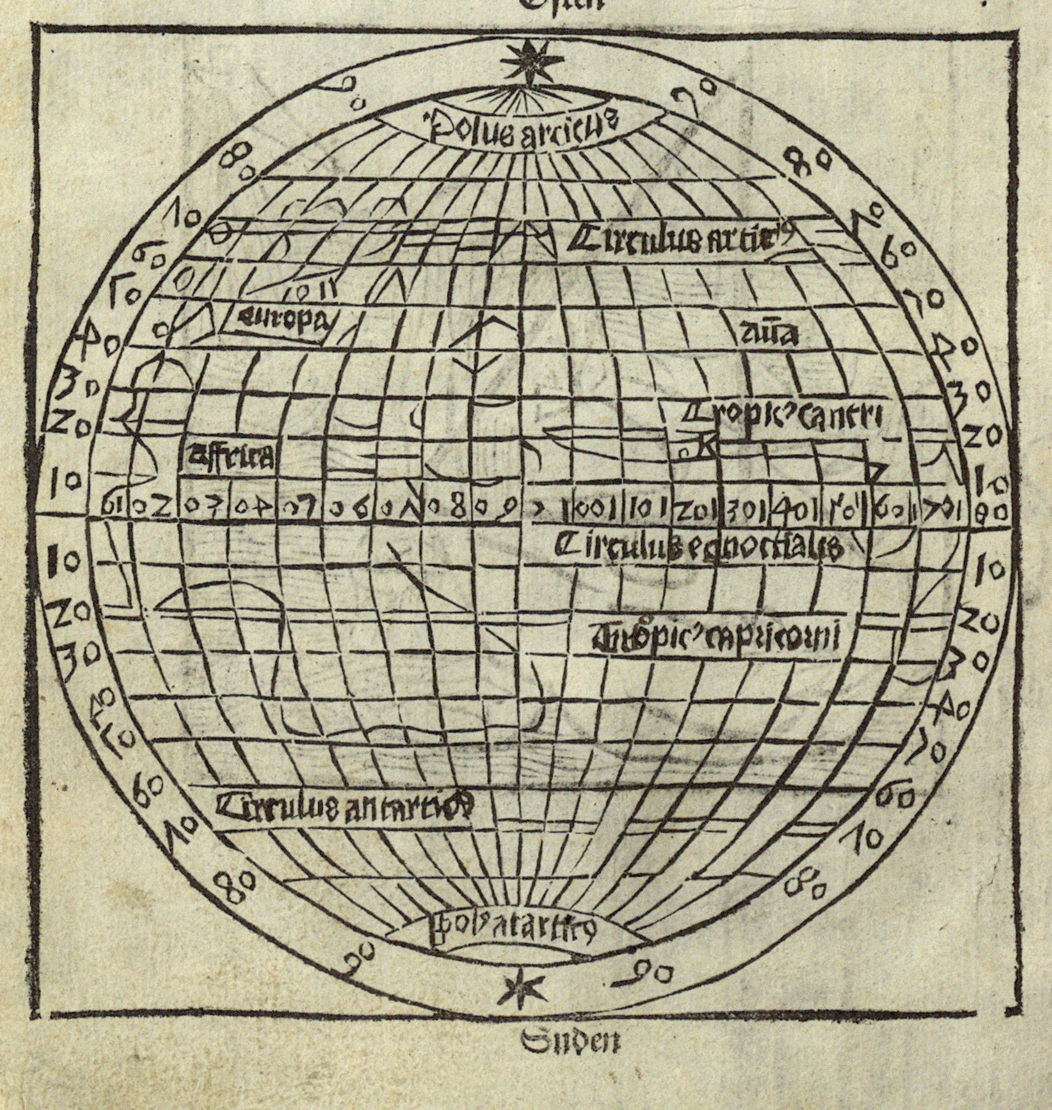

Suden

116

DIE MERFART (THE SEA VOYAGE)

Balthasar Springer
Woodcuts attributed to **Wolf Traut**
Oppenheim: Jakob Köbel, 1509

Post-incunable, 14 leaves, woodcut illustrations

H. 21 cm; W. 15 cm (each leaf)

Bayerische Staatsbibliothek, Munich, shelf mark Rar. 470

Open to fols. 2v–3r: the Triumphal Procession of the King of Gutzin

References:
Erhard and Ramminger 1998; Borowka-Clausberg 1999, pp. 44–56, 197–214 (transcription); Horst 2006; Bujok 2018; Exh. cat. Frankfurt and Vienna 2023, pp. 138–41, cat. no. 1.21 (Heidrun Lange-Krach).

Balthasar Springer's *Merfart* (Sea Voyage) was printed in 1509 and consists of fourteen pages of text supplemented by fifteen full-page woodcuts. It describes the first great Portuguese expedition to India, an undertaking that involved trading firms from Augsburg and Nuremberg.[1] Together with several Italian families, the Welsers, Fuggers, Höchstetters, Imhoffs, Gossembrots, and Hirschvogels were investors in the venture. They sought profit from the import of spices and the eventual export of precious metals,[2] and they probably anticipated that acts of plunder along the route would add to their riches. The German investors equipped three of the fleet's twenty ships, which set sail from Lisbon in March 1505 under the command of Francisco de Almeida (d. 1510) |**see fig. p. 95**|. Springer, a native of Vils in Tyrol, sailed aboard the *Lionarda*, and he returned to Lisbon on November 15, 1506.

In his first-person account, Springer describes his experiences on the outward and return journeys, devoting the final pages to portrayals of the people he encountered. This ethnographic interest marks a turning point in the genre of the travelogue, because it breaks with the "tradition of depicting monstrous foreignness, which since ancient times had been associated with India nearly in the manner of a topos."[3] At the same time, Springer's text makes plain the brutal measures that the future colonial powers were taking against their perceived adversaries in pursuit of expansionist interests. Flourishing trading cities such as Kilwa Kisiwani and Mombasa on the eastern coast of Africa were destroyed, plundered, and occupied, as Springer reports without a hint of empathy.[4]

The illustrations accompanying the text make no reference to those colonial endeavors and their associated injustices. Instead, they present the reader mostly with isolated depictions of inhabitants of the regions visited by Springer in Africa and the Indian subcontinent |**see fig. p. 23**|. In addition to these illustrations, the report contains two identical woodcuts of a tree and the scene of the "King of Gutzin" being carried in procession, accompanied by musicians and warriors. The latter woodcut, a fold-out piece, forms the visual highlight of the travelogue. Since 1911, the woodcuts have been attributed in part to the Nuremberg painter and block cutter Wolf Traut.[5] They are based on works by the Augsburg artist Hans Burgkmair. The year before the *Merfart* was published, Burgkmair had created several woodcuts that include short texts by Springer. These images, which are considered "the earliest printed representations of an overseas indigenous population,"[6] are interpreted in different ways with regard to tradition and innovation. On the one hand, they break with the tradition of depicting unknown parts of the world as places of mythical creatures and monsters, as in Schedel's *Nuremberg Chronicle* |**cat. no. 4**|. On the other hand, they reinforce a worldview shaped by cultural biases: by showing people scantily clothed or naked, they not only emphasize cultural differences but also construct presumed hierarchies.

Sven Jakstat

1 Pohle 2000, pp. 189–204, documents two earlier expeditions with German participation.
2 Häberlein 1998, p. 28.
3 Translated from the German in Dharampal-Frick 1994, p. 29.
4 See Erhard and Ramminger 1998, pp. 98–107, 117–28; see the essay by Elgidius E. B. Ichumbaki and Dominicus Z. Makukula in the present volume.
5 The attribution goes back to Dodgson 1911, p. 72. He ascribed only the following prints to Traut: Springer's coat of arms, the Guinean family, the eastern African family, and the royal procession. Dodgson regarded the woodcuts as the work of an unknown printmaker.
6 Translated from the German in Pohle 2000, p. 206.

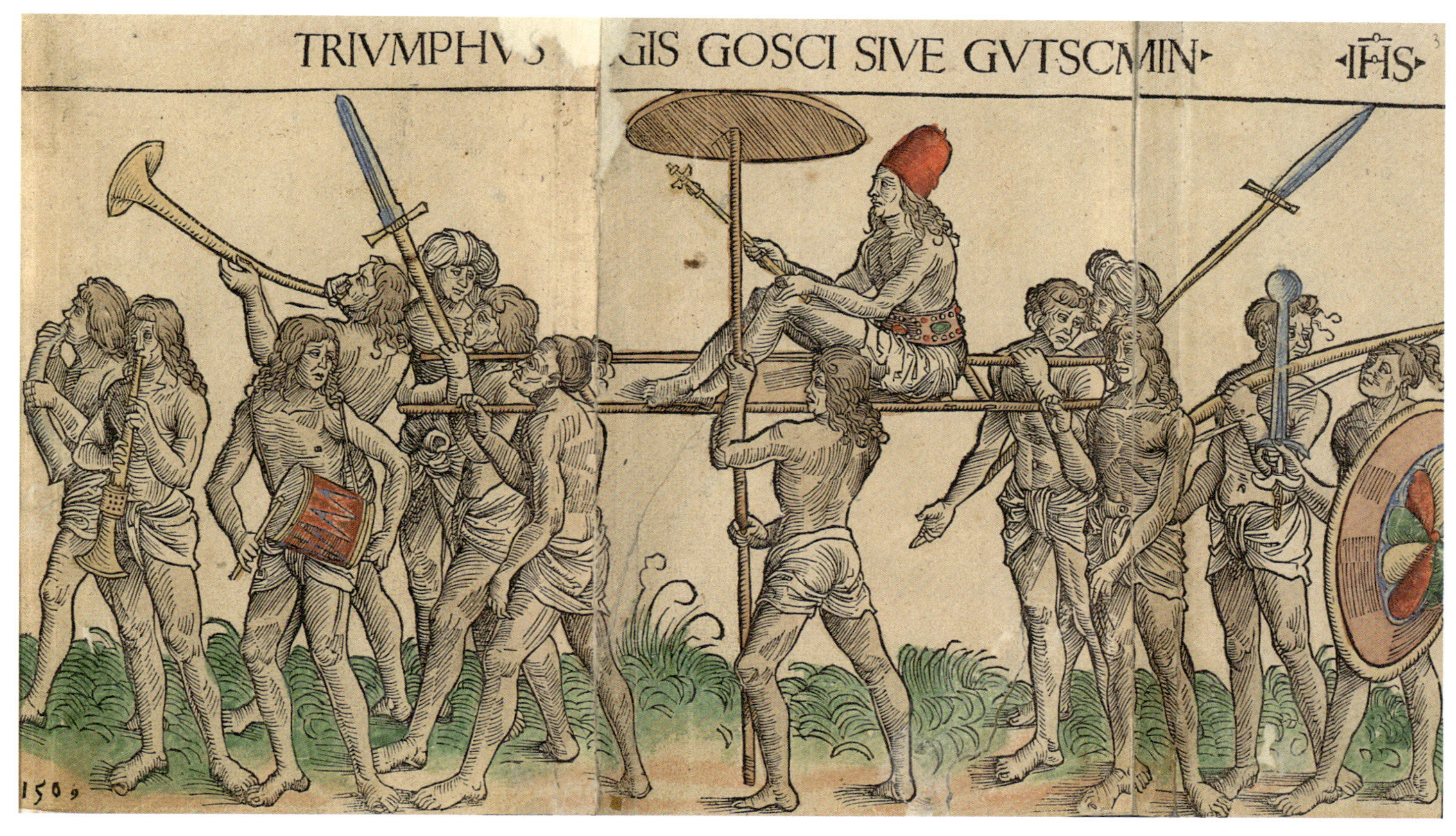
TRIVMPHVS GIS GOSCI SIVE GVTSCMIN
IHS
1509

117

THE KING OF GUTZIN

Georg Glockendon (after Hans Burgkmair)

Nuremberg, 1511

117.1–3 Three woodblocks, each cut on both sides

Wood

117.1: H. 27.4 cm; W. 39.4 cm;

117.2: H. 27 cm; W. 40.5 cm;

117.3: H. 27.6 cm; W. 39.5 cm

Kupferstichkabinett, Staatliche Museen zu Berlin, inv. no. Derschau 182,1–3

117.4 Impression made in 1810

From Derschau and Becker 1810

Woodcut in five sections

H. 28.5 cm; W. 188 cm

GNM, inv. no. H179

References:
Kroll 1974, pp. 42–43; Massing 1995, pp. 39–40; Borowka-Clausberg 1999, pp. 28, 42–44; McDonald 2003, pp. 242–43; Leitch 2010, pp. 148–50.

In 1508, Hans Burgkmair created a series of woodcuts depicting various peoples of Africa and India. These were based on Balthasar Springer's eyewitness account of Francisco de Almeida's expedition to India in 1505–6, a venture that involved Nuremberg trading firms, among other investors |**cat. no. 116**|. The woodcuts could be assembled into a frieze almost two meters long.

The Nuremberg block cutter Georg (Jörg) Glockendon (d. 1514) copied and reissued the frieze with minor changes in 1509 and 1511.[1] The present three woodblocks are attributed to Glockendon based on an impression from them that is now found in the collections of the Fugger Foundations (Fuggersche Stiftungen) in Augsburg, signed "Jorg Glogkendon" and dated 1509.[2] In addition, in 1541, Glockendon's son Albrecht wrote a rhymed version of Springer's text, and those verses are pasted under the Augsburg impression of the frieze. The aforementioned signature appears at the lower left edge, under the dancing boy.[3] On the corresponding woodblock, the upper flourish of the letter *J* from "Jorg" is still visible; the rest of the signature has been cut away. Evidence that these illustrations circulated in Nuremberg in the sixteenth century is provided by the costume book of Sigmund Heldt, which was created in Nuremberg and borrows figures from the frieze.[4] Apart from the impression in Augsburg, Glockendon's version of the woodcut frieze is known only from nineteenth-century impressions made from the original woodblocks, which had come into the possession of Hans Albrecht von Derschau (1755–1824).[5]

In the frieze, composed of five parts, one can trace Springer's itinerary along the African coast to India based on the people represented.[6] The first four parts depict families accompanied by inscriptions that locate them in western, southern, and eastern Africa and on the western coast of India: "IN GENNEA," "IN ALLAGO," "IN ARABIA," and "DAS GROS INDIA." The fifth section shows the King of Gutzin ("KVNIG VON GVTZIN") being carried on a sedan chair, accompanied by warriors and musicians. The term "Gutzin" refers to present-day Kochi (formerly Cochin) on the Malabar Coast of southern India, where the Portuguese established their first trading post in 1502.

The novelty of this iconography, with its focus on people's appearance and clothing habits, is underscored by comparison with other, near-contemporary depictions of the parts of the world traveled by Springer. On the Behaim Globe |**cat. no. 1**| and in Schedel's *Nuremberg Chronicle* |**cat. no. 4**|, these regions are in part shown to be populated by monstrous creatures.[7] Although the imagery of the frieze is often postulated as being objective in character, it nevertheless conveys stereotypes. This is apparent in a detail missing from Burgkmair's version and included in Glockendon's: at the center of the frieze, there is a tree in the background hung with a severed human leg and head. A fire blazes below. In sensationalistic manner, this addition, derived from published reports about the Indigenous peoples of the Americas, exploits prejudices based on the supposed cannibalism of the faraway "Other."[8]

Sven Jakstat

1 On the differences between the versions, see Hümmerich 1918, pp. 56–58.
2 Dodgson 1911, p. 71; Ruge 1916, p. 90; Borowka-Clausberg 1999, pp. 42–43, 216–20. This impression was deaccessioned from the Landesmuseum in Gotha in 1948 and acquired by the Fugger Foundations on the art market in 1951.
3 Illustrated in Borowka-Clausberg 1999, p. 216.
4 Album of Sigmund Heldt, Kunstbibliothek, Staatliche Museen zu Berlin, Lipp Aa 3 mtl R. See Massing 1995, pp. 48–50.
5 Derschau and Becker 1810, pl. B 26.
6 Leitch 2009, p. 143.
7 See Bujok 2018, esp. p. 372.
8 Leitch 2010, p. 149; West 2010, p. 108.

WING PANELS OF THE ROSARY ALTARPIECE FROM THE ROCHUSKAPELLE IN NUREMBERG

118

Hans Burgkmair

Augsburg, 1522

The patrician Imhoff family amassed great wealth through trade in spices from South Asia, among other sources of revenue |**see cat. no. 38**|. Their trading firm contributed 3,000 cruzados to the royal Portuguese expedition to India in 1505–6, an early colonial venture headed by Francisco de Almeida |**see cat. no. 116**|.[1] The family's high standing enabled it to build a chapel in Nuremberg's new Rochusfriedhof (Saint Roch's Cemetery), a graveyard not far outside the city walls that was consecrated in 1519. For the chapel's southern side altar, the Imhoffs commissioned a Renaissance-style retable in Augsburg with a shrine relief devoted to the Rosary prayer and a predella relief on the subject of purgatory. The wing paintings—scenes from the life of the Virgin attached to the shrine, Christ in Limbo and the Resurrection attached to the predella—display great artistic ingenuity. On the exteriors of the predella wings, patron saints represent the four Imhoff brothers and their wives involved in the commission.

The Imhoff Archive at the Germanisches Nationalmuseum contains a list of receipts for the Rosary Altarpiece with the following heading: "Das Ist die taffel so In der Cappelen auff Dem gozacker Vnd zu augspurg gemacht worden ist" (This is the panel [i.e., altarpiece] that was made in Augsburg for the chapel at the cemetery).[2] In 1520, initial payments were made to the Augsburg sculptor Sebastian Loscher (d. 1548) and to the cabinetmaker Thomas Hebendanz. The date of 1521 written on the shrine's rear wall, covered by the relief, suggests that Loscher's and Hebendanz's work was completed that year.[3] In 1522, the *Maller* (painter) received 60 guldens. His signature and the date appear in the depiction of the Meeting at the Golden Gate, on the column pedestal at the left: "MDXXII IOAN. BURGKMAIR AUGUSTAE VINDELICORUM FACIEBAT" (1522. Johannes [Hans] Burgkmair from Augsburg made this). Also in 1522, a blacksmith was paid to "mount" (*peschlagen*) what are called "boards" (*preder*), which probably refers to attaching hinges to the wings.[4] Roughly cut recesses in the upper portions of the wings were required to allow them to open freely, since the shrine's projecting cornice would otherwise block their movement. All this suggests that in 1521 the retable was delivered without wings, and that they were added in 1522. Apparently, given the deep cuts in the wings, the coordination between Nuremberg and Augsburg was not completely clear.

The fact that the paintings were commissioned in Augsburg—the home of two of the married couples involved in the commission—can probably be explained by the quality of workmanship available from Hans Burgkmair (1473–1531). The inventiveness of his compositions is particularly noteworthy—for example, the almost choreographic staging of the Adoration of the Magi, in which three servants present the precious golden gifts above the heads of the kneeling kings. Burgkmair's use of light has an ethereal quality. In the aureole around the risen Christ in the scene of Christ Appearing to His Mother, the golden burst of light, the translucent banner of the Resurrection, and the surrounding cloud of blue angels' heads merge into a transcendent apparition. The vine scroll decoration in gold and black on the inner surfaces of the wings' frames is almost three-dimensional in appearance.

The Rosary Altarpiece is an impressive example of how capital from global trade flowed into commissions of sacred art in Nuremberg. It is worth noting that, in the person of Hans Burgkmair, the Imhoffs employed the same artist who, after the Portuguese expedition to India in 1505–6, had designed a woodcut containing stereotypical depictions of Africans and Indians, a print reissued in Nuremberg by Georg Glockendon |**cat. no. 117**|.

Benno Baumbauer

Paint on limewood

Left wing of the shrine: H. 139 cm; W. 42.5 cm; right wing of the shrine: H. 139.3 cm; W. 42.8 cm; left wing of the predella: H. 62.6 cm; W. 40.8 cm; right wing of the predella: H. 62.4 cm; W. 40.2 cm

Friedhofskapelle Sankt Rochus, Nuremberg, property of the Alt-Conrad von Imhoff'sche Familienstiftung

References:
Falk 1968, pp. 74, 117–18, no. 68; Pilz 1984, pp. 160–62; Weniger 2018, pp. 439–45; Riestra 2021, pp. 12–15, ill. pp. 20–23.

1 See Jahnel 1950, pp. 101–52, esp. p. 102.
2 GNM, Historisches Archiv, FM-IMH-1 34.04a.6. Transcription in Falk 1968, pp. 117–18, no. 68; corrected partial transcription in Eikelmann 1994, p. 22, n. 63.
3 Documented in the restoration report by Eike Oellermann, May 1984, p. 2. BLfD, Munich.
4 "preder dar czu / auch dem schmid zü / peschlagen."

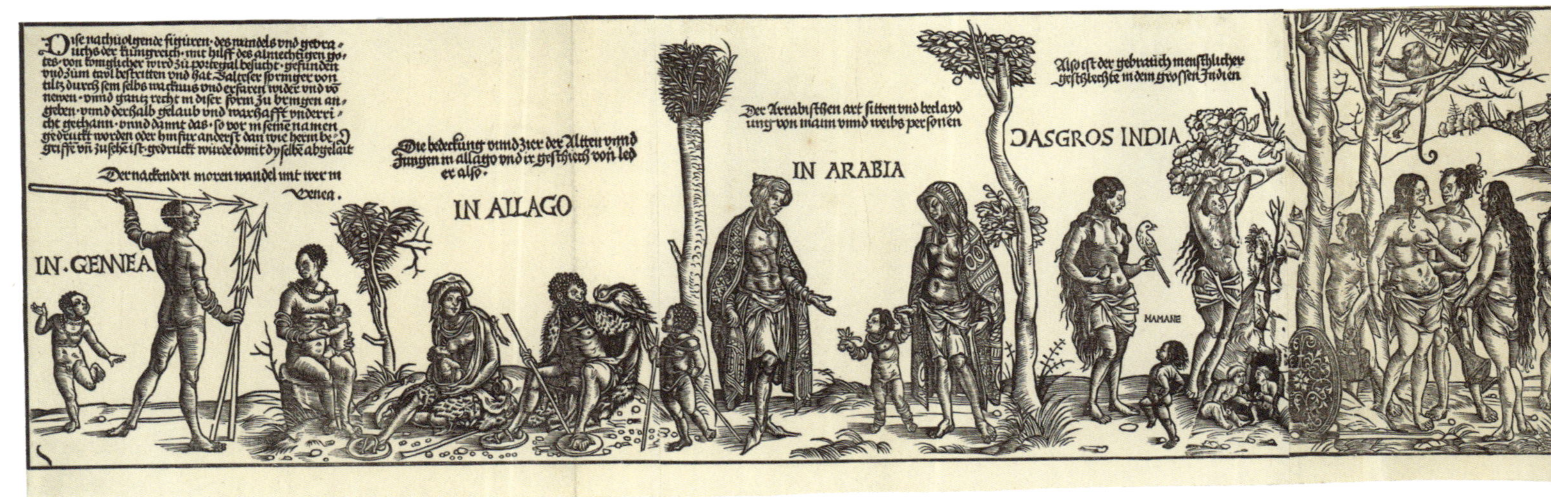

cat. no. 117.4

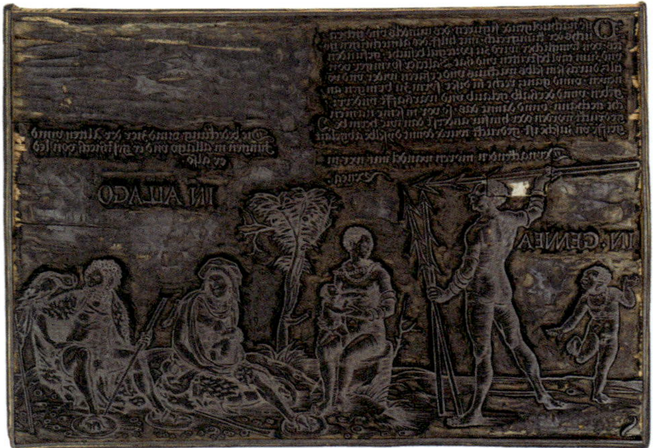

cat. no˙ 117.3
Derschau 182,3 verso

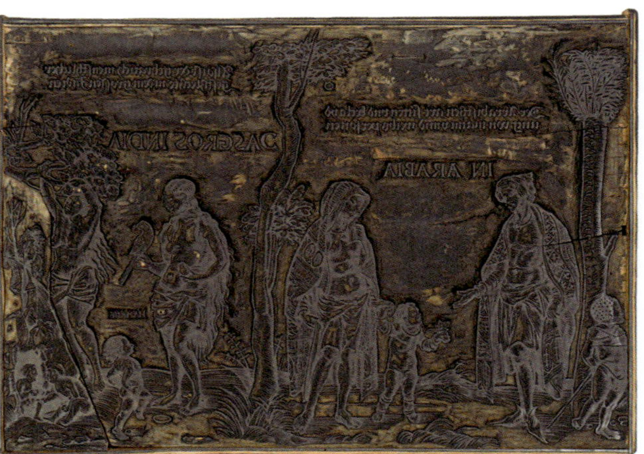

cat. no. 117.3
Derschau 182,3

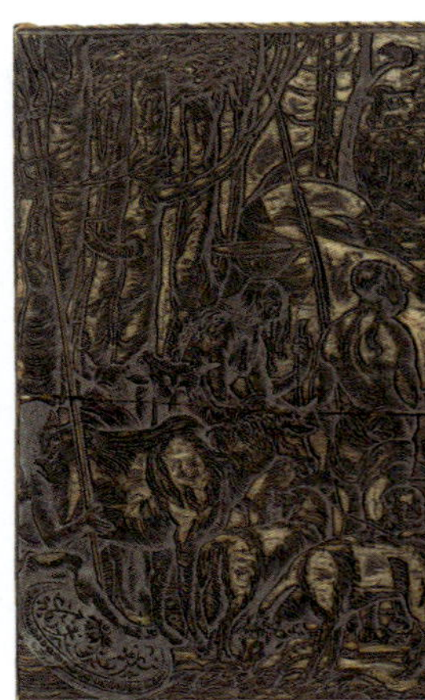

cat. no. 117.2
Derschau 182,2

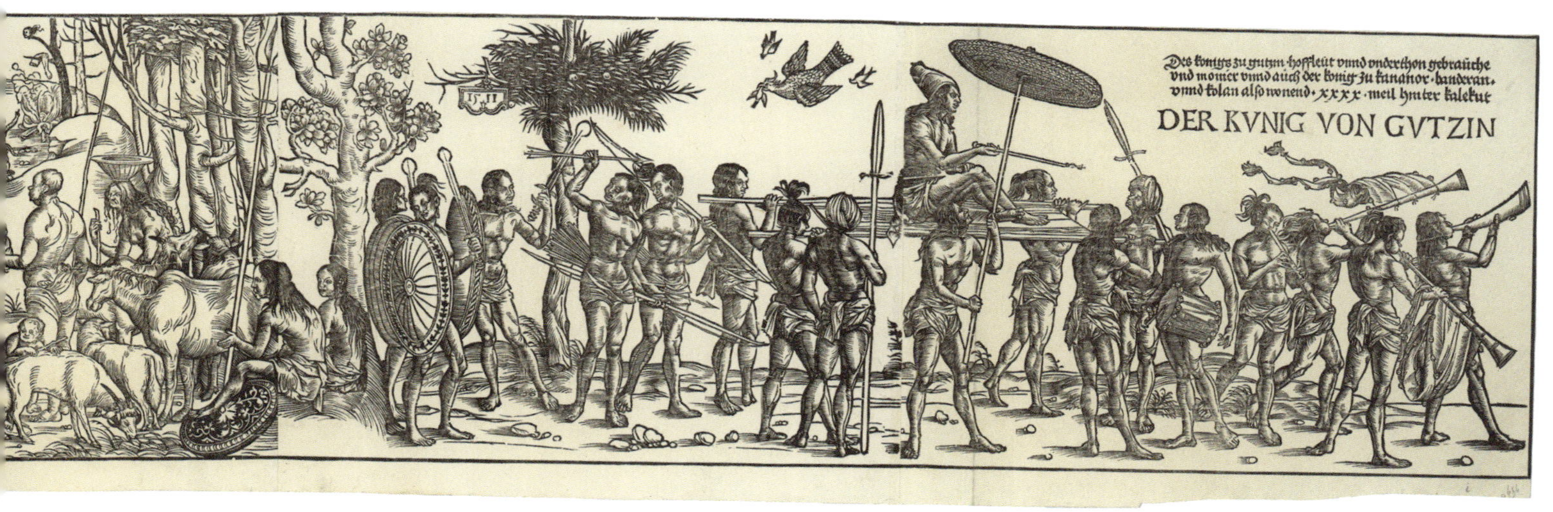

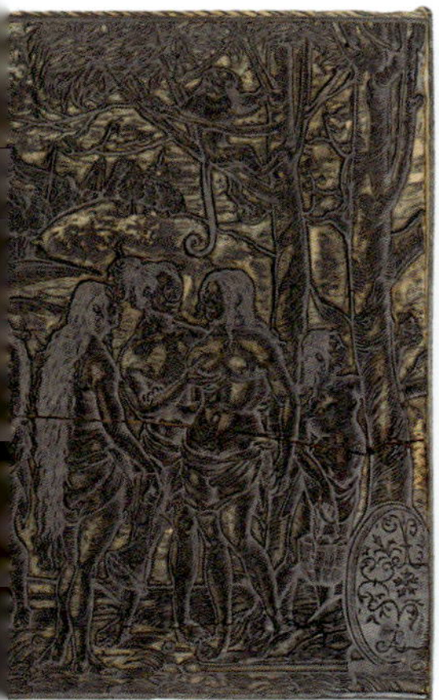

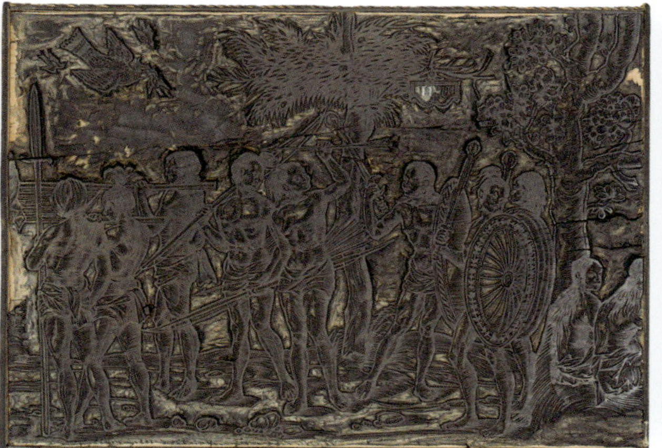

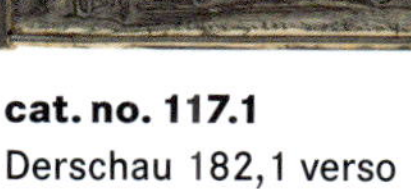

cat. no. 117.1
Derschau 182,1 verso

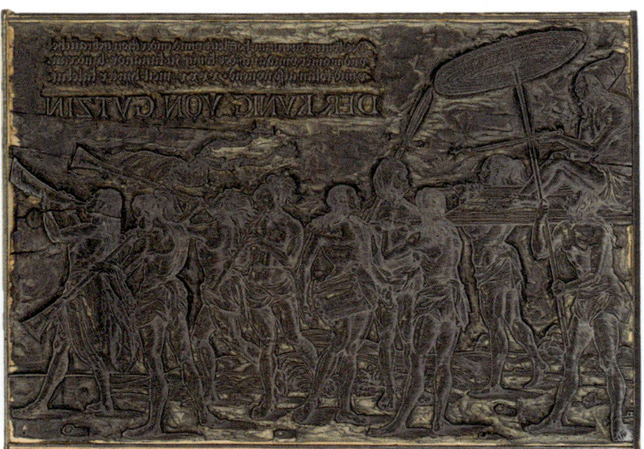

cat. no. 117.1
Derschau 182,1

cat. no. 118
Wings of the shrine

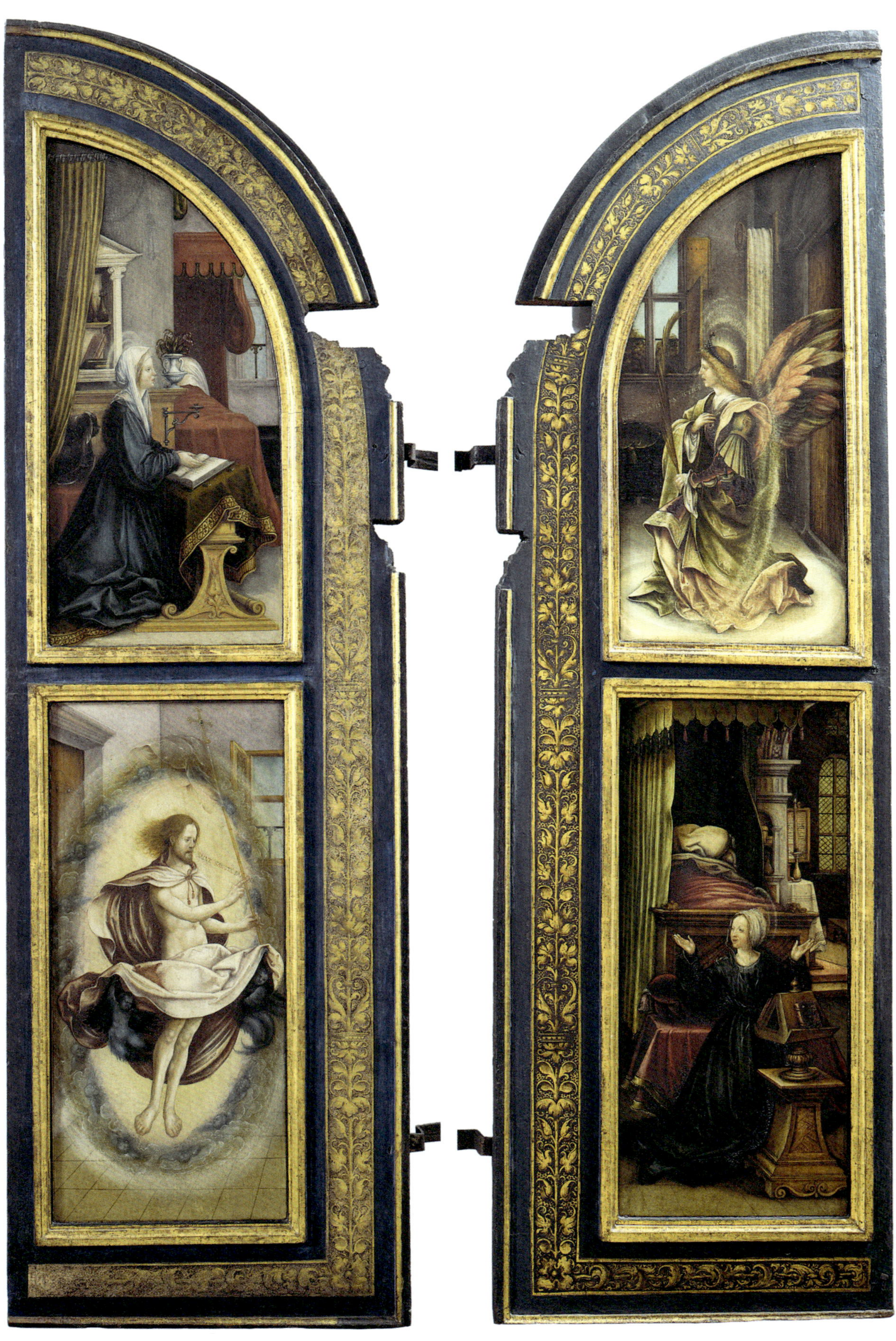

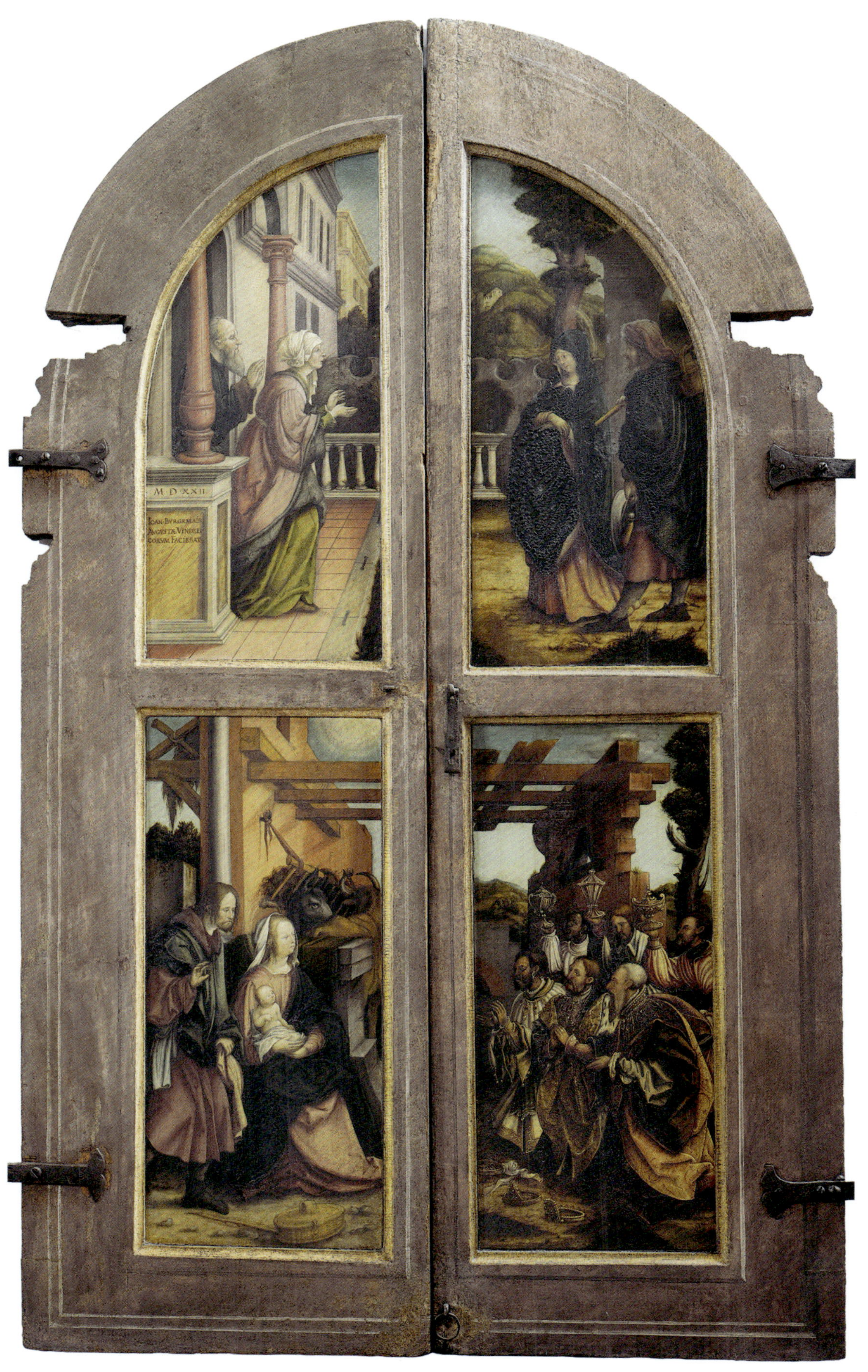
M D XXII
IOAN·BVRGKMAIR
AVGVSTÆ VINDELI
CORVM FACIEBAT

cat. no. 118
Wings of the predella

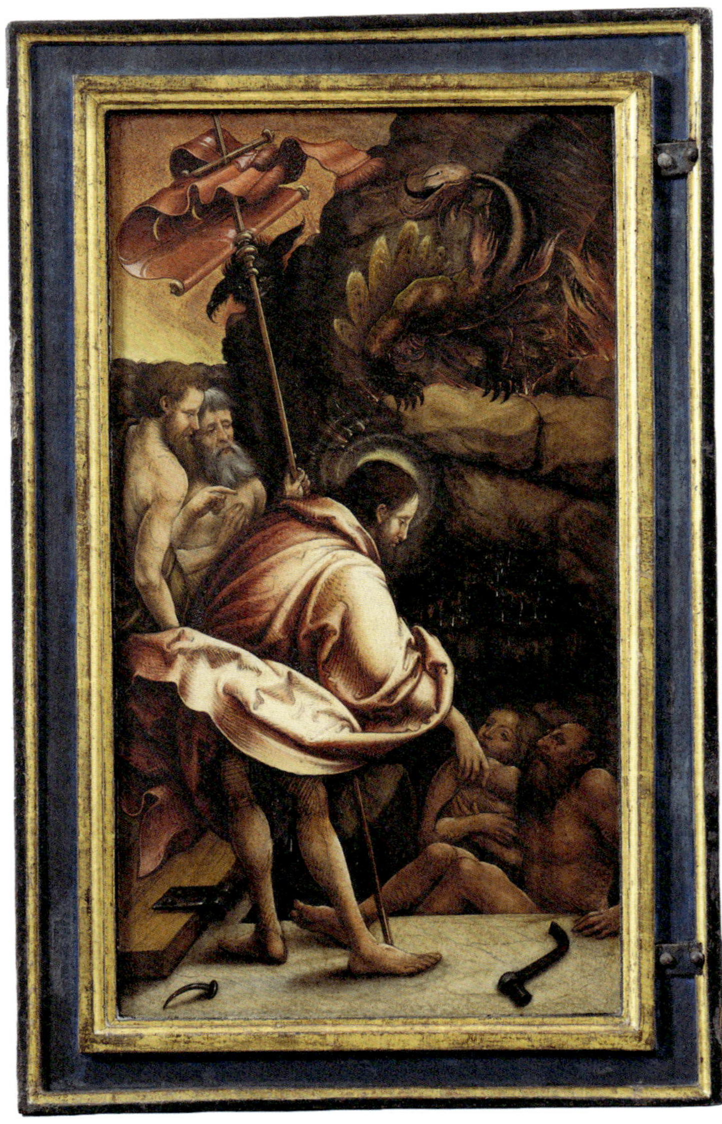

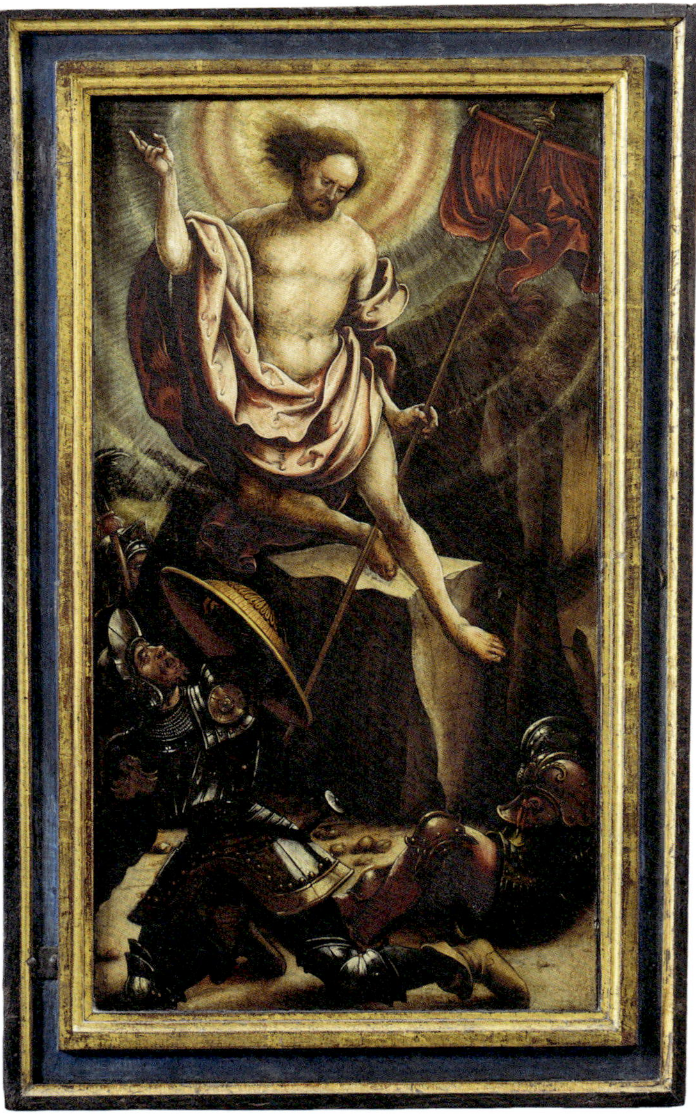

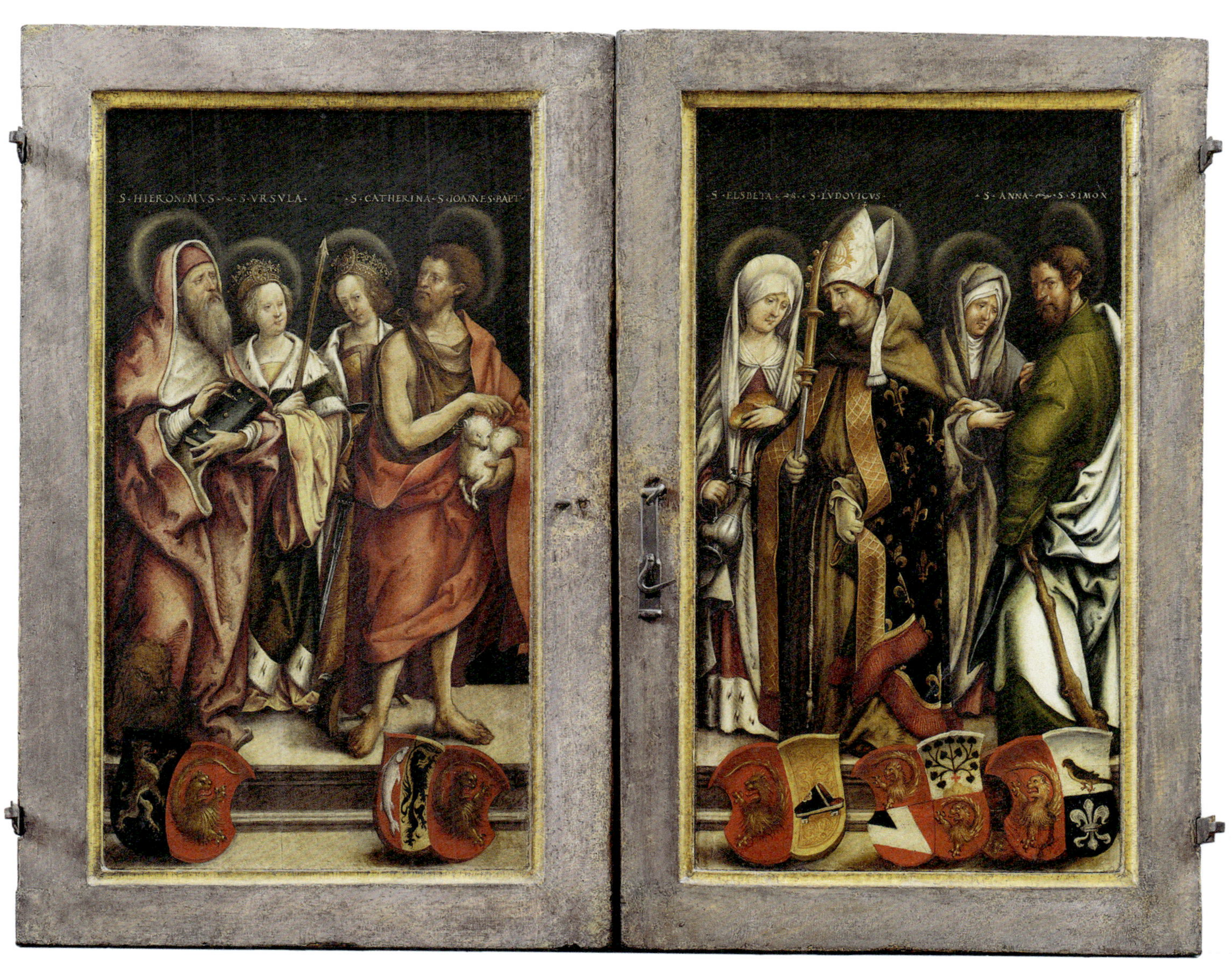
S·HIERONIMVS·S·VRSVLA·
·S·CATHERINA·S·IOANNES·BAPT·
·S·ELSBETA·S·LVDOVICVS·
·S·ANNA·S·SIMON

119

RHINOCEROS

Albrecht Dürer

Nuremberg, 1515

Woodcut and letterpress

119.1

H. 24.8 cm; W. 30.2 cm

GNM, inv. no. H7589, on long-term loan from the Sammlung Bernhard Hausmann

119. 2 (not illustrated)

H. 21.2 cm; W. 29.8 cm

Universitätsbibliothek Erlangen-Nürnberg, Erlangen, inv. no. H 62/AH 266

References:
Schoch, Mende, and Scherbaum 2002, pp. 420–24, cat. no. 241 (Yasmin Doosry).

More than almost any other work of art, Albrecht Dürer's *Rhinoceros* woodcut epitomizes Nuremberg's global connectedness in the early modern period. The Indian rhinoceros that is the subject of this print was shipped as a diplomatic gift from Goa to Lisbon in May 1515. It caused a sensation at the royal court of Portugal. No living rhinoceros had been seen in Europe since antiquity; they were known only from hearsay and ancient texts. That same year, Dürer created his iconic *Rhinoceros* based on a description sent from Lisbon to Nuremberg, presumably accompanied by a sketch.

Dürer, who never encountered this nor any other rhinoceros firsthand, depicted the animal in profile. Above its head, he placed the title "RHINOCERVS," the year of the woodcut's creation, and his famous "AD" monogram, which identifies him as the author of the image. The rhinoceros is framed tightly against the border lines. It appears to stand motionless, its powerful hooves firmly planted on the patch of ground below. Bold lines describe the textures and patterning of the armor-like plates covering the animal's body. The profile view and absence of a background cause the viewer to focus on the subject's physical features. For that reason, scholarship has repeatedly raised the question of whether Dürer's main interest lay in creating a zoologically accurate depiction, or rather in spreading the spectacular story surrounding the animal. That story took a dramatic turn when, after surviving the long journey from India to Portugal, this rhinoceros drowned in a shipwreck on its way to Rome.

It is unsurprising that news of the sensational diplomatic gift reached Nuremberg in just a few weeks and was then quickly disseminated in the medium of woodcut. In 1505–6, Nuremberg trading firms had been involved in a major expedition to India organized by the Portuguese crown |**see cat. no. 116**|. In the same years, hastily printed pamphlets advertising Indian travel and trade were issued to attract investors for further ventures |**cat. no. 115**|. Prints published in Nuremberg supplied the public with projections of what the people there looked like |**cat. no. 117**|. Nurembergers were always well informed about current events in Lisbon and the global enterprises initiated there, thanks to intermediaries such as the cartographer Martin Behaim |**see cat. nos. 1, 114**| and the printer Valentim Fernandes, the latter being the one who sent news of the rhinoceros to Nuremberg. With the help of Dürer's woodcut, which has the character of an illustrated broadsheet, the sensational story of the Indian rhinoceros spread like wildfire, reaching far beyond Nuremberg and southern Germany. Renditions of the motif in other visual media are found as far away as the Colombian Andes |**fig. p. 29**|.[1]

Sven Jakstat

1 See the essay by Benno Baumbauer and Sven Jakstat in the present volume.

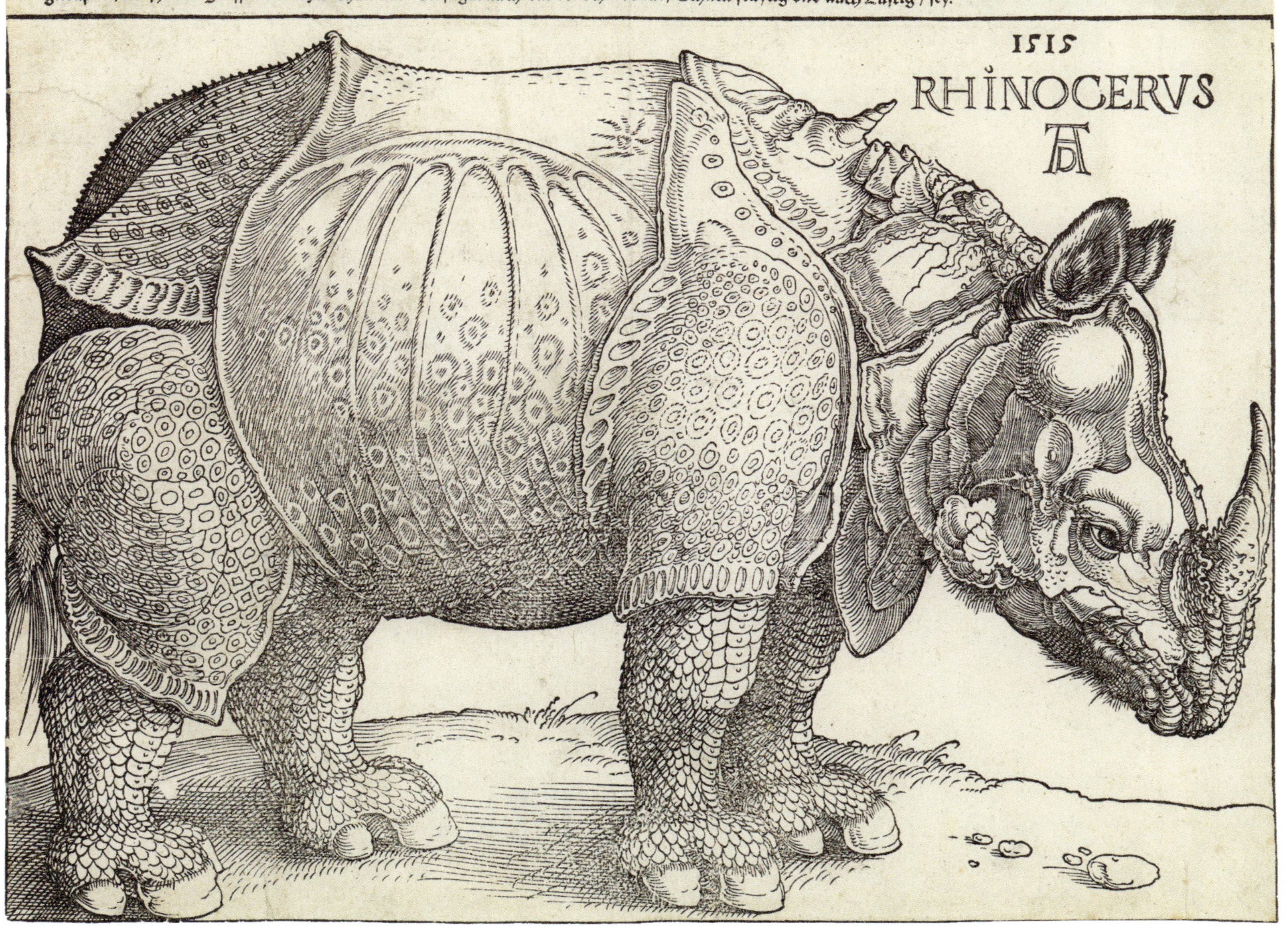
Nach Choistiegeburt/1513. Jar Adi 1. May hat man dem großmechtigisten König Emanuel von Portugal/gen Lysabona aus India pracht/
ain solch lebendig Thier. das nennen sie Rhinocerus/Das ist hie mit all seiner gestalt Abconterfect. Es hat ein farb wie ein gepsreckelte schildkrot/vnd ist von dicken scha-
len vberleget sehr fest/vnd ist in der größ als der Heilffandt/aber niderichter von baynen vnd sehr wehrhafftig es hat ein scharff starck Horn vorn auff der l lassen /das be-
gundt es zu wetzen wo es bey staynen ist / das da ein Sieg Thir ist/des Heilffandten Todtfeyndt. Der Heilffandt fürchts fast vbel /den wo es Jhn ankompt/so laufft Jhm
das Thir mit dem kopff zwischen die fordern bayn /vnd reist den Heilffanten vnten am bauch auff/vnd er würget jhn/des mag er sich nicht erwehren. dann das Thier ist also
gewapnet/das jhm der Jeilffandt nichts Thun kan/ Sie sagen auch/das der Rhinocerus/Schnell fraytig vnd auch Lustig / sey.
1515
RHINOCERVS
AD

cat. no. 119.1

120

TURBAN SHELL CUP

Friedrich Hillebrandt

Nuremberg, 1595

Silver, gilded, cast, repoussé, chased, engraved, etched, punched; turban shell; pearl

H. 39.1 cm; W. 13.9 cm; D. 12.5 cm

GNM, inv. no. HG2147, on long-term loan from the Johann Carl von Schlüsselfelder'sche Familienstiftung

References:
Tiedtke 2009, pp. 75–78, cat. no. 16; Exh. cat. Ansbach 2022, pp. 214–15 (Birgit Schübel).

This cup's gently shimmering bowl was fashioned from the shell of a large turban snail. The stem is formed by a kneeling figure of the ancient hero Hercules. Foliate and floral motifs decorate the foot. Three intricately ornamented straps hold the shell in place. The lip of the bowl, attached at the shell's opening, is engraved with hunting scenes separated by medallions displaying etched floral designs. The shell's marine origin is reflected in the lid decoration, which shows fantastic sea creatures swimming among waves. The lid is surmounted by a figure of Neptune holding a trident and blowing a conch horn. He holds the reins of three hippocampi, legendary sea creatures with the hindparts of a fish and the foreparts of a horse. The underside of the lid is etched with the date 1595 and with the coats of arms of the Nuremberg patrician families Schlüsselfelder and Löffelholz. It has not yet been determined for what occasion this magnificent cup was commissioned.

In addition to turban snail shells, sometimes referred to as "turbo shells," nautilus shells were also made into vessels. And small mother-of-pearl sections obtained from the shells of various bivalve sea mollusks were used to adorn elaborately designed basins and cups |**see cat. no. 2**|. The Nuremberg goldsmith Friedrich Hillebrandt (1555–1608) seems to have specialized in the use of these materials. At least that is the impression given by his surviving works: of the thirty-six works that are extant or preserved in photographs, twenty-six were made with these "exotic" natural materials, seven of them with turban shells. Unfortunately, none of the known archival records provide information about how Hillebrandt acquired these materials.

The calcareous shell of the turban snail, a marine gastropod mollusk, coils in a right-handed spiral and is lined with mother-of-pearl. When such shells were made into precious vessels, their often heavily textured outer layer was removed. This was achieved using nitric acid, with the shells being either boiled or worked with files and grinding wheels.[1] To this day, it remains unclear which types of laborers carried out the arduous work of exposing the mother-of-pearl layer and thus bringing the shells to a semi-finished state of processing. Where this procedure was carried out is also unknown.

Seashells appear in works of goldsmithing as early as the Middle Ages. Such vessels found their way into church treasuries and, later on, into art and curiosity cabinets. Along with other goods from Asia, the shells were initially brought by land to the eastern Mediterranean and then by sea to Venice. From there, merchants transported them across the Alps. In 1498, Vasco da Gama (d. 1524) of Portugal discovered the sea route to India, simplifying the transport of goods from Asia. The shells of mussels and sea snails native to the Indo-Pacific may have been brought to Nuremberg by patrician families and merchants involved in long-distance trade, such as the Imhoffs and Hirschvogels, who first invested in an expedition to Kochi in India in 1505–6 |**see cat. no. 116**|.[2]

Birgit Schübel and Sabine Tiedtke

1 See Krünitz 1773–1858, vol. 98 (1805), p. 228.
2 Imhoff 1987b, pp. 11–44; Pohle 2000, esp. pp. 122–34, 205–11; Horst 2009.

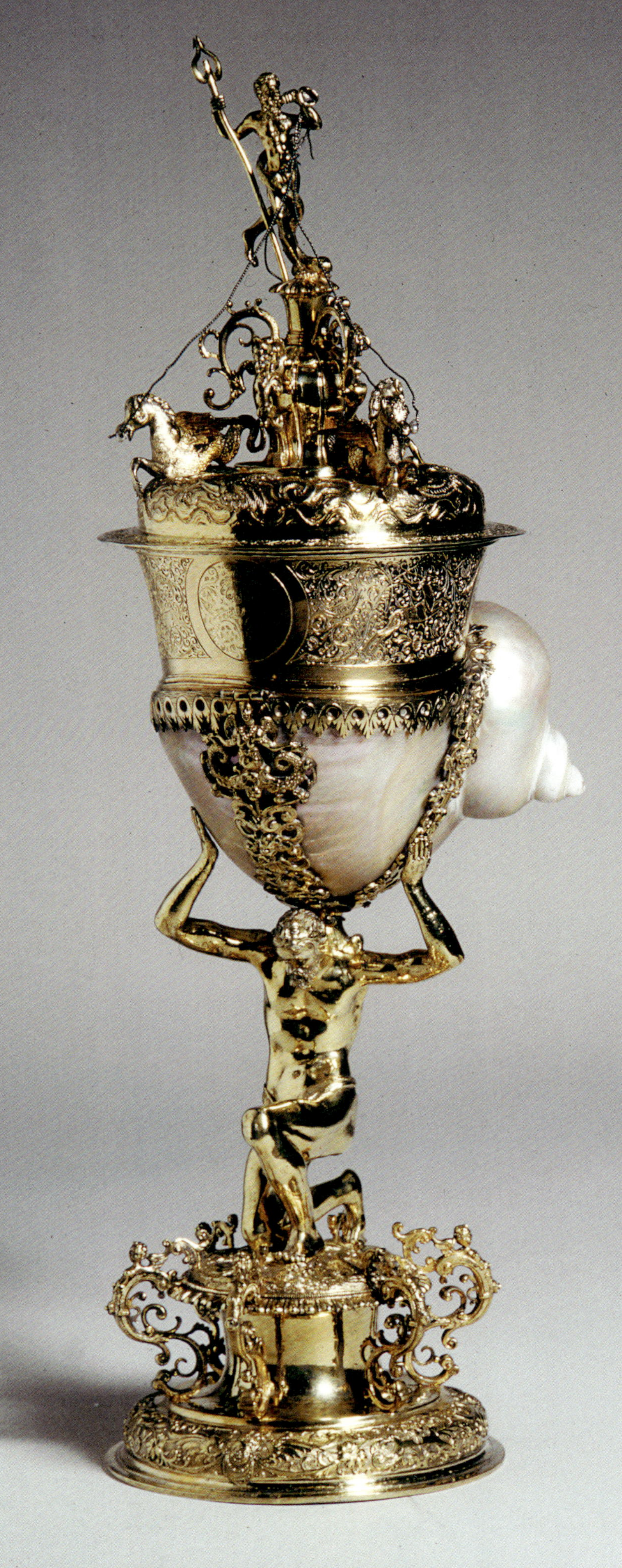

121

IVORY CASKET WITH ALBRECHT DÜRER'S *BAGPIPER*

121.1 Ivory Casket

Sri Lanka, former Kingdom of Kotte, ca. 1551 (?)

Ivory, carved; lock and gemstone settings of gold filigree; handle of gilded bronze; set with rubies and sapphires

H. 11.5 cm; W. 23.5 cm; D. 13 cm

Private collection

References:
Exh. cat. Zurich 2010, pp. 60–63, cat. no. 12 (Annemarie Jordan Gschwend); Vassallo e Silva 2013, p. 94; Saviello 2018a, pp. 337–39.

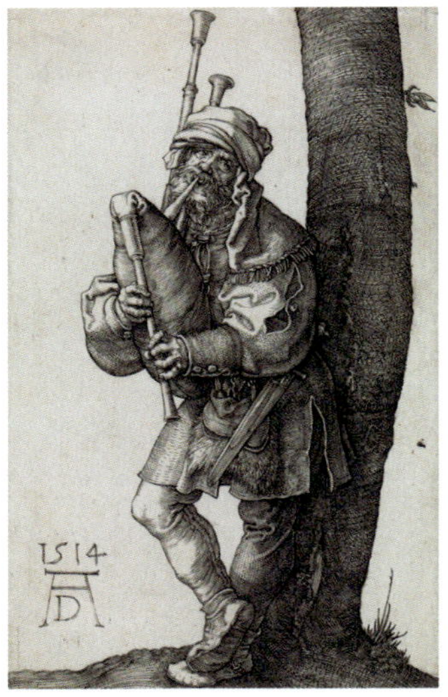

121.2 The Bagpiper

Albrecht Dürer, Nuremberg, 1514

Engraving

H. 11.6 cm; W. 7.4 cm

GNM, inv. no. StN2192, on long-term loan from the Museen der Stadt Nürnberg

This work belongs to a group of about twelve similar ivory caskets created in Sri Lanka (formerly Ceylon) in the sixteenth and seventeenth centuries. Modeled on European reliquaries and jewelry boxes, they all have the same basic architectural form and similar divisions of the decorated panels.[1] In addition, some of them combine European motifs with local figurative traditions. The caskets are now mainly in European collections. Three of them are documented as diplomatic gifts to the king of Portugal from Kotte and Sitavaka, two of the rival kingdoms on the island of Ceylon.[2] The present example is thought to have arrived in Europe in the same context.

This casket is a work of great opulence. Gold filigree and settings of sapphires and rubies decorate the lock, handle, and framing elements. Figural and vegetal carvings cover the outer surfaces of the sides and lid. These include European motifs. A figure based on Albrecht Dürer's *The Bagpiper* engraving appears on the right of the lid. Nearby are figures from a printed book of hours issued in Paris by the Kerver family of printers: four small warriors on the right front and, on the back, two unicorns, a nursing woman, a hunting party (right), and putti surrounded by banderoles (in the narrow border panels).[3] The two large panels on the sides of the casket borrow motifs from Lucas van Leyden—on the left, Christ in Limbo; on the right, Saint Luke with his ox attribute.[4]

The models were probably brought to Ceylon either by Sri Ramaraksa Pandita, the envoy of the king of Kotte (now Colombo) at the royal court in Lisbon, or by Christian missionaries. Sri Ramaraksa Pandita is said to have received books and prints from the Portuguese royal library as gifts. In this scenario, motifs adopted from Portuguese gifts were integrated into gifts used for Sinhalese diplomacy, as is assumed for this casket. The Kotte kings Bhuvanekubahu VII (r. 1521–51) and Dharmapala (r. 1551–97) sought military backing from the Portuguese, who had been present on the island since 1505. Kotte's rulers were engaged in a struggle for supremacy over the other kings of Ceylon, especially the monarchs of Sitavaka. In return for their support, the Portuguese pressed for the traditionally Buddhist kings to convert to Christianity. Whereas Bhuvanekubahu VII successfully held out, his grandson and successor Dharmapala accepted conversion.

The inclusion of Christian subject matter on this casket is suggestive of a diplomatic rapprochement with the Portuguese. Nevertheless, traditional Sinhalese motifs and symbols of power predominate. This applies to the two depictions of the ruler wearing a broad headband (*chinnapattikadhatu*) and riding a royal elephant (*mangala hatthi*) that appear centrally on the lid and the back. At the back center of the lid, the representation of a Hindu deity flanked by European riders on rearing horses would seem to allude to the king of Kotte asserting political and religious sovereignty against the wishes of his allies.

The Christian motifs were not simply copied by the creators of the casket, but instead appropriated for use within their own world of imagery. Unlike in the prototype, the ox of Saint Luke wears an ornate necklace. While this type of adornment is unprecedented for the symbolic animal of the biblical evangelist, it does appear in the Hindu tradition—namely, in depictions of the bull Nandi, the mount (*vahana*) of the god Shiva.

Alberto Saviello

1 See Gall 1965, p. 126.
2 See Biedermann 2018, pp. 88–98.
3 See Saviello 2018a, p. 338.
4 Exh. cat. Zurich 2010, pp. 60–63, cat. no. 12 (Annemarie Jordan Gschwend).

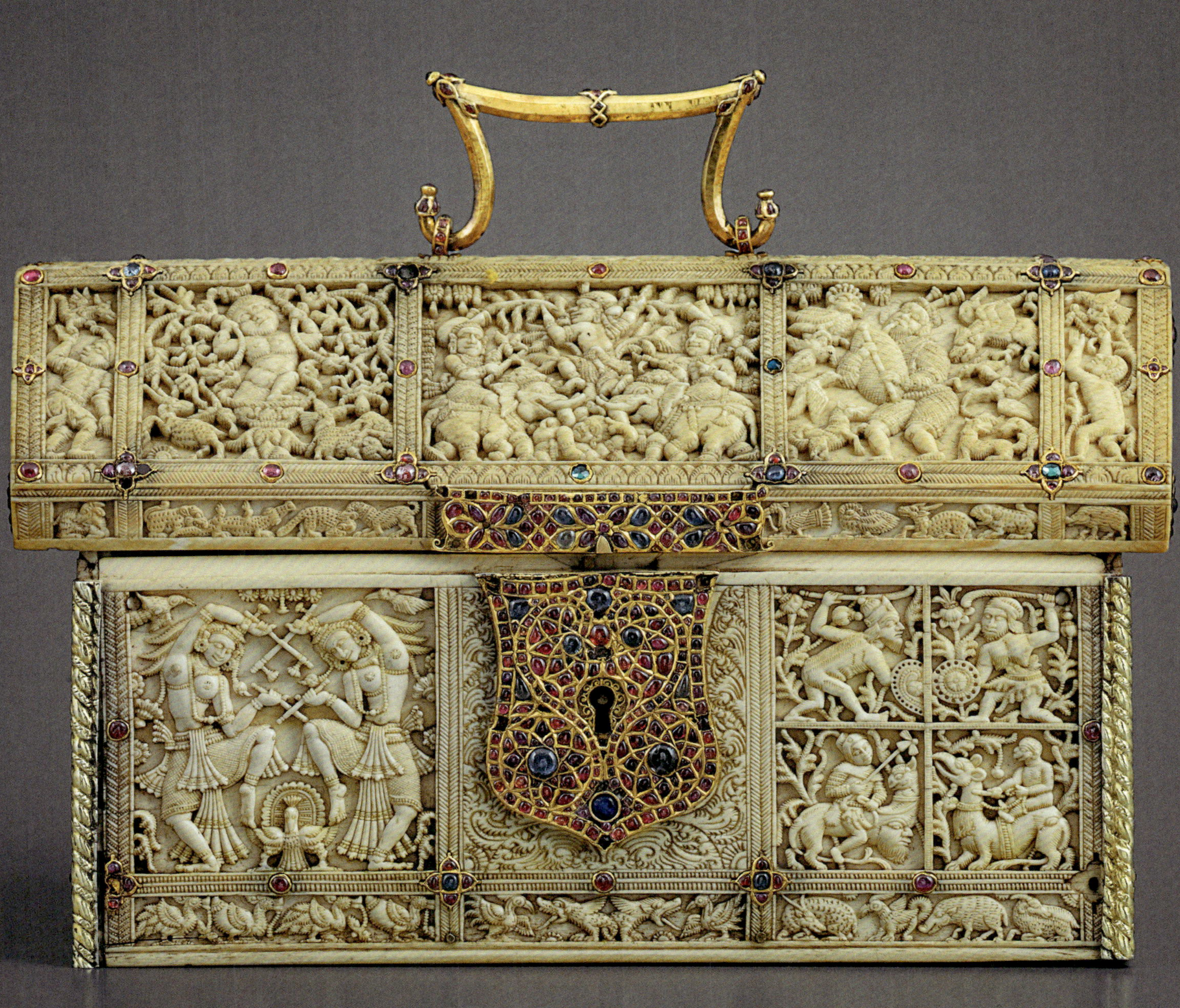

122

JAHANGIR ALBUM

122.1–3 Three pages from the Jahangir Album

India, Agra (?), ca. 1608–18

Ink, gold, and watercolor on paper, engraving

Each H. 42.2 cm; W. 26.5 cm

Staatsbibliothek zu Berlin, Preußischer Kulturbesitz, Orientalische Handschriften, Libri picturati A 117, fols. 5a, 9a,11b

References:
Grebe 2014, pp. 396–98; Natif 2018, pp. 74, 107–9; Saviello 2022, pp. 46–49.

122.4 The Crucifixion
(fig. p. 26)

Albrecht Dürer, Nuremberg, 1511

Engraving

H. 11.7 cm; W. 7.4 cm

GNM, inv. no. StN2081, on long-term loan from the Museen der Stadt Nürnberg, Kunstsammlungen

These three pages belong to a set of fifty referred to as the Jahangir Album, now at the Staatsbibliothek (State Library) in Berlin. The set, originally consisting of twenty-five folios, was brought to Berlin by the Egyptologist Heinrich Karl Brugsch, who had acquired it in Persia in 1860 or 1861. All twenty-five folios were later split front from back, creating the present fifty pages. They were originally part of a larger album that is now divided among various collections. The largest part, known as the Gulshan Album, is kept at the Golestan Palace Library in Tehran.

The album was created in stages from 1599 to 1619 under the patronage of the Mughal ruler Prince Salim, the later Emperor Jahangir (r. 1605–1627). It contains calligraphy, illuminations, drawings, and prints of various origin. These include motifs by Albrecht Dürer and other European printmakers. The individual works were arranged into new compositions on album leaves richly decorated with gold paint. In the original ordering, facing pages of calligraphy—mostly Persian poetry—were followed by facing pages with figural representations. The Mughal court painters designed the illuminated margins to alternate between figural scenes (on the pages with calligraphic centerpieces) and combinations of vegetal ornaments and birds (on the pages with figurative representations as centerpieces). Interestingly, the European prints are placed in the album in ways that associate them with calligraphy.

The tradition of creating such albums (*muraqqa*) traces back to fifteenth-century Herat, at the court of the Timurids, from whom the Mughal dynasty descended.[1] In courtly culture, albums were used individually or in groups, providing a basis for reflections on beauty, style, and meaning. They testify to their owners' connoisseurship and sophistication. As a museum in book form, so to speak, an album documented artistic traditions; as a "think tank for allegory,"[2] it served as a source of inspiration.

The Jahangir Album is distinguished by its integration and adaptation of a large number of European works and individual figures. This reflects the Muslim emperor's great interest in European art. In addition to Christian subjects, there are depictions of nobles dressed in European clothing (fol. 11b, top) as well as figures of commoners, such as a dancing peasant couple (fol. 11b, left). The dancing couple is based on "The Peasants' Feast" series of engravings by the Nuremberg-born printmaker Sebald Beham. The motif was adapted to local courtly tastes and viewpoints.

Jahangir and his court appear to have been particularly fond of the works of Albrecht Dürer.[3] In one example of a calligraphy page, an engraved reverse copy of the monkey from Dürer's *Virgin and Child with the Monkey* appears together with a detail of Saint John the Evangelist from an engraving by Raphael Sadeler (fol. 9a). On another page, the marginal illuminations show three adaptations from Dürer's works: a Virgin and Child, a figure of Saint Peter seen from behind, and the Saint John from Dürer's *Crucifixion* engraving of 1511 (fol. 5a). This borrowing can be seen as an expression of homage to the Nuremberg master. Dürer seems to have been viewed as a kind of benchmark for quality and as an exemplar of genius whose talents emerged at an early age. In the oeuvre of the court painter Abu'l Hasan (1589 – ca. 1630), whom Emperor Jahangir praised as one of the greatest artists of his time, there is a drawing after the same Saint John by Dürer that is copied in the Jahangir Album. According to that drawing's inscription, Abu'l Hasan made it at the age of thirteen |**fig. p. 26**|.[4] Thus, in a kind of artistic competition that took place some 6,000 kilometers away from Nuremberg, Dürer served as both exemplar and rival.

Alberto Saviello

1 See Roxburgh 2001, p. 3.
2 Koch 2010.
3 See also Grebe 2014.
4 See Natif 2018, p. 106; Saviello 2022, with references to earlier literature. See also the essay by Benno Baumbauer and Sven Jakstat in the present volume.

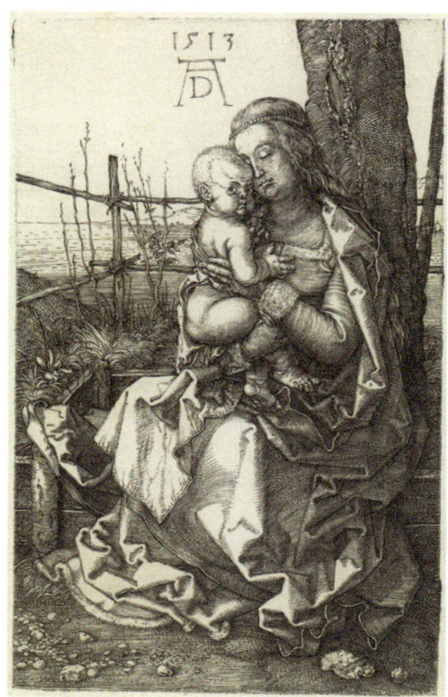

122.5 Virgin and Child Seated by a Tree

Albrecht Dürer, Nuremberg, 1513

Engraving

H. 17 cm; W. 11.9 cm

GNM, inv. no. StN2095, on long-term loan from the Museen der Stadt Nürnberg, Kunstsammlungen

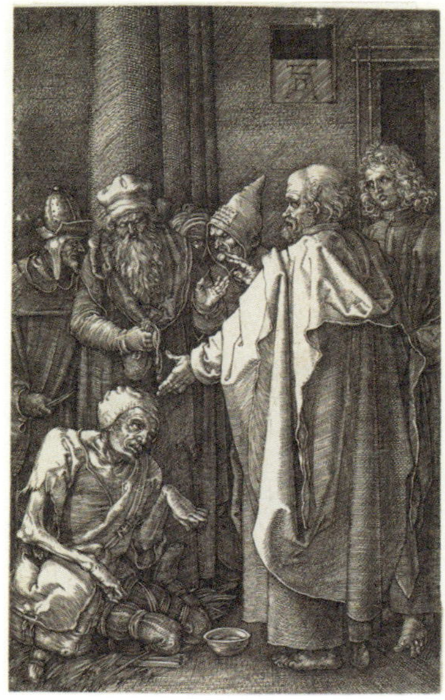

122.6 Saint Peter and Saint John at the Gate of the Temple

Albrecht Dürer, Nuremberg, 1513

Engraving

H. 11.5 cm; W. 7.3 cm

GNM, inv. no. StN2086, on long-term loan from the Museen der Stadt Nürnberg, Kunstsammlungen

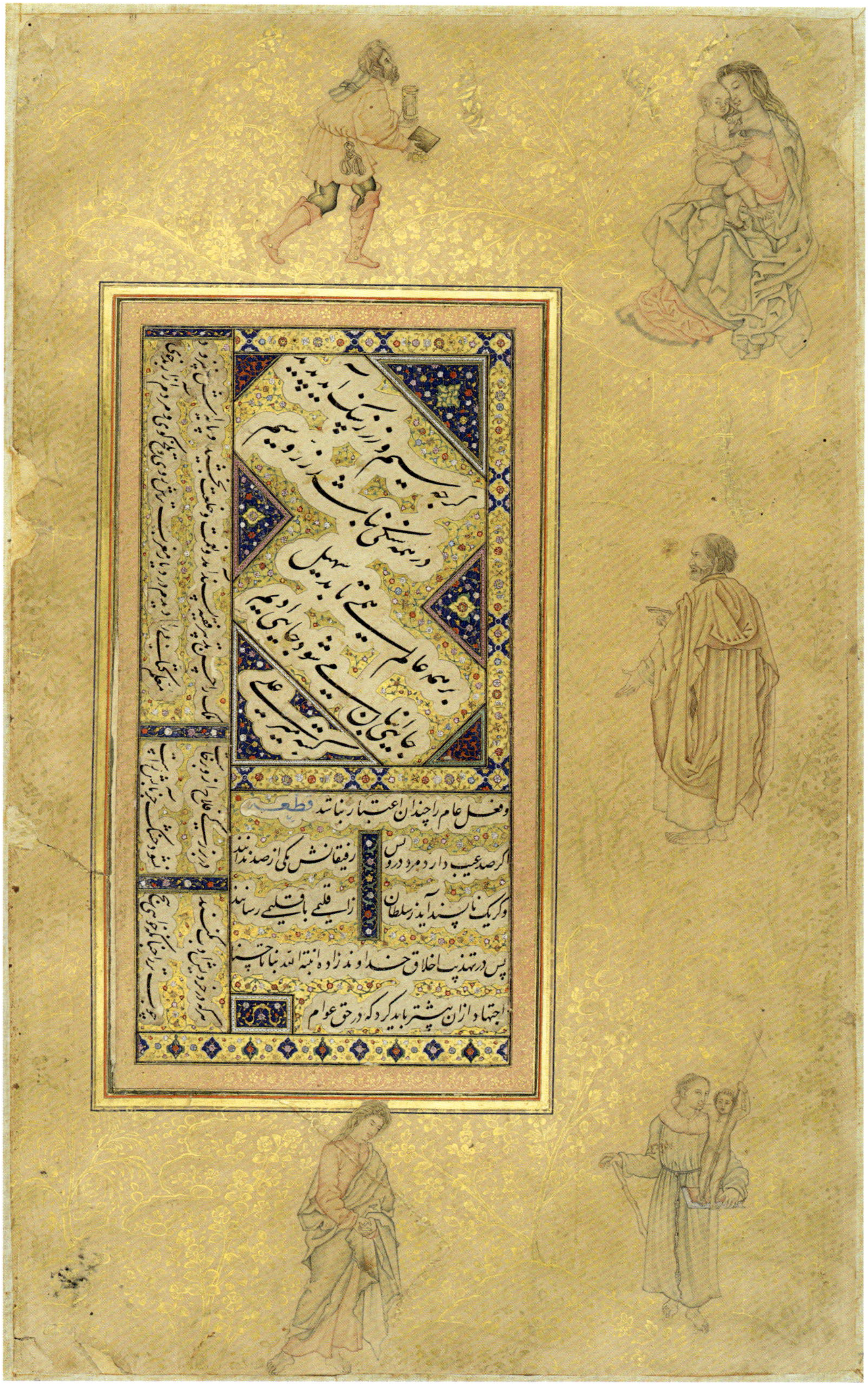

cat. no. 122.1 fol. 5a

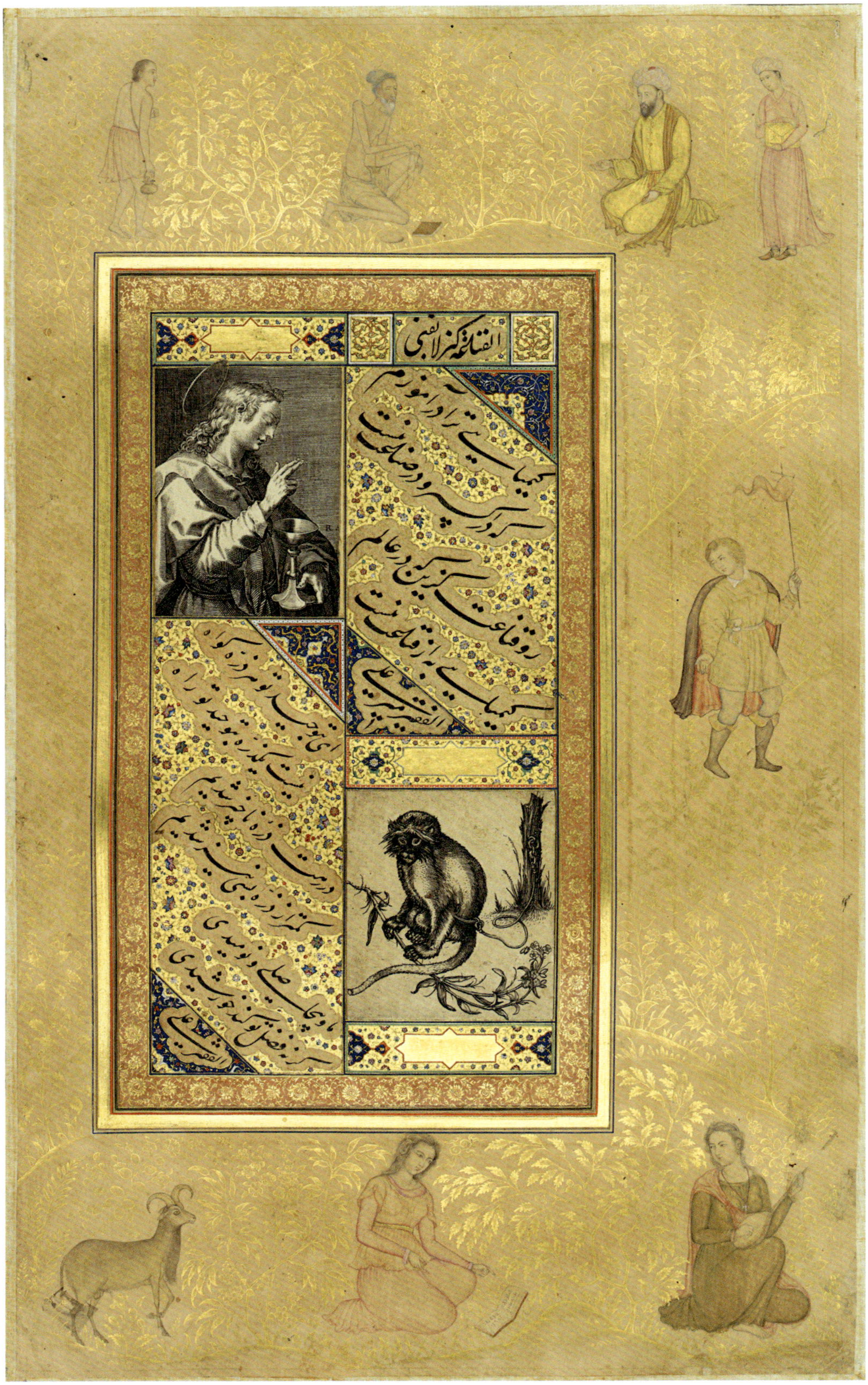

cat. no. 122.2 fol. 9a

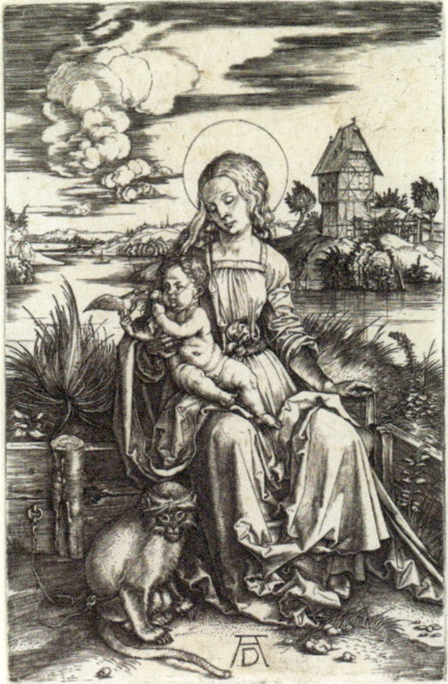

122.7 Virgin and Child with the Monkey

Albrecht Dürer, Nuremberg, ca. 1498

Engraving

H. 19.3 cm; W. 12.6 cm

GNM, inv. no. StN2102, on long-term loan from the Museen der Stadt Nürnberg, Kunstsammlungen

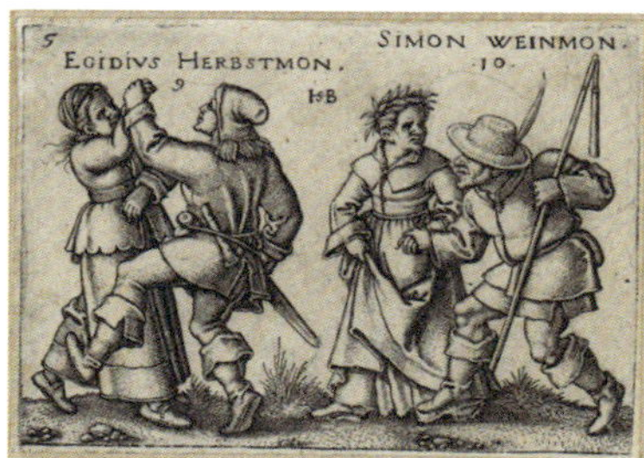

122.8 September and October from "The Peasants' Feast"

Sebald Beham, Frankfurt am Main, 1546–47

Engraving

H. 5 cm; W. 7.4 cm

GNM, inv. no. StN624b, on long-term loan from the Museen der Stadt Nürnberg, Kunstsammlungen

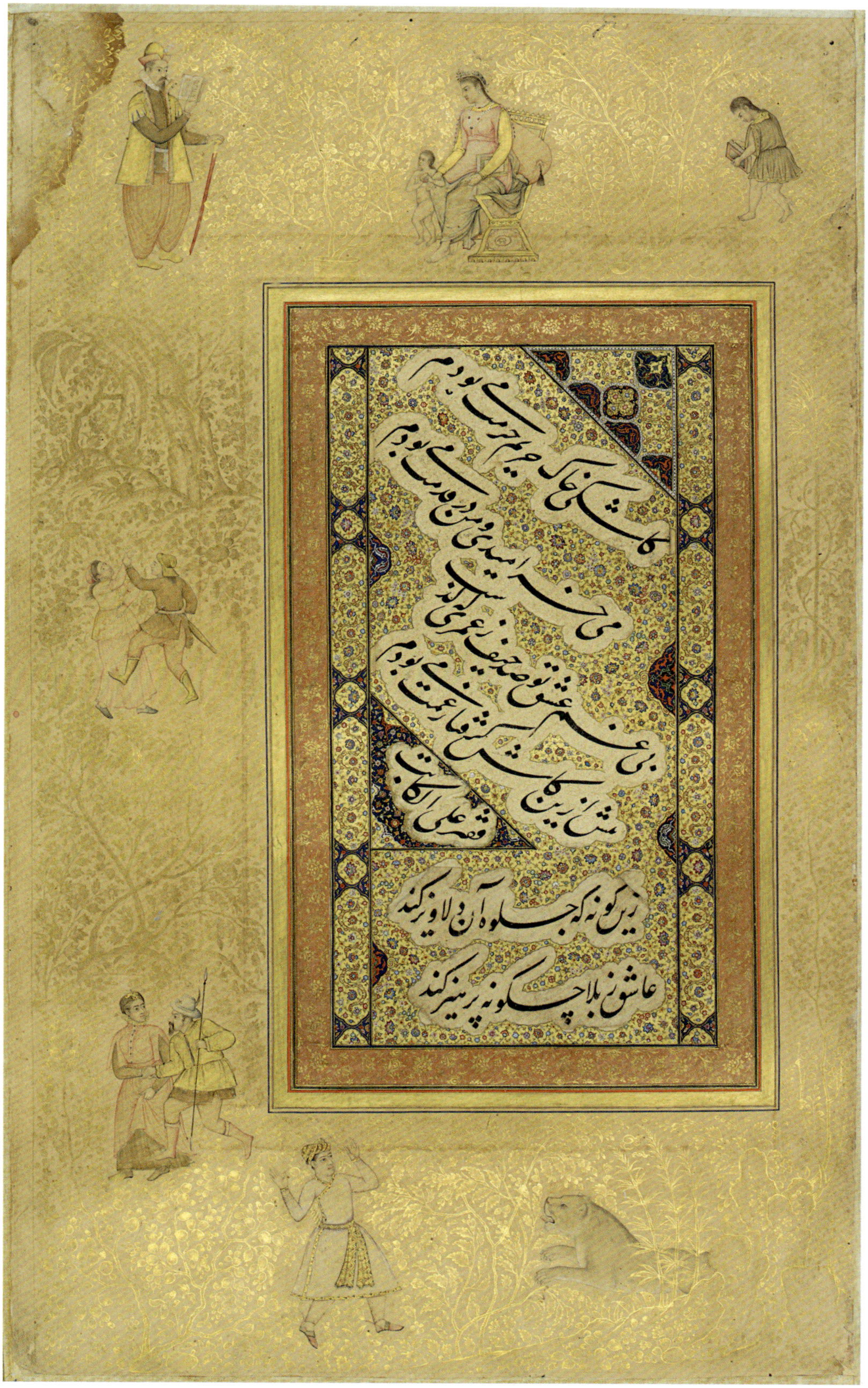

cat. no. 122.3 fol. 11b

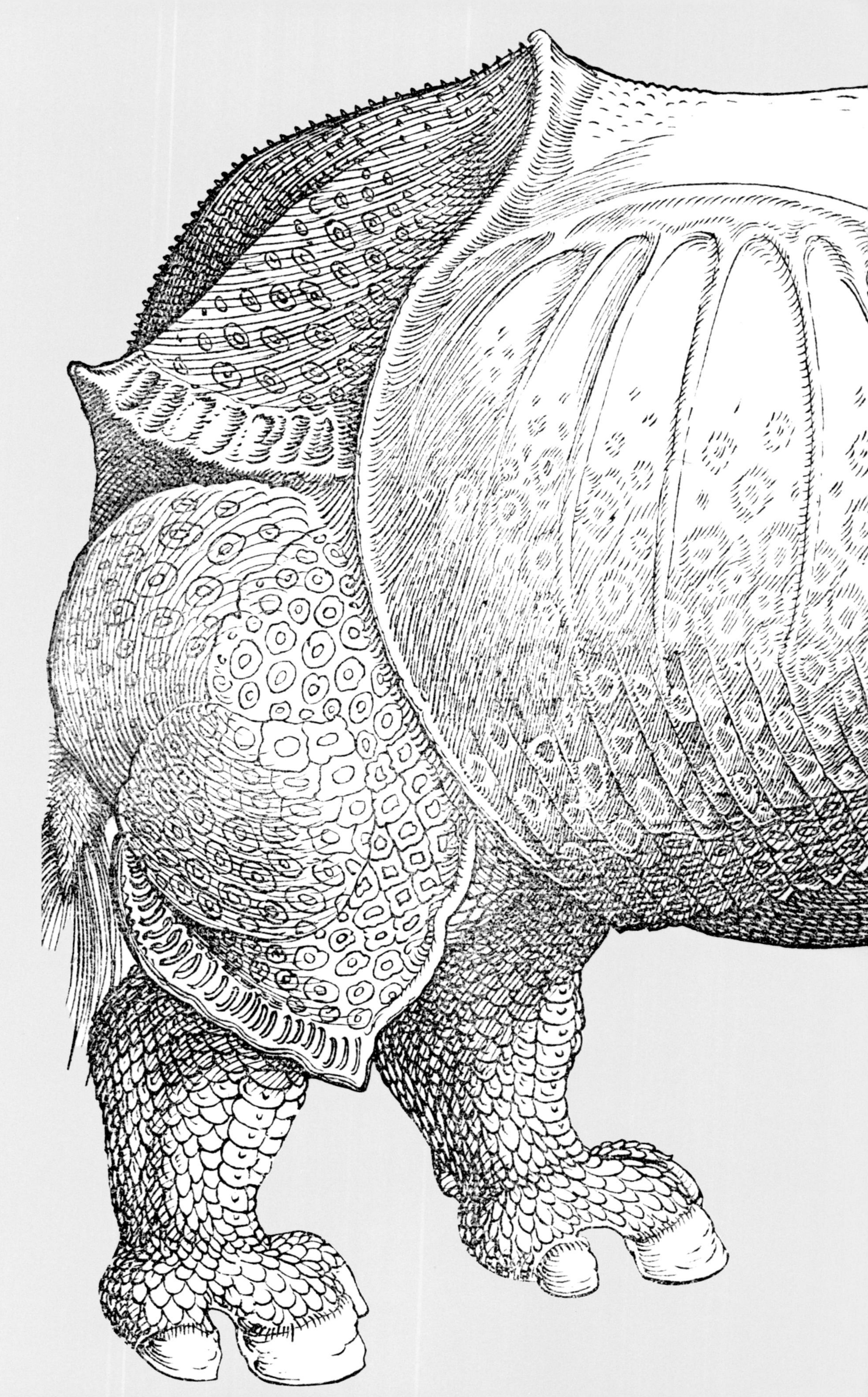

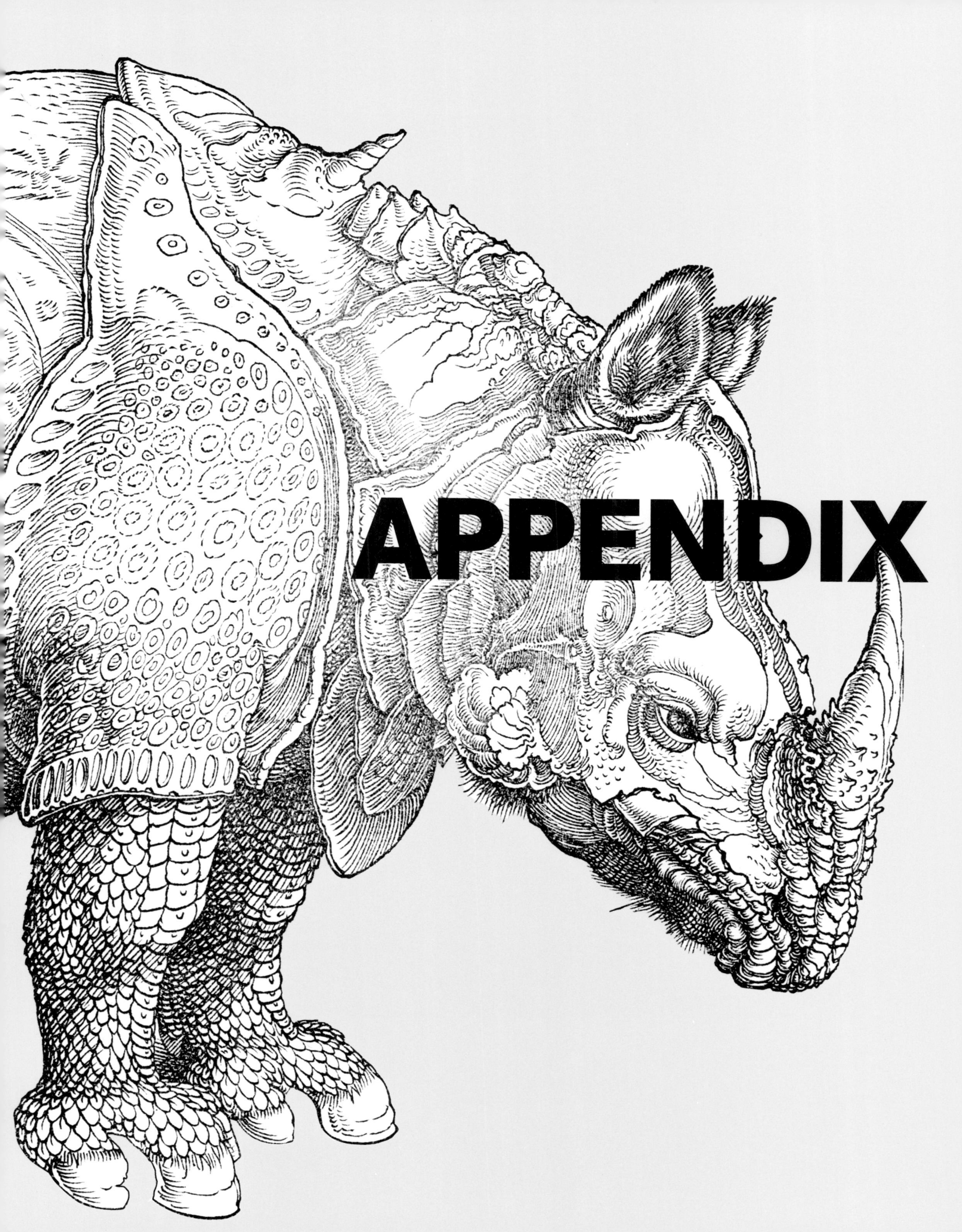

APPENDIX

BIBLIOGRAPHY

Abul Fazl and Blochmann 2001 Abul Fazl 'Allami. *The Ain I Akbari: Text and Translation*. Translated by Heinrich Blochmann. 2 vols. Delhi, 2001.

Achilles-Syndram 1994a Achilles-Syndram, Katrin, comp. *Die Kunstsammlung des Paulus Praun: Die Inventare von 1616 und 1719*. Quellen zur Geschichte und Kultur der Stadt Nürnberg 25. Nuremberg, 1994.

Achilles-Syndram 1994b Achilles-Syndram, Katrin. "'... und sonderlich von großen stuckhen nichts bey mihr vorhanden ist.': Die Sammlung Praun als kunst- und kulturgeschichtliches Dokument." In Exh. cat. Nuremberg 1994, pp. 35–55.

Acosta Cuellar 2022 Acosta Cuellar, Handy. "Manteniendo la fragua encendida: esclavizados africanos y tecnología de fundición de cobre en Cuba (1540–1767)." *Perspectivas Afro* 1, no. 2 (2022), pp. 128–48.

Adıgüzel 2021 Adıgüzel, Hatice. "Imitation and Adaptation of the Exotic: The Ottoman Influence on Italian Pottery Production (16th–19th Centuries)." In Kontogiannis, Böhlendorf-Arslan, and Yenişehirlioğlu 2021, pp. 355–86.

Aertsen and Pickavé 2002 Aertsen, Jan A., and Martin Pickavé, eds. *Ende und Vollendung: Eschatologische Perspektiven im Mittelalter*. Miscellanea mediaevalia 29. Berlin, 2002.

Aign 1961 Aign, Theodor. *Die Ketzel: Ein Nürnberger Handelsherren- und Jerusalempilgergeschlecht*. Neustadt/Aisch, 1961.

Al-Farghānī and al-Battānī 1537 Al-Farghānī and al-Battānī. *Rvdimenta astronomica ...* . Edited by Regiomontanus and Philip Melanchthon. Nuremberg, 1537.

Alraum, Holndonner, and Lehner 2016 Alraum, Claudia, Andreas Holndonner, and Hans-Christian Lehner, eds. *Zwischen Rom und Santiago: Festschrift für Klaus Herbers zu seinem 65. Geburtstag*. Bochum, 2016.

Amin 2013 Amin, Abbas. *Ägyptomanie und Orientalismus: Ägypten in der deutschen Reiseliteratur (1175–1663); Mit einem kommentierten Verzeichnis der Reiseberichte (383–1845)*. Berlin and Boston, 2013.

Anderson 2009 Anderson, Jaynie, ed. *Crossing Cultures: Conflict, Migration and Convergence*. Melbourne, 2009.

Andrews 2022 Andrews, Noam. *The Polyhedrists: Art and Geometry in the Long Sixteenth Century*. Cambridge, MA, and London, 2022.

Angelini 2012 Angelini, Alessandro. "Qualità, devozione e pratica." In Fattorini et al. 2012, pp. 14–21.

Ankenbauer 2010 Ankenbauer, Norbert. *"das ich mochte meer newer dyng erfaren": Die Versprachlichung des Neuen in den "Paesi novamente retrovati" (Vicenza, 1507) und in ihrer deutschen Übersetzung (Nürnberg, 1508)*. Romanistik 5. Berlin, 2010.

Amburger 1931 Amburger, Hannah S. M. "Die Familiengeschichte der Koeler: Ein Beitrag zur Autobiographie des 16. Jahrhunderts." *MVGN* 30 (1931), pp. 161–289.

Ammann 1970 Ammann, Hektor. "Deutsch-spanische Wirtschaftsbeziehungen bis zum Ende des 15. Jahrhunderts." In Kellenbenz 1970b, pp. 132–55.

Anzelewsky 1983 Anzelewsky, Fedja. *Dürer-Studien: Untersuchungen zu den ikonographischen und geistesgeschichtlichen Grundlagen seiner Werke zwischen den beiden Italienreisen*. Berlin, 1983.

Anzelewsky 1991 Anzelewsky, Fedja. *Albrecht Dürer: Das malerische Werk; Neuausgabe; Text- u. Tafelband*. Berlin, 1991.

Arad 2020 Arad, Peninah. *Christian Maps of the Holy Land: Images and Meanings*. Turnhout, 2020.

Armstrong 1996 Armstrong, Lilian. "Benedetto Bordon, 'Miniator,' and Cartography in Early Sixteenth-Century Venice." *Imago Mundi* 48 (1996), pp. 65–92.

Ashcroft 2017 Ashcroft, Jeffrey. *Albrecht Dürer: Documentary Biography; Dürer's Personal and Aesthetic Writings; Words on Pictures; Family, Legal and Business Documents; The Artist in the Writings of Contemporaries*. Edited, translated, and with commentary by Jeffrey Ashcroft. 2 vols. New Haven, CT, 2017.

Asmussen 2016 Asmussen, Tina. "The Kux as a Site of Meditation: Economic Practices and Material Desires in the Early Modern German Mining Industry." In Burghartz, Burkart, and Göttler 2016, pp. 159–82.

Asmussen 2020 Asmussen, Tina. "Spirited Metals and the Oeconomy of Early Modern European Mining." *Earth Sciences History* 39 (2020), pp. 371–88.

Astorga Poblete 2021 Astorga Poblete, Daniel. "Tiempo y espacio en el plano de Tenochtitlan de 1524." *Revista de Estudios Hispánicos* 55, no. 3 (2021), pp. 727–51.

Astorga Poblete 2025 Astorga Poblete, Daniel. "El Nuevo Mundo iluminado para el Archiduque Fernando: El Plano de Tenochtitlan de 1524 en la Biblioteca Nacional de Austria." *Hipogrifo* 13, no. 2 (2025) (forthcoming).

Asutay-Effenberger and Rehm 2009 Asutay-Effenberger, Neslihan, and Ulrich Rehm, eds. *Sultan Mehmet II: Eroberer Konstantinopels – Patron der Künste*. Cologne, Weimar, and Vienna, 2009, pp. 59–75.

Augustyn and Söding 2021 Augustyn, Wolfgang, and Ulrich Söding, eds. *Bildnis – Memoria – Repräsentation: Beiträge zur Erinnerungskultur im Mittelalter und in der Frühen Neuzeit*. Veröffentlichungen des Zentralinstituts für Kunstgeschichte in München 56. Passau, 2021.

Augustyn and Teget-Welz 2018 Augustyn, Wolfgang, and Manuel Teget-Welz, eds. *Hans Burgkmair: Neue Forschungen*. Passau, 2018.

Aurenhammer and Bohde 2015 Aurenhammer, Hans, and Daniela Bohde, eds. *Räume der Passion: Raumvisionen, Erinnerungsorte und Topographien des Leidens Christi in Mittelalter und Früher Neuzeit*. Bern, 2015.

Aveni, Calnek, and Hartung 1988 Aveni, Anthony, Edward E. Calnek, and Horst Hartung. "Myth, Environment, and the Orientation of the Templo Mayor of Tenochtitlan." *American Antiquity* 53 (1988), pp. 287–309.

Avrin 2010 Avrin, Leila. *Scribes, Script, and Books: The Book Arts from Antiquity to the Renaissance*. Chicago, 2010.

Baader and Wolf 2010 Baader, Hannah, and Gerhard Wolf, eds. *Das Meer, der Tausch und die Grenzen der Repräsentation*. Zurich, 2010.

Baader and Wolf 2014 Baader, Hannah, and Gerhard Wolf. "Ästhetiken der Schwelle: Sieben Aspekte der Morphologie und Topologie von Hafenstädten im nachantiken Mittelmeerraum." In Ladstätter, Pirson, and Schmidts 2014, pp. 17–44.

Backmann 2010 Backmann, Sibylle. "Der Fondaco dei Tedeschi in Venedig: Inklusion und Exklusion oberdeutscher Kaufleute in Wirtschaft und Gesellschaft (1550–1650)." PhD diss., Universität Zürich, 2010.

Bailey 1999 Bailey, Gauvin Alexander. *Art on the Jesuit Missions in Asia and Latin America, 1542–1773*. Toronto, Buffalo, and London, 1999.

Barbe, Caselli, and Dantan 2019 Barbe, Françoise, Letizia Caselli, and Marie-Elsa Dantan, eds. *I rami smaltati detti veneziani del Rinascimento italiano / Les cuivres émaillés dits* *vénitiens de la Renaissance italienne.* 2 vols. Vol. 1, *Atti del convegno internazionale di studi / Actes du colloque international d'études.* Vol. 2, *Corpus delle opere nelle collezioni pubbliche e private / Corpus des œuvres en collections publiques et privées.* Milan, 2019.

Barzen 2011 Barzen, Rainer Josef. "Das Nürnberger Memorbuch / The Memorbook of Nuremberg: An Introduction." In *Corpus der Quellen zur mittelalterlichen Geschichte der Juden im Reichsgebiet*, edited by Alfred Haverkamp and Jörg R. Müller. 2011. http://www.medieval-ashkenaz.org/quellen/nuernberger-memorbuch/einleitung.html.

Bauernfeind 2009 Bauernfeind, Walter. "Jacob Welser (1468–1541) als 'homo novus' in der Reichsstadt Nürnberg." In Westermann and Welser 2009, pp. 225–54.

Bauernfeind 2018 Bauernfeind, Walter. "Totengedenken durch Stiftung von Altären, Seelmessen und Ewiglichtern in vorreformatorischer Zeit." *Norica: Berichte und Themen aus dem Stadtarchiv Nürnberg* 14 (2018), pp. 92–99.

Baumbauer 2014 Baumbauer, Benno. "Veit Wirsbergers Pappenheim-Retabel und seine Stellung in der niederländisch-oberrheinischen Hofkunst Kaiser Friedrichs III." In Fajt and Hörsch 2014, pp. 247–77.

Baumbauer 2019 Baumbauer, Benno. "'Die Vereinigung der Holzbildnerei und Malerkunst in ihrem höchsten Glanze'? Bildschnitzer in Kooperation mit der Wolgemut-Werkstatt." In Exh. cat. Nuremberg 2019b, pp. 101–11.

Baumbauer 2021 Baumbauer, Benno. *Die Kirche von Eichstätt unter Fürstbischof Wilhelm von Reichenau 1464–1496: Selbstverständnis und visuelle Repräsentation eines spätmittelalterlichen Hochstifts.* Studia Jagellonica Lipsiensia 21. Vienna, Cologne, and Weimar, 2021.

Baumgärtner 2014 Baumgärtner, Ingrid. *Fürstliche Koordination: Landesvermessung und Herrschaftsvisualisierung um 1600.* Schriften zur sächsischen Geschichte und Volkskunde 46. Leipzig, 2014.

Beach 1965 Beach, Milo Cleveland. "The Gulshan Album and Its European Sources." *Bulletin of the Museum of Fine Arts* 63, no. 332 (1965), pp. 63–91.

Becksmann 2005 Becksmann, Rüdiger, ed. *Glasmalerei im Kontext: Bildprogramme und Raumfunktionen.* Wissenschaftliche Beibände zum Anzeiger des Germanischen Nationalmuseums 25. Nuremberg, 2005.

Beer 2000 Beer, Helmut. "Herrentrinkstube." In Diefenbacher and Endres 2000, p. 441.

Behringer 2023 Behringer, Wolfgang. *Der große Aufbruch: Globalgeschichte der Frühen Neuzeit.* Munich, 2023.

Beier, Juckes, and Pinkus 2021 Beier, Christine, Tim Juckes, and Assaf Pinkus, eds. *How Do Images Work? Strategies of Visual Communication in Medieval Art: Proceedings from a Conference in Honour of Michael Viktor Schwarz.* Turnhout, 2021.

Beit-Arié 1985 Beit-Arié, Malachi, ed. *The Worms Mahzor: Introductory Volume Facsimile Edition.* London, 1985.

Bell 2015 Bell, Peter. "Alltägliches im Ereignis – Fremdes im Eigenen: Zigeunergenre bei Burgkmair, van Leyden und Bruegel." In Münch and Müller 2015, pp. 247–64.

Belting 2012 Belting, Hans. *Florenz und Bagdad: Eine westöstliche Geschichte des Blicks.* Munich, 2012.

Belting 2018 Belting, Hans. "A Venetian Artist at the Ottoman Court: An Encounter of Two Worlds." *Convivium* 5, no. 2 (2018), pp. 14–31.

Bendikowski 2016 Bendikowski, Tillmann. "Der Schatz der Neuen Welt: Wie die Europäer das Silber Amerikas raubten / The Treasures of the New World: How the Europeans Looted America's Silver." In Exh. cat. Lübeck 2016, pp. 16–25.

Bentley, Subrahmanyam, and Weisner-Hanks 2015 Bentley, Jerry H., Sanjay Subrahmanyam, and Merry E. Weisner-Hanks, eds. *The Construction of a Global World 1400–1800 CE: Foundations.* The Cambridge World History, vol. 6, no. 1. Cambridge, 2015.

Bergau 1871 Bergau, Rudolf. *Der Schöne Brunnen zu Nürnberg: Geschichte und Beschreibung.* Berlin, 1871.

Bergdolt 2011 Bergdolt, Klaus. *Deutsche in Venedig: Von den Kaisern des Mittelalters bis zu Thomas Mann.* Darmstadt, 2011.

Berger 2013 Berger, Frank. *Der Erdglobus des Johannes Schöner von 1515.* Kunststücke des historischen Museums Frankfurt 3. Frankfurt am Main, 2013.

Bergstraesser 1969 Bergstraesser, Dorothea. "Herberstein, Sigmund Freiherr von." *NDB* 8 (1969), pp. 579–80. https://www.deutsche-biographie.de/pnd118710656.html#ndbcontent.

Bernecker 2000 Bernecker, Walther L. "Nürnberg und die überseeische Expansion im 16. Jahrhundert." In Neuhaus 2000, pp. 185–218.

Bernecker and Pietschmann 2005 Bernecker, Walther L., and Horst Pietschmann. *Geschichte Spaniens: Von der frühen Neuzeit bis zur Gegenwart.* 4th ed. Stuttgart, 2005.

Besler 1616 Besler, Basilius. *Fasciculus rariorum et aspectu dignorum varii generis / quae collegit at suis impensis aeri ad vivum incidi curavit atque evulgavit Basilius Besler.* Nuremberg, 1616.

Bevilacqua and Pfeifer 2013 Bevilacqua, Alexander, and Helen Pfeifer. "Turquerie: Culture in Motion, 1650–1750." *Past & Present* 221 (2013), pp. 75–118.

Beyin et al. 2025 Beyin, Amanuel, et al. "Late Quaternary Human Occupation of the Kilwa Coast (Tanzania): OSL Ages and Paleoenvironmental Proxies from Isotope Geochemistry." *Journal of Archaeological Science: Reports* 61 (2025), p. 16.

Bezzel 1995 Bezzel, Irmgard. "News from Portugal in 1506 and 1507, as Printed by Johann Weissenburger in Nuremberg." In Flood and Kelly 1995, pp. 31–44.

Biedermann 2018 Biedermann, Zoltán. "Diplomatic Ivories: Sri Lankan Caskets and the Portuguese-Asian Exchange in the Sixteenth Century." In Biedermann, Gerritsen, and Riello 2018, pp. 88–118.

Biedermann, Gerritsen, and Riello 2018 Biedermann, Zoltán, Anne Gerritsen, and Giorgio Riello, eds. *Global Gifts: The Material Culture of Diplomacy in Early Modern Eurasia.* Cambridge, 2018.

Bieker, Kraus, and Schröder 2018 Bieker, Ulrike, Michael Kraus, and Ingo W. Schröder, eds. *Ich durfte den Jaguar am Waldrand sprechen: Festschrift für Mark Münzel zum 75. Geburtstag.* Marburg, 2018.

Biersack 2010 Biersack, Martin. *Mediterraner Kulturtransfer am Beginn der Neuzeit: Die Rezeption der italienischen Renaissance in Kastilien zur Zeit der Katholischen Könige.* Munich, 2010.

Bikker 2007 Bikker, Jonathan, ed. *Dutch Paintings of the Seventeenth Century in the Rijksmuseum Amsterdam.* Vol. 1, no. 1, *Artists Born between 1570 and 1600.* Amsterdam, 2007.

Billion et al. 2009 Billion, Philipp, et al., eds. *Weltbilder im Mittelalter: Perceptions of the World in the Middle Ages.* Bonn, 2009.

Blackbourn 2024 Blackbourn, David. *Die Deutschen in der Welt: Siedler, Händler, Philosophen; Eine globale Geschichte vom Mittelalter bis heute.* Munich, 2024.

Blick and Tekippe 2005 Blick, Sarah, and Rita Tekippe, eds. *Art and Architecture of the Late Medieval Pilgrimage in Northern Europe and the British Isles.* Studies in Medieval and Reformation Traditions 104. Leiden et al., 2005.

Bloch 1959 Bloch, Ernst. *Das Prinzip Hoffnung.* 5 vols. Frankfurt am Main, 1959.

Bobzin 2010 Bobzin, Hartmut. "Von Luther zu Rückert: Der Koran in Deutschland; Ein weiter Weg von der Polemik zur poetischen Übersetzung." *Akademie Aktuell: Zeitschrift der Bayerischen Akademie der Wissenschaften* 32 (2010), pp. 14–17.

Bock 2005 Bock, Sebastian. *Ova struthionis: Die Straußeneiobjekte in den Schatz-, Silber- und Kunstkammern Europas.* Freiburg im Breisgau et al., 2005.

Böckel 1990 Böckel, Annamaria. *Heilig-Geist in Nürnberg: Spitalstiftung und Aufbewahrungsort der Reichskleinodien.* Nürnberger Schriften 4. Nuremberg, 1990.

Böckem 2012 Böckem, Beate. "Der Frühe Dürer und Italien: Italienerfahrungen und Mobilitätsprozesse um 1500." In Exh. cat. Nuremberg 2012, pp. 52–64.

Böckem 2016 Böckem, Beate. *Jacopo de' Barbari: Inszenierung einer Künstlerpersönlichkeit;*

Künstlerschaft und Hofkultur um 1500. Studien zur Kunst 32. [PhD diss., Universität Basel, 2010.] Cologne, Weimar, and Vienna, 2016.

Bohms 2024 Bohms, Ingrid. *Vögel in der altägyptischen Literatur*. 2 vols. Berlin, 2024.

Bohn 2021 Bohn, Babette. *Women Artists, Their Patrons, and Their Publics in Early Modern Bologna*. University Park, PA, 2021.

Böning-Weis, Emmerling, and Hemmeter 1994 Böning-Weis, Susanne, Erwin Emmerling, and Karlheinz Hemmeter, eds. *Der heilige Alexius im Augsburger Maximilianmuseum*. Arbeitshefte des Bayerischen Landesamtes für Denkmalpflege 67. Munich, 1994.

Boone 2011 Boone, Elizabeth Hill. "This New World Now Revealed: Hernán Cortés and the Presentation of Mexico to Europe." *Word & Image: A Journal of Verbal/Visual Enquiry* 27 (2011), pp. 31–46.

Born 2024 Born, Robert. "Zwischen Faszination und Furcht: Orientbilder im Spätmittelalter und in der Frühen Neuzeit." In Exh. cat. Heidelberg 2024, pp. 49–69.

Born and Jagodzinski 2014 Born, Robert, and Sabine Jagodzinski, eds. *Türkenkriege und Adelskultur in Ostmitteleuropa vom 16. bis zum 18. Jahrhundert*. Studia Jagellonica Lipsiensia 14. Ostfildern, 2014.

Bornfleth 1989 Bornfleth, Elisabeth, ed. *Das Gewerbemuseum der LGA im Germanischen Nationalmuseum*. Nuremberg, 1989.

Borobia 2008 Borobia, Mar, ed. *El siglo de Durero: Problemas historiográficos*. Madrid, 2008.

Borowka-Clausberg 1999 Borowka-Clausberg, Beate. *Balthasar Sprenger und der frühneuzeitliche Reisebericht*. [PhD diss., Universität Kassel, 1996.] Munich, 1999.

Borrelli 2019 Borrelli, Luciano. "L'araldica nei rami smaltati detti veneziani del Rinascimento italiano." In Barbe, Caselli, and Dantan 2019, vol. 2, pp. 23–47.

Bracker 1997 Bracker, Jörger, eds. *Bauen nach der Natur – Palladio: Die Erben Palladios in Nordeuropa*. Ostfildern, 1997.

Braun 1982 Braun, Karl, ed. *"Sie suchen nach dem Gold wie Schweine": Die Eroberung Mexiko-Tenochtitlans aus indianischer Sicht; Zusammengestellt und bearbeitet nach Bildern und Texten von Bernardino de Sahagún*. Tübingen, 1982.

Bräunlein 2018 Bräunlein, Peter J. "Hieronymus Köler d. Ä. (1507–1573) und die Neue Welt: Eine imaginäre Begegnung." In Bieker, Kraus, and Schröder 2018, pp. 309–58.

Bräutigam 1961 Bräutigam, Günther. "Gmünd – Prag – Nürnberg: Die Nürnberger Frauenkirche und der Prager Parlerstil vor 1360." *Jahrbuch der Berliner Museen* 3 (1961), pp. 38–75.

Brielle et al. 2023 Brielle, Esther S., et al. "Entwined African and Asian Genetic Roots of Medieval Peoples of the Swahili Coast." *Nature* 615 (2023), pp. 866–73. https://doi.org/10.1038/s41586-023-05754-w.

Briesemeister 1992 Briesemeister, Dietrich. "Die frühe Verarbeitung von Nachrichten über die 'Neue Welt'." *Weimarer Beiträge* 38 (1992), pp. 196–213.

Brotton 2014 Brotton, Jerry. *Die Geschichte der Welt in zwölf Karten*. 2nd ed. Munich, 2014.

Bruck 1903 Bruck, Robert. *Friedrich der Weise als Förderer der Kunst*. Strasbourg, 1903.

Brückner 2010 Brückner, Wolfgang. *Die Sprache christlicher Bilder*. Kulturgeschichtliche Spaziergänge im Germanischen Nationalmuseum 12. Nuremberg, 2010.

Bruhn and Hemken 2008 Bruhn, Matthias, and Kai-Uwe Hemken, eds. *Modernisierung des Sehens: Sehweisen zwischen Künsten und Medien*. Bielefeld, 2008.

Brühne 1992 Brühne, Wolfgang. "Kreuzzug und Asienhandel: Genua, Portugal und die europäische Expansion 1290–1520." *Periplus* 2 (1992), pp. 142–51.

Bruscoli 1999 Bruscoli, Francesco Guido. "Der Handel mit Seidenstoffen und Leinengeweben zwischen Florenz und Nürnberg in der ersten Hälfte des 16. Jahrhunderts." *MVGN* 86 (1999), pp. 81–113.

Budde 1987 Budde, Hendrik. "Jakob Welser, Kaufmann und Montanherr, 1468–1541." In Imhoff 1987a, pp. 79–81.

Budde 1996 Budde, Hendrik. *Die Kunstsammlung des Nürnberger Patriziers Willibald Imhoff unter besonderer Berücksichtigung der Werke Albrecht Dürers*. UNI PRESS Hochschulschriften 90. Münster, 1996.

Buisseret 2007 Buisseret, David. "Spanish Colonial Cartography, 1450–1700." In Woodward 2007, pp. 1143–71.

Bujok 2018 Bujok, Elke. "Illustrationen zu Balthasar Springers Ostiendienfahrt und Indianerdarstellungen." In Augustyn and Teget-Welz 2018, pp. 367–93.

Buono 2015 Buono, Amy J. "'Their Treasures are the Feathers of Birds': Tupinambá Featherwork and the Image of America." In Russo, Wolf, and Fane 2015, pp. 179–89.

Burghartz, Burkart, and Göttler 2016 Burghartz, Susanna, Lucas Burkart, and Christine Göttler, eds. *Sites of Meditation: Connected Histories of Places, Processes, and Objects in Europe and Beyond, 1450–1650*. Leiden and Boston, 2016.

Burghartz et al. 2021 Burghartz, Susanna, et al., eds. *Materialized Identities in Early Modern Culture, 1450–1750: Objects, Affects, Effects*. Amsterdam, 2021.

Burmester and Krekel 1998 Burmester, Andreas, and Christoph Krekel. "Von Dürers Farben." In Goldberg, Heimberg, and Schawe 1998, pp. 54–101.

Burschel 2009 Burschel, Peter. "Verlorene Söhne: Bilder osmanischer Gefangenschaft in der frühen Neuzeit." In Emich and Signori 2009, pp. 157–82.

Buttaroni and Musiał 2003 Buttaroni, Susanna, and Stanislaw Musiał, eds. *Ritualmord: Legenden in der europäischen Geschichte*. Vienna, Cologne, and Weimar, 2003.

Büttner 2008 Büttner, Nils. "Die 'Turckische Frawe' und ihr Bad: Wahrheit und Fiktion eines topischen Elements europäischer Orientreiseberichte." In Ilg 2008, pp. 95–133, 287–91.

Butts 2006 Butts, Barbara. "The Drawings of Hans Süss von Kulmbach." *Master Drawings* 44 (2006), pp. 127–212.

Carbach 1733 Carbach, Johann Jacob. *Nürnbergisches Zion, das ist wahrhaffte Beschreibung aller Kirchen und Schulen in- und außerhalb der Reichsstadt Nürnberg*. Nuremberg, 1733.

Cary and Warmington 1963 Cary, Max, and Eric H. Warmington. *The Ancient Explorers*. Harmondsworth, 1963.

Casson 1989 Casson, Lionel. *The Periplus Maris Erythreai: Text with Introduction, Translation, and Commentary*. Princeton, NJ, 1989.

Catalogue Glasgow 1882–83 *Catalogue of the Italian Art Loan Exhibition Held in the Corporation Galleries*. Glasgow, 1882–83.

Cattaneo 2010 Cattaneo, Angelo. "Venedig, 1450: Ozean – Meer – Seefahrt – Welthandelsrouten – Schiffbrüche." In Baader and Wolf 2010, pp. 263–92.

Cavaciocchi 2007 Cavaciocchi, Simonetta, ed. *Relazioni economiche tra Europa e mondo islamico secc. XIII–XVIII*. Grassina, 2007.

Cermann 2010 Cermann, Regina. "Über den Export deutschsprachiger Stundenbücher von Paris nach Nürnberg." *Codices manuscripti: Zeitschrift für Handschriftenkunde* 75 (2010), pp. 9–24.

Chakrabarty 2010 Chakrabarty, Dipesh. *Europa als Provinz: Perspektiven postkolonialer Geschichtsschreibung*. Frankfurt am Main, 2010.

Chinellato 2017 Chinellato, Alberto. "Il ponte di Rialto a Norimberga." In Sapio 2017, pp. 71–77.

Chittick 1968 Chittick, Neville. "Two Traditions About the Early History of Kilwa." *Azania: Archaeological Research in Africa* 3, no. 1 (1968), pp. 197–200.

Chittick 1974 Chittick, Neville. *Kilwa: An Islamic Trading City on East African Coast*. 2 vols. Nairobi, 1974.

Chroust and Proesler 1934 Chroust, Anton, and Hans Proesler, eds. *Das Handlungsbuch der Holzschuher in Nürnberg von 1304–1307*. Veröffentlichungen der Gesellschaft für Fränkische Geschichte, vol. 10, no. 1. Erlangen, 1934.

Chrzanowski 1986 Chrzanowski, Tadeusz. "Die Grabplastik in Polen zur Jagiellonenzeit." In Exh. cat. Schallaburg 1986, pp. 137–46.

Cipolla 1965 Cipolla, Carlo M. *Guns and Sails in the Early Phase of European Expansion 1400–1700*. London, 1965.

Classen 2003 Classen, Albrecht. "Die Iberische Halbinsel aus der Sicht eines humanistischen Nürnberger Gelehrten: Hieronymus Münzer, Itinerarium Hispanicum (1494–1495).” *Mitteilungen des Instituts für Österreichische Geschichtsforschung* 111, no. 4 (2003), pp. 317–40.

Clough 1995 Clough, Cecil H. “Art as Power in the Decoration of the Study of an Italian Renaissance Prince: The Case of Federico da Montefeltro.” *Artibus et Historiae* 16, no. 31 (1995), pp. 19–50.

Colin 1988 Colin, Susi. *Das Bild des Indianers im 16. Jahrhundert*. Beiträge zur Kunstgeschichte 102. Idstein, 1988.

Colin 1992 Colin, Susi. “Holzfäller und Kannibalen: Brasilianische Indianer auf frühen Karten.” In Exh. cat. Munich 1992, pp. 175–81.

Coquery-Vidrovitch and Mesnard 2019 Coquery-Vidrovitch, Catherine, and Éric Mesnard. *Être esclave. Afrique-Amériques. XVe–XIXe siècle*. Paris, 2019.

Cordez et al. 2018 Cordez, Philippe, et al., eds. *Object Fantasies: Experience and Creation*. Berlin and Boston, 2018.

Cordus 1561 Cordus, Valerius. *Annotationes in Pedacij Dioscoridis Anazarbei de Medica materia libros V. Straßburg*. Iosias Rihelius, 1561.

Cortés 1998 Cortés, Hernán. *Letters from Mexico*. Translated by Anthony Pagden. New York, 1998.

Coulon 2002 Coulon, Damien. *Barcelone et le grand commerce d’Orient au Moyen Âge: Un siècle de relations avec l’Égypte et la Syrie-Palestine (ca. 1330 – ca. 1430)*. Madrid and Barcelona, 2002.

Dackerman 2011 Dackerman, Susan. “The Rhinoceros – Dürer’s Indexical Fantasy: The Rhinoceros and Printmaking.” In Exh. cat. Cambridge, MA 2011, pp. 164–84.

Dackerman 2024 Dackerman, Susan. *Dürer’s Knots: Early European Print and the Islamic East*. Princeton, NJ, 2024.

Däubler-Hauschke and Weingärtner n.d. Däubler-Hauschke, Claudia, and Helge Weingärtner. “The Limoges Service of the Tucher Family.” *bavarikon*. https://www.bavarikon.de/object/bav:BSB-CMS-0000000000005994?lang=en.

Dekker 2007 Dekker, Elly. “Globes in Renaissance Europe.” In Harley 2007, pp. 135–73.

Denzer 2005 Denzer, Jörg. *Die Konquista der Augsburger Welser-Gesellschaft in Südamerika, 1528–1556: Historische Rekonstruktion, Historiografie und lokale Erinnerungskultur in Kolumbien und Venezuela*. Munich, 2005.

Denzler 2023 Denzler, Alexander. *Straßen im 16. Jahrhundert: Erhalt – Nutzung – Wahrnehmung*. Ding, Materialität, Geschichte 5. Cologne, 2023.

Derschau and Becker 1810 Becker, Rudolf Zacharias, ed. *Holzschnitte alter deutscher Meister in den Original-Platten gesammelt von Hans Albrecht von Derschau: Als ein Beitrag zur Kunstgeschichte herausgegeben & mit einer Abhandlung über die Holzschneidekunst & deren Schicksale begleitet von Rud. Zachar. Becker*. Vol. 2. Gotha, 1810.

Dettenthaler 1976 Dettenthaler, Josef. “Hans Springinklee als Maler.” *MVGN* 63 (1976), pp. 145–82.

Dharampal-Frick 1994 Dharampal-Frick, Gita. *Indien im Spiegel deutscher Quellen der frühen Neuzeit (1500–1750): Studien zu einer interkulturellen Konstellation*. Tübingen, 1994.

Di Carlo et al. 2024 Di Carlo, Laura, et al., eds. *Andere Ästhetik meets Andere Ästhetik: Visualisierungen von Antiken nördlich der Alpen in der frühneuzeitlichen Druckgraphik*. Andere Ästhetik: Studien 5. Berlin and Boston, 2024.

Dickel 2014 Dickel, Hans, ed. *Zeichnen seit Dürer: Die süddeutschen und schweizerischen Zeichnungen der Renaissance in der Universitätsbibliothek Erlangen*. Petersberg, 2014.

Diefenbacher 2000 Diefenbacher, Michael. “Fernhandelsstraßen.” In Diefenbacher and Endres 2000, pp. 281–82.

Diefenbacher and Endres 2000 Diefenbacher, Michael, and Rudolf Endres, eds. *Stadtlexikon Nürnberg*. 2nd ed. Nuremberg, 2000.

Diener-Schönberg 1905 Diener-Schönberg, Alfons. “Knebel an Jagdblankwaffen.” *Zeitschrift für Historische Waffenkunde* 3, no. 12 (1905), pp. 235–57.

Dienst 2002 Dienst, Barbara. *Der Kosmos des Peter Flötner: Eine Bildwelt der Renaissance*. Munich, 2002.

Dilherr 1662 Dilherr, Johann Michael. *Propheten-Schul: Das ist Christliche Anweisung zu Gottseliger Betrachtung des Lebens und der Lehre Heiliger Propheten Altes Testaments ...* . Nuremberg, 1662.

Dix and Schübel 2020 Dix, Annika, and Birgit Schübel. “Blumen, Eidechsen und ein Schiff: Farbfassungen auf Goldschmiedearbeiten im Germanischen Nationalmuseum.” In Witting and Weinhold 2020, pp. 54–69.

Dodgson 1911 Dodgson, Campbell. *Catalogue of Early German and Flemish Woodcuts Preserved in the Department of Prints and Drawings in the British Museum*. Vol. 2. London, 1911.

Doering 1901 Doering, Oscar. *Des Augsburger Patriciers Philipp Hainhofer Reisen nach Innsbruck und Dresden*. Vienna, 1901.

Döring 2013 Döring, Karoline Dominika. *Türkenkrieg und Medienwandel im 15. Jahrhundert*. Husum, 2013.

Dyballa 2014 Dyballa, Katrin. *Georg Pencz: Künstler zu Nürnberg*. Jahresgabe des Deutschen Vereins für Kunstwissenschaft 2013. Berlin, 2014.

Earle and Lowe 2005 Earle, Thomas F., and Kate J. P. Lowe, eds. *Black Africans in Renaissance Europe*. Cambridge et al., 2005.

Eberl 2021 Eberl, Oliver. *Naturzustand und Barbarei: Begründung und Kritik staatlicher Ordnung im Zeichen des Kolonialismus*. Hamburg, 2021.

Egyeki-Szabó 2008 Egyeki-Szabó, Tamás. *Beckenschlägerschüsseln (15.–16. Jahrhundert)*. Budapest, 2008.

Eichberger 2002 Eichberger, Dagmar. *Leben mit Kunst, Wirken durch Kunst: Sammelwesen und Hofkunst unter Margarete von Österreich, Regentin der Niederlande*. Burgundica 5. Turnhout, 2002.

Eikelmann 1994 Eikelmann, Renate. “Der heilige Alexius von Sebastian Loscher.” In Böning-Weis, Emmerling, and Hemmeter 1994, pp. 7–23.

Eikelmann and Bauer 2006 Eikelmann, Renate, and Ingolf Bauer, eds. *Das Bayerische Nationalmuseum, 1855–2005; 150 Jahre Sammeln, Forschen, Ausstellen*. Munich, 2006.

Eiximenis 1496 Eiximenis, Francesc. *Libro de la vida de nuestro senor ihesu christo ...* . Granada, 1496.

Elkiss 1973 Elkiss, Terry H. “Kilwa Kisiwani: The Rise of an East African City-State.” *African Studies Review* 16, no. 1 (1973), pp. 119–30.

Elliott 1989 Elliott, John H. *Spain and Its World 1500–1700: Selected Essays*. New Haven, CT, and London, 1989.

Emich and Signori 2009 Emich, Birgit, and Gabriela Signori, eds. *Kriegs/Bilder in Mittelalter und Früher Neuzeit*. Zeitschrift für Historische Forschung, supplement no. 42. Berlin, 2009.

Enenkel and Zittel 2013 Enenkel, Karl, and Claus Zittel, eds. *Die Vita als Vermittlerin von Wissenschaft und Werk: Form- und Funktionsanalytische Untersuchungen zu frühneuzeitlichen Biographien von Gelehrten, Wissenschaftlern, Schriftstellern und Künstlern*. Scientia universalis, vol. 1, no. 1. Münster, 2013.

Erffa 1976 Erffa, Hans Martin von. “Der Nürnberger Stadtpatron auf italienischen Gemälden.” *Mitteilungen des Kunsthistorischen Institutes in Florenz* 20, no. 1 (1976), pp. 1–12.

Erhard and Ramminger 1998 Erhard, Andreas, and Eva Ramminger, eds. *Die Meerfahrt: Balthasar Springers Reise zur Pfefferküste; Mit einem Faksimile des Buches von 1509*. Innsbruck, 1998.

Erichsen 2024 Erichsen, Johannes. “Beobachtungen zum sogenannten Trachtenbuch des Christoph Weiditz.” *Anzeiger des Germanischen Nationalmuseums* 2017 (2024), pp. 30–74.

Eser 2002 Eser, Thomas. “Ein Leuchter, drei Rätsel, ein Kartenspiel: Nürnberger Kunst in Italien.” In Exh. cat. Nuremberg 2002, pp. 45–71.

Eser 2010a Eser, Thomas. “Gewürze auf dem Behaim-Globus: Venture-Capital-Akquise um 1500.” In Holl 2010, pp. 134–45.

Eser 2010b Eser, Thomas. “Weltbild in Bewegung: Zwei Globen und ein Silberschiff.” In Hess and Hirschfelder 2010, pp. 32–45.

Eser 2013 Eser, Thomas. “Der Nürnberger Schöner-Globus von 1520.” In Berger 2013, pp. 74–79. http://archiv.ub.uni-heidelberg.de/artdok/volltexte/2015/3065.

Eser 2014 Eser, Thomas. *Die älteste Taschenuhr der Welt? Der Henlein-Uhrenstreit.* Kulturgeschichtliche Spaziergänge im Germanischen Nationalmuseum 16. Nuremberg, 2014.

Esposito 2003 Esposito, Anna. "Das Stereotyp des Ritualmordes in den Trienter Prozessen und die Verehrung des 'Seligen' Simone." In Buttaroni and Musiał 2003, pp. 131–72.

Essenwein 1877 Essenwein, August von. *Quellen zur Geschichte der Feuerwaffen.* Leipzig, 1877.

Essenwein 1883 Essenwein, August von. "Trabantenwaffen des 16.–18. Jahrhunderts." *Anzeiger für Kunde der deutschen Vorzeit*, new series 30, no. 1 (1883), cols. 1–6.

Exh. cat. Ansbach 2022 *Typisch Franken? Katalog zur Bayerischen Landesausstellung 2022.* Edited by Christof Paulus et al. Exh. cat. Haus der Bayerischen Geschichte, Ansbach. Regensburg, 2022.

Exh. cat. Antwerp 1991 *America: Bride of the Sun; 500 years Latin America and the Low Countries.* Edited by J. Fred Muggs, Ine Pisters, and Frank Vanhaecke. Exh. cat. Royal Museum of Fine Arts, Antwerp. Ghent, 1991.

Exh. cat. Augsburg 1955 *Ausstellung Augsburger Renaissance.* Compiled by Norbert Lieb, Hannelore Müller, and Günther Thiem. Exh. cat. Schaezler-Haus Maximilianstrasse, Augsburg. Augsburg, 1955.

Exh. cat. Augsburg 1997 *"… wider Laster und Sünde": Augsburgs Weg in der Reformation.* Edited by Josef Kirmeier, Wolfgang Jahn, and Evamaria Brockhoff. Exh. cat. St. Anna, Augsburg. Augsburg, 1997.

Exh. cat. Augsburg 2019 *Maximilian I. 1459–1519: Kaiser. Ritter. Bürger zu Augsburg.* Edited by Heidrun Lange-Krach. Exh. cat. Maximilianmuseum, Augsburg. Regensburg, 2019.

Exh. cat. Baltimore and Princeton 2012 *Revealing the African Presence in Renaissance Europe.* Edited by Joaneath Spicer. Exh. cat. The Walters Art Museum, Baltimore, and Princeton University Art Museum, Princeton, NJ. Baltimore, 2012.

Exh. cat. Berlin 1982 *Mythen der Neuen Welt: Zur Entdeckungsgeschichte Lateinamerikas.* Edited by Karl-Heinz Kohl. Exh. cat. Martin-Gropius-Bau, West Berlin. Berlin, 1982.

Exh. cat. Berlin 1993 *Japan und Europa: 1543–1929.* Edited by Doris Croissant and Lothar Ledderose. Exh. cat. Martin-Gropius-Bau, Berlin. Berlin, 1993.

Exh. cat. Berlin 2007 *Novos Mundos – Neue Welten: Portugal und das Zeitalter der Entdeckungen.* Edited by Michael Kraus. Exh. cat. Deutsches Historisches Museum, Berlin. Berlin, 2007.

Exh. cat. Berlin 2023 *Dürer für Berlin: Eine Spurensuche im Kupferstichkabinett.* Edited by Michael Roth. Exh. cat. Kupferstichkabinett, Staatliche Museen zu Berlin. Berlin, 2023.

Exh. cat. Berlin and Karlsruhe 2015 *Double Vision: Albrecht Dürer / William Kentridge.* Edited by Klaus Krüger, Andreas Schallhorn, and Elke Anna Werner. Exh. cat. Kulturforum, Berlin, and Staatliche Kunsthalle, Karlsruhe. Berlin, 2015.

Exh. cat. Besançon, Colmar, and Dijon 2024 *Altdeutsche Malerei in den französischen Sammlungen (1370–1550).* Edited by Isabelle Dubois-Brinkmann and Aude Briau. Exh. cat. Musée des Beaux-Arts et d'Archéologie, Besançon, Musée Unterlinden, Colmar, and Musée des Beaux-Arts, Dijon. Dijon, 2024

Exh. cat. Bochum 1990 *Meisterwerke bergbaulicher Kunst vom 13. bis 19. Jahrhundert.* Edited by Rainer Slotta and Christoph Bartels. Exh. cat. Deutsches Bergbau-Museum, Bochum. Bochum, 1990.

Exh. cat. Braunschweig 2019 *Dressed for Success: Matthäus Schwarz; Ein Modetagebuch des 16. Jahrhunderts.* Edited by Martina Minning, Nadine Rottau, and Thomas Richter. Exh. cat. Herzog Anton Ulrich-Museum, Braunschweig. Dresden, 2019.

Exh. cat. Brussels 2000 *Âge d'or bruxellois: Tapisseries de la couronne d'Espagne.* Edited by Arlette Smolar-Meynart. Exh. cat. Cathédrale des Saints Michel et Gudule, Brussels. Brussels, 2000.

Exh. cat. Brussels and Kraków 2015 *The Sultan's World: The Ottoman Orient in Renaissance Art.* Exh. cat. Centre for Fine Arts, Brussels, and National Museum, Kraków. Ostfildern, 2015.

Exh. cat. Cambridge, MA 2011 *Prints and the Pursuit of Knowledge in Early Modern Europe.* Edited by Susan Dackerman. Exh. cat. Harvard Art Museums, Cambridge, MA. New Haven, CT, and London, 2011.

Exh. cat. Dresden and Bonn 1995 *Im Lichte des Halbmonds: Das Abendland und der türkische Orient.* Compiled by Alfred Auer et al. Exh. cat. Staatliche Kunstsammlungen Dresden, Dresden, and Kunst- und Ausstellungshalle der Bundesrepublik Deutschland, Bonn. Leipzig, 1995.

Exh. cat. Frankfurt 2013 *Dürer: Kunst, Künstler, Kontext.* Edited by Jochen Sander. Exh. cat. Städel Museum, Frankfurt am Main. Munich, 2013.

Exh. cat. Frankfurt 2019 *Meisterstücke – vom Handwerk der Maler.* Edited by Wolfgang P. Cilleßen and Andreas Tacke. Exh. cat. Historisches Museum, Frankfurt am Main. Frankfurt am Main, 2019.

Exh. cat. Frankfurt and Hamburg 2013 *Verwandlung der Welt: Die romantische Arabeske.* Edited by Werner Busch, Petra Maisak, and Sabine Weisheit. Exh. cat. Goethemuseum, Frankfurt am Main, and Kunsthalle, Hamburg. Petersberg, 2013.

Exh. cat. Frankfurt and Vienna 2014 *Fantastische Welten: Albrecht Altdorfer und das Expressive in der Kunst um 1500.* Edited by Stefan Roller and Jochen Sander. Exh. cat. Städel-Museum, Frankfurt am Main, and Kunsthistorisches Museum, Vienna. Munich, 2014.

Exh. cat. Frankfurt and Vienna 2023 *Renaissance im Norden: Holbein, Burgkmair und die Zeit der Fugger.* Edited by Guido Messling and Jochen Sander. Exh. cat. Städel Museum, Frankfurt am Main, and Kunsthistorisches Museum, Vienna. Munich, 2023.

Exh. cat. Füssen and Augsburg 2010 *Bayern – Italien.* Edited by Rainhard Riepertinger et al. Exh. cat. Ehemaliges Kloster St. Mang, Füssen, Maximilianmuseum, Augsburg, and Staatliches Textil- und Industriemuseum, Augsburg. Veröffentlichungen zur Bayerischen Geschichte und Kultur 58. Augsburg, 2010.

Exh. cat. Göttingen 2013 *Abgekupfert: Roms Antiken in den Reproduktionsmedien der Frühen Neuzeit.* Edited by Manfred Luchterhandt, Lisa Roemer, Johannes Bergemann, and Daniel Graepler. Exh. cat. Kunstsammlung und Sammlung der Gipsabdrücke, Universität Göttingen. Petersberg, 2013.

Exh. cat. Heidelberg 2024 *Die Erfindung des Fremden in der Kunst.* Compiled by Julia Carrasco. Exh. cat. Kurpfälzisches Museum, Heidelberg. Petersberg, 2024.

Exh. cat. Hildesheim and Munich 1986 *Glanz und Untergang des alten Mexiko: Die Azteken und ihre Vorläufer.* Edited by Arne Eggebrecht. Exh. cat. Roemer- und Pelizaeus-Museum, Hildesheim, and Haus der Kunst, Munich. 2 vols. Mainz, 1986.

Exh. cat. Kiel 2013 *Münzen – Banknoten – Notgeld – Medaillen: Schätze aus dem Münzkabinett der Schleswig-Holsteinischen Landesbibliothek.* Edited by Jens Ahlers. Exh. cat. Schleswig-Holsteinische Landesbibliothek, Kiel. Kiel, 2013.

Exh. cat. Kraków 2018 *Mistrz i Katarzyna: Hans von Kulmbach i jego dzieła dla Krakowa.* Edited by Mirosław P. Kruk. Exh. cat. Nationalmuseum Krakau, Kraków. Kraków, 2018.

Exh. cat. Kronach 2022 *Renaissance in Franken: Hans von Kulmbach und die Kunst um Dürer.* Edited by Manuel Teget-Welz and Hans Dickel. Exh. cat. Fränkische Galerie, Kronach. Petersberg, 2022.

Exh. cat. Lisbon 2017 *A Cidade Global: Lisboa no Renascimento.* Edited by Annemarie Jordan Gschwend and Kate J. P. Lowe. Exh. cat. Museu Nacional de Arte Antiga, Lisbon. Lisbon, 2017.

Exh. cat. London, Berlin, and Bonn 2003 *Azteken.* Compiled by Jürgen Geiger. Exh. cat. Royal Academy of Arts, London, Martin-Gropius-Bau, Berlin, and Kunst- und Ausstellungshalle der Bundesrepublik Deutschland, Bonn. Cologne, 2003.

Exh. cat. London and Boston 2005 *Bellini and the East.* Edited by Caroline Campbell and Alan Chong. Exh. cat. The National Gallery, London, and Isabella Stewart Gardener Museum, Boston. London, 2005.

Exh. cat. Lübeck 2016 *Silberglanz und Silbergier: Der Silberschatz aus Bergen / Silver's Shine and Silver Greed: The Bergen Silver Treasure*. Edited by Felicia Sternfeld. Exh. cat. Europäisches Hansemuseum, Lübeck. Lübeck, 2016.

Exh. cat. Lüneburg and Stade 2020 *Pilgerspuren: Wege in den Himmel; Von Lübeck an das Ende der Welt*. Compiled by Hartmut Kühne. Exh. cat. Museum Lüneburg, Lüneburg, and Museum Schwedenspeicher, Stade. Petersberg, 2020.

Exh. cat. Madrid 2006 *El trazo oculto: Dibujos subyacentes en pinturas de los siglos XV y XVI*. Edited by Gabriele Finaldi and Carmen Garrido. Exh. cat. Museo Nacional del Prado, Madrid. Madrid, 2006.

Exh. cat. Madrid 2011 *La huella de Leonardo en España: Los Hernandos y Leonardo*. Compiled by Pedro Miguel Ibáñez Martínez. Exh. cat. Canal de Isabel II. Comunidad de Madrid, Madrid. Madrid, 2011.

Exh. cat. Magdeburg 2008 *Spektakel der Macht: Rituale im alten Europa 800–1800*. Edited by Barbara Stollberg-Rilinger. Exh. cat. Kulturhistorisches Museum, Magdeburg. Darmstadt, 2008.

Exh. cat. Manchester 2023 *Albrecht Dürer's Material World*. Edited by Edward H. Wouk and Jennifer Spinks. Exh. cat. Whitworth Art Gallery, The University of Manchester. Manchester, 2023.

Exh. cat. Massa Marittima 2024 *Il Sassetta e il suo tempo: Uno sguardo sull'arte senese del primo Quattrocento*. Edited by Alessandro Bagnoli. Exh. cat. Museo di San Pietro all'Orto, Massa Marittima. Florence, 2024.

Exh. cat. Memmingen 1998 *Geld und Glaube: Leben in evangelischen Reichsstädten*. Edited by Wolfgang Jahn et al. Exh. cat. Antonierhaus, Memmingen. Veröffentlichungen zur Bayerischen Geschichte und Kultur 37. Munich, 1998.

Exh. cat. Munich 1984 *Wallfahrt kennt keine Grenzen*. Edited by Thomas Raff. Exh. cat. Bayerisches Nationalmuseum, Munich. Regensburg, 1984.

Exh. cat. Munich 1992 *America: Das frühe Bild der Neuen Welt*. Exh. cat. Bayerische Staatsbibliothek, Munich. Compiled by Hans Wolff. Munich, 1992.

Exh. cat. Munich 2014 *Welten des Wissens: Die Bibliothek und die Weltchronik des Nürnberger Arztes Hartmann Schedel (1440–1514)*. Compiled by Bettina Wagner. Exh. cat. Bayerische Staatsbibliothek, Munich. Munich, 2014.

Exh. cat. Munich 2024 *Traumschiffe der Renaissance: Schiffspokale und Seefahrt um 1600*. Edited by Frank Matthias Kammel. Exh. cat. Bayerisches Nationalmuseum, Munich. Munich, 2024.

Exh. cat. New York 1970 *Before Cortés: Sculpture of Middle America*. Compiled by Elizabeth Kennedy Easby and John F. Scott. Exh. cat. The Metropolitan Museum of Art, New York. New York, 1970.

Exh. cat. New York 2011 *Wonder of the Age: Master Painters of India, 1100–1900*. Edited by John Guy and Jorrit Britschgi. Exh. cat. The Metropolitan Museum of Art, New York. New York and New Haven, CT, 2011.

Exh. cat. New York 2015 *The World in Play: Luxury Cards 1430–1540*. Compiled by Timothy B. Husband. Exh. cat. The Metropolitan Museum of Art, New York. New York, 2015.

Exh. cat. Nuremberg 1971 *Albrecht Dürer: 1471–1971*. Edited by Leonie von Wilckens. Exh. cat. Germanisches Nationalmuseum, Nuremberg. Nuremberg, 1971.

Exh. cat. Nuremberg 1979 *Reformation in Nürnberg: Umbruch und Bewahrung*. Exh. cat. Germanisches Nationalmuseum, Nuremberg. Vol. 1. Schriften des Kunstpädagogischen Zentrums im Germanischen Nationalmuseum Nürnberg 9. Nuremberg, 1979.

Exh. cat. Nuremberg 1984 *Aus dem Wirtshaus zum Wilden Mann: Funde aus dem mittelalterlichen Nürnberg*. Edited by Rainer Kahsnitz and Rainer Brandl. Exh. cat. Germanisches Nationalmuseum, Nuremberg. Nuremberg, 1984.

Exh. cat. Nuremberg 1985 *Wenzel Jamnitzer und die Nürnberger Goldschmiedekunst 1500–1700*. Compiled by Klaus Pechstein et al. Exh. cat. Germanisches Nationalmuseum, Nuremberg. Munich, 1985.

Exh. cat. Nuremberg 1986 *Der Traum vom Raum: Gemalte Architektur aus 7 Jahrhunderten; Eine Ausstellung der Albrecht-Dürer-Gesellschaft Nürnberg in Zusammenarbeit mit der Kunsthalle Nürnberg*. Edited by Kurt Löcher. Exh. cat. Kunsthalle Nürnberg, Nürnberg. Marburg, 1986.

Exh. cat. Nuremberg 1989 *650 Jahre Hospital zum Heiligen Geist in Nürnberg 1339–1989*. Edited by Michael Diefenbacher. Exh. cat. Stadtarchiv Nürnberg. Nuremberg, 1989.

Exh. cat. Nuremberg 1992 *FOCUS BEHAIM-GLOBUS*. Edited by Gerhard Bott. Exh. cat. Germanisches Nationalmuseum, Nuremberg. 2 vols. Nuremberg, 1992.

Exh. cat. Nuremberg 1993 *Altdeutsche Spielkarten, 1500–1650*. Compiled by Detlef Hoffmann. Exh. cat. Germanisches Nationalmuseum, Nuremberg. Nuremberg, 1993.

Exh. cat. Nuremberg 1994 *Das Praunsche Kabinett: Kunst des Sammelns; Meisterwerke von Dürer bis Carracci*. Edited by Katrin Achilles-Syndram. Exh. cat. Germanisches Nationalmuseum, Nuremberg. Nuremberg, 1994.

Exh. cat. Nuremberg 1996 *Dreiecks-Verhältnisse: Architektur- und Ingenieurzeichnungen aus vier Jahrhunderten*. Edited by G. Ulrich Großmann. Exh. cat. Germanisches Nationalmuseum, Nuremberg. Nuremberg, 1996.

Exh. cat. Nuremberg 2000a *Albrecht Dürer – ein Künstler in seiner Stadt*. Edited by Matthias Mende. Exh. cat. Stadtmuseum Fembohaus, Nuremberg. Nuremberg, 2000.

Exh. cat. Nuremberg 2000b *Spiegel der Seligkeit: Privates Bild und Frömmigkeit im Spätmittelalter*. Edited by Frank Matthias Kammel. Exh. cat. Germanisches Nationalmuseum, Nuremberg. Nuremberg, 2000.

Exh. cat. Nuremberg 2002 *Quasi Centrum Europae: Europa kauft in Nürnberg 1400–1800*. Edited by Hermann Maué et al. Exh. cat. Germanisches Nationalmuseum, Nuremberg. Nuremberg, 2002.

Exh. cat. Nuremberg 2004 *Faszination Meisterwerk: Dürer – Rembrandt – Riemenschneider*. Edited by G. Ulrich Großmann. Exh. cat. Germanisches Nationalmuseum, Nuremberg. Nuremberg, 2004.

Exh. cat. Nuremberg 2007 *Verborgene Schönheit: Spätgotische Schätze aus der Klarakirche in Nürnberg*. Compiled by Frank Matthias Kammel. Exh. cat. Germanisches Nationalmuseum, Nuremberg. Nuremberg, 2007.

Exh. cat. Nuremberg 2008a *100 Meisterzeichnungen aus der Graphischen Sammlung der Universität Erlangen-Nürnberg*. Edited by Rainer Schoch. Exh. cat. Germanisches Nationalmuseum, Nuremberg. Nuremberg, 2008.

Exh. cat. Nuremberg 2008b *Enthüllungen: Restaurierte Kunstwerke von Riemenschneider bis Kremser Schmidt*. Compiled by Frank Matthias Kammel. Exh. cat. Germanisches Nationalmuseum, Nuremberg. Nuremberg, 2008.

Exh. cat. Nuremberg 2012 *Der frühe Dürer*. Edited by Daniel Hess and Thomas Eser. Exh. cat. Germanisches Nationalmuseum, Nuremberg. Nuremberg, 2012.

Exh. cat. Nuremberg 2013 *Kaiser – Reich – Stadt: Die Kaiserburg Nürnberg*. Edited by Katharina Heinemann. Exh. cat. Bayerische Verwaltung der Staatlichen Schlösser, Gärten und Seen, Kaiserburg Nürnberg, Nuremberg. Nuremberg, 2013.

Exh. cat. Nuremberg 2014a *Peter Flötner: Renaissance in Nürnberg*. Edited by Thomas Schauerte and Manuel Teget-Welz. Exh. cat. Museen der Stadt Nürnberg, Nuremberg. Petersberg, 2014.

Exh. cat. Nuremberg 2014b *Von nah und fern: Zuwanderer in die Reichsstadt Nürnberg*. Edited by Brigitte Korn, Michael Diefenbacher, and Steven M. Zahlaus. Exh. cat. Stadtmuseum Fembohaus, Nuremberg. Petersberg, 2014.

Exh. cat. Nuremberg 2015a *Deutschlands Auge & Ohr: Nürnberg als Medienzentrum der Reformationszeit*. Edited by Thomas Schauerte. Exh. cat. Stadtmuseum Fembohaus, Nuremberg. Nuremberg, 2015.

Exh. cat. Nuremberg 2015b *In Mode: Kleider und Bilder aus Renaissance und Frühbarock*. Edited by Jutta Zander-Seidel. Exh. cat. Germanisches Nationalmuseum, Nuremberg. Nuremberg, 2015.

Exh. cat. Nuremberg 2015c *In Nürnberg illuminiert: Die Reichsstadt als Zentrum der Buchmalerei im Zeitalter Johannes Gutenbergs*. Compiled by Christine Sauer. Exh. cat. Stadtbibliothek Nürnberg, Nuremberg. Zehn Stationen zur mitteleuropäischen Buchmalerei 7. Nuremberg, 2015.

Exh. cat. Nuremberg 2017 *Luther, Kolumbus und die Folgen: Welt im Wandel 1500–1600*. Edited by Stephanie Armer and Thomas Eser. Exh. cat. Germanisches Nationalmuseum, Nuremberg. Nuremberg, 2017.

Exh. cat. Nuremberg 2018 *Adam Kraft: Der Kreuzweg*. Edited by Frank Matthias Kammel. Exh. cat. Germanisches Nationalmuseum, Nuremberg. Nuremberg, 2018.

Exh. cat. Nuremberg 2019a *Helden Märtyrer Heilige: Wege ins Paradies*. Edited by Daniel Hess and Markus Prummer. Exh. cat. Germanisches Nationalmuseum, Nuremberg. Nuremberg, 2019.

Exh. cat. Nuremberg 2019b *Michael Wolgemut: Mehr als Dürers Lehrer*. Edited by Benno Baumbauer, Dagmar Hirschfelder, and Manuel Teget-Welz. Exh. cat. Albrecht-Dürer-Haus, Nuremberg, Germanisches Nationalmuseum, Nuremberg, Museum Tucherschloss, Nuremberg, and Stadtkirchen in Nuremberg and Schwabach. Regensburg, 2019.

Exh. cat. Nuremberg 2024 *Hello Nature: Wie wollen wir zusammenleben?* Edited by Susanne Thürigen, Daniel Hess, and Alexandra Böhm. Exh. cat. Germanisches Nationalmuseum, Nuremberg. Nuremberg, 2024.

Exh. cat. Nuremberg and New York 1986 *Nürnberg 1300–1550: Kunst der Gotik und Renaissance*. Edited by Gerhard Bott. Exh. cat. Germanisches Nationalmuseum, Nuremberg, and The Metropolitan Museum of Art, New York. Munich, 1986.

Exh. cat. Potsdam 2013 *Europa Jagellonica: Kunst und Kultur Mitteleuropas unter der Herrschaft der Jagiellonen 1386–1572*. Edited by Jiří Fajt. Exh. cat. Haus der Brandenburgisch-Preußischen Geschichte, Potsdam. Potsdam, 2013.

Exh. cat. Prague 2006 *Albrecht Dürer: The Feast of the Rose Garlands 1505–2006*. Edited by Olga Kotková. Exh. cat. Nationalgalerie, Prague. Prague, 2006.

Exh. cat. Rome 2024 *Roma pittrice: Artiste al lavoro tra XVI e XIX secolo*. Edited by Ilaria Miarelli Mariani and Raffaella Morselli. Exh. cat. Palazzo Braschi, Rome. Rome, 2024.

Exh. cat. Rome and Berlin 2008 *Raffaels Grazie – Michelangelos Furor: Sebastiano del Piombo 1485–1547*. Edited by Bernd Wolfgang Lindemann and Claudio Strinati. Exh. cat. Palazzo di Venezia, Rome, and Gemäldegalerie, Berlin. Berlin, 2008.

Exh. cat. Schallaburg 1977 *Das Wiener Bürgerliche Zeughaus: Rüstungen und Waffen aus fünf Jahrhunderten*. Edited by Günter Düriegl. Exh. cat. Schallaburg. Vienna, 1977.

Exh. cat. Schallaburg 1986 *Polen im Zeitalter der Jagiellonen 1386–1572*. Edited by Franciszek Stolot. Exh. cat. Schollach, Schallaburg. Vienna, 1986.

Exh. cat. Schallaburg 2018 *Byzanz und der Westen: 1000 Jahre vergessene Geschichte*. Edited by Falko Daim and Dominik Heher. Exh. cat. Schollach, Schallaburg. Schallaburg, 2018.

Exh. cat. Siena 2010 *Da Jacopo della Quercia a Donatello: Le arti a Siena nel primo Rinascimento*. Edited by Max Seidel. Exh. cat. Santa Maria della Scala, Siena, Opera della Metropolitana, Siena, and Pinacoteca Nazionale, Siena. Milan, 2010.

Exh. cat. Stuttgart 2024 *Carpaccio, Bellini und die Frührenaissance in Venedig*. Edited by Annette Hojer and Christine Follmann. Exh. cat. Staatsgalerie Stuttgart. Munich, 2024.

Exh. cat. Stuttgart, Vienna, and Leiden 2019 *Azteken: Edited by Doris Kurella, Martin Berger, Inés de Castro*. Exh. cat. Linden-Museum Stuttgart, Weltmuseum Wien, Vienna, and Museum Volkenkunde, Leiden. Munich, 2019.

Exh. cat. Tübingen 2014 *1514: Macht Gewalt Freiheit; Der Vertrag zu Tübingen in Zeiten des Umbruchs*. Edited by Götz Adriani and Andrea Schmauder. Exh. cat. Kunsthalle Tübingen. Tübingen, 2014.

Exh. cat. Tübingen 2018 *Antike im Druck: Zwischen Imagination und Empirie*. Edited by Johannes Lipps and Anna Pawlak. Exh. cat. Museum der Universität Tübingen (MUT). Tübingen, 2018.

Exh. cat. Ulm 1995 *Bilder aus Licht und Farbe: Meisterwerke spätgotischer Glasmalerei; "Straßburger Fenster" in Ulm und ihr künstlerisches Umfeld*. Edited by Michael Roth. Exh. cat. Ulmer Museum, Ulm. Ulm, 1995.

Exh. cat. Venice 1999a *A volo d'uccello: Jacopo de' Barbari e le rappresentazioni di città nell'Europa del Rinascimento*. Edited by Giandomenico Romanelli. Exh. cat. Musei Civici Veneziani, Venice. Venice, 1999.

Exh. cat. Venice 1999b *Renaissance Venice and the North: Crosscurrents in the Time of Bellini, Dürer and Titian*. Edited by Bernard Aikema and Beverly Louise Brown. Exh. cat. Palazzo Grassi, Venice. Milan, 1999.

Exh. cat. Vienna 1994 *Albrecht Dürer im Kunsthistorischen Museum*. Edited by Karl Schütz. Exh. cat. Kunsthistorisches Museum, Vienna. Vienna, 1994.

Exh. cat. Vienna 2000 *Exotica: Portugals Entdeckungen im Spiegel fürstlicher Kunst- und Wunderkammern der Renaissance*. Edited by Wilfried Seipel. Exh. cat. Kunsthistorisches Museum, Vienna. Milan, 2000.

Exh. cat. Vienna 2019 *Albrecht Dürer*. Edited by Christof Metzger. Exh. cat. Albertina, Vienna. Munich, London, and New York, 2019.

Exh. cat. Washington 1991 *Circa 1492: Art in the Age of Exploration*. Edited by Jay A. Levenson. Exh. cat. National Gallery of Art, Washington, DC. New Haven, CT, and London, 1991.

Exh. cat. Washington and New York 1999 *Tilman Riemenschneider: Master Sculptor of the Late Middle Ages*. Compiled by Julien Chapuis and Michael Baxandall. Exh. cat. National Gallery of Art, Washington, DC, and The Metropolitan Museum of Art, New York. New Haven, CT, 1999.

Exh. cat. Washington and Nuremberg 2005 *Die Anfänge der europäischen Druckgraphik: Holzschnitte des 15. Jahrhunderts und ihr Gebrauch*. Compiled by Peter Parshall and Rainer Schoch. Exh. cat. National Gallery of Art, Washington, DC, and Germanisches Nationalmuseum, Nuremberg. Nuremberg, 2005.

Exh. cat. Wolfenbüttel 1976 *Die Neue Welt in den Schätzen einer alten europäischen Bibliothek*. Compiled by Yorck A. Haase and Harold Jantz. Exh. cat. Herzog August Bibliothek, Wolfenbüttel. Wolfenbüttel, 1976.

Exh. cat. Wrocław 2019 *Migrations: Late Gothic Art in Silesia*. Edited by Agnieszka Patała. With contributions by Jan Gromadzki et al. Exh. cat. Muzeum Narodowe, Wrocław. Wrocław, 2019.

Exh. cat. Zurich 2010 *Elfenbeine aus Ceylon: Luxusgüter für Katharina von Habsburg (1507–1578)*. Edited by Annemarie Jordan Gschwend and Johannes Beltz. Exh. cat. Museum Rietberg, Zurich. Zurich, 2010.

Fabri 1998 Fabri, Felix. *Evagatorium über die Pilgerreise ins Heilige Land, nach Arabien und Ägypten*. Edited by Konrad Dietrich Haßler. Translated by Herbert Wiegandt and Herbert Kraus. Ulm, 1998.

Fajt 2019 Fajt, Jiří. *Nürnberg als Kunstzentrum des Heiligen Römischen Reichs: Höfische und städtische Malerei in der Zeit Kaiser Karls IV. 1346–1378*. Berlin, Munich, and Prague, 2019.

Fajt and Hörsch 2014 Fajt, Jiří, and Markus Hörsch, eds. *Niederländische Kunstexporte nach Nord- und Ostmitteleuropa vom 14. bis 16. Jahrhundert: Forschungen zu ihren Anfängen, zur Rolle höfischer Auftraggeber, der Künstler und ihrer Werkstattbetriebe*. Studia jagellonica lipsiensia 15. Ostfildern, 2014.

Fajt and Hörsch 2018 Fajt, Jiří, and Markus Hörsch, eds. *Vom Weichen über den Schönen Stil zur Ars Nova: Neue Beiträge zur europäischen Kunst zwischen 1350 und 1470*. Studia Jagellonica Lipsiensia 19. Vienna, Cologne, and Weimar, 2018.

Fajt, Hörsch, and Jaeger 2011 Fajt, Jiří, Markus Hörsch, and Susanne Jaeger. "Im Zeichen der Goldwaage: Das Europa der Jagiellonen." *Mitropa: Jahresheft des Geisteswissenschaftlichen Zentrums Geschichte und Kultur Ostmitteleuropas (GWZO)* (2011), pp. 13–17.

Fajt, Hörsch, and Winzeler 2019 Fajt, Jiří, Markus Hörsch, and Marius Winzeler, eds. *Nürnbergs Glanz: Studien zu Architektur und Ausstattung seiner Kirchen in Mittelalter und Früher Neuzeit*. Studia Jagellonica Lipsiensia

20. Vienna, Cologne, and Weimar, 2019. https://www.vr-elibrary.de/doi/pdf/10.7788/9783412518691.

Fajt and Jaeger 2018 Fajt, Jiří, and Susanne Jaeger, eds. *Das Expressive in der Kunst 1500–1550: Albrecht Altdorfer und seine Zeitgenossen.* Munich, 2018.

Falk 1968 Falk, Tilman. *Hans Burgkmair: Studien zu Leben und Werk des Augsburger Malers.* Munich, 1968.

Falk 1987 Falk, Tilman. “Frühe Rezeption der Neuen Welt in der graphischen Kunst.” In Reinhard 1987, pp. 37–64.

Faroqhi 2016 Faroqhi, Suraiya. *A Cultural History of the Ottomans.* London, 2016.

Farrenkopf et al. 2022 Farrenkopf, Michael, et al., eds. *Alte Dinge – Neue Werte: Musealisierung und Inwertsetzung von Objekten.* Wert der Vergangenheit 6. Göttingen, 2022.

Fattorini et al. 2012 Fattorini, Gabriele, et al., eds. *Sano di Pietro: Qualità, devozione e pratica nella pittura senese del Quattrocento.* LAB / Fondazione Musei Senesi 2. Cinisello Balsamo, 2012.

Feest 1990 Feest, Christian F. “Vienna's Mexican Treasures: Aztec, Mixtec and Tarascan Works from 16th Century Austrian Collections.” *Archiv für Völkerkunde* 44 (1990), pp. 1–64.

Feest 1992 Feest, Christian F. “‘Seltzam ding von gold da von vill ze schreiben were’: Bewertungen amerikanischer Handwerkskunst im Europa des frühen 16. Jahrhunderts.” *Pirckheimer-Jahrbuch* 7 (1992), pp. 105–26.

Feest 2013 Feest, Christian F. “Von Kalikut nach Amerika: Dürer und die ‘wunderliche Künstlich ding’ aus dem ‘neuen gulden land’.” In Exh. cat. Frankfurt 2013, pp. 366–71.

Fehrenbach, Felfe, and Leonhard 2018 Fehrenbach, Frank, Robert Felfe, and Karin Leonhard, eds. *Kraft, Intensität, Energie: Zur Dynamik der Kunst.* Berlin, 2018.

Felten 2002 Felten, Franz J., ed. *Ein gefüllter Willkomm: Festschrift für Knut Schulz zum 65. Geburtstag.* Aachen, 2002.

Fey 2006 Fey, Carola. “Wallfahrtserinnerungen an spätmittelalterlichen Fürstenhöfen in Bild und Kult.” In Fey, Krieb, and Rösener 2006, pp. 141–65.

Fey, Krieb, and Rösener 2006 Fey, Carola, Steffen Krieb, and Werner Rösener, eds. *Mittelalterliche Fürstenhöfe und ihre Erinnerungskulturen.* Göttingen, 2006.

Firth 2014 *Doctor Hieronymus Münzer's “Itinerary (1494 and 1495) and Discovery of Guinea.”* Translated into English with detailed notes by James Firth. London, 2014.

Fischer 2020 Fischer, Doris, ed. *Fürstliche Feste: Höfische Festkultur zwischen Zeremoniell und Amüsement.* Jahrbuch der Stiftung Thüringer Schlösser und Gärten 23. Petersberg, 2020.

Fleischmann 2008 Fleischmann, Peter. *Rat und Patriziat in Nürnberg: Die Herrschaft der Ratsgeschlechter vom 13. bis zum 18. Jahrhundert.* 3 vols. Augsburg, 2008.

Fleisher 2004 Fleisher, Jeffrey. “Behind the Sultan of Kilwa's ‘Rebellious Conduct’: Local Perspectives on an International East African Town.” In Reid and Lane 2004, pp. 91–123.

Fleisher et al. 2012 Fleisher, Jeffrey, et al. “Geophysical Survey at Kilwa Kisiwani, Tanzania.” *Journal of African Archaeology* 10 (2012), pp. 207–20.

Flood and Kelly 1995 Flood, John L., and William A. Kelly, eds. *The German Book 1450–1750: Studies Presented to David L. Paisey in His Retirement.* London, 1995.

Flores 2015 Flores, Jorge. “The Iberian Empires, 1400 to 1800.” In Bentley, Subrahmanyam, and Weisner-Hanks 2015, pp. 271–96.

Flurschütz da Cruz 2014 Flurschütz da Cruz, Andreas. *Zwischen Füchsen und Wölfen: Konfession, Klientel und Konflikte in der fränkischen Reichsritterschaft nach dem Westfälischen Frieden.* Konflikte und Kultur 29. Constance, 2014.

Flurschütz da Cruz, Vroom, and Zander-Seidel 2017 Flurschütz da Cruz, Andreas, Wim Vroom, and Jutta Zander-Seidel. “Die spätmittelalterliche Familientafel der Wolf (von Wolfsthal): Genealogische Legitimation und sozialer Aufstieg im Kontext vorreformatorischer Memorialkultur.” *MVGN* 104 (2017), pp. 25–54.

Folgado García 2011 Folgado García, Jesús R. “Un instrumento usado en la evangelización de la Granada nazarí: La ‘Breve doctrina’ de Hernando de Talavera.” *Toletana: cuestiones de teología e historia* 24 (2011), pp. 291–307.

Frank 1967 Frank, Karl Friedrich von. *Standeserhebungen und Gnadenakte für das Deutsche Reich und die Österreichischen Erblande bis 1806 ...* . Vol. 1, *A–E.* Schloss Senftenberg, 1967.

Freigang 2009 Freigang, Christian. “Margaretes Paradiesvogel: Vereinnahmungen des Fremden und Wunderbaren aus der Neuen Welt im frühneuzeitlichen Kunstdiskurs.” In Grenzmann et al. 2009, pp. 73–99.

Freigang 2015 Freigang, Christian. “Bildskeptische Nachbildungsmodi der Passionstopographie Christi im Spätmittelalter – der Görlitzer Kalvarienberg.” In Aurenhammer and Bohde 2015, pp. 117–50.

French 2021 French, Howard W. *Born in Blackness: Africa, Africans, and the Making of the Modern World, 1471 to the Second World War.* New York, 2021.

French 2023 French, Howard W. *Afrika und die Entstehung der modernen Welt: Eine Globalgeschichte.* Stuttgart, 2023.

Friedman 2008 Friedman, John Block. “The Art of the Exotic: Robinet Testard's Turbans and Turban-like Coiffure.” In Netherton and Owen-Crocker 2008, pp. 173–91.

Friedrich and Schunka 2012 Friedrich, Markus, and Alexander Schunka, eds. *Orientbegegnungen deutscher Protestanten in der Frühen Neuzeit.* Zeitsprünge: Forschungen zur Frühen Neuzeit, vol. 16, nos. 1, 2. Frankfurt am Main, 2012.

Fritz 1983 Fritz, Rolf. *Die Gefäße aus Kokosnuß in Mitteleuropa 1250–1800.* Mainz, 1983.

Fromann 1875 Fromann, Georg Karl. “Israelitische Grabsteine in Nürnberg.” *Anzeiger für Kunde der deutschen Vorzeit* 22 (1875), cols. 181–83.

Frübis 2001 Frübis, Hildegard. “‘Der wilde Mann und die Freiheit in der Wildnis’: Zur Rezeption der Entdeckung Amerikas im deutschsprachigen Kulturraum des 16. Jahrhunderts.” In Janz 2001, pp. 107–25.

Fumasoli 2017 Fumasoli, Beat. *Wirtschaftserfolg zwischen Zufall und Innovativität: Oberdeutsche Städte und ihre Exportwirtschaft im Vergleich (1350–1550).* Stuttgart, 2017.

Fürer von Haimendorff 1646 Fürer von Haimendorff, Christoph. *Christoph Fürers von Haimendorff ... Reis-Beschreibung: In Egypten, Arabien, Palästinam, Syrien, etc.* Nuremberg, 1646.

Füssel 1987 Füssel, Stephan, ed. *Reiseberichte der Frühen Neuzeit: Wirtschafts- und kulturhistorische Quellen.* Pirckheimer-Jahrbuch 2 [1986]). Munich, 1987.

Gaitán 2005 Gaitán, Andrés, ed. *Los límites del cuerpo – o lo bello en el horror.* Bogotá, 2005.

Gall 1965 Gall, Günter. *Leder im europäischen Kunsthandwerk: Ein Handbuch für Sammler und Liebhaber.* Braunschweig, 1965.

Gast and Syrer 2020 Gast, Uwe, and Christa Syrer. “Zwei Glasgemälde mit den Wappen Albertinelli und Giorgini in Coburg und der ‘Mohrenkopfpokal’ von Christoph Jamnitzer: Italienische Kauf- und Handelsleute um 1600 in Nürnberg, ihr Netzwerk und ihre Kunstaufträge.” *Zeitschrift des Deutschen Vereins für Kunstwissenschaft* 74 (2020), pp. 9–32.

Gebert 1917 Gebert, Carl Friedrich. “Die Nürnberger Rechenpfennigschlager.” *Mitteilungen der Bayerischen Numismatischen Gesellschaft* 35 (1917), pp. 1–128.

Gebhardt and Zöllner 2021 Gebhardt, Johannes, and Frank Zöllner, eds. *Paragone: Leonardo in Comparison.* Petersberg, 2021.

Geisberg 1974 Geisberg, Max. *The German Single-Leaf Woodcut: 1500–1550.* Revised and edited by Walter L. Strauss. Vol. 4. New York, 1974.

Gerber 2014 Gerber, Stefan, ed. *Zwischen Stadt, Staat und Nation: Bürgertum in Deutschland; Hans-Werner Hahn zum 65. Geburtstag.* Vol. 1. Göttingen, 2014.

Gessner 1555 Gessner, Conrad. *Historia animalium liber III. qui est de avium natura.* Zurich, 1555.

Gessner 1561 Gessner, Conrad. “Horti Germaniae.” In Cordus 1561, fols. 236v–287v.

Gessner 1606 Gessner, Conrad. *Thierbuch: Das ist Außführliche beschreibung und lebendige ja auch eigentliche Contrafactur und Abmahlung* *aller Vierfüssigen thieren, so auff der Erden und in Wassern wohnen …* . Heidelberg, 1606.

Gewecke 1986 Gewecke, Frauke. *Wie die neue Welt in die alte kam*. Munich, 1986.

Gilbert 2024 Gilbert, Claire. "Morisco Catechisms: Religious Incorporation and Differentiation in Early Modern Spain." *Religions* 15 (2024), pp. 1–23.

Glaser 2000 Glaser, Silvia. *Majolika: Die italienischen Fayencen im Germanischen Nationalmuseum; Bestandskatalog*. Kataloge des Germanischen Nationalmuseums. Nuremberg, 2000.

Glaser 2004 Glaser, Silvia, ed. *Italienische Fayencen der Renaissance: Ihre Spuren in internationalen Museumssammlungen*. Nuremberg, 2004.

Gleixner and Dos Santos Lopes 2021 Gleixner, Ulrike, and Marília dos Santos Lopes, eds. *Things on the Move – Dinge unterwegs: Objects in Early Modern Cultural Transfer*. Wolfenbüttler Forschungen 165. Wolfenbüttel, 2021.

Gmelin 1961 Gmelin, Hans Georg. "Georg Pencz als Maler." PhD diss., Universität Freiburg, Freiburg im Breisgau, 1961.

Goldberg, Heimberg, and Schawe 1998 Goldberg, Gisela, Bruno Heimberg, and Martin Schawe, eds. *Albrecht Dürer: Die Gemälde der Alten Pinakothek*. Munich, 1998.

Göllner 1961–78 Göllner, Carl. *Tvrcica: Die europäischen Türkendrucke des XVI. Jahrhunderts*. 3 vols. Bucharest, Berlin, and Baden-Baden, 1961–78.

Göllner 1983 Göllner, Carl. *Chronica vnnd beschreibung der Türckey mir eyner vorrhed D. Martini Lutheri: Unveränderter Nachdruck der Ausgabe Nürnberg 1530 sowie fünf weiterer "Türkendrucke" des 15. und 16. Jahrhunderts*. Cologne et al., 1983.

Grafetstätter 2013 Grafetstätter, Andrea. *Ludus compleatur: Theatralisierungsstrategien epischer Stoffe im spätmittelalterlichen und frühneuzeitlichen Spiel*. Imagines Aevi: Interdisziplinäre Beiträge zur Mittelalterforschung 33. Wiesbaden, 2013.

Granda and Schreiber 2013 Granda, Jeanette, and Jürgen Schreiber, eds. *Perspektiven durch Retrospektiven: Wirtschaftsgeschichtliche Beiträge; Festschrift für Rolf Walter zum 60. Geburtstag*. Cologne, Weimar, and Vienna, 2013.

Grebe 2005 Grebe, Anja. "Pilgrims and Fashion: The Functions of Pilgrims' Garments." In Blick and Tekippe 2005, pp. 3–27.

Grebe 2014 Grebe, Anja. "Albrecht Dürer in Asian Art: Paradigms of Cross-Cultural Reproduction and Transformation." In Osano 2014, pp. 389–402.

Green 2006 Green, Nile. "Ostrich Eggs and Peacock Feathers: Sacred Objects as Cultural Exchange between Christianity and Islam." *Al-Masāq: Islam and the Medieval Mediterranean* 18, no. 1 (2006), pp. 27–78.

Grenzmann et al. 2009 Grenzmann, Ludger, et al., eds. *Wechselseitige Wahrnehmung der Religionen im Spätmittelalter und in der Frühen Neuzeit*. Part 1, *Konzeptionelle Grundfragen und Fallstudien*. Abhandlungen der Akademie der Wissenschaften zu Göttingen (new series) 4. Berlin and New York, 2009.

Gresle-Pouligny 1999 Gresle-Pouligny, Dominique. *Un plan pour Mexico-Tenochtitlan: Les representations de la cite et l'imaginaire Européen (XVIe–XVIIIe siècles)*. Paris, 1999.

Grieb 2007 Grieb, Manfred H., ed. *Nürnberger Künstlerlexikon: Bildende Künstler, Kunsthandwerker, Gelehrte, Sammler, Kulturschaffende und Mäzene vom 12. bis zur Mitte des 20. Jahrhunderts*. 4 vols. Munich, 2007.

Griffin 1988 Griffin, Clive. *The Crombergers of Seville: The History of a Printing and Merchant Dynasty*. Oxford, 1988.

Grimmsmann 2016 Grimmsmann, Damaris. *Krieg mit dem Wort: Türkenpredigten des 16. Jahrhunderts im Alten Reich*. Berlin, 2016.

Groenendijk and Levinson 2015 Groenendijk, Freek, and Robert A. Levinson. *Rechenpfennige*. Vol. 2, *Die Familie Lauffer ca. 1554–1712*. Kataloge / Staatliche Münzsammlung München – Museum für Geldgeschichte. Munich, 2015.

Grote 1961 Grote, Ludwig. *Die Tucher: Bildnis einer Patrizierfamilie*. Bibliothek des Germanischen Nationalmuseums Nürnberg zur deutschen Kunst- und Kulturgeschichte 15–16. Munich, 1961.

Grote 1998 Grote, Ludwig. *Albrecht Dürer: Reisen nach Venedig*. Munich and New York, 1998.

Gruzinski 2014 Gruzinski, Serge. *Drache und Federschlange: Europas Griff nach Amerika und China 1519/20*. Frankfurt am Main, 2014.

Gulyás 2014 Gulyás, Borbála. "'gegen den Bluedthunden und Erbfeindt der Christenhait': Die Thematisierung der Türkengefahr in Wort und Bild im Rahmen der höfischen Feste der Habsburger in der zweiten Hälfte des 16. Jahrhunderts." In Born and Jagodzinski 2014, pp. 217–36.

Gümbel 1906 Gümbel, Albert. "Meister Heinrich der Parlier der Ältere und der Schöne Brunnen." *Jahresbericht des Historischen Vereins für Mittelfranken* 53 (1906), pp. 49–86.

Guthmüller and Kühlmann 2000 Guthmüller, Bodo, and Wilhelm Kühlmann, eds. *Europa und die Türken in der Renaissance*. Tübingen, 2000.

Häberlein 1998 Häberlein, Mark. "Die Welser-Vöhlin-Gesellschaft: Fernhandel, Familienbeziehungen und sozialer Status an der Wende vom Mittelalter zur Neuzeit." In Exh. cat. Memmingen 1998, pp. 17–37.

Häberlein 2010 Häberlein, Mark. "Schwarz, Matthäus." *NDB* 24 (2010), pp. 2–3. https://www.deutsche-biographie.de/pnd118762958.html#ndbcontent.

Häberlein 2016 Häberlein, Mark. *Aufbruch ins Globale Zeitalter: Die Handelswelt der Fugger und Welser*. Darmstadt, 2016.

Häberlein 2021 Häberlein, Mark. "Connected Histories: South German Merchants and Portuguese Expansion in the Sixteenth Century." *RiMe: Rivista dell'Istituto di Storia dell'Europa Mediterranea* 9/II n.s. (2021), pp. 35–53.

Häberlein and Burkhardt 2002 Häberlein, Mark, and Johannes Burkhardt, eds. *Die Welser: Neue Forschungen zur Geschichte und Kultur des oberdeutschen Handelshauses*. Colloquia Augustana 16. Munich, 2002.

Habich 1906 Habich, Georg. "Studien zur deutschen Renaissancemedaille, T. 1: Hans Schwarz." *Jahrbuch der Königlich Preußischen Kunstsammlungen* 27 (1906), pp. 30–69.

Habich 1929 Habich, Georg, ed. *Die deutschen Schaumünzen des XVI. Jahrhunderts, T. 1*. Vol. 1, no. 1. Munich, 1929.

Habich 1931 Habich, Georg, ed. *Die deutschen Schaumünzen des XVI. Jahrhunderts, T. 1*. Vol. 1, no. 2. Munich, 1931.

Häbler 1900 Häbler, Konrad. "Deutsche Buchdrucker in Spanien und Portugal." In Hartwig 1900, pp. 488–504.

Haedeke 1963 Haedeke, Hanns Ulrich. *Zinn: Ein Handbuch für Sammler und Liebhaber*. Bibliothek für Kunst- und Antiquitätenfreunde 16. Braunschweig, 1963.

Hagen 2001 Hagen, Friedrich von. "Viten." In Tacke 2001a, pp. 343–632.

Hamacher and Karnehm 1994 Hamacher, Bärbel, and Christl Karnehm, eds. *Pinxit, sculpsit, fecit: Kunsthistorische Studien; Festschrift für Bruno Bushart*. Munich, 1994.

Hamm, Taube, and Lorenz 2008 Hamm, Johannes, Elisabeth Taube, and Anke Lorenz. "Wertvolles Kunstgut aus der Nürnberger Frauenkirche." In Exh. cat. Nuremberg 2008b, pp. 50–63.

Hampe 1927 Hampe, Theodor, ed. *Das Trachtenbuch des Christoph Weiditz von seinen Reisen nach Spanien (1529) und den Niederlanden (1531/32): Nach der in der Bibliothek des Germanischen Nationalmuseums zu Nürnberg aufbewahrten Handschrift*. Historische Waffen und Kostüme 2. Berlin and Leipzig, 1927.

Hanke 2012 Hanke, Lewis. *The Imperial City of Potosí: An Unwritten Chapter in the History of Spanish America*. First edition, The Hague, 1956. Dordrecht, 2012.

Hanß 2017 Hanß, Stefan. *Lepanto als Ereignis: Dezentrierende Geschichte(n) der Seeschlacht von Lepanto (1571)*. Göttingen, 2017.

Hanß 2019 Hanß, Stefan. "Die Universität Tübingen und die Anfänge osmanischer Sprachstudien im 16. und 17. Jahrhundert." In Mährle 2019, pp. 119–46.

Hanß 2021a Hanß, Stefan. "Making Featherwork in Early Modern Europe." In Burghartz et al. 2021, pp. 137–85.

Hanß 2021b Hanß, Stefan. "New World Feathers and the Matter of Early Modern Ingenuity:

Digital Microscopes, Period Hands, and Period Eyes." In Oosterhoff, Marcaida, and Marr 2021, pp. 189–303.

Hanß 2021c Hanß, Stefan. "Ottoman Language Learning in Early Modern Germany." *Central European History* 54, no. 1 (2021), pp. 1–33.

Hanß 2021d Hanß, Stefan. "A Shared Taste? Material Culture and Intellectual Curiosity in the Habsburg Mediterranean." In Hanß and McEwan 2021, pp. 257–77.

Hanß and McEwan 2021 Hanß, Stefan, and Dorothea McEwan, eds. *The Habsburg Mediterranean, 1500–1800*. Vienna, 2021.

Hantzsch 1897 Hantzsch, Viktor. "Wild, Johannes." *ADB* 42 (1897), pp. 487–88. https://www.deutsche-biographie.de/pnd120141620.html#adbcontent.

Harley 2007 Harley, John Brian, ed. *The History of Cartography*. Vol. 3, part 1, *Cartography in the European Renaissance*. Chicago, 2007.

Harreld 2004 Harreld, Donald J. *High Germans in the Low Countries: German Merchants and Commerce in Golden Age Antwerp*. The Northern World 14. Leiden, 2004.

Harris 2019 Harris, Max. *Christ on a Donkey: Palm Sunday, Triumphal Entries, and Blasphemous Pageants*. Amsterdam, 2019.

Harsdorf 1958 Harsdorf, Karl von. "Der Kupferhammer zu Enzendorf bei Rupprechtstegen." *MVGN* 48 (1958), pp. 26–50.

Hartwig 1900 Hartwig, Otto, ed. *Festschrift zum fünfhundertjährigen Geburtstage von Johann Gutenberg*. Leipzig, 1900.

Haug 2021 Haug, Henrike. *imitatio – artificium: Goldschmiedehandwerk und Naturbetrachtung im 16. Jahrhundert*. Interdependenzen 7. Vienna and Cologne, 2021.

Hauschild 2004 Hauschild, Stephanie. "Spiegelbild und Schatten: Bildnisse des Sebald Schirmer und des Jakob Hofmann von Georg Pencz." *Anzeiger des Germanischen Nationalmuseums* (2004), pp. 105–14.

Hauschke 2002 Hauschke, Sven. "Globen und Wissenschaftliche Instrumente: Die europäischen Höfe als Kunden Nürnberger Mathematiker." In Exh. cat. Nuremberg 2002, pp. 364–89.

Hauschke 2006 Hauschke, Sven. *Die Grabdenkmäler der Nürnberger Vischerwerkstatt 1453–1544*. Denkmäler deutscher Kunst: Bronzegeräte des Mittelalters 6. Berlin and Petersberg, 2006.

Haussherr 1987–88 Haussherr, Reiner. "Spätgotische Ansichten der Stadt Jerusalem (Oder: War der Hausbuchmeister in Jerusalem?)." *Jahrbuch der Berliner Museen* 29–30 (1987–88), pp. 47–70.

Hegel 1862 Hegel, Carl, ed. *Die Chroniken der fränkischen Städte: Nürnberg*. Vol. 1, Die Chroniken der deutschen Städte vom 14. bis ins 16. Jahrhundert 1. Leipzig, 1862.

Heher 2018 Heher, Dominik. "1000 vergessene Jahre?" In Exh. cat. Schallaburg 2018, pp. 44–46.

Heller and Talmon 2001 Heller, Jan, and Shemaryahu Talmon, eds. *The Old Testament as Inspiration in Culture*. Prague, 2001.

Hellwig 1970 Hellwig, Barbara. *Inkunabelkatalog des Germanischen Nationalmuseums Nürnberg: Nach einem Verzeichnis von Walter Matthey*. Kataloge des Germanischen Nationalmuseums Nürnberg. Wiesbaden, 1970.

Hendrich 2007 Hendrich, Yvonne. *Valentim Fernandes: Ein deutscher Buchdrucker in Portugal um die Wende vom 15. zum 16. Jahrhundert und sein Umkreis*. Frankfurt am Main, 2007.

Henkelmann 2021 Henkelmann, Vera. "In ewigem Angedenken: Inschriften ausgewählter Funeraltücher und Funeralteppiche des Spätmittelalters." In Kohwagner-Nikolai, Päffgen, and Steininger 2021, pp. 305–25.

Hentschel 2018 Hentschel, Judith. "Porträtdeckel mit Wildem Mann." *KulturGUT: Aus der Forschung des Germanischen Nationalmuseums* 57 (2nd Quarter 2018), pp. 3–7.

Herberger 1851 Herberger, Theodor. *Conrad Peutinger in seinem Verhältnisse zum Kaiser Maximilian I: Ein Beitrag zur Geschichte ihrer Zeit, mit besonderer Berücksichtigung der literarisch-artistischen Bestrebungen Peutingers und des Kaisers nach bisher unbenützten archivalischen Quellen bearbeitet*. Augsburg, 1851.

Herbers 2000 Herbers, Klaus. "'Murcia ist so groß wie Nürnberg': Nürnberg und Nürnberger auf der iberischen Halbinsel; Eindrücke und Wechselbeziehungen." In Neuhaus 2000, pp. 151–83.

Herbers 2020 Herbers, Klaus. *Der Reisebericht des Hieronymus Münzer: Ein Nürnberger Arzt auf der "Suche nach der Wahrheit" in Westeuropa (1494/95)*. Tübingen, 2020.

Herbers and Plötz 1996 Herbers, Klaus, and Robert Plötz. *Nach Santiago zogen sie: Berichte von Pilgerfahrten ans "Ende der Welt."* Munich, 1996.

Herberstein 2007 Herberstein, Sigismund von. *Rerum Moscoviticarum commentarii: Synoptische Edition der lateinischen und der deutschen Fassung letzter Hand*. Basel, 1556, and Vienna, 1557. Compiled by Eva Maurer and Andreas Fülberth under the direction of Frank Kämpfer. Redacted and edited by Hermann Beyer-Thoma. Munich, 2007.

Hermens and Van Laar 2024 Hermens, Emma, and Paul J. C. van Laar. "Technical Art History, Itineraries, Networks and Interdisciplinary Collaboration: The Curious History of the Green 'Soup' Turtle." In Sauge and Ford 2024, pp. 69–80.

Herrero Carretero 2004 Herrero Carretero, Concha. *Tapices de Isabel la Católica: Origen de la colección real española*. Madrid, 2004.

Herz 1997 Herz, Randall. "Briefe Hans Tuchers d. Ä. aus dem Heiligen Land und andere Aufzeichnungen." *MVGN* 84 (1997), pp. 61–90.

Herz 1999 Herz, Randall. "Wanckel, Nikolaus." *VL* 10 (1999), cols. 703–4.

Herz 2002 Herz, Randall. *Die "Reise ins Gelobte Land" Hans Tuchers des Älteren (1479–1480): Untersuchungen zur Überlieferung und kritische Edition eines spätmittelalterlichen Reiseberichts*. Wiesbaden, 2002.

Herz 2005 Herz, Randall. *Studien zur Drucküberlieferung der "Reise ins Gelobte Land" Hans Tuchers des Älteren: Bestandsaufnahme und historische Auswertung der Inkunabeln unter Berücksichtigung der späteren Drucküberlieferung*. Nuremberg, 2005.

Herz 2018 Herz, Randall. "Der Arzt und Frühhumanist Hieronymus Münzer († 1508) aus Feldkirch: Sein Leben und sein Wirken im Nürnberger Humanistenkreis." *MVGN* 105 (2018), pp. 99–215.

Herz 2019 Herz, Randall. "Michael Wolgemut und die Schedel'sche Weltchronik." In Exh. cat. Nuremberg 2019b, pp. 122–31.

Hess 2014 Hess, Daniel. "Kaiser und Reich." In Zander-Seidel and Kregeloh 2014, pp. 248–61.

Hess 2019 Hess, Daniel. "Heilige: Schutz, Beistand und Vorbild." In Exh. cat. Nuremberg 2019a, pp. 76–103.

Hess 2022 Hess, Daniel. "Museale Sammlungen unter neuen Perspektiven: Vom Germanischen zu einem europäischen Museum." In Farrenkopf et al. 2022, pp. 37–53.

Hess and Hirschfelder 2010 Hess, Daniel, and Dagmar Hirschfelder, eds. *Renaissance, Barock, Aufklärung: Kunst und Kultur vom 16. bis zum 18. Jahrhundert*. Die Schausammlungen des Germanischen Nationalmuseums 3. Nuremberg, 2010.

Hess, Hirschfelder, and Baum 2019 Hess, Daniel, Dagmar Hirschfelder, and Katja von Baum, eds. *Die Gemälde des Spätmittelalters im Germanischen Nationalmuseum*. Vol. 1, *Franken*, 2 parts. Bestandskataloge des Germanischen Nationalmuseums. Regensburg, 2019.

Hess and Kammel 2010 Hess, Daniel, and Frank Matthias Kammel. "Zwischen Renaissance und Barock: Die Ungleichzeitigkeit des Gleichzeitigen." In Hess and Hirschfelder 2010, pp. 296–308.

Hess et al. 2007 Hess, Daniel, et al. *Mittelalter: Kunst und Kultur von der Spätantike bis zum 15. Jahrhundert*. Die Schausammlungen des Germanischen Nationalmuseums 2. Edited by G. Ulrich Großmann. Nuremberg, 2007.

Hessler 2013 Hessler, John W. *A Renaissance Globemaker's Toolbox: Johannes Schöner and the Revolution of Modern Science 1475–1550*. Washington, DC, 2013.

Hildebrandt 1972 Hildebrandt, Rainer. "Augsburger und Nürnberger Kupferhandel 1500–1619." *Zeitschrift für Wirtschafts- und Sozialwissenschaften (ZWS) – Vierteljahresschrift der Gesellschaft für Wirtschafts- und Sozialwissenschaften, Verein für Socialpolitik* 92, no. 1 (1972), pp. 1–31.

Hildebrandt 1977 Hildebrandt, Reinhard. "Augsburger und Nürnberger Kupferhandel 1500–1619." In Kellenbenz 1977, pp. 191–224.

Hirschfelder 2014 Hirschfelder, Dagmar. “Hans Pleydenwurff: Ein Nürnberger Maler aus Bamberg.” In Exh. cat. Nuremberg 2014, pp. 79–84.

Höfert 2003a Höfert, Almut. *Den Feind beschreiben: “Türkengefahr” und europäisches Wissen über das Osmanische Reich 1450–1600.* Frankfurt am Main, 2003.

Höfert 2003b Höfert, Almut. “Ist das Böse schmutzig? Das Osmanische Reich in den Augen europäischer Reisender des 15. und 16. Jahrhunderts.” *Historische Anthropologie* 11, no. 2 (2003), pp. 176–92.

Holl 2010 Holl, Frank, ed. *Gewürze – sinnlicher Genuss, lebendige Geschichte: Begleitbuch zur Sonderausstellung.* Rosenheim, 2010.

Hollstein German 47 *Hollstein's German Engravings, Etchings and Woodcuts.* Vol. 47, *Erhard Schön.* Compiled by Ursula Mielke. Rotterdam, 2000.

Hollstein German 48 *Hollstein's German Engravings, Etchings and Woodcuts.* Vol. 48, *Erhard Schön (Fortsetzung).* Compiled by Ursula Mielke. Rotterdam, 2000.

Hommers 2021 Hommers, Jeannet. “‘Instrumenti di mirabile efficacia’? Leonardo und Dürer als Militärtechniker.” In Gebhardt and Zöllner 2021, pp. 72–83.

Hoppe 2002 Hoppe, Jens. *Jüdische Geschichte und Kultur in Museen: Zur nichtjüdischen Museologie des Jüdischen in Deutschland.* Münster et al., 2002.

Hoppe 2014 Hoppe, Stephan. “Die vermessene Stadt: Kleinräumige Vermessungskampagnen im Mitteleuropa des 16. Jahrhunderts und ihr funktionaler Kontext.” In Baumgärtner 2014, pp. 251–73.

Horodowich and Markey 2017 Horodowich, Elizabeth, and Lia Markey, eds. *The New World in Early Modern Italy, 1492–1750.* Cambridge, 2017.

Hörsch 2019 Hörsch, Markus. “Nürnbergs repräsentative Architektur in der Zeit Kaiser Karls IV. und ihre Bedeutung: Architekturikonografische Überlegungen am Beispiel der Frauenkirche und des Ostchors der Sebalduskirche.” In Fajt, Hörsch, and Winzeler 2019, pp. 63–88.

Horst 2006 Horst, Thomas. “‘Am Anfang war das Gewürz’: Vor 500 Jahren kehrte der Allgäuer Balthasar Sprenger von einer Indienfahrt zurück. Er hinterließ einen eindrucksvollen Reisebericht.” *Literatur in Bayern* 85 (2006), pp. 13–21.

Horst 2009 Horst, Thomas. “The Voyage of the Bavarian Explorer Balthasar Sprenger to India (1505/1506) at the Turning Point between the Middle Ages and the Early Modern Times: His Travelogue and the Contemporary Carthography as Historical Sources.” In Billion et al. 2009, pp. 167–97.

Horton and Middleton 2000 Horton, Marc C., and John Middleton. *The Swahili: The Social Landscape of a Mercantile Society.* Oxford, 2000.

Huffman 2024 Huffman, Kristin L., ed. *A View of Venice: Portrait of a Renaissance City.* Durham, NC, and London, 2024.

Humfrey 2024 Humfrey, Peter. “Venezianische Malerei im Zeitalter von Giovanni Bellini und Vittore Carpaccio.” In Exh. cat. Stuttgart 2024, pp. 29–41.

Hümmerich 1918 Hümmerich, Franz. *Quellen und Untersuchungen zur Fahrt der ersten Deutschen nach dem portugiesischen Indien 1505/6.* Munich, 1918.

Husband 2015 Husband, Timothy B. “The World in Play: Luxury Cards 1430–1540.” In Exh. cat. New York 2015, pp. 13–131.

Husung 1925–26 Husung, Max J. “Ein jüdischer Lederschnittkünstler.” *Soncino-Blätter: Beiträge zur Kunde des jüdischen Buches* 1 (1925–26), pp. 29–43.

Ichumbaki and Munisi 2024 Ichumbaki, Elgidius, and Neema Munisi. “Kilwa and Its Environs.” *Oxford Research Encyclopedia of African History* (2024).

Ichumbaki and Pollard 2021 Ichumbaki, Elgidius, and Edward Pollard. “The Swahili Civilization in Eastern Africa.” *Oxford Research Encyclopedia of Anthropology* (2021).

Ilg 2008 Ilg, Ulrike, ed. *Text und Bild in Reiseberichten des 16. Jahrhunderts.* Studi e ricerche 3. Venice, 2008.

Ilg 2024 Ilg, Ulrike. “Venedig und das Mittelmeer – Praktiken des Kulturtransfers um 1500 am Beispiel Bellinis und Carpaccios.” In Exh. cat. Stuttgart 2024, pp. 91–103.

Imhoff 1974 Imhoff, Christoph von. “Imhof(f).” *NDB* 10 (1974), pp. 146–48. https://www.deutsche-biographie.de/sfz36365.html#ndbcontent.

Imhoff 1975 Imhoff, Christoph von. “Die Imhoff – Handelsherren und Kunstliebhaber: Überblick über eine 750 Jahre alte Nürnberger Ratsfamilie.” *MVGN* 62 (1975), pp. 1–42.

Imhoff 1987a Imhoff, Christoph von, ed. *Berühmte Nürnberger aus neun Jahrhunderten.* Nuremberg, 1987.

Imhoff 1987b Imhoff, Christoph von. “Nürnbergs Indienpioniere: Reiseberichte von der ersten oberdeutschen Handelsfahrt nach Indien (1505/1506).” In Füssel 1987, pp. 11–44.

Irmscher 1984 Irmscher, Günter. *Kleine Kunstgeschichte des europäischen Ornaments seit der frühen Neuzeit (1400–1900).* Darmstadt, 1984.

Isler 2019 Isler, Andreas. *Alles Derwische? Anschauungen, Begriffe, Bilder: Zur Darstellung von islamischen Ordensleuten in westlichen Orientwerken der frühen Neuzeit.* Zurich, 2019.

Jahnel 1950 Jahnel, Helga. “Die Imhoff: Eine Nürnberger Patrizier- und Großkaufmannsfamilie; Eine Studie zur reichsstädtischen Wirtschaftspolitik und Kulturgeschichte an der Wende vom Mittelalter zur Neuzeit (1351–1579).” PhD diss., Universität Würzburg, 1950.

Jakob 2007 Jakob, Reinhard. “Wer war Martin Behaim? Auf den Spuren seines Lebens.” *NORICA: Berichte und Themen aus dem Stadtarchiv Nürnberg* 3 (2007), pp. 32–47.

Jakstat 2024 Jakstat, Sven. “Leerstellen: Hans Tetzels Totenschild und der Bergbau auf Kuba im 16. Jahrhundert im Kontext der Ausstellung Nürnberg GLOBAL 1300–1600.” *KulturGUT: Aus der Forschung des Germanischen Nationalmuseums* 83 (4th Quarter 2024), pp. 12–18.

Jansen and Perez Jimenez 2019 Jansen, Maarten E.R.G.N., and Gabina Aurora Perez Jimenez. “Opfer im Alten Mexiko.” In Exh. cat. Stuttgart, Vienna, and Leiden 2019, pp. 255–66.

Janz 2001 Janz, Rolf-Peter, ed. *Faszination und Schrecken des Fremden.* Frankfurt am Main, 2001.

Jaspert 2002 Jaspert, Nikolas. “Ein Leben in der Fremde: Deutsche Handwerker und Kaufleute im Barcelona des 15. Jahrhunderts.” In Felten 2002, pp. 435–62.

Jaspert 2016 Jaspert, Nikolas. “Hieronymus Münzers deutsche Gastgeber auf der Iberischen Halbinsel: Archivnotizen und Ergänzungen.” In Alraum, Holndonner, and Lehner 2016, pp. 79–98.

Johanek 1983 Johanek, Peter. “Meister Jörg von Nürnberg.” In Ruh and Keil 1983, cols. 867–69.

Johnson 2011 Johnson, Carina L. *Cultural Hierarchy in Sixteenth-Century Europe: The Ottomans and Mexicans.* Cambridge, 2011.

Johnston 2013 Johnston, Mark D. “Gluttony and Convivencia: Hernando de Talavera's Warning to the Muslims of Granada in 1496.” *eHumanista* 25 (2013), pp. 107–26.

Jones 2017 Jones, Ann Rosalind. “Cesare Vecellio's Floridians in the Venetian Book Market: Beautiful Imports.” In Horodowich and Markey 2017, pp. 248–69.

Jones and King 2002 Jones, Julie, and Heidi King. “Gold of the Americas.” *The Metropolitan Museum of Art Bulletin* 59, no. 4 (2002).

Jordan Gschwend and Lowe 2015 Jordan Gschwend, Annemarie, and Kate J. P. Lowe, eds. *The Global City: On the Streets of Renaissance Lisbon.* London, 2015.

Jörg von Nürnberg ca. 1482–83 Jörg von Nürnberg. *Geschicht von der Turckey.* Memmingen, ca. 1482–83.

Juckes 2021 Juckes, Tim. “Eye of the Donkey: Visual Strategies on the Choir Threshold of St. Laurence's in Nuremberg.” In Beier, Juckes, and Pinkus 2021, pp. 177–98.

Juneja 2023 Juneja, Monica. *Can Art History be Made Global? Meditations from the Periphery.* Berlin and Boston, 2023.

Junquera de Vega and Herrero Carretero 1986 Junquera de Vega, Paulina, and Concha Herrero Carretero, eds. *Catalogo de tapices del Patrimonio Nacional.* Vol. 1, *Siglo XVI.* Madrid, 1986.

Kahsnitz 1983 Kahsnitz, Rainer, ed. *Veit Stoß in Nürnberg: Werke des Meisters und seiner Schule in Nürnberg und Umgebung*. Munich, 1983.

Kahsnitz 1984 Kahsnitz, Rainer. "Ein 'syro-fränkisches' Glas aus dem Wirtshaus Zum Wilden Mann in Nürnberg." *Monatsanzeiger Museen und Ausstellungen in Nürnberg* 40 (1984), pp. 318–19.

Kaiser 2005 Kaiser, Christiane. "Die Fleischbrücke in Nürnberg: 1596–1598." 3 vols. PhD diss., BTU Cottbus, 2005. https://opus4.kobv.de/opus4-btu/frontdoor/index/index/docId/151.

Kalus 2010 Kalus, Maximilian. *Pfeffer, Kupfer, Nachrichten: Kaufmannsnetzwerke und Handelsstrukturen im europäisch-asiatischen Handel am Ende des 16. Jahrhunderts*. Augsburg, 2010.

Kammel 1997 Kammel, Frank Matthias. "Ein polnischer Ritter und sein Grabmal aus Nürnberg: Zu einem neuerworbenen Gußmodell." *Monatsanzeiger Museen und Ausstellungen in Nürnberg* 195 (1997), pp. 12–13.

Kammel 2007 Kammel, Frank Matthias. "Ornament und Bildmagie: Mittelalterliche Bauskulptur." In Hess et al. 2007, pp. 214–27.

Kammel 2010a Kammel, Frank Matthias. "Natur und Antike: Pole einer erneuerten Kunst." In Hess and Hirschfelder 2010, pp. 232–43.

Kammel 2010b Kammel, Frank Matthias. "Skulptur der Dürerzeit: Traditionelle Motive und neue Formen." In Hess and Hirschfelder 2010, pp. 61–73.

Kammel 2018 Kammel, Frank Matthias. "Spur der Steine: Zu den jüdischen Grabdenkmalen im Germanischen Nationalmuseum." *KulturGUT: Aus der Forschung des Germanischen Nationalmuseums* 58 (3rd Quarter 2018), pp. 13–16.

Kammel et al. 2020 Kammel, Frank Matthias, et al., eds. *Die Nürnberger Totenschilde des Spätmittelalters im Germanischen Nationalmuseum: Jenseitsvorsorge und ständische Repräsentation städtischer Eliten*. 2 vols. Nuremberg, 2020.

Karner and Stelzl-Marx 2021 Karner, Stefan, and Barbara Stelzl-Marx, eds. *Sigmund von Herberstein: Moscovia; Die Reisen nach Moskau; Bedeutung und Erbe*. Vienna, 2021.

Kastenholz 2006 Kastenholz, Richard. *Hans Schwarz: Ein Augsburger Bildhauer und Medailleur der Renaissance*. Kunstwissenschaftliche Studien 126. Munich and Berlin, 2006.

Katzenstein 1982 Katzenstein, Ursula E. "Mair Jaffe and Bookbinding Research." *Studies in Bibliography and Booklore* 14 (1982), pp. 17–28.

Kaufmann 2008 Kaufmann, Thomas. *"Türckenbüchlein": Zur christlichen Wahrnehmung "türkischer Religion" in Spätmittelalter und Reformation*. Göttingen, 2008.

Keating 2018 Keating, Jessica. *Animating Empire: Automata, the Holy Roman Empire, and the Early Modern World*. University Park, PA, 2018.

Kehrer 1953 Kehrer, Hugo. *Deutschland in Spanien: Beziehung, Einfluss und Abhängigkeit*. Munich, 1953.

Kellenbenz 1967 Kellenbenz, Hermann. "Die Beziehungen Nürnbergs zur Iberischen Halbinsel, besonders im 15. und in der ersten Hälfte des 16. Jahrhunderts." In Stadtarchiv Nürnberg 1967, vol. 1, pp. 456–93.

Kellenbenz 1970a Kellenbenz, Hermann. "Nürnberger Safranhändler." In Kellenbenz 1970b, pp. 197–225.

Kellenbenz 1970b Kellenbenz, Hermann, ed. *Fremde Kaufleute auf der Iberischen Halbinsel*. Kölner Kolloquien zur internationalen Sozial- und Wirtschaftsgeschichte 1. Cologne and Vienna, 1970.

Kellenbenz 1977 Kellenbenz, Hermann. *Schwerpunkte der Kupferproduktion und des Kupferhandels in Europa 1500–1650*. Cologne, 1977.

Kellenbenz 1986 Kellenbenz, Hermann, ed. *Handbuch der europäischen Wirtschafts- und Sozialgeschichte*. Vol. 3, *Europäische Wirtschafts- und Sozialgeschichte vom ausgehenden Mittelalter bis zur Mitte des 17. Jahrhunderts*. Stuttgart, 1986.

Kellenbenz and Walter 2001 Kellenbenz, Hermann, and Rolf Walter, eds. *Oberdeutsche Kaufleute in Sevilla und Cadiz (1525–1560): Eine Edition von Notariatsakten aus den dortigen Archiven*. Stuttgart, 2001.

Kern 1862 Kern, Theodor von. "Chronik aus Kaiser Sigmund's Zeit bis 1434 mit Fortsetzung bis 1441." In Hegel 1862, pp. 313–414.

Keupp et al. 2009 Keupp, Jan, et al. *"... die keyserlichen zeychen ...": Die Reichskleinodien – Herrschaftszeichen des Heiligen Römischen Reiches*. Regensburg, 2009.

Kiening 2006 Kiening, Christian. *Das wilde Subjekt: Kleine Poetik der Neuen Welt*. Göttingen, 2006.

Kiening 2016 Kiening, Christian. *Fülle und Mangel: Medialität im Mittelalter*. Zurich, 2016.

Kiesewetter 2022 Kiesewetter, Arndt. *Der Hauptaltar in der St. Annenkirche zu Annaberg und die Augsburger Daucher-Werkstatt*. Arbeitshefte des Landesamtes für Denkmalpflege Sachsen 31. Dresden, 2022.

Kießling 1997 Kießling, Rolf. "Augsburg in der Reformationszeit." In Exh. cat. Augsburg 1997, pp. 17–43.

Kießling and Müller 2018 Kießling, Rolf, and Gernot Michael Müller, eds. *Konrad Peutinger: Ein Universalgelehrter zwischen Spätmittelalter und Früher Neuzeit; Bestandsaufnahme und Perspektiven*. Colloquia Augustana 35. Berlin and Boston, 2018.

Kim 2006 Kim, David Y. "Uneasy Reflections: Images of Venice and Tenochtitlan in Benedetto Bordone's Isolario." *RES: Anthropology and Aesthetics* 49–50 (2006), pp. 80–91.

Kim 2024 Kim, Dascl. "Muslim, Sub-Saharan African, and Native American Bodies as European Furnishings, 1500–1700." PhD diss., Rice University, Houston, TX, 2024 [manuscript].

King 2002 King, Heidi. "Gold in Ancient America." In Jones and King 2002, pp. 6–8.

Klein 2007 Klein, Bruno, ed. *Gotik: Geschichte der bildenden Kunst in Deutschland*. Vol. 3. Munich, 2007.

Klingelhöfer 1972 Klingelhöfer, Hans, ed. *Peter Martyr von Anghiera: Acht Dekaden über die Neue Welt*. Vol. 1, *Dekaden I–IV*. Texte zur Forschung 5. Darmstadt, 1972.

Knabe and Noli 2012 Knabe, Wolfgang, and Dieter Noli. *Die versunkenen Schätze der Bom Jesus: Sensationsfund eines Indienseglers aus der Frühzeit des Welthandels*. Berlin, 2012.

Koch 2010 Koch, Ebba. "The Mughal Emperor as Solomon, Majnun, and Orpheus or the Album as a Think Tank for Allegory." *Muqarnas* 27 (2010), pp. 277–311.

Kogman-Appel 1994 Kogman-Appel, Katrin. "The Second Nuremberg Haggadah and the Yahuda Haggadah: Were They Made by the Same Artist?" *World Congress of Jewish Studies* (1994), pp. 25–32.

Kogman-Appel 2001 Kogman-Appel, Katrin. "The Iconography of the Biblical Cycle of the Second Nuremberg and the Yahuda Haggadot: Tradition and Innovation." In Heller and Talmon 2001, pp. 118–31.

Kohlhaussen 1968 Kohlhaussen, Heinrich. *Nürnberger Goldschmiedekunst des Mittelalters und der Dürerzeit 1240 bis 1540*. Berlin, 1968.

Kohwagner-Nikolai, Päffgen, and Steininger 2021 Kohwagner-Nikolai, Tanja, Bernd Päffgen, and Christine Steininger, eds. *Über Stoff und Stein: Knotenpunkte von Textilkunst und Epigraphik*. Wiesbaden, 2021.

Kollinger and Pommeranz 2001 Kollinger, Andrea, and Johannes Pommeranz. "Fernando Colóns Buchkäufe in Nürnberg im Winter 1521/1522." *Anzeiger des Germanischen Nationalmuseums* (2001), pp. 86–111.

Kollmann 2024 Kollmann, Nancy S. *Visualizing Russia in Early Modern Europe*. Cambridge, 2024.

König 1935 König, Arthur. "Die Nürnberger Rechenpfennigschlager." *Mitteilungen der Bayerischen Numismatischen Gesellschaft* 53 (1935), pp. 4–16.

König and Stalzer 1989 König, Arthur, and Franz Stalzer. *Rechenpfennige*. Vol. 1, *Nürnberg: Signierte und zuweisbare Gepräge; 1. Lieferung; Die Familien Schultes, Koch und Krauwinckel*. Kataloge / Staatliche Münzsammlung München – Museum für Geldgeschichte. Munich, 1989.

Kontogiannis, Böhlendorf-Arslan, and Yenişehirlioğlu 2021 Kontogiannis, Nikos D., Beate Böhlendorf-Arslan, and Filiz Yenişehirlioğlu, eds. *Glazed Wares as Cultural Agents in the Byzantine, Seljuk, and Ottoman Lands*. Istanbul, 2021.

Koschatzky and Strobl 1971 Koschatzky, Walter, and Alice Strobl. *Die Dürer Zeichnungen der Albertina*. Salzburg, 1971.

Kovács 2018 Kovács, Péter E. *König Sigismund in Siena*. Budapest, 2018.

Krause and Schellewald 2011 Krause, Karin, and Barbara Schellewald, eds. *Bild und Text im Mittelalter*. Sensus: Studien zur mittelalterlichen Kunst 2. Cologne, 2011.

Krauß 1732 Krauß, Johann Werner. *Eißfeldische Brand- und Gedächtnispredigt. Bey Erinnerung der vor hundert Jahren Anno 1632. D.I.Octobr. Erlittenen totalen Einäscherung Der Stadt Eißfeld Am XVII. Sonntag nach Trinit*. Hildburghausen, 1732.

Krebs 2021 Krebs, Verena. *Medieval Ethiopian Kingship, Craft, and Diplomacy with Latin Europe*. Cham (CH), 2021.

Kreslin 1597 Kreslin, Georg. *Berg-Practica oder Prognosticon diß Bergwerck bawens*. Nuremberg: Valentin Fuhrmann, 1597.

Kroell 1980 Kroell, Anne. "Le voyage de Lazarus Nürnberger en Inde (1517–1518)." *Bulletin des Études Portugaises et Brésiliennes* 41 (1980), pp. 59–87.

Kroll 1974 Kroll, Renate. *Hans Burgkmair 1473–1531: Holzschnitte, Zeichnungen, Holzstöcke*. Berlin, 1974.

Kröner 2023 Kröner, Marius. *Vom Höllenfeuer zum Exportschlager: Nürnbergs Rotschmiede und buntmetallverarbeitende Handwerke im Spätmittelalter und in der Frühen Neuzeit*. Arbeiten zur Archäologie Süddeutschlands 34. Büchenbach, 2023.

Krünitz 1773–1858 Krünitz, Johann Georg. *Oekonomische Encyklopädie oder allgemeines System der Staats-, Stadt-, Haus und Landwirthschaft in alphabetischer Ordnung*. 242 vols. Brünn and Berlin, 1773–1858.

Kügelgen 2002 Kügelgen, Helga von, ed. *Herencias indígenas, tradiciones europeas, y la mirada europea / Indigenes Erbe, europäische Traditionen und der europäische Blick*. With Gabriele Schulze. Ars Iberica et Americana 7. Frankfurt am Main, 2002.

Kuhl 2008 Kuhl, Isabel. "Cesare Vecellios Habiti et antichi moderni: Ein Kostüm-Fachbuch des 16. Jahrhunderts." PhD diss., Universität zu Köln, Cologne, 2008. http://nbn-resolving.de/urn:nbn:de:hbz:38-28786.

Kühlmann et al. 2016 Kühlmann, Wilhelm, et al., eds. *Literaturwissenschaftliches Verfasserlexikon: Frühe Neuzeit in Deutschland 1520–1620*. Vol. 5. Berlin, 2016.

Kuhn 2010 Kuhn, Christian. *Genealogie als Grundbegriff einer historischen Geschichtskultur: Die Nürnberger Tucher im langen 16. Jahrhundert*. Göttingen, 2010.

Kula 2014 Kula, Gülbeyaz. "Vom Wissen um die Leserschaft: Zur Bedeutung der Apodemik für die Reisebeschreibungen von Salomon Schweigger und Johann Wild am Beispiel des türkischen Bades (Hamam)." *Zeitschrift für Germanistik* 24 (2014), pp. 10–24.

Kunstmann 1861 Kunstmann, Friedrich. *Die Fahrt der ersten Deutschen nach dem Portugiesischen Indien*. Munich, 1861.

Kunz 2014 Kunz, Tobias. *Bildwerke nördlich der Alpen 1050 bis 1380: Kritischer Bestandskatalog der Berliner Skulpturensammlung*. Petersberg, 2014.

Kunz 2019 Kunz, Tobias. *Bildwerke nördlich der Alpen und im Alpenraum 1380–1440: Kritischer Bestandskatalog; Skulpturensammlung und Museum für Byzantinische Kunst, Staatliche Museen zu Berlin*. Petersberg, 2019.

Kupper 2006 Kupper, Christine, ed. *Erwerbungen zur Kunst des Mittelalters: Ziborium aus Kloster Tennenbach, zwei Nürnberger Bildteppiche*. Patrimonia 165. Berlin, 2006.

Kurmann 2002 Kurmann, Peter. "Zur Vorstellung des Himmlischen Jerusalem und zu den eschatologischen Perspektiven in der Kunst des Mittelalters." In Aertsen and Pickavé 2002, pp. 293–300.

Kusimba 1999 Kusimba, Chapurukha M. *The Rise and Fall of Swahili States*. Walnut Creek, CA, 1999.

Kusimba 2024 Kusimba, Chapurukha M. *Swahili Worlds in Globalism*. Cambridge, 2024.

Lacroix 1998 Lacroix, W. F. G. *Africa in Antiquity*. Nimwegen, 1998.

Ladstätter, Pirson, and Schmidts 2014 Ladstätter, Sabine, Felix Pirson, and Thomas Schmidts, eds. *Häfen und Hafenstädte im östlichen Mittelmeerraum von der Antike bis in byzantinische Zeit*. Byzas 19. Istanbul, 2014.

Landois 2020 Landois, Antonia. "Zum Entstehungshintergrund der Meldeman-Rundansicht in Nürnberg." In Opll and Scheutz 2020, pp. 167–79.

Lane 2019 Lane, Kris. *Potosí: The Silver City that Changed the World*. Oakland, CA, 2019.

Lang 2020 Lang, Heinrich. *Wirtschaften als kulturelle Praxis: Die Florentiner Salviati und die Augsburger Welser auf den Märkten in Lyon (1507–1559)*. Stuttgart, 2020.

Lange 1896 Lange, Konrad. "Peter Flötner als Bildschnitzer." *Jahrbuch der Preuszischen Kunstsammlungen* 17 (1896), pp. 162–80, 221–35.

Lange 1897 Lange, Konrad. *Peter Flötner: Ein Bahnbrecher der deutschen Renaissance*. Berlin, 1897.

Lange-Krach 2018a Lange-Krach, Heidrun. *Das Gebetbuch Kaiser Maximilians I: Meisterhafte Zeichnungen der deutschen Renaissance. München, Bayerische Staatsbibliothek, 2 L.impr. membr. 64, Besançon, Bibliothèque municipale, Étude 67633*. 2 vols. Lucerne, 2018.

Lange-Krach 2018b Lange-Krach, Heidrun. "Illustrationen im Gebetbuch Kaiser Maximilians I." In Augustyn and Teget-Welz 2018, pp. 315–32.

Lange-Krach 2018c Lange-Krach, Heidrun. "Konrad Peutingers Kunstsammlung." In Kießling and Müller 2018, pp. 107–35.

Lange-Krach 2025 Lange-Krach, Heidrun. *Das Neue Gebetbuch Kaiser Maximilians I. in seiner Entstehung*. Berlin, 2025 (forthcoming).

Las Casas 1992 Las Casas, Bartolomé de. *A Short Account of the Destruction of the Indies*. Edited and translated by Nigel Griffin, with an introduction by Anthony Pagden. London, 1992.

Laue 2018 Laue, Georg, ed. *Perspectiva: A Nuremberg Renaissance Casket for the Marquesses of Lothian*. London, 2018.

Laue 2023 Laue, Georg, ed. *Silberne Trinkspiele an den Höfen Europas / Drinking Games in Silver at European Courts*. Munich, 2023.

Leader 2018 Leader, Anne, ed. *Memorializing the Middle Classes in Medieval and Renaissance Europe*. Studies in Medieval and Early Modern Culture 60. Kalamazoo, MI, 2018.

Lehfeldt and Voss 1907 Lehfeldt, Paul, and Georg Voss. *Landrathsamt Coburg*. Bau- und Kunst-Denkmäler Thüringens: Herzogthum Sachsen-Coburg und Gotha IV. Jena, 1907.

Lehner 2019 Lehner, Julia, ed. *Politik. Macht. Kultur. Nürnberg und Lauf unter Kaiser Karl IV. und seinen Nachfolgern*. Schriften des Kulturreferats der Stadt Nürnberg 5. Nuremberg, 2019.

Leibnitz 1674 Leibnitz, Johann Jacob. *Inclutae Bibliothecae Norimbergensis Memorabilia ...* . Nuremberg, 1674.

Leitch 2009 Leitch, Stephanie. "Burgkmair's Peoples of Africa and India (1508) and the Origins of Ethnography in Print." *The Art Bulletin* 91 (2009), pp. 134–58.

Leitch 2010 Leitch, Stephanie. *Mapping Ethnography in Early Modern Germany: New Worlds in Print Culture*. New York, 2010.

Leitch 2013 Leitch, Stephanie. "Vespucci's Triangle and the Shape of the World." *Cadernos de Letras* 29 (2013), pp. 86–111.

Lessmann 2004 Lessmann, Johanna. "Italienische Majolika in Nürnberg." In Glaser 2004, pp. 235–64.

Liesegang 1972 Liesegang, Gerhard. "Archaeological Sites in the Bay of Sofala." *Azania: Archaeological Research in Africa* 7 (1972), pp. 147–59.

Litterscheid 1989 Litterscheid, Claus, ed. *Aus der Welt der Azteken: Die Chronik des Fray Bernardino de Sahagún*. Frankfurt am Main, 1989.

Löcher 1997 Löcher, Kurt. *Die Gemälde des 16. Jahrhunderts: Germanisches Nationalmuseum Nürnberg; Kataloge des Germanischen Nationalmuseums*. With Carola Gries and Anna Bartl. Ostfildern-Ruit, 1997.

Löcher 1999 Löcher, Kurt. *Barthel Beham: Ein Maler aus dem Dürerkreis*. Munich, 1999.

Löhlein 1963–64 Löhlein, Georg. "Die Gründungsurkunde des Nürnberger Heilig-Geistspitals von 1339." *MVGN* 52 (1963–64), pp. 65–79.

Loose 1877 Loose, Wilhelm, ed. *Anton Tuchers Haushaltbuch (1507 bis 1517)*. Bibliothek des litterarischen Vereins in Stuttgart 134. Tübingen, 1877.

López Camarillas 2021 López Camarillas, José A. "La tabla perdida de Yañez que nunca desapareció: Origen de la Santa Generación del

Prado." *Archivo de arte valenciano* 102 (2021), pp. 51–60.

Lowe 2005 Lowe, Kate. The Stereotyping of Black Africans in Renaissance Europe. In Earle and Lowe 2005, pp. 17–47.

Lowe 2012 Lowe, Kate. "The Lives of African Slaves and People of African Descent in Renaissance Europe." In Exh. cat. Baltimore and Princeton 2012, pp. 12–33.

Lutz 2007 Lutz, Gerhard. "Repräsentation und Affekt: Skulptur von 1250 bis 1430." In Klein 2007, pp. 327–97.

Madar 2023 Madar, Heather. *Albrecht Dürer and the Depiction of Cultural Differences in Renaissance Europe*. New York and London, 2023.

Maimon, Breuer, and Guggenheim 1995 Maimon, Arye, Mordechai Breuer, and Jacov Guggenheim, eds. *Germania Judaica*. Vol. 3, *1350–1519*. Part 2, *Ortschaftsartikel Mährisch-Budwitz – Zwolle*. Tübingen, 1995.

Mährle 2019 Mährle, Wolfgang, ed. *Spätrenaissance in Schwaben: Wissen, Literatur, Kunst*. Stuttgart, 2019.

Malcolm 2019 Malcolm, Noel. *Useful Enemies: Islam and the Ottoman Empire in Western Political Thought, 1450–1750*. Oxford, 2019.

Mathew 1963 Mathew, Gervase. "The East African Coast until the Coming of the Portuguese." In Oliver and Mathew 1963, pp. 94–127.

Maué 1989 Maué, Hermann. "Nürnberger Medaillenkunst zur Zeit Dürers." *Médailles & Antiques* 1 (1989), pp. 23–30.

Maugham 1906 Maugham, Reginald C. F. *Portuguese East Africa: The History, Scenery, and Great Game of Manica and Sofala*. New York, 1906.

Martin 1994 Martin, Andrew John. "Anton Kolb und Jacopo de' Barbari: Venedig im Jahre 1500." In Hamacher and Karnehm 1994, pp. 84–121.

Martínez 1990 Martínez, José Luis. *Documentos cortesianos*. Mexico City, 1990.

Martire d'Anghiera 1912 Martire d'Anghiera, Peter. *De Orbe Novo*. Translated by Francis Augustus MacNutt. New York, 1912.

Maruska 2008 Maruska, Monika. "Johannes Schöner – 'Homo est nescio qualis': Leben und Werk eines fränkischen Wissenschafters [*sic*] an der Wende vom 15. zum 16. Jahrhundert." PhD diss., Universität Wien, Vienna, 2008. http://othes.univie.ac.at/1354/1/2008-08-07_8001863.pdf.

Māshā'allāh and Heller 1549 Māshā'allāh ibn Atharī. *De elementis et orbibvs coelestibvs …* . Edited by Joachim Heller. Nuremberg, 1549.

Massing 1991 Massing, Jean Michel. "Early European Images of America: The Ethnographic Approach." In Exh. cat. Washington 1991, pp. 515–20.

Massing 1995 Massing, Jean Michel. "Hans Burgkmair's Depiction of Native Africans." *RES: Anthropology and Aesthetics* 27 (1995), pp. 39–51.

Massing 2016 Massing, Jean Michel. "The Origin of the Iconography of Cannibalism in the Early Modern Period." *Print Quarterly* 33 (2016), pp. 3–10.

Mathesius 1562 Mathesius, Johannes. *Sarepta oder Bergpostill sampt der Jochimssthalischen kurtzen Chroniken*. Nuremberg, 1562.

Matos Moctezuma 2009 Matos Moctezuma, Eduardo. *Tenochtitlan*. Mexico City, 2009.

Matos Moctezuma 2011 Matos Moctezuma, Eduardo. "Reflexiones acerca del Plano de Tenochtitlan publicado en Nuremberg en 1524." *Caravelle* 76 (2011), pp. 183–95.

Matthew 1999 Matthew, Louisa C. "Working Abroad: Northern Artists in the Venetian Ambient." In Exh. cat. Venice 1999b, pp. 61–69.

Maué 2002 Maué, Hermann. "In Nürnberg gedruckte Bücher." In Exh. cat. Nuremberg 2002, pp. 320–63.

Mauntel 2021 Mauntel, Christoph, ed. *Geography and Religious Knowledge in the Medieval World*. Berlin and Boston, 2021.

Maxwell 2022 Maxwell, Andrea Kibler. "Painting and Persecution: Anti-Jewish and Anti-Protestant Visual Rhetoric in Northern Italy, 1475–1550." PhD diss., University of Pittsburgh, 2022. https://d-scholarship.pitt.edu/42381/.

Mazzei 1999 Mazzei, Rita. *Itinera mercatorum: Circolazione di uomini e beni nell'Europa centro-orientale 1550–1650*. Lucca, 1999.

McConnell and McConnell 2009 McConnell, Karen, and Winder McConnell, eds. *"Er ist ein wol gevriunder man": Essays in Honor of Ernst S. Dick on the Occasion of His Eightieth Birthday*. Hildesheim, 2009.

McDonald 2003 McDonald, Mark P. "Burgkmair's Woodcut Frieze of the Natives of Africa and India." *Print Quarterly* 20 (2003), pp. 227–44.

McDonald 2004 McDonald, Mark P. *The Print Collection of Ferdinand Columbus (1488–1539): A Renaissance Collector in Seville*. 2 vols. London, 2004.

Meier 2006 Meier, Esther. *Die Gregorsmesse: Funktionen eines spätmittelalterlichen Bildtypus*. Cologne et al., 2006.

Meier 2021 Meier, Esther. "Standesrepräsentation und ihre Memorialsysteme am Beispiel der Gedächtnistafel des Heinrich Wolff von Wolffsthal und der Katharina Mayr." In Augustyn and Söding 2021, pp. 261–75.

Meißner 2018 Meißner, Friedemann. "Das Nürnberger Schenkbuch 1400–1451: Ein Beitrag zur Erforschung von Schenkpraxis und symbolischer Kommunikation im Spätmittelalter." *MVGN* 105 (2018), pp. 1–97.

Mejía 2005 Mejía, Juan. "Rinocerontes colombianos: Mirada a unos animales en el arte." In Gaitán 2005, pp. 53–110.

Méndez Rodríguez 2013 Méndez Rodríguez, Luis. *La aventura de Jerónimo Köler*. First edition, Sevilla, 1533. Madrid and Sevilla, 2013.

Merkl 1999 Merkl, Ulrich. *Buchmalerei in Bayern in der ersten Hälfte des 16. Jahrhunderts: Spätblüte und Endzeit einer Gattung*. Regensburg, 1999.

Messerli 2008 Messerli, Alfred. "Bilder verstehen, so gut es geht: Frühneuzeitliche Bildrezeption zwischen visueller Vorgabe und individuellen Erwartungshorizont." In Bruhn and Hemken 2008, pp. 158–77.

Messling 2015 Messling, Guido. "The Northern View: Albrecht Dürer and the Ottomans." In Exh. cat. Brussels and Kraków 2015, pp. 53–55.

Meurer 2001 Meurer, Peter H. *Corpus der älteren Germania-Karten: Ein annotierter Katalog der gedruckten Gesamtkarten des deutschen Raumes von den Anfängen bis 1650*. 2 vols. Alphen aan den Rijn, 2001.

Meyer 2009 Meyer, Carla. *Die Stadt als Thema: Nürnbergs Entdeckung in Texten um 1500*. Mittelalter-Forschungen 26. Ostfildern, 2009.

Meyer zur Capellen 1985 Meyer zur Capellen, Jürg. *Gentile Bellini*. Stuttgart, 1985.

Michelfelder 1967 Michelfelder, Gottfried. "Die wirtschaftliche Tätigkeit der Juden Nürnbergs im Spätmittelalter." In Stadtarchiv Nürnberg 1967, pp. 237–60.

Monteleone 2024 Monteleone, Cosimo. "A Perspectival Investigation of Jacopo de' Barbari's View of Venice." In Huffman 2024, pp. 50–61.

Mordtmann 1921–22 Mordtmann, Johannes Heinrich. "Zwei osmanische Paßbriefe aus dem XVI. Jahrhundert." *Mitteilungen zur osmanischen Geschichte* 1 (1921–22), pp. 172–202.

Morel 2020 Morel, Thomas. "De Re Geometrica: Writing, Drawing, and Preaching Mathematics in Early Modern Mines." *Isis* 101, no. 1 (2020), pp. 22–45.

Morselli 2024 Morselli, Raffaella. "Roma: la gloria delle donne tra Cinquecento e Seicento." In Exh. cat. Rome 2024, pp. 17–31.

Mory 1975 Mory, Ludwig. *Schönes Zinn: Geschichte, Formen und Probleme*. 5th ed. Munich, 1975.

Motture, Jones, and Zikos 2013 Motture, Peta, Emma Jones, and Dimitrios Zikos, eds. *Carvings, Casts & Collectors: The Art of Renaissance Sculpture*. London, 2013, pp. 120–33.

Mozzati 2020 Mozzati, Tomasso. "Una tabla inédita de Fernando Yañez y nueva luz sobre su estancia en la Almedina (1518–1525)." *Archivo de arte valenciano* 101 (2020), pp. 115–26.

Mraz 1983 Mraz, Gottfried. "Risse der Rüstungen und Handfeuerwaffen für die Türkenverehrung 1590." *Jahrbuch der kunsthistorischen Sammlungen in Wien* 79 (1983), pp. 107–25.

Müller 1907 Müller, Johannes. "Nürnbergs Botschaft nach Spanien zu Kaiser Karl V. im Jahre 1519." *Historische Zeitschrift* 98 (1907), pp. 302–28.

Müller 1986 Müller, Hannelore. *European Silver: The Thyssen-Bornemisza Collection*. London, 1986.

Müller 2002 Müller, Heidi. *Tand und Nürnberger Waren*. In Exh. cat. Nuremberg 2002, pp. 73–79.

Müller 2005 Müller, Ralf C. *Franken im Osten: Art, Umfang, Struktur und Dynamik der Migration aus dem lateinischen Westen in das Osmanische Reich des 15./16. Jahrhunderts auf der Grundlage von Reiseberichten*. Leipzig, 2005.

Müller 2009a Müller, Jörg R. "Sexual Relationships between Christians and Jews in Medieval Germany, According to Christian Sources." *Iggud: Selected Essays in Jewish Studies* 2 (2009), pp. 19–32.

Müller 2009b Müller, Ulrich. "'Mich lustet vil sêre daz wir in das bat gân': Die erste Beschreibung eines türkischen Bades (Hamam) in deutscher Sprache; Salomon Schweigger 1608." In McConnell and McConnell 2009, pp. 275–93.

Müller, Spieß, and Friedrich 2013 Müller, Matthias, Karl-Heinz Spieß, and Udo Friedrich, eds. *Kulturtransfer am Fürstenhof: Höfische Austauschprozesse und ihre Medien im Zeitalter Kaiser Maximilians I*. Berlin, 2013.

Müllner 2003 Müllner, Johannes. *Die Annalen der Reichsstadt Nürnberg von 1623*. Edited by Michael Diefenbacher with Walter Gebhardt. Part 3, *1470–1544*. Quellen und Forschungen zur Geschichte und Kultur der Stadt Nürnberg 32. Nuremberg, 2003.

Mummenhoff 1891 Mummenhoff, Ernst. *Das Rathaus in Nürnberg*. Nuremberg, 1891.

Münch and Müller 2015 Münch, Birgit Ulrike, and Jürgen Müller, eds. *Peraikos' Erben: Die Genese der Genremalerei bis 1550*. Wiesbaden, 2015.

Mundy 1998 Mundy, Barbara. "Mapping the Aztec Capital: The 1524 Nuremberg Map of Tenochtitlan, Its Sources and Meanings." *Imago Mundi* 50 (1998), pp. 1–22.

Munro 2007 Munro, John H. "South German Silver, European Textiles, and Venetian Trade with the Levant and Ottoman Empire, c. 1370 to c. 1720." In Cavaciocchi 2007, pp. 905–60.

Münzer and Herbers 2020 Münzer, Hieronymus. *Itinerarium*. Edited by Klaus Herbers. MGH: Reiseberichte des Mittelalters 1. Wiesbaden, 2020.

Murr 1778 Murr, Christoph Gottlieb von. *Beschreibung der vornehmsten Merkwürdigkeiten in des H. R. Reichs freyen Stadt Nürnberg und auf der hohen Schule zu Altdorf: Nebst einem chronologischen Verzeichnisse der von Deutschen, insonderheit Nürnbergern, erfundenen Künste, vom XIII Jahrhunderte bis auf jetzige Zeiten; Mit Kupfern*. Nuremberg, 1778.

Murr 1801 Murr, Christoph Gottlieb von. *Beschreibung der vornehmsten Merkwürdigkeiten in der Reichsstadt Nürnberg in deren Bezirke und auf der Universität Altdorf; Nebst einem Anhange*. 2nd ed. Nuremberg, 1801.

MVGN *Mitteilungen des Vereins für Geschichte der Stadt Nürnberg*. vols. 1ff. Nuremberg, 1879ff.

Nagel and Pericolo 2010 Nagel, Alexander, and Lorenzo Pericolo, eds. *Subject as Aporia in Early Modern Art*. Farnham, 2010.

Narciß 1988 Narciß, Georg A., ed. *Geschichte der Eroberung von Mexiko: Von Bernal Diaz del Castillo*. Insel Taschenbuch 1067. Frankfurt am Main, 1988.

Natif 2018 Natif, Mika. *Mughal Occidentalism: Artistic Encounters between Europe and Asia at the Courts of India, 1580–1630*. Studies in Persian Cultural History 15. Leiden, 2018.

NDB *Neue Deutsche Biographie*. Edited by Historische Kommission bei der Bayerischen Akademie der Wissenschaften. Berlin, 1953ff.

Necipoğlu and Payne 2016 Necipoğlu, Gülru, and Alina Payne, eds. *Histories of Ornament: From Global to Local*. Princeton, NJ, 2016.

Nehring 1897 Nehring, Alfred. *Über Herberstain und Hirsfogel: Beiträge zur Kenntnis ihres Lebens und ihrer Werke*. Berlin, 1897.

Netherton and Owen-Crocker 2008 Netherton, Robin, and Gale R. Owen-Crocker, eds. *Medieval Clothing and Textiles*. Vol. 4. Woodbridge, 2008.

Neuber 2000 Neuber, Wolfgang. "Grade der Fremdheit: Alteritätskonstruktion und experientia-Argumentation in deutschen Turcica der Renaissance." In Guthmüller and Kühlmann 2000, pp. 262–64.

Neudörfer and Lochner 1875 *Des Johann Neudörfer Schreib- und Rechenmeisters zu Nürnberg Nachrichten von Künstlern und Werkleuten daselbst aus dem Jahre 1547: Nebst der Fortsetzung des Andreas Gulden; Nach der Handschrift und mit Anmerkungen hrsg. von Georg Wolfgang Karl Lochner*. Quellenschriften für Kunstgeschichte und Kunsttechnik des Mittelalters und der Renaissance 10. Vienna, 1875.

Neuhaus 1935 Neuhaus, August. "Das Federbarett des Christoph Kress von Kressenstein: Eine Neuerwerbung des Germanischen Nationalmuseums." *Zeitschrift für Historische Waffen- und Kostümkunde* (new series) 5 (1935), pp. 34–38.

Neuhaus 2000 Neuhaus, Helmut, ed. *Nürnberg: Eine europäische Stadt in Mittelalter und Neuzeit*. Nürnberger Forschungen 2. Nuremberg, 2000.

Nevinson 1967 Nevinson, John L. "Origin and Early History of the Fashion Plate." *United States National Museum Bulletin* 60 (1967), pp. 65–92.

New Hollstein German 5, no. 2 *The New Hollstein German*. Vol. 5, no. 2, *Jost Amman*. Compiled by Gero Seelig. Rotterdam, 2001.

New Hollstein German 7 *The New Hollstein German*. Vol. 7, *Jörg Breu the Elder and the Younger*. Compiled by Guido Messling. Rotterdam, 2008.

NGK 2007 *Nürnberger Goldschmiedekunst 1541–1868*. Vol. 1, *Meister, Werke, Marken*. Part 1, *Textband*. Part 2, *Tafeln*. Compiled by Karin Tebbe et al. Vol. 2, *Goldglanz und Silberstrahl*. Begleitband zur Ausstellung im Germanischen Nationalmuseum, Nuremberg. Edited by Karin Tebbe. Nuremberg, 2007.

Nickel 1995 Nickel, Helmut. "The Seven Shields of Behaim: New Evidence." *Metropolitan Museum Journal* 30 (1995), pp. 29–51.

Nicolay 1572 Nicolay, Nicolas de. *Von der Schiffart vnnd Raiß in die Türckeÿ ...* . Nuremberg, 1572.

Nirenberg 2007 Nirenberg, David. "Vom Verschwinden des Judentums: Das christliche Spanien im Zeitalter der Massenkonversionen." In Stollberg-Rilinger and Weller 2007, pp. 105–22.

Noehles-Doerk 1996 Noehles-Doerk, Gisela, ed. *Kunst in Spanien im Blick des Fremden: Reiseerfahrungen vom Mittelalter bis in die Gegenwart*. Ars Iberica 2. Frankfurt am Main, 1996.

Northemann 2011 Northemann, Yvonne. *Zwischen Vergessen und Erinnern: Die Nürnberger Klöster im medialen Geflecht*. Petersberg, 2011.

Novgorod Geography 2022 Novgorod Geography. "Point on the Map: Small-Scale Maps of Russia." 2022. https://novgeo.graphics/en/tochka-na-karte/exhibit.

Nowotny 1947 Nowotny, Karl A. "Die Gastgeschenke des Motecuhçoma an Cortes." *Archiv für Völkerkunde* 2 (1947), pp. 210–21.

Nowotny 1960 Nowotny, Karl A. *Mexikanische Kostbarkeiten aus Kunstkammern der Renaissance*. Vienna, 1960.

Oakes 2009 Oakes, Simon P. "'Hieronymo Thodesco' and the Fondaco dei Tedeschi: A Reappraisal of the Documents and Sources Relating to a German Architect in Early Sixteenth-Century Venice." *Zeitschrift für Kunstgeschichte* 72, no. 4 (2009), pp. 479–96.

Obermeier 2003 Obermeier, Franz. "Die frühen illustrierten Einblattdrucke zu Amerika und ihre Verbreitung im zeitgenössischen Pressewesen." *Wolfenbütteler Notizen zur Buchgeschichte* 28 (2003), pp. 3–29.

O'Flanagan 2008 O'Flanagan, Patrick. *Port Cities of Atlantic Iberia, c. 1500–1900*. Aldershot, Burlington, 2008.

Olariu 2023 Olariu, Dominic. *Georg Öllingers Kräuterbuch: Ein Nürnberger Apotheker erforscht die Pflanzenwelt der Renaissance*. Darmstadt, 2023.

Oliver and Mathew 1963 Oliver, Roland, and Gervase Mathew, eds. *History of East Africa*. Vol. 1. Oxford, 1963.

Oosterhoff, Marcaida, and Marr 2021 Oosterhoff, Richard J., José Ramón Marcaida, and Alexander Marr, eds. *Ingenuity in the Making: Matter and Technique in Early Modern Europe*. Pittsburgh, 2021.

Opll and Scheutz 2020 Opll, Ferdinand, and Martin Scheutz, eds. *Die Osmanen vor Wien: Die Meldeman-Rundansicht von 1529/30; Sensation, Propaganda und Stadtbild.* Vienna, 2020.

Ortuño Molins 2002 Ortuño Molins, Milagros. "Dürer in Spanien." *Anzeiger des Germanischen Nationalmuseums* (2002), pp. 253–63.

Osano 2014 Osano, Shigetoshi, ed. *Between East and West: Reproductions in Art.* Kraków, 2014.

Otte 1963–64 Otte, Heinrich. "Jakob und Hans Cromberger und Lazarus Nürnberger, die Begründer des deutschen Amerikahandels." *MVGN* 52 (1963–64), pp. 129–62.

Özsoy 2024 Özsoy, Ergün. "Cultural and Religious Diversity in Istanbul in the Sixteenth Century: Through the Eyes of German Travellers." *Journal of Balkan and Black Sea Studies* 7 (2024), pp. 57–76.

Paehr 2018 Paehr, Sabine. "Kupfer-, Blei- und Silbergewinnung: Mitteleuropäisches Hüttenwesen in der Frühen Neuzeit; Eine vergleichende Darstellung wissenschaftlicher Fachliteratur." PhD diss., Leibniz Universität Hannover, 2018.

Palm 1956 Palm, Erwin Walter. "Dürer's Ganda and a XVI Century APOTHEOSIS OF HERCULES at Tunja." *Gazette des Beaux-Arts* series 6, no. 48 (1956), pp. 65–74.

Panofsky 1971 Panofsky, Erwin. *The Life and Art of Albrecht Dürer.* 4th ed. Princeton, NJ, 1971.

Pápay 2021 Pápay, Gyula. "Amerigo Vespucci's Contribution to the Modernization of Cartographic Representation." *KN: Journal of Cartography and Geographic Information* 71 (2021), pp. 3–13.

Pappas 2008 Pappas, Nicholas J. C. "Stradioti: Balkan Mercenaries in Fifteenth and Sixteenth Century Italy." Sam Houston State University, Huntsville, TX, 2008. https://www.academia.edu/835267/Stradioti_Balkan_Mercenaries_in_Fifteenth_and_Sixteenth_Century_Italy.

Parker and Prottengeier 1956 *From Lisbon to Calicut.* Translated by Alvin E. Prottengeier. Commentary and notes by John Parker. Minneapolis, 1956.

Patała 2018a Patała, Agnieszka. *Pod znakiem świętego Sebalda: Rola Norymbergii w kształtowaniu późnogotyckiego malarstwa tablicowego na Śląsku.* Wrocław, 2018.

Patała 2018b Patała, Agnieszka. "Nuremberg Merchants in Breslau (1440–1520): Commemoration as Assimilation." In Leader 2018, pp. 49–74.

Patała 2019 Patała, Agnieszka. "Hans Pleydenwurff and Wrocław Contexts." In Exh. cat. Wrocław 2019, pp. 83–93.

Patterson 2009 Patterson, Angus. *Fashion and Armour in Renaissance Europe.* London, 2009.

Paulicelli 2008 Paulicelli, Eugenia. "Mapping the World: The Political Geography of Dress in Cesare Vecellio's Costume Books." *The Italianist* 28 (2008), pp. 24–53.

Pechstein 1975 Pechstein, Klaus. "'Allerlei Visierungen und Abriss wegen der Fleischbrücken 1595'." *Anzeiger des Germanischen Nationalmuseums* (1975), pp. 72–89.

Pereda 2007 Pereda, Felipe. *Las imágenes de la discordia: Política y poética de la imagen sagrada en la España del cuatrocientos.* Madrid, 2007.

Peters 1994 Peters, Lambert F. *Der Handel Nürnbergs am Anfang des Dreißigjährigen Krieges – eine quantitative Analyse.* Vierteljahrschrift für Sozial- und Wirtschaftsgeschichte: Beihefte 112. Stuttgart, 1994.

Pfisterer 2013 Pfisterer, Ulrich. "Traurige Musen: Jacopo de' Barbari zu Malerei, Dichtung und Kulturtransfer im Norden." In Müller, Spieß, and Friedrich 2013, pp. 189–217.

Pfisterer 2018 Pfisterer, Ulrich. "Die Kraft der Libido: Peter Flötners Holzschuher-Pokal und der Fortschritt der Kunst." In Fehrenbach, Felfe, and Leonhard 2018, pp. 123–46.

Pfotenhauer 2016 Pfotenhauer, Bettina. *Nürnberg und Venedig im Austausch: Menschen, Güter und Wissen an der Wende vom Mittelalter zur Neuzeit.* Schriftenreihe des Deutschen Studienzentrums in Venedig Centro Tedesco di Studi Veneziani, new series 14. Regensburg, 2016.

Pickl 1970 Pickl, Othmar. "Geadelte Kaufherren: Untersuchung zum Übertritt reicher steirischer Kaufleute des 15. und 16. Jahrhunderts in den Adelsstand." *Blätter für Heimatkunde* 44 (1970), pp. 20–28.

Piechocki 2019 Piechocki, Katharina N. *Cartographic Humanism: The Making of Early Modern Europe.* Chicago, 2019.

Pietrzak and Schilling 2018 Pietrzak, Ewa, and Michael Schilling, eds. *Die Sammlung des Kunstmuseums Moritzburg in Halle a. S.* Deutsche illustrierte Flugblätter des 16. und 17. Jahrhunderts 9. Berlin and Boston, 2018.

Pilz 1974 Pilz, Kurt. "Die Allegorie des Handels aus der Werkstatt des Jost Amman: Ein Holzschnitt von 1585." *Scripta Mercaturae* 1–2 (1974), pp. 25–60.

Pilz 1984 Pilz, Kurt. *St. Johannis und St. Rochus in Nürnberg: Die Kirchhöfe mit den Vorstädten St. Johannis und Gostenhof.* Nuremberg, 1984.

Pittioni 1969 Pittioni, Richard. *Der Holzschuher-Petzolt-Pokal des Jahres 1626.* Studien zur Industrie-Archäologie 2 / Österreichische Akademie der Wissenschaften: Philosophisch-Historische Klasse; Sitzungsberichte, vol. 264, no. 4. Vienna et al., 1969.

Ploss 1967 Ploss, Emil. *Ein Buch von alten Farben: Technologie der Textilfarben im Mittelalter mit einem Ausblick auf die festen Farben.* Munich, 1967.

Pohl 1992 Pohl, Horst. *Willibald Imhoff, Enkel und Erbe Willibald Pirckheimers.* Quellen zur Geschichte und Kultur der Stadt Nürnberg 24. Nuremberg, 1992.

Pohle 2000 Pohle, Jürgen. *Deutschland und die überseeische Expansion Portugals im 15. und 16. Jahrhundert.* Münster, 2000.

Pokorny 2009 Pokorny, Erwin. "The Gypsies and Their Impact on Fifteenth-Century Western European Iconography." In Anderson 2009, pp. 597–601.

Pollard 2016 Pollard, Edward. "Interpreting Medieval to Post-Medieval Seafaring in South East Tanzania Using 18th- to 20th-Century Charts and Sailing Directions." *Les Cahiers d'Afrique de l'Est / The East African Review* 51 (2016), pp. 99–125. https://doi.org/10.4000/eastafrica.332.

Pollard and Ichumbaki 2017 Pollard, Edward, and Elgidius Ichumbaki. "Why Land Here? Ports and Harbours in Southeast Tanzania in the Early Second Millennium AD." *Journal of Island and Coastal Archaeology* 12, no. 4 (2017), pp. 459–89.

Pollard et al. 2016 Pollard, Edward, et al. "Shipwreck Evidence from Kilwa, Tanzania." *International Journal of Nautical Archaeology* 45, no. 2 (2016), pp. 352–69.

Pommeranz 2002 Pommeranz, Johannes. "Fernando Colóns Buchkäufe in Nürnberg im Winter 1521/1522: Zum Vertrieb des Nürnberger Buchhandels im Zeitalter der Fugger." In Exh. cat. Nuremberg 2002, pp. 305–19.

Praun 1916–17 Praun, Friedrich. "'Was sich auf meiner Reise zugetragen, da ich Stephan Praun von Nürnbergkh, den 20. Jenner bis 31. May, Ao 1569 mit Kaysers Maximillian Pottschafft, dem Herrn Kaspar von Minckwitz von Wien zu Landt nach Constantinoppol mit dem Tribut gezogen': Mitgeteilt nach den Manuskripten und Tagebüchern im Archiv des von Praun'schen Gesamtgeschlechts." *Mitteilungen aus dem Germanischen Nationalmuseum* (1916), pp. 45–62, and (1917), pp. 49–58.

Press and Bauch 2013 Press, Werner, and Wolfgang Bauch. "Von Adam Ries bis Bordesholm: Rechenpfennige aus Nürnberg." In Exh. cat. Kiel 2013, pp. 80–92.

Priebsch 1901 Priebsch, Robert. *Deutsche Handschriften in England.* Vol. 2, *Das British Museum: Mit einem Anhang über die Guildhall-Bibliothek.* Erlangen, 1901.

Priesterjahn 2024 Priesterjahn, Maike. "Schiffstypen in der Renaissance: Der Schiffbau nimmt Kurs auf die hohe See." In Exh. cat. Munich, 2024, pp. 134–59.

Prinzing 2009 Prinzing, Günter. "Zu Jörg von Nürnberg, dem Geschützgießer Mehmets II., und seiner Schrift 'Geschicht von der Turckey'." In Asutay-Effenberger and Rehm 2009, pp. 59–75.

Prummer 2016 Prummer, Markus. "Der Rosenkranz: Marienminne, Memorationshilfe, Modeaccessoire." *KulturGUT: Aus der Forschung des Germanischen Nationalmuseums* 51 (4th Quarter 2016), pp. 8–12.

Purin and Selheim 2025 Purin, Bernhard, and Claudia Selheim. *Judaica – Menschen und*

Objekte: Bestandskatalog des Germanischen Nationalmuseums; Mit einem Beitrag von Susanna Brogi. Nuremberg, 2025.

Putzer 2020a Putzer, Katja. "Wer bekam einen Totenschild? Voraussetzungen, Berechtigung, Ausschlusskriterien." In Kammel et al. 2020, vol. 1, pp. 228–45.

Putzer 2020b Putzer, Katja. "Herrschaft und Memoria: Der Nürnberger Rat und sein Einfluss auf Repräsentation und Erinnerungskultur." In Kammel et al. 2020, vol. 1, pp. 276–97.

Radway 2023 Radway, Robyn D. *Portraits of Empires: Habsburg Albums from the German House in Ottoman Constantinople*. Bloomington, IN, 2023.

Rasmussen 1974 Rasmussen, Jörg. *Die Nürnberger Altarbaukunst der Dürerzeit*. Hamburg, 1974.

Ravenstein 1908 Ravenstein, Ernest George. *Martin Behaim: His Life and His Globe; With a Facsimile of the Globe Printed in Colours; Eleven Maps and Seventeen Illustrations*. London, 1908. http://dl.ub.uni-freiburg.de/diglit/ravenstein1908.

Reichert 1988 Reichert, Folker. "Columbus und Marco Polo – Asien in Amerika: Zur Literaturgeschichte der Entdeckungen." *Zeitschrift für Historische Forschung* 15 (1988), pp. 1–63.

Reichert 1993 Reichert, Folker. "Zipangu – Japans Entdeckung im Mittelalter." In Exh. cat. Berlin 1993, pp. 25–36.

Reid and Lane 2004 Reid, Andrew, and Paul Lane, eds. *African Historical Archaeologies: Contributions to Global Historical Archaeology*. New York, 2004.

Reinhard 1987 Reinhard, Wolfgang, ed. *Humanismus und Neue Welt*. Mitteilung 15 der Kommission für Humanismusforschung. Weinheim, 1987.

Reinhard 2018 Reinhard, Wolfgang. *Die Unterwerfung der Welt: Globalgeschichte der europäischen Expansion 1415–2015*. 4th ed. Munich, 2018.

Reither 2009 Reither, Hans. "Die Reichskleinodien: Beschreibung der Hauptstücke." In Keupp et al. 2009, pp. 23–58.

Resines 1993 Resines, Luis. *La "Breve doctrina" de Hernando de Talavera*. Granada, 1993.

Reske 2000 Reske, Christoph. *Die Produktion der Schedelschen Weltchronik in Nürnberg / The Production of Schedel's Nuremberg Chronicle*. Mainzer Studien zur Buchwissenschaft 10. Wiesbaden, 2000.

Rice 2009 Rice, Yael. "The Brush and the Burin: Mogul Encounters with European Engravings." In Anderson 2009, pp. 305–10.

Riello 2006 Riello, Giorgio. *A Foot in the Past: Consumers, Producers and Footwear in the Long Eighteenth Century*. Oxford, 2006.

Riello 2019 Riello, Giorgio. "The World in a Book: The Creation of the Global in Sixteenth-Century European Costume Books." *Past & Present* 242 (2019), pp. 281–317. https://doi.org/10.1093/pastj/gtz047.

Riese 2011 Riese, Berthold. *Das Reich der Azteken: Geschichte und Kultur*. Munich, 2011.

Riestra 2021 Riestra, Pablo de la. *Rochuskapelle Nürnberg*. Lindenberg im Allgäu, 2021.

Rinke 2022 Rinke, Stefan. *Conquistadoren und Azteken: Cortés und die Eroberung Mexikos*. Munich, 2022.

Rodriguez 2019 Rodriguez, Raül Barrera. "Der Huei Tzompantli, der Ballspielplatz und der Tempel des Ehecatl-Quetzalcoatl: Eine Trilogie der neuesten Entdeckungen." In Exh. cat. Stuttgart, Vienna, and Leiden 2019, pp. 255–66.

Roque 2017 Roque, Ana Cristina. "The Sofala Coast (Mozambique) in the 16th Century: Between the African Trade Routes and Indian Ocean Trade." In Walker, Ramos, and Kaarsholm 2017, pp. 19–36.

Rose 1929 Rose, Walther. "Behördliche Beschau-, Sarwürcher- und Eigentümermarken auf okzidentalischen Maschenpanzern." *Zeitschrift für historische Waffen- und Kostümkunde* 12 (1929), pp. 77–84, 99a–104.

Rothermund 1998 Rothermund, Dietmar. "Der Seeweg nach Indien." *Periplus* 8 (1998), pp. 1–7.

Rothermund 2004 Rothermund, Dietmar. "Der Blick vom Westen auf den Indischen Ozean vom 'Periplus' bis zur 'Summa Oriental'." In Rothermund and Weigelin-Schwiedrzik 2004, pp. 9–35.

Rothermund and Weigelin-Schwiedrzik 2004 Rothermund, Dietmar, and Susanne Weigelin-Schwiedrzik, eds. *Der Indische Ozean: Das afro-asiatische Mittelmeer als Kultur- und Wirtschaftsraum*. Vienna, 2004.

Röttinger 1921 Röttinger, Heinrich. "Die Zeichner der Nürnberger Flugblätter zur Ersten Wiener Türkenbelagerung." *Monatsblatt des Vereins für Geschichte der Stadt Wien* 3 (1921), pp. 126–27.

Röttinger 1925 Röttinger, Heinrich. *Erhard Schön und Niklas Stör, der Pseudo-Schön: Zwei Untersuchungen zur Geschichte des alten Nürnberger Holzschnittes*. Strasbourg, 1925.

Roxburgh 2001 Roxburgh, David J. *Prefacing the Image: The Writing of Art History in Sixteenth-Century Iran*. Leiden et al., 2001.

Rubach 2013 Rubach, Birte. "Rom als Kategorie in der italienischen Druckgraphik des 16. Jahrhunderts." In Exh. cat. Göttingen 2013, pp. 61–74.

Rubach 2016 Rubach, Birte. *Ant. Lafreri Formis Romae: Der Verleger Antonio Lafreri und seine Druckgraphikproduktion*. Berlin, 2016.

Rublack 2010 Rublack, Ulinka. *Dressing Up: Cultural Identity in Renaissance Europe*. Oxford, 2010.

Rublack 2013 Rublack, Ulinka. "Matter in the Material Renaissance." *Past & Present* 219 (2013), pp. 41–85.

Rublack 2021 Rublack, Ulinka. "Befeathering the European: The Matter of Feathers in the Material Renaissance." *The American Historical Review* 126 (2021), pp. 19–53.

Rublack 2022 Rublack, Ulinka. *Die Geburt der Mode: Eine Kulturgeschichte der Renaissance*. Stuttgart, 2022.

Rudy 2001 Rudy, Kathryn. "Northern European Visual Responses to Holy Land Pilgrimage, 1453–1550." PhD diss., Columbia University, New York, 2001.

Ruge 1916 Ruge, Walther. *Aelteres kartographisches Material in deutschen Bibliotheken*. Vol. 5, *Fünfter Bericht über die Jahre 1910–1913*. Berlin, 1916.

Ruh and Keil 1983 Ruh, Kurt, and Gundolf Keil, eds. *Die deutsche Literatur des Mittelalters: Verfasserlexikon*. Vol. 4. Berlin et al., 1983.

Rupprich 1934 Rupprich, Hans, ed. *Der Briefwechsel des Konrad Celtis*. Veröffentlichungen der Kommission zur Erforschung der Geschichte der Reformation und Gegenreformation: Humanistenbriefe 3. Munich, 1934.

Rupprich 1956 Rupprich, Hans, ed. *Dürer: Schriftlicher Nachlass*. Vol. 1, *Autobiographische Schriften, Briefwechsel, Dichtungen. Beischriften, Notizen und Gutachten: Zeugnisse zum persönlichen Leben*. Berlin, 1956.

Rusam 2000 Rusam, Herbert. "Georgskirche Kraftshof." In Diefenbacher and Endres 2000, pp. 331–32.

Russo, Wolf, and Fane 2015 Russo, Alessandra, Gerhard Wolf, and Diana Fane, eds. *Images Take Flight: Feather Art in Mexico and Europe 1400–1700*. Munich, 2015.

Sachs 1568 Sachs, Hans. *Eygentliche Beschreibung Aller Stände auff Erden. Hoher vnd Nidriger, Geistlicher vnd Weltlicher. Aller Künsten, Handwercken vnd Händeln etc. Vom grösten biß zum kleinesten. Auch von jrem Vrsprung, Erfindung vnd Gebreuchen*. Frankfurt am Main, 1568.

Sachs 1895 Sachs, Hans. *Werke*. Edited by Adelbert von Keller and Edmund Goetze. Vol. 23. Tübingen, 1895.

Salfeld and Stern 1894–96 Salfeld, Siegmund, and Moritz Stern, eds. *Die israelitische Bevölkerung der deutschen Städte*. Nürnberg im Mittelalter 3 (Sources, sections 1 and 2). Kiel, 1894–96.

Salinas 1903 Salinas, Martín de. *El emperador Carlos V y su corte según las cartas de Don Martín de Salinas embajador del infante Don Fernando*. Edited by Antonio Rodríguez. Madrid, 1903.

Sandrart 1679 Sandrart, Joachim von. *L'Academia Todesca della architectura, scultura & pittura oder Teutsche Academie der edlen Bau-, Bild- und Mahlerey-Künste*. Vol. 2, no. 3, *Der Edlen Mahler-Kunst rechten Grund, Eigenschafften und Geheimnisse ... erörtert*. Nuremberg, 1679.

Sapio 2017 Sapio, Maria, ed. *Il restauro del Ponte di Rialto a Venezia*. Naples, 2017.

Sauer 2021a Sauer, Christine. "Die Memorabilien in der Stadtbibliothek Nürnberg." In Sauer 2021b, pp. 17–96.

Sauer 2021b Sauer, Christine, ed. *Wunderkammer im Wissensraum: Die Memorabilien der Stadtbibliothek Nürnberg im Kontext städtischer Sammlungskulturen.* Beiträge zur Geschichte und Kultur der Stadt Nürnberg 27. Wiesbaden, 2021.

Sauge and Ford 2024 Sauge, Birgitte, and Thierry Ford, eds. *Bridging the Gap: Synergies between Art History and Conservation.* London and Oslo, 2024.

Saviello 2018a Saviello, Alberto. "'Beziehungskästchen': Die Übersetzung europäischer Bildvorlagen am singhalesischen Elfenbeinkästchen des Berliner Museums für Asiatische Kunst." *Zeitschrift für Kunstgeschichte* 81, no. 3 (2018), pp. 328–55.

Saviello 2018b Saviello, Julia. "Schildkröte – The Turtle's Shield." In Cordez et al. 2018, pp. 107–23.

Saviello 2022 Saviello, Alberto. "Inter-Pictorial Religious Discourse in Mughal Paintings: Translations and Interpretations of Marian Images." *Journal of Transcultural Studies* 13, nos. 1–2 (2022), pp. 32–55.

Saville 1920 Saville, Marshall H. *The Goldsmith's Art in Ancient Mexico.* New York, 1920.

Schäfer, Eydinger, and Rekow 2016 Schäfer, Bernd, Ulrike Eydinger, and Matthias Rekow, eds. *Fliegende Blätter: Die Sammlung der Einblattholzschnitte des 15. und 16. Jahrhunderts der Stiftung Schloss Friedenstein Gotha.* 2 vols. Gotha and Stuttgart, 2016.

Schatz 2002 Schatz, Michael. "La recepción de los grabados europeos en los murales de la época colonial temprana en el Nuevo Reino de Granada." In Kügelgen 2002, pp. 123–66.

Schauerte 2012 Schauerte, Thomas. *Dürer: Das ferne Genie; Eine Biographie.* Stuttgart, 2012.

Schauerte 2014 Schauerte, Thomas. "Albrecht Dürer der Ältere." In Exh. cat. Nuremberg 2014b, pp. 74–78.

Schedel 1493 Schedel, Hartmann. *Das buch der Chronicken vnd gedechtnus wirdigern geschichte[n] ...* . Nuremberg, 1493.

Scherner 2023 Scherner, Antje. "'Gestern bin ich voll gewest': Alkohol und Trinkspiele in der Frühen Neuzeit / 'Yesterday I was cup-shot': Spirits and Drinking Games in the Early Modern Age." In Laue 2023, pp. 8–35.

Schewe and Goll 2019 Schewe, Roland, and Jürg Goll. "Die Zeit in der Tasche: Die älteste, in Europa erhaltene hölzerne Klappsonnenuhr aus dem Kloster Müstair, Schweiz." *Zeitschrift für schweizerische Archäologie und Kunstgeschichte* 76, nos. 1–2 (2019), pp. 5–30.

Schiedlausky 1973 Schiedlausky, Günter. "Die Taufgarnitur des Dr. Christoph Scheurl." *Mitteilungen der Keramikfreunde der Schweiz* 85 (1973), pp. 5–16.

Schiermeier 2006 Schiermeier, Franz. *Stadtatlas Nürnberg: Karten und Modelle von 1492 bis heute.* Nuremberg, 2006.

Schilling 1990 Schilling, Michael. *Bildpublizistik der frühen Neuzeit: Aufgaben und Leistungen des illustrierten Flugblatts in Deutschland um 1700.* Studien und Texte zur Sozialgeschichte der Literatur 29. Tübingen, 1990.

Schleif 1999 Schleif, Corine. "*Das pos weyb* Agnes Frey Dürer: Geschichte ihrer Verleumdung und Versuche der Ehrenrettung." *MVGN* 86 (1999), pp. 47–79.

Schmidt-Linsenhoff 2010 Schmidt-Linsenhoff, Viktoria. *Ästhetik der Differenz: Postkoloniale Perspektiven vom 16. bis 21. Jahrhundert.* 2 vols. Marburg, 2010.

Schmieder 2021 Schmieder, Felicitas. "The Globe as Mappa Mundi? Reflections on Terrestrial Globes from around 1500." In Mauntel 2021, pp. 163–78.

Schmitz-Esser 2023 Schmitz-Esser, Romedio. *Um 1500: Europa zur Zeit Albrecht Dürers.* Darmstadt, 2023.

Schneider 2004 Schneider, Ute. *Die Macht der Karten: Eine Geschichte der Kartographie vom Mittelalter bis heute.* Darmstadt, 2004.

Schoch 1993 Schoch, Rainer. "Aller Laster Anfang: Zur Ikonographie der Nürnberger Künstlerspielkarten." In Exh. cat. Nuremberg 1993, pp. 55–80.

Schoch, Mende, and Scherbaum 2001 Schoch, Rainer, Matthias Mende, and Anna Scherbaum, eds. *Albrecht Dürer: Das druckgraphische Werk.* Vol. 1, *Kupferstiche, Eisenradierungen und Kaltnadelblätter.* Munich et al., 2001.

Schoch, Mende, and Scherbaum 2002 Schoch, Rainer, Matthias Mende, and Anna Scherbaum, eds. *Albrecht Dürer: Das druckgraphische Werk.* Vol. 2, *Holzschnitte und Holzschnittfolgen.* Munich et al., 2002.

Schock-Werner 1986 Schock-Werner, Barbara. "Bamberg ist Jerusalem: Architekturporträt im Mittelalter." In Exh. cat. Nuremberg 1986, pp. 43–55.

Scholz 1995 Scholz, Hartmut. "Die Straßburger Werkstattgemeinschaft: Ein historischer und kunsthistorischer Überblick." In Exh. cat. Ulm 1995, pp. 13–26.

Scholz 2005 Scholz, Hartmut. "Eine Glasgemälde-Stiftung der Behaim aus dem Nürnberger Dominikanerinnenkloster St. Katharina: Die kurze Geschichte einer Wiederentdeckung." In Becksmann 2005, pp. 274–81.

Scholz 2013 Scholz, Hartmut. *Die mittelalterlichen Glasmalereien in Nürnberg: Sebalder Stadtseite.* Corpus vitrearum medii aevi: Deutschland, vol. 10, no. 2. Berlin, 2013.

Scholz 2019 Scholz, Hartmut. *Die Glasmalereien des Mittelalters und der Frühen Neuzeit in Nürnberg: Lorenzer Stadtseite.* 2 vols. Corpus vitrearum medii aevi: Deutschland, vol. 10, no. 3. Berlin, 2019.

Schommers 2024 Schommers, Annette. "Die goldene Flotte: Süddeutsche Schiffe für die Tafel." In Exh. cat. Munich 2024, pp. 27–71.

Schöntag 2023 Schöntag, Roger. "Testimonios del mercader Hans Tetzel (1518–1571) de Núremberg en Cuba: Un análisis histórico y socio-lingüístico." *Islas* 65, no. 204 (2023), pp. 1–23.

Schottenloher 1910 Schottenloher, Karl. *Die Entwicklung der Buchdruckerkunst in Franken bis 1530.* Würzburg, 1910.

Schreyl 1990 Schreyl, Karl Heinz. *Hans Schäufelein: Das druckgraphische Werk; Text- und Tafelband.* Nördlingen, 1990.

Schröck, Klein, and Bürger 2013 Schröck, Katja, Bruno Klein, and Stefan Bürger, eds. *Kirche als Baustelle: Große Sakralbauten des Mittelalters.* Cologne, Weimar, and Vienna, 2013.

Schuler and Metzner 1869 Schuler, Stephan. *Stephan Schuler's Saalbuch der Frauenkirche in Nürnberg.* Bericht über das Wirken und den Stand des historischen Vereins zu Bamberg 32. Edited by Joseph Metzner. Bamberg, 1869.

Schultheiß 1955 Schultheiß, Werner. "Die Reichsstadt Nürnberg und die Entdeckung Amerikas." *Jahrbuch für fränkische Landesforschung* 15 (1955), pp. 171–99.

Schulz 1924 Schulz, Fritz Traugott. "Der Oelberg der Clarakirche in Nürnberg, ein Werk der Adam Kraft-Schule." *Anzeiger des Germanischen Nationalmuseums.* Nuremberg, 1922–23 (1924), pp. 33–37.

Schulz 2015 Schulz, Johann. "Ereignisraum Jerusalem: Zur Konstitution eines Sakralraumes vor den Mauern der Stadt Nürnberg." In Aurenhammer and Bohde 2015, pp. 83–116.

Schulze 1978 Schulze, Winfried. *Reich und Türkengefahr im späten 16. Jahrhundert: Studien zu den politischen und gesellschaftlichen Auswirkungen einer äußeren Bedrohung.* Munich, 1978.

Schunka 2012 Schunka, Alexander. "Die Konfessionalisierung der Osmanen: Protestantische Berichte über den Orient im ausgehenden 16. Jahrhundert." In Friedrich and Schunka 2012, pp. 8–46.

Schunka 2016 Schunka, Alexander. "Schweigger, Salomon." In Kühlmann et al. 2016, cols. 590–98.

Schürer 2002 Schürer, Ralf. "Vom alten Ruhm der Goldschmiedearbeit: Nürnberger Silber in Europa." In Exh. cat. Nuremberg 2002, pp. 174–97.

Schürer 2010 Schürer, Ralf. "Die Kunst- und Wunderkammer." In Hess and Hirschfelder 2010, pp. 256–69.

Schwarz 1917 Schwarz, Karl. *Augustin Hirschvogel: Ein deutscher Meister der Renaissance; Mit einem Selbstbildnis Hirschvogels in Handpressenkupferdruck und siebenundsiebzig Abbildungen in Tonätzung.* Berlin, 1917.

Schweigger 1616 Schweigger, Salomon. *Alcoranus Mahometicus, Das ist. Der Türcken Alcoran, Religion vnd Aberglauben.* Nuremberg: Simon Halbmayern, 1616.

Schwemmer 1949 Schwemmer, Wilhelm. "Aus der Geschichte der Kunstsammlungen der Stadt Nürnberg." *MVGN* 40 (1949), pp. 97–206.

Schwemmer 1977 Schwemmer, Wilhelm. *Die Stadt Nürnberg: Kurzinventar.* Bayerische Kunstdenkmale 10. Munich, 1977.

Seelig 2006 Seelig, Lorenz. "Schatzkunst, Goldschmiedekunst und Schmuck." In Eikelmann and Bauer 2006, pp. 382–401.

Seidl 1983 Seidl, Günter Heinz. "Die Denkmäler des mittelalterlichen Jüdischen Friedhofs in Nürnberg." *MVGN* 70 (1983), pp. 28–74.

Servais 2024 Servais, Anne. "How do Pigment Recipes Demonstrate their Authors' Technical and Artistical Know-How? Brazilwood Colour Recipes from the Twelfth to Fifteenth Centuries." In *Proceedings of the 9th Symposium of the ICOM-CC Working Group on Art Technological Source Research*, Paris, November 24–25, 2022. Downloadable on the ICOM-CC Online-Publikation 2024 website: https://www.icom-cc-publications-online.org/.

Seyller 1995 Seyller, John. "Farrukh Beg in the Deccan." *Artibus Asiae* 55, nos. 3–4 (1995), pp. 319–41.

Shalem 2016 Shalem, Avinoam. "The Poetics of Portability." In Necipoğlu and Payne 2016, pp. 250–61.

Siebenhüner 2018 Siebenhüner, Kim. *Die Spur der Juwelen: Materielle Kultur und transkontinentale Verbindungen zwischen Indien und Europa in der Frühen Neuzeit.* Ding, Materialität, Geschichte 3. Cologne and Weimar, 2018.

Siebenhüner 2021 Siebenhüner, Kim. "Paternoster: Religiöse Objekte zwischen Transkulturalität und Konfessionalisierung." In Gleixner and Dos Santos Lopes 2021, pp. 73–97.

Silva Maroto 2008 Silva Maroto, Pilar. "En torno a las relaciones entre Durero y España." In Borobia 2008, pp. 181–209.

Simmer 2000 Simmer, Götz. *Gold und Sklaven: Die Provinz Venezuela während der Welser-Verwaltung (1528–1556).* Berlin, 2000.

Singer and Jopp 1967 Singer, Ronald, and Werner Jopp. "The Earliest Illustration of Hottentots: 1508." *The South African Archaeological Bulletin* 22, no. 85 (1967), pp. 15–19.

Skelton 1957 Skelton, Robert. "The Mughal Artist Farrukh Beg." *Ars Orientalis* 2 (1957), pp. 393–411.

Slenczka 2002 Slenczka, Eberhard. "Die Weltchronik des Hartmann Schedel aus Nürnberg." In Exh. cat. Nuremberg 2002, pp. 285–303.

Sloterdijk 2001 Sloterdijk, Peter. *Nicht gerettet: Versuche nach Heidegger.* Frankfurt am Main, 2001.

Sloterdijk 2024 Sloterdijk, Peter. *Der Kontinent ohne Eigenschaften: Lesezeichen im Buch Europa.* Berlin, 2024.

Slotta 1990 Slotta, Rainer. "Der Beitrag des Bergbaus zur Kunst." In Exh. cat. Bochum 1990, pp. 34–56.

Smith 1983 Smith, Jeffrey Chipps. *Nuremberg: A Renaissance City, 1500–1618.* Austin, TX, 1983.

Smith 1990–91 Smith, Jeffrey Chipps. "Netherlandish Artists and Art in Renaissance Nuremberg." *Netherlands Quarterly for the History of Art* 20, nos. 2–3 (1990–91), pp. 153–67.

Smith 2013 Smith, Jeffrey Chipps. "Hans Vischer and the Challenges of the 1530s." In Motture, Jones, and Zikos 2013, pp. 120–33.

Söding 2023 Söding, Beatrize. *Hans Peisser und die Nürnberger Bronzeplastik.* Munich, 2023.

Speel 2008 Speel, Erika. "Limousiner Maleremail: Die Materialien und ihre Anwendungstechniken als bestimmende Faktoren für die stilistischen Entwicklungen." In Weinhold 2008, pp. 150–57.

Spenlé 2018 Spenlé, Virginie. "The Court Casket Owned by the Marquesses of Lothian: A Masterpiece of Nuremberg Perspective." In Laue 2018, pp. 6–69.

Spinks 2023 Spinks, Jennifer. "Objects in Motion: Albrecht Dürer's *Nemesis*." In Exh. cat. Manchester 2023, pp. 35–47.

Sporhan-Krempel 1968 Sporhan-Krempel, Lore. *Nürnberg als Nachrichtenzentrum zwischen 1400 und 1700.* Nuremberg, 1968.

Sporhan-Krempel and Stromer 1962 Sporhan-Krempel, Lore, and Wolfgang von Stromer. "Wolf Jacob Stromer 1561–1614: Ratsbaumeister zu Nürnberg; Amt – Leben – Werk; Ein Beitrag zur Baugeschichte der Renaissance." *MVGN* 51 (1962), pp. 273–310.

Šprajc 1999 Šprajc, Ivan. "Alineamientos astronómicos en el Templo Mayor de Tenochtitlan." *Arqueología* 21 (1999), pp. 73–98.

Srovnal 2019 Srovnal, Filip. "Der Triumphbogen für den kommenden Herrscher: Zur Ikonographie, Symbolik und Bedeutung der Skulpturenausstattung der Nürnberger Frauenkirche." *Umění: Časopis Ústavu Dějin Umění Akademie Věd České Republiky / Art: Journal of the Institute of Art History, Czech Academy of Sciences* 67, no. 5 (2019), pp. 378–95.

Stadtarchiv Nürnberg 1967 *Beiträge zur Wirtschaftsgeschichte Nürnbergs.* Edited by Stadtarchiv Nürnberg. 2 vols. Nuremberg, 1967.

Stahlschmidt 1971 Stahlschmidt, Rainer. *Die Geschichte des eisenverarbeitenden Gewerbes in Nürnberg von den 1. Nachrichten im 12.–13. Jahrhundert bis 1630.* Nuremberg, 1971.

Staub 2021 Staub, Martial. "Trust, Globalization and Citizenship in Renaissance Europe: The Case of the South German Merchants of Lisbon around 1500." *Archiv für Kulturgeschichte* 103, no. 1 (2021), pp. 83–112.

Stauber 2000 Stauber, Reinhard. "Nürnberg und Italien in der Renaissance." In Neuhaus 2000, pp. 123–49.

Stazzone 2024 Stazzone, Alessandra. "D'eau et de sang: Le Nouveau Monde au XVIe siècle à travers l'Isolario de Benedetto Bordone." *Perspektiven auf die Romania* 13 (2024), pp. 8–22. https://doi.org/10.15460/apropos.13.2322.

Steimann 2019 Steimann, Ilona. "'Das es dasselb puch sey': The Book as Protagonist in the Ceremony of the Jewry-Oath." *European Journal of Jewish Studies* 13, no. 1 (2019), pp. 77–102.

Stein 1987 Stein, Heidi. "Das türkische Sprachmaterial in Salomon Schweiggers Reisebuch (1608)." *Acta Orientalia (Academiae Scientiarum Hungaricae)* 41 (1987), pp. 217–66.

Steinhilper 2016 Steinhilper, Diantha. "An Emperor's Heraldry, a Pope's Portrait, and the 'Cortés Map of Tenochtitlan': The 'Praeclara Ferdinadi Cortessi' as an Evangelical Announcement." *The Sixteenth Century Journal* 47 (2016), pp. 371–99.

Steinschneider 1895 Steinschneider, Moritz. *Die hebraeischen Handschriften der K. Hof- und Staatsbibliothek in München.* Catalogus codicum manu scriptorum Bibliothecae Regiae Monacensis, vol. 1, no. 1. 2nd edition, largely revised and expanded. Munich, 1895.

Stern 1916 Stern, Dorothea. *Der Nürnberger Bildhauer Adam Kraft: Stilentwicklung und Chronologie seiner Werke.* Studien zur deutschen Kunstgeschichte 191. Strasbourg, 1916.

Stern von Labach and Meldemann 1530 Stern von Labach, Peter, and Nicolaus Meldemann. *Warhafftige handlung Wie vnd welchermasen der Türck die stat Ofen und Wienn belegert/ Erstlich durch Kü. Ma. zů Hungern vnd Behem etc. kriegß secretari/ herrn Peter Stern von Labach k[ue]rtzlich begriffen und beschriben. Nachuolgend durch Niclausen Meldeman, burger zů N[ue]renberg mit merer anzeigung, was von tag zů tag sich zutragen hat .../ gemert und erlengert/ sampt einer contrafactur der stat Wienn außgangen* [Nuremberg, 1530].

Sternthal, Cohen-Mushlin, and Levy 2009–14 Sternthal, Michal, Aliza Cohen-Mushlin, and Yaffa Levy. "13th-Century Ashkenazi Pentateuch and Its Binding of [the] 1470s." *The Bezalel Narkiss Index of Jewish Art* (2009–14). Published online. https://cja.huji.ac.il/browser.php?mode=set&id=22119.

Steyn 2023 Steyn, Gerald. "The Architectural Development of the Mosques on the East African Coast: A Sharing of Critical Observations." *South African Journal of Art History* 38, no. 2 (2023), pp. 60–84.

Stollberg-Rilinger and Weller 2007 Stollberg-Rilinger, Barbara, and Thomas Weller, eds. *Wertekonflikte – Deutungskonflikte: Internationales Kolloquium des Sonderforschungsbereichs 496 an der Westfälischen Wilhelms-Universität Münster, 19.–20. Mai 2006.* Münster, 2007.

Stolz 2007 Stolz, Georg. "Veni Sancte Spiritus – Komm Heiliger Geist: Spitalkapelle – Schatzkammer – Pfarrkirche – Haus zum Heiligen Geist." In *St. Lorenz + Heilig-Geist.* St. Lorenz / Verein zur Erhaltung der St.-Lorenzkirche in

Nürnberg, new series 56. Nuremberg, 2007, pp. 3–66.

Strandes 1989 Strandes, Justus. *The Portuguese Period in East Africa*. Nairobi, 1989.

Strauss 1975 Strauss, Walter Leopold. *The German Single-Leaf Woodcut 1550–1600: A Pictorial Catalogue*. 3 vols. New York, 1975.

Strauss 1984 Strauss, Walter L. *German Masters of the Sixteenth Century: Erhard Schoen, Niklas Stoer*. The Illustrated Bartsch, vol. 13, no. 2. New York, 1984.

Strieder 1993 Strieder, Peter. *Tafelmalerei in Nürnberg 1350–1550*. Königstein im Taunus, 1993.

Stromer 1963 Stromer, Wolfgang von. *Die Nürnberger Handelsgesellschaft Gruber-Podmer-Stromer im 15. Jahrhundert*. Nürnberger Forschungen 7. Nuremberg, 1963.

Stromer 1967 Stromer, Wolfgang von. "Das Schriftwesen der Nürnberger Wirtschaft vom 14. bis zum 16. Jahrhundert: Zur Geschichte oberdeutscher Handelsbücher." In Stadtarchiv Nürnberg 1967, vol. 2, pp. 751–99.

Stromer 1970 Stromer, Wolfgang von. "Oberdeutsche Unternehmen im Handel mit der Iberischen Halbinsel im 14. und 15. Jahrhundert." In Kellenbenz 1970b, pp. 156–74.

Stromer 1975 Stromer, Wolfgang von. "Nürnberg-Breslauer Wirtschaftsbeziehungen im Spätmittelalter." *Jahrbuch für fränkische Landesforschung* 34–35 (1975), pp. 1079–1100.

Stromer 1978 Stromer, Wolfgang von. "Die Metropole im Aufstand gegen König Karl IV: Nürnberg zwischen Wittelsbach und Luxemburg Juni 1348 – September 1349." *MVGN* 65 (1978), pp. 55–90.

Stromer 1997 Stromer, Wolfgang von. "Palladio nördlich der Alpen: Nürnberg unter Wolf-Jacob Stromer (Ratsbaumeister 1561–1614)." In Bracker 1997, pp. 170–79.

Stromer 2002 Stromer, Wolfgang von. "Welser Augsburg und Welser Nürnberg: Zwei Unternehmen und ihre Standorte." In Häberlein and Burkhardt 2002, pp. 215–22.

Stummvoll, Gibson, and Unterkircher 1960 Stummvoll, Josef, Charles Gibson, and Franz Unterkircher, eds. *Cartas de relación de la conquista de la Nueva España: Escritas por Hernán Cortés al Emperador Carlos V y otros Documentos relativos a la conquista, años de 1519–1527; Codex Vindobonensis S. N. 1600*. CODICES SELECTI 2. Graz, 1960.

Sturm and Teget-Welz 2022 Sturm, Isabella, and Manuel Teget-Welz. "Kollegen oder Konkurrenten? Die Kooperationen des Hans von Kulmbach." In Exh. cat. Kronach 2022, pp. 87–103.

Subrahmanyam 2013 Subrahmanyam, Sanyam. *L'empire portugais d'Asie 1500–1700*. Paris, 2013.

Suckale 2009 Suckale, Robert. *Die Erneuerung der Malkunst vor Dürer*. 2 vols. Schriftenreihe / Historischer Verein Bamberg für die Pflege der Geschichte des Ehemaligen Fürstbistums e. V. 44. Petersberg, 2009.

Tacke 1995 Tacke, Andreas. *Die Gemälde des 17. Jahrhunderts im Germanischen Nationalmuseum. Bestandskatalog*. Kataloge des Germanischen Nationalmuseums. Mainz, 1995.

Tacke 2001a Tacke, Andreas, eds. *"Der Mahler Ordnung und Gebräuch in Nürnberg": Die Nürnberger Maler(zunft)bücher ergänzt durch weitere Quellen, Genealogien und Viten des 16., 17. und 18. Jahrhunderts*. Munich and Berlin, 2001.

Tacke 2001b Tacke, Andreas. "Johann Hauer: Nürnberger Flach- und Ätzmaler, Kunsthändler, Verleger und Dürerforscher des 17. Jahrhunderts; Eine Fallstudie zur handwerksgeschichtlichen Betrachtung des Künstlers im Alten Reich." In Tacke 2001a, pp. 11–141.

Tacke et al. 2020 Tacke, Andreas, et al., eds. *Künstlerreisen: Fallbeispiele vom Mittelalter bis zur Gegenwart*. Kunsthistorisches Forum Irsee 7. Petersberg, 2020.

Tammen 1996 Tammen, Silke. "Kunsterfahrung spätmittelalterlicher Spanienreisender." In Noehles-Doerk 1996, pp. 49–71.

Tammen 2014 Tammen, Silke. "Tod und Tuch: Grabteppiche." Lecture at the international conference STROMATA: The Carpet as Artifact, Concept and Metaphor, November 3–5, 2014, Kunsthistorisches Institut in Florenz, Florence. https://www.uni-giessen.de/de/fbz/fb04/institute/kunstgeschichte/institut/team/tammen-silke/Grabteppiche_Vortrag.pdf.

Tafur and Pérez Priego 2018 Tafur, Pero. *Andanzas y viajes*. Letras hispánicas 802. Edited by Miguel Angel Pérez Priego. Madrid, 2018.

Taube, Sanyova, and Roth 2023 Taube, Elisabeth, Jana Sanyova, and Astrid Roth. "Red Glazes from Brazilwood Dye: Findings in Late Medieval Polychromy." In *Working Towards a Sustainable Past*, edited by Janet Bridgland. ICOM-CC 20th Triennial Conference Preprints, Valencia, September 18–22, 2023. Paris, 2023. https://www.icom-cc-publications-online.org/search?wg=0&vy=2023+Valencia&t=0&page=6.

Tebbe 2003 Tebbe, Karin. "Wertvolle Jagdbeute: Eine Nürnberger Goldschmiedearbeit in der Eremitage in St. Petersburg." *Monatsanzeiger Museen und Ausstellungen in Nürnberg* 270 (2003), pp. 2–3.

Tebbe 2007 Tebbe, Karin. "Nürnberger Goldschmiedekunst: Formtypen und stilistische Entwicklung." *NGK* 2 (2007), pp. 120–204.

Teget-Welz 2020 Teget-Welz, Manuel. "Wir waren schon da! Deutsche Künstler vor Dürer in der Republik Venedig." In Tacke et al. 2020, pp. 10–25.

Teget-Welz 2021 Teget-Welz, Manuel, ed. *Albrecht Dürer: Spurensuche in Nürnberg*. Historische Spaziergänge 18. Nuremberg, 2021.

Teget-Welz 2022 Teget-Welz, Manuel. "Hans von Kulmbach: Ein Nürnberger Maler macht Karriere." In Exh. cat. Kronach 2022, pp. 31–47.

Teply 1964 Teply, Karl, ed. *Johann Wild: Reysbeschreibung eines gefangenen Christen anno 1604*. Stuttgart, 1964.

Teter 2020 Teter, Magda. *Blood Libel: On the Trail of an Antisemitic Myth*. Cambridge, MA, and London, 2020.

Thackston 1999 Thackston, Wheeler M., ed. *The Jahangirnama: Memoirs of Jahangir, Emperor of India*. New York, 1999.

Thomas 2022 Thomas, Andrew L. *The Apocalypse in Reformation Nuremberg: Jews and Turks in Andreas Osiander's World*. Ann Arbor, MI, 2022.

Tiedemann 2018 Tiedemann, Klaus. *Nürnberger Beckenschlägerschüsseln: Nuremberg Alms Dishes*. 2nd ed. Dettelbach, 2018.

Tiedtke 2009 Tiedtke, Sabine. "Der Nürnberger Goldschmied Friedrich Hillebrandt und seine Werkstatt: Ein Werkkatalog." Master's thesis, Friedrich-Alexander-Universität Erlangen-Nürnberg, 2009.

Timann 1993 Timann, Ursula. *Untersuchungen zu Nürnberger Holzschnitt und Briefmalerei in der ersten Hälfte des 16. Jahrhunderts: Mit besonderer Berücksichtigung von Hans Guldenmund und Niclas Meldeman*. Kunstgeschichte 18. Münster and Hamburg, 1993.

Timann 1996 Timann, Ursula. "Das Grabmal des Magnaten Mikołaj Herburt-Odnowski im Dom zu Lemberg, gegossen 1551 von Pankraz Labenwolf zu Nürnberg." *Anzeiger des Germanischen Nationalmuseums* (1996), pp. 93–114.

Timann 2005 Timann, Ursula. "Unveröffentlichtes Vortragsmanuskript zur Ikone von Konstantin und Helena. XXVIII. Deutscher Kunsthistorikerkongress Bonn 2005." Nuremberg, GNM, Sammlung Malerei bis 1800 und Glasmalerei, image file Gm507.

Timann 2007a Timann, Ursula. "Die Handwerker des Behaim-Globus." *Norica: Berichte und Themen aus dem Stadtarchiv Nürnberg* 3 (2007), pp. 59–64.

Timann 2007b Timann, Ursula. "Zur Handwerksgeschichte der Nürnberger Goldschmiede." *NGK* 2 (2007), pp. 33–69.

Timann 2020 Timann, Ursula. "Sebald Beham (1500–1550) und Jacob Seisenegger (1505–1567), die geheimnisvollen 'Schöpfer' der Meldemann-Rundansicht?" In Opll and Scheutz 2020, pp. 61–84.

Tipton 1996 Tipton, Susan. *Res publica bene ordinata: Regentenspiegel und Bilder vom guten Regiment; Rathausdekorationen in der frühen Neuzeit*. Hildesheim, Zurich, and New York, 1996.

Toch 2003a Toch, Michael. "Der jüdische Geldhandel in der Wirtschaft des deutschen Spätmittelalters: Nürnberg 1350–1499." In Toch 2003c, pp. 283–310.

Toch 2003b Toch, Michael. "Die soziale und demographische Struktur der jüdischen Gemeinde Nürnbergs im Jahre 1489." In Toch 2003c, pp. 80–91.

Toch 2003c Toch, Michael, ed. *Peasants and Jews in Medieval Germany*. Aldershot, Hampshire, 2003.

Toch 2008a Toch, Michael. "Economic Activities of German Jews in the Middle Ages." In Toch 2008b, pp. 181–210.

Toch 2008b Toch, Michael, ed. *Wirtschaftsgeschichte der mittelalterlichen Juden: Fragen und Einschätzungen*. Berlin and Boston, 2008, pp. 181–210.

Tolias 2007 Tolias, George. "'Isolarii,' Fifteenth to Seventeenth Century." In Woodward 2007, pp. 263–84.

Tolias 2012 Tolias, George. "The Politics of the Isolario: Maritime Cosmography and Overseas Expansion During the Renaissance." *The Historical Review / La Revue Historique* 9 (2012), pp. 27–52. https://doi.org/10.12681/hr.287.

Topkaya 2020 Topkaya, Yiğit. "Eingekreiste Zeugen, auf den Kopf gestellte Märtyrer: Bilder des Grauens in Niclas Meldemans Rundansicht." In Opll and Scheutz 2020, pp. 241–55.

Treue 1996 Treue, Wolfgang. *Der Trienter Judenprozeß: Voraussetzungen – Abläufe – Auswirkungen (1475–1588)*. Forschungen zur Geschichte der Juden, series A, no. 4. Hannover, 1996.

Tripps 2000 Tripps, Johannes. *Das handelnde Bildwerk in der Gotik*. 2nd ed. Berlin, 2000.

Tyrakowski 1997 Tyrakowski, Konrad. "México-Tenochtitlan um 1520: Kartographisch-stadtgeographische Analyse des sogenannten Cortés-Plans, der ersten europäischen Darstellung der alt-aztekischen Metropole." *Die Alte Stadt* 24 (1997), pp. 85–109.

Uhlirz 1894 Uhlirz, Karl. "Der Wiener Bürger Wehr und Waffen (1426–1648): Auszüge aus den städtischen Kämmerei-Rechnungen." *Berichte und Mittheilungen des Alterthums-Vereines zu Wien* 30 (1894), pp. 106–29.

Unverfehrt 2007 Unverfehrt, Gerd. *"Da sah ich viel köstliche Dinge": Albrecht Dürers Reise in die Niederlande*. Göttingen, 2007.

Valentin 2019 Valentin, Elke. "Gemalte Meisterstücke im Nürnberger Rathaus: Von Pflicht, Kür und Repräsentation." In Exh. cat. Frankfurt 2019, pp. 76–81.

Vandenbroeck 1991 Vandenbroeck, Paul. "Amerindian Art and Ornamental Objects in Royal Collections: Brussels, Mechelen, Duurstede, 1520–1530." In Exh. cat. Antwerp 1991, pp. 99–120.

Van Dijk 2020 Van Dijk, Casper J. "A New Halberd Typology (1500–1800): Based on the Collection of the National Military Museum, The Netherlands." *Arms & Armour* 17, no. 1 (2020), pp. 1–26.

Vassallo e Silva 2013 Vassallo e Silva, Nuno. "'Engenho e primor': A arte do marfim no Ceilão / 'Ingenuity and Excellence': Ivory Art in Ceylon." In Vassallo e Silva, Bailey, and Massing 2013, pp. 87–142.

Vassallo e Silva, Bailey, and Massing 2013 Vassallo e Silva, Nuno, Gauvin A. Bailey, and Jean-Michel Massing, eds. *Marfins no Império Português / Ivories in the Portuguese Empire*. Lisbon, 2013.

Vázquez de Prada 1986 Vázquez de Prada, Valentín. "Spanien 1350–1660." In Kellenbenz 1986, pp. 706–35.

Veit 1960 Veit, Ludwig. *Handel und Wandel mit aller Welt: Aus Nürnbergs großer Zeit*. Bibliothek des Germanischen National-Museums Nürnberg zur deutschen Kunst- und Kulturgeschichte 14. Munich, 1960.

Vespucci 1916 Vespucci, Amerigo. *Mundus Novus: Letter to Lorenzo Pietro Di Medici*. Translated by George Tyler Northup. Vespucci Reprints, Texts, and Studies 5. Princeton, NJ, 1916.

Veth and Muller 1918 Veth, Jan, and Samuel Muller. *Albrecht Dürers niederländische Reise*. 2 vols. Berlin and Utrecht, 1918.

Vincke 1959 Vincke, Johannes. "Zu den Anfängen der deutsch-spanischen Kultur- und Wirtschaftsbeziehungen." *Spanische Forschungen. Reihe 1. Gesammelte Aufsätze zur Kulturgeschichte Spaniens* 14 (1959), pp. 111–82.

VL Keil, Gundolf, et al., eds. *Die deutsche Literatur des Mittelalters: Verfasserlexikon*. 2nd fully revised new edition. Berlin and New York, 1978–2008.

Vlachos 2018 Vlachos, Stavros. "Vorläufer des Frühen Realismus in der Malerei um 1400." In Fajt and Hörsch 2018, pp. 243–65.

Wagner 1929 Wagner, Henry R. "Three Accounts of the Expedition of Fernando Cortés, Printed in Germany Between 1520 and 1522." *The Hispanic American Historical Review* 9 (1929), pp. 176–212.

Walczak 2018 Walczak, Marek. "Krakau und Nürnberg: Verbindungen auf dem Gebiet der Kunst an der Wende vom Mittelalter zur Renaissance." In Exh. cat. Kraków, 2018, pp. 107–35.

Walde 2018 Walde, Benno Jakobus. "Albrecht Altdorfer – Hans Burgkmair d. Ä. – Erhard Schön: Kaiser Maximilian I. und Kolumbus' Santa Maria als Ikone des habsburgischen Machtbereichs." In Fajt and Jaeger 2018, pp. 363–78.

Walker, Ramos, and Kaarsholm 2017 Walker, Iain, Manuel João Ramos, and Preben Kaarsholm, eds. *Fluid Networks and Hegemonic Powers in the Western Indian Ocean*. Lisbon, 2017.

Walleit 2020 Walleit, Lisa. "Nürnberger Patrizier in Santiago: Die Pilgerberichte von Peter Rieter und Sebald Rieter dem Älteren – eine Neubewertung; Überlieferungsgeschichte und kritische Edition." *Archiv für Kulturgeschichte* 102, no. 2 (2020), pp. 341–80.

Wallisch 2012 Wallisch, Robert, eds. *Der "Mundus Novus" des Amerigo Vespucci: Text, Übersetzung und Kommentar*. Edition Woldan 5. Vienna, 2012.

Walter 2001 Walter, Rolf. "Einleitung: Oberdeutsche Kaufleute und Genuesen in Sevilla und Cadiz (1525–1560)." In Kellenbenz and Walter 2001, pp. 11–64.

Walter 2014 Walter, Rolf. "Was könnte Proto-Globalisierung bedeuten? Auf den Spuren oberdeutscher Fernhändler in der Frühen Neuzeit." In Gerber 2014, pp. 51–72.

Ward 2015 Ward, Rachel. "Coincidental Developments? The Aldrevandin Glasses and Ayyubid-Mamluk Glass." *Journal of Glass Studies* 57 (2015), pp. 137–46.

Warren 2019 Warren, Jeremy. "'Venetian' Enamels: The Case for Florence?" In Barbe, Caselli, and Dantan 2019, vol. 1, pp. 55–70.

Weber 1983 Weber, Gerhard. "Das Praun'sche Kunstkabinett." *MVGN* 70 (1983), pp. 125–95.

Weber 2022 Weber, Andreas. *Die Nürnberger Judengemeinde 1349–1499: Politische Handlungsspielräume jüdischer Akteure im Spätmittelalter*. Nuremberg, 2022.

Weigel 1577 Weigel, Hans. *Habitus præcipvorvm popvlorum …* . Nuremberg, 1577.

Weihrauch 1944 Weihrauch, Hans Robert. "Bronze, Bronzeguß, Bronzeplastik." *RDK* 2 (1944), pp. 1182–1216. https://www.rdklabor.de/wiki/Bronze,_Bronzegu%C3%9F,_Bronzeplastik.

Weilandt 2007 Weilandt, Gerhard. *Die Sebalduskirche in Nürnberg: Bild und Gesellschaft im Zeitalter der Gotik und Renaissance*. Studien zur internationalen Architektur- und Kunstgeschichte 47. Petersberg, 2007.

Weilandt 2013 Weilandt, Gerhard. "Der ersehnte Thronfolger: Die Bildprogramme der Frauenkirche in Nürnberg zwischen Herrschaftspraxis und Reliquienkult im Zeitalter Karls IV." In Schröck, Klein, and Bürger 2013, pp. 224–42.

Weilandt 2019 Weilandt, Gerhard. "Der Schöne Brunnen auf dem Nürnberger Hauptmarkt: Bildprogramm und Bedeutung." In Lehner 2019, pp. 115–37.

Weingärtner 2008 Weingärtner, Helge. "Das Tucherservice." *MVGN* 95 (2008), pp. 63–92.

Weingärtner 2020 Weingärtner, Helge. "Zwei Kreuzwege in St. Johannis, das 'Kleebergerkreuz' und die Holzschuherkapelle als Begräbnisort." In *MVGN* 107 (2020), pp. 135–74.

Weinhold 2008 Weinhold, Ulrike, ed. *Maleremail aus Limoges im Grünen Gewölbe*. Munich and Berlin, 2008.

Weinhold and Witting 2024 Weinhold, Ulrike, and Theresa Witting. *Goldschmiedekunst im Grünen Gewölbe: Die Werke des 16. bis 19. Jahrhunderts*. 3 vols. Dresden, 2024.

Welser 1874 Welser, Johann Michael Freiherr von. "Aus Hieronymus Kölers Aufzeichnungen." *Zeitschrift des Historischen Vereins für Schwaben und Neuburg* 1 (1874), pp. 321–33.

Weniger 2018 Weniger, Matthias. "Hans Burgkmair und Sebastian Loscher." In Augustyn and Teget-Welz 2018, pp. 439–64.

Wenninger 2016 Wenninger, Markus J. "als etlich kristen lüt … mit dien Juden getantzet hant: Über die Teilnahme von Christen an jüdischen Festen im Mittelalter." *Aschkenas* 26 (2016), pp. 37–68.

Werner 1961 Werner, Theodor Gustav. "Das Kupferhüttenwerk Hans Tetzels aus Nürnberg auf Kuba (1545–1571)." *Vierteljahrschrift für Sozial- und Wirtschaftsgeschichte* 48, no. 3 (1961), pp. 289–328, 444–502.

Werner 1967 Werner, Theodor Gustav. "Die Beteiligung der Nürnberger Welser und der Augsburger Fugger an der Eroberung des Rio de la Plata und der Gründung von Buenos Aires." In Stadtarchiv Nürnberg 1967, vol. 1, pp. 494–592.

Werner 1967–68 Werner, Theodor Gustav. "Zur Geschichte Tetzelscher Hammerwerke bei Nürnberg und des Kupferhüttenwerks Hans Tetzels auf Kuba." *MVGN* 55 (1967–68), pp. 214–25.

Werner 2015 Werner, Elke. "Bilder auf Wanderung und in Verwandlung / Pictures Migrating and Mutating." In Exh. cat. Berlin and Karlsruhe 2015, pp. 80–90.

Werz 2015 Werz, Bruno E. J. S. "Saved from the Sea: The Shipwreck of the 'Bom Jesus' (1533) and Its Material Culture." In Jordan Gschwend and Lowe 2015, pp. 89–93.

West 2010 West, Ashley D. "Between Artistry and Documentation: A Passage to India and the Problem of Representing New Global Encounters." In Nagel and Pericolo 2010, pp. 87–114.

Westermann 2002 Westermann, Ekkehard. "Die Nürnberger Welser und der mitteldeutsche Saigerhandel des 16. Jahrhunderts in seinen europäischen Verflechtungen." In Häberlein and Burkhardt 2002, pp. 240–64.

Westermann 2009 Westermann, Ekkehard. "Auftakt zur Globalisierung: Die 'Novos Mundos' Portugals und Valentim Fernandes als ihr Mittler nach Nürnberg und Augsburg; Korrekturen – Ergänzungen – Anfragen." *Vierteljahrschrift für Sozial- und Wirtschaftsgeschichte* 96, no. 1 (2009), pp. 44–58.

Westermann 2013a Westermann, Ekkehard. "Der Brief des Valentim Fernandes des Moravia vom 6. Juni 1510: Aus Lissabon an Stefan Gabler in Nürnberg; Eine Edition." In Granda and Schreiber 2013, pp. 37–46.

Westermann 2013b Westermann, Ekkehard. "'Die versunkenen Schätze der "Bom Jesus"' von 1533: Die Bedeutung der Fracht des portugiesischen Indienseglers für die internationale Handelsgeschichte; Würdigung und Kritik." *Vierteljahrschrift für Sozial- und Wirtschaftsgeschichte* 100 (2013), pp. 459–78.

Westermann and Welser 2009 Westermann, Angelika, and Stefanie von Welser, eds. *Einblicke in die Geschichte des Handelshauses Welser.* Neunhofer Dialog 1. St. Katharinen, 2009.

Westphal 2024 Westphal, Herbert H. *Saufedern und Bäreneisen: Zur historischen Entwicklung von Jagdspießen.* Horn-Bad Meinberg, 2024.

Wilckens 1983 Wilckens, Leonie von. "Der Holzschuhersche Grabteppich mit der Gregorsmesse." *Monatsanzeiger Museen und Ausstellungen in Nürnberg* 26 (1983), pp. 205–6.

Wild 1613 Wild, Johannes. *Neue Reysbeschreibung eines Gefangenen Christen ... .* Nuremberg: Balthasar Scherff, 1613.

Wilder 1824 Wilder, Johann Christoph Jakob. *Der schöne Brunnen zu Nürnberg: Andeutungen über seinen Kunstwerth, sowie über seine Geschichte, zum Andenken der Aufdeckung desselben, nach erfolgter gänzlicher Wiederherstellung am 12. October 1824.* Nuremberg, 1824.

Willers 2002 Willers, Johannes. "Nürnberger Waffen: Herstellung und Verkauf." In Exh. cat. Nuremberg 2002, pp. 138–57.

Williams 2003 Williams, Alan. *The Knight and the Blast Furnace: A History of the Metallurgy of Armour in the Middle Ages & the Early Modern Period.* History of Warfare 12. Boston et al., 2003.

Winkler 1936–39 Winkler, Friedrich. *Die Zeichnungen Albrecht Dürers.* 4 vols. Berlin, 1936–39.

Witting and Weinhold 2020 Witting, Theresa, and Ulrike Weinhold, eds. *Farbfassungen auf Gold und Silber.* Dresden, 2020.

Witting and Weinhold 2024 Witting, Theresa, and Ulrike Weinhold. "Außereuropäische Konchylien im Grünen Gewölbe: Prozesse der Aneignung in den Werkstätten deutscher Goldschmiede." In Weinhold and Witting 2024, vol. 1, pp. 56–65.

Wolder and Neudörffer 1558 Wolder, Simon, and Johannes Neudörffer. *Neu Türkenbüchlein ... .* Frankfurt am Main, 1558.

Woodward 2007 Woodward, David, ed. *The History of Cartography.* Vol. 3, part 1, *Cartography in the European Renaissance.* Chicago, 2007.

World Congress of Jewish Studies 1994 World Congress of Jewish Studies, ed. *Proceedings of the Eleventh World Congress of Jewish Studies, Jerusalem 1993, Division D.* Vol. 2. Jerusalem, 1994.

Worm 2011 Worm, Andrea. "Text – Bild – Kontext: Jerusalem in Hartmann Schedels Liber Chronicarum." In Krause and Schellewald 2011, pp. 175–203.

Worm 2021 Worm, Andrea. *Geschichte und Weltordnung: Graphische Modelle von Zeit und Raum in Universalchroniken vor 1500.* Jahresgabe des Vereins für Kunstwissenschaft 2016. Berlin, 2021.

Wouk 2023 Wouk, Edward H. "Albrecht Dürer's Landscape with a Cannon of 1518." In Exh. cat. Manchester 2023, pp. 99–112.

Wynne-Jones 2016 Wynne-Jones, Stephanie. *A Material Culture: Consumption and Materiality on the Coast of Precolonial East.* Oxford, 2016.

Yoon 2024 Yoon, Rangsook. "Jacopo de' Barbari, a Wandering Court Artist in the North: Changing Perspectives on His Role in Northern Renaissance Art." In Huffman 2024, pp. 150–59.

Yuval 1981 Yuval, Israel Jacob. "Alms from Nuremberg to Jerusalem (1375–1392)" [Hebrew]. *Zion* 46 (1981), pp. 182–97.

Yuval 2006 Yuval, Israel Jacob. *Two Nations in Your Womb: Perceptions of Jews and Christians in Late Antiquity and the Middle Ages.* Berkeley, 2006.

Zalamea 2019 Zalamea, Patricia. "En diálogo con un mundo antiguo: Las pinturas de las casas coloniales de Tunja en el marco de un Renacimiento global." *Historia y sociedad* 36 (2019), pp. 161–94.

Zander-Seidel 1997 Zander-Seidel, Jutta. "Teilstück eines Festbehangs für die Kirche St. Sebald in Nürnberg." *Anzeiger des Germanischen Nationalmuseums* (1997), pp. 184–87.

Zander-Seidel 1990 Zander-Seidel, Jutta. *Textiler Hausrat: Kleidung und Haustextilien in Nürnberg von 1500–1650.* Munich, 1990.

Zander-Seidel 2006 Zander-Seidel, Jutta. "Nürnberger Bildteppiche: Nürnberger Bildwirkerei im 15. Jahrhundert." In Kupper 2006, pp. 37–68.

Zander-Seidel 2010 Zander-Seidel, Jutta. "Pilgerfahrt und Prestige: Reisen nach Jerusalem und Santiago de Compostela." In Hess and Hirschfelder 2010, pp. 166–77.

Zander-Seidel and Kregeloh 2014 Zander-Seidel, Jutta, and Anja Kregeloh, eds. *Geschichtsbilder: Die Gründung des Germanischen Nationalmuseums und das Mittelalter.* Nuremberg, 2014.

Zeuske 2004 Zeuske, Michael. *Schwarze Karibik: Sklaven, Sklavereikultur und Emanzipation.* Zurich, 2004.

Ziegler 2020 Ziegler, Hendrik. "'Alla turca' – Osmanen als Bezwungene und Bezwinger im höfischen Fest des Barock." In Fischer 2020, pp. 123–42.

Zils 1927 Zils, Wilhelm, ed. *Bayerisches Handwerk in seinen alten Zunftordnungen: Ein Beitrag zur Geschichte des bayerischen Handwerks und Zunftwesen.* Munich, 1927.

Zink 1968 Zink, Fritz. *Die Handzeichnungen bis zur Mitte des 16. Jahrhunderts.* Kataloge des Germanischen Nationalmuseums Nürnberg: Die deutschen Handzeichnungen 1. Nuremberg, 1968.

Zinner 1967 Zinner, Ernst. *Deutsche und niederländische astronomische Instrumente des 11. bis 18. Jahrhunderts.* Munich, 1967.

Zittlau 1992 Zittlau, Reiner. *Heiliggrabkapelle und Kreuzweg: Eine Bauaufgabe in Nürnberg um 1500.* Nuremberg, 1992.

INDEX OF PERSONS

Compiled by Birgit Schübel in collaboration with Leona Fernkorn and Ana Griza

INDEX OF PLACES AND OBJECTS

Compiled by Birgit Schübel in collaboration with Leona Fernkorn and Ana Griza

Main articles are marked by numbers in bold.

IMAGE CREDITS

Bachmann, Thomas: p. 56

Berlin, bpk / Kupferstichkabinett, SMB / Dietmar Katz: p. 40 (top, bottom)

Berlin, SBB-PK: pp. 18, 84, 283, 307, 370 (cat. no. 122.1), 371 (cat. no. 122.2), 372 (cat. no. 122.3)

Berlin, Staatliche Museen zu Berlin, Kupferstichkabinett / Markus Hilbich, Public Domain Mark 1.0: pp. 356–57 (cat. nos. 117.1–117.3)

Cambridge, Trinity College: p. 60

Coburg, Kunstsammlungen der Veste Coburg: p. 241

Doha, Museum of Islamic Art, photo: Marc Pelletreau: p. 86

Dresden, © Grünes Gewölbe, Staatliche Kunstsammlungen Dresden, photo: Jürgen Karpinski: p. 44

Dresden, © Grünes Gewölbe, Staatliche Kunstsammlungen Dresden, photo: Paul Kuchel: pp. 104, 106

Erlangen, Universitätsbibliothek der FAU Erlangen-Nürnberg: pp. 20, 183 (top left, top right, bottom left, bottom right), 187, 295 (left, right), 341 (top left, top right, bottom left, bottom center, bottom right)

GNM: pp. 38, 63, 69, 70

GNM / Annette Kradisch: pp. 58, 289

GNM / Carolin Merz: pp. 149 (cat. nos. 22.1–22.9), 321

GNM / Dirk Meßberger: pp. 117 (left, right), 159, 191, 195, 267, 313

GNM, Photoabteilung: pp. 16, 21, 115, 119, 142, 155, 209, 323 (left, right)

GNM / Georg Janßen: pp. 65, 107 (cat. nos. 3.1, 3.3–3.9), 122, 123, 135, 138, 143, 157 (left), 165, 170, 171, 172–73, 176 (cat. nos. 34.1–34.3), 177, 178, 180, 181, 199 (left, right), 203, 221 (top, bottom), 225, 228, 235, 237, 243, 245, 251 (bottom), 255 (top, bottom), 261, 262–63 (cat. nos. 74.1–74.5), 293, 307, 311, 333, 335, 349 (top, bottom), 363, 370 (cat. no. 122.6), 371 (cat. no. 122.7)

GNM / Jens Voskamp: pp. 88, 89, 147, 167, 301 (cat. nos. 92.1–92.5), 357–58 (cat. no. 117.4), 372 (cat. no. 122.8)

GNM / Jürgen Musolf: pp. 103, 139, 151, 207, 211, 297

GNM / Klaus Schmidt: p. 223 (cat. nos. 55.2–55.4)

GNM / Monika Runge: pp. 45, 46, 48, 107 (cat. no. 3.2), 125 (left, right), 126, 127, 133, 156, 157 (right), 163, 185, 231, 236 (left, right), 239, 244, 277, 287, 291, 301 (cat. no. 92.6), 347, 365, 370 (cat. no. 122.5)

GNM / Scan: pp. 111 (top, bottom), 131, 197, 218–19, 233, 251 (top), 259, 281, 285, 325, 337

GNM / Sebastian Tolle: pp. 257, 366

GNM / Simone Hänisch: p. 36

GNM / Ursula Teichmann: p. 223 (cat. no. 55.1)

GNM / Ute Bock: p. 26 (left)

Gotha, Friedenstein Stiftung Gotha (CC BY 4.0): pp. 188–89, 253, 271, 273, 275

Ichumbaki, Elgidius B: pp. 90, 93, 97

Jerusalem, © The Israel Museum: p. 33

Jerusalem, The National Library of Israel: pp. 30, 34

Lisbon, Academia das Ciências de Lisboa: p. 95

London, British Library: pp. 28, 339 (top, bottom)

London, © Victoria and Albert Museum: p. 42

Madrid, Photographic Archive, Museo Nacional del Prado: p. 307

Madrid, Thyssen-Bornemisza Collections: pp. 41 (top, bottom), 161

Munich, Bayerisches Nationalmuseum, Bastian Krack: pp. 326, 327

Munich, Bayerische Staatsbibliothek: pp. 23, 35, 72, 74, 129, 279, 305, 319, 331, 353

Munich, Bayerische Verwaltung der staatlichen Schlösser, Gärten und Seen: p. 76

Munich, Bibliothek des Herzoglichen Georgianums: p. 205 (top, bottom)

Munich, Universitätsbibliothek der LMU München: pp. 81, 314, 317, 350, 351

Nuremberg, © Museen der Stadt Nürnberg, Kunstsammlungen, photo: Martin Ammon: pp. 59, 113

Nuremberg, © Museen der Stadt Nürnberg, Kunstsammlungen, photo: Roland Schewe, GNM: p. 373

Nuremberg, Stadtarchiv Nürnberg: p. 57

Nuremberg, Stadtbibliothek im Bildungscampus: p. 121

Nuremberg, Tucher Kulturstiftung, photo: Liliana M. Frevel – Designfrevel, Dieter Ertel – Dieter Ertel Photographie: pp. 47, 54, 215, 249

Oxford, © Ashmolean Museum, University of Oxford: p. 26 (right)

Oxford, © Bodleian Libraries, University of Oxford: p. 32

Prague, © National Gallery Prague 2025: p. 53

Private collection: p. 367

Ravenstein 1908: p. 66

Rome, Bibliotheca Hertziana / Creative Commons (CC BY-NC 4.0): p. 29

Runge, Monika: pp. 358 (left, right), 359, 360 (left, right), 361

Siena, Banca Monte dei Paschi di Siena, photo: Lensini Siena: p. 153

Venice, Archivio fotografico G.A.VE – su concessione del Ministero della Cultura – Gallerie dell'Accademia di Venezia: pp. 51, 52

Warsaw, from the collection of the Polish Army Museum in Warsaw: p. 299

Warsaw, National Museum in Warsaw: p. 201

Vienna, © Albertina: pp. 77, 229, 269

Vienna, © KHM-Museumsverband: p. 75

Vienna, Österreichische Nationalbibliothek, Kartensammlung und Globenmuseum: pp. 78, 329

Wikimedia Commons: p. 83

Wikimedia Commons / Piero Falchetta: p. 50

Wolfenbüttel, Herzog August Bibliothek: pp. 213, 315

Zurich, Zentralbibliothek Zürich, Graphische Sammlung: p. 64

EXHIBITION CATALOGUES, GERMANISCHES NATIONALMUSEUM, NUREMBERG

Director General Daniel Hess

Head of Department "Transfer / Special Exhibitions" Heike Zech

COLOPHON

EXHIBITION

Project Lead Benno Baumbauer

Curators Benno Baumbauer, Marie-Therese Feist, Sven Jakstat

Curatorial Assistant Laura Di Carlo

Exhibition Assistant Marie-Therese Feist, Barbara Rök, Birgit Schübel, Sabine Tiedtke

Student Internships Mona Freitag, Leona Fernkorn

Conservators Institut für Kunsttechnik und Konservierung (IKK), Oliver Mack, Markus Raquet, Annegret Alesi, Michele Cristale, Roland Damm, Annika Dix, Maria Ellinger-Gebhardt, Bettina Guggenmos, Simone Hänisch, Frank Heydecke, Petra Kreß, Sabine Martius, Benjamin Rudolph, Louise Schaufel, Alexandra Scheld, Elisabeth Taube, Jens Wagner

Registrar Arabelle Herkner

Technical Services Frank Stolpmann, Robert Dechet and the Teams of the Estates and Technical Services Department and the Exhibition and Transport Services (ATD)

Museum Learning and Education Jessica Mack-Andrick, Gesa Büchert, Regina Rüdebusch, Lena Schmiedl, Pirko Schröder, and the Team of the Education Department of the Museums in Nuremberg (KPZ)

Exhibition Media Laura Di Carlo and Design Practice, Darmstadt

Digital Story Laura Di Carlo, Dominik von Roth, and ip plus, Düsseldorf

Video Screen Meyrav Levy, Munich; Maria Sagolla, Sabrina Zierhut, and endlosMedia, Erlangen

Audio Guide Regina Rüdebusch and Soundgarden, Munich

Marketing, Social Media, Events Andrea Langer and the Team of the Department

Press and Medien Sonja Mißfeldt, Jens Voskamp, Thomas Spindler, CAB-Artis

Design 3D Bach Dolder, Darmstadt

Design 2D Design Practice, Darmstadt

Translations Büro LS Anderson, Berlin

Lighting Design Josef Wollinger, München

Special Object Installations Matthias Förster, Berlin; Monolith Steinrestaurierung, Bamberg

Design for Marketing Campaign BOROS, Berlin

CATALOGUE

Editors Benno Baumbauer, Marie-Therese Feist, Sven Jakstat

Contributors Florian Abe, Tina Asmussen, Daniel Astorga Poblete, Benno Baumbauer, Fabian Brenker, Laura Di Carlo, Britta Dümpelmann, Marie-Therese Feist, Uwe Gast, Johannes Gebhardt, Stefan Hanß, Vera Henkelmann, Judith Hentschel, Daniel Hess, Markus T. Huber, Elgidius E. B. Ichumbaki, Sven Jakstat, Monica Juneja, Henry Kaap, Marie-Luise Kosan, Meyrav Levy, Dominicus Z. Makukula, Alexander Rácz, Adelheid Rasche, Alberto Saviello, Barbara Schellewald, Birgit Schübel, Verena Suchy, Elisabeth Taube, Manuel Teget-Welz, Susanne Thürigen, Sabine Tiedtke, Theresa Witting, Heike Zech

Translation Joshua Waterman

Copyediting and Proofreading (GNM) Benno Baumbauer, Laura Di Carlo, Marie-Therese Feist, Sven Jakstat

Copyediting (DKV) Dawn Michelle d'Atri

Image Editing Laura Di Carlo, Mona Freitag

Photography GNM, Monika Runge and Georg Janßen, as well those separately credited

Cover Illustration Albrecht Dürer, Rhinocerus, Nuremberg, 1515, cat. no. 119
Collage based on BOROS, Berlin

Design and Typesetting Edgar Endl, booklab, Munich

Scans and Image Processing LVD Gesellschaft für Datenverarbeitung mbH, Berlin

Printing and Binding Beltz Grafische Betriebe GmbH, Bad Langensalza

Typefaces Corporate S/E Pro

Paper 135 g/m² Magno Volume

Project Management (GNM) Christine Dippold

Project Management (DKV) Martina Kupiak

Processing (DKV) Gianfranco de Felice

Verlag und Vertrieb
Deutscher Kunstverlag
Ein Verlag der Walter de Gruyter GmbH
Genthiner Straße 13, 10785 Berlin

www.gnm.de · www.deutscherkunstverlag.de · www.degruyterbrill.com

Questions on general product safety:
productsafety@degruyterbrill.com

Bibliographic information published by the Deutsche Nationalbibliothek
The Deutsche Nationalbibliothek lists this publication in the Deutsche Nationalbibliografie; detailed bibliographic data are available on the internet at http://dnb.dnb.de abrufbar.

ISBN 978-3-422-80341-1
ISBN 978-3-98501-383-8 (PDF)

Library of Congress Control Number: 2025950779

German edition: "Nürnberg GLOBAL 1300–1600"
Deutscher Kunstverlag, 2025
ISBN 978-3-422-80321-3
ISBN 978-3-98501-382-1 (PDF)

The electronic open access version of this work is permanently available at
https://www.arthistoricum.net
urn: urn:nbn:de:bsz:16-ahn-artbook-1669
doi: https://doi.org/10.11588/arthistoricum.1669
as well as for the German Edition
urn: urn:nbn:de:bsz:16-ahn-artbook-1668
doi: https://doi.org/10.11588/arthistoricum.1668
Published by Heidelberg University / Heidelberg University Library, 2026
arthistoricum.net – Specialised Information Service Art · Photography · Design
Grabengasse 1, 69117 Heidelberg, Germany
https://www.uni-heidelberg.de/en/imprint
e-mail: ub@ub.uni-heidelberg.de

FULL-PAGE ILLUSTRATIONS

Page 2
Terrestrial Globe from the Ayrer Kunstkammer, 1566, GNM, inv. no. WI3, on long-term loan from the Museen der Stadt Nürnberg, Kunstsammlungen, detail (cat. no. 107). Photo: GNM / Georg Janßen

Pages 6–7
The Hauptmarkt in Nuremberg, from the Baumeisterbuch I of Wolf Jacob Stromer, ca. 1600, Staatsarchiv, Nuremberg, Archiv der Freiherren Stromer von Reichenbach, B15, no. 200. Photo: Staatsarchiv Nürnberg

Page 12
Erhard Etzlaub, *Road Map of the Holy Roman Empire*, 1533, GNM, inv. no. La217 (cat. no. 25.2). Photo: Fotoabteilung GNM

Page 100
Unknown artisan from Gujarat, India, and Nicolaus Schmidt, *Lavabo Set with Mother-of-Pearl*, ca. 1540–80 and ca. 1592–94, Staatliche Kunstsammlungen Dresden, Grünes Gewölbe, inv. nos. IV 157, IV 248 (cat. no. 2). Photo: © Grünes Gewölbe, Staatliche Kunstsammlungen Dresden. Photo: Paul Kuchel

Page 108
Master of Perspective, *Casket*, 1565, GNM, inv. no. Z1289, detail of lid (cat. no. 20). Photo: GNM / Georg Janßen

Page 144
Jost Amman, *Allegory of Trade*, 1585 (Augsburg impression from 1622), GNM, inv. no. H128, detail (cat. no. 21). Photo: GNM / Jens Voskamp

Page 168
Nutmeg Seeds and Flowers, from Georg Öllinger, *Magnarum medicine partium herbariae et zoographiae imagines*, ca. 1553, Universitätsbibliothek der FAU Erlangen-Nürnberg, Erlangen, shelf mark H62/B 164, pl. 14, detail (cat. no. 38). Photo: Universitätsbibliothek der FAU Erlangen-Nürnberg, Erlangen

Page 192
Pierre Reymond, *Basin from the Tucher Table Service*, 1558, on long-term loan from the Tucher Kulturstiftung to the Museum Tucherschloss und Hirsvogelsaal, Museen der Stadt Nürnberg, inv. no. HI Kh 009, detail (cat. no. 52). Photo: Liliana M. Frevel - Designfrevel, Dieter Ertel - Dieter Ertel Photographie

Page 216
Albrecht Dürer, *The Holzschuher Lamentation*, ca. 1499, GNM, inv. no. Gm165, on long-term loan from the Bayerische Staatsgemäldesammlungen, detail (cat. no. 57). Photo: GNM / Georg Janßen

Page 246
Pilgrimage Panel of Frederick the Wise, after 1503, Stiftung Schloss Friedenstein, Gotha, inv. no. SG77, detail (cat. no. 69). Photo: Friedenstein Stiftung Gotha (CC BY 4.0)

Page 264
Kunz Lochner, *Round Shield of King Sigismund II Augustus*, ca. 1555, Muzeum Wojska Polskiego, Warsaw, inv. no. MWP 34385, detail (cat. no. 91). Photo: From the collection of the Polish Army Museum in Warsaw

Page 302
Terrestrial Globe from the Ayrer Kunstkammer, 1566, GNM, inv. no. WI3, on long-term loan from the Museen der Stadt Nürnberg, Kunstsammlungen, detail (cat. no. 107). Photo: GNM / Georg Janßen

Page 345
Ivory Casket, Sri Lanka, former Kingdom of Kotte, ca. 1551 (?), private collection, detail of the back (cat. no. 121). Photo: private collection